PHILIP'S

STREET ATLAS
Derbyshire

First published in 1995 by

Philip's, a division of
Octopus Publishing Group Ltd
2-4 Heron Quays, London E14 4JP

Second colour edition 2002
Third impression with revisions 2004

ISBN 0-540-08115-9 (spiral)

© Philip's 2004

Ordnance Survey®

This product includes mapping data licensed
from Ordnance Survey® with the permission of
the Controller of Her Majesty's Stationery Office.
© Crown copyright 2004. All rights reserved.
Licence number 100011710.

No part of this publication may be reproduced,
stored in a retrieval system or transmitted in any
form or by any means, electronic, mechanical,
photocopying, recording or otherwise, without
the permission of the Publishers and the
copyright owner.

To the best of the Publishers' knowledge, the
information in this atlas was correct at the time
of going to press. No responsibility can be
accepted for any errors or their consequences.

The representation in this atlas of a road, track
or path is no evidence of the existence of a right
of way.

Ordnance Survey and the OS Symbol are
registered trademarks of Ordnance Survey, the
national mapping agency of Great Britain.

Printed and bound in Spain
by Cayfosa-Quebecor

Contents

III   **Key to map symbols**

IV   **Key to map pages**

VI   **Route planning**

VIII   **Administrative and Postcode boundaries**

1   **Street maps** at 3½ inches to 1 mile

266   **Street maps of centres of Chesterfield and Derby** at 7 inches to 1 mile

268   **Town maps** of Mansfield, Nottingham, Stafford and Stoke-on-Trent

270   **Index** of towns and villages

271   **Index** of streets, hospitals, industrial estates, railway stations, schools, shopping centres, universities and places of interest

Digital Data

The exceptionally high-quality mapping found in this atlas is available as digital data in TIFF format, which is easily convertible to other bitmapped (raster) image formats.

The index is also available in digital form as a standard database table. It contains all the details found in the printed index together with the National Grid reference for the map square in which each entry is named.

For further information and to discuss your requirements, please contact Philip's on 020 7644 6932 or james.mann@philips-maps.co.uk

the Sheffield College

Peaks Learning Resource Centre

Acc. No. ~~500000~~ ~~0586~~

WITHDRAWN

Class	Loan Category
912.4251	QREF

Motorway with junction number (22a)	
Primary route – dual/single carriageway	
A road – dual/single carriageway	
B road – dual/single carriageway	
Minor road – dual/single carriageway	
Other minor road – dual/single carriageway	
Road under construction	
Pedestrianised area	
DY7 **Postcode boundaries**	
County and unitary authority boundaries	
Railway, railway under construction	
Tramway, tramway under construction	
Miniature railway	
Rural track, private road or narrow road in urban area	
Gate or obstruction to traffic (restrictions may not apply at all times or to all vehicles)	
Path, bridleway, byway open to all traffic, road used as a public path	

The representation in this atlas of a road, track or path is no evidence of the existence of a right of way

58
230
237   **Adjoining page indicators**

The map area within the pink band is shown at a larger scale on the page indicated by the red block and arrow

Abbr	Full	Abbr	Full
Acad	**Academy**	Mkt	**Market**
Allot Gdns	**Allotments**	Meml	**Memorial**
Cemy	**Cemetery**	Mon	**Monument**
C Ctr	**Civic Centre**	Mus	**Museum**
CH	**Club House**	Obsy	**Observatory**
Coll	**College**	Pal	**Royal Palace**
Crem	**Crematorium**	PH	**Public House**
Ent	**Enterprise**	Recn Gd	**Recreation Ground**
Ex H	**Exhibition Hall**	Resr	**Reservoir**
Ind Est	**Industrial Estate**	Ret Pk	**Retail Park**
IRB Sta	**Inshore Rescue Boat Station**	Sch	**School**
		Sh Ctr	**Shopping Centre**
Inst	**Institute**	TH	**Town Hall/House**
Ct	**Law Court**	Trad Est	**Trading Estate**
L Ctr	**Leisure Centre**	Univ	**University**
LC	**Level Crossing**	Wks	**Works**
Liby	**Library**	YH	**Youth Hostel**

■ The small numbers around the edges of the maps identify the 1 kilometre National Grid lines ■ The dark grey border on the inside edge of some pages indicates that the mapping does not continue onto the adjacent page

Walsall	**Railway station**
	Private railway station
West Bromwich Central	**Metro station**
	Tram stop
	Bus, coach station
	Ambulance station
	Coastguard station
	Fire station
	Police station
	Accident and Emergency entrance to hospital
H	**Hospital**
+	**Place of worship**
i	**Information Centre** (open all year)
P	**Parking**
P&R	**Park and Ride**
PO	**Post Office**
X	**Camping site**
	Caravan site
	Golf course
	Picnic site
Prim Sch	**Important buildings, schools, colleges, universities and hospitals**
River Medway	**Water name**
	River, stream
	Lock, weir
	Water
	Tidal water
	Woods
	Houses
Church	**Non-Roman antiquity**
ROMAN FORT	**Roman antiquity**

The scale of the maps on the pages numbered in blue is 5.52 cm to 1 km • 3½ inches to 1 mile • 1: 18103

0	¼	½	¾	1 mile
0	250 m	500 m	750 m	1 kilometre

The scale of the maps on pages numbered in red is 11.04 cm to 1 km • 7 inches to 1 mile • 1: 9051.4

0	220 yards	440 yards	660 yards	½ mile
0	125 m	250 m	375 m	½ kilometre

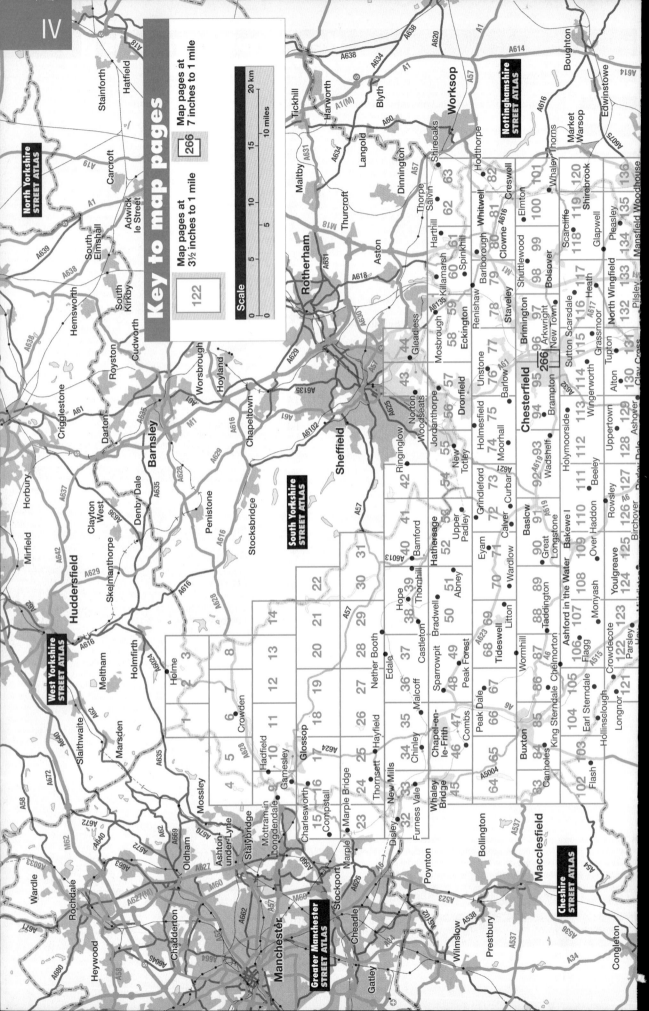

Route planning

Scale

0 1 2 3 4 5 6 7 8 km

0 1 2 3 4 5 miles

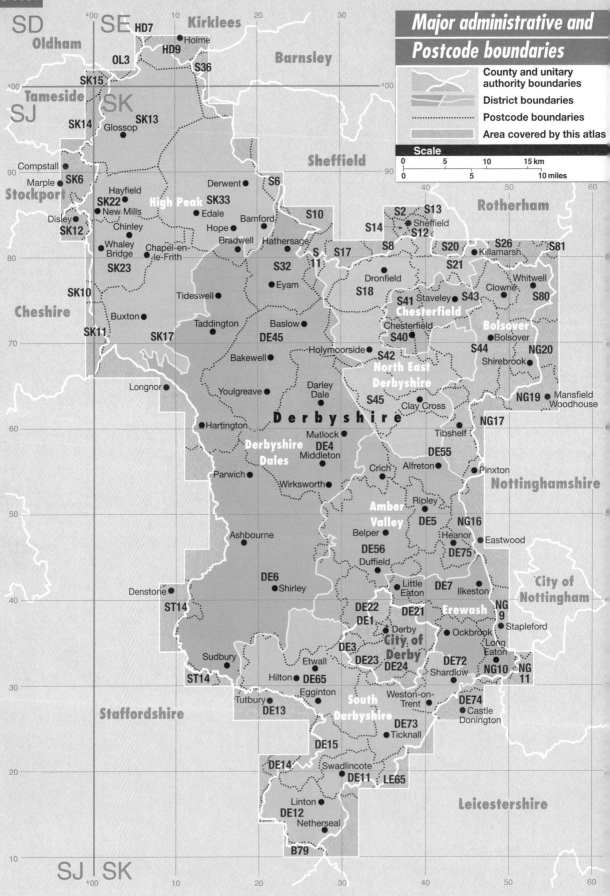

Major administrative and Postcode boundaries

County and unitary authority boundaries

District boundaries

Postcode boundaries

Area covered by this atlas

Scale

| 0 | 5 | 10 | 15 km |
| 0 | 5 | | 10 miles |

SD
Oldham
SE
HD7
Kirklees
Holme
HD9
S36
Barnsley
OL3
SK15
SJ
Tameside
SK
SK14
Glossop
SK13
Sheffield
Compstall
90
Marple
SK6
Stockport
Hayfield
SK22
New Mills
Disley
Chinley
SK12
Whaley Bridge
Chapel-en-le-Frith
SK23
Derwent
S6
High Peak
SK33
Edale
Hope
Bamford
Bradwell
Hathersage
S10
S2
S13
Sheffield
S14
S12
S8
S20
Killamarsh
S26
S81
80
SK10
S
11
S32
S17
S21
Eyam
S18
Dronfield
S41
Staveley
S43
Whitwell
Clowne
S80
Cheshire
Tideswell
Chesterfield
S40
Bolsover
Bolsover
Buxton
Taddington
DE45
Baslow
Holymoorside
S42
S44
NG20
Shirebrook
SK11
70
SK17
Bakewell
North East Derbyshire
Longnor
Youlgreave
Darley Dale
S45
Clay Cross
NG19
Mansfield Woodhouse
Hartington
Derbyshire
60
Matlock
DE4
Tibshelf
NG17
Derbyshire Dales
Middleton
Crich
Alfreton
DE55
Pinxton
Parwich
Wirksworth
Ripley
Nottinghamshire
50
Amber Valley
Belper
DE5
NG16
Heanor
Eastwood
DE56
Duffield
DE75
Ashbourne
DE6
Little Eaton
DE7
Ilkeston
City of Nottingham
Denstone
Shirley
40
ST14
DE22
DE21
NG9
Erewash
DE1
Stapleford
Derby
Ockbrook
Long Eaton
DE3
City of Derby
DE72
NG10
NG11
Sudbury
DE23
Shardlow
Etwall
DE24
ST14
Hilton
DE65
Weston-on-Trent
DE74
30
Tutbury
Egginton
South Derbyshire
Castle Donington
DE13
DE73
Ticknall
DE15
Staffordshire
DE14
Swadlincote
20
DE11
LE65
DE12
Linton
Leicestershire
Netherseal
B79
10
SJ SK

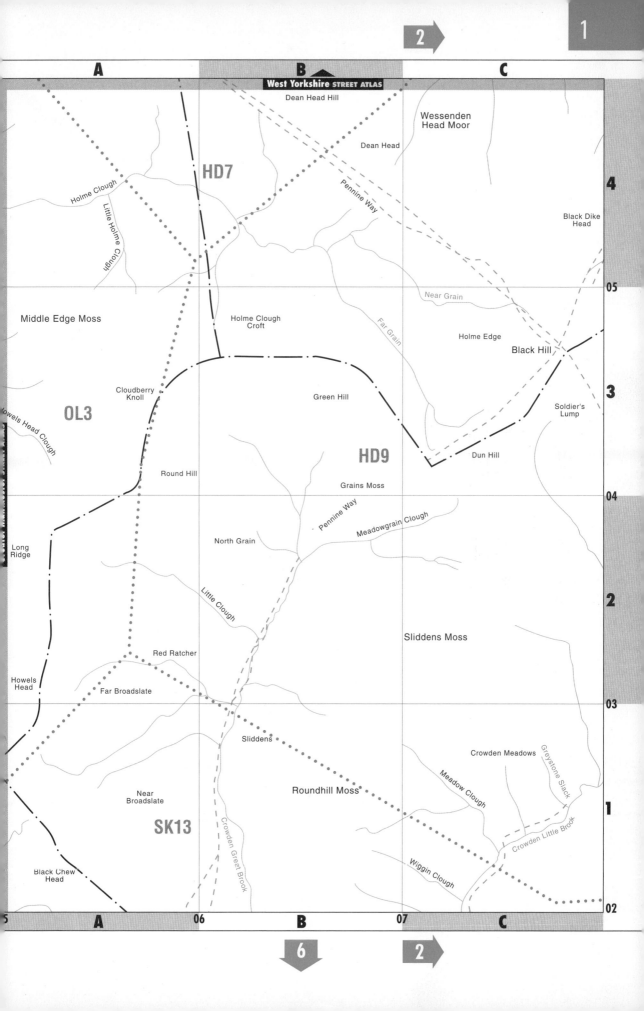

West Yorkshire STREET ATLAS

A   **B**   **C**

4

05

3

04

2

03

1

02

HD7

OL3

HD9

SK13

Dean Head Hill

Wessenden
Head Moor

Dean Head

Pennine Way

Black Dike
Head

Holme Clough

Little Holme Clough

Middle Edge Moss

Holme Clough
Croft

Near Grain

Far Grain

Holme Edge

Black Hill

Howels Head Clough

Cloudberry
Knoll

Green Hill

Soldier's
Lump

Round Hill

Dun Hill

Grains Moss

Pennine Way

Meadowgrain Clough

North Grain

Long
Ridge

Little Clough

Sliddens Moss

Howels
Head

Red Ratcher

Far Broadslate

Sliddens

Roundhill Moss

Crowden Meadows

Greystone Slack

Meadow Clough

Near
Broadslate

Crowden Great Brook

Crowden Little Brook

Wiggin Clough

Black Chew
Head

1

A
B
C
West Yorkshire STREET ATLAS
A6024 Holmfirth
Pennine Way
Hey Clough
Issues Road
Cliff Rd
The Whams
Holme
Watery Lane
The Fleece (PH)
Meal Hill Rd
Round Hill Flat
Round Hill
Lane
Hart Hill Dyke
Issue Edge
Hart Hill
Gill Hey Bridge
Rake Dike
Cliff Edge
Ings Bridge
Issues Clough
Rake Head Rd
Old Gate
Cow Close
A6024
Burley Bank La
Great Hill
Heyden Head
Holme Woods La
High Brow
Kaye Edge
Woodhead Rd
Netherley Clough
Kiln Bent Rd
Holme Moss
Holme Woods
Little Hey
Kiln Bent Bridge
Causeway Holes
Boggery Dike
Gusset Dike
Mast
Great Hey
Tooleyshaw Moss
Holme Moss Television Station
Lightens
Fern Hill
HD9
Upper Heyden
Lightens Edge
Wilmer Hill
Lightens Moss
Tooleyshaw Moor
Bleakmires Rushes
Heydon Brook
Stable Clough
Bleakmires Moss
Binns Moss
Whitelow Slack
Mound and Stake
Binns
Britland Edge Hill
West Withens Clough
White Low
Heyden Moor
SK13
A6024
4
05
3
04
2
03
1
02
08
09
10

1
7

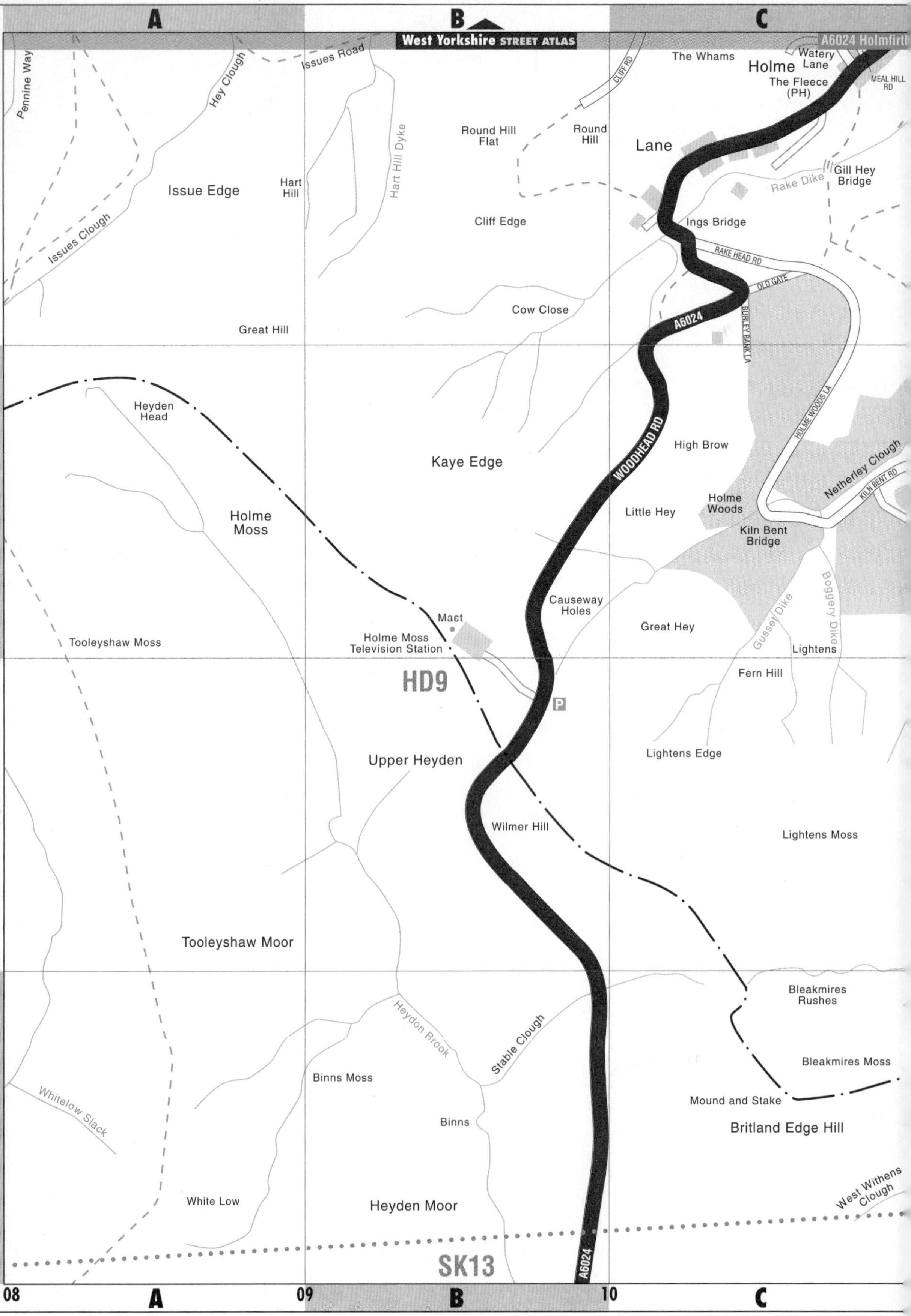

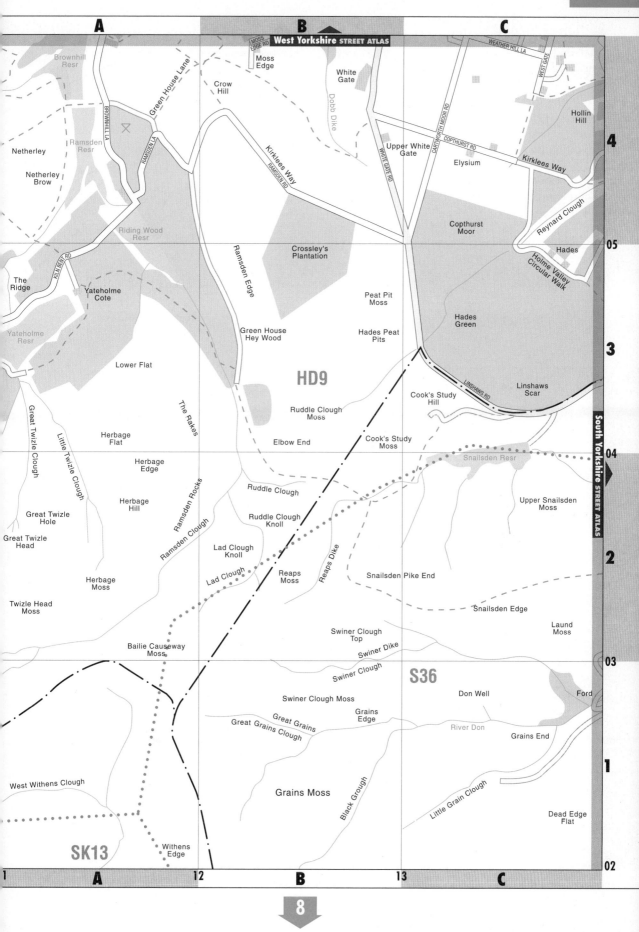

A   B   C

4

05

3

04

2

03

1

02

South Yorkshire STREET ATLAS

Brownhill Resr

Moss Edge

MOSS EDGE RD

WEATHER HILL LA

WEST GATE

White Gate

Hollin Hill

Netherley

Crow Hill

Green House Lane

BROWNHILL LA

RAMSDEN LA

Ramsden Resr

Dobb Dike

Upper White Gate

WHITE GATE RD

CARTWORTH MOOR RD

COPTHURST RD

Elysium

Kirklees Way

Netherley Brow

Kirklees Way

RAMSDEN RD

Reynard Clough

KILN BENT RD

Riding Wood Resr

Crossley's Plantation

Copthurst Moor

Hades

The Ridge

Ramsden Edge

Holme Valley Circular Walk

Yateholme Cote

Peat Pit Moss

Hades Green

Yateholme Resr

Green House Hey Wood

Hades Peat Pits

Lower Flat

HD9

Linshaws Scar

Great Twizle Clough

Little Twizle Clough

The Rakes

Ruddle Clough Moss

Cook's Study Hill

LINSHAWS RD

Herbage Flat

Elbow End

Cook's Study Moss

Snailsden Resr

Great Twizle Hole

Herbage Edge

Ruddle Clough

Upper Snailsden Moss

Great Twizle Head

Herbage Hill

Ramsden Rocks

Ruddle Clough Knoll

Ramsden Clough

Lad Clough Knoll

Reaps Dike

Snailsden Pike End

Herbage Moss

Lad Clough

Reaps Moss

Snailsden Edge

Twizle Head Moss

Laund Moss

Bailie Causeway Moss

Swiner Clough Top

Swiner Dike

S36

Swiner Clough

Don Well

Ford

Swiner Clough Moss

Grains Edge

West Withens Clough

Great Grains

Great Grains Clough

River Don

Grains End

Black Grough

Grains Moss

Little Grain Clough

Dead Edge Flat

SK13

Withens Edge

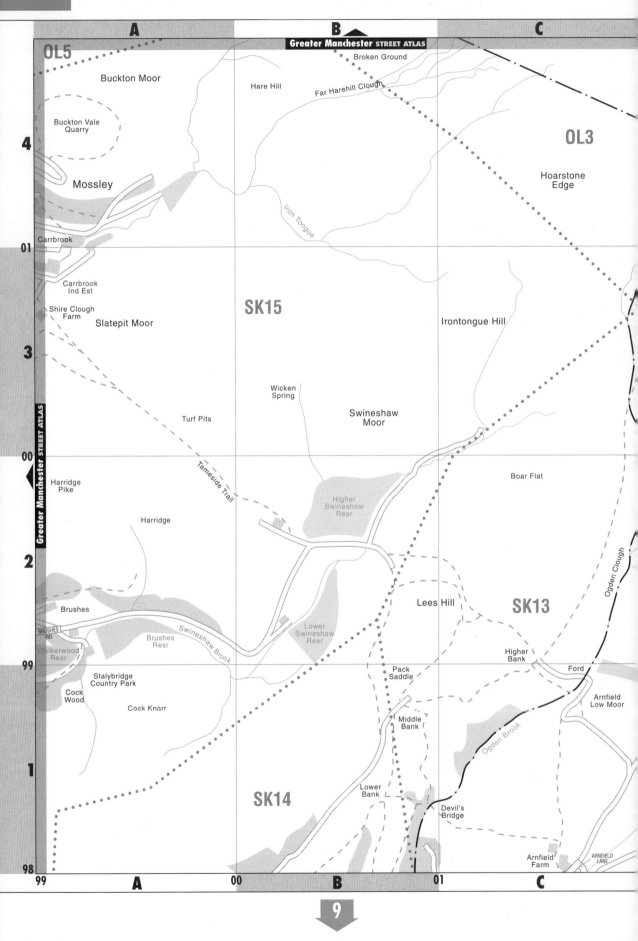

OL5

A

B

C

Broken Ground

Buckton Moor

Hare Hill

Far Harehill Clough

OL3

Buckton Vale
Quarry

4

Hoarstone
Edge

Mossley

Iron Tongue

Carrbrook

01

Carrbrook
Ind Est

SK15

Irontongue Hill

Shire Clough
Farm

Slatepit Moor

3

Wicken
Spring

Swineshaw
Moor

Turf Pits

Tameside Trail

00

Harridge
Pike

Boar Flat

Higher
Swineshaw
Resr

Harridge

2

Lees Hill

SK13

Brushes

Swineshaw Brook

Lower
Swineshaw
Resr

Ogden Clough

BRUSHES
RD

Brushes Resr

Walkerwood
Resr

Higher
Bank

Ford

99

Stalybridge
Country Park

Pack
Saddle

Arnfield
Low Moor

Cock
Wood

Cook Knarr

Middle
Bank

Ogden Brook

1

SK14

Lower
Bank

Devil's
Bridge

Arnfield
Farm

ARNFIELD
LANE

98

99

A

00

B

01

C

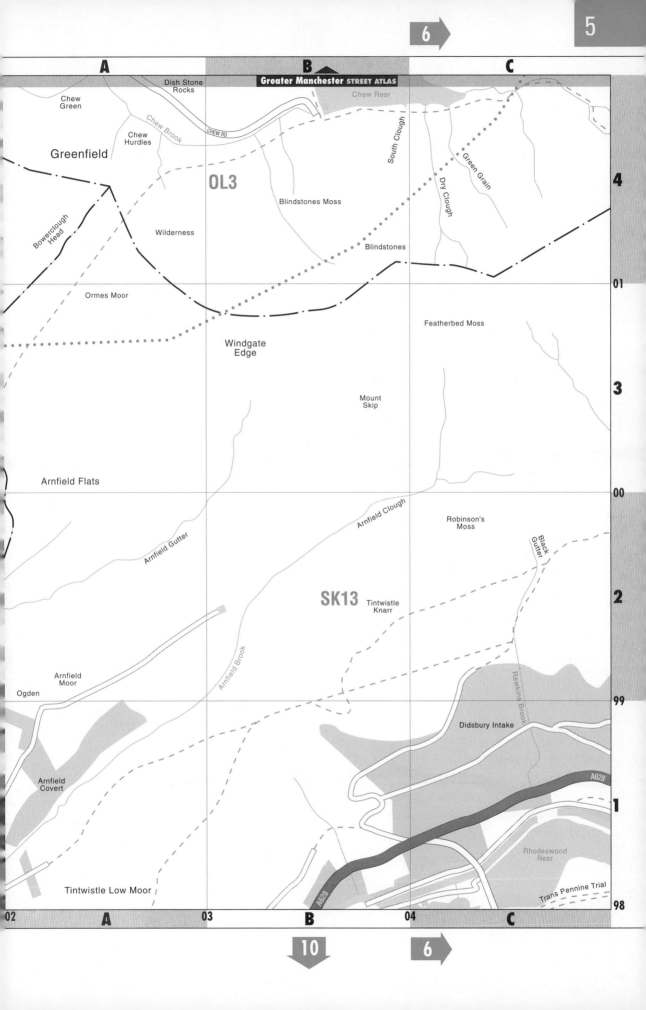

Greater Manchester STREET ATLAS

A · B · C

Chew Green

Dish Stone Rocks

Chew Hurdles

Chew Brook

CHEW RD

Chew Resr

Greenfield

OL3

Bowerclough Head

Wilderness

Blindstones Moss

South Clough

Dry Clough

Green Grain

Ormes Moor

Blindstones

Windgate Edge

Featherbed Moss

Mount Skip

Arnfield Flats

Arnfield Clough

Robinson's Moss

Black Gutter

Arnfield Gutter

SK13

Tintwistle Knarr

Arnfield Brook

Arnfield Moor

Ogden

Rawkins Brook

Didsbury Intake

Arnfield Covert

A628

Rhodeswood Resr

Tintwistle Low Moor

A628

Trans Pennine Trial

02 · A · 03 · B · 04 · C · 98

4

01

3

00

2

99

1

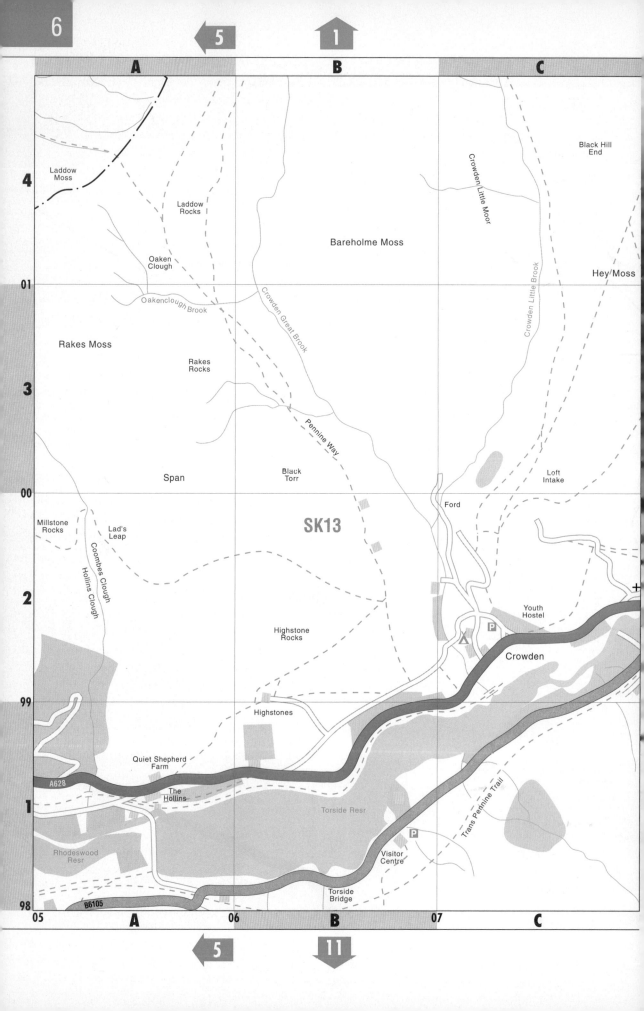

A · B · C

4

Laddow
Moss

Laddow
Rocks

Bareholme Moss

Crowden Little Moor

Black Hill
End

Oaken
Clough

01

Oakenclough Brook

Crowden Great Brook

Crowden Little Brook

Hey Moss

Rakes Moss

Rakes
Rocks

3

Pennine Way

Span

Black
Torr

Loft
Intake

00

SK13

Ford

Millstone
Rocks

Lad's
Leap

Coombes Clough

Hollins Clough

2

Highstone
Rocks

Youth
Hostel

Crowden

99

Highstones

Quiet Shepherd
Farm

A628

The
Hollins

Torside Resr

Trans Pennine Trail

1

Rhodeswood
Resr

Visitor
Centre

98

Torside
Bridge

B6105

05 · A · 06 · B · 07 · C

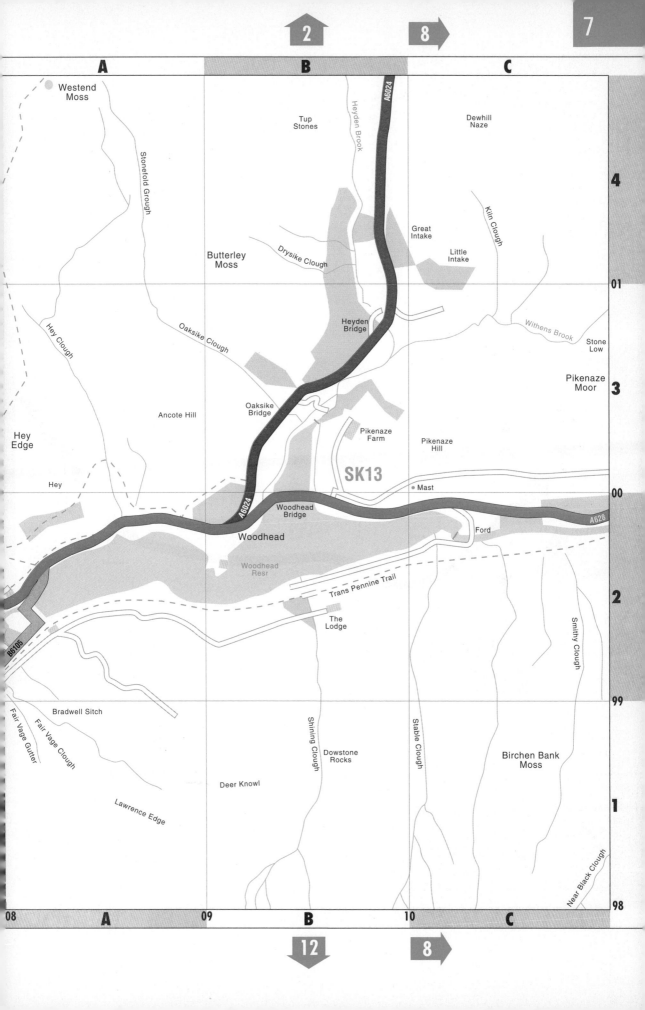

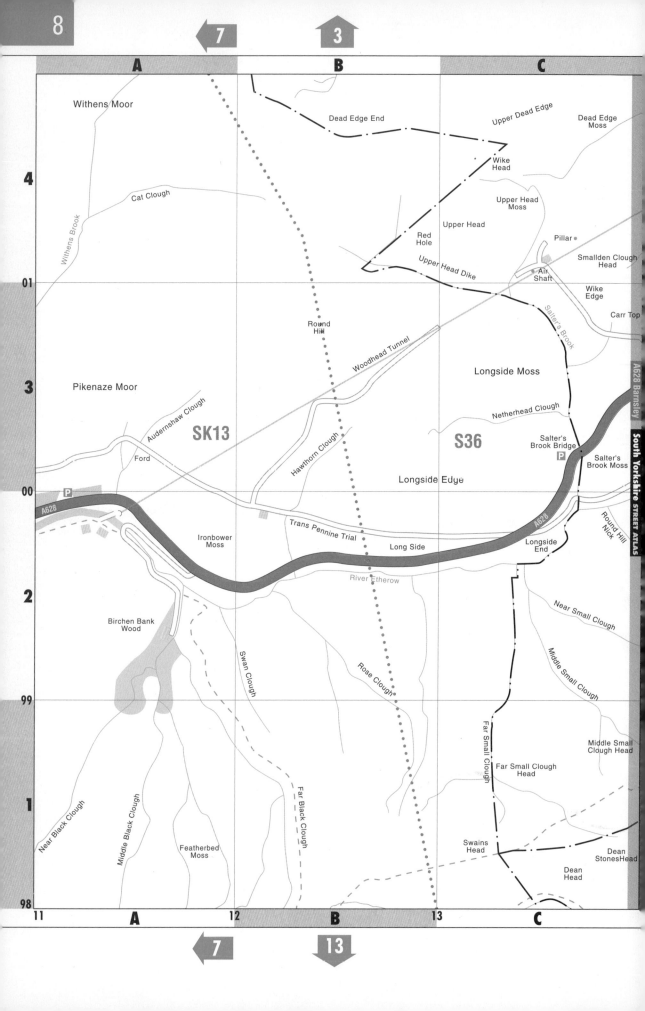

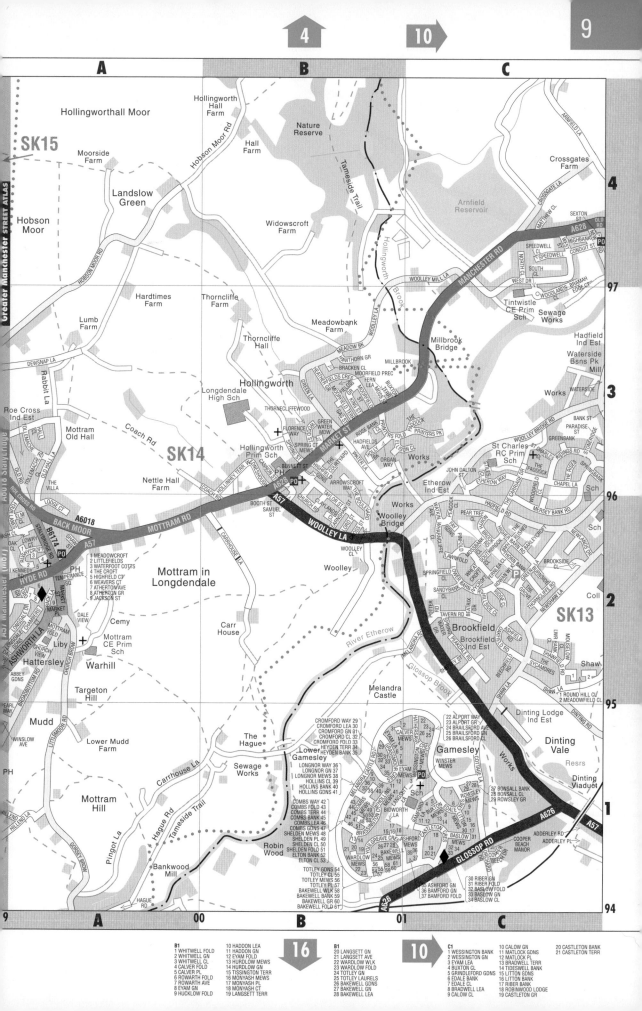

A B C

Greater Manchester STREET ATLAS

Hollingworthall Moor

SK15

Moorside Farm

Landslow Green

Hobson Moor

Hollingworth Hall Farm

Hall Farm

Hobson Moor Rd

Nature Reserve

Tameside Trail

Hollingworth Brook

Crossgates Farm

4

Hardtimes Farm

Thorncliffe Farm

Widowscroft Farm

Meadowbank Farm

Woolley La

Woolley Mill La

MANCHESTER RD A628

Arnfield Reservoir

ARNFIELD LA

CROSSGATE LA

MATTHEW CL

SEXTON ST

OLD RD

WEST ST

SPEEDWELL

PO

NORTH CL

SOUTH CL

CONDUIT ST

WEST DR

WOODLANDS

BRAMAH

EDGE CL

97

Lumb Farm

DEWSNAP LA

Rabbit La

Roe Cross Ind Est

Mottram Old Hall

Coach Rd

SK14

Thorncliffe Hall

Longdendale High Sch

Hollingworth Prim Sch

Hollingworth

Longdendale

Thorncliffewood

MEADOW BK

HAWTHORN GR

HEATHERFIELDS CRES

MOORFIELD PREC

BRACKEN CL

FERN LEA

MILLBROOK

Millbrook Bridge

MOSS ST

BUXTON RD

THE PADDOCK

Works

PRINTERS PK

Tintwistle CE Prim Sch

Sewage Works

Hadfield Ind Est

Waterside Bsns Pk Mill

WATERSIDE

Works

WATERSIDE

3

THE VILLA

Nettle Hall Farm

GREEN WATER MDW

FLORENCE WAY

THORNCLIFFEWOOD

GREEN LA

MOORFIELD ST

HADFIELDS AVE

ROSE BANK

HOLLY

ROSE BANK

BANK ST

PARADISE ST

GREENBANK

WOOLLEY BRIDGE RD

STONEBRIDGE

St Charles RC Prim Sch

ST CHARLES ST

RIDINGS RD

THE PADDOCK

Sch

96

TOLLEMACHE

OLD HALL LA

LODGE CT

A6018 STALYBRIDGE

A6018

BACK MOOR

MOTTRAM RD

A57

CARRHOUSE LA

SPRING CT

BENNETT ST

BOOTH ST

SAMUEL ST

CHURCH RD

HIGHFIELD

WINTER LA

ORGAN WAY

JOHN DALTON ST

CHAPEL LA

MERSEY BANK RD

A57

WOOLLEY LA

Woolley Bridge

Works

ETHEROW WAY

Etherow Ind Est

PEAR TREE

THE CARRIAGE DR

MOSSGATE

PINFOLD

PEACOCK

WATKIN

HADFIELD RD

HIGH ST

SOUTHBROOK

THORN BANK

BARLEYCROFT

NEWGATE RD

BROOKSIDE

96

HYDE RD

J KENNEDY

STALYBRIDGE RD

ASHWORTH LA

A57 Manchester (M67)

PH TEMPERANCE SQ

DALE VIEW

Mottram in Longdendale

WOOLLEY CL

Woolley

River Etherow

SPRINGFIELD

SANDYBANK

WHEAT BARN

PENLEA

ROWAN MT

THE GROVE

THORNCLIFFE RD

P

Coll

SK13

Shaw

LWR BANK RD

MOUSELOW CL

SHAWFIELD RD

THE SYCAMORES

SHAW LA

1 Round Hill Cl
2 Meadowfield Cl

95

Hattersley

Warhill

Mottram CE Prim Sch

Cemy

Carr House

MELANDRA CASTLE RD

Brookfield

Brookfield Ind Est

GLOSSOP BROOK

Melandra Castle

WATER LA

POTTER

TAVERN RD

RIDGE CL

HILL SIDE CL

BETHIX

ASHFIELD RD

WHITFIELD RD

BEECHFIELD

SHAW LA

Dinting Lodge Ind Est

DINTING RD

Mudd

Targeton Hill

ABBEY GDNS

Lower Mudd Farm

Carrhouse La

The Hague

Sewage Works

Lower Gamesley

Tameside Trail

CROMFORD WAY 29
CROMFORD LEA 30
CROMFORD GN 31
CROMFORD CL 32
CROMFORD FOLD 33
HEYDEN TERR 34
HEYDEN BANK 35

LONGNOR WAY 36
LONGNOR GN 37
LONGNOR MEWS 38
HOLLIS CL 39
HOLLINS BANK 40
HOLLINS GDNS 41

Gamesley

HATHERSAGE CRES

CALVER MEWS

EYAM LA

GRASSMOOR CRES

WINSTER MEWS

22 ALPORT WAY
23 ALPORT GR
24 BRAILSFORD AVE
25 BRAILSFORD GN
26 BRAILSFORD CL

PO

Sch

27 BONSALL BANK
28 BONSALL CL
29 ROWSLEY GR

Dinting Vale

Resrs

Dinting Viaduct

95

PEARL WAY

LITTLEMOOR RD

PH

Mottram Hill

Pingot La

GRASSY BROW

Hague Rd

Robin Wood

Bankwood Mill

Hague Rd

COMBS WAY 42
COMBS FOLD 43
COMBS TERR 44
COMBS BANK 45
COMBS LEA 46
COMBS GDNS 47
SHELDEN MEWS 48
SHELDEN PL 49
SHELDEN CL 50
SHELDEN FOLD 51
ELTON BANK 52
ELTON CL 53

TOTLEY GDNS 54
TOTLEY CL 55
TOTLEY MEWS 56
TOTLEY PL 57
BAKEWELL WLK 58
BAKEWELL BANK 59
BAKEWELL GR 60
BAKEWELL FOLD 61

MELANDRA CASTLE RD

BRISSENDEN GREEN

YOULGREAVE CRES

ASHFORD MEWS

BIDWORTH LA

CASTLETON CRES

BAMFORD LA

BUXTON MEWS

EDALE CRES

BASLOW MEWS

GLOSSOP RD

A626

A57

A626

Cooper Beach Manor

ADDERLEY RD

ADDERLEY PL

30 RIBER GN
31 RIBER FOLD
32 BASLOW FOLD
33 BASLOW GN
34 BASLOW CL

35 ASHFORD GN
36 BAMFORD GN
37 BAMFORD FOLD

94

9

A 00 B 01 C

16
10

B1
1 WHITWELL FOLD
2 WHITWELL GN
3 WHITWELL CL
4 CALVER FOLD
5 CALVER PL
6 ROWARTH FOLD
7 ROWARTH AVE
8 EYAM GN
9 HUCKLOW FOLD

10 HADDON LEA
11 HADDON GN
12 EYAM FOLD
13 HURDLOW MEWS
14 HURDLOW GN
15 TISSINGTON TERR
16 MONYASH MEWS
17 MONYASH PL
18 MONYASH CT
19 LANGSETT TERR

B1
20 LANGSETT GN
21 LANGSETT AVE
22 WARDLOW WLK
23 WARDLOW FOLD
24 TOTLEY GN
25 TOTLEY LAURELS
26 BAKEWELL GDNS
27 BAKEWELL GN
28 BAKEWELL LEA

C1
1 WESSINGTON BANK
2 WESSINGTON GN
3 EYAM LEA
4 BUXTON CL
5 GRINDLEFORD GDNS
6 EDALE BANK
7 EDALE CL
8 BRADWELL LEA
9 CALOW CL

10 CALOW GN
11 MATLOCK GDNS
12 MATLOCK PL
13 BRADWELL TERR
14 TIDESWELL PL
15 LITTON GDNS
16 LITTON BANK
17 RIBER BANK
18 ROBINWOOD LODGE
19 CASTLETON GR

20 CASTLETON BANK
21 CASTLETON TERR

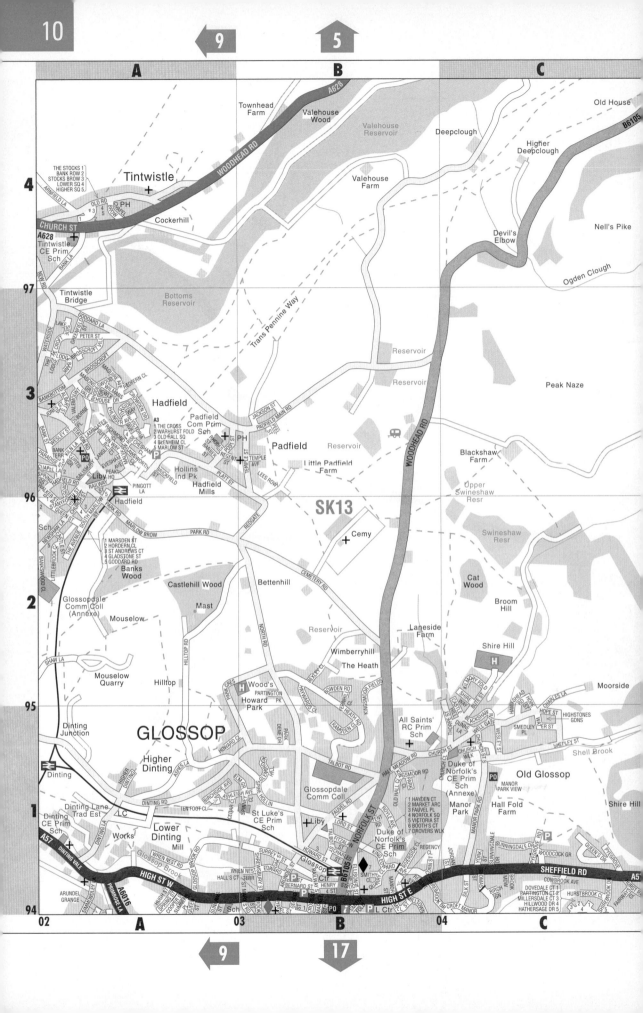

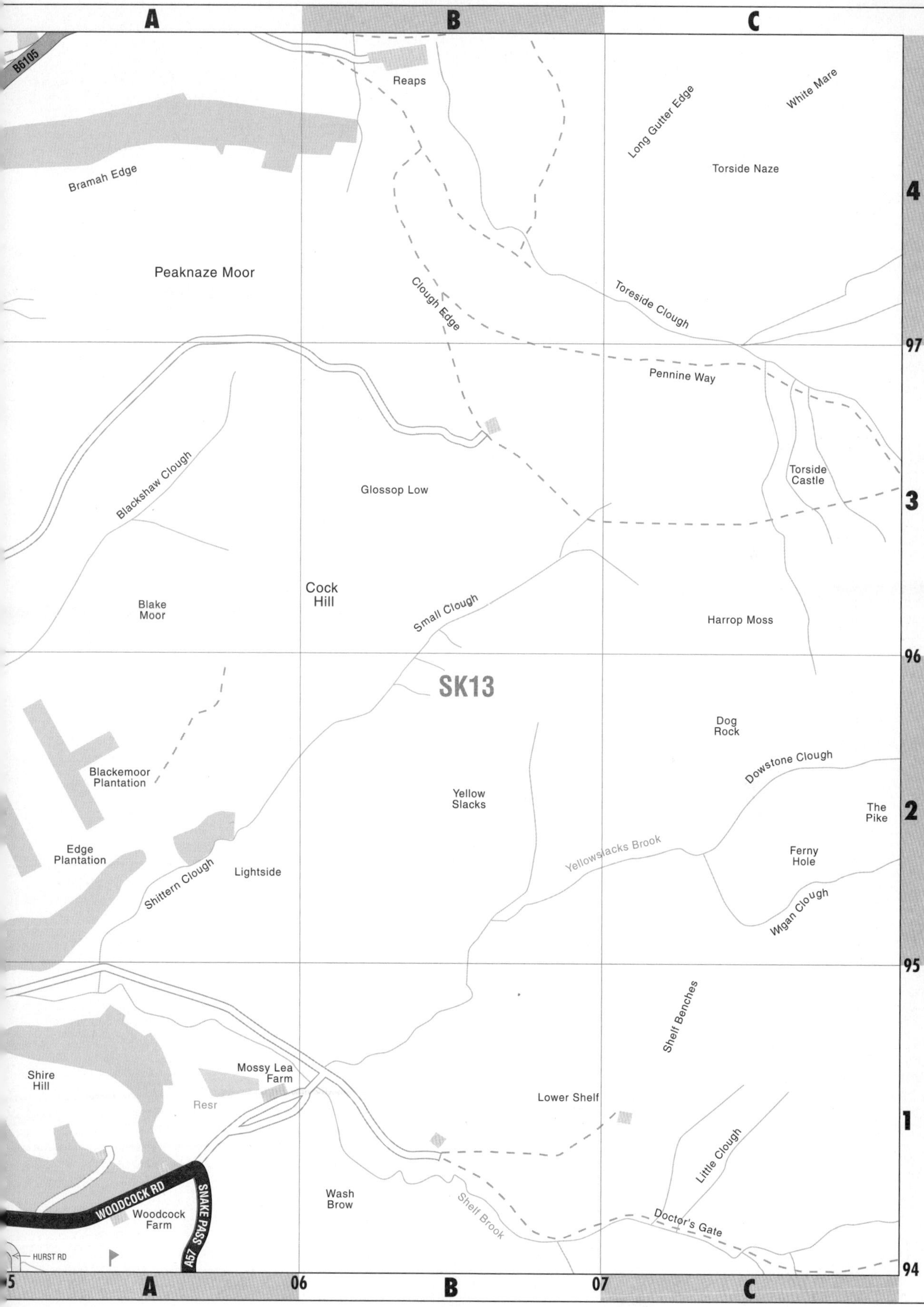

A   **B**   **C**

B6105

Reaps

Long Gutter Edge   White Mare

Bramah Edge   Torside Naze

4

Peaknaze Moor

Clough Edge

Toreside Clough

97

Pennine Way

Blackshaw Clough

Glossop Low   Torside
Castle

3

Cock
Hill   Small Clough   Harrop Moss

Blake
Moor

96

SK13

Dog
Rock

Blackemoor
Plantation   Dowstone Clough

The
Pike   **2**

Yellow
Slacks

Edge
Plantation   Ferny
Hole

Shittern Clough   Lightside   Yellowslacks Brook

Wigan Clough

95

Shelf Benches

Shire
Hill   Mossy Lea
Farm

Resr   Lower Shelf   **1**

Little Clough

Wash
Brow   Doctor's Gate

WOODCOCK RD   Shelf Brook

SNAKE PASS A57

Woodcock
Farm

HURST RD

94

5   **A**   06   **B**   07   **C**

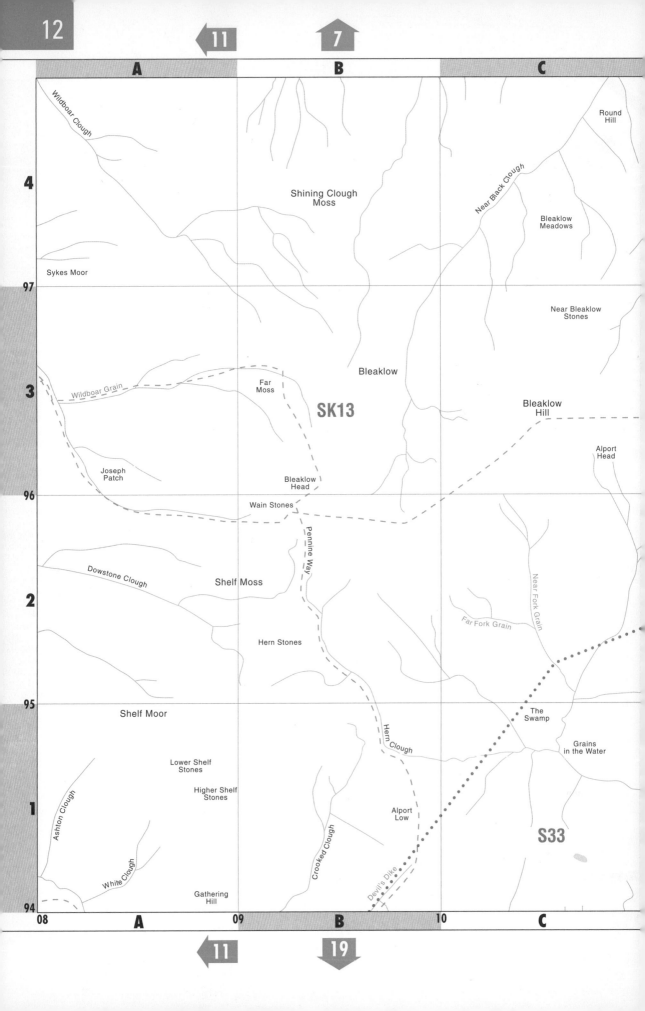

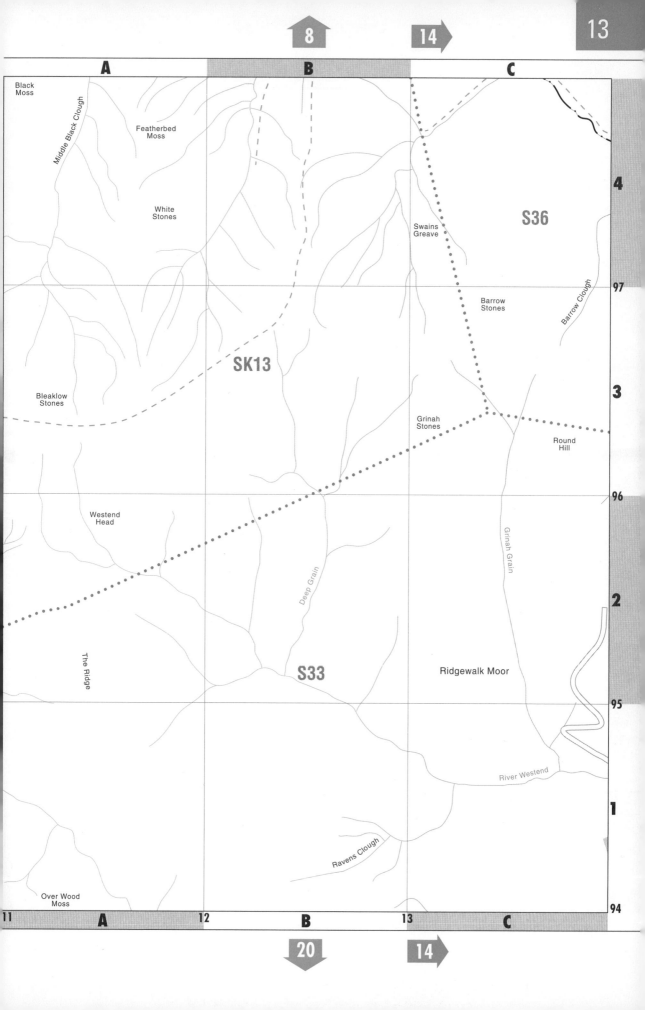

A **B** **C**

Black Moss

Middle Black Clough

Featherbed Moss

White Stones

4

Swains Greave

S36

97

Barrow Stones

Barrow Clough

SK13

Bleaklow Stones

3

Grinah Stones

Round Hill

96

Westend Head

Grinah Grain

Deep Grain

2

The Ridge

S33

Ridgewalk Moor

95

River Westend

1

Ravens Clough

Over Wood Moss

94

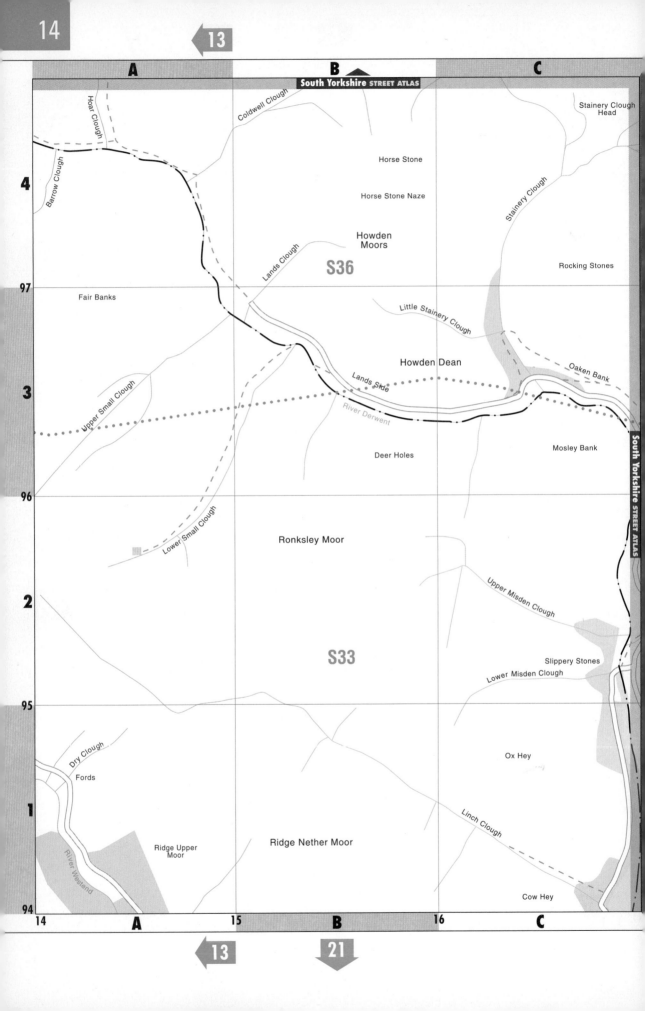

A   **B**   **C**

South Yorkshire STREET ATLAS

Hoar Clough

Coldwell Clough

Stainery Clough Head

Barrow Clough

Horse Stone

4

Horse Stone Naze

Stainery Clough

Howden Moors

Rocking Stones

Lands Clough

S36

97

Fair Banks

Little Stainery Clough

Howden Dean

Upper Small Clough

Lands Side

Oaken Bank

3

River Derwent

Deer Holes

Mosley Bank

96

Lower Small Clough

Ronksley Moor

Upper Misden Clough

2

Slippery Stones

S33

Lower Misden Clough

95

Ox Hey

Dry Clough

Fords

1

Linch Clough

River Westend

Ridge Upper Moor

Ridge Nether Moor

Cow Hey

94

14   **A**   **15**   **B**   **16**   **C**

South Yorkshire STREET ATLAS

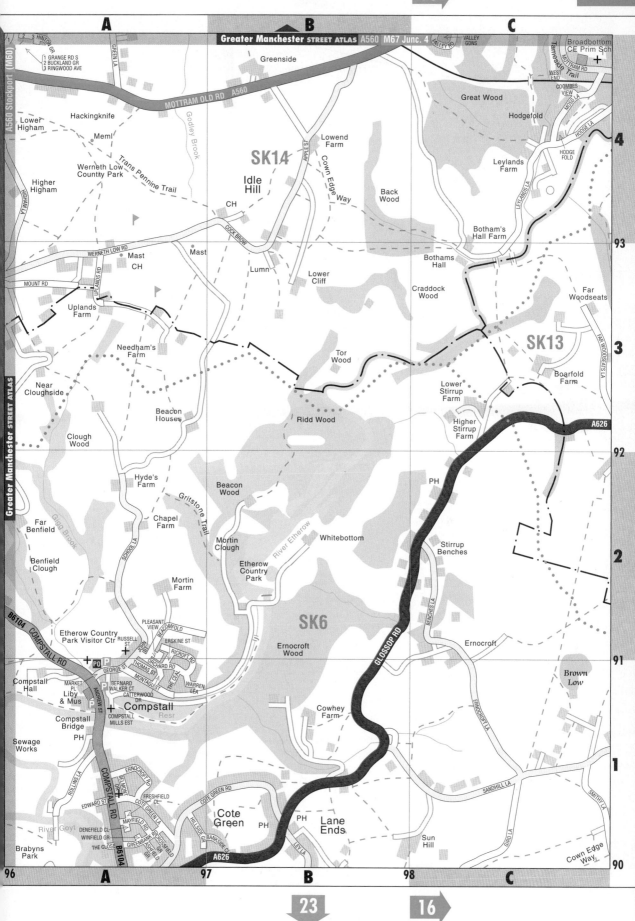

Greater Manchester STREET ATLAS A560 M67 Junc. 4

A **B** **C**

1 GRANGE RD S
2 BUCKLAND GR
3 RINGWOOD AVE

Greenside

MOTTRAM OLD RD A560

Broadbottom
CE Prim Sch

Tameside Trail
WEST END
COOMBES VIEW

Great Wood

Hackingknife

Lower Higham
Meml

SK14

Lowend Farm

Hodgefold

HODGE LA

4

Higher Higham

Werneth Low Country Park

Trans Pennine Trail

Idle Hill

Leylands Farm

HODGE FOLD

HIGHAM LA

CH

Botham's Hall Farm

93

Mast CH

Mast

Lumn

Bothams Hall

WERNETH LOW RD

DOCK BROW

Lower Cliff

Craddock Wood

Far Woodseats

MOUNT RD

UPLANDS RD

Uplands Farm

Needham's Farm

Tor Wood

SK13

FAR WOODSEATS LA

Boarfold Farm

3

Near Cloughside

Lower Stirrup Farm

Clough Wood

Beacon Houses

Ridd Wood

Higher Stirrup Farm

A626

92

Hyde's Farm

Beacon Wood

PH

Far Benfield

GIGG BROOK

Gritstone Trail

Chapel Farm

Mortin Clough

Whitebottom

River Etherow

Stirrup Benches

BENCHES LA

2

Benfield Clough

Mortin Farm

Etherow Country Park

SK6

Ernocroft Wood

Ernocroft

ERNOCROFT LA

Brown Low

B6104

COMPSTALL RD

Pleasant View

BEACOMFOLD

RUSSELL ST

Erskine St

RICROFT RD

ORCHARD RD

Etherow Country Park Visitor Ctr

GLOSSOP RD

91

Compstall Hall

MARKET PL

Liby & Mus

BERNARD WALKER CT

GEORGE ST

THOMAS ST

MONTAGU ST

CATTERWOOD DR

THE CREA

WARREN LEA

Compstall

Compstall Resr

Cowhey Farm

Ernocroft

Compstall Bridge

PH

ANDREW ST

Compstall Mills Est

1

Sewage Works

ROLLINS LA

BELMONT

ERNOCROFT RD

FRESHFIELD CT

SANDHILL LA

SMITHY LA

GIRL LA

Brabyns Park

River Goyt

EDWARD ST

COMPSTALL RD

B6104

DENEFIELD CL
WINFIELD GR
THE CLOSE

MAYFIELD

GREENBANK RD
CROSSHILL
ASHFIELD GR

COTE GREEN LA

HILLSIDE GR

BANKSIDE CL

Cote Green

PH

PH

Lane Ends

LEY LA

Sun Hill

Cown Edge Way

A626

90

96 **A** 97 **B** 98 **C**

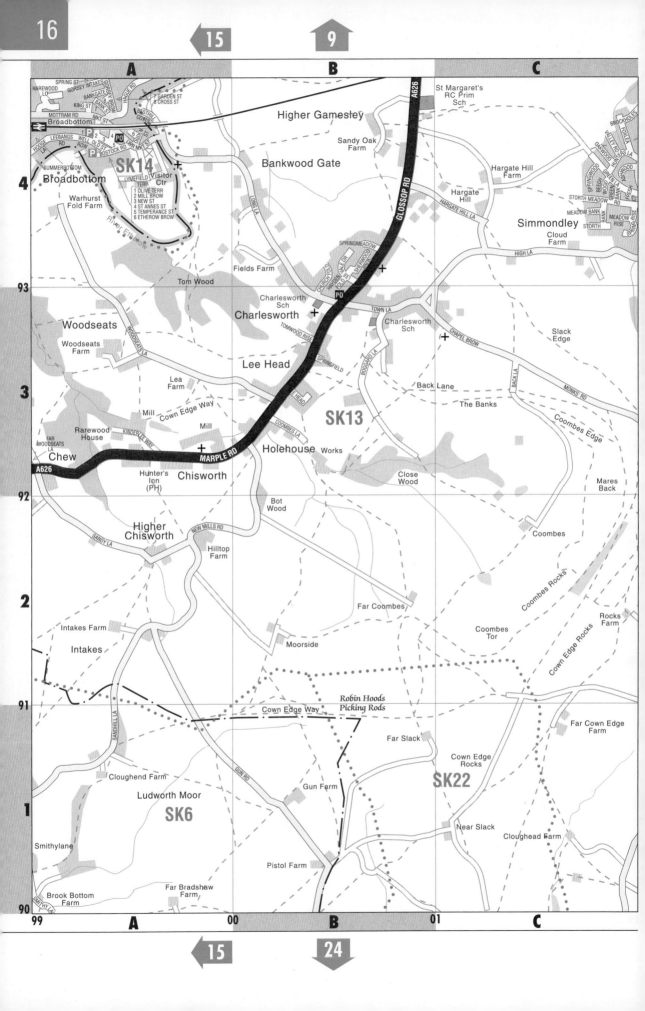

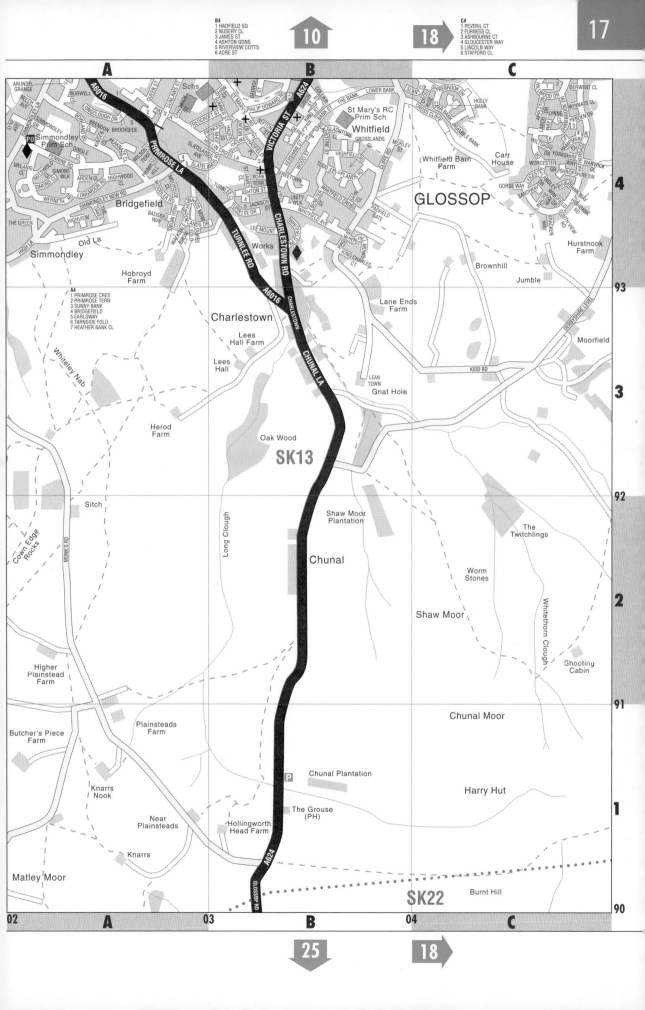

B4
1 HADFIELD SQ
2 NUSERY CL
3 JAMES ST
4 ASHTON GDNS
5 RIVERVIEW COTTS
6 ACRE ST

10

18

C4
1 PEVERIL CT
2 FURNESS CL
3 ASHBOURNE CT
4 GLOUCESTER WAY
5 LINCOLN WAY
6 STAFFORD CL

A B C

A4
1 PRIMROSE CRES
2 PRIMROSE TERR
3 SUNNY BANK
4 BRIDGEFIELD
5 EARLSWAY
6 TARNSIDE FOLD
7 HEATHER BANK CL

ARUNDEL GRANGE
BURWELL CL
BEECH AVE
LYNE AVE
Simmondley PO
Prim Sch
Simmondley
MELANIE CL
COTSWOLD
SIMONS WLK
WERNETH
Bridgefield
HIGHVIEW
Old La
Simmondley
THE GREEN
HIGH LA
PRIMROSE LA
A6016

Hobroyd Farm

Whiteley Nab

Sitch

Cown Edge Rocks

MONK'S RD

Higher Plainstead Farm

Butcher's Piece Farm

Knarrs Nook

Near Plainsteads

Knarrs

Matley Moor

Schs
QUEEN ST
PIKE'S LA
Brookside
TURNLEE RD
Works
Charlestown
Lees Hall Farm
Lees Hall

Herod Farm

Oak Wood

SK13

Long Clough

Plainsteads Farm

Chunal

Shaw Moor Plantation

Chunal Plantation

The Grouse (PH)

Hollingworth Head Farm

A624
GLOSSOP RD

SK22

VICTORIA ST
A624
St Mary's RC Prim Sch
Whitfield
CROSSLANDS CL
HIGHFIELD RD
Whitfield Cross
CHARLESTOWN RD
A6016
CHARLESTOWN
King Charles CT
Lane Ends Farm
LEAN TOWN
Gnat Hole
KIDD RD
CHUNAL LA

Burnt Hill

GLOSSOP

Whitfield Barn Farm

Carr House

Hurstnook Farm

Brownhill

Jumble

Moorfield

DERBYSHIRE LEVEL

The Twitchlings

Worm Stones

Shaw Moor

Whitethorn Clough

Shooting Cabin

Chunal Moor

Harry Hut

HOLLY BANK
DERWENT CL
WINNATS CL
WARWICK DR

4

93

3

92

2

91

1

90

02 A 03 B 04 C

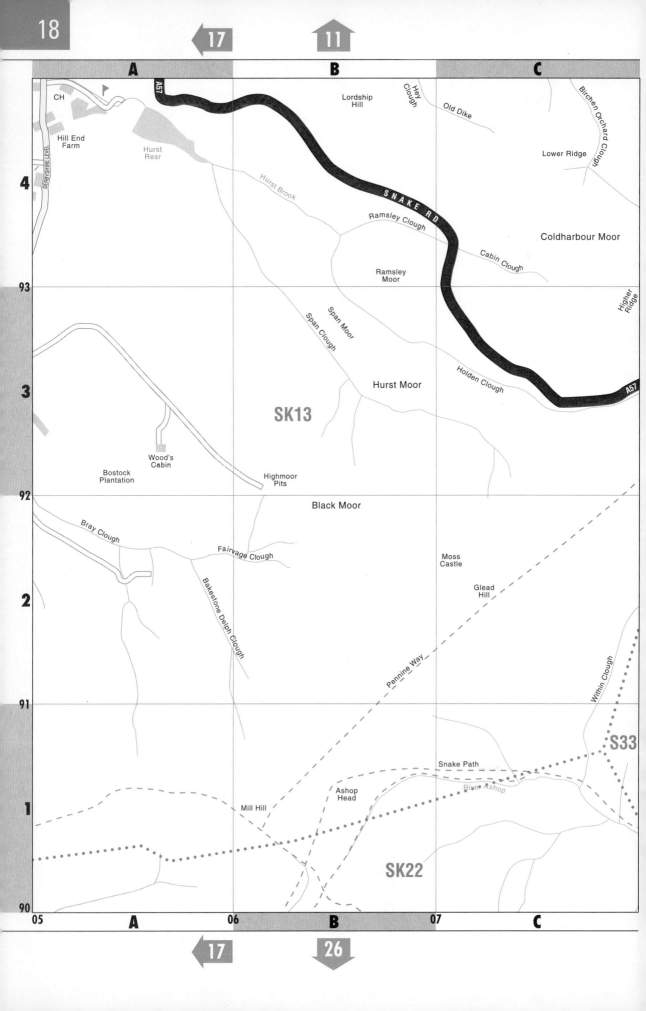

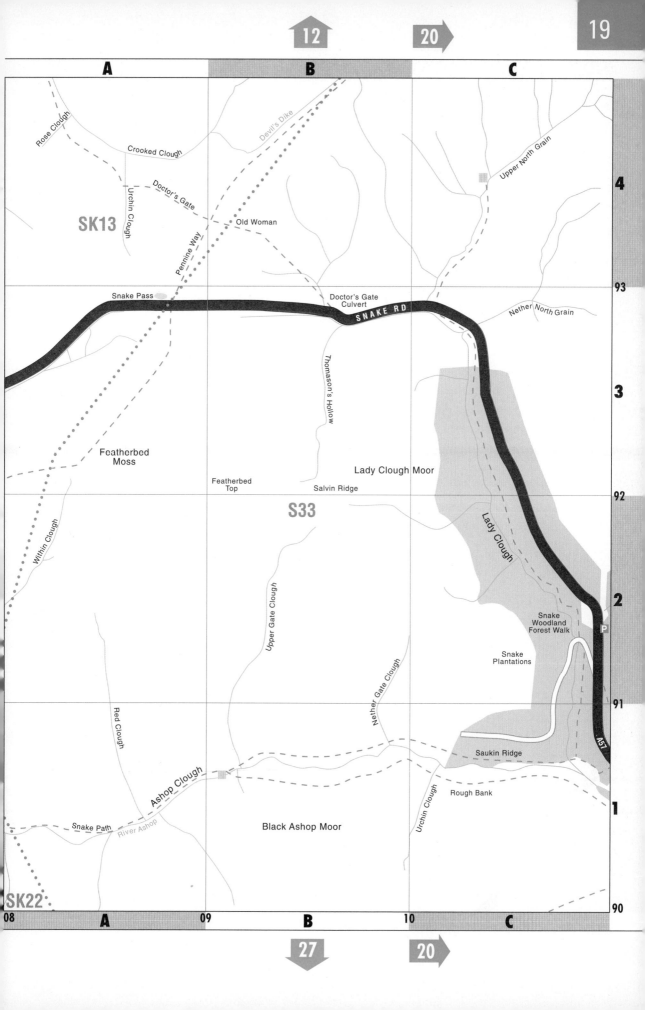

A   B   C

SK13

Rose Clough

Crooked Clough

Doctor's Gate

Urchin Clough

Pennine Way

Devil's Dike

Old Woman

Upper North Grain

4

Snake Pass

Doctor's Gate
Culvert

SNAKE RD

Nether North Grain

93

Thomason's Hollow

Featherbed
Moss

Lady Clough Moor

3

Within Clough

Featherbed
Top

Salvin Ridge

S33

Lady Clough

92

Upper Gate Clough

Snake
Woodland
Forest Walk

2

P

Snake
Plantations

Nether Gate Clough

Red Clough

91

Ashop Clough

Saukin Ridge

A57

Snake Path

River Ashop

Black Ashop Moor

Urchin Clough

Rough Bank

1

SK22

90

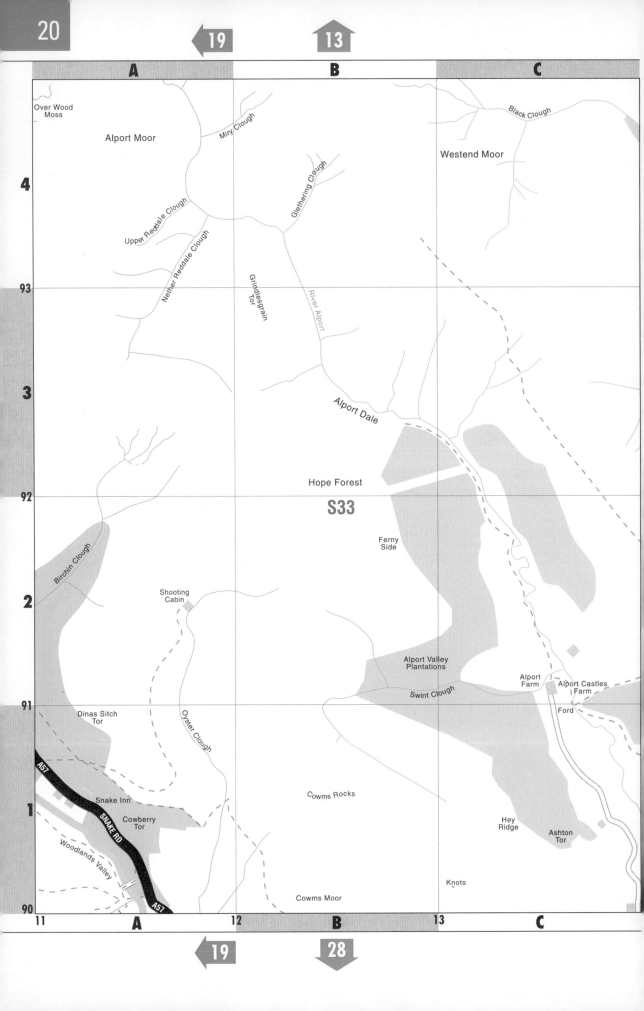

Over Wood Moss

Alport Moor

Miry Clough

Black Clough

Westend Moor

Glethering Clough

4

Upper Reddale Clough

Nether Reddale Clough

Grindlesgrain Tor

River Alport

93

3

Alport Dale

Hope Forest

92

S33

Ferny Side

Birchin Clough

Shooting Cabin

2

Alport Valley Plantations

Alport Farm

Alport Castles Farm

Swint Clough

91

Dinas Sitch Tor

Oyster Clough

Ford

A57

Snake Inn

Cowberry Tor

SNAKE RD

Cowms Rocks

1

Hey Ridge

Ashton Tor

Woodlands Valley

Knots

A57

Cowms Moor

90

A **B** **C**

Ridge Nether Moor

Banktop Hey

Ford

Upper Wood

Ronksley South Plantation

Ridge Clough

Nether Wood Plantation

River Westend

Ridge Wood

4

Banktop Plantation

Howden Resr

Fagney Plantation

Hern Side

93

Fagney Clough

Ditch Clough Plantation

Fox's Piece

West Cable Tip Plantation

3

Ditch Clough

Beaver's Croft

Green Clough

Chapel Plantation

Birchin Hat

S33

Bank Clough

92

Birchinlee Pasture

Upper Derwent Valley

Calfhey Wood

Birchinlee

Birchinlee East Plantation

Derwent Resr

2

Alport Castles

Cote Clough

Little Moor

Castles Wood

91

Ouzelden Clough

Gores Farm

Hucklow Lees Barn

Birchinlee New Piece

Alport Grain

Gores Heights

Gores Plantation

1

Whitefield Pits

Rowlee Pasture

Nabs Wood

90

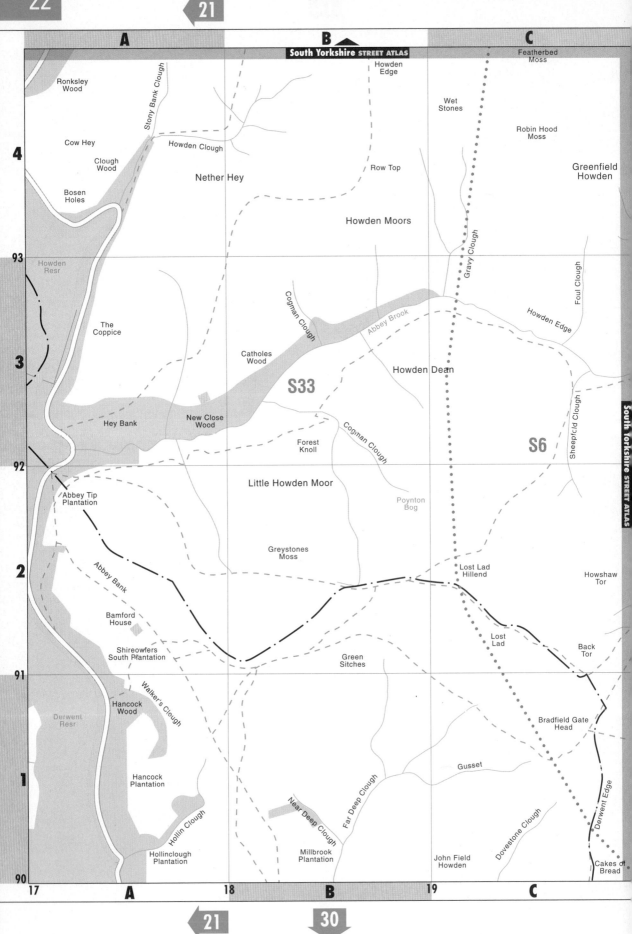

A | B | C

4

Ronksley
Wood

Howden
Edge

Featherbed
Moss

Stony Bank Clough

Cow Hey

Howden Clough

Wet
Stones

Robin Hood
Moss

Clough
Wood

Nether Hey

Row Top

Greenfield
Howden

Bosen
Holes

Howden Moors

93

Howden
Resr

The
Coppice

Cogman Clough

Abbey Brook

Gravy Clough

Foul Clough

Howden Edge

3

Catholes
Wood

Howden Dean

Hey Bank

New Close
Wood

S33

Sheepfcld Clough

S6

Forest
Knoll

Cogman Clough

92

Little Howden Moor

Poynton
Bog

Abbey Tip
Plantation

Greystones
Moss

2

Abbey Bank

Lost Lad
Hillend

Howshaw
Tor

Bamford
House

Lost
Lad

Back
Tor

Shireowlers
South Plantation

Green
Sitches

91

Walker's Clough

Hancock
Wood

Bradfield Gate
Head

Derwent
Resr

1

Hancock
Plantation

Gusset

Derwent Edge

Hollin Clough

Near Deep Clough

Far Deep Clough

Dovestone Clough

Hollinclough
Plantation

Millbrook
Plantation

John Field
Howden

Cakes of
Bread

90

17 | A | 18 | B | 19 | C

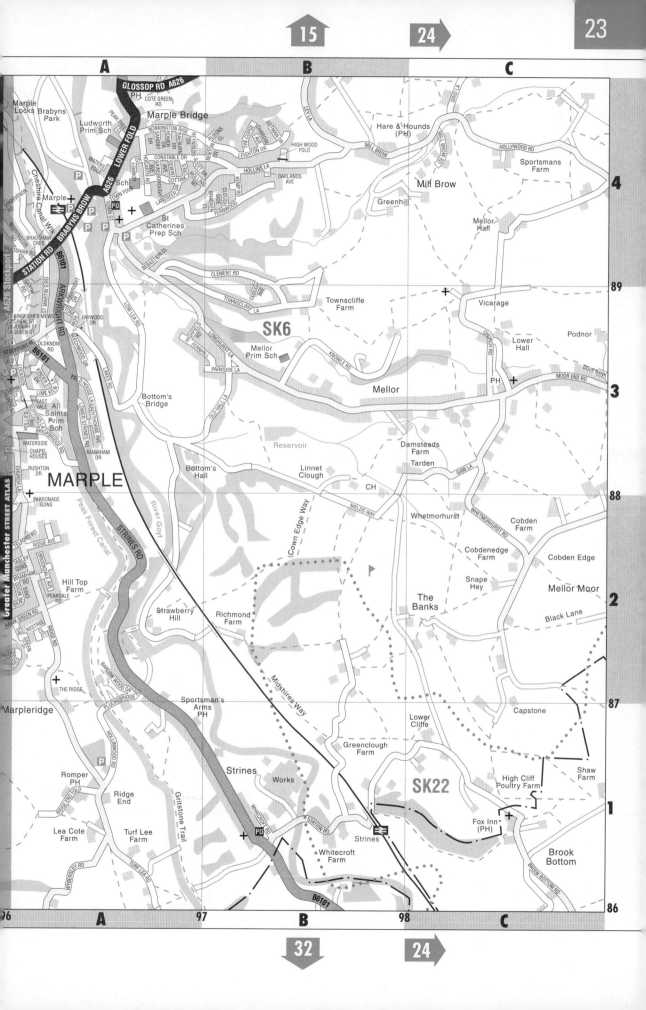

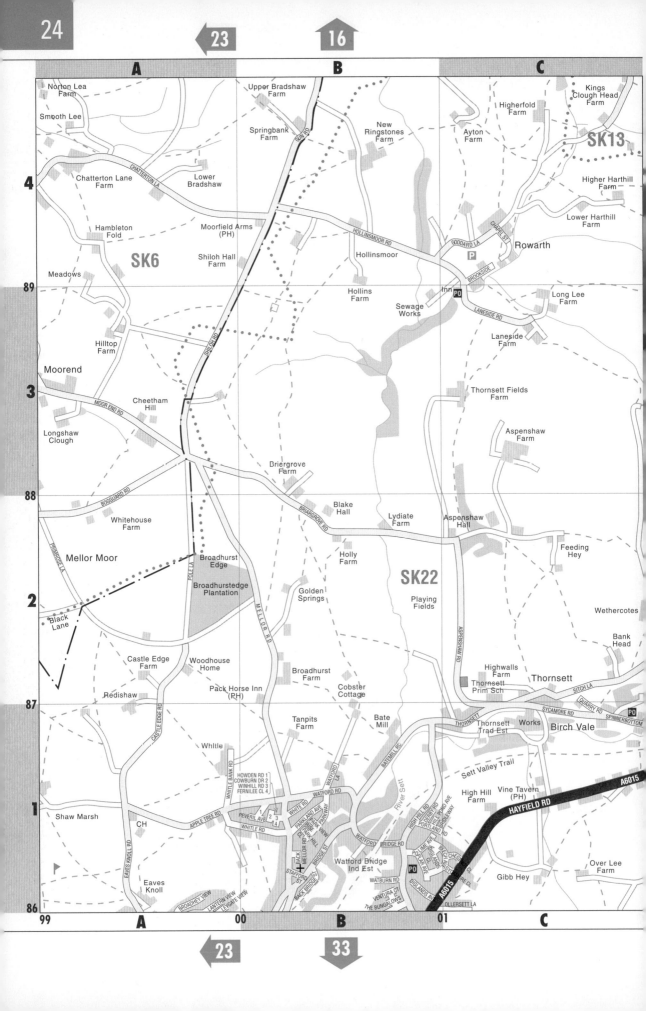

A   B   C

Norton Lea
Farm

Smooth Lee

CHATTERTON LA

Chatterton Lane
Farm

Lower
Bradshaw

Upper Bradshaw
Farm

SUN RD

Springbank
Farm

New
Ringstones
Farm

Ayton
Farm

Higherfold
Farm

Kings
Clough Head
Farm

SK13

4

Higher Harthill
Farm

Lower Harthill
Farm

Hambleton
Fold

Moorfield Arms
(PH)

HOLLINSMOOR RD

Hollinsmoor

GODDARD LA

CHAPEL ST

Rowarth

SK6

Shiloh Hall
Farm

Hollins
Farm

P

Meadows

89

Inn

PO

BROOKSIDE

Long Lee
Farm

Sewage
Works

LANESIDE RD

Hilltop
Farm

SHAW RD

Laneside
Farm

Moorend

Cheetham
Hill

Thornsett Fields
Farm

3

MOOR END RD

Longshaw
Clough

Aspenshaw
Farm

Driergrove
Farm

BRIARGROVE RD

Blake
Hall

Lydiate
Farm

Aspenshaw
Hall

88

BOGGUARD RD

Whitehouse
Farm

Feeding
Hey

PRIMROSE LA

Mellor Moor

POLE LA

Broadhurst
Edge

Holly
Farm

SK22

Wethercotes

Broadhurstedge
Plantation

MELLOR RD

Golden
Springs

Playing
Fields

Bank
Head

2

Black
Lane

Castle Edge
Farm

Woodhouse
Home

Broadhurst
Farm

Cobster
Cottage

ASPENSHAW RD

Highwalls
Farm

Thornsett
Prim Sch

Thornsett

SITCH LA

Redishaw

CASTLE EDGE RD

Pack Horse Inn
(PH)

Bate
Mill

Thornsett
Trad Est

Works

SYCAMORE RD

QUARRY RD

SPINNERBOTTOM

PO

87

Whitle

WHITE BANK RD

Tanpits
Farm

THORNSETT

Birch Vale

Shaw Marsh

CH

APPLE TREE RD

Howden Rd 1
Cowburn Dr 2
Winhill Rd 3
Fernilee Cl 4

PEVERIL AVE

WHITLE RD

1 2 3
4

WATFORD RD

WATFORD LA

Sett Valley Trail

High Hill
Farm

Vine Tavern
(PH)

HAYFIELD RD

A6015

River Sett

HIGH HILL RD

PARKLAND AVE

1

PARKLAND NEW PARKWAY

BACK MELLOR RD

BRIDGE ST

STAFFORD ST

BACK BRIDGE

Watford Bridge
Ind Est

WATFORD RD

BRIDGE RD

PO

WATBURN RD

VENTURA DT

THE BUNGALOWS

PORTLAND AVE

DIGLANDS AVE

OLLERSETT LA

A6015

Gibb Hey

Over Lee
Farm

Eaves Knoll

EAVES KNOLL RD

BROADHEY VIEW

LANTERN VIEW

LEYGATE VIEW

86

A | B | C

4

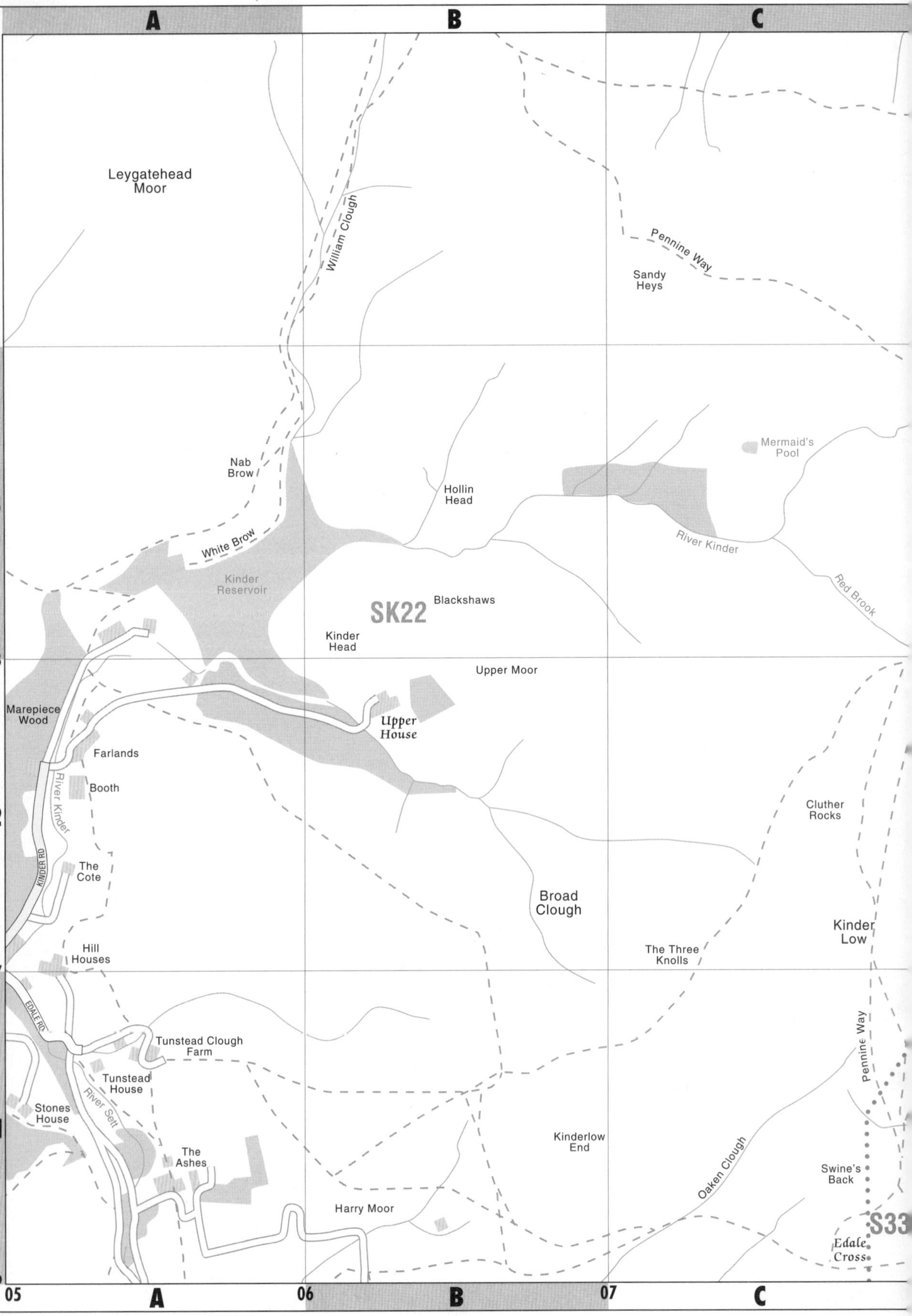

Leygatehead
Moor

William Clough

Pennine Way

Sandy
Heys

89

Mermaid's
Pool

Nab
Brow

3

Hollin
Head

White Brow

River Kinder

Red Brook

Kinder
Reservoir

SK22 Blackshaws

Kinder
Head

88

Upper Moor

Marepiece
Wood

Upper
House

River Kinder

Farlands

Cluther
Rocks

Booth

2

Kinder
Low

KINDER RD

The
Cote

Broad
Clough

The Three
Knolls

Hill
Houses

87

Pennine Way

EDALE RD

Tunstead Clough
Farm

Tunstead
House

River Sett

Stones
House

1

Kinderlow
End

Oaken Clough

Swine's
Back

The
Ashes

S33

Harry Moor

Edale
Cross

86

05 | A | 06 | B | 07 | C

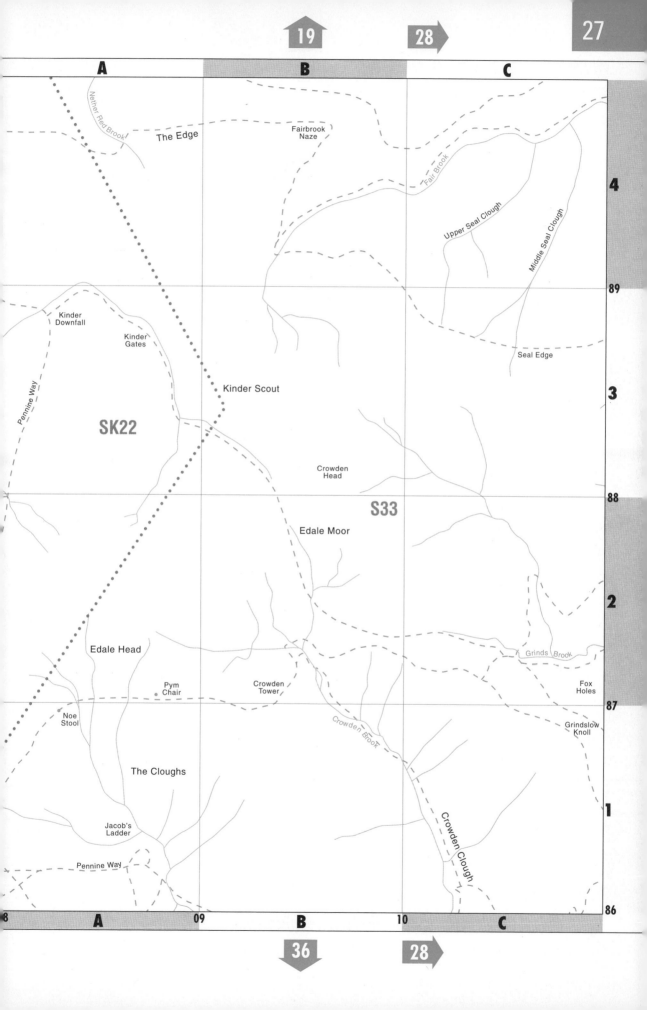

A   B   C

Nether Red Brook

The Edge

Fairbrook Naze

Fair Brook

Upper Seal Clough

Middle Seal Clough

4

Kinder Downfall

Kinder Gates

Seal Edge

89

Pennine Way

Kinder Scout

3

SK22

Crowden Head

88

S33

Edale Moor

2

Grinds Brook

Edale Head

Fox Holes

Pym Chair

Crowden Tower

87

Noe Stool

Grindslow Knoll

Crowden Brook

The Cloughs

1

Jacob's Ladder

Crowden Clough

Pennine Way

86

27
20

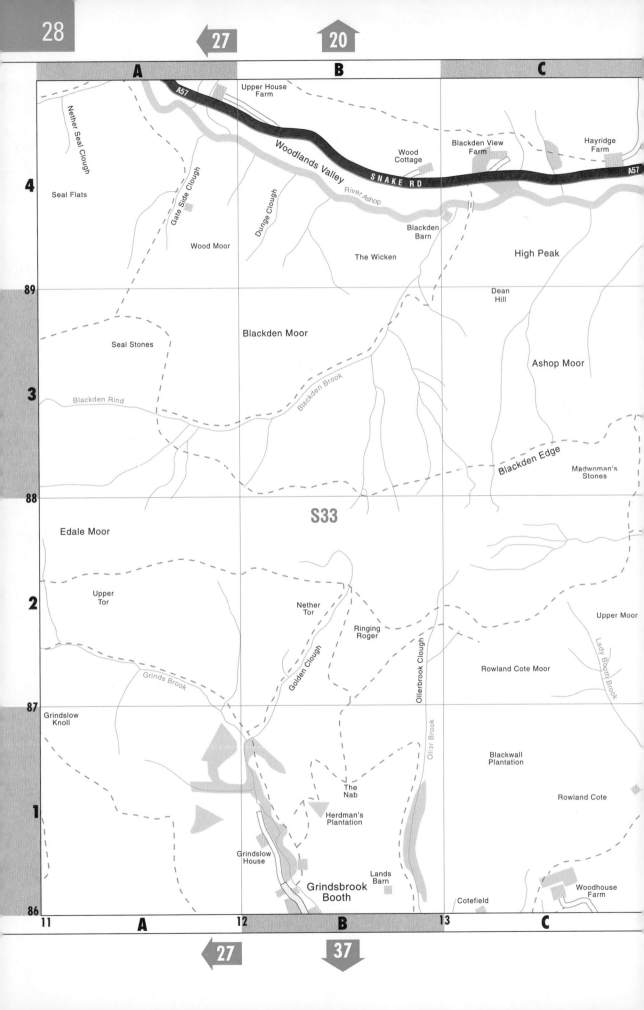

A

B

C

Upper House Farm

Nether Seal Clough

A57

Woodlands Valley

Wood Cottage

Blackden View Farm

Hayridge Farm

A57

SNAKE RD

Seal Flats

Gate Side Clough

Dunge Clough

River Ashop

Blackden Barn

High Peak

4

Wood Moor

The Wicken

89

Dean Hill

Seal Stones

Blackden Moor

Ashop Moor

Blackden Rind

Blackden Brook

3

Blackden Edge

Madwoman's Stones

88

S33

Edale Moor

2

Upper Tor

Nether Tor

Ringing Roger

Upper Moor

Golden Clough

Ollerbrook Clough

Rowland Cote Moor

Lady Booth Brook

Grinds Brook

87

Grindslow Knoll

Ollar Brook

Blackwall Plantation

1

The Nab

Rowland Cote

Herdman's Plantation

Grindslow House

Lands Barn

Woodhouse Farm

86

Grindsbrook Booth

Cotefield

27
37

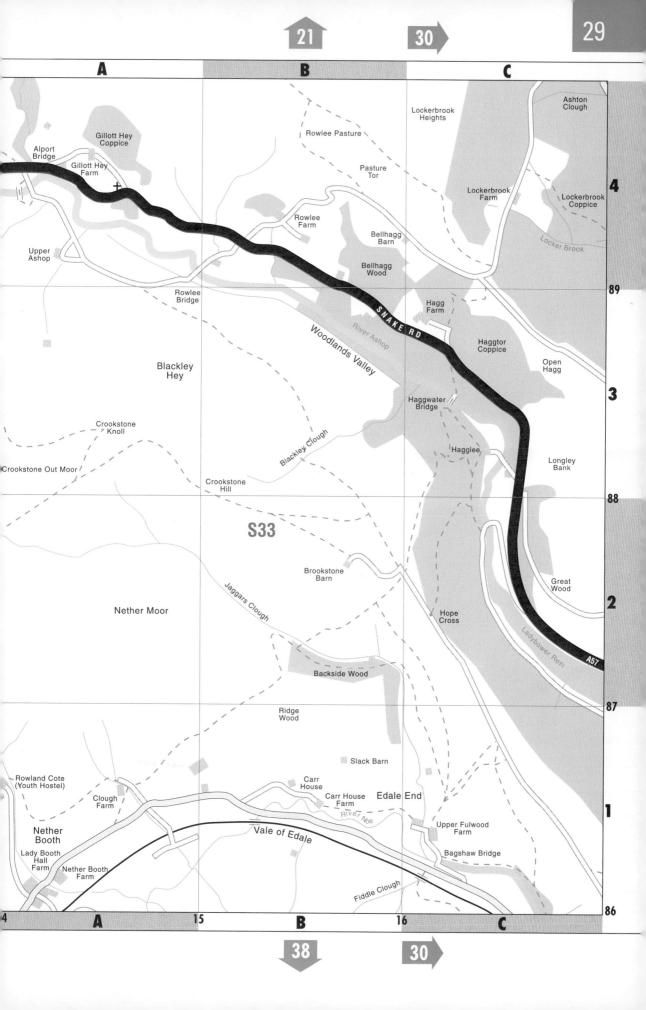

A   B   C

4

Ashton
Clough

Lockerbrook
Heights

Rowlee Pasture

Alport
Bridge

Gillott Hey
Coppice

Pasture
Tor

Lockerbrook
Farm

Lockerbrook
Coppice

Gillott Hey
Farm

Locker Brook

Upper
Ashop

Rowlee
Farm

Bellhagg
Barn

89

Rowlee
Bridge

Bellhagg
Wood

SNAKE RD

Hagg
Farm

River Ashop

Woodlands Valley

Haggtor
Coppice

Open
Hagg

Blackley
Hey

3

Haggwater
Bridge

Crookstone
Knoll

Blackley Clough

Hagglee

Longley
Bank

Crookstone Out Moor

Crookstone
Hill

88

S33

Brookstone
Barn

Nether Moor

Jaggars Clough

Great
Wood

Hope
Cross

2

Ladybower Rest

A57

Backside Wood

87

Ridge
Wood

Slack Barn

Rowland Cote
(Youth Hostel)

Carr
House

Clough
Farm

Carr House
Farm

Edale End

1

Upper Fulwood
Farm

Nether
Booth

River Noe

Vale of Edale

Bagshaw Bridge

Lady Booth
Hall Farm

Nether Booth
Farm

Fiddle Clough

86

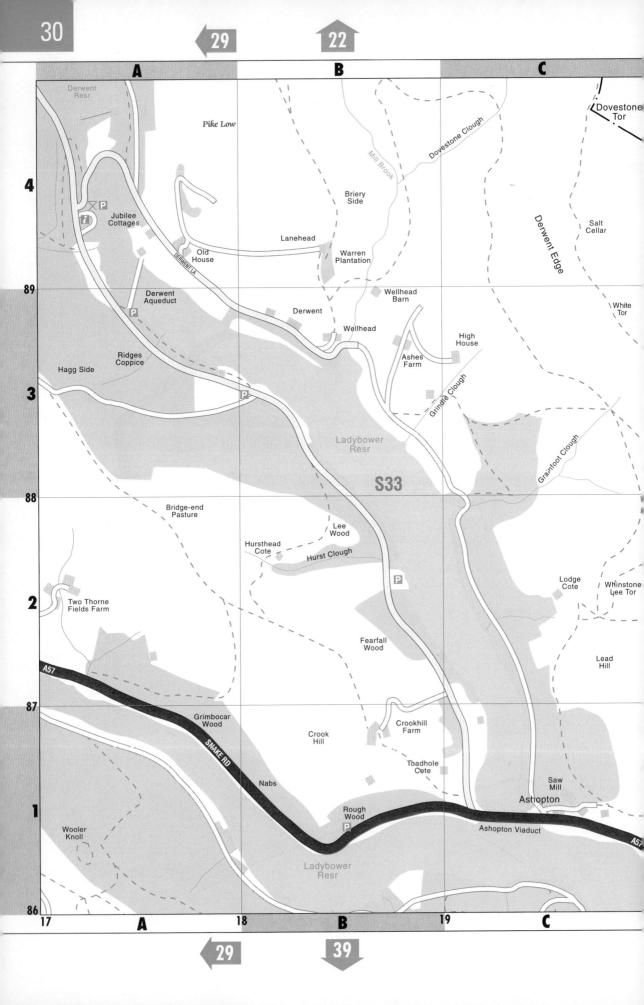

A   B   C

Derwent
Resr

Pike Low

Mill Brook

Dovestone Clough

Dovestone
Tor

Salt
Cellar

4

Briery
Side

Derwent Edge

Lanehead

P

Jubilee
Cottages

i

Old
House

Warren
Plantation

White
Tor

DERWENT LA.

89

Derwent
Aqueduct

P

Derwent

Wellhead
Barn

Wellhead

High
House

Ashes
Farm

Ridges
Coppice

Grindle Clough

Hagg Side

3

P

Grainfoot Clough

Ladybower
Resr

S33

88

Bridge-end
Pasture

Lee
Wood

Hurst Clough

Hursthead
Cote

Lodge
Cote

Whinstone
Lee Tor

2

Two Thorne
Fields Farm

P

Fearfall
Wood

Lead
Hill

A57

87

Grimbocar
Wood

Crookhill
Farm

SNAKE RD

Crook
Hill

Saw
Mill

Nabs

Toadhole
Cote

Ashopton

1

Wooler
Knoll

Rough
Wood

P

Ashopton Viaduct

A57

Ladybower
Resr

86

17   A   18   B   19   C

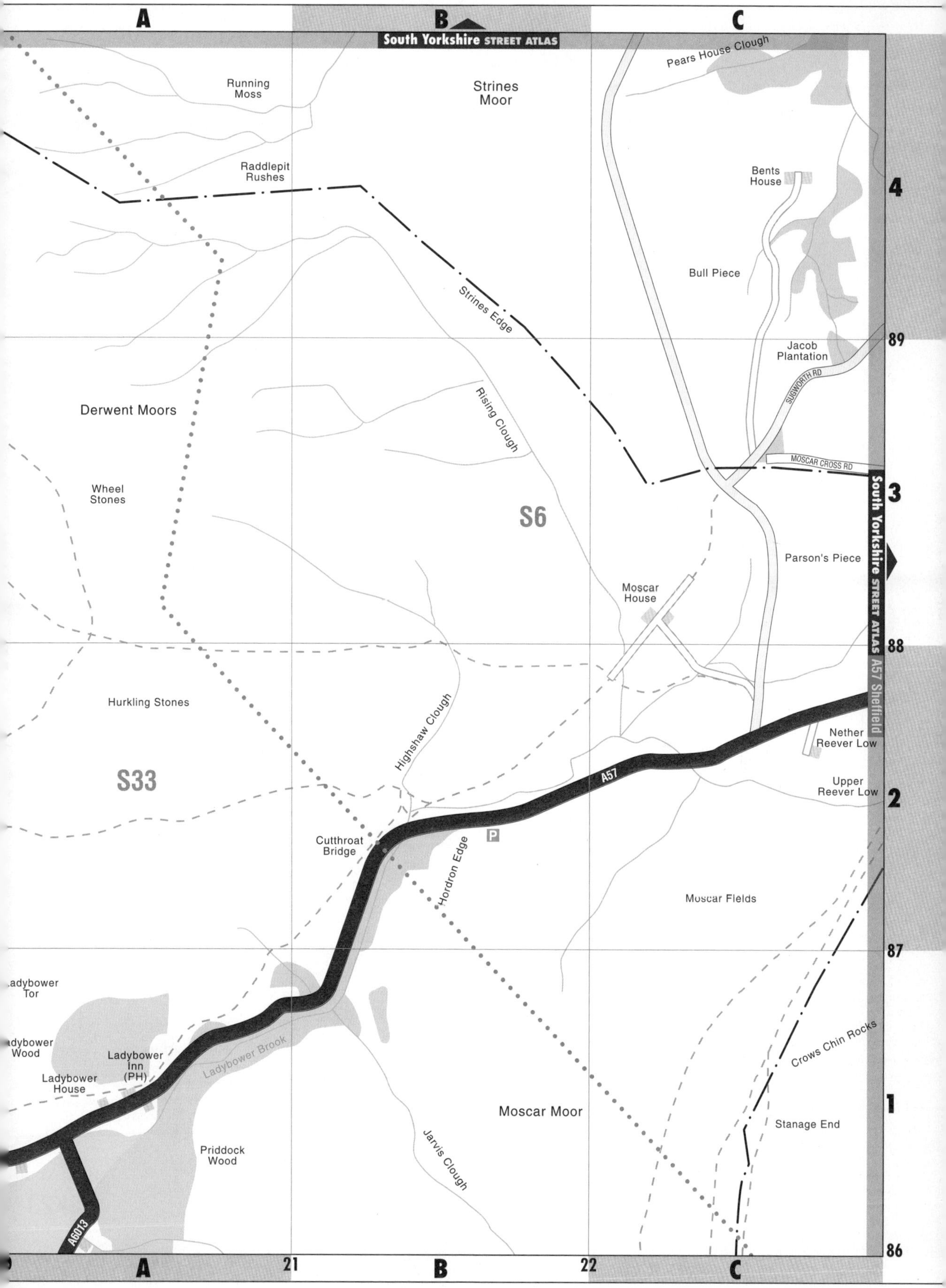

A
B
C
South Yorkshire STREET ATLAS
Pears House Clough
Running Moss
Strines Moor
Raddlepit Rushes
Bents House
4
Bull Piece
Strines Edge
89
Jacob Plantation
SUGWORTH RD
Derwent Moors
Rising Clough
MOSCAR CROSS RD
Wheel Stones
S6
3
Parson's Piece
Moscar House
South Yorkshire STREET ATLAS
A57 Sheffield
88
Hurkling Stones
Highshaw Clough
Nether Reever Low
S33
A57
Upper Reever Low
2
Cutthroat Bridge
P
Hordron Edge
Moscar Fields
87
Ladybower Tor
Ladybower Wood
Ladybower Inn (PH)
Ladybower Brook
Ladybower House
Crows Chin Rocks
1
Moscar Moor
Stanage End
Priddock Wood
Jarvis Clough
A6013
86
A
21
B
22
C

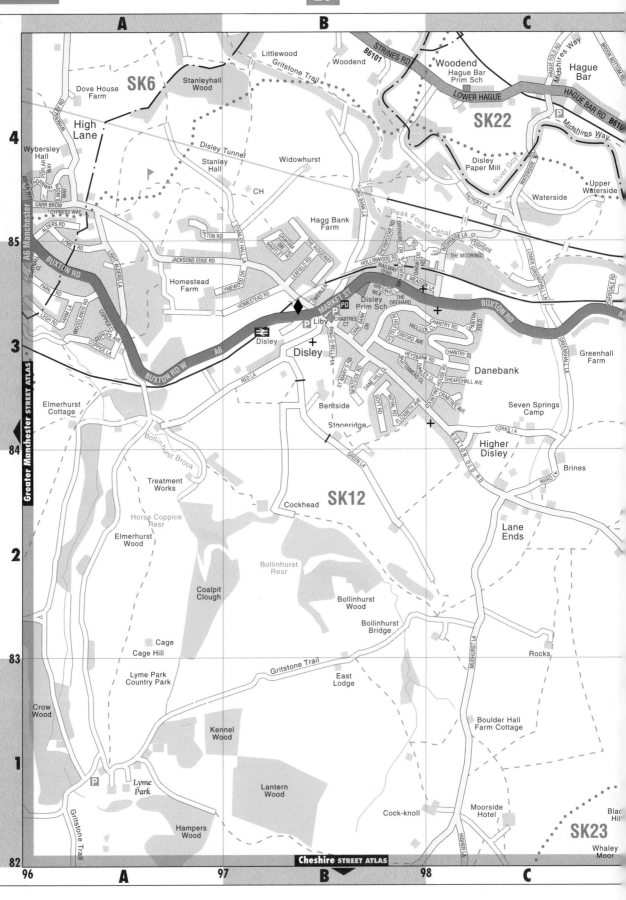

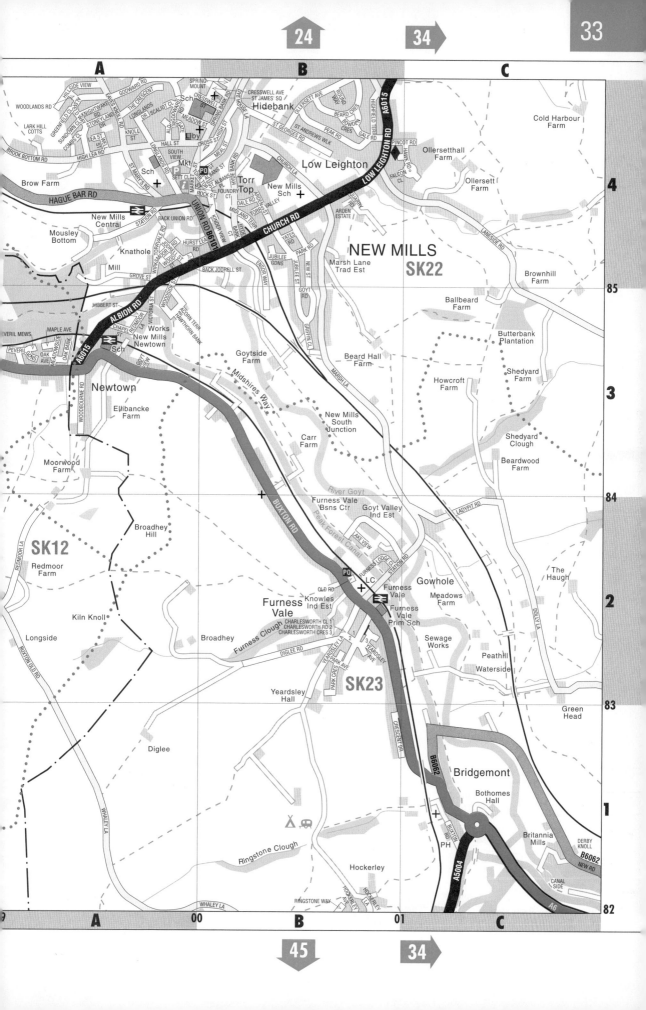

A B C

4

Moor
Lodge

Piece
Farm

Ollersett
SK22

Foxholes Clough

Far
Phoside

Newhouse
Farm

A624

The
Heys

HIGHGATE RD

CHAPEL RD

Higher
Heys
Farm

Peep-o-Day

85

LANESIDE
RD

Higher Hills
Farm

Whiterakes

Red
Mires

Lower
Ashen
Clough

Higher
Ashen
Clough

HAYFIELD RD

Chinley
Head

3

Shedyard
Piece

OVER HILL RD

New
Allotments

MAYNESTONE RD

Monk's
Meadows

Greenacres
Farm

84

Clappersgate

Otter Brook

Hollands

2

Cloughhead

Throstle
Bank

Chinley
Churn

SK23

Cracken
Edge

The
Naze

Mosley
House

Alders
Farm

Laneside
Farm

Hill
Farm

83

Ancoats

Dryclough

Cotebank

Tithe
Barn

Stubbins

Stubbins

LYME PARK

ALDERS LA

Chinley
Houses

DOLLY LA

STUBBINS LA

RUTLAND WAY

Alpha
RD

Hotel

ALDER BROOK

BUXTON RD

B606

1

Brierley
Green

Buxworth

Knowltop

DOLLY
WOOD CL

BRIERLEY
PK

Hollin
Wood

Chinley

STATION RD

CRACKEN CL

MANNERS
CL

PORTLAND
DR

Princes RD

PIKE
VIEW
CL

ALDER
BROOK

ALDERS AVE

STOCKTON DR

Chinley

Leaden
Knowle

White Hall

LOWER LA

DEVONSHIRE
DR

DERWENT DR

BELGRADE AVE

HANTHORN
CL

ASH GR

GRANBY
AVE

B6062

NEW RD

STATION RD

BROOKSIDE

Buxworth
Prim Sch

JANE LA

Works

Black Brook

WHITEHALL
TERR

WHITEHOUGH HEAD LA

Inn

GREEN LA

HARTINGTON DR

HUNTERS
GN

FORGE
TERR

Mill

82

Inn

A6

02 A 03 B 04 C

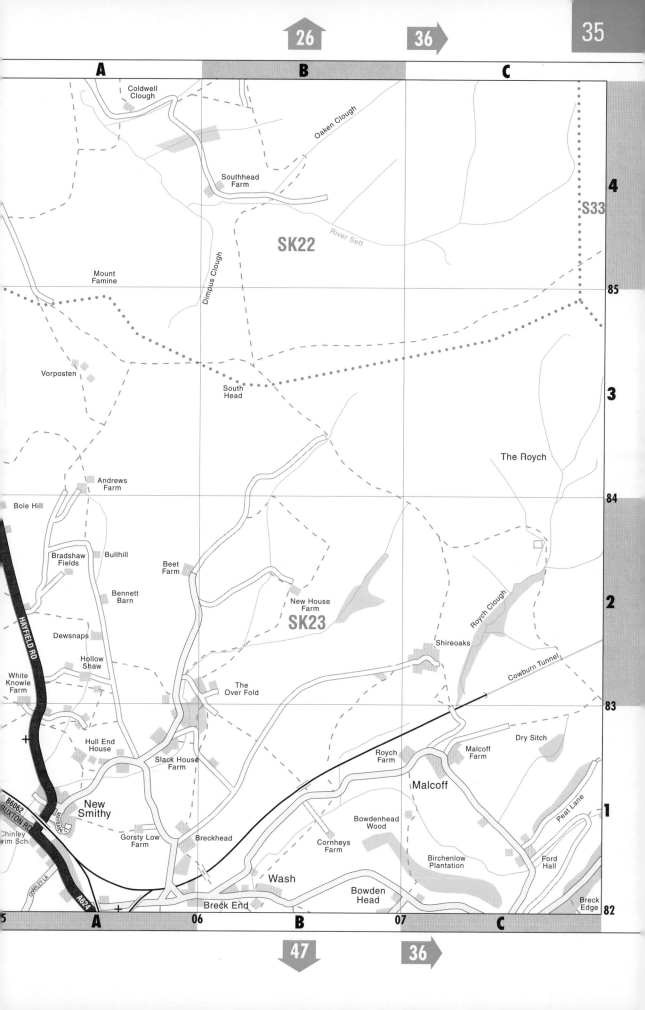

A
B
C

Coldwell Clough
Oaken Clough
Southhead Farm
River Sett
4
S33
SK22
Dimpus Clough
Mount Famine
85
Vorposten
South Head
3
The Roych
Andrews Farm
Bole Hill
84
Bradshaw Fields
Bullhill
Beet Farm
New House Farm
Roych Clough
2
Bennett Barn
SK23
Dewsnaps
Shireoaks
Hollow Shaw
Cowburn Tunnel
White Knowle Farm
The Over Fold
83
HAYFIELD RD
Dry Sitch
Hull End House
Roych Farm
Malcoff Farm
Slack House Farm
Malcoff
B6062
BUXTON RD
New Smithy
MAYBANK
Bowdenhead Wood
Peat Lane
1
Chinley Prim Sch
Gorsty Low Farm
Breckhead
Cornheys Farm
Birchenlow Plantation
Ford Hall
CHARLEY LA
A624
Wash
Bowden Head
Breck Edge
Breck End
82

A
06
B
07
C

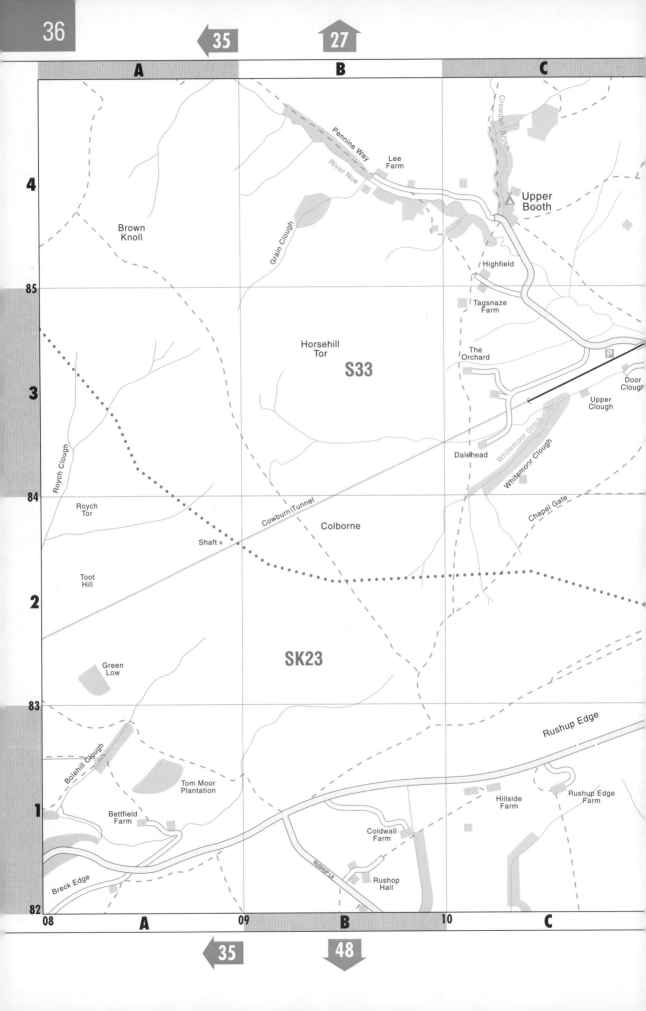

A B C

Crowden Brook

Pennine Way

River Noe

4

Brown
Knoll

Grain Clough

Lee
Farm

Upper
Booth

Highfield

85

Tagsnaze
Farm

Horsehill
Tor

S33

The
Orchard

3

P

Door
Clough

Roych Clough

Upper
Clough

Whitemoor Stitch

Dalehead

Whitemoor Clough

84

Roych
Tor

Cowburn Tunnel

Colborne

Chapel Gate

Shaft

Toot
Hill

2

SK23

Green
Low

83

Rushup Edge

Bolehill Clough

Tom Moor
Plantation

Hillside
Farm

Rushup Edge
Farm

1

Bettfield
Farm

Coldwall
Farm

Breck Edge

RUSHUP LA

Rushop
Hall

82

08 A 09 B 10 C

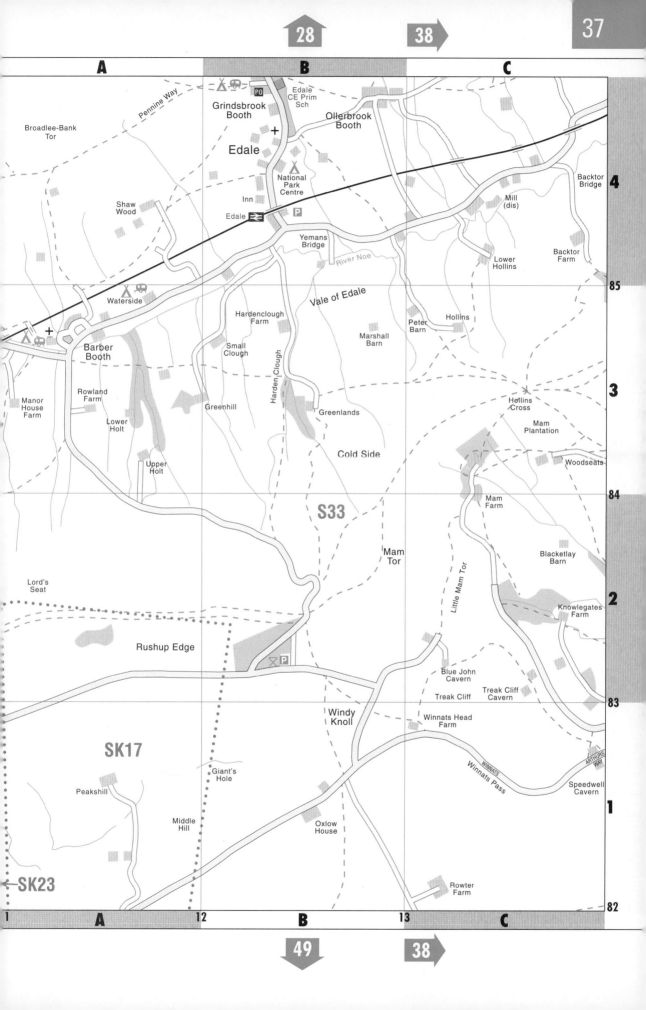

A
B
C

Pennine Way

Broadlee-Bank Tor

Grindsbrook Booth

Edale CE Prim Sch

Ollerbrook Booth

Edale

National Park Centre

Backtor Bridge

4

Shaw Wood

Inn

Mill (dis)

Edale

Lower Hollins

Backtor Farm

Yemans Bridge

River Noe

85

Waterside

Vale of Edale

Peter Barn

Hollins

Hardenclough Farm

Marshall Barn

Barber Booth

Small Clough

Harden Clough

Hollins Cross

3

Rowland Farm

Greenhill

Greenlands

Mam Plantation

Manor House Farm

Lower Holt

Cold Side

Woodseats

Upper Holt

84

S33

Mam Farm

Mam Tor

Blacketlay Barn

Lord's Seat

Little Mam Tor

Knowlegates Farm

2

Rushup Edge

Blue John Cavern

Treak Cliff Cavern

83

Treak Cliff

SK17

Windy Knoll

Winnats Head Farm

Winnats Pass

ARTHURS WAY

Speedwell Cavern

Giant's Hole

Peakshill

Middle Hill

Oxlow House

1

SK23

Rowter Farm

82

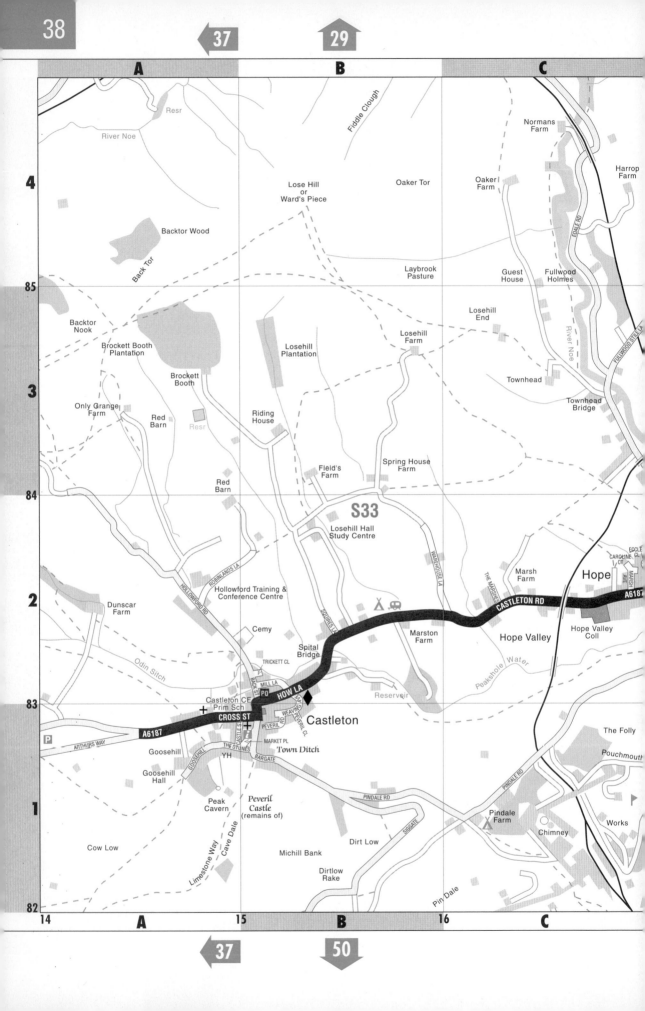

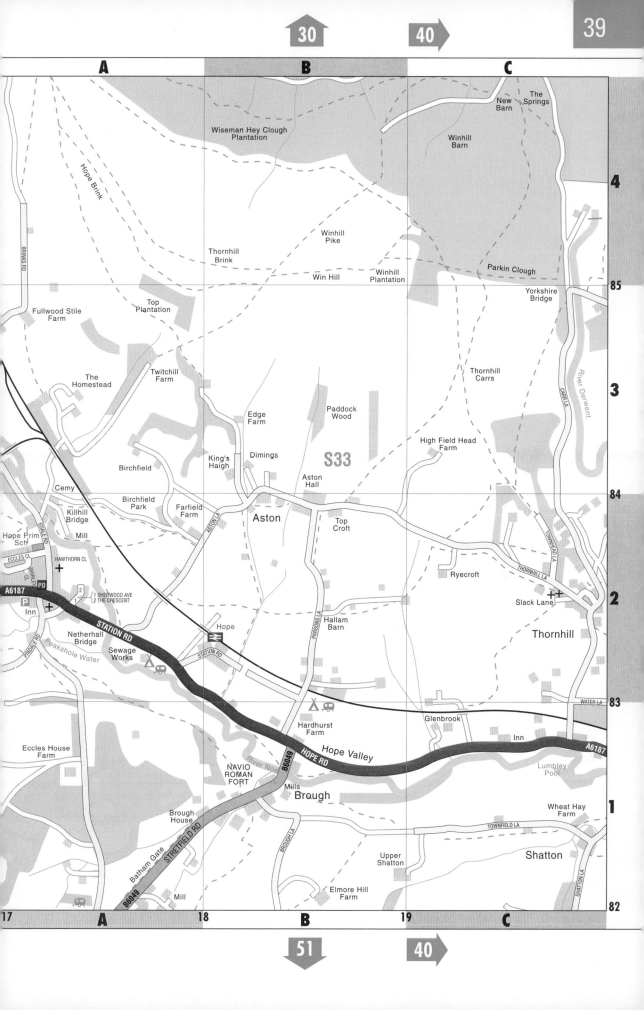

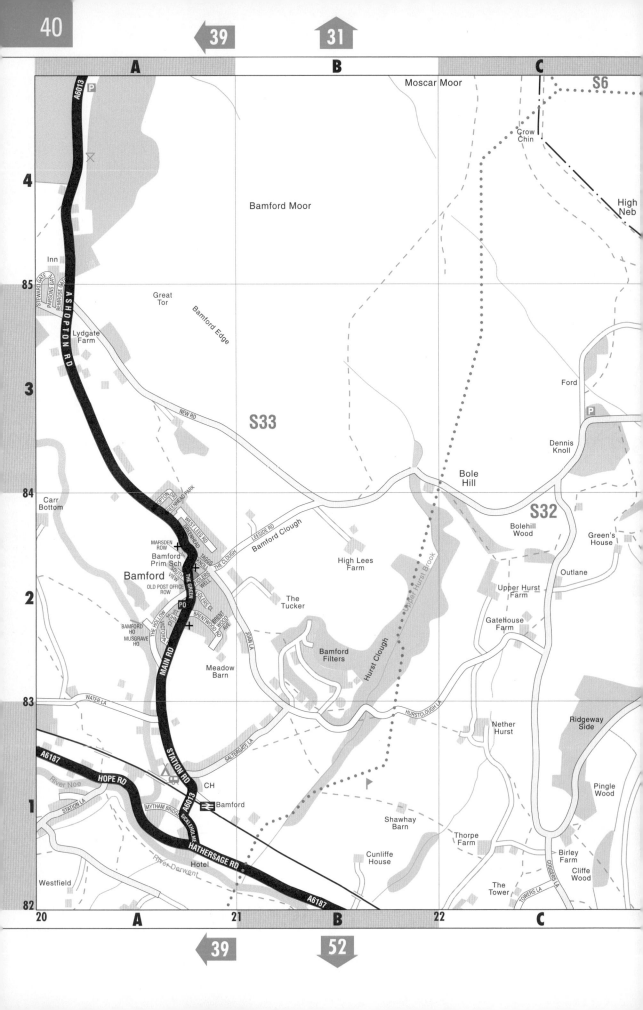

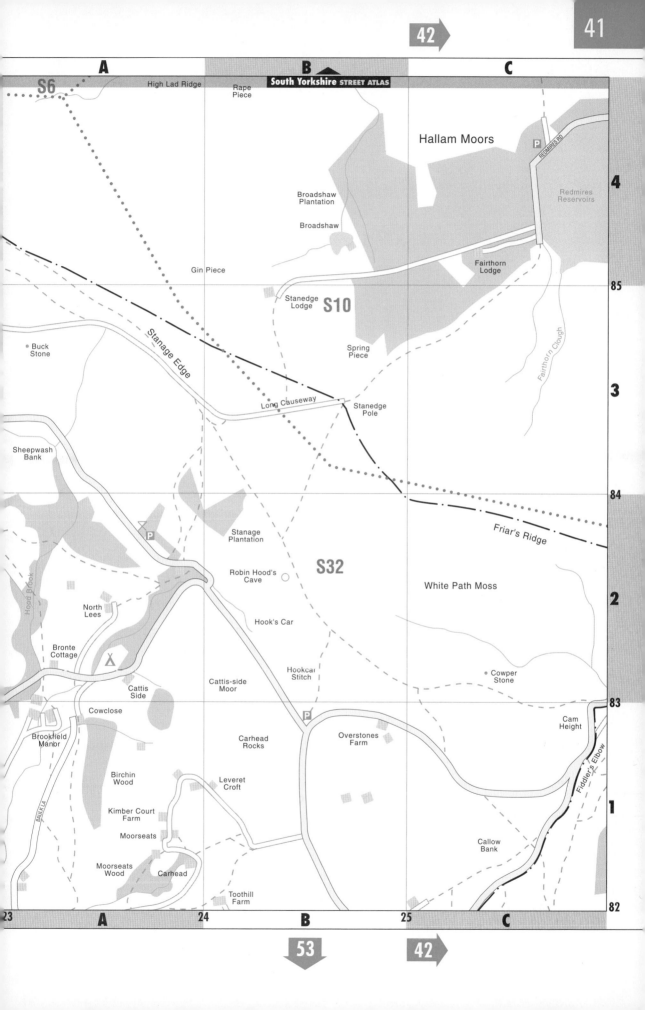

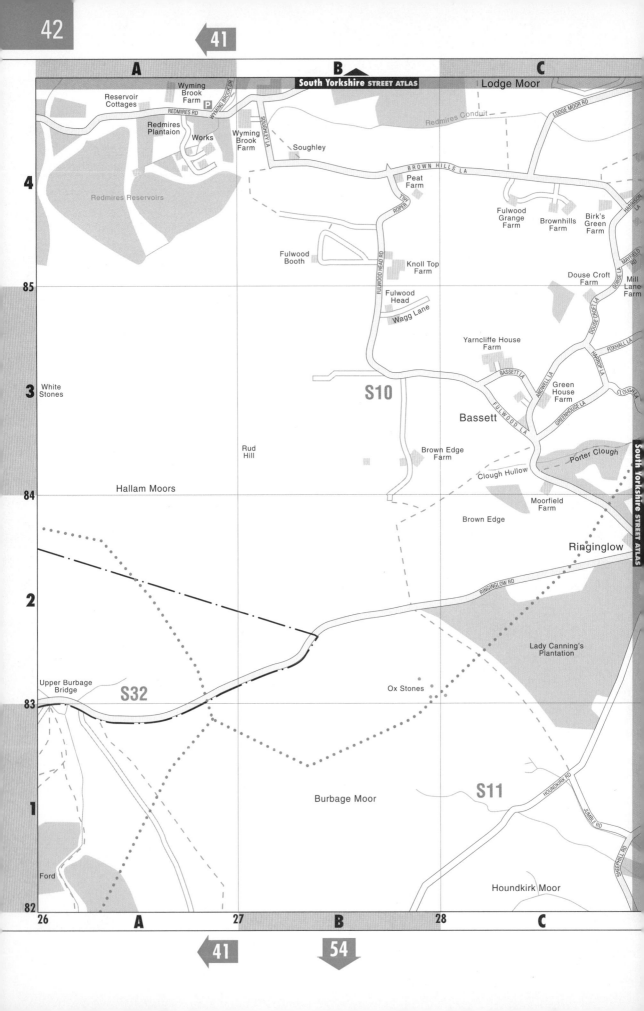

A B C

Lodge Moor

Reservoir Cottages

Wyming Brook Farm

REDMIRES RD

Redmires Plantaion

Works

Wyming Brook Farm

SOUGHLEY LA

Soughley

Redmires Conduit

LODGE MOOR RD

BROWN HILLS LA

Peat Farm

Fulwood Grange Farm

Brownhills Farm

Birk's Green Farm

HARRISON LA

4

Redmires Reservoirs

Fulwood Booth

FULWOOD HEAD RD

ROPER

Knoll Top Farm

Douse Croft Farm

MAYFIELD RD

Mill Lane Farm

85

Fulwood Head

Wagg Lane

GORSE LA

DOUSE CROFT LA

Yarncliffe House Farm

FOXHALL LA

HARROP LA

3

White Stones

Rud Hill

S10

BASSETT LA

ANDWELL A

Green House Farm

CLOUGH LA

Bassett

FULWOOD LA

GREENHOUSE LA

Brown Edge Farm

Porter Clough

Hallam Moors

Clough Hullow

Moorfield Farm

84

Brown Edge

Ringinglow

RINGINGLOW RD

2

Lady Canning's Plantation

Upper Burbage Bridge

S32

Ox Stones

83

HOUNDKIRK RD

S11

JUMBLE RD

1

Burbage Moor

SHEEPHILL RD

Ford

Houndkirk Moor

82

26 A 27 B 28 C

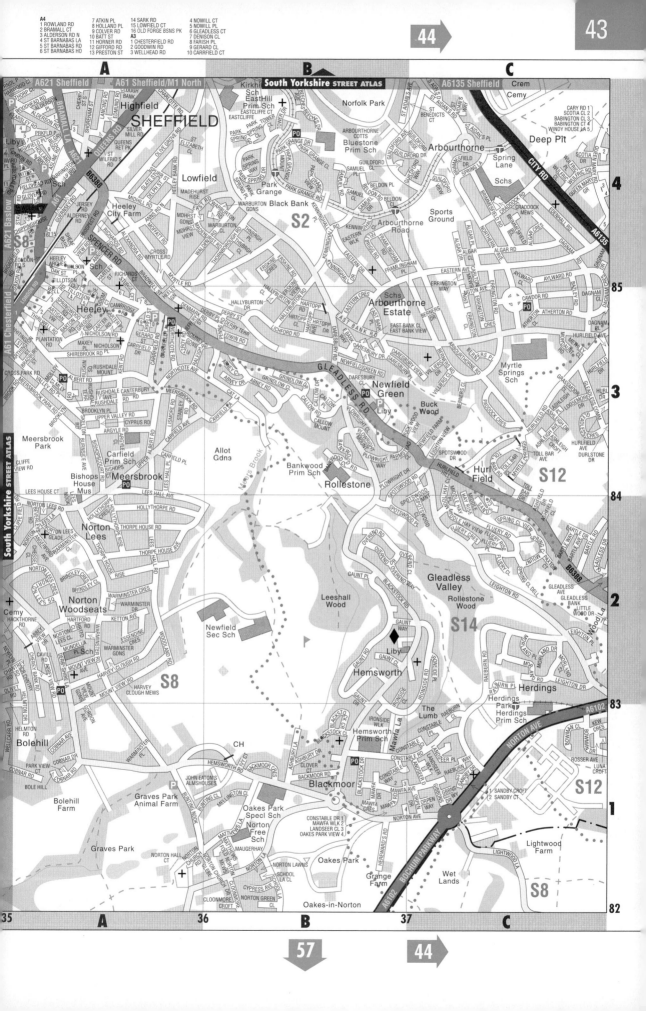

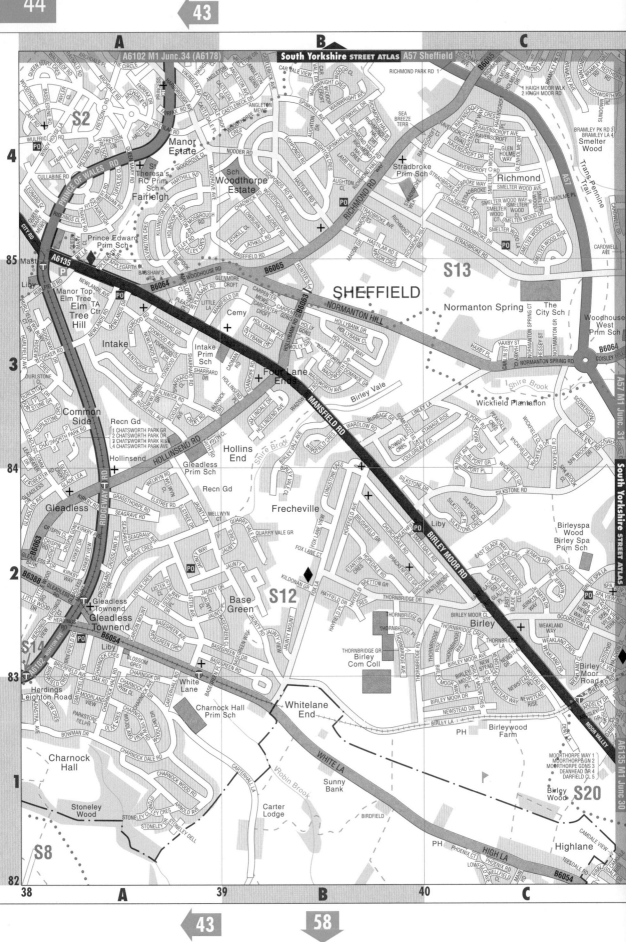

SHEFFIELD

S2

Manor Estate

Woodthorpe Estate

Richmond

Smelter Wood

S13

Normanton Spring

Elm Tree Hill

Intake

Four Lane Ends

Birley Vale

Wickfield Plantation

Common Side

Hollins End

Frecheville

Gleadless

S14

Base Green

S12

Birley

Gleadless Townend

White Lane

Charnock Hall Prim Sch

Whitelane End

Birleywood Farm

Birley Moor Road

Charnock Hall

Stoneley Wood

Sunny Bank

Carter Lodge

Birley Wood

S20

Highlane

S8

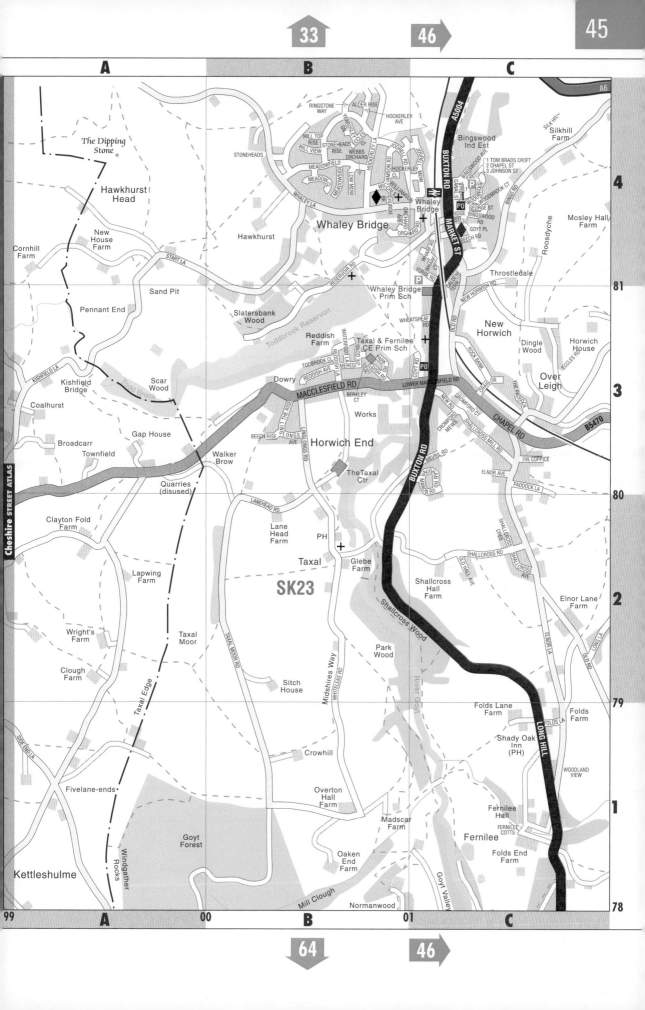

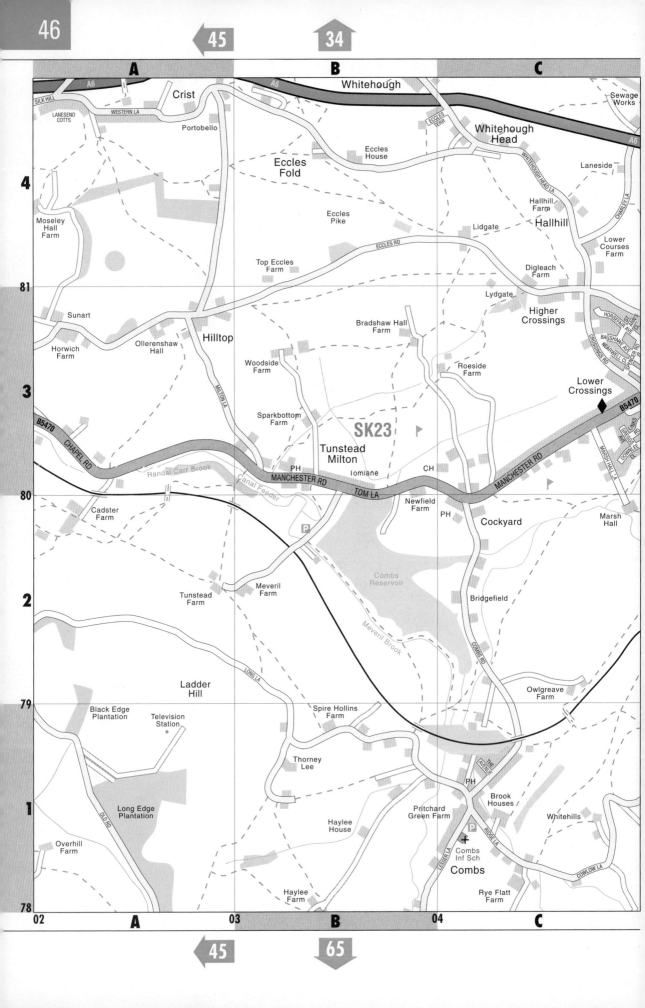

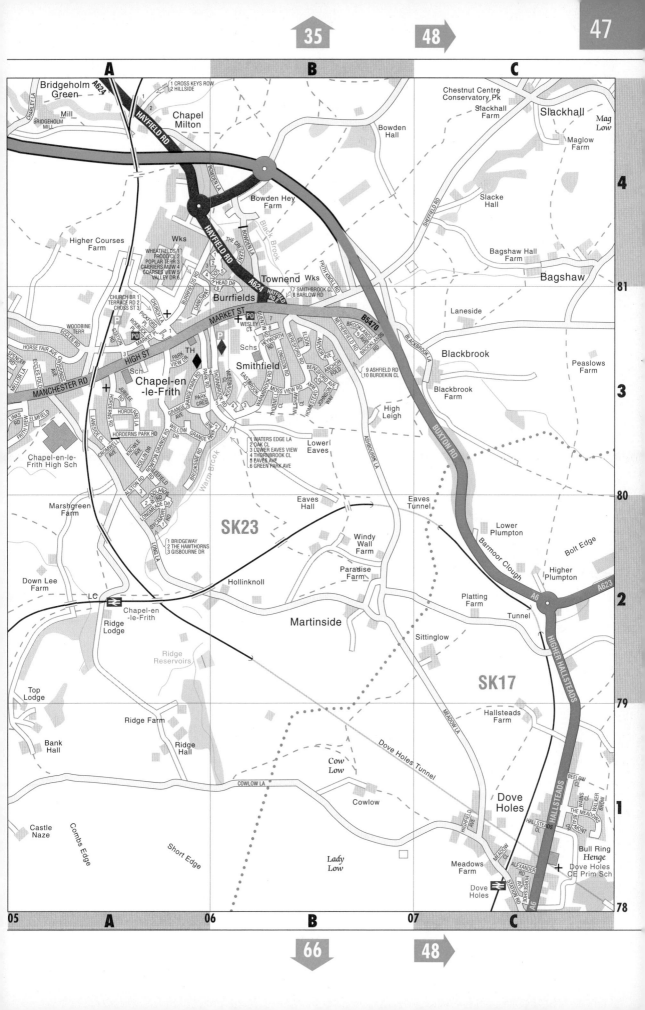

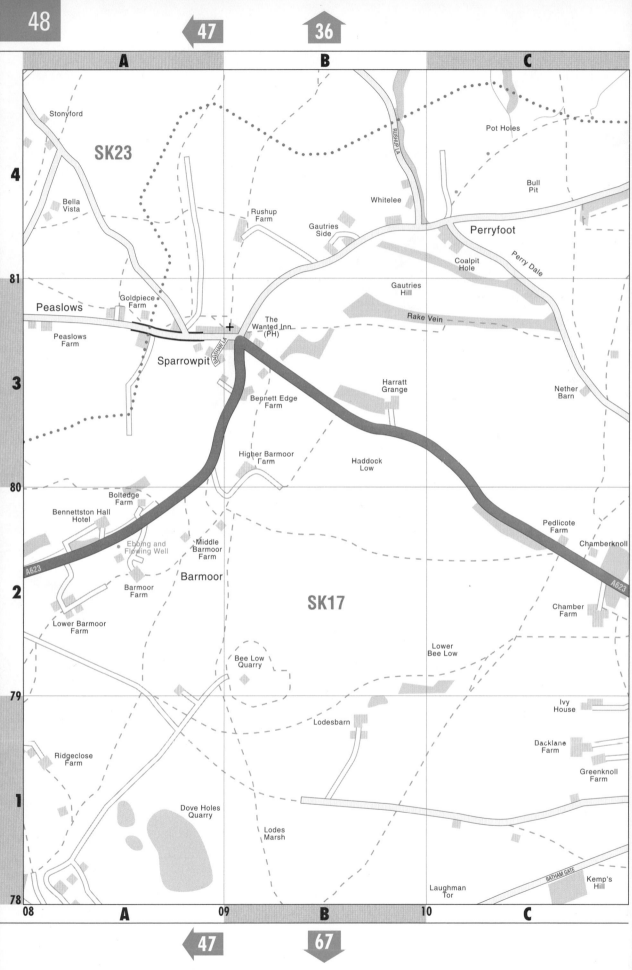

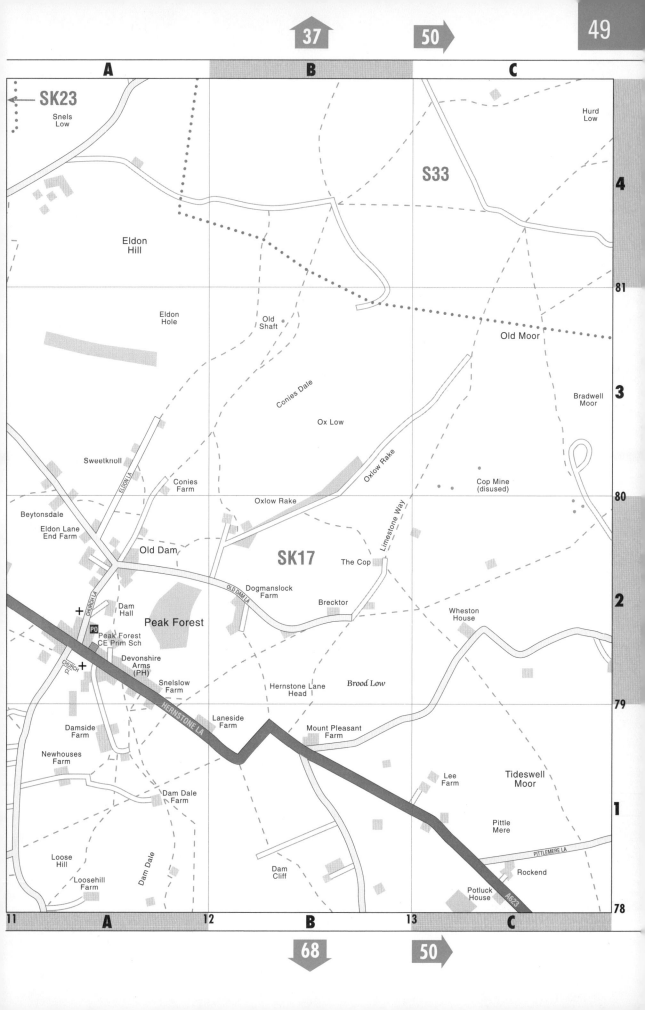

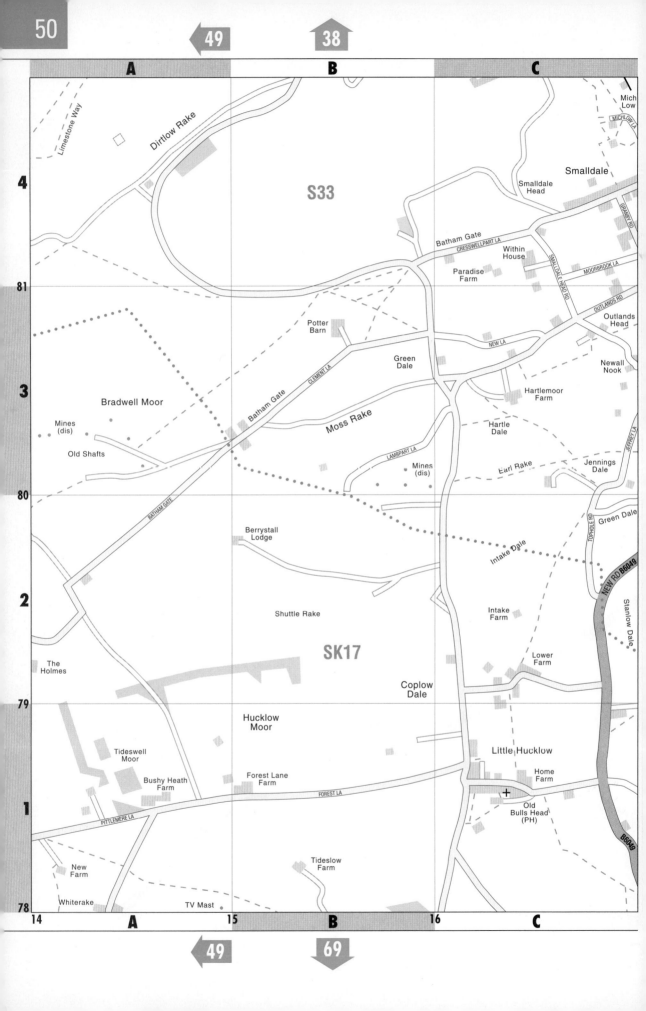

A
B
C

Mich
Low

Limestone Way

Dirtlow Rake

MICHLOW LA

Smalldale

4

Smalldale
Head

S33

Batham Gate
CRESSWELLPART LA

GRANBY RD

Within
House

SMALLDALE HEAD RD

MOORBROOK LA

Paradise
Farm

81

OUTLANDS RD

Potter
Barn

Outlands
Head

NEW LA

Green
Dale

Newall
Nook

3

Bradwell Moor

Batham Gate

CLEMENT LA

Hartlemoor
Farm

JEFFREY LA

Mines
(dis)

Moss Rake

Hartle
Dale

Old Shafts

LAMBPART LA

Mines
(dis)

Earl Rake

Jennings
Dale

80

BATHAM GATE

TOPHOLE RD

Green Dale

Berrystall
Lodge

Intake Dale

NEW RD B6049

Stanlow Dale

2

Shuttle Rake

Intake
Farm

SK17

Lower
Farm

The
Holmes

Coplow
Dale

79

Hucklow
Moor

Little Hucklow

Tideswell
Moor

Home
Farm

Bushy Heath
Farm

Forest Lane
Farm

1

FOREST LA

Old
Bulls Head
(PH)

PITTLEMERE LA

B6049

New
Farm

Tideslow
Farm

78

Whiterake

TV Mast

14
A
15
B
16
C

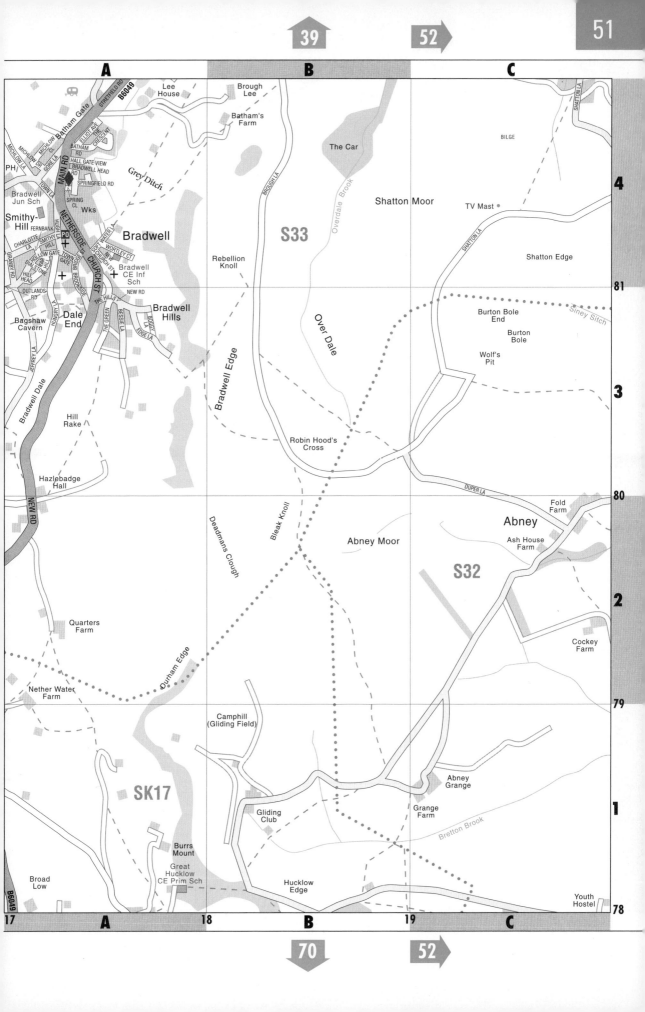

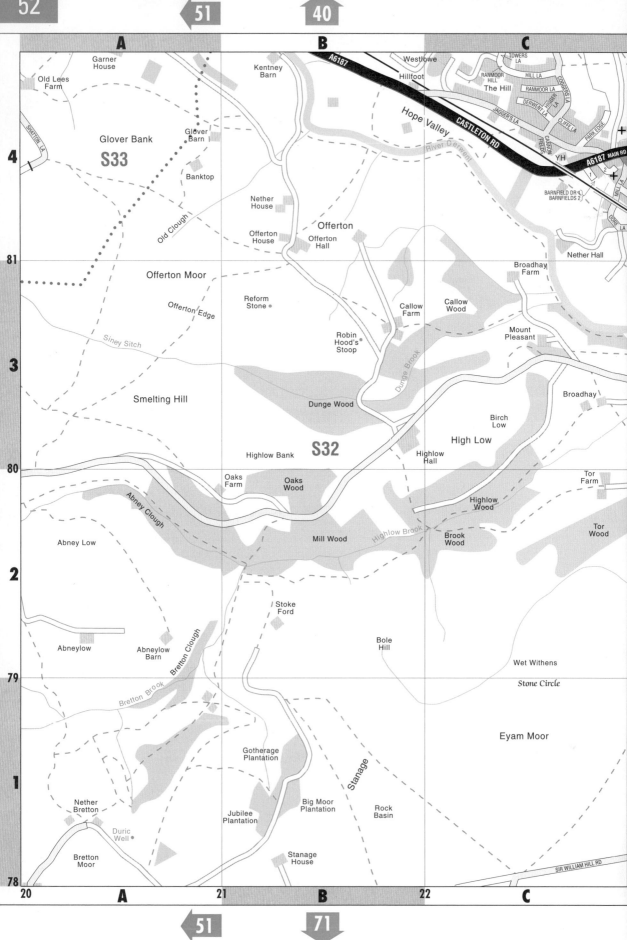

A **B** **C**

4

Old Lees Farm

Garner House

Kentney Barn

Westlowe

Hillfoot

TOWERS LA

HILL LA

RANMOOR HILL

The Hill   RANMOOR LA

HILL LA

JAGGER'S LA

DERWENT LA

LUGGER LA

CLIFFE LA

PARK EDGE

A6187

SHATTON LA

Glover Bank

S33

Glover Barn

Banktop

A6187 MAIN RD

Hope Valley CASTLETON RD

River Derwent

YH

BARNFIELD DR

BARNFIELDS 2

DORE LA

MILL LA

Old Clough

Nether House

Offerton House

Offerton

Offerton Hall

Nether Hall

81

Offerton Moor

Reform Stone

Broadhay Farm

Offerton Edge

Callow Farm

Callow Wood

Siney Sitch

Robin Hood's Stoop

Mount Pleasant

3

Smelting Hill

Dunge Wood

Dunge Brook

Birch Low

Broadhay

S32

Highlow Bank

High Low

Highlow Hall

Highlow Wood

Tor Farm

80

Oaks Farm

Oaks Wood

Abney Clough

Mill Wood

Highlow Brook

Brook Wood

Tor Wood

Abney Low

2

Abneylow

Abneylow Barn

Bretton Clough

Stoke Ford

Bole Hill

Wet Withens

79

Bretton Brook

Stone Circle

Gotherage Plantation

Stanage

Eyam Moor

1

Nether Bretton

Jubilee Plantation

Big Moor Plantation

Rock Basin

Duric Well

Bretton Moor

Stanage House

SIR WILLIAM HILL RD

78

20 **A** **21** **B** **22** **C**

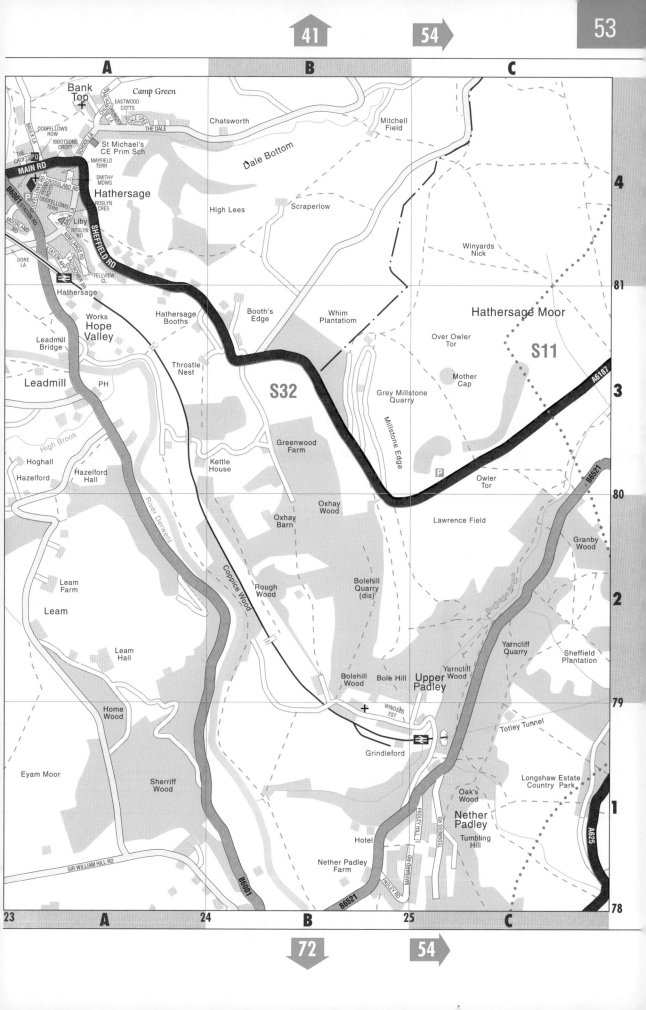

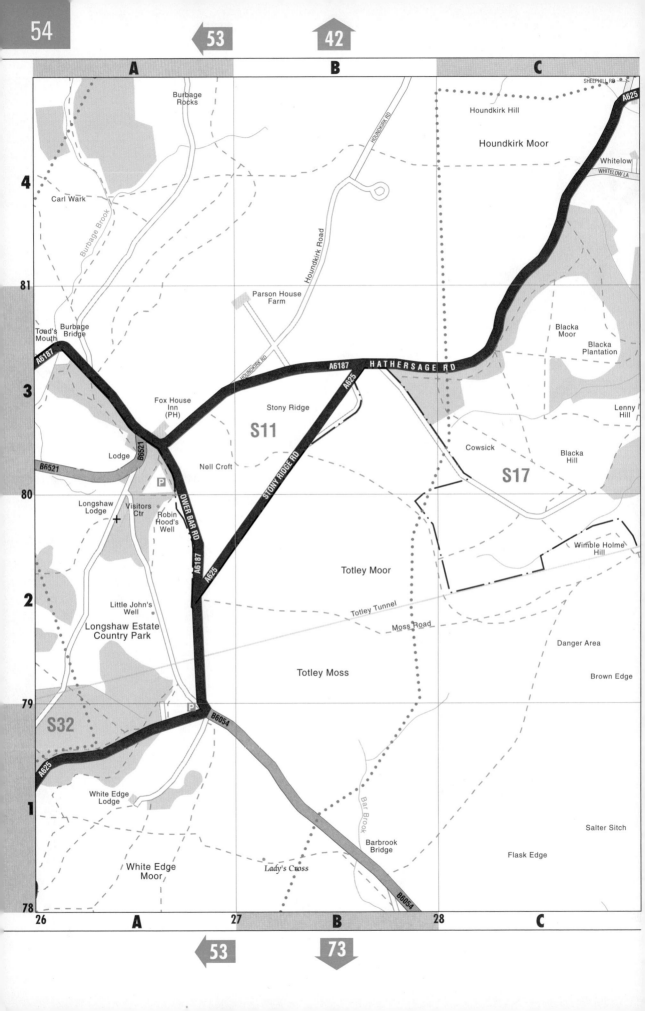

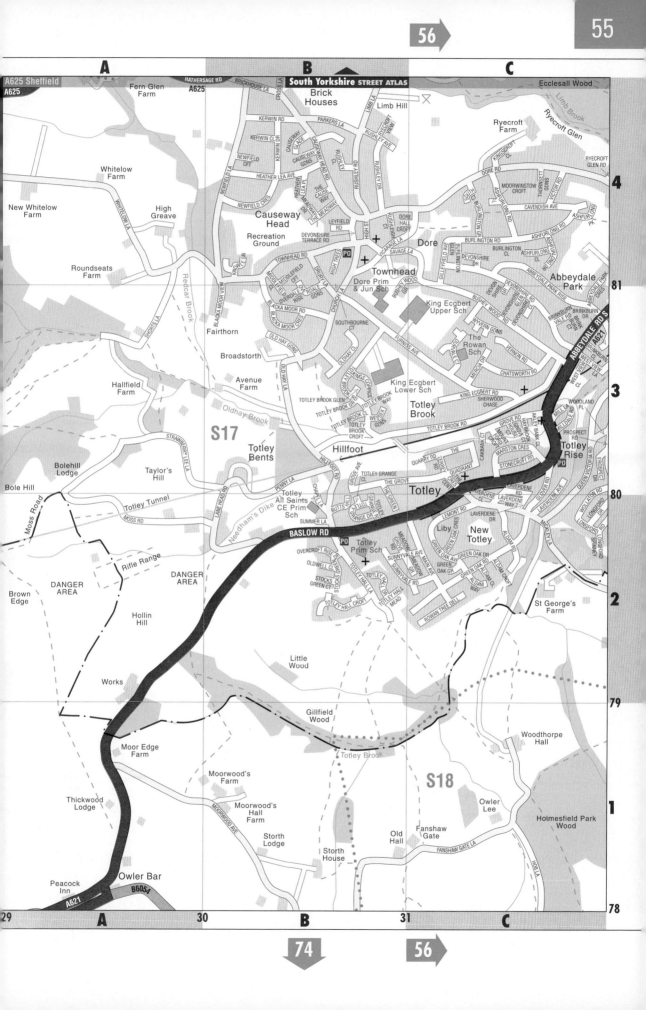

55

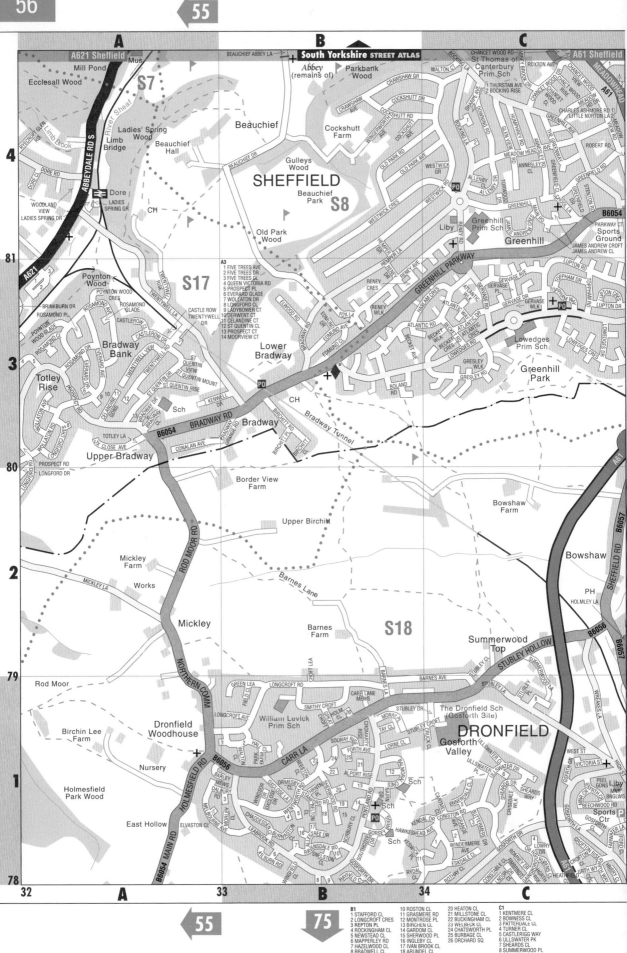

A3
1 FIVE TREES AVE
2 FIVE TREES DR
3 FIVE TREES CL
4 QUEEN VICTORIA RD
5 PROSPECT PL
6 EVERARD GLADE
7 WOLLATON DR
8 LONGFORD CL
9 LADYBOWER CL
10 DERWENT CT
11 CELANDINE CT
12 ST QUENTIN CL
13 PROSPECT CT
14 MOORVIEW CT

B1
1 STAFFORD CL
2 LONGCROFT CRES
3 REPTON PL
4 ROCKINGHAM CL
5 NEWSTEAD CL
6 MAPPERLEY RD
7 HAZELWOOD CL
8 BRADWELL CL
9 ASHFORD RD
10 ROSTON CL
11 GRASMERE RD
12 MONTROSE PL
13 BIRCHEN CL
14 GARDOM CL
15 SHERWOOD PL
16 INGLEBY CL
17 IVAN BROOK CL
18 ARUNDEL CL
19 LYNWOOD CL
20 HEATON CL
21 MILLSTONE CL
22 BUCKINGHAM CL
23 WELBECK CL
24 CHATSWORTH CL
25 BURBAGE CL
26 ORCHARD SQ

C1
1 KENTMERE CL
2 BOWNESS CL
3 PATTERDALE CL
4 TURNER CL
5 CASTLERIGG WAY
6 ULLSWATER PK
7 SHEARDS CL
8 SUMMERWOOD PL

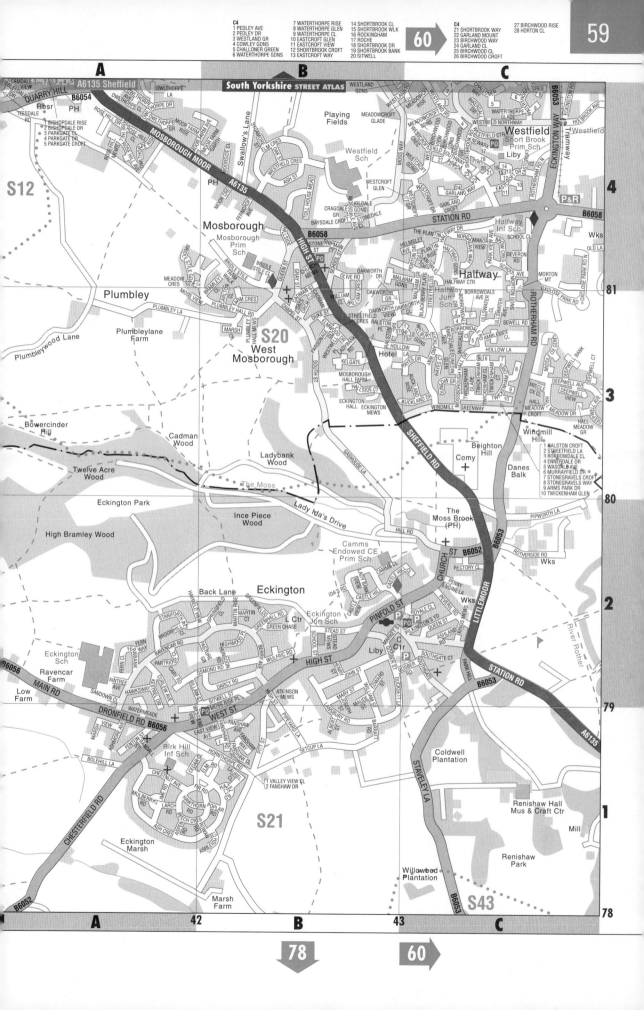

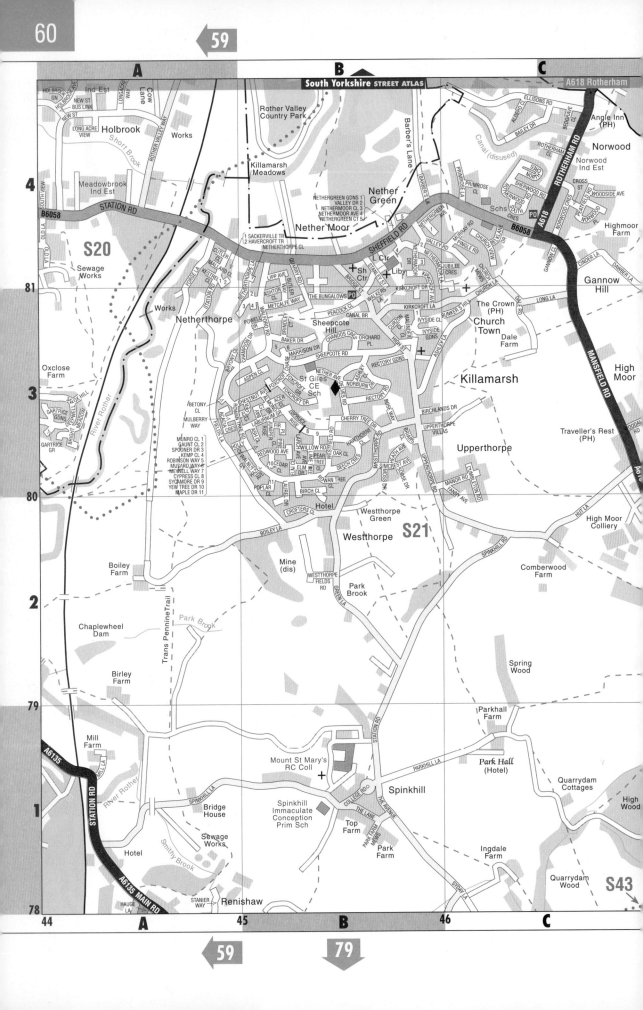

South Yorkshire STREET ATLAS

A618 Rotherham

Holbrook

HOLBROOK
GN
NEW ST
BUS LINK
LONGACRE WAY
ROTHER VALLEY WAY
NEW ST
LONG ACRE
VIEW
Ind Est
Cow Lane
Works

Ellisons Rd
Aldred Cl
Bedgrave Dr
Bailey Dr
Angle Inn (PH)
Rotherham Cl
Norwood
Norwood Ind Est
Sherwood Nor
Cross St
Sherwood Cres
Redfield Rd
Woodside Ave
Highmoor Farm

Rother Valley
Country Park

Barber's Lane

Killamarsh
Meadows

Meadowbrook
Ind Est

SOUTH VIEW

4

B6058
STATION RD

Nethergreen Gdns 1
Valley Dr 2
Nethermoor Cl 3
Nethermoor Ave 4
Nethergreen Ct 5

**Nether
Green**

Primrose Cl
Primrose Cl
Schs
PO
A618
B6058

OLD LA

S20

Sewage
Works

OLD LA

Nether Moor

1 Sackerville Tr
2 Havercroft Tr
Netherthorpe Cl

Sheffield Rd
L Ctr
Sh Ctr
Liby

Nethergreen Ave
Valley Rd
Pingle Rd
Murray Rd
Church View
Jubilee Cres
Church La

Gannow Cl
Cinder La
Dwber La
**Gannow
Hill**

81

Works

Netherthorpe

Forge La
Mallard Cl
Cutler La
Nestfield Cl
Lipp Ave
Ashton La
Metcalfe Way
Walford Rd
Powell Rd
Butler Way
Delves Rd

The Bungalows
PO
Peacock Cl
Canal Br
Kirkcroft Dr
Kirkcroft La
Bunker's Hill
Ivyside Cl
Ivyside Gdns
Astle La
The Crown (PH)
**Church
Town**
Dale Farm

Long La

Dwber La

3

Oxclose
Farm

RIVER ROTHER

GARTRICE GDNS
FOX HILL
DEEPWELL
BRIGHT MEADOW
GARTRICE GR

Bat Cul Cl
Champion Dr
Aspen Cl
Baker Dr
Marrison Dr
Chandos Cres
Orchard Pl
Sheepcote Rd
Rectory Gdns

**Sheepcote
Hill**

Nether Ave
Norburn Dr
Rectory Rd
Rose Way
Birchlands Dr
Upperthorpe
Villas

Killamarsh

High St
Ashley La

Dale Farm

**High
Moor**

Mansfield Rd

Travellers Rest (PH)

Betony Cl
Mulberry Way

Chestnut Cl
Foxcroft Cl
Foxcroft Dr
Alder La
Acacia Cres
Holly Cl
Rowan Tree Dell
Laburnum Gr
Juniper Cl
Ash Cl
Fir Cl
Spruce Rise
Cherry Tree La
Hawthorne Rd
Westthorpe Rd
Keith Ave
Simcrest Ave
Manor Rd
Fanny Ave
Hut La

Munro Cl 1
Gaunt Cl 2
Spooner Dr 3
Kemp Cl 4
Robinson Way 5
Musard Way 6
Mevrell Way 7
Cypress Cl 8
Sycamore Dr 9
Yew Tree Dr 10
Maple Dr 11

Redwood Ave
Willow La
Pear Tree Cl
Oak Cl
Lime Cl
Elm Cl
Deech Cres
Crocus Dr
Tumbleton Rd

Cedar Cl
Poplar
Birch Cl
Rowan Tree
Laurel Dr
Crofters Cl

Upperthorpe

High Moor
Colliery

80

Hotel
Westthorpe
Green

Boiley La
Boiley
Farm

Westthorpe

S21

Spinkhill Rd

Comberwood
Farm

2

Chaplewheel
Dam

Trans Pennine Trail

Park Brook

Mine
(dis)

Westthorpe
Fields Rd

Green La

Park
Brook

Spring
Wood

Birley
Farm

79

Parkhall
Farm

Park Hall (Hotel)

Quarrydam
Cottages

**High
Wood**

Mill Farm

Station Rd

1

A6135
Station Rd

River Rother

Mill La
Spinkhill La
Bridge
House

Mount St Mary's
RC Coll

College Rd

Parkhill La
Spinkhill
The Lane
The Avenue
Park Farm Mews

Sewage
Works

Smithy Brook

Spinkhill
Immaculate
Conception
Prim Sch

Top Farm
Park Farm

Ingdale
Farm

Quarrydam
Wood

S43

Hotel

A6135 MAIN RD

HAUGE
LA

STANIER
WAY

Renishaw

Stoat La

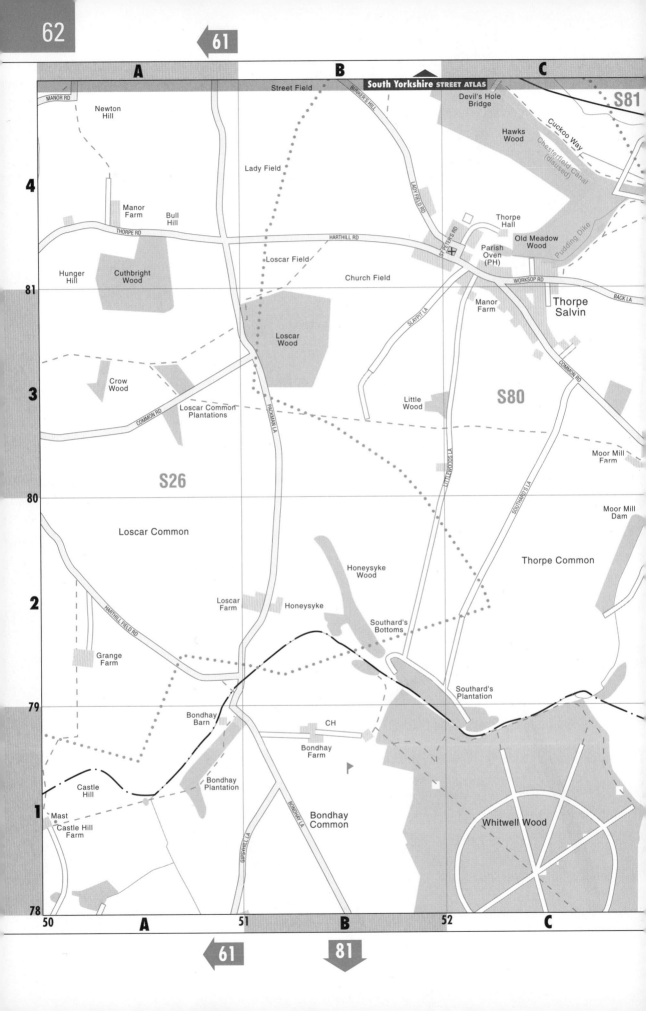

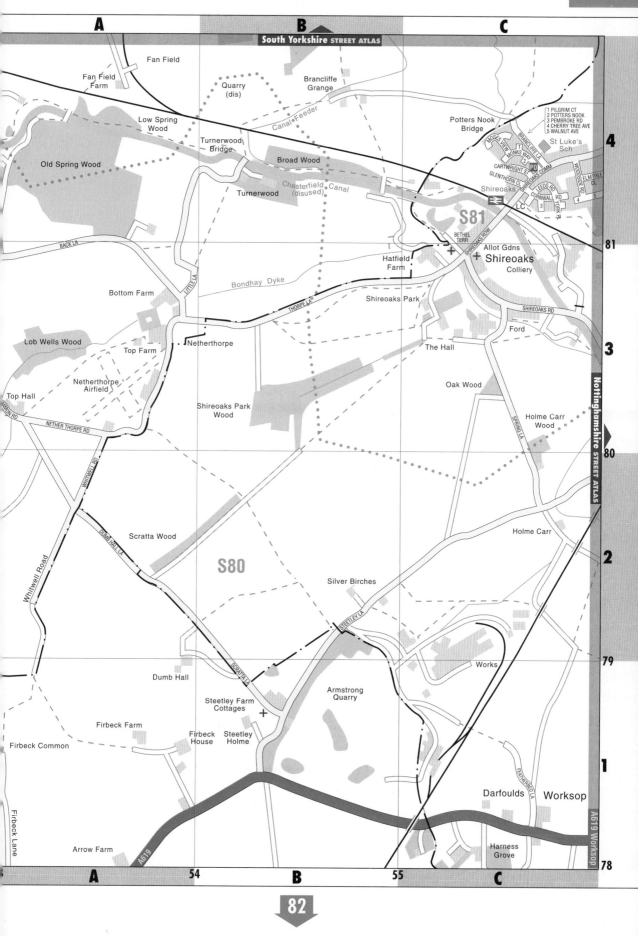

Fan Field

Fan Field Farm

Quarry (dis)

Brancliffe Grange

Canal Feeder

Low Spring Wood

Potters Nook Bridge

1 PILGRIM CT
2 POTTERS NOOK
3 PEMBROKE RD
4 CHERRY TREE AVE
5 WALNUT AVE

St Luke's Sch

Turnerwood Bridge

Broad Wood

Old Spring Wood

MONKS VIEW
MONKS WAY
PO
BRANCLIFFE LA
SHIREOAKS COMM
WOODSIDE RD
ELMTREE CL

Turnerwood

Chesterfield Canal (disused)

CARTWRIGHT ST
GLENTHORN CL
LEEDS RD
CORNWALL RD
YORK PL

Shireoaks

S81

LC

BACK LA

BETHEL TERR

Hatfield Farm

Allot Gdns

Shireoaks Colliery

LITTLE LA

Bottom Farm

Bondhay Dyke

THORPE LA

Shireoaks Park

SHIREOAKS RD

Shireoaks Rd

Ford

Lob Wells Wood

Top Farm

Netherthorpe

The Hall

Netherthorpe Airfield

Oak Wood

Top Hall

Shireoaks Park Wood

Holme Carr Wood

FITTON RD

NETHER THORPE RD

WHITWELL RD

SPRING LA

80

DUME HALL LA

Scratta Wood

Holme Carr

Whitwell Road

S80

Silver Birches

STEETLEY LA

79

SCRATTA LA

Dumb Hall

Works

Steetley Farm Cottages

Armstrong Quarry

Firbeck Farm

Firbeck House

Steetley Holme

Firbeck Common

FEATHERBED LA

Firbeck Lane

Darfoulds

Worksop

Arrow Farm

A619

Harness Grove

A619 Worksop

78

82

Nottinghamshire STREET ATLAS

A   B   C

Browtop Farm

Oldfield

Wks

River Goyt

A5004

LONG HILL

A5004

4

Hodgel Brook

Ladbitch Wood

Hoo Moor

SK23

Goyt Valley

Fernilee Reservoir

77

Goyt Forest

Midshires Way

Pymchair Farm

P

Pym Chair

EMBRIDGE CSWY

Calfhay Wood

3

Oldgate Nick

Jep Clough

THE STREET

Cheshire STREET ATLAS

76

Cats Tor

Withinleach Moor

SK10

The Street Forest Walks

Bunsal Cob

Sailing Club

Foxlow Edge

Errwood Reservoir

SK17

2

The Tors

75

Errwood Hall

Errwood Forest Walks

GOYT'S LA

Shooter's Clough

1

SK11

River Goyt

Stake Side

74

99   A   00   B   01   C

A B C

Pye Greave Farm

Lower Hay Lee

Wythen Lache

SK23

Greave House

Allston Lee Farm

Bag House Farm

Allston Lee

Hazelhurst Farm

RIDGE LA

Wainstones

Combshead Farm

Broadlee Farm

Hanging Rock

Combs Edge

White Hall Centre North Lodge

OLD RD

LONG HILL

Round the Bend

Midshires Way

Rake End

Combs Moss

Hogshaw Brook

SK17

OLD LONGHILL RD

Mon

GOYT'S LA

P

Brookfield

Moss House Farm

Cuckoo Tors

Longhill Farm

Cold Springs Farm

Wildmoorstone Brook

Watford Moor

Coldspring Plantation

Wild Moor

MANCHESTER RD A5004

Gadley House

Nithen End Farm

The Beet

Watford Wood

Watford Farm

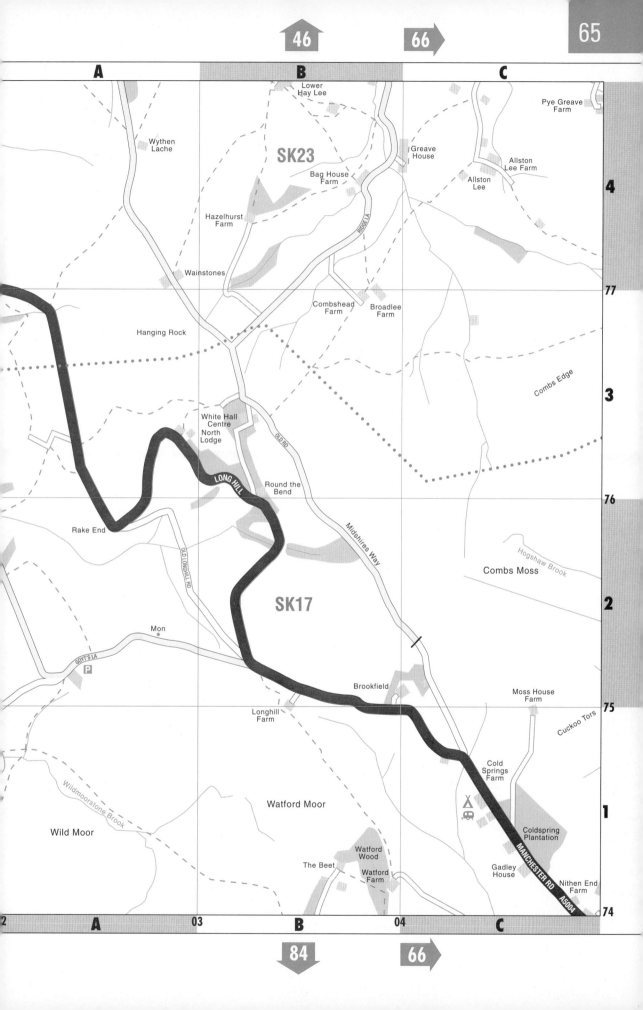

A   B   C

4

SK23

Pyegreave Brook

Hob Tor

Resrs

Ashpiece Farm

Buxton Rd

A6

PO
PH

1 STATION RD
1,2 HALLSTEADS

PH

LONGRIDGE LA

DALE RD

P

Bibbington

77

Combs Moss

Black Edge

3

Blackedge Resr

Blackedge Farm

Field Farm

Tom Thorn Farm

BATHAM GATE

76

SK17

Thorn Head Farm

Batham Gate

Tomthorn

WATERSWALLOWS LA

Hogshaw Brook

2

Television Station

Brownedge Plantation

Resr

Turner Lodge

High Peak Nurseries

Lightwood Resr

Light Wood

Frome Lodge

Brookhouse Farm

Brook House

Breezemount Farm

Waterswallows Green

75

Works

The Barms Farm

WATERSWALLOWS RD

DAISYMERE LA

Hogshaw Brook

1

LIGHTWOOD RD

NURSERY DR

BROWN EDGE RD

LADYCROFT

Fairfield Common

Nunsfield Farm

Corbar Hill

John Duncan Sch

CORBAR RD

BIRCH CL

CHESTNUT CL

ASPEN CL

WILLIAMSON AVE

LANSDOWNE RD

NUNSFIELD RD

GLENMOOR RD

BARMS WAY

ST PETER'S RD

FAIRFIELD NORTH RD

A6

CROSS ST

CHERRY TREE DR

MONTPELIER PL

ASHWOOD RD

WATERSWALLOWS MEWS

DAKIN CT

TOWN END

LESSER LA

Townend Farm

Corbar Woods

CORBAR WOODS LA

SYCAMORE CL

LASCELLES RD

St Anne's RC Prim Sch

FAIRFIELD RD

DAKIN

CH

74

05   A   06   B   07   C

A
B
C

Sewage Works

Dove Holes Quarry

Lodes La

BATHAM GATE

Smalldale

Heath Farm

SMALLDALE COTTS

Works

Middle Hill

Gorsey Nook

SMALLDALE RD

Dale Rd

Doveholes Dale

PH

SMALL KNOWLE END

77

Higher Bibbington

BATHAM GATE RD

CHURCH AVE

Peak Dale

SCHOOL RD

MEADOW AVE

PO

HIGHFIELDS

Peak Dale Prim Sch

Withered Low

Wormhill Moor

3

Ppg Sta

Thornheyes Farm

Upper End

NEW ST

Sewage Works

SK17

Longbridge La

FERNDALE AVE

FERNDALE RD

SPRING BANK

UPPER END RD

Broadlow Farm

76

Buxton Bridge

Bole Hill

2

Great Rocks Lees

Taylor Farm

WATERSWALLOWS LA

WATERSWALLOWS LA

Hardybarn

Tunstead

DAISYMERE LA

Water Swallows

75

Waterswallows Green

GREEN LA

Waterswallows Quarry

Green La

Green La

Great Rocks Tunnel

Greenfairfield Farm

Green Fairfield

1

Daisymere Farm

REDGAP LA

Tunstead Works

4

74

8
A
09
B
10
C

A | B | C

Kempshill Farm

Lower Kempshill Farm

Stone Lea Farm

Dam Dale

A623

4

77

Hay Dale

Dale Head Farm

Dale Head

WATER LA

Bottom Farm

Wheston

3

Sitch House

Hall

The Top Farm

76

Peter Dale

SK17

Limestone Way

Cherryslack

Monksdale House

2

Hargatewall

Hayward Farm

Wind Low

Hargate Hall

75

Hill Top Farm

Wormhill Hill

MONKSDALE LA

Monk's Dale

Old Hall Farm

Wormhill

Nature Reserve

1

✝

Wormhill Hall

74

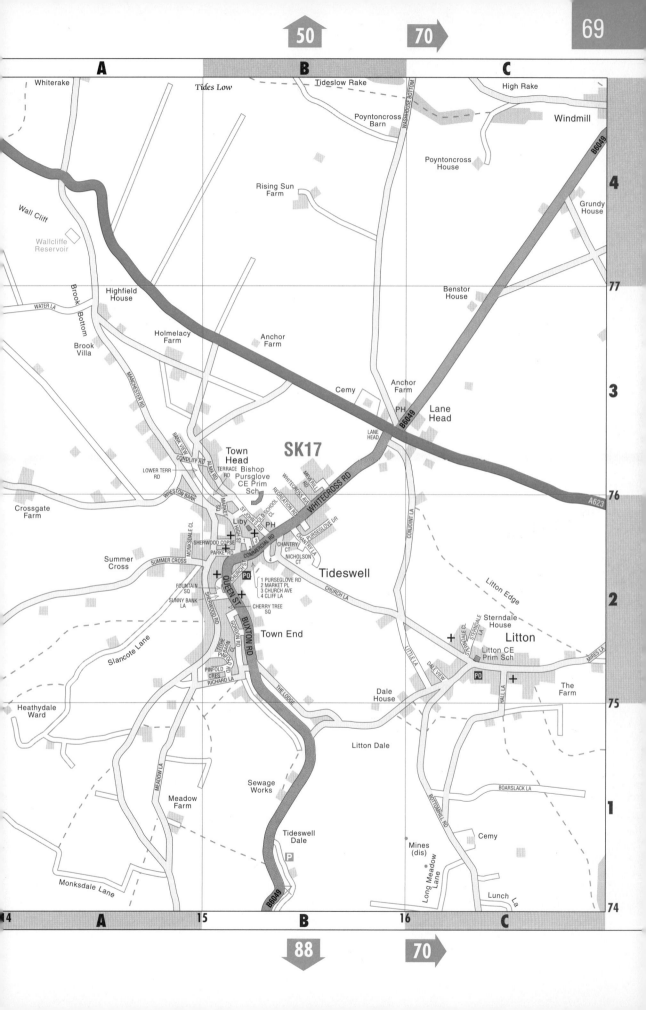

A B C

Whiterake

Tides Low

Tideslow Rake

Poyntoncross Barn

High Rake

Windmill

Poyntoncross House

Rising Sun Farm

4

Wall Cliff

Wallcliffe Reservoir

Grundy House

Highfield House

WATER LA

Brook Bottom

Holmelacy Farm

Anchor Farm

Benstor House

77

Brook Villa

Cemy

Anchor Farm

MANCHESTER RD

PH

Lane Head

3

Crossgate Farm

BANK VIEW

CONDLIFF RD

LOWER TERR RD

WHESTON BANK

Town Head

TERRACE RD

Bishop Pursglove CE Prim Sch

SK17

LANE HEAD

Lane Head

B6049

ALMA RD

MARKET SQ

ST JOHNS RD

OLD SCHOOL CL

PH

Liby

HIGH ST

RECREATION RD

WHITECROSS AVE

IMVERILL RD

WHITECROSS RD

76

A623

Summer Cross

MONKSDALE CL

PARKE RD

SHERWOOD COPSE

SUMMER CROSS

COMMERCIAL RD

PURSGLOVE DR

CHANTRY LA

CHANTRY CT

NICHOLSON CT

Tideswell

CONDUIT LA

Litton Edge

2

FOUNTAIN SQ

SUNNY BANK LA

SHERWOOD RD

QUEEN ST

GORDON RD

BUXTON RD

CHURCH'S RD

P.O

CHERRY TREE SQ

CLIFF LA

1 PURSGLOVE RD
2 MARKET PL
3 CHURCH AVE
4 CLIFF LA

CHURCH LA

Sterndale House

STERNDALE CL

Litton

MIRES LA

Slancote Lane

TITHE BARN RD

PINWELL RD

PINFOLD CRES

RICHARD LA

THE LODGE

Town End

Dale House

DALE VIEW

LITTLE LA

Litton CE Prim Sch

P.O

HALL LA

The Farm

Heathydale Ward

Litton Dale

75

MEADOW LA

Meadow Farm

Sewage Works

BOARSLACK LA

BOTTOMHILL RD

Cemy

1

Monksdale Lane

Tideswell Dale

P

B6049

Mines (dis)

Long Meadow Lane

Lunch La

74

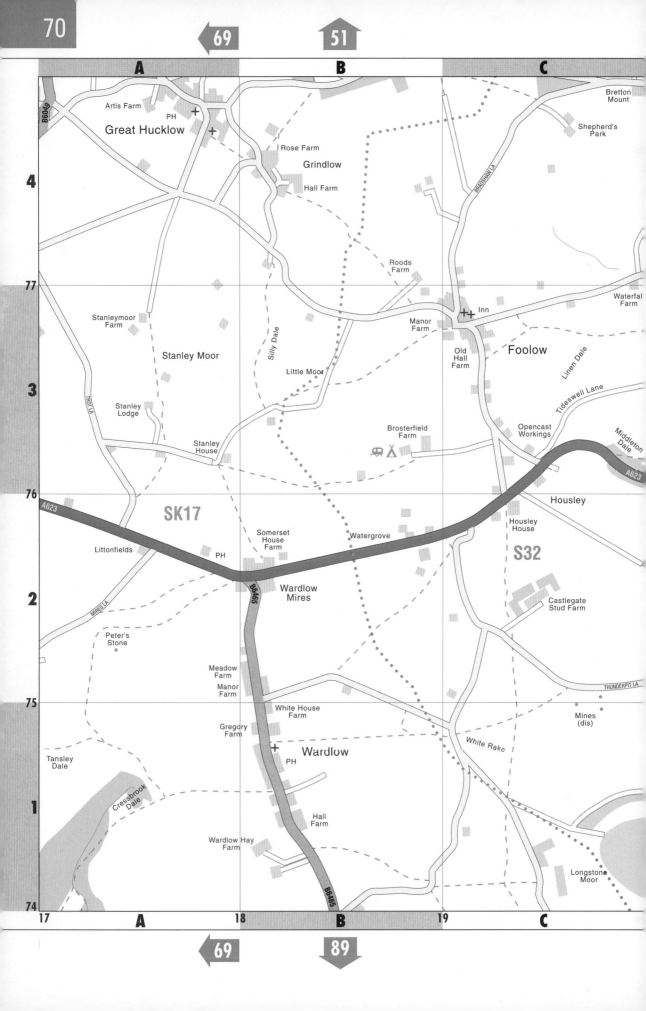

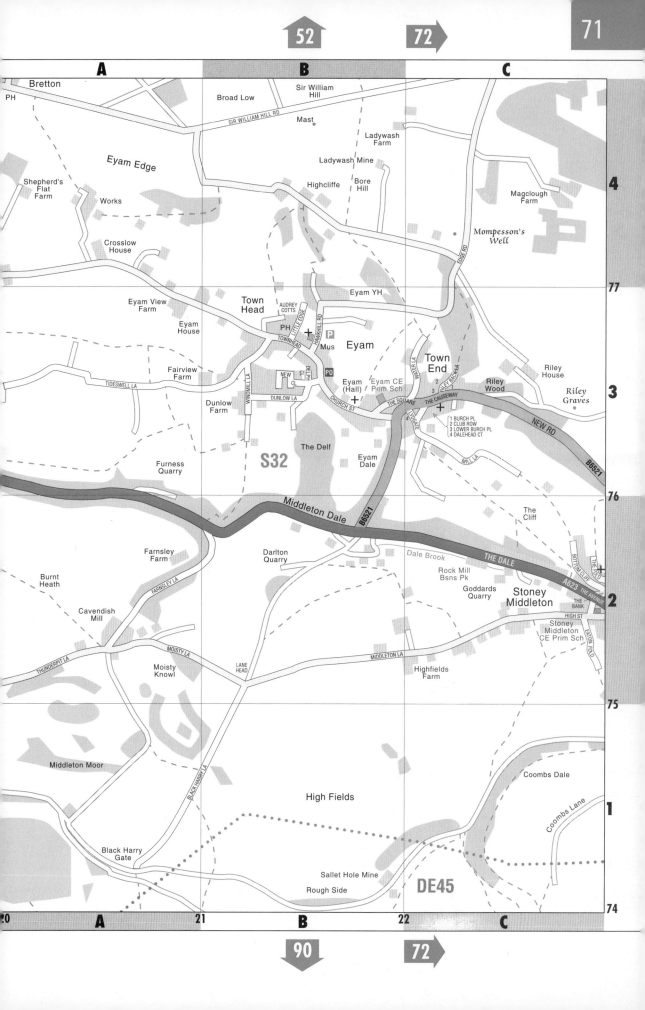

Bretton

PH

Broad Low

Sir William Hill

SIR WILLIAM HILL RD

Mast

Ladywash Farm

Eyam Edge

Ladywash Mine

Highcliffe

Bore Hill

Shepherd's Flat Farm

Works

Magclough Farm

Mompesson's Well

4

Crosslow House

77

Eyam YH

Eyam View Farm

Town Head

AUDREY COTTS

Eyam House

PH

TOWNHEAD

Mus

Eyam

Town End

Riley House

WELL LA

Fairview Farm

P

PO

Riley Wood

Riley Graves

3

TIDESWELL LA

NEW CL

Eyam (Hall)

Eyam CE Prim Sch

RILEY BACK LA

Riley Graves

Dunlow Farm

WINDMILL LA

DUNLOW LA

CHURCH ST

THE SQUARE

THE CAUSEWAY

NEW RD

LYDGATE

1 BURCH PL
2 CLUB ROW
3 LOWER BURCH PL
4 DALEHEAD CT

B6521

Furness Quarry

S32

The Delf

Eyam Dale

MILL LA

76

Middleton Dale

B6521

The Cliff

Farnsley Farm

BOTTOM CLIFF

THE FOLD

Burnt Heath

Darlton Quarry

Dale Brook

THE DALE

A623

THE AVENUE

2

Cavendish Mill

Rock Mill Bsns Pk

Goddards Quarry

Stoney Middleton

THE BANK

HIGH ST

FARNSLEY LA

Stoney Middleton CE Prim Sch

EATON FOLD

THUNDERPIT LA

MOISTY LA

LANE HEAD

MIDDLETON LA

Moisty Knowl

Highfields Farm

75

Middleton Moor

BLACK HARRY LA

Coombs Dale

High Fields

Coombs Lane

1

Black Harry Gate

Sallet Hole Mine

Rough Side

DE45

74

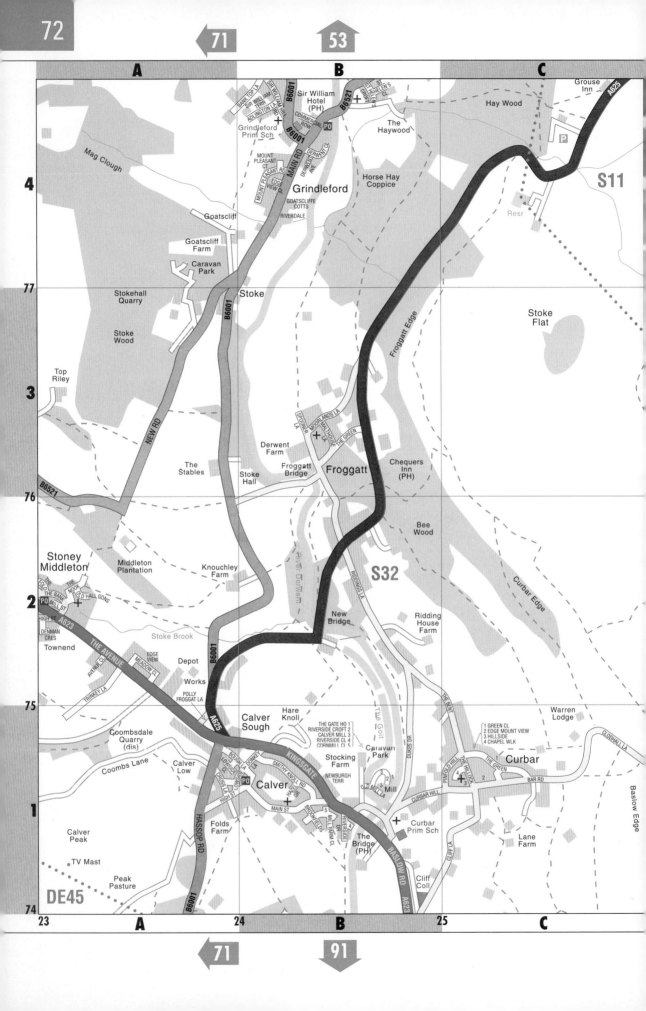

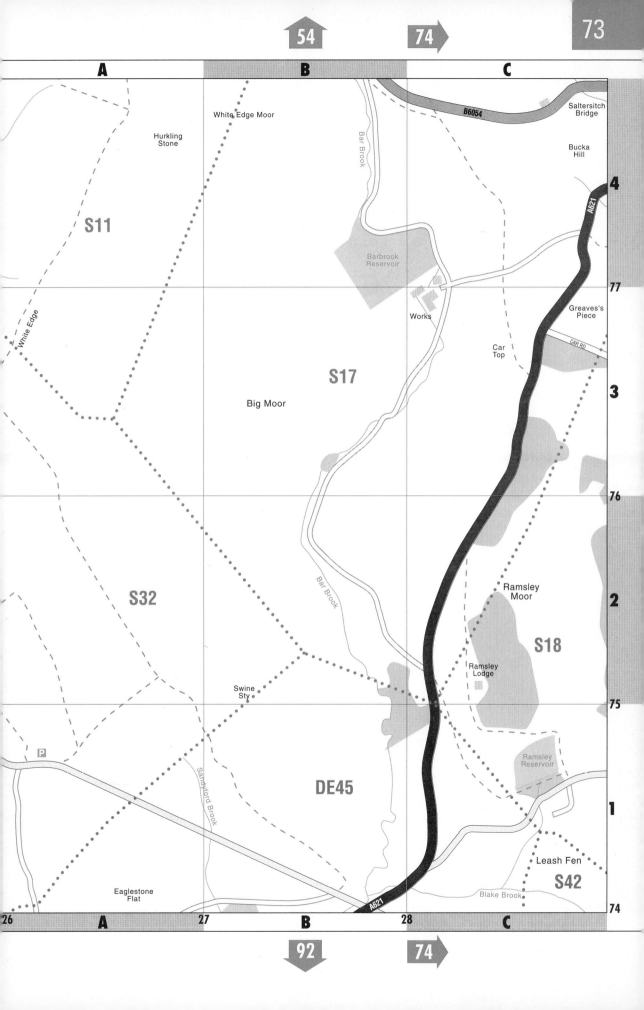

A
B
C

White Edge Moor

Hurkling
Stone

Bar Brook

B6054

Saltersitch
Bridge

Bucka
Hill

S11

4

A621

White Edge

Barbrook
Reservoir

77

Works

Greaves's
Piece

CAR RD

Car
Top

S17

3

Big Moor

76

Bar Brook

S32

Ramsley
Moor

2

S18

Ramsley
Lodge

Swine
Sty

75

DE45

Ramsley
Reservoir

P

Sandyford Brook

1

Leash Fen

S42

Eaglestone
Flat

A621

Blake Brook

74

26
A
27
B
28
C

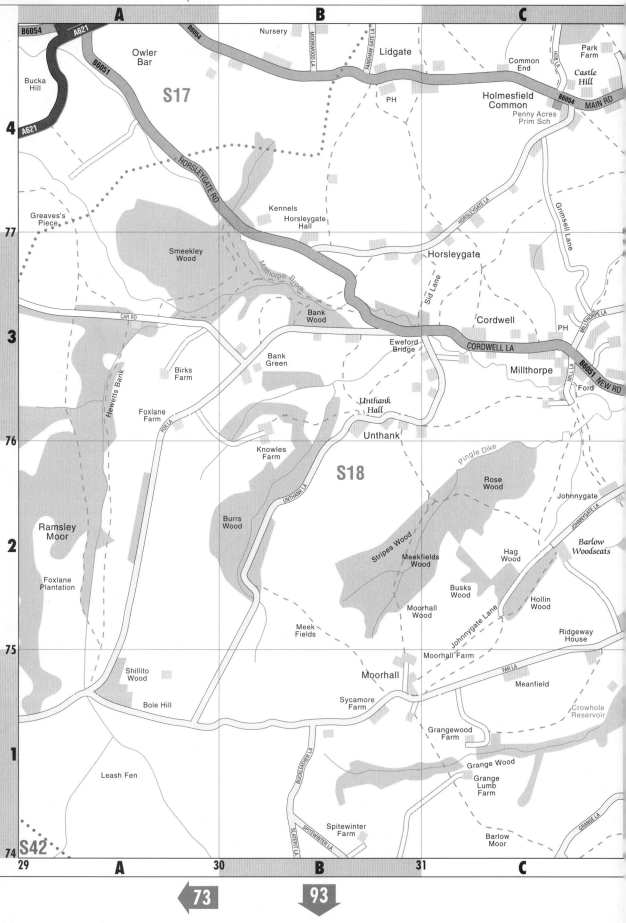

A   B   C

B6054   A621
B6054
Nursery
MOORWOOD LA
FANSHAW GATE LA
Lidgate
Common End
HOB LA
Park Farm
Owler Bar
B6051
Castle Hill
Bucka Hill
S17
PH
Holmesfield Common
B6054   MAIN RD
A621
4
Penny Acres Prim Sch
HORSLEYGATE RD
Grimsell Lane
Greaves's Piece
Kennels
Horsleygate Hall
HORSLEYGATE LA
77
Smeekley Wood
Horsleygate
Millthorpe Brook
Sid Lane
Cordwell
MILLTHORPE LA
Bank Wood
PH
3
CAR RD
Eweford Bridge
CORDWELL LA
Millthorpe
B6051 NEW RD
Hewetts Bank
Birks Farm
Bank Green
MILL LA
Ford
Foxlane Farm
FOX LA
Unthank Hall
76
Knowles Farm
Unthank
Pingle Dike
S18
Rose Wood
Johnnygate
Ramsley Moor
Burrs Wood
UNTHANK LA
Stripes Wood
Meekfields Wood
Hag Wood
JOHNNYGATE LA
Barlow Woodseats
2
Foxlane Plantation
Busks Wood
Hollin Wood
Moorhall Wood
Ridgeway House
Meek Fields
Johnnygate Lane
Moorhall Farm
FAR LA
Meanfield
75
Shillito Wood
Crowhole Reservoir
Bole Hill
Moorhall
Sycamore Farm
Grangewood Farm
1
BUCKLEATHER LA
Grange Wood
Leash Fen
Grange Lumb Farm
GRANGE LA
SLATEPIT LA
Spitewinter Farm
SPITEWINTER LA
Barlow Moor
74
S42

29   A   30   B   31   C

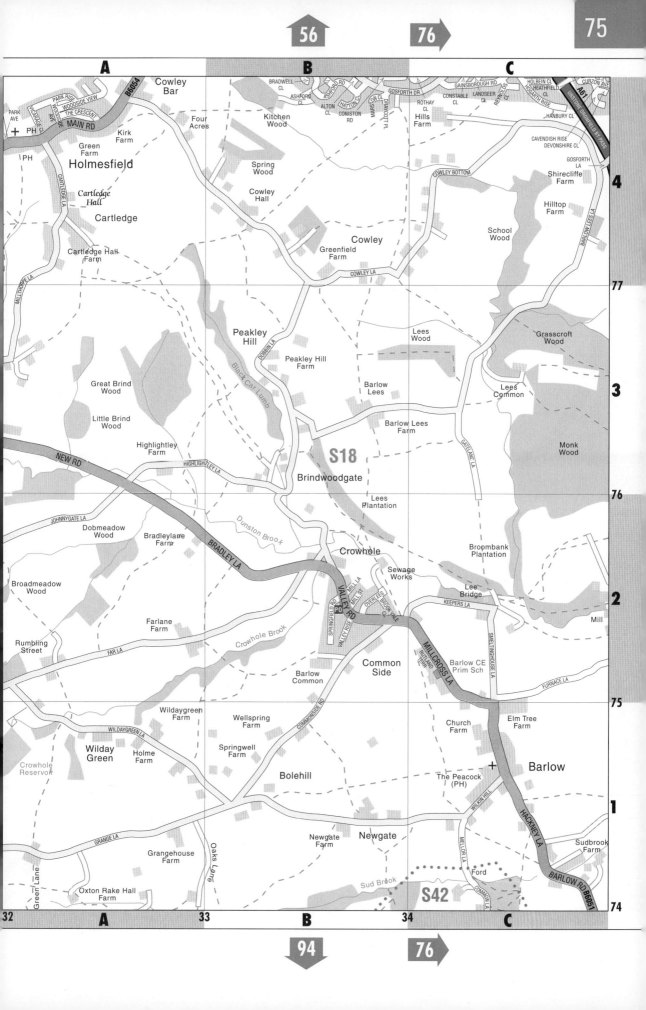

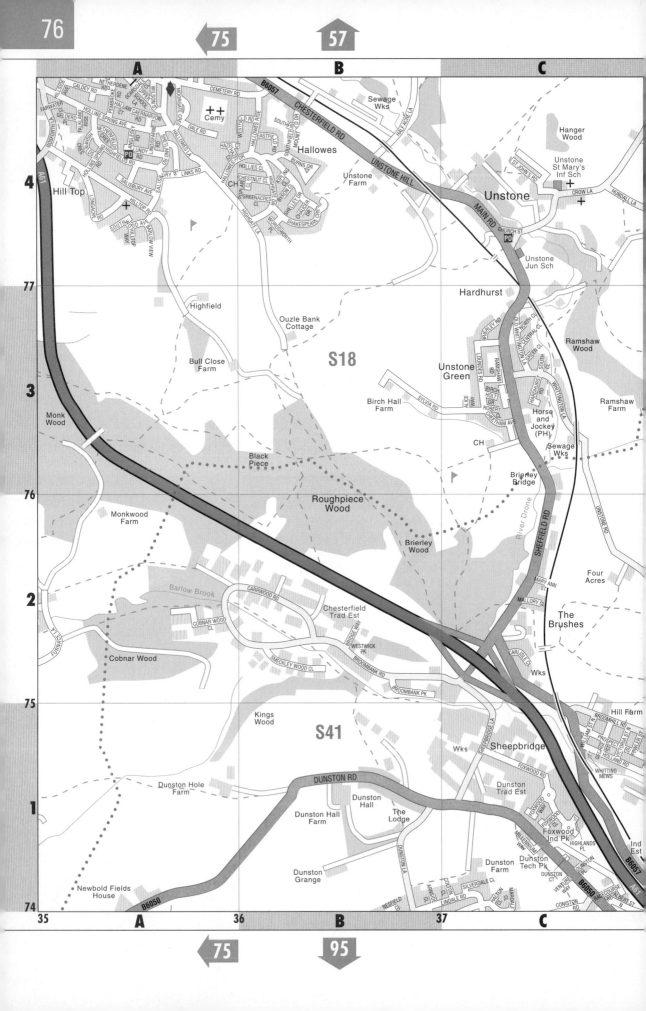

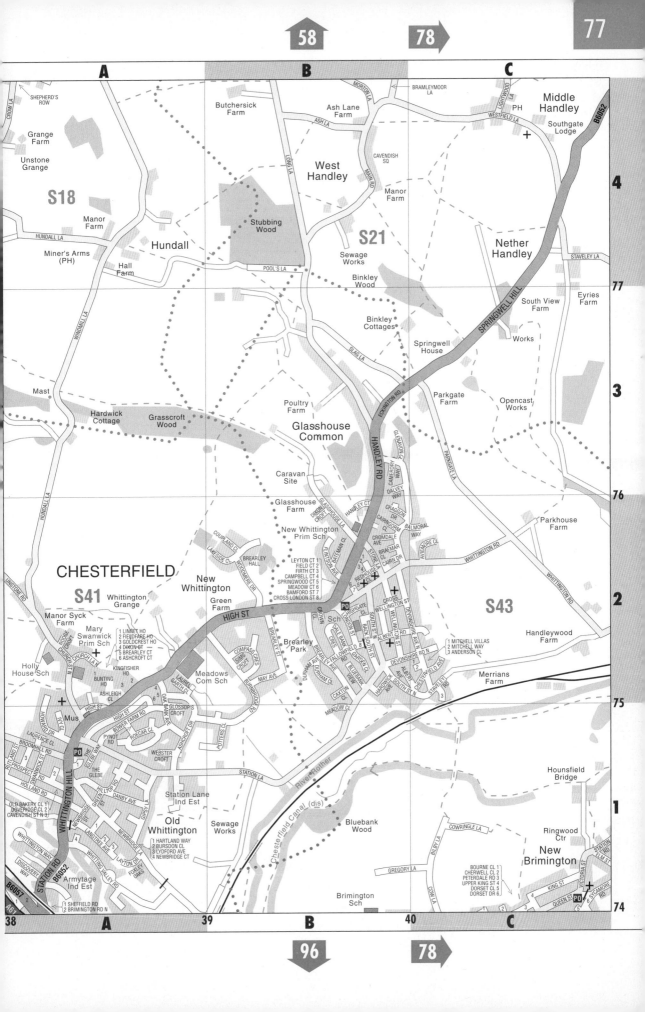

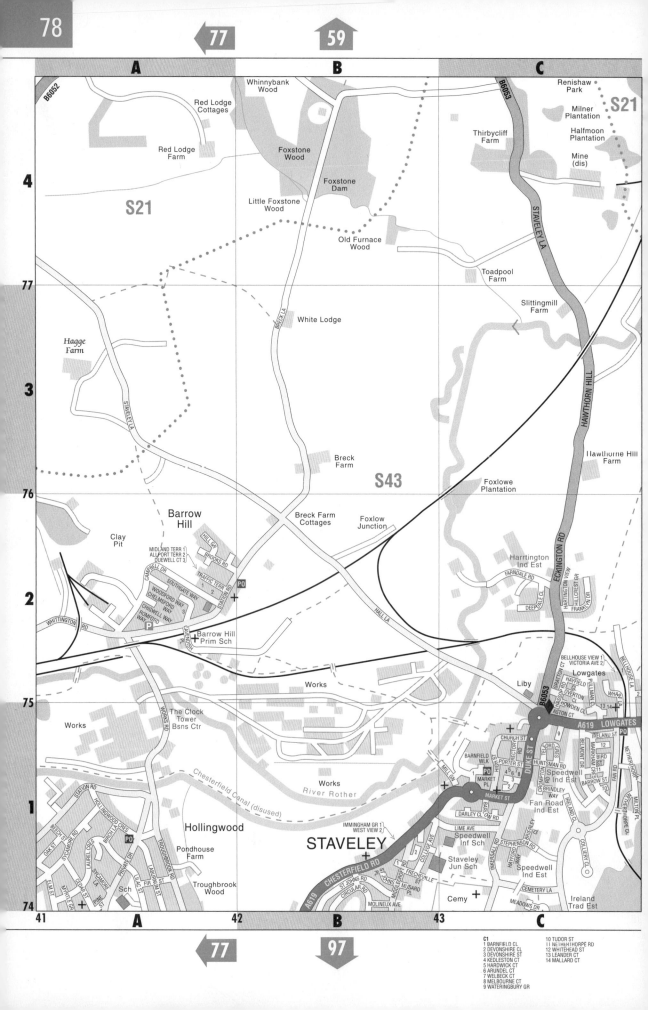

A   B   C

B6052

Red Lodge
Cottages
Whinnybank
Wood
Red Lodge
Farm

S21

Foxstone
Wood

Foxstone
Dam

4

Little Foxstone
Wood

Old Furnace
Wood

B6053

Renishaw
Park
Milner
Plantation
Halfmoon
Plantation

S21

Thirbycliff
Farm

Mine
(dis)

STAVELEY LA

Toadpool
Farm

77

Hagge
Farm

BRECK LA

White Lodge

Slittingmill
Farm

HAWTHORN HILL

STAVELEY LA

3

Hawthorne Hill
Farm

Breck
Farm

S43

Foxlowe
Plantation

76

Barrow
Hill

Breck Farm
Cottages

Foxlow
Junction

ECKINGTON RD

Clay
Pit

MIDLAND TERR 1
ALLPORT TERR 2
DUEWELL CT 3

HILL GR
BROOKS RD

Harrtington
Ind Est

FARNDALE RD

DEEPDALE CL

HILLCREST GR
FRANKW DR

2

CAMPBELL DR

SOUTHGATE WAY

CHELMSFORD
WAY 3
WOODFORD WAY

TRAFFIC TERR

STATION RD

PO

WHITTINGTON RD

CHIGWELL WAY

ROMFORD
WAY

P

CAVENDISH
PL

Barrow Hill
Prim Sch

HALL LA

HARTINGTON VIEW

DEEPDALE CL

HILLCREST GR

BELLHOUSE VIEW 1
VICTORIA AVE 2

GRATTON CT
BRINDLEY
HASSOP CL
HOWDEN CL

Lowgates

HAYFIELD
CL
OVERTON
PULLMAN CL

WHARF
13 14

BELLHOUSE LA

B6053

Liby

ASTON CT

75

Works

The Clock
Tower
Bsns Ctr

WORKS RD

Works

A619 LOWGATES

LOWGATES

PO

Works

CHURCH ST

RECTORY RD

DUKE ST

FORD CRES

BELMONT RD

Speedwell
Ind Est

MARKHAM RD

IRELAND ST

BIRD ST

NETHERTHORPE RD

MILTON ST

Works

Station Rd

HOLLINGWOOD CRES

BIRCH LA
PRIVATE DR

PO

TROUGHBROOK RD

LILAC ST

LABURNUM ST

Chesterfield Canal (disused)

River Rother

Works

BARNFIELD
WLK

PO

MARKET
PL

ST JOHNS
ST JOSEPH
PORTER ST

4 5 6
7 8

Huntsman St

CRAMPTON
ST

BARROW HILL

FAN RD

COLLIERY CL

IRELAND ST

1

Hollingwood

Pondhouse
Farm

OAK ST
BEECH LA
SYCAMORE CRES
LAUREL CRES
GEORGE ST
SYCAMORE
FIR ST
PINE ST

ELM ST
MYRTLE ST

Sch

Troughbrook
Wood

STAVELEY

IMMINGHAM GR 1
WEST VIEW 2

MILL GN

MARKET ST

BARROW RD

DARLEY CL

LIME AVE

Speedwell
Inf Sch

Staveley
Jun Sch

Speedwell
Ind Est

STENHENSON RD

HAYFORD
CRES

BRIERLEY
WAY

Fan Road
Ind Est

BRINDLEY
WAY

CEMETERY LA

Ireland
Trad Est

74

A619 CHESTERFIELD RD

ST JOHNS RD
CIRCULAR RD
MOLINEUX AVE

FRECHEVILLE
ST

COLLEGE AVE

MIDDLECROFT RD

Cemy

MEADOWS DR

41   A   42   B   43   C

C1
1 BARNFIELD CL
2 DEVONSHIRE CL
3 DEVONSHIRE ST
4 KEDLESTON CT
5 HARDWICK CT
6 ARUNDEL CT
7 WELBECK CT
8 MELBOURNE CT
9 WATERINGBURY GR
10 TUDOR ST
11 NETHERTHORPE RD
12 WHITEHEAD ST
13 LEANDER CT
14 MALLARD CT

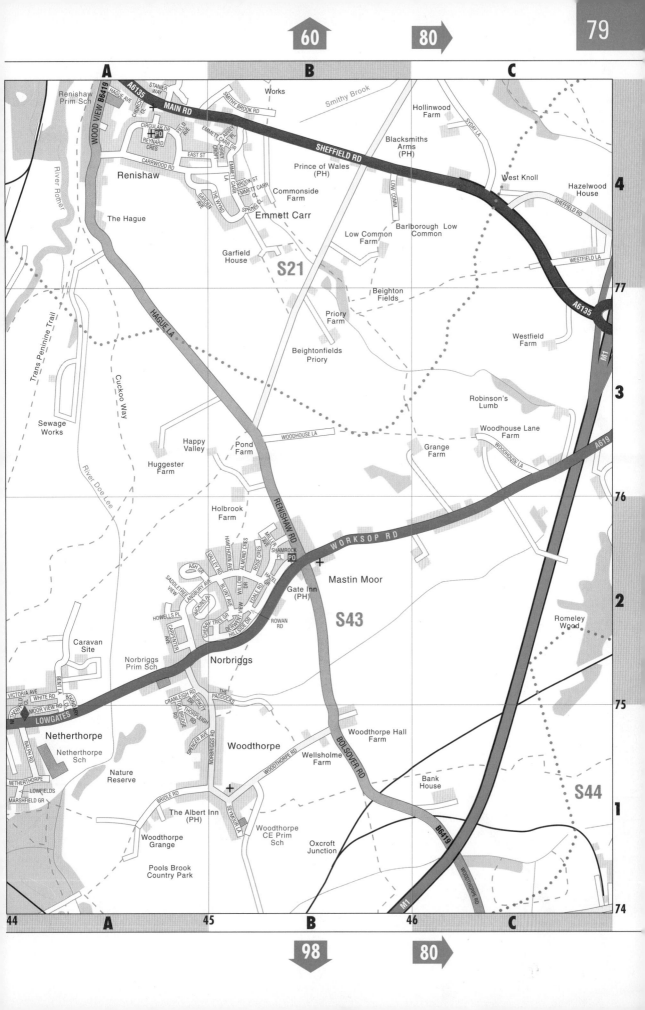

A B C

Renishaw Prim Sch
WOOD VIEW B6619
A6135
STANIER WAY
HAGUE AVE
CHURCH CL
MAIN RD
SMITHY BROOK RD
Works
Smithy Brook
Hollinwood Farm
SYDAL LA
FIELD AVE
ABBEY PL
CIRCULAR DR
PO
REYNARD CRES
EAST ST
EMMETT CARR LA
EMMETT CARR CL
ABBEY CROFT
BROOK ST
SPRING CL
CARRWOOD RD
THE WYND
GARDEN AVE
SHEFFIELD RD
Blacksmiths Arms (PH)
West Knoll
Hazelwood House
4

Renishaw
The Hague
Prince of Wales (PH)
Commonside Farm
Commonside Farm
Emmett Carr
Garfield House
LOW COMM
Low Common Farm
Barlborough Low Common
SHEFFIELD RD
WESTFIELD LA

S21
77

HAGUE LA
Beighton Fields
Priory Farm
Westfield Farm
A6135
M1
Trans Pennine Trail
Beightonfields Priory
Robinson's Lumb
A619
3

Cuckoo Way
Sewage Works
Happy Valley
Huggester Farm
Pond Farm
WOODHOUSE LA
Grange Farm
Woodhouse Lane Farm
WOODHOUSE LA
A619

River Doe Lee
Holbrook Farm
76

Caravan Site
HAWTHORN AVE
ASH GR
VALLEY RD
ALMOND CRES
MILLER AVE
SHAMROCK PL
ROSE CRES
HAZEL GR
PO
Renishaw RD
WORKSOP RD
SADDLETREE VIEW
LANSBURY AVE
BLUNT AVE
WILLOW DR
EDALE RD
Mastin Moor
Romeley Wood
2

Norbriggs Prim Sch
HOWELLS PL
MACKINLAY AVE
CHERRY TREE GR
HILLSIDE DR
DERWENT VIEW
CARPENTER AVE
Gate Inn (PH)
ROWAN RD
S43

Norbriggs
BENTLA
VICTORIA AVE
WHITE RD
MOOR VIEW RD
BONDAL RD
CRANLEIGH RD
BLUNT DR
THORPELEIGH RD
TOTLEY BRIDGE
THE PADDOCKS
75

NETHERKERRY CL
LOWGATES
Netherthorpe
Netherthorpe Sch
RALPH RD
NETHERTHORPE
LOWFIELDS
MARSHFIELD GR
Nature Reserve
SPENCER AVE
NORBRIGGS RD
SIGSBROOK RD
Woodthorpe
WOODTHORPE RD
Wellsholme Farm
Woodthorpe Hall Farm
BOLSOVER RD
Bank House
S44
1

BRIDLE RD
The Albert Inn (PH)
Woodthorpe Grange
ST MAUR LA
Woodthorpe CE Prim Sch
Oxcroft Junction
B6419
WOODTHORPE RD

Pools Brook Country Park
M1
74

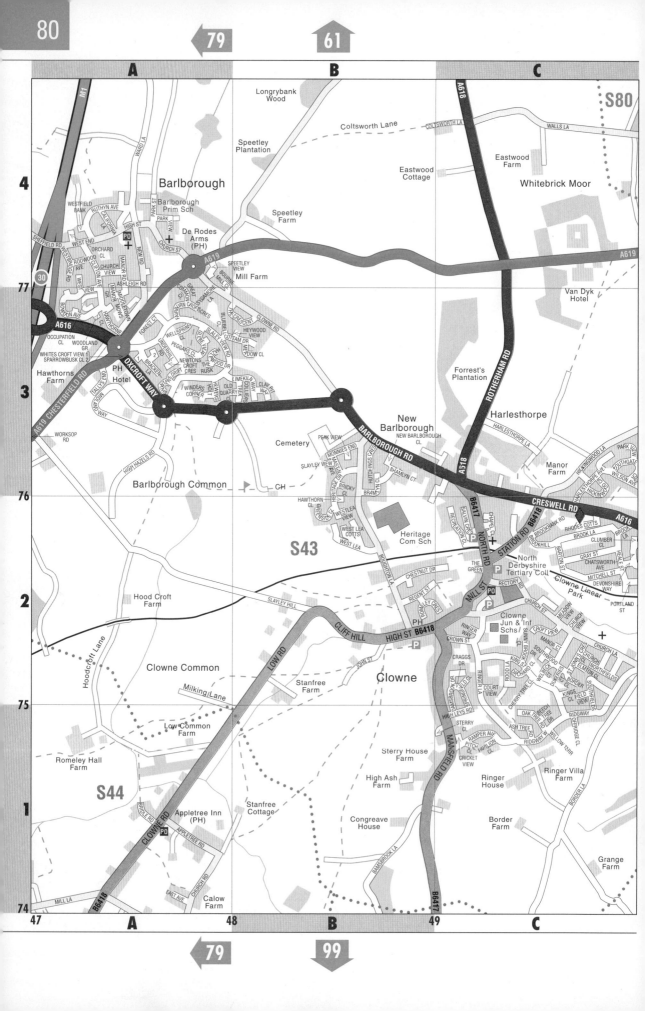

A   B   C

North Walls

South Walls

WALLS LA

Gipsyhill Farm

GIPSYHILL LA

Cinders Farm

Springfield Farm

Hawthorn Fields

Commonside Farm

Whitwell Common

BONDHAY LA

Woodnook

PH

B6043

Whitwell Wood

Rob Nook

CLINTHILL LA

A619

B6043

Whitwell Hall

OLD HALL LA

HIGH ST

WORKSOP RD

GREENWAY

4

77

Hickin Wood

GAPSICK LA

Hickingwood Farm

HICKINGWOOD LA

ASHLEA WLK

Highwood Farm

HIGHWOOD LA

Ash Tree Cave

Bakestone Moor

Whitwell

Claylands

PORTLAND ST

MANOR FARM

SCOTLAND

Liby

PORTLAND CT

MASON ST

HILLSIDE CL

HILLSIDE ST

PORTLAND

TITCHFIELD ST

BUTT HILL

SOUTH VIEW

JUBILEE RD

JUBILEE GDNS

LAWRENCE VIEW

JUBILEE CRES

BAKESTONE MOOR

FRANKLIN CRES

SCYTHEFIELD CL

LONGHURST VIEW

THORPE AVE

SANDY CL

NEW ST

CLAYLANDS PL

CLAYLANDS RD

CLAYLANDS GR

PLANTATION CL

3

76

CLUNE ST

EAST ST

ROSE AVE

WEST ST

WILSON AVE

PO

JAGO AVE

MARKLAND CRES

JUBILEE CRES

S43

CRESWELL RD

DUKE ST

HADDON AVE

CAVENDISH DR

BATTINCK DR

PORTLAND ST

DEVONSHIRE WAY

HOLLIN HILL

Works

Highfield House

Archaeological Trail

Gorse Covert

Hollin Hill

S80

Peter More

PETER MORE HILL

Tunnel

2

1 CHATSWORTH AVE
2 THORESEY AVE
3 HARDWICK CL
4 HARTINGTON CT
5 WOODLAND GR

Hollinhill Grips

Mill Cottages

Upper Mill Farm

SHEFFIELD RD

North Derbyshire Tertiary Coll (Markland Campus)

Lower Mill Farm

Butcher's Wood

75

Markland Farm

HAZELMERE RD

Hazelmere Farm

MARKLAND VIEW

NOBEL DR

HAWTHORN AVE

CHESTNUT DR

SYCAMORE

HALDANE CL

MAPLE DR

LINDEN CL

ROWAN CL

ORCHARD DR

Brookside Farm

P

Creswell

MARKLAND LA

Markland Grips

Markland Plantation

Archaeological Trail

ROGERS AVE

TENNYSON RD

SHAKESPEARE AVE

EYRE ST

WEST ST

SHERWOOD AVE

PORTLAND AVE

BANK CL

Cemy

SKINNER ST

JOHN ST

ELMTON RD

Creswell CE Inf Sch

GYPSY LA

Creswell

BAKER ST

QUEENS CT

DUKE ST

QUEEN ST

PO

PH

Liby

L Ctr

MANSFIELD RD

CHURCH ST

1 WILLOW CL
2 CRAGS VIEW
3 DUCHESS ST

Bank House Farm

CRAGS RD

A616

1

BENTINK CL 1
THE BIRCHILLS 2
COMPTON DR 3
CAVENDISH CL 4
MANSE AVE 5
MANSE CL 6

DEVONSHIRE DR

HARTINGTON DR

BEELEY CL

CHATSWORTH RD

WOOD AVE

WEST ST

MILL BECK

Enterprise Ct

ANN ST

WELBECK ST

Sch

MODEL VILLAGE

Victoria Ho

VICTORIA ST

LABURNUM RD

FIELDINGS RD

BEECH ST

PINE ST

B6042

74

50   A   51   B   52   C

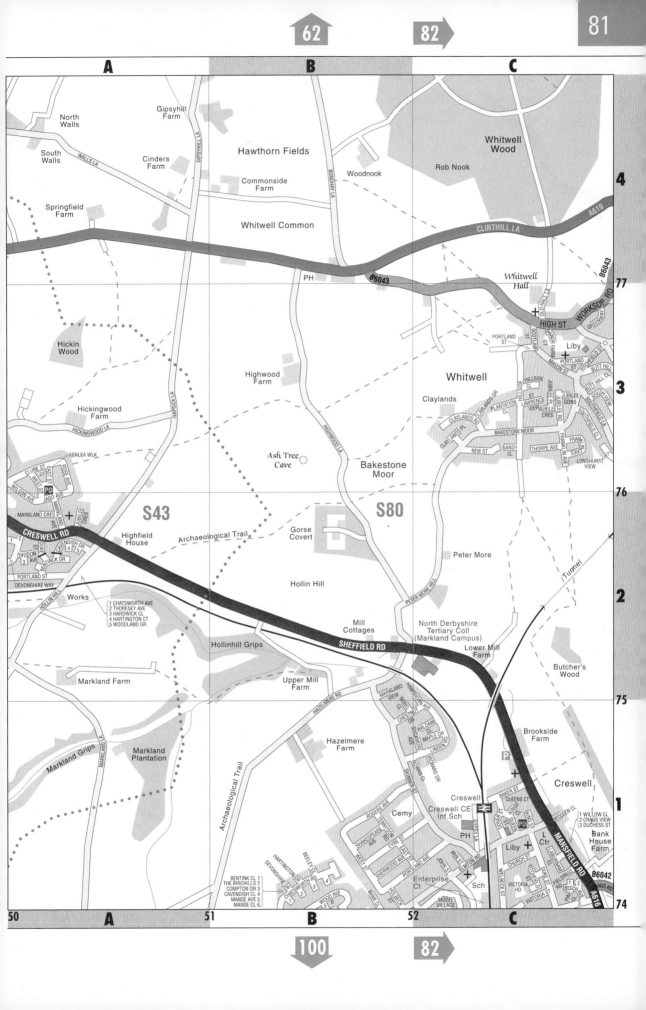

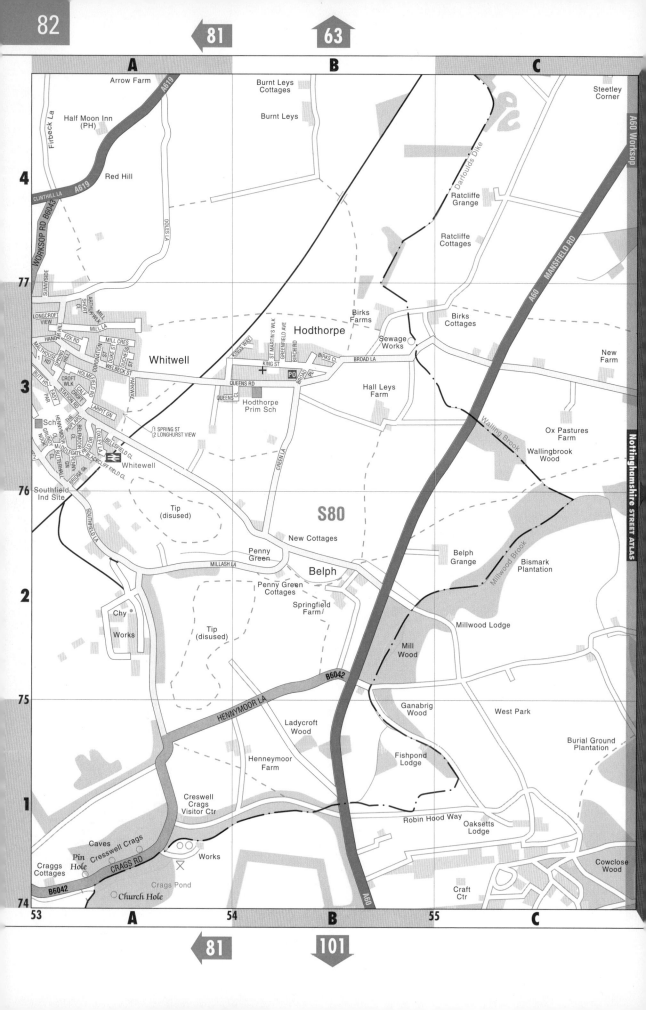

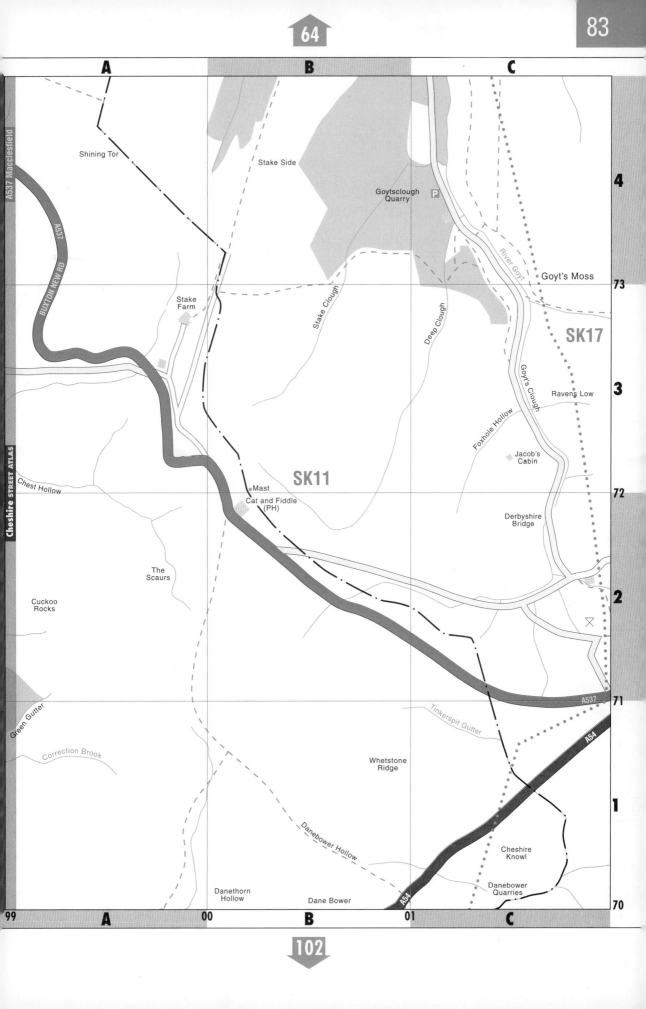

A

B

C

4

Shining Tor

Stake Side

Goytsclough
Quarry

P

River Goyt

Goyt's Moss

73

A537 Macclesfield

A537

BUXTON NEW RD

Stake Farm

Stake Clough

Deep Clough

SK17

Goyt's Clough

3

Ravens Low

Foxhole Hollow

Jacob's
Cabin

Chest Hollow

SK11

Mast

Cat and Fiddle
(PH)

72

Derbyshire
Bridge

Cheshire STREET ATLAS

The Scaurs

Cuckoo
Rocks

2

A537

71

Green Gutter

Tinkerspit Gutter

A54

Correction Brook

Whetstone
Ridge

1

Danebower Hollow

Cheshire
Knowl

A54

Danethorn
Hollow

Dane Bower

Danebower
Quarries

70

99

A

00

B

01

C

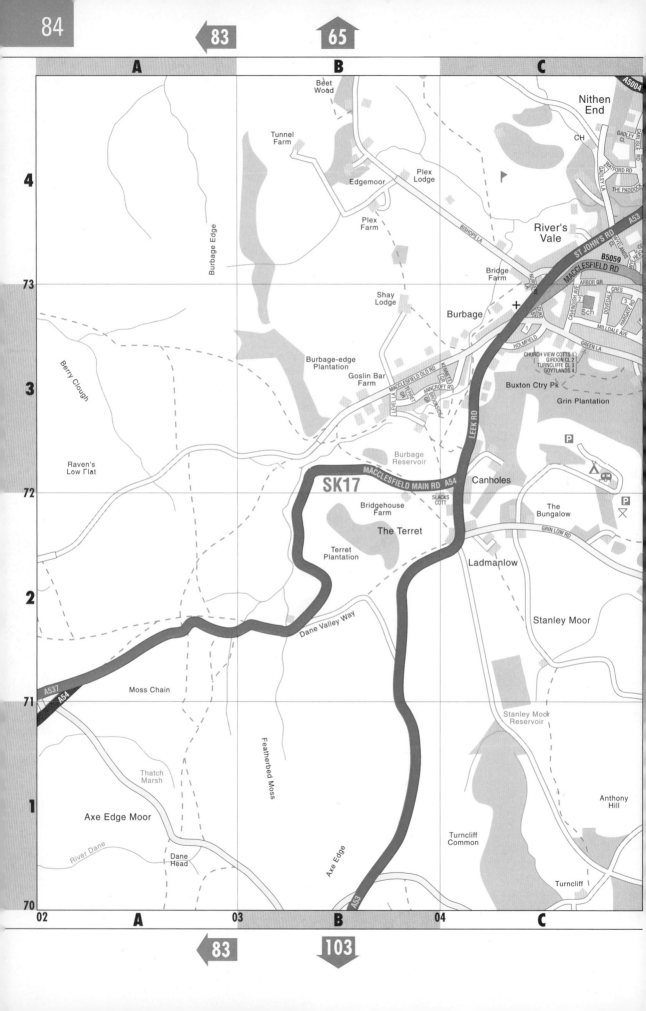

A   B   C

Nithen
End

A5004

Beet
Wood

Tunnel
Farm

CH

GADLEY
CL

CARLISLE
RD

Edgemoor

Plex
Lodge

WATFORD RD

GADLEY LA

THE PADDOCK

4

Burbage Edge

Plex
Farm

BISHOPS LA

River's
Vale

St JOHN'S RD

A53

Plex
Farm

Bridge
Farm

NURSERY LA

MACCLESFIELD RD

B5059

WYE HEAD CL

73

Shay
Lodge

Burbage

ARBOR GR

CAVENDISH AVE

DOVEDALE

CRES

2

Sch

DUKE ST

1

HOLMFIELD

GREEN LA

HARTGATE RD

MILLDALE AVE

Berry Clough

Burbage-edge
Plantation

Goslin Bar
Farm

MACCLESFIELD OLD RD

LEVEL LA

TERRET GR

KENNET GR

ANNCROFT RD

BROWNSIDE GR

CHURCH VIEW COTTS 1
GIRDON CL 2
TURNCLIFFE CL 3
GOYTLANDS 4

Buxton Ctry Pk

Grin Plantation

3

Raven's
Low Flat

Burbage
Reservoir

LEEK RD

P

72

SK17

MACCLESFIELD MAIN RD

A54

SLACKS
COTT

Canholes

The
Bungalow

P

Bridgehouse
Farm

The Terret

Ladmanlow

GRIN LOW RD

Terret
Plantation

Dane Valley Way

Stanley Moor

2

A537

A54

Moss Chain

Stanley Moor
Reservoir

71

Featherbed Moss

Anthony
Hill

Axe Edge Moor

Turncliff
Common

1

River Dane

Dane
Head

Axe Edge

A53

Turncliff

70

02   A   03   B   04   C

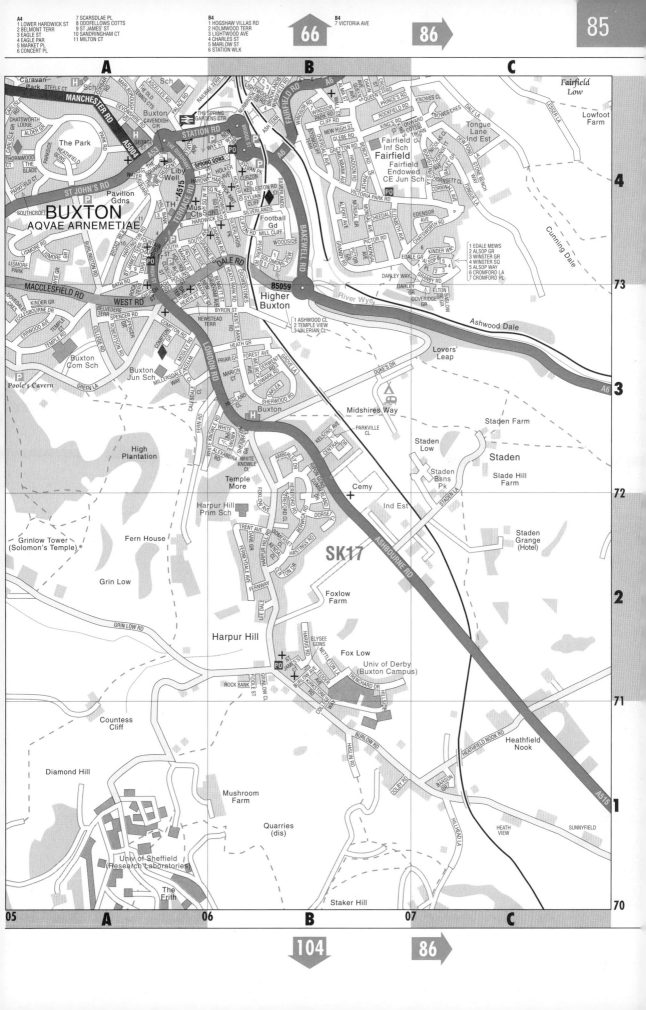

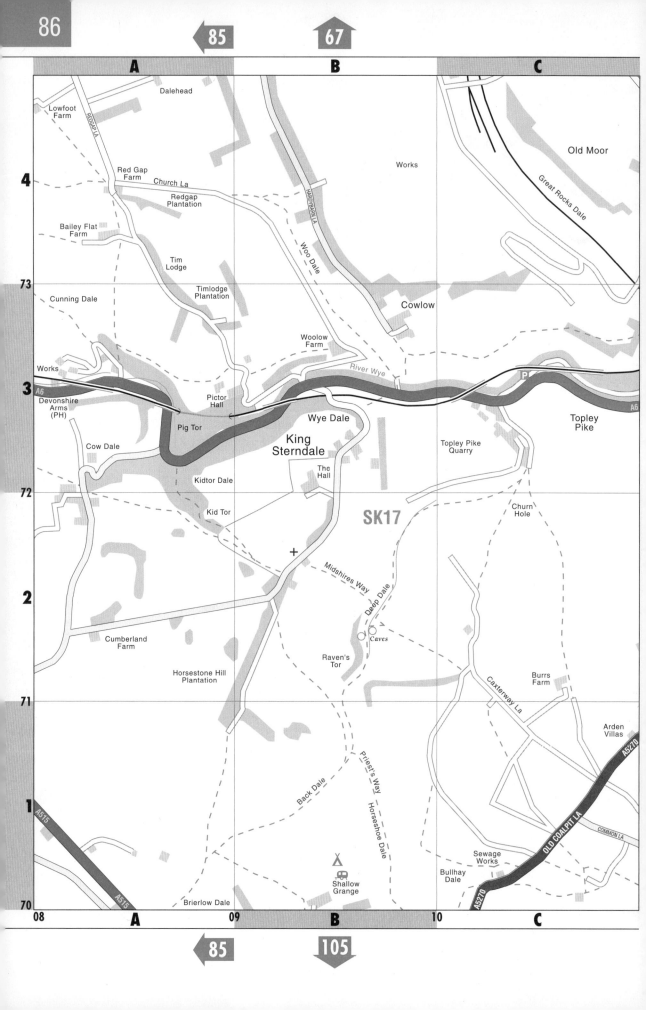

A **B** **C**

Lowfoot Farm

Dalehead

REDGAP LA

Red Gap Farm

Church La

Redgap Plantation

4

Bailey Flat Farm

Cunning Dale

Tim Lodge

Timlodge Plantation

73

HARDYBARN LA

Woo Dale

Works

Old Moor

Great Rocks Dale

Cowlow

Woolow Farm

River Wye

Works

A6

3

Devonshire Arms (PH)

Pictor Hall

Wye Dale

P

A6

Topley Pike

Pig Tor

Cow Dale

King Sterndale

Kidtor Dale

Kid Tor

The Hall

Topley Pike Quarry

Churn Hole

72

+

SK17

Midshires Way

Deep Dale

2

Cumberland Farm

Horsestone Hill Plantation

Raven's Tor

Caves

Caxterway La

Burrs Farm

Arden Villas

A5270

71

Back Dale

Priest's Way

Horseshoe Dale

OLD COALPIT LA

COMMON LA

A515

1

A515

Sewage Works

Bullhay Dale

A5270

Shallow Grange

70

08

A

09

B

10

C

Brierlow Dale

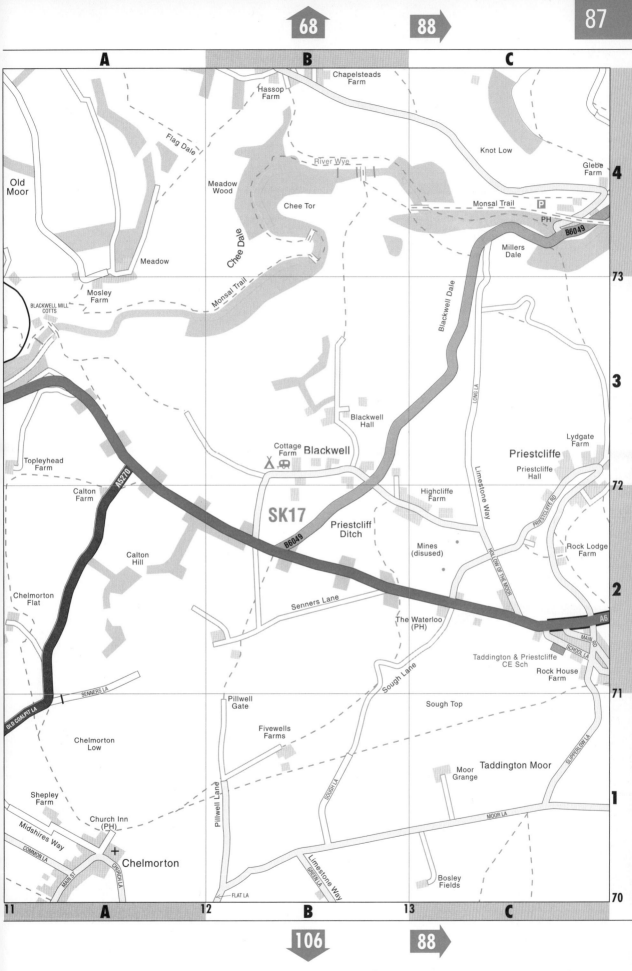

A
B
C

Chapelsteads Farm

Hassop Farm

Flag Dale

Meadow Wood

River Wye

Knot Low

Glebe Farm

4

Old Moor

Chee Tor

Monsal Trail

P

PH

B6049

Chee Dale

Millers Dale

73

Meadow

Monsal Trail

Blackwell Dale

Mosley Farm

BLACKWELL MILL COTTS

3

Blackwell Hall

Lydgate Farm

Topleyhead Farm

Cottage Farm

Blackwell

Priestcliffe

Priestcliffe Hall

A5270

Calton Farm

SK17

72

Highcliffe Farm

Limestone Way

Priestcliffe Rd

B6049

Priestcliff Ditch

Rock Lodge Farm

Calton Hill

Mines (disused)

Hollow of the Moor

Chelmorton Flat

2

A6

Senners Lane

The Waterloo (PH)

Main Rd

School La

Taddington & Priestcliffe CE Sch

Rock House Farm

Senners La

71

Old Coalpit La

Pillwell Gate

Sough Lane

Sough Top

Shepley Farm

Chelmorton Low

Fivewells Farms

Moor Grange

Taddington Moor

Slipperlow La

1

Church Inn (PH)

Pillwell Lane

Sough La

Moor La

Midshires Way

Common La

Main St

Church La

Chelmorton

Limestone Way

Green La

Bosley Fields

Flat La

70

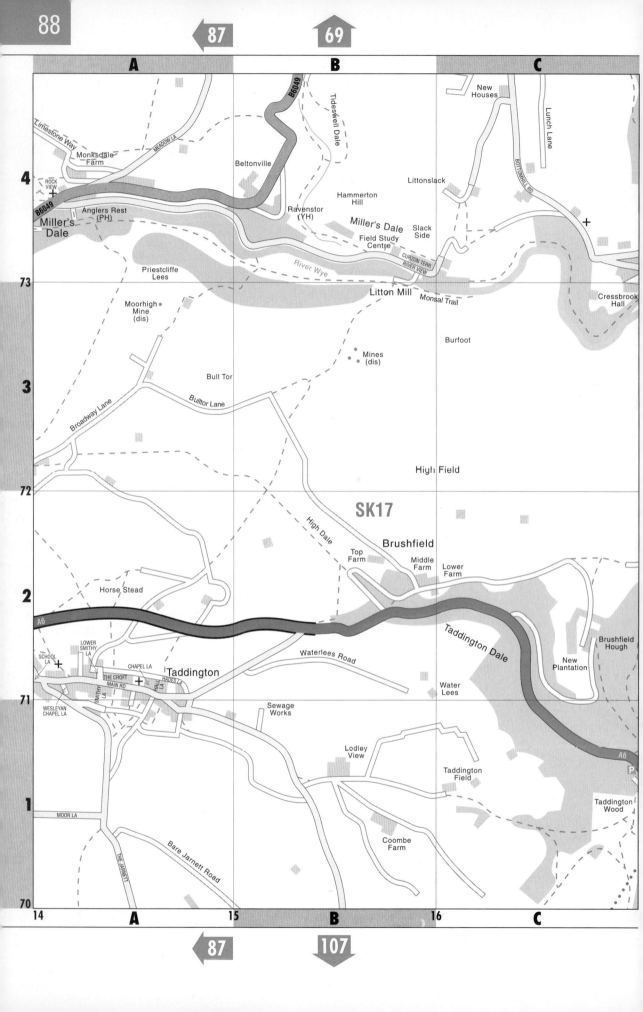

A **B** **C**

Limestone Way

MEADOW LA

Monksdale
Farm

ROCK
VIEW

B6049

Miller's
Dale

Anglers Rest
(PH)

Priestcliffe
Lees

Moorhigh
Mine
(dis)

Bull Tor

Bulltor Lane

Broadway Lane

Beltonville

Tideswell Dale

B6049

Ravenstor
(YH)

Hammerton
Hill

Field Study
Centre

River Wye

River View

Curzon Terr

Litton Mill

Monsal Trail

Mines
(dis)

New
Houses

Lunch Lane

Littonslack

Bottomhill Rd

Miller's Dale

Slack
Side

Cressbrook
Hall

Burfoot

4

73

3

72

High Field

SK17

Brushfield

High Dale

Top
Farm

Middle
Farm

Lower
Farm

Taddington Dale

Brushfield
Hough

New
Plantation

Horse Stead

A6

2

SCHOOL
LA

LOWER
SMITHY
LA

THE CROFT

CHAPEL LA

MAIN RD

SMITHY
LA

HALL LA

HADES LA

Taddington

Waterlees Road

Water
Lees

71

WESLEYAN
CHAPEL LA

Sewage
Works

Lodley
View

Taddington
Field

A6

P

1

MOOR LA

THE JARNETT

Bare Jarnett Road

Coombe
Farm

Taddington
Wood

70

14 15 16

A **B** **C**

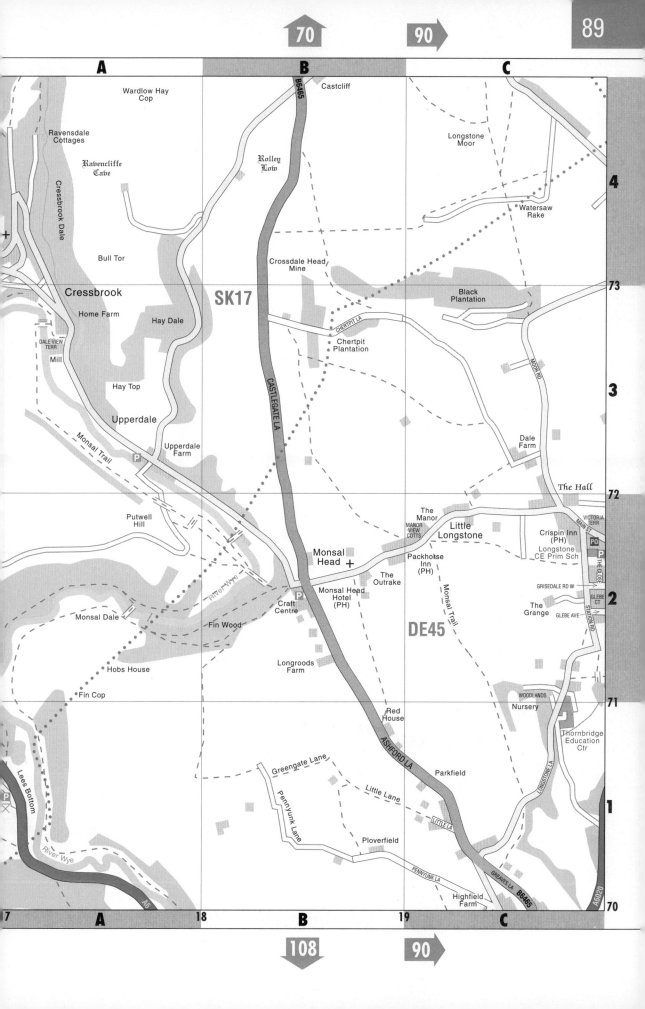

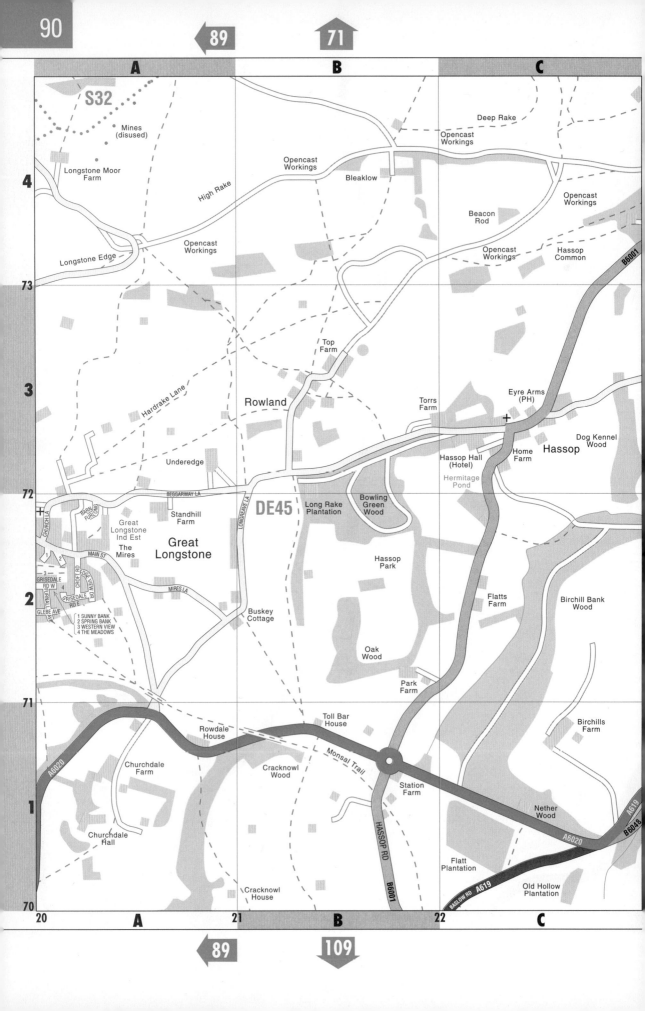

A   **B**   **C**

S32

Mines
(disused)

Longstone Moor
Farm

High Rake

4

Deep Rake

Opencast
Workings

Bleaklow

Opencast
Workings

Beacon
Rod

Opencast
Workings

Hassop
Common

B6001

Longstone Edge

Opencast
Workings

73

Top
Farm

3

Hardrake Lane

Rowland

Torrs
Farm

Eyre Arms
(PH)

Dog Kennel
Wood

Hassop

Underedge

Hassop Hall
(Hotel)

Home
Farm

Hermitage
Pond

72

BEGGARWAY LA

DE45

Long Rake
Plantation

Bowling
Green
Wood

CHURCH LA

BARN
FURLONG

Standhill
Farm

LONGREAK LA

Great
Longstone Ind Est

The Mires

**Great
Longstone**

Hassop
Park

MAIN ST

EDGE VIEW DR

CROFT RD

1 2

GRISEDALE
RD W

3

GRISEDALE
RD E

FURNALL AVE

GLEBE AVE

MIRES LA

Buskey
Cottage

Flatts
Farm

Birchill Bank
Wood

2

1 SUNNY BANK
2 SPRING BANK
3 WESTERN VIEW
4 THE MEADOWS

Oak
Wood

Park
Farm

71

A6020

Toll Bar
House

Monsal Trail

Station
Farm

Birchills
Farm

Rowdale
House

Churchdale
Farm

Cracknowl
Wood

HASSOP RD

Nether
Wood

A619

B604B

1

Churchdale
Hall

Flatt
Plantation

A6020

Old Hollow
Plantation

Cracknowl
House

B6001

BASLOW RD A619

70

20   **A**   **21**   **B**   **22**   **C**

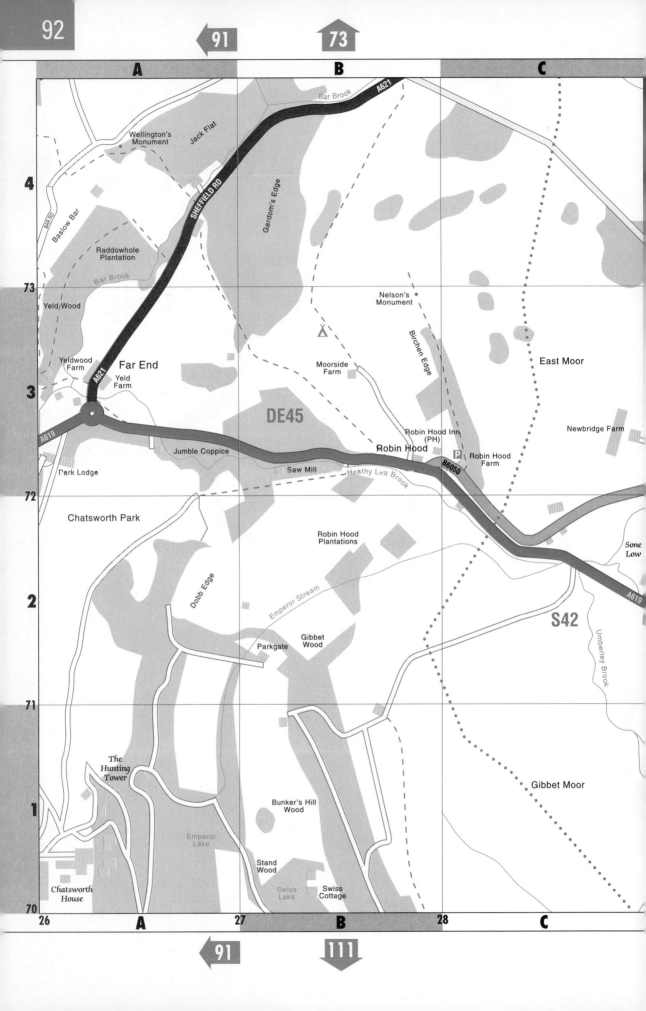

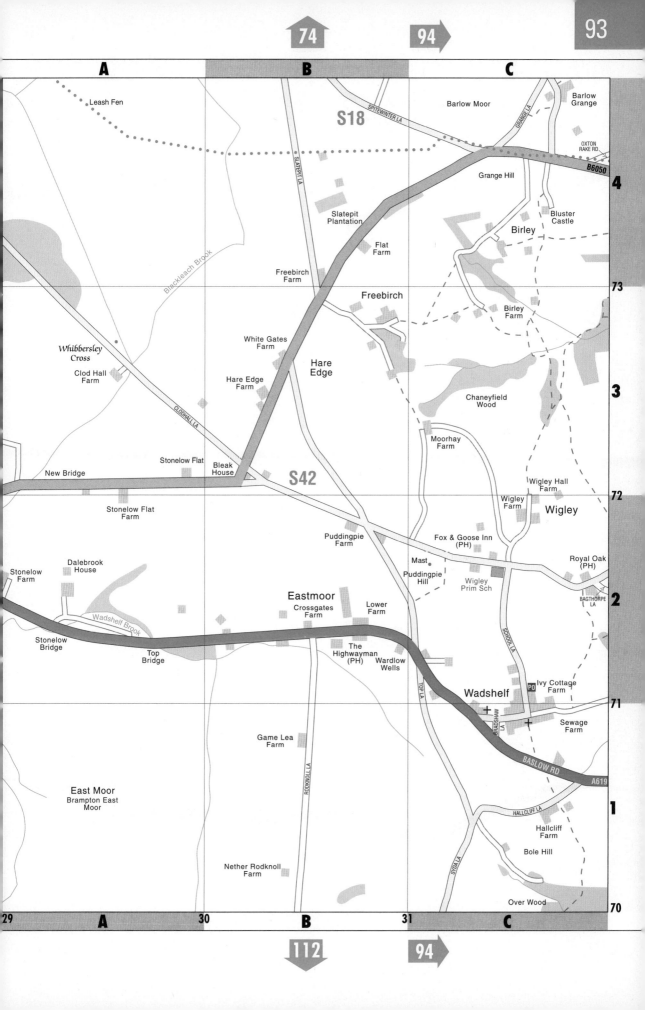

A
B
C

Leash Fen

SPITEWINTER LA
S18
Barlow Moor
Barlow Grange

SLATEPIT LA
GRANGE LA
OXTON RAKE RD
B6050
4

Grange Hill

Slatepit Plantation
Birley
Bluster Castle

Flat Farm

Freebirch Farm
Freebirch
Birley Farm
73

Blackleach Brook

White Gates Farm
Whibbersley Cross
Hare Edge
Chaneyfield Wood
3

Clod Hall Farm
Hare Edge Farm

CLODHALL LA

Moorhay Farm

Stonelow Flat
New Bridge
Bleak House
S42
Wigley Hall Farm
72

Wigley Farm
Wigley

Stonelow Flat Farm
Puddingpie Farm
Fox & Goose Inn (PH)
Royal Oak (PH)

Stonelow Farm
Dalebrook House
Mast
Puddingpie Hill
Wigley Prim Sch
BAGTHORPE LA
2

Wadshelf Brook
Eastmoor
Crossgates Farm
Lower Farm

SCHOOL LA

Stonelow Bridge
Top Bridge
The Highwayman (PH)
Wardlow Wells
Wadshelf
Ivy Cottage Farm
PO
71

BRADSHAW LA
Sewage Farm

Game Lea Farm
BASLOW RD
A619

RODKNOLL LA
East Moor
Brampton East Moor
Hallcliff Farm
HALLCLIFF LA
1

TOP LA
SYDA LA
Bole Hill

Nether Rodknoll Farm
Over Wood
70

29
A
30
B
31
C

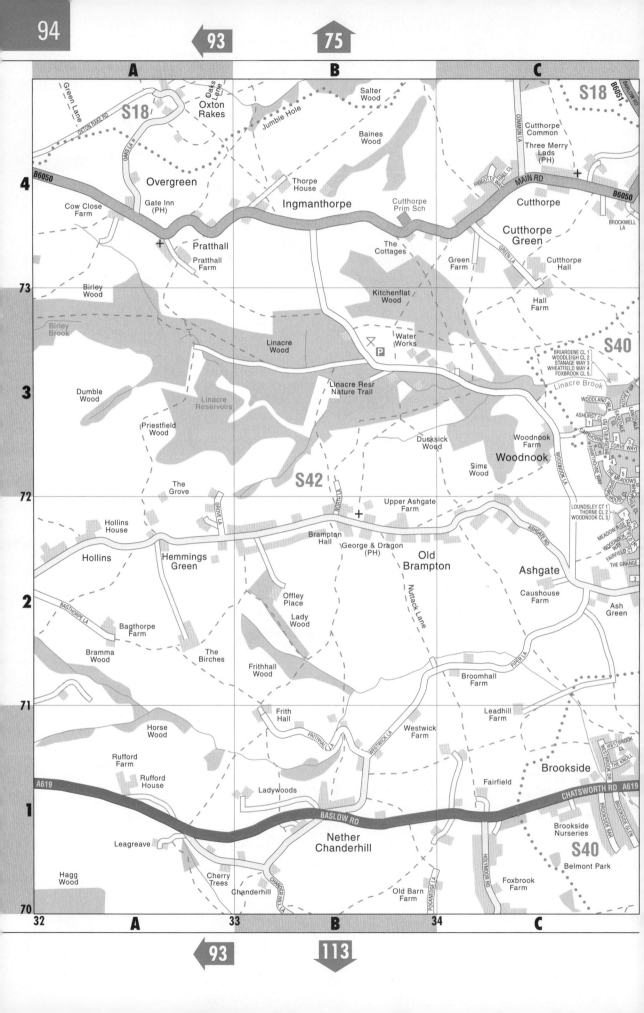
A B C

S18
Green Lane
OXTON RAKE RD
Oaks Lane
Oxton Rakes
Salter Wood
S18
BARLOW RD
B6051
COMMON LA
Cutthorpe Common
Three Merry Lads (PH)
OAKS LA
S18
Jumble Hole
Baines Wood

4
B6050
Overgreen
Thorpe House
Ingmanthorpe
Cutthorpe Prim Sch
RIGGOTTS PINFALL CL
MAIN RD
Cutthorpe
B6050
Gate Inn (PH)
Cow Close Farm
+
Pratthall
Pratthall Farm
The Cottages
BROCKWELL LA
Cutthorpe Green
Green Farm
GREEN LA
Cutthorpe Hall

73
Birley Wood
Kitchenflat Wood
Hall Farm

Birley Brook
Linacre Wood
Water Works
S40
BRIARDENE CL 1
WOODLEIGH CL 2
STANAGE WAY 3
WHEATFIELD WAY 4
FOXBROOK CL 5
P
Linacre Brook
ROTHEY GR
FASCEME
LANGDALE

3
Dumble Wood
Priestfield Wood
Linacre Reservoirs
Linacre Resr Nature Trail
Ducksick Wood
Woodnook Farm
Woodnook
Sims Wood
WOODLAND WALK
ASHURST CL
CARTHORPE RD
CORVE WAY
HAWTHORNE WAY
OLD HILL
SHRUB
THE MEADOWS
FAIRFIELD CL
THE SPRINGS CL
MEADOW RISE
HOUSE CL

72
The Grove
GROVE LA
NORTH LA
S42
Upper Ashgate Farm
+
LOUNDSLEY CT 1
THORNE CL 2
WOODNOOK CL 3
WOODNOOK WAY
FAIRFIELD CT
THE GRANGE

Hollins House
Brampton Hall
George & Dragon (PH)
Old Brampton
ASHGATE RD
Ashgate

2
BAGTHORPE LA
Hollins
Hemmings Green
Offley Place
Lady Wood
Caushouse Farm
Ash Green

Bagthorpe Farm
The Birches
Nuttack Lane
PIPER LA

Bramma Wood
Frithhall Wood
Broomhall Farm

71
Frith Hall
Leadhill Farm
Horse Wood
FRITHHALL LA
WESTWICK LA
Westwick Farm
WESTBROOK CL
THE KNOLL
WESTBROOK GR
Brookside

Rufford Farm
Rufford House
A619
Ladywoods
Fairfield
CHATSWORTH RD
A619
BROOKSIDE BAR
BROOKSIDE GLEN

1
BASLOW RD
Brookside Nurseries
Belmont Park
S40
Leagreave
Nether Chanderhill
HOLYMOOR RD
Foxbrook Farm

Hagg Wood
Cherry Trees
Chanderhill
CHANDER HILL LA
Old Barn Farm
POCKNEDGE LA

70
32 A 33 B 34 C

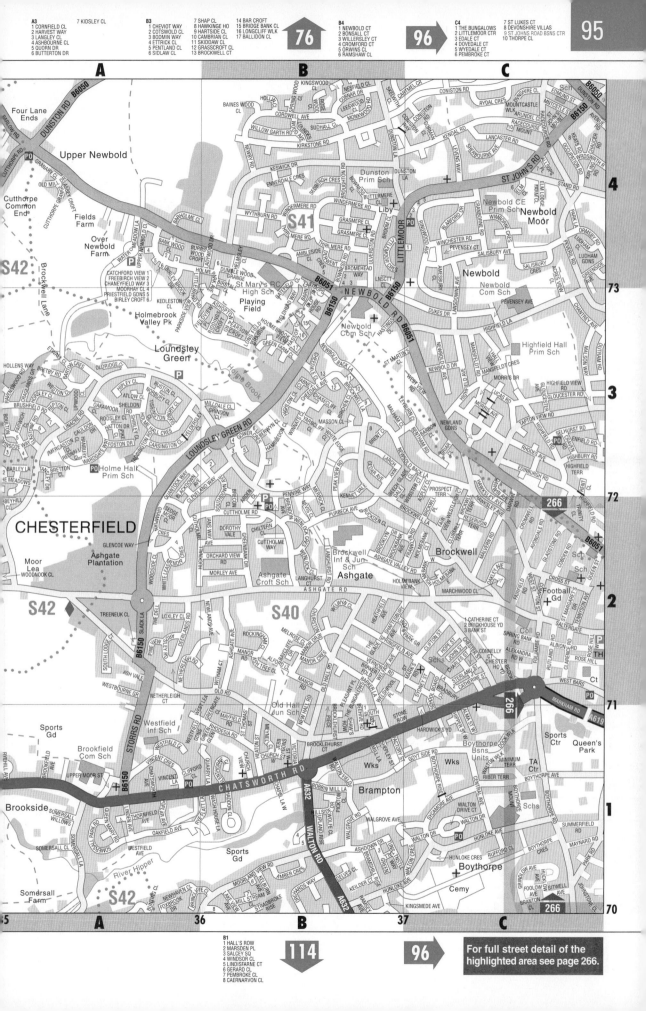

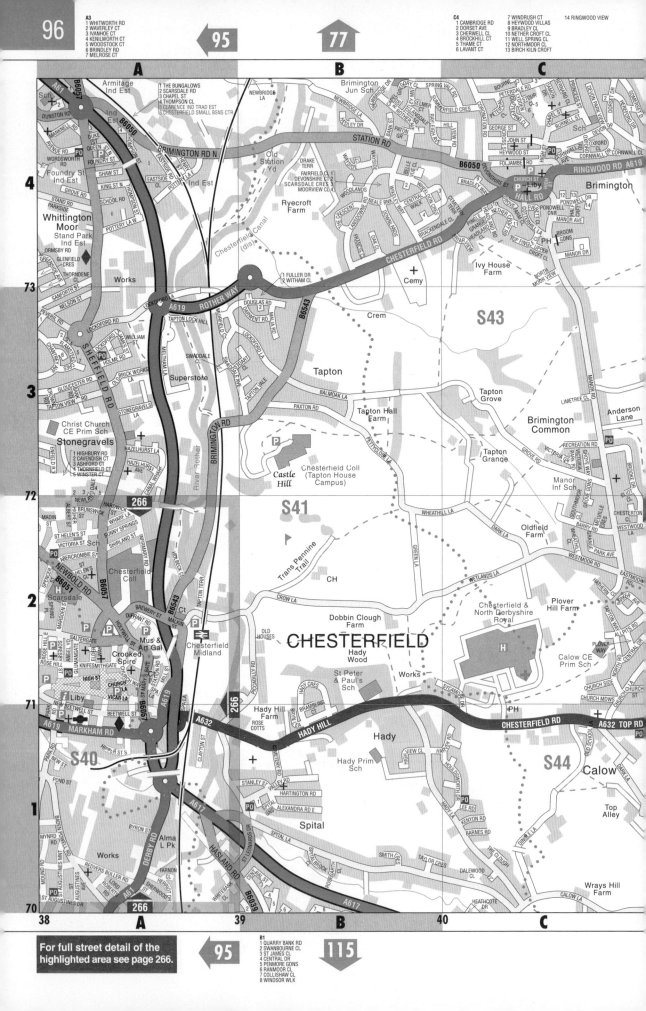

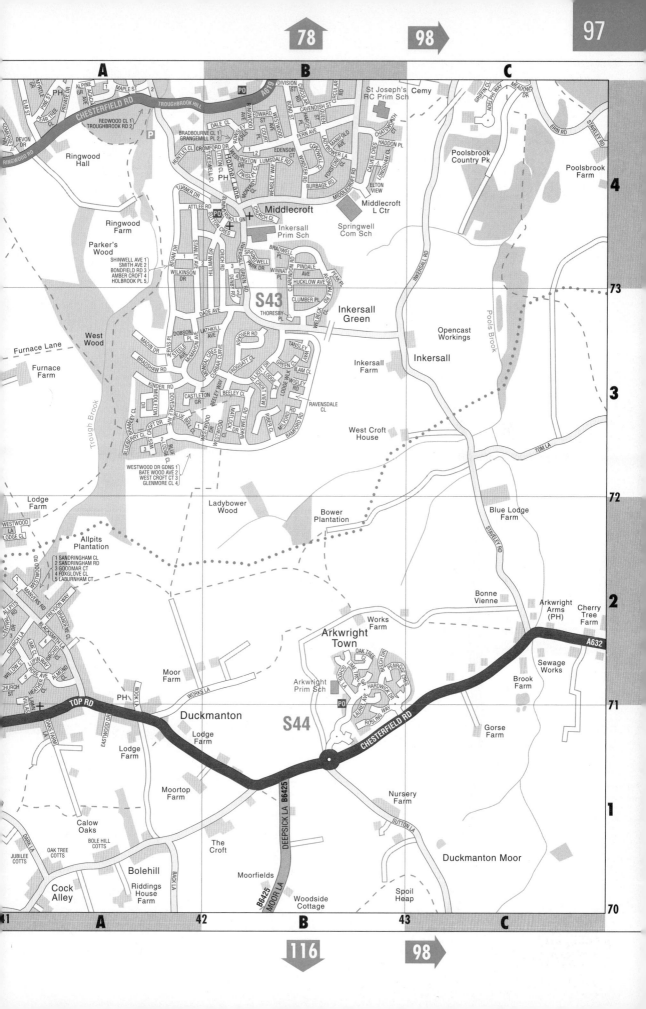

A B C

Seymour Junction

Poolsbrook Country Pk

POOLSBROOK VIEW AVE
POOLSBROOK AVE
STAVELEY RD
THE GROVE
POOLSBROOK CRES
COTTAGE CL
POOLSBROOK SQ
Poolsbrook Prim Sch
P
Poolsbrook
PH

S43

4

73
Opencast Workings

B6419
MILL LA
Lodge Farm

WOODTHORPE RD
BENTINCK RD
Woodside
Shuttlewood Common
Brockley Prim Sch
CLOWNE RD
Shuttlewood
WOODTHORPE CL
PH
ADIN AVE
PRETORIA ST
VIVIAN ST
PATTISON
PO
BOLSOVER RD
SHUTTLEWOOD RD
BROCKLEY AVE
NORTON AVE
B6419

ERIN RD

Sch
NORTH CL
NORTH CRES
EAST CRES
WEST CRES
POOLSBROOK RD
TOM LA
PH
PO
DUCKMANTON RD
POOLSBROOK SOUTH CRES
MARKHAM RD
The Oaks
Duckmanton
Middle Farm
+

The Nunnery
CHESTERFIELD RD
Nunnery Farm
Wyandotte Farm

Woodhouse Farm
Bolsover Woodhouse

3

Poplar Farm
OLD PEVERIL RD
Resr
RECTORY RD
ROBERTSON'S AVE
CHERRY TREE DR
BEECH GR
ST PETERS CL
+
Manor Farm
MANOR FARM MEWS
RECTORY CL

72
Sewage Works
Works
S44

M1 Commerce Pk
MARKHAM LA

Nether Woodhouse Farm

WOODHOUSE LA
NETHER SPRINGS RD 1
BRIAR BRIGGS RD 2
MANOR COURT RD 3
HARVEY CT 4
HASLAM CT 5
BOLSOVER HILL 6.

2
A632
CHESTERFIELD RD
B6418

Long Duckmanton

Works

River Doe Lea

BUTTERMILK LA

Over Woodhouse
BLIND LA
IRON CLIFF RD
PEVERIL RD
FARMFIELDS CL
HOUFTON CRES
NURSERY DR
MOULDSWORTH
HYNDLEY RD
SPRINGFIELD CRES
DAVEY CT
HALDANE CL

71
Railway Cottages
Lea-Holme
Mill Farm
Bsns Pk
P
RIVERSIDE WAY
INTAKE RD
Bsns Pk
Castle Ind Est
STATION RD
A632
VILAS RD

LONGCOURSE LA

Longcourse House

1
Longcourse Farm

Burton Barn

The Goit

The Goit
Sewage Works

New Bolsover
PO
New Bolsover Prim Sch
RUTLAND AVE 1
KESWICK CL 2
AMBLESIDE DR 3
ESKDALE CL 4.
NEW STATION RD
CHAPEL RD
CARR VALE RD
BAINBRIDGE RD
CASTLE
DUMBLES RD

70
NORTH VIEW ST

44 A 45 B 46 C

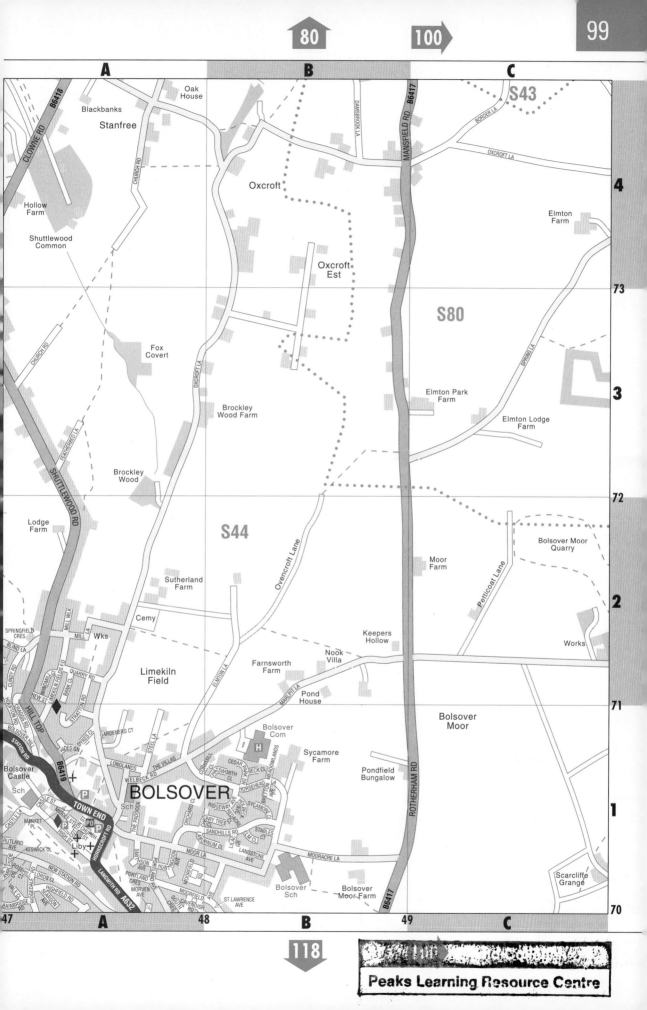

A   **B**   **C**

S43

CLOWNE RD
B6418

Blackbanks
Oak House
Stanfree

Hollow Farm

Shuttlewood Common

CHURCH RD

Oxcroft

DAMSBROOK LA

MANSFIELD RD
B6417

BORDER LA

OXCROFT LA

Elmton Farm

4

Oxcroft Est

73

S80

Fox Covert

OXCROFT LA

CHURCH RD

FEATHERBED LA

Brockley Wood Farm

Elmton Park Farm

SPRING LA

Elmton Lodge Farm

3

Brockley Wood

SHUTTLEWOOD RD

72

Lodge Farm

S44

Ovencroft Lane

Moor Farm

Bolsover Moor Quarry

Petticoat Lane

2

Sutherland Farm

Cemy

SPRINGFIELD CRES

BLIND LA

MILL WLK

MILL LA

Wks

MILL

Keepers Hollow

Works

ELMTON LA

Farnsworth Farm

Nook Villa

QUARRY RD

STATION RD

BANK CL

MICKLN FIELDS FD

WINDMILL CL

NEW ST

Limekiln Field

MARLPIT LA

Pond House

71

CUNDY RD

HOUFTON RD

CRAGGS RD

BOLSOVER HILL

HIDES GN

GARDENERS CT

Gardeners Ct

STEEL LA

Bolsover Com

[H]

Sycamore Farm

Bolsover Moor

Bolsover Castle

Sch

B6419

P

LONGLANDS

THE VILLAS

WELBECK RD

CHURCH

Pondfield Bungalow

ROTHERHAM RD

BOLSOVER

P

TOWN END

Sch

CASTLE LA

MARKET PL

MIDDLE ST

HIGH ST

P

Liby

P

HORNSCROFT RD

THE PADDOCK

ORCHARD CL

RIDGEWAY

COTMANHAY

CHATSWORTH CL

CEDAR PARK DR

HORSEHEAD

BRETTON

SYCAMORE AVE

MEADOWLANDS

1

RUTLAND AVE

KESWICK CL

SANDHILLS RD

LILAC CL

LABURNUM CL

BARRY TREE

STABLES CT

ROSEHILL RD

RIDGEDALE RD

LORDS CL

HIGHFIELD RD

NEW STATION RD

AMBLESIDE

CASTLE LA

VALE CT

BAINBRIDGE RD

SEASON ST

LANGWITH RD
A632

JASON AVE

PORTLAND CRES

MORVEN AVE

MOORFIELD SQ

MOOR LA

Langstone Ave

LANGSTONE AVE

Bolsover Sch

ST LAWRENCE AVE

CAVENDISH

SOUTH CRES

MOORACRE LA

Bolsover Moor Farm

B6417

Scarcliffe Grange

70

47   **A**   **48**   **B**   **49**   **C**

Peaks Learning Resource Centre

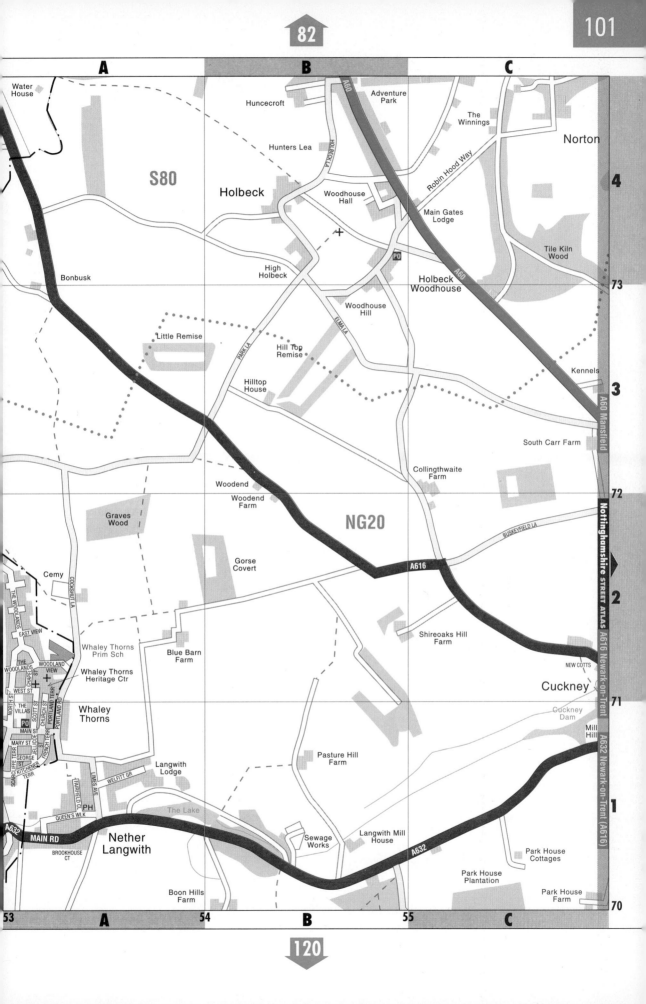

A B C

Water House

Huncecroft

Adventure Park

The Winnings

Norton

Hunters Lea

Robin Hood Way

S80

Holbeck

Woodhouse Hall

Main Gates Lodge

4

HOLBECK LA

A60

PO

Tile Kiln Wood

Bonbusk

High Holbeck

Holbeck Woodhouse

A60

73

Little Remise

Woodhouse Hill

Kennels

Hill Top Remise

ELMA LA

PARK LA

Hilltop House

South Carr Farm

3

A60 Mansfield

Woodend

Collingthwaite Farm

72

Woodend Farm

NG20

BUSKEYFIELD LA

Graves Wood

Gorse Covert

A616

Cemy

COCKSHUT LA

Shireoaks Hill Farm

2

Nottinghamshire STREET ATLAS A616 Newark-on-Trent

THE WOODLANDS

EAST VIEW

Whaley Thorns Prim Sch

Blue Barn Farm

NEW COTTS

THE WOODLANDS

CHAPEL ST

WOODLAND VIEW

Whaley Thorns Heritage Ctr

Cuckney

WEST ST

Whaley Thorns

Cuckney Dam

71

NORTH ST

THE VILLAS

GEORGE ST

SCOTT ST

CHURCH ST

PORTLAND TERR

PORTLAND RD

Mill Hill

A632 Newark-on-Trent (A616)

MARY ST

SLOCIE ST

FRENCH TERR

MAIN ST

PO

Langwith Lodge

Pasture Hill Farm

SPARCLIFFE TERR

KITCHENER TERR

Langwith Lodge

Langwith Mill House

FAIRFIELD CL

LIMES AVE

WELFITT GR

PH

A632

QUEEN'S WLK

The Lake

1

A632

MAIN RD

Nether Langwith

Sewage Works

Boon Hills Farm

Park House Cottages

Park House Plantation

Park House Farm

70

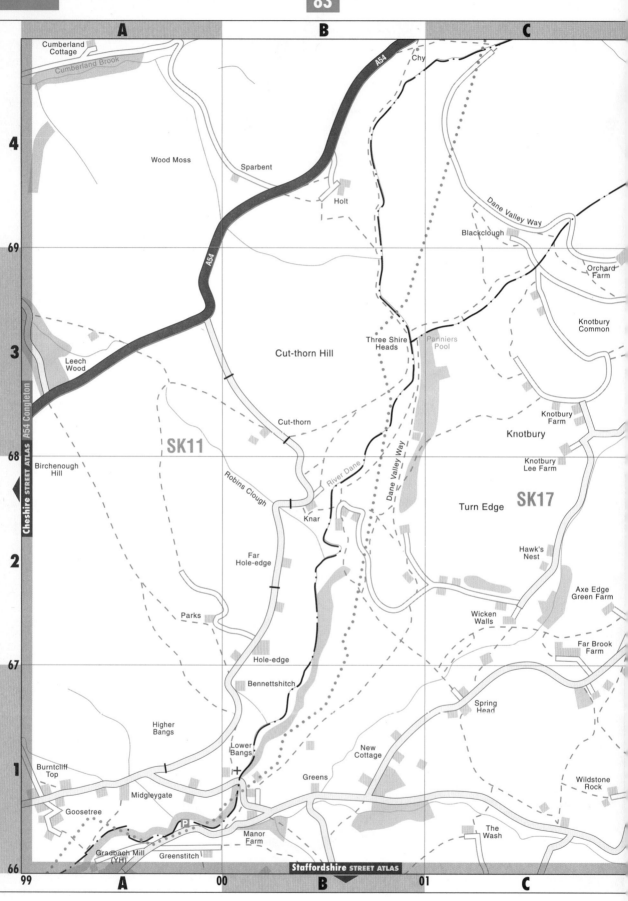

Cumberland
Cottage

Cumberland Brook

A54

Chy

Wood Moss

Sparbent

Holt

Dane Valley Way

Blackclough

Orchard
Farm

4

A54

69

Cut-thorn Hill

Three Shire
Heads

Panniers
Pool

Knotbury
Common

Leech
Wood

3

Knotbury
Farm

Knotbury

SK11

Cut-thorn

68

Birchenough
Hill

Robins Clough

River Dane

Dane Valley Way

Knotbury
Lee Farm

Turn Edge

SK17

Cheshire STREET ATLAS   A54 Congleton

Knar

Far
Hole-edge

Hawk's
Nest

Axe Edge
Green Farm

2

Parks

Wicken
Walls

Far Brook
Farm

Hole-edge

67

Bennettshitch

Spring
Head

Higher
Bangs

Lower
Bangs

New
Cottage

Wildstone
Rock

1

Burntcliff
Top

Midgleygate

Greens

Goosetree

P

The
Wash

Gradbach Mill
(YH)

Greenstitch

Manor
Farm

66

99   A   00   B   01   C

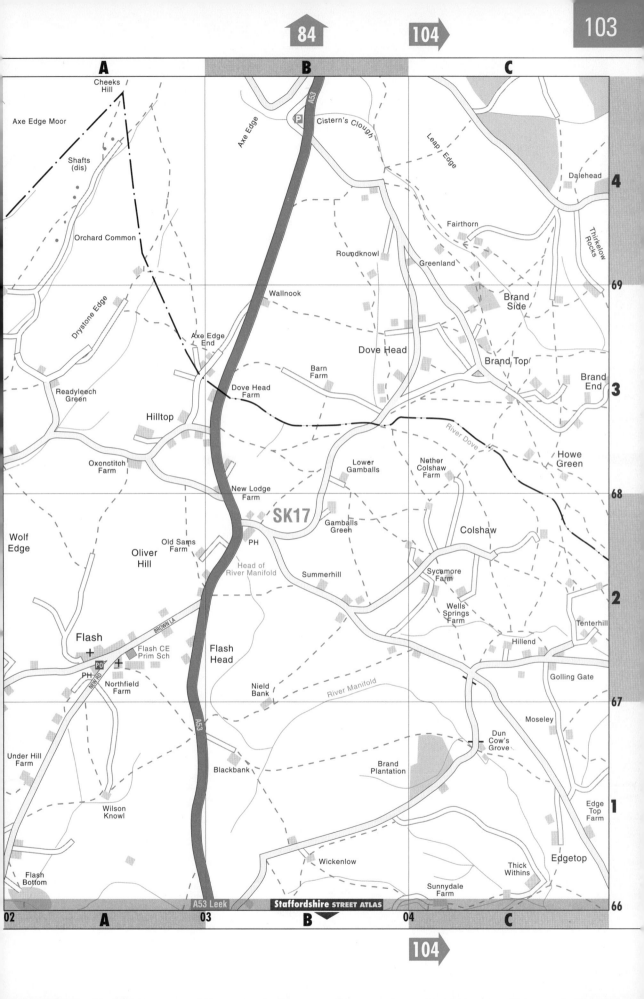

Cheeks Hill

Axe Edge Moor

Shafts (dis)

Orchard Common

Axe Edge

Cistern's Clough

Leap Edge

Dalehead

4

Thirkelow Rocks

Fairthorn

Roundknowl

Greenland

Drystone Edge

Wallnook

69

Brand Side

Dove Head

Readyleech Green

Axe Edge End

Barn Farm

Brand Top

Brand End

3

Hilltop

Dove Head Farm

River Dove

Howe Green

Oxonstitch Farm

Lower Gamballs

Nether Colshaw Farm

New Lodge Farm

68

Wolf Edge

SK17

Gamballs Green

Colshaw

Old Sams Farm

PH

Oliver Hill

Head of River Manifold

Summerhill

Sycamore Farm

2

Wells Springs Farm

Tenterhill

Flash

Hillend

BROWN LA

Flash CE Prim Sch

Flash Head

Golling Gate

+
PO
PH
NEW RD
Northfield Farm

Nield Bank

River Manifold

67

Under Hill Farm

Moseley

Dun Cow's Grove

A53

Blackbank

Brand Plantation

Edge Top Farm

1

Wilson Knowl

Edgetop

Flash Bottom

Wickenlow

Thick Withins

Sunnydale Farm

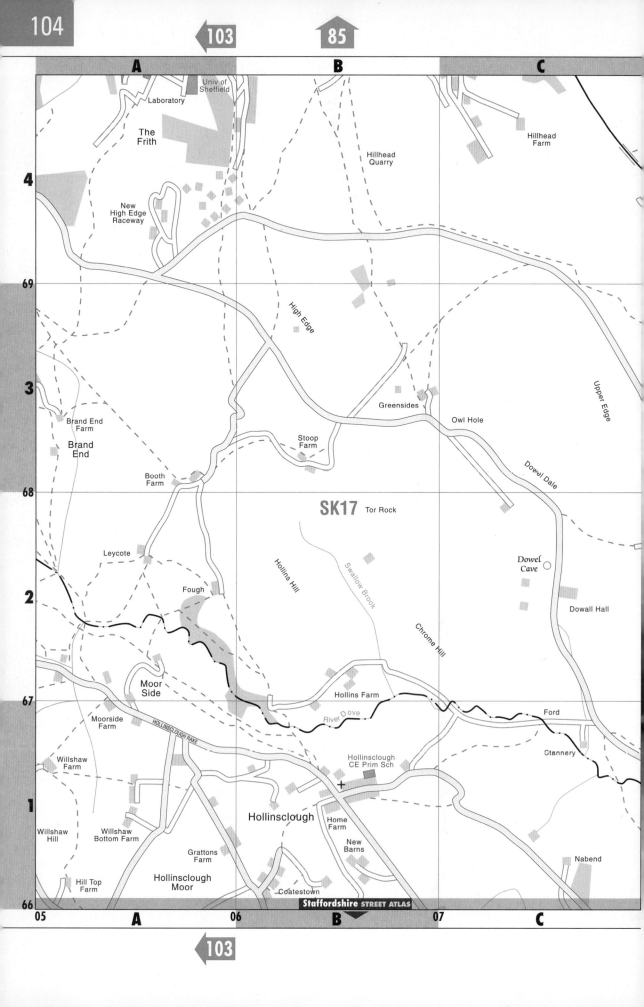

A   B   C

4

Univ of
Sheffield

Laboratory

The
Frith

Hillhead
Quarry

Hillhead
Farm

New
High Edge
Raceway

69

High Edge

3

Brand End
Farm

Greensides

Owl Hole

Upper Edge

Brand
End

Stoop
Farm

Booth
Farm

Dowel Dale

68

SK17   Tor Rock

Leycote

Hollins Hill

Swallow Brook

Dowel
Cave

Fough

Dowall Hall

2

Chrome Hill

Moor
Side

Hollins Farm

Ford

67

Moorside
Farm

HOLLINSCLOUGH RAKE

River Dove

Stannery

Willshaw
Farm

Hollinsclough
CE Prim Sch

1

Willshaw
Hill

Willshaw
Bottom Farm

Hollinsclough

Home
Farm

New
Barns

Nabend

Grattons
Farm

Hill Top
Farm

Hollinsclough
Moor

Coatestown

66

05   A   06   B   07   C

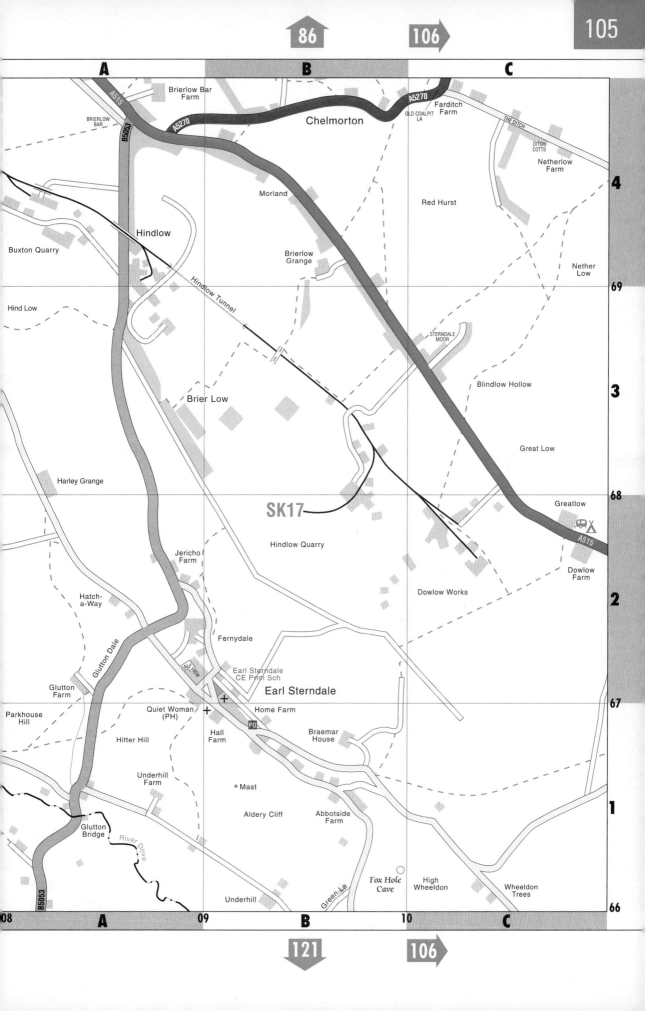

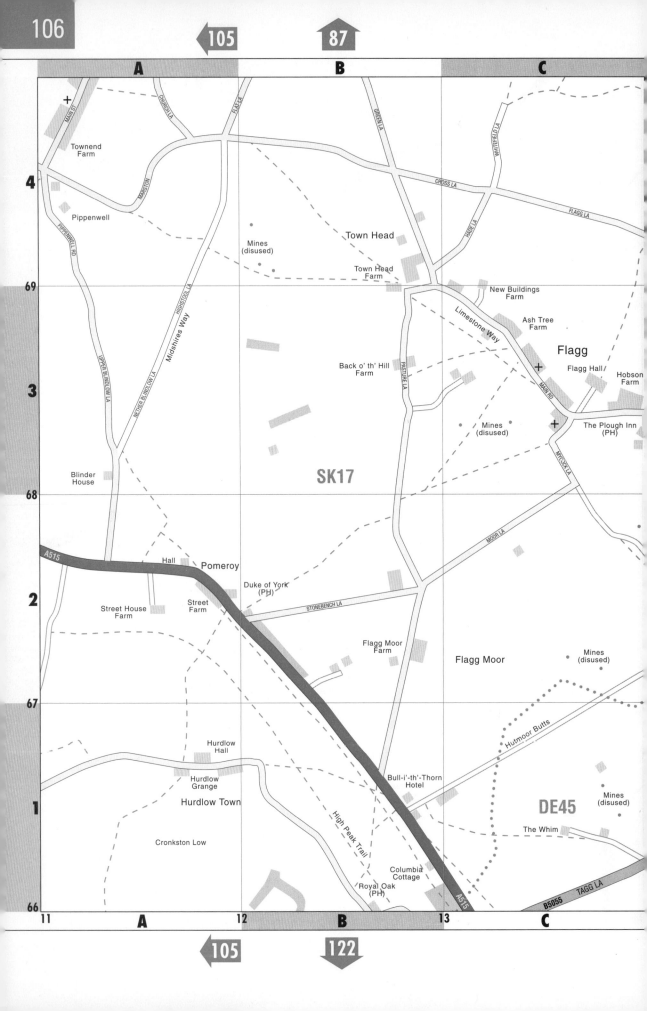

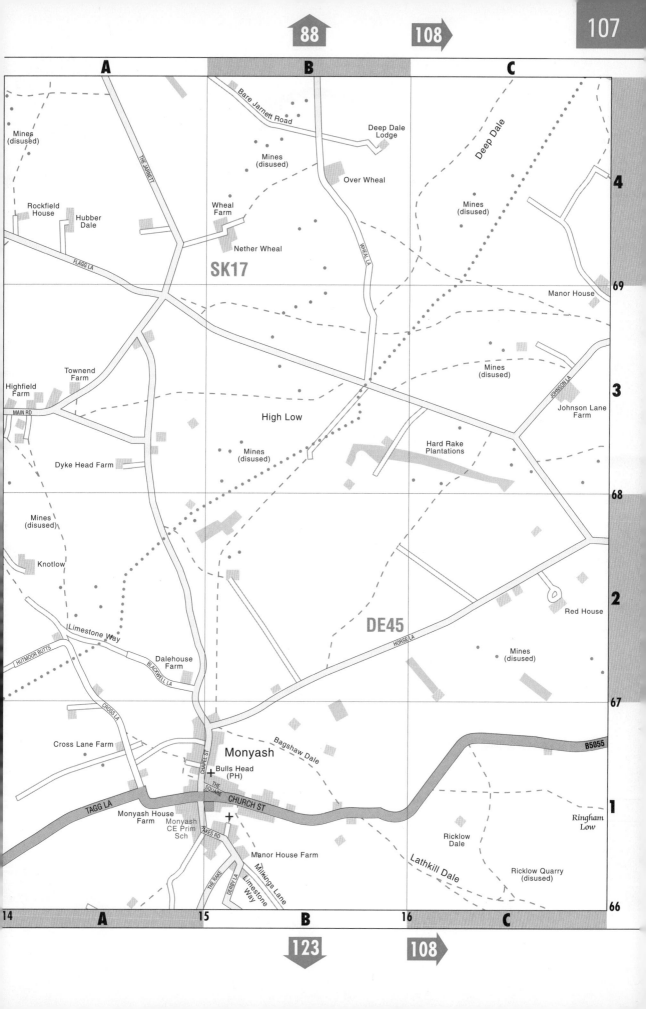

88
108
123
108

Mines
(disused)

Bare Jarnett Road

Deep Dale
Lodge

Deep Dale

Mines
(disused)

Over Wheal

4

Rockfield
House

Wheal
Farm

Hubber
Dale

Mines
(disused)

THE JARNETT

Nether Wheal

WHEAL LA

Mines
(disused)

FLAGG LA

SK17

Manor House

69

Townend
Farm

Mines
(disused)

JOHNSON LA

3

Highfield
Farm

High Low

Johnson Lane
Farm

MAIN RD

Dyke Head Farm

Mines
(disused)

Hard Rake
Plantations

68

Mines
(disused)

Knotlow

2

Limestone Way

Red House

HUTMOOR BUTTS

DE45

HORSE LA

Mines
(disused)

Dalehouse
Farm

BLACKWELL LA

67

CROSS LA

B5055

Cross Lane Farm

Bagshaw Dale

Monyash

CHAPEL ST

Bulls Head
(PH)

THE SQUARE

TAGG LA

CHURCH ST

1

Monyash House
Farm

Monyash
CE Prim
Sch

Ringham
Low

Manor House Farm

Ricklow
Dale

THE RAKE

JAKES RD

DERBY LA

Limestone Way

Milkings Lane

Lathkill Dale

Ricklow Quarry
(disused)

66

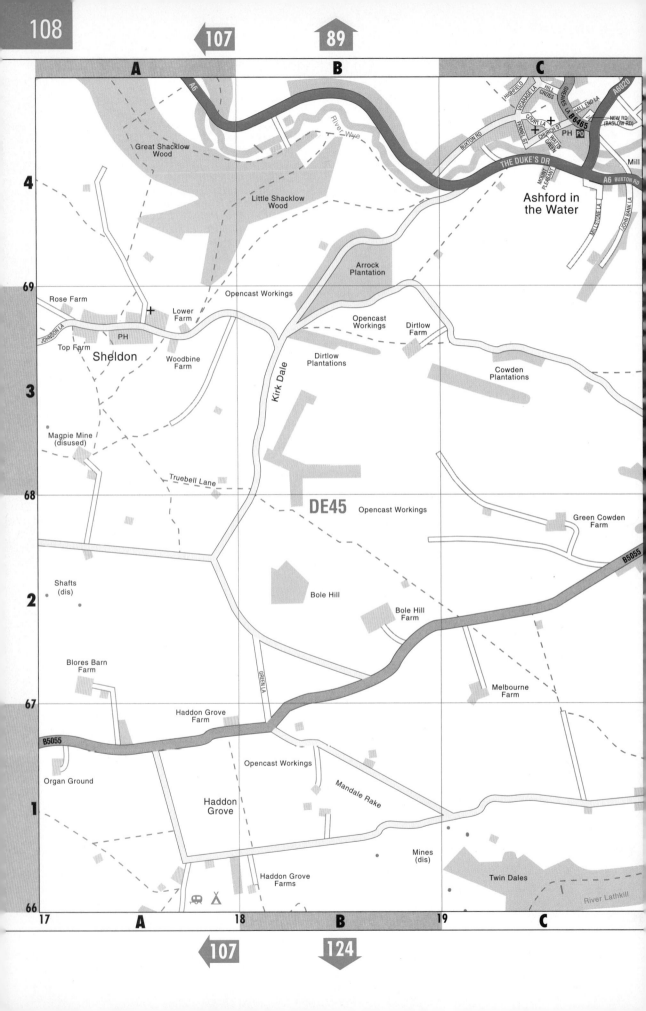

A   **B**   **C**

4

Great Shacklow Wood

Little Shacklow Wood

River Wye

A6

Arrock Plantation

I HIGHFIELD
VICARAGE LA
HILL CROSS
BREAKS LA
HALL END LA
B6465
NEW RD (BASLOW RD)
A6020
COURT LA
FENNEL ST
CHURCH ST
WALTS GREEN
PH
PO
BUXTON RD
THE DUKE'S DR
MOUNT PLEASANT
A6 BUXTON RD
MILLSTONE LA
JOHN BANK LA
Mill

Ashford in the Water

69

Rose Farm

Opencast Workings

Opencast Workings

Dirtlow Farm

Cowden Plantations

JOHNSON LA
Top Farm
PH
Lower Farm
Woodbine Farm

Sheldon

Dirtlow Plantations

3

Kirk Dale

Magpie Mine (disused)

Truebell Lane

68

DE45   Opencast Workings

Green Cowden Farm

B5055

Shafts (dis)

Bole Hill

Bole Hill Farm

2

Blores Barn Farm

GREEN LA

Melbourne Farm

67

Haddon Grove Farm

B5055

Organ Ground

Opencast Workings

Mandale Rake

Haddon Grove

1

Mines (dis)

Twin Dales

Haddon Grove Farms

River Lathkill

66

17   **A**   **18**   **B**   **19**   **C**

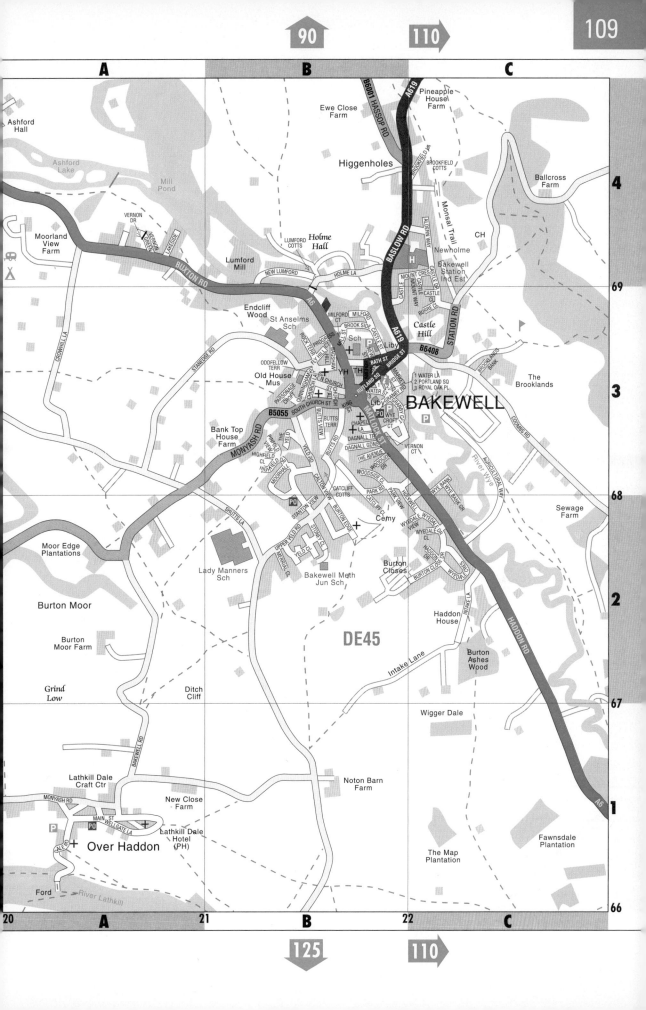

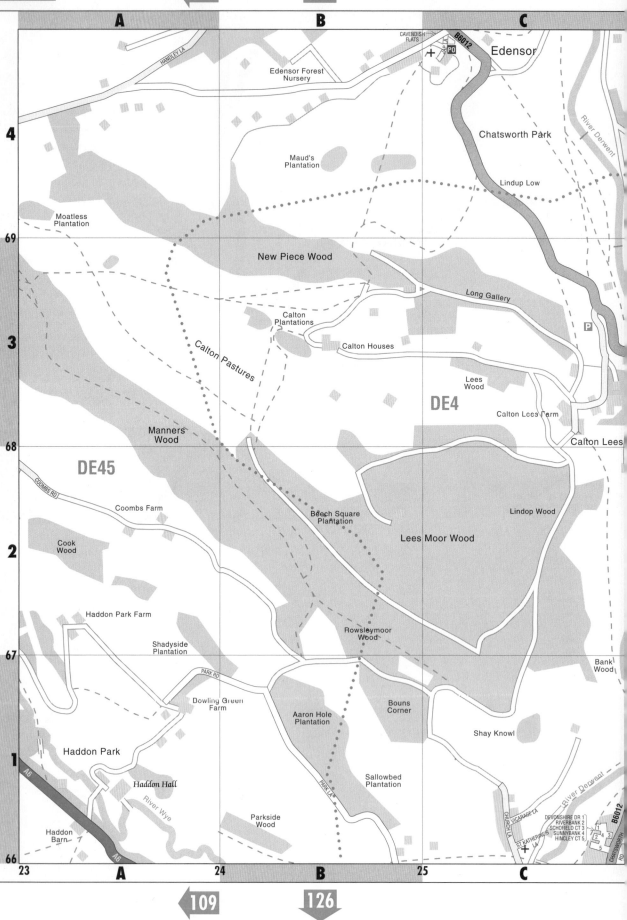

A   B   C

HANDLEY LA

CAVENDISH FLATS

B6012

Edensor

P0

Chatsworth Park

River Derwent

Edensor Forest Nursery

4

Maud's Plantation

Lindup Low

Moatless Plantation

69

New Piece Wood

Long Gallery

Calton Plantations

P

Calton Houses

3

Calton Pastures

Lees Wood

DE4

Calton Lees Farm

Manners Wood

Calton Lees

68

DE45

COOMBS RD

Coombs Farm

Beech Square Plantation

Lindop Wood

Cook Wood

2

Lees Moor Wood

Haddon Park Farm

Shadyside Plantation

Bank Wood

67

PARK RD

Dowling Green Farm

Rowsleymoor Wood

Bouns Corner

Aaron Hole Plantation

Shay Knowl

Haddon Park

1

A6

Haddon Hall

River Wye

PARK LA

Sallowbed Plantation

River Derwent

B6012

Haddon Barn

A6

Parkside Wood

CHURCH LA

VICARAGE LA

ST KATHERINE'S LA

DEVONSHIRE DR 1
RIVERBANK 2
SCHOFIELD CT 3
SUNNYBANK 4
HINCLEY CT 5

CHATSWORTH RD

66

23   A   24   B   25   C

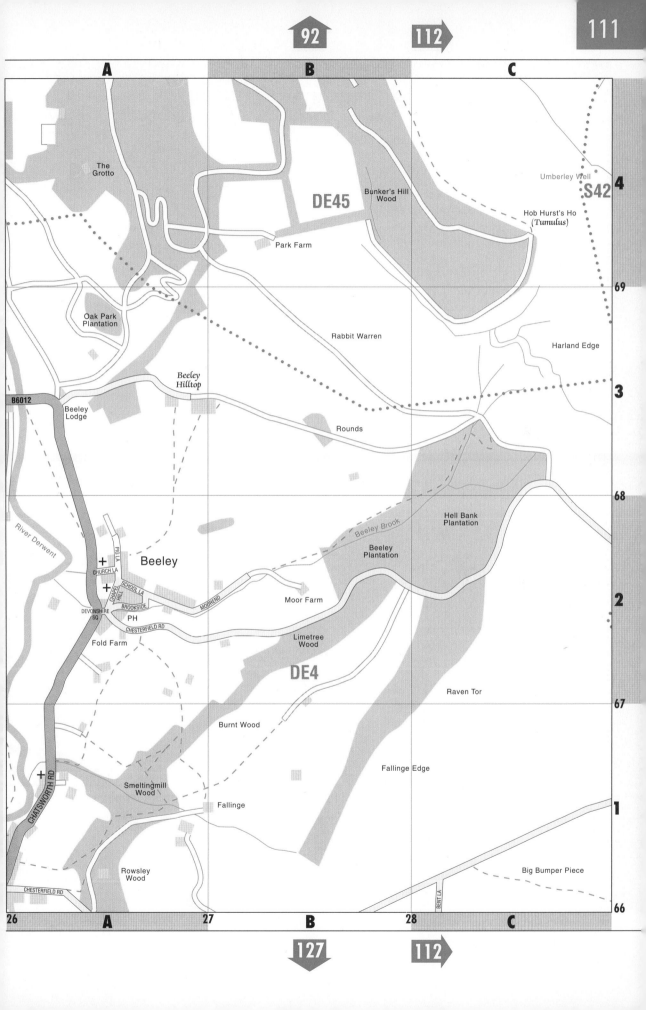

A   B   C

The Grotto

DE45

Bunker's Hill Wood

Umberley Well

S42   4

Hob Hurst's Ho (Tumulus)

Park Farm

69

Oak Park Plantation

Rabbit Warren

Harland Edge

Beeley Hilltop

B6012

Beeley Lodge

3

Rounds

68

River Derwent

Beeley Brook

Hell Bank Plantation

Beeley Plantation

Beeley

PIG LA

CHURCH LA

SCHOOL LA

CHAPEL HILL

Moor Farm

2

DEVONSHIRE SQ

PH

BROOKSIDE

MOOREND

CHESTERFIELD RD

Fold Farm

Limetree Wood

DE4

Raven Tor

67

Burnt Wood

Fallinge Edge

CHATSWORTH RD

Smeltingmill Wood

Fallinge

1

Big Bumper Piece

Rowsley Wood

BENT LA

CHESTERFIELD RD

66

26   A   27   B   28   C

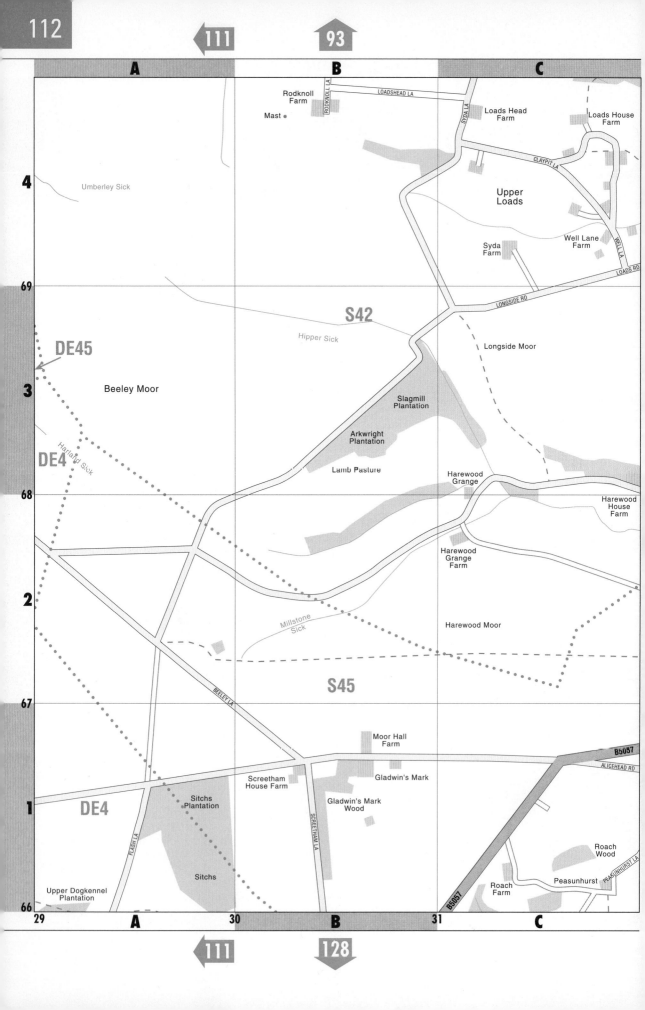

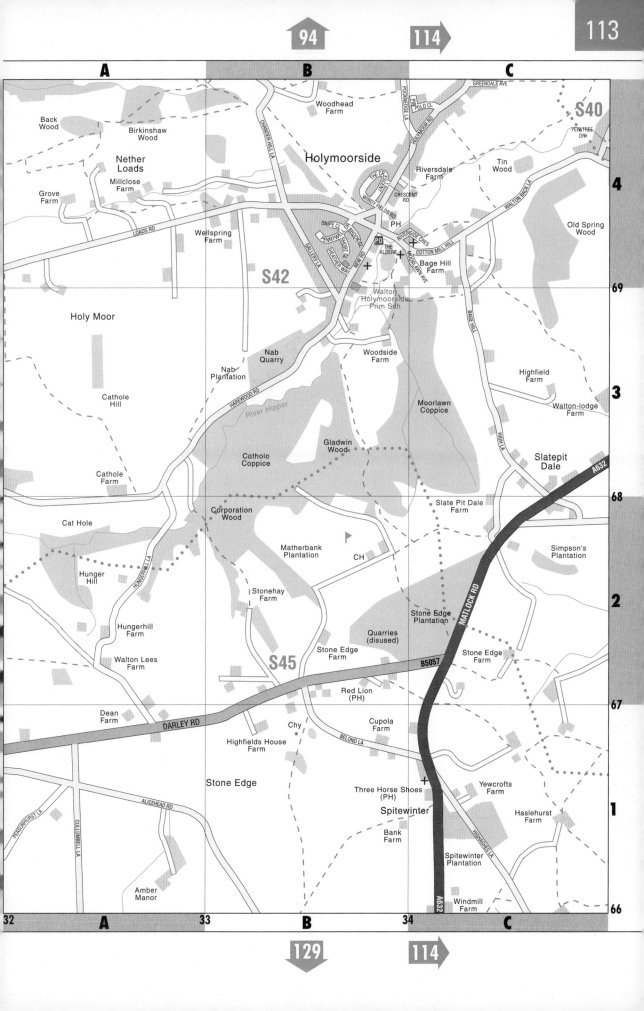

← **113**
95

A   B   C

Nether House Farm
CALOW LA
HALL FLASH LA
Calow Green
Calow Green Farm
BACK LA
MOOR LA
B6425
Spoil Heap
Sutton Lane Farm

4

Woodnook Farm
Bull Paddock Farm
SUTTON LA

S44

69

Calow Brook
HASSOCKY LA
Sutton Springs Wood
Hall Farm
ROCK LA
Yewtree Farm
SHIRE LA

3
A617
S41

Hill Farm
Muster Brook
Springwood Farm
68
B6039
B6425
Temple Normanton Prim Sch
POSTMANS LA
High House Farm
Temple Normanton Bsns Pk
Bond's Main
SPRINGWOOD ST
M ST
S42
Grassmoor Country Park

2
Cemy
CHURCH LA
Temple Normanton
BIRKIN LA
P
MANSFIELD RD
Musterbrook Bridge
A617

67
Philadelphia

High Top Poultry Farm
CHESTERFIELD RD
Holmewood Bsns Pk
Williamthorpe Ind Pk
Williamthorpe Ponds (Nature Reserve)
SLACK LA
MOORLAND DR
LILAC CL
GORSE BANK
HEATHER CL
BRACKEN AVE
BRAMBLE CL
Heath Prim Sch

1
Lings Farm
ENTERPRISE DR WAY
MOORE CL
TUPTON WAY
WOODSOME PK
Holmewood Ind Pk
PARK RD
Sewage Works
FERN CL
HEATH RD
A6175
Pavilion Workshops
Works
QUEENS WLK
DEVONSHIRE TERR
RAILWAY COTTS
Holmewood
WOOD ST
HUNLOKE
QUEENSWAY
Hardwick View Rd
CHESTERFIELD RD
B6038
P
SHELLEY CL
TENNYSON
SHAW CL
LAWRENCE AVE
SHAKESPEARE ST
MASEFIELD AVE
B6039
DICKENS DR
FISHER WATERS
COMPTON ST
ASTWITH CL
STAINSBY
A6175

66

41   A   42   B   43   C

A

B

C

4

69

3

68

2

67

1

66

Park Gate Cottages

Pond Plantation

The Goit

NORTH VIEW ST

SPENCER ST

CHARLESWORTH ST

SUTTON HALL RD

SCARSDALE ST

MAIN ST

PO

GREENAWAY DR

BATHURST RD

SHERWOOD ST

ORCHARD ST

Carr Vale

WATER LA

P

Doe Lea Bridge

PALTERTON LA

CARR LA

Sutton Scarsdale Hall

Deepdale Farm

MILL HILL

Sutton Scarsdale

Park Farm

Rylah

RYLAH HILL

Wrang Plantation

Rylah Farm

Owlcotes

S44

Sewage Works

Stockley Farm

River Doe Lea

Stockley

Church (remains of)

CHURCH LA

Mansfield Rd

PH

Motel

Ivy Farm

CHURCH LA

A617

A6175

29

A617

Heath

VICARAGE CL

MAIN RD

PO

WILSON LA

Stockley LA

NUTTALL TERR

CROSS ST

Gildage Farm

WEST ST

CENTRE ST

EAST ST

OLD SCHOOL CL

NORTH ST

JACKSON RD

GARDEN ROW

MANSFIELD RD

PH

Chapel Hill

MILL LA

Doe Lea

STANHOPE ST

CAMBRIDGE CRES

Sch

BRAMLEY RD

LANCASTER ST

PO

CAMBRIDGE CRES

ORCHID RD

WATERLOO ST

A617 THE HILL

S42

Bramley-Vale

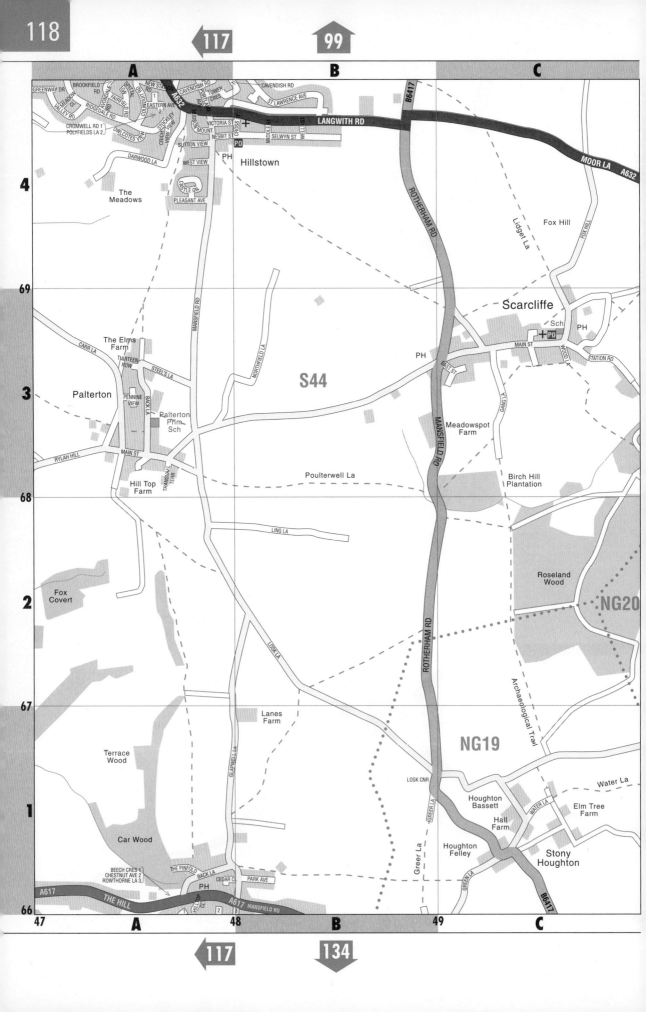

A B C

Greenway Dr
Brookfield Rd
Meadow Cl
Valley Rd
Avondale Rd
Fairfield Rd
Ridgedale Rd
New Station
Spital Dr
Littlewood
Eastern Ave
A632
Cavendish Rd
Cavendish Rd
St Lawrence Ave
Tower Cres
LANGWITH RD
B6417

Cromwell Rd 1
Polyfields La 2
Owlcotes View
Crags
Stockley View
Victoria St
North St
Mount
Nesbit St
Cross St
Middle St
Selwyn St
Wells St
+
PO

Darwood La
Sutton View
West View
PH
Hillstown

The Meadows
Castle Cl
Pleasant Ave

MOOR LA A632

4

Lidget La
Fox Hill
Fox Hill

69

Carr La
The Elms Farm
Thirteen Row
Steels La
Mansfield Rd
Northfield La
S44
Scarcliffe
Sch
+PO
PH
Main St
Wood La
Station Rd

PH
East St
Gang La

Palterton
Pennine View
Back La
Palterton Prim Sch
Meadowspot Farm

3

Rylah Hill
Main St
Transval Terr
Poulterwell La
Birch Hill Plantation

Hill Top Farm

68

Ling La

Fox Covert
Roseland Wood

2

NG20

Loss La

67

Lanes Farm

Terrace Wood
NG19

Archaeological Trail

Water La
Losk Cnr

1

Glapwell La
Greer La
Houghton Bassett
Hall Farm
Elm Tree Farm
Water La

Car Wood
Houghton Felley
Stony Houghton

Beech Cres 1
Chestnut Ave 2
Rowthorne La 3
The Pinfold
Back La
Cedar Cl
Park Ave
PH
Green La
B6417

A617
THE HILL
A617 Mansfield Rd

66

47   A   48   B   49   C

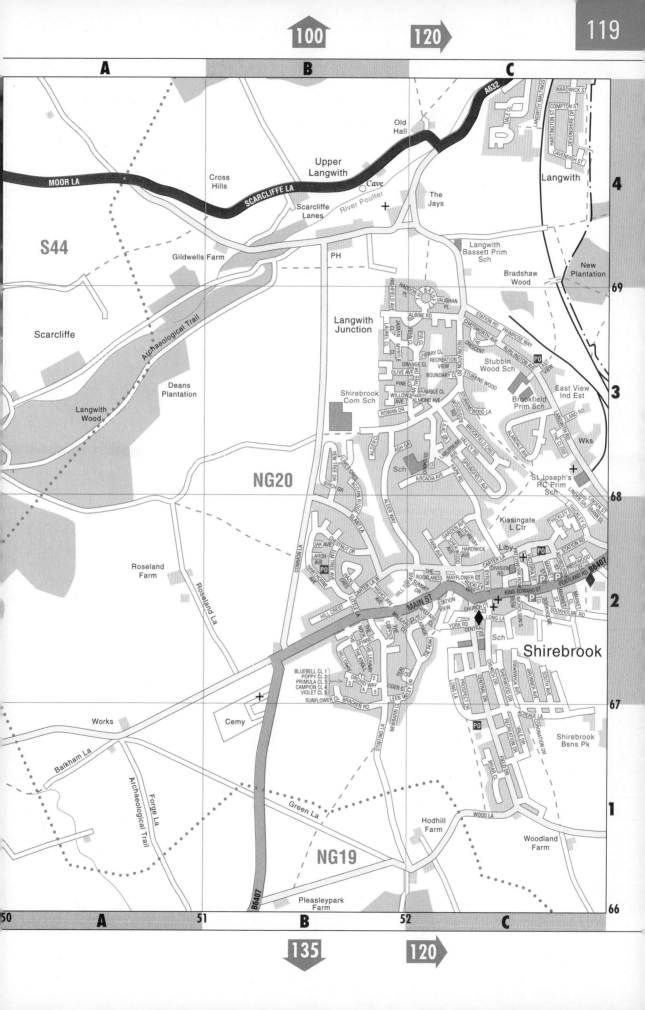

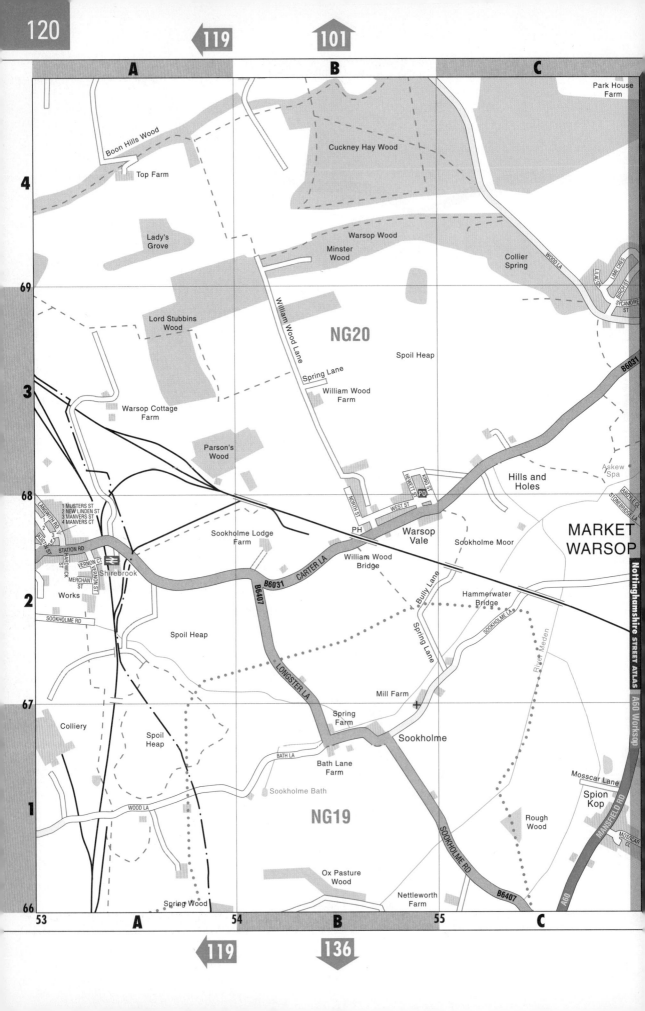

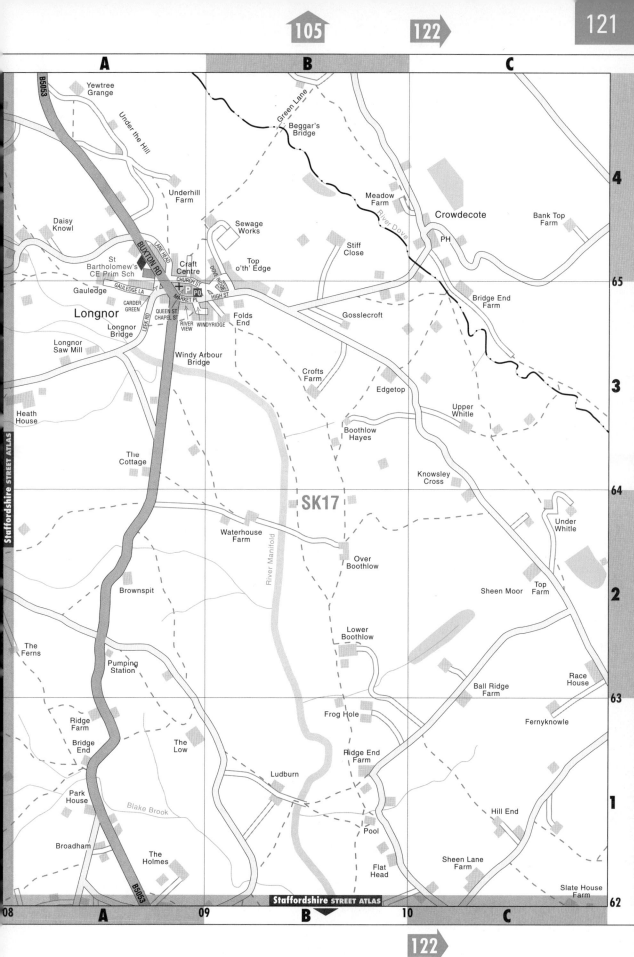

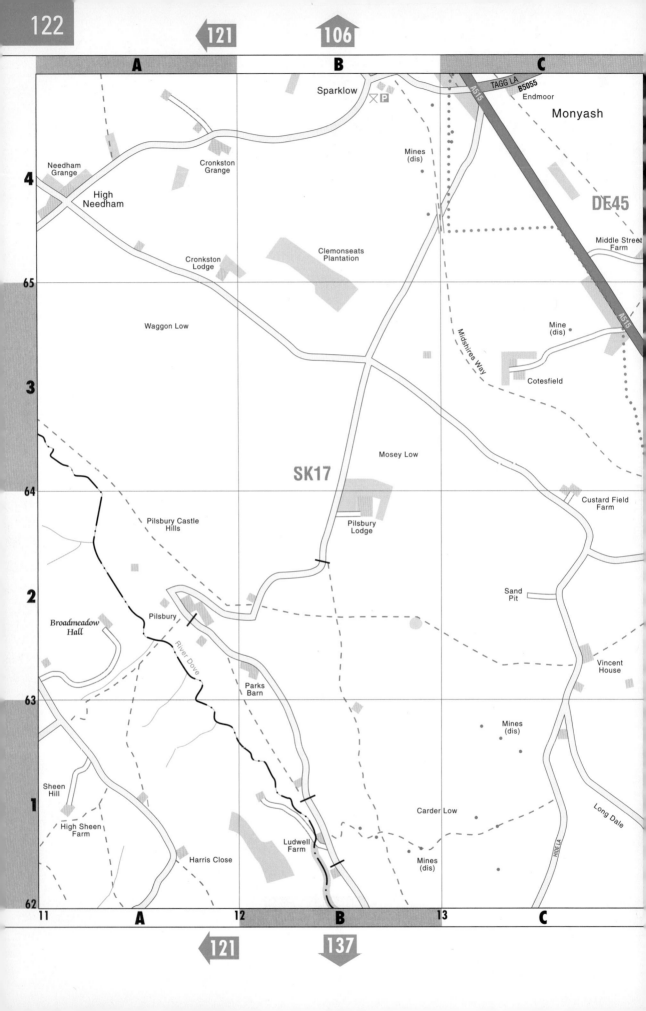

A **B** **C**

Sparklow

Monyash

TAGG LA

B5055

Endmoor

Mines
(dis)

DE45

4

Needham
Grange

Cronkston
Grange

High
Needham

Middle Street
Farm

Cronkston
Lodge

Clemonseats
Plantation

65

Waggon Low

Midshires Way

Mine
(dis)

A515

Cotesfield

3

Mosey Low

SK17

64

Custard Field
Farm

Pilsbury Castle
Hills

Pilsbury
Lodge

2

Broadmeadow
Hall

Pilsbury

Sand
Pit

River Dove

Vincent
House

63

Parks
Barn

Mines
(dis)

1

Sheen
Hill

Carder Low

Long Dale

High Sheen
Farm

HIDE LA

Ludwell
Farm

Mines
(dis)

Harris Close

62

11 **A** **12** **B** **13** **C**

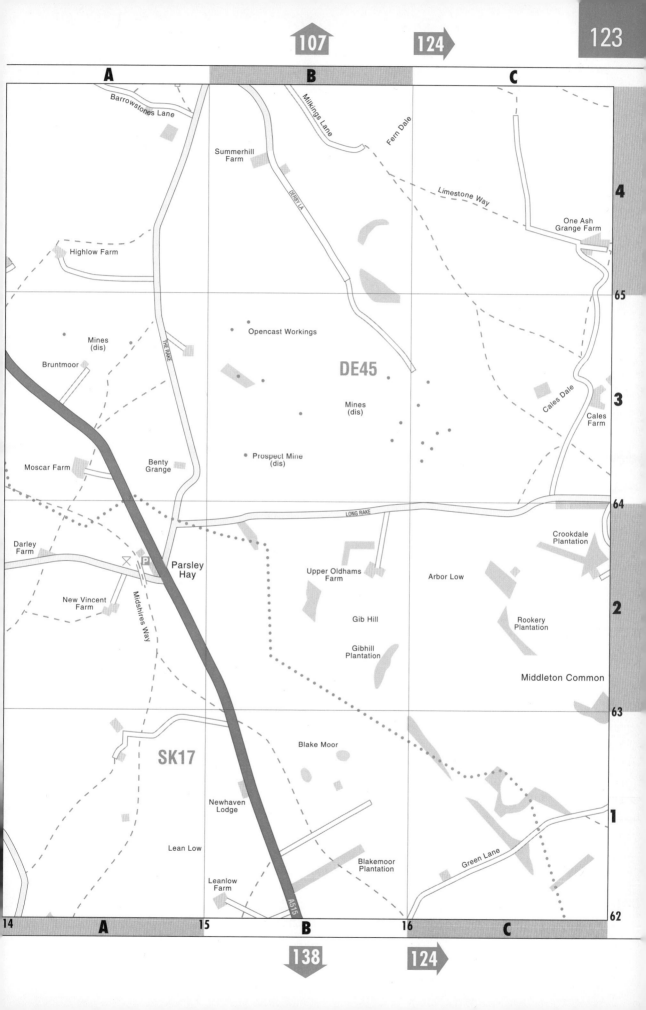

A
B
C

Barrowstones Lane

Milkings Lane

Fern Dale

Summerhill Farm

DERBY LA.

Limestone Way

One Ash Grange Farm

4

Highlow Farm

THE RAKE

Opencast Workings

65

Mines (dis)

DE45

Bruntmoor

Cales Dale

Mines (dis)

3

Cales Farm

Moscar Farm

Benty Grange

Prospect Mine (dis)

LONG RAKE

64

Darley Farm

Crookdale Plantation

Parsley Hay

Upper Oldhams Farm

Arbor Low

New Vincent Farm

Midshires Way

Gib Hill

Rookery Plantation

2

Gibhill Plantation

Middleton Common

63

SK17

Blake Moor

Newhaven Lodge

1

Lean Low

Blakemoor Plantation

Green Lane

Leanlow Farm

A515

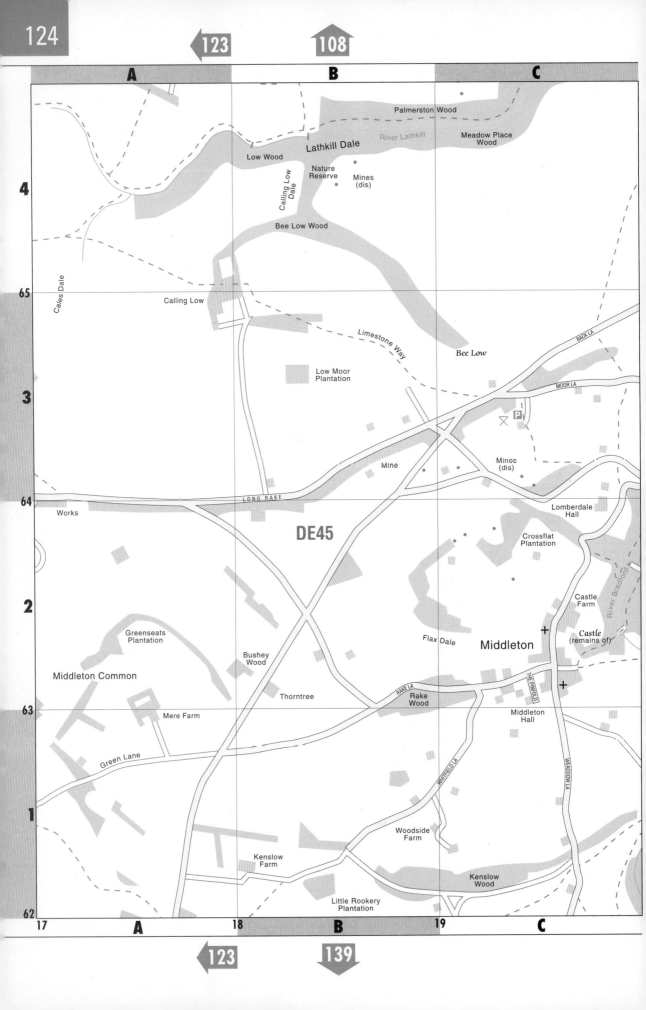

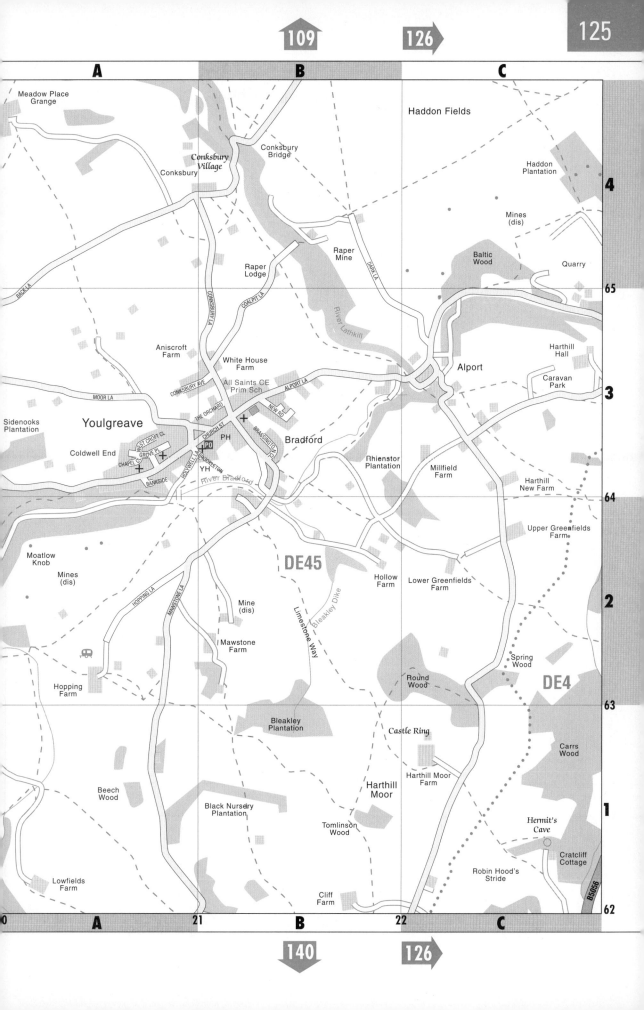

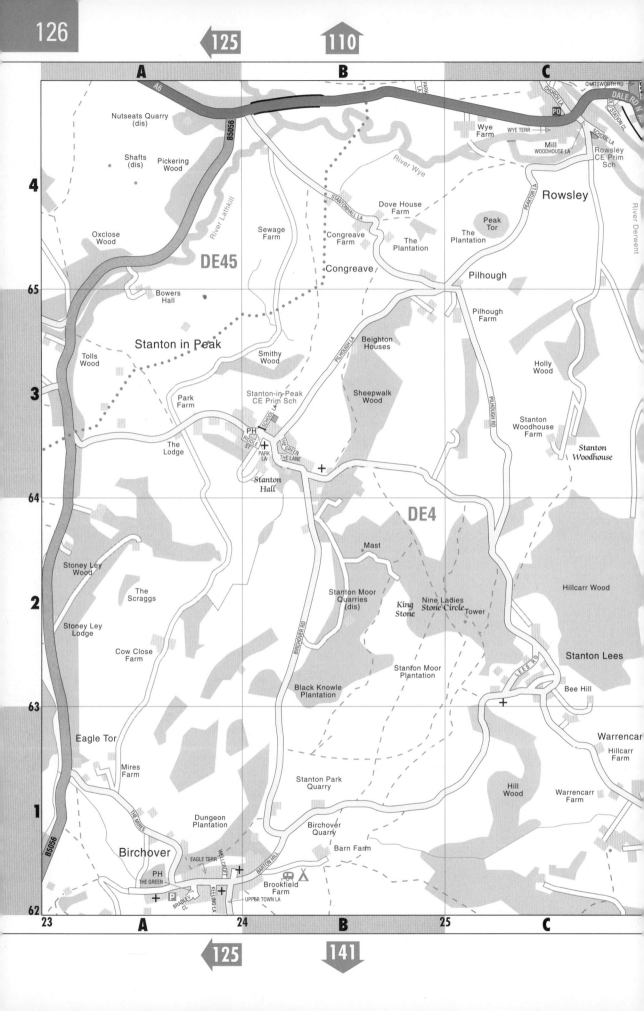

A

B

C

Nutseats Quarry (dis)

Wye Farm

CHATSWORTH RD

PARK LA

CHURCH LA

PO

OLD STATION CL

DALE RD N

Shafts (dis)

Pickering Wood

Mill

WYE TERR

WOODHOUSE LA

SCHOOL LA

Rowsley CE Prim Sch

A6

B5056

4

Oxclose Wood

River Lathkill

DE45

Sewage Farm

STANTON HALL LA

River Wye

Dove House Farm

Congreave Farm

The Plantation

The Plantation

Peak Tor

PEAK TOR LA

Rowsley

River Derwent

Bowers Hall

Congreave

Pilhough

65

Stanton in Peak

Pilhough Farm

Tolls Wood

Smithy Wood

PILHOUGH LA

Beighton Houses

Holly Wood

3

Park Farm

Stanton-in-Peak CE Prim Sch

SCHOOL LA

Sheepwalk Wood

PILHOUGH RD

Stanton Woodhouse Farm

The Lodge

PH

RIDDLE ST

PARK LA

THE GREEN

THE LANE

Stanton Woodhouse

Stanton Hall

DE4

64

Mast

Stoney Ley Wood

Hillcarr Wood

2

The Scraggs

Stanton Moor Quarries (dis)

King Stone

Nine Ladies Stone Circle

Tower

Stoney Ley Lodge

Stanton Lees

Cow Close Farm

BIRCHOVER RD

Stanton Moor Plantation

LEES RD

Bee Hill

63

Black Knowle Plantation

Warrencar

Eagle Tor

Hillcarr Farm

Mires Farm

Stanton Park Quarry

Hill Wood

Warrencarr Farm

1

Dungeon Plantation

Birchover Quarry

Birchover

THE MIRES

B5056

EAGLE TERR

WELLCROFT

BARTON HILL

Barn Farm

PH

THE GREEN

P

BRADLEY CL

KEELING LA

Brookfield Farm

UPPER TOWN LA

62

23

A

24

B

25

C

A   B   C

CHESTERFIELD RD
Rowsley
Wood

Falling
Edge

Little Bumper
Piece

Whitesprings
Plantation

4

Copy
Wood

Bumper
Castle

Wayne
Piece

Copywood

HARRISON
WAY

Tinkersley

Tinkersley
Farm

Black Hill

Wayne Corner
Plantation

65

COTE HILL LOC

Northwood
Carr

Sitch
Plantation

Halldale Brook

Woodside
Farm

BENT LA

DERWENT
LA

CARLTON AVE

NORTHWOOD LA
THORNCLIFFE AVE

Northwood

Burley Fields
Farm

Halldale Wood

Hall Dale

3

DALE RD N

Peak Railway

Rowsley
South

Stancliffe
Hall Sch

Newtonlot
Plantation

DE4

BACK LA

B5057

BUTCHER'S LA

Stancliffe
Quarries

Playing
Field

Darley Hillside

64

Abbey
Farm

Stancliffe View

STANTON
CL

Molyneaux
Bsns Pk

Vineyard
Terr

MOOR LA

1 PEVERIL CL
2 ARKWRIGHT CL
3 OLD HALL CL
4 NEWELL WAY
5 JOHN TURNER RD
6 BOWLER RD

Hallmoor
Wood

Cock's Head
Wood

Hazel
Farm

SYDNOPE HILL

Potter
Dam

Fancy
Dam

2

HALLDALE LA

Darley
Churchtown CE
Prim Sch

BUTTS RD

LC

Two
Dales

KNAB RD

Churchtown

Rectory
Farm

Broadmeadow

CHESTERFIELD RD

Holt
Farm

LADY GROVE RD

63

River Derwent

B5057
PO

Darley
Dale

Darley Dale
Prim Sch

Holt
Wood

Darley
Dale

STATION RD
LC

HOLT RD

1

FOUR LANE
ENDS

OLD RD

DALE RD S

Redhouse Stables
Working Carriage Mus

St Elphins
Sch

Judy Hill

Works

Bridge
Farm

MAIN RD

Flatts
Farm

Normanhurst
PK

A6

BLIND LA

DAKEYNE

62

6   A   27   B   28   C

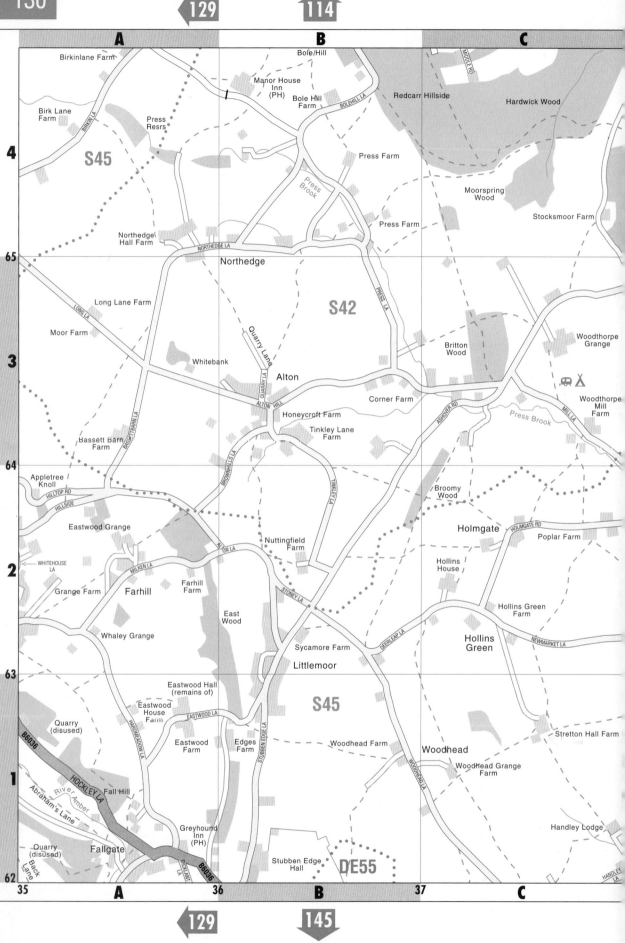

A   **B**   **C**

Birkinlane Farm

Bole/Hill

Manor House
Inn
(PH)

Bole Hill
Farm

Redcarr Hillside

Hardwick Wood

Birk Lane
Farm

Press
Resrs

BIRKIN LA

BOLEHILL LA

MIDDLE RD

4

S45

Press Farm

Moorspring
Wood

Press
Brook

Press Farm

Stocksmoor Farm

Northedge
Hall Farm

NORTHEDGE LA

65

Northedge

S42

PRESS LA

Long Lane Farm

Woodthorpe
Grange

LONG LA

Moor Farm

Britton
Wood

Quarry Lane

Whitebank

Woodthorpe
Mill
Farm

3

Alton

QUARRY LA

Corner Farm

Press Brook

MILL LA

ALTON HILL

Honeycroft Farm

ASKOVER RD

Bassett Barn
Farm

BASSETT BARN LA

Tinkley Lane
Farm

64

Appletree
Knoll

HILLTOP RD

Broomy
Wood

HILLSIDE

BROOMHILLS LA

Eastwood Grange

TINKLEY LA

Holmgate

HOLMGATE RD

Poplar Farm

Nuttingfield
Farm

ALTON LA

WHITEHOUSE
LA

Hollins
House

2

MILKEN LA

Grange Farm

Farhill
Farm

Farhill

Hollins Green
Farm

East
Wood

STONEY LA

Whaley Grange

NEWMARKET LA

Sycamore Farm

DEERLEAP LA

Hollins
Green

Littlemoor

63

Eastwood Hall
(remains of)

S45

Eastwood
House
Farm

EASTWOOD LA

HARDMEADOW LA

Quarry
(disused)

Stretton Hall Farm

Edges
Farm

Woodhead Farm

B6036

Eastwood
Farm

STUBBEN EDGE LA

Woodhead

HOCKLEY LA

River Amber

Fall Hill

Woodhead Grange
Farm

WOODHEAD LA

1

Abraham's Lane

Greyhound
Inn
(PH)

Handley Lodge

Quarry
(disused)

Fallgate

Back Lane

BLACKANT LA

B6036

Stubben Edge
Hall

DE55

HANDLEY LA

62

35   **A**   **36**   **B**   **37**   **C**

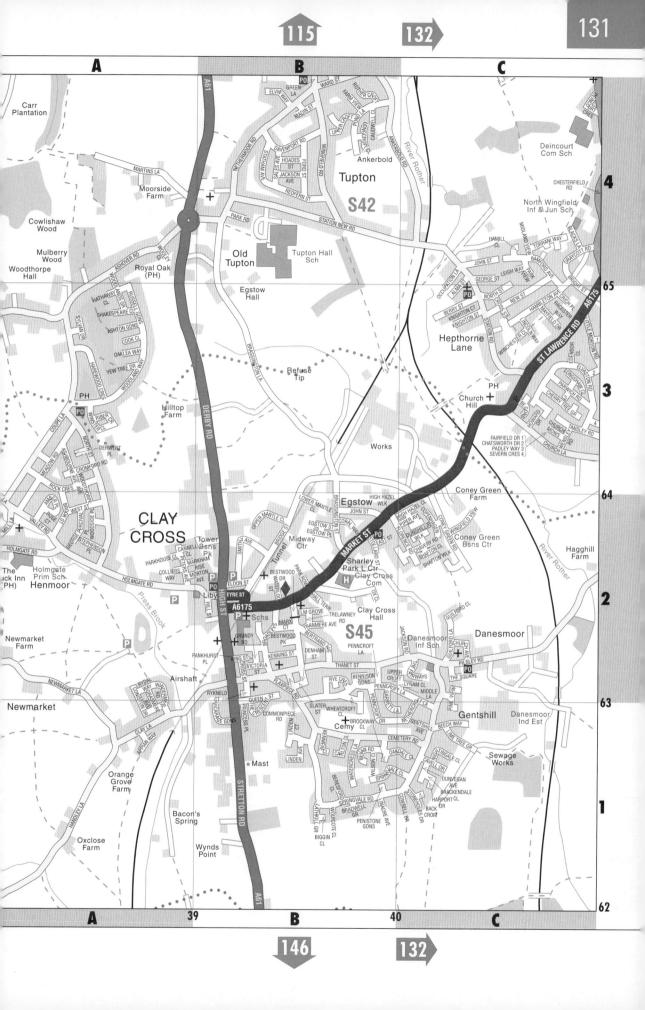

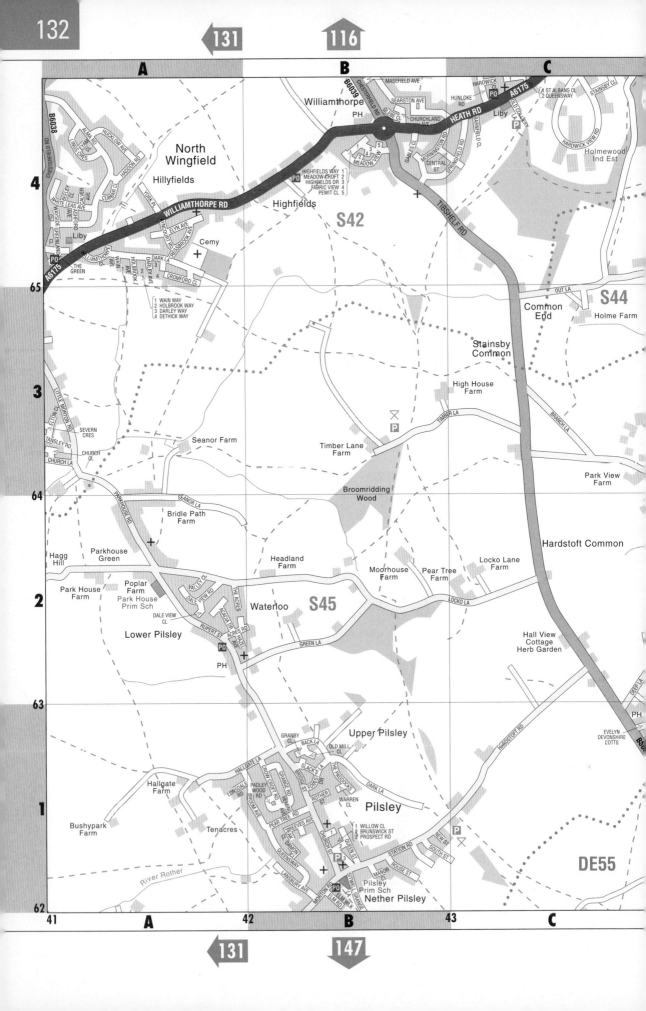

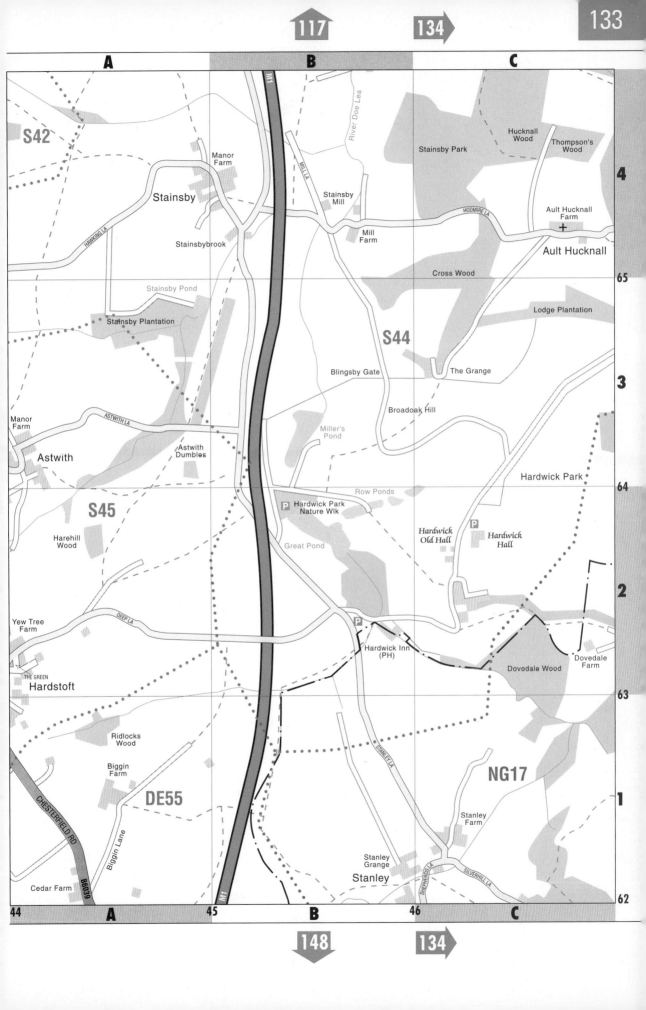

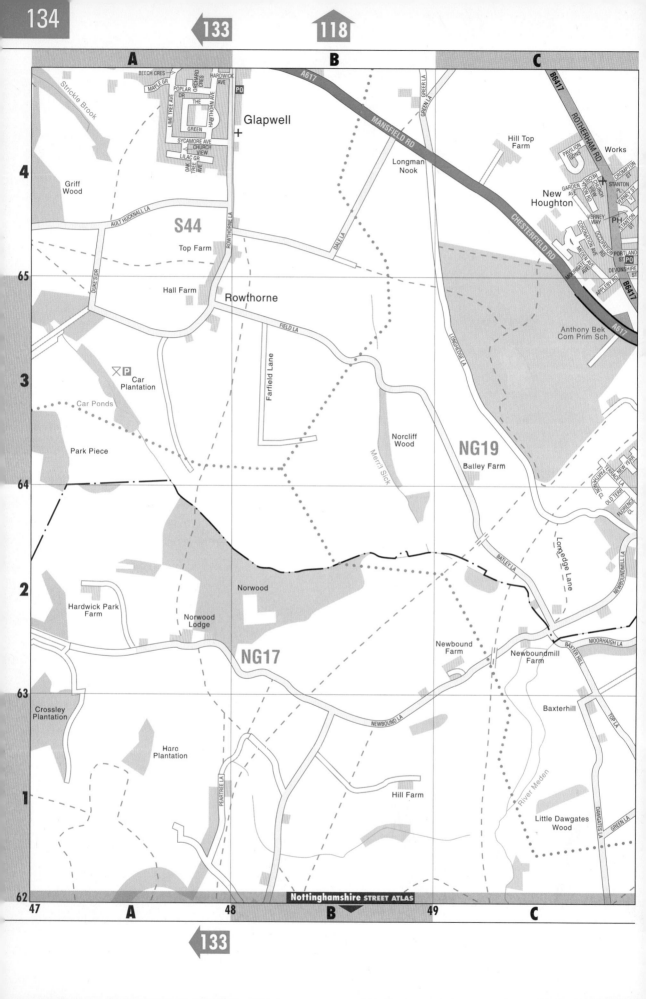

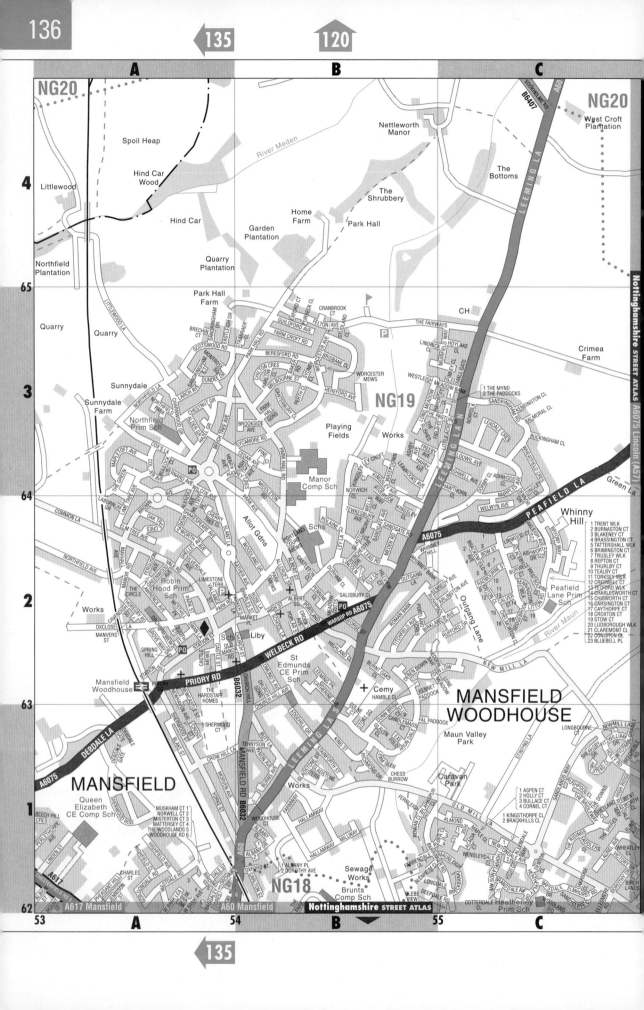

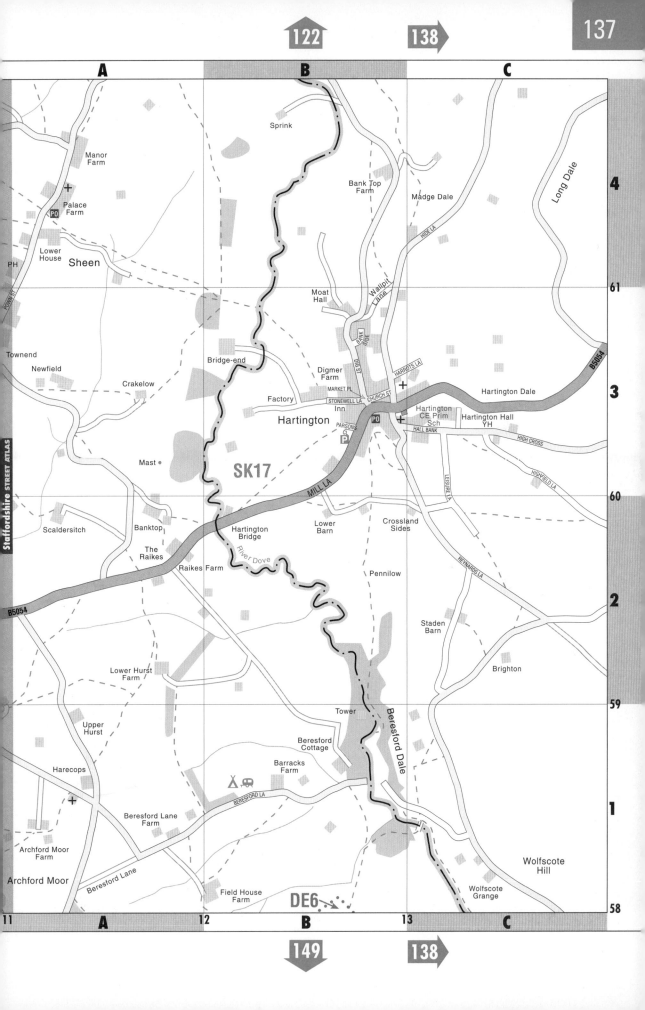

A
B
C

4

Long Dale

Manor
Farm

+

Palace
Farm

PO

Lower
House

Sheen

PH

61

Townend

Newfield

Crakelow

Bridge-end

Digmer
Farm

MARKET PL

Factory

STONEWELL LA

Hartington

Inn

CHURCH ST

PO

Sprink

Bank Top
Farm

Madge Dale

HIDE LA

Moat
Hall

Wallpit
Lane

BANK SIDE

DIG ST

HARROTS LA

+

Hartington Dale

Hartington
CE Prim
Sch

+

Hartington Hall
YH

HALL BANK

HIGH CROSS

HIGHFIELD LA

B5054

3

SK17

PARSONS
CL

P

Mast

MILL LA

Lower
Barn

Crossland
Sides

LEISURE LA

60

Scaldersitch

Banktop

The
Raikes

Raikes Farm

Hartington
Bridge

River Dove

Pennilow

REYNARDS LA

Staden
Barn

Brighton

B5054

2

Lower Hurst
Farm

Tower

Beresford
Cottage

Barracks
Farm

Beresford Dale

59

Upper
Hurst

Harecops

+

Beresford Lane
Farm

BERESFORD LA

Wolfscote
Hill

1

Archford Moor
Farm

Archford Moor

Beresford Lane

Field House
Farm

DE6

Wolfscote
Grange

58

11
A
12
B
13
C

Staffordshire STREET ATLAS

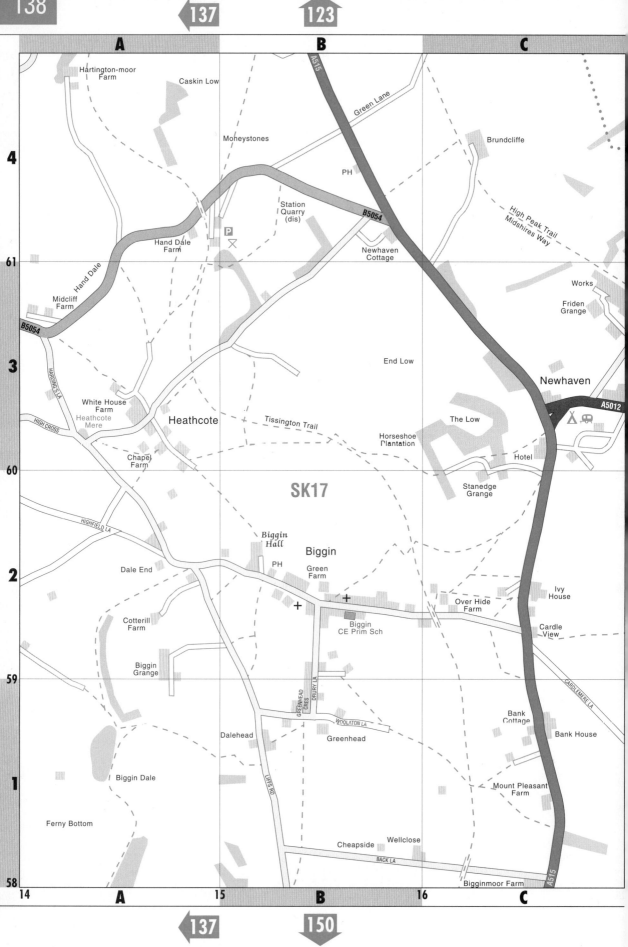

A   B   C

4

Hartington-moor
Farm

Caskin Low

Moneystones

Brundcliffe

PH

B5054

Station
Quarry
(dis)

High Peak Trail
Midshires Way

P
Hand Dale
Farm

Newhaven
Cottage

61

Hand Dale

Works

Midcliff
Farm

Friden
Grange

B5054

3

End Low

Newhaven

HARDINGS LA

White House
Farm

The Low

A5012

High Cross

Heathcote
Mere

Heathcote

Tissington Trail

Horseshoe
Plantation

Hotel

Chapel
Farm

60

SK17

Stanedge
Grange

HIGHFIELD LA

Biggin
Hall

Biggin

Dale End

PH

Green
Farm

Ivy
House

2

Over Hide
Farm

Cotterill
Farm

Biggin
CE Prim Sch

Cardle
View

Biggin
Grange

GREENHEAD CRES

DRURY LA

59

WOOLATON LA

CARDLEMERE LA

Dalehead

Greenhead

Bank
Cottage

Bank House

LIFFS RD

1

Biggin Dale

Mount Pleasant
Farm

Ferny Bottom

Cheapside

Wellclose

BACK LA

58

Bigginmoor Farm

A515

14   A   15   B   16   C

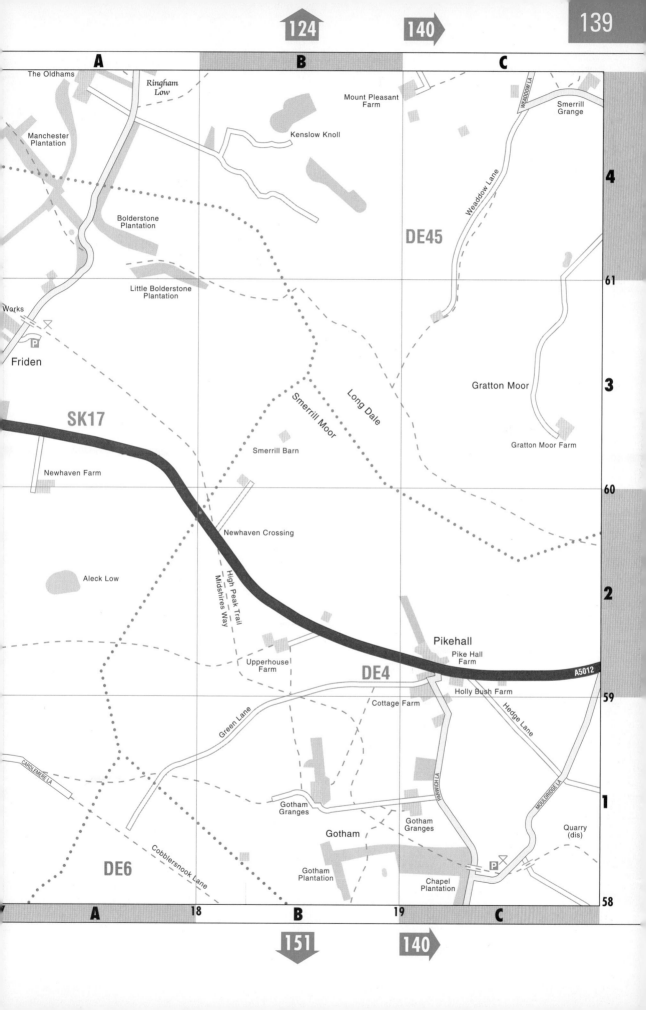

A
B
C

The Oldhams

Ringham Low

Mount Pleasant Farm

Smerrill Grange

WEADDOW LA

Manchester Plantation

Kenslow Knoll

Weaddow Lane

4

Bolderstone Plantation

DE45

Little Bolderstone Plantation

61

Works

Gratton Moor

3

Friden

SK17

Smerrill Moor

Long Dale

Gratton Moor Farm

Newhaven Farm

Smerrill Barn

60

Newhaven Crossing

Aleck Low

High Peak Trail
Midshires Way

2

Pikehall

Pike Hall Farm

DE4

Upperhouse Farm

A5012

Holly Bush Farm

59

Green Lane

Cottage Farm

Hedge Lane

CAROLEMERE LA

PARWICH LA

MOULDRIDGE LA

1

Gotham Granges

Gotham Granges

Quarry (dis)

Gotham

DE6

Cobblersnook Lane

Gotham Plantation

Chapel Plantation

58

A
B
C

18
19

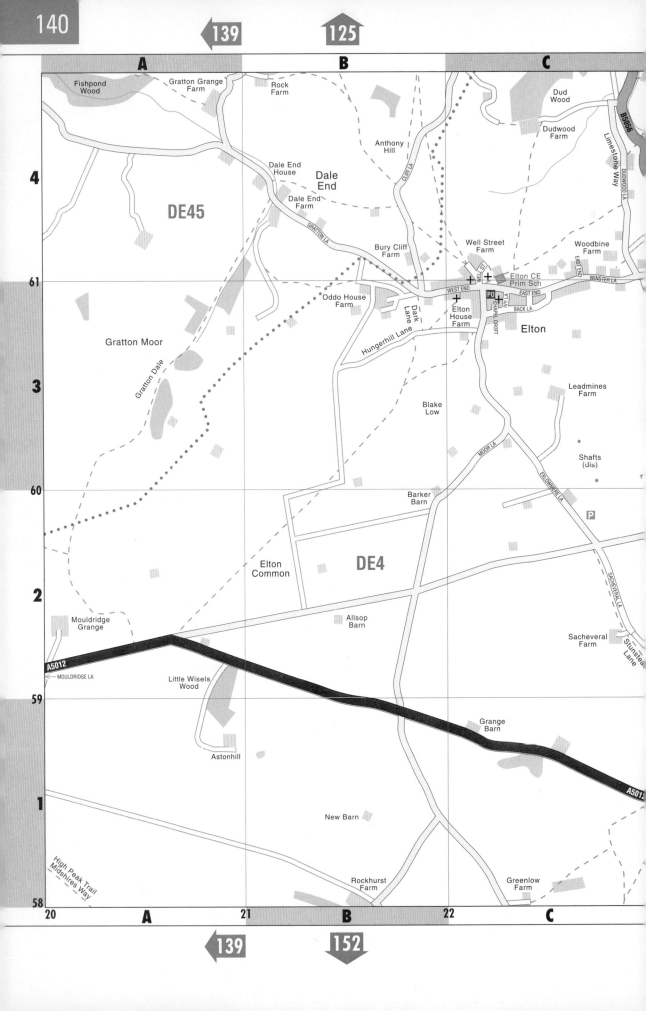

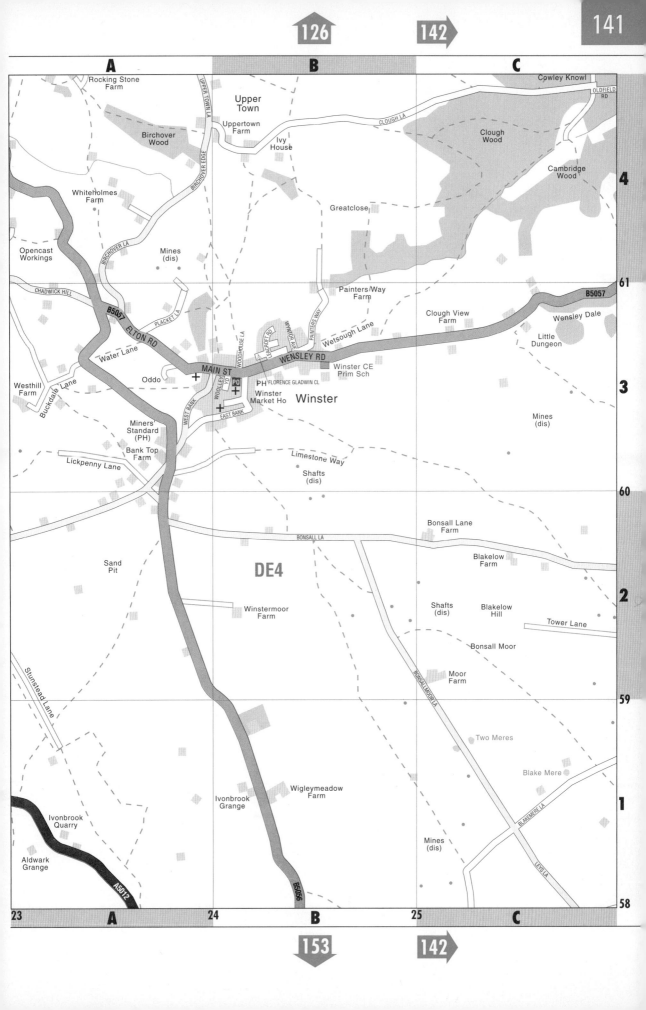

Rocking Stone Farm

Upper Town

Uppertown Farm

Birchover Wood

Ivy House

Clough La

Clough Wood

Cowley Knowl

OLDFIELD RD

Cambridge Wood

Whiteholmes Farm

Greatclose

Birchover La

Birchover Edge

Upper Town La

Mines (dis)

Opencast Workings

B5057

Chadwick Hill

Elton Rd

Placket La

Water Lane

Painters Way Farm

Wetsough Lane

Wetsough Lane

Clough View Farm

Wensley Dale

B5057

Little Dungeon

Leacroft Rd

Wyntor Ave

Painters Way

Woodhouse La

Wensley Rd

Main St

Winster CE Prim Sch

Oddo

PO

PH

Florence Gladwin Cl

West Bank

Woolley Yd

Winster Market Ho

Winster

Mines (dis)

Westhill Farm

Buckdale Lane

Miners' Standard (PH)

East Bank

Bank Top Farm

Limestone Way

Bonsall Lane Farm

Lickpenny Lane

Shafts (dis)

Bonsall La

Blakelow Farm

DE4

Sand Pit

Shafts (dis)

Blakelow Hill

Tower Lane

Bonsall Moor

Winstermoor Farm

Bonsall Moor La

Moor Farm

Stunstead Lane

Two Meres

Blake Mere

Wigleymeadow Farm

Ivonbrook Grange

Blakemere La

Leys La

Ivonbrook Quarry

Mines (dis)

Aldwark Grange

A5012

B5056

141
127

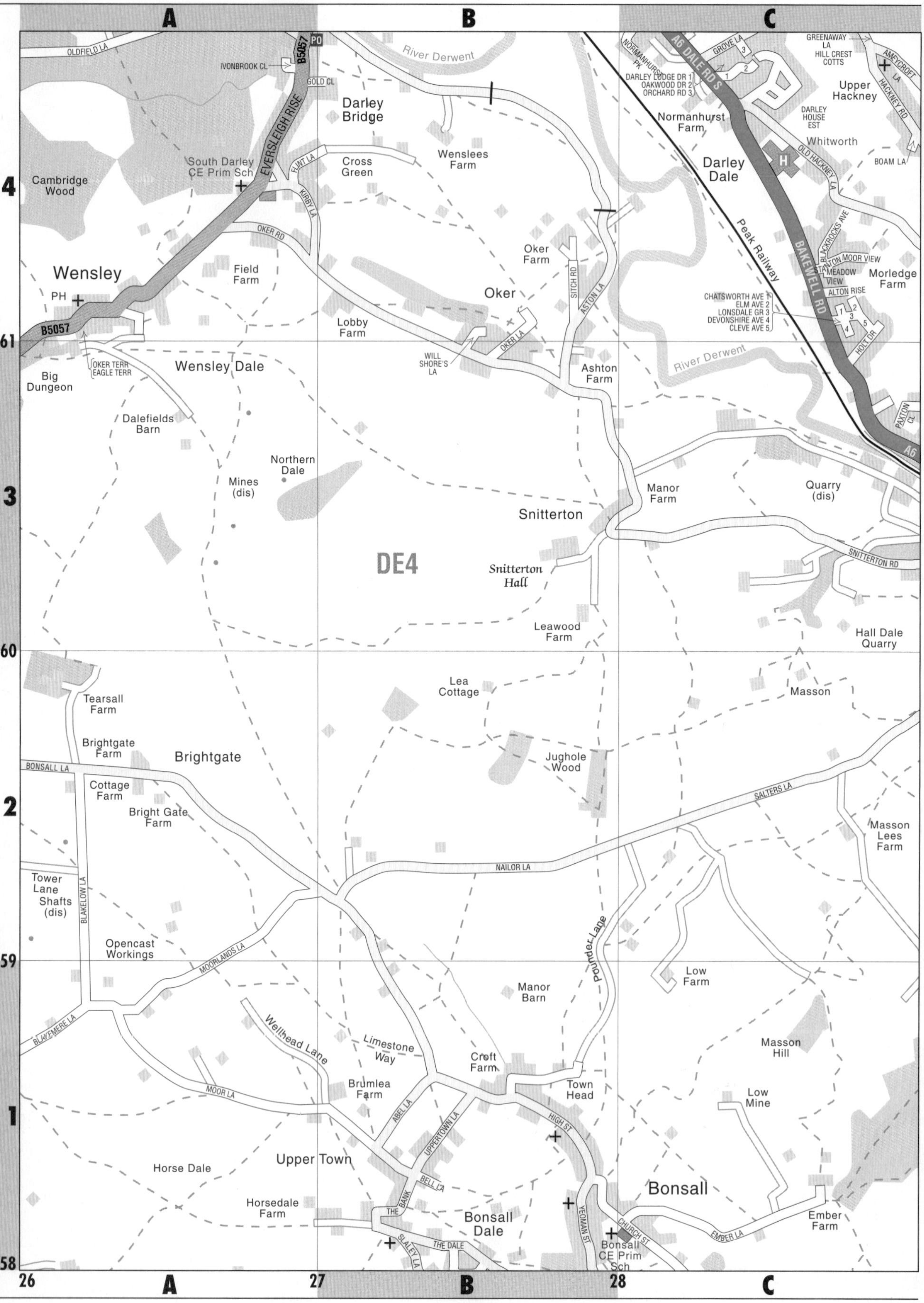
A
B
C
4
3
2
1
61
60
59
58
26
27
28
OLDFIELD LA
IVONBROOK CL
B5057
PO
GOLD CL
EVERSLEIGH RISE
River Derwent
Darley Bridge
Cambridge Wood
South Darley CE Prim Sch
FLINT LA
Cross Green
Wenslees Farm
KIRBY LA
OKER RD
Wensley
PH
Field Farm
Oker Farm
SITCH RD
ASTON LA
Oker
Lobby Farm
OKER LA
WILL SHORE'S LA
OKER TERR
EAGLE TERR
Big Dungeon
Wensley Dale
Ashton Farm
Dalefields Barn
Northern Dale
Mines (dis)
Snitterton
DE4
Snitterton Hall
Leawood Farm
Manor Farm
Quarry (dis)
SNITTERTON RD
Hall Dale Quarry
NORMANHURST PK
A6 DALE RD S
GROVE LA
DARLEY LODGE DR 1
OAKWOOD DR 2
ORCHARD RD 3
Normanhurst Farm
GREENAWAY LA
HILL CREST COTTS
AMEYCROFT LA
HACKNEY RD
Upper Hackney
DARLEY HOUSE EST
Whitworth
H
OLD HACKNEY LA
BOAM LA
Darley Dale
Peak Railway
BAKEWELL RD
BLACKROCKS AVE
STANTON MOOR VIEW
MEADOW VIEW
ALTON RISE
Morledge Farm
CHATSWORTH AVE 1
ELM AVE 2
LONSDALE GR 3
DEVONSHIRE AVE 4
CLEVE AVE 5
HOLT DR
River Derwent
PAXTON CL
A6
Tearsall Farm
Lea Cottage
Masson
Brightgate Farm
Brightgate
Jughole Wood
BONSALL LA
Cottage Farm
Bright Gate Farm
SALTERS LA
Masson Lees Farm
NAILOR LA
Tower Lane Shafts (dis)
BLAKELOW LA
Opencast Workings
MOORLANDS LA
Pounder Lane
Low Farm
Manor Barn
BLAKEMERE LA
Wellhead Lane
Limestone Way
Croft Farm
Masson Hill
MOOR LA
Brumlea Farm
Town Head
Low Mine
ABEL LA
UPPERTOWN LA
HIGH ST
Horse Dale
Upper Town
BELL LA
Bonsall
THE BANK
YEOMAN ST
Horsedale Farm
THE
Bonsall Dale
CHURCH ST
Ember Farm
SLALEY LA
THE DALE
EMBER LA
Bonsall CE Prim Sch

141
154

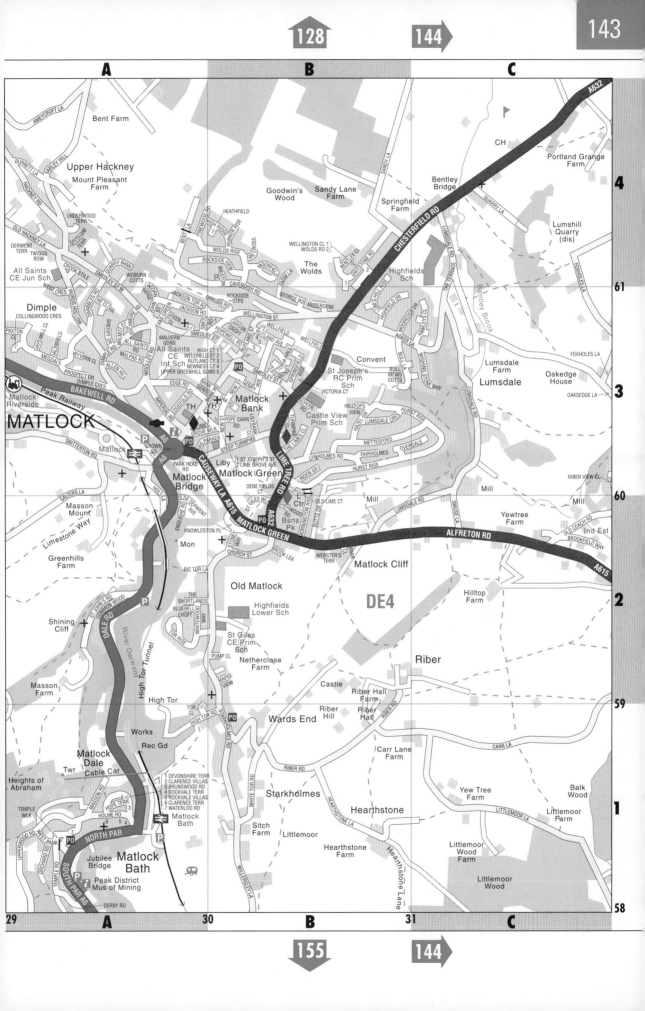

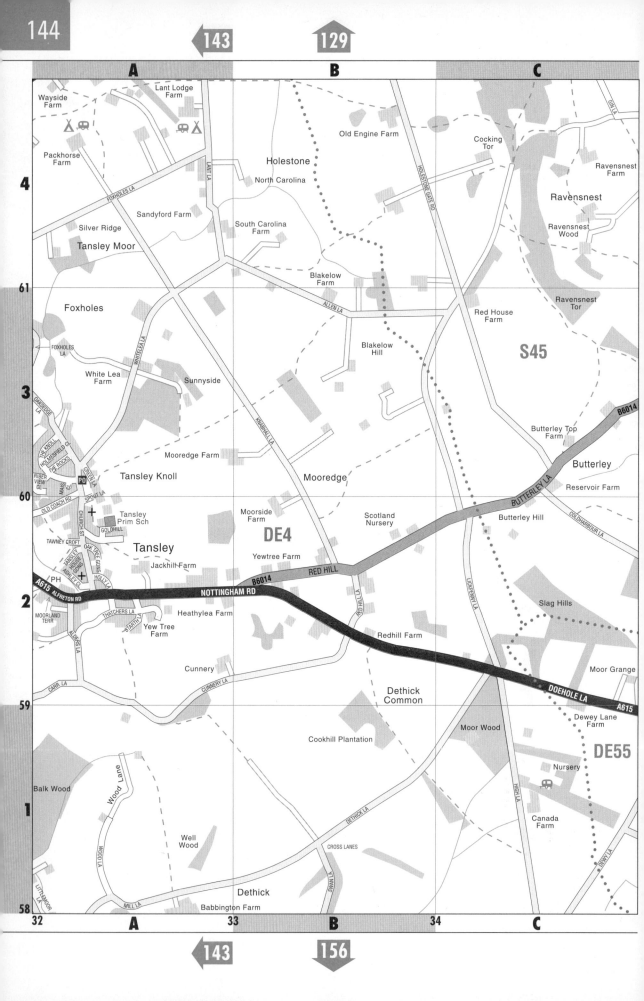

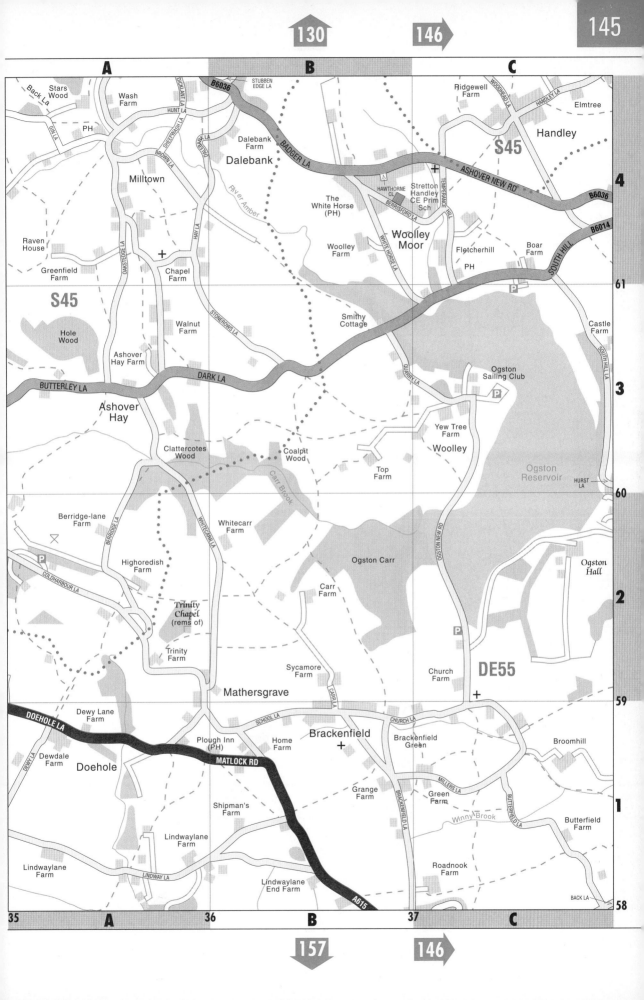

A   B   C

Back La
Stars Wood
Gin La
Wash Farm
PH
HUNT LA
DICKLAND LA
STUBBEN EDGE LA
B6036
Ridgewell Farm
WOODHEAD LA
Elmtree
HANDLEY LA
Handley
S45

SHEEPWASH LA
DALEBANK LA
BROWN LA
Dalebank Farm
Dalebank
BADGER LA
Ashover New Rd
HAWTHORNE CL
Stretton Handley CE Prim Sch
TEMPERANCE HILL
B6036

Milltown
River Amber
The White Horse (PH)
BERRISFORD LA
Woolley Moor
B6014

OAKSTEDGE LA
HAY LA
Chapel Farm
Woolley Farm
WHITE HORSE LA
Fletcherhill
PH
Boar Farm
SOUTH HILL

Raven House
Greenfield Farm
4

S45
Walnut Farm
STONEROWS LA
Smithy Cottage
P
61

Hole Wood
Ashover Hay Farm
DARK LA
QUARRY LA
Ogston Sailing Club
P
Castle Farm
SOUTH HILL LA

BUTTERLEY LA
Ashover Hay
Yew Tree Farm
Woolley
3

Clattercotes Wood
Coalpit Wood
CARR BROOK
Top Farm
Ogston Reservoir
HURST LA

Berridge-lane Farm
BERRIDGE LA
Whitecarr Farm
WHITECARR LA
60

P
Highoredish Farm
Ogston Carr
OGSTON NEW RD
Ogston Hall

COLDHARBOUR LA
Trinity Chapel (rems of)
Carr Farm
P
2

Trinity Farm
Sycamore Farm
CARR LA
Church Farm
DE55

Mathersgrave
SCHOOL LA
CHURCH LA
59

DOEHOLE LA
Dewy Lane Farm
Plough Inn (PH)
Home Farm
Brackenfield
Brackenfield Green
MILLERS LA
Broomhill

DEWY LA
Dewdale Farm
Doehole
MATLOCK RD
Grange Farm
BRACKENFIELD LA
Green Farm
BUTTERFIELD LA
Butterfield Farm
1

Shipman's Farm
Winny Brook

Lindwaylane Farm
Lindwaylane Farm
LINDWAY LA
Lindwaylane End Farm
A615
Roadnook Farm
BACK LA
58

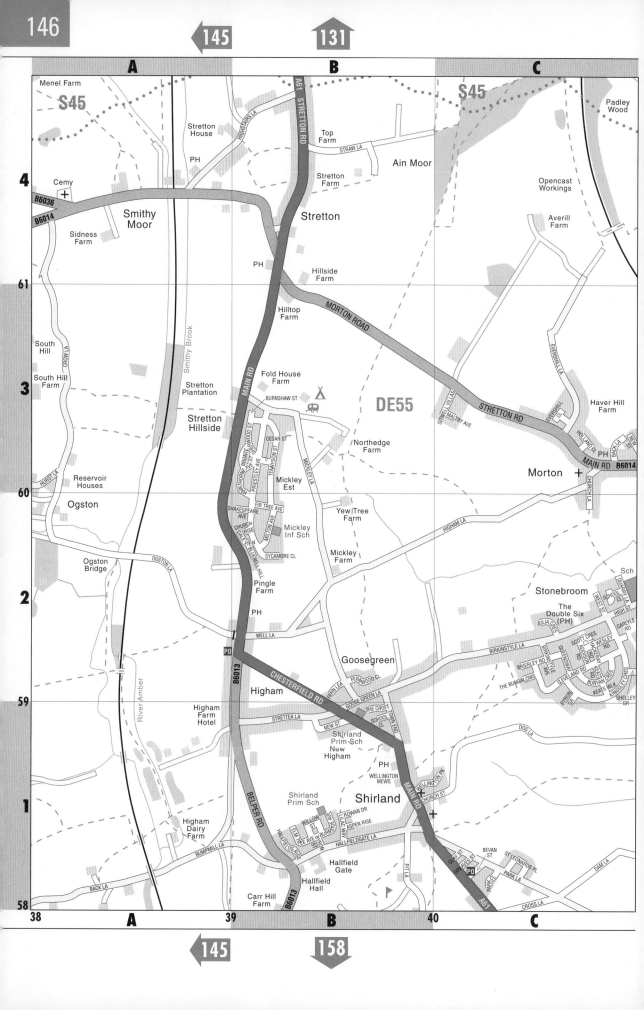

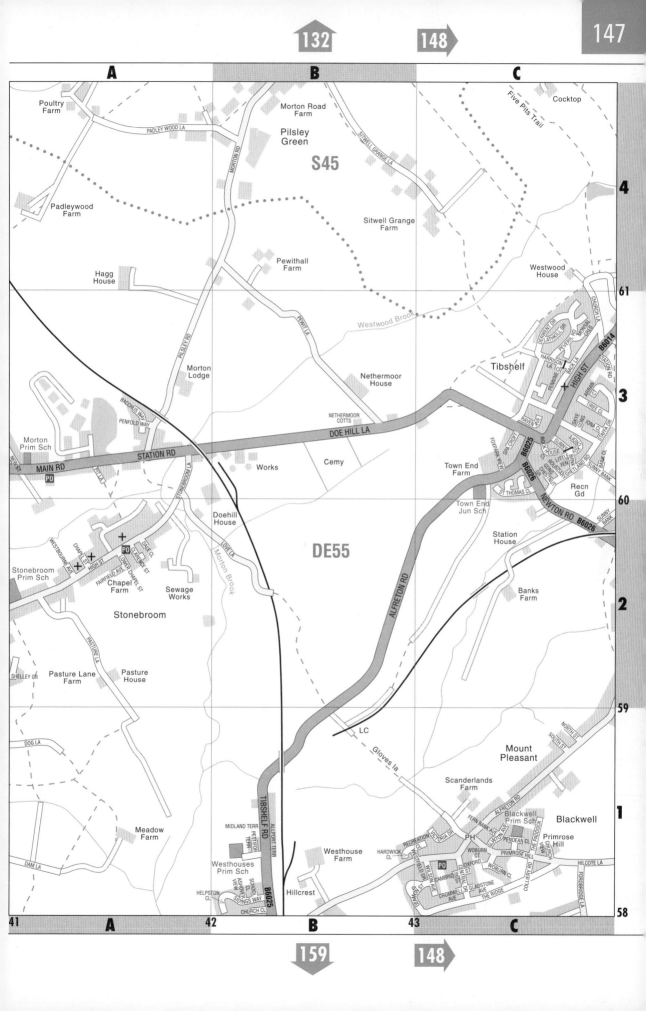

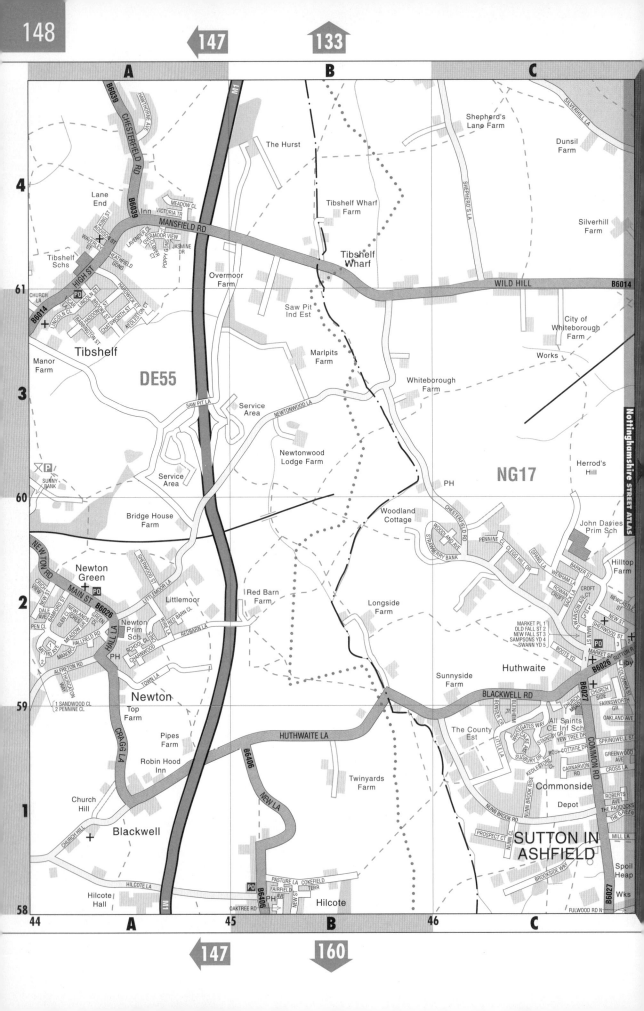

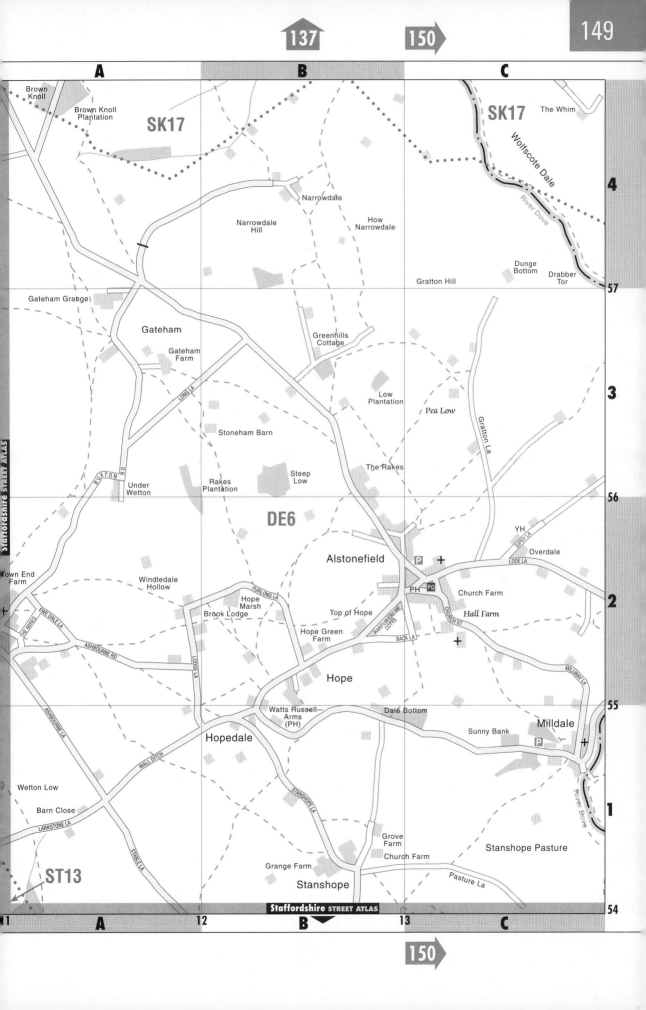

SK17

Brown Knoll

Brown Knoll Plantation

The Whim

SK17

Wolfscote Dale

River Dove

4

Narrowdale

Narrowdale Hill

How Narrowdale

Gateham Grange

Dunge Bottom

Drabber Tor

Gratton Hill

57

Gateham

Greenhills Cottage

Gateham Farm

LONG LA

Low Plantation

3

Pea Low

Gratton La

Stoneham Barn

Staffordshire STREET ATLAS

The Rakes

BUXTON RD

Rakes Plantation

Steep Low

Under Wetton

DE6

56

YH

GIPSY LA

Overdale

LODE LA

Alstonefield

P

Town End Farm

Windledale Hollow

FURLONG LA

Hope Marsh

Brook Lodge

Top of Hope

PH PO

Church Farm

Hall Farm

2

THE MIRES

EWE DALE LA

ASHBOURNE RD

LODGE LA

HARPUR-CREWE COTTS

Hope Green Farm

BACK LA

CHURCH ST

MILLWAY LA

Hope

ASHBOURNE LA

55

Watts Russell Arms (PH)

Dale Bottom

Sunny Bank

Milldale

P

WALL DITCH

Hopedale

P

River Dove

Wetton Low

STANSHOPE LA

1

Barn Close

LARKSTONE LA

Grove Farm

STABLE LA

Church Farm

Stanshope Pasture

ST13

Grange Farm

Stanshope

Pasture La

54

11 A 12 B 13 C

149
138

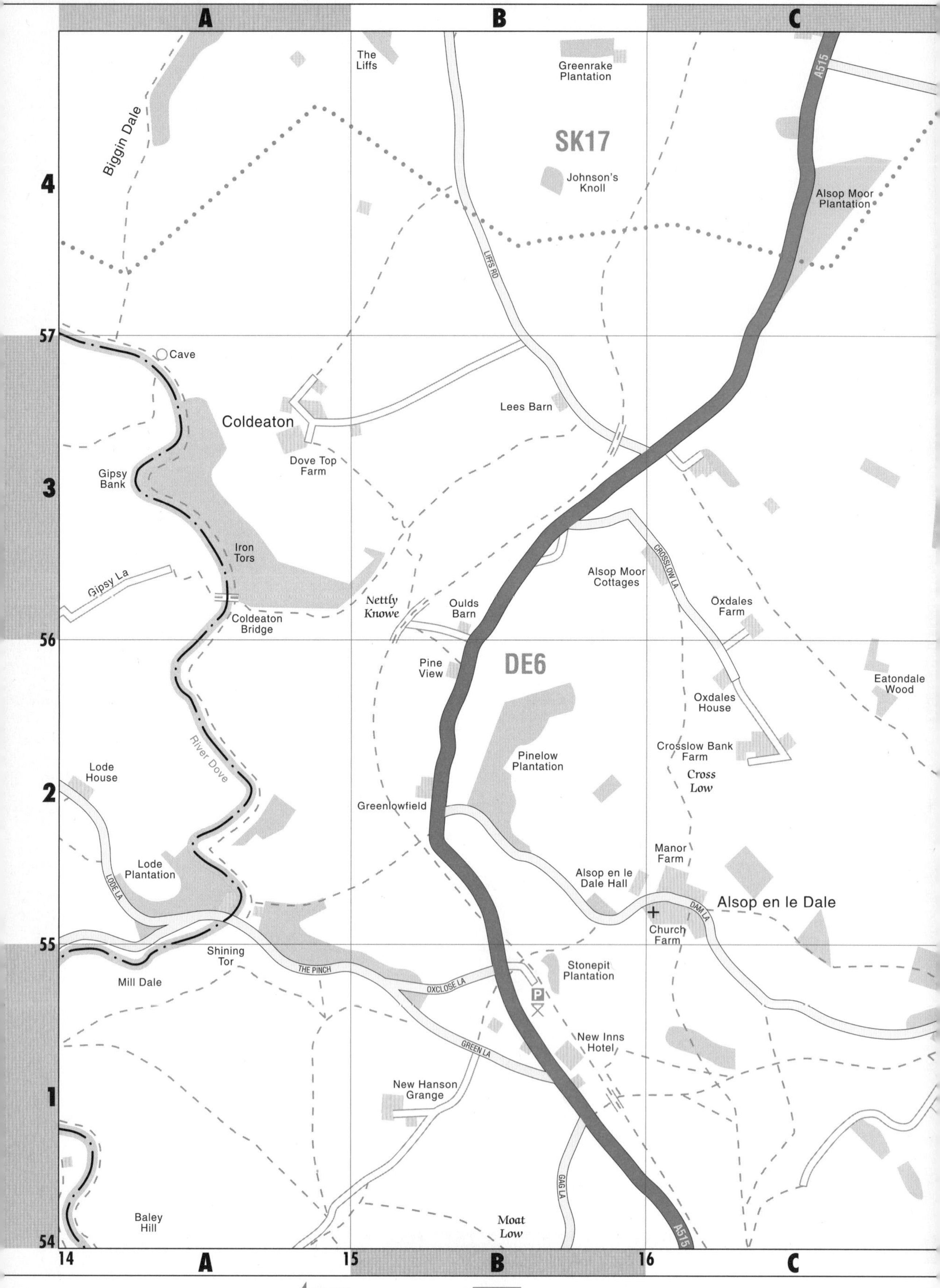

A **B** **C**

Biggin Dale

The Liffs

Greenrake Plantation

SK17

Johnson's Knoll

A515

Alsop Moor Plantation

4

LIFFS RD

Cave

Lees Barn

Coldeaton

Dove Top Farm

57

Gipsy Bank

Iron Tors

3

Gipsy La

Coldeaton Bridge

Alsop Moor Cottages

CROSSLOW LA

Oxdales Farm

Nettly Knowe

 Oulds Barn

56

Pine View

DE6

Eatondale Wood

Oxdales House

Pinelow Plantation

Crosslow Bank Farm

Cross Low

River Dove

Lode House

Greenlowfield

2

Manor Farm

Alsop en le Dale Hall

Alsop en le Dale

DAM LA

Lode Plantation

LODE LA

Church Farm

Shining Tor

THE PINCH

Stonepit Plantation

55

Mill Dale

OXCLOSE LA

P

New Inns Hotel

GREEN LA

New Hanson Grange

1

6AG LA

Baley Hill

Moat Low

A515

54

14 **A** **15** **B** **16** **C**

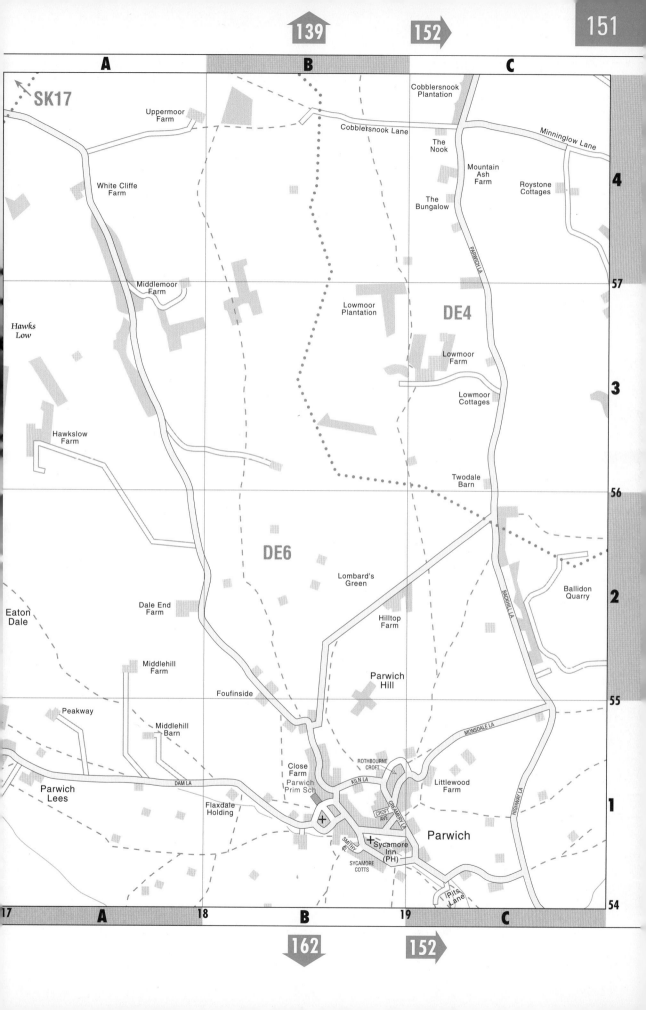

A
B
C

SK17

Uppermoor
Farm

Cobblersnook
Plantation

Cobblersnook Lane

Minninglow Lane

The
Nook

White Cliffe
Farm

Mountain
Ash
Farm

Royston
Cottages

4

The
Bungalow

Middlemoor
Farm

57

Hawks
Low

Lowmoor
Plantation

DE4

Lowmoor
Farm

Lowmoor
Cottages

3

Hawkslow
Farm

DE6

Twodale
Barn

56

Lombard's
Green

Ballidon
Quarry

2

Eaton
Dale

Dale End
Farm

Hilltop
Farm

Parwich
Hill

Middlehill
Farm

Foufinside

55

Peakway

Middlehill
Barn

MONSDALE LA

Close
Farm

ROTHBOURNE
CROFT

Littlewood
Farm

Parwich Lees

DAM LA

Parwich
Prim Sch

KILN LA

Flaxdale
Holding

CREAMERY LA

CROFT AVE

1

Sycamore
Inn
(PH)

Parwich

SMITHY
LE

SYCAMORE
COTTS

Pits
Lane

54

17
A
18
B
19
C

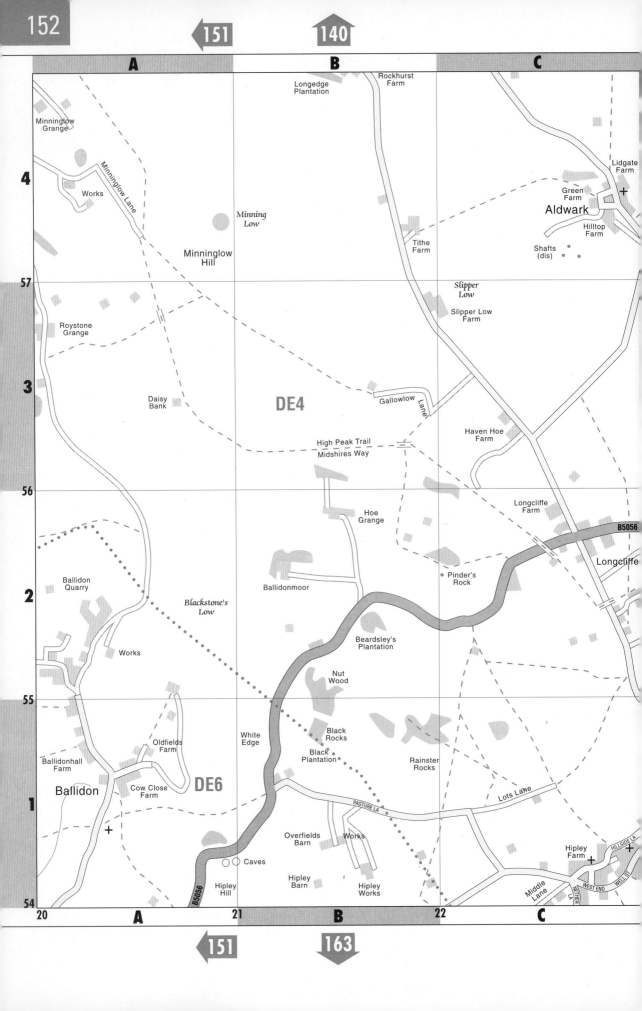

A **B** **C**

4

Minninglow
Grange

Minninglow Lane

Works

Longedge
Plantation

Rockhurst
Farm

Minning
Low

Lidgate
Farm

Green
Farm

Aldwark

Hilltop
Farm

Minninglow
Hill

Tithe
Farm

Shafts
(dis)

57

Roystone
Grange

Slipper
Low

Slipper Low
Farm

3

Daisy
Bank

DE4

Gallowlow Lane

Haven Hoe
Farm

High Peak Trail
Midshires Way

56

Longcliffe
Farm

B5056

Hoe
Grange

Longcliffe

2

Ballidon
Quarry

Blackstone's
Low

Ballidonmoor

Pinder's
Rock

Works

Beardsley's
Plantation

Nut
Wood

55

White
Edge

Black
Rocks

Black
Plantation

Rainster
Rocks

Lots Lane

Ballidonhall
Farm

Oldfields
Farm

DE6

Ballidon

Cow Close
Farm

Overfields
Barn

Works

Hipley
Farm

HILLSIDE LA

PASTURE LA

1

Caves

Hipley
Hill

B5056

Hipley
Barn

Hipley
Works

Middle
Lane

NETHER LA

WEST END

WELL ST

54

20 **A** **21** **B** **22** **C**

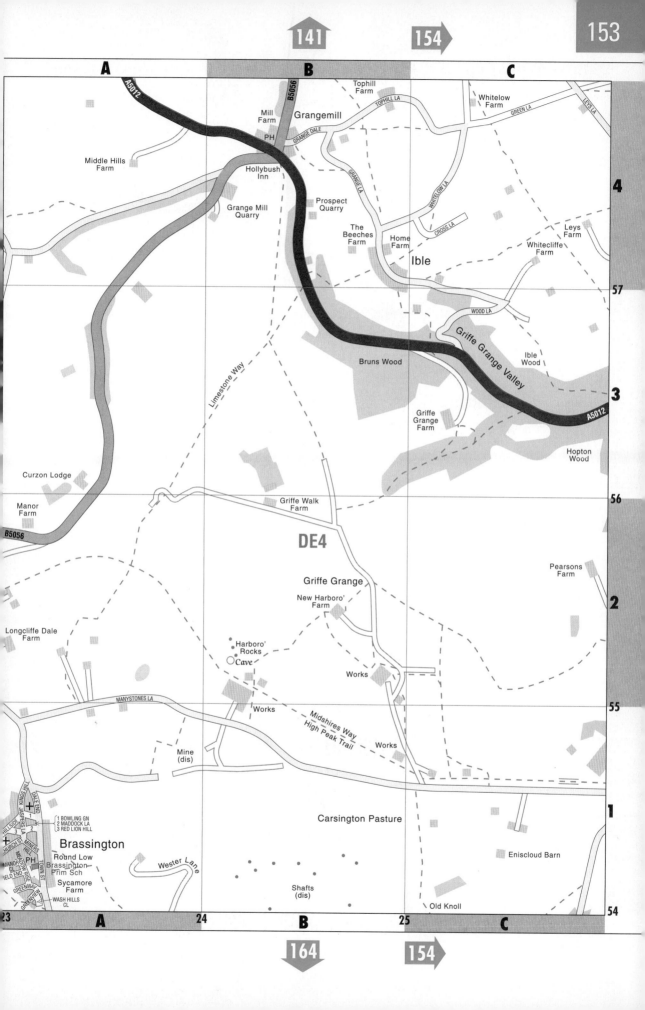

153
142

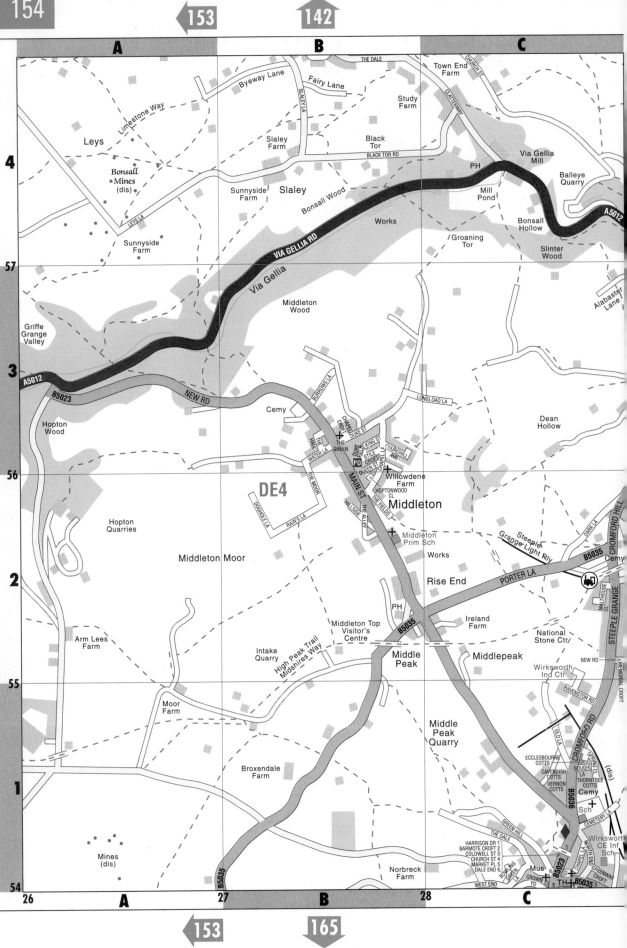

153
165

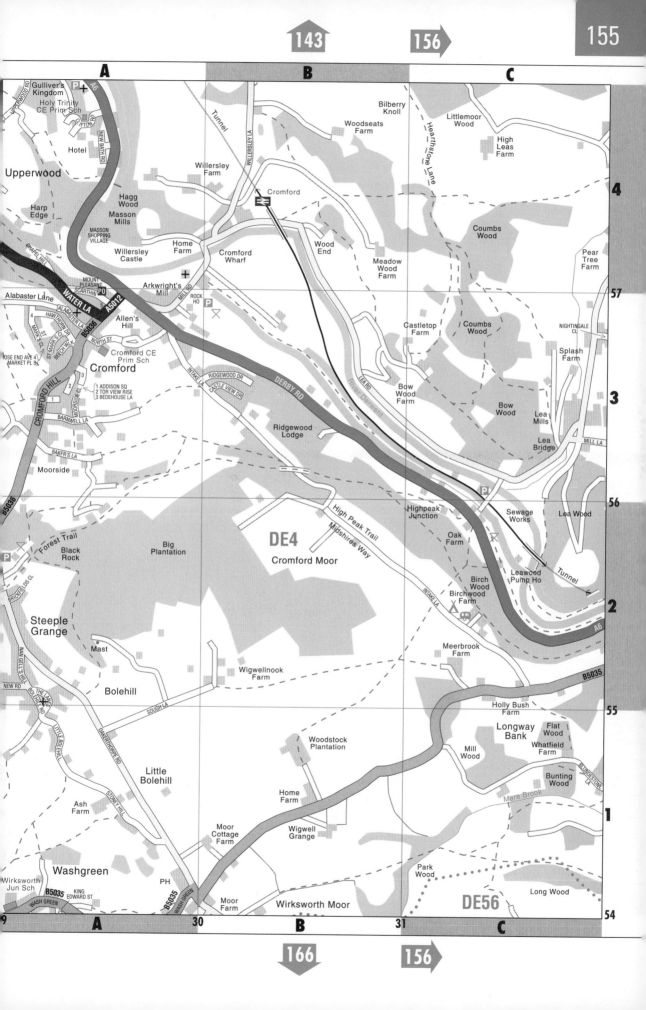

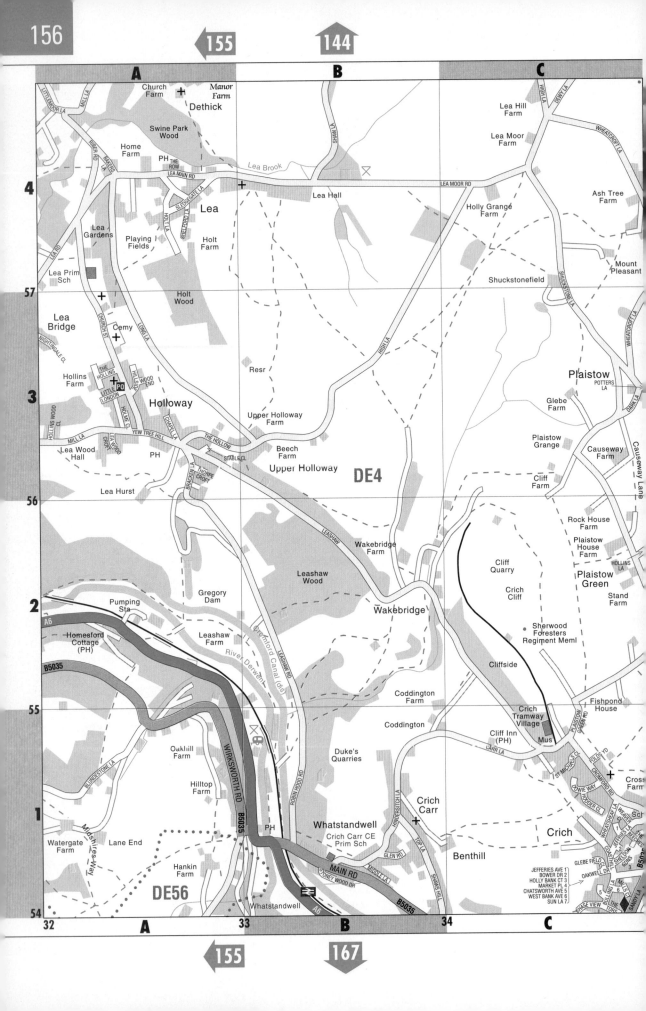

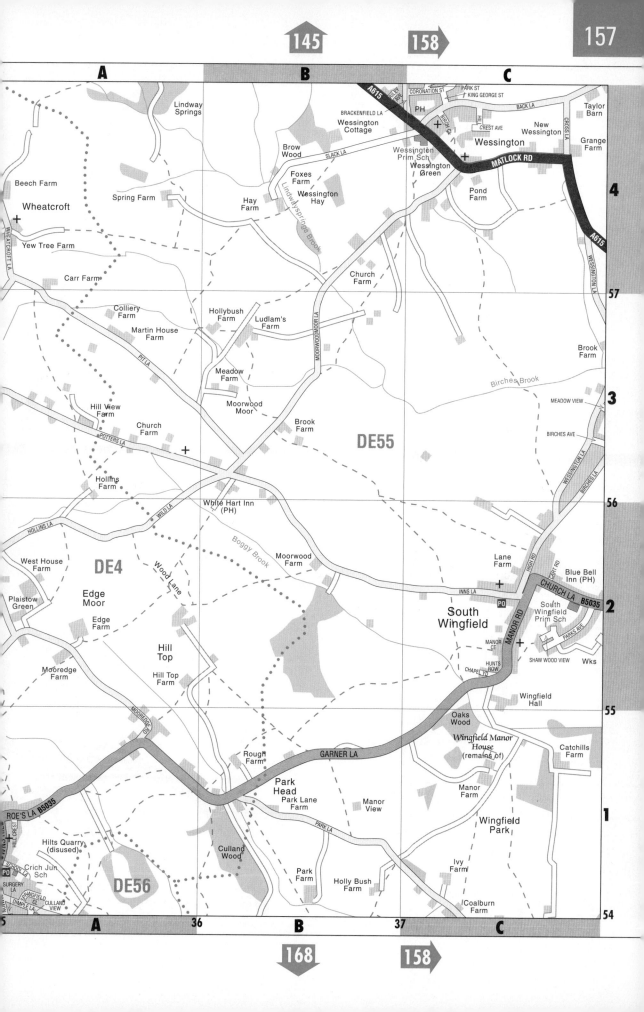

A   B   C

4
57
3
56
2
55
1
54

A   36   B   37   C

Wessington

A615
RILEY AVE
CORONATION ST
PARK ST
KING GEORGE ST
PH
BIRCH CL
CREST AVE
BACK LA
HILL
TAYLOR Barn
New Wessington
CROSS LA
Grange Farm
MATLOCK RD
A615
WESSINGTON LA

Lindway Springs
BRACKENFIELD LA
Wessington Cottage
Brow Wood
SLACK LA
Wessington Prim Sch
Wessington Green
Wessington Hay
Foxes Farm
Hay Farm
Lindwaysprings Brook

Beech Farm
Wheatcroft
Spring Farm
Yew Tree Farm
WHEATCROFT LA
Carr Farm

Pond Farm

Church Farm

Colliery Farm
Hollybush Farm
Ludlam's Farm
MOORWOODMOOR LA
Church Farm
Brook Farm

Martin House Farm
PIT LA
Meadow Farm

Birches Brook
MEADOW VIEW
BIRCHES AVE
Brook Farm

Hill View Farm
Church Farm
POTTERS LA
Moorwood Moor
Brook Farm
DE55
WESSINGTON CA LA
BIRCHES LA
3

Hollins Farm
WILD LA
White Hart Inn (PH)
56

HOLLINS LA
Boggy Brook
Moorwood Farm
Lane Farm
HIGH RD
CART RD
Blue Bell Inn (PH)
CHURCH LA
B5035
2

DE4
West House Farm
Wood Lane
INNS LA
MANOR RD
South Wingfield Prim Sch
PARKS AVE

Plaistow Green
Edge Moor
Edge Farm
South Wingfield
PO
MANOR CT
Shaw Wood View
Wks

Mooredge Farm
Hill Top
Hill Top Farm
HUNTS ROW
CHAPEL YD
Wingfield Hall
55

MOOREDGE RD
Oaks Wood
Catchills Farm

Rough Farm
GARNER LA
Wingfield Manor House (remains of)
Manor Farm

ROE'S LA B5035
Park Head
Park Lane Farm
PARK LA
Manor View
Wingfield Park
1

HILL CREST
Hilts Quarry (disused)
Culland Wood
Park Farm
Holly Bush Farm
Ivy Farm

SCHOOL LA
PO
Crich Jun Sch
DE56
Coalburn Farm
54

SURGERY LA
WINGFIELD
DIMPLE LA
CL
CULLAND VIEW

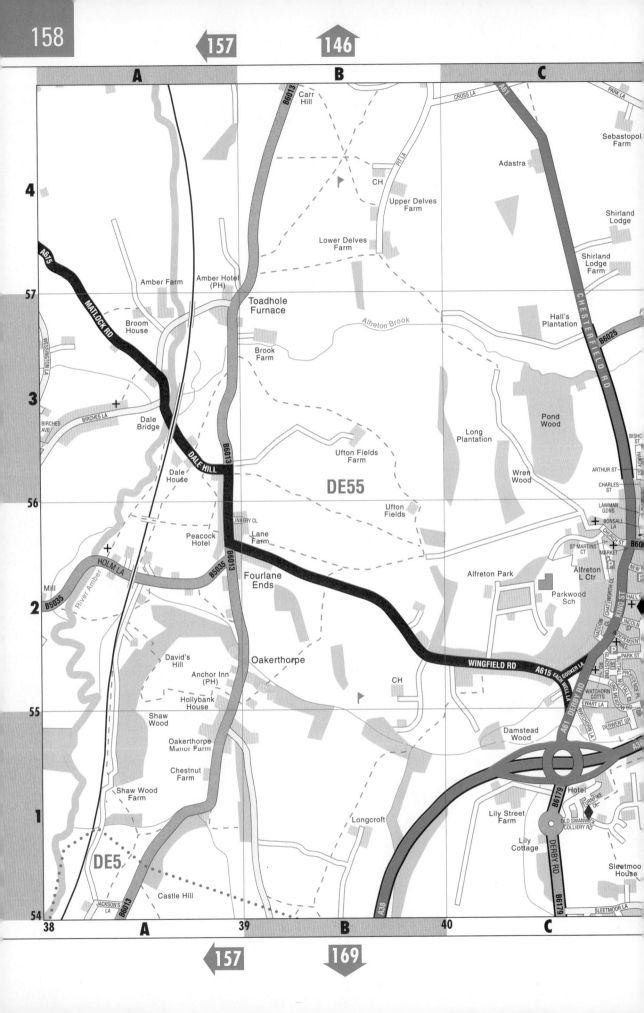

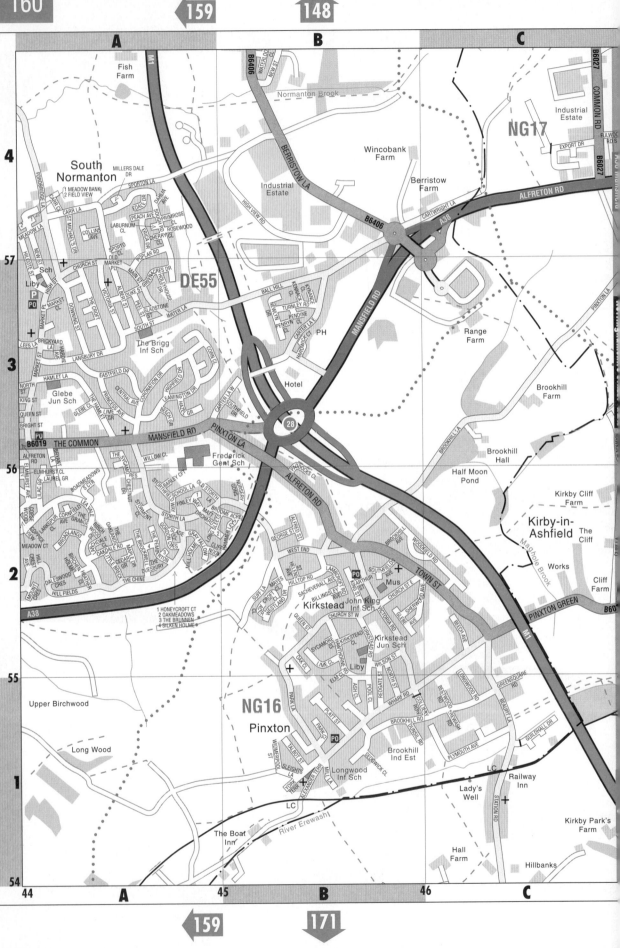

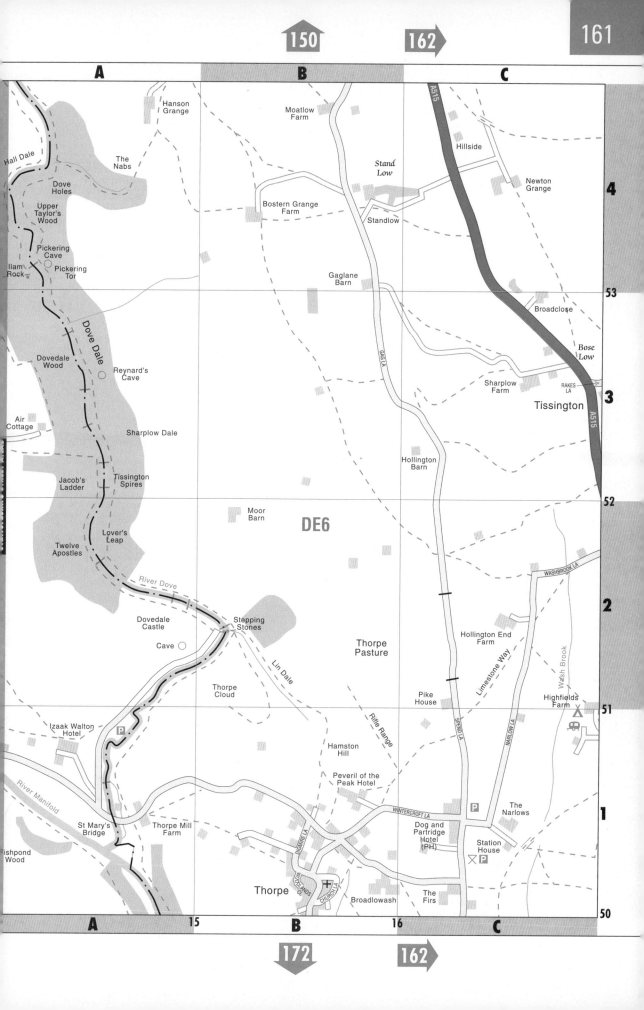

A B C

4

53

3

52

2

51

1

50

Hall Dale

The Nabs

Hanson Grange

Moatlow Farm

Stand Low

Hillside

A515

Newton Grange

Dove Holes

Upper Taylor's Wood

Bostern Grange Farm

Standlow

Pickering Cave

Pickering Tor

Ilam Rock

Gaglane Barn

Broadclose

Dove Dale

Bose Low

Dovedale Wood

Reynard's Cave

Sharplow Farm

RAKES LA

Tissington

Air Cottage

Sharplow Dale

GAG LA

Jacob's Ladder

Tissington Spires

Hollington Barn

Moor Barn

DE6

Twelve Apostles

Lover's Leap

River Dove

Dovedale Castle

Stepping Stones

Thorpe Pasture

WASHBROOK LA

Hollington End Farm

Highfields Farm

Wash Brook

Cave

Lin Dale

Pike House

Limestone Way

Izaak Walton Hotel

Thorpe Cloud

Rifle Range

SPEND LA

MARLOW LA

River Manifold

Hamston Hill

Peveril of the Peak Hotel

WINTERCROFT LA

The Narlows

St Mary's Bridge

Thorpe Mill Farm

Dog and Partridge Hotel (PH)

Station House

Fishpond Wood

PIKEHIRE LA

WOODLANDS CL

CHURCH LA

Thorpe

Broadlowash

The Firs

A B C

The Thorns

4

Crakelow
Farm

Crake
Low

Shaw's
Farm

Bletch Brook

Sitterlow
Farm

Rushycliffe
Barn

White
Meadow

53

Hunger
Hill

Tissington Trail

High
Flats

Gorsehill
Farm

RAKES LA

3

Town Head
Farm

CHAPEL LA

Tissington

Wibben Hill

Bent
Farm

Tissington
Hall

BENT LA

THE GREEN

THE AVENUE

Keepers
Cottage

Lea Cottage
Farm

P

52

A515

WASHBROOK
LA

DARFIELD LA

B50

Square
Plantation

DE6

Lea Hall

Bluebell
Inn
(PH)

Mill Pond
Plantation

Horsley
Farm

Darfield
Plantation

Bradbourne Brook

2

Bassett Wood
Farm

Choughriddins

Tissington Wood
Farm

51

Brookwood
Farm

Woodeaves
Farm

Woodside

Bentley
Hall

1

Lees Farm

The
Priory

Firs Farm

Woodeaves
Mill

Fenny
Bentley

Bentley Brook

Ravenscliffe

Fitzherbert CE
Prim Sch

Cherry Orchard
Farm

ASHES LA

A515

Bentley Old Hall

Riddings
Park

SCHOOL CL

Coach and Horses
(PH)

50

B5056

17 A 18 B 19 C

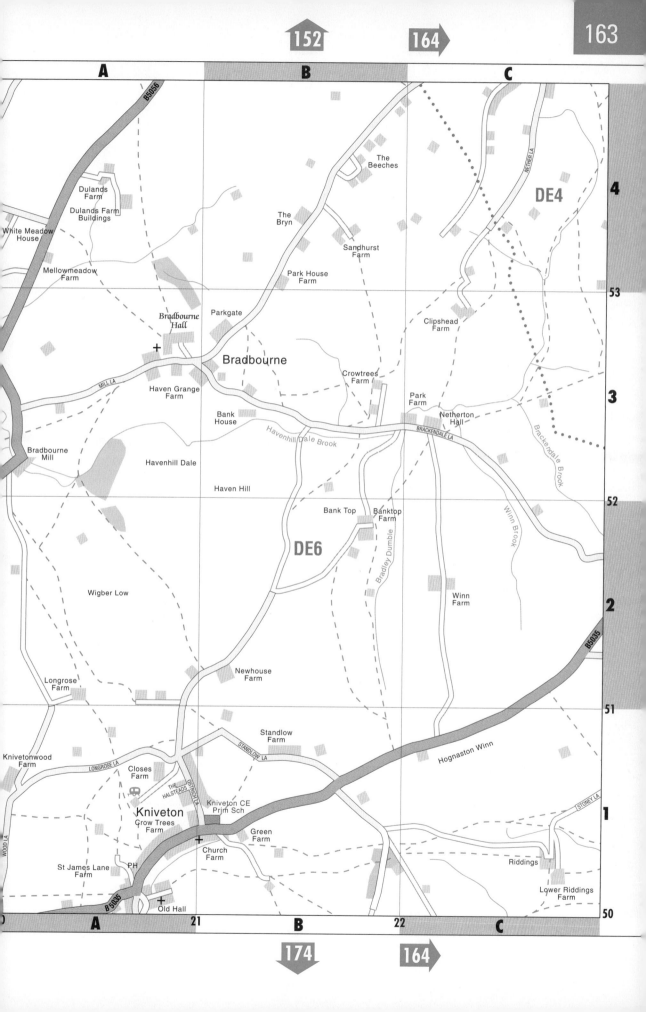

A   B   C

4

DE4

NETHER LA

53

B5056

Dulands
Farm
Dulands Farm
Buildings

White Meadow
House

Mellowmeadow
Farm

The Beeches

The Bryn

Sandhurst
Farm

Park House
Farm

Parkgate

Bradbourne
Hall

+

Bradbourne

MILL LA

Haven Grange
Farm

Bank
House

Bradbourne
Mill

Havenhill Dale

Haven Hill

Havenhill Dale Brook

Clipshead
Farm

Crowtrees
Farm

Park
Farm

Netherton
Hall

BRACKENDALE LA

Brackendale Brook

3

52

Bank Top

Banktop
Farm

DE6

Wigber Low

Bradley Dumble

Winn Brook

Winn
Farm

B5035

2

Longrose
Farm

Newhouse
Farm

51

Knivetonwood
Farm

LONGROSE LA

Closes
Farm

THE HALSTEADS

DISTRICT LA

STANDLOW LA

Standlow
Farm

Hognaston Winn

STONEY LA

1

WOOD LA

Kniveton
Crow Trees
Farm

Kniveton CE
Prim Sch

+

Green
Farm

Riddings

St James Lane
Farm

PH

Church
Farm

Lower Riddings
Farm

B5035

+

Old Hall

50

A   21   B   22   C

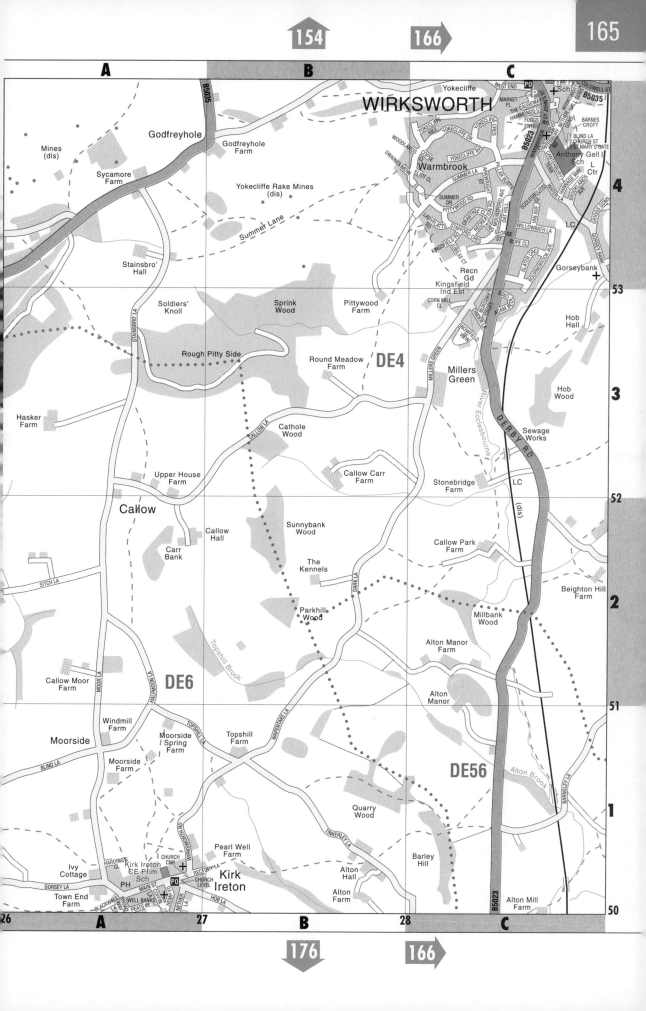

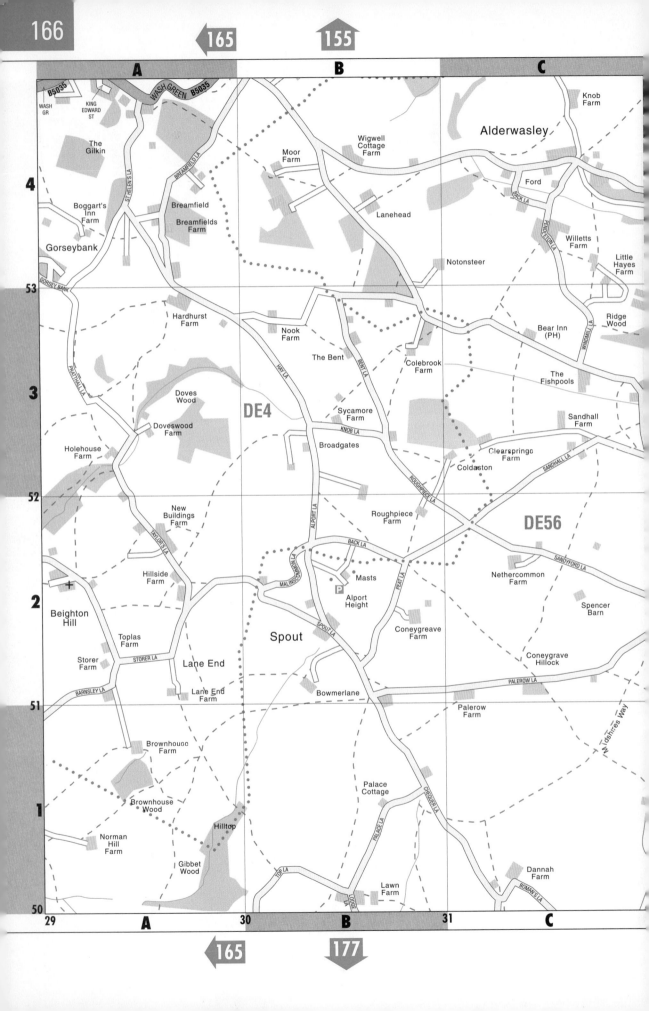

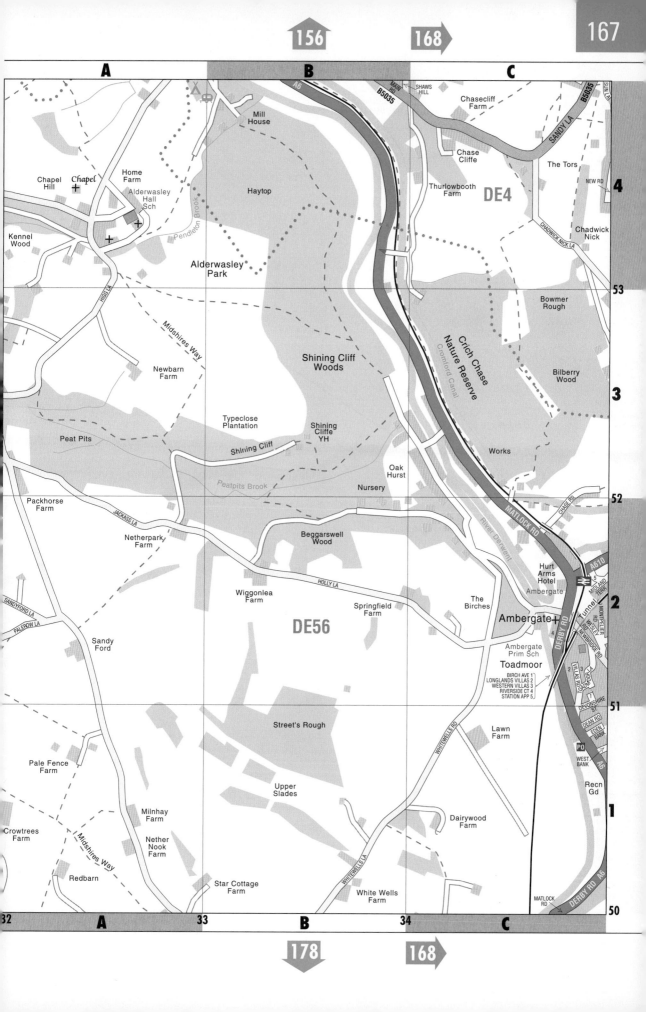

156
168

A   **B**   **C**

MAIN RD

Mill
House

B5035

SHAWS
HILL

Chasecliff
Farm

B5035

SANDY LA

SUN LA

Chapel
Hill

Chapel

Home
Farm

Alderwasley
Hall Sch

Haytop

Chase
Cliffe

Thurlowbooth
Farm

DE4

The Tors

NEW RD

4

Kennel
Wood

CHADWICK NICK LA

Chadwick
Nick

Pendleton Brook

HIGG LA

Alderwasley
Park

53

Midshires Way

Newbarn
Farm

Shining Cliff
Woods

Crich Chase
Nature Reserve

Cromford Canal

Bowmer
Rough

Bilberry
Wood

3

Peat Pits

Typeclose
Plantation

Shining Cliff

Shining
Cliffe
YH

Shining Cliffe
YH

Oak
Hurst

Works

Peatpits Brook

Nursery

River Derwent

MATLOCK RD

CHASE RD

52

Packhorse
Farm

JACKASS LA

Netherpark
Farm

Beggarswell
Wood

HOLLY LA

Hurt
Arms
Hotel

A610

MIDLAND
TERR

Ambergate

MONPELIER RD

2

SANDYFORD LA

Wiggonlea
Farm

Springfield
Farm

The
Birches

Ambergate

DERBY RD

WEST
NEWBRIDGE RD

Tunnel

PALEROW LA

DE56

Sandy
Ford

Ambergate
Prim Sch

Toadmoor

BIRCH AVE 1
LONGLANDS VILLAS 2
WESTERN VILLAS 3
RIVERSIDE CT 4
STATION APP 5

VILLAS RD

RADHAI

DEVONSHIRE
ST

51

Pale Fence
Farm

Street's Rough

WHITEWELLS RD

Lawn
Farm

DEAN RD

EGEN
BANK

A6

PO

WEST
BANK

Crowtrees
Farm

Midshires Way

Milnhay
Farm

Nether
Nook
Farm

Upper
Slades

Dairywood
Farm

Recn
Gd

1

Redbarn

Star Cottage
Farm

WHITEWELLS LA

White Wells
Farm

MATLOCK
RD

DERBY RD A6

50

32   **A**   33   **B**   34   **C**

178
168

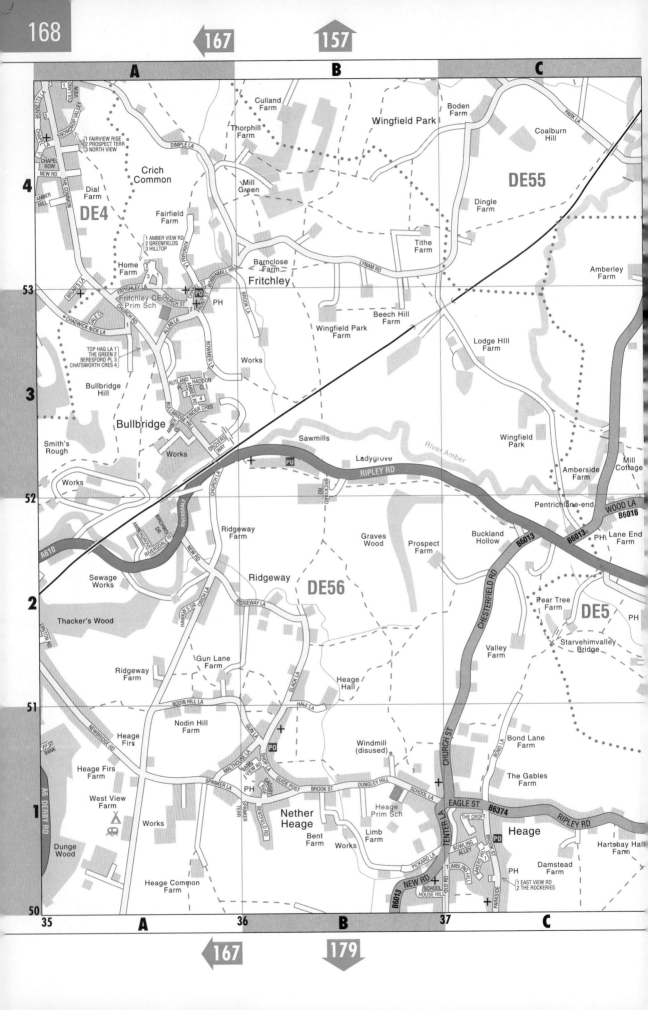

A   **B**   **C**

Culland Farm

Thorphill Farm

Wingfield Park

Boden Farm

Coalburn Hill

1 FAIRVIEW RISE
2 PROSPECT TERR
3 NORTH VIEW

Crich Common

Mill Green

DE55

Dial Farm

DE4

Dingle Farm

4

Fairfield Farm

1 AMBER VIEW RD
2 GREENFIELDS
3 HILLTOP

Home Farm

Barnclose Farm

Fritchley

Tithe Farm

Amberley Farm

Lynam Rd

Fritchley CE Prim Sch

PO

PH

Wingfield Park Farm

Beech Hill Farm

Lodge Hill Farm

53

TOP HAG LA 1
THE GREEN 2
BERESFORD PL 3
CHATSWORTH CRES 4

Works

RUTLAND PL

HADDON CL

Bullbridge Hill

Wingfield Park

3

Smith's Rough

Bullbridge

Works

Sawmills

Ladygrove

River Amber

Amberside Farm

Mill Cottage

Works

PU

RIPLEY RD

Pentrichlane-end

WOOD LA

B6016

52

A610

Ridgeway Farm

Graves Wood

Prospect Farm

Buckland Hollow

B6013

B6013

PH

Lane End Farm

Sewage Works

Ridgeway

DE56

Pear Tree Farm

DE5

PH

Thacker's Wood

Ridgeway Farm

Gun Lane Farm

RIDGEWAY LA

Valley Farm

Starvehimvalley Bridge

2

Nodin Hill Farm

SLACK LA

HALL LA

Heage Hall

Bond Lane Farm

51

Heage Firs

NODIN HILL LA

PO

Windmill (disused)

The Gables Farm

WEST ST BANK

Heage Firs Farm

Heage Prim Sch

SCHOOL LA

West View Farm

PH

GUIDE POST

BROOK ST

DUNGLEY HILL

EAGLE ST

B6374

Heage

A6 DERBY RD

Works

Nether Heage

Bent Farm

Limb Farm

Works

THE CROFT

RIPLEY RD

Hartshay Hall Farm

1

Dunge Wood

Heage Common Farm

PICKARD LA

NEW RD

TUMBLING HILL

BOWLING ALLEY

PO

PH

Damstead Farm

1 EAST VIEW RD
2 THE ROCKERIES

PARKSIDE

50

35   **A**   **36**   **B**   **37**   **C**

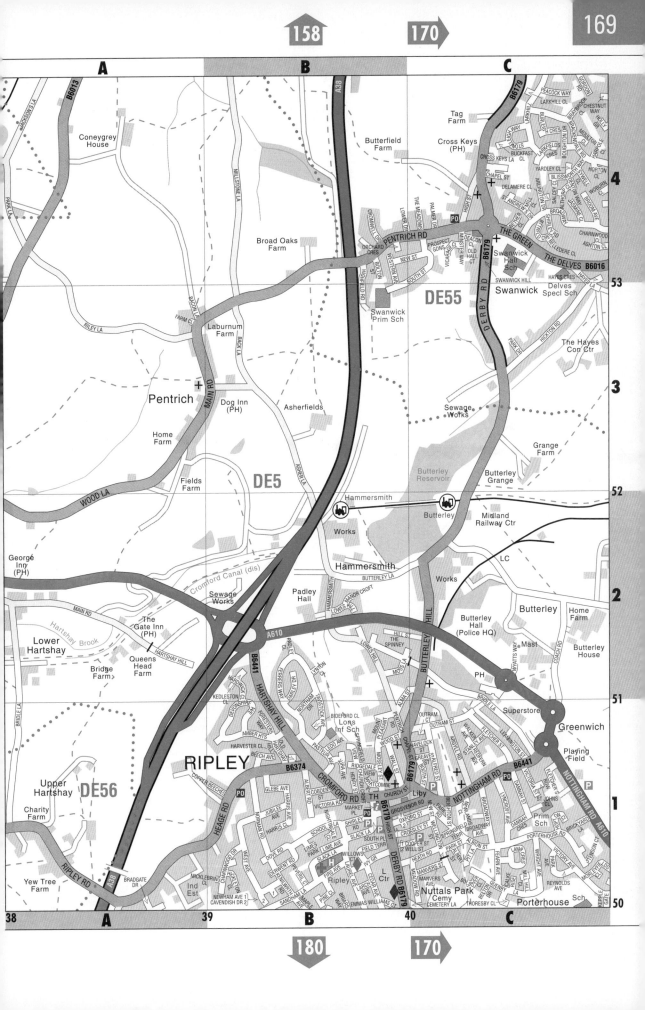

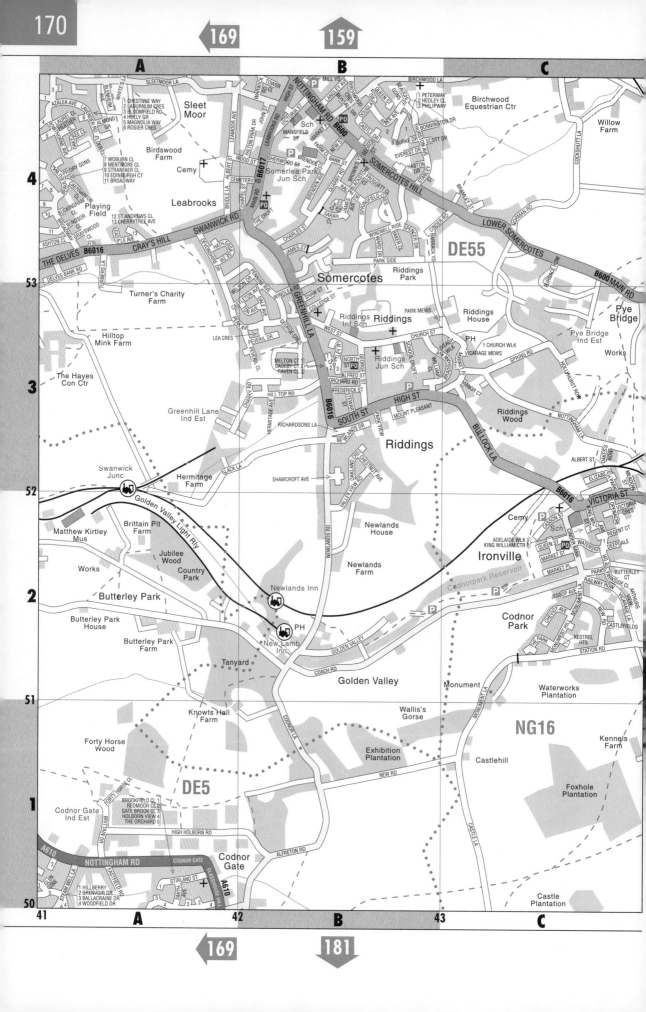

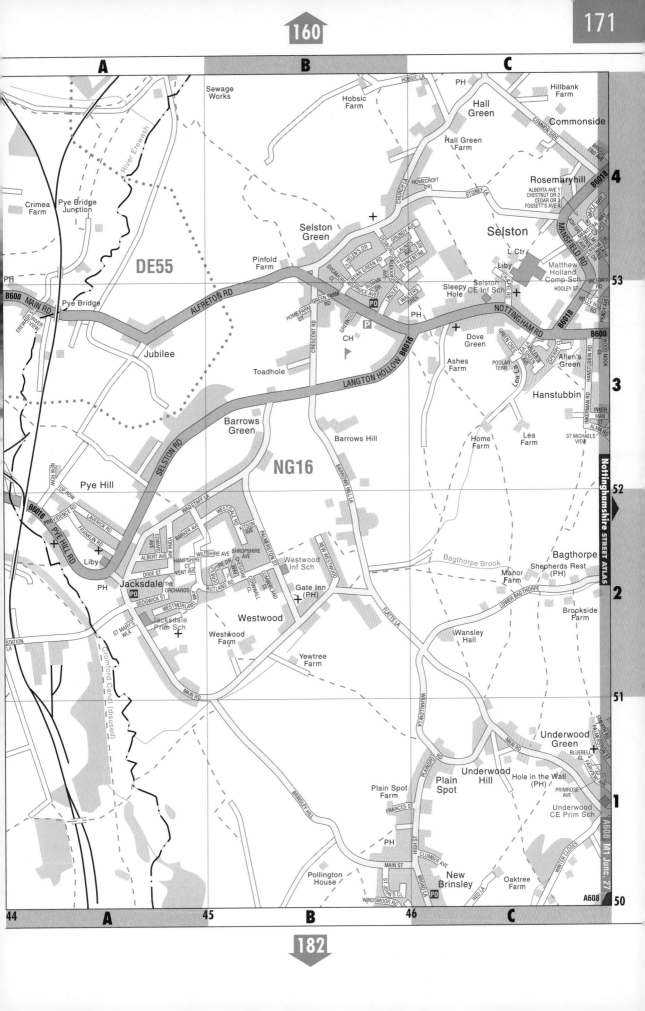

Nottinghamshire STREET ATLAS

A   **B**   **C**

Sewage Works

Hobsic Farm

HOBSIC LA

PH

Hall Green

Hillbank Farm

COMMON SIDE

Commonside

Hall Green Farm

CHURCH LA

HOMECROFT DR

STONEY LA

Rosemaryhill

B6018

ALBERTA AVE 1
CHESTNUT DR 2
CEDAR DR 3
FOSSETT'S AVE 4

4

Crimea Farm

Pye Bridge Junction

River Erewash

DE55

PH

B600

MAIN RD

EREWASH ST
RIVER VIEW

Pye Bridge

Jubilee

Pinfold Farm

ALFRETON RD

Selston Green

HELEN'S DR
BRYAN GREEN RD
DESBOROUGH RD
GRUNDY AVE
LAUNDS AVE
ALEXANDRA ST
DE VALENTINE
LINDLEY ST

SYCAMORE CT
SPRUCE AVE
ROWAN DR
GREEN FARM RD
HOME FARM CT
CRESCENT RD
GREENSIDE

PO

P
CH

Selston

L Ctr

Liby

Selston CE Inf Sch

Sleepy Hole

PH

Matthew Holland Comp Sch

MANSFIELD RD
MAPLE VALE
MANITOBA WAY
ANNVILLE STH
SASKATCHEWAN

HOOLEY ST
VICTORIA RD
HOLLY HILL

53

Dove Green

GREEN CRES
POOLAR TERR

NOTTINGHAM RD

B6018

B600

Allen's Green

WOOD NOOK

HANSTUBBIN RD

Toadhole

LANGTON HOLLOW B6016

Ashes Farm

Hanstubbin

INKERMAN RD
INKER MAN ST
ALMA RD
ST MICHAELS VIEW

3

Barrows Green

Barrows Hill

BARROWS HILL LA

Home Farm

Lea Farm

52

Pye Hill

NG16

NEW ROW
TOP ROW
PROVIDENCE RD
LAVERICK RD
FRANKLIN RD

B6016

PYE HILL RD

Liby

PH

Jacksdale

PO

SELSTON RD

WAGSTAFF LA
BARKER AVE
YORK AVE
EDWARD AVE
ALBERT AVE
DIXIE ST
KENT AVE

WESTDALE RD
KITSON AVE
WILTSHIRE AVE
HAMPSHIRE CT
CHESHIRE DR
BRISTOL
RUTLAND RD
SHROPSHIRE AVE
CORNWALL
CUMBERLAND CL

PALMERSTON ST

NEW WESTWOOD

Westwood Inf Sch

Gate Inn (PH)

Bagthorpe Brook

Manor Farm

Bagthorpe

Shepherds Rest (PH)

Brookside Farm

2

STATION LA

Cromford Canal (disused)

ST MARY'S WLK
SEDGWICK ST
WESTMORLAND
THE ORCHARDS

Jacksdale Prim Sch

Westwood

Westwood Farm

Yewtree Farm

MAIN RD

FLATTS LA

Wansley Hall

LOWER BAGTHORPE

51

BRINSLEY HILL

WILLMOTHALE LA
MOTHALE LA

PLAINSPOT RD

MAIN RD

Plain Spot

Underwood Hill

Underwood Green

BLUEBELL CL

SMEATH RD
PALMERSTON ST
FAIRVIEW
PRIMROSE AVE

Hole in the Wall (PH)

A608 M1 Junc 27

1

Plain Spot Farm

FRANCES ST

HIGH ST

CLUMBER AVE

New Brinsley

RED LA

Underwood CE Prim Sch

WINTER CLOSES

A608

Pollington House

ST JOHN'S CL

WINDSMOOR RD

MAIN ST

BROAD LA

PO

Oaktree Farm

50

44   **A**   45   **B**   46   **C**

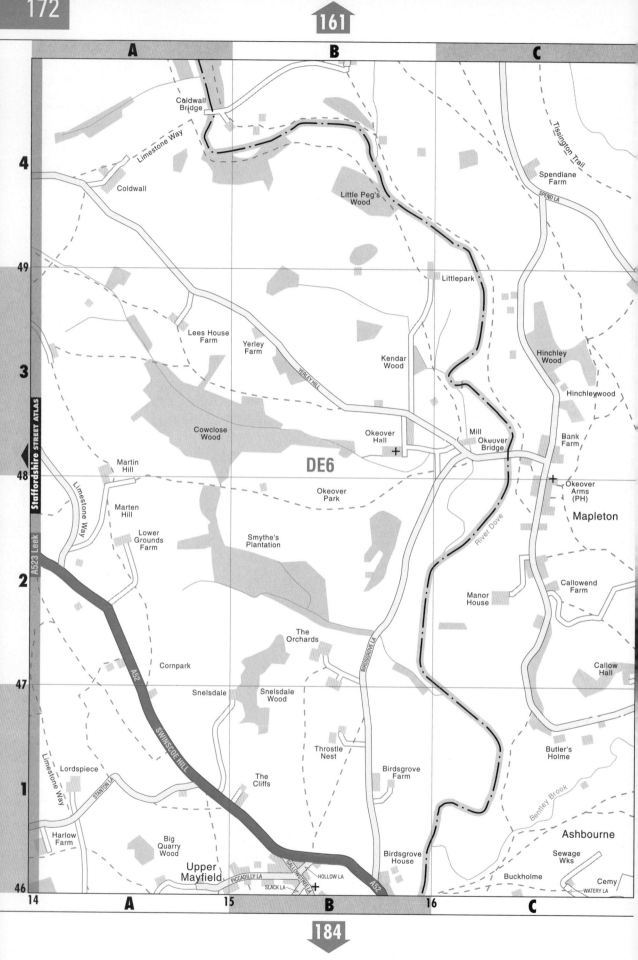

A   B   C

Coldwall Bridge

Limestone Way

4

Coldwall

Little Peg's Wood

Tissington Trail

Spendlane Farm

SPEND LA

Littlepark

49

Lees House Farm

Yerley Farm

YERLEY HILL

Kendar Wood

Hinchley Wood

Hinchleywood

3

Cowclose Wood

Okeover Hall

Mill Okeover Bridge

Bank Farm

Staffordshire STREET ATLAS

Martin Hill

DE6

Okeover Park

Okeover Arms (PH)

48

Marten Hill

Mapleton

Limestone Way

Lower Grounds Farm

Smythe's Plantation

River Dove

Callowend Farm

A523 Leek

2

Cornpark

The Orchards

Manor House

Callow Hall

A52

SWINSCOE HILL

47

Snelsdale

Snelsdale Wood

BIRDSGROVE LA

Butler's Holme

Lordspiece

STANTON LA

Throstle Nest

Birdsgrove Farm

Bentley Brook

1

Limestone Way

The Cliffs

Ashbourne

Harlow Farm

Big Quarry Wood

Birdsgrove House

Sewage Wks

Buckholme

Cemy

Upper Mayfield

PICCADILLY LA

GALLOWSTREE LA

HOLLOW LA

A52

WATERY LA

46

SLACK LA

14   A   15   B   16   C

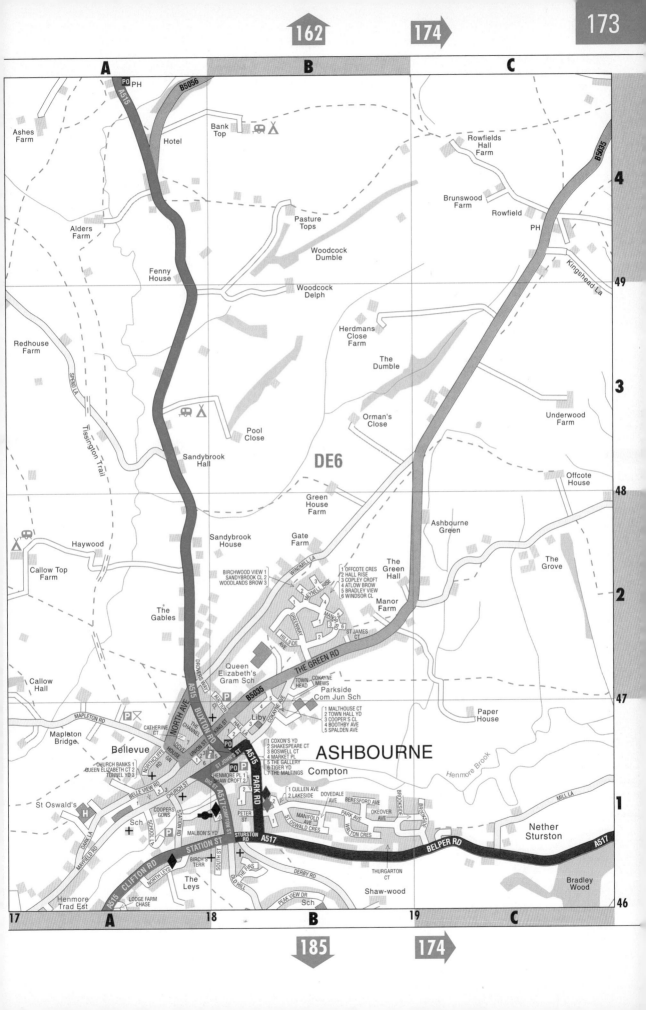

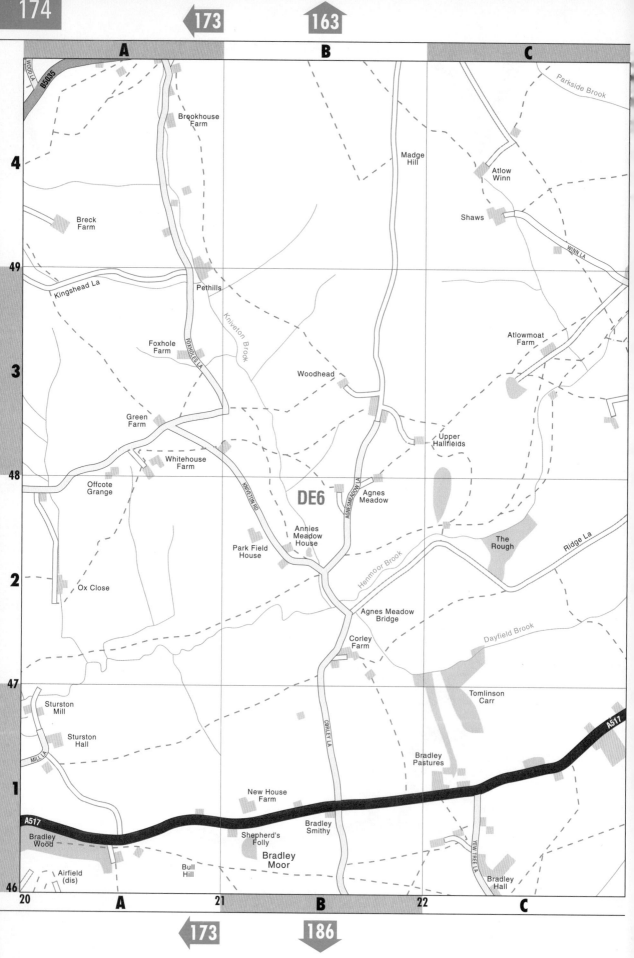

A B C

4

Brookhouse Farm

Madge Hill

Atlow Winn

Breck Farm

Shaws

WINN LA

49

Kingshead La

Pethills

Atlowmoat Farm

3

Foxhole Farm

Woodhead

Green Farm

Upper Hallfields

Whitehouse Farm

48

Offcote Grange

DE6

Agnes Meadow

The Rough

Ridge La

Annies Meadow House

Park Field House

2

Ox Close

Agnes Meadow Bridge

Dayfield Brook

Corley Farm

47

Tomlinson Carr

Sturston Mill

Sturston Hall

Bradley Pastures

A517

1

New House Farm

A517

Bradley Smithy

Bradley Wood

Shepherd's Folly

Bull Hill

Bradley Moor

YEW TREE LA

Bradley Hall

Airfield (dis)

46

20 A 21 B 22 C

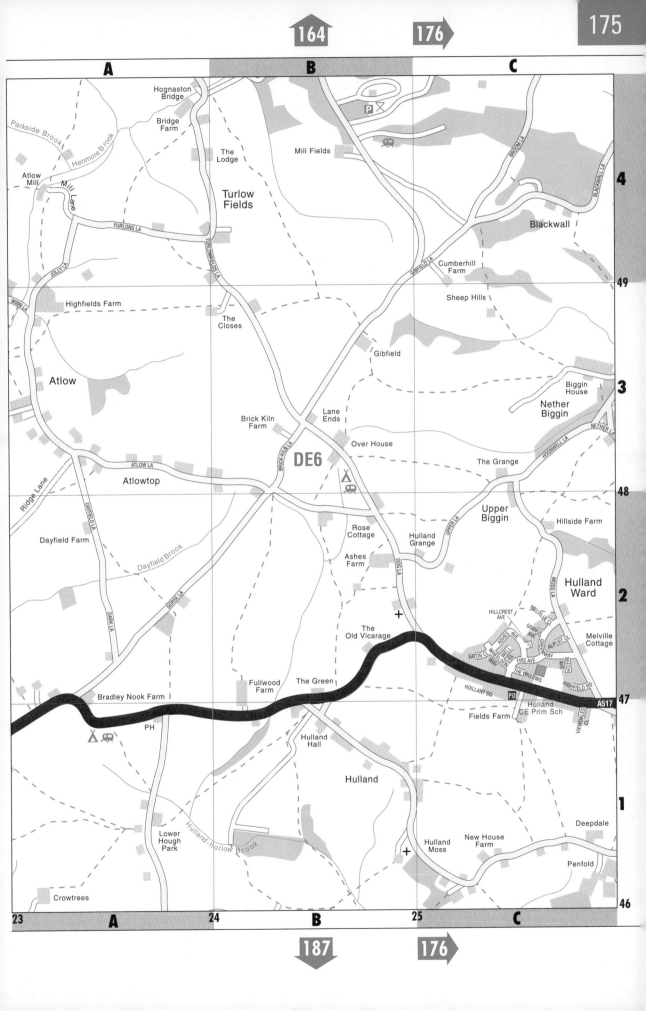

A
B
C

4
49
3
48
2
47
1
46

Parkside Brook
Hognaston Bridge
Bridge Farm
Henmore Brook
Atlow Mill
Mill Lane
Jolly La
Furlong La
WINN LA
The Lodge
Mill Fields
Turlow Fields
TURLOWFIELDS LA
P
Highfields Farm
The Closes
Atlow
Atlow La
Atlowtop
Ridge Lane
DAYFIELD LA
Dayfield Farm
Dayfield Brook
GORSE LA
DARK LA
Brick Kiln Farm
BRICK-KILN LA
Lane Ends
DE6
Over House
Gibfield
GIBFIELD LA
Cumberhill Farm
Sheep Hills
Blackwall
BROOM LA
BLACKWALL LA
Biggin House
Nether Biggin
NETHER LA
PROONWELL LA
The Grange
Upper Biggin
UPPER LA
Hillside Farm
MOSS LA
Hulland Ward
Melville Cottage
Rose Cottage
Ashes Farm
Hulland Grange
DOG LA
HILLCREST AVE
MELVILLE CL
GRANGE AVE
GREENWAY
ALPORT CL
ASHES AVE
WHEELDON WAY
WELL MEAD
EATON CL
FIRS AVE
THE WILLOWS
BEECH AVE
HIGHFIELD RD
The Old Vicarage
Bradley Nook Farm
PH
Fullwood Farm
The Green
Hulland Hall
HOILLANT SQ
PO
Hulland CE Prim Sch
Fields Farm
VIEWDALES CL
A517
Lower Hough Park
Hulland-hollow Brook
Hulland
Hulland Moss
New House Farm
Hulland CE Prim Sch
Deepdale
Penfold
Crowtrees

23
24
B
25
C
46

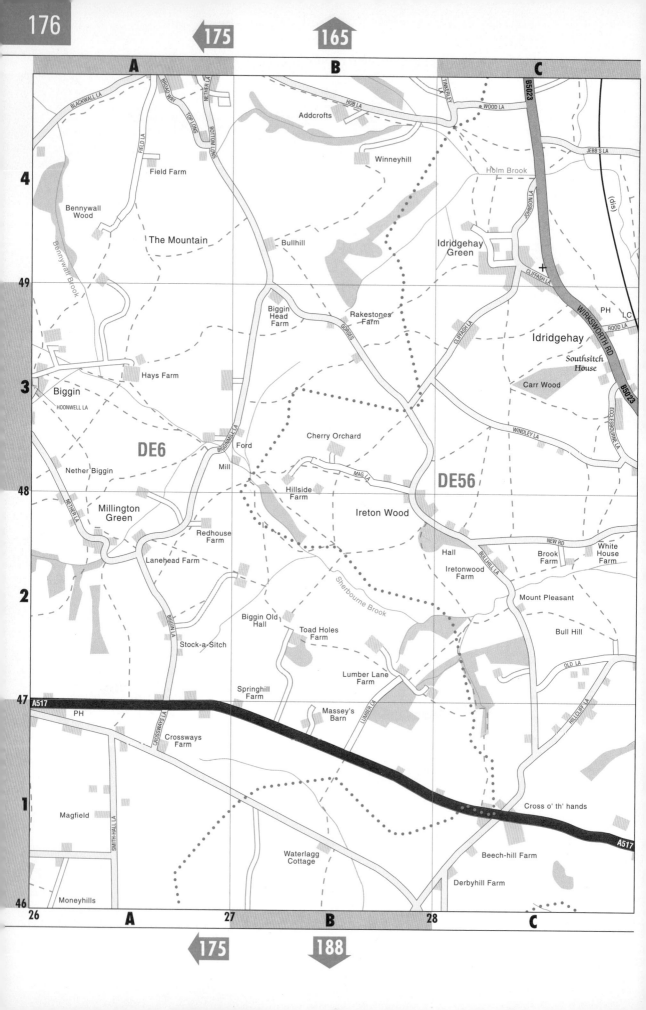

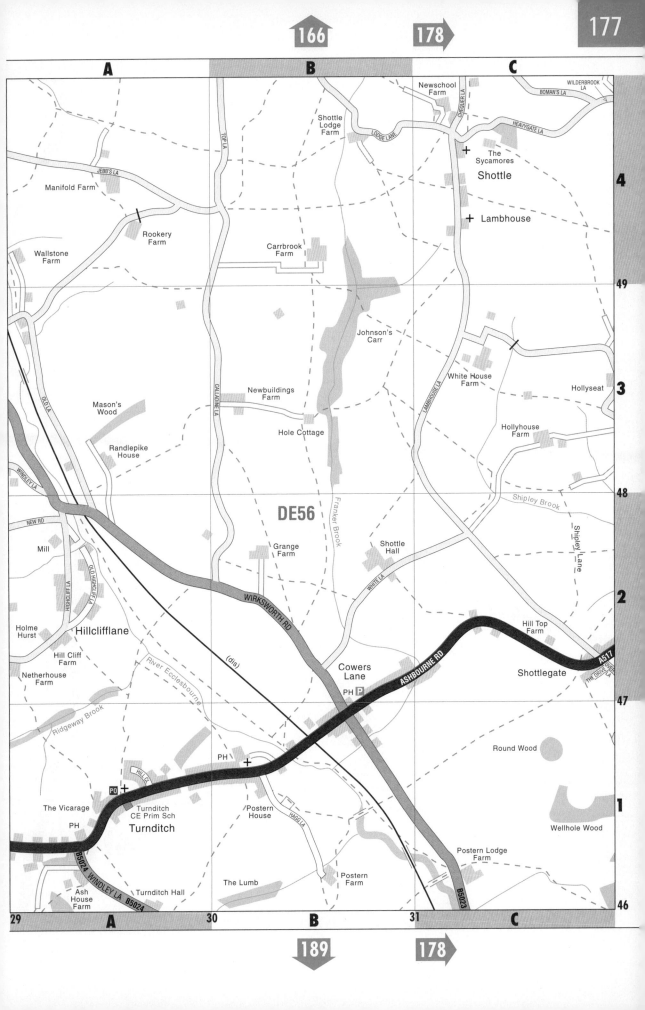

4

49

3

48

2

47

1

46

DE56

Newschool Farm

WILDERBROOK LA

BOMAN'S LA

CHEQUER LA

HEAVYGATE LA

Shottle Lodge Farm

LODGE LANE

TOP LA

The Sycamores

Shottle

Lambhouse

JEBB'S LA

Manifold Farm

Carrbrook Farm

Rookery Farm

Wallstone Farm

White House Farm

Hollyseat

LAMBHOUSE LA

CALLADINE LA

Johnson's Carr

Mason's Wood

Newbuildings Farm

Hollyhouse Farm

OLD LA

Hole Cottage

Randlepike House

Shipley Brook

WINDLEY LA

Shipley Lane

Franker Brook

NEW RD

Mill

Grange Farm

Shottle Hall

HIGHCLIFF LA

OLD HIGHCLIFF LA

WIRKSWORTH RD

WHITE LA

Holme Hurst

Hillclifflane

Hill Top Farm

Hill Cliff Farm

(dis)

River Ecclesbourne

Cowers Lane

ASHBOURNE RD

Shottlegate

A517

THE DRIVE

FERN LA

Netherhouse Farm

PH P

Round Wood

Ridgeway Brook

PH

Wellhole Wood

HILL CT

The Vicarage

PO

Turnditch CE Prim Sch

Postern House

HAGG LA

PH

Turnditch

B5024

WINDLEY LA B5024

Ash House Farm

Turnditch Hall

The Lumb

Postern Farm

Postern Lodge Farm

B5023

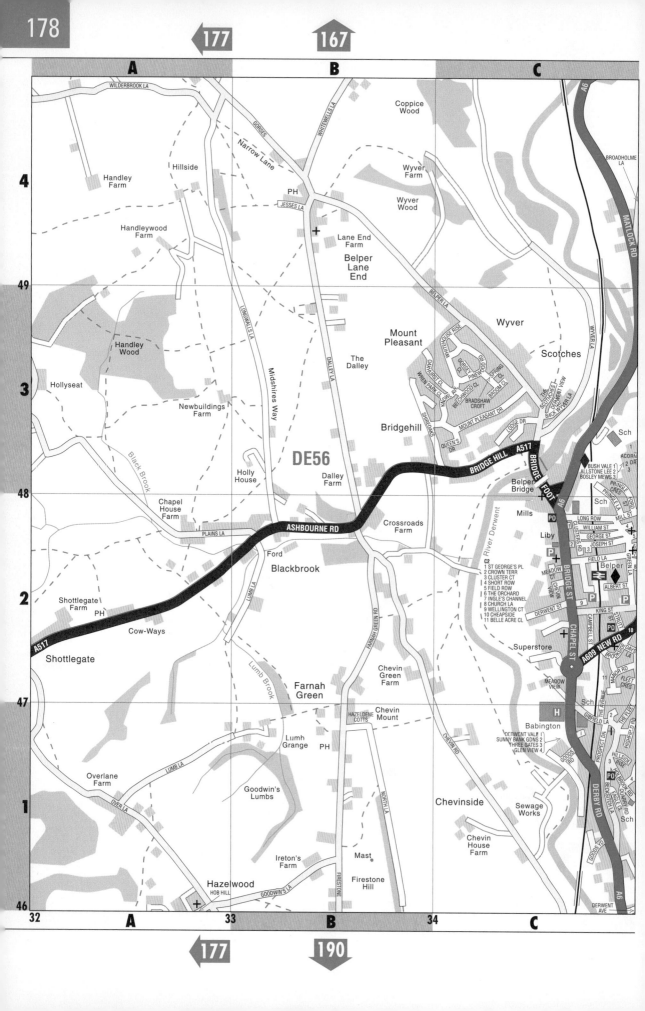

A **B** **C**

WILDERBROOK LA

Handley Farm

Hillside

Narrow Lane

Coppice Wood

GORSES

WHITEWELLS LA

4

Wyver Farm

Handleywood Farm

PH

JESSES LA

Lane End Farm

Wyver Wood

Belper Lane End

49

BELPER LA

Handley Wood

LONGWALLS LA

The Dalley

Mount Pleasant

Wyver

Scotches

DERWENT VIEW

Hollyseat

Midshires Way

3

Newbuildings Farm

DALLEY LA

Bradshaw Croft

Bridgehill

Mount Pleasant DR

QUEEN'S DR

LODGE DR

BACK WYVER LA

Sch

ACORN

BUSH VALE 1
ALLSTONE LEE 2
BOSLEY MEWS 3

PRINGLE

Black Brook

Holly House

Dalley Farm

DE56

BRIDGE HILL **A517**

BRIDGE FOOT

Belper Bridge

PO

Sch

LONG ROW

MILL LA

48

Chapel House Farm

PLAINS LA

ASHBOURNE RD

Crossroads Farm

River Derwent

Mills

Liby

WILLIAM ST

GEORGE ST

JOSEPH ST

FIELD LA

GREEN LA

48

Ford

Blackbrook

LUMB LA

C2
1 ST GEORGE'S PL
2 CROWN TERR
3 CLUSTER CT
4 SHORT ROW
5 FIELD ROW
6 THE ORCHARD
7 INGLE'S CHANNEL
8 CHURCH LA
9 WELLINGTON CT
10 CHEAPSIDE
11 BELLE ACRE CL

P

Belper

ALBERT ST

BRIDGE ST

MEADOW VIEW

CHEVIN

DERWENT ST

KING ST

P

PO

STRUTT ST

2

Shottlegate Farm

PH

Cow-Ways

A517

Shottlegate

FARNAH GREEN RD

Chevin Green Farm

Superstore

CHAPEL ST

A609 NEW RD

MANOR RD

FLEET CRES

Lumb Brook

Farnah Green

HAZELDENE COTTS

Chevin Mount

GIBFIELD LA

THE AVENUE

H

Sch

MEADOW VIEW

47

Lumh Grange

PH

CHEVIN RD

Babington

DERWENT VALE 1
SUNNY BANK GDNS 2
THREE GATES 3
GLEN VIEW 4

PROSPECT DR

HILLSIDE RISE

PO

Overlane Farm

LUMB LA

Goodwin's Lumbs

NORTH LA

Chevinside

Sewage Works

DERBY RD

EAGLE CL

Sch

1

OVER LA

Ireton's Farm

FIRESTONE

Mast

Chevin House Farm

GOODS YD

Hazelwood

HOB HILL

GOODWIN'S LA

Firestone Hill

DERWENT AVE

46

32 **A** **33** **B** **34** **C**

A6

MATLOCK RD

BROADHOLME LA

WYVER LA

Sch

A6

GREEN LA

GOODS RD

A6

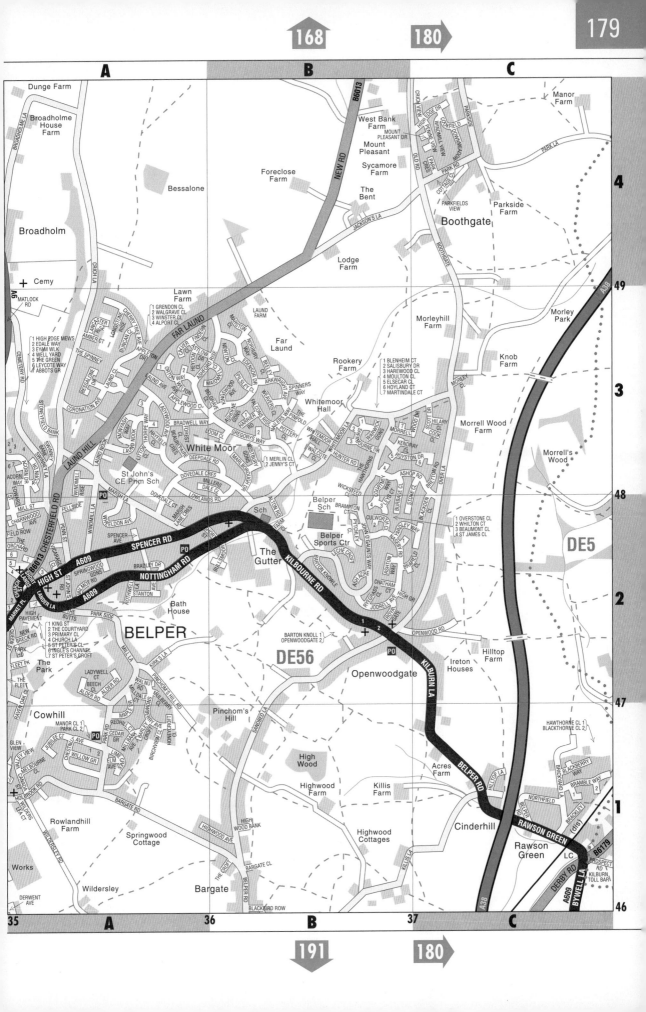

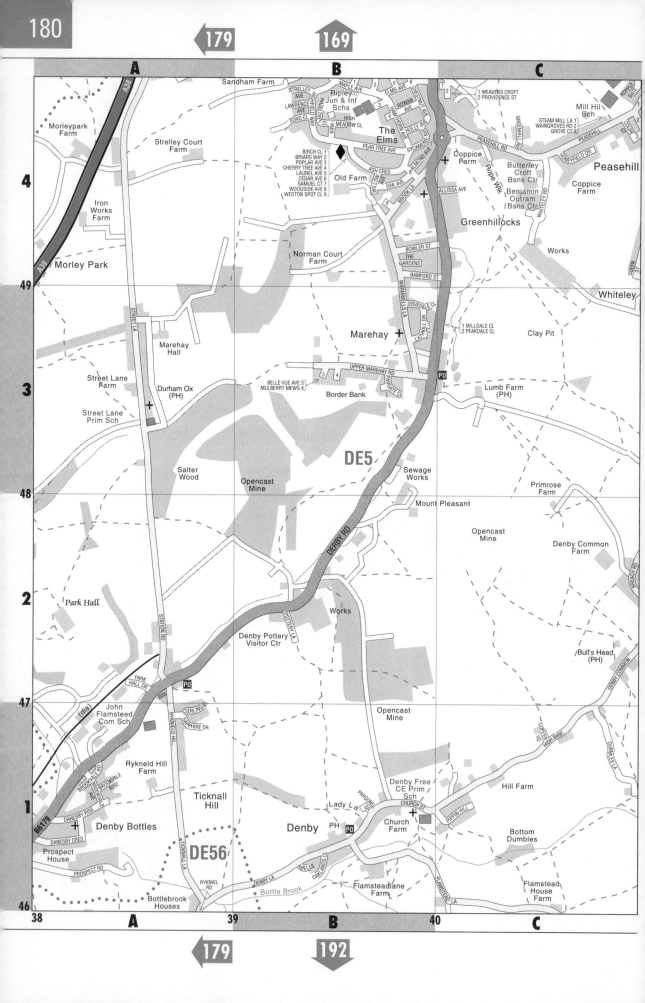

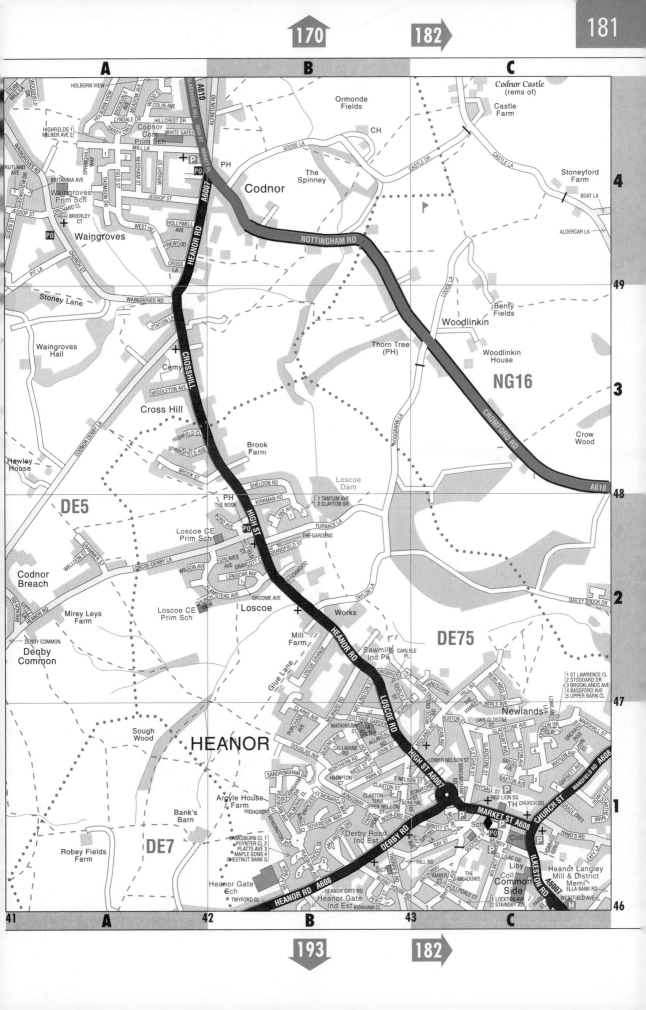

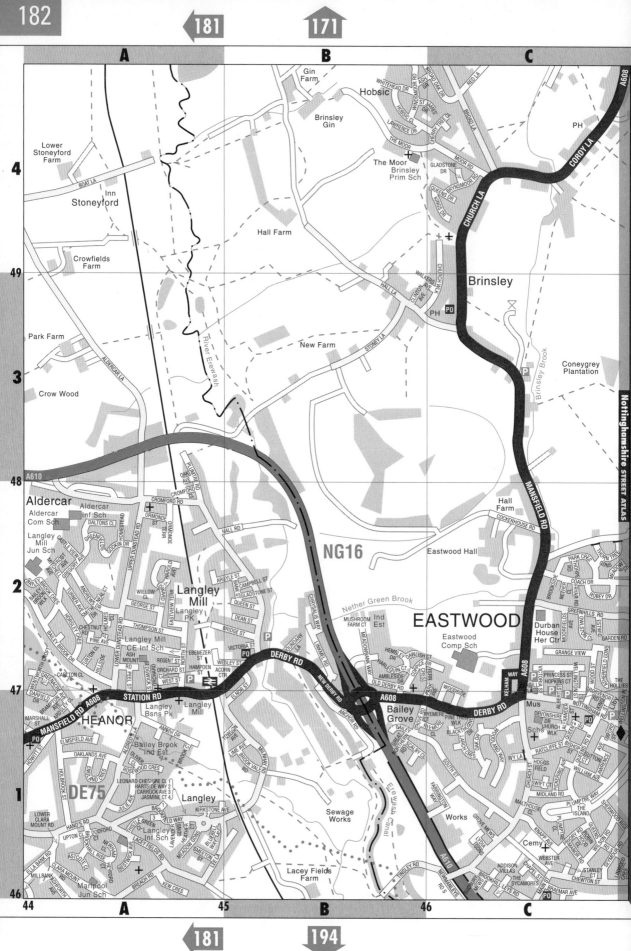

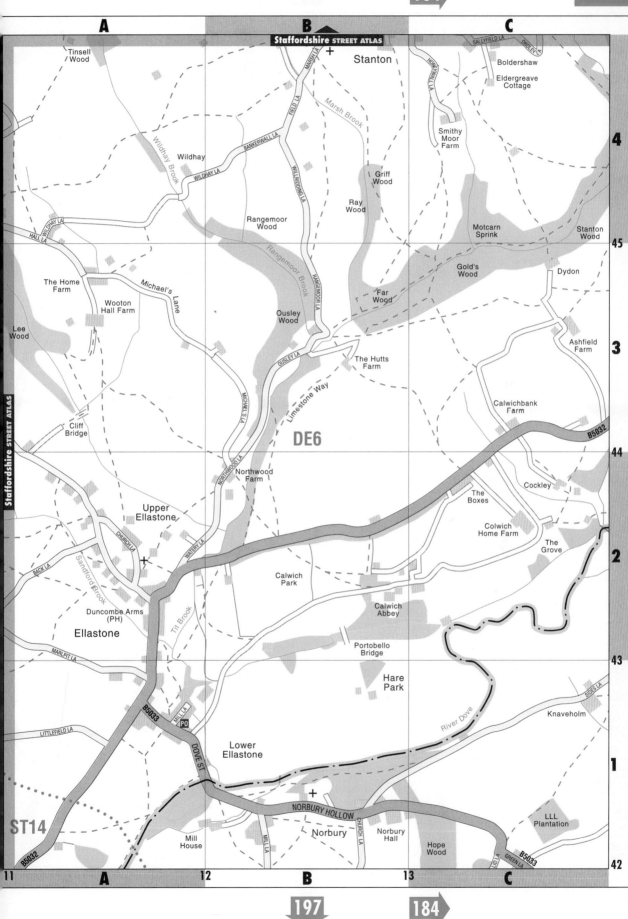

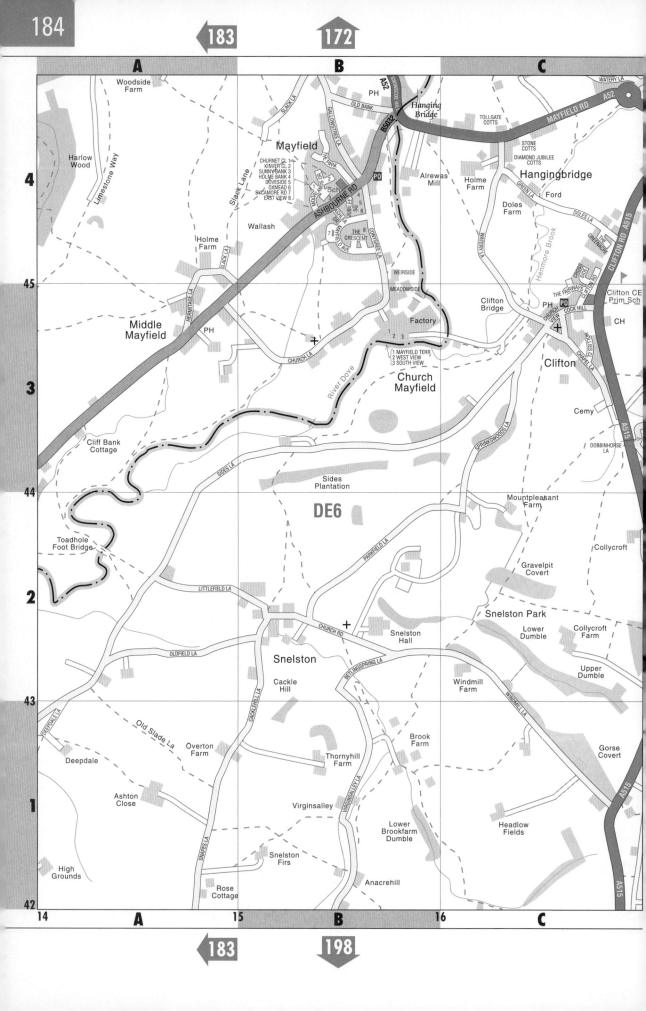

173
186

A   **B**   **C**

MAYFIELD RD

LODGE FARM CHASE
GEORGE ST
MARGERY CL
LODGE AVE
HIGHFIELD RD

CLIFTON RD

A515

OLD HILL
PEAK VIEW DR
Sch

MUMFORD DR
SPRINGFIELD AVE
ROADMEADOW

BURNASH DR
CAVENDISH DR
MILLDALE CT
ILAM CT
STANTON RD
SHARDON CT

OAKHILL
BUSCOT DR
HARBORD CL
PLUMBER CL
NORTHWOOD AVE
PREMIER AVE
ROYSTON
RISE
HAMBLETON
FORSHAW CL
BRUCKNING

SPENCER CL
WEAVER CL
BRICKYARD COTTS

OLD DERBY RD
LABOURNE AVE
ASHMEADOW CT

DERBY RD

LATHKILL DR

WHITLEY WAY

MOOR FARM RD W
MOOR FARM RD E
BLENHEIM RD

George Dutton Ind Pk

Airfield (dis)

Westwood

Lodge Farm

NETHERFIELD CL
Hill Top Inf Sch
Spitalhill

POPLAR CRES
HAZEL CT
LIME GR
PINE
OAK CRES

ROWAN
BEECH DR
TREE CL
WYASTON RD
WILLOW
CHESTNUT DR

1 DERWENT GDNS
2 HAWTHORN CL
3 MAPLE DR

4

CH

Bank Cottages

Hilltop

SNIPESMOOR LA

45

A52

Whitemeadow

The Hollies

WYASTON RD

Blake House

Centenary Way
Bonnie Prince Charlie Wlk

MOOR LA

3

Briery House

DOBBINHORSE LA

Tinker's Inn

Osmaston Fields Farm

Glebe House

New House Farm

44

DE6

The Holts

Osmaston CE Prim Sch
CHURCH LA
Osmaston

New Buildings Farm

A515

Osmaston Pastures

QUILOW LA

Quilow Farm

2

Scardale Covert

43

Wyaston Brook

Copse Hill

EDLASTON LA

Edlaston Hall

PH

Edlaston

Church Farm

Wyaston

Wyaston Grove

1

Airfield (dis)

ORCHARD LA

The Hole

RODSLEY LA

42

A   **B**   **C**

Bradley Moor

Park Farm

Hole in the Wall

Lady's Pond

Bradley

Bradley CE Prim Sch

Moorend

HADLEY LA

Brook Farm

PINFOLD LA

4

Lady Hole

Ladyhole Farm

Firs Farm

Old Hall Farm

MILLIAM LA

Knoll Lodge

45

Airfield (disused)

DOGBENNEL LA

YELDERSLEY LA

Bradley Brook

A52

War Farm

Home Stead Farm

3

CHURCH LA

Yeldersley Home Farm

PAINTER'S LA

Yeldersley Hall

Boat House

ROUGH LA

44

Yeldersley Hollies

DE6

Hazelwell Farm

The Hollies Farm

PH

Ian's Oak

PO

The Mount

QUILOW LA

Madge La

Shirley Bridge

2

The Rookery

Oak Covert

Home Farm

Bonnie Prince Charlie Wlk

East Deer Park

Shirleycommon Farm

Corner Farm

43

Centenary Way

Osmaston Park

Shirley Common

1

A52

Ednaston Home Farm

Shirleypark Farm

BRICK-KILN LA

Shirley Park

PARK LA

HALL LA

The Vicarage

Wyaston Brook

Shirley House

42

A   B   C

PINFOLD LA

The Knob

Brunswood Cottage

BRUNSWOOD LA

Houghpark

Hulland-Hollow Brook

Black Carr Farm

Common End Farm

Scout Lane

4

Parkside

Ends Bridge

Spinnyford Brook

Gun Hill

45

Mansell Park Farm

Bradley Park Farm North

Spinney Farm

Spinnyford Brook

Mansell Meadows

Burton Shutts Farm

3

Bradley Oldpark

Gaskin's Carr

Park Farm

Cuscas

CUSCAS LA

44

Bradley Oldpark South

DE6

Bradley Brook

The Far Carr

Hollies Farm

Crystal Springs Farm

Coppice Farm

NORTH LA

Sandy's

2

North Farms

Knowles Farm

North Farm House

Alder Carr

Cave Farm

43

CARPER LA

YELDERSLEY LA

Brook Cottage

Brailsford Brook

Wood Farm

Ednaston Lodge Farm

Dam Farm

Monk's Pond

Brailsford Gorse

King's Grove

1

St Mary's Home

EDNASTON CT

Birch House

SLACK LA

Ednaston Manor

Fiddler's Folly

LUKE LA

A52

DERBY LA

Commonside

42

3   A   24   B   25   C

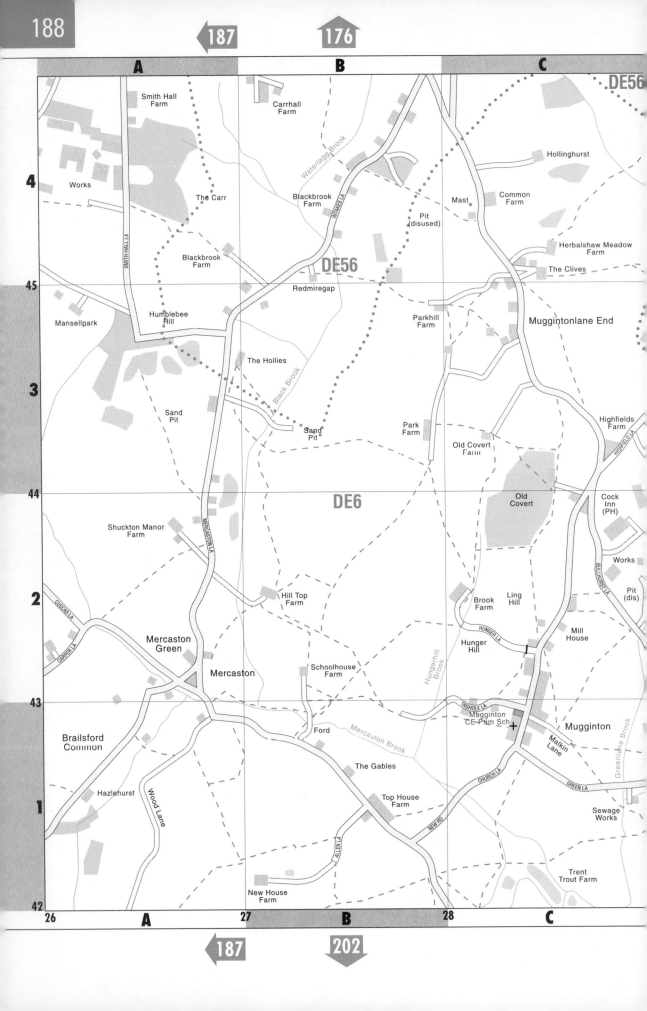

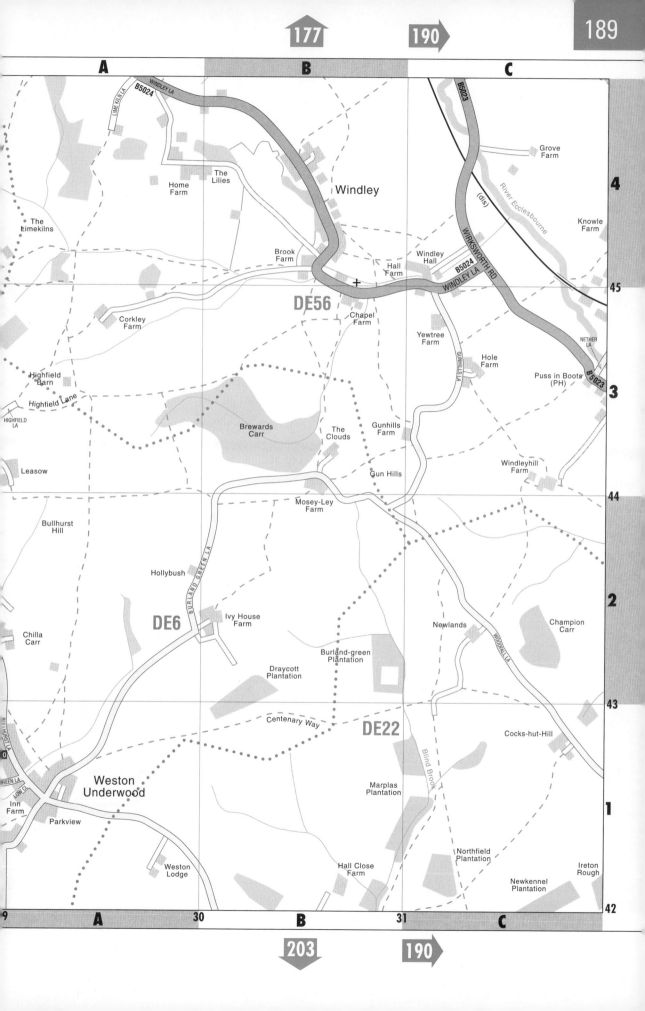

A

B

C

B5024
WINDLEY LA
LIME KILN LA

B5023

Grove Farm

4

Home Farm

The Lilies

Windley

(dis)

River Ecclesbourne

Knowle Farm

The Limekilns

Brook Farm

Hall Farm

Windley Hall

WIRKSWORTH RD

45

DE56

Chapel Farm

B5024 WINDLEY LA

Corkley Farm

Yewtree Farm

NETHER LA

Highfield Barn

GUNHILLS LA

Hole Farm

Puss in Boots (PH)

B5023

Highfield Lane

Brewards Carr

The Clouds

Gunhills Farm

3

HIGHFIELD LA

Leasow

Gun Hills

Windleyhill Farm

44

Mosey-Ley Farm

Bullhurst Hill

BURLAND GREEN LA

Hollybush

2

DE6

Ivy House Farm

Newlands

WOODALL LA

Champion Carr

Chilla Carr

Burland-green Plantation

Draycott Plantation

43

Centenary Way

DE22

Cocks-hut-Hill

RII HURST LA

Blind Brook

0

GREEN LA

LOW CL

Weston Underwood

Marplas Plantation

1

Inn Farm

Parkview

Weston Lodge

Hall Close Farm

Northfield Plantation

Ireton Rough

Newkennel Plantation

42

9

A

30

B

31

C

42

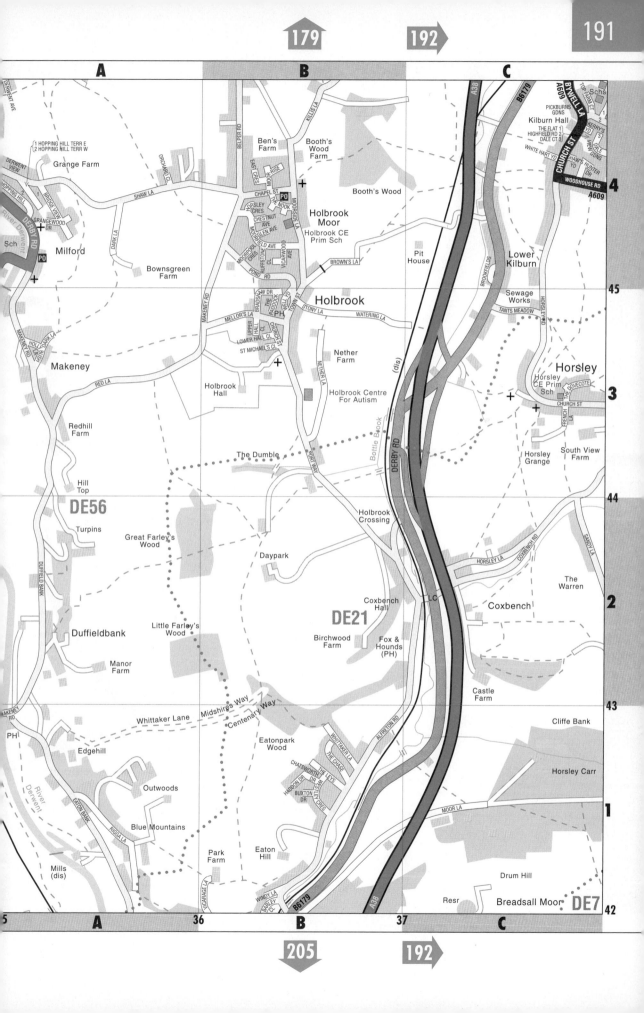

A   **B**   **C**

DERWENT AVE

1 HOPPING HILL TERR E
2 HOPPING HILL TERR W

DERWENT VIEW

Grange Farm

HOPPING HILL

BRIDGE VIEW

GRANGEWOOD DR

River Derwent

DERBY RD

Sch

PO

Milford

PO

SHAW LA

ORCHARD CL

DARK LA

Bownsgreen Farm

BELPER RD

WILLIS LA

Ben's Farm

Booth's Wood Farm

EAST CRES

MOOR RISE

CHAPEL ST

PO

THE NOOK

MOORSIDE LA

Booth's Wood

HORSLEY CRES

CHESTNUT AVE

GLEN LA

MUDFIELD AVE

Holbrook Moor

Holbrook CE Prim Sch

MOORPOOL CRES

RUFFSTONE CL

VICARWOOD AVE

POND RD

BROWN'S LA

Pit House

A38

B6179

BYWELL LA

Schs

PICKBURNS GDNS

Kilburn Hall

THE FLAT 1
HIGHFIELD RD 2
DALE CT 3

A609

KERRY'S YD

DYLE

NEW GUNS

WHITE HART YD

CHURCH ST

SHAW'S

HUNTER DR

YD

WOODHOUSE RD

A609

Lower Kilburn

BROOKFIELDS

Sewage Works

HORSLEY RD

TANTS MEADOW

4

45

Makeney

MAKENEY RD

HOLLY BUSH

DARK LA

RED LA

Redhill Farm

Hill Top

DE56

Turpins

Great Farley's Wood

DUFFIELD BANK

Little Farley's Wood

Duffieldbank

Manor Farm

EATON BANK

RIGGA LA

MAKENEY RD

PH

Edgehill

River Derwent

Outwoods

Blue Mountains

Mills (dis)

5

MELLOR'S LA

UPPER HALL

LOWER HALL CL

BRADSHAW DR

THE PADDOCK

CHURCH ST

WELL LTD

ST MICHAEL'S CL

TOWN ST

STONY LA

PH

Holbrook

WATERING LA

NETHER LA

Nether Farm

Holbrook Hall

PORT WAY

The Dumble

Holbrook Centre For Autism

Bottle Brook

DERBY RD

(dis)

Horsley CE Prim Sch

THE DOVECOTE

Horsley

FRENCH LA

CHURCH ST

Horsley Grange

South View Farm

3

44

Holbrook Crossing

Daypark

DE21

Coxbench Hall

Birchwood Farm

Fox & Hounds (PH)

LC

HORSLEY LA

COXBENCH RD

Coxbench

SANDY LA

The Warren

Castle Farm

2

43

Whittaker Lane

Midshires Way

Centenary Way

Eatonpark Wood

WHITTAKER LA

THE CHASE

CHATSWORTH DR

THE LEYS

HADDON DR

WESTLEY CRES

BUXTON DR

ALFRETON RD

Cliffe Bank

Horsley Carr

MOOR LA

1

Park Farm

Eaton Hill

VICARAGE LA

WINDY LA

BARLEY CL

B6179

A38

Resr

Drum Hill

Breadsall Moor

DE7

42

A 36   **B** 37   **C**

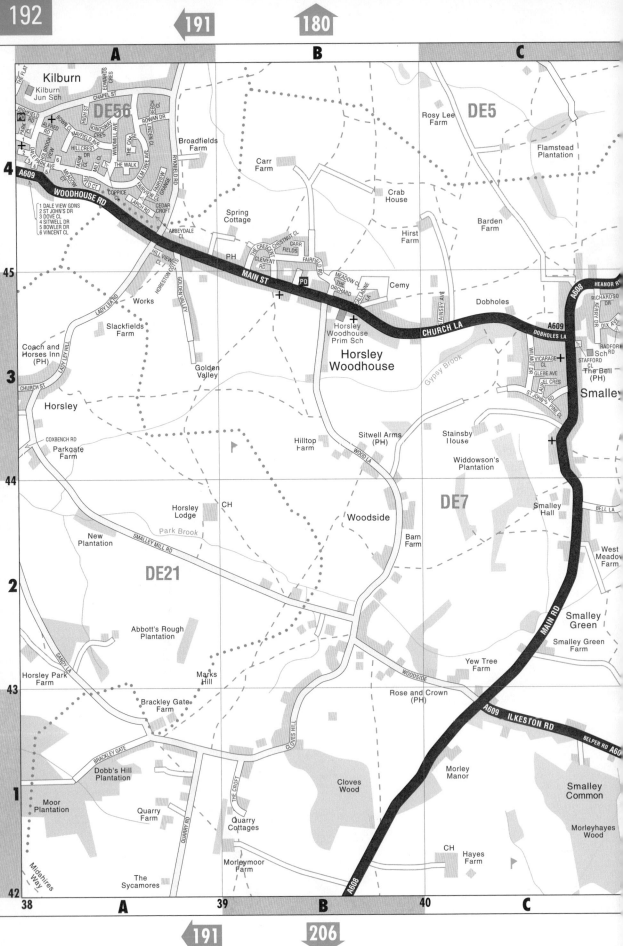

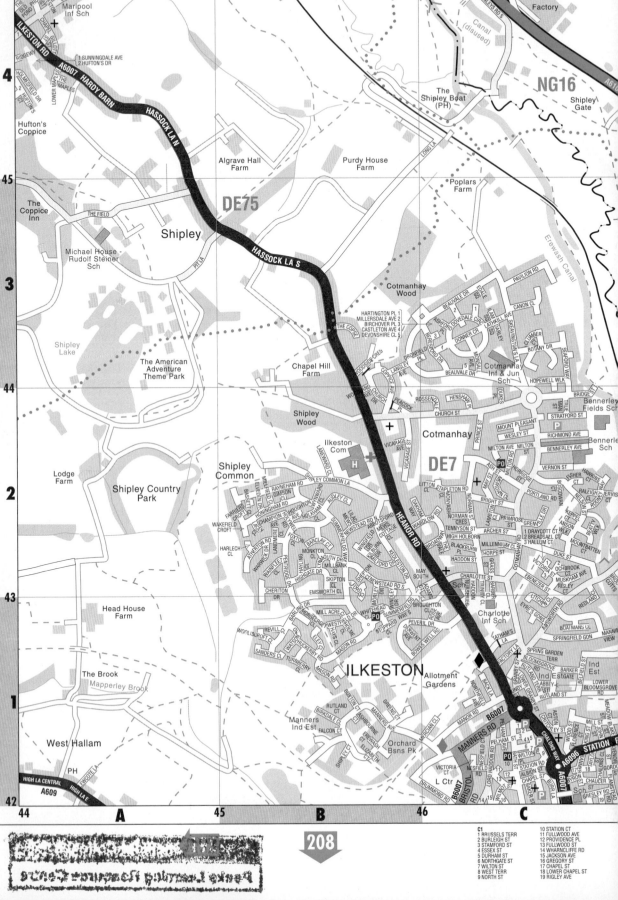

C1
1 RRUSSELS TERR
2 BURLEIGH ST
3 STAMFORD ST
4 ESSEX ST
5 DURHAM ST
6 NORTHGATE ST
7 WILTON ST
8 WEST TERR
9 NORTH ST
10 STATION CT
11 FULLWOOD AVE
12 PROVIDENCE PL
13 FULLWOOD ST
14 WHARNCLIFFE RD
15 JACKSON AVE
16 GREGORY ST
17 CHAPEL ST
18 LOWER CHAPEL ST
19 RIGLEY AVE

Parke Learning Resource Centre

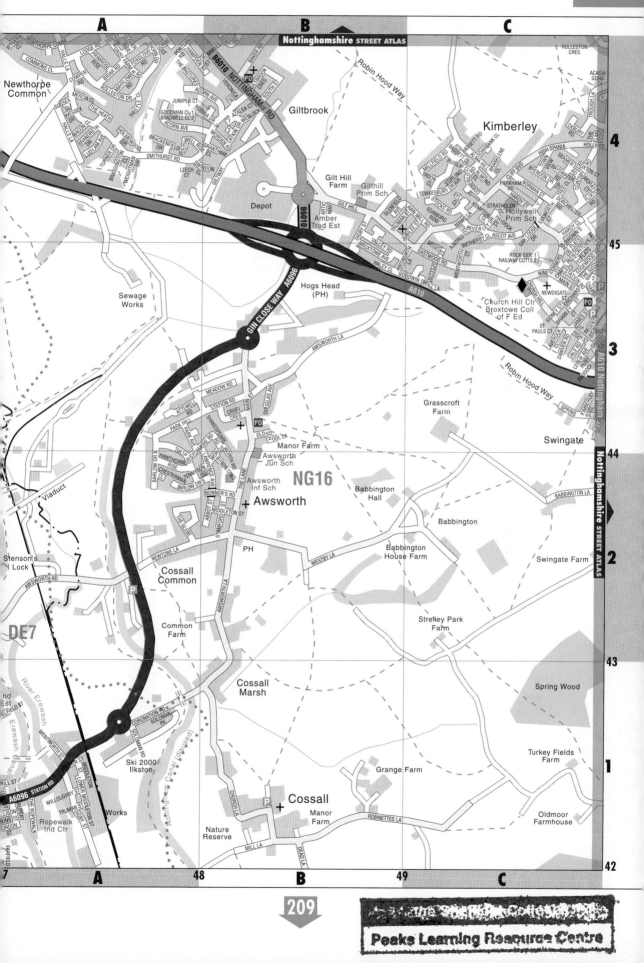

A   B   C

Newthorpe
Common

Giltbrook

Gilt Hill
Farm

Gilthill
Prim Sch

Kimberley

Hollywell
Prim Sch

Depot

Amber
Trad Est

4

45

Sewage
Works

Hogs Head
(PH)

Church Hill Ctr
Broxtowe Coll
of F Ed

Robin Hood Way

Robin Hood Way

3

Grasscroft
Farm

Swingate

Meadow Rd

Manor Farm

Awsworth
Jun Sch

Awsworth
Inf Sch

NG16

Babbington
Hall

44

Viaduct

Awsworth

Babbington

Swingate Farm

Stenson's
Lock

Cossall
Common

PH

Westby La

Babbington
House Farm

Stretley Park
Farm

2

DE7

Common
Farm

43

Cossall
Marsh

Spring Wood

Ski 2000
Ilkston

Turkey Fields
Farm

1

Works

Nature
Reserve

Cossall

Manor
Farm

Robinettes La

Grange Farm

Oldmoor
Farmhouse

Ropewalk
Ind Ctr

Mill La

42

7   A   48   B   49   C

209 ▼

The Sheffield College
Peaks Learning Resource Centre

ST10

A

B

C

Holbrook Farm

Saltersford Lane

Folly Farm

Alverton Hall Farm

4

QUIXHILL LA

QUIXHILL BANK

PRESTWOOD LA

B5032

QUIXHILL LA

Quixhill

DENSTONE LA

Quixhill Bridge

Windyharbour

41

Little Park Farm

Oliver's Green

THE WEAVERS

B5031

Denstone Hall

Staffordshire Way

Manor Farm

GREENFIELDS 1
ST CHAD'S CL 2
CROFTSTEAD AVE 3

MARLPIT LA

NARROW LA

ALTON RD

The Tavern (PH)

Denstone Hall

Nabb Farm

HOLLIS LA

COLLEGE RD

THE WESTLANDS

BIRCH CL

PO

ELM VIEW

HAWTHORN CL

Denstone

All Saints CE Fst Sch

OAK RD

LADY MEADOW

BENNION GR

MEADOW CL

3

COLLEGE RD

Harper Meadow

ST14

Denstone Coll

STUBWOOD HOLLOW

Stubwood Farm

40

Hallriddings

Smalley

TAYLORS LA

Rycroft CE Mid Sch

B5031

B5030

Nabb Brook

Riddings

Stubwood

River Churnet

NABB LA

Works

2

Woodhouse Farm

STUBWOOD LA

JARDINES LA

Armitage

Churnet Bridge

HIGH ST

ASHBOURNE RD

ELMS FARM DR

EATON RD

RIVERSFIELD DR

ATKINS WAY

DOVEDALE

PO

SOUTH VIEW WLK

MILL ST 1
WESTGATE CL 2
ABBEY RD 3
CHURCH LA 4
WHITAKER MEWS 5
NORTHFIELD AVE 6

Woodhouse Field Farm

Woodhouse Fields

39

Alders

New Plantation

Banks Farm

Woottons Farm

Alders Brook

Woodseat

1

Pit Holes Plantation

Ford

Cornhill Farm

Field Head Farm

DE6

River Dove

Nothill Brook

B5030

38

08

A

09

B

10

C

Staffordshire STREET ATLAS

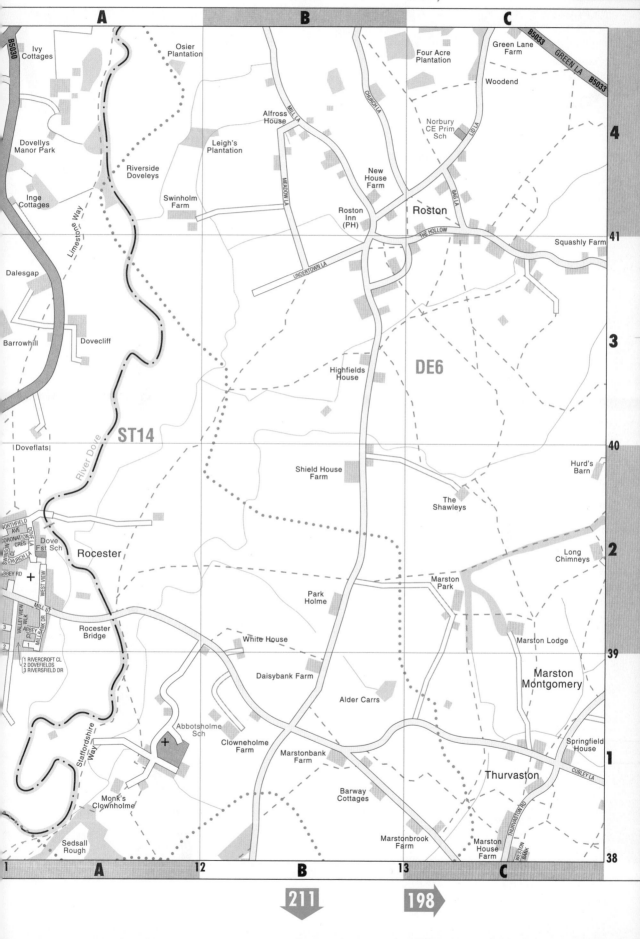

197
184

A | B | C

Shepherdswood

Chapel House

Queen Adelaide Arms (PH)

Snelston Common

Old Queen Farm

Cindershills Wood

Flat Covert

Darley Moor

B5033

GREEN LA

SNAPES LA

VIRGINS ALLEY LA

COCKSHEAD LA

B5033

A515

Common Farm

Quarry (dis)

John Roe's Covert

Grange Cottage

Top Stydd

Grange Farm

Manor House

Birchwood Park

Cubley Brook

Roston Common

Birchwoodmoor

Cubley Wood Farm

Accession Wood

DE6

HOLLIES LA

Marstoncommon Farm

Wood Hay Farm

The Hollies

Side Gate

Sammy's Wood

Broad Lane

Sandhills Farm

Cubley Covert

Cubley Common

Whiterley

Holme Lea

Cubley Cottage Farm

Common Farm

Mountpleasant Farm

Gorse Covert

Rough Grounds

Great Cubley

Birch Field Farm

SHAW LA

CUBLEY LA

The Spinney

Brookside Farm

DERBY LA

LONG MEADOW

Howard Arms (PH)

Cubley Fields Farm

A515

PO

14 | A | 15 | B | 16 | C

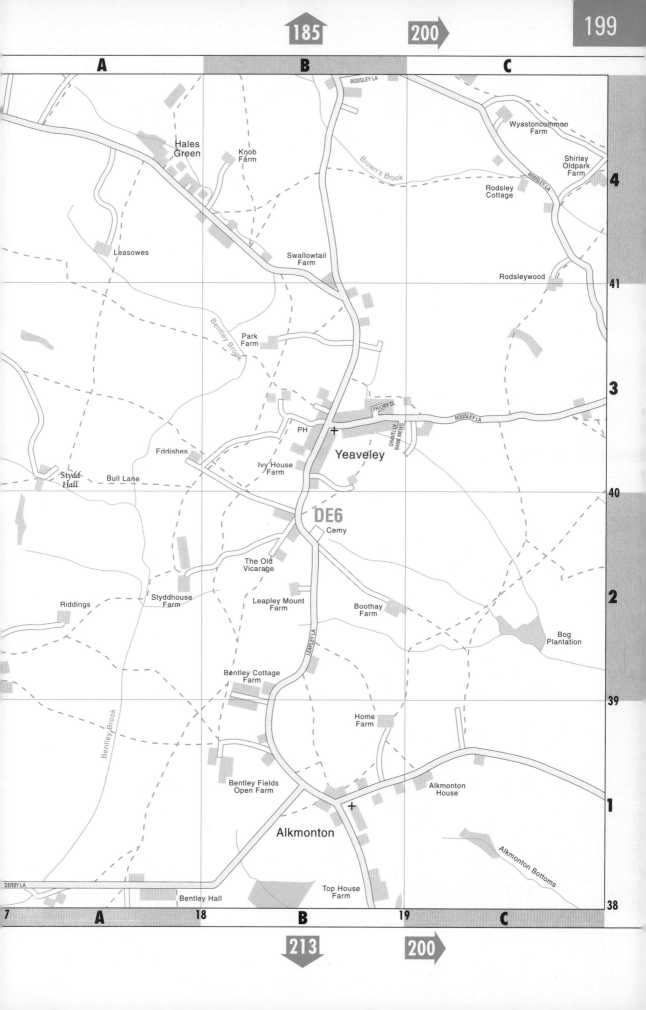

A
B
C

RODSLEY LA

Wyastoncommon Farm

Hales Green

Knob Farm

Brown's Brook

Shirley Oldpark Farm

RODSLEY LA

Rodsley Cottage

4

Leasowes

Swallowtail Farm

Rodsleywood

41

Bentley Brook

Park Farm

3

RODSLEY LA

PH

PRIORY CL

GRAVELLY BANK MEWS

Eddishes

Yeaveley

Stydd Hall

Bull Lane

Ivy House Farm

40

DE6

Cemy

The Old Vicarage

2

Riddings

Styddhouse Farm

Leapley Mount Farm

Boothay Farm

Bog Plantation

LEAPLEY LA

Bentley Cottage Farm

Home Farm

39

Bentley Brook

Bentley Fields Open Farm

Alkmonton House

1

Alkmonton

Alkmonton Bottoms

DERBY LA

Bentley Hall

Top House Farm

38

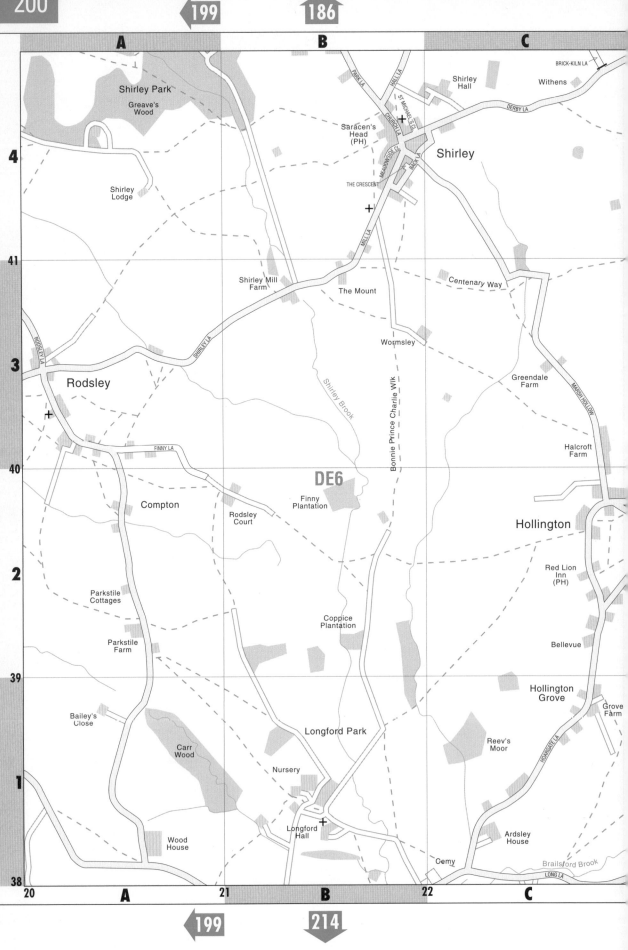

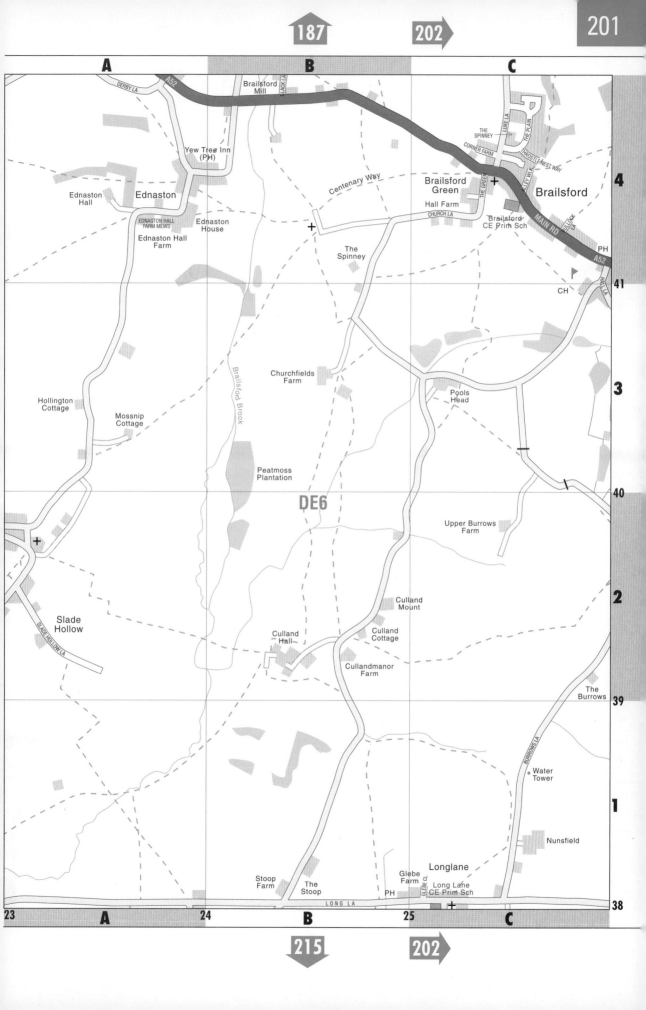
A B C

DERBY LA
A52
Brailsford Mill
SLACK LA

THE SPINNEY
LUKE LA
THE PLAIN
CORNER FARM
THROSTLE NEST WAY
Yew Tree Inn (PH)
Centenary Way
Brailsford Green
THE GREEN
Brailsford
Ednaston Hall
Ednaston
Hall Farm
VALLEY WLK
Ednaston House
EDNASTON HALL FARM MEWS
CHURCH LA
Brailsford CE Prim Sch
MAIN RD
Ednaston Hall Farm
BULLOCK LA
The Spinney
PH
A52
HALL LA
4
CH
41

Churchfields Farm
Brailsford Brook
Pools Head
3

Hollington Cottage
Mossnip Cottage
Upper Burrows Farm
Peatmoss Plantation
40

DE6

Culland Mount
Slade Hollow
SLADE HOLLOW LA
Culland Hall
Culland Cottage
Cullandmanor Farm
2

The Burrows
39

BURROWS LA
Water Tower
1

Nunsfield

Stoop Farm
The Stoop
Glebe Farm
GLEBE CL
Longlane
Long Lane CE Prim Sch
PH
LONG LA
38

23 **A** 24 **B** 25 **C**

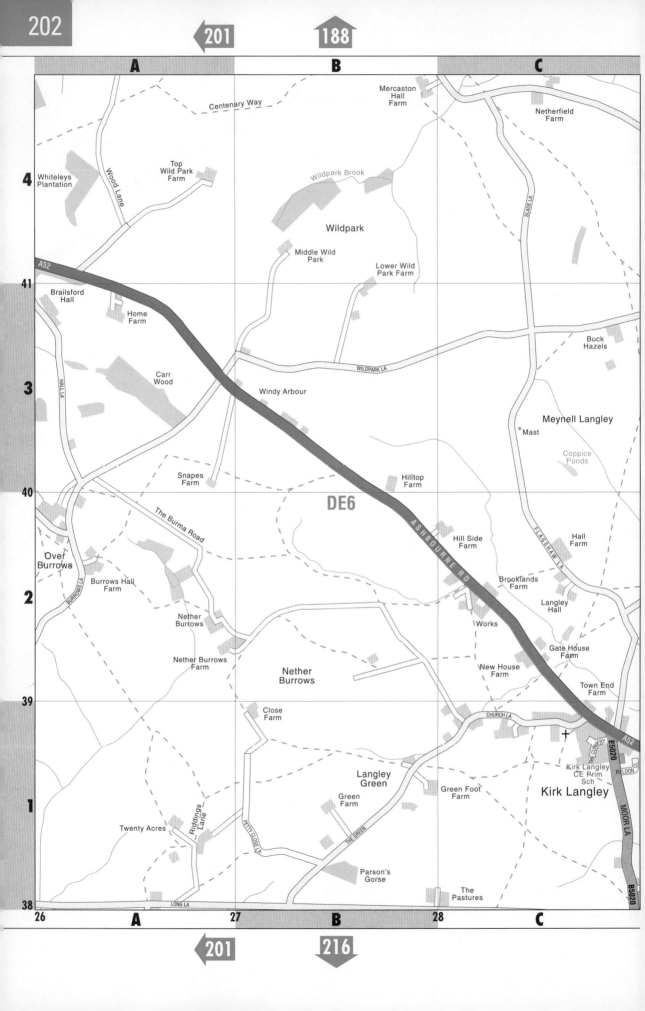

A   B   C

4

Whiteleys Plantation

Centenary Way

Mercaston Hall Farm

Netherfield Farm

Wood Lane

Top Wild Park Farm

Wildpark Brook

Wildpark

Slade La

41

A52

Brailsford Hall

Home Farm

Middle Wild Park

Lower Wild Park Farm

Buck Hazels

3

HALL LA

Carr Wood

Windy Arbour

WILDPARK LA

Meynell Langley

Mast

Coppice Ponds

Snapes Farm

Hilltop Farm

DE6

40

The Burma Road

Over Burrows

BURROWS LA

Burrows Hall Farm

ASHBOURNE RD

Hill Side Farm

FLAGSHAW LA

Hall Farm

Brooklands Farm

2

Nether Burrows

Langley Hall

Works

Nether Burrows Farm

Nether Burrows

New House Farm

Gate House Farm

Town End Farm

39

Close Farm

CHURCH LA

THE CUMBERY

B5020

Kirk Langley CE Prim Sch

FIELDON

Langley Green

Green Foot Farm

Kirk Langley

Riddings Lane

Green Farm

1

Twenty Acres

PETTY CLOSE LA

THE GREEN

MOOR LA

Parson's Gorse

The Pastures

B5020

38

LONG LA

26   A   27   B   28   C

189
204

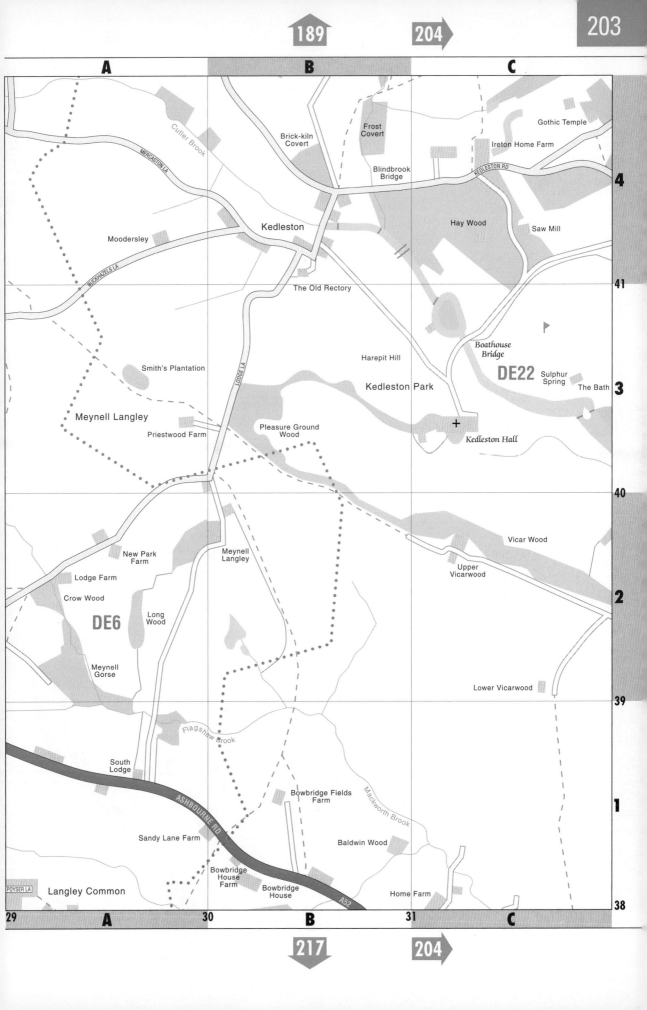

A B C

4

41

3

40

2

39

1

38

Cutler Brook

MERCASTON LA

Brick-kiln Covert

Frost Covert

Blindbrook Bridge

Gothic Temple

Ireton Home Farm

KEDLESTON RD

Kedleston

Hay Wood

Saw Mill

Moodersley

BUCKHAZELS LA

The Old Rectory

Harepit Hill

Boathouse Bridge

DE22

Sulphur Spring

The Bath

Smith's Plantation

LODGE LA

Kedleston Park

Meynell Langley

Priestwood Farm

Pleasure Ground Wood

Kedleston Hall

New Park Farm

Meynell Langley

Vicar Wood

Lodge Farm

Upper Vicarwood

Crow Wood

DE6

Long Wood

Meynell Gorse

Lower Vicarwood

Flagshaw Brook

South Lodge

Mackworth Brook

Bowbridge Fields Farm

Sandy Lane Farm

Baldwin Wood

POYSER LA

Langley Common

Bowbridge House Farm

Bowbridge House

ASHBOURNE RD

A52

Home Farm

29 A 30 B 31 C

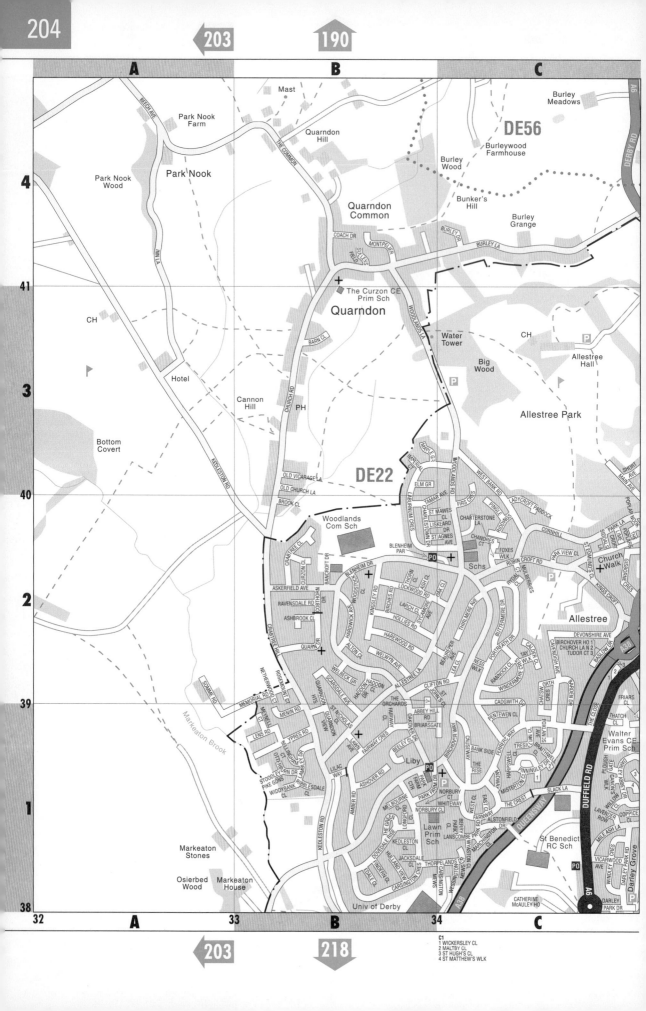

A B C

4

41

Quarndon

3

2

40

DE56

Burley
Meadows

Burleywood
Farmhouse

Burley
Wood

Bunker's
Hill

Burley
Grange

CH

Allestree
Hall

Allestree Park

DE22

Allestree

Park Nook
Farm

Quarndon
Hill

Quarndon
Common

Park Nook
Wood

Park Nook

Mast

BEECH AVE

THE COMMON

INN LA

COACH DR

MONTPELIER

FIELD SLYDES

The Curzon CE
Prim Sch

CH

Hotel

Cannon
Hill

PH

CHURCH RD

BARN CL

KEDLESTON RD

Bottom
Covert

Water
Tower

Big
Wood

BURLEY DR

BURLEY LA

WOODLANDS LA

DERBY RD
A6

P

P

P

OLD VICARAGE LA

OLD CHURCH LA

BROOK CL

Woodlands
Com Sch

CRABTREE CL

CURZON CL

BANCROFT DR

BLENHEIM DR

WOODSTOCK DR

CORBTHORN

MAYLE GR

MEMORIAL RD

ELM GR

LABURNUM CRES

TAMAR AVE

ST MAWES
CL

LISKEARD
DR

ST AGNES
AVE

CHARLESTON DR

FIRS CRES

CHARTERSTONE
LA

RIDDINGS

PINGLE

LADYCROFT PADDOCK

CHANDRES
CT

FOXES
WLK

CORNHILL

ROBIN CROFT RD

PARK VIEW CL

RYDAL

MILLBERRIES

PO

Schs

Church
Walk

ST EDMUND'S CL

KINGS CROFT

POPLAR AVE

LIME AVE

CROWN CRES

PARK LA

SIDDALS

MAIN AVE

SHORT
AVE

2

39

1

38

ASKERFIELD AVE

RAVENSDALE RD

ASHBROOK CL

CRABTREE HILL

NETHERWOOD CT

SOMME RD

Markeaton Brook

QUARN

ROSSMORE CT

HARDWICK AVE

KINGSLEY RD

BIRCHES RD

LARCH CL

HOLLIES RD

HAREWOOD RD

ALTON CL

WELWYN AVE

BEAUREPER AVE

THIRLMERE AVE

LEA CL

NESS
WLK

PORTREATH DR

BUTTERMERE DR

WINDERMERE CRES

RAMNOCH CL

TAY CL

CALDER CL

P

WELBECK GR

HADDON
DR

SCARSDALE AVE

QUARNDON
HTS

ST NICHOLAS

QUARNDON
VIEW

ALLESTREE LA

CLIFTON RD

JOHN'S CL

CADGWITH DR

ORTH
WLK

BASLOW DR

A38

NETHERWOOD CT

MEMORIAL RD

MENIN RD

YPRES RD

LENS RD

BELLINGHAM CL

OTTERBURN DR

PIKE GDNS

WIDDYBANK
CL

KEDLESTON RD

STOODLEY CL

RIBBLESDALE
CL

AMBER RD

LILAC
WAY

ASHOVER RD

MELBOURNE

OLD CHUROT
THE
ORCHARDS

FAIRWAY

DAOVER DR

ABBEY HILL

BRIARSGATE

FAIRWAY CRES

BEELEY CL

LINN
AVE

Liby

BIRCHOVER WAY

CAUSEWAY

THE
FIRS

BANK SIDE

FERNDENE WAY

PENTEWEN CL

TRESL

FOXLAND CL

BROUGHT AVE

THE CLOSE

FRIARS
CL

THATCH
CL

Walter
Evans CE
Prim Sch

PO

P

NORBURY
CT

WHITEWAY

NORBURY CL

PARK FARM
CTR

THE
RISE

BANK SIDE

HARPSWELL

WEST CL

EAST CL

FARWAY

MISTERTON CL

THE CREST

INNINGLEY CL

SLACK LA

KEDLESTON
CL

Lawn
Prim
Sch

DOVEDALE RIDGE

FINDERN CL

EDALE CL

HILLAND VIEW

JACKSDALE

CARSINGTON CRES

THORPELANDS
DR

LANSCOMBE PARK RD

BERRY
PARK
CL

MARCHINGTON
CL

ALSTONEFIELD
DR

NEWS 1ST ND 2

CARSINGTON
MEWS

QUEENSWAY

A38

DUFFIELD RD

A6

St Benedict
RC Sch

CATHERINE
McAULEY HO

Univ of Derby

Markeaton
Stones

Osierbed
Wood

Markeaton
House

DEVONSHIRE AVE

BIRCHOVER HO 1
CHURCH LA N 2
TUDOR CT 3

Darley
Park Dr

DARLEY PARK RD

VICARWOOD
AVE

WINDLEY
CRES

MILE ASH LA

COPPICE
CL

LAVENDER
ROW

PLOUGH
GATE

WILLOW
CROFT

ABBEY DR

CANNING
WAY

A Darley Grove

P

A B C

C1
1 WICKERSLEY CL
2 MALTBY CL
3 ST HUGH'S CL
4 ST MATTHEW'S WLK

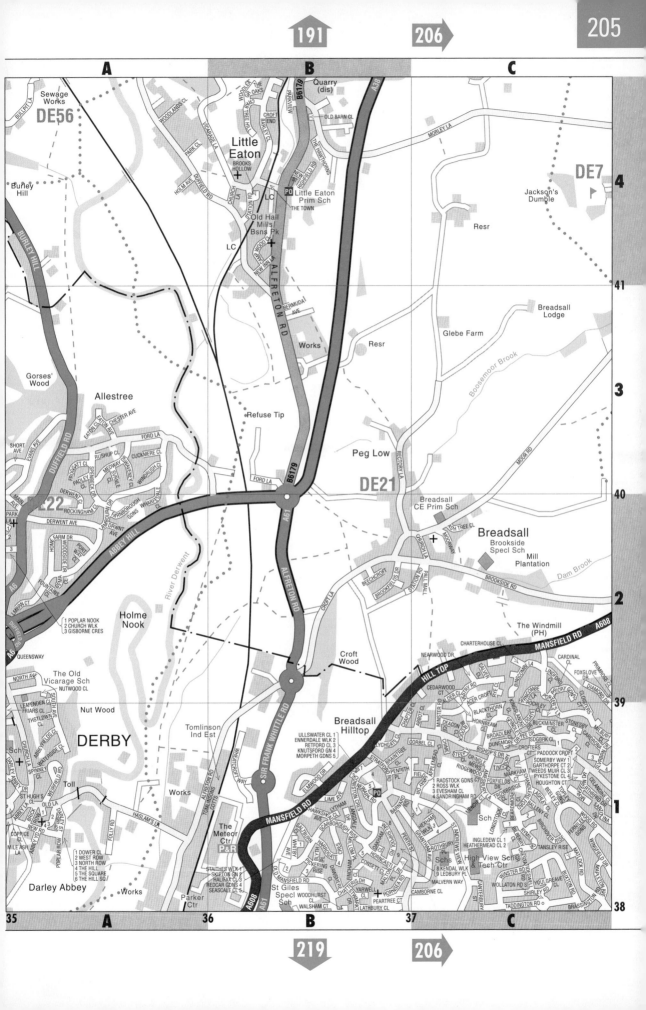

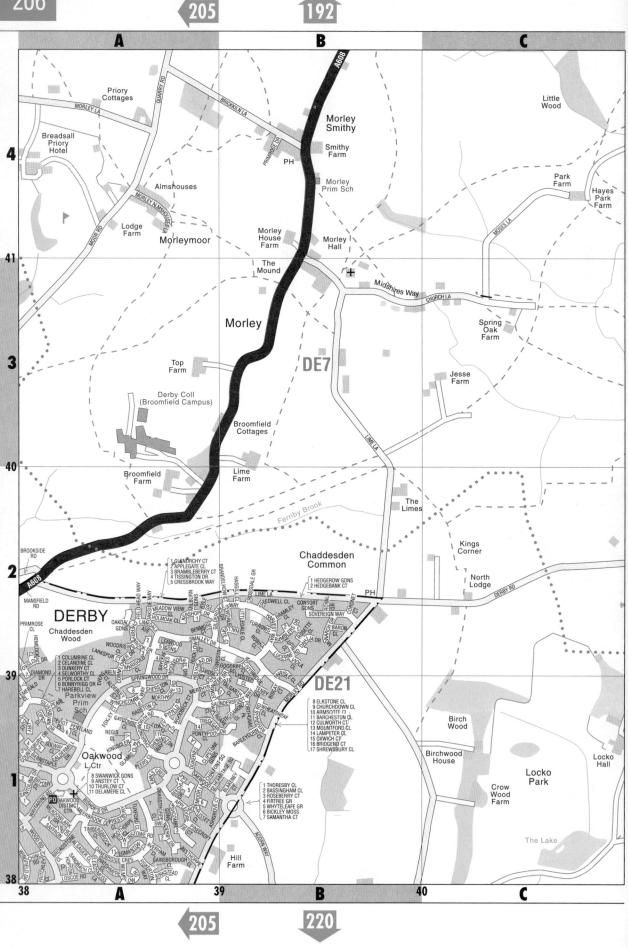

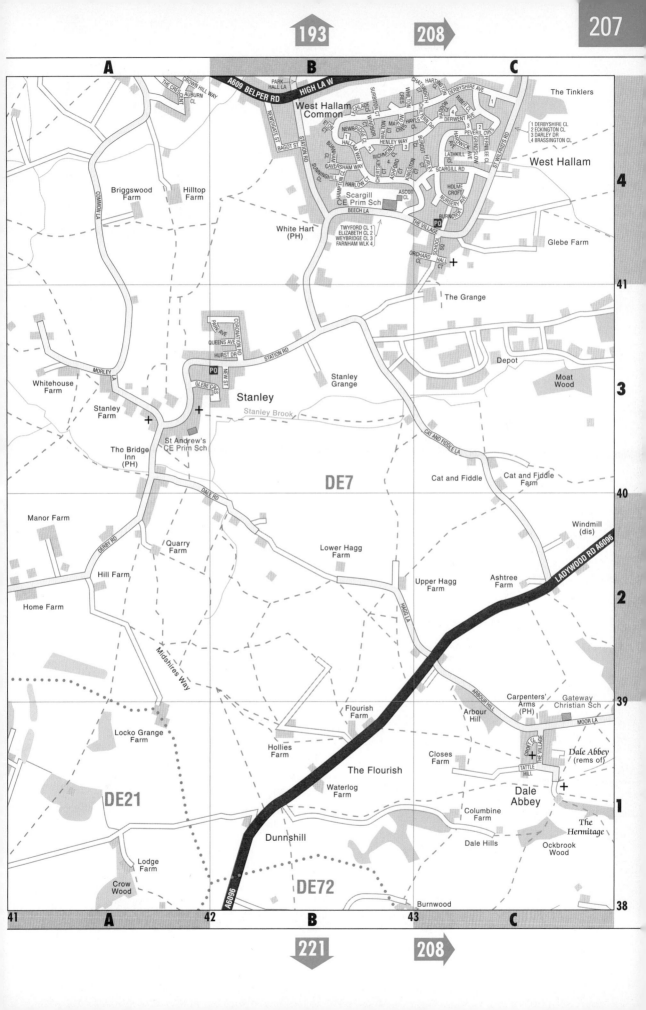

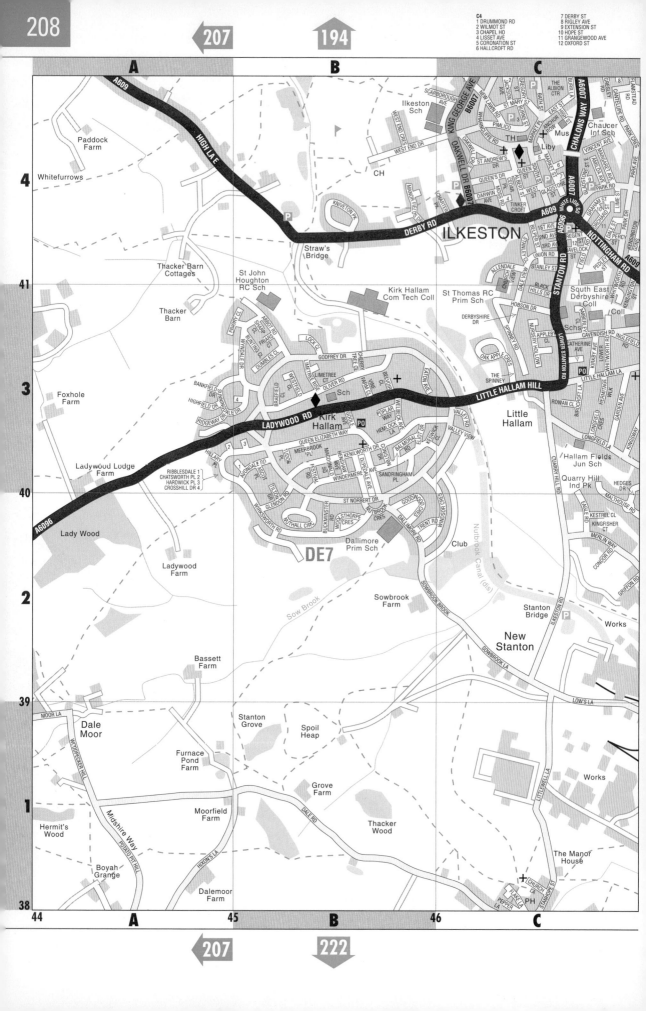

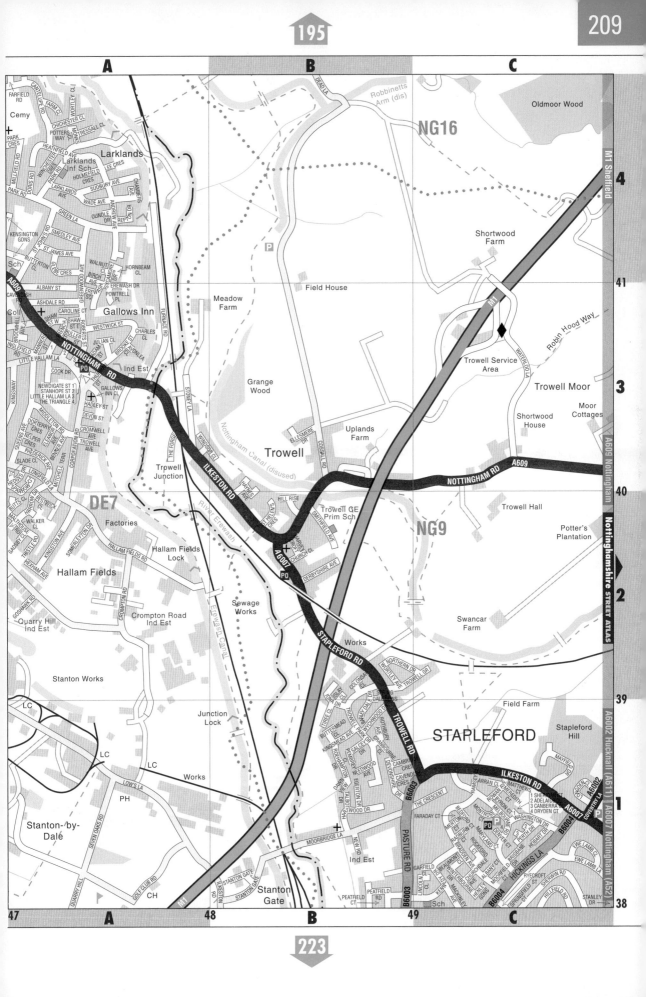

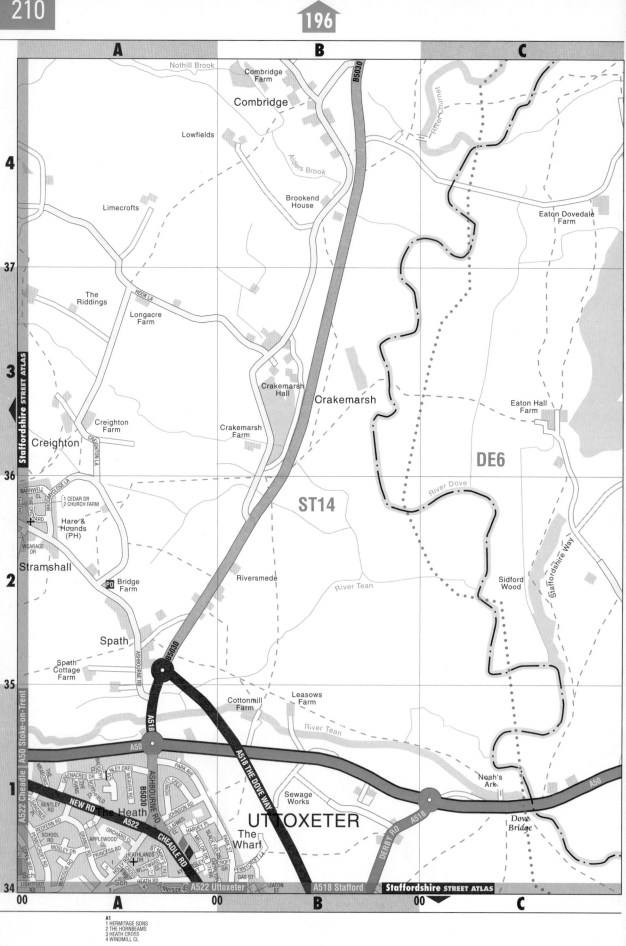

A1
1 HERMITAGE GDNS
2 THE HORNBEAMS
3 HEATH CROSS
4 WINDMILL CL

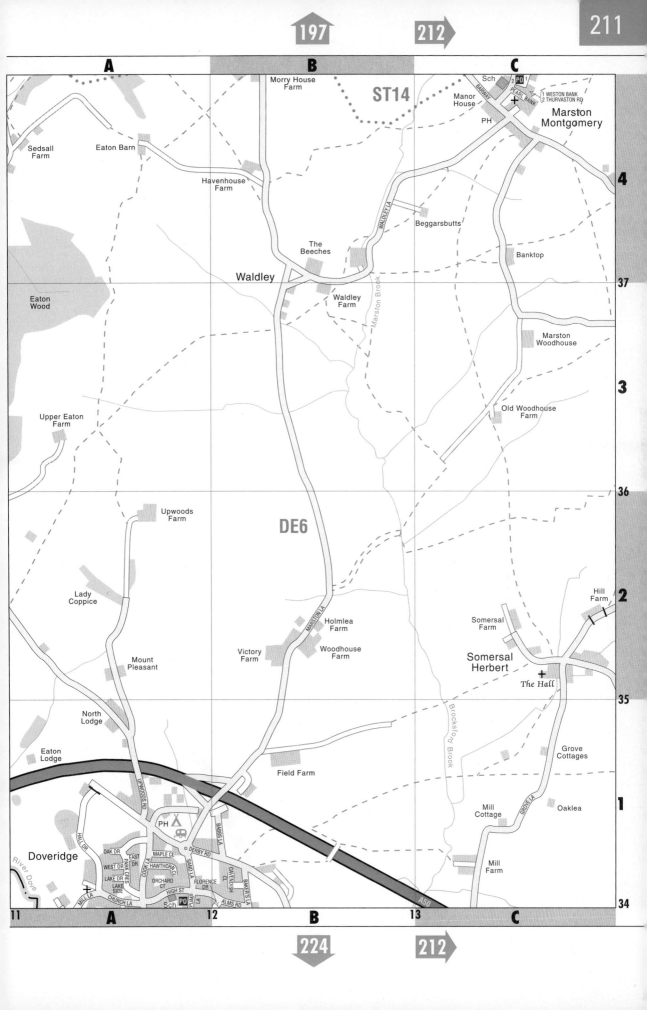

A
B
C

Morry House Farm

ST14

Sch
Manor House
BARWAY
PEARL BANK
2 PO 1
1 WESTON BANK
2 THURVASTON RD

Marston Montgomery

PH

Sedsall Farm
Eaton Barn

Havenhouse Farm

4

WALDLEY LA

Beggarsbutts

The Beeches

Banktop

Waldley

37

Waldley Farm

Marston Woodhouse

Eaton Wood

Marston Brook

Upper Eaton Farm

Old Woodhouse Farm

3

36

Upwoods Farm

DE6

MARSTON LA

Lady Coppice

Hill Farm

2

Holmlea Farm

Somersal Farm

Mount Pleasant

Victory Farm

Woodhouse Farm

Somersal Herbert

The Hall

35

North Lodge

Brocksford Brook

Grove Cottages

Eaton Lodge

UPWOODS RD

Field Farm

GROVE LA

Mill Cottage

Oaklea

1

PH

Mill Farm

BABBS LA

Doveridge

HALL DR
OAK DR
EAST DR
PARK CRES
WEST DR
COOK LA
MAPLE CL
HAWTHORN CL
SAND LA
DERBY RD
CAVENDISH CL
FLORENCE DR
BAKER'S LA

River Dove

MILL LA
LAKE DR
LAKE SIDE
ORCHARD CT
HIGH ST
PUMP LA
ALMS RD

Sch PO

A50

34

11
A
12
B
13
C

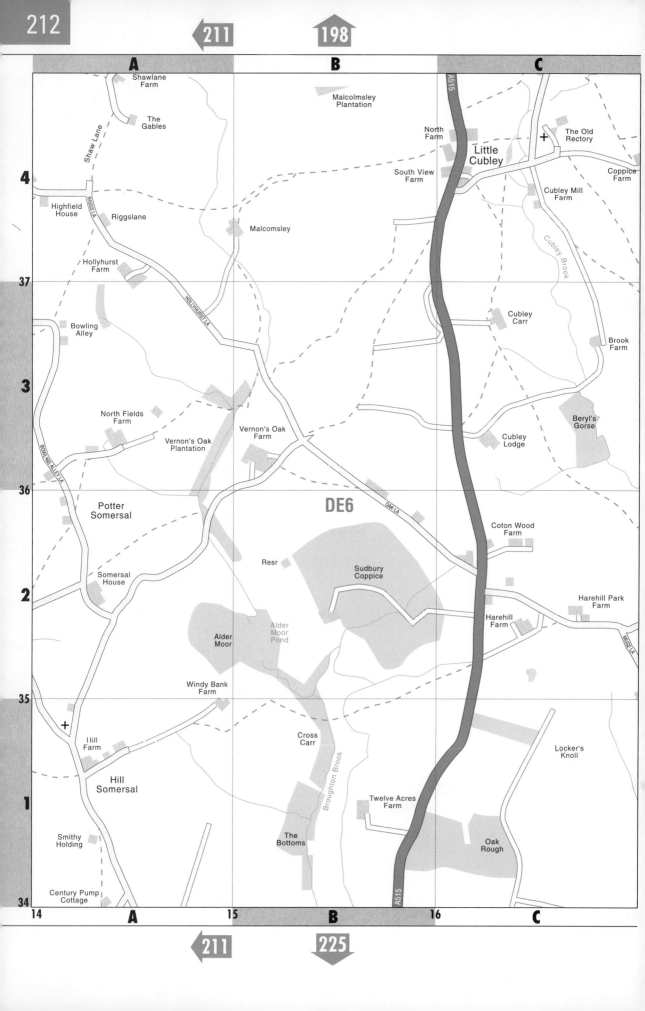

A B C

Shawlane Farm

The Gables

Shaw Lane

4

Highfield House

RIGGS LA

Riggslane

Malcomsley Plantation

North Farm

South View Farm

Little Cubley

The Old Rectory

A515

Cubley Mill Farm

Coppice Farm

Malcomsley

37

Hollyhurst Farm

HOLLYHURST LA

Cubley Brook

Cubley Carr

Brook Farm

Bowling Alley

3

North Fields Farm

Vernon's Oak Plantation

Vernon's Oak Farm

Beryl's Gorse

Cubley Lodge

BOWLING ALLEY LA

36

Potter Somersal

DE6

OAK LA

Coton Wood Farm

Resr

Sudbury Coppice

Somersal House

2

Alder Moor

Alder Moor Pond

Harehill Farm

Harehill Park Farm

RUSSE LA

Windy Bank Farm

35

Hill Farm

Cross Carr

Broughton Brook

Locker's Knoll

Hill Somersal

1

Twelve Acres Farm

Smithy Holding

The Bottoms

Oak Rough

A515

Century Pump Cottage

34

14 A 15 B 16 C

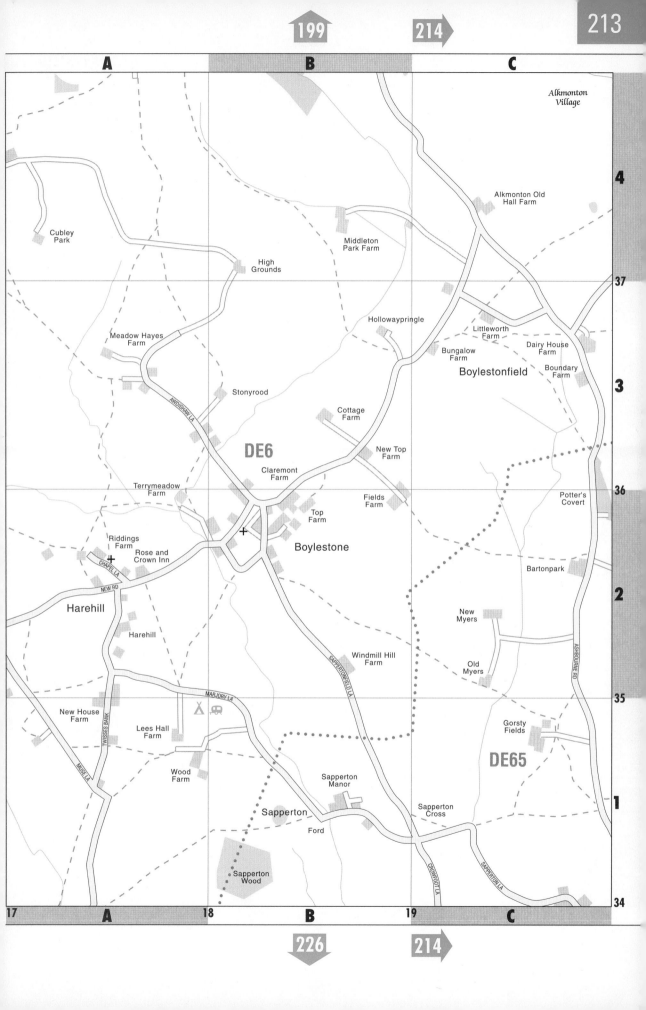

213
200

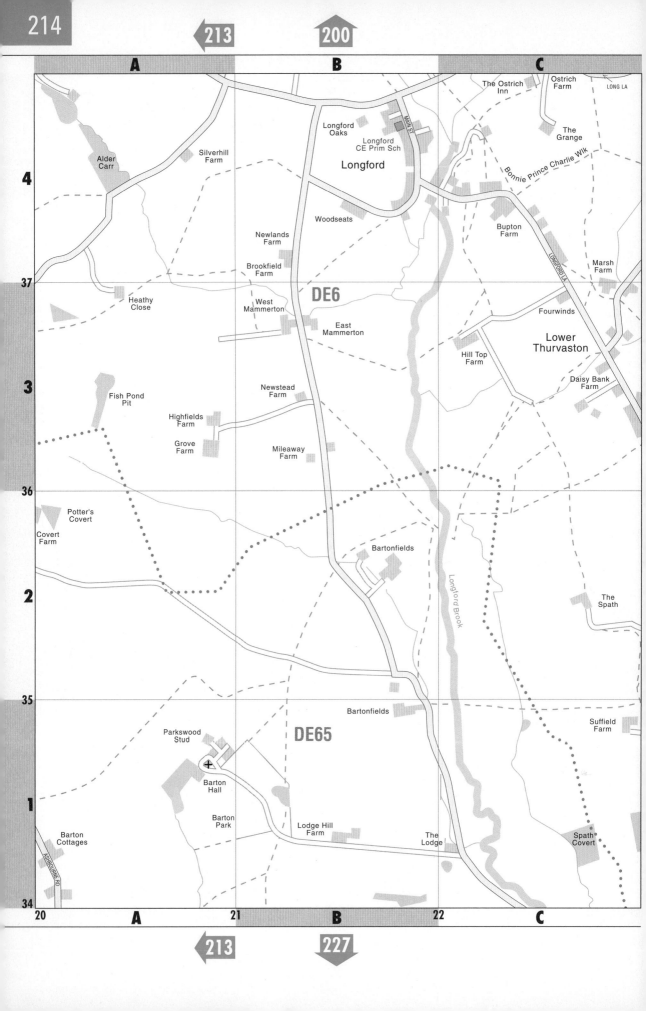

213
227

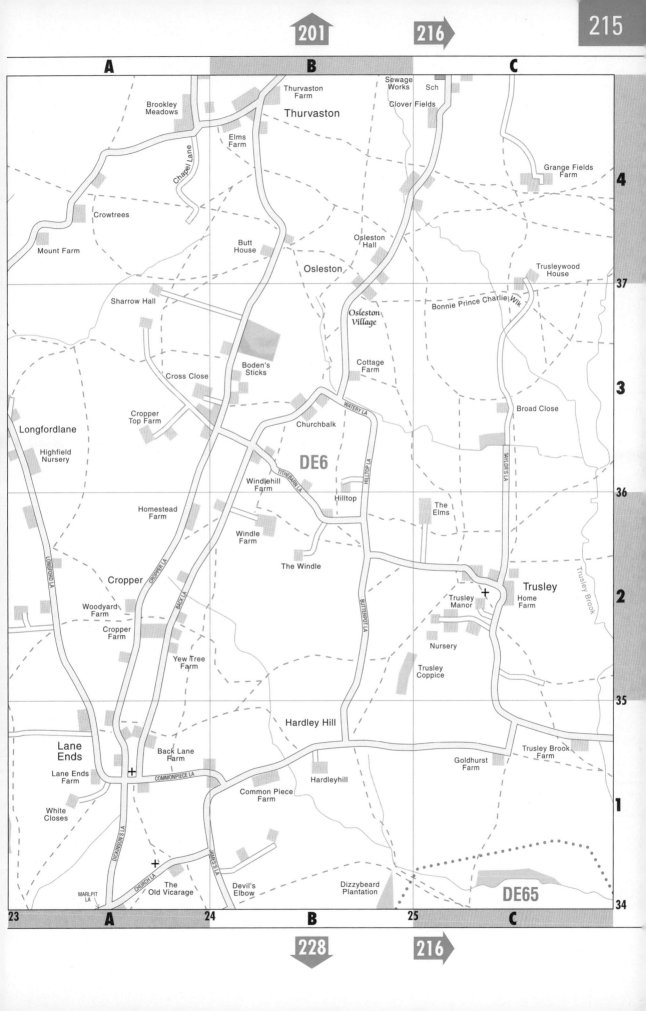

Thurvaston Farm

Thurvaston

Sewage Works

Sch

Clover Fields

Brookley Meadows

Elms Farm

Chapel Lane

Grange Fields Farm

4

Crowtrees

Butt House

Osleston Hall

Osleston

Mount Farm

Trusleywood House

37

Sharrow Hall

Osleston Village

Bonnie Prince Charlie Wlk

Cross Close

Boden's Sticks

Cottage Farm

Broad Close

3

Cropper Top Farm

Churchbalk

WATERY LA

DE6

Longfordlane

Highfield Nursery

Windlehill Farm

TITHEBARN LA

HILLTOP LA

TAYLOR'S LA

36

Homestead Farm

Windle Farm

Hilltop

The Elms

Woodyard Farm

CROPPER LA

LONGFORD LA

The Windle

Cropper

BACK LA

BUTTERPOT LA

Trusley Manor

Trusley

Home Farm

2

Cropper Farm

Nursery

Trusley Brook

Yew Tree Farm

Trusley Coppice

35

Lane Ends

Back Lane Farm

Hardley Hill

Goldhurst Farm

Trusley Brook Farm

Lane Ends Farm

COMMONPIECE LA

Hardleyhill

White Closes

Common Piece Farm

1

DICKINSON'S LA

JAMES'S LA

Devil's Elbow

Dizzybeard Plantation

DE65

MARLPIT LA

CHURCH LA

The Old Vicarage

34

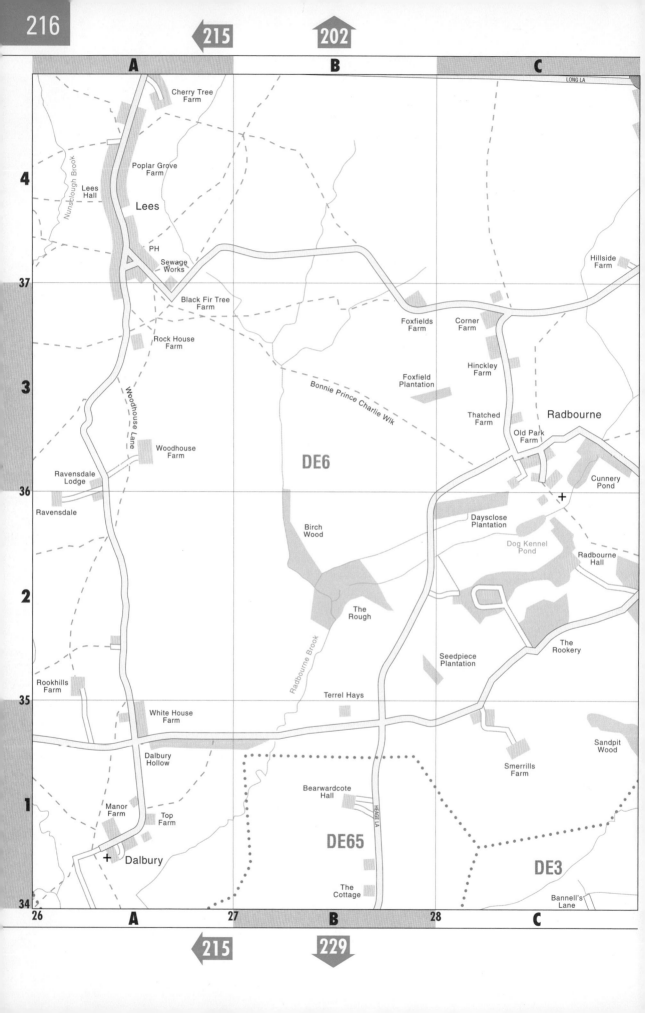

A   **B**   **C**

LONG LA

Cherry Tree Farm

Nunsblough Brook

Poplar Grove Farm

4

Lees Hall

Lees

Hillside Farm

PH

37

Sewage Works

Black Fir Tree Farm

Rock House Farm

Foxfields Farm

Corner Farm

Woodhouse Lane

Foxfield Plantation

Hinckley Farm

Bonnie Prince Charlie Wlk

3

Thatched Farm

Radbourne

DE6

Old Park Farm

Woodhouse Farm

Ravensdale Lodge

Cunnery Pond

36

Daysclose Plantation

Ravensdale

Birch Wood

Dog Kennel Pond

Radbourne Hall

2

Radbourne Brook

The Rough

The Rookery

Seedpiece Plantation

Rookhills Farm

Terrel Hays

35

White House Farm

Sandpit Wood

Smerrills Farm

Dalbury Hollow

1

Manor Farm

Top Farm

Bearwardcote Hall

HEAGE LA

DE65

DE3

Dalbury

The Cottage

Bannell's Lane

34

26   **A**   27   **B**   28   **C**

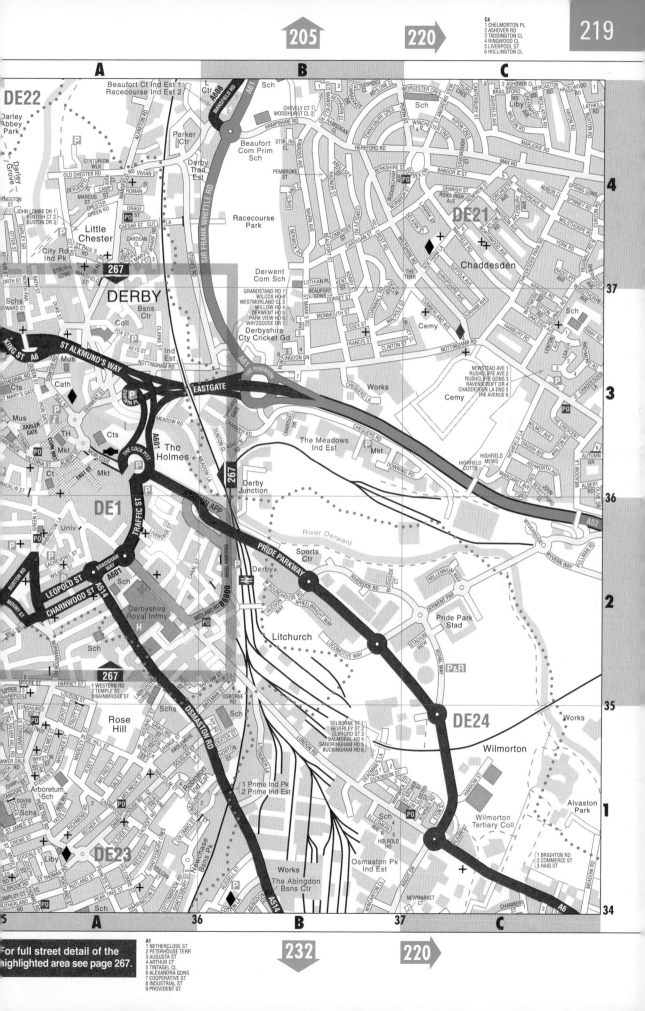

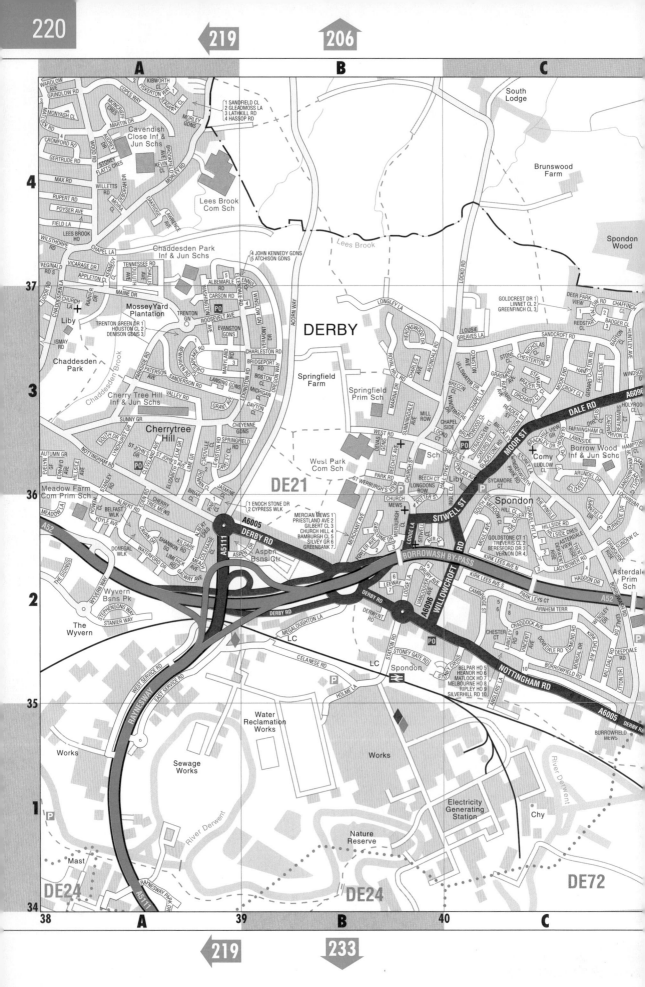

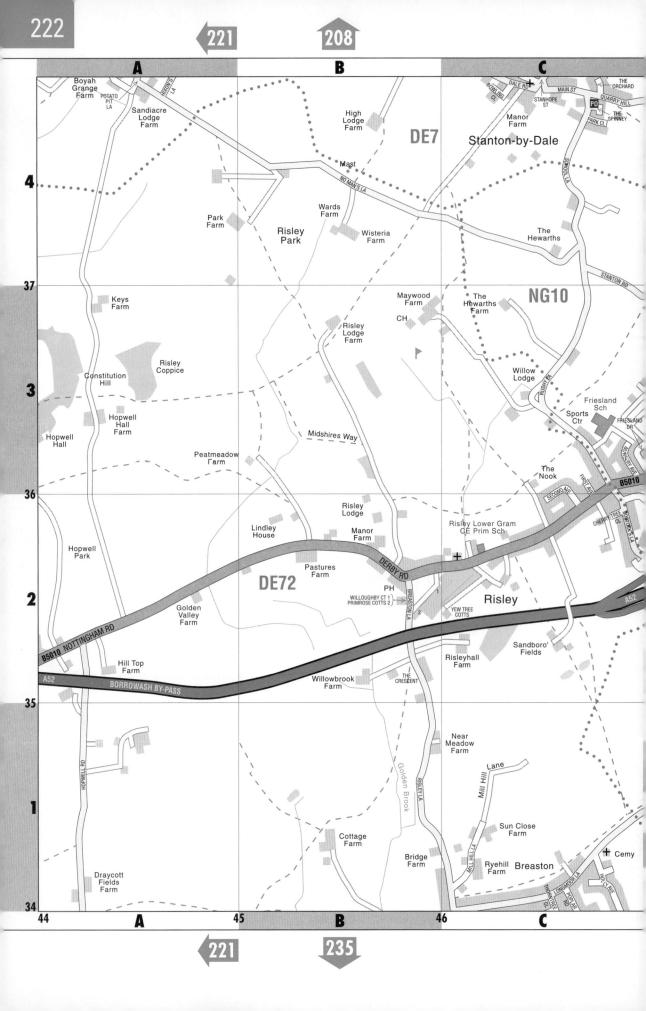

221 208

221 235

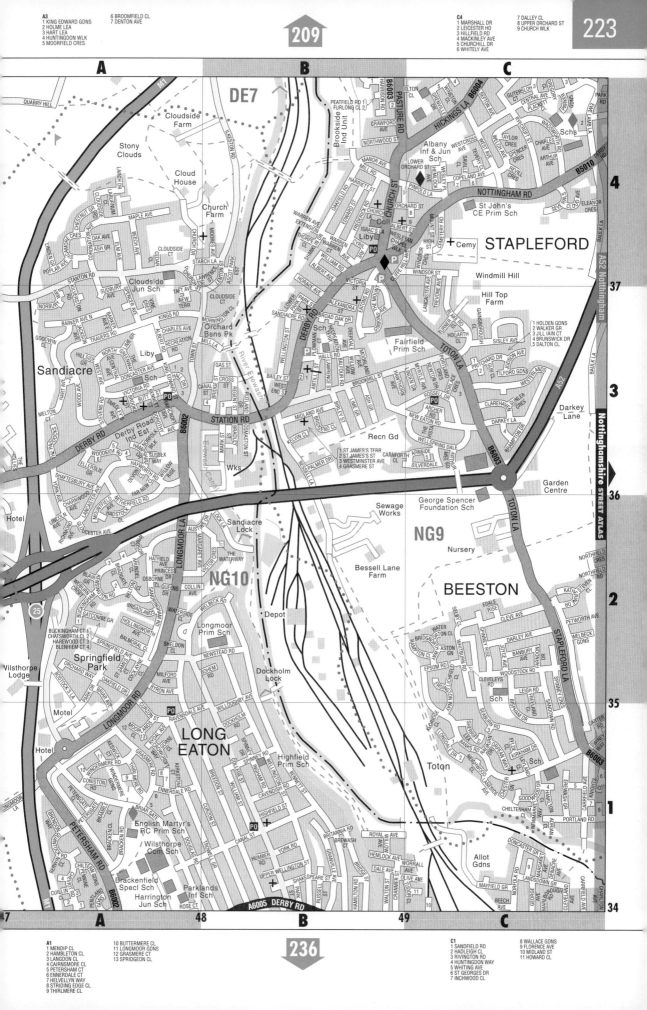

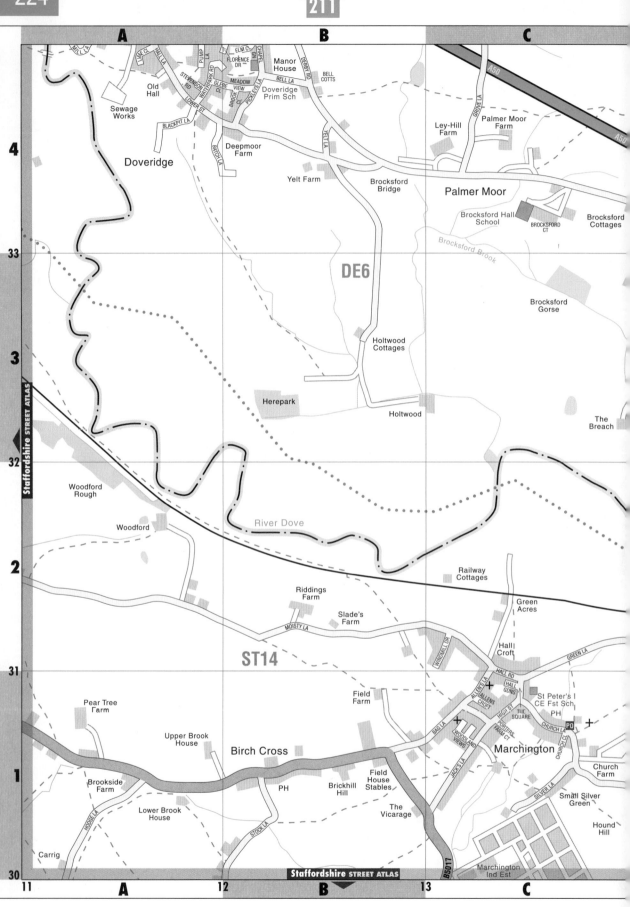

A   B   C

4

33

DE6

3

32

2

31

1

30

11   A   12   B   13   C

Doveridge

Old Hall

Sewage Works

MILL LA

LYKE CL

HALL LA

PUMP

STEVENSON RD

GLEBE CL

WATERPARK RD

LOWER ST

BLACKPIT LA

BATCH LA

ELM CL

FLORENCE DR

MEADOW

BROOK CL

CHAPEL

GN

PICKLEY LA

Manor House

Bell La

DERBY RD

BELL COTTS

Doveridge Prim Sch

Deepmoor Farm

Yelt Farm

FELT LA

Brocksford Bridge

Ley-Hill Farm

GROVE LA

A50

Palmer Moor Farm

Palmer Moor

Brocksford Hall School

BROCKSFORD CT

Brocksford Cottages

Brocksford Brook

Brocksford Gorse

Holtwood Cottages

The Breach

Herepark

Holtwood

Woodford Rough

Woodford

River Dove

Riddings Farm

Slade's Farm

MOISTY LA

ST14

Railway Cottages

Green Acres

Hall Croft

WINDMILL LA

GREEN LA

Pear Tree Farm

Field Farm

Upper Brook House

Birch Cross

Brookside Farm

Lower Brook House

HODGE LA

Carrig

PH

STOCK LA

Brickhill Hill

Field House Stables

The Vicarage

B5017

HALL RD

ALLENS LA

ALLENS CROFT

HALL GDNS

St Peter's CE Fst Sch

HIGH ST

PORTERS FARM CT

BAG LA

THE SQUARE

PH

WOODLAND VIEWS

JACK'S LA

Marchington

CHURCH LA

PO

Church Farm

SILVER LA

Small Silver Green

Hound Hill

Marchington Ind Est

Staffordshire STREET ATLAS

A

B

C

Cave
Cottage

Heath House
Farm

Somersal
Heath

Merefield
Gorse

Parkside

Sudbury Park

Brickyard
Farm

Oaks
Green

Sudbury Park
Farm

4

A50

Gorse
Covert

Flacketts Lane
Farm

Grove
Plantation

Halfway
House

33

The Grove

West
Broughton

HM
Prison

Sewage
Works

Portway
Head

Deercote

DE6

3

Home
Farm

Fiddlers
Farm

Oak
Cottage

Square
Pond

West Broughton
Farm

The
Decoy

P

✝
Sudbury
Hall

PH

Mus

32

Aston

MAIN RD A50

Sudbury

Sudbury
Prim Sch

Rectory
Farm

Aston
House
Farm

Dovebank

LEATHERSLEY LA

2

Weir
Plantation

River Dove

Dovefields
Crossing

Aston
Bridge

LC

31

GREEN LA

ST14

LC

Sudbury
Dairy

Hotel

Houndhill
Farm

Dove
Fields

Moat
Farm

1

Draycott
Mill

Densey
Lodge

30

A B C

Church Broughton

SAPPERTON LA
ASHBOURNE RD
CHURCH RD
AUDEN CL
BROUGHTON CL
BOGGY LA
TIPPER'S LA
CHAPEL LA
MAIN ST
OLD HALL LA
PH

Church Broughton CE Prim Sch

1 2
1 FEARN CL
2 MEADOW RISE

Badder Green Farm

Badder Green

Bent Brook

Bent House

Sutton Heath

Longford Brook

COMMON LA

DE6

4

Broughton House Farm

LITTLEFIELD RD

The Bent

SUTTON RD

Mount Pleasant

SCHOOLPIECE LA

COTE BOTTOM LA
WOODYARD LA

Littlemeadow La

Claypit Hill

Limbersitch Brook

33

Heathtop

Heath Top Farm

Dark La

BENT LA

Birchill's Farm

DE65

CH

Hatton Fields Farm

LIMBERSITCH LA

Limbersitch Farm

Hatton Fields

3

Dove Valley Pk

PARK AVE

Airfield (dis)

PACKENHAM BLVD

A511

Heath House

MIRY LA

Heath Cottage Farm

Pennywaste Wood

Hoon Drive Farm

32

UTTOXETER RD

Heath Farm

CHURCH BROUGHTON RD

Works

Sycamore Farm

Newlands Farm

Hockley Farm

Hatton House

SUTTON LA

Hoon Mount Farm

A50

2

Guinea Farm

BROOK LA

BREACH LA

MALTHOUSE LA

Hoon Hall Farm

31

UTTOXETER RD

SAWPIT LA

Yew Tree Farm

PH

DERBY RD

PH

NETHERCLOSE LA

SCROPTON RD

The Firs Farm

THE SHIELING
BRADSHAW MDW
COOPERS CROFT
FLAX CROFT
RUSSET CL
BRAMLEY CT

THE HAYS
BROOK CL
YEW TREE RD
GRANVILLE CL
LEY CROFT
WOODMANS CROFT
HOLME CL
SCALE TREE RD
HEATH WAY
FIELD AVE

STATION RD

Birch Gr
LIME CL
RYE FLATS LA
ROGERS CT
PETERS CT
EATON CL
HANBURY AVE
HASSALL MEWS
CHURCH CROFT

The Fields

Cherry Cottage

Heath Fields Prim Sch

A511

1

30

A B C

A B C

DE6

Highfield

Highwall
Lodge

HEAGE LA

Bannell's Farm

DE3

Bannell's Lane Farm

BANNELL'S LA

Bearwardcote
Farm

A516

4

Highfields Farm

Hepnalls

Marsh Farm

DEE LA

33

Oakdene

Ashe
Hall

The Marsh

ASH LA

SUTTON LA

Marsh
Cottage
Farm

Burnaston LA

Greenacres

The
Lawns

ETWALL LA

TINDERBOX LA

MANOR FARM MEWS

MAIN ST

WALNUT CL

3

Burnaston

Etwall Brook

ALMSHOUSES

CHURCH HILL

John Port
Sch

PO

BLENHEIM
MEWS

WILLINGTON RD

MAIN ST

PORTLAND

KILN CROFT

PARK

AVON

LAWN AVE

SLADE CL

SANDYPITS LA

Sandypits Farm

RISBOROW CL

GREEN LA

32

Derby Rd

HILTON RD

Liby

OLD STATION CL

MEADOW
WAY

MANSFIELDS

ORBIT

ETTA'S WAY

Etwall
Prim
Sch

JOHN PORT

PINFOLD CL

OAKLANDS RD

LODGE

WILLINGTON RD

DE65

ASHE BANCROFT

MILL

CHESTNUT GR

ASH VIEW
CL

BLAKELOW
DR

WINDMILL CL

LABURNUM
WAY

COURTLAND DR

ELMS GR

BEECH
DR

GERMAIN GR

BELFIELD CL

SYCAMORE
CL

Etwall

Lodge Farm

New Close Farm

New Gorse
Fox Covert

2

Friary Farm

BELFIELD CT 1
BELFIELD TERR 2

SPRINGFIELD RD

MELVILLE
CL

WILLINGTON RD

Marlpit
Plantation

Sewage
Works

COMMON END

PK

GROVE

EGGINTON RD

JACKSONS LA

Broomhill
Cottages

31

DE1

TYNEFIELD
MEWS

BLAKELEY LA

TYNEFIELD CT

Etwall Common

Works

1

Blakeley Lodge

OLDFIELD LA

Egginton
Common

A50

30

26 A 27 B 28 C

A **B** **C**

Bunkers Wood

Hotel

Littleover
Com Sch

KIPLING
DR
Sch
BLENCATHRA
DR
BRIERFIELD WAY
GABLE
CT

A516

WELNEY CL
THORNDON
INGHAM DR
HEDINGHAM WAY
THE HOLLOW

ROUGHTON CL 1
ARDLEIGH CL 2
WRETHAM CL 3

WOODCOCK
SQ

WILSON CL

The Grange

MALLARD WLK

PASTURES HILL
PASTURES AVE

1 MALCOLM GR
2 GREGORY WLK
3 RODNEY WLK

4

Field House

GRASSY
CT

HOSPITAL LA
EDMUND'S
SQ

LINNET CL

FINCH CR

MERLIN WAY

ALLAN
AVE
RONALD
CL
MAYPO
MATTHEW CL
DENNIS CL

WOODHALL
CT
ANDREW CL
PRITCHETT
DR
LESLIE CL
WELLS CT

RIVENHALL
CL
CALLOW
CLOSE WAY

RESCORL
CL
WITHERS
WITHERN
RETWIN
NEBULE
PALATINE
ROXMORE
Sch

PLOVER
WAY
FISHER
CL
WREN WAY
LARK HILL
KESTREL
CL
SANDERLING
HEATH
DUESBURY
CL
MERLIN WAY

Sch

HAVEN BAULK LA
HAVEN BAULK AVE

1 GAYTON THORPE CL
2 SPOONLEY WOOD CL
3 COX GREEN CT
4 LAKESIDE DR

DE3

WATERGO
LA

Staker Flats

LATIMER CL

CHERITON
GDNS
JENSON
GDNS
OXENPRESS
PENDLESIDE WAY
CMGLESHAW DR
MICKLEROFT
GDNS
RYKNELD
RYKNELD
CL
CRAMHILL CL

ATWORTH GR
CHESTERFORD
H

33

Bushy
Cottage

STAKER LA

E Midlands
Nuffield

DE23

PH

RYKNELD WAY

RYKNELD WAY

HOLLY BROOK WAY

WOODALE CL
KILNSEY CT

KIRKSTEAD
CL
GERBER
WHITEGREEN DR
WHITEGREEN DR

COMFREY CL 1
CRANBERRY GR 2
MEADOW BROOK CL 3

3

Millway House

Micklemeadow

BURGHLEY
WAY

Hotel

Highfield's Farm

Burnaston

MAIN ST
GREEN LA

Hill Farm

New Buildings
Farm

32

Nursery

Thurston

Blakemere
Farm

FINDERN LA

BAKEACRE LA

2

Depot

Park
House

Fields Farm

Landown Farm

Nursery

DE65

DOLES LA

31

BARN CL
WALL
FIELDS CL
FIELDS LA

CARDALES CL

MEADOW CL

Findern

DE1

BURTON RD

Mill Farm

EAST
LAWN
WEST
LAWN
CROMWELL
AVE
LAWNS
CL
WILLOW FARM
CT

Green Way

HAZEL CL
SYCAMORE DR
LWR

Doles Brook

Hell Brook

1

Works

THRUSHTON
CL
HILLSIDE
CL
CLOVERSLADE
THE HAYES
WREN PARK
CL
MILL CL
LAWN
AULTS CL
CASTLE
HILL
PORTER'S LA
MAIN ST
THE GREEN
PH
PO
BROOK CL
LOWER
THE GREEN
GREEN

COMMON PIECE LA

A50

Rumenco Farm

ALDERSLEY CL
LONGLANDS LA
GORSEY LEYS
WILLOWSLAND CL
HEATH LA

Sewage
Works

A38

A50

DE73

30

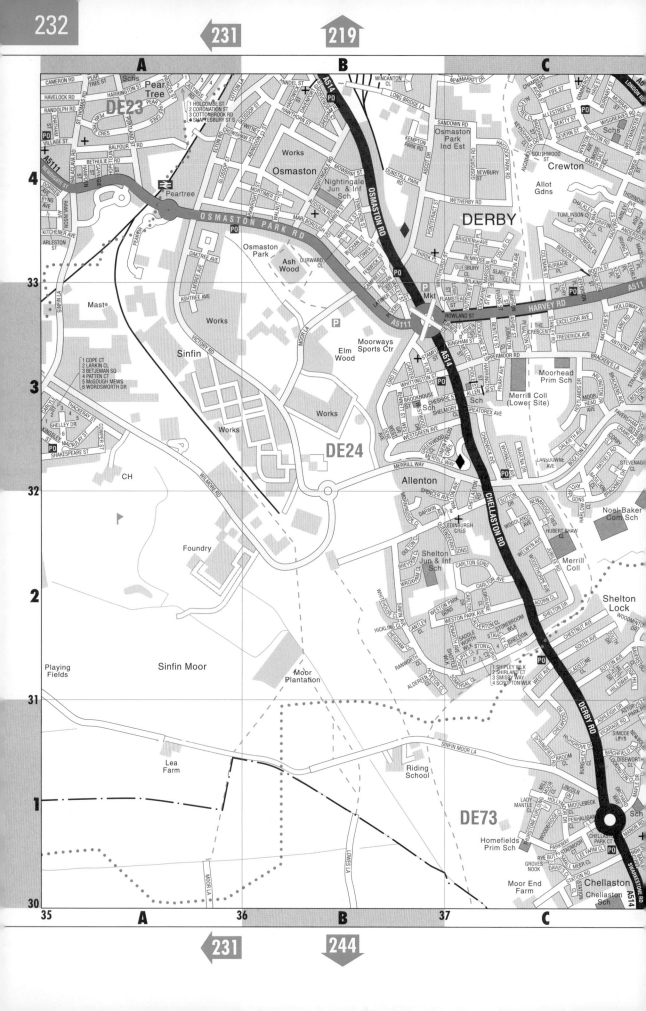

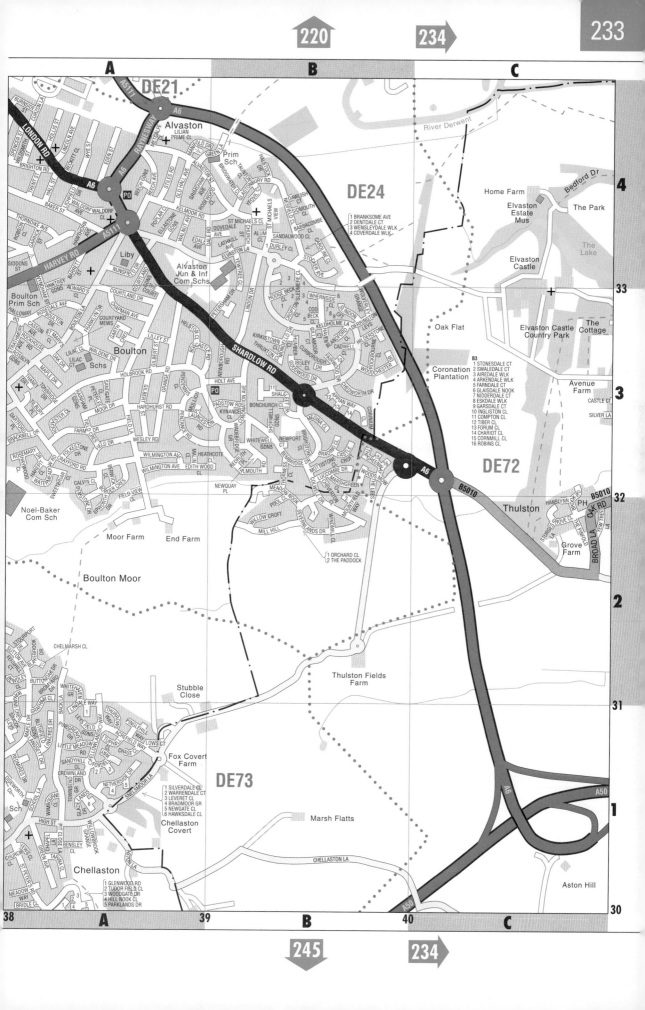

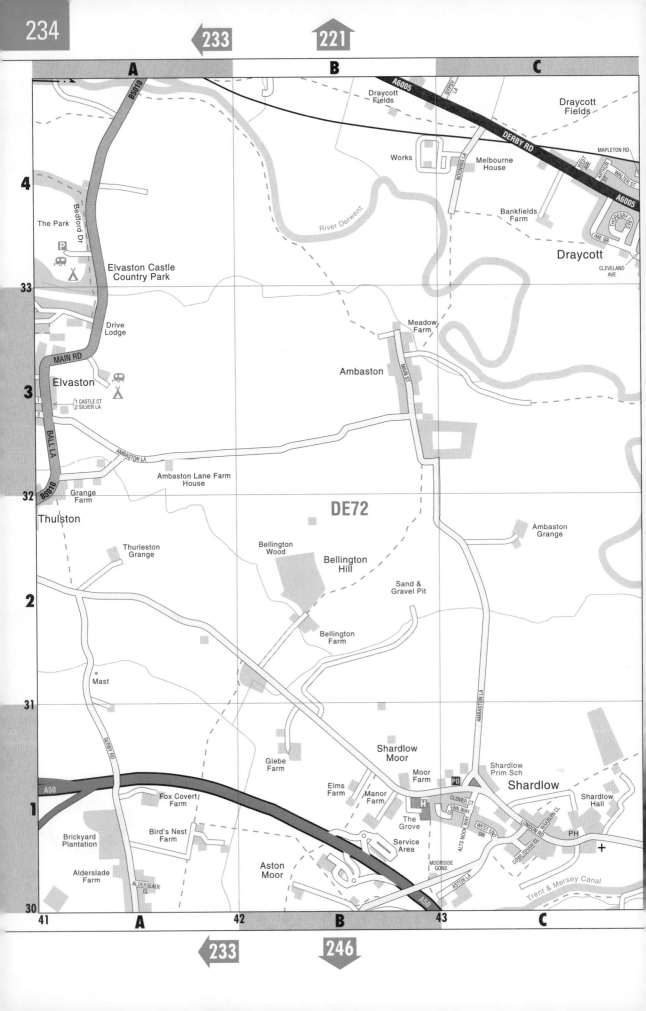

233
221

A B C

B5010

Draycott
Fields

Draycott
Fields

DERBY RD

A6005

GYPSY LA

Works

NOONING LA

Melbourne
House

MAPLETON RD

WEST AVE

ARTHUR ST

WALTER ST

A6005

THORESBY CRES

LIME GR

4

Bedford Dr

The Park

River Derwent

Bankfields
Farm

Draycott

P

Elvaston Castle
Country Park

Cleveland
AVE

33

Drive
Lodge

Meadow
Farm

MAIN ST

MAIN RD

Ambaston

3

Elvaston

1 CASTLE CT
2 SILVER LA

1
2

BALL LA

AMBASTON LA

B5010

Ambaston Lane Farm
House

DE72

Ambaston
Grange

32

Grange
Farm

Thulston

Thurleston
Grange

Bellington
Wood

Bellington
Hill

Sand &
Gravel Pit

2

Mast

Bellington
Farm

AMBASTON LA

31

DERBY RD

Shardlow
Moor

Glebe
Farm

Moor
Farm

Shardlow
Prim Sch

Shardlow

A50

Fox Covert
Farm

Elms
Farm

Manor
Farm

PO

Shardlow
Hall

H

CLOVER CT

WEST END
DR

LONDON RD

WAKELIN CL

PH

1

Brickyard
Plantation

Bird's Nest
Farm

The
Grove

ALTS NOOK WAY

FENN WAY

COWLISHAW CL

+

Alderslade
Farm

ALDERSLADE CL

Aston
Moor

Service
Area

MOORSIDE
GDNS

ASTON LA

Trent & Mersey Canal

A50

30

41 A 42 B 43 C

233
246

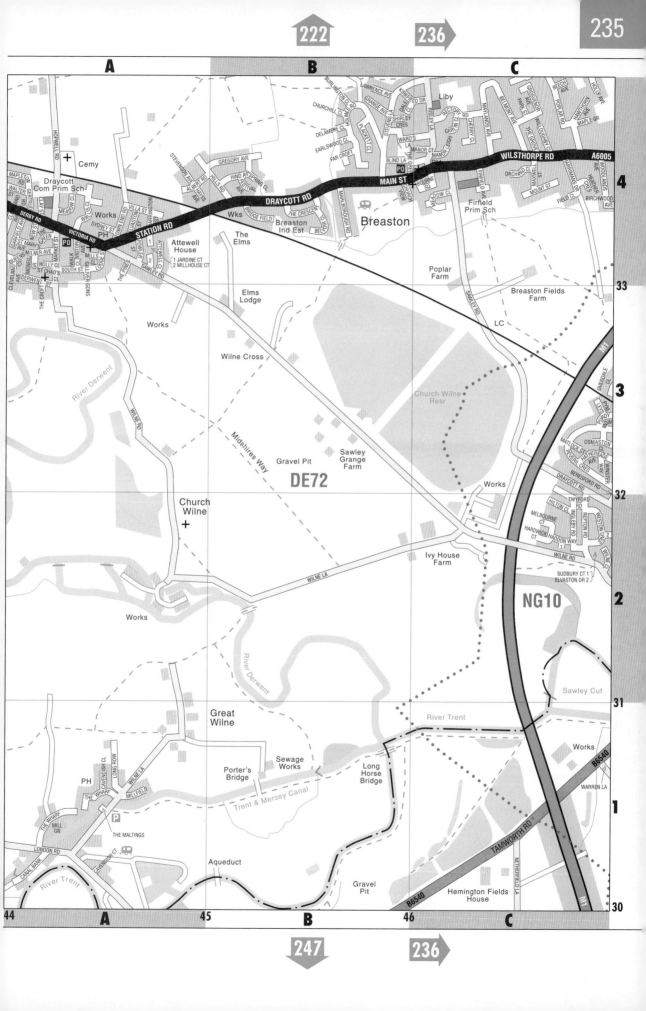

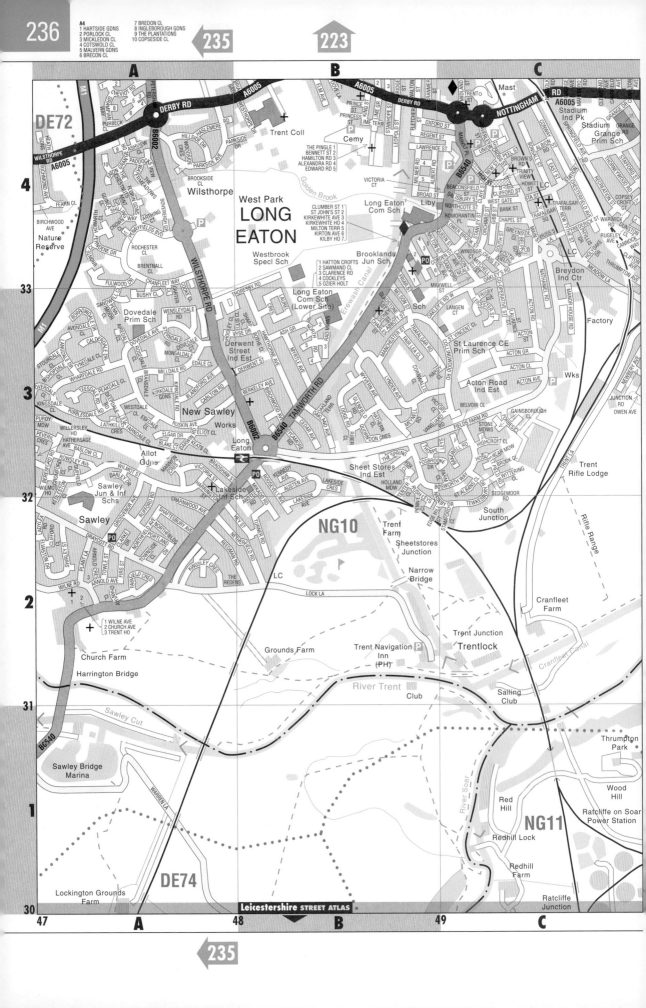

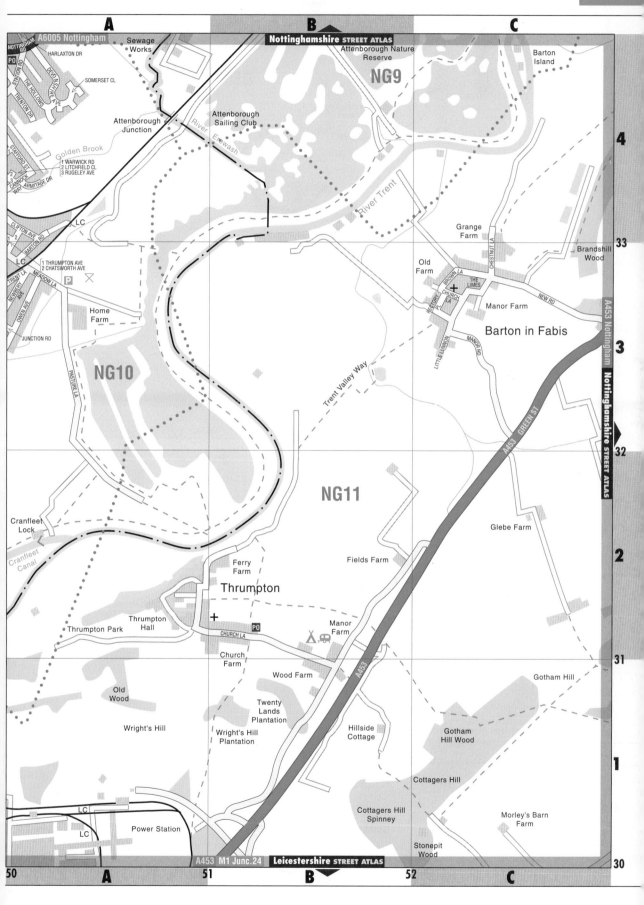

A6005 Nottingham

NOTTINGHAM RD

PO

HARLAXTON DR

STATION RD

THE ROLLONS

DEVONSHIRE AVE

TRENTON DR

SOMERSET CL

Sewage Works

Attenborough Nature Reserve

Barton Island

NG9

4

Attenborough Junction

River Erewash

Attenborough Sailing Club

River Trent

33

Grange Farm

Brandshill Wood

STAFFORD ST

Golden Brook

1 WARWICK RD
2 LITCHFIELD CL
3 RUGELEY AVE

CANNOCK WAY

ARMITAGE DR

Old Farm

CHESTNUT LA

CLIFTON AVE

BARTON RD

LC

Home Farm

TRENT LA

MEADOW LA

NEWBERY AVE

OWEN AVE

1 THRUMPTON AVE
2 CHATSWORTH AVE

P

RECTORY PL

BROWN LA

CHURCH LA

THE LIMES

NEW RD

Manor Farm

Barton in Fabis

A453 Nottingham

3

JUNCTION RD

LITTLE LUNNON

MANOR RD

Nottinghamshire STREET ATLAS

NG10

PASTURE LA

Trent Valley Way

A453 GREEN ST

32

NG11

Glebe Farm

Cranfleet Lock

Cranfleet Canal

Ferry Farm

Fields Farm

2

Thrumpton

Thrumpton Hall

Thrumpton Park

CHURCH LA

PO

Manor Farm

31

Church Farm

Wood Farm

Gotham Hill

A453

Old Wood

Twenty Lands Plantation

Hillside Cottage

Gotham Hill Wood

Wright's Hill

Wright's Hill Plantation

1

Cottagers Hill

Cottagers Hill Spinney

Morley's Barn Farm

LC

LC

Power Station

Stonepit Wood

30

50

A

51

B

52

C

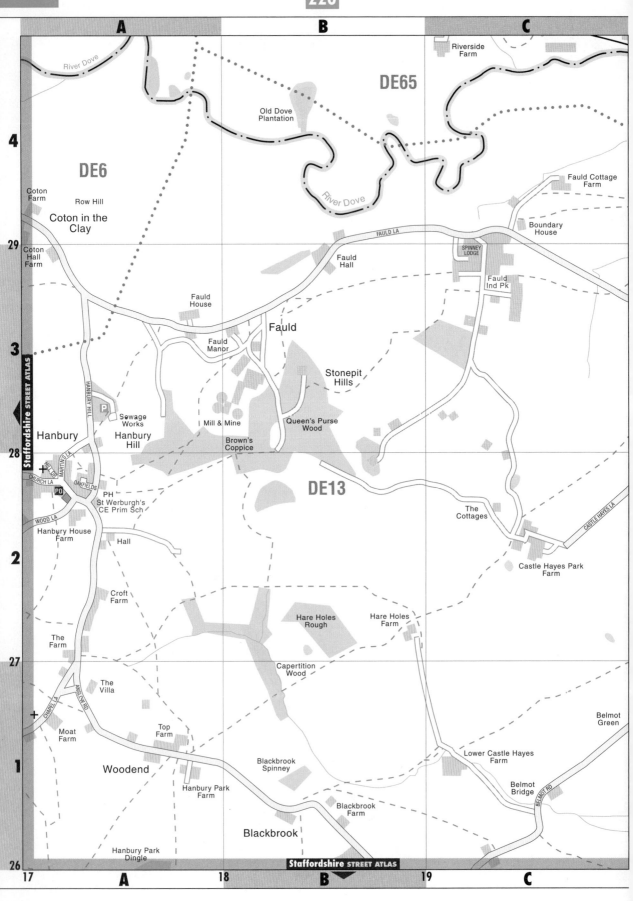

Staffordshire STREET ATLAS

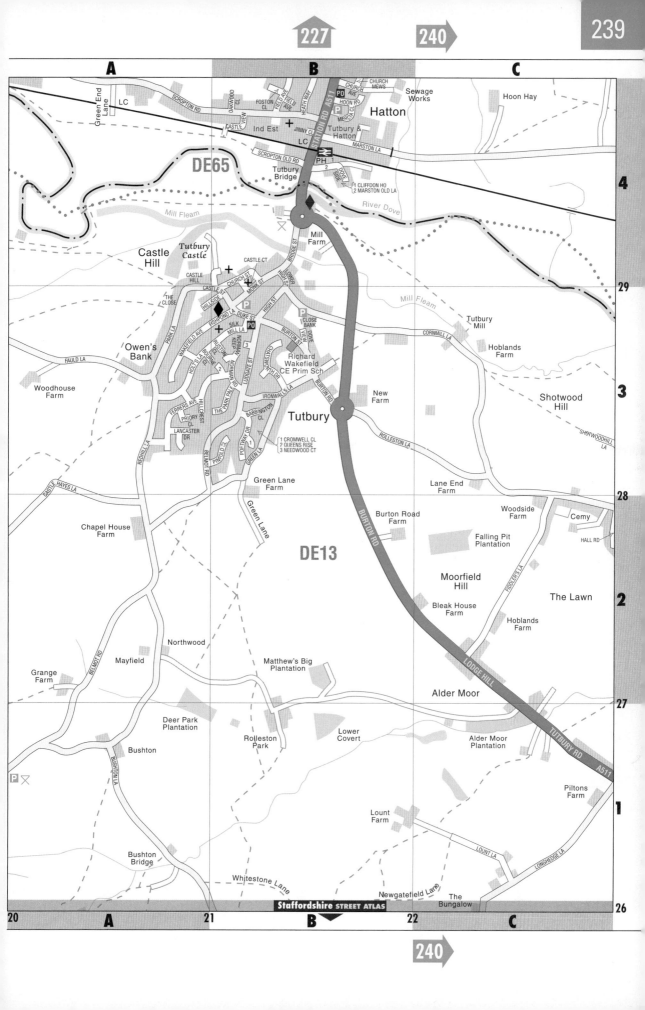

A   B   C

Green End Lane
LC
SCROPTON RD
OAKWOOD CL
FOSTON CL
FIELD AVE
HEATH WAY
FOSTON CL
CASTLE VIEW
Ind Est
JINNY CL
MERCIA CL
HOON RD
STATION RD A511
PO
P
CHURCH AVE
CHURCH MEWS
Sewage Works
Hoon Hay

Hatton

Tutbury & Hatton
LC
MARSTON LA
SCROPTON OLD RD
PH
1
2
DOVE SIDE
1 CLIFFDON HO
2 MARSTON OLD LA

DE65

Tutbury Bridge

River Dove

4

Mill Fleam

Mill Farm

Castle Hill

Tutbury Castle

CASTLE CT
CASTLE HILL
THE CLOSE
CASTLE ST
CHURCH ST
MONK ST
HIGH ST
LOWER HIGH ST
BRIDGE ST

HILLSIDE
P
FISHPOND LA
DUKE ST
HIGH ST
SILK MILL LA
DOVE VIEW
CLOSE BANK
PO
P

Mill Fleam

Tutbury Mill

29

Owen's Bank

FAULD LA

PARK LA
WAKEFIELD AVE
HOLTS LA
BOURNE CT
MONK ST
LUDGATE ST
OAKSWORD
CRANSWICK
KEEP NEWTON
BURTON ST
ARTHUR
IRONWALLS LA
BURTON RD

Richard Wakefield CE Prim Sch

CORNMILL LA

Hoblands Farm

Woodhouse Farm

FERRERS AVE
HILLCREST
PRIORY CL
LANCASTER DR
REDHILL
THE FARR PALE
PINFOLD CL
BELMOT RD
PATHWAY DR
GREEN LA
BABBINGTON CL

Tutbury

1 CROMWELL CL
2 QUEENS RISE
3 NEEDWOOD CT

New Farm

Shotwood Hill

SHOTWOODHILL LA

3

Green Lane Farm

ROLLESTON LA

Lane End Farm

28

CASTLE HAYES LA

GREEN LANE

DE13

Burton Road Farm

Woodside Farm

Cemy

HALL RD

Chapel House Farm

Falling Pit Plantation

BURTON RD

Moorfield Hill

RIDDLER'S LA

The Lawn

2

Northwood

Matthew's Big Plantation

Bleak House Farm

Hoblands Farm

Mayfield

BELMOT RD

Grange Farm

LODGE HILL

Alder Moor

27

P

Deer Park Plantation

Rolleston Park

Lower Covert

Alder Moor Plantation

TUTBURY RD
A511

Bushton

BUSHTON LA

Piltons Farm

1

Lount Farm

Bushton Bridge

Whitestone Lane

Newgatefield Lane

LOUNT LA

LONGHEDGE LA

The Bungalow

26

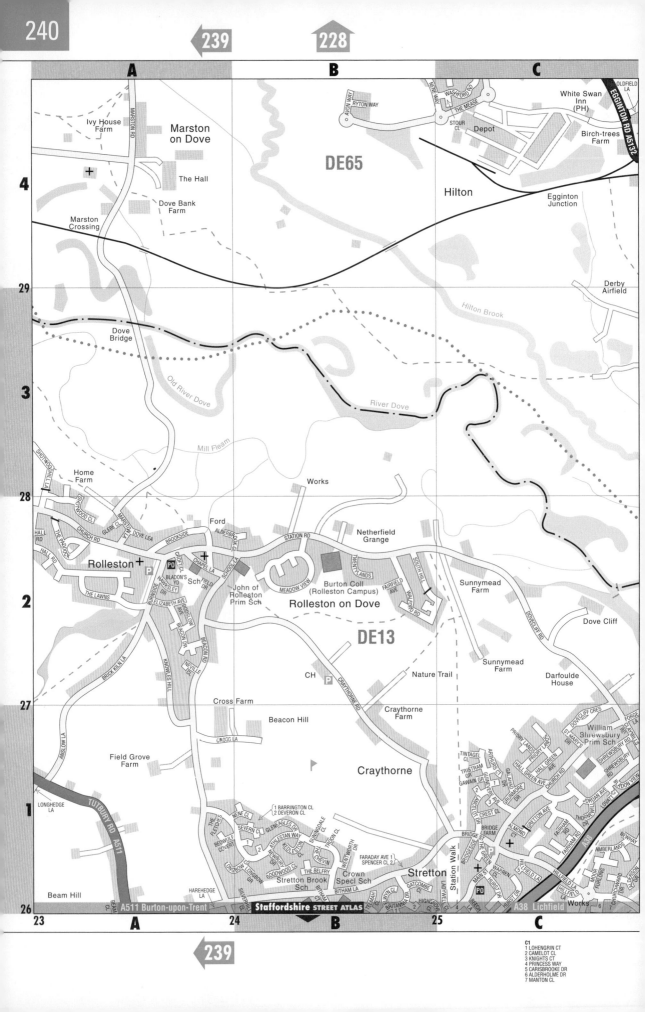

C1
1 LOHENGRIN CT
2 CAMELOT CL
3 KNIGHTS CT
4 PRINCESS WAY
5 CARISBROOKE DR
6 ALDERHOLME DR
7 MANTON CL

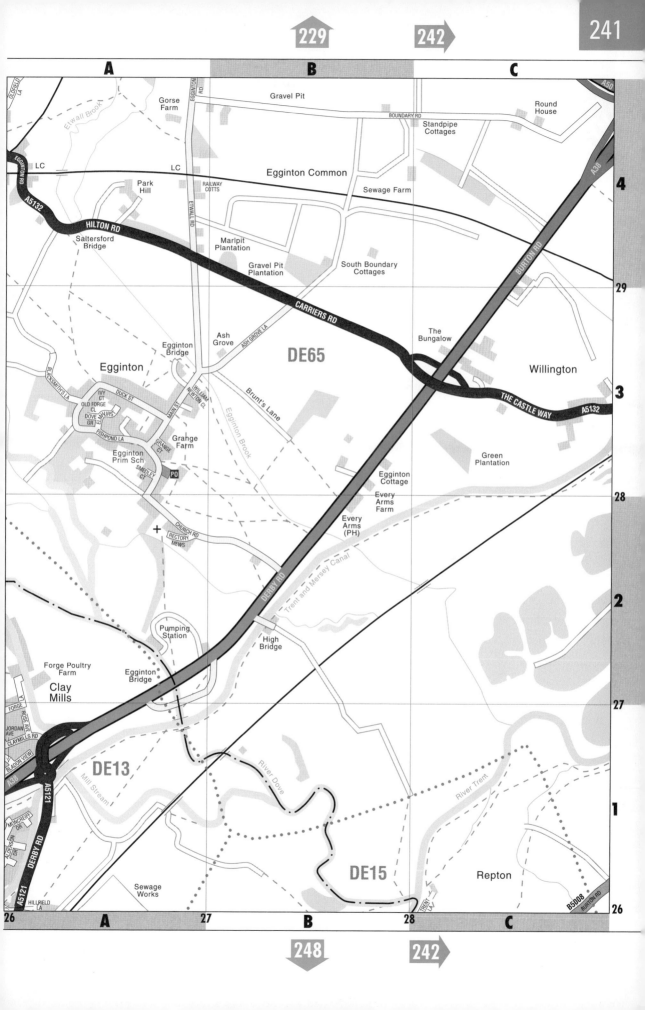

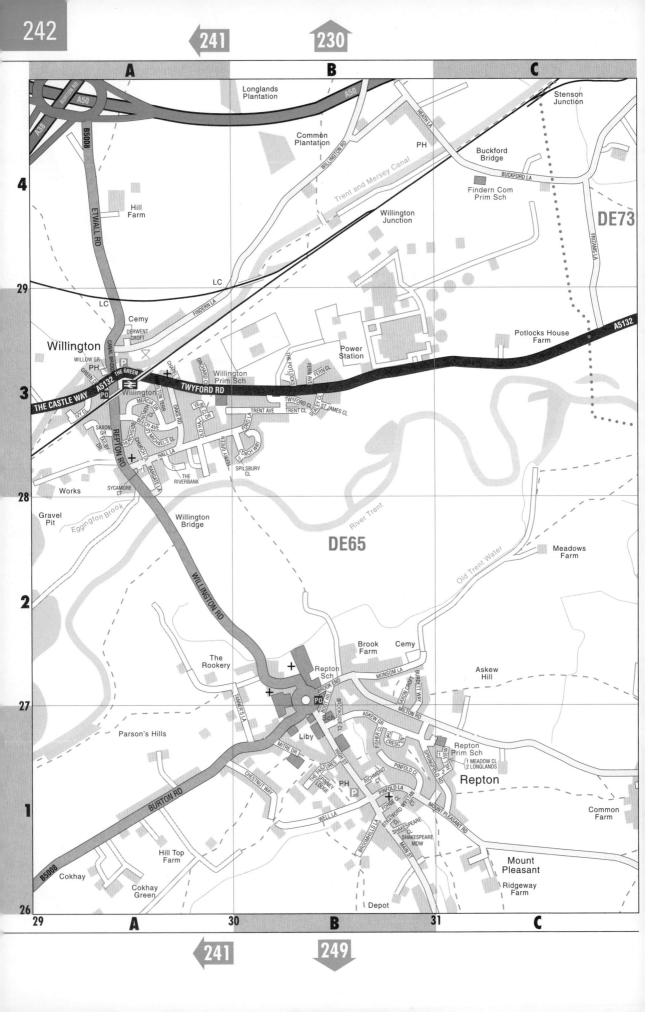

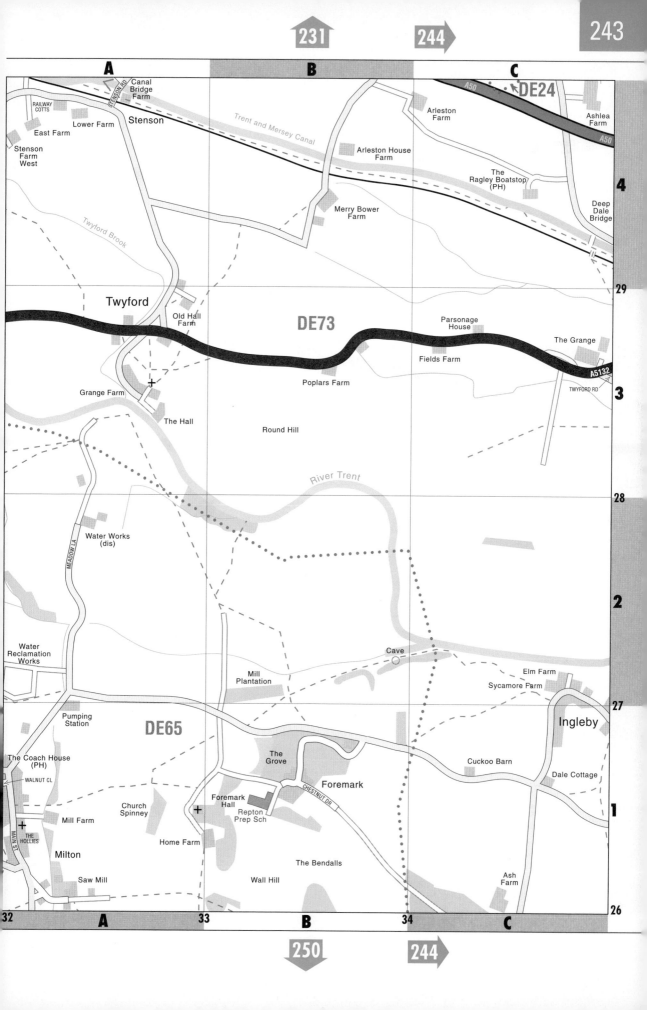

243
232

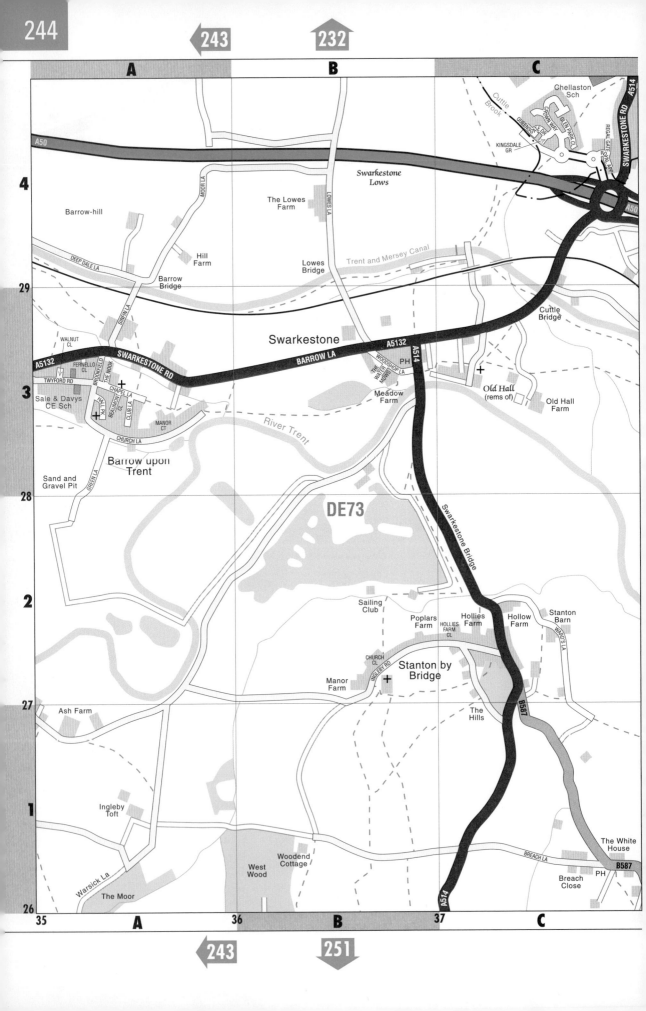

243
251

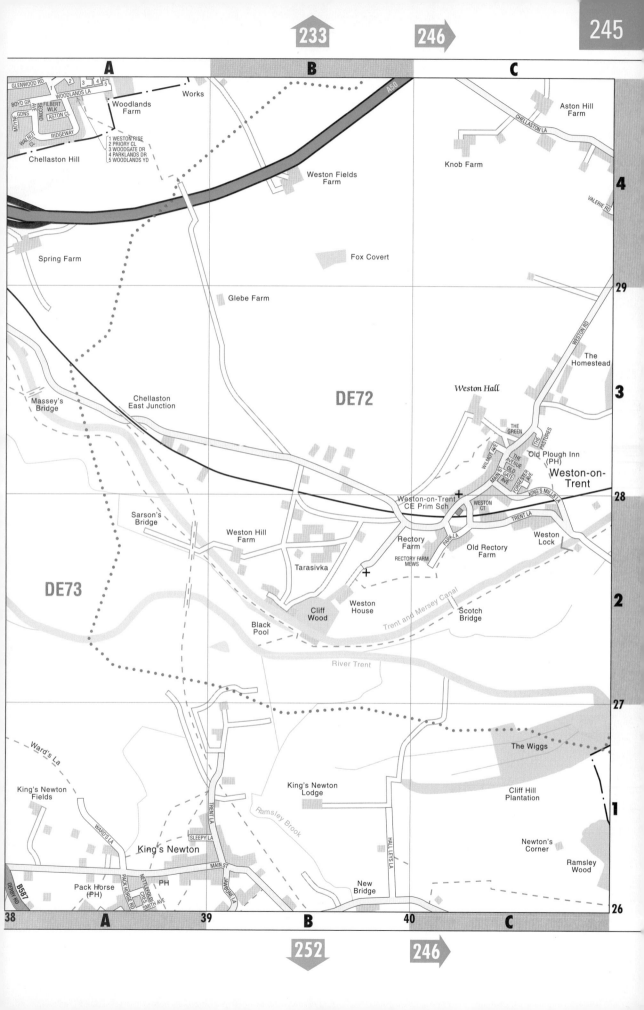

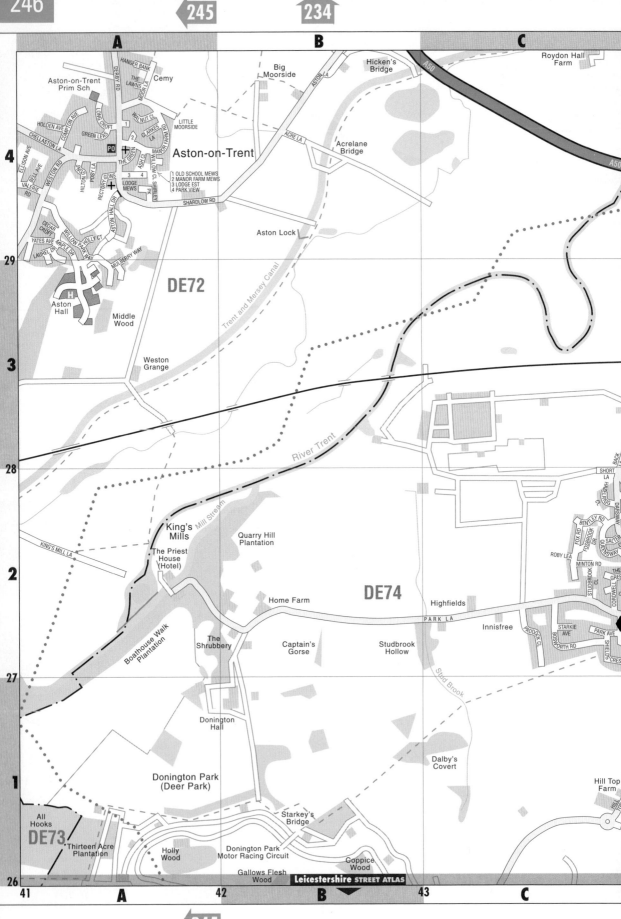

A   B   C

HANGER BANK
THE LAWNS
Cemy
DERBY RD
MOOR LA
Big Moorside
Hicken's Bridge
A50
Roydon Hall Farm

Aston-on-Trent Prim Sch
LONG CROFT
WALNUT CL
CLARKES LA
LITTLE MOORSIDE
ACRE LA
ASTON LA
Acrelane Bridge

HOLDEN AVE
COMPTON AVE
GREEN LEYS
MANOR FARM RD
ASH CL
Aston-on-Trent
A50

CHELLASTON LA
WESTON RD
HILTON RD
POSEY LA
THE GREEN
WILLOW CL SHIRLEY
PK
1 OLD SCHOOL MEWS
2 MANOR FARM MEWS
3 LODGE EST
4 PARK VIEW

ELLISON AVE
BELL AVE
VALERIE RD
RECTORY GDNS
ASTON HALL DR
LODGE MEWS
3 4
SHARDLOW RD

4

CEDAR CROFT
YATES AVE
MAPLE DR
WILLOW PARK WAY
HOLLY CT
MULBERRY WAY
Aston Lock

LAUREL DR

29

Aston Hall
Middle Wood
DE72

Weston Grange
Trent and Mersey Canal

3

28

River Trent

King's Mills
Mill Stream
Quarry Hill Plantation
DE74
SHORT LA
BACK LA
HARTLEY RD

KING'S MILL LA
The Priest House (Hotel)

2

FOX RD
BENTLEY RD
FOSBROOK DR
SALTER CL
QUEENSWAY
ROBY LEA
MINTON RD
THE GREEN
STUDBROOK CL
COTSWOLD
Home Farm
Highfields
PARK LA
Innisfree
PADDOCK CL
STARKIE AVE
PARK AVE
SHIELDS CRES

Boathouse Walk Plantation
The Shrubbery
Captain's Gorse
Studbrook Hollow
Stud Brook
BUSWORTH RD

27

Donington Hall
Dalby's Covert

1

Donington Park (Deer Park)
Hill Top Farm

All Hooks
DE73
Thirteen Acre Plantation
Holly Wood
Starkey's Bridge
Donington Park Motor Racing Circuit
Coppice Wood
HILL TOP

26

Gallows Flesh Wood
Leicestershire STREET ATLAS

41   A   42   B   43   C

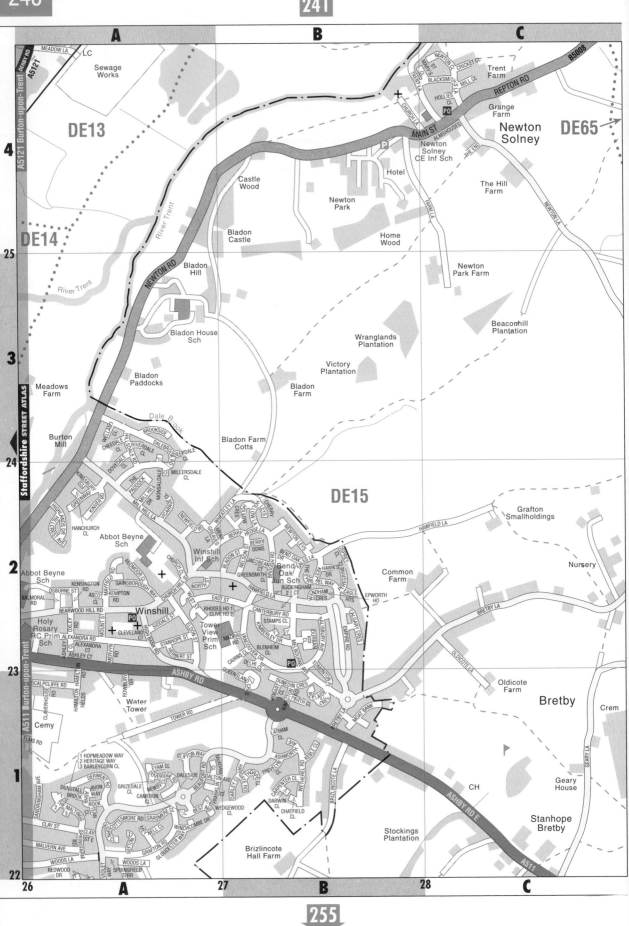

A
B
C

Cockey Barn Farm

Bank House Farm

New Inn (PH)

MAIN ST

Lawn Bridge

ROBIN'S CROSS LA

4

DE65

HARTSHORNE RD

GRAVEL PIT HILL

Park Pond

25

Dale Farm

Broken Flatts

The Hayes

RED LA

Loscoe Farm

3

Little Rough

Repton Park Farm

NEWTON LA

KNIGHT'S LA

Hill Farm Cottages

Hill Farm

Repton Park

Repton Common

Newton Lane Farm

24

Shades Farm

Town Farm

DE15

Repton Lodge

Cherry Tree Cottage

2

THE SQUARE

Bretby

Mill (dis)

Repton Shrubs

BRETBY LA

MOUNT RD

Castle Farm

WATERY LA

The Dower House

23

GEARY LA

BRETBY MEWS

Philosopher's Wood

Noah's Ark

White Hollow

Greysich Farm

The Decoy

Bretby Hall

REPTON RD

1

Bretby Park

The Gorse

Hoofies Wood

Common Plantation

DE11

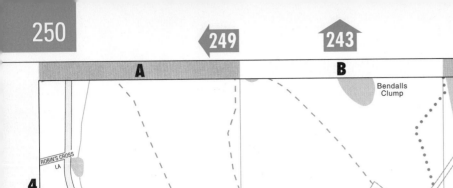

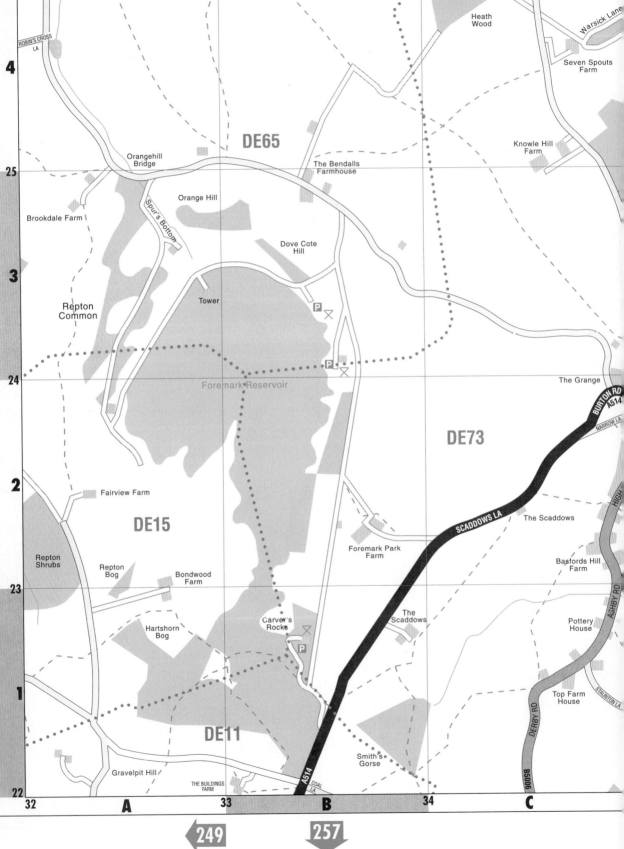

A B C

Bendalls
Clump

Heath
Wood

Warsick Lane

ROBIN'S CROSS
LA

Seven Spouts
Farm

4

DE65

Knowle Hill
Farm

Orangehill
Bridge

The Bendalls
Farmhouse

25

Orange Hill

Brookdale Farm

Spur's Bottom

Dove Cote
Hill

3

Tower

Repton
Common

Foremark Reservoir

The Grange

24

BURTON RD
A514

NARROW LA

DE73

Fairview Farm

2

DE15

SCADDOWS LA

The Scaddows

HIGH

Foremark Park
Farm

Repton
Shrubs

Repton
Bog

Bondwood
Farm

Basfords Hill
Farm

ASHBY RD

23

Hartshorn
Bog

Carver's
Rocks

The
Scaddows

Pottery
House

1

DERBY RD

Top Farm
House

STAUNTON LA

DE11

Smith's
Gorse

Gravelpit Hill

THE BUILDINGS
FARM

A514

COAL
LA

B5006

22

32 A 33 B 34 C

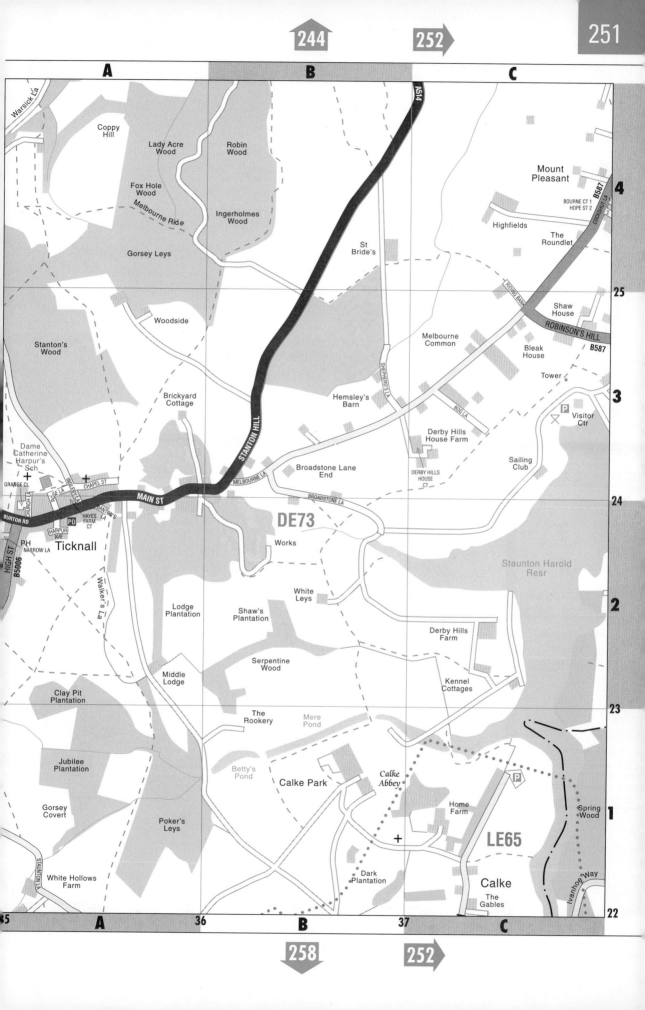

A B C

4

25

3

24

23

2

1

22

A5114

Warsick La

Coppy
Hill

Lady Acre
Wood

Robin
Wood

Fox Hole
Wood

Melbourne Ride

Ingerholmes
Wood

Gorsey Leys

St
Bride's

Mount
Pleasant

BOURNE CT 1
HOPE ST 2

Highfields

The
Roundlet

B587

DOCKSIDE LA

Woodside

Stanton's
Wood

RIDING BANK

Shaw
House

ROBINSON'S HILL

B587

Melbourne
Common

Bleak
House

Tower

Brickyard
Cottage

STANTON HILL

Hemsley's
Barn

SHEPHERD'S LA

BOG LA

Derby Hills
House Farm

P

Visitor
Ctr

Dame
Catherine
Harpur's
Sch

GRANGE CL

INGLEBY LA

CHAPEL ST

MELBOURNE LA

Broadstone Lane
End

DERBY HILLS
HOUSE
CT

Sailing
Club

CHURCH LA

ROSE LA

STANTON'S
FARM
CT

MAIN ST

BROADSTONE LA

DE73

BURTON RD

PO

HARPUR
AVE

HAYES
FARM
CT

Works

PH

NARROW LA

Ticknall

HIGH ST

B5006

White
Leys

Staunton Harold
Resr

Walker's La

Lodge
Plantation

Shaw's
Plantation

Derby Hills
Farm

Middle
Lodge

Serpentine
Wood

Kennel
Cottages

Clay Pit
Plantation

The
Rookery

Mere
Pond

Jubilee
Plantation

Betty's
Pond

Calke Park

Calke
Abbey

P

Home
Farm

Spring
Wood

Gorsey
Covert

Poker's
Leys

LE65

STAUNTON LA

White Hollows
Farm

Dark
Plantation

Calke

The
Gables

Ivanhoe Way

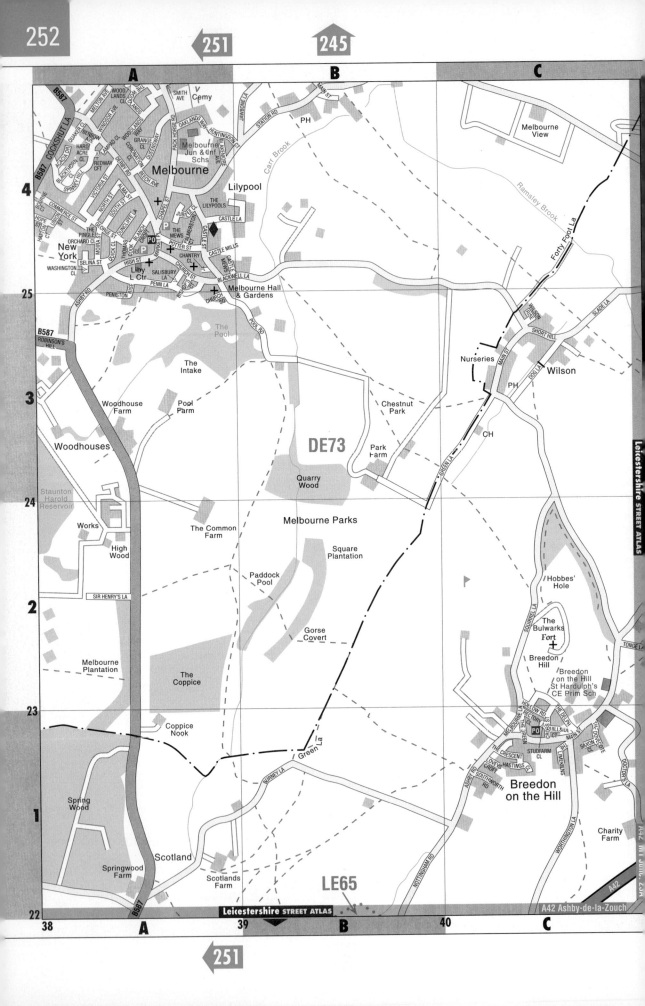

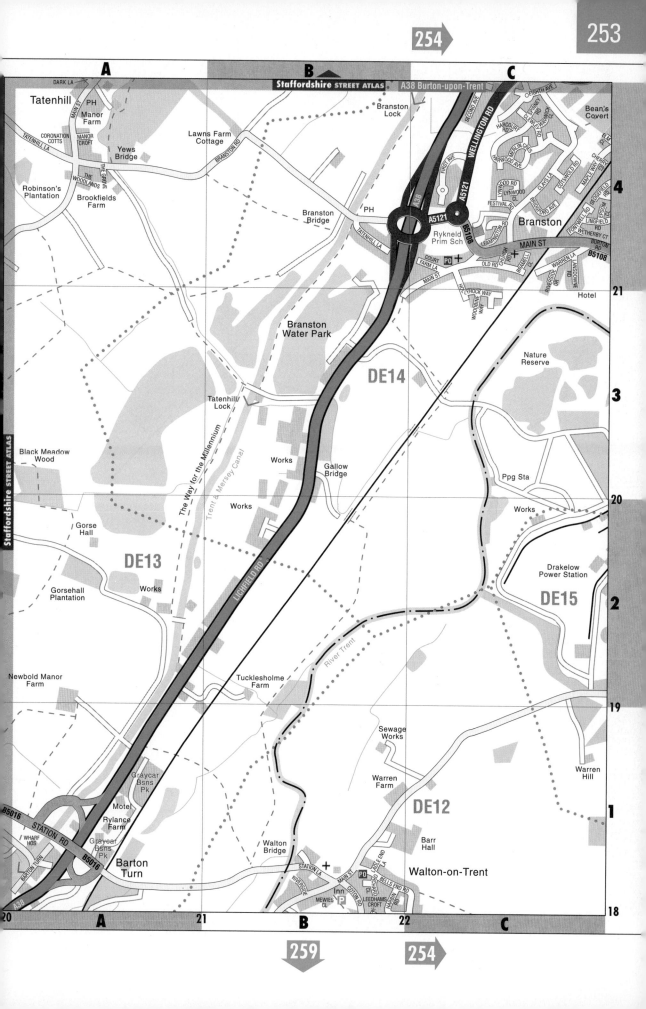

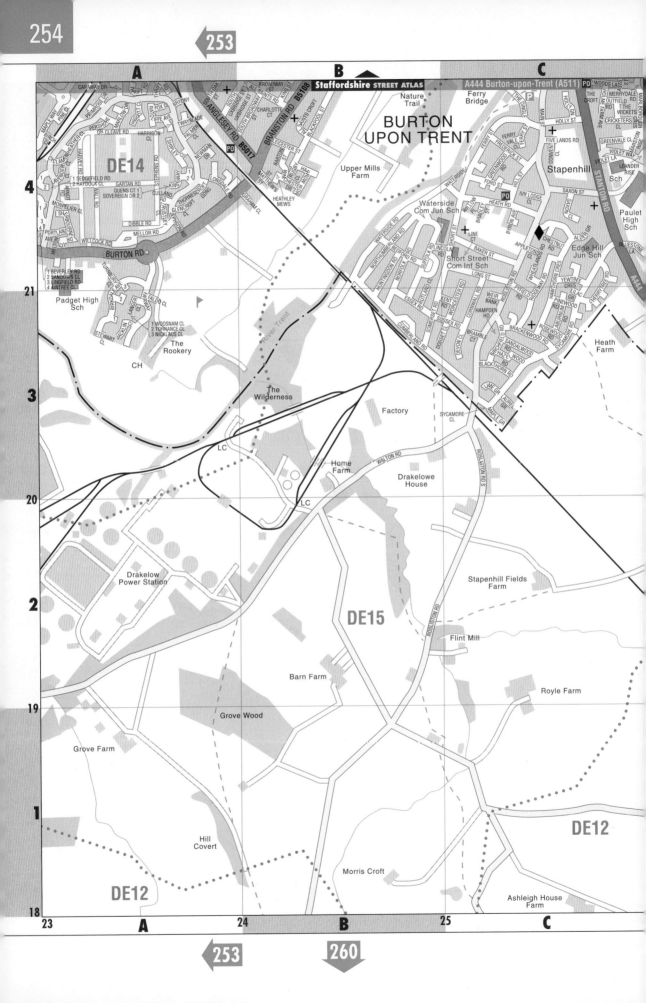

BURTON UPON TRENT

Stapenhill

DE14

DE15

DE12

DE12

Drakelow Power Station

Drakelowe House

Stapenhill Fields Farm

Flint Mill

Barn Farm

Royle Farm

Grove Wood

Grove Farm

Hill Covert

Morris Croft

Ashleigh House Farm

The Rookery

The Wilderness

Home Farm

Factory

Upper Mills Farm

Waterside Com Jun Sch

Short Street Com Inf Sch

Padget High Sch

Paulet High Sch

Edge Hill Jun Sch

Heath Farm

Nature Trail

Ferry Bridge

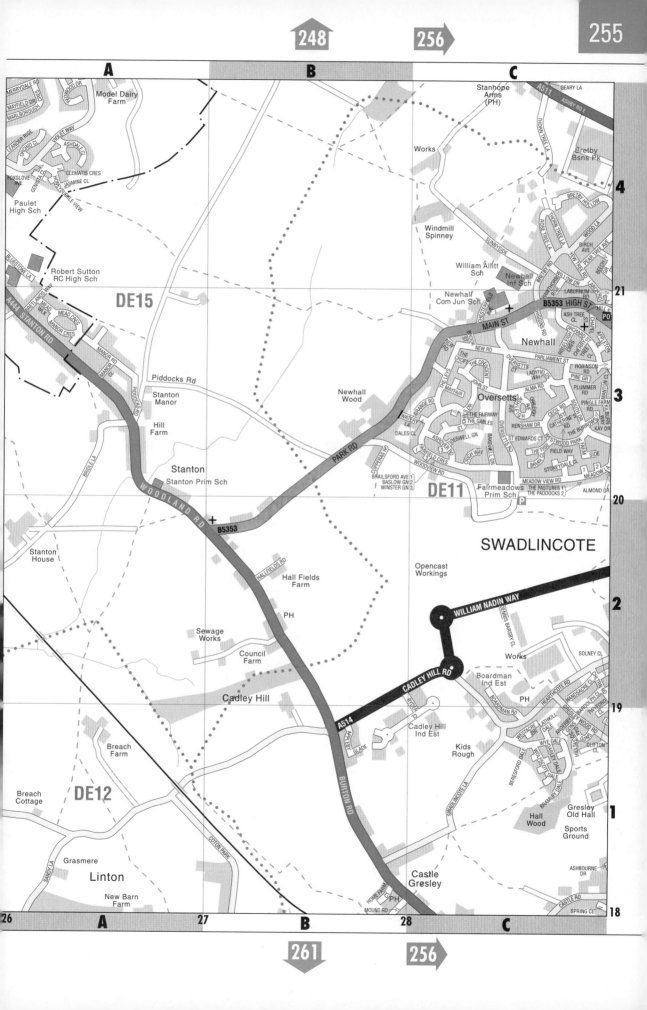

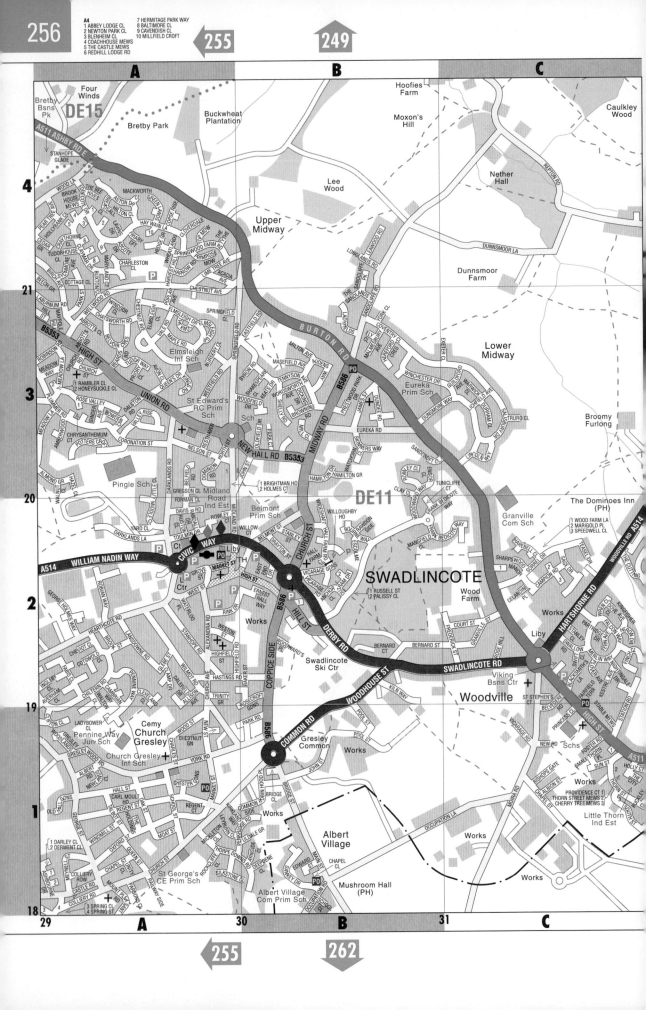

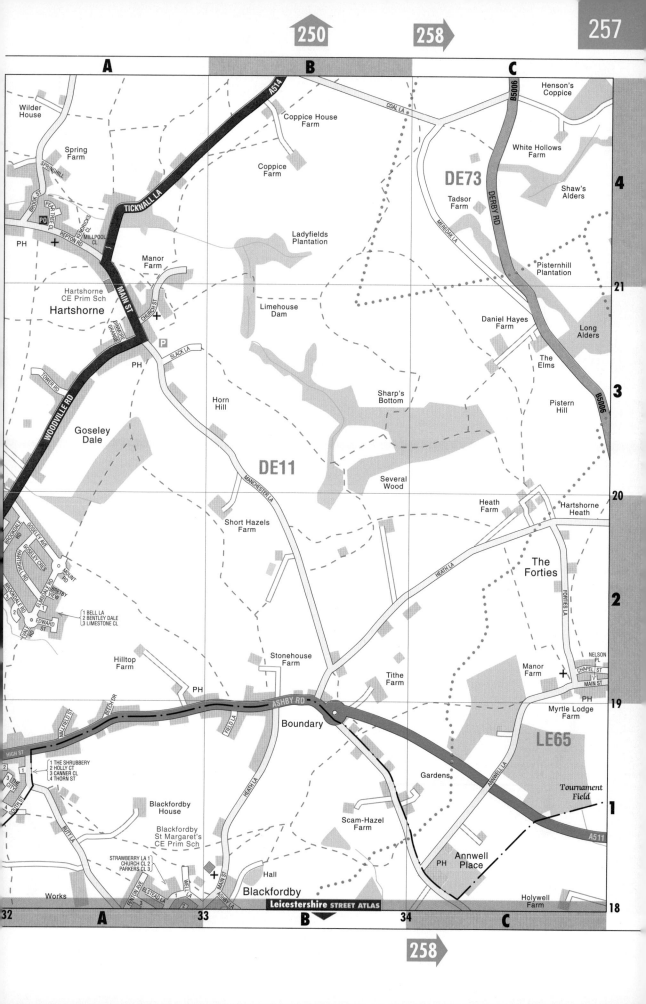

A
B
C

4

Wilder House

Spring Farm

Coppice House Farm

COAL LA

B5006

Henson's Coppice

DE73

White Hollows Farm

Shaw's Alders

SPRINGHILL

BRICK ST

PEAR TREE CL

PO

PH

KENDRICKS CL

REPTON RD

MILLPOOL CL

Coppice Farm

Tadsor Farm

MEROAK LA

DERBY RD

Pisternhill Plantation

TICKNALL LA

Ladyfields Plantation

Manor Farm

21

Hartshorne CE Prim Sch

MAIN ST

CHURCH ST

Hartshorne

Limehouse Dam

Daniel Hayes Farm

Long Alders

P

The Elms

PH

SLACK LA

Sharp's Bottom

Pistern Hill

B5006

3

TOWER RD

WOODVILLE RD

PINFORE GRANGE

PH

Horn Hill

Goseley Dale

DE11

MANCHESTER LA

Several Wood

Heath Farm

Hartshorne Heath

20

BROOKVALE RD

GOSELEY AVE

GOSELEY CRES

HARTSHILL RD

ELMSDALE RD

IBRETBY VIEW

MOUNT RD

Short Hazels Farm

The Forties

FORTIES LA

2

BROOKDALE RD

TYVALE

EDWARD ST

1 BELL LA
2 BENTLEY DALE
3 LIMESTONE CL

NELSON PL

Manor Farm

CHAPEL ST

MAIN ST

PH

Hilltop Farm

PH

BEECH DR

Stonehouse Farm

Tithe Farm

HEATH LA

Myrtle Lodge Farm

19

MILLFIELD ST

FIELD LA

ASHBY RD

Boundary

ANNWELL LA

LE65

HIGH ST

1 THE SHRUBBERY
2 HOLLY CT
3 CANNER CL
4 THORN ST

THE CITY

SOUTH ST

HEATH LA

Gardens

Tournament Field

1

BUTT LA

Blackfordby House

Blackfordby St Margaret's CE Prim Sch

Scam-Hazel Farm

Annwell Place

A511

FENTON AVE

ELSTEAD LA

STRAWBERRY LA 1
CHURCH CL 2
PARKERS CL 3

WELL LA

ASHBY LA

Hall

PH

Holywell Farm

Works

Blackfordby

32
A
33
B
34
C
18

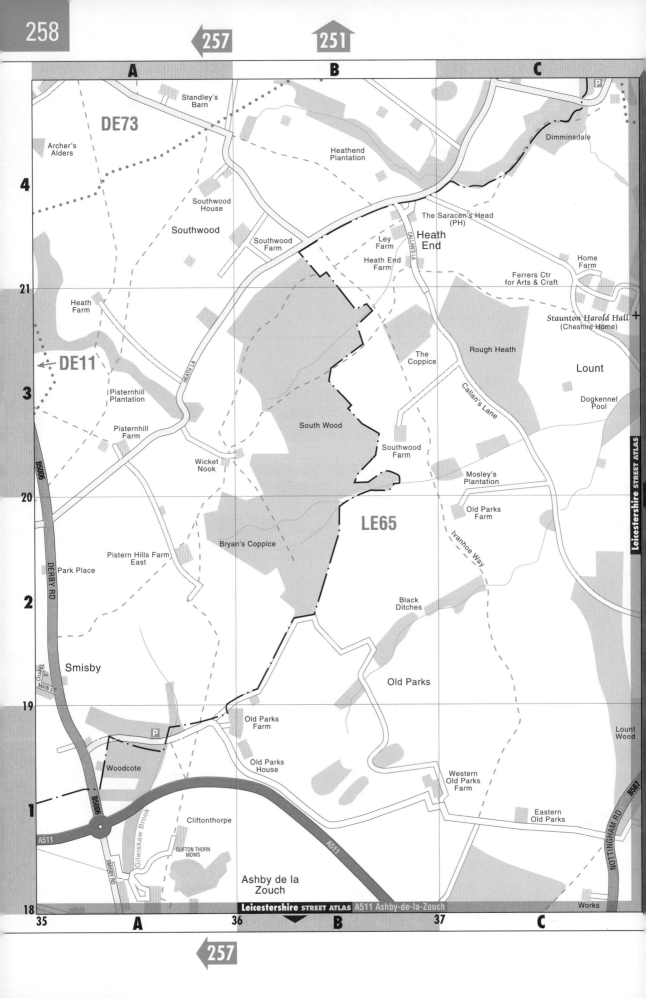

A B C

DE73

Standley's
Barn

Archer's
Alders

Heathend
Plantation

Dimminsdale

4

Southwood
House

The Saracen's Head
(PH)

Southwood

Ley
Farm

Heath
End

Home
Farm

Southwood Farm

Heath End
Farm

Ferrers Ctr
for Arts & Craft

21

Heath
Farm

Staunton Harold Hall
(Cheshire Home)

DE11

The
Coppice

Rough Heath

Lount

3

Pisternhill
Plantation

Callan's Lane

Dogkennel
Pool

Pisternhill
Farm

South Wood

Wicket
Nook

Southwood
Farm

Mosley's
Plantation

20

Bryan's Coppice

LE65

Old Parks
Farm

Pistern Hills Farm
East

Ivanhoe Way

Park Place

2

Black
Ditches

Smisby

Old Parks

Lount
Wood

19

Old Parks
Farm

Woodcote

Old Parks
House

Western
Old Parks
Farm

1

Cliftonthorpe

Eastern
Old Parks

CLIFTON THORN
MDWS

A511

Ashby de la
Zouch

18

Works

35 A 36 B 37 C

Leicestershire STREET ATLAS

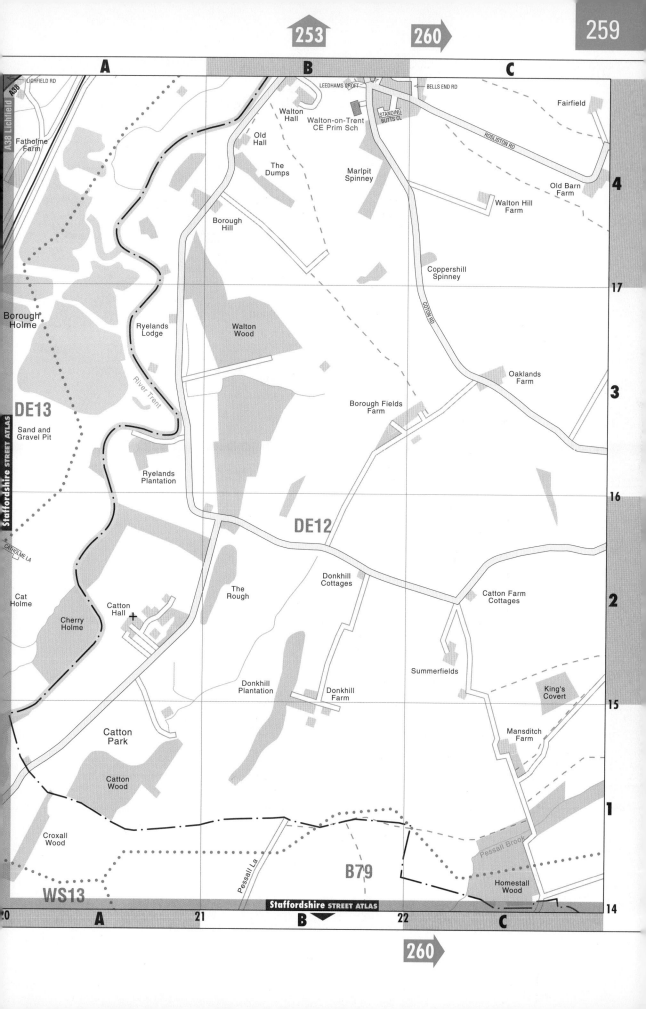
A   B   C

LICHFIELD RD

A38 Lichfield

LEEDHAMS CROFT

BELLS END RD

Fatholme Farm

Walton Hall

Walton-on-Trent CE Prim Sch

STANDING BUTTS CL

Fairfield

Old Hall

ROSLISTON RD

The Dumps

Marlpit Spinney

Old Barn Farm

4

Walton Hill Farm

Borough Hill

Coppershill Spinney

17

Borough Holme

Ryelands Lodge

Walton Wood

COTTON RD

Oaklands Farm

3

DE13

Borough Fields Farm

Sand and Gravel Pit

Ryelands Plantation

River Trent

16

DE12

CATHOLME LA

Donkhill Cottages

Catton Farm Cottages

2

Cat Holme

The Rough

Cherry Holme

Catton Hall

Summerfields

King's Covert

Donkhill Plantation

Donkhill Farm

15

Mansditch Farm

Catton Park

Catton Wood

1

Croxall Wood

Pessall Brook

Pessall La

B79

Homestall Wood

WS13

14

Staffordshire STREET ATLAS

20   A   21   B   22   C

Staffordshire STREET ATLAS

A   B   C

DE15

4

Nursery

Rosliston
Forestry
Ctr

Corner
Farm

ROSLISTON RD

Walton Lane
Farm

Fox
Covert

The
Royal Oak
(PH)

Priory
Farm

SANDY LA

Caldwell

Calves Croft
Farm

MAIN ST

CHURCH LA

Manor
Farm

Pegasus
Sch

17

Moonraker

THE CHASE

BURTON RD

The
Bull's Head
(PH)

HOLDON CROFT

Rosliston

Rosliston CE
Prim Sch

Caldwell
Covert

PO

THE GLEBE

VICARAGE WLK

GARAGE WLK

YEW TREE RD

YEW TREE
GDNS

MAIN ST

NEW ST

CAULDWELL RD

3

CATTON LA

STRAWBERRY LA

LINTON RD

Blakenhall
Farm

16

COTON RD

Field House
Farm

DE12

Beehive
Farm

COTON LA

Lads Grave

Longfurlong
Farm

P

2

Coton in the Elms

BURTON RD

Pessall Brook

Overfields
Farm

Church
Farm

CHURCH CROFT

PO

ELMS RD

CHAPMANS
CROFT

Coton in the
Elms CE Prim
Sch

GREENACRE
PK

CHURCH ST

GLEBE
CL

ELMS EA
AVE

NEW RD

MAIN ST

CHAPEL ST

Queen's Head
Inn (PH)

MILL ST

COALPIT LA

15

MILL GREEN CL

Pessall Brook

Malt House
Farm

P

Garland's
Wood

Church Flatts
Farm

1

Pessall Brook

Little
Liverpool

The Crosses

Grafton
House

14

B79

23   A   24   B   25   C

A **B** **C**

Sch

THE CLOSE

Littleworth

Boothorpe

MOIRA RD

MUSHROOM LA

DE11

Spoil Heaps and
Clay Pits

4

Gresley Tunnel

OCCUPATION RD

COVERT PL

P

RESERVOIR HILL

Swainspark

17

PARK RD

Gorse La

Hanging
Hill

P

Hanging Hill
Farm

BURTON RD

A444

3

Works

SPRING COTTAGE RD

MILLENIUM
AVE

RAWDON RD

MARQUIS DR

Spring
Cottage

PH

Conkers
Discovery

MARQUIS
CT

16

DE12

Works

BRITON
LODGE CL

EDWARD ST

ALEXANDRA
RD

STANLEIGH
RD

HADLEY'S
CL

SLACKEY LA

Conkers
Waterside

STATION
DR

CORONATION ST

WOODVILLE RD

Overseal
Prim Sch

Visitors
Ctr

ASHBY RD

PO

WOODLANDS
CRES

WOODLANDS RD

FOREST
VIEW

P

Gorsey
Leys

Blencathra

BATH LA

FOREST
LEA

2

Overseal

LULLINGTON
MEWS

DAISY LA

HALLCROFT AVE

Overseal
Manor Sch

MOIRA RD

Brooklands
Farm

Moira

FURNACE LA

Furnace
Lane Ind Est

Warren House
Farm

Ashby-de-la-Zouch Canal

LULLINGTON RD

CLIFTON

BRAMBLE
WALK

JACKSON
CL

SHORTGATE

SHORT
HEATH RD

Moira
Furnace
Mus

MEASHAM RD

BAILS

IVY AVE

MAIN ST

ASHLEY
CL

VALLEY RD

PO

SHORT

DONISTHORPE LA

PARK RD

SCHOOL ST

15

Sewage
Works

SQUIRREL WALK

Grange
Farm

Short
Heath

POPLAR AVE

Rookery
Farm

Shortheath
Farm

IVANHOE WAY

P

ACRESFORD RD

FINNEY
CL

JUBILEE
TERR

MOIRA RD

1

Cadborough
Hill

Hooborough Brook

Sewage
Works

DAWKINS RD

HILL ST

DAISY
CL

BUTTERCUP AVE

SICLET CL

COWSLIP CL

Donisthorpe

ASHLAR
DR

Church Way

GREENSIDE
CL

BLUEBELL CL

FOXGLOVE
AVE

Cemy

Cadborough
Farm

SEALS RD

NEW ST

CHAPEL ST

BARKLAM
CL

IVY CL

PO

CHURCH ST

14

A444

A **B** **C**

Leicestershire STREET ATLAS

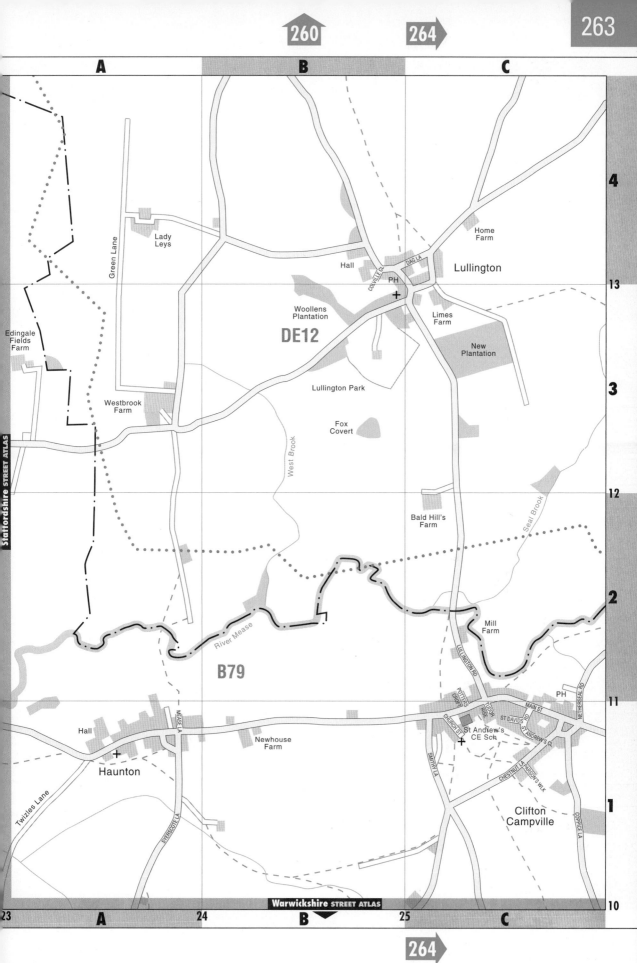

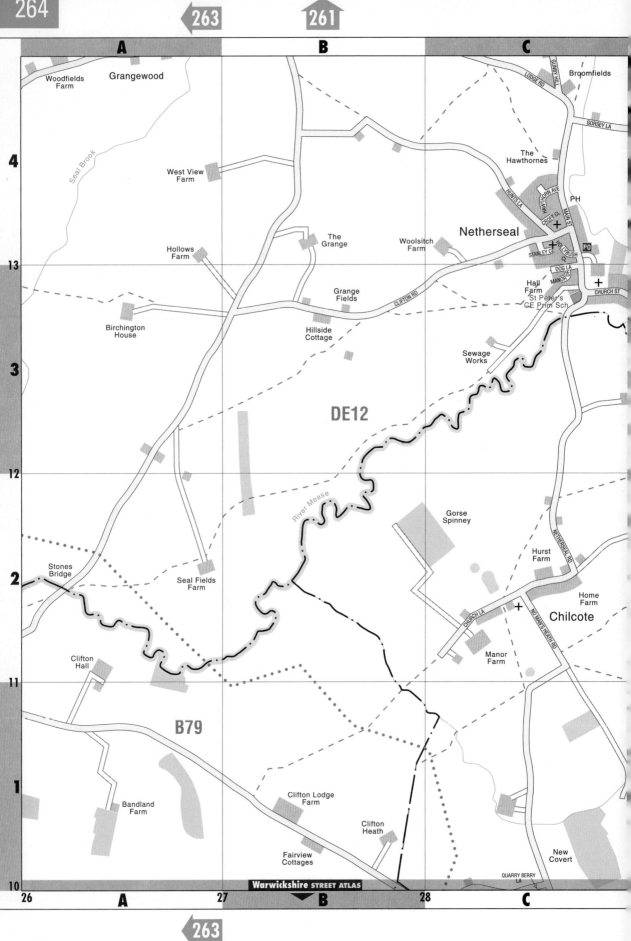

A

B

C

Woodfields Farm

Grangewood

Seal Brook

4

West View Farm

Hollows Farm

The Grange

Woolsitch Farm

Netherseal

Lodge Rd

Gunby Hill

Broomfields

Gorsey La

The Hawthornes

Hunt's La

Hawthorn Ave

Croft Cl

Main St

PH

Hollybush Cl

Stanley Cl

Manor Dr

Dog La

Church St

PO

Hall Farm

St Peter's CE Prim Sch

13

Birchington House

Grange Fields

Hillside Cottage

Sewage Works

3

DE12

12

River Mease

Gorse Spinney

Netherseal Rd

Hurst Farm

Stones Bridge

2

Seal Fields Farm

Home Farm

Chilcote

Church La

No Man's Heath Rd

Clifton Hall

Manor Farm

11

B79

Bandland Farm

1

Clifton Lodge Farm

Clifton Heath

New Covert

Quarry Berry La

10

26

A

27

B

28

C

Fairview Cottages

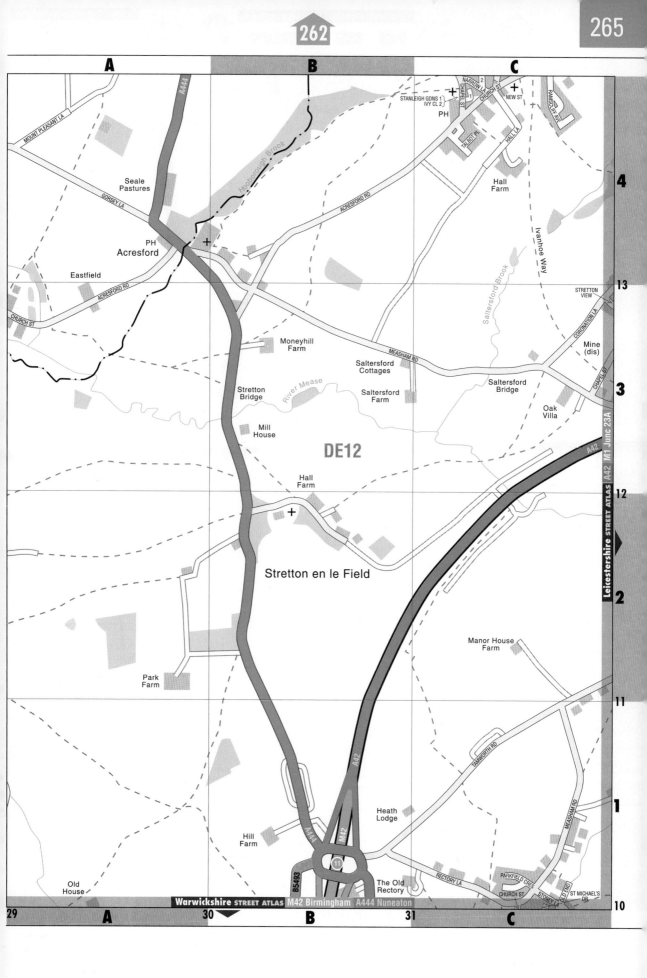

Warwickshire STREET ATLAS M42 Birmingham A444 Nuneaton

Leicestershire STREET ATLAS A42 M1 Junc 23A

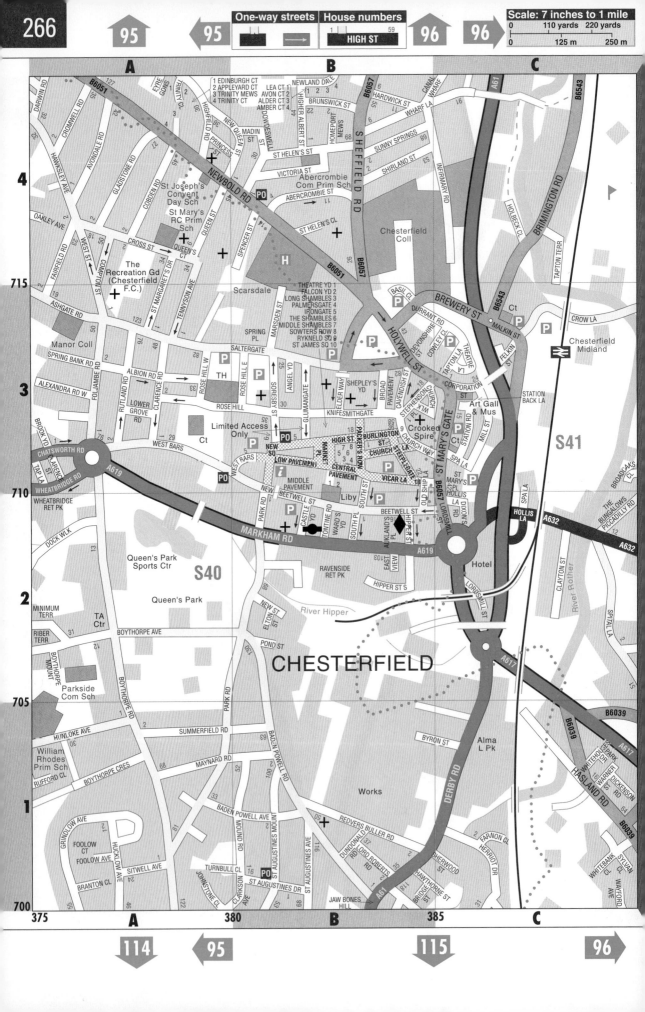

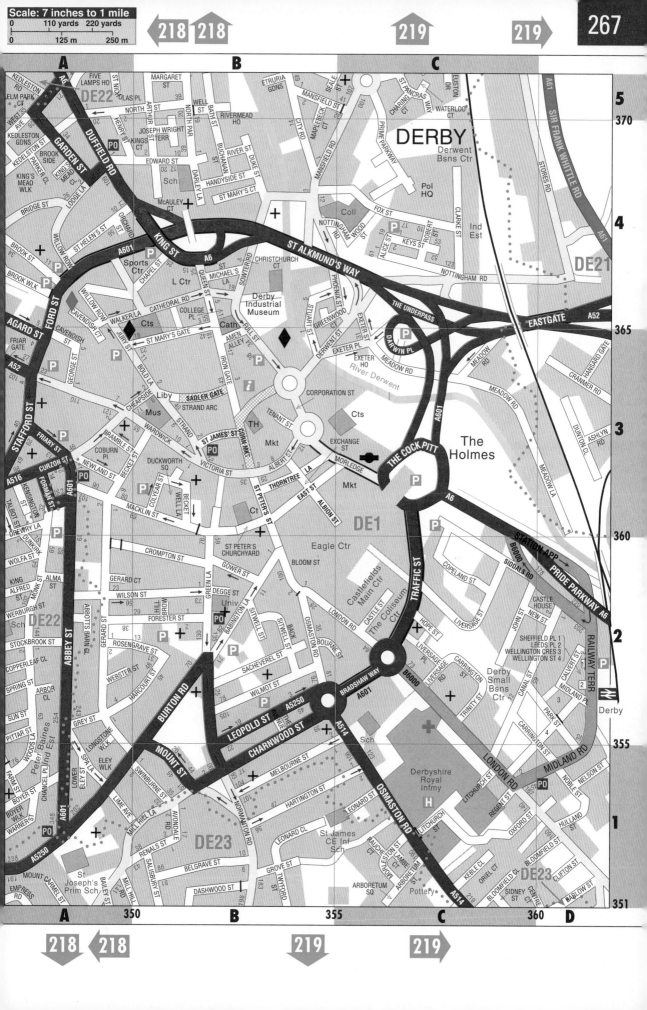

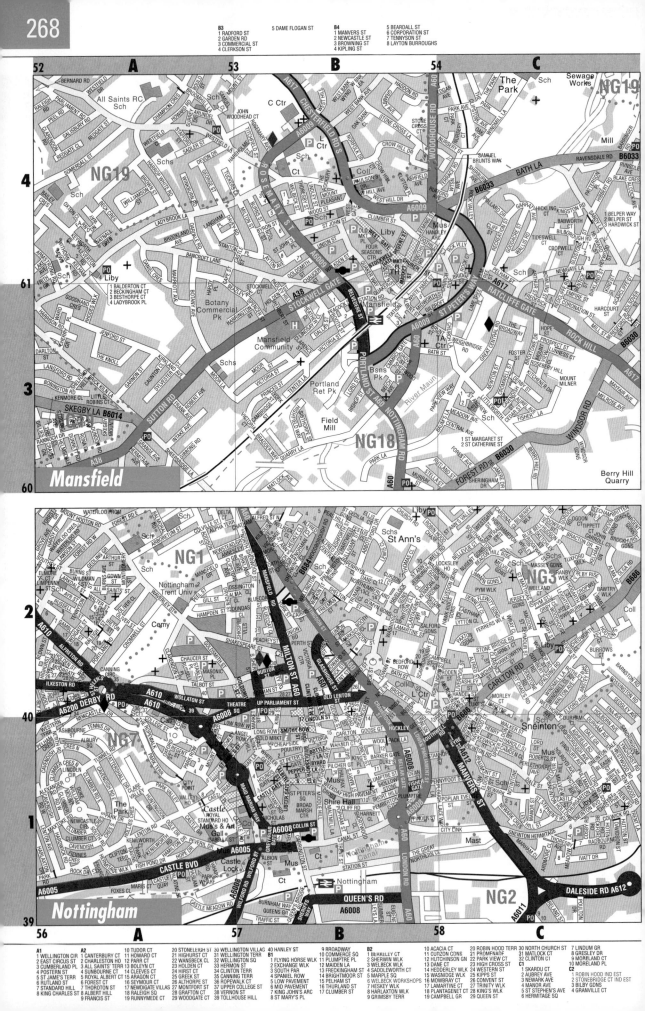

Mansfield

Nottingham

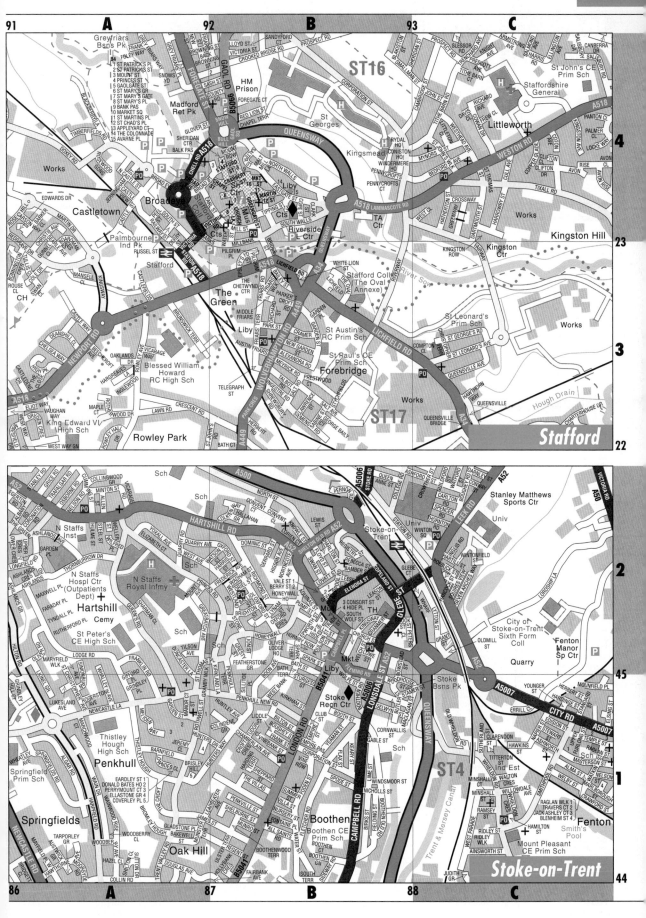

Stafford

Stoke-on-Trent

Index

Church Rd **6** Beckenham BR2..........**53** C6

Place name	**Location number**	**Locality, town or village**	**Postcode district**	**Page and grid square**
May be abbreviated on the map	Present when a number indicates the place's position in a crowded area of mapping	Shown when more than one place has the same name	District for the indexed place	Page number and grid reference for the standard mapping

Public and commercial buildings are highlighted in **magenta** **Places of interest** are highlighted in blue with a star★

Abbreviations used in the index

Acad	**Academy**	Comm	**Common**	Gd	**Ground**	L	**Leisure**	Prom	**Prom**
App	**Approach**	Cott	**Cottage**	Gdn	**Garden**	La	**Lane**	Rd	**Road**
Arc	**Arcade**	Cres	**Crescent**	Gn	**Green**	Liby	**Library**	Recn	**Recreation**
Ave	**Avenue**	Cswy	**Causeway**	Gr	**Grove**	Mdw	**Meadow**	Ret	**Retail**
Bglw	**Bungalow**	Ct	**Court**	H	**Hall**	Meml	**Memorial**	Sh	**Shopping**
Bldg	**Building**	Ctr	**Centre**	Ho	**House**	Mkt	**Market**	Sq	**Square**
Bsns, Bus	**Business**	Ctry	**Country**	Hospl	**Hospital**	Mus	**Museum**	St	**Street**
Bvd	**Boulevard**	Cty	**County**	HQ	**Headquarters**	Orch	**Orchard**	Sta	**Station**
Cath	**Cathedral**	Dr	**Drive**	Hts	**Heights**	Pal	**Palace**	Terr	**Terrace**
Cir	**Circus**	Dro	**Drove**	Ind	**Industrial**	Par	**Parade**	TH	**Town Hall**
Cl	**Close**	Ed	**Education**	Inst	**Institute**	Pas	**Passage**	Univ	**University**
Cnr	**Corner**	Emb	**Embankment**	Int	**International**	Pk	**Park**	Wk, Wlk	**Walk**
Coll	**College**	Est	**Estate**	Intc	**Interchange**	Pl	**Place**	Wr	**Water**
Com	**Community**	Ex	**Exhibition**	Junc	**Junction**	Prec	**Precinct**	Yd	**Yard**

Index of localities, towns and villages

Abney .51 C2
Aldercar .182 A2
Alderwasley .166 C4
Alfreton .159 B2
Alkmonton .199 B1
Alsop en le Dale .150 C2
Alstonefield .149 B2
Alton .130 B3
Ambergate .167 C2
Apperknowle .58 A1
Ashbourne .173 B2
Ashby-de-la-Zouch .258 B1
Ashford in the Water .108 C4
Ashover .129 C2
Aston-on-Trent .246 A4
Atlow .175 A3
Ault Hucknall .133 C4
Awsworth .195 B2
Bakewell .109 C3
Bamford .40 A2
Barlborough .80 A4
Barlow .75 C1
Barrow Hill .78 A2
Barrow upon Trent .244 A3
Barton in Fabis .237 C3
Barton Turn .253 A1
Baslow .91 C3
Beeley .111 A2
Beeston .223 C2
Belper .179 A2
Biggin .138 B2
Birchover .126 A1
Blackfordby .257 B1
Blackwell .147 C1
Bolsover .99 A1
Bonsall .142 C1
Borrowash .221 B1
Boylestone .213 B2
Brackenfield .145 B1
Bradbourne .163 B3
Bradley .186 C4
Bradwell .51 A4
Brailsford .201 C4
Bramley-Vale .117 C1
Branston .253 C4
Brassington .153 A1
Breadsall .205 C2
Breaston .235 B4
Breedon on the Hill .252 C1
Bretby .249 A2
Brimington .96 C4
Brinsley .182 C3
Broadbottom .16 A4
Bullbridge .168 A3
Burnaston .229 C3
Burton upon Trent .254 B2
Buxton .85 A4
Caldwell .260 C4
Calow .96 C1
Calver .72 B1
Carsington .164 C4
Castle Donington .247 B2
Castleton .38 B1
Chapel-en-le-Frith .47 A3
Chelmorton .87 A1
Chesterfield .96 B2
Chinley .34 C1
Church Broughton .227 A4
Clay Cross .131 A2
Clifton .184 C3
Clifton Campville .263 C1
Clowne .80 B2
Codnor .181 B4
Compstall .15 A1
Cossall .195 B1
Coton in the Elms .260 B2
Creswell .81 C1
Crich .156 C1
Cromford .155 A3
Curbar .72 C1
Dale Abbey .207 C1
Darley Dale .127 B1
Denby .180 B1
Denstone .196 B3
Derby .219 A3
Derwent .30 B3
Disley .32 B3
Donisthorpe .262 C1
Dore .55 C4
Dove Holes .47 C1
Doveridge .211 A1
Draycott .234 C4
Dronfield .56 C1
Duffield .190 C2
Earl Sterndale .105 B2
Eastwood .182 C2
Eckington .59 B2
Edale .37 B4
Egginton .241 A3
Ellastone .183 A2
Elmton .100 A4
Elton .140 C3
Elvaston .234 A3
Etwall .229 B2
Eyam .71 B3
Fenny Bentley .162 A1
Fenton .269 C1
Findern .230 B1
Flagg .106 C3
Flash .103 A2
Fritchley .168 B4
Gamesley .9 C1
Glapwell .134 B4
Glossop .10 A1
Grassmoor .115 C2
Great Cubley .198 C1
Great Hucklow .70 A4
Great Longstone .90 A2
Grindleford .72 B4
Hanbury .238 A3
Harthill .61 C3
Hartington .137 B3
Hartshorne .257 A3
Hassop .90 C3
Hathersage .53 A4
Hatton .239 B4
Hayfield .25 B1
Hazelwood .190 A4
Heage .168 C1
Heanor .181 B1
Heath .117 A1
High Lane .32 A4
High Peak .28 C4
Hilcote .148 B1
Hilton .228 B1
Hognaston .164 A1
Holbeck .101 B4
Holbrook .191 B3
Hollington .200 C2
Hollingworth .9 B3
Hollinsclough .104 B1
Holloway .156 A3
Holme .2 C4
Holmesfield .75 A4
Holmewood .116 C1
Holymoorside .113 B4
Hope .38 C2
Horsley .191 C3
Hulland Ward .175 C2
Ible .153 C4
Idridgehay .176 C3
Ilkeston .208 C4
Ironville .170 C2
Kettleshulme .45 A1
Kilburn .192 A4
Killamarsh .60 C3
Kimberley .195 C4
King's Newton .245 A1
Kirby-in-Ashfield .160 C2
Kirk Ireton .165 B1
Kirk Langley .202 C1
Kniveton .163 A1
Langley Mill .182 A2
Langwith .119 C4
Linton .261 B3
Little Eaton .205 B4
Lockington .247 C3
Long Duckmanton .98 A2
Long Eaton .236 B4
Longford .214 B4
Longnor .121 A3
Lount .258 C3
Lullington .263 C4
Mackworth .217 C4
Mansfield .136 A1
Mansfield .268
Mansfield Woodhouse .136 C1
Mapperley .193 C2
Marchington .224 C1
Market Warsop .120 C2
Marple .23 A3
Marston Montgomery .211 C4
Mastin Moor .79 B2
Matlock .143 A3
Matlock Bath .143 A1
Mayfield .184 B4
Melbourne .252 A4
Middleton .124 C2
Middleton (Nr Wirksworth) .154 B2
Moira .262 C2
Monyash .107 B1
Morley .206 B3
Mosborough .59 B4
Mossley .4 A4
Mottram in Longdendale .9 A2
Nether Heage .168 B1
Nether Padley .53 C1
Netherseal .264 C4
New Houghton .134 C4
New Mills .33 B4
Newton .148 A2
Newton Solney .248 C4
North Wingfield .132 A4
Northedge .130 B3
Northwood .127 A3
Nottingham .268
Ockbrook .221 B3
Old Brampton .94 B2
Osmaston .185 C2
Over Haddon .109 A1
Overseal .262 A2
Palterton .118 A3
Parwich .151 C1
Peak Forest .49 A2
Pikehall .139 C2
Pilsley (Nr Baslow) .91 B2
Pilsley (Nr Clay Cross) .132 B1
Pinxton .160 B1
Pleasley .135 A3
Poolsbrook .98 A4
Quarndon .204 B3
Renishaw .79 A4
Repton .242 C1
Ridgeway .168 B2
Ringinglow .42 A3
Ripley .169 B1
Risley .222 C2
Rocester .197 A2
Rodsley .200 A3
Rolleston .240 A2
Rosliston .260 B3
Roston .197 C4
Sandiacre .223 A3
Scarcliffe .118 C3
Scropton .226 C1
Selston .171 C4
Shardlow .234 C1
Sheffield .44 B3
Shipley .194 A3
Shirebrook .119 C2
Shireoaks .63 C3
Shirland .146 B1
Shirley .200 C4
Shottle .177 C4
Smalley .192 C3
Smisby .258 A2
Snelston .184 B2
Somercotes .170 B4
Somersal Herbert .211 C2
South Normanton .160 A4
South Wingfield .157 C2
Spout .166 B2
Stafford .269
Stanley .207 B3
Stanton-by-Dale .222 C4
Stapleford .223 C4
Staveley .78 B1
Stoke-on-Trent .269
Stonebroom .146 C2
Stoney Middleton .71 C2
Stretton en le Field .265 B2
Strines Moor .31 B4
Sudbury .225 C2
Sutton in Ashfield .148 C1
Sutton on the Hill .228 A4
Swadlincote .256 B2
Swanwick .169 C3
Taddington .88 A2
Tansley .144 A2
Thornhill .39 C2
Thorpe .161 B1
Thorpe Salvin .62 C3
Thrumpton .237 B2
Thurvaston .215 B4
Tibshelf .148 A3
Ticknall .251 A2
Tideswell .69 B2
Tissington .162 A3
Toadmoor .167 C2
Totley .55 C3
Trowell .209 B3
Trusley .215 C2
Tupton .131 B4
Turnditch .177 A1
Tutbury .239 B3
Underwood Green .171 C1
Unstone .76 C4
Uttoxeter .210 B1
Walton-on-Trent .253 C1
Wensley .142 A4
Wessington .157 C4
West Hallam .207 C4
Weston Underwood .189 A1
Weston-on-Trent .245 C3
Westwood .171 B2
Whaley Bridge .45 B4
Whaley Thorns .101 A1
Whitwell .81 C3
Willington .242 A3
Windley .189 B4
Wingerworth .114 C2
Winster .141 B3
Wirksworth .165 C4
Woodville .256 C2
Workop .63 C1
Wyaston .185 B1
Yeaveley .199 B3
Youlgreave .125 A3

1
1st Ave DE7 208 C4

2
2nd Ave DE7 208 C4

3
3rd Ave DE7 208 C4

A
Abba Cl NG16 195 C4
Abbey Brook Dr S8 56 C4
Abbey Cl ST14 197 A2
Abbey Croft
 Chesterfield S40 95 A4
 Renishaw S21 79 B4
Abbey Gdns SK14 9 A2
Abbey Hill DE21, DE22 205 A2
Abbey Hill Rd DE22 204 B1
Abbey La DE22 205 A1
Abbey Lodge Cl 1 DE11 256 A4
Abbey Pl S21 79 B4
Abbey St
 Derby DE1, DE22 267 A2
 Ilkeston DE7 194 C1
Abbey View Dr S8 43 A2
Abbey View Rd S8 43 A2
Abbey Yd DE22 205 A1
Abbeydale Cl DE56 192 A4
Abbeydale Park Cres S17 55 C3
Abbeydale Park Rise S17 55 C3
Abbeydale Rd S8 43 A4
Abbeydale Rd S S17 56 A4
Abbeyfields Cl DE22 205 A1
Abbeyhill Cl S42 95 A2
Abbot Beyne Sch DE15 248 A2
Abbot Cl DE21 205 C1
Abbot Rd DE7 208 B3
Abbot St NG16 195 B2
Abbots Gr DE56 179 A3
Abbotsford Dr NG3 268 B2
Abbotsford Mews DE7 194 B2
Abbotsholme Sch ST14 197 A1
Abbott Rd DE55 159 A2
Abbott St Heanor DE75 181 C1
 Long Eaton NG10 236 B3
Abbotts Barn Cl DE22 267 A2
Abbotts Cl DE11 256 A3
Abbotts Croft NG19 135 C1
Abbotts Rd DE11 256 A3
Abel La DE4 142 B1
Abells DE5 180 B1
Abercrombie Com Prim Sch S41 266 B4
Abercrombie St S41 266 B4
Aberdare Cl DE21 206 A1
Aberdeen St NG3 268 C2
Abingdon Bsns Ctr The DE24 219 B1
Abingdon St DE24 232 B4
Abney Cl Chesterfield S40 95 B3
 Derby DE3 217 C1
 Sheffield S14 43 B3
Abney Dr S14 43 B3
Abney Rd S14 43 B3
Acacia Ave Brimington S43 97 A4
 Derby DE3 217 C1
 Swadlincote DE11 256 A4
Acacia Cres S21 60 A3
Acacia Ct
 Mansfield NG19 136 C1
 10 Nottingham NG3 268 B2
Acacia Dr
 Melbourne DE73 252 A4
 Pilsley S45 132 A2
Acacia Gdns NG16 195 C4
Acer Cl Killamarsh S21 60 B3
 Pinxton NG16 160 B2
Acer Croft DE21 205 C2
Ackwright's Mill★ DE4 155 A4
Acorn Ave NG16 195 B4
Acorn Bsns Pk NG18 268 B3
Acorn Cl DE24 232 C2
Acorn Ctr NG16 182 B2
Acorn Dr DE56 179 A3
Acorn Ridge
 Chesterfield S40 114 A4
 Matlock DE4 143 A3
 Shirebrook NG20 119 B3
Acorn Terr SK22 33 A3
Acorn Way Belper DE56 179 A3
 Derby DE21 220 B3
Acre La DE72 246 B4
Acre St 6 SK13 17 B4
Acreage La NG20 119 C1
Acrefield Way DE73 233 A1
Acres Rd S45 132 A2
Acres The S45 132 A2
Acres View Cl S41 95 C4
Acresford Rd
 Donisthorpe DE12 265 B4
 Netherseal DE12 265 A3
 Overseal DE12 262 A1
Acton Ave NG10 236 C3
Acton Cl NG10 236 C3
Acton Gr NG10 236 C3
Acton Rd Derby DE22 217 C3
 Long Eaton NG10 236 C3
Acton Road Ind Est NG10 236 C3
Acton St NG10 236 C3
Adale Rd DE7 193 A4
Adam Bede Cres DE4 165 C3
Adam St DE7 209 A3
Adam's Rd DE6 217 A4
Adams Cl DE75 193 B4
Adams Ct DE7 194 C2
Adastral Ave S12 44 A1
Adderley Pl SK13 9 C1
Adderley Rd SK13 9 C1
Addison Dr DE55 159 A2
Addison Rd Derby DE24 232 B4
 Stonebroom DE55 146 C2
Addison Sq DE4 155 A3
Addison St
 Nottingham NG1 268 A2
 Tibshelf DE55 148 A4
Addison Villas NG16 182 C1
Adelaide Cl Derby DE3 217 C2
 Stapleford NG9 209 C1
Adelaide Cres DE15 248 B1
Adelaide Wlk NG16 170 C2
Adelphi Cl DE23 231 A3
Adelphi Way S43 97 C4
Adin Ave S44 98 C3
Adlington Ave S42 115 B1
Adlington La S32 72 B4
Admiral Cl DE75 181 B1
Adrian Cl NG9 223 C1
Adrian St DE24 232 B3
Adwick Cl DE3 217 B1
Agard St DE1 218 C3
Agnesmeadow La DE6 174 B2
Agricultural Way DE45 109 C3
Aimploy Ct DE23 219 A1
Ainley Cl DE24 232 C4
Ainsworth Dr DE23 231 C4
Ainsworth St ST4 269 C1
Aintree Ave S21 59 A2
Aintree Cl
 Burton u T DE14 254 A4
 Kimberley NG16 195 C4
Airedale Cl NG10 236 A3
Airedale Wlk 3 DE24 233 B3
Akley Bank Cl S17 55 C3
Alabaster La DE4 155 A3
Alandale Ave NG20 119 C3
Albany Cl NG19 136 B1
Albany Ct NG9 209 C1
Albany Dr NG19 136 B1
Albany Inf & Jun Schs NG9 223 C4
Albany Inf Sch NG9 209 C1
Albany Pl NG19 136 B1
Albany Rd Derby DE22 218 B2
 Stoke-on-T ST4 269 A2
Albany St DE7 209 A3
Albemarle Rd DE21 220 A4
Albert Ave
 Chesterfield S43 77 B2
 Stapleford NG9 223 B4
 Westwood NG16 171 A2
Albert Cres DE21 220 A2
Albert Hill 8 NG7 268 A2
Albert Rd Breaston DE72 235 A4
 Chesterfield S43 77 B2
 Derby DE21 220 A2
 Long Eaton NG10 236 B4
 Ripley DE5 169 B1
 Sandiacre NG10 223 A3
 Sheffield S8 43 A3
 Swadlincote DE11 256 A1
Albert St Belper DE56 178 C2
 Derby DE1 267 B3
 Eastwood NG16 182 C2
 Eckington S21 59 B1
 Glossop SK13 10 A3
 Ilkeston DE7 208 C4
 Ironville NG16 170 C3
 Mansfield NG18 268 B3
 Mansfield Woodhouse NG19 136 B2
 Nottingham NG1 268 B1
 Ripley DE5 169 C1
 Somercotes DE55 170 A4
 South Normanton DE55 160 A3
 Stapleford NG9 223 B4
Albert St N S41 76 C1
Albert Village Com Prim Sch DE11 256 B1
Alberta Ave NG16 171 C4
Albine Rd NG20 119 C3
Albion Ctr The DE7 208 C4
Albion Rd
 Chesterfield S40 266 A3
 Long Eaton NG10 236 C4
 New Mills SK22 33 A3
Albion St Derby DE1 267 B3
 Ilkeston DE7 194 C1
 Mansfield NG19 135 C1
 Nottingham NG1 268 B1
 Ripley DE5 169 C1
 Woodville DE11 256 C1
Albrighton Ave DE24 231 B1
Albury Sq NG7 268 A1
Alcock Ave NG18 268 C4
Aldam Cl S17 55 C2
Aldam Croft S17 55 C2
Aldam Rd S17 55 C2
Aldam Way S17 55 C2
Alder Brook SK23 34 C1
Alder Cl Derby DE21 205 C2
 Mansfield NG19 136 C1
 Shirebrook NG20 119 B3
Alder Ct Chesterfield S41 266 B4
 Derby DE1 219 A4
Alder Gr Burton u T DE15 254 C4
 Buxton SK17 85 A4
 Mansfield Woodhouse NG19 136 A3
Alder Rd DE56 179 A2
Alder Rise SK23 45 B4
Alder Way NG20 119 B2
Alderbrook Cl DE13 240 A2
Aldercar Com Sch NG16 182 A2
Aldercar Inf Sch NG16 182 A2
Aldercar La NG16 182 A3
Alderd Cl S21 60 C4
Alderfen Cl DE24 232 B2
Alderholme Dr 6 DE13 240 C1
Alderley Ct DE21 206 A1
Aldern Way DE45 109 C4
Alderney Rd S2 43 A4
Alders Ave SK23 34 C1
Alders Brook DE65 228 B1
Alders La Chinley SK23 34 C1
 Tansley DE4 144 A2
Alders Rd SK12 32 A4
Alders The S42 113 B4
Aldersgate Derby DE22 217 C4
 New Mills SK22 33 A4
Alderslade Cl DE72 234 A1
Aldersley Cl DE65 230 B1
Alderson Dr DE13 240 C1
Alderson Pl S2 43 A4
Alderson Rd S2 43 A4
Alderson Rd N 3 S2 43 A4
Alderwashley Hall Sch DE56 167 A4
Aldred's La DE75, NG16 182 A1
Aldridge Cl NG9 223 C1
Aldwark Rd SK17 85 B3
Aldwych DE22 218 A3
Alexander Ave NG16 171 B4
Alexander Rd
 Dove Holes SK17 47 C1
 Nottingham NG7 268 A1
Alexander St NG16 182 C1
Alexander Terr NG16 160 B1
Alexandra Ave NG19 136 A3
Alexandra Ct DE15 248 A2
Alexandra Gdns 6 DE23 219 A1
Alexandra Rd
 Burton u T DE15 248 A2
 Buxton SK17 85 B3
 Dronfield S18 57 A1
 Long Eaton NG10 236 B4
 Overseal DE12 262 A2
 Sheffield S2 43 A4
 Stafford ST17 269 B3
 Swadlincote DE11 256 A2
Alexandra Rd E S41 96 B1
Alexandra Rd W S40 266 A3
Alexandra St NG9 223 B3
Alexandre Cl DE23 231 B3
Alford Cl S40 95 B2
Alfred Cl NG3 268 B2
Alfred Ct NG18 268 B4
Alfred Rd DE56 192 A4
Alfred St Alfreton DE55 158 C2
 Pinxton NG16 160 B2
 Ripley DE5 169 C1
 Somercotes DE55 170 B3
 South Normanton DE55 159 C3
Alfred St Central NG3 268 B2
Alfred St N NG1,NG3 268 B2
Alfred St S NG3 268 C2
Alfreton & Mansfield Parkway Sta DE55 159 B3
Alfreton L Ctr DE55 158 C2
Alfreton Motorway Link Ind Est DE55 159 A1
Alfreton Rd
 Blackwell DE55 147 C1
 Breadsall DE21 205 B3
 Codnor DE5 170 B1
 Holbrook DE21 191 B1
 Little Eaton DE21 205 B3
 Matlock DE4 143 C2
 Nottingham NG7 268 A2
 Pinxton NG16 160 B2
 Selston DE55, NG16 171 B3
 Tibshelf DE55 147 B2
Alfreton Trad Est DE55 159 A1
Algar Cl S2 43 C4
Algar Cres S2 43 C4
Algar Dr S2 43 C4
Algar Pl S2 43 C4
Algar Rd Sheffield S2 43 C4
 Stoke-on-T ST4 269 A1
Alice St DE1 267 C4
Alice Way S18 76 C3
Alicehead Rd S45 113 A1
Alison Cl DE21 219 C4
All Saints CE Fst Sch ST14 196 C3
All Saints CE Inf Sch
 Matlock DE4 143 A3
 Sutton in A NG17 148 C1
All Saints CE Jun Sch DE4 143 A4
All Saints CE Prim Sch DE45 125 B3
All Saints Croft DE14 254 B4
All Saints Ct DE3 217 B1
All Saints Prim Sch SK6 23 A3
All Saints RC Sch NG19 268 A4
All Saints Rd
 Burton u T DE14 254 B4
 Stoke-on-T ST4 269 B1
All Saints' RC Prim Sch SK13 10 B1
All Saints' Rd DE4 143 A3
All Saints' St NG7 268 A2
All Saints' Terr 3 NG7 268 A2
Allan Ave DE23 230 C4
Allan La DE56 168 A3
Allandale Rd DE75 181 B1
Allcroft St NG19 136 B2
Allen Hill DE4 143 A3
Allen La Ashover DE4 144 B3
 Weston Underwood DE6 188 B1
Allen St Derby DE24 232 C3
 Stoke-on-T ST4 269 A2
Allen's Green Ave NG16 171 C3
Allen's La ST14 224 C1
Allenby Cl S8 56 C4
Allenby Dr S8 56 C4
Allendale DE7 208 C4
Allendale Rd S42 114 C2
Allendale Way NG19 136 C1
Allenpark Inf Sch DE24 232 C3
Allens Croft ST14 224 C1
Allenton Com Prim Sch DE24 232 B3
Allestree Cl DE24 232 C4
Allestree Dr S18 56 B1
Allestree La DE22 204 B2
Allestree Park★ DE22 204 C3
Allestree St DE24 232 C4
Alley The DE4 154 B2
Alley Wlk DE6 201 C4
Allison Ave DE11 256 A2
Allison Gdns DE7 195 A1
Allissa Ave DE5 180 C4
Allpits Rd S44 96 C2
Allport Terr
 Barrow Hill S43 78 A2
 Blackwell DE55 147 B1
Allsops Pl S41 95 C4
Allstone Lee DE56 178 C3
Alma Cl NG1 268 B2
Alma Cres S18 57 A2
Alma Hill NG16 195 C4
Alma Hts DE3 217 C1
Alma Rd
 North Wingfield S42 132 A4
 Nottingham NG3 268 C2
 Selston NG16 171 C3
 Swadlincote DE11 255 C3
 Tideswell SK17 69 B3
Alma St Alfreton DE55 159 A2
 Buxton SK17 85 B4
 Derby DE22 267 A2
 Fenton ST4 269 C1
 Melbourne DE73 252 A4
 North Wingfield S42 131 C3
 Ripley DE5 169 B2
Alma St W S40 95 C1
Almond Ave Ripley DE5 180 B4
 Shirebrook NG20 119 C3
Almond Cl Calow S44 97 A2
 Kimberley NG16 195 C4
Almond Cres S43 79 B2
Almond Ct DE13 240 C1
Almond Dr S21 60 B3
Almond Gr
 Swadlincote DE11 256 A3
 Swanwick DE55 170 A4
Almond Rise NG19 136 C1
Alms Rd DE6 211 B1
Almshouses Etwall DE65 229 A3
 Newton Solney DE15 248 C4
Alnwick Dr S12 44 A3
Alnwick Rd S12 44 A3
Alpha Rd SK23 34 C1
Alpha Terr NG1 268 A2
Alpine Gr S43 97 A4
Alport Ave Buxton SK17 85 B4
 Sheffield S12 44 C3
Alport Cl Belper DE56 179 A3
 Hulland Ward DE6 175 C2
Alport Dr S12 44 C3
Alport Gr Gamesley SK13 9 C1
 Sheffield S12 44 C3
Alport La Spout DE4,DE56 166 B2
 Youlgreave DE45 125 B3
Alport Pl S12 44 C3
Alport Rd S12 44 C3
Alport Rise S18 56 B1
Alport Way SK13 9 C1
Alsager Cl DE21 206 A1
Alsfeld Way SK22 33 A4
Alsop Gr SK17 85 C4
Alsop Pl SK17 85 C4
Alsop Way SK17 85 C4
Alston Rd SK23 47 A3
Alstonefield YH★ DE6 149 C2
Alstonfield Dr DE22 204 C1
Althorp Cl DE55 169 C4
Althorpe St 26 NG7 268 A2
Alton Cl Chesterfield S40 114 A4
 Derby DE22 204 B2
 Dronfield S18 75 B4
Alton Hill S42 130 B3
Alton La S45 130 B2
Alton Rd Belper DE56 179 B2
 Denstone ST14 196 B3
Alton Rise DE4 142 C4
Alts Nook Way DE72 234 C1
Alum Chine Cl S41 115 B4
Alum Cl DE24 233 B4
Alvaston Inf Sch DE24 233 B4
Alvaston Jun Com Sch DE24 233 B4
Alvaston St DE24 233 A4
Alvenor St DE7 194 C1
Alverton Cl DE3 217 B1
Alward's Cl DE24 233 A3
Ambaston La
 Elvaston DE72 234 A3
 Shardlow DE72 234 C2
Amber Bldgs DE55 159 A3
Amber Cl DE56 168 A3
Amber Cres S40 95 B1
Amber Croft S43 97 B4
Amber Ct Belper DE56 179 A3
 Chesterfield S41 266 B4
 Heanor DE75 181 C1
Amber Dr NG16 182 A1
Amber Gr DE55 158 C1
Amber Hill DE4 168 A4
Amber Hts DE5 169 B1
Amber La S45 129 B2
Amber Pl S45 131 A2
Amber Rd
 Bullbridge DE56 168 A3
 Derby DE22 204 B1
Amber St DE24 232 B4
AMber Trad Est NG16 195 B4
Amber View Rd DE56 168 A4
Amberdene DE4 143 B3
Ambergate Prim Sch DE56 167 C2
Ambergate Sta DE56 167 C2
Ambergrove DE56 168 A2
Amberlands DE13 240 C1
Amberley Cl DE7 208 C3
Amberley Dr Buxton SK17 85 B3
 Derby DE24 231 C3
Ambervale Cl DE23 231 A3
Amberwood DE11 256 A3
Ambleside Cl
 Chesterfield S41 95 B4
 Mosborough S20 59 C3
Ambleside Dr
 Bolsover S44 98 C1
 Eastwood NG16 182 B2
Ambrose Terr DE1 218 C3
Amen Alley DE1 267 B3
American Adventure Theme Pk The★ DE75 194 A3
Amesbury Cl S41 95 C4
Amesbury La DE21 205 C1
Ameycroft La DE4 143 A4
Amilda Ave DE7 208 C4
Amy St DE22 218 C2
Anchor Ave SK23 47 B3
Anchor Cl DE11 256 B2
Anchor Fold SK23 47 B3
Anchor Rd NG16 182 B1
Anchor Row DE7 208 C4
Anchor Sq DE45 109 B3
Ancient High House Mus★ ST16 269 B4
Anderby Gdns DE11 255 C1
Anderson Cl S43 77 C2
Anderson Sch The SK17 85 A4
Anderson St DE24 232 C4
Andrew Ave DE7 209 A4
Andrew Cl DE23 230 C4
Andrew St SK6 15 A1
Andrews Dr
 Langley Mill NG16 182 A2
 Stanley DE7 193 A1
Andwell La S10 42 C3
Angel Row NG1 268 B1
Angel Yd S40 266 B3
Angerford Ave S8 43 A2
Anglers' La DE21 220 C2
Anglesey Rd
 Burton u T DE14 254 A4
 Dronfield S18 76 A4
Anglesey St DE21 219 B4
Angleton Ave S2 44 B4
Angleton Cl S2 44 B4
Angleton Gdns S2 44 B4
Angleton Gn S2 44 B4
Angleton Mews S2 44 B4
Ankerbold Rd S42 131 B4
Ann St S80 81 C1
Anncroft Rd SK17 84 B3
Anne Potter Cl DE72 221 B3
Annesley Cl
 Chesterfield S41 115 B4
 Sheffield S8 56 C4
Annesley Gr NG1 268 A2
Annesley Rd S8 56 C4
Anns Grove Prim Sch S2 43 A4
Anns Rd S2 43 A4
Anns Rd N S2 43 A4
Annwell La LE65 257 C1
Anslow La DE13 240 A1
Anslow Rd DE13 238 A1
Anson Wlk DE7 194 C2
Anstee Rd NG10 236 B3
Anstey Ct DE21 206 A1
Anstey Rise NG3 268 C2
Anthony Bek Com Prim Sch NG19 134 C3
Anthony Cres DE24 232 C3
Anthony Dr DE24 232 C3
Anthony Gell Sch DE4 165 C4
Antill St NG9 223 B3
Apiary Gate DE74 247 A2
Apperknowle Jun Sch S18 58 A1
Appian Cl DE72 221 B1
Appian Way
 Clay Cross S45 131 B1
 Derby DE24 233 B3
Apple St SK14 15 B4
Apple Tree Rd SK22 24 A1
Appleby Cl DE7 208 C3

Appleby Ct DE22 ....218 C2
Appleby Glade DE11 ...255 B1
Appleby Rd NG19 ....134 C3
Applecross Ct DE24 ...231 C2
Appledore Dr DE21 ..206 A1
Appledown Way DE23 ..231 A3
Applegarth Cl S12 .....44 A3
Applegarth Dr S12 ....44 A3
Applegate Cl DE21 ...206 A2
Applemead Cl DE21 ...205 C1
Appleton Cl
  Burton u T DE15 ....254 C4
  Derby DE21 ....220 A4
  Swadlincote DE11 ...255 C3
Appleton Dr Belper DE56 179 A3
  Glossop SK13 ....17 C4
Appletree Cl DE72 ...221 B1
Appletree Dr S18 .....57 A1
Appletree Rd
  Bolsover S44 ....80 A1
  Hatton DE65 ....227 B1
Appletree Wlk S18 .....57 A1
Applewood Cl
  Belper DE56 ....179 A3
  Uttoxeter ST14 .....210 A1
Appleyard Ct
  Chesterfield S41 ....266 A4
  █Stafford ST16 ....269 B4
Aquinas St ST4 ....269 B2
Aragon Ct █ NG7 ...268 A2
Arbor Cl DE22 ....267 A2
Arbor Gr SK17 ....84 C4
Arbor Low (Henge)★
  DE45 ....123 C2
Arboretum Prim Sch
  DE23 ....219 A1
Arboretum Sq DE23 ...267 C1
Arboretum St
  Derby DE23 ....267 C1
  Nottingham NG1,NG7 ..268 A2
Arbour Cl S41 ....115 B3
Arbour Hill DE7 ......207 C1
Arbourthorne Cotts S2 .43 B4
Arbourthorne Jun Sch
  S2 ....43 B3
Arbourthorne Rd
  Sheffield S2 ....43 B4
  Sheffield S2 ....43 C3
Arcadia Ave NG20 ....119 C3
Archdale Cl S2 ....44 A4
Archdale Pl S2 ....44 A4
Archdale Rd S2 ....44 A4
Archer Rd NG9 ....223 C3
Archer St Derby DE24 ..219 C1
  Ilkeston DE7 ....194 C2
Arden Cl Chesterfield S40 .95 B3
  Derby DE23 ....218 C1
  Glossop SK13 ....17 A4
Arden Est SK22 ....33 B4
Arden St SK22 ....33 B4
Ardleigh Cl DE3 .....230 B4
Ardmore Cl S42 ......268 C1
Ardsley Cl Heanor DE75 .182 A1
  Sheffield S20 ....44 C1
Ardsley Dr S20 ....44 C1
Ardsley Gr S20 ....44 C1
Ardsley Rd S40 ....95 A2
Argyle Cl
  Market Warsop NG20 ..120 C2
  Sheffield S8 ....43 A3
Argyle Rd S8 ....43 A3
Argyle St Derby DE22 ..218 C2
  Langley Mill NG16 ...182 B2
Argyll Cl DE21 ....220 C3
Argyll Rd DE5 ....169 C1
Arkendale Wlk █ DE24 .231 C2
Arkwright Cl DE4 ....127 B2
Arkwright Dr SK6 .....23 A3
Arkwright Prim Sch S44 .97 B2
Arkwright Rd SK6 .....23 A3
Arkwright St Derby DE24 232 B4
  Wirksworth DE4 ....165 C4
Arleston La DE24 ....231 C4
Arleston St DE23 ....231 C4
Arlington Ave NG19 ..136 C2
Arlington Dr Derby DE24 232 C3
  Swanwick DE55 .....169 C4
Arlington Rd DE23 ...218 B1
Armitage Dr NG10 ...237 A4
Arms Park Dr S20 .....59 C3
Armscote Cl DE21 ...206 A1
Armstrong Ave ST16 ..269 C4
Armstrong Rd NG19 ..268 A4
Armytage Ind Est S41 ..77 A1
Arnfield La SK13 ......9 C4
Arnhem Terr DE21 ...220 C2
Arnold & Carlton Coll of F Ed
  NG1 ....268 B2
Arnold Ave
  Long Eaton NG10 ....236 A2
  Sheffield S12 ....44 A1
Arnold Cl DE11 ......261 C4
Arnold Cres NG10 ....236 A2
Arnold St DE22 ......218 B3
Arnot Rd DE14 ....254 A4
Arnside NG9 ....223 C3
Arnside Cl
  Chesterfield S41 .....76 B1
  Swadlincote DE11 ...256 B1
Arran Cl Derby DE24 ..231 C2
  Stapleford NG9 .....209 C1
Arran Ct DE55 ....159 B1
Arridge Rd DE21 .....219 C3

Arrowscroft Way SK14 ...9 B3
Arthington St S8 ......43 A3
Arthur Ave NG9 ......223 C4
Arthur Ct █ DE23 ....219 A1
Arthur Hind Cl DE22 ..218 C4
Arthur Mee Ctr (Coll of F Ed)
  The NG9 ....223 B4
Arthur Mee Rd NG9 ..223 C3
Arthur Short Cl S80 ...82 A3
Arthur St Alfreton DE55 .159 A3
  Derby DE1 ....267 B5
  Draycott DE72 .....234 C4
  Linton DE11 ....261 C4
  Mansfield NG18 ....268 C3
  Nottingham NG7 ....268 A2
  Pinxton NG16 ......160 B2
Arthurs Ct DE13 .....240 C1
Arthurs View DE56 ....56 B1
Arthurs Way S33 ......38 A1
Artic Way NG16 .....195 B4
Artisan View S8 ......43 A3
Arun Dale NG19 .....136 B1
Arundel Ave DE3 ....217 C1
Arundel Cl
  Chesterfield S41 .....95 C4
  █Dronfield S18 ......56 B1
  Sandiacre NG10 ....223 A2
Arundel Ct █ S43 ....78 C1
Arundel Dr Derby DE21 .220 C3
  Mansfield NG18 ....268 A4
Arundel Grange SK13 ...17 A4
Arundel St Derby DE22 .218 B2
  Glossop SK13 ....10 B1
  Nottingham NG7 ....268 A2
Ascot Ave NG16 .....195 C4
Ascot Cl Burton u T DE15 .248 A2
  West Hallam DE7 ...207 B4
Ascot Dr DE24 ....232 B4
Ascot Park Est NG10 ..223 B4
Ascot Pl DE7 ....208 B3
Ascott Dr DE11 ......256 A4
Ascroft Ct S41 ....77 A2
Ash Acre DE56 ......179 B2
Ash Cl Aston-on-T DE72 .246 A4
  Derby DE22 ....204 B2
  Killamarsh S21 ......60 B3
  Mottram in L SK14 ....9 A2
  Pinxton NG16 ......160 B1
Ash Cres Eckington S21 .59 A1
  Ripley DE5 ....180 B4
Ash Croft Prim Sch
  DE24 ....231 C1
Ash Ct DE55 ....159 B2
Ash Gr Brinsley NG16 ..182 B4
  Chinley SK23 ....34 C1
  Long Eaton NG10 ...236 B3
  Mastin Moor S43 ....79 A2
  Sandiacre NG10 ....223 A4
  Selston NG16 ......171 C4
  Shirebrook NG20 ...119 C3
  Stapleford NG9 ....223 B3
Ash Grove La DE65 ..241 B3
Ash La Chesterfield S21 ..77 B4
  Eckington S18 ....57 C2
  Sutton on t H DE6,DE65 .228 C4
Ash Mount Rd NG16 ..182 A2
Ash St Buxton SK17 ...85 A3
  Ilkeston DE7 ....194 C2
  Mosborough S20 .....59 B4
Ash Terr SK17 ....85 B4
Ash Tree Ave NG19 ..136 B3
Ash Tree Cl
  Breadsall DE21 .....205 C2
  Chesterfield S40 .....95 B2
  Duffield DE56 ......190 C3
  Swadlincote DE11 ...255 C3
Ash Tree Rd S43 ......80 C1
Ash Vale S40 ....95 A2
Ash View Cl DE55 ....229 A2
Ashbourne Ave
  Derby DE22 ....218 A3
  █Glossop SK13 ......17 C4
  Ilkeston DE7 ....194 B1
Ashbourne Cl █ S40 ...95 A3
Ashbourne Ct
  Derby DE22 ....218 C3
  █Glossop SK13 ......17 C4
  Ilkeston DE7 ....194 B1
Ashbourne Dr DE11 ..256 A1
Ashbourne La
  Alstonefield DE6 ....149 A1
  Chapel-en-le-F SK23 ..47 B3
Ashbourne Rd
  Alstonefield DE6 ....149 A2
  Belper DE56 ....178 B2
  Buxton SK17 ....85 B2
  Church Broughton DE65 .213 C2
  Derby DE22 ....218 A4
  Kirk Langley DE6 ...202 B2
  Mackworth DE22 ...217 C4
  Mayfield DE6 ....184 B4
  Rocester ST14 .....196 C2
  Shottle DE56 ....177 B2
  Uttoxeter ST14 .....210 A1
Ashbourne St
  Nottingham NG7 ....268 A2
  Scarcliffe NG20 .....119 C3
Ashbrook DE15 ......248 A1
Ashbrook Ave DE72 ..221 B1
Ashbrook Cl DE22 ...204 B2
Ashbrook Inf & Jun Sch
  DE72 ....221 B1
Ashbury Dr S8 ....43 B1
Ashbury La S8 ....43 B1
Ashby Ave NG19 .....136 B3
Ashby La DE11 ....257 B1
Ashby Rd
  Blackfordby DE11,LE65 .257 B1
  Breedon on t H DE73 .252 C1
  Burton u T DE15 ....248 A1
  Melbourne DE73 ....252 A3

Ashby Rd continued
  Moira DE12 ....262 C2
Ashby Rd E DE15 ....248 C1
Ashby St DE24 ....232 C3
Ashcombe Gdns DE21 .206 A1
Ashcroft Cl DE24 ....232 C4
Ashcroft Dr S41 ......77 A1
Ashdale Cl DE15 ....255 A4
Ashdale Rd DE7 .....209 A3
Ashdene Gdns DE56 ..179 B3
Ashdown Dr S40 ......95 B1
Ashe Pl DE23 ....218 C1
Asher La DE5 ....169 B3
Asher La DE6 ....175 C2
Ashes La
  Fenny Bentley DE6 ..162 A1
  Glossop SK13 ....10 A1
Ashfield Ave Derby DE21 219 C4
  Mansfield NG18 ....268 B4
  Somercotes DE55 ...159 B1
Ashfield Cl S12 ....43 C2
Ashfield Dr S12 ......43 C2
Ashfield Gr SK6 ......15 A1
Ashfield Rd
  Chapel-en-le-F SK23 ..47 B3
  Chesterfield S41 ...115 B4
  Glossop SK13 ....9 C2
  Nottingham NG2 ...268 C1
Ashford Ave S42 .....132 A4
Ashford Cl S18 ....75 B4
Ashford Ct
  West Hallam DE7 ...207 B4
  Chesterfield S41 .....96 A3
Ashford Gn SK13 ......9 C1
Ashford La DE45 ......89 B1
Ashford Mews SK13 ...9 B1
Ashford Pl DE7 ......194 C3
Ashford Rd S18 ......75 B4
Ashford Rise DE56 ..179 B3
Ashford St ST4 ......269 C2
Ashforth Ave DE75 ..194 A4
Ashforth St NG3 ....268 B2
Ashfurlong Cl S17 ....55 C4
Ashfurlong Dr S17 ...55 C4
Ashfurlong Rd S17 ...55 C4
Ashgate Ave S40 ......95 B2
Ashgate Croft Sch S40 .95 B2
Ashgate Prim Sch DE22 218 B3
Ashgate Rd S40 ......95 B2
Ashgate Valley Rd S40 .95 B2
Ashgrove Ct DE21 ...206 A1
Ashland Rd S21 ......59 C2
Ashlands Ave ST4 ....269 A2
Ashlands Cres ST4 ...269 A2
Ashlands Gr ST4 .....269 A2
Ashlands Rd ST4 .....269 A2
Ashlar Dr DE12 ......262 C1
Ashlea Dr DE6 ......184 B4
Ashlea Wlk S43 ....81 A3
Ashleigh Ave
  Glossop SK13 ....10 A1
  Sheffield S12 ....43 C3
  Swadlincote DE11 ...255 C3
Ashleigh Cl S41 ......77 A2
Ashleigh Croft S12 ...43 C3
Ashleigh Ct S21 ......59 B1
Ashleigh Dr Derby DE73 .232 C1
  Sheffield S12 ....43 C3
Ashleigh Pl S12 ......43 C3
Ashleigh Rd S43 ......80 A4
Ashleigh Wlk S8 ......56 C3
Ashley Cl Killamarsh S21 .60 B3
  Overseal DE12 .....262 A2
  Tansley DE4 ....144 A2
Ashley Ct DE15 .....248 A2
Ashley La S21 ....60 B3
Ashley St Derby DE22 ..218 B3
  Nottingham NG3 ...268 C2
Ashlyn Rd DE7 ......267 D3
Ashmeadow DE7 ....207 A4
Ashmeadow Ct DE6 ..185 B4
Ashmore Ave S21 .....59 A1
Ashop Rd DE56 .....179 B3
Ashopton Ave DE23 ..231 C4
Ashopton Dr S33 .....40 A2
Ashopton Rd Bamford S33 40 A3
  Chesterfield S41 .....95 B3
Ashover Cl DE21 ....219 C4
Ashover New Rd DE55,
  S45 ....145 C4
Ashover Prim Sch S45 .129 C2
Ashover Rd Alton S45 ..130 C3
  Ashover S45 ....129 C2
  Derby DE22 ....204 B1
  █Derby, Chaddesden
    DE21 ....219 C4
  Staveley S43 ....97 B3
  Swadlincote DE11 ...255 C3
  Tupton S42 ....131 A4
Ashover View DE55 ..147 B1
Ashton Cl
  Chesterfield S40 ....114 B4
  Derby DE3 ....217 B2
  Killamarsh S21 ......60 B3
  Swanwick DE55 ....170 A4
Ashton Gdns
  Clay Cross S42 .....131 A3
  █Glossop SK13 ......17 A4
Ashton St SK13 ....17 A4
Ashton Way DE56 ...179 B2
Ashtree Ave DE24 ...232 A4
Ashurlong Pk S17 ....55 C4
Ashurst Cl S40 ....94 C3
Ashview Cl NG10 ....236 A4
Ashwater Cl DE24 ...231 C1
Ashwell Ave NG19 ...136 C3
Ashwood SK13 ....16 C4
Ashwood Cl Buxton SK17 .85 B4

Ashwood Cl continued
  Mansfield Woodhouse
    NG19 ....136 C3
Ashwood Rd Buxton SK17 .66 C1
  Disley SK12 ....32 B3
Ashworth Ave
  Burton u T DE15 ....248 B1
  Derby DE21 ....219 C3
Ashworth Dr NG19 ..136 C2
Ashworth La SK14 ....9 A2
Ashworth St ST4 ....269 C1
Asker La DE4 ....143 B3
Askerfield Ave DE22 ..204 B2
Askew Gr DE65 .....242 B1
Askew Rd S2 ....43 A4
Asline Rd S2 ....43 A4
Aspen Bsns Ctr DE21 ..220 A2
Aspen Cl Buxton SK17 ..66 A1
  Killamarsh S21 ......60 B3
Aspen Ct NG19 .....136 C1
Aspen Dr DE21 ......220 B2
Aspen Rd S21 ....59 A1
Aspen Rise DE55 ....146 B1
Aspen Way SK6 ....32 A4
Aspenshaw Rd SK22 ..24 C2
Aspley Cl S40 ....95 C3
Astcote Cl DE75 ....182 A1
Asterdale Prim Sch
  DE21 ....220 C2
Asterdale View DE21 .220 C2
Astil St S45 ....254 C4
Astlow Dr DE56 .....179 A3
Aston Cl Derby DE73 ..245 A4
  Dronfield S18 ....57 B2
Aston Ct Ilkeston DE7 ..194 C1
  Staveley S43 ....78 C1
Aston Dr DE11 ......256 A4
Aston Gn NG9 ......223 C2
Aston Hall Dr DE72 ..246 A4
Aston Hall Hospl DE72 246 A3
Aston La Derby DE73 ..233 A1
  Hope S33 ....39 B2
  Shardlow DE72 ....234 C1
  Sudbury DE6 ....226 A3
  Wensley DE4 ....142 B4
Aston Rd DE23 ......231 B3
Aston-on-Trent Prim Sch
  DE72 ....246 A4
Astorville Park Rd DE73 232 C1
Astwith Cl S44 ......116 C1
Astwith La S44,S45 ..133 A3
Atchison Gdns DE21 ..59 B2
Atherfield Gdns NG16 .182 C2
Atherton Ave SK14 ...9 A2
Atherton Cl S2 ....43 C3
Atherton Gr SK14 ....9 A2
Atherton Rd
  Ilkeston DE7 ....194 B2
  Sheffield S43 ....43 C3
Athlestan Way DE13 ..240 B1
Athlone Cl DE21 ....219 B4
Athol Cl Chesterfield S40 .114 A4
  Derby DE24 ....231 C2
Atkin Pl █ S2 ....43 A4
Atkins Way ST14 ....196 B2
Atkinson Mews S21 ..59 B2
Atlantic Cres S8 ......56 C3
Atlantic Dr S8 ....56 C3
Atlantic Rd S8 ....56 C3
Atlantic Way S8 ......56 C3
Atlantic Wlk S8 ......56 C3
Atlow Brow DE6 ....173 B2
Atlow Cl S40 ....95 A3
Atlow La DE6 ....175 A4
Atlow Rd DE21 ......219 C4
Attenborough Nature
  Reserve★ NG9 ....237 B4
Attewell Cl DE72 ....235 A4
Attewell Rd NG16 ...195 A4
Attlebridge Cl DE21 ..219 B4
Attlee Rd S43 ....97 C4
Atworth Gr DE23 ....230 C4
Aubrey Ave █ NG2 ..268 C1
Auburn Cl DE7 ......207 A4
Auckland Cl DE3 ....217 C2
Auckland Dr S20 .....59 C3
Auckland Rise S20 ...59 C3
Auckland Way S20 ...59 C3
Auction Cl DE6 .....173 B1
Auden Cl DE65 .....227 A4
Audley Cl DE7 ......194 B2
Audrey Cres NG19 ..136 B3
Audrey Dr DE21 ....220 A4
Audrey Rd S13 ....44 B4
Aughton Cl S13 ......44 B4
Aughton Cres S13 ...44 B4
Aughton Dr S13 ......44 B4
Augusta St █ DE23 ..219 A1
Aukland's Pl S40 ....266 B2
Ault Hucknall La S44 .134 C4
Aults Cl DE65 ......230 B1
Austen Ave Derby DE23 .231 A4
  Long Eaton NG10 ...236 B3
Austin Friars ST17 ..269 B3
Austin Sq DE23 ....231 C4
Austin St NG20 ....120 A2
Austins Dr NG10 ...223 A2
Austwick Gr ST4 ....269 A1
Autumn Gr DE21 ...219 C3
Avarne Pl █ ST16 ..269 B4
Avenue 1 S41 ....115 A4
Avenue 2 S41 ....115 A4
Avenue 3 S41 ....115 A4
Avenue 4 S41 ....115 A4
Avenue 5 S41 ....115 A4
Avenue 6 S41 ....115 A4
Avenue 7 S41 ....115 A4

Avenue 8 S41 ....115 A4
Avenue 12 S41 ....72 A2
Avenue E NG3 ......268 C1
Avenue Rd
  Chesterfield S41 .....96 A4
  Duffield DE56 .....190 C3
Avenue The
  Bakewell DE45 .....109 A3
  Belper DE56 ....178 C1
  Chapel-en-le-F SK23 ..46 C1
  Derby DE1 ....267 B2
  Derby, Chaddesden DE21 219 C3
  Dronfield S18 ....57 A1
  Glossop SK13 ....10 A2
  Killamarsh S21 ......60 B1
  Northwood DE4 ....127 A3
  Stoney Middleton S32 .72 A2
  Tissington S32 .....162 A3
  Weston-on-T DE72 ..245 C3
Averham Cl Derby DE21 .206 A1
  Swadlincote DE11 ...256 A2
Aviemore Cl S43 ......77 C2
Aviemore Way DE24 ..231 C2
Avis Ave DE75 ......193 C4
Avocet Ct █ DE24 ..231 B2
Avon Cl Derby DE24 ..231 B1
  Dronfield S18 ....57 A2
  Stafford ST16 .....269 C4
  Swadlincote DE11 ...256 A4
Avon Ct S41 ....266 B4
Avon Rise ST16 .....269 C4
Avon St DE24 ....232 C4
Avon Way
  Burton u T DE15 ....248 A1
  Hilton DE65 ....228 C1
  Marston on D DE65 .240 B4
Avondale Cl NG10 ...236 A3
Avondale Rd
  Bolsover S44 ....118 A4
  Chesterfield S40 ....266 A4
  Derby DE23 ....267 B1
  Derby, Spondon DE21 .220 B3
  Ilkeston DE7 ....208 B3
  Staveley S43 ....97 B4
Avonlea Cl DE7 .....209 A3
Avonmouth Dr DE24 .232 C4
Awdishaw La DE6 ...213 B3
Awsworth Inf Sch NG16 195 B2
Awsworth Jun Sch
  NG16 ....195 B2
Awsworth La NG16 ..195 B2
Awsworth Rd DE7 ...194 C1
Aycliffe Gdns DE24 ..232 C2
Aylesbury Ave DE21 .219 C4
Aylward Cl S2 ....43 C4
Aylward Rd S2 ....43 C4
Ayncourt Rd S42 ...132 A4
Ayr Cl DE21 ....220 B2
Ayr St NG7 ....268 A2
Azalea Ave DE55 ...170 A4
Azalea Cl DE55 .....159 C2
Azalea Ct NG16 ....195 B4

B

Babbacombe Cl DE24 .233 B4
Babbington Cl DE13 ..239 B3
Babbington La NG16 ..195 C2
Babbington St DE55 ..148 A3
Babbs La DE6 ......211 B1
Babington Cl S2 ......43 C4
Babington Ct S2 .....43 C4
Babington Hospl DE56 .178 C1
Babington La DE1 ...267 B2
Babworth Ct NG18 ..268 A4
Bacchus Way DE55 ..147 A3
Back Bridge St SK22 ..24 C1
Back Browning St ST16 269 A4
Back Croft S45 .....131 C4
Back Jodrell St SK22 .33 A4
Back La
  Alderwasley DE56 ..166 C3
  Alstonefield DE6 ...149 C2
  Biggin SK17 ....138 C1
  Brackenfield DE55 ..146 A1
  Calow S44 ....116 A4
  Castle Donington DE74 .247 A3
  Darley Dale DE4 ...127 C2
  Derby DE73 ....233 A1
  Ellastone DE6 .....183 A2
  Elton DE4 ....140 C3
  Glapwell S44 ....118 A1
  Glossop SK13 ....16 C3
  Hathersage S32 .....53 A4
  Hilton DE65 ....228 B1
  Ilkeston DE7 ....194 C1
  Mottram in L SK14 ....9 A2
  Palterton S44 ......118 A3
  Pilsley S45 ....132 B1
  Ripley DE5 ....169 B3
  Shirley DE6 ....200 B4
  Spout DE4 ....166 B2
  Stonebroom DE55 ..146 A2
  Sutton in A NG17 ..148 C2
  Thorpe Salvin S80 ...63 A3
  Thurvaston DE6 ...215 A2
  Tibshelf DE55 .....147 C3
  Unstone S18 ....57 C1
  Wessington DE55 ..157 C4
  Youlgreave DE45 ..125 C4
Back Mellor Rd SK22 ..24 B1
Back Moor SK14 ......9 A2
Back Rd S18 ....57 C1
Back Sitwell St DE1 .267 B2
Back South St S43 ....77 B2
Back St S33 ....38 B2
Back Union Rd SK22 ..33 B4

Back Wyver La DE56 ....178 C3
Backhill La DE6 ....151 C2
Backhouse La DE72 ....221 B3
Backmoor Cres S8 ....43 B1
Backmoor Rd S8 ....43 B1
Bacon Cl NG16 ....195 A4
Bacon La DE5 ....169 A3
Bacons La S40 ....115 A4
Baden Powell Ave S40 ...266 B1
Baden Powell Rd S40 ....266 B1
Badger Cl
  Chesterfield S40 ....114 A4
  Derby DE21 ....220 C3
Badgers Way SK13 ....17 A4
Badgery Cl ST14 ....210 A1
Bag La Marchington ST14 .224 C1
  Roston DE6 ....197 C4
Bage Hill S42 ....113 C3
Baggaley Cres NG19 ......136 A1
Bagot St DE7 ....207 B4
Bagshaw Cavern★ S33 ......52 C1
Bagshaw Hill DE45 ....109 B3
Bagshaw La SK17 ....48 A3
Bagshaw St Derby DE24 ...232 C4
  Pleasley NG19 ....135 A2
Bagshaw's Rd S12 ....44 A3
Bagshawe Ave SK23 ....46 C3
Bagthorpe La S42 ....94 A2
Bailey Ave DE12 ....262 A2
Bailey Brook Cres NG16 .182 A2
Bailey Brook Dr NG16 ...182 A2
Bailey Brook Ind Est
  NG16 ....182 A1
Bailey Brook Wlk NG16 ..182 A2
Bailey Cres NG19 ....268 A4
Bailey Dr S21 ....60 C4
Bailey Gr SK17 ....85 C4
Bailey Grove Rd NG16 ...182 B1
Bailey St Derby DE23 ....267 A1
  Stafford ST17 ....269 B3
  Stapleford NG9 ....223 B3
Bainbridge Rd S44 ....98 C1
Bainbridge St DE23 ......219 A2
Baines Wood Cl S41 ....94 B4
Bains Dr DE72 ....221 B1
Bakeacre La DE65 ....230 C2
Baker Ave DE75 ....193 C4
Baker Cl
  Somercotes DE55 ....170 B4
  Stanley DE7 ....193 A4
Baker Dr S21 ....60 B3
Baker Rd Eastwood NG16 .195 B4
  Mansfield Woodhouse
  NG19 ....136 B3
Baker St Burton u T DE15 .254 C4
  Creswell S80 ....81 C1
  Derby DE24 ....232 C4
  Ilkeston DE7 ....194 C1
  Swadlincote DE11 ......256 B2
Baker's La Cromford DE4 .155 A3
  Doveridge DE6 ....211 B1
Bakers La DE4 ....156 A4
Bakestone Moor S80 ....81 C3
Bakewell Bank SK13 ....9 B1
Bakewell CE Inf Sch
  DE45 ....109 B3
Bakewell Dr DE74 ....247 A1
Bakewell Fold SK13 ....9 B1
Bakewell Gdns 26 SK13 ....9 B1
Bakewell Gn
  27 Gamesley SK13 ....9 B1
  Swadlincote DE11 ......255 C3
Bakewell Gr SK13 ....9 B1
Bakewell Lea 28 SK13 .....9 B1
Bakewell Meth Jun Sch
  DE45 ....109 B2
Bakewell Mews SK13 ....9 B1
Bakewell Rd Baslow DE45 .91 C2
  Buxton SK17 ....85 B4
  Darley Dale DE4 ....142 C4
  Long Eaton NG10 ......236 C3
  Matlock DE4 ....143 A3
  Over Haddon DE45 .....109 A1
  Staveley S43 ....97 B3
Bakewell St Derby DE22 ..218 C4
  Stoke-on-T ST4 ....269 A1
Bakewell Station Ind Est
  DE45 ....109 C4
Bakewell Wlk SK13 ....9 B1
Balaclava Rd DE23 ....232 A4
Balderton Cl NG19 ......268 A4
Baldwin St NG7 ....268 A2
Balfour Rd Derby DE23 ...232 A4
  Stapleford NG9 ....223 B3
Balham Wlk DE22 ....218 A3
Balk Pas ST16 ....269 A4
Ball Hill DE55 ....160 B3
Ball La DE72 ....234 A3
Ballacraine Dr DE5 .....169 C1
Ballards Way DE72 ......221 B1
Ballater Cl Derby DE24 ..231 C2
  Mansfield NG19 ....135 C1
Balleny Cl DE21 ....205 C1
Ballidon Cl 17 S41 ....95 B3
Balliol St ST4 ....269 B2
Balmoak La S41 ....96 B3
Balmoral Cl Derby DE23 .218 A1
  Heanor DE75 ....181 B1
  Mansfield Woodhouse
  NG19 ....136 C3
  Sandiacre NG10 ....223 A2
Balmoral Cres S18 ....56 B1
Balmoral Dr NG19 ....135 C1
Balmoral Ho DE24 ....219 B1
Balmoral Rd
  Borrowash DE72 ....221 B1

Balmoral Rd continued
  Burton u T DE15 ....248 A2
  Ilkeston DE7 ....208 B3
  Nottingham NG1 ....268 A2
Balmoral Way S43 ....77 C2
Baltimore Cl 8 DE11 ....256 A4
Bamber St ST4 ....269 B2
Bamburgh Cl DE21 ....220 B2
Bamford Ave
  Derby DE23 ....231 C4
  North Wingfield S42 ...131 C4
Bamford Fold SK13 ....9 C1
Bamford Gn SK13 ....9 C1
Bamford Ho S33 ....40 A2
Bamford La SK13 ....9 C1
Bamford Prim Sch S33 ....40 A2
Bamford Rd S43 ....97 B3
Bamford St
  Chesterfield S43 ....77 B2
  Newton DE55 ....148 A2
  Ripley DE5 ....180 B4
Bamford Sta S33 ....40 A1
Bamsbrook La S43 ....80 B1
Banbury Ave NG9 ....223 C2
Banchory Cl NG19 ......135 C1
Bancroft Cl DE65 ....228 B1
Bancroft Dr DE22 ......204 B2
Bancroft La NG18 ......268 A4
Bangor St DE21 ....219 C4
Bank Bldgs DE56 ....190 C4
Bank Cl Bolsover S44 ....99 A2
  Creswell S80 ....100 B4
  Shirebrook NG20 ......119 C2
  Tibshelf DE55 ....147 C3
Bank Gdns DE4 ....143 A3
Bank House Ct DE6 .....164 A1
Bank La SK13 ....10 A4
Bank Pas 9 ST16 ....269 A4
Bank Rd Chesterfield S41 .96 A3
  Matlock DE4 ....143 B3
Bank Row SK13 ....10 A4
Bank Side Derby DE22 ...204 C1
  Hartington SK17 ....137 B3
Bank St Brimington S43 ...96 B4
  Broadbottom SK14 ......16 A4
  Chesterfield S40 ....95 C2
  Glossop SK13 ....17 B4
  Glossop, Hadfield SK13 ..10 A3
  Hayfield SK22 ....25 B2
  Langley Mill NG16 ....182 B2
  Long Eaton NG10 ......236 C3
  Somercotes DE55 ......170 A4
  Swadlincote DE11 ......262 A4
Bank Terr SK13 ....10 A3
Bank The Bonsall DE4 ...142 B1
  Glossop SK13 ....17 B4
  Stoney Middleton S32 ..71 C2
Bank Top La S32 ....72 B4
Bank Vale Rd SK22 ....25 B2
Bank View SK17 ....69 A3
Bank View Rd
  Derby DE22 ....218 C4
  Nether Heage DE56 ....168 B1
Bank Wood Cl S40 ....95 A4
Bankbottom SK13 ....10 A3
Bankerwall La DE6 .....183 B4
Bankfield Dr Derby DE21 220 C2
  Ilkeston DE7 ....208 A3
Bankgate SK14 ....16 A4
Bankholmes Cl DE24 ....231 C1
Banks Rd NG9 ....223 C1
Banksburn Cl DE75 .....181 B1
Bankside DE45 ....125 A3
Bankside Cl SK6 ....15 B1
Bankswood Cl SK13 ....10 A2
Bankwood Cl S14 ....43 B3
Bankwood Rd S14 ....43 B3
Bannell's La DE3 ....229 C4
Bannels Ave DE23 ......231 A4
Banton's La DE73 ......251 A2
Banwell Cl DE3 ....217 B2
Bar Croft 18 S40 ....95 B3
Bar Rd Baslow DE45 ......91 C3
  Curbar S32 ....72 C1
Barber Cl DE7 ....194 C2
Barber St SK13 ....10 A3
Barber's La S21 ....60 B4
Barbon Cl S40 ....95 C3
Barchester Cl DE21 .....206 A1
Barclay Ct DE7 ....194 B2
Barden Dr DE22 ....204 C2
Bardolph Cl DE11 ......255 C2
Bare La DE72 ....221 B3
Barf Cl DE3 ....217 C1
Bargate DE65 ....179 B1
Bargate La DE65 ....242 A3
Bargate Rd DE56 ....179 A1
Barholme Cl S41 ....95 A4
Barker Ave E NG10 .....223 B3
Barker Ave N NG10 .....223 A3
Barker Cl ST16 ....269 A4
Barker Fold S40 ....95 B2
Barker Gate
  Ilkeston DE7 ....194 C1
  Nottingham NG1 ....268 B1
Barker La S40 ....95 B2
Barker St NG17 ....148 C2
Barklam Cl DE12 ....262 C1
Barlborough Hall Sch
  S43 ....61 A1
Barlborough Prim Sch
  SK43 ....80 A4
Barlborough Rd S43 ......80 B3

Barley Cft Derby DE73 ...232 C1
  South Normanton DE55 .160 A2
Barley Cl DE21 ....205 B4
Barley Croft DE56 ......179 A1
Barley Dale Dr NG9 .....209 B1
Barley La S42 ....95 A3
Barley Mews S18 ....56 A1
Barleycorn Cl
  Burton u T DE15 ....248 A1
  Derby DE21 ....206 B1
Barleycroft SK13 ....9 C2
Barling Dr DE7 ....194 B1
Barlow CE Prim Sch S18 .75 C2
Barlow Dr N NG16 ......195 A4
Barlow Dr S NG16 ......195 A4
Barlow Lees La S18 ......75 C4
Barlow Rd Barlow S18,S42 94 C4
  Chapel-en-le-F SK23 ....47 B3
  Staveley S43 ....78 C1
Barlow St DE1,DE23 .....267 C1
Barlow View S18 ....76 A4
Barlow Wood Dr SK6 .....23 A2
Barmote Croft DE4 .....154 C1
Barms Way SK17 ....66 B1
Barn Cl
  Castle Donington DE74 .247 A2
  Chesterfield S41 ....95 B3
  Findern DE65 ....230 B1
  Glossop SK13 ....17 A4
  Quarndon DE22 ....204 B3
Barn Furlong DE45 ....90 A2
Barnard Ave S18 ....57 B2
Barnard Rd DE21 ....205 B1
Barnes Ave S18 ....56 C1
Barnes Croft
  Heanor DE75 ....193 B4
  Wirksworth DE4 ....165 C4
Barnes Gn DE22 ....218 A4
Barnes La S18 ....56 B1
Barnes Rd S41 ....96 C1
Barnfield ST4 ....269 A1
Barnfield
  Holmewood S42 ....132 C4
  1 Staveley S43 ....78 C1
Barnfield Dr S32 ....52 C4
Barnfield Wlk S43 ....78 C1
Barnfields S32 ....52 C4
Barnham Cl S40 ....114 A4
Barnhill Gr S20 ....59 B4
Barnsfold Ct SK22 ....25 B2
Barnsley La DE4,DE56 ...165 C1
Barnstaple Cl DE21 .....206 A1
Barnston Rd NG2 ......268 C2
Barnwell Cl ST14 ......210 A2
Barnwell La DE4 ....155 A3
Barnwood Cl DE3 ....217 B1
Baron Cl DE21 ....206 B2
Barrack Rd S18 ....58 A1
Barrack Yd DE55 ....170 B4
Barratt Rd S21 ....59 B1
Barrett St DE24 ....233 A4
Barrie Dr DE21 ....231 C3
Barringer Rd NG19 .....136 B1
Barrington Cl DE13 ....240 B1
Barron's Way DE72 .....221 B1
Barroon The DE74 .....247 A2
Barrow Hill Prim Sch
  S43 ....78 A2
Barrow La DE73 ....244 B3
Barrow St S43 ....78 C1
Barrows Hill La NG16 ...171 B3
Barry Rd S43 ....96 C2
Barson Gr SK17 ....85 C1
Bartle Ave S12 ....43 C2
Bartle Dr S12 ....43 C2
Bartle Rd S12 ....43 C2
Bartle Way S12 ....43 C2
Barton Cl DE21 ....220 C3
Barton Cres S40 ....95 A3
Barton Hill DE4 ....126 B1
Barton Knoll DE56 .....179 B2
Barton Knowle DE56 ...179 B2
Barton Rd
  Long Eaton NG10 .....237 A3
  Sheffield S8 ....43 A3
Barton St
  Burton u T DE14 ......254 B4
  Clowne S43 ....80 C2
Barton Turn DE13 .....253 A1
Barway DE6 ....211 C4
Basegreen Ave S12 ......44 A2
Basegreen Cl S12 ....44 B2
Basegreen Cres S12 .....44 A2
Basegreen Dr S12 ....44 A2
Basegreen Pl S12 ....44 A2
Basegreen Rd S12 ....44 B2
Basegreen Way S12 .....44 B2
Basil Cl S41 ....266 B3
Basildon Cl DE24 ......232 C3
Basingwerke Ct S42 .....25 B2
Baslow Cl Gamesley SK13 .9 C1
  Long Eaton NG10 .....236 A3
Baslow Dr DE22 ....204 C2
Baslow Fold SK13 ....9 C1
Baslow Gn Gamesley SK13 .9 C1
  Swadlincote DE11 ......255 C3
Baslow Gr SK17 ....85 C3
Baslow Mews SK13 ....9 C1
Baslow Rd
  Bakewell DE45 ....109 B4
  Curbar S32 ....72 B1
  Holymoorside S42 ......94 B1
  Totley S17 ....55 B2
Bass St DE22 ....218 B3
Bass's Cres DE11 ......261 C4
Bassett Cl Ilkeston DE7 .194 B3
  Kimberley NG16 ......195 C4
Bassett La S10 ....42 C3

Bassett Rd NG16 ....195 C4
Bassett The NG20 ......119 B3
Bassettbarn La S42 ....130 A3
Bassingham Cl DE21 ...206 A1
Bassington Cl DE21 ....206 A1
Batch La DE6 ....224 A4
Bate Wood Ave S43 ......97 A3
Bateman Cl S43 ....77 B2
Bateman St DE23 ......219 B2
Batemill Rd SK22 ....24 B1
Batemoor Cl S8 ....57 A3
Batemoor Dr S8 ....57 A3
Batemoor Pl S8 ....57 A3
Batemoor Rd S8 ....57 A3
Batemoor Wlk S8 ....57 A3
Bath Ct ST17 ....269 B3
Bath La Ashover S45 ....129 C3
  Mansfield NG18 ....268 C4
  Market Warsop NG19 ..120 B1
  Moira DE12 ....262 B2
Bath Rd Buxton SK17 ....85 A3
  Derby DE3 ....217 C1
Bath St Bakewell DE45 .109 B3
  Derby DE1 ....267 B4
  Ilkeston DE7 ....194 C1
  Mansfield NG18 ....268 C2
  Nottingham NG1 ......268 B2
  Stoke-on-T ST4 ......269 B2
Bath Terr ST4 ....269 B2
Batham Gate
  Bradwell SK17 ....50 A2
  Peak Forest SK17 .....48 C1
Batham Gate Rd SK17 ...67 C3
Batham Rd S33 ....51 A4
Bathurst Rd S44 ......117 C4
Bathurst Terr NG20 ...100 C1
Batley La NG19 ....134 C2
Batt St 10 S8 ....43 A4
Baulk La Beeston NG9 ..223 C4
  Hathersage S32 ....41 A1
Baum's La NG18 ....268 C3
Baverstock Cl DE73 ....232 C2
Bawtry Wlk NG3 ....268 C2
Baxter Hill NG19 ......134 C2
Baxter Sq DE23 ....231 C3
Bay Ct S21 ....60 B3
Baycliffe Dr S40 ....95 B2
Bayleaf Cres DE21 .....206 A2
Baysdale Croft S20 ......59 B4
Baysdale Dr NG19 .....136 C1
Bayswater Cl DE22 ....217 C3
Bayswater Rd NG16 ...195 C4
Bazley Rd S2 ....43 C3
Beacomfold SK6 ....15 A2
Beacon Dr DE13 ......240 A2
Beacon Hill Rise NG3 ..268 C2
Beaconsfield St NG10 ..236 C4
Beard Cres SK22 ....33 B4
Beardall St NG18 .....268 B4
Beardmore Cl DE21 ....205 C1
Beards Rd DE11 ....256 A4
Bearwood Hill Rd DE15 248 A2
Beast Market Hill NG1 ..268 B1
Beatrix Dr SK13 ....9 C2
Beatty St DE24 ....232 C4
Beatty Wlk DE7 ......194 C2
Beauchief Abbey La S8 ..56 C4
Beauchief Dr S8,S17 ....56 B4
Beauchief Gdns S55 ....170 A4
Beaufit La NG16 ......160 C1
Beaufort Com Prim Sch
  DE21 ....219 B4
Beaufort Ct Ind Est
  DE21 ....219 B4
Beaufort Gdns DE21 ...219 B4
Beaufort Rd
  Burton u T DE15 ......248 A1
  Derby DE24 ....231 B1
Beaufort St DE21 .....219 B4
Beaulieu Way DE55 ....170 A4
Beaumaris Ct DE21 ....220 C3
Beaumont Cl
  Barrow u T DE73 .....244 A3
  Belper DE56 ....179 B2
  Stapleford NG9 ......209 C1
Beaumont Dr SK17 .....47 C1
Beaumont St NG2 .....268 C1
Beaumont Wlk DE23 ..231 C3
Beaurepaire Cres DE56 179 A3
Beaureper Ave DE7 ...204 C2
Beauvale Dr DE7 .....194 C3
Beazley Ave NG18 ....268 A4
Becher St DE23 ......219 A1
Beck Cl S44 ....99 B1
Beck Cres NG19 ......268 A4
Beck St NG1 ....268 B2
Beckenham Way DE22 .218 A3
Becket Ave S8 ....56 B3
Becket Cres S8 ....56 C3
Becket Prim Sch DE22 218 C2
Becket Rd S8 ....56 C3
Becket St DE1 ....267 B3
Becket Well La DE1 ...267 B3
Becket Wlk S8 ....56 C3
Beckett Ave NG19 ....135 C1
Beckford Rd NG2 .....268 C1
Beckingham Ct NG19 ..268 A4
Beckitt Cl DE24 ......233 A4
Becksitch La DE56 ....178 C1
Bedehouse La DE4 ....155 A3
Bedford Ave ST16 ....269 C4
Bedford Ct NG9 ......209 C1
Bedford Rd DE15 .....254 B4
Bedford Row NG1 ....268 B2
Bedford St DE22 .....218 B2

Bedgrave Cl S21 ....60 C4
Bee Hives The DE11 ...256 A4
Beech Ave Alfreton DE55 159 A3
  Borrowash DE72 ....221 B2
  Breaston DE72 ....235 C4
  Creswell S80 ....81 C1
  Derby DE24 ....233 A4
  Glossop SK13 ....17 A4
  Hulland Ward DE6 ....175 C2
  Long Eaton NG10 .....223 C1
  Mansfield NG18 ......268 B3
  Melbourne DE73 ......252 A4
  New Mills SK22 ....24 B1
  Pinxton NG16 ....160 C2
  Quarndon DE22 ......204 A3
  Ripley DE5 ....169 B1
  Sandiacre NG10 ......223 A4
  Willington DE65 ......242 A3
Beech Cl Belper DE56 ..179 A2
  Kilburn DE56 ....192 A4
Beech Cres Eckington S21 .59 A1
  Glapwell S44 ....134 A4
  Killamarsh S21 ....60 B3
Beech Ct DE21 ....220 B3
  Derby DE24 ....218 C4
  Etwall DE65 ....229 B2
  Findern DE65 ....230 C1
Beech Dr Ashbourne DE6 185 B4
Beech Gdns DE24 .....233 A4
Beech Gr
  Long Duckmanton S44 ..98 A2
  South Normanton DE55 160 A3
  Swadlincote DE11 .....255 C3
Beech Hill Ave NG19 ..135 C1
Beech Hill Cres NG19 ..135 C1
Beech Hill Dr NG19 ...135 C1
Beech Hill Specl Sch
  NG19 ....135 C1
Beech La
  Burton u T DE13 ......240 C1
  Dove Holes SK17 ......66 C4
  West Hallam DE7 .....207 B4
Beech Rd SK23 ....45 C4
Beech Rise SK23 ....45 B3
Beech St S43 ....78 A1
Beech Tree Ave S43 ...136 A3
Beech Tree Dr S43 .....80 C3
Beech Way
  Clay Cross S45 ....131 C1
  Dronfield S18 ....57 A2
Beech Wlk Cromford DE4 155 A3
  Derby DE23 ....218 B1
Beecham Ave NG3 ....268 C2
Beechcroft DE21 ......205 B4
Beechcroft Ave ST17 ..269 A3
Beechdale Cl S40 ....95 B2
Beechdale Rd
  Alfreton DE55 ....159 B2
  Mansfield NG19 ......136 C1
Beeches Ave Derby DE21 220 B3
  Sheffield S2 ....43 B4
Beeches Dr S2 ....43 B4
Beeches The Crich DE4 .156 C1
  Heanor DE75 ....193 B4
Beechfield Rd SK13 .....9 C2
Beechley Dr DE21 .....206 A1
Beechway SK13 ....16 C4
Beechwood Cl DE56 ...178 C3
Beechwood Cres DE23 231 B4
Beechwood Dr SK6 .....23 A3
Beechwood Rd S18 .....56 C1
Beehive Rd S40 ....95 B1
Beeley Cl Belper DE56 .179 B3
  Creswell S80 ....81 B1
  Derby DE22 ....204 B3
  Derby, Oakwood DE21 ..205 C1
  North Wingfield S42 ...132 A4
  Staveley S43 ....97 B3
Beeley La DE4 ....112 A2
Beeley View S40 ....114 A4
Beeley Way S43 ....97 B3
Beelow Cl SK17 ....47 C1
Beeston Cl S18 ....56 B1
Beetwell St S40 ....266 B2
Beggarway La DE45 ....90 A3
Beighton St DE5 ......169 C1
Beldon Cl S2 ....43 B4
Beldon Pl S2 ....43 B4
Beldon Rd S2 ....43 B4
Belfast Wlk DE21 .....220 A2
Belfield Ct Etwall DE65 229 A2
  Heanor DE75 ....181 C1
Belfield Gdns NG10 ...236 C4
Belfield Rd Etwall DE65 229 B2
  Swadlincote DE11 .....256 A3
Belfield St DE7 ....194 C1
Belfield Terr DE65 ....229 A2
Belfit Dr S42 ....114 C1
Belfmoor Cl S80 ....82 A3
Belfry Cl DE3 ....217 C1
Belfry The DE13 ......240 B1
Belgrade Ave SK23 ....34 C1
Belgrave Cl DE56 .....179 B3
Belgrave Sq S2 ....43 A4
Belgrave St DE23 .....267 B1
Belklane Dr S21 ....60 C4
Bell Ave DE72 ....246 A4
Bell Cotts DE6 ....224 C4
Bell La Bonsall DE4 ...142 B1
  Doveridge DE6 ....224 B4
  Hartshorne DE11 .....257 A2
Bellar Gate NG1 ......268 B1
Belle Acre Cl 11 DE56 .178 C2

Belle View Rd DE6 .....173 A1
Belle Vue Ave DE5 .....180 B3
Belle Vue Cl S43 .....96 B4
Belledere Cl DE55 .....169 C4
Bellevue Ct NG3 .....268 C2
Bellhouse La S43 .....78 C2
Bellhouse View S43 .....78 C2
Bellingham Ct DE22 .....204 B1
Bells End Rd DE12 .....253 B1
Bellsfield Cl S80 .....82 A3
Belmont Ave DE72 .....235 C4
Belmont Dr
　Borrowash DE72 .....221 A1
　Marple SK6 .....15 A1
　Staveley S43 .....78 C1
Belmont Prim Sch DE11 256 B2
Belmont St DE11 .....256 B2
Belmont Terr [2] SK17 .....85 A4
Belond La S45 .....113 B1
Belper Ho DE21 .....220 C2
Belper La DE56 .....178 C3
Belper Rd
　Ashbourne DE6 .....173 C1
　Derby DE1 .....218 C4
　Holbrook DE56 .....191 B4
　Kilburn DE56 .....179 C1
　Morley DE7 .....192 C1
　Shirland DE55 .....146 B1
　Stanley DE7 .....193 A1
　West Hallam DE7 .....207 B4
Belper Sch DE56 .....179 B2
Belper Sports Ctr DE56 179 B2
Belper St Ilkeston DE7 .....208 C4
　Mansfield NG18 .....268 C4
Belper Sta DE56 .....178 C2
Belper Way NG18 .....268 C4
Belsize Cl DE22 .....217 C3
Belton Dronfield S18 .....56 B1
　Sandiacre NG10 .....223 A2
Belton Dr DE5 .....169 C1
Belvedere Ave S40 .....114 C4
Belvedere Cl
　Chesterfield S40 .....114 A4
　Derby DE3 .....217 B2
Belvedere Rd DE11 .....256 C1
Belvedere St NG18 .....268 B3
Belvedere Terr SK17 .....85 A3
Belvoir Cl Breaston DE72 235 B4
　Ilkeston DE7 .....208 B3
　Long Eaton NG10 .....236 C3
Belvoir Cres DE11 .....256 A3
Belvoir Hill NG2 .....268 C1
Belvoir St DE23 .....218 C1
Belvoir Way DE55 .....159 B1
Bembridge Dr DE24 .....233 B4
Bemrose Com Sch
　DE22 .....218 B2
Bemrose Gate S33 .....40 A3
Bemrose Mews DE22 ..218 B2
Bemrose Rd DE24 .....232 C4
Benbow Ave DE73 .....252 A4
Bench Rd SK17 .....85 B4
Benches La SK6 .....15 C2
Bend Oak Dr S18 .....248 B2
Bend Oak Jun Sch DE15 248 B2
Bendall Gn DE23 .....231 B3
Beninmoor Way S40 .....114 C4
Benjamin Outram Bsns Ctr
　DE5 .....180 C4
Benmore Ct DE21 .....206 A2
Benner Ave DE7 .....209 A3
Bennerley Ave DE7 .....194 C2
Bennerley Fields Sch
　DE7 .....194 C2
Bennerley Sch DE7 .....194 C2
Bennett St Buxton SK17 .....85 B3
　Derby DE24 .....232 B3
　Hollingworth SK14 .....9 B3
　Long Eaton NG10 .....223 B1
　Sandiacre NG10 .....223 A3
Bennetts La DE4 .....168 A4
Bennington Wlk NG19 .136 C2
Bennion Gr ST14 .....196 C3
Bennison Gdns S45 .....131 B2
Bensley Cl DE73 .....233 A1
Benson Ct DE24 .....232 C4
Bent La
　Church Broughton DE65 .....227 B3
　Darley Dale DE4 .....127 B3
　Matlock DE4 .....143 A4
　Spout DE4,DE56 .....166 B3
　Staveley S43 .....79 A2
　Tissington DE6 .....162 B3
Bent The S32 .....72 C2
Bent's La S18 .....57 B1
Bentfield Rd DE56 .....168 B1
Bentham Rd S40 .....95 C3
Bentick St NG18 .....268 C4
Bentinch Dr S43 .....81 A2
Bentinck Rd S44 .....98 C4
Bentink Cl S80 .....81 B1
Bentley Brook S28 .....228 C1
Bentley Cl Alfreton DE55 159 C4
　Matlock DE4 .....143 B4
Bentley Dale DE11 .....257 A2
Bentley Fields Open Farm*
　DE6 .....199 B1
Bentley Rd
　Castle Donington DE74 .246 C2
　Uttoxeter ST14 .....210 A1
Bentley St DE24 .....232 C3
Benton Dr SK6 .....23 B4
Bents Cres S18 .....57 B2
Bents La S18 .....57 B2

Bentside Rd SK12 .....32 B3
Beowulf Covert DE13 .240 A1
Beresford Ave
　Ashbourne DE6 .....173 B1
　Chapel-en-le-F SK23 .....47 B3
Beresford Cl S45 .....131 B1
Beresford Dale DE11 .255 C1
Beresford Dr
　Derby DE21 .....220 C2
　Ilkeston DE7 .....194 C3
Beresford La SK17 .....137 B1
Beresford Pl DE56 .....168 A3
Beresford Rd
　Chapel-en-le-F SK23 .....47 B3
　Long Eaton NG10 .....236 A3
　Mansfield Woodhouse
　NG19 .....136 B3
Beresford St NG18 .....268 C3
Berkeley Ave NG10 .....236 B3
Berkeley Cl DE23 .....231 B4
Berkeley Cl [1] NG1 .....268 B2
Berkley Ct SK23 .....45 B3
Berkshire St DE21 .....219 B4
Berle Ave DE75 .....181 C1
Bermuda Ave DE21 .....205 B3
Bernard Ave NG19 .....136 A3
Bernard Cl S43 .....96 C4
Bernard Ct DE11 .....256 B2
Bernard Rd NG19 .....268 A4
Bernard St Glossop SK13 .10 B1
　Swadlincote DE11 .....256 B2
Bernard Walker Ct SK6 .15 A1
Berners Cl S2 .....43 C3
Berners Dr S2 .....43 C3
Berners Pl S2 .....43 C3
Berners Rd S2 .....43 C3
Berridge La S45 .....145 A2
Berrisford La DE55 .....145 B4
Berristow La DE55 .....160 B4
Berry Ave S21 .....59 B2
Berry Gdns DE15 .....248 B2
Berry Hedge La DE15 .248 B2
Berry Hill Rd NG18 .....268 C4
Berry Park Cl DE22 .....204 C1
Berry St
　North Wingfield S42 .....131 C3
　Stoke-on-T ST4 .....269 B2
Bertrand Ave S45 .....131 B2
Berwick Ave
　Chesterfield S40 .....114 C4
　Derby DE21 .....219 B4
Berwick Cl DE24 .....233 A3
Berwick Dr DE24 .....231 B2
Berwick Rd SK17 .....85 B2
Borwin Cl NG10 .....223 A1
Berwyn Cl S40 .....95 B3
Bessalone Dr DE56 .....179 A3
Bessell La NG9 .....223 B3
Bessie La S33 .....51 A3
Best Ave DE15 .....248 A1
Besthill Cotts SK14 .....16 A4
Besthorpe Cl DE21 .....206 A1
Besthorpe Ct NG19 .....268 A4
Bestwick Ave DE75 .....182 A1
Bestwick Cl DE7 .....209 A2
Bestwood Dr S45 .....131 B2
Bestwood Pk S45 .....131 B3
Bestwood Rd NG16 .....160 C1
Bethel Terr S80 .....63 C4
Bethulie Rd DE23 .....232 A4
Betjeman Sq DE24 .....232 A3
Betlingspring La DE6 ..184 B2
Betony Cl S21 .....60 A3
Bevan Dr S43 .....97 A4
Bevan Rd S45 .....131 B1
Bevan St DE55 .....146 C1
Beverley Dr NG16 .....195 C4
Beverley Rd DE14 .....254 A4
Beverley St DE24 .....219 B1
Beverleys Rd S8 .....43 C4
Bewdley Cl DE73 .....233 A2
Bexley Cl S14 .....10 B2
Bicester Ave DE24 .....231 B1
Bickley Moss DE21 .....206 A1
Bideford Cl DE5 .....169 B1
Bideford Dr DE23 .....231 B3
Bidston Cl DE4 .....143 B4
Bidworth La SK13 .....9 B1
Biggin CE Prim Sch
　SK17 .....138 B2
Biggin Cl S45 .....131 B1
Biggin La DE6 .....176 A2
Biggin The DE74 .....247 A2
Bigginmill La DE6 .....176 B3
Bilberry Cl DE21 .....205 C1
Bilberry Wlk NG3 .....268 C2
Bilby Gdns [3] NG3 .....268 C2
Bilby La S43 .....77 C1
Billam St S21 .....59 A2
Billingsley Ave NG16 .160 B2
Bilton St ST4 .....269 B1
Bingham St DE24 .....232 C4
Bings Rd SK23 .....45 C4
Bingswood Ave SK23 ..45 C4
Bingswood Ind Est SK23 .45 C4
Bingswood Rd SK23 ....45 C4
Binscombe La DE21 .....205 C2
Birch Ave Ilkeston DE7 .209 A4
　Swadlincote DE11 .....256 A4
　Toadmoor DE56 .....167 C2
Birch Cl Alfreton DE55 .159 A3
　Burton u T DE14 .....254 A4
　Buxton SK17 .....66 A1
　Denstone ST14 .....196 B3
　Derby DE21 .....221 A3
　Grassmoor S42 .....115 C2
　Killamarsh S21 .....60 B3
　Ripley DE5 .....180 B4

Birch Cl continued
　Wessington DE55 .....157 C4
Birch Farm Ave S8 .....57 A4
Birch Gn SK13 .....10 C1
Birch Gr Hatton DE65 .227 B1
　Shirebrook NG20 .....119 B3
Birch Hall Cl SK22 .....25 A1
Birch Holt Gr S18 .....76 C3
Birch Kiln Croft [13] S43 .96 C4
Birch La S43 .....78 A1
Birch Rd S80 .....82 B3
Birch St NG20 .....120 C3
Birch Vale Ind Est SK22 .25 A1
Birch View Ct S41 .....218 C4
Birch's Terr DE6 .....173 A1
Birchen Cl
　Chesterfield S40 .....95 B3
　[13] Dronfield S18 .....56 B1
Birchen Holme DE55 ...160 A2
Birches Ave DE55 .....157 C3
Birches Fold S18 .....57 B2
Birches La Dronfield S18 .57 B2
　South Wingfield DE55 ...158 A3
Birches Rd DE22 .....204 B2
Birches The SK22 .....25 B1
Birchfield Cl DE73 .....232 C1
Birchfield Pk DE75 .....193 C4
Birchfield Rd DE15 .....254 C3
Birchills The S80 .....81 B1
Birchitt Cl S17 .....56 B3
Birchitt Pl S17 .....56 B3
Birchitt Rd S17 .....56 B3
Birchitt View S18 .....57 A2
Birchlands NG19 .....136 C1
Birchlands Dr S21 .....60 B3
Birchover Edge DE4 ...141 A4
Birchover Ho DE22 .....204 C2
Birchover La DE4 .....141 A4
Birchover Pl DE7 .....194 C3
Birchover Rd
　Birchover DE4 .....126 B2
　Youlgreave DE4 .....126 B2
Birchover Rise DE21 ...205 C1
Birchover Way DE22 ...204 C1
Birchside Ave SK13 .....10 A1
Birchvale Rd S12 .....44 C2
Birchview Cl DE56 .....179 A1
Birchwood Ave
　Derby DE23 .....231 B3
　Long Eaton, Breaston
　NG10 .....236 A4
　Long Eaton, New Sawley
　NG10 .....236 B3
Birchwood Cl
　[25] Mosborough S20 .....59 C4
　South Normanton DE55 .160 C2
Birchwood Cres
　Chesterfield S40 .....114 C4
　Somercotes DE55 .....170 A4
Birchwood Croft [26] S20 .59 C4
Birchwood Ct S40 .....114 C4
Birchwood Dr DE56 .....168 A2
Birchwood Gdns S20 ..59 C4
Birchwood Gr S20 .....59 C4
Birchwood La
　Pinxton DE55 .....159 C2
　Somercotes DE55 .....159 C2
　South Normanton DE55 .159 C2
Birchwood Rd DE55 .....159 B2
Birchwood Rise [27] S20 .59 C4
Birchwood View
　Ashbourne DE6 .....173 B2
　Mosborough S20 .....59 C4
Birchwood Way
　[28] Mosborough S20 .....59 C4
　Somercotes DE55 .....159 B1
Bircumshaw's Rd DE75 .181 C1
Bird St S43 .....78 C1
Birdcage Wlk DE22 .....217 C3
Birdcroft La DE7 .....208 C3
Birdfield S12 .....44 B1
Birdholme Cres S40 ...115 A4
Birdholme Inf Sch S40 .115 A4
Birding St NG19 .....136 A1
Birdsgrove La
　Ashbourne DE6 .....172 B2
　Mayfield DE6 .....172 B2
Birdwood St DE23 .....218 C1
Birk Hill Inf Sch S21 ...59 A1
Birkdale Ave DE14 .....254 A3
Birkdale Cl Derby DE3 .218 A1
　Ilkeston DE7 .....194 B1
Birkdale Dr S40 .....114 B4
Birkin Ave S42 .....115 B1
Birkin La Grassmoor S42 .115 C1
　Holmewood S42 .....116 A2
　Wingerworth S40,S42 ...114 B1
Birkin La W S42 .....115 C1
Birkinstyle La DE55 .....146 C2
Birkinstyle La DE55 .....146 C2
Birkland Ave
　Mansfield Woodhouse
　NG19 .....136 B2
　Nottingham NG1 .....268 B2
Birkland St NG18 .....268 C4
Birks Cl S80 .....82 B3
Birks St ST4 .....269 B1
Birley Brook Dr S40 .....95 A4
Birley Com Coll S12 ....44 B2
Birley Croft S41 .....95 A4
Birley La S12 .....44 C1
Birley Moor Ave S12 ...44 C2
Birley Moor Cl S12 .....44 C2
Birley Moor Cres S12 ..44 C1
Birley Moor Dr S12 .....44 C1
Birley Moor Pl S12 .....44 C1

Birley Moor Rd
　Sheffield S12 .....44 C2
　Sheffield S13 .....44 C1
Birley Moor Way S12 ...44 C1
Birley Spa La S12 .....44 C1
Birley Spa Prim Sch S12 44 C2
Birley St NG9 .....223 B3
Birley Vale Ave S12 .....44 B3
Birley Vale Cl S12 .....44 B3
Birstall Cl S41 .....95 B4
Biscay Ct DE21 .....206 B1
Bishop Lonsdale CE Prim Sch
　DE22 .....218 C2
Bishop Pursglove CE Prim
　Sch SK17 .....69 B2
Bishop St Alfreton DE55 .159 A3
　Eastwood NG16 .....182 C1
　Mansfield NG18 .....268 B3
Bishop Stamer CE Prim Sch
　ST4 .....269 B1
Bishop's Ct DE73 .....252 A4
Bishop's Dr DE21 .....205 C1
Bishopdale Cl NG10 ....236 A3
Bishopdale Dr S20 .....59 A4
Bishopdale Rise S20 ...59 A4
Bishops Ct S8 .....43 A3
Bishopberry Flats S20 ..59 C4
Bishops Gate DE11 .....256 C1
Bishops House Mus* S8 43 A2
Bishops La SK17 .....84 C1
Bishopscourt Rd S8 .....43 A3
Bispham Dr NG9 .....223 B1
Bitham Ct DE13 .....240 B1
Bitham La DE13 .....240 B1
Blaby Cl DE23 .....231 C3
Black Harry La S32 .....71 A1
Black Hills Dr DE7 .....208 C3
Black Rock* DE4 .....155 A2
Black Tor Rd DE4 .....154 B4
Blacka Moor Cres S17 ..55 B3
Blacka Moor Rd S17 ....55 B3
Blacka Moor View S17 ..55 B3
Blackberry Flats S20 ...59 C4
Blackberry La S16 .....269 A1
Blackberry Way DE56 ..179 C1
Blackbird Row DE56 ...179 B4
Blackbrook La SK23 .....47 C3
Blackburn Pl DE7 .....194 C2
Blackcliff Field Cl S80 ..82 A3
Blackden Cl DE56 .....179 C2
Blackdown Ave S40 .....95 A3
Blackfordby St Margaret's CE
　Prim Sch DE11 .....257 A1
Blackmore St DE23 .....231 C4
Blackmount Ct [7] DE24 .231 B2
Blackpit La DE6 .....224 A4
Blackpool St DE14 .....254 B4
Blackrocks Ave DE4 ...142 C4
Blacks La S42 .....131 C4
Blackshaw Rd SK13 .....10 C1
Blacksmith La S44 .....97 A2
Blacksmith's La
　Egginton DE65 .....241 A3
　Newton Solney DE15 ...248 C4
　Woodville DE11 .....256 C2
Blacksmiths Yd DE4 .....127 C1
Blackstock Cl S14 .....43 B1
Blackstock Cres S14 ....43 B1
Blackstock Dr S14 .....43 B1
Blackstock Rd S14 .....43 B1
Blackstone Cl DE55 .....170 B4
Blackthorn Cl
　Chesterfield S41 .....115 B4
　Derby DE21 .....205 C1
　Melbourne DE73 .....252 A4
Blackthorn Dr S20 .....59 C4
Blackthorne Cl DE56 ...179 C1
Blackwall La S42 .....176 A4
Blackwell La
　Melbourne DE73 .....252 A4
　Monyash DE45 .....107 A2
Blackwell Mill Cotts
　SK17 .....87 A3
Blackwell Prim Sch
　DE55 .....147 C1
Blackwell Rd NG17 .....148 C2
Bladon House Sch
　DE15 .....248 A3
Bladon St DE15 .....248 A3
Bladon View DE13 .....241 A1
Bladon's Yd DE13 .....240 A1
Blagdon Cl DE4 .....127 B2
Blagreaves Ave DE23 ..231 B3
Blagreaves La DE23 ....231 B3
Blair Gr NG10 .....223 A3
Blair Ho DE23 .....231 B1
Blake Cres NG18 .....268 C4
Blake Rd NG9 .....223 C3
Blake St Ilkeston DE7 ...194 C1
　Mansfield Woodhouse
　NG19 .....136 A1
Blakebrook Dr DE73 ....233 A2
Blakeley La DE65 .....229 A1
Blakelow Dr DE65 .....229 A2
Blakelow La DE4 .....142 A2
Blakemere La DE4 .....141 C1
Blakemore Ave DE73 ...252 A4
Blakeney Ct Derby DE21 .206 B1
　Mansfield Woodhouse
　NG19 .....136 C2
Blakiston St ST16 .....269 B4
Blanch Croft DE73 .....252 A4
Blandford Ave NG10 ...236 A3
Blandford Cl DE24 .....233 B3
Blandford Dr S41 .....95 C4
Blankney Cl DE24 .....231 B1
Bleasby St NG2 .....268 C1
Blencathra Dr DE3 .....230 C4

Blenheim Ave DE55 ....170 A4
Blenheim Cl
　Burton u T DE15 .....248 B2
　[4] Glossop SK13 .....10 A1
　Mansfield NG19 .....136 B1
　[3] Swadlincote DE11 ...256 A4
Blenheim Dr DE21 .....204 B2
Blenheim Mews DE65 ..229 B2
Blenheim Par DE22 .....204 B2
Blenheim Pl NG17 .....148 C2
Blenheim Rd DE6 .....185 C4
Blenheim St ST4 .....269 C1
Blenhiem Ct Belper DE56 179 B3
　Sandiacre NG10 .....223 A2
Blessed William Howard RC
　High Sch ST17 .....269 A3
Blind La Bolsover S44 ..98 C2
　Breaston DE72 .....235 B4
　Darley Dale DE4 .....127 C1
　Kirk Ireton DE6 .....165 A1
　Wirksworth DE4 .....165 C4
Blissworth Way DE55 ..169 C4
Blithe Cl DE65 .....228 C1
Blithfield Gdns DE73 ...233 A1
Bloom St DE1 .....267 B3
Bloomfield Cl Derby DE1 267 C1
　Hilton DE65 .....228 B1
Bloomfield Rd DE55 .....170 A4
Bloomfield St DE1 .....267 D1
Bloomgrove Rd DE7 ...194 C1
Blore Cl DE6 .....185 B4
Blossom Cres S12 .....44 A2
Blue Bell Cl S43 .....169 C2
Blue Bell Hill Jun & Inf Schs
　NG3 .....268 C2
Blue Bell Hill Rd NG3 ..268 C2
Blue John Cavern* S33 .37 C2
BLue Lodge S43 .....77 B2
Bluebank View S43 .....77 B2
Bluebell Cl
　Barlborough S43 .....80 A3
　Derby DE24 .....231 B1
　Donisthorpe DE12 .....262 C1
　Hayfield SK22 .....25 B2
　Shirebrook NG20 .....119 B3
　Somercotes DE55 .....159 C1
　Underwood Green NG16 .171 C1
Bluebell Croft DE4 .....143 A2
Bluebell Hill DE55 .....146 B2
Bluebell Pl NG19 .....136 C2
Bluebell Way DE75 .....182 A1
Blueberry Cl S43 .....97 A3
Bluebird Ct DE24 .....231 B2
Bluecoat Cl NG1 .....268 B2
Bluecoat St NG1 .....268 B2
Bluestone La DE15 .....255 A4
Bluestone Prim Sch S2 .43 B4
Blundestone La DE4 ....156 A1
Blunt Ave S43 .....79 B2
Blunt St DE7 .....193 A1
Blyth Cl Chesterfield S40 .114 A4
　Mansfield NG19 .....135 B2
Blyth Pl DE21 .....205 B1
Boadmeadows S Ctr
　DE55 .....160 A2
Boam La DE4 .....142 C4
Boardman Cres ST16 ..269 A4
Boardman Ind Est DE11 255 C2
Boardman Rd DE11 .....255 C1
Boarslack La SK17 .....85 C4
Boat La NG16 .....182 A4
Boatmans Cl DE7 .....194 C1
Bobbin Mill La S40 .....95 B1
Bobbinmill Hill DE56 ...168 A4
Bochum Parkway S8 ....57 B4
Bocking La S8 .....56 C4
Bocking Rise S8 .....56 C4
Boden St DE23 .....219 A1
Bodmin Cl DE24 .....231 B2
Bodmin Way [3] S40 .....95 B3
Bog La DE73 .....251 C3
Boggard La SK13 .....16 B3
Bogguard Rd SK6 .....24 A3
Boggy La Bradwell S33 ..51 A3
　Church Broughton DE65 .227 A4
Bohem Rd NG10 .....223 B2
Boiley La S21 .....60 B2
Boland Rd S8 .....56 B3
Bold La DE1 .....267 B3
Bole Hill S8 .....43 A1
Bole Hill Cotts S44 .....97 A1
Bolehill La Eckington S21 .59 C1
　Eckington, Marsh Lane S21 .58 C1
　Northedge S42 .....130 B4
　Wingerworth S42 .....114 B1
Bolehill Rd DE4 .....155 C4
Boleyn Ct [15] NG7 .....268 A2
Bolsover Castle* S44 ...99 A1
Bolsover CE Jun Sch
　S44 .....99 A1
Bolsover Cl DE5 .....169 C1
Bolsover Com Hospl S44 99 B1
Bolsover Hill S44 .....99 A1
Bolsover Inf Sch S44 ...99 A1
Bolsover Rd Bolsover S44 .98 C3
　Mastin Moor S43 .....79 B1
Bolsover Sch S44 .....99 A1
Bolsover St NG18 .....268 C3
Bolton St DE5 .....169 B4
Boman's La DE56 .....177 C4
Bonchurch Cl DE24 .....233 B3
Bond La DE56 .....168 C1
Bond St Nottingham NG2 .268 C1
　Staveley S43 .....97 B4
Bondgate DE74 .....247 A2
Bondhay La S80 .....62 B1

Bonington Rd NG19 ...268 A3
Bonner's Rd NG16 .....195 B2
Bonnington Cres ST16 .269 A3
Bonnington Dr DE55 ...170 B4
Bonnington Rise SK6 ...23 A4
Bonnyrigg Dr DE21 ...206 A1
Bonsall Bank SK13 ......9 C1
Bonsall CE Prim Sch
DE4 ....142 C1
Bonsall Cl SK13 ....9 C1
Bonsall Ct 2 S41 ......95 B4
Bonsall Dr Derby DE3 ..217 C2
Somercotes DE55 .....170 B4
Bonsall La Alfreton DE55 158 C2
Bonsall DE4 ....141 B2
Winster DE4 ....141 B2
Bonsall St NG10 ......236 C4
Bonsallmoor La DE4 ...141 C1
Bonsalt Dr DE55 ......170 B4
Bonser Cres NG17 .....148 C3
Boon Ave ST4 ....269 B2
Boot Hill DE65 ....242 B2
Booth Ave NG19 .....135 A3
Booth Cl NG3 ....268 B2
Booth Cres NG19 .....135 B1
Booth St Derby DE24 ..232 C4
Hollingworth SK14 ......9 B3
Mansfield Woodhouse
NG19 ....136 A2
Ripley DE5 ....169 C1
Stoke-on-T ST4 ....269 B1
Booth's Ct SK13 ......10 B1
Boothby Ave DE6 .....173 B1
Boothen CE Prim Sch
ST4 ....269 B1
Boothen Ct ST4 ......269 B1
Boothen Gn ST4 ......269 B1
Boothen Old Rd ST4 ..269 B1
Boothen Rd ST4 ......269 B1
Boothenwood Terr ST4 269 B1
Boothgate DE56 ......179 C4
Boots Yd NG17 ....148 C2
Border Cl S43 ....80 C2
Border Cres DE24 .....233 A4
Border La S80 ....80 C2
Borlace Cres NG9 .....223 C3
Borough St DE74 ......247 A2
Borrow Wood Inf & Jun Schs
DE21 ....220 C4
Borrowash By-pass
Borrowash DE72 ......221 B2
Derby DE21 ....220 B2
Borrowash Rd DE21 ...220 C2
Borrowdale Ave S20 ...59 C3
Borrowdale Cl S20 .....59 C3
Borrowdale Dr
Long Eaton NG10 ......236 A3
Mosborough S20 ....59 C3
Borrowdale Rd S20 ....59 C3
Borrowfield Rd DE21 ..220 C2
Borrowfields DE21 ....221 A1
Boscastle Rd DE24 ....233 A4
Boscowan Ct DE7 .....194 C2
Bosley Mews DE56 ....178 C3
Bosnall Ave DE23 .....231 B4
Bostock Rd SK14 ......16 A4
Bostock's La
Risley DE7,DE72 ......222 C2
Sandiacre NG10 ....223 A2
Boston Cl DE21 ....220 B3
Boston St NG1 ....268 B2
Boswell Ct DE6 ....173 A1
Boswell Sq DE23 .....231 C3
Bosworth Ave DE23 ...231 C3
Bosworth Rd DE74 ....246 C2
Bosworth Way NG10 ..236 C2
Botany Ave NG18 .....268 A4
Botany Commercial Pk
NG18 ....268 A4
Botany Dr DE7 ....194 C3
Bothe Cl NG10 ....236 B3
Bottle La NG1 ....268 B1
Bottom Cliff S32 ......71 C2
Bottom Lons DE6 .....176 A4
Bottom Rd S42 ....114 C1
Bottomhill Rd SK17 ....69 C1
Bough La S32 ....72 A1
Boughey Rd ST4 .....269 C2
Boughey St ST4 ......269 B1
Boughton Dr DE55 ....169 C4
Boughton La S43 ....80 B2
Bould St NG19 ....135 C1
Boulevard The SK14 ....9 B2
Boulton Cl S40 ....95 A4
Boulton Dr DE24 .....233 A3
Boulton La
Derby, Allenton DE24 ..232 C3
Derby, Boulton DE24 ..233 A3
Boulton Prim Sch DE24 233 A3
Boundary Cl
Shirebrook NG20 ......119 C3
Staveley S43 ....79 A2
Boundary Gdns DE55 ..147 C3
Boundary La NG16 ....182 C2
Boundary Rd
Derby DE22 ....218 C2
Egginton DE65 ....241 B4
Boundary Wlk NG20 ..100 C1
Bourne Cl Brimington S43 .96 C4
Tutbury DE13 ....239 A3
Bourne Ct DE73 ......251 C4
Bourne Mill Cl S43 .....80 A4
Bourne Sq DE72 .....235 C4
Bourne St DE1 ....267 B2
Bourne Way DE11 ....256 B2
Bournebrook Ave DE4 ..165 C4
Bow St NG19 ....136 C2
Bowbank Cl DE23 .....231 A3

Bowbridge Ave DE23 ..231 B3
Bowden Cl Hayfield SK22 ..25 B2
Swadlincote DE11 .....256 A3
Bowden Cres SK22 .....33 B4
Bowden La S23 ....47 B4
Bowden La SK13 ....10 C1
Bowden Rd SK13 ......10 C1
Bowdon Ave S43 ....80 A3
Bower Dr DE4 ....156 C1
Bower Farm Rd S41 ....77 A1
Bower St DE24 ....232 C4
Bowes Well Rd DE7 ...194 C1
Bowland Cl DE3 ......217 C1
Bowland Dr S40 ......114 A4
Bowland Rd SK13 ......17 A4
Bowlees Ct DE23 .....230 C4
Bowler Dr DE56 ......192 A4
Bowler Rd DE4 ....127 B2
Bowler St DE5 ....180 B4
Bowling Alley DE6 ....168 C1
Bowling Alley La DE6 ..212 A3
Bowling Cl DE7 ......222 C4
Bowling Gn DE4 ......153 A1
Bowling Green La DE4 ..154 C1
Bowling St NG18 .....268 C3
Bowman Cl S12 ....43 C1
Bowman Dr S12 ....44 A1
Bowmer La DE56 .....168 A3
Bowmer Rd DE24 .....219 C1
Bown Cl DE56 ....192 A4
Bowness Cl
Chesterfield S41 ......95 B4
2 Dronfield S18 ....56 C1
Bowness Rd S41 ....95 B4
Bowns Hill DE4 ......157 A1
Bowshaw Ave S8 ......57 A3
Bowshaw Cl S8 ....57 A3
Bowshaw View S8 .....57 A3
Bowstead St ST4 .....269 B2
Boxmoor Cl DE23 .....230 C4
Boyd Gr DE73 ....245 A4
Boyer St DE22 ....267 A1
Boyer Wlk DE22 .....267 A1
Boylestone Rd DE23 ..231 B3
Boythorpe Ave S40 ...266 C4
Boythorpe Bsns Units
S40 ....95 C1
Boythorpe Cres S40 ..266 A1
Boythorpe Mount S40 .266 A2
Boythorpe Rd S40 ....266 A2
Boythorpe Rise S40 ...95 C1
Brabyns Brow SK6 .....23 A4
Bracken Ave S44 .....116 C1
Bracken Cl
Hollingworth SK14 ......9 B3
Long Eaton NG10 ......223 B1
Marple SK6 ....23 B4
Bracken La
Barlborough S43 ....80 A3
Holloway DE4 ....156 A4
Bracken Rd
Long Eaton NG10 ......223 A1
Shirebrook NG20 ......119 B2
Bracken Way SK13 .....17 C4
Bracken's La DE24 ....232 C3
Brackendale Cl
Brimington S43 ....96 B4
Clay Cross S45 ....131 C1
Brackendale La DE6 ...163 C3
Brackendale Rd DE55 ..169 C4
Brackenfield Ave NG16 .136 C2
Brackenfield Dr NG16 ..195 A4
Brackenfield Gr S12 ....44 B2
Brackenfield La
Brackenfield DE55 ....145 B1
Wessington DE55 .....157 B4
Brackenfield Specl Sch
NG10 ....223 A1
Brackens Ave DE24 ...232 C3
Brackensdale Ave DE22 218 A3
Brackensdale Inf Sch
DE22 ....218 A3
Brackensdale Jun Sch
DE22 ....218 A3
Brackenwood Rd DE15 254 C3
Brackley DE55 ....179 C1
Brackley Dr DE21 ....220 C3
Bracknell Dr DE24 ....232 C3
Bracon Dr NG3 ......268 C2
Bradbourne Cl S41 ....97 B4
Bradbourne Ct DE22 ..218 C2
Bradbury Cl
Borrowash DE72 ......221 B1
Chesterfield S40 ......95 C2
Bradbury Dr S42 .....114 C2
Bradbury St S8 ....43 A3
Bradden Ave NG9 ....209 C1
Bradder Way NG18 ...268 B3
Bradgate Cl NG10 ....223 A2
Bradgate Croft S41 ...115 B4
Bradgate Ct DE23 ....231 C3
Bradgate Dr DE5 .....169 A1
Brading Rd DE24 .....233 B3
Bradley CE Prim Sch
DE6 ....186 A4
Bradley Cl Birchover DE4 126 A1
9 Brimington S43 .....96 C4
Bradley Dr DE56 .....179 B4
Bradley La S18 ....75 B2
Bradley St
Burton u T DE15 ......254 C4
Derby DE22 ....218 C4
Sandiacre NG10 ......223 B3
Bradley View DE6 ....173 B2
Bradley Way S43 ......96 C4
Bradmoor Gr DE73 ...233 A1
Bradshaw Ave DE55 ..170 C3

Bradshaw Cres SK6 ....23 A4
Bradshaw Croft DE56 .178 C3
Bradshaw Dr DE56 ...191 B3
Bradshaw La
Old Brampton S42 .....93 C1
Stoney Middleton S32 ..70 C4
Bradshaw Mdw Marple SK6 ..23 A3
Staveley S43 ....97 A3
Bradshaw St NG10 ...236 A3
Bradshaw Way DE1 ...267 C2
Bradway Cl S17 ....56 A3
Bradway Dr S17 ......56 A3
Bradway Grange Rd S17 .56 B3
Bradway Rd S17 ......56 B3
Braeburn Ct DE23 ....218 C1
Braefield Cl DE7 .....208 B3
Braemar Ave NG16 ...182 C1
Braemar Cl
Chesterfield S43 ....77 B2
12 Dronfield S18 ......56 C1
Brafield Cl DE56 .....179 B2
Brailsford Ave
Gamesley SK13 ....9 C1
Swadlincote DE11 .....255 C3
Brailsford CE Prim Sch
DE6 ....201 C4
Brailsford Cl SK13 ......9 C1
Brailsford Gn SK13 .....9 C1
Brailsford Rd DE21 ...219 C4
Braintree Cl DE21 ....205 B3
Braithwell Cl DE22 ...204 C1
Bramah Edge Ct SK13 ..9 C4
Bramall Ct 2 S2 ......43 A4
Bramall La S2 ....43 A4
Bramble Bank SK13 ....17 C4
Bramble Cl
Holmewood S44 ......116 C1
Long Eaton NG10 .....223 A1
Shirebrook NG20 .....119 C3
Bramble Ct DE15 .....254 C3
Bramble Mews DE3 ...217 B1
Bramble St DE1 ......267 A3
Bramble Way DE56 ...179 C1
Bramble Wlk DE12 ...262 A2
Brambleberry Ct DE21 .206 A2
Bramblewick Dr DE23 .231 A3
Brambling Ct S41 .....96 B1
Bramell Cl DE14 .....253 C4
Bramfield Ave DE22 ..218 C2
Bramfield Ct DE22 ...218 C2
Bramham Rd SK6 ......23 A2
Bramley Ave S13 ......44 C4
Bramley Cl Derby DE21 .206 B2
Mosborough S20 ......59 B4
Staveley S43 ....97 A3
Bramley Ct Hatton DE65 .227 B1
Kimberley NG16 ......195 C3
Bramley Dale DE11 ...255 C1
Bramley Hall Rd S13 ...44 C4
Bramley La Baslow DE45 .91 B4
Sheffield S13 ....44 C4
Bramley Park Cl S13 ...44 C4
Bramley Park Rd S13 ..44 C4
Bramley Pk Caravan Site
S21 ....58 C2
Bramley Rd
Bramley-Vale S44 .....117 C1
Eckington S21 ....58 C1
Bramley St DE55 .....170 C4
Bramley Vale Prim Sch
S44 ....117 C1
Bramleymoor La S21 ...58 C1
Bramlyn Cl S43 ....80 B3
Bramlyn Ct S43 ....80 B3
Brampton Ave DE75 ..182 A1
Brampton Cl DE3 .....217 B2
Brampton Ct DE56 ...179 B2
Brampton Dr NG9 ....223 C3
Brampton Prim Sch S40 .95 C2
Bramshill Rise S40 ....95 B1
Branch La S45 ....132 C3
Brancliffe La S81 ......63 C4
Brandelhow Ct DE21 ..206 B2
Brandene Cl S44 ......97 A2
Brandreth Dr NG16 ...195 A4
Branklene Cl NG16 ...195 C4
Branksome Ave DE23 .233 B4
Branksome Chine Ave
S41 ....115 B4
Bransdale Ave NG19 ..136 C1
Bransdale Cl NG10 ...236 A3
Branston Rd
Branston DE13,DE14 ..253 B4
Burton u T DE14 .....254 B4
Branston Water Pk
DE14 ....253 B3
Branton Cl S40 ......266 A1
Brassington Cl
Eastwood NG16 ......195 A4
West Hallam DE7 .....207 C3
Youlgreave DE45 .....125 B3
Brassington Cres SK13 ...9 B1
Brassington Ct NG19 .136 C2
Brassington La S42,S45 .131 B3

Brassington Prim Sch
DE4 ....153 A1
Brassington Rd DE21 ..205 C1
Brassington St S45 ...131 B2
Braybrook Cl DE55 ...169 C4
Brayfield Ave DE23 ...231 B4
Brayfield Rd DE23 ....231 B4
Breach La
Barrow-u-T DE73 .....244 C1
Hatton DE65 ....227 B2
Scropton DE6 ....226 B3
Breach Rd Denby DE5 .181 A2
Heanor DE75 ....194 A4
Breadsall CE Prim Sch
DE21 ....205 C2
Breadsall Cl DE11 ....256 A4
Breadsall Ct DE7 .....194 C2
Breadsall Hill Top Inf Sch
DE21 ....205 C1
Breadsall Hill Top Jun Sch
DE21 ....205 C1
Breamfield La DE4 ...166 A4
Brearley Ave S43 ......77 B2
Brearley Ct S41 ....77 A2
Brearley Hall S41 .....77 A2
Brearley St S41 ....77 B2
Breaston Ind Est DE72 .235 A4
Breaston La DE72 ....222 B2
Brechin Ct NG19 .....136 A3
Breck La S21,S43 ......78 B3
Breckbank NG19 .....136 C1
Breckland Rd S40,S42 .114 A4
Brecon Cl Chesterfield S40 95 B3
Derby DE21 ....220 C3
6 Long Eaton NG10 ..236 A4
Bredon Cl 7 NG10 ...236 A4
Breedon Ave DE23 ...231 B3
Breedon Hill Rd DE23 .218 C2
Breedon on the Hill St
Hardulph's CE Prim Sch
DE73 ....252 C1
Breedon St NG10 ....223 B1
Bren Way DE65 ......228 C3
Brenden Ave DE55 ...170 B4
Brenden Cl DE55 .....170 B4
Brendon Ave S40 ......95 B2
Brendon Cl SK13 ......17 A4
Brendon Dr NG16 ....195 C4
Brendon Way NG10 ...223 A1
Brent Cl S40 ....95 B3
Brentford Dr DE22 ...218 A3
Brentnall Cl NG10 ....236 A4
Brentwood Ave S33 ...40 A2
Brentwood Rd S33 ....40 A2
Bretby Bsns Pk DE15 .255 C4
Bretby Hollow DE11 ..255 C4
Bretby La Bretby DE15 .248 C3
Burton u T DE15 .....248 B1
Bretby Mews DE15 ...249 A1
Bretby Rd Chesterfield S40 95 A3
Swadlincote DE11 .....255 C4
Bretby Sq DE23 ......231 B3
Bretby View DE11 ....257 A2
Bretlands Way DE15 ..255 C4
Bretton Ave Bolsover S44 .99 B1
Derby DE23 ....218 B1
Bretton Cl S40 ....95 A3
Bretton Gr S12 ....44 B2
Bretton Rd DE56 .....179 C3
Brewash Ct NG10 ....223 B1
Brewery St
Chesterfield S41 ......266 C3
Kimberley NG16 ......195 C3
Brewhouse Yd (Mus of
Nottingham Life)*
NG7 ....268 A1
Breydon Ct DE24 .....232 B2
Breydon Ind Ctr NG10 .236 C4
Briar Ave NG10 ......223 A2
Briar Briggs Rd S44 ...98 C2
Briar Cl Alfreton DE55 .159 B2
Borrowash DE72 .....221 B1
Chesterfield S41 ......95 C3
Derby DE21 ....220 A3
Swadlincote DE11 .....255 C4
Briar Gate NG10 .....223 A1
Briar Lea DE23 ......231 C2
Briar Rd NG16 ....195 A4
Briar View S43 ....96 C4
Briar's La DE4 ....168 A4
Briardene Cl S40 ......94 C3
Briargrove Rd SK22 ...24 B2
Briars Cl S21 ....60 B3
Briars Way DE5 ......180 B4
Briarsgate DE22 .....204 B1
Briarwood Cres SK6 ...23 A2
Briarwood Way DE23 .231 B3
Brick Kiln La
Mansfield NG19 ......268 A4
Rolleston DE13 ......240 A2
Brick Row DE22 .....205 A1
Brick-kiln La
Brailsford DE6 ....186 C1
Hulland Ward DE6 ...175 B3
Brickbridge Rd SK6 ...23 A3
Brickfield St SK13 .....10 A3
Brickfields Cl DE4 ....155 C4
Brickhouse La S17 ....55 B4
Brickhouse Yd S40 ....95 C2
Brickkiln La DE7 .....206 B3
Bricky Cl S43 ....80 B3
Brickyard Cotts DE6 ..185 C3
Brickyard
Kilburn DE56 ....179 C2
Ripley DE5 ....169 C1
South Normanton DE55 .160 A3
Brickyard Rd DE56 ...168 B3

Brickyard The DE7 ....193 A1
Bridge Bank Cl 15 S40 .95 B3
Bridge Cl
Swadlincote DE11 .....256 B1
Whitwell S80 ....82 A3
Bridge End Ave NG16 .171 C4
Bridge Farm DE7 .....240 C1
Bridge Field DE72 ....235 B4
Bridge Foot DE56 ....178 C3
Bridge Hill DE56 .....178 C3
Bridge St Bakewell DE45 .109 B3
Belper DE56 ....178 C2
Bradwell S33 ....51 A4
Burton u T, Stretton DE13 .240 C1
Buxton SK17 ....85 B4
Chesterfield S40 .....266 B1
Clay Cross S45 ......131 B2
Derby DE1 ....218 C3
Ilkeston DE7 ....194 C1
Killamarsh S21 ....60 B4
Langley Mill NG16 ...182 B2
Linton DE11 ....261 C4
Long Eaton NG10 ....223 B1
Mansfield NG18 .....268 C4
New Mills SK22 ....24 B1
Pilsley S45 ....132 B1
Sandiacre NG10 .....223 B3
Stafford ST16 ....269 B3
Swadlincote DE11 ....256 B1
Tupton S42 ....115 B1
Tutbury DE13 ....239 B4
Whaley Bridge SK23 ...45 C4
Bridge View DE56 ....191 A4
Bridge Way S41 ....76 B2
Bridgefield 4 SK13 ....17 A4
Bridgeholm Mill SK23 ..47 A4
Bridgend Cl NG9 .....223 B3
Bridgend Ct DE21 ....206 B1
Bridgeness Rd DE22 ..230 C3
Bridgeport Rd DE21 ..220 B3
Bridgeside DE13 .....240 C1
Bridgett Cl ST4 ......269 A1
Bridgewater St S42 ...115 B1
Bridgeway SK23 ....47 A2
Bridgford Ave DE14 ..253 C4
Bridgnorth Way NG9 ..223 C2
Bridgwater Cl DE24 ..233 A4
Bridle Cl DE73 ....233 A1
Bridle La
Ripley, Greenwich DE5 .169 C1
Ripley, Lower Hartshay
DE5, DE55 ....169 A1
Somercotes DE55 ....170 A4
Swadlincote DE15 ....255 A3
Bridle Rd Bolsover S44 ..80 C1
Staveley S43 ....79 A1
Bridle Stile S20 ....59 B4
Bridle Stile Cl S20 .....59 B4
Bridle Stile Gdns S20 ..59 A4
Bridlesmith Gate NG1 .268 B1
Bridleway SK22 ....24 C1
Bridleway The NG19 ..136 C1
Brierfield Ave S12 .....44 A2
Brierfield Cres S12 ....44 A2
Brierfield Way DE3 ...230 C4
Brierley Cl S43 ....78 C1
Brierley Pk SK23 ......34 A1
Brierley Rd
Stonebroom DE55 ...146 C2
Unstone S18 ....76 C3
Brierlow Bar SK17 ...105 A4
Brigden Ave DE24 ...232 C4
Brigg Inf Sch The The
DE55 ....160 A3
Bright Mdw S20 ......60 A3
Bright Side NG16 ....195 C3
Bright Sq NG19 ......135 B1
Bright St Derby DE22 .218 B3
Ilkeston DE7 ....194 C1
North Wingfield S42 ..131 C3
South Normanton DE55 .159 C3
Brightman Ho DE11 ..256 A3
Brightmoor St 14 NG1 .268 B1
Brighton Cl DE24 ....232 C4
Brighton St S4 ......269 C2
Brightstone Cl DE24 ..233 B4
Brigmor Wlk DE22 ...218 B3
Brimington Ct NG19 ..136 C2
Brimington Jun Sch
Brimington S43 ....96 C4
Brimington S43 ....96 C4
Brimington Rd S41 ...96 A4
Brimington Rd N S41 ..96 A4
Brimmesfield Dr S2 ...43 C4
Brimmesfield Rd S2 ...43 C4
Brincliffe Cl S40 ......95 A1
Brindle Way DE23 ....231 A3
Brindley Cl S8 ....43 A2
Brindley Cres S8 ......43 A2
Brindley Ct S21 ....60 B3
Brindley Rd 6 S41 ....96 A4
Brindley Way S43 .....78 C1
Brindley Wlk DE24 ...231 C1
Brinkburn Cl S17 .....55 C3
Brinkburn Ct S17 .....55 C3
Brinkburn Dr S17 .....55 C3
Brinkburn Vale Rd S17 .55 C3
Brinks Rd S33 ....39 A4
Brinsley Hill NG16 ...171 B1
Brinsley Prim Sch NG16 182 B4
Brisbane Cl NG19 ....136 B3
Brisbane Dr NG9 .....209 C1
Brisbane Rd DE3 .....217 C2

Briset Cl DE24 ... 231 C1
Brisley Hill ST4 ... 269 A1
Bristol Dr DE3 ... 217 C1
Bristol Rd DE7 ... 194 C1
Britannia Ave DE5 ... 181 A4
Britannia Dr DE13 ... 240 B1
Britannia Rd
Chesterfield S40 ... 115 A4
Long Eaton NG10 ... 223 B1
Briton Lodge Cl DE12 ... 262 C2
Brittain Dr DE5 ... 170 A1
Brittain Pit Farm* DE5 170 A2
Britten Gdns NG3 ... 268 C2
Brizlincote La DE15 ... 248 B1
Broad Bank DE22 ... 218 C4
Broad Eye ST16 ... 269 A4
Broad La Brinsley NG16 ... 182 C4
Creswell S80 ... 82 B3
Elvaston DE72 ... 233 C2
Broad Marsh Ctr NG1 ... 268 B1
Broad Oak Dr
Brinsley NG16 ... 182 C4
Stapleford NG9 ... 223 B3
Broad Pavement S40 ... 266 B3
Broad Pl S80 ... 82 B3
Broad St
Long Eaton NG10 ... 236 B4
Nottingham NG1 ... 268 B1
Stafford ST16 ... 269 A4
Broad Way DE6 ... 176 A4
Broad Wlk Buxton SK17 ... 85 A4
Darley Dale DE4 ... 127 B2
Broadbottom CE Prim Sch
SK14 ... 15 C4
Broadbottom Rd SK14 ... 9 A2
Broadbottom Sta SK14 ... 16 A4
Broadfield Rd S8 ... 43 A4
Broadfields Cl DE22 ... 218 C4
Broadgorse Cl S40 ... 114 C4
Broadhey View SK22 ... 24 A1
Broadholme La DE56 ... 179 A4
Broadlands
Sandiacre NG10 ... 223 A2
South Normanton DE55 ... 160 A2
Broadleaf Cl DE21 ... 205 C1
Broadleys S45 ... 131 B2
Broadmeadow DE4 ... 127 B2
Broadoaks Cl S41 ... 266 C3
Broadstairs Rd NG9 ... 223 C1
Broadstone Cl DE21 ... 206 A1
Broadstone La DE73 ... 251 B2
Broadway Derby DE22 ... 218 C4
Duffield DE56 ... 190 C1
Heanor DE75 ... 181 C1
Ilkeston DE7 ... 194 C2
9 Nottingham NG1 ... 268 B1
Ripley DE5 ... 169 C1
Swanwick DE55 ... 169 C4
Broadway Ave DE5 ... 169 C1
Broadway Park Cl DE22 218 C4
Broadway St DE14 ... 254 B4
Broadway The NG18 ... 268 C3
Brockhall Rise DE75 ... 182 A1
Brockhill Ct 4 S43 ... 96 C4
Brockholes SK13 ... 16 C4
Brockhurst Gdns NG3 ... 268 C2
Brockhurst La S45 ... 129 B3
Brocklehurst Ave S8 ... 57 B4
Brocklehurst Ct S40 ... 95 B1
Brocklehurst Piece S40 ... 95 B1
Brockley DE21 ... 220 C3
Brockley Ave S44 ... 98 C3
Brockley Prim Sch S44 ... 98 C4
Brocksford Ct DE6 ... 224 C4
Brocksford Hall Sch
DE6 ... 224 C4
Brockway Cl S45 ... 131 B1
Brockwell Ct 13 S41 ... 95 B3
Brockwell Inf & Jun Sch
S40 ... 95 B2
Brockwell La Barlow S42 ... 94 C4
Chesterfield S40 ... 95 B2
Brockwell Pl S40 ... 95 C2
Brockwell Terr S40 ... 95 C2
Brockwell The DE55 ... 160 A2
Bromehead Way S41 ... 95 B4
Bromley Hough ST4 ... 269 A1
Bromley Pl NG1 ... 268 A1
Bromley St DE22 ... 218 C4
Brompton Rd DE22 ... 217 C3
Bromyard Dr DE73 ... 233 A2
Bronte Cl NG10 ... 236 A4
Bronte Pl DE23 ... 231 A4
Bronte St DE55 ... 146 B3
Brook Ave DE55 ... 159 A2
Brook Bottom Rd SK22 ... 33 A4
Brook Cl Alfreton DE55 ... 159 A2
Doveridge DE6 ... 224 B4
Findern DE65 ... 230 B1
Hatton DE65 ... 227 B1
Holymoorside S42 ... 113 B4
Long Eaton NG10 ... 236 C3
Quarndon DE22 ... 204 B2
Brook Cotts DE7 ... 194 C2
Brook Ct NG16 ... 182 A1
Brook End DE65 ... 242 B2
Brook House Mews
DE11 ... 256 A4
Brook La Alfreton DE55 ... 159 A2
Clowne S43 ... 80 C2
Crich DE56 ... 168 B3
Hatton DE65 ... 227 B2
Ripley DE5 ... 180 B4
Sutton on t H DE6 ... 228 A4
Brook Lea DE4 ... 143 B2
Brook Mdw SK13 ... 10 C1
Brook Rd
Borrowash DE72 ... 221 A1
Elvaston DE72 ... 233 C2
Sheffield S8 ... 43 A3
Brook Side DE45 ... 109 B3
Brook St Clay Cross S45 ... 131 A2
Derby DE1 ... 267 A4
Glossop SK13 ... 10 B1
Hartshorne DE11 ... 257 A4
Heage DE56 ... 168 C1
Heanor DE75 ... 181 A3
Nether Heage DE56 ... 168 B1
Nottingham NG1 ... 268 B2
Renishaw S21 ... 79 B4
Stoke-on-T ST4 ... 269 B2
Swadlincote DE11 ... 256 A2
Swadlincote, Newhall
DE11 ... 255 C3
Tibshelf DE55 ... 148 A3
Brook Vale Cl S18 ... 75 B2
Brook Vale Rd NG16 ... 182 B1
Brook Wlk DE1 ... 267 A4
Brook Yd S40 ... 266 A3
Brookbank Ave S40 ... 95 B2
Brookbank Rd S43 ... 80 C2
Brookdale Ave SK6 ... 23 A2
Brookdale Dr DE23 ... 231 A3
Brookdale Rd DE11 ... 257 A2
Brooke Dr S43 ... 96 C3
Brooke St Ilkeston DE7 ... 209 A3
Sandiacre NG10 ... 223 A3
Brookfield DE73 ... 244 A3
Brookfield Ave
Chesterfield S40 ... 95 A1
Derby, Chaddesden DE21 ... 220 A4
Derby, Littleover DE23 ... 231 B3
Brookfield Cl DE5 ... 170 A1
Brookfield Com Sch S40 ... 95 A1
Brookfield Cres NG20 ... 119 C3
Brookfield Ind Est SK13 ... 9 C2
Brookfield La DE45 ... 109 C4
Brookfield Park Ind Est
DE4 ... 143 C2
Brookfield Prim Sch
Derby DE3 ... 230 B4
Shirebrook NG20 ... 119 C3
Brookfield Rd S44 ... 118 A4
Brookfield Way
Heanor DE75 ... 182 A1
Tansley DE4 ... 143 C2
Brookfields Calver S32 ... 72 B1
Horsley DE56 ... 191 C4
Brookfields Dr DE21 ... 205 B2
Brookhill S43 ... 80 C2
Brookhill Ave NG16 ... 160 B2
Brookhill Ind Est NG16 ... 160 B1
Brookhill La NG16 ... 160 C3
Brookhill Leys Rd NG16 182 C1
Brookhill Rd NG16 ... 160 B1
Brookhill St NG9 ... 223 B3
Brookhouse Ct
Hayfield SK22 ... 25 B2
Whaley Thorns NG20 ... 101 A1
Brookhouse St DE24 ... 232 B3
Brookland Ave NG18 ... 268 A4
Brooklands SK17 ... 85 B4
Brooklands Ave
Chapel-en-le-F SK23 ... 47 B3
Heanor DE75 ... 181 C1
Wirksworth DE4 ... 165 C4
Brooklands Bank DE45 ... 109 C3
Brooklands Dr
Derby DE23 ... 231 B4
Glossop SK13 ... 17 A4
Brooklands Inf Sch
NG10 ... 236 B3
Brooklands Jun Sch
NG10 ... 236 B4
Brooklands Rd SK23 ... 47 B3
Brookleton DE45 ... 125 B3
Brooklyn Dr S40 ... 95 B2
Brooklyn Pl S8 ... 43 A3
Brooklyn Rd S8 ... 43 A3
Brooks Hollow DE21 ... 205 B4
Brooks Rd S43 ... 78 A2
Brookside
Ashbourne DE6 ... 173 B1
Beeley DE4 ... 111 A2
Belper DE56 ... 178 C2
Bradwell S33 ... 51 A4
Burton u T DE15 ... 248 A3
Chapel-en-le-Frith SK23 ... 34 A1
Derby DE1 ... 267 A4
Eastwood NG16 ... 182 C2
Glossop SK13 ... 17 A4
New Mills SK22 ... 24 C4
Rolleston DE13 ... 240 A2
Brookside Ave NG19 ... 136 B3
Brookside Bar S40 ... 94 C1
Brookside Cl Derby DE1 ... 218 C4
Glossop SK13 ... 9 C2
Long Eaton NG10 ... 236 A4
Repton DE65 ... 242 B1
Brookside Glen S40 ... 94 C1
Brookside Gr SK17 ... 84 B3
Brookside Ind Unit NG9 223 B3
Brookside Rd
Breadsall DE21 ... 205 C2
Chapel-en-le-F SK23 ... 47 A3
Brookside Specl Sch
DE21 ... 205 C2
Brookside Way NG17 ... 148 C1
Brookvale Ave
Codnor DE5 ... 181 A4
Denby DE5 ... 180 A1
Brookvale Rd DE5 ... 180 A1
Brookvale Rise DE5 ... 180 A1
Brookview Ct S18 ... 57 A2
Broom Ave Pilsley S45 ... 132 B1
Swanwick DE55 ... 169 C4
Broom Cl Belper DE56 ... 178 C3
Chesterfield S41 ... 95 B4
Derby, Chellaston DE73 ... 232 C1
Derby, Sinfin DE73 ... 231 C1
Duffield DE56 ... 190 B2
Broom Dr S42 ... 115 C1
Broom Gdns S43 ... 96 C4
Broom La DE6 ... 175 C4
Broom's La DE6 ... 226 A1
Broombank Pk S41 ... 76 B2
Broombank Rd S41 ... 76 B2
Broome Acre DE55 ... 160 B2
Broomfield Ave S41 ... 115 B4
Broomfield Cl 6 NG10 ... 223 A3
Broomhill Ave DE7 ... 209 A3
Broomhill Cl Derby DE3 ... 217 B2
Eckington S21 ... 59 A2
Broomhill Fst Sch NG19 268 A4
Broomhill La NG19 ... 268 A4
Broomhill Rd S41 ... 76 C1
Broomhills La DE65 ... 242 B1
Broomyclose La ST14 ... 210 A2
Brosscroft SK13 ... 10 A3
Brosscroft Village SK13 ... 10 A3
Brough La S33 ... 51 B4
Brough Rd DE15 ... 248 B2
Brough St DE22 ... 218 B3
Brougham Ave NG19 ... 135 B1
Broughton Ave DE23 ... 218 B1
Broughton Cl
Church Broughton DE65 ... 227 A4
Ilkeston DE7 ... 194 B1
Broughton Rd S41 ... 95 B4
Brow Cres S20 ... 59 C4
Brown Ave NG19 ... 136 A2
Brown Edge Rd SK17 ... 66 B1
Brown Hills La S10 ... 42 B4
Brown La Ashover S45 ... 145 A4
Barton in F NG11 ... 237 C3
Dronfield S18 ... 57 B2
Flash SK17 ... 103 A2
Brown St NG19 ... 268 A4
Brown's Flats NG16 ... 195 C3
Brown's La DE56 ... 191 B4
Brown's Rd NG10 ... 236 C4
Brown's Yd DE55 ... 170 B4
Brownhill La HD9 ... 3 A4
Brownhills La S42 ... 130 B2
Browning Cir DE23 ... 231 C4
Browning Rd DE11 ... 256 B3
Browning St Derby DE23 231 C4
3 Mansfield NG18 ... 268 B4
Stafford ST16 ... 269 A4
Brownlow Rd NG19 ... 135 C1
Broxtowe Ave NG16 ... 195 B3
Broxtowe Dr NG18 ... 268 C3
Brun La DE6,DE22 ... 217 A4
Brunnen The DE55 ... 160 A2
Brunner Ave NG20 ... 119 C2
Brunswick Dr NG9 ... 223 C3
Brunswick St
Chesterfield S41 ... 266 B4
Derby DE23 ... 231 C4
Pilsley S45 ... 132 B1
Brunswick Terr ST16 ... 269 A3
Brunswood Cl DE21 ... 220 C3
Brunswood La DE6 ... 187 B4
Brunswood Rd DE4 ... 143 A1
Brunt St NG18 ... 268 C3
Brunton Cl DE3 ... 217 B1
Brunts Comp Sch NG19 136 B1
Brushes Rd SK15 ... 4 A2
Brushfield Gr S12 ... 44 B2
Brushfield Rd S40,S42 ... 94 C3
Brussels Terr 1 DE7 ... 194 C1
Bryant La DE55 ... 160 A2
Bryn Lea S41 ... 96 B1
Brynsmoor Rd NG16 ... 182 C4
Bryony DE14 ... 254 A4
Bryony Cl Derby DE21 ... 206 A1
Killamarsh S21 ... 60 A3
Bryony Way NG19 ... 136 C2
Bubnell Rd DE45 ... 91 B3
Buchan St DE24 ... 232 B4
Buchanan St DE1 ... 267 B4
Buck Wood View S12 ... 43 B3
Buckden Cl S40 ... 95 B2
Buckfast Cl DE55 ... 169 C4
Buckford La DE65,DE73 ... 242 C4
Buckhazels La DE6,DE22 203 A4
Buckingham Ave DE21 ... 219 B4
Buckingham Cl
22 Dronfield S18 ... 56 B1
Mansfield Woodhouse
NG19 ... 136 C3
Swanwick DE55 ... 170 A4
Buckingham Ct
Burton u T DE15 ... 248 B2
Sandiacre NG10 ... 223 A2
Buckingham Dr DE75 ... 181 B1
Buckingham Ho DE24 ... 219 B1
Buckingham Rd NG10 ... 223 A2
Buckland Cl DE1 ... 218 C3
Buckland Gr SK14 ... 15 A4
Buckleather La S18 ... 74 B1
Buckley Cl DE11 ... 256 C1
Buckminster Cl DE21 ... 205 C1
Buckminster Rd DE7 ... 208 B2
Bull Farm Fst & Mid Sch
NG19 ... 135 B1
Bull Hill ST16 ... 269 B4
Bull La DE4 ... 143 B3
Bull Mews Cotts DE4 ... 143 B3
Bullace Ct NG19 ... 136 C1
Bullbridge Hill DE56 ... 168 A3
Buller St Derby DE23 ... 218 C1
Ilkeston DE7 ... 209 A3
Bullhill La DE56 ... 176 C2
Bullhurst La DE6 ... 188 C2
Bulling La DE4 ... 156 C1
Bullivant Ave S80 ... 100 B4
Bullivant St NG3 ... 268 B2
Bullock Cl NG19 ... 136 A3
Bullock La Brailsford DE6 201 C4
Ironville NG16, DE55 ... 170 C3
Bullpit La DE56 ... 205 A4
Bulls Mews Cotts DE4 ... 143 B3
Bullsmoor DE56 ... 179 B2
Bumpmill La DE55 ... 146 A1
Bun Alley DE45 ... 91 B2
Bungalows The
Chesterfield, Brampton S40 ... 95 B2
Chesterfield, Hady S41 ... 266 C2
1 Chesterfield, Newbold
S41 ... 95 C4
Chesterfield, Whittington Moor
S41 ... 96 A4
Killamarsh S21 ... 60 B3
New Mills SK22 ... 24 B1
Stonebroom DE55 ... 146 C2
Bunker S Hill S21 ... 60 C3
Bunker's Hill S80 ... 62 B4
Bunting Cl
Chesterfield S42 ... 95 A1
Ilkeston DE7 ... 208 B3
Sheffield S8 ... 43 A1
Bunting Ho S41 ... 77 A2
Bunting Nook S8 ... 43 A1
Buntingbank Cl DE55 ... 159 C2
Buntingfield La S45 ... 129 A4
Buntings Cl DE3 ... 218 A2
Bunyan Cres DE55 ... 146 C2
Bunyan Green Rd NG16 ... 171 B4
Burbage Cl Belper DE56 ... 179 B3
25 Dronfield S18 ... 56 B1
Burbage Gr S12 ... 44 B3
Burbage Pl DE24 ... 232 C4
Burbage Prim Sch SK17 ... 84 C3
Burbage Rd S43 ... 97 B4
Burch Pl S32 ... 71 C3
Burcot Cl DE7 ... 207 C4
Burdekin Cl SK23 ... 47 B3
Burdett Way DE65 ... 242 B2
Burdock Cl DE21 ... 205 C1
Burgess Cl S41 ... 115 B4
Burghley Cl DE73 ... 232 C1
Burghley Way DE23 ... 230 C3
Burke Dr DE55 ... 170 B4
Burkitt Dr S43 ... 79 A2
Burland Green La DE6 ... 189 A2
Burleigh Cres DE55 ... 169 C4
Burleigh Dr DE22 ... 218 C4
Burleigh St 2 DE7 ... 194 C1
Burley Bank La HD7 ... 2 C4
Burley Cl S40 ... 115 A4
Burley Dr DE22 ... 204 C4
Burley Hill DE22, DE56 ... 205 A4
Burley La DE22 ... 204 C4
Burlington Ave NG20 ... 119 C3
Burlington Cl
Breaston DE72 ... 235 B4
Dore S17 ... 55 C4
Burlington Dr NG19 ... 135 C1
Burlington Glen S17 ... 55 C4
Burlington Gr S17 ... 55 C4
Burlington Rd
Buxton SK17 ... 85 A4
Derby DE22 ... 217 C3
Dore S17 ... 55 C4
Burlington St S40 ... 266 B3
Burlington Way DE3 ... 217 B1
Burlow Ave SK17 ... 85 B2
Burlow Rd SK17 ... 85 B1
Burnaby St DE24 ... 232 C4
Burnage Ct DE22 ... 218 C2
Burnaston Cl S18 ... 56 B1
Burnaston Ct NG19 ... 136 C2
Burnaston La DE65 ... 229 B3
Burnbridge Rd S41 ... 77 B2
Burncroft DE7 ... 207 C4
Burnell St S43 ... 96 C4
Burnett La DE4 ... 143 A4
Burney La DE73 ... 252 B1
Burnham Cl DE7 ... 207 B4
Burnham Dr DE3 ... 217 B1
Burnham Way NG2 ... 268 B1
Burns Ave
Mansfield Woodhouse
NG19 ... 136 B1
Nottingham NG7 ... 268 A2
Burns Cl Chesterfield S40 114 C4
Derby DE23 ... 231 A4
Burns Dr Dronfield S18 ... 76 B4
Grassmoor S42 ... 115 C2
Burns St Ilkeston DE7 ... 208 C4
Mansfield NG18 ... 268 B4
Nottingham NG7 ... 268 A2
Burnshaw St DE55 ... 146 B3
Burnside Glossop SK13 ... 9 C2
Rolleston DE13 ... 240 A2
Burnside Ave Sheffield S8 ... 43 A3
Shirland DE55 ... 146 B1
Burnside Cl DE24 ... 231 B2
Burnside Dr Derby DE21 ... 220 C2
Mansfield NG19 ... 135 C1
Burnside St DE24 ... 233 A4
Burnt House Rd DE75 ... 181 B1
Burnt Oaks Cl NG19 ... 136 B2
Burr La DE7 ... 194 C1
Burre Cl DE45 ... 109 C3
Burrfields Rd SK23 ... 47 A3
Burrowfield Mews
DE21 ... 220 C1
Burrows Ct NG3 ... 268 C2
Burrows La
Brailsford DE6 ... 201 C1
Middleton (Nr Wirksworth)
DE4 ... 154 B3
Burrows The DE11 ... 255 C3
Burrs Wood Croft S41 ... 95 B4
Bursdon Cl S41 ... 77 A1
Burton Close Dr DE45 ... 109 C2
Burton Edge DE45 ... 109 B2
Burton Rd
Burton u T DE14 ... 254 A4
Coton in t E DE12 ... 260 B2
Derby DE23 ... 218 B1
Findern DE65 ... 230 B2
Linton DE11 ... 255 B1
Overseal DE12 ... 262 A2
Repton DE15,DE65 ... 242 A1
Rosliston DE12 ... 260 B3
Swadlincote DE11 ... 256 B3
Tutbury DE13 ... 239 B2
Willington DE65 ... 241 C4
Burton St Heanor DE75 ... 181 C1
Nottingham NG1 ... 268 B2
Tutbury DE13 ... 239 B3
Burton Tech Coll (Rolleston
Campus) DE13 ... 240 B2
Burwell Cl SK13 ... 17 A4
Burwell Ct NG19 ... 136 C2
Buscott Dr DE6 ... 185 A4
Bush Vale DE56 ... 178 C3
Bushey Wood Gr S17 ... 55 B3
Bushey Wood Rd S17 ... 55 C3
Bushton La DE13 ... 239 A1
Bushy Cl NG10 ... 236 A3
Buskeyfield La NG20 ... 101 C2
Butcher's La DE4 ... 127 C2
Bute St SK13 ... 10 C2
Butler Cres NG19 ... 135 B1
Butler St ST4 ... 269 B1
Butler Way S21 ... 60 B3
Butt Hill S80 ... 81 C3
Butt Hill Cl S80 ... 81 C3
Butt La Blackfordby DE11 ... 257 A1
Mansfield Woodhouse
NG19 ... 136 B1
Butt St NG10 ... 223 A3
Buttercup Ave DE12 ... 262 C1
Butterfield Cres DE55 ... 169 C4
Butterfield La DE55 ... 145 C1
Butterhall Cl S80 ... 82 A3
Butterley Croft Bsns Ctr
DE5 ... 180 C4
Butterley Ct NG16 ... 170 C2
Butterley Hill DE5 ... 169 C2
Butterley La
Ashover DE4,S45 ... 144 C3
Ripley DE5 ... 169 B2
Butterley Sta DE5 ... 169 C2
Buttermead Cl NG9 ... 209 B1
Buttermere Cl
Chesterfield S41 ... 95 B4
10 Long Eaton NG10 ... 223 A1
Buttermere Dr
Derby DE22 ... 204 C2
Dronfield S18 ... 56 C1
Buttermilk La S44 ... 98 B2
Butterpot La DE6 ... 215 B2
Butterton Cl DE7 ... 209 A4
Butterton Dr 6 S40 ... 95 A3
Butterwick Cl DE23 ... 231 C3
Buttonoak Dr DE73 ... 233 A2
Butts Cl DE7 ... 209 A2
Butts Dr DE4 ... 143 B2
Butts Hill S17 ... 55 B2
Butts Rd Ashover S45 ... 129 C2
Bakewell DE45 ... 109 B3
Darley Dale DE4 ... 127 A2
Butts Terr DE45 ... 109 B3
Butts The DE56 ... 179 A2
Butts View DE45 ... 109 B3
Buxton Ave DE75 ... 193 C4
Buxton Cl
4 Gamesley SK13 ... 9 C1
Swadlincote DE11 ... 256 A4
Buxton Com Sch SK17 ... 85 A3
Buxton Ct DE7 ... 194 B1
Buxton Ctry Pk* SK17 ... 84 C3
Buxton Dr Derby DE3 ... 217 C2
Little Eaton DE21 ... 191 B1
Buxton Gn DE75 ... 193 C4
Buxton Hospl SK17 ... 85 B3
Buxton Inf Sch SK17 ... 85 B4
Buxton Jun Sch SK17 ... 85 A3
Buxton Mews SK13 ... 9 C1
Buxton Mus & Art Gal*
SK17 ... 85 A4
Buxton New Rd SK11 ... 83 A3
Buxton Old Rd SK12 ... 32 C2
Buxton Rd
Alstonefield DE6 ... 149 A3
Ashbourne DE6 ... 173 A1
Ashford in t W DE45 ... 108 C4
Bakewell DE45 ... 109 A4
Chapel-en-le-F SK17,SK23 ... 47 C3
Chinley SK23 ... 34 C1
Derby DE21 ... 219 C4
Disley SK12 ... 32 C3
Dove Holes SK17 ... 66 C4
High Lane SK12 ... 32 A3
Longnor SK17 ... 121 A4
Mansfield NG19 ... 135 B1
New Mills SK22,SK23 ... 33 B2
Tideswell SK17 ... 69 B2
Whaley Bridge SK23 ... 33 C1
Whaley Bridge, New Horwich
SK23 ... 45 C3
Buxton Rd W SK12 ... 32 A3

Buxton Sta SK17 ... 85 A4
Buxton Terr SK14 ... 9 B3
Buxworth Prim Sch SK23 34 A1
Byard La NG1 ... 268 B1
Byfield Cl DE21 ... 206 A1
Byng Ave DE23 ... 231 C4
Byron Ave Alfreton DE55 . 159 A2
Burton u T DE15 ... 254 C4
Long Eaton NG10 ... 223 A2
Mansfield Woodhouse
NG19 ... 136 B1
Byron Cl Dronfield S18 ... 76 B4
Grassmoor S42 ... 115 C2
Byron Cres NG16 ... 195 B2
Byron Ct NG9 ... 209 C1
Byron Gr DE55 ... 146 C2
Byron Rd
Chesterfield S40 ... 115 A4
Swadlincote DE11 ... 256 B3
Byron St Buxton SK17 ... 85 B3
Chesterfield S40 ... 266 B1
Derby DE23 ... 218 C1
Ilkeston DE7 ... 194 C1
Mansfield NG18 ... 268 B4
Shirebrook NG20 ... 119 C2
Shirland DE55 ... 146 B1
Bywell La DE56 ... 179 C1

C

Cacklehill La DE6 ... 184 B1
Cadeby Ct DE55 ... 170 B3
Cadgwith Dr DE22 ... 204 C2
Cadley Hill Ind Est
DE11 ... 255 C1
Cadley Hill Rd DE11 ... 255 C2
Cadman Ct S20 ... 59 B3
Cadman Rd S12 ... 44 B3
Cadman St S20 ... 59 B3
Cadwell Cl DE24 ... 233 B3
Caerhays Ct DE24 ... 231 B2
Caernarfon Cl DE55 ... 170 A4
Caernarvon Cl
8 Chesterfield S40 ... 95 B1
Derby DE21 ... 220 C3
Caernarvon Rd S18 ... 76 A4
Caesar St DE1 ... 219 A4
Cairn Dr S43 ... 77 B2
Cairngorm Cl S43 ... 77 B2
Cairngorm Dr DE24 ... 231 B2
Cairns Cl Burton u T DE15 248 B2
Derby DE3 ... 217 C2
Cairns St NG1 ... 268 B2
Cairnsmore Cl 4 NG10 . 223 A1
Caldene Terr SK23 ... 45 C4
Calder Cl Derby DE22 ... 204 C2
Hilton DE65 ... 228 B1
Calderdale Dr NG10 ... 236 A3
Caldermill Dr DE21 ... 206 A1
Caldey Rd S18 ... 76 A4
Calesdale Cl SK17 ... 85 A3
Calf Croft S80 ... 82 A3
Calgary Cres DE15 ... 248 B2
California Gdns DE22 ... 218 B2
California La S43 ... 80 A4
Calke Abbey★ LE65 ... 251 B1
Calke Ave NG17 ... 148 C1
Calke Rise DE5 ... 169 C1
Calladine La
Horsley Woodhouse DE7 .. 192 B3
Shottle DE56 ... 177 B3
Calladine Rd DE75 ... 181 B1
Callan's La LE65 ... 258 B4
Callow Dr S14 ... 43 B3
Callow Hill Way DE23 ... 231 A4
Callow La DE4,DE6 ... 165 B3
Callow Mount S14 ... 43 B3
Callow Pl S14 ... 43 B3
Callow Rd S14 ... 43 B3
Callywhite La S18 ... 57 B1
Calow Brook Dr S41 ... 115 C4
Calow CE Prim Sch S44 . 96 C2
Calow Cl 9 SK13 ... 9 C1
Calow Gn 10 SK13 ... 9 C1
Calow La Calow S41,S44 .. 96 C1
Chesterfield S41 ... 115 C4
Calow La Ind Est S41 ... 115 C4
Calton View DE45 ... 109 B3
Calver Ave S42 ... 132 A4
Calver Cl Belper DE56 ... 179 A3
Derby DE21 ... 205 C2
Calver Cres S43 ... 97 B4
Calver Fold 4 SK13 ... 9 B1
Calver Mews SK13 ... 9 C1
Calver Mill S32 ... 72 B1
Calver Pl 5 SK13 ... 9 B1
Calver Rd DE45 ... 91 B3
Calver St NG19 ... 136 C2
Calvert St DE1 ... 267 D2
Calverton Cl DE24 ... 232 C2
Calvin Cl DE24 ... 233 A3
Camberwell Ave DE22 ... 218 A3
Camborne Cl DE21 ... 205 C1
Cambria Rd NG19 ... 135 B2
Cambrian Cl 10 S40 ... 95 B3
Cambrian Way DE11 ... 256 A2
Cambridge Cres
Bramley-Vale S44 ... 117 C1
Stapleford NG9 ... 209 B1
Cambridge Rd
1 Brimington S43 ... 96 C4
Sheffield S8 ... 43 A3
Cambridge St
Blackwell DE55 ... 147 C1
Derby, Rose Hill DE23 ... 219 A1
Derby, Spondon DE21 ... 220 C2
Mansfield NG18 ... 268 B3
Cambridge St *continued*
Stafford ST16 ... 269 C4
Camdale Rise S12 ... 44 C1
Camdale View S12 ... 44 C1
Camden Cl NG2 ... 268 C1
Camden St DE22 ... 218 B2
Camellia Cl DE3 ... 217 B2
Camelot Cl 2 DE13 ... 240 C1
Cameron Cl DE15 ... 248 A1
Cameron Rd DE23 ... 231 C4
Camerory Way S43 ... 77 B3
Camms Cl S21 ... 59 B2
Camms Endowed CE Prim
Sch S21 ... 59 B2
Camp St DE1 ... 219 A4
Camp Wood Cl DE21 ... 205 B4
Campbell Ct S43 ... 77 B2
Campbell Dr S43 ... 78 A2
Campbell Gr 19 NG3 ... 268 B2
Campbell Pl ST4 ... 269 B2
Campbell Rd ST4 ... 269 B1
Campbell St Belper DE56 178 C2
Derby DE24 ... 232 B4
Langley Mill NG16 ... 182 B2
Nottingham NG3 ... 268 B2
Campion Cl NG20 ... 119 B2
Campion Hill DE74 ... 247 A2
Campion Rd DE11 ... 256 C2
Campion St DE22 ... 218 B3
Campsie Ct 6 DE24 ... 231 B2
Canada St DE56 ... 179 A1
Canal Bank DE72 ... 235 A1
Canal Br S21 ... 60 B3
Canal Bridge DE65 ... 242 A3
Canal Mus NG1 ... 268 B1
Canal Side SK23 ... 33 C1
Canal St Derby DE1 ... 267 C2
Ilkeston DE7 ... 195 A1
Long Eaton NG10 ... 223 B1
Marple SK6 ... 23 A3
Nottingham NG1 ... 268 B1
Sandiacre NG10 ... 223 B3
Whaley Bridge SK23 ... 45 C4
Canal Wharf S41 ... 96 A3
Canberra Cl Derby DE3 ... 217 C1
Stapleford NG9 ... 209 C1
Canberra Dr ST16 ... 269 C4
Candlemass Ct NG19 ... 136 B1
Cannell Cl S45 ... 131 A2
Canner Cl DE11 ... 257 A1
Canning Cir NG7 ... 268 A2
Canning Terr 35 NG7 ... 268 A2
Cannock Way NG10 ... 237 A4
Cannon Fields S32 ... 52 C4
Cannon St SK14 ... 9 B3
Canon Cl DE7 ... 194 C3
Canon's Wlk DE22 ... 204 C1
Cantelupe Rd DE7 ... 209 A4
Canterbury Cl
Duffield DE56 ... 190 C2
Mansfield Woodhouse
NG19 ... 136 B3
Canterbury Ct 1 NG1 ... 268 A2
Canterbury Rd
Burton u T DE15 ... 248 B2
Sheffield S8 ... 43 A3
Wirksworth DE4 ... 165 C4
Canterbury St DE21 ... 219 C4
Canterbury Terr DE4 ... 165 C4
Cantley Cl DE24 ... 232 B2
Cantley Rd DE55 ... 170 B3
Cape St NG18 ... 268 A4
Capel Rise S43 ... 96 B4
Capthorne Cl S40 ... 94 C3
Car Rd S18 ... 74 A3
Car Vale Dr S13 ... 44 B4
Car Vale View S13 ... 44 B4
Caraway Dr DE14 ... 254 A4
Cardale Rd NG19 ... 135 B2
Cardales Cl DE65 ... 230 B1
Cardean Cl DE1 ... 219 A4
Carder Gn SK17 ... 121 A3
Cardiff St NG3 ... 268 C2
Cardigan St DE21 ... 219 B4
Cardinal Cl Derby DE21 . 205 C1
Nottingham NG3 ... 268 C2
Cardlemere La SK17 ... 138 C1
Cardrona Cl DE21 ... 205 C1
Cardwell Ave S13 ... 44 C4
Cardwell Dr S13 ... 44 C4
Carfield Ave S8 ... 43 A3
Carfield La S8 ... 43 B3
Carfield Pl S8 ... 43 A3
Carfield Prim Sch S8 ... 43 A3
Carisbrooke Dr 5 DE13 240 C1
Carisbrooke Gdns DE23 231 B3
Carl Moult Ho DE11 ... 256 A1
Carlin Cl DE72 ... 235 C4
Carlin St S13 ... 44 C3
Carlisle Ave DE23 ... 231 A4
Carlisle Cl S41 ... 76 C2
Carlisle Gr SK17 ... 85 A4
Carlisle Rd SK17 ... 84 C4
Carlton Ave Derby DE24 . 232 C2
Northwood DE4 ... 127 A3
Carlton Cl Clay Cross S45 131 B1
Heanor DE75 ... 182 A2
Mosborough S20 ... 59 B3
Carlton Dr DE24 ... 232 C2
Carlton Gdns DE24 ... 232 C2
Carlton Mews S2 ... 43 C4
Carlton Rd
Chesterfield S40 ... 115 A3
Derby DE23 ... 218 C1
Long Eaton NG10 ... 236 A3
Nottingham NG1,NG3 ... 268 C2
Stoke-on-T ST4 ... 269 C2
Carlton St
Mansfield Woodhouse
NG19 ... 136 B1
Nottingham NG1 ... 268 B1
Carlyle Inf Sch DE23 ... 231 A4
Carlyle Pl DE75 ... 181 B2
Carlyle Rd DE55 ... 146 C2
Carlyle St Derby DE24 ... 231 C3
Heanor DE75 ... 181 B2
Carlyon Gdns S40 ... 114 C4
Carnarvon Rd NG17 ... 148 C1
Carnegie St DE23 ... 232 A4
Carnfield Hall★ DE55 ... 159 B3
Carnfield Hill DE55 ... 159 B3
Carnforth Cl Derby DE3 . 217 C1
Stapleford NG9 ... 223 B3
Carnival Way DE74 ... 247 A2
Carnoustie Ave S40 ... 114 B4
Carnoustie Cl DE3 ... 217 C1
Carol Cres DE21 ... 219 C3
Caroline Cl DE24 ... 233 B4
Caroline Ct Hope S33 ... 38 C2
Ilkeston DE7 ... 209 A3
Carpenter Ave
Mansfield NG19 ... 135 B1
Mastin Moor S43 ... 79 A2
Carpenter Cl DE15 ... 248 B1
Carpenter Croft S12 ... 44 B3
Carpenter Gdns S12 ... 44 B3
Carpenter Mews S12 ... 44 B3
Carper La DE6 ... 187 C1
Carr Bank SK13 ... 17 C4
Carr Brow SK6 ... 32 A4
Carr Cl DE55 ... 160 A4
Carr Fields DE7 ... 192 B4
Carr La Brackenfield DE55 145 B2
Crich DE4 ... 156 C1
Dronfield S18 ... 56 B1
Matlock DE4 ... 143 C1
Scarcliffe S44 ... 117 C4
South Normanton DE55 . 160 A4
Thornhill S33 ... 39 C3
Carr Lane Mews S18 ... 56 B1
Carr Vale Rd S44 ... 98 C1
Carrbrook Ind Est SK15 ... 4 A3
Carrfield Ave NG10 ... 223 C1
Carrfield Ct 10 S8 ... 43 A3
Carrfield Dr S8 ... 43 A3
Carrfield La S8 ... 43 A3
Carrfield Rd S8 ... 43 A3
Carrfield St S8 ... 43 A3
Carrhouse La SK14 ... 9 B2
Carriage Dr The SK13 ... 9 C3
Carriers Mdw SK23 ... 47 A4
Carriers Rd DE65 ... 241 B3
Carrington Ct Ind Est
DE1 ... 218 C3
Carrington St Derby DE1 267 C2
Nottingham NG1 ... 268 B1
Carrock Ave DE75 ... 182 A1
Carron Cl DE24 ... 231 C2
Carrs Cl DE74 ... 247 A2
Carrwood Rd
Chesterfield S41 ... 76 B2
Renishaw S21 ... 79 A4
Carsington & Hopton CE
Prim Sch DE4 ... 164 C4
Carsington Cl S40 ... 95 A3
Carsington Cres DE22 . 204 B1
Carsington Ct NG19 ... 136 C2
Carsington Mews DE22 . 204 C1
Carsington Water Visitor
Ctr★ DE6 ... 164 B2
Carson Croft DE4 ... 143 B3
Carson Mount S12 ... 44 A2
Carson Rd DE21 ... 220 A3
Carson Way ST16 ... 269 A4
Cart Rd DE55 ... 157 C2
Carter Cl NG10 ... 236 A3
Carter La
Market Warsop NG20 ... 120 B2
Shirebrook NG20 ... 119 C2
Carter La E DE55 ... 160 B3
Carter La W
Shirebrook NG20 ... 119 B3
South Normanton DE55 . 160 B3
Carter Pl S8 ... 43 A3
Carter Rd Beeston NG9 . 223 C1
Sheffield S8 ... 43 A3
Carter St DE24 ... 232 B3
Carterhall La S12 ... 44 B1
Carterhall Rd S12 ... 44 A1
Cartledge La S18 ... 75 A4
Cartmel Cl S18 ... 56 C1
Cartmel Cres S41 ... 95 C4
Cartworth Moor Rd HD9 .. 3 C4
Cartwright La DE55 ... 160 C4
Cartwright St S81 ... 63 C4
Carver Cl S26 ... 61 C3
Carver Way S26 ... 61 C3
Cary Rd Eckington S21 ... 59 A2
Sheffield S2 ... 44 A4
Cascade Gr DE23 ... 231 A4
Casson Ave DE24 ... 233 A3
Casson Dr S26 ... 61 C4
Casson St NG16 ... 170 C2
Castings Rd DE23 ... 232 A4
Castle Bvd NG7 ... 268 A1
Castle Cl Bakewell DE45 . 109 C3
Borrowash DE72 ... 221 B1
Castle Croft DE24 ... 233 B3
Castle Ct Elvaston DE72 . 234 A3
Tutbury DE13 ... 239 B4
Castle Donington Com Coll
DE74 ... 247 A2
Castle Dr Bakewell DE45 . 109 C4
Codnor NG16 ... 181 C4
Somercotes DE55 ... 170 B4
Castle Edge Rd SK22 ... 24 A1
Castle Gate NG1 ... 268 B1
Castle Gn S44 ... 118 A4
Castle Gr NG7 ... 268 A1
Castle Gresley Inf Sch
DE11 ... 261 C4
Castle Hayes La DE13 ... 239 A3
Castle Hill
Castle Donington DE74 ... 247 A2
Duffield DE56 ... 190 C2
Eckington S21 ... 59 B2
Findern DE65 ... 230 B1
Glossop SK13 ... 10 C1
Tutbury DE13 ... 239 A4
Castle Hill Cl S21 ... 59 B2
Castle Ho DE1 ... 267 D2
Castle Ind Est S44 ... 98 C1
Castle La Bolsover S44 ... 99 A1
Ironville NG16 ... 170 C1
Melbourne DE73 ... 252 A4
Castle Meadow Rd NG2 268 A1
Castle Mews
Mansfield Woodhouse
NG19 ... 136 A2
Melbourne DE73 ... 252 A4
Castle Mews The 5
DE11 ... 256 A4
Castle Mills DE73 ... 252 A4
Castle Mount Cres
DE45 ... 109 B4
Castle Mount Way DE45 109 C4
Castle Mus & Art Gall
NG7 ... 268 A1
Castle Orch DE56 ... 190 C2
Castle Pl NG1 ... 268 A1
Castle Quay NG7 ... 268 A1
Castle Rd
Nottingham NG1 ... 268 B1
Swadlincote DE11 ... 255 C1
Castle Row S17 ... 56 A3
Castle St Bakewell DE45 . 109 B3
Bolsover S44 ... 99 A1
Castleton S33 ... 38 A1
Derby DE1 ... 267 C2
Glossop SK13 ... 10 A2
Mansfield NG18 ... 268 B4
Mansfield Woodhouse
NG19 ... 136 A2
Melbourne DE73 ... 252 A4
Nottingham NG2 ... 268 C1
Stafford ST16 ... 269 A4
Tutbury DE13 ... 239 B3
Castle View
Aldercar NG16 ... 182 A2
Duffield DE56 ... 190 C2
Eckington S21 ... 59 B2
Hatton DE65 ... 239 B4
Stafford ST16 ... 269 A4
Castle View Dr DE4 ... 155 B3
Castle View Prim Sch
DE4 ... 143 B3
Castle Way ST16 ... 269 A3
Castle Way The DE65 ... 241 C3
Castle Yd S40 ... 266 B2
Castlebeck Ave S2 ... 44 B3
Castlebeck Dr S2 ... 44 B4
Castlecraig Ct DE24 ... 231 C1
Castledale Croft S2 ... 44 A4
Castledale Gr S2 ... 44 B4
Castledale Pl S2 ... 44 A4
Castledene Dr ST16 ... 269 A3
Castlefields
Ironville NG16 ... 170 C2
Stafford ST16 ... 269 A3
Castlefields Main Ctr
DE1 ... 267 C2
Castlegate La SK17,DE45 . 89 B3
Castlerigg Way 5 S18 ... 56 C1
Castlerow Cl S17 ... 56 A3
Castlerow Dr S17 ... 56 A3
Castleshaw Dr DE23 ... 230 C4
Castleton Ave
Derby DE23 ... 231 C4
Ilkeston DE7 ... 194 C3
Somercotes DE55 ... 170 B3
Castleton Bank 20 SK13 ... 9 C1
Castleton CE Prim Sch
S33 ... 38 B1
Castleton Cl NG19 ... 136 B2
Castleton Cres SK13 ... 9 C1
Castleton Gr
19 Gamesley SK13 ... 9 C1
Staveley S43 ... 97 A3
Castleton Rd
Hathersage S32 ... 52 C4
Hope S33 ... 38 C2
Castleton Terr 21 SK13 ... 9 C1
Castleton Tourist Information
Ctr★ S33 ... 38 B1
Castleton YH★ S33 ... 38 A1
Cat & Fiddle La DE7 ... 207 C3
Cat La S14 ... 43 B3
Catchford View S40 ... 95 A4
Catcliff Cl DE45 ... 109 B2
Catcliff Cotts DE45 ... 109 B3
Cathedral of All Saints★
DE1 ... 267 B4
Cathedral Rd DE1 ... 267 B4
Cathedral View DE22 ... 218 B1
Catherine Ave
Ilkeston DE7 ... 208 C3
Mansfield Woodhouse
NG19 ... 136 B2
Catherine Ct
Ashbourne DE6 ... 173 A1
Chesterfield S40 ... 95 C2
Catherine McAuley Ho
DE22 ... 204 C1
Catherine St
Alfreton DE55 ... 159 B2
Chesterfield S40 ... 95 C2
Derby DE23 ... 219 A1
Catkin Dr NG16 ... 195 B4
Cator Rd NG19 ... 135 B2
Catterick Dr DE3 ... 217 B1
Catterwood Dr SK6 ... 15 A1
Catton La DE12 ... 260 A3
Caudwell's Mill & Working
Craft Ctr★ DE4 ... 126 C4
Caudwell Cl S42 ... 131 B4
Cauldon Dr S40 ... 95 A3
Cauldwell Rd DE12 ... 261 A3
Caunton Cl NG18 ... 268 A3
Causeway DE22 ... 204 C1
Causeway Gdns S17 ... 55 B4
Causeway Glade S17 ... 55 B4
Causeway Head Rd S17 . 55 B4
Causeway La DE4 ... 143 B3
Causeway The
Ashover S45 ... 129 B2
Dore S17 ... 55 B4
Eyam S32 ... 71 C3
Wirksworth DE4 ... 165 C4
Cavan Dr DE21 ... 220 A2
Cavell Dr S45 ... 131 C1
Cavendish Ave
Buxton SK17 ... 84 C3
Derby DE22 ... 204 C2
Dore S17 ... 55 C4
Cavendish Cir SK17 ... 85 A4
Cavendish Cl
Castle Donington DE74 ... 247 A1
Creswell S80 ... 81 B1
Doveridge DE6 ... 211 B1
Duffield DE56 ... 190 B1
Holmewood S42 ... 116 C1
Shardlow DE72 ... 235 A1
9 Swadlincote DE11 ... 256 A4
Cavendish Close Inf & Jun
Schs DE21 ... 220 A4
Cavendish Cotts DE4 ... 154 C1
Cavendish Cres NG9 ... 209 B1
Cavendish Cres N NG7 . 268 A1
Cavendish Cres S NG7 . 268 A1
Cavendish Ct
Chesterfield S41 ... 96 A3
Derby DE1 ... 267 A4
Shardlow DE72 ... 235 A1
Cavendish Dr
Ashbourne DE6 ... 185 B4
Clowne S43 ... 81 A2
Ripley DE5 ... 169 B1
Cavendish Flats DE45 ... 110 C4
Cavendish Hospl The
SK17 ... 85 A4
Cavendish Jun Sch S41 . 95 C4
Cavendish Pl S43 ... 78 A2
Cavendish Rd
Bolsover S44 ... 99 A1
Ilkeston DE7 ... 208 C3
Long Eaton NG10 ... 223 B1
Matlock DE4 ... 143 B4
Cavendish Rd E NG7 ... 268 A1
Cavendish Rd W NG7 ... 268 A1
Cavendish Rise S18 ... 75 C4
Cavendish Sq S21 ... 77 B4
Cavendish St
Chesterfield S40 ... 266 B3
Derby DE1 ... 267 A3
Langwith NG20 ... 119 C4
Mansfield NG18 ... 268 C3
Mansfield Woodhouse
NG19 ... 136 A2
Staveley S43 ... 97 B4
Cavendish St N S41 ... 77 A1
Cavendish Way DE3 ... 217 C1
Caversfield Cl DE23 ... 231 A4
Caversham Way DE7 ... 207 B4
Cavill Rd S8 ... 43 A2
Cawdor Rd S2 ... 43 C3
Caxton Cl S43 ... 77 B2
Caxton St
Derby, Littleover DE23 ... 231 C3
Derby, Normanton DE23 . 231 C4
Caythorpe Ct NG19 ... 136 C2
Ceal The SK6 ... 15 A1
Cecil Ave S18 ... 57 A1
Cecil Rd Dronfield S18 ... 57 A1
Swadlincote DE11 ... 255 C3
Cecil St DE22 ... 218 B3
Cedar Ave Alfreton DE55 . 159 A3
Chesterfield S40 ... 95 B3
Long Eaton NG10 ... 236 B3
Mansfield Woodhouse
NG19 ... 136 B3
Ripley DE5 ... 169 B1
Cedar Cl Ashbourne DE6 . 185 B4
Eckington S21 ... 59 A1
Glapwell S44 ... 118 A1
Glossop SK13 ... 10 A1
Killamarsh S21 ... 60 B3
Sandiacre NG10 ... 223 A4
Cedar Croft
Aston-on-T DE72 ... 246 A4
Kilburn DE56 ... 192 A4
Cedar Dr Ockbrook DE72 . 221 B2
Selston NG16 ... 171 C4
Uttoxeter ST14 ... 210 A2
Cedar Gr Belper DE56 ... 179 A1
Linton DE12 ... 261 B3
South Normanton DE55 . 160 A2
Swadlincote DE11 ... 256 A4
Cedar Park Dr S44 ... 99 B1

Cedar Pk DE7 . . . . .208 C4
Cedar Rd
 Castle Donington DE74 . .247 A1
 Linton DE11 . . . . .261 C4
Cedar St Brimington S43 . . .78 A1
 Derby DE22 . . . . .218 C4
 Mansfield NG18 . . . . . . .268 C3
 Shirland DE55 . . . . .146 B3
Cedarwood Ct DE21 . . . .205 C1
Celandine Cl DE21 . . . . .206 A1
Celandine Ct 11 S17 . . .56 A3
Celandine Gdns S17 . . . .56 A3
Celandine Pl DE11 . . . .256 C2
Celanese Rd DE22 . . . . .220 B2
Cemetery La Ripley DE5 .169 C1
 Staveley S43 . . . . .78 C1
 Wirksworth DE4 . . . . . . .154 C1
Cemetery Rd
 Belper DE56 . . . . .179 A3
 Chesterfield S41 . . . . . . .96 B1
 Clay Cross S45 . . . . .131 C1
 Dronfield S18 . . . . .76 A4
 Glossop SK13 . . . . .10 B2
 Somercotes DE55 . . . . . .170 B4
 Stapleford NG9 . . . . . . .223 C4
Cemetery Terr S43 . . . . .96 C4
Central Ave
 Borrowash DE72 . . . . . . .221 A1
 Chesterfield S40 . . . . . . .95 C1
 Creswell S80 . . . . .100 B4
 Mansfield NG18 . . . . . . .268 C3
 Sandiacre NG10 . . . . . . .223 A3
 South Normanton DE55 . .160 A3
 Stapleford NG9 . . . . . . .223 C4
Central Cl
 Shirebrook NG20 . . . . . .119 C2
 Unstone S18 . . . . .76 C3
Central Dr
 Blackwell DE55 . . . . . . .147 C1
 Buxton SK17 . . . . .85 B3
 Calow S44 . . . . .96 C2
 Chesterfield S41 . . . . . . .96 B1
 Shirebrook NG20 . . . . . .119 C2
 Wingerworth S42 . . . . . .114 C4
Central Pavement S40 .266 B3
Central Rd DE55 . . . . . .159 A2
Central St Chesterfield S41 96 B1
 Holmewood S42 . . . . . . .132 C4
 Nottingham NG3 . . . . . . .268 C2
Central Wlk S43 . . . . . . .96 B4
Centre Ct DE1 . . . . .267 C1
Centre St S44 . . . . .117 B1
Centurion Wlk DE1 . . . .219 A4
Chaddesden Cl S18 . . . . .56 B1
Chaddesden La DE21 . . .220 A3
Chaddesden Lane End
 DE21 . . . . .219 C3
Chaddesden Park Inf & Jun
 Schs DE21 . . . . .220 A4
Chaddesden Park Rd
 DE21 . . . . .219 C4
Chadfield Rd DE56 . . . . .190 C3
Chadwick Ave DE24 . . . .232 C3
Chadwick Hill DE4 . . . . .141 A3
Chadwick Nick La DE4 .167 C4
Chadwick Rd S13 . . . . . . .44 B4
Chadwick St SK13 . . . . . .17 A4
Chaffinch Cl DE21 . . . . .220 C4
Chain La DE3 . . . . .218 A1
Chalfont Sq DE21 . . . . . .206 A1
Chalkley Cl DE24 . . . . . .232 C4
Challands Cl S41 . . . . . .115 B4
Challands Way S41 . . . . .115 B4
Challis Ave DE21 . . . . . .220 A4
Challoner Gn 5 S20 . . . .59 C4
Challoner Way S20 . . . . .59 C4
Chalons Cl DE7 . . . . . . .194 C1
Chalons Way DE7 . . . . . .208 C4
Chamberlain Ave ST4 . .269 B1
Chambers Ave DE7 . . . . .209 A4
Chambers Ct SK14 . . . . . .9 A2
Chambers St DE24 . . . . .219 C1
Champion Ave DE7 . . . . .194 B2
Champion Cres NG19 . . .268 A4
Champion Dr S21 . . . . . . .60 B3
Champion Hill DE56 . . . .190 C2
Chancel Pl DE22 . . . . . .267 A1
Chancery La DE22 . . . . . .218 A3
Chancet Wood Cl S8 . . .56 C4
Chancet Wood Dr S8 . . .56 C4
Chancet Wood Rd S8 . . .56 C4
Chancet Wood Rise S8 . .56 C4
Chancet Wood View S8 .56 C4
Chander Hill La S42 . . . .113 B4
Chandlers Ford DE21 . . .205 C1
Chandos Cres S21 . . . . . .60 B3
Chandos Pole St DE22 . .218 B3
Chandres Ct DE22 . . . . .204 C2
Chaneyfield Way S40 . . .95 A4
Channel The DE6 . . . . . .173 A1
Chantrey Ave S41 . . . . . .96 C4
Chantrey Rd S8 . . . . .43 A2
Chantry Cl Derby DE3 . . .217 B1
 Disley SK12 . . . . .32 C3
 Long Eaton NG10 . . . . . .236 A2
 Melbourne DE73 . . . . . . .252 A4
Chantry Ct SK17 . . . . . . .69 B2
Chantry Fold SK12 . . . . . .32 C3
Chantry La SK17 . . . . . . .69 B2
Chantry Rd SK12 . . . . . . .32 C3
Chapel Bar NG1 . . . . . . .268 A1
Chapel Brow
 Broadbottom SK13 . . . . . .16 C3
 Glossop SK13 . . . . .10 A4
Chapel Cl Clowne S43 . . . .80 C2

Chapel Cl *continued*
 Moira DE11 . . . . .256 B1
 Willington DE65 . . . . . . .242 A3
 Youlgreave DE45 . . . . . .125 A3
Chapel Croft Elton DE4 . .140 C3
 Middleton (Nr Wirksworth)
 DE4 . . . . .154 B3
Chapel Ct DE7 . . . . .194 C1
Chapel Gn DE6 . . . . .224 B4
Chapel Hill Ashover S45 .129 C2
 Beeley DE4 . . . . .111 A2
 Cromford DE4 . . . . .155 A4
Chapel Ho 3 DE7 . . . . .208 C4
Chapel Houses SK6 . . . . .23 A3
Chapel Inf Sch SK23 . . . .47 A3
Chapel La
 Apperknowle S18 . . . . . . .58 A1
 Bakewell DE45 . . . . .109 B3
 Barrow u T DE73 . . . . . .244 A3
 Boylestone DE6 . . . . . . .213 A2
 Church Broughton DE65 . .227 A4
 Clifton DE6 . . . . .184 C3
 Crich DE4 . . . . .168 A4
 Derby DE73 . . . . .233 A1
 Derby, Chaddesden DE21 .220 A4
 Derby, Spondon DE21 . . .220 C3
 Glossop SK13 . . . . .9 C3
 Hanbury DE13 . . . . .238 A1
 Holloway DE4 . . . . .156 A3
 Middleton (Nr Wirksworth)
 DE4 . . . . .154 B3
 Rolleston DE13 . . . . . . .240 A2
 Taddington SK17 . . . . . . .88 A2
 Tissington DE6 . . . . .162 A3
 Totley S17 . . . . .55 B2
 Wirksworth DE4 . . . . . . .154 C1
Chapel La E S41 . . . . . . .115 B4
Chapel La W S40 . . . . . . .95 B1
Chapel Pl NG16 . . . . . . .195 C3
Chapel Rd Bolsover S44 . .98 C1
 Grassmoor S42 . . . . .115 C2
 Hayfield SK22 . . . . .25 B1
 Selston NG16 . . . . .171 C3
 Whaley Bridge SK23 . . . . .45 C3
Chapel Row
 Borrowash DE72 . . . . . . .221 A1
 Crich DE4 . . . . .168 A4
Chapel Side DE21 . . . . . .220 C3
Chapel St Alfreton DE55 .159 A2
 Belper DE56 . . . . .178 C2
 Brimington S43 . . . . .96 C4
 Buxton SK17 . . . . .85 A4
 Chesterfield S41 . . . . . . .96 A4
 Coton in t E DE12 . . . . . .260 B2
 Derby DE1 . . . . .267 B4
 Derby, Spondon DE21 . . .220 C3
 Donisthorpe DE12 . . . . . .265 C4
 Duffield DE56 . . . . .190 C2
 Eastwood NG16 . . . . . . .182 C1
 Fritchley DE56 . . . . .168 A3
 Glossop SK13 . . . . .10 B1
 Hayfield SK22 . . . . .25 B1
 Heanor DE75 . . . . .194 A4
 Holbrook DE56 . . . . .191 B4
 17 Ilkeston DE7 . . . . . . .194 C1
 Kilburn DE56 . . . . .192 A4
 Kimberley NG16 . . . . . . .195 C3
 Linton DE11 . . . . .261 C4
 Long Eaton NG10 . . . . . .236 C4
 Longnor SK17 . . . . .121 A3
 Melbourne DE73 . . . . . . .252 A4
 Monyash DE45 . . . . .107 A1
 Mosborough S20 . . . . . . .59 B3
 New Mills SK22 . . . . .33 A3
 New Mills, Rowarth SK22 . .24 C4
 Ripley DE5 . . . . .169 B1
 Smisby LE65 . . . . .257 C2
 Somercotes DE55 . . . . . .170 B4
 Stafford ST16 . . . . .269 A4
 Stonebroom DE55 . . . . . .147 A2
 Stretton en le F DE12 . . .265 C3
 Swadlincote, Church Gresley
 DE11 . . . . .256 A1
 Swadlincote, Newhall
 DE11 . . . . .255 C3
 Swanwick DE55 . . . . . . .169 C4
 Ticknall DE73 . . . . .251 A3
 Whaley Bridge SK23 . . . . .45 C4
 Whaley Thorns NG20 . . .101 A2
 Woodville DE11 . . . . . . .256 C1
Chapel Terr ST16 . . . . . .269 B4
Chapel Way S42 . . . . . . .115 B1
Chapel Wlk
 Alfreton DE55 . . . . .159 A2
 Curbar S32 . . . . .72 C1
Chapel Yd Dronfield S18 . .57 A1
 Harthill S26 . . . . .61 C3
 South Wingfield DE55 . . .157 C2
Chapel-en-le-Frith CE Inf
 Sch SK23 . . . . .47 B3
Chapel-en-le-Frith High Sch
 SK23 . . . . .47 A3
Chapel-en-le-Frith Sta
 SK23 . . . . .47 A2
Chapman Ave DE24 . . . .233 A3
Chapman La S42 . . . . . . .115 C2
Chapmans Croft DE12 . .260 B2
Chapter Cl DE21 . . . . . .205 B1
Chardin Ave SK6 . . . . . . .23 A4
Charing Ct DE1 . . . . . . .267 C5
Charingworth Rd DE21 .206 A1
Chariot Ct 14 DE24 . . . .233 B3
Charity Rd DE55 . . . . . . .170 B3
Charlbury Cl DE23 . . . . .231 A4
Charles Ashmore Rd S8 .57 A4
Charles Ave Derby DE21 .220 B3
 Sandiacre NG10 . . . . . . .223 A4
 Stapleford NG9 . . . . . . .223 C4

Charles Cl DE7 . . . . .209 A3
Charles La SK13 . . . . .10 C2
Charles St Alfreton DE55 .159 A3
 4 Buxton SK17 . . . . .85 B4
 Chesterfield S40 . . . . . . .95 C2
 Glossop SK13 . . . . .10 B1
 Long Eaton NG10 . . . . . .236 B3
 Mansfield NG19 . . . . . . .136 A1
 Mansfield Woodhouse
 NG19 . . . . .136 B2
 Somercotes DE55 . . . . . .170 B4
 Swadlincote DE11 . . . . . .256 B4
Charleston Cl DE11 . . . .256 A4
Charleston Ho 2 NG1 . .268 A2
Charleston Rd DE21 . . . .220 B3
Charlestown SK13 . . . . . .17 B3
Charlestown Dr DE22 . . .204 B2
Charlestown Rd SK13 . . . .17 B4
Charlesworth Cl S43 . . . .33 B2
Charlesworth Cres SK23 .33 B2
Charlesworth Ct NG19 . .136 C2
Charlesworth Rd SK23 . . .33 B2
Charlesworth Sch SK13 . .16 B3
Charlesworth St S44 . . . .117 C4
Charley La SK23 . . . . .47 A4
Charlotte Ct DE14 . . . . . .254 B4
Charlotte La S33 . . . . .51 A4
Charlotte Rd S2 . . . . .43 A4
Charlotte St Derby DE23 .219 A1
 Ilkeston DE7 . . . . .194 C2
Charlton Ave NG10 . . . . .223 C1
Charlton Cl DE12 . . . . . .261 B3
Charlton St ST4 . . . . .269 B2
Charnock Ave S12 . . . . . .44 A2
Charnock Cres S12 . . . . . .44 A2
Charnock Dale Rd S12 . .44 A1
Charnock Dr S12 . . . . . . .44 A2
Charnock Gr S12 . . . . . . .44 A1
Charnock Hall Prim Sch
 S12 . . . . .44 A1
Charnock Hall Rd S12 . . .44 A1
Charnock View Rd S12 . .44 A1
Charnock Wood Rd S12 .44 A1
Charnwood Ave
 Belper DE56 . . . . .179 A2
 Borrowash DE72 . . . . . . .221 B1
 Castle Donington DE74 . .247 B2
 Derby DE23 . . . . .231 B3
 Long Eaton NG10 . . . . . .236 A2
 Sandiacre NG10 . . . . . . .223 A2
Charnwood Cl DE55 . . . .169 C4
Charnwood Cres DE55 . .148 A2
Charnwood Dr DE5 . . . . .169 B1
Charnwood Gr NG19 . . . .136 A3
Charnwood St DE1 . . . . .267 B1
Charter Pk DE7 . . . . .208 C4
Charterhouse Cl DE21 . .205 C2
Charterhouse Dr ST17 . .269 C3
Charterstone La DE22 . .204 C2
Chartwell Ave S42 . . . . .114 B3
Chartwell Dr DE21 . . . . .219 B3
Chase Cl DE73 . . . . .233 A1
Chase Rd DE56 . . . . .167 C2
Chase The Derby DE24 . .231 C2
 Kilburn DE56 . . . . .192 A4
 Little Eaton DE21 . . . . . .191 B1
 Rosliston DE12 . . . . .260 B3
Chase View DE4 . . . . . . .156 C1
Chasecliff Cl S40 . . . . . . .95 B3
Chatfield Cl DE15 . . . . . .248 B1
Chatham Ave DE55 . . . . .159 B2
Chatham Cl DE56 . . . . . .179 B2
Chatham St Derby DE23 .232 A4
 Nottingham NG1 . . . . . . .268 B2
Chatsworth Ave
 Chesterfield S40 . . . . . . .95 A1
 Clowne S43 . . . . .80 C2
 Crich DE4 . . . . .156 C1
 Darley Dale DE4 . . . . . . .142 C4
 Long Eaton NG10 . . . . . .237 A3
 Shirebrook NG20 . . . . . .119 C3
Chatsworth Cl
 Alfreton DE55 . . . . .158 C2
 Bolsover S44 . . . . .99 B1
 Sandiacre NG10 . . . . . . .223 A2
Chatsworth Cres
 Bullbridge DE56 . . . . . . .168 A3
 Derby DE22 . . . . .204 C2
Chatsworth Ct
 Derby DE24 . . . . .231 C2
 Staveley S43 . . . . .97 B4
 West Hallam DE7 . . . . . .207 C4
Chatsworth Dr
 Derby DE3 . . . . .217 C2
 Little Eaton DE21 . . . . . .191 B1
 North Wingfield S42 . . . .131 C3
 Tutbury DE13 . . . . .239 B3
Chatsworth Ho * DE45 . .92 A1
Chatsworth Lodge SK17 .85 A4
Chatsworth Park Ave
 S12 . . . . .44 A3
Chatsworth Park Dr S12 .44 A3
Chatsworth Park Gr S12 .44 A3
Chatsworth Park Rd S12 44 A3
Chatsworth Park Rise
 S12 . . . . .44 A3
Chatsworth Pl
 24 Dronfield S18 . . . . . . .56 B1
 Ilkeston DE7 . . . . .208 A3
Chatsworth Rd
 Buxton SK17 . . . . .85 C4
 Chesterfield S40 . . . . . . .95 B1
 Creswell S80 . . . . .81 B1
 Darley Dale DE4 . . . . . . .111 A4
 Dore S17 . . . . .55 C3
 Swadlincote DE11 . . . . . .256 A3

Chatsworth St
 Derby DE23 . . . . .218 C1
 Tibshelf DE55 . . . . .148 A3
Chatteris Dr DE21 . . . . .205 B1
Chatterton La SK6 . . . . . .24 A4
Chaucer Dr S18 . . . . .76 B4
Chaucer Inf Sch DE7 . . .194 C1
Chaucer Jun Sch DE7 . .194 C1
Chaucer Rd S41 . . . . .95 C4
Chaucer St Ilkeston DE7 .194 C1
 Mansfield NG18 . . . . . . .268 B4
 Nottingham NG1 . . . . . . .268 A2
Chavery Rd S45 . . . . .131 C2
Cheadle Cl DE23 . . . . . . .218 A1
Cheadle Rd ST14 . . . . . . .210 A1
Cheam Cl DE22 . . . . .217 C3
Cheapside
 10 Belper DE56 . . . . . . .178 C2
 Derby DE1 . . . . .267 B3
 Nottingham NG1 . . . . . . .268 C2
Chedworth Cl NG3 . . . . .268 C2
Chedworth Dr DE24 . . . .233 A3
**Cheedale SK17 . . . . .85 B4
Cheedale Ave S40 . . . . . .95 B3
Cheedale Cl
 Burton u T DE15 . . . . . . .248 A3
 Chesterfield S40 . . . . . . .95 B3
Cheetham Ave S18 . . . . . .76 C3
Chell Rd ST16 . . . . .269 A4
Chellaston Inf Sch
 DE73 . . . . .233 A1
Chellaston Jun Sch
 DE73 . . . . .232 C1
Chellaston La DE72,
 DE73 . . . . .233 A1
Chellaston Park Ct
 DE73 . . . . .232 C1
Chellaston Rd DE24 . . . .232 C2
Chellaston Sch DE73 . . .232 C1
Chelmarsh Cl DE73 . . . .233 A2
Chelmorton Cl NG19 . . .136 C2
Chelmorton Pl 1 DE21 .219 C4
Chelmsford Cl DE3 . . . . .217 B2
Chelmsford Way S43 . . . .78 A2
Chelsea Cl DE22 . . . . . . .217 C3
Chelsea Way ST16 . . . . . .269 A3
Cheltenham Cl NG9 . . . .223 C1
Chelwood Rd DE73 . . . . .232 C1
Chendre Cl SK22 . . . . .25 B2
Chepstow Cl S40 . . . . . . .114 C4
Chepstow Gdns S40 . . . .114 C4
Chequer La DE56 . . . . . . .166 B1
Chequers La DE21 . . . . . .219 B3
Chequers Rd DE21 . . . . . .219 B3
Cheribough Rd DE74 . . . .247 A2
Cheriton Cl NG19 . . . . . .135 C1
Cheriton Dr DE7 . . . . . . .194 B2
Cheriton Gdns DE23 . . . .230 C4
Cherry Bank Rd S8 . . . . . .43 A2
Cherry Cl Breaston DE72 .235 C4
 Shirebrook NG20 . . . . . .119 C3
 South Normanton DE55 . .160 A4
Cherry Ct DE14 . . . . .253 C4
Cherry Garth DE65 . . . . .228 B1
Cherry Gr NG18 . . . . .268 A3
Cherry Leys DE15 . . . . . .248 B2
Cherry St S S2 . . . . .43 A4
Cherry Tree Ave
 Belper DE56 . . . . .179 A3
 Ripley DE5 . . . . .180 B4
 Shireoaks S81 . . . . .63 C4
Cherry Tree Cl
 Barlborough S43 . . . . . . .80 A4
 Bolsover S44 . . . . .99 B1
 Brinsley NG16 . . . . .182 C4
 Derby DE22 . . . . .218 A2
 Hilton DE65 . . . . .228 B1
 Ilkeston DE7 . . . . .208 B3
 Mansfield Woodhouse
 NG19 . . . . .136 A2
 Risley DE72 . . . . .222 C2
 Swadlincote DE11 . . . . . .255 C3
Cherry Tree Dr
 Buxton SK17 . . . . .66 B1
 Killamarsh S21 . . . . .60 B3
 Long Duckmanton S44 . . .98 C2
Cherry Tree Gr
 Mastin Moor S43 . . . . . . .79 B2
 North Wingfield S42 . . . .131 C3
Cherry Tree Hill Inf & Jun
 Schs DE21 . . . . .220 A3
Cherry Tree Mews
 Derby DE21 . . . . .220 A2
 Woodville DE11 . . . . . . .256 C1
Cherry Tree Sq SK17 . . . .69 B2
Cherrybrook Dr DE21 . . .206 A2
Cherrydale Ct DE23 . . . .231 A3
Cherrytree Ave DE55 . . .170 A4
Cherrytree Rd DE15 . . . .254 C4
Chertpit La SK17,DE45 . . .89 B3
Chertsey Cl S40 . . . . .114 C4
Chertsey Ct DE7 . . . . . . .207 B4
Chertsey Rd DE3 . . . . . . .217 B1
Cherwell Ct 3 S43 . . . . .96 C4
Chesapeake Rd DE21 . . .220 A3
Chesham Cl SK13 . . . . . . .10 A3
Cheshire St DE24 . . . . . .232 C3
Cheshire Way NG16 . . . .171 B2
Chess Burrow NG19 . . . .136 B1
Chessel Cl S8 . . . . .43 A2
Chester Ave DE22 . . . . . .205 A3
Chester Ct DE21 . . . . . . .220 C2
Chester Gdns DE11 . . . . .256 A1
Chester Gn NG9 . . . . . . .223 C1
Chester Green Rd DE1 . .219 A4
Chester Ho S40 . . . . .95 C4
Chester St
 Chesterfield S40 . . . . . . .95 C4

Chester St *continued*
 Mansfield NG19 . . . . . . .135 C1
Chesterfield & North
 Derbyshire Royal Hospl
 S41 . . . . .96 C2
Chesterfield Art Gall & Mus★
 S41 . . . . .266 C3
Chesterfield Ave
 Chesterfield S43 . . . . . . .77 C3
 Long Eaton NG10 . . . . . .236 C4
 Swadlincote DE11 . . . . . .255 C5
Chesterfield Coll S41 . . .266 B4
Chesterfield Coll (Tapton
 House Campus) S41 . . . .96 B3
Chesterfield Dr DE12 . . .261 B3
Chesterfield Midland Sta
 S41 . . . . .266 C3
Chesterfield Rd
 Alfreton DE55 . . . . .158 C3
 Barlborough S43 . . . . . . .80 A3
 Beeley DE4 . . . . .111 A2
 Belper DE56 . . . . .179 A2
 Bolsover S44 . . . . .98 C3
 Brimington, Middlecroft S43 97 A4
 Brimington, Tapton S41,
 S43 . . . . .96 B4
 Calow S41,S44 . . . . .96 C1
 Darley Dale DE4 . . . . . . .127 B1
 Dronfield S18 . . . . .57 A1
 Eckington S21 . . . . .59 A1
 Grassmoor S42 . . . . .115 C1
 Heage DE56 . . . . .168 C2
 Holmewood S42 . . . . . . .116 B1
 Long Duckmanton S44 . . .98 B2
 Matlock DE4 . . . . .143 B4
 New Houghton NG19 . . . .134 C4
 North Wingfield S42 . . . .132 A4
 Pilsley DE55 . . . . .133 B1
 Pleasley NG19 . . . . .135 A3
 1 Sheffield S8 . . . . .43 A3
 Shirland DE55 . . . . .146 B2
 Sutton in A NG17 . . . . . .148 C2
Chesterfield Rd N NG19 135 B2
Chesterfield Rd S
 Mansfield NG18,NG19 . . .268 B4
 Sheffield S8 . . . . .57 A3
Chesterfield Small Bsns Ctr
 S41 . . . . .96 A4
Chesterfield Trad Est
 S41 . . . . .76 B2
Chesterford Ct DE23 . . .230 C3
Chesterman Cl NG16 . . .195 A4
Chesterton Ave DE23 . . .231 C4
Chesterton Cl S43 . . . . . .96 C2
Chesterton Rd DE21 . . . .220 C3
Chestnut Ave
 Belper DE56 . . . . .179 A1
 Derby DE3 . . . . .217 B2
 Derby, Chellaston DE73 . .232 C2
 Derby, Rose Hill DE23 . . .219 A1
 Eckington S21 . . . . .59 A1
 Holbrook DE56 . . . . .191 B4
 Killamarsh S21 . . . . .60 B3
 Ripley DE5 . . . . .180 B4
 Somercotes DE55 . . . . . .170 B3
 Swadlincote DE11 . . . . . .256 A3
Chestnut Bank DE75 . . . .181 B1
*Chestnut Centre
 Conservatory Pk★* SK23 47 C4
Chestnut Cl Buxton SK17 .66 C1
 Dronfield S18 . . . . .76 B4
 Duffield DE56 . . . . .190 C1
 Horsley Woodhouse DE7 .192 B4
 New Mills SK22 . . . . .24 C1
Chestnut Ctr★ SK23 . . . . .47 C4
Chestnut Dr
 Ashbourne DE6 . . . . .185 B4
 Clowne S43 . . . . .80 B2
 Creswell S80 . . . . .81 B1
 Repton DE65 . . . . .243 B4
 Selston NG16 . . . . .171 C4
 Shirebrook NG20 . . . . . .119 B2
 South Normanton DE55 . .160 A2
Chestnut Gn DE11 . . . . . .256 A1
Chestnut Gr
 Borrowash DE72 . . . . . . .221 B2
 Etwall DE65 . . . . .229 A2
 Mansfield Woodhouse
 NG19 . . . . .136 A3
 Sandiacre NG10 . . . . . . .223 A4
 Tibshelf DE55 . . . . .147 C3
Chestnut La
 Barton in F NG11 . . . . . .237 C3
 Clifton Campville B79 . . .263 C4
Chestnut Rd
 Burton u T DE15 . . . . . . .254 C4
 Langley Mill NG16 . . . . .182 A2
Chestnut Way
 Repton DE65 . . . . .242 B1
 Swanwick DE55 . . . . . . .170 A4
Chestnuts The NG10 . . .236 A4
Chetwynd Ctr The ST17 .269 B3
Chevely Ct DE21 . . . . . . .219 B4
Cheverton Ct DE24 . . . . .233 B3
Chevin Alley DE56 . . . . .190 C4
Chevin Ave
 Borrowash DE72 . . . . . . .221 B2
 Derby DE3 . . . . .217 C1
Chevin Bank DE56 . . . . .190 B3
Chevin Pl DE22 . . . . .218 C4
Chevin Rd
 Belper, Chevinside DE56 .178 C2
 Belper, Milford DE56 . . . .190 C4
 Derby DE1 . . . . .267 A3
 Duffield DE56 . . . . .190 C3
Chevin The DE13 . . . . . . .240 B1
Chevin Vale DE56 . . . . . .190 C3

Chevin View DE56 ......**178** C2
Cheviot Ave NG16 ....**170** C2
Cheviot Cl DE11 ......**256** C1
Cheviot Rd NG10 ......**223** A1
Cheviot St DE22 ......**218** B3
Cheviot Way ◼ S40 ....**95** A3
Chew Rd OL3 ....**5** B4
Chewton St NG16 ......**182** C1
Cheyenne Gdns DE21 ..**220** B3
Cheyne Wlk DE22 ......**218** B3
Chichester Cl DE7 ....**209** A4
Chigwell Way S43 ......**78** A2
Chilson Dr DE3 ......**217** B2
Chiltern Cl
   Chesterfield S40 ......**95** B1
   Grassmoor S42 ......**115** C2
Chiltern Dr DE7 ......**207** C4
Chiltern Gdns NG10 ..**223** A1
Chiltern Rd DE11 ......**256** A1
Chilton Cres NG19 ....**136** B3
Chime Cl DE21 ....**205** C1
Chine The DE55 ....**160** A2
Chingford Ct DE7 ......**218** A3
Chinley Prim Sch SK23 ..**35** A1
Chinley Rd DE21 ......**206** A1
Chinley Sta SK23 ......**34** B1
Chippinghouse Rd S8 ....**43** A4
Chiswick Cl DE7 ......**217** C3
Chisworth Ct NG19 ....**136** C2
Chiverton Cl S18 ......**57** A1
Chorlton Terr ST14 ....**210** B1
Christ Church CE Prim Sch
   S41 ....**96** A3
Christ the King RC Prim Sch
   DE55 ....**159** A3
Christchurch Ct DE1 ..**267** B4
Christie Ave ST16 ....**269** A4
Christopher Terr ST17 ..**269** C3
Chrysalis Way NG16 ..**182** B2
Chrysanthemum Ct
   DE11 ....**256** A3
Chunal La SK13 ....**17** B3
Church Alley DE45 ....**109** B3
Church Ave Buxton SK17 ..**67** A3
   Clay Cross S45 ......**131** C2
   Hatton DE65 ....**239** B4
   Long Eaton NG10 ....**236** A2
   Swadlincote DE11 ....**256** A2
   Tideswell SK17 ......**69** B2
Church Bank S32 ......**53** A4
Church Banks DE6 ....**173** A1
Church Bk SK23 ....**45** B1
Church Broughton CE Prim
   Sch DE65 ....**227** A4
Church Broughton Rd
   DE65 ....**227** B2
Church Brow
   Chapel-en-le-F SK23 ..**47** A3
   Mottram in L SK14 ....**9** A2
Church Cl
   Barrow-u-T DE73 ......**244** B2
   Blackfordby DE11 ....**257** A1
   Blackwell DE55 ......**147** B1
   Burton u T DE15 ......**248** A2
   Clowne S43 ....**80** C2
   Derby DE73 ....**233** A1
   Glossop SK13 ....**10** C1
   Marchington ST14 ....**224** C1
   North Wingfield S45 ..**132** A3
   Nottingham NG3 ......**268** B2
   Peak Forest SK17 ....**49** A2
   Renishaw S21 ....**79** A4
   Staveley S43 ....**97** A3
   Trowell NG9 ....**209** B2
   Willington DE65 ......**242** A3
   Wingerworth S42 ....**115** A2
Church Cnr DE6 ......**165** A1
Church Croft
   Coton in t E DE12 ....**260** B2
   Ripley DE5 ....**169** B1
Church Ct NG10 ......**119** C2
Church Dr Ilkeston DE7 ..**194** B3
   Sandiacre NG10 ......**223** A4
   Shirebrook NG20 ....**119** C2
Church Farm ST14 ....**210** A2
Church Fold SK13 ......**16** B4
Church Gdns NG19 ....**136** B2
Church Gresley Inf Sch
   DE11 ....**256** A1
Church Hill Derby DE21 ..**220** B2
   Etwall DE65 ....**229** A3
   Kimberley NG16 ......**195** C3
   Mansfield Woodhouse
   NG19 ....**136** B2
   Newton DE55 ....**148** A1
Church Hill Ave NG19 ..**136** B2
Church Hill Ctr Broxtowe Coll
   of F Ed NG16 ......**195** C3
Church Hill St DE15 ..**248** A2
Church La Bakewell DE45 **109** B3
   Barrow u T DE73 ......**244** A3
   Barton in F NG11 ....**237** C3
   Baslow DE45 ....**91** C3
   Beeley DE4 ....**111** A2
   Belper DE56 ....**179** A2
   Brackenfield DE55 ..**145** B1
   Brailsford DE6 ......**201** C4
   Breadsall DE21 ......**205** C2
   Brinsley NG16 ......**182** C4
   Caldwell DE12 ......**260** C4
   Calow S44 ....**97** A2
   Castle Donington DE74 ..**247** A2
   Castle Donington, Hemington
   DE74 ....**247** C2
   Chapel-en-le-F SK23 ..**47** A3
   Chelmorton SK17 ....**106** A4
   Chesterfield S40 ....**266** B3
   Clowne S43 ....**80** C2

Church La continued
   Cossall NG16 ....**195** B1
   Darley Dale DE4 ......**110** C1
   Derby, Chaddesden DE21 ..**220** A3
   Derby, Darley Abbey DE22 **205** A1
   Dore S17 ....**55** B3
   Doveridge DE6 ......**211** A1
   Ellastone DE6 ......**183** A2
   Fritchley DE56 ......**168** A3
   Great Longstone DE45 ..**90** A1
   Hanbury DE13 ....**238** A2
   Heath DE55 ....**117** A2
   Heath, Stockley S44 ..**117** B2
   Holmewood S42 ......**116** A2
   Horsley Woodhouse DE7 **192** C3
   Killamarsh S21 ......**60** C3
   Kirk Langley DE6 ....**202** C1
   Little Eaton DE21 ....**205** B4
   Mackworth DE22 ....**217** C4
   Mansfield NG18 ......**268** C3
   Marchington ST14 ....**224** C1
   Marple SK6 ....**23** A3
   Mayfield DE6 ....**184** B3
   Morley DE7 ....**206** C3
   Netherseal DE12 ....**264** C2
   New Mills SK22 ......**33** B4
   Newton Solney DE15 ..**248** B4
   North Wingfield S42 ..**131** C3
   Osmaston DE6 ......**186** A3
   Peak Forest SK17 ....**49** A2
   Pleasley NG19 ......**135** A3
   Rocester ST14 ......**197** A2
   Roston DE6 ....**197** B4
   Selston NG16 ....**171** B4
   Shirley DE6 ....**200** B4
   South Wingfield DE55 ..**157** C2
   Stafford ST16 ....**269** B4
   Stanton-by-D DE7 ....**208** C1
   Stapleford NG9 ......**223** B4
   Stonebroom DE55 ....**146** C3
   Sutton on t H DE6 ....**215** A1
   Thorpe DE6 ....**161** B1
   Thrumpton NG11 ....**237** B2
   Tibshelf DE55 ......**147** C3
   Ticknall DE73 ......**251** A2
   Tideswell SK17 ......**69** B2
   Weston Underwood DE6 **188** C1
Church La N
   Chesterfield S41 ....**77** A2
   Derby DE22 ....**204** C2
Church Level DE6 ....**165** A1
Church Mdws Calow S44 ..**96** C2
   North Wingfield S42 ..**131** C3
Church Mead NG17 ....**148** C2
Church Mews
   Derby DE21 ....**220** B2
   Hatton DE65 ....**227** B1
   Killamarsh S21 ......**60** C4
   Mosborough S20 ....**59** B4
Church Rd Bolsover S44 ..**99** A4
   Branston DE14 ......**253** C4
   Burton u T DE13 ....**240** C1
   Church Broughton DE65 **227** A4
   Darley Dale DE4 ....**127** A1
   Egginton DE65 ......**241** A2
   Fritchley DE56 ......**168** A3
   Hollingworth SK14 ....**9** B2
   Marple SK6 ....**23** A3
   New Mills SK22 ......**33** B4
   Nottingham NG3 ....**268** B2
   Quarndon DE22 ......**204** B3
   Rolleston DE13 ......**240** A2
   Snelston DE6 ....**184** B2
   Swadlincote DE11 ....**256** A3
Church Rise DE55 ....**146** B2
Church Side Calow S44 ..**96** C2
   Mansfield NG18 ......**268** C3
   Sutton in A NG17 ....**148** C2
Church Sq Heanor DE75 ..**181** C1
   Melbourne DE73 ....**252** A4
Church St Alfreton DE55 **158** C2
   Alstonefield DE6 ....**149** C2
   Ashbourne DE6 ......**173** A1
   Ashford in t W DE45 ..**108** C4
   Ashover S45 ....**129** C2
   Barlborough S43 ....**80** A4
   Baslow DE45 ....**91** C3
   Belper DE56 ....**179** A2
   Bolsover S44 ....**99** A1
   Bonsall DE4 ....**142** B1
   Bradwell S33 ....**51** A4
   Brassington DE4 ....**153** A1
   Brimington S43 ......**96** C4
   Buxton SK17 ....**85** A3
   Calow S44 ....**96** C2
   Clifton Campville B79 **263** C1
   Clowne S43 ....**80** C2
   Coton in t E DE12 ....**260** B2
   Creswell S80 ....**81** C1
   Denby DE5 ....**180** B1
   Derby DE23 ....**218** B4
   Derby, Alvaston DE24 **233** B4
   Derby, Rose Hill DE23 **219** A1
   Donisthorpe DE12 ....**262** C1
   Dronfield S18 ......**57** A1
   Eastwood NG16 ......**182** C1
   Eckington S21 ......**59** C2
   Eyam S32 ....**71** B3
   Fritchley DE56 ......**168** A3
   Glossop SK13 ....**10** B1
   Glossop, Hadfield SK13 ..**10** B2
   Glossop, Tintwistle SK13 ..**10** A4
   Hartington SK17 ....**137** B3
   Hartshorne DE11 ....**257** A3
   Hayfield SK22 ......**25** B1
   Heage DE56 ....**168** C2
   Heanor DE75 ....**181** C1

Church St continued
   Holbrook DE56 ......**191** B3
   Holloway DE4 ....**156** A3
   Horsley DE21 ....**191** C3
   Ilkeston DE7 ....**194** C2
   Kilburn DE56 ....**191** C4
   Lockington DE74 ....**247** C2
   Longnor SK17 ......**121** C3
   Mansfield NG18, NG19 **268** B4
   Mansfield Woodhouse
   NG19 ....**136** B2
   Marple SK6 ....**23** A3
   Matlock DE4 ....**143** B2
   Melbourne DE73 ....**252** A4
   Monyash DE45 ......**107** B1
   Netherseal DE12 ....**264** C3
   Ockbrook DE72 ......**221** B2
   Pilsley S45 ....**132** B1
   Pleasley NG19 ......**135** A2
   Ripley DE5 ....**169** B1
   Ripley, Waingroves DE5 **181** A4
   Sandiacre NG10 ......**223** A4
   Shirland DE55 ......**146** B1
   Somercotes DE55 ....**170** B3
   South Normanton DE55 **160** A3
   Stapleford NG9 ......**223** B4
   Staveley S43 ....**78** C1
   Stoke-on-T ST4 ......**269** B2
   Stretton en le F DE12 **265** C1
   Swadlincote DE11 ....**256** A1
   Swadlincote, Lower Midway
   DE11 ....**256** B2
   Swadlincote, Newhall
   DE11 ....**256** A3
   Tansley DE4 ....**144** A2
   Tideswell SK17 ......**69** B2
   Tutbury DE13 ......**239** B4
   Unstone S18 ....**76** C4
   Whaley Thorns NG20 **101** A1
   Wirksworth DE4 ....**165** C4
   Youlgreave DE45 ....**125** B3
Church St E NG16 ....**160** B2
Church St N S41 ......**77** A2
Church St S
   Chesterfield S40 ....**115** A4
   Glossop SK13 ....**10** C1
Church St W
   Chesterfield S40 ....**95** B1
   Pinxton NG16 ......**160** B2
Church View
   Barlborough S43 ....**80** A4
   Breaston DE72 ......**235** B4
   Chesterfield S40 ....**95** B1
   Clifton DE6 ....**184** C3
   Clowne S43 ....**80** C2
   Duffield DE56 ......**190** C1
   Glapwell S44 ....**134** A4
   Heanor DE75 ....**181** A2
   Ilkeston DE7 ....**208** C4
   Killamarsh S21 ......**60** C4
   Mottram in L SK14 ....**9** A2
   New Houghton NG19 ..**134** C4
Church View Cotts S43 ..**84** C3
Church View Dr DE45 ..**91** C3
Church Way S40 ......**266** B3
Church Wlk
   Brinsley NG16 ......**182** C4
   Chesterfield S40 ....**266** B3
   Derby DE22 ....**205** A2
   Duffield DE56 ......**190** C1
   Eastwood NG16 ......**182** C1
   Glossop SK13 ....**10** C1
   Somercotes DE55 ....**170** C3
   ◼ Stapleford NG9 ....**223** C4
Churchdale Ave NG9 ..**209** C3
Churchdale Rd S12 ....**44** B2
Churchdown Cl DE21 ..**206** A1
Churchill Ave DE4 ....**154** B3
Churchill Cl DE72 ....**235** B4
Churchill Dr Hilton DE65 **228** C1
   ◼ Stapleford NG9 ....**223** C4
Churchland Ave S42 ..**132** B4
Churchside
   Grassmoor S41 ......**115** B3
   Willington DE65 ....**242** A3
Churchside La S41 ....**115** B3
Churchside Wlk DE22 ..**218** C2
Churchward Dr DE13 ..**240** C1
Churnet Cl DE6 ......**184** B4
Churston Rd S40 ......**95** B2
Cinder Bank DE7 ....**170** C2
Cinder La Killamarsh S21 ..**60** C4
   Wirksworth DE4 ....**165** C3
Cinder Rd DE55 ......**170** B4
Cinderhill La S8 ......**57** B4
Circle The Derby DE24 ..**231** C4
   Mansfield Woodhouse
   NG19 ....**136** A2
   Sheffield S2 ....**44** A4
Circular Dr S21 ......**79** A4
Circular Rd
   Chesterfield S40 ....**115** A4
   Staveley S43 ....**78** B1
City Link NG2 ....**268** C1
City of Stoke-on-Trent Sixth
   Form Coll ST4 ....**269** C2
City Point NG7 ......**268** A1
City Rd Derby DE1 ....**219** A4
   Fenton ST4 ....**269** C1
   Sheffield S2 ....**43** C4
City Rd Ind Pk DE1 ..**219** A4
City Sch The S13 ....**44** C3
City The Woodville DE11 **256** C1
   Woodville, Blackfordby
   DE11 ....**257** A1
Civic Ctr S18 ....**57** A1
Civic Way DE11 ......**256** A1
Clamp Dr DE11 ......**256** A1

Clapgun St DE74 ......**247** A2
Clara Mount Rd DE75 ..**182** A1
Clare Valley NG7 ......**268** A1
Clarehaven NG9 ......**223** C3
Claremont Cl NG19 ....**136** C2
Clarence Ind Trad Est
   S41 ....**96** A4
Clarence Rd
   Chesterfield S40 ....**266** A3
   Derby DE23 ....**218** C1
   Long Eaton NG10 ....**236** B3
Clarence St
   Chesterfield S40 ....**266** A3
   Mansfield NG18 ......**268** B3
   Mansfield, Moorhaigh
   NG19 ....**135** B2
   Nottingham NG3 ....**268** C2
   Stonebroom DE55 ....**147** A2
Clarence Terr DE4 ....**143** A1
Clarence Villas DE4 ..**143** A1
Clarendon Rd
   Mansfield NG18 ......**268** A4
   Staveley S43 ....**97** A3
Clarendon St Fenton ST4 **269** C1
   Nottingham NG1 ....**268** A2
Clark St ST16 ....**269** B4
Clarke Ave DE75 ......**181** B1
Clarke Dr NG10 ......**236** A2
Clarke St DE1 ....**267** C4
Clarkes Cl ST14 ......**210** A1
Clarkes La DE72 ......**246** A4
Clarkson Ave S40 ....**266** B1
Clatterway DE4 ......**154** C4
Claverhouse Rd DE15 **248** A1
Claxton St DE75 ......**181** B1
Claxton Terr DE75 ....**181** B1
Clay Cl DE11 ....**256** B3
Clay Cross Com Hospl
   S45 ....**131** B2
Clay Cross Inf & Jun Sch
   S45 ....**131** B2
Clay La Clay Cross S45 ..**131** A1
   Heanor DE75 ....**181** C1
Clay Pit Way S43 ......**80** B3
Clay St Burton u T DE15 **248** A1
   Draycott DE72 ......**235** A4
   Shirland DE55 ......**146** C1
Clay St E DE15 ......**248** A1
Claye St NG10 ......**236** C4
Claylands Cl SK14 ....**9** B2
Claylands Gr S80 ......**81** C3
Claylands Pl S80 ......**81** C3
Claylands Rd S80 ......**81** C3
Claymar Dr DE11 ....**256** A4
Claymills Rd DE13 ....**241** A1
Claypit La S42 ......**112** C4
Clays La DE14 ......**253** C4
Clayton Gr DE75 ......**181** B2
Clayton St S41 ......**266** C2
Cleave Rd DE14 ......**254** A4
Cleeves Ct ◼◼ NG7 ....**268** A2
Clegg Hill Dr NG17 ..**148** C2
Clematis Cres DE15 ..**255** A4
Clement La S33 ....**50** B3
Clement Rd
   Horsley Woodhouse DE7 **192** B4
   Marple SK6 ....**23** B4
Clerkson St ◼ NG18 ..**268** B3
Clerkson's Alley NG18 **268** B3
Cleve Ave Beeston NG9 **223** C1
   Darley Dale DE4 ....**142** C4
Cleveland Ave
   Derby DE21 ....**220** A3
   Draycott DE72 ......**235** A4
   Long Eaton NG10 ....**223** C1
Cleveland Cl DE11 ....**256** A2
Cleveland Ct DE15 ....**248** A2
Cleveland Rd DE55 ....**146** C2
Cleveland Way S40 ....**95** B3
Cleveleys Rd NG9 ....**223** C2
Clewley Rd DE14 ......**253** C4
Cliff Bvd NG16 ......**195** C4
Cliff Coll S32 ....**91** C3
Cliff La Curbar S32 ....**72** C1
   Elton DE45 ....**140** B4
   Kirby-in-A NG16 ....**160** C2
   Tideswell SK17 ......**69** B2
Cliff Nook DE55 ......**160** A2
Cliff Rd Buxton SK17 ..**85** B4
   Holme HD7 ....**2** C4
   Nottingham NG1 ....**268** B1
Cliff St NG18 ....**268** C4
Cliffash La DE56 ......**176** C3
Cliffdon Ho DE65 ....**239** B4
Cliffe Field Rd S8 ....**43** A2
Cliffe Hill Ave NG9 ..**223** B4
Cliffe La S32 ....**52** C4
Cliffe Rd S43 ....**33** A4
Cliffe View Rd S8 ....**43** A3
Clifford Cl
   Chesterfield S40 ....**95** A1
   Long Eaton NG10 ....**236** A2
Clifford St Derby DE24 **219** B1
   Long Eaton NG10 ....**236** C4
Clifton Ave
   Barlborough S43 ....**80** A4
   Long Eaton NG10 ....**237** A4
Clifton CE Prim Sch
   DE6 ....**184** C3
Clifton Cl Overseal DE12 **262** A2
   Stafford ST16 ......**269** C4
   Swadlincote DE11 ....**256** A1
Clifton Dr Buxton SK17 ..**85** B2
   Derby DE3 ....**217** C2
   Stafford ST16 ......**269** C4
Clifton Pl NG18 ......**268** B4
Clifton Rd
   Ashbourne DE6 ......**185** A4

Clifton Rd continued
   Buxton SK17 ....**85** B4
   Derby DE22 ....**204** B2
   Matlock Bath DE4 ....**155** A4
   Netherseal DE12 ....**264** B3
Clifton St Chesterfield S40 **95** C2
   Derby DE1 ....**267** D1
Clifton Terr NG7 ......**268** A1
Clifton Thorn Mdws
   LE65 ....**258** A1
Clifton Way DE15 ....**248** A1
Clinthill La S80 ....**81** C4
Clinton Ave NG16 ....**182** B3
Clinton Ct ◼◼ NG1 ....**268** B2
Clinton St DE21 ......**219** B3
Clinton St E NG1 ......**268** B2
Clinton St W NG1 ......**268** B2
Clinton Terr ◼◼ NG7 ..**268** A1
Clipstone Ave
   Mansfield NG18 ......**268** C4
   Nottingham NG1 ....**268** B2
Clipstone Gdns DE21 ..**206** A1
Clive Ho DE55 ....**159** C2
Clock Tower Bsns Ctr The
   S43 ....**78** A1
Clodhall La Curbar S32 ..**72** C1
   Old Brampton S42 ....**93** A3
Cloisters Ct DE21 ....**205** C2
Cloonmore Croft S8 ..**43** B1
Cloonmore Dr S8 ......**43** B1
Close Bank DE13 ......**239** B3
Close Jun Sch The ST4 **269** A2
Close The
   Derby, Allestree DE22 **204** C1
   Derby, Normanton Park
   DE23 ....**218** B1
   Great Longstone DE45 ..**89** C2
   Linton DE12 ....**261** B3
   Marple SK6 ....**15** A1
   Matlock DE4 ....**143** A3
   Moira DE11 ....**262** B4
   Shirebrook NG20 ....**119** C3
   Stafford, Rowley Park
   ST16 ....**269** A3
   Tutbury DE13 ......**239** A3
Cloud Ave NG9 ......**223** C4
Cloudside Ct NG10 ....**223** A4
Cloudside Jun Sch
   NG10 ....**223** A4
Cloudside Rd NG10 ....**223** A4
Cloudwood Cl DE21 ..**218** A1
Clough Ave SK6 ......**23** B3
Clough Bank S2 ......**43** A4
Clough La Hayfield SK22 ..**25** B3
   Birchover DE4 ......**141** B4
   Ringinglow S10 ......**42** C3
   Wensley DE4 ....**141** B4
Clough Side SK6 ......**23** B4
Clough St SK17 ....**85** A4
Clough The Bamford S33 ..**40** A2
   Chesterfield S41 ....**96** C1
Cloughside SK12 ......**32** C3
Clover Cl DE21 ......**220** C3
Clover Ct Shardlow DE72 **234** C1
   Sheffield S8 ....**43** B1
   Tibshelf DE55 ......**148** A4
Clover Nook Ind Est
   DE55 ....**159** C2
Clover Nook Rd
   Pinxton NG16 ......**159** C2
   Somercotes DE55 ....**159** C2
   South Normanton DE55 **159** C2
Clover Rise NG16 ....**195** A4
Cloverdale DE11 ......**256** A4
Cloverdale Dr DE24 ..**231** C1
Cloverslade DE65 ....**230** B1
Cloves Hill DE7 ......**192** B1
Clowne Jun & Inf Schs
   S43 ....**80** C2
Clowne Rd
   Barlborough S43 ....**80** B3
   Bolsover S44 ....**99** A4
Club La DE73 ....**244** A3
Club Row S32 ....**71** C3
Club St ST4 ....**269** B1
Clubmill Terr S40 ....**95** C2
Clumber Ave
   Ashbourne DE6 ......**185** A4
   Clowne S43 ....**80** C2
Clumber Cl
   Long Eaton NG10 ....**236** A2
   Mansfield NG19 ......**268** B4
   ◼◼ Nottingham NG1 ..**268** B1
Clumber Cres N NG7 ..**268** A1
Clumber Cres S NG7 ..**268** A1
Clumber Ct Ilkeston DE7 **194** C3
   Mansfield NG19 ......**135** C1
   Nottingham NG1 ....**268** A1
Clumber Dr NG19 ....**135** C1
Clumber Pl S43 ....**97** B3
Clumber Rd E NG7 ....**268** A1
Clumber Rd W NG7 ....**268** A1
Clumber St
   Long Eaton NG10 ....**236** B4
   Mansfield NG18 ......**268** B4
   ◼◼ Nottingham NG1 ..**268** B1
Clun Ct NG19 ....**136** B1
Clune St S43 ....**81** A3
Cluster Ct ◼ DE56 ..**178** C2
Cluster Rd DE56 ......**178** C2
Co-operative St
   Derby DE23 ....**218** C1
   Long Eaton NG10 ....**236** C3
Coach Dr Eastwood NG16 **182** C2
   Quarndon DE22 ......**204** B4
Coach Rd Hollingworth SK14 **9** B3
   Ironville DE55 ......**170** B2
   Ripley DE5 ....**169** C2

Coach Way DE65 ....242 B3
Coachhouse Mews 4
DE11 ....256 A4
Coachways DE7 ....193 C2
Coal La DE11,DE73 ......257 B4
Coalpit La
Coton in t E DE12 ....260 C2
Youlgreave DE45 ....125 B3
Coarses View SK23 .....47 B4
Coasthill DE4 ....156 C1
Coatsby Rd NG16 ......195 C4
Cobden Pl NG19 ....135 C1
Cobden Rd
Chesterfield S40 ....266 A4
Matlock DE4 ....143 B3
Cobden St Derby DE22 ..218 B3
Long Eaton NG10 ....236 C4
Ripley DE5 ....169 B1
Cobham Cl DE24 ....231 B2
Cobnar Ave S8 ....43 A1
Cobnar Dr
Chesterfield S41 ....95 B4
Sheffield S8 ....43 A1
Cobnar Rd S8 ....43 A1
Cobnar Wood Cl S18 ....76 A2
Cobthorn Dr DE22 .....204 B2
Coburn Pl DE1 ....267 A3
Cock Ayne Cl NG10 ....223 A2
Cock Brow SK14 ....15 B4
Cock Hill Baslow DE45 ...91 C3
Clifton DE6 ....184 C3
Cock Pitt The DE1 .....267 C3
Cockayne La DE6 ......164 A1
Cockayne St N DE24 ...232 C3
Cockayne St S DE24 ...232 C3
Cockerhouse Rd NG16 ..182 C2
Cockleys NG10 ....236 B3
Cockshead La DE6 .....198 B4
Cockshut La
Holbeck NG20 ....101 A2
Melbourne DE73 ....251 C4
Whaley Thorns NG20 .....101 A2
Cockshutt Ave S8 ....56 B4
Cockshutt Dr S8 ....56 B4
Cockshutt La DE55 .....170 C4
Cockshutt Rd S8 ....56 B4
Cod Beck Cl DE24 ......233 B3
Codnor Com Prim Sch
DE5 ....181 A4
Codnor Denby La DE5 ..181 A3
Codnor Gate DE5 ......170 A1
Codnor Gate Ind Est
DE5 ....170 A1
Codnor La DE5 ....170 B1
Coffin La DE6 ....165 A1
Coggers La S32 ....52 C4
Coisley Hill S13 ....44 C3
Cokayne Ave DE6 ......173 B1
Cokayne Mews DE6 ....173 B2
Coke St DE22 ....218 B3
Cokefield Terr DE55 ....148 B1
Coldharbour La S45 ....145 A2
Coldstream Wlk DE24 ..231 C2
Coldwell St DE4 ....154 C1
Cole Dr ST16 ....269 A3
Cole La DE72 ....221 B2
Coleman St DE24 ......232 C4
Coleraine Cl DE21 .....220 A2
Coleridge St
Derby, Littleover DE23 ...231 C3
Derby, Normanton DE23 ..231 C4
Colin Ave DE5 ....181 A4
Colin St DE55 ....159 A2
Colindene Gr ST4 ......269 B1
Coliseum Ctr The DE1 ..267 C2
Colledge St DE55 ......170 B3
College Ave S43 ....78 B1
College Mews DE1 .....218 C3
College Pl DE1 ....267 B4
College Rd Buxton SK17 ..85 A3
Denstone ST14 ....196 B3
Killamarsh S21 ....60 B1
Stoke-on-T ST4 ....269 B2
College St
Long Eaton NG10 ....223 B1
Nottingham NG1 ....268 A1
College Way SK17 ....85 B1
Collier Ave NG19 ....136 A3
Collier La DE72 ....221 B2
Collier St SK13 ....17 B4
Colliers Trek S43 ....80 B3
Colliers Way S45 ....131 A2
Colliery Cl S43 ....78 C1
Colliery La DE12 ....261 B2
Colliery Rd
Blackwell DE55 ....147 C1
Swadlincote DE11 ....256 A1
Colliery Row
Alfreton DE55 ....159 A3
Pinxton NG16 ....160 B1
Swadlincote DE11 ....256 A1
Collin Ave NG10 ....223 A2
Collin Rd ST4 ....269 A1
Collin St NG1 ....268 B1
Collingham Gdns DE22 .218 A3
Collingham Rd NG19 ...135 B1
Collingwood Cres DE4 ..143 A3
Collingwood Gr ST4 ...269 A2
Collingwood Rd NG10 ..236 C3
Collins Ave DE55 ......160 A4
Collis Cl DE24 ....232 C4
Collishaw Cl S41 ....96 B1
Collumbell Ave DE72 ...221 B3
Colne Ct NG19 ....136 B1
Colombo St DE23 ......219 A1
Colonnade The 14 ST16 .269 B4
Colonsay Cl NG9 ....209 B2
Colton Cl S41 ....76 C1
Coltsfoot Dr DE24 .....231 C1
Coltsworth La S43 ....80 C4
Columbell Way DE4 ....127 B1
Columbia St NG17 .....148 C2
Columbine Cl DE21 .....206 A1
Colver Rd 9 S2 ....43 A4
Colvile St DE22 ....218 B3
Colville Cl DE12 ....263 B4
Colville St NG1 ....268 A2
Colwell Dr DE24 ....233 B3
Colwick Cl NG19 ....135 C1
Colwick Rd NG2 ....268 C1
Colwyn Ave DE23 ......218 B1
Colyear St DE1 ....267 B3
Combs Bank SK13 ....9 B1
Combs Cl SK22 ....33 A4
Combs Fold SK13 ....9 B1
Combs Gdns SK13 ....9 B1
Combs Inf Sch SK23 .....46 C1
Combs Lea SK13 ....9 B1
Combs Mews SK13 ....9 B1
Combs Rd SK23 ....46 C2
Combs Terr SK13 ....9 B1
Combs Way SK13 ....9 B1
Comfrey Cl DE23 ....230 C3
Commerce Sq 10 NG1 ..268 B1
Commerce St
Derby DE24 ....232 C4
Melbourne DE73 ....252 A4
Commercial Gate NG18 .268 B3
Commercial Rd SK17 ....69 B2
Commercial Row S32 ...72 B4
Commercial St 3 NG18 268 B3
Common End DE65 .....229 A2
Common La
Chelmorton SK17 ....87 A1
Mansfield Woodhouse
NG19 ....136 A2
Old Brampton S42 ....94 C4
Pleasley NG20 ....119 B2
Scarcliffe NG20 ....119 B2
Shirebrook NG20 ....119 B2
Stanley DE7 ....207 A4
Sutton on t H DE6 ....228 A4
Common Piece La DE65 230 C1
Common Rd Harthill S26 .62 A3
Sutton in A NG17 ....148 C1
Swadlincote DE11 ....256 B1
Thorpe Salvin S80 ....62 C3
Common Side
Selston NG16 ....171 C4
Swadlincote DE11 ....256 B1
Common The Crich DE4 .168 A4
Quarndon DE22 ....204 B4
South Normanton DE55 ..160 A3
Common Wood DE4 ....143 A2
Commonpiece La DE6 ..215 A1
Commonpiece Rd S45 ..131 B2
Commons Cl NG16 .....195 A4
Commonside Rd S18 ....75 B1
Compass Cres S41 ......77 B2
Compstall Mills Est SK6 .15 A1
Compstall Rd
Compstall SK6 ....15 A2
Marple SK6 ....15 A1
Compton Ave DE72 .....246 A4
Compton Cl
11 Derby DE24 ....233 B3
Stafford ST17 ....269 C3
Compton Dr S80 ....81 B1
Compton Gr SK17 ....85 A3
Compton Rd SK17 ....85 A3
Compton St
Ashbourne DE6 ....173 B1
Chesterfield S40 ....266 A4
Holmewood S42 ....116 C1
Langwith NG20 ....119 C4
Comyn Gdns NG3 ......268 B2
Conalan Ave S17 ....56 A3
Concert Pl 6 SK17 ......85 A4
Condliff Rd SK17 ....69 A3
Conduit St SK13 ....9 C4
Coney Green Bsns Ctr
S45 ....131 C2
Coney Green Rd S45 ...131 C2
Coniston Ave DE21 .....220 C3
Coniston Cl NG19 ......136 C2
Coniston Cres DE21 ....205 B1
Coniston Dr
Clay Cross S45 ....131 A1
Ilkeston DE7 ....208 B3
Coniston Ho ST16 ......269 B4
Coniston Rd
Chesterfield S41 ....95 C4
Dronfield S18 ....56 C1
Long Eaton NG10 ....223 A1
Coniston Way S41 ....95 C4
Conkers Discovery*
DE12 ....262 B3
Conkers Waterside*
DE12 ....262 B2
Conksbury Ave DE45 ...125 B3
Conksbury La DE45 ....125 B3
Connaught Ct DE55 ....159 A2
Connaught Rd DE22 ....218 B2
Connelly Ct S40 ....95 C2
Consett Cl DE21 ....205 B1
Consort Gdns DE21 .....206 B2
Consort St ST4 ....269 B2
Constable Ave DE23 ....218 B1
Constable Cl
Dronfield S18 ....56 C1
Sheffield S14 ....43 C1
Constable Dr
Derby DE23 ....218 A1
Constable Dr *continued*
Marple SK6 ....23 A4
Sheffield S14 ....43 B1
Constable La DE23 .....218 B2
Constable Pl S14 ....43 C1
Constable Rd S14 ....43 B1
Constable Way S14 .....43 B1
Convent Cl
Burton u T DE15 ....254 C4
Stoke-on-T ST4 ....269 B2
Convent Ct ST4 ....269 B2
Convent St 26 NG1 .....268 B2
Conway Ave DE72 ......221 B1
Conway St
Long Eaton NG10 ....236 C4
Stoke-on-T ST4 ....269 C2
Conygree La DE6 ......184 B4
Cook Cl Belper DE56 ...179 C3
Clay Cross S42 ....131 A3
Cook Dr DE7 ....209 A3
Cook La DE6 ....211 A1
Cooke Cl NG10 ....236 A3
Cookfield DE56 ....179 C4
Cookham Cl DE3 ....217 B1
Cooks Ave DE74 ....247 A2
Coombes La SK13 ....16 B3
Coombes View SK14 ....15 C4
Coombs Rd DE45 ......109 C3
Cooper St Derby DE22 ..218 B3
Glossop SK13 ....10 A1
Ripley DE5 ....169 B1
Cooper's Cl DE6 ....173 B1
Coopers Cl DE72 ....221 B1
Coopers Croft DE65 ....227 B1
Coopers Gdns DE6 .....173 A1
Cope Ct DE24 ....232 A3
Cope St ST16 ....269 B4
Copeland Ave NG9 .....223 C4
Copeland St Derby DE1 .267 C2
Stoke-on-T ST4 ....269 B2
Copenhagen Rd S45 ...131 C2
Copes Way Derby DE21 ..220 A4
Uttoxeter ST14 ....210 A1
Copley Croft DE6 ......173 B2
Coplow La DE65 ....226 B3
Copper Beach Manor
SK13 ....9 C1
Copper Beech Dr SK13 ...9 C1
Copper Beeches DE5 ...169 B1
Copper Glade ST16 ....269 C4
Copper Yd DE5 ....180 C1
Copperas Rd DE11 .....255 B3
Copperleaf Cl DE22 ....267 A2
Coppice Ave
High Lane SK12 ....32 A3
Ilkeston DE7 ....194 B3
Coppice Cl
Chesterfield S41 ....115 B3
Derby DE22 ....204 C1
High Lane SK12 ....32 A3
Kilburn DE56 ....192 A4
Coppice Ct DE75 ....193 C4
Coppice Dr
Eastwood NG16 ....182 B2
Heanor DE75 ....193 C4
Coppice La
Clifton Campville B79 ....263 C1
High Lane SK12 ....32 A3
Coppice Prim Sch DE75 193 C4
Coppice Side DE11 ....256 B2
Coppice The
Shirebrook NG20 ....119 B2
Whaley Bridge SK23 ......45 C3
Coppice View DE55 ....160 A2
Coppicewood Dr DE23 .218 A1
Copse Cl DE4 ....165 C4
Copse Gr DE23 ....231 A4
Copse Rise DE11 ....256 A4
Copse The Ilkeston DE7 ..194 B3
Marple SK6 ....23 B4
Copseside Cl 10 NG10 ..236 A4
Copsewood DE55 ......160 A2
Copsey Croft Ct NG10 ..236 C4
Copthorne Com Inf Sch
DE55 ....159 A3
Copthurst Rd HD9 ....3 C4
Coral Way S45 ....131 B2
Corbar Rd SK17 ....66 A1
Corbarwoods La SK17 ...66 A1
Corbel Cl DE21 ....205 C1
Corbridge Gr DE23 .....231 A4
Corden Ave DE3 ....218 A1
Corden St DE23 ....219 A1
Cordville Cl DE21 ......220 A3
Cordwell Ave S41 ....95 B4
Cordwell Cl
Castle Donington DE74 ...246 C2
Staveley S43 ....97 B4
Cordwell La S18 ....74 C3
Cordy La Brinsley NG16 ..182 C4
Selston NG16 ....182 C4
Corfe Cl DE23 ....231 B3
Corfield Ave DE75 .....193 C4
Corfield CE Inf Sch
DE75 ....181 B1
Coriander Gdns DE23 ..231 B2
Corinium Cl DE24 ......233 B3
Corker Rd S12 ....44 A3
Corks La SK12 ....32 C3
Corley La DE6 ....174 B1
Corn Cl DE55 ....160 A3
Corn Mill Cl DE4 ......165 C3
Corn Mkt DE1 ....267 B3
Corn St SK13 ....10 B1
Corner Farm DE6 ......201 C4
Cornfield Ave DE55 ....160 A2
Cornfield Cl 1 S42 ......95 A3
Cornfield Rd NG16 .....195 C4
Cornflower Dr DE21 ....206 A2
Cornhill DE22 ....204 C2
Cornhill Dr DE55 ......159 A2
Cornmill Cl Bolsover S44 .99 A1
Calver S32 ....72 B1
15 Derby DE72 ....233 B3
Cornmill La DE13 ......239 C3
Cornwall Ave
Brimington S43 ....96 C4
Buxton SK17 ....85 C4
Cornwall Cl
Brimington S43 ....96 C4
Westwood NG16 ....171 B2
Cornwall Dr
Brimington S43 ....96 C4
Grassmoor S42 ....115 C2
Cornwall Rd
Burton u T DE15 ....254 C3
Derby DE21 ....219 B3
Shireoaks S81 ....63 C4
Cornwallis Cl NG10 ....236 B3
Cornwallis St ST4 ......269 B1
Coronation Ave
Belper DE56 ....179 A3
Derby DE24 ....233 B3
New Houghton NG19 ....134 C4
Sandiacre NG10 ....223 A4
Coronation Cl DE73 ....252 A4
Coronation Cotts DE13 .253 A4
Coronation Cres ST14 ..197 A2
Coronation Dr
Shirebrook NG20 ....119 C1
South Normanton DE55 ..160 A3
Coronation La DE12 ...265 C3
Coronation Rd
Brimington S43 ....96 C4
Cossall DE7, NG16 ......195 A1
Mapperley DE7 ....193 C2
Stanley DE7 ....207 B3
Stoke-on-T, Hartshill ST4 .269 A2
Coronation St
Derby DE23 ....232 A4
5 Ilkeston DE7 ....208 C4
Mansfield NG18 ....268 C3
Overseal DE12 ....262 A2
Swadlincote DE11 ....256 A3
Whitwell S80 ....82 A3
Coronet Ct DE21 ....206 B2
Corporation Rd DE7 ...209 A3
Corporation St
Chesterfield S41 ....266 C3
Derby DE1 ....267 B3
6 Mansfield NG18 ....268 B4
Stafford ST16 ....269 B4
Stoke-on-T ST4 ....269 B1
Corve Way S40 ....94 C3
Cosby Rd NG2 ....268 C1
Cossall Rd NG9 ....209 B3
Cote Bottom La DE65 ..227 A4
Cote Green La SK6 .....15 A1
Cote Green Rd SK6 .....15 B1
Cote Hilloc DE4 ....127 A3
Cote La SK22 ....25 B2
Cotes Park Ind Est
DE55 ....159 B1
Cotes Park La DE55 ....159 B1
Cotgrave Rd NG19 .....135 C1
Cotman Dr SK6 ....23 B4
Cotmanhay Inf & Jun Sch
DE7 ....194 C3
Cotmanhay Rd DE7 ....194 C2
Coton Ave ST16 ....269 C4
Coton Cl NG19 ....136 C2
Coton in the Elms CE Prim
Sch DE12 ....260 B2
Coton La DE12 ....260 B3
Coton Pk DE12 ....255 B1
Coton Rd Derby DE23 ..219 A1
Walton-on-T DE12 ....259 C3
Cotswold Cl
2 Chesterfield S40 ....95 B3
Derby DE23 ....231 B4
Glossop SK13 ....17 A4
4 Long Eaton NG10 .....236 A4
Swadlincote DE11 ....256 A2
Cotswold Dr S42 ....115 C2
Cotswold Rd DE14 .....253 C4
Cottage Cl Heage DE56 ..179 C4
Ilkeston DE7 ....194 B2
Poolsbrook S43 ....98 A4
Swadlincote DE11 ....256 A4
Cottage Garden La
DE75 ....181 B1
Cottage La SK13 ....9 C1
Cottam Cres SK6 ....23 A4
Cottam Dr S43 ....80 B3
Cotterdale Cl NG19 ....136 C1
Cotterhill La S43 ....96 C4
Cottesmore Rd DE15 ...248 A1
Cottisford Cl DE23 ....231 A4
Cotton La DE24 ....219 B1
Cotton Mill Hill S42 ...113 C4
Cotton St S44 ....99 A1
Counduit Rd S44 ......118 A4
Counting House Rd SK12 32 C3
Countisbury Dr DE21 ..206 A1
County Est The NG17 ..148 C1
County Rd ST16 ....269 B4
Coupe La S42, S45 .....131 A3
Coupe St DE5 ....180 C4
Coupland Cl S41 ....77 B2
Coupland Pl DE55 .....159 B1
Court Farm La DE14 ...253 C4
Court La DE45 ....108 C4
Court Pl S43 ....97 B4
Court St DE11 ....256 C2
Court The DE24 ....233 A3
Court View S43 ....80 C2
Courtland Dr DE24 ....233 A3
Courtland Gdns DE24 ..233 A4
Courtland Rd DE65 ....229 B2
Courtney Way DE56 ...179 B3
Courtyard Mews DE24 .233 A3
Courtyard The
Belper DE56 ....179 A2
Darley Dale DE4 ....127 B2
Hollingworth SK14 ....9 B3
Coventry Cl DE11 .....256 B3
Coventry La NG9 ......209 C1
Coverdale Wlk DE24 ..233 B4
Coverley Pl ST4 ....269 A1
Covert Pl DE11 ....262 B4
Covert The DE21 ......220 C2
Cow La S43 ....77 C1
Cowan Dr ST16 ....269 C4
Cowan St NG1 ....268 B2
Cowbrook Ave SK13 ....10 C1
Cowburn Dr SK22 ......24 B1
Cowdray Cl DE24 ......231 B1
Cowham Cl DE55 ......159 B2
Cowley Bottom S18 .....75 C4
Cowley Cl S41 ....266 C3
Cowley Gdns 4 S20 .....59 C4
Cowley La S18 ....75 B4
Cowley St DE22 ....218 C4
Cowlishaw Cl DE72 ....234 C1
Cowlow La SK17,SK23 ....47 B1
Cowper Rd NG16 ......195 A4
Cowper St DE24 ....232 A3
Cowringle La S43 ....77 C1
Cowsell Dr S45 ....131 C1
Cowsley Rd DE21 ......219 B4
Cowslip Cl DE12 ......262 C1
Cox Green Ct DE23 ....230 C4
Cox's La NG19 ....136 A3
Coxbench Rd DE21 ....191 C2
Coxon St DE21 ....220 C3
Coxon's Yd DE6 ....173 A1
Coyt Rd SK23 ....45 C3
Crab Tree Hill DE21 ...205 B4
Crabbery St ST16 .....269 B4
Crabtree Ave SK12 ......32 C3
Crabtree Cl
Castle Donington DE74 ...247 A1
Derby DE22 ....204 B2
Wirksworth DE4 ....165 C4
Crabtree Ct SK12 ....32 B3
Crabtree Hill DE22 ....204 B2
Cracken Cl SK23 ....34 B1
Craddock Ave DE21 ...220 C2
Craddock Mews S2 .....43 C4
Craddock Rd S2 ....43 C4
Cragdale Gr S20 ....59 B4
Cragg La DE55 ....148 A1
Craggon Dr S43 ....77 B2
Craggs Dr S43 ....80 C2
Craggs Rd S44 ....99 A1
Craglands Gr S40 ....95 A3
Crags Bsns Pk S80 ....100 C4
Crags Rd S80 ....82 A1
Crags View S80 ....81 C1
Craig Dr SK23 ....45 C3
Craig St NG10 ....236 C4
Craiglee Ct DE24 ......231 B2
Craigs Gn NG18 ....268 A3
Cramer St ST17 ....269 B3
Cranberry Gr DE23 ....230 C3
Cranborne Rd S41 ......95 C4
Cranbourne Cl NG9 ...209 B1
Cranbrook Ct NG19 ...136 B3
Cranbrook St NG1 ....268 B1
Cranfleet Way NG10 ..236 A4
Cranhill Cl DE23 ......230 C3
Cranleigh Rd S43 ....79 A2
Cranmer Gr NG19 ....135 B2
Cranmer Rd DE21 .....267 D3
Cranmer St Ilkeston DE7 194 C1
Long Eaton NG10 ....223 B1
Stoke-on-T ST4 ....269 B2
Craven Rd S41 ....95 C3
Crawford Ave NG9 ....223 B4
Crawford St ST4 ......269 C1
Crawley Rd DE24 .....232 C3
Crawshaw Ave S8 ......56 B4
Crawshaw Gr S8 ....56 B4
Cray's Hill DE55 ......170 A4
Crayford Rd DE24 ....233 A3
Craythorne Cl DE11 ...256 A4
Craythorne Rd DE13 ...240 B2
Creamery La DE6 .....151 B1
Crecy Cl DE22 ....218 B2
Creighton La ST14 ....210 A3
Crescent S26 ....61 C3
Crescent Dr SK23 ......33 B1
Crescent Rd Ashover S42 113 B1
Selston NG16 ....171 B3
Stafford ST17 ....269 A3
Crescent The
Alfreton DE55 ....159 A2
Barlborough S43 ....80 B3
Bradwell S33 ....51 A4
Breaston DE72 ....235 B4
Breedon on t H DE73 ....252 C1
Brimington S43 ....96 B4
Buxton SK17 ....85 A4
Chapel-en-le-F SK23 ......47 B4
Clay Cross S45 ....131 B1
Derby, Boulton DE24 ....232 C3
Derby, Chaddesden DE21 .219 C3
Hayfield SK22 ....25 A1
Holmesfield S18 ....75 A4
Holymoorside S42 ....113 B4
Hope S33 ....39 A2
Horsley Woodhouse DE7 ..192 B4
Mayfield DE6 ....184 B4
New Mills SK22 ....33 A4

Crescent The *continued*
Repton DE65 242 B1
Risley DE72 222 B2
Shirebrook NG20 119 C3
Shirley DE6 200 B4
Stanley DE7 207 A4
Stapleford NG9 209 C1
Swadlincote DE11 255 C3
Totley S17 55 C3
Cressbrook Ave S42 132 A4
Cressbrook Way DE21 206 A2
Cresswell Ave SK22 33 B4
Cresswell St SK22 33 B4
Cresswellpart La S33 50 C4
Cressy Rd DE55 159 A2
Crest Cl DE13 240 C1
Crest The Derby DE22 204 C1
Linton DE12 261 B3
Cresta Gr DE21 205 C1
Creswell Bsns Pk S80 100 C4
Creswell CE Inf Sch S80 81 C1
Creswell Crags Visitor Ctr★
S80 82 A1
Creswell Ct NG19 136 C2
Creswell Jun Sch S80 81 C1
Creswell Rd S43 80 C2
Creswell Sta S80 81 C1
Creswick Cl S40 114 A4
Crewe St DE23 218 C1
Crewton Way DE24 232 C4
Crich Ave DE23 218 B1
Crich Carr CE Prim Sch
DE4 156 B1
Crich CE Inf Sch DE4 156 C1
Crich Cir DE23 218 B1
Crich Jun Sch DE4 157 A1
Crich La Belper DE56 179 A4
Ridgeway DE56 168 A2
Crich Pl S42 131 C3
Crich Rd S43 97 B4
Crich Tramway Vilage★
DE4 156 C1
Crich View Bolsover S44 118 A4
Heage DE56 179 C4
Newton DE55 148 A2
Crich Way DE11 255 C3
Cricket Cl DE15 248 C4
Cricket View S43 80 C1
Cricketers Cl DE15 254 C4
Cricketers Ct DE23 231 B4
Cricklewood Rd DE22 218 A3
Cringle Mews DE21 205 C1
Cripton La S45 129 C3
Crispin Cl S12 44 A2
Crispin Dr S12 44 A2
Crispin Gdns S12 44 A2
Crispin Rd S12 44 A2
Critch's Flats NG16 195 C3
Critchley St DE7 194 C1
Croft Ave DE6 151 B1
Croft Cl Dale Abbey DE7 207 C1
Derby DE21 220 C3
Netherseal DE12 264 C4
Ockbrook DE72 221 B2
Pinxton NG16 160 B2
Rolleston DE13 240 A2
Croft Cres
Awsworth NG16 195 B3
Stoke-on-T ST4 269 B1
Croft Ct NG17 148 C2
Croft End DE21 205 B4
Croft Gr ST14 210 B1
Croft Inf Sch DE55 159 A2
Croft La DE21 205 B2
Croft Lea S18 56 B1
Croft Manor SK13 10 C1
Croft Rd
Great Longstone DE45 90 A2
Sheffield S12 44 A3
Croft The Belper DE56 179 B1
Burton u T DE15 254 B4
Derby DE23 231 B4
Draycott DE72 235 A3
Glossop SK13 10 A3
Heage DE56 168 C1
Morley DE7 192 B1
Mottram in L SK14 9 A2
Shirland DE55 146 B1
Somercotes DE55 170 B4
South Normanton DE55 160 A3
Stoke-on-T ST4 269 A1
Swadlincote DE11 255 C3
Taddington SK17 88 A2
Croft View Clowne S43 80 C2
Staveley S43 97 B3
Croft Wlk S80 82 A3
Crofters Cl S21 60 B2
Crofters Ct DE21 205 C1
Crofton Cl S18 56 C1
Crofton Rise S18 56 C1
Crofts The S32 53 A4
Croftstead Ave ST14 196 B3
Cromarty Cl DE24 231 C2
Cromarty Rise S18 56 B1
Cromdale Ave S43 77 B2
Cromer Cl DE3 217 B1
Cromford CE Prim Sch
DE4 155 A3
Cromford Cl
Aldercar NG16 182 A2
Gamesley SK13 9 B1
Long Eaton NG10 236 A3
North Wingfield S42 132 A4
Cromford Ct
4 Chesterfield S41 95 B4
Whaley Bridge SK23 45 C3
Cromford Dr Derby DE3 217 C2
Staveley S43 97 B4
Cromford Fold SK13 9 B1
Cromford Gn SK13 9 B1
Cromford Hill DE4 155 A3
Cromford La SK17 85 C4
Cromford Lea SK13 9 B1
Cromford Mews SK23 45 C3
Cromford Pl SK17 85 C4
Cromford Rd
Aldercar NG16 181 C3
Clay Cross S45 131 A3
Crich DE4 156 C1
Derby DE21 220 A4
Langley Mill NG16 182 A2
Ripley DE5 169 B1
Wirksworth DE4 154 C1
Cromford Sta DE4 155 B4
Cromford Way SK13 9 B1
Cromford Wharf★ DE4 155 B4
Crompton Rd
Ilkeston DE7 209 A2
Mansfield NG19 135 B2
Staveley S43 78 C1
Crompton Road Ind Est
DE7 209 A2
Crompton St Derby DE1 267 B2
New Houghton NG19 134 C4
Cromwell Ave
Blackwell DE55 147 C1
Chapel-en-le-F SK23 47 A3
Findern DE65 230 B1
Ilkeston DE7 209 A3
Cromwell Cl DE13 239 B3
Cromwell Dr DE55 169 B4
Cromwell Rd
Bolsover S44 118 A4
Chesterfield S40 266 A4
Derby DE23 218 C1
Cromwell St
Eastwood NG16 195 B4
Mansfield NG18 268 C3
Nottingham NG7 268 A2
Crook Stile DE4 143 A4
Crook's Ave NG19 136 B2
Crooked Bridge Rd
ST16 269 B4
Crookes Ave NG19 135 A3
Cropper La DE6 215 A2
Cropston Cl S41 115 B4
Cropton Cl DE24 233 B3
Cropwell Ct NG18 268 C4
Cropwell Gn NG3 268 C2
Crosby St DE22 218 B2
Cross Chantrey Rd S8 43 A2
Cross Cl DE23 231 B4
Cross Cliffe SK13 17 C4
Cross Keys La DE55 169 C4
Cross Keys Row SK23 47 A4
Cross La Calver S32 72 A1
Codnor DE5 181 A4
Dore S17 55 B4
Dronfield, Coal Aston S18 57 B2
Dronfield, Quoit Green S18 57 A1
Flagg SK17 106 C4
Ible DE4 153 C4
Monyash DE45 107 A1
Rolleston DE13 240 A1
Shirland DE55 158 C4
Sutton in A NG17 148 C1
Wessington DE55 157 C4
Cross Lanes DE4 144 B1
Cross London St S43 77 B2
Cross Myrtle Rd S2 43 A4
Cross Park Rd S8 43 A3
Cross Rd ST14 210 A1
Cross Rise SK13 17 C4
Cross Side DE6 184 C4
Cross St Bolsover S44 118 B4
Bramley-Vale S44 117 B1
Breedon on t H DE73 252 C1
Brimington S43 96 C4
Broadbottom SK14 16 A4
Buxton SK17 85 B4
Castleton S33 38 A1
Chapel-en-le-F SK23 47 A3
Chesterfield S40 266 A4
Clay Cross S45 131 B2
Derby DE22 218 B3
Glossop SK13 10 B1
Glossop, Hadfield SK13 10 A3
Grassmoor S42 115 C2
Hollingworth SK14 9 B2
Killamarsh S21 60 C4
Linton DE11 261 C4
Long Eaton NG10 236 C4
Mansfield Woodhouse
NG19 136 A1
New Mills SK22 33 B4
North Wingfield S42 131 C3
Sandiacre NG10 223 B3
Cross The 1 SK13 10 A3
Cross Wellington St S43 77 B2
Crossdale Gr DE21 206 B2
Crossfield Gr SK6 15 A1
Crossgate La SK13 9 C4
Crosshill DE5 181 A3
Crosshill Dr DE7 208 B3
Crossings Ave SK23 47 A3
Crossings Rd SK23 46 C3
Crossland Dr S12 44 A2
Crossland Pl S12 44 A2
Crossland Rd S32 53 A4
Crosslands Cl SK13 17 B4
Crossley St DE5 169 B1
Crosslow La DE6 150 C3
Crossway ST16 269 C4
Crossways La DE6 176 A1
Crow Croft Rd S45 132 B1
Crow Hill NG19 135 A3
Crow Hill Ct NG18 268 B4
Crow Hill Dr NG18 268 B4
Crow Hill La NG19 136 A1
Crow La Chesterfield S41 96 B2
Shirland DE55 146 A3
Unstone S18 76 C4
Crowcroft Way NG10 223 A1
Crowden Dr SK13 10 A3
Crowden in Longendale YH★
SK13 6 C2
Crowestones SK17 85 B3
Crowfoot La DE65 226 C4
Crowhill La DE45 109 A3
Crown Cl Chesterfield S43 77 B2
Long Eaton NG10 236 A4
Crown Hill Way DE7 207 A4
Crown Mews DE22 218 C2
Crown Rd S41 96 A3
Crown Specl Sch DE13 240 B1
Crown Sq DE4 143 A3
Crown St Clowne S43 80 C2
Derby DE22 218 C2
Duffield DE56 190 C2
Crown Terr 2 DE56 178 C2
Crown Way DE73 244 C4
Crown Yd DE4 154 C1
Crownland Dr DE73 233 A1
Crowshaw St DE24 232 A4
Crowstones Rd DE4 127 A2
Crowther St ST4 269 C2
Croxton Ct NG19 136 C2
Croydon Wlk DE22 217 C3
Cruck Cl S18 56 C1
Cubley La DE6 198 B1
Cuckmere Cl DE22 205 A3
Cuckoostone La DE4 128 C1
Cuillin Cl NG10 223 A1
Cull Ave ST16 269 C4
Cullabine Rd S2 44 A4
Culland Rd DE14 254 A4
Culland View DE4 168 A4
Cullen Ave DE6 173 B1
Cullumbell La S45 129 A4
Culworth Cl DE56 179 B2
Culworth Ct DE21 206 A1
Cumberhills Rd DE22,
DE56 190 B1
Cumberland Ave DE21 219 C3
Cumberland Cl NG16 171 B2
Cumberland Cres DE72 221 A1
Cumberland Dr SK17 85 B2
Cumberland Pl 3 NG1 268 A1
Cumberland Rd DE15 254 B3
Cumbria Wlk DE3 217 B1
Cumming St ST4 269 A2
Cummings St DE23 219 A1
Cundy Rd S44 99 A2
Cunliffe St S18 57 B2
Cunnery La DE4 144 A2
Cunnery The DE6 202 C1
Cunningham Pl DE45 109 B3
Curbar Cl S42 132 A4
Curbar Curve S43 97 B3
Curbar Hill S32 72 B1
Curbar Prim Sch S32 72 B1
Curborough Dr DE24 233 B3
Curlew Ave S21 59 A2
Curlew Cl 1 DE24 231 B2
Curtis Gr SK13 10 A3
Curzon Ave S18 75 C4
Curzon CE Prim Sch The
DE22 204 B3
Curzon Cl Derby DE22 204 B2
Killamarsh S21 60 B3
Curzon Ct Duffield DE56 190 C2
Nottingham NG3 268 B2
Curzon Gdns 11 NG3 268 B2
Curzon La Derby DE24 233 A4
Duffield DE56 190 B2
Curzon Rd Buxton SK17 85 B4
Derby DE21 219 C4
Curzon St Derby DE1 267 A3
Long Eaton NG10 223 A1
Nottingham NG3 268 B2
Curzon Terr SK17 88 B4
Cuscas La DE6 187 C2
Cut La DE1,DE21 219 A4
Cutholme Cl S40 95 A2
Cutler Cl S21 60 A4
Cuttholme Rd S40 95 B2
Cuttholme Way S40 95 B2
Cutthorpe Grange S40 95 A4
Cutthorpe Prim Sch S42 94 B4
Cutthorpe Rd S40 95 A4
Cutting The DE11 256 C2
Cuttlebrook Cl DE23 231 C3
Cyclamen Cl DE14 254 A4
Cypress Ave S8 43 B1
Cypress Cl S21 60 B3
Cypress Way SK6 32 A4
Cypress Wlk DE21 220 A3
Cyprus Rd S8 43 A3
Cyril Ave NG9 223 B4

D

D H Lawrence Mus★
NG16 182 C2
Dade Ave S43 97 B3
Dag La DE12 263 C4
Dagnall Gdns DE45 109 B3
Dagnall Terr DE45 109 B3
Dagnam Cl S2 43 C3
Dagnam Cres S2 43 C3
Dagnam Dr S2 43 C4
Dagnam Pl S2 43 C3
Dagnam Rd S2 43 C4
Dahlia Ave DE55 160 A4
Dahlia Dr DE21 206 B2
Dairy House Rd DE23 219 A1
Daisy Cl DE12 262 C1
Daisy Farm Rd NG16 195 A4
Daisy La DE12 262 A2
Daisymere La SK17 67 A1
Dakeyne Cl DE4 127 C1
Dakeyne St NG3 268 C2
Dakin Ave SK17 85 B4
Dakin Ct SK17 66 C1
Dalbury Rd S18 56 B1
Dalbury Wlk DE23 231 B3
Dale Ave
Long Eaton NG10 223 B1
Newton DE55 148 A2
Somercotes DE55 170 B3
Dale Bank Cres S43 77 B2
Dale Brook DE65 228 C1
Dale Cl Breaston DE72 235 B4
Fritchley DE56 168 A3
Langwith NG20 119 C4
Staveley S43 97 B4
Stonebroom DE55 147 A2
Whaley Thorns NG20 100 C1
Dale Com Prim Sch
DE23 218 C1
Dale Cres Hathersage S32 53 A4
Tupton S42 115 B1
Dale Ct DE56 191 C4
Dale End
Brassington DE4 153 A1
Wirksworth DE4 154 C1
Dale End Rd DE65 228 B1
Dale Gr NG2 268 C1
Dale Hill DE55 158 A3
Dale La Ault Hucknall S44 134 B4
Buxton SK17 85 C4
Dale Park Ave DE56 192 A4
Dale Rd Buxton SK17 85 B4
Dale Abbey DE21,DE72 221 A3
Derby DE23 218 C1
Derby, Alvaston DE24 233 B4
Derby, Spondon DE21 220 C3
Dove Holes SK17 67 A4
Dronfield S18 76 A4
Killamarsh S21 60 C3
Kimberley NG16 195 C3
Matlock Bath DE4 143 A2
New Mills SK22 33 B4
Over Haddon DE45 109 A1
Stanley DE7 207 B2
Stanton-by-D DE7 208 B1
Tupton S42 115 B1
Dale Rd N
Darley Dale DE4 127 A3
Northwood DE4 127 A3
Dale Rd S DE4 127 B1
Dale Side SK17 85 A4
Dale St Ilkeston DE7 208 C4
Mansfield NG19 136 A1
Nottingham NG2 268 C1
Dale Terr SK17 85 A3
Dale The Bonsall DE4 142 B1
Hathersage S32 53 A4
Stoney Middleton S32 71 C2
Wirksworth DE4 154 C1
Dale View
Earl Sterndale SK17 105 A2
Ilkeston DE7 208 C4
Mottram in L SK14 9 A2
Shirland DE55 146 B2
Tideswell SK17 69 C2
Dale View Cl S45 132 A2
Dale View Gdns DE56 191 C4
Dale View Rd S45 132 A2
Dale View Terr SK17 89 A3
Daleacre Ave DE74 247 C3
Dalebank La S45 145 A4
Dalebrook Rd DE15 248 A3
Dalefield Dr DE11 256 A2
Dalehead Ct S32 71 C3
Dales Cl DE11 255 C3
Dalesfield DE4 143 A3
Dalesgate Cl DE23 231 B3
Daleside DE15 248 A1
Dalestorth Ave NG19 135 B1
Daleswood Cres DE55 160 A2
Dalewood Cl S41 96 C1
Dalkieth Ave DE24 232 C3
Dallas St NG18 268 B3
Dalley Cl 7 NG9 223 C4
Dalley La DE56 178 B3
Dallimore Prim Sch
DE7 208 B2
Dallimore Rd DE7 208 B2
Dalness Ct 4 DE24 231 B2
Dalston Rd DE11 256 A3
Dalton Ave
Burton u T DE15 248 A1
Derby DE22 218 B2
Dalton Cl NG9 223 C3
Daltons Cl NG16 182 A2
Dalvey Way S43 77 B3
Dam La Alsop en le D DE6 150 C2
Shirland DE55 146 C1
Dame Catherine Harpur's Sch
DE73 251 A3
Dame Flogan St 5
NG18 268 B3
Damon Cl S45 132 B1
Damon Dr S43 96 C4
Damsbrook Dr S43 80 C2
Danbury Gr S42 115 C2
Danby Ave S41 77 A1
Dane Bank Dr SK12 32 B3
Dane Cl NG3 268 B2
Dane Ct 13 NG3 268 B2
Dane Gr SK17 85 B2
Dane Hill Cl SK12 32 B3
Danebridge Cres DE21 206 A1
Danesby Cres DE5 180 A1
Danesby Rise DE5 180 A1
Danesmoor Ind Est S45 131 C1
Danesmoor Inf Sch S45 131 C2
Danesway SK23 47 A3
Daniel Cres NG18 268 A4
Dannah Cres DE5 169 C1
Dannah St DE5 169 C1
Darby St DE23 218 C1
Darcy Rd S21 59 B2
Daresbury Cl S2 43 B3
Daresbury Dr S2 43 B3
Daresbury Pl S2 43 B3
Daresbury Rd S2 43 B3
Daresbury View S2 43 B3
Darfield Ave S20 44 C1
Darfield Cl S20 44 C1
Darfield Dr DE75 182 A1
Darfield La DE6 162 B2
Dark La Ashbourne DE6 173 A1
Ashover DE55 145 B3
Bradley DE6 175 A2
Branston DE13 253 A4
Calow S44 96 C1
Chesterfield S44 96 C2
Crich DE4 156 C3
Cromford DE4 154 C2
Holbrook DE56 191 A4
North Wingfield S42 132 A4
Pilsley S45 132 B1
Wirksworth DE4,DE56 165 B2
Youlgreave DE45 125 B4
Darkey La NG9 223 C3
Darklands La DE11 256 A2
Darklands Rd DE11 256 A3
Darley Abbey Dr DE22 204 C1
Darley Ave Beeston NG9 223 C2
Darley Dale DE4 127 B2
North Wingfield S42 132 A4
Darley Churchtown CE Prim Sch DE4 127 A2
Darley Cl Burton u T DE15 248 B1
Harthill S26 61 C3
Staveley S43 78 C1
Swadlincote DE11 256 A1
Darley Dale DE11 255 C1
Darley Dale Prim Sch
DE4 127 C1
Darley Dale Sta★ DE4 127 B1
Darley Dr
Long Eaton NG10 236 A3
Ripley DE5 169 B2
West Hallam DE7 207 C4
Darley Gr Buxton SK17 85 B3
Derby DE1 219 A4
Darley House Est DE4 142 C4
Darley La DE1 267 B4
Darley Lodge Dr DE4 142 C4
Darley Park Dr DE22 204 C1
Darley Park Rd DE22 204 C1
Darley Rd S45 113 A1
Darley Sq DE7 194 C3
Darley St DE22 205 A1
Darley Way Buxton SK17 85 C4
North Wingfield S42 132 A4
Darlton St NG19 268 A3
Darnley St ST4 269 C2
Darsway DE74 246 C2
Dartford Pl DE24 233 A3
Dartmouth St ST16 269 C4
Dartnall Cl SK12 32 A3
Darwent Rd S41 96 B3
Darwin Ave Buxton SK17 85 B4
Chesterfield S40 95 C3
Derby DE24 232 B2
Ilkeston DE7 208 C4
Darwin Cl DE15 248 B1
Darwin Pl DE1 267 C3
Darwin Rd
Chesterfield S40 266 A4
Derby DE3 217 C2
Long Eaton NG10 236 A3
Darwood La S44 118 A4
Dashwood St DE23 267 B1
Datchet Cl DE23 231 A4
Daveham Ave SK17 85 B3
Davenport Rd
Derby DE24 232 B4
Tupton S42 131 B4
Daventry Cl DE3 217 B2
Davey Ct S44 98 C2
Davey Rd NG18 268 B4
Davian Way S40 114 C4
David's Cl DE73 232 C1
Davids Dr S42 114 C2
Davidson St NG2 268 C1
Davis Cl ST16 269 C4
Davis Rd DE11 256 A2
Dawber La S21 60 C4
Dawgates La NG17,NG19 134 C1
Dawkins Rd DE12 262 C1
Dawlish Ct Derby DE24 233 B4
Eastwood NG16 182 B2
Dawn View NG9 209 B1
Dawsmere Cl DE21 205 B1
Dawver Rd NG16 195 C3
Day Gr SK14 9 A2
Dayfield La DE6 175 A2
Daylesford Cl DE23 231 A4
Days La DE56 178 C2
Days Mill Cl DE4 143 A3
Dayton Cl DE21 220 B3

De Sutton Pl S26 ....**61** C3
De Warren Pl S26 ....**61** C3
Deacon Cl Derby DE21 ..**205** C1
 Swanwick DE55 ....**169** C4
Dead La NG16 ....**195** B1
Deadman's La DE24 ....**219** B1
Deamon St DE55 ....**147** C1
Dean Cl DE23 ....**218** A1
Dean Ct DE23 ....**218** C1
Dean Rd DE56 ....**167** C1
Dean St Derby DE22 ....**218** C2
 Langley Mill NG16 ....**182** B2
 Nottingham NG1 ......**268** B1
Deanhead Dr S20 ....**44** C1
Deans Dr DE72 ....**221** A1
Deansgate NG19 ......**135** A3
Deanshill Cl ST16 ......**269** A3
Debdale Gate NG19 ....**136** A1
Debdale La NG19 ......**136** A1
Deben Cl S40 ....**114** B4
Deben Down NG19 .....**136** B2
Deborah Dr DE21 ......**220** A4
Dee Cl DE24 ....**231** C2
Dee La DE65 ....**229** C3
Deep Dale La
 Barrow u T DE73 ......**244** A4
 Derby DE24, DE73 .....**231** C1
Deepdale NG16 ....**170** C4
Deepdale Ave
 Borrowash DE72 ....**221** B1
 Stapleford NG9 ....**223** B3
Deepdale Cl
 Burton u T DE15 ......**248** A3
 Staveley S43 ....**78** C4
Deepdale Ct DE75 .....**181** C1
Deepdale La DE6 ......**184** A1
Deepdale Rd
 Belper DE56 ....**179** A3
 Bolsover S44 ....**98** C2
 Derby DE21 ....**220** C2
 Long Eaton NG10 .....**236** A3
 Mansfield NG19 ......**136** C1
Deepdene Cl DE11 .....**256** B1
Deepsick La S44 ....**97** B1
Deepwell Ave
 Killamarsh S20 ....**60** A3
 Mosborough S20 ....**59** C3
Deepwell Bank S20 ....**59** C3
Deepwell Ct S20 ....**59** C3
Deepwell View S20 ....**59** C3
Deer Park Prim Sch
 S42 ....**114** C2
Deer Park View DE21 ..**220** C3
Deerlands Rd
 Chesterfield S40 ....**95** A2
 Wingerworth S42 .....**114** C1
Deerleap La S42 ....**130** B2
Deerpark Cres S42 ....**114** C2
Degge St DE1 ....**267** B2
Deincourt Cl DE21 ....**221** A3
Deincourt Com Sch
 S42 ....**131** C4
Deincourt Cres S42 ...**131** C4
Delamere Cl
 Breaston DE72 ....**235** B4
 Derby DE21 ....**206** A1
 Swanwick DE55 ....**169** C4
Delamere Dr NG18 ....**268** C3
Delhi Cl DE15 ....**248** B2
Dell The S40 ....**95** A2
Delph Bank S40 ....**114** C4
Delph Cl S32 ....**71** B3
Delph St S2 ....**43** A4
Delph The DE73 ....**252** C1
Delta Cl NG1 ....**268** A2
Delven La DE74 ....**247** A2
Delves Bank Rd DE55 ..**170** A4
Delves Cl S40 ....**95** B1
Delves Ct DE75 ....**193** C4
Delves Rd DE75 ......**193** B4
Delves Specl Sch DE55 **169** C4
Delves The DE55 ......**169** C4
Denacre Ave NG10 ....**223** C1
Denacre La DE4 ....**127** C2
Denarth Ave DE24 ....**232** C2
Denbigh St DE21 ......**219** C4
Denby Comm DE5 .....**180** C2
Denby Free CE Prim Sch
 DE5 ....**180** B1
Denby La DE5, DE56 ...**180** B1
Denby Pottery Visitor Ctr★
 DE5 ....**180** B2
Denby Rd S43 ....**97** B4
Dene Fields Ct DE4 ...**143** B3
Denefield Cl SK6 ......**15** A1
Denham St S45 ....**131** B2
Denison Cl **7** S2 ......**43** A3
Denison Gdns DE21 ...**220** A3
Denman Cres S32 ......**72** A2
Denmark Rd S2 ....**43** A3
Dennett Cl NG3 ......**268** C2
Dennis Barsby Cl DE11 .**255** C2
Dennis Cl DE23 ....**230** C4
Dennor Dr NG19 ......**136** C3
Denstone Coll ST14 ...**196** A3
Denstone Dr DE24 ....**233** A2
Denstone La ST14 ....**196** B4
Denstone Rd NG3 ....**268** C2
Dent La S20, S12 ......**44** C1
Dentdale Ct DE24 ....**233** B4
Denton Ave **7** NG10 .**223** A4
Denton Cl NG19 ......**136** C1
Denton Way DE55 .....**169** C4
Denver Ct NG9 ....**209** C1

Denver Rd DE3 ....**217** B2
Depedale Ave DE7 ....**208** B3
Depot St DE23 ....**219** A1
Derby Cath DE1 ......**267** B4
Derby City Hospl DE23 .**218** A1
Derby Coll (Broomfield
 Campus) DE7 ....**206** A3
Derby High Sch DE23 ..**218** A1
Derby Hills House Ct
 DE73 ....**251** C3
Derby Ind Gram Sch for Boys
 DE23 ....**230** C4
Derby Industrial Mus★
 DE1 ....**267** B3
Derby Knoll SK23 ......**33** C1
Derby La Brailsford DE6 .**201** A4
 Derby DE23 ....**231** C4
 Great Cubley DE6 ....**198** C1
 Monyash DE45 ....**123** B4
 Shirley DE6 ....**200** C4
Derby Moor Com Sch
 DE23 ....**231** A4
Derby Mus & Art Gallery★
 DE1 ....**267** B3
Derby Pl S2 ....**43** B3
Derby Rd
 Alderwasley DE56 ....**167** C1
 Alfreton DE55 ....**158** C2
 Ambergate DE56 ....**167** C2
 Ashbourne DE6 ......**185** C4
 Aston-on-T DE72 ....**234** A1
 Belper DE56 ....**190** C4
 Borrowash DE21, DE72 .**221** A1
 Burton u T DE13 .....**241** A1
 Clay Cross S45, S42 ...**131** B3
 Cromford DE4 ....**155** B3
 Dale Abbey DE7, DE21 .**206** C2
 Derby, Chellaston DE73 .**232** C1
 Derby, Spondon DE21 .**220** B2
 Doveridge DE6 ....**211** A1
 Draycott DE72 ....**234** C4
 Duffield DE56 ....**190** C1
 Eastwood NG16 ......**182** C1
 Egginton DE65 ......**241** B2
 Hatton DE65 ....**227** C1
 Heanor DE75 ....**181** B1
 Hilton DE65 ....**228** C2
 Horsley DE21, DE56 ..**191** B3
 Ilkeston DE7 ....**208** B4
 Kilburn DE56 ....**179** C1
 Langley Mill NG16 ...**182** B2
 Long Eaton NG10 ....**236** A4
 Marston on D DE65 ..**228** A1
 Melbourne DE73 ....**252** A4
 New Mills SK22 ......**24** B1
 Nottingham NG7 ....**268** A2
 Ripley DE5 ....**180** B2
 Risley DE72 ....**222** B2
 Sandiacre NG10 .....**223** A3
 Smisby LE65 ....**258** A2
 Stanley DE7 ....**207** A2
 Stapleford NG9 ......**223** B3
 Swadlincote DE11 ...**256** B2
 Swanwick DE5, DE55 .**169** C3
 Ticknall DE11, DE73 ..**257** C4
 Uttoxeter ST14 ......**210** B1
 Wingerworth S42 ....**115** A3
 Wirksworth DE4 .....**165** C3
Derby Road Ind Est
 Heanor DE75 ....**181** B1
 Sandiacre NG10 ....**223** A3
Derby Small Bsns Ctr
 DE1 ....**267** C2
Derby St Glossop SK13 ..**17** B4
 7 Ilkeston DE7 ....**208** C4
 Mansfield NG18 ....**268** C3
 Nottingham NG1 ....**268** A2
 Sheffield S2 ....**43** B3
 Stafford ST16 ....**269** A4
Derby Sta DE1 ....**219** B2
Derby Terr S2 ....**43** B3
Derby Trad Est DE21 ..**219** A4
Derby Univ (Mickleover Site)
 DE3 ....**217** C2
Derbyshire Ave
 Trowell NG9 ....**209** B2
 West Hallam DE7 ....**207** A4
Derbyshire Cl DE7 ....**207** A4
Derbyshire Cty Cricket Gd
 DE21 ....**219** B3
Derbyshire Dr
 Ilkeston DE7 ....**208** C3
 Westwood NG16 ....**171** B2
Derbyshire La S8 ....**43** A2
Derbyshire Level SK13 .**17** C3
Derbyshire Royal Infmy
 DE1 ....**267** C1
Derrington Leys DE24 .**233** B3
Derventio Cl DE1 .....**219** A4
Derwent Ave
 Belper DE56 ....**179** A4
 Borrowash DE72 ....**221** B2
 Darley Dale DE4 ....**127** B2
 Derby DE72 ....**205** A2
 Grindleford S32 ......**72** B4
 Ilkeston DE7 ....**194** B1
 West Hallam DE7 ....**207** C4
Derwent Bsns Ctr DE1 .**267** C4
Derwent Cl Derby DE22 .**205** A2
 Dronfield S18 ....**57** A2
 Glossop SK13 ....**17** C4
 Grindleford S32 ......**72** B4
 Swadlincote DE11 ...**256** A1
Derwent Com Sch DE21 **219** B4
Derwent Cres S41 ......**95** B4
Derwent Croft DE55 ..**242** A3
Derwent Ct **10** S17 ..**56** A3
Derwent Dr Baslow DE45 **91** B3

Derwent Dr continued
 Chinley SK23 ....**34** C1
 Derby DE24 ....**231** B1
 Tibshelf DE55 ....**147** C3
Derwent Gdns DE6 ...**185** B4
Derwent Gr DE55 .....**158** C1
Derwent Ho DE21 ....**219** B3
Derwent La Derwent S33 .**30** A4
 Hathersage S32 ....**52** C4
 Northwood DE4 .....**127** A3
Derwent Par DE21, DE24 .**219** C2
Derwent Pl S45 ......**131** A3
Derwent Rd
 Burton u T DE15 ....**248** A1
 Buxton SK17 ....**85** B3
 Derby DE21 ....**220** B2
 Dronfield S18 ....**57** A2
 Ripley DE5 ....**169** B1
Derwent Rise DE21 ...**220** C2
Derwent Sq SK23 ......**34** C1
Derwent St Belper DE56 .**178** C2
 Derby DE1 ....**267** B3
 Draycott DE72 ......**235** A4
 Long Eaton NG10 ...**236** B3
Derwent Street Ind Est
 NG10 ....**236** B3
Derwent Terr DE4 ....**143** A4
Derwent Vale DE56 ...**178** C1
Derwent View
 Baslow DE45 ....**91** C3
 Belper, Milford DE56 .**191** A4
 Belper, Mount Pleasant
  DE56 ....**178** C3
 Mastin Moor S43 .....**79** B2
Desborough Rd NG16 .**171** B4
Dethick Dr DE4 ......**144** B1
Dethick Way S42 .....**132** A4
Devas Gdns DE21 ....**220** B3
Deveron Cl DE13 .....**240** B1
Deveron Rd S20 ....**59** C4
Devizes Cl S40 ....**114** C4
Devon Cl Burton u T DE15 **254** C3
 Derby DE21 ....**219** B4
 Grassmoor S42 ......**115** C1
 Sandiacre NG10 ....**223** A3
Devon Dr Brimington S43 .**96** C4
 Mansfield NG19 ....**268** A4
Devon Park View S43 ..**96** C4
Devon St Ilkeston DE7 .**209** A3
 Nottingham NG3 ....**268** C2
Devonish Royal Hospl The
 SK17 ....**85** A4
Devonshire Ave
 Borrowash DE72 ....**221** B1
 Darley Dale DE4 ....**142** C4
 Derby DE72 ....**204** C2
 Long Eaton NG10 ...**237** A4
Devonshire Ave E S41 .**115** B4
Devonshire Ave N S43 ..**77** C2
Devonshire Cl
 Chesterfield S41 ......**95** C4
 Dore S17 ....**55** C3
 Dronfield S18 ....**75** C4
 Ilkeston DE7 ....**194** C3
 2 Staveley S43 ......**78** C1
Devonshire Ct S43 .....**96** B4
Devonshire Dr
 Chinley SK23 ....**34** B1
 Creswell S80 ....**81** B1
 Darley Dale DE4 ....**110** C1
 Derby DE3 ....**217** C2
 Dore S17 ....**55** C4
 Duffield DE56 ....**190** B2
 Eastwood NG16 ....**182** C1
 Langwith NG20 .....**119** C4
 Somercotes DE55 ...**170** A4
 Stapleford NG9 .....**209** B1
Devonshire Glen S17 ...**55** C3
Devonshire Gr S17 .....**55** C3
Devonshire Rd
 Buxton SK17 ....**85** A4
 Dore S17 ....**55** C3
Devonshire Rd E S41 ..**115** B4
Devonshire Rd N S43 ..**77** B2
Devonshire Sq DE4 ...**111** A2
Devonshire St
 Brimington S43 ....**96** C4
 Chesterfield S41 .....**266** B3
 New Houghton NG19 .**135** A4
 3 Staveley S43 ....**78** C1
Devonshire Terr
 Holmewood S42 .....**116** C1
 Matlock Bath DE4 ...**143** A1
Devonshire Terrace Rd
 S17 ....**55** B4
Devonshire Villas **8** S41 **95** C4
Devonshire Way S43 ...**81** A2
Dew Pond La SK17 .....**85** B4
Dewchurch Dr DE23 ..**231** C3
Dewint Ave SK6 ....**23** A4
Dewsnap La SK14 ......**9** A3
Dewy La DE4, DE55 ...**144** C1
Dexter St DE23 ......**219** B1
Dialstone S33 ....**51** A4
Diamond Dr DE21 ....**205** C2
Diamond Jubilee Cotts
 DE6 ....**184** C4
Dibble Rd DE14 ......**254** A4
Dickens Dr
 Holmewood S42 .....**116** B1
 Swadlincote DE11 ...**256** B3
Dickens Sq DE23 .....**231** C4
Dickenson Rd S41 ....**266** B3
Dickinson St DE24 ...**219** B1
Dickinson's La DE6 ...**215** A1
Dicklant La S45 ......**145** A4
Didcot Cl S40 ....**114** C4

Didsbury Terr SK22 ....**25** C1
Dig St Ashbourne DE6 ..**173** B1
 Hartington SK17 ....**137** B3
Digby St Cossall DE7 ..**195** A1
 Kimberley NG16 ....**195** B4
Diglands Ave SK22 .....**24** B1
Diglands Cl SK22 ......**24** B1
Diglee Rd SK23 ....**33** B2
Digmire La DE6 ......**161** B1
Dimple Cres DE4 .....**143** A3
Dimple La DE56 ......**168** A4
Dimple Rd DE4 ......**143** A3
Dingle Cl SK13 ....**17** A4
Dingle La S41, S44 .....**96** C1
Dingley Cl NG16 ......**136** C3
Dinmore Grange DE11 .**257** A3
Dinting CE Prim Sch
 SK13 ....**10** A1
Dinting La SK13 ....**10** A1
Dinting Lane Trad Est
 SK13 ....**10** A1
Dinting Lodge Ind Est
 SK13 ....**9** C1
Dinting Rd SK13 ......**10** A1
Dinting Sta SK13 ......**10** A1
Dinting Vale SK13 .....**10** A1
Discovery Way S41 .....**77** A1
Diseworth Rd DE74 ..**247** A1
Dish La DE6, DE65 ...**228** A3
Dishwell La S26 ....**61** C3
Disley Prim Sch SK12 ..**32** B3
Disley Sta SK12 ....**32** B3
Ditch Cotts SK17 .....**105** C4
Ditch The SK17 ......**105** C4
Division Rd NG20 ....**119** C2
Division St S43 ....**97** B4
Dix Ave DE7 ....**192** C3
Dixie St NG16 ....**171** A2
Dixon Croft S43 ......**77** B2
Dixon Ct S41 ....**77** A2
Dixon's Rd S41 ......**266** C2
Dobbin La S18 ....**75** B3
Dobbinhorse La DE6 ..**185** A3
Dobholes La DE7 .....**192** C3
Dobson Pl S43 ....**97** A3
Dock Wlk S40 ....**266** A2
Dockholm Rd NG10 ..**223** B1
Doctor La S26 ....**61** C3
Doctor's La DE73 ....**252** C1
Dodburn Ct DE24 ...**231** B2
Dodford Ct DE75 ....**182** A1
Dodslow Ave DE13 ...**240** A2
Doe Hill La DE55 ....**147** B3
Doehole La
 Ashover DE4, DE55 ..**144** C2
 Brackenfield DE55 ..**145** A1
Dog La
 Breedon on t H DE73 **252** C3
 Hulland Ward DE6 ..**175** B2
 Netherseal DE12 ...**264** C3
 Stonebroom DE55 ..**146** C1
Doghole La DE4 .....**154** B2
Dogkennel La DE6 ...**186** C4
Dolby Rd SK17 ....**85** B1
Doles La Clifton DE6 ..**184** C4
 Findern DE65 ....**230** B2
 Whitwell S80 ....**82** A4
Dolly La Chinley SK23 ..**34** A1
 Whaley Bridge SK23 ..**33** C2
Dolly Wood Cl SK23 ...**34** A1
Dolphin Cl DE21 ......**221** A3
Dominic St ST4 ......**269** A2
Dominion Rd DE11 ...**256** A3
Dominoe Gr S12 ......**44** B3
Donald Bates Ho ST4 .**269** A1
Donald Hawley Way
 DE56 ....**190** C2
Doncaster Ave NG10 ..**223** A3
Doncaster Gr NG10 ..**223** C1
Doncaster La ST4 ....**269** A2
Donegal Wlk DE21 ...**220** A2
Donington La DE72, DE74 **247** B4
Donington Dr DE23 ..**231** C3
Donington Dr DE23 ..**231** C3
Dorchester Ave DE21 .**219** C4
Dorchester Rd NG16 .**195** C4
Dore Cl S17 ....**56** A4
Dore Hall Croft S17 ...**55** B4
Dore La S32 ....**53** A4
Dore Prim & Jun Sch
 S17 ....**55** B3
Dore Rd S17 ....**55** C4
Dore Sta S17 ....**56** A4
Doris Rd DE7 ....**209** A4
Dorking Rd DE22 ....**218** A3
Dormy Cl NG19 ......**136** C3
Dorothy Ave
 Mansfield Woodhouse
  NG19 ....**136** B1
 Sandiacre NG10 ....**223** A3
Dorothy Dr NG19 ....**136** C1
Dorothy Vale S40 .....**95** B2
Dorrien Ave DE23 ...**232** A4
Dorset Ave **2** S43 ...**96** C4
Dorset Cl Brimington S43 .**77** C1
 Burton u T DE15 ....**254** C3
 Buxton SK17 ....**85** B2
Dorset Dr S43 ....**96** C4
Dorset St DE21 ......**219** B3
Dorterry Cres DE7 ...**209** A4
Douglas Ave
 Awsworth NG16 ....**195** B3
 Heanor DE75 ......**181** B1
 Stoke-on-T ST4 ....**269** A1

Douglas Rd
 Chesterfield S41 ......**96** B3
 Long Eaton NG10 ...**223** A1
 Somercotes DE55 ...**170** B4
Douglas St DE23 .....**219** A1
Douse Croft La S10 ...**42** C3
Dove Bk SK6 ....**23** C3
Dove Cl Derby DE3 ...**218** A2
 Kilburn DE56 ....**192** A4
 Woodville DE11 ....**256** C2
Dove Fst Sch ST14 ...**197** A2
Dove Gr DE65 ....**241** B3
Dove Holes CE Prim Sch
 SK17 ....**47** C1
Dove Holes Sta SK17 ..**47** C1
Dove House Gn DE6 ..**173** A1
Dove La Long Eaton NG10 **236** B4
 Rocester ST14 ......**197** A2
Dove Lea DE13 ......**240** A2
Dove Rd DE5 ....**169** B1
Dove Ridge SK17 ....**121** B3
Dove Rise DE65 .....**228** B1
Dove Side DE65 .....**239** B4
Dove St DE6 ....**183** A1
Dove Valley Pk DE65 .**227** A3
Dove View DE13 ....**239** B3
Dove Way The ST14 ..**210** B1
Dovecliff Cres DE13 .**240** C1
Dovecliff Rd DE13 ...**240** C2
Dovecote DE74 ......**247** A2
Dovecote Dr DE21 ...**221** A1
Dovecote The
 Breedon on t H DE73 .**252** C1
 Horsley DE21 ......**191** C3
Dovecotes S45 ......**129** C2
Dovedale Ave
 Ashbourne DE6 ....**173** B4
 Derby DE24 ....**233** B4
 Long Eaton NG10 ..**236** A3
 Staveley S43 ....**97** A3
Dovedale Cir DE7 ...**194** C3
Dovedale Cl
 Burton u T DE15 ...**248** A3
 Ripley DE5 ....**180** B3
Dovedale Cres
 Belper DE56 ....**179** A3
 Buxton SK17 ....**84** C3
Dovedale Ct Belper DE56 **179** A2
 4 Chesterfield S41 ...**95** C4
 Glossop SK13 ....**10** C1
 Long Eaton NG10 ..**236** A3
Dovedale Prim Sch
 NG10 ....**236** B3
Dovedale Rd DE21 ..**220** C2
Dovedale Rise DE22 .**204** B1
Dovefields ST14 ....**196** C2
Dover Ct DE23 ......**219** A1
Dover St Creswell S80 .**81** C1
 Derby DE23 ....**219** A1
Doveridge Cl S41 .....**77** A1
Doveridge Gr SK17 ...**85** C3
Doveridge Prim Sch
 Doveridge DE6 ......**211** A1
 Doveridge, Manor House
  DE6 ....**224** B4
Doveridge Rd DE15 ..**248** A1
Doveridge Wlk DE23 .**231** B3
Doveside DE6 ....**184** B4
Dovewood Cl DE23 ..**231** A4
Dowcarr La S26 ......**61** B2
Dowdeswell St S41 ..**266** B4
Dower Cl DE22 ......**205** A1
Dowie Way DE4 ....**156** C1
Downham Cl DE3 ...**217** C1
Downing Cl DE22 ...**217** C3
Downing Rd Derby DE21 .**219** B3
 Sheffield S8 ....**56** C4
Downing St DE55 ....**160** A3
Downings The S26 ....**61** C3
Downlands S43 ......**96** B4
Downlee Cl SK23 ....**46** C3
Downmeadow DE56 .**179** C4
Downs The NG19 ...**136** C1
Dowson St NG3 .....**268** C2
Doxey Rd ST16 .....**269** A4
Dr John Bingham Prim Sch
 S8 ....**57** A3
Drabbles Rd DE4 ...**143** A3
Drage St DE1 ....**219** A4
Drake Terr S43 ......**96** B4
Draycott Cl DE75 ...**181** B2
Draycott Com Prim Sch
 DE72 ....**235** A4
Draycott Ct DE7 ...**194** C2
Draycott Dr DE3 ...**217** B2
Draycott Pl S18 .....**75** C2
Draycott Rd
 Borrowash DE72 ...**221** B1
 Breaston DE72 ....**235** B4
 Long Eaton NG10 .**236** A2
 North Wingfield S42 .**131** C4
Drayton Ave Derby DE22 **217** C3
 Mansfield NG19 ...**135** B3
Drayton St DE11 ....**256** B2
Dresden Cl DE3 ....**217** B1
Drewry Ct DE1 .....**218** C3
Drewry La DE22 ....**218** C2
Dreyfus Cl DE21 ....**220** C3
Drive The DE6 ......**184** B4
Dronfield Holmesdale Inf Sch
 S18 ....**57** B1
Dronfield Inf & Jun Sch
 S18 ....**57** A1
Dronfield Pl DE7 ....**194** C3
Dronfield Rd S21 ....**59** A1
Dronfield Sch (Gosforth Site)
 The S18 ....**56** C1
Dronfield Sch The S18 .**57** A1

Dronfield Sta S18 ....57 A1
Drovers Way
Ashbourne DE6 ....173 A2
Bullbridge DE56 ....168 A3
Drovers Wlk SK13 ....10 B1
Drummond Rd DE7 ....194 C1
Drury Ave DE21 ....220 B2
Drury La Biggin SK17 ....138 B1
Dore S17 ....55 B4
Dronfield S18 ....57 B2
Dryden Ave S40 ....115 A4
Dryden Cres ST17 ......269 A3
Dryden Ct NG9 ....209 C1
Dryden St Derby DE23 ...231 C4
Nottingham NG1 ....268 A2
Dryhurst Dr SK12 ....32 B3
Dryhurst La SK12 ....32 B3
Drysdale Rd DE3 ....217 B2
Duchess St Creswell S80 ..81 C1
Whitwell S80 ....82 A3
Duck Row DE45 ....91 B2
Duck St DE65 ....241 A3
Duckmanton Prim Sch
S44 ....98 A3
Duckmanton Rd S44 ....98 A3
Ducksett La S21 ....59 B2
Duckworth Sq DE1 .....267 B3
Dudwood La DE4 ....140 C4
Duesbury Cl DE24 ......232 C4
Duesbury Ct DE3 ......230 A4
Duesbury The DE55 ....160 A2
Duewell Ct S43 ....78 A2
Duffield Bank DE56 ....191 A2
Duffield Cl NG10 ....236 A3
Duffield Ct DE56 ....190 C2
Duffield Rd DE22 ....205 A3
Duffield Sta DE56 ......190 C2
Duke Field DE4 ....154 B3
Duke of Norfolk's CE Prim
Sch SK13 ....10 B1
Duke of Norfolk's CE Prim
Sch (Annexe) SK13 .....10 C1
Duke St Buxton SK17 .....84 C3
Chesterfield S41 ....96 A4
Clowne S43 ....81 A2
Creswell S80 ....81 C1
Derby DE1 ....267 B4
Ilkeston DE7 ....194 C2
Middleton (Nr Wirksworth)
DE4 ....154 B3
Mosborough S20 ....59 B3
South Normanton DE55 ..160 A3
Staveley S43 ....78 C1
Tutbury DE13 ....239 B3
Whitwell S80 ....82 A3
Duke William Mount
NG7 ....268 A1
Duke's Dr
Ault Hucknall S44 ....134 A4
Buxton SK17 ....85 B3
Duke's Dr The DE45 ....108 C4
Duke's Pl NG1 ....268 B1
Dukeries Ct S43 ....80 C2
Dukeries La DE21 ....206 A1
Dukes Cl S42 ....116 C1
Dukes Dr Chesterfield S41 .95 C3
Curbar S32 ....72 B1
Dukes Fold SK13 ....17 A4
Dukes Pl DE7 ....194 C2
Dukes St SK13 ....17 B4
Duluth Ave DE21 ....220 A4
Dulverton Ave DE24 ....231 B1
Dulwich Rd DE22 ....217 C3
Dumb Hall La S80 ....63 A2
Dumble Wood Grange
S41 ....95 B4
Dumbles Cl DE7 ....208 B3
Dumbles La DE5 ....180 C1
Dumbles Rd S44 ....98 C1
Dumbleton Rd S21 ....60 C3
Dunbar Cl DE24 ....231 C1
Duncan Cl DE56 ....179 A3
Duncan Rd DE23 ....231 C4
Duncliffe La DE73 ......252 A4
Duncombe Dr DE6 ......185 B4
Dundas Cl NG1 ....268 B2
Dundee Dr NG19 ....136 A3
Dundee Rd DE11 ....256 B3
Dundonald Rd S40 ......266 B1
Dunedin Cl DE3 ....217 C2
Dunedin Cres DE15 .....248 B1
Dunedin Glen S20 ....59 C3
Dunedin Gr S20 ....59 C3
Dungley Hill DE56 ......168 B1
Dungreave Ave DE4 .....127 A3
Dunkery Ct DE21 ....206 A1
Dunkirk DE22 ....267 A2
Dunlow La S32 ....71 B3
Dunn Brigg NG19 ....136 B1
Dunne La SK13 ....10 C1
Dunnett Rd NG19 ....268 A3
Dunnsmoor La DE11 ....256 C4
Dunoon Cl DE24 ....231 C2
Dunoon Rd NG18 ....268 A3
Dunsa La DE45 ....91 B1
Dunsford Rd DE55 ......159 A3
Dunshill Wlk S45 ....131 C2
Dunsil Rd NG16 ....160 B1
Dunsmore Dr DE21 ......205 C1
Dunsmore Way DE11 ....256 B3
Dunstall Brook DE15 ....248 A1
Dunstall Park Rd DE24 .232 B4
Dunston Cl NG10 ....236 C4
Dunston Ct S41 ....76 C1
Dunston La S41 ....95 B4
Dunston Pl S41 ....76 C1
Dunston Prim Sch S41 ..95 B4
Dunston Rd S41 ....76 B1
Dunston Tech Pk S41 ....76 C1
Dunston Trad Est S41 ...76 C1
Dunton Cl DE21 ....267 D3
Dunvegan Ave S45 ......131 C1
Dunvegan Cl DE24 ......231 B1
Duper La S32 ....51 C3
Durban Cl DE15 ....248 B2
Durban House Her Ctr★
NG16 ....182 C2
Durham Ave
Chesterfield S43 ....77 B2
Derby DE21 ....219 C3
Grassmoor S42 ....115 C1
Nottingham NG2 ....268 C1
Durham Cl
Chesterfield S43 ....77 B2
Mansfield Woodhouse
NG19 ....136 B2
Nottingham NG2 ....268 C1
Swadlincote DE11 ......256 C3
Durham St 5 DE7 ......194 C1
Durley Chine Dr S41 ...115 B4
Durley Cl DE24 ....233 B4
Durlstone Cl S12 ....44 A3
Durlstone Cres S12 .....44 A3
Durlstone Dr S12 ....44 A3
Durlstone Gr S12 ....44 A3
Durrant Rd S41 ....266 B3
Durvale Ct S17 ....55 C3
Durward Cl DE24 ....232 B4
Dyche Cl S8 ....57 A3
Dyche Dr S8 ....57 A3
Dyche La S8,S18 ....57 A3
Dyche Pl S8 ....57 A3
Dyche Rd S8 ....57 A3
Dye House La SK22 ......33 B4
Dyke Vale Rd S12 ....44 C3
Dykes Cl S44 ....99 A1
Dymond Gr S42 ....115 C2
Dystelegh Rd SK12 ......32 B3

E

Each Well La DE55 .....158 C2
Eagle Cl DE56 ....178 C1
Eagle Ctr DE1 ....267 B2
Eagle Hts DE15 ....248 B2
Eagle Par 4 SK17 ....85 A4
Eagle Rd DE7 ....208 C2
Eagle St 3 Buxton SK17 ..85 A4
Heage DE56 ....168 C1
Eagle Terr Birchover DE4 .126 A1
Wensley DE4 ....142 A4
Ealing Cl DE22 ....218 A3
Eardley Cl DE21 ....220 A3
Eardley St ST4 ....269 A1
Earl St ST16 ....269 B4
Earl Sterndale CE Prim Sch
SK17 ....105 B2
Earls Cres DE21 ....206 A1
Earlsway 5 SK13 ....17 A4
Earlswood Cl DE72 .....235 B4
Earlswood Dr DE3 ......217 C2
Earnshaw St SK14 ....9 B2
Easedale Cl S40 ....94 C3
East Ave Bolsover S44 ....80 A1
Derby DE3 ....217 C2
East Bank DE4 ....141 B3
East Bank Cl S2 ....43 B3
East Bank Pl S2 ....43 B3
East Bank Rd S2 ....43 B3
East Bank View S2 ......43 B3
East Bank Way S2 ....43 B3
East Circus St 2 NG1 ..268 A1
East Cl DE22 ....204 C1
East Cres Holbrook DE56 .191 B4
Long Duckmanton S44 .....98 A3
East Croft Ave DE23 ...231 B3
East Dr DE6 ....211 A1
East End Dr DE11 ....256 B2
East Glade Ave S12 ......44 C2
East Glade Cl S12 ....44 C2
East Glade Cres S12 ....44 C2
East Glade Pl S12 ....44 C2
East Glade Rd S12 ....44 C2
East Glade Sq S12 ....44 C2
East Glade Way S12 .....44 C2
East Hill Primt Sch S2 ..43 B4
East Lawn DE65 ....230 B1
East Midlands International
Airport DE74 ....247 B1
East Midlands Nuffield Hospl
DE23 ....230 C3
East Nelson St DE75 ...181 C1
East Rd S2 ....43 A4
East Service Rd DE21 ..220 A2
East St Bramley-Vale S44 .117 B1
Burton u T DE15 ....248 B2
Clay Cross S45 ....131 B2
Clowne S43 ....81 A3
Creswell S80 ....81 B1
Derby DE1 ....267 B3
Heanor DE75 ....194 A4
Ilkeston DE7 ....208 C4
Long Eaton NG10 ....236 C4
Nottingham NG1 ....268 B2
Renishaw S21 ....79 A4
Scarcliffe S44 ....118 C3
East Vale SK6 ....23 A3
East View
Chesterfield S40 ....266 B2
Mayfield DE6 ....184 B4
Shirebrook NG20 ....119 C3
Whaley Thorns NG20 ....101 A2
East View Ave S21 ......59 B1
East View Ind Est NG20 .119 C3
East View Rd DE56 .....168 C1
Eastbrae Rd DE23 ....231 B4
Eastbrook Cl SK23 ....47 B3
Eastcliffe S2 ....43 B4
Eastcliffe Ct S2 ....43 B4
Eastcroft Cl S20 ....59 C4
Eastcroft Dr S20 ....59 C4
Eastcroft Glen 10 S20 ...59 C4
Eastcroft View 11 S20 ...59 C4
Eastcroft Way 13 S20 ....59 C4
Eastern Ave
Bolsover S44 ....118 A4
Sheffield S2 ....43 C4
Eastern Cres S2 ....43 B3
Eastern Dr S2 ....43 B4
Eastern Wlk S2 ....43 B4
Eastfield Dr DE55 ....160 A3
Eastfield Rd Dronfield S18 76 B4
Ripley DE5 ....170 A1
Swadlincote DE11 ......256 B3
Eastgate DE1, DE21 ....267 D4
Eastgate St ST16 ....269 B4
Eastham Cl NG3 ....268 C2
Eastleigh Ct S41 ....115 B4
Eastleigh Dr Derby DE3 .217 C1
Mansfield Woodhouse
NG19 ....136 A3
Eastmoor Rd S43 ....96 C2
Eastside Cl S41 ....96 A4
Eastside Rd S41 ....96 A4
Eastview Terr NG16 .....182 A2
Eastway DE74 ....247 A2
Eastwood Ave DE23 .....218 B1
Eastwood Cl S41 ....115 B4
Eastwood Comp Sch
NG16 ....182 C2
Eastwood Cotts S32 .....53 A4
Eastwood Dr Calow S44 ..97 A1
Derby DE23 ....218 B1
Eastwood Jun & Inf Schs
NG16 ....182 C1
Eastwood La S45 ....130 A1
Eastwood Park Dr S41 .115 B4
Eastwood Rd NG16 .....195 C3
Easy Par S80 ....82 A3
Eather Ave NG19 ....136 B2
Eaton Ave Derby DE22 ...205 A3
Ilkeston DE7 ....208 B3
Eaton Bank DE56 ....191 A1
Eaton Cl Derby DE22 ....205 A3
Hatton DE65 ....227 B1
Hulland Ward DE6 ......175 C2
Eaton Ct Derby DE1 .....218 C3
Duffield DE56 ....190 C1
Eaton Dr DE45 ....91 C3
Eaton Fold S32 ....71 C2
Eaton Grange Dr NG10 .236 A4
Eaton Hill DE45 ....91 C3
Eaton Pl DE45 ....91 C3
Eaton Rd
Castle Donington DE74 ..247 A2
Rocester ST14 ....196 C2
Eaton St ST14 ....210 B1
Eatons Rd NG9 ....223 B3
Eaves Ave SK23 ....47 B3
Eaves Knoll Rd SK22 ....33 A4
Ebenezer St Glossop SK13 17 B4
Ilkeston DE7 ....194 C2
Langley Mill NG16 ......182 A2
Eccles Cl Hope S33 ......39 A2
Whaley Bridge SK23 .....45 B4
Eccles Fold SK23 ....47 A3
Eccles Rd
Chapel-en-le-F, Higher Crossings
SK23 ....47 A3
Chapel-en-le-F, Hilltop SK23 46 B4
Eccles Terr SK23 ....46 B4
Ecclesbourne Ave DE56 190 C2
Ecclesbourne Cl
Duffield DE56 ....190 C2
Wirksworth DE4 ....165 C4
Ecclesbourne Cotts
DE4 ....154 C1
Ecclesbourne Dr SK17 ..85 A3
Ecclesbourne La DE56 .176 C3
Ecclesbourne Pk DE55 .159 B1
Ecclesbourne Sch The
DE56 ....190 C2
Eckington Cl DE7 ....207 C4
Eckington Hall S20 ......59 B3
Eckington Jun Sch S21 ..59 B2
Eckington Mews S20 ....59 B3
Eckington Rd
Dronfield S18 ....57 B2
Mosborough S20 ....59 C4
Staveley S43 ....78 C2
Unstone S43 ....77 B3
Eckington Sch S21 ......59 A2
Eckington Way S20 ......59 C4
Eclipse Yd NG18 ....268 B4
Edale Ave Derby DE23 ..218 C1
Derby, Alvaston DE24 ....233 A4
Derby, Mickleover DE3 ...217 B1
Edale Bank 6 SK13 ......9 C1
Edale CE Prim Sch S33 ..37 B4
Edale Cl Derby DE22 ....204 B1
7 Gamesley SK13 ....9 C1
Long Eaton NG10 ....236 A3
Edale Cres SK13 ....9 C1
Edale Ct 3 S41 ....95 C4
Edale Dr Derby DE21 ....220 C2
South Normanton DE55 ..160 A4
Edale Gr SK17 ....85 C4
Edale Rd Hayfield SK22 ...26 A1
Hope S33 ....38 C4
Mastin Moor S43 ....79 B2
Edale Rise NG9 ....223 C2
Edale Sq DE7 ....194 C3
Edale Sta S33 ....37 B4
Edale Way DE56 ....179 A3
Edale YH★ S33 ....29 A1
Eden Bank DE56 ....167 C1
Eden Low NG19 ....136 C2
Eden Rd DE21 ....220 A2
Eden St Derby DE24 .....233 A4
Wingerworth S42 ....114 C2
Edenhall Rd S2 ....43 C4
Edensor Ave SK17 ....85 C4
Edensor Cl S42 ....131 C3
Edensor Ct S43 ....97 B4
Edensor Dr DE56 ....179 B3
Edensor Sq DE22 ....218 C2
Edes Farm Dr ST14 .....196 C2
Edgar Ave NG18 ....268 C4
Edgbaston Ct DE23 .....231 B4
Edge Hill DE73 ....232 C2
Edge Hill Ct NG10 ......236 B2
Edge Hill Jun Sch DE15 254 C4
Edge La S33 ....51 A3
Edge Mount View S32 ...72 C1
Edge Rd Eyam S32 ....71 C4
Matlock DE4 ....143 A3
Edge View S32 ....72 A2
Edge View Cl S32 ....72 B4
Edge View Dr DE45 ....90 A2
Edgecote Dr DE11 ....256 A4
Edgefold Rd DE4 ....143 A3
Edgehill Gr NG19 ....136 B1
Edgelaw Ct 10 DE24 ....231 B2
Edgewood Rd NG16 .....195 C3
Edgware Rd DE22 ....217 C3
Edinboro Row NG16 .....195 C4
Edinburgh Cres DE24 ..232 C2
Edinburgh Ct
Chesterfield S41 ....266 A4
Swanwick DE55 ....170 A4
Edinburgh Rd
Chesterfield S41 ....95 C3
Wingerworth S42 ....114 C2
Edision St ST4 ....269 C1
Edith Wood Cl DE24 ...233 A3
Edlaston La DE6 ....185 A1
Edmonton Pl DE15 ......248 B1
Edmund Ave S17 ....56 B3
Edmund Cl S17 ....56 B3
Edmund Dr S17 ....56 B3
Edmund Rd Derby DE21 .220 C2
Sheffield S2 ....43 A4
Edmund St S41 ....95 C4
Edmund's Sq DE3 ....230 A4
Ednaston Ave DE23 .....231 B3
Ednaston Hall Farm Mews
DE6 ....201 A4
Edward Ave Derby DE21 .220 A3
Westwood NG16 ....171 A2
Edward Rd NG10 ....236 B4
Edward St Aldercar NG16 182 A2
Belper DE56 ....179 A2
Derby DE1 ....267 B4
Eckington S21 ....59 B2
Glossop SK13 ....10 B1
Hartshorne DE11 ....257 A2
Marple SK6 ....15 A1
Moira DE11 ....256 B1
Overseal DE12 ....262 A2
Stapleford NG9 ....223 B4
Staveley S43 ....97 B4
Edward Wlk S42 ....115 B1
Edwards Cres DE56 .....192 A4
Edwards Dr ST16 ....269 A4
Edwin Ave S40 ....114 B4
Edwin Rd S2 ....43 B3
Edwinstowe Rd DE21 ...206 A1
Egerton Dr NG9 ....209 B1
Egerton Rd Dronfield S18 .57 A1
Stoke-on-T ST4 ....269 A2
Eggesford Rd DE24 ....231 B1
Egginton Prim Sch
DE65 ....241 A3
Egginton Rd Etwall DE65 229 A1
Hilton DE65 ....228 C1
Egmanton Cl DE21 ......206 A1
Egreaves Ave DE75 .....181 B2
Egstow Pl S45 ....131 B2
Egstow St S45 ....131 B2
Ehlinger Ave SK13 ....10 A3
Eider Cl NG20 ....119 B2
Eighth Ave DE14 ....253 C4
Eland Cl DE21 ....221 A3
Eland Rd NG20 ....119 C3
Elder Cl DE55 ....170 A4
Elder Ct S21 ....60 B3
Elder Way S40 ....266 B3
Eldon Cl SK23 ....47 B3
Eldon La SK17 ....49 A3
Eldon St Burton u T DE15 .248 B2
Clay Cross S45 ....131 B2
Eleanor Ave DE7 ....209 A3
Eleanor Cres NG9 ......223 C4
Elenora St ST4 ....269 B2
Eley Cl DE7 ....194 B1
Eley Wlk DE22 ....267 A1
Elford Rise NG3 ....268 C2
Elgar Dr NG10 ....236 A3
Elgin Ave DE23 ....218 A1
Elgin Cl S40 ....114 B4
Eliot Cl Calow S43 ....96 C3
Long Eaton NG10 ....236 A3
Wirksworth DE4 ....165 C4
Eliot Dr DE7 ....208 B3
Eliot Rd DE23 ....231 A4
Eliot Way ST17 ....269 A3
Elizabeth Ave
Buxton SK17 ....85 B4
Disley SK12 ....32 B3
Rolleston DE13 ....240 A2
Elizabeth Cl Derby DE21 .220 A3
Elizabeth Cl *continued*
West Hallam DE7 ....207 B4
Elizabeth Ct Ilkeston DE7 194 B1
Stoke-on-T ST4 ....269 A2
Elizabeth Pk NG16 .....170 C3
Elkstone Cl DE21 ......206 A1
Elkstone Rd S40 ....95 A3
Ella Bank Rd DE75 .....182 A1
Ellastone Gdns DE24 ...233 A4
Ellastone Gr ST4 ....269 A1
Ellendale Rd DE21 .....220 A4
Ellerslie Gr NG10 ......223 A3
Ellesmere Ave
Alfreton DE55 ....159 A2
Derby DE24 ....219 B1
Ellesmere Dr NG9 ......209 B3
Ellington Ave ST16 .....269 C4
Elliot Ave S33 ....51 A4
Elliott Dr S43 ....97 B3
Elliott St NG7 ....268 A2
Ellis Cl NG10 ....236 B3
Ellis Ct NG3 ....268 B2
Ellison Ave DE72 ....246 A4
Ellison Cl SK14 ....9 B3
Ellison St SK13 ....10 B1
Elm Ave Belper DE56 ....179 A1
Darley Dale DE4 ....142 C4
Long Eaton NG10 ....236 B4
Sandiacre NG10 ....223 A4
Elm Cl Bolsover S44 ......99 B1
Branston DE14 ....253 C4
Chesterfield S41 ....95 C4
Doveridge DE6 ....224 B4
Killamarsh S21 ....60 B3
Mottram in L SK14 ....9 A2
Pinxton NG16 ....160 B2
Elm Cres S20 ....59 B4
Elm Dr Hilton DE65 .....228 B1
Killamarsh S21 ....60 B3
Elm Gr Clay Cross S45 ...131 B2
Derby DE22 ....204 B3
Derby, Cherrytree Hill
DE21 ....220 A3
Glossop SK13 ....10 B1
Elm Lodge Farm Cl S41 .95 C4
Elm Park Ct DE1 ....267 A5
Elm Rd Eckington S21 .....59 B1
Pilsley S45 ....132 B1
Elm St Borrowash DE72 ..221 A1
Brimington S43 ....97 A4
Holmewood S42 ....116 A2
Elm Tree Ave
Kilburn DE56 ....192 A4
Mansfield Woodhouse
NG19 ....136 A2
Shirebrook NG20 ....119 B2
Shirland DE55 ....146 B1
Elm Tree Cres S18 ......57 A2
Elm Tree Dr S42 ....114 C2
Elm Tree St NG18 ......268 C4
Elm View ST14 ....196 C3
Elm Wlk S45 ....132 B1
Elma La S80 ....101 B3
Elmfield SK23 ....47 A3
Elmhurst DE65 ....241 A3
Elmhurst Ave DE55 .....160 A2
Elmhurst Cl DE55 ......160 A2
Elmhurst Rd NG19 ......136 C1
Elmore Ct NG7 ....268 A2
Elms Ave Alfreton DE55 ..159 A2
Derby DE23 ....218 A1
Ripley DE5 ....180 B4
Elms Cl DE55 ....159 A2
Elms Dr DE23 ....218 A1
Elms Farm Way DE23 ..231 A4
Elms Gr DE65 ....229 B2
Elms Rd Burton u T DE15 .248 A1
Coton in t E DE12 ....260 B2
Elms St DE1 ....218 C4
Elms The NG16 ....195 C4
Elmsdale Rd DE11 ......257 A2
Elmsfield Ave DE75 .....182 A1
Elmslea Ave DE12 ......260 B2
Elmsleigh Cl DE11 .....256 A3
Elmsleigh Dr DE11 .....256 A3
Elmsleigh Gr DE11 .....256 A3
Elmsleigh Inf Sch DE11 256 A3
Elmton Cl Clowne S43 ...80 C2
Creswell S80 ....100 B4
Elmton La S44 ....99 B2
Elmton Rd S80 ....81 C1
Elmtree Ave Derby DE24 .232 A4
Selston NG16 ....171 C4
Elmtree Cl S81 ....63 C4
Elmwood Dr Derby DE21 205 B1
Mosborough S20 ....59 B3
Elnor Ave SK23 ....45 C3
Elnor La SK23 ....45 C2
Elnor St NG16 ....182 B2
Elsecar Cl DE56 ....179 B3
Elsing St ST4 ....269 C1
Elstead La DE11 ....257 A1
Elston Cl NG19 ....135 B1
Elstree Dr S12 ....44 A2
Elstree Rd S12 ....44 A2
Elton Bank SK13 ....9 B1
Elton CE Prim Sch DE4 .140 C3
Elton Cl Gamesley SK13 ....9 B1
North Wingfield S42 .....132 A3
Stapleford NG9 ....223 B4
Elton Gr SK17 ....85 C3
Elton Rd Derby DE24 ....232 A4
Winster DE4 ....141 A3
Elton St S40 ....266 B2
Elton View S43 ....97 B4

Elvaston Castle★ DE21 233 C4
Elvaston Castle Ctry Pk DE21 233 C3
Elvaston Cl S18 56 A1
Elvaston Dr NG10 236 A2
Elvaston Estate Mus★ DE72 233 C4
Elvaston La DE24 233 B4
Elvaston Rd S42 131 C3
Elvaston St DE72 235 A4
Elveden Dr DE7 194 B2
Elvin Way S42 131 B4
Elwood Rd S17 56 B3
Elwyn Cl DE13 240 B1
Ely Cl
Mansfield Woodhouse NG19 136 B2
Swadlincote DE11 256 B3
Elyn Ave S42 132 A4
Elysee Gdns SK17 85 B2
Embankment Cl DE22 217 C4
Ember La DE4 142 C1
Embridge Cswy SK10, SK17 64 A3
Emerald Cl Derby DE21 206 A1
Mansfield NG19 135 C1
Emerson Sq DE23 231 C3
Emery Cl DE12 261 B3
Emmas Williams Ct DE5 169 B1
Emmet Field Cl S40 114 C4
Emmett Carr Cl S21 79 B4
Emmett Carr Dr S21 79 B4
Emmett Carr La S21 79 B4
Empire Pas ST4 269 B1
Empire Rd DE15 248 B2
Empire St
Mansfield NG18 268 C3
Stoke-on-T ST4 269 B1
Empress Rd DE23 267 A1
Emsworth Cl DE7 194 B2
Ena Ave NG2 268 C2
End The DE15 248 C4
Endland Ind Est DE1 218 B3
Endowood Rd S40 114 A4
Endsleigh Gdns DE22 217 C3
Enfield Cl DE65 228 C1
Enfield Rd
Chesterfield S41 96 A3
Derby DE22 218 A3
England Cres DE75 182 A1
English Martyrs RC Prim Sch NG10 223 A1
Englishe Rd DE4 143 A2
Ennerdale Ave S20 59 C3
Ennerdale Cl S18 56 C1
Ennerdale Cres S41 95 B4
Ennerdale Ct 6 NG10 223 A1
Ennerdale Dr S20 59 C3
Ennerdale Rd NG10 223 A1
Ennerdale Wlk DE21 205 B1
Ennis Cl DE21 220 B4
Enoch Stone Dr DE21 220 A2
Enslet La DE6 164 A2
Ensor Cl DE11 256 B3
Ensor Way SK22 33 B4
Enterprise Cl NG19 135 C1
Enterprise Ct S80 81 C1
Enterprise Dr S42 116 B1
Enterprise Way NG19 135 C2
Epping Cl DE22 217 C3
Epsley's Yd ST16 269 B3
Epsom Cl DE14 253 C4
Epsom Rd NG9 223 C2
Epworth Dr DE24 233 A2
Epworth Ho DE15 248 B2
Epworth St ST4 269 B2
Erdington Way NG9 223 C2
Erewash Ct DE7 194 B1
Erewash Dr DE7 209 A3
Erewash Gr NG9 223 C1
Erewash Mus★ DE7 208 C4
Erewash Rd NG16 160 C1
Erewash Sq DE7 209 A3
Erewash St DE55 171 A3
Erica Dr DE55 160 A4
Erin Rd S43,S44 98 A4
Ernest Hall Way DE11 256 B2
Ernocroft La SK6 15 C1
Ernocroft Rd SK6 15 A1
Errill Cl ST4 269 C1
Errington Ave S2 43 C3
Errington Cl S2 43 C3
Errington Cres S2 43 C3
Errington Rd
Chesterfield S40 114 B4
Sheffield S2 43 C3
Errington Way S2 43 C4
Errwood Ave SK17 85 A3
Errwood Forest Walks★ SK17 64 C1
Erskine Cres S2 43 B4
Erskine Rd S2 43 B4
Erskine St SK6 15 A2
Erskine View S2 43 B4
Escolme Cl DE11 256 B2
Eskdale Cl Bolsover S44 98 C1
Dronfield S18 56 C1
Long Eaton NG10 236 A3
Eskdale Wlk 8 DE24 233 B3
Essendine Cres S8 43 A2
Essex Rd DE15 254 B3
Essex St Derby DE21 219 B3
4 Ilkeston DE7 194 C1
Estwic Ave NG16 182 C2
Ethel Wainwright Fst & Mid Schs NG19 268 A4
Etherow Brow SK14 16 A4
Etherow Ctry Pk SK6 15 B2
Etherow Ctry Pk Visitor Ctr SK6 15 A2
Etherow Ind Est SK13 9 C3
Etherow Way SK13 9 C3
Eton Ct DE7 207 B4
Eton St DE24 219 C1
Etruria Gdns DE1 267 B5
Etta's Way DE65 229 A2
Ettrick Cl 4 S40 95 B3
Ettrick Dr DE24 231 C1
Etwall Cl S40 95 A3
Etwall La DE65 229 C3
Etwall Prim Sch DE65 229 A2
Etwall Rd Derby DE3 217 B1
Egginton DE65 241 A4
Willington DE65 242 A4
Etwall St DE22 218 C3
Eugene St NG2 268 B1
Eureka Prim Sch DE11 256 B3
Eureka Rd DE11 256 B3
Euston Dr DE1 267 C5
Evans Ave DE22 205 A3
Evans St DE24 232 C3
Evanston Gdns DE21 220 A3
Evelyn Devonshire Cotts S45 132 C1
Evelyn Gr DE21 220 A3
Evelyn St NG1 268 C1
Everard Ave S17 56 A3
Everard Dr S17 56 A3
Everard Glade 6 S17 56 A3
Everest Dr DE55 170 B4
Everett Cl S43 96 C4
Evergreen Cl DE21 206 A2
Evershill Cl DE55 146 C3
Evershill La DE55 146 C3
Eversleigh Rise DE4 142 A4
Everton St NG19 135 C1
Evesham Ave SK13 10 A3
Evesham Cl DE21 205 C1
Ewart La DE55 158 C2
Ewe Dale La DE6 149 A2
Ewe Lamb Cl NG9 209 C1
Ewe Lamb La NG9 209 C1
Excelsior Ave DE24 232 C3
Exchange St DE1 267 B3
Exchange Wlk 2 NG1 268 B1
Exe Fold NG19 136 B1
Exeter Cl DE11 256 C3
Exeter Ho DE1 267 C3
Exeter Pl DE1 267 C3
Exeter St DE1 267 C4
Exford Ct NG19 136 B3
Exlowmere La DE4 140 C3
Export Dr NG17 160 C4
Extension St 9 DE7 208 C4
Eyam CE Prim Sch S32 71 B3
Eyam Cl Burton u T DE15 248 A1
North Wingfield S42 132 A4
Eyam Fold 12 SK13 9 B1
Eyam Gn 8 SK13 9 B1
Eyam Hall★ S32 71 B3
Eyam La SK13 9 B1
Eyam Lea 3 SK13 9 C1
Eyam Mews SK13 9 C1
Eyam Mus★ S32 71 B3
Eyam Wlk DE56 179 A3
Eyam YH★ S32 71 B3
Eyes Ct DE56 190 C2
Eyre Gdns S40 266 A4
Eyre St Clay Cross S45 131 B2
Creswell S80 81 B1
Nottingham NG2 268 C1
Eyre St E S41 115 B4
Eyre's Gdns DE7 194 C1
Eyrie The
Burton u T DE15 248 B2
Derby DE24 231 C1

F

Fabis Cl DE11 256 A2
Fabric View S42 132 B4
Factory La Disley SK12 32 C4
Ilkeston DE7 194 C1
Factory St S40 95 B1
Fair Lea Cl NG10 236 B3
Fair View S40 95 C2
Fairbank Ave ST4 269 B1
Fairbourne Dr DE3 217 B2
Fairburn Croft Cres S43 80 A3
Faircroft Ave NG10 223 A3
Fairdene DE23 218 C1
Faire St DE22 218 C2
Faires Cl DE72 221 B1
Fairfax Dr S2 44 A4
Fairfax Rd Derby DE23 218 C1
Sheffield S2 44 A4
Fairfield Ave
Borrowash DE72 221 B2
Hilcote DE55 148 B1
Rolleston DE13 240 B2
Stonebroom DE55 147 A2
Fairfield Cl Brimington S43 96 B4
Whaley Thorns NG20 101 A1
Fairfield Cres
Long Eaton NG10 236 A2
Swadlincote DE11 255 C3
Fairfield Ct S42 94 C2
Fairfield Dr S42 94 C2
Fairfield Endowed CE Jun Sch SK17 85 C4
Fairfield Inf Sch SK17 85 B4
Fairfield Prim Sch NG9 223 B3
Fairfield Rd
Bolsover S44 118 A4
Buxton SK17 85 B4
Chesterfield S40 266 A4
Derby DE23 218 C1
Horsley Woodhouse DE7 192 B4
Fairfield Terr DE11 256 C2
Fairford Cl S40 114 C4
Fairford Gdns DE23 231 A3
Fairham Rd DE13 240 C1
Fairholme Dr NG19 135 C1
Fairholmes DE4 143 B3
Fairisle Cl DE21 206 B2
Fairlawns DE56 190 B2
Fairleigh S2 44 A4
Fairmeadows Prim Sch DE11 255 C3
Fairview Ave NG16 171 C1
Fairview Cl Derby DE23 231 A4
Kilburn DE56 192 A4
Fairview Grange DE56 192 A4
Fairview Rd S18 57 A2
Fairview Rise DE4 168 A4
Fairway Burton u T DE14 254 A3
Stafford ST16,ST17 269 C3
Fairway Cl DE22 204 B1
Fairway Cres DE22 204 B1
Fairway The Clifton DE6 184 C3
Swadlincote DE11 255 C3
Fairways Cl SK13 10 C1
Fairways The
Clay Cross S45 131 C2
Mansfield Woodhouse NG19 136 B3
Fairwinds Cl S18 57 A1
Fairwood Dr DE24 233 B3
Fairy Bank Cres SK22 25 B2
Fairy Bank Rd SK22 25 B2
Fal Paddock NG19 136 B1
Falaise Way DE65 228 C1
Falcon Cl SK22 33 B4
Falcon Ct DE7 194 B1
Falcon Rd S18 57 B2
Falcon Rise S18 57 B2
Falcon Way Derby DE24 231 C1
Woodville DE11 256 C2
Falcon Yd S40 266 B3
Falcons Rise DE56 179 B3
Faldo Cl DE14 254 A3
Falkland Rise S18 76 A4
Fall Rd DE75 181 C2
Fallow Rd DE21 220 C3
Fallowfield Rd S43 77 B2
Falmouth Rd DE24 233 B3
Fan Rd S43 78 C1
Fan Road Ind Est S43 78 C1
Fanny Ave S21 60 C3
Fanshaw Ave S21 59 B1
Fanshaw Bank S18 57 A1
Fanshaw Cl S21 59 B1
Fanshaw Dr S21 59 B1
Fanshaw Gate La S18 55 C1
Fanshaw Rd Dronfield S18 57 A1
Eckington S21 59 B1
Fanshaw Way S21 59 B1
Far Croft DE72 235 B4
Far Cross DE4 143 B4
Far Gn DE4 143 A3
Far Hill S33 51 A4
Far La Barlow S18 75 A2
Ockbrook DE72 221 B3
Far Laund DE56 179 A3
Far New Cl NG10 223 A3
Far Woodseats La SK13 15 C3
Faraday Ave DE13 240 B1
Faraday Ct NG9 209 C1
Faraday Pl ST4 269 A2
Farfield Rd DE7 209 A4
Farish Pl 8 S2 43 A3
Farley Hill DE4 143 A4
Farley La DE4 128 A2
Farley Rd DE23 218 B1
Farm Cl Belper DE56 179 B2
Chesterfield S40 114 C3
Dronfield S18 57 A2
Hilton DE65 228 B1
Ilkeston DE7 209 A4
Kilburn DE56 192 A4
Long Eaton NG10 236 C3
Ripley DE5 169 A3
Sheffield S12 44 A1
Somercotes DE55 170 B4
Farm Cres S20 59 B3
Farm Croft Rd NG19 136 B3
Farm Dr DE24 233 A3
Farm La High Lane SK12 32 A3
Matlock DE4 143 B4
Newton Solney DE15 248 C4
Farm Side DE11 255 C3
Farm St DE22 218 C2
Farm View S42 131 B4
Farm Wlk S20 59 B4
Farmfields Cl S44 98 C2
Farmhouse Rd DE24 231 C1
Farmilo Cres NG19 135 C1
Farmilo Prim Sch NG19 135 B2
Farmlands La DE23 231 A3
Farmstead Cl S14 43 B3
Farmway NG19 136 B1
Farnah Green Rd DE56 178 B2
Farnborough Gdns DE22 205 A2
Farncombe La DE21 205 C2
Farndale Ave S40 114 A4
Farndale Cl NG10 236 A3
Farndale Ct 5 DE24 233 B3
Farndale Rd S43 78 C2
Farndon Dr NG9 223 C2
Farndon Way NG19 268 A4
Farneworth Rd DE3 217 B1
Farnham Cl DE3 217 B1
Farnham Wlk DE7 207 B4
Farningham Cl DE21 220 C3
Farnon Cl S40 266 C1
Farnsley La S32 71 A2
Farnsworth Gr NG17 148 C2
Farnsworth St S41 115 B4
Farnway DE22 204 C1
Farrendale Cl NG19 136 B1
Farrier Gdns DE23 231 A4
Farriers Croft DE7 194 B2
Farringdon Cl DE22 217 C3
Farrington Way NG16 182 C1
Farthing Ct NG10 236 A4
Farwater Cl S18 76 A4
Farwater La S18 56 C1
Fauld Ind Pk DE13 238 C3
Fauld La Tutbury DE13 239 A3
Tutbury, Fauld DE13 238 B4
Fauvel Pl SK13 10 B1
Fauvel Rd SK13 10 B1
Faversham Cl DE24 232 C3
Fawn Cl S42 114 C2
Fay Gdns SK13 9 C2
Faywood Dr SK6 23 A3
Fearn Ave DE5 169 C1
Fearn Cl
Church Broughton DE65 227 A4
Long Eaton DE72 236 A4
Featherbed La
Bolsover S44 99 A3
Whitwell S80 63 C1
Featherstone Gr ST4 269 B2
Felkin St S41 266 C3
Fellbrigg Rd S2 43 B4
Fellowlands Way DE73 233 A1
Fellside Belper DE56 179 A2
Derby DE21 220 C3
Fellview Cl S32 53 A4
Felton Ave NG19 136 B3
Fenchurch Wlk DE22 218 A4
Fenland Way S40 114 C4
Fennel St DE45 108 C4
Fenton Ave DE11 257 A1
Fenton Rd DE3 217 B1
Fenton St S21 59 A1
Fenwick St DE24 232 B4
Ferguson Ave NG19 136 A2
Fern Ave Staveley S43 97 B4
Willington DE65 242 B3
Fern Bank Ave DE55 147 C1
Fern Cl Eckington S21 59 A2
Holmewood S44 116 C1
Shirebrook NG20 119 C3
Willington DE65 242 B3
Fern Cres NG16 182 B2
Fern Lea Hollingworth SK14 9 B3
Shirland DE55 146 B2
Fern Rd SK17 85 A3
Fern Royd S32 53 A4
Fern Way S21 59 A2
Fernbank S33 51 A4
Fernbank Dr S21 59 A2
Ferncroft Ave S20 59 B4
Ferndale Ave SK17 67 B2
Ferndale Cl S18 57 B2
Ferndale Rd Buxton SK17 67 B2
Dronfield S18 57 B2
Ferndale Rise S18 57 B2
Ferndene Dr NG10 236 A4
Fernello Cl DE73 244 A3
Ferneydale Ave SK17 85 B2
Fernhill SK6 23 A3
Fernhill Cl SK13 10 B2
Fernhill Ct DE73 233 A2
Fernilee Cl New Mills SK22 24 B1
West Hallam DE7 207 C4
Fernilee Cotts SK23 45 C1
Fernlea Cl SK13 9 C2
Fernleigh Rise NG19 136 B1
Fernway SK17 85 B2
Fernwood SK6 23 B4
Fernwood Cl
Chesterfield S41 115 C4
Derby DE23 231 B4
Shirland DE55 146 B2
Ferrers Ave DE13 239 A3
Ferrers Cl DE74 247 A2
Ferrers Cres DE56 190 B2
Ferrers Ctr for Arts & Crafts★ LE65 258 C4
Ferrers Way Derby DE22 204 C1
Ripley DE5 169 B2
Ferrers Wlk NG3 268 C2
Ferry Gn DE65 242 A3
Ferry St DE15 254 C4
Ferry Vale Cl DE15 254 C4
Festival Ave DE72 235 B4
Festival Rd
Branston DE14 253 C4
Ilkeston DE7 208 B3
Festus Cl NG3 268 B2
Fiddle St SK17 85 B2
Fiddler's La DE13 239 C2
Fidlers Cl S33 40 A2
Fidlers Well S33 40 A2
Field Ave Hatton DE65 239 B4
Renishaw S21 79 A4
Field Cl Borrowash DE72 221 A2
Breaston DE72 235 C4
Dronfield S18 56 B1
Hilton DE65 228 B1
Mansfield Woodhouse NG19 136 B3
Field Cres DE24 233 A3
Field Ct Chesterfield S43 77 B2
Kilburn DE56 192 A4
Field Dr Derby DE24 233 A3
Rolleston DE13 240 A2
Shirebrook NG20 119 C1
Field End DE4 153 A1
Field Head Way DE21 206 A2
Field House Inf Sch DE7 208 C3
Field House La SK6 23 A3
Field La
Ault Hucknall NG19,S44 134 B3
Belper DE56 178 C2
Blackfordby DE11 257 B1
Derby, Boulton DE24 233 A3
Derby, Chaddesden DE21 220 A4
Kirk Ireton DE6 176 A4
Mayfield DE6 183 B4
Field Rd DE7 208 C4
Field Rise DE23 231 B4
Field Row 5 DE56 178 C2
Field St DE5 181 A4
Field Terr DE5 169 B1
Field The DE75 194 A3
Field View
Chesterfield S40 115 A4
Clowne S43 80 C2
South Normanton DE55 160 A4
Field View Cl DE24 233 A3
Field Way DE11 255 C3
Fielden Ave NG19 135 B1
Fieldfare Ct DE23 231 A3
Fieldfare Ho S41 77 A2
Fieldgate Dr DE21 205 C1
Fieldhead Rd S8 43 A4
Fieldhead Way S41 95 B3
Fielding St ST4 269 B1
Fieldings Rd S80 81 C1
Fieldon Cl DE6 202 C1
Fields Cres SK14 9 B3
Fields Farm Rd NG10 236 C3
Fields Gr SK14 9 B3
Fields La Killamarsh S21 60 A3
Linton DE11 261 C3
Fields The DE4 154 B2
Fieldsway Dr DE21 205 C1
Fieldview Pl S41 95 B3
Fiennes Cres NG7 268 A1
Fife St DE24 232 C4
Filbert Wlk DE73 245 A4
Finch Cl DE11 256 C2
Finch Cres DE3 230 B4
Fincham Cl DE21 205 B1
Finchley Ave DE22 217 C3
Findern Cl Belper DE56 179 A3
Derby DE22 204 B1
Findern Com Prim Sch DE65 242 C4
Findern La
Burnaston DE65 230 A2
Willington DE65 242 A3
Findern St DE22 218 B3
Finley Way DE55 160 A2
Finmere Cl DE23 231 A4
Finney Cl DE12 262 C1
Finningley Dr DE22 204 C1
Finny La DE6 200 A3
Finsbury Ave
Derby DE22 218 A3
Nottingham NG2 268 C1
Finsley Wlk DE23 231 C3
Fir Cl NG20 119 B3
Fir Pl S21 60 B3
Fir Rd S21 59 B1
Fir St S43 78 A1
Fir Tree Ave DE55 146 B2
Firestone DE56 178 B1
Firfield Ave DE72 235 C4
Firfield Prim Sch DE72 235 C4
Firs Ave Alfreton DE55 159 A3
Hulland Ward DE6 175 C2
Ripley DE5 169 B1
Firs Cres DE22 204 C2
Firs Estate Prim Sch DE22 218 C2
Firs Gdns DE55 159 A2
Firs Par DE4 143 B3
Firs St NG10 236 A2
Firs The DE6 173 B1
First Ave Branston DE14 253 C4
Risley NG10 222 C3
Firth Ct S43 77 B2
Firthwood Ave S18 57 B2
Firthwood Cl S18 57 B2
Firthwood Rd S18 57 B2
Firtree Gr DE21 206 A1
Firvale S26 61 C3
Firvale Rd S40 114 A4
Fish Pond Dr NG7 268 A1
Fisher Cl
Chesterfield S40 114 C4
Repton DE65 242 B1
Fisher Ct DE7 194 C2
Fisher Gate NG1 268 B1
Fisher La Duffield DE56 190 C2
Mansfield NG18 268 C3
Fisher St DE24 232 C3
Fishers Bridge SK22 25 B1
Fishpond La
Egginton DE65 241 A3
Tutbury DE13 239 B3
Fishponds Cl S42 115 A2
Fishponds Rd S13 44 B4
Fishponds Rd W S13 44 B4
Fiskerton Way DE21 206 A1
Fitzalan St SK13 10 B1
Fitzherbert CE Prim Sch DE6 162 A1

Fitzhubert Rd S2 ....44 A4
Fitzroy Rd S2 ....43 A3
Fitzwilliam Dr NG19 ...136 C1
Five Lamps Ct DE1 .....218 C3
Five Lamps Ho DE1 .....267 A5
Five Lands Rd DE15 ....254 C4
Five Trees Ave **1** S17 ...56 A3
Five Trees Cl **3** S17 ....56 A3
Five Trees Dr **2** S17 ....56 A3
Flackets La DE6 ....225 A4
Flagg La SK17 ....106 C4
Flagshaw La DE6 ......202 C2
Flake La DE7 ....208 C1
Flamstead Ave DE5 ....181 B2
Flamstead La DE5 .....180 C1
Flamstead Rd DE7 .....194 C1
Flamstead St DE24 ....232 C3
Flamsteed Cres S41 .....96 A3
Flash CE Prim Sch
  SK17 ....103 A2
Flash La DE4 ....128 A4
Flat La SK17 ....106 B4
Flat The DE56 ....191 C4
Flatts La NG16 ....171 B2
Flax Croft DE65 ....227 B1
Flax St ST4 ....269 B1
Flaxholme Ave DE56 ...190 C1
Flaxpiece Rd S45 ......131 B2
Fleet Cres DE56 ....178 C2
Fleet Jun Sch DE56 ....178 C1
Fleet Pk DE56 ....179 A2
Fleet St DE23 ....219 A1
Fleet The DE56 ....178 C1
Fleming Rd ST4 ....269 B2
Fletcher Ave S18 ....57 A1
Fletcher Rd S8 ....43 B4
Fletcher St Heanor DE75 181 C1
  Long Eaton NG10 .....236 B4
  Ripley DE5 ....169 C1
Fletcher's Row DE5 ....169 C1
Fletches The DE13 .....240 A1
Flewitt Gdns NG3 .....268 C2
Flint Ave NG19 ....136 C1
Flint La DE4 ....142 A4
Flint St DE24 ....232 B3
Flintson Ave S43 ....77 B2
Flixton Rd NG16 ......195 C4
Flood St DE72 ....221 B2
Florence Ave **9** NG10 ..223 C1
Florence Cl
  Chesterfield S40 .....114 C3
  Pleasley NG19 ....134 C1
Florence Ct DE7 ....194 C1
Florence Dr DE6 ....224 B4
Florence Gladwin Cl
  DE4 ....141 B3
Florence Rd
  Clay Cross S45 ......131 C2
  Wingerworth S42 ....114 C2
Florence Way SK14 ......9 B3
Florin Gdns NG10 .....236 A4
Flowery Leys La DE55 .159 B2
Floyd St ST4 ....269 B2
Fluery Cl S14 ....43 C2
Fluery Cres S14 ....43 C2
Fluery Pl S14 ....43 C2
Fluery Rd S14 ....43 C2
Fluery Rise S14 ....43 C2
Fly Hill DE45 ....109 B3
Flying Horse Wlk **1**
  NG1 ....268 B1
Foden St ST4 ....269 B1
Foggs Entry DE4 ......165 C4
Fold The S32 ....71 C2
Folds La SK23 ....45 C2
Folds Yd DE4 ....156 C1
Foljambe Ave S40 .....114 B4
Foljambe Rd
  Brimington S43 ....96 C4
  Chesterfield S40 .....266 A3
Folkestone Dr DE24 ...233 A3
Folly Rd DE22 ....205 A1
Fontaine Pl ST4 ....269 B1
Foolow Ave S40 ....266 A1
Foolow Ct S40 ....266 A1
Forbes Cl NG10 ....236 C3
Ford Ave DE75 ....181 B2
Ford Cl Dronfield S18 ...56 C1
  Ripley DE5 ....180 B4
Ford Gr SK14 ....9 A2
Ford La Breadsall DE21 .205 B3
  Derby DE22 ....205 A3
  Ridgeway S12 ....58 C3
  Willington DE65 .....242 B3
Ford Rd S21 ....58 C2
Ford St Belper DE56 ...178 C2
  Burton u T DE15 .....254 C4
  Derby DE1 ....218 C3
  Tupton S42 ....131 B4
Fordbridge La DE55 ....160 A4
Fordwells Cl DE23 .....231 A4
Foregate Ct ST16 ......269 A4
Foregate St ST16 ......269 A4
Foremark Ave DE23 ....231 C4
Forest Cl Barlborough S43 .80 A3
  6 Nottingham NG7 ..268 A2
Forest Dr S45 ....132 B1
Forest Gr NG7 ....268 A2
Forest La S41 ....50 B1
Forest Lea DE12 ......262 C2
Forest Rd NG18 ....268 C3
Forest Rd E NG1,NG7 ..268 A2
Forest Rd W NG7 ......268 A2

Forest View DE12 .....262 A2
Forester St DE1 ....267 B2
Foresters Way DE5 ....169 B1
Forge Cl DE65 ....242 B1
Forge La Burton u T DE13 241 A1
  Killamarsh S21 ....60 A4
Forge Rd S43 ....45 C4
Forge Terr SK23 ....34 C1
Forge The NG9 ....209 A3
Forman Cl DE11 ....256 A2
Forman St
  Derby DE1, DE22 .....267 A3
  Nottingham NG1 .....268 B2
Forrester Ave DE72 ...245 C3
Forrester's La S18 .....57 B2
Forshaw Cl DE6 ....185 B4
Forth Ave S18 ....56 B1
Forties La LE65 ....257 C2
Forty Foot La DE5 ....170 A1
Forum Cl **18** DE24 .....233 B3
Fosbrook Dr DE74 ....246 C2
Fosbrooke Dr NG10 ...236 B3
Fosse Cl DE72 ....221 B1
Fossett's Ave NG16 ...171 C4
Foster Rd DE11 ....256 C1
Foster St NG18 ....268 C3
Foston Cl DE65 ....239 B4
Foston Dr S40 ....95 A3
Foundry Ct SK22 ......33 B4
Foundry La DE56 .....190 C4
Foundry St S41 ....96 A4
Foundry Street Ind Est
  S41 ....96 A4
Fountain Sq SK17 .....69 B2
Fountain St SK17 .....85 A4
Fountains Cl DE22 ....205 A2
Four Lanes End DE4 ..127 B1
Four Lanes SK14 ......9 A2
Four Seasons Ctr NG18 268 B4
Fowler Ave DE55 .....159 B2
Fowler St Chesterfield S41 76 C1
  Derby DE22 ....218 C3
  Draycott DE72 ....235 A4
Fox Cl Burton u T DE14 .254 A4
  Derby DE21 ....231 B1
  Long Eaton NG10 ....236 B3
Fox Croft DE55 ....147 C3
Fox Hill S44 ....118 C3
Fox La Holmesfield S18 ..74 A3
  Sheffield S8,S17 ......56 B3
  Sheffield, Frecheville S12 ..44 B2
Fox Lane Cl S12 ....44 B2
Fox Lane View S12 ....44 B2
Fox Rd
  Castle Donington DE74 .246 C4
  Whitwell S80 ....82 A3
Fox St DE1 ....267 C4
Foxbrook Cl
  Chesterfield S42 ......94 C3
  Derby S41 ....231 A4
Foxbrook Dr S40 ......95 A1
Foxcote Way S40 ......114 A4
Foxcroft Chase S21 ...60 B3
Foxcroft Dr S21 ....60 B3
Foxcroft Gr S21 ......60 B3
Foxdale Ave S12 ....44 A3
Foxdell Way DE73 ....233 A1
Foxes Cl NG7 ....268 A1
Foxes Wlk DE22 ......204 C1
Foxes Yd SK17 ....66 B1
Foxfields Dr DE21 ....205 C1
Foxglove Ave
  Burton u T DE15 .....255 A4
  Donisthorpe DE12 ...262 C1
Foxglove Cl S44 ....97 C2
Foxglove Rd NG16 ...195 A4
Foxhall La S10 ....42 C3
Foxholes La
  Kniveton DE6 ....174 A3
  Tansley DE4 ....144 A4
Foxlands Ave DE22 ...204 C1
Foxlea SK13 ....16 C4
Foxley Ct DE21 ....206 A1
Foxley Oaks S41 ......77 A1
Foxlow Ave SK17 ......85 B2
Foxpark View DE55 ...147 C3
Foxstone Cl S43 ....97 B4
Foxton Cl DE7 ....194 B2
Foxwood Ave S12 ......44 A3
Foxwood Cl
  Chesterfield S41 .....115 B3
  Chesterfield, Sheepbridge
  S41 ....76 C1
Foxwood Ct S40 ......114 A4
Foxwood Dr
  Chesterfield S40 .....114 A4
  Sheffield S12 ....44 A3
Foxwood Gr S12 ....44 A3
Foxwood Ind Pk S41 ...76 C1
Foxwood Rd
  Chesterfield S41 .....76 C1
  Sheffield S12 ....44 A3
Foxwood Way S41 .....76 C1
Foyle Ave DE21 ......220 A2
Framlingham Pl S2 ....43 B4
Framlingham Rd S2 ...43 B4
Frampton Gdns DE23 .230 C3
Frances Dr S42 ......114 C2
Frances St NG16 ......171 B1
Franchise St DE22 ....218 C2
Francis Cl S43 ....96 B4
Francis St Derby DE21 ..219 B3
  9 Nottingham NG7 ..268 A2
Frank Ave NG18 ......268 A4
Frank Bedicote Way
  DE11 ....256 B2
Frank Foley Way ST16 .269 A4
Frank St ST4 ....269 B1

Franklin Ave S80 ....81 C3
Franklin Cl DE15 .....248 A1
Franklin Cres S80 .....81 C3
Franklin Rd
  Stoke-on-T ST4 .....269 A4
  Westwood NG16 .....171 A4
Franklyn Dr Derby DE24 .233 A3
  Staveley S43 ....78 C2
Franklyn Rd S40 ....95 C2
Frazer Cl DE21 ....220 C3
Frecheville St S43 .....78 B1
Freckingham St **1** NG1 268 B1
Frederic Ave DE75 ....193 C4
Frederick Ave
  Derby DE24 ....232 C3
  Ilkeston DE7 ....209 A3
  Stoke-on-T ST4 .....269 B2
Frederick Gent Sch
  DE55 ....160 A4
Frederick Harrison Inf Sch
  NG9 ....223 C4
Frederick Rd NG9 ....223 B4
Frederick St
  Alfreton DE55 ....159 A3
  Burton u T DE15 .....254 C4
  Derby DE22 ....218 B3
  Grassmoor S42 ......115 C2
  Long Eaton NG10 ....236 C4
  Mansfield NG18 .....268 C3
  Somercotes DE55 ....170 B3
  Swadlincote DE11 ...256 C2
Freebirch View S40 ....95 A4
Freeby Ave NG19 .....136 B3
Freehold St DE22 .....218 C2
Freeland Cl NG9 ......223 C2
Freeman Ave DE23 ...231 C3
Freemantle Rd DE3 ...217 C2
Freesia Cl DE3 ....217 C1
Freetown SK13 ....17 B4
French La DE21 ......191 C3
French St Derby DE23 .218 C1
  Ilkeston DE7 ....209 A3
French Terr NG20 ....101 A1
Fresco Dr DE23 ......230 C4
Fresh Ct SK13 ....16 C4
Freshfield Cl SK6 ......15 A1
Freshwaters S42 ......116 B1
Fretson Cl S2 ....44 A4
Fretson Gn S2 ....44 A4
Fretson Rd S2 ....44 A4
Frew Cl ST16 ....269 C4
Freydon Way S44 .....97 A2
Friar Gate DE1 ....218 C3
Friar Gate Ct DE1 ...218 C3
Friar Gate House Sch
  DE1 ....218 C3
Friar Gr SK17 ....85 B3
Friar La NG1 ....268 A1
Friar St Long Eaton NG10 236 B4
  Stafford ST16 ....269 A4
Friars Ct DE22 ....205 A1
Friars Ct Ilkeston DE7 .208 B3
  Nottingham NG7 ....268 A1
Friars' Rd ST17 ......269 B3
Friars' Terr ST17 .....269 B3
Friars' Wlk ST17 .....269 B3
Friary Ave DE24 ......232 C3
Friary Croft DE11 ....256 A4
Friary St DE1 ....267 B3
Friesland Dr NG10 ...222 C3
Friesland Sch NG10 ..222 C3
Frinton Cl S40 ....114 C4
Frisby Ave NG10 .....236 C3
Fritchley CE Prim Sch
  DE56 ....168 A3
Fritchley Cl DE21 ....206 A1
Fritchley La DE56 ....168 A4
Frith Cl S12 ....44 A3
Frith Gr NG19 ....268 A4
Frith Knoll Rd SK23 ...47 B4
Frith Rd S12 ....44 A3
Frith View S23 ....47 A3
Frithall La S42 ....94 B1
Frithwood La S80 ....100 B4
Frizams La DE73 .....242 C4
Froggatt Cl Derby DE22 205 A3
  Staveley S43 ....97 B3
Froggett Cl DE55 ....170 B4
Frogmore St NG1 .....268 B2
Front St DE56 ....168 A3
Frood Cl S43 ....47 B4
Frost Ave NG16 ......182 A2
Fryar Rd NG16 ....182 C2
Fulbrook Rd DE23 ...231 A4
Fulford Cl S40 ....114 B4
Fulforth St NG1 ......268 B2
Fulham Rd DE22 .....218 C3
Full St DE1 ....267 B3
Fuller Dr S41 ....96 B3
Fullwood Ave **11** DE7 .194 C1
Fullwood St **13** DE7 ..194 C1
Fulmar Cl DE3 ....218 A2
Fulwood Dr NG10 ....236 A4
Fulwood Head Rd S10 .42 B4
Fulwood La S10 ....42 C3
Fulwood Rd N NG17 ..148 C1
Fulwood Rd S NG17 ..160 C4
Furlong Cl NG9 ......223 C2
Furlong La
  Alstonefield DE6 ....149 B2
  Atlow DE6 ....175 A4
Furnace Cl S42 ......115 C1
Furnace La Barlow S18 ..75 C2
  Heanor DE75 ....181 B2
  Moira DE12 ....262 C2
Furnace Lane Ind Est
  DE12 ....262 C2
Furnace Rd DE7 .....209 A3

Furnace Row DE55 ...170 C4
Furnall Ave DE45 ......90 A2
Furness Cl **2** SK13 ...17 C4
Furness Lodge Cl SK23 .33 B2
Furness Vale Bsns Ctr
  SK23 ....33 B2
Furness Vale Prim Sch
  SK23 ....33 B2
Furness Vale Sta SK23 .33 B2
Furniss Ave S17 ....55 B3
Furrows Cl DE21 .....206 B2
Fyfield Rd DE15 ......254 C3
Fylde NG9 ....223 C1

G

Gable Ct DE3 ....230 C4
Gable St ST4 ....269 B1
Gables Cl S42 ....132 B4
Gables The DE11 .....255 C3
Gadley Cl SK17 ....84 C3
Gadley La SK17 ......84 C4
Gadsby Cl DE7 ....209 A2
Gadsby Rise DE56 ...168 B1
Gag La DE6 ....161 B3
Gainsborough Cl DE21 206 A1
Gainsborough Ave SK6 .23 A4
Gainsborough Cl
  Long Eaton NG10 ....236 C3
  Stapleford NG9 ......223 C3
Gainsborough Rd S18 ..75 C4
Gainsborough Way
  DE15 ....248 A2
Gairloch Cl DE24 ....231 B1
Galahad Dr DE13 ....240 C1
Gale Rd S21 ....33 B4
Gallery La S42 ....113 B4
Gallery The DE6 .....173 B1
Gallows Inn Cl DE7 ..209 A3
Gallowstree La DE6 ..184 B4
Galway Ave DE21 ....220 A2
Gamble St NG7 ......268 A2
Gamesley Com Prim Sch
  SK13 ....9 C1
Gang La S44 ....118 C3
Gannow Cl S21 ....60 C4
Gaol Rd ST16 ....269 B4
Gaol Sq ST16 ....269 B4
Goalgate St **5** ST16 ..269 B4
Gapsick La S43,S80 ...81 A3
Garden Ave Ilkeston DE7 208 C3
  New Houghton NG19 .134 C4
  Renishaw S21 ....79 A4
  Shirebrook NG20 ....119 C2
Garden Cl S43 ....77 B2
Garden Cr DE55 ......159 C2
Garden Cres DE24 ...247 A2
Garden Pl Stafford ST17 269 B3
  Stoke-on-T ST4 .....269 A2
Garden Rd
  Eastwood NG16 .....182 C1
  2 Mansfield NG18 ..268 B3
Garden Row S44 .....117 B1
Garden St
  Broadbottom SK14 ...16 A4
  Derby DE1 ....267 A4
  Stafford ST16 ....269 B3
  Stoke-on-T ST4 .....269 A1
Gardeners Ct S44 .....99 A1
Gardens The
  Heanor DE75 ....181 B2
  Ripley DE5 ....180 B4
Gardner Pl ST14 .....210 A1
Gardom Cl **14** S18 ....56 B1
Garfield Ave DE72 ...235 A4
Garfield Cl Derby DE23 231 B3
  Stapleford NG9 .....209 C1
Garland Cl **2** S80 ....59 C4
Garland Croft S20 ....59 C4
Garland Mount **22** S20 59 C4
Garland Way S20 .....59 C4
Garner La DE4,DE55 ..157 B1
Garnet Ct NG3 ....268 C2
Garnett Ave DE75 ....181 C1
Garnham Cl DE55 ....159 B1
Garnon St NG18 .....268 A3
Garrard Way S41 .....96 B3
Garratt La S35 ....131 B1
Garrick Dr S24 ......233 A4
Garry Cl DE24 ....231 B1
Garsdale Ct **9** DE24 ..233 B3
Gartan Rd DE14 .....254 A4
Garth Cres DE24 ....233 A3
Garth Rd SK6 ....23 A3
Garth Way S18 ....56 C1
Garth Way Cl S18 ....56 C1
Garthorpe Ct DE21 ..205 C1
Gartrice Gdns S20 ....60 A3
Gartrice Gr S21 ....60 A3
Gary Cl DE23 ....231 B1
Gas St Hollingworth SK14 9 A3
  Sandiacre NG10 .....223 B3
  Uttoxeter ST14 ......210 A1
Gascoine Dr DE21 ...220 B2
Gashouse La S20 ......59 B3
Gaskell Ave S24 ......231 C4
Gasny Ave DE74 .....247 A3
Gatcombe Cl
  Burton u T DE13 ....240 B1
  Derby DE21 ....206 A1
Gatcombe Gr NG10 ..223 A2
Gate Brook Cl DE55 ..170 A1
Gate Ho The S32 .....72 B1
Gatefield Cl S41 ......95 B4
Gateland La S18 ......75 C2
Gateway Christian Sch
  DE7 ....207 C2

Fit – Gis 285

Gauledge La SK17 ....121 A3
Gaunt Cl Killamarsh S21 .60 B3
  Sheffield S14 ....43 B2
Gaunt Dr S14 ....43 B2
Gaunt Pl S14 ....43 B2
Gaunt Rd S14 ....43 B2
Gaunt Way S14 ....43 B2
Gawain Gr DE13 .....240 C1
Gawsworth Cl SK13 ...10 A3
Gayton Ave DE23 ....231 B3
Gayton Com Jun Sch
  DE23 ....231 B3
Gayton Thorpe Cl DE23 230 C4
Geary La DE55 ......248 C1
Gedling Gr NG7 ......268 A2
Gedling St NG1 ......268 B1
Geen St ST4 ....269 B2
Geer La S12 ....58 B3
Gelderd Pl S18 ....76 A4
Gema Cl DE22 ....205 A2
Genista Cl DE15 .....255 A4
Gentshill Ave S45 ....131 C1
George Ave NG10 ....223 C1
George Baily Ct S17 .269 B3
George Cres DE55 ...170 B2
George Dutton Ind Pk
  DE6 ....185 C4
George Holmes Way
  DE11 ....256 A2
George Percival Pl S45 131 A2
George Rd S41 ......143 B3
George Spencer Foundation
  Sch NG9 ....223 C3
George St Alfreton DE55 159 A2
  Alfreton, Riddings DE55 .170 B3
  Ashbourne DE6 .....185 A4
  Belper DE56 ....178 C2
  Brimington S43 ......96 C4
  Buxton SK17 ....85 A4
  Chesterfield S41 .....76 C1
  Compstall SK6 ......15 A1
  Derby DE1 ....267 A3
  Glossop SK13 ....17 B4
  Langley Mill NG16 ..182 A2
  Mansfield NG18, NG19 268 A4
  Mansfield Woodhouse
  NG19 ....136 B2
  Melbourne DE73 ....252 A4
  North Wingfield S42 131 C4
  Nottingham NG1 ....268 B2
  Pinxton NG16 ....160 B2
  Somercotes DE55 ...170 B4
  South Normanton DE55 159 C3
  Swadlincote DE11 ...256 A1
  Whaley Bridge SK23 ..45 C4
  Whaley Thorns NG20 101 A1
Georgina Ct DE74 ...247 A2
Gerard Cl
  6 Chesterfield S40 ...95 B1
  Derby DE21 ....220 C3
  9 Sheffield S8 ....43 A3
Gerard Ct DE1 ....267 A2
Gerard Gr DE65 .....229 B2
Gerard St Derby DE1 .267 A2
  Sheffield S8 ....43 A3
Gerrard St ST4 ......269 B2
Gertrude Rd Derby DE21 220 A4
  Draycott DE72 ......235 A4
Gervase Ave S8 ....56 C3
Gervase Dr S8 ....56 C3
Gervase Pl S8 ....56 C3
Gervase Rd S8 ....56 C3
Gervase Wlk S8 ......56 C3
Gibb La Marple SK6 ...23 C3
  Sudbury DE6 ....225 C3
Gibb St NG10 ....236 C4
Gibbons Ave NG9 ....223 B3
Gibbons Dr S14 ....43 C1
Gibbons Rd NG18 ....268 A3
Gibbons Way S14 ....43 C1
Gibfield La Belper DE56 178 C1
  Kirk Ireton DE6 .....175 C4
Gifford Pl S14 ....269 A1
Gifford Rd **12** S8 .....43 A4
Gilbert Ave S40 ......114 B4
Gilbert Cl DE21 ......220 B2
Gilbert Cres DE56 ...190 C1
Gilbert Heathcote Inf Sch
  S41 ....96 A4
Gilbert St DE24 ......233 A3
Gilcroft St NG18 ....268 C3
Gilderdale Way DE21 206 A2
Gill La DE4 ....127 B2
Gill St NG1 ....268 B2
Gill's La S42 ....115 C1
Gillamoor Ct DE24 ..233 B3
Gilleyfield Ave S17 ...55 C4
Gillies The NG19 ....268 B3
Gilliver Gdns DE72 ..235 A4
Gillott St DE75 ......194 A4
Gilt Hill NG16 ....195 B4
Giltbrook Cres NG16 195 B4
Gilthill Prim Sch NG16 195 B4
Giltway NG16 ....195 B4
Gimson Cl DE7 ......194 B2
Gin Close Way NG16 195 B3
Gin La S45 ....144 C4
Gipsy La Alstonefield DE6 149 C2
  Apperknowle S18 ....58 A1
  Chesterfield S41 .....77 A1
Gipsyhill La S80 ......81 A4
Gird La SK6 ....15 C3
Girdon Cl SK17 ....84 C3
Gisborne Cl DE7 ....217 C2
Gisborne Cres DE22 .204 C2

Gisborne Gn DE1 .....218 C3
Gisbourne Dr SK23 .....47 A3
Glade Cl S40 .....95 C3
Glade Croft S12 .....44 A2
Glade Lands Dr DE73 ...233 A1
Glade Lea S12 .....44 A2
Glade The Buxton SK17 ...85 A4
Chesterfield S40 .....95 B2
Gladstone Ave
Blackwell DE55 .....147 C1
Heanor DE75 .....181 C1
Gladstone Cl Derby DE73 232 C2
Glossop SK13 .....17 B4
Gladstone Dr NG16 ....182 A2
Gladstone Pl ST4 .....269 A1
Gladstone Rd
Alfreton DE55 .....158 C2
Chesterfield S40 .....266 A4
Derby DE21 .....220 C3
Gladstone St Derby DE23 218 C1
Glossop SK13 .....17 B4
Glossop, Hadfield SK13 ....10 A2
Heanor DE75 .....181 C1
Ilkeston DE7 .....208 C4
Langley Mill NG16 .....182 B2
Long Eaton NG10 .....236 B3
Mansfield NG18 .....268 C4
Mansfield Woodhouse
NG19 .....136 B1
South Normanton DE55 ..160 A3
Gladstone St E DE7 ....208 C4
Gladstone Terr NG19 ...136 B1
Gladwin Gdns S40 .....114 B4
Glaisdale Nook 6 DE24 233 B3
Glamis Cl DE21 .....206 A1
Glapwell La S44 .....118 A1
Glasshouse Hill DE5 ...181 A4
Glasshouse La S43 .....77 B2
Glasshouse St NG1 .....268 B2
Glastonbury Cl NG19 ...136 B2
Glastonbury Rd DE24 ...233 B4
Glaven Cl NG19 .....136 B1
Gleadless Ave S12 .....44 A2
Gleadless Bank S12 .....43 C2
Gleadless Comm S12 ....44 A4
Gleadless Cres S12 .....43 C3
Gleadless Ct 6 S2 .....43 A3
Gleadless Dr S12 .....43 C2
Gleadless Mount S12 ....44 A2
Gleadless Prim Sch S12 .44 A3
Gleadless Rd S2 .....43 B3
Gleadless Townend S12 .44 A2
Glebe Ave
Great Longstone DE45 ....90 A2
Harthill S26 .....61 C4
Pinxton NG16 .....160 B2
Ripley DE5 .....169 B1
Smalley DE7 .....192 C3
Glebe Cl
Coton in t E DE12 .....260 B2
Doveridge DE6 .....224 A4
Holmewood S42 .....132 B4
Rolleston DE13 .....240 A2
South Normanton DE55 ..160 A3
Thurvaston DE6 .....201 C1
Glebe Cres Ilkeston DE7 .209 A4
Stanley DE7 .....207 A3
Glebe Ct
Great Longstone DE45 ....89 C2
Stoke-on-T ST4 .....269 C2
Glebe Farm Cl S26 .....61 C4
Glebe Field Cl DE4 .....156 C1
Glebe Gdns S42 .....131 C3
Glebe Jun Sch DE55 ...160 A3
Glebe Rd SK17 .....85 B4
Glebe Rise DE23 .....218 B1
Glebe St Stoke-on-T ST4 .269 B2
Swadlincote DE11 .....256 A2
Glebe The
Awsworth NG16 .....195 A2
Chesterfield S41 .....77 A1
Rosliston DE12 .....260 B3
Glebe View S43 .....80 A3
Glebe Way The S41 .....77 A1
Gledhill Cl S18 .....57 A1
Glen Ave DE56 .....191 B4
Glen Cl DE55 .....148 A2
Glen Park Cl DE73 .....244 C4
Glen Rd DE4 .....156 B1
Glen View DE56 .....178 C1
Glen View Rd S8 .....56 C4
Glen Vine DE5 .....170 A1
Glenavon Cl S43 .....77 B3
Glenbrook Hill SK13 .....10 B1
Glencoe Way S40 .....95 A2
Glencroft Cl DE14 .....254 A4
Glencroft Dr DE24 .....231 B2
Glendale Dr DE21 .....220 C3
Glendon Rd Derby DE24 .231 B2
Ilkeston DE7 .....208 B2
Glendon St DE7 .....193 A1
Gleneagles Cl
Chesterfield S40 .....114 B4
Derby DE3 .....217 C1
Gleneagles Dr DE13 ...240 B1
Glenfield Ave NG16 ....195 B4
Glenfield Cres
Chesterfield S41 .....96 A4
Derby DE3 .....217 B1
Glenfield Rd NG10 .....236 B3
Glengarry Way DE24 ...231 C2
Glenholme Dr S13 .....44 C4
Glenholme Pl S13 .....44 C4
Glenholme Way S13 .....44 C4
Glenmoor Rd SK17 .....66 B1
Glenmore Cl S43 .....97 A3
Glenmore Croft S12 .....44 B3
Glenmore Dr DE24 .....231 B2
Glenmoy Cl DE23 .....231 B4
Glenn Way DE72 .....234 C1
Glenorchy Ct DE21 .....206 A2
Glenthorn Cl S81 .....63 C4
Glenthorne Cl S40 .....95 B1
Glenwood Rd DE73 ....245 A4
Glinton Ave DE55 .....147 C1
Glossop Brook Rd SK13 .10 A1
Glossop Central Sta
SK13 .....10 B1
Glossop Heritage Ctr*
SK13 .....10 B1
Glossop Rd Hayfield SK22 .25 B3
Broadbottom SK13 .....16 B4
Gamesley SK13 .....9 C1
Marple SK6 .....15 B2
Glossop St DE24 .....232 A4
Glossop's Croft S41 .....77 A1
Glossopdale Comm Coll
SK13 .....10 B1
Glossopdale Comm Coll
(Annexe) SK13 .....10 A2
Gloster St DE24 .....219 C1
Gloucester Ave
Chesterfield S41 .....95 C3
Sandiacre NG10 .....223 A2
Gloucester Rd S41 .....95 C3
Gloucester Way
Burton u T DE15 .....248 A1
4 Glossop SK13 .....17 C4
Glover Rd Sheffield S8 ....43 A4
Totley S17 .....55 C3
Glover St ST16 .....269 A4
Gloves La DE55 .....147 B1
Glumangate S40 .....266 B3
Goathland Rd DE24 .....231 B1
Goatscliffe Cotts S32 .....72 B4
Goddard La Glossop SK13 .10 A3
New Mills SK22 .....24 C4
Goddard Rd SK13 .....10 A1
Godfrey Dr DE7 .....208 B3
Godfrey St DE75 .....181 C1
Godkin Dr NG16 .....182 A2
Godward Rd SK22 .....33 A4
Gold Cl DE4 .....142 A4
Gold La DE22 .....217 C4
Goldcrest Dr DE21 .....220 C3
Goldcrest Rd S41 .....77 A2
Golden Valley
Horsley Woodhouse DE7 ..192 A3
Somercotes DE55 .....170 B2
Golders Green Wlk
DE22 .....218 A3
Goldhill DE4 .....144 A2
Goldsmith St
Mansfield NG18 .....268 B4
Nottingham NG1 .....268 B2
Goldstone Ct DE21 .....220 C2
Golf Cl DE23 .....218 A1
Golf Club Rd DE7 .....209 A1
Golf La DE56 .....190 C3
Gomersal La S18 .....57 A1
Goodacre St NG18 .....268 C4
Goodale St DE23 .....219 A1
Goodhand Cres NG18 ...268 A3
Goodman Cl NG16 .....195 B4
Goodmar Ct S44 .....97 A2
Goodrington Rd DE21 ...206 B2
Goods Rd DE56 .....178 C1
Goods Yd DE56 .....178 C1
Goodsmoor Rd DE23,
DE24 .....231 C3
Goodwin Cl NG10 .....223 A3
Goodwin Dr NG16 .....195 C3
Goodwin Rd 2 S8 .....43 A3
Goodwin St NG7 .....268 A2
Goodwin's La DE56 .....178 B1
Goodwood Cl DE13 .....240 B1
Goodwood Cres DE7 ...208 B2
Goodwood Dr
Beeston NG9 .....223 C1
Derby DE24 .....233 B3
Gooker La DE55 .....158 C2
Goole Ave DE7 .....208 B3
Goose Gate NG1 .....268 B1
Goose Green La DE55 ...146 B2
Goose Green View DE45 .91 C3
Goose La DE5 .....181 B4
Goosehill S33 .....38 A1
Gordon Ave S8 .....43 A1
Gordon Cres DE55 .....160 A2
Gordon Rd
Borrowash DE72 .....221 A1
Derby DE23 .....218 C2
Nottingham NG3 .....268 C2
Swanwick DE55 .....169 C4
Tideswell SK17 .....69 B2
Gordon St DE7 .....195 A1
Gordondale Rd NG19 ...136 A1
Gore La S33 .....51 A4
Gorman Cl S41 .....95 C4
Gorse Bank S44 .....116 C1
Gorse Cl Derby DE23 ....231 B3
Eastwood NG16 .....195 A4
Long Eaton NG10 .....223 A1
Gorse Dr S21 .....60 B3
Gorse La Bradley DE6 ...175 A2
Ringinglow S10 .....42 C4
Gorse Ridge Dr DE45 ....91 C3
Gorse Valley Rd S41 ...115 C4
Gorse Valley Way S41 ...115 C4
Gorse Way SK13 .....17 C4
Gorsebank La DE45 .....91 C4
Gorsehill Gr DE23 .....231 A4
Gorses Alderwasley DE56 .178 B4
Gorses *continued*
Idridgehay DE6 .....176 B3
Gorsey Bank DE4 .....165 C4
Gorsey Brigg S18 .....56 B1
Gorsey Brow SK14 .....9 A1
Gorsey Cl DE56 .....178 C3
Gorsey Intakes SK14 ....16 A4
Gorsey La
Kirk Ireton DE6 .....165 A1
Netherseal DE12 .....265 A4
Gorseybrigg Inf Sch S18 .56 B1
Gorseybrigg Jun Sch
S18 .....56 B1
Gorsty Leys DE65 .....230 B1
Gosber Rd S21 .....59 C2
Gosber St S21 .....59 B2
Goseley Ave DE11 .....257 A2
Goseley Cres DE11 .....257 A2
Gosforth Cl S18 .....56 C1
Gosforth Cres S18 .....56 C1
Gosforth Dr S18 .....56 C1
Gosforth Gn S18 .....56 C1
Gosforth La S18 .....56 C1
Gosforth Rd DE24 .....232 C4
Goshawk Rd DE7 .....209 A2
Gower Cres S40 .....95 B3
Gower St DE1 .....267 B2
Goyt Pl SK23 .....45 C4
Goyt Rd Disley SK12 .....32 B3
New Mills SK22 .....33 B3
Goyt Side Rd S40 .....95 C1
Goyt Valley Ind Est SK23 .33 B2
Goyt View SK22 .....33 A3
Goyt's La SK17 .....65 A2
Goytlands SK17 .....84 C3
Grace Cres DE75 .....181 C1
Gradbach Mill* SK17 ..102 A1
Grafham Cl DE73 .....233 A2
Grafton Ct 28 NG7 .....268 A2
Grafton Rd DE15 .....248 A1
Grafton St DE23 .....218 C1
Graham Cl DE14 .....254 B4
Graham Dr SK12 .....32 B3
Graham St DE7 .....208 C4
Grammer St DE5 .....181 A2
Grampian Cres S40 .....95 A2
Grampian Prim Sch
DE24 .....231 B2
Grampian Way
Derby DE24 .....231 C2
Long Eaton NG10 .....236 A4
Granary Cl S40 .....95 A4
Granby Ave Chinley SK23 .34 C1
Mansfield NG18 .....268 B4
Granby Cl S45 .....132 B1
Granby Croft DE45 .....109 B3
Granby Jun Sch DE7 ...194 C2
Granby Rd
Bakewell DE45 .....109 B3
Bradwell S33 .....50 C4
Buxton SK17 .....85 B4
Granby St DE7 .....194 C1
Granby Wlk ST4 .....269 A1
Grandfield St DE75 .....181 B2
Grandstand Rd DE21 ...219 B3
Grange Ave
Breaston DE72 .....235 B4
Chapel-en-le-F SK23 .....47 A3
Derby DE23 .....231 C4
Dronfield S18 .....56 C1
Hulland Ward DE6 .....175 C2
Mansfield NG18 .....268 A3
Grange Cl
Melbourne DE73 .....252 A4
Somercotes DE55 .....159 C1
Ticknall DE73 .....251 A2
Grange Ct DE65 .....241 A3
Grange Dale DE4 .....153 B4
Grange Dr
Castle Donington DE74 ...247 A2
Long Eaton NG10 .....236 C4
Grange Farm Cl DE74 ...247 B3
Grange La Barlow S18 ....75 A1
Darley Dale DE4 .....127 C1
Ible DE4 .....153 B4
Grange Park Ave
Calow S43 .....96 C2
Chapel-en-le-F SK23 .....47 A3
Grange Park Rd SK23 ...47 A3
Grange Prim Sch NG10 .236 C4
Grange Rd Buxton SK17 ...85 B4
Derby DE24 .....233 A3
Long Eaton NG10 .....236 C4
Pilsley S45 .....132 B1
Swadlincote DE11 .....255 C3
Uttoxeter ST14 .....210 A1
Grange Rd S SK14 .....15 A4
Grange St Alfreton DE55 .159 A2
Derby DE23 .....219 A1
Grange The
Old Brampton S42 .....94 C2
Smalley DE75 .....193 B4
South Normanton DE55 ..160 A2
Grange View NG16 .....182 C2
Grange Wlk S42 .....115 C1
Grangemill Pl S43 .....97 B4
Grangewood Ave 11
DE7 .....208 C4
Grangewood Ct S40 ...114 C4
Grangewood Dr DE56 ...191 A4
Grangewood Rd S40 ...114 C4
Gransden Way S40 .....114 B4
Grant Ave DE21 .....220 A3
Grant St ST4 .....269 C2
Grantham Ave DE21 ....205 C1
Grantham Cl NG16 .....195 B4
Granville Ave NG10 .....223 B1
Granville Cl
Chesterfield S41 .....115 B4
Duffield DE56 .....190 C2
Hatton DE65 .....227 B1
Granville Com Sch
DE11 .....256 C2
Granville Ct 4 NG3 ....268 C2
Granville St Derby DE1 ..218 C3
Swadlincote DE11 .....256 C2
Grasmere Ave
Clay Cross S45 .....131 A2
Derby DE21 .....220 C3
Grasmere Cl
Burton u T DE15 .....248 A1
Chesterfield S41 .....95 B4
Grasmere Cres DE24 ....231 C2
Grasmere Ct 12 NG10 ..223 A1
Grasmere Rd
11 Dronfield S18 .....56 B1
Long Eaton NG10 .....223 A1
Grasmere St NG10 .....223 B3
Grass St DE7 .....194 C2
Grasscroft Cl 12 S40 .....95 B3
Grassdale View S12 .....44 C2
Grassmoor Cl S12 .....43 C3
Grassmoor Cres SK13 ....9 B1
Grassmoor Ctry Pk*
S42,S41 .....116 A2
Grassmoor Prim Sch
S42 .....115 C1
Grassthorpe Cl DE21 ...206 A1
Grassthorpe Rd S12 .....44 A2
Grassy Ct DE3 .....230 A4
Gratton Ct S43 .....78 C2
Gratton La DE45 .....140 B4
Gravel Pit Hill DE65 ....249 C4
Gravel Pit La DE21 .....220 C2
Gravelly Bank Mews
DE6 .....199 B3
Graves Park Animal Farm*
S8 .....43 A1
Graves Tennis & L Ctr
S8 .....57 A4
Graves Trust Homes S8 ..57 A4
Gray Fallow DE55 .....160 A2
Gray St Clowne S43 .....80 C2
Mosborough S20 .....59 B4
Graycar Bsns Pk DE13 ..253 A1
Grayling St DE23 .....219 A1
Grays Cl DE74 .....247 A2
Grayswood Cl DE55 ....170 A4
Great Central Rd NG18 .268 C3
Great Common Cl S43 ...80 A3
Great Croft S18 .....56 B1
Great Freeman St NG1,
NG3 .....268 B2
Great Hucklow CE Prim Sch
SK17 .....51 A1
Great Longstone Ind Est
DE45 .....90 A2
Great Northern Cl The
NG2 .....268 B1
Great Northern Cotts
NG19 .....135 A3
Great Northern Rd
Derby DE1 .....218 C3
Eastwood NG16 .....182 B1
Greatbatch Ave ST4 ....269 A2
Greatorex Ave DE24 ....232 C3
Greaves La DE45 .....108 C4
Greaves St Ripley DE5 ...169 C1
Shirland DE55 .....146 C1
Greek St 25 NG7 .....268 A2
Green Ave DE73 .....233 A1
Green Bank SK13 .....16 C4
Green Chase S21 .....59 B2
Green Cl Curbar S32 .....72 C1
Matlock DE4 .....143 A3
Newton DE55 .....148 A2
Staveley S43 .....97 B3
Unstone S18 .....76 C3
Willington DE65 .....242 A3
Green Cres NG16 .....171 C3
Green Cross S18 .....57 A1
Green Farm Cl S40 .....95 B3
Green Farm Rd NG16 ...171 B3
Green Glen S40 .....95 B1
Green Hill DE4 .....154 C1
Green Inf Sch The DE55 160 A3
Green La
Alsop en le D DE6 .....150 B1
Bakewell DE45 .....108 B2
Barrow u T DE73 .....244 A3
Belper DE56 .....178 C2
Bonsall DE4 .....153 C4
Breedon on t H DE73 ....252 C3
Burnaston DE65 .....230 A2
Buxton SK17 .....85 A3
Buxton, Water Swallows
SK17 .....67 B1
Chelmorton SK17 .....106 B4
Chesterfield S41 .....96 B2
Chinley SK23 .....34 C1
Clifton DE6 .....184 C4
Compstall SK14 .....15 A4
Creswell S80 .....82 B3
Darley Dale DE4 .....127 A2
Derby DE1 .....267 B2
Derby, Alvaston DE24 ....233 B4
Disley SK12 .....32 B2
Dronfield S18 .....57 A1
Glossop SK13 .....16 C4
Glossop, Brookfield SK13 ...9 C2
Hognaston DE6 .....164 A1
Hollingworth SK14 .....9 B3
Ilkeston DE7 .....209 A4
Killamarsh S21 .....60 B2
Mansfield NG19 .....135 A1
Green La *continued*
Marchington ST14 .....225 A1
Ockbrook DE72 .....221 B3
Old Brampton S42 .....94 C4
Overseal DE12 .....261 C2
Pilsley S45 .....132 B2
Pleasley S44 .....134 B4
Roston DE6 .....197 C4
Tansley DE4 .....144 A3
Tupton S42 .....115 B1
Tutbury DE13 .....239 B3
Weston Underwood DE6 ..188 C1
Green Lands DE11 .....256 A4
Green Lea S18 .....56 B1
Green Leas DE72 .....246 A4
Green Oak Ave S17 .....55 C2
Green Oak Cres S17 .....55 C2
Green Oak Dr S17 .....55 C2
Green Oak Gr S17 .....55 C2
Green Oak Rd S17 .....55 C2
Green Park Ave SK23 ....47 B3
Green Pk DE22 .....218 A3
Green Rd The DE6 .....173 B2
Green St
Barton in F NG11 .....237 C3
Chesterfield S41 .....77 A1
Green The Alfreton DE55 .159 A2
Aston-on-T DE72 .....246 A4
Bamford S33 .....40 A2
Belper DE56 .....179 A3
Birchover DE4 .....126 A1
Bradwell S33 .....51 A3
Brailsford DE6 .....201 C4
Breaston DE72 .....235 B4
Breedon on t H DE73 ....252 C1
Burton u T DE13 .....240 C1
Castle Donington DE74 ...247 A2
Chesterfield S41 .....115 B4
Clowne S43 .....80 C2
Curbar S32 .....72 C1
Derby DE22 .....204 B1
Derby, Mickleover DE3 ...217 B1
Draycott DE72 .....235 A4
Findern DE65 .....230 B1
Fritchley DE56 .....168 A3
Glapwell S44 .....134 A4
Glossop SK13 .....17 A4
Kirk Langley DE6 .....202 B1
Mansfield Woodhouse
NG19 .....136 A3
Marple SK6 .....23 A2
Middleton (Nr Wirksworth)
DE4 .....154 B3
North Wingfield S42 .....132 A4
Pilsley S45 .....133 A2
Stoke-on-T ST4 .....269 A2
Stoney Middleton S32 .....72 B3
Sutton in A NG17 .....148 C1
Swanwick DE55 .....169 C4
Tissington DE6 .....162 A3
Totley S17 .....55 B2
Weston-on-T DE72 .....245 C3
Willington DE65 .....242 A3
Youlgreave DE4 .....126 B3
Green Water Mdw SK14 ...9 B3
Green Way Findern DE65 .230 B1
Wingerworth S42 .....115 B1
Greenacre Ave DE75 ....182 A2
Greenacre Pk DE12 .....260 B2
Greenacre The DE6 .....184 C4
Greenacres DE23 .....231 A4
Greenacres Cl S18 .....76 B4
Greenacres Dr
South Normanton DE55 ..160 A3
Uttoxeter ST14 .....210 A1
Greenaway La DE4 .....127 C1
Greenbank Derby DE21 ..220 B2
Hollingworth SK13 .....9 C3
Greenbank Dr S40 .....95 B2
Greenbank Rd SK6 .....15 A1
Greenburn Cl DE23 ....231 B3
Greendale Ave S42 ....113 C4
Greendale Ct S18 .....57 A1
Greendale Sh Ctr S18 ...57 A1
Greenfell Ave DE23 ....231 C3
Greenfield Ave S80 .....82 B3
Greenfield Cl
New Mills SK22 .....33 A4
Sheffield S8 .....56 C4
Greenfield Dr
Linton DE12 .....261 B3
Sheffield S8 .....56 C4
Greenfield Rd S8 .....56 C4
Greenfield St SK13 .....10 A3
Greenfields
Aldercar NG16 .....182 A2
Denstone ST14 .....196 B3
Eckington S21 .....59 B2
Fritchley DE56 .....168 A4
Greenfields Ave DE23 ..231 A4
Greenfinch Cl DE21 ....220 C3
Greengate Cl S40 .....95 B1
Greengate St ST16 .....269 B4
Greenhall Rd S21 .....59 B2
Greenhead S33 .....40 A2
Greenhead Cres SK17 ..138 B1
Greenhead Pk S33 .....40 A2
Greenhill Ave Ripley DE5 180 C4
Sheffield S8 .....56 C4
Greenhill La DE55 .....170 B3
Greenhill Lane Ind Est
DE55 .....170 A3
Greenhill Main Rd S8 ...56 C4
Greenhill Parkway S8 ...56 C3
Greenhill Prim Sch S8 ..56 C4
Greenhill Wlk SK12 .....32 B3
Greenhills Rd NG16 ....182 C2
Greenhouse La S10 .....42 C3

Greenland Ave DE22 ...218 A3
Greenland Cl S42 ...132 A4
Greenmount Cl DE23 ...231 A3
Greens Ct DE7 ...194 B1
Greens La NG16 ...195 C3
Greenshall La SK12 ...32 C3
Greenside NG16 ...171 B3
Greenside Ave S41 ...96 A4
Greenside Cl
Barlborough S43 ...80 B2
Donisthorpe DE12 ...262 C1
Long Eaton NG10 ...236 C4
Greenside Ct DE3 ...217 B1
Greensmith Cl DE15 ...248 B2
Greensquare Rd NG16 ..160 C1
Greenvale Cl DE15 ...254 C4
Greenview DE4 ...153 A1
Greenway Ashbourne DE6 173 B2
Brassington DE4 ...153 A1
Burton u T DE15 ...248 A2
Hulland Ward DE6 ...175 C2
Stafford ST16 ...269 C4
Whitwell S80 ...81 C3
Greenway Cl DE72 ...221 A2
Greenway Croft DE4 ..154 C1
Greenway Dr
Bolsover S44 ...118 A4
Derby DE23 ...218 A1
Greenway The
Derby DE72 ...233 B3
Sandiacre NG10 ...223 A3
Sheffield S8 ...56 C4
Greenways S40 ...114 B4
Greenwich Dr N DE22 ..218 B3
Greenwich Dr S DE22 ..218 A3
Greenwood Ave
Derby DE21 ...219 C4
Ilkeston DE7 ...209 A4
Mansfield Woodhouse
NG19 ...136 A2
Sutton in A NG17 ...148 C1
Greenwood Cl DE24 ...232 B3
Greenwood Ct DE1 ...267 B4
Greenwood Rd DE15 ..254 C4
Greer La S44 ...118 B1
Gregg Ave DE75 ...181 C1
Greggs Ave SK23 ...46 C3
Gregory Ave
Aldercar NG16 ...182 A2
Breaston DE72 ...235 B4
Langley Mill NG16 ...182 A2
Gregory Cl Brimington S43 96 B4
Stapleford NG9 ...223 C4
Gregory La S43 ...77 B1
Gregory Rd S8 ...43 A3
Gregory St DE7 ...208 C4
Gregory Wlk DE23 ...230 C4
Gregorys Way DE56 ...179 B3
Gregson Cl DE11 ...256 A3
Grendon Cl DE56 ...179 A3
Grenville Dr
Ilkeston DE7 ...194 C2
Stapleford NG9 ...223 C4
Grenvoir Dr DE5 ...170 A1
Gresham Rd DE24 ...232 B4
Gresley Dr 8 NG2 ...268 C1
Gresley Rd Ilkeston DE7 .194 C1
Sheffield S8 ...56 C3
Gresley Wlk S8 ...56 C3
Gresley Wood Rd
Swadlincote DE11 ...255 C1
Woodville DE11 ...256 A1
Gresley Woodlands
DE11 ...256 A1
Gresty St ST4 ...269 B2
Gretton Ave DE13 ...240 C1
Gretton Rd SK17 ...85 B4
Grey Friars Way ST16 ..269 A4
Grey Friars' Pl ST16 ...269 A4
Grey St DE22 ...267 A2
Greyfriar Gate NG1 ...268 B1
Greyfriars Bsns Pk
ST16 ...269 A4
Greystones Ct S26 ...61 B3
Grice Rd ST4 ...269 A2
Griffe Field Prim Sch The
DE23 ...231 A3
Griffin Cl Derby DE24 ..232 C4
New Mills SK22 ...33 B3
Staveley S43 ...97 C4
Griggs Gdns DE4 ...165 C4
Grimsby Terr 9 NG3 ...268 B2
Grimshaw Ave DE24 ...233 A4
Grin Low Rd SK17 ...85 A2
Grindleford Gdns 5 SK13 .9 C1
Grindleford Prim Sch
S32 ...72 B4
Grindleford Sta S32 ...53 C1
Grindley Hill Ct ST4 ...269 A1
Grindley Pl ST4 ...269 A1
Grindlow Ave S40 ...266 A1
Grindlow Cl S14 ...43 B3
Grindlow Dr S14 ...43 B3
Grindlow Rd DE21 ...220 A4
Grindon Cl S40 ...95 B3
Grindslow Ave DE7 ...207 C4
Grinlow Cl SK17 ...85 B2
Grinton Wlk S40 ...114 C4
Grisedale Rd E DE45 ...90 A2
Grisedale Rd W DE45 ...90 A2
Grisedale Wlk S18 ...56 C1
Gritstone Rd DE4 ...143 B4
Grizedale Cl DE15 ...248 A1
Groombridge Cres
DE23 ...231 A3
Groome Ave DE75 ...181 B2
Grosvenor Ave
Breaston DE72 ...235 C4
Grosvenor Ave *continued*
Long Eaton NG10 ...236 A2
Grosvenor Dr DE23 ...231 A3
Grosvenor Rd
Eastwood NG16 ...182 C1
Marple SK6 ...23 A4
Ripley DE5 ...169 B1
Grosvenor St DE24 ...232 B4
Grove Ave
Nottingham NG7 ...268 A2
Totley S17 ...55 B3
Grove Cl DE72 ...233 C2
Grove Ct DE5 ...180 C4
Grove Farm Cl S43 ...96 C4
Grove Gdns S43 ...96 C3
Grove Hospl The DE72 ..234 B1
Grove House Ct S17 ...55 C3
Grove La Buxton SK17 ...85 B3
Darley Dale DE4 ...127 C1
Old Brampton S42 ...94 A2
Somersal Herbert DE6 ..211 C1
Grove Mews NG16 ...182 C1
Grove Pk DE65 ...229 A1
Grove Pl DE45 ...125 A3
Grove Rd Calow S43 ...96 C3
Chesterfield S41 ...96 A4
Totley S17 ...55 C3
Grove St Chesterfield S41 115 B4
Derby DE23 ...267 B1
Mansfield Woodhouse
NG19 ...136 A2
New Mills SK22 ...33 A4
Swadlincote DE11 ...256 A2
Grove The
Branston DE13 ...253 A4
Breaston DE72 ...235 C4
Derby DE3 ...217 C1
Glossop SK13 ...9 C2
Poolsbrook S43 ...98 A4
Totley S17 ...55 B3
Grove Way Calow S43 ...96 C3
Mansfield Woodhouse
NG19 ...136 A2
Grovebury Dr DE23 ...231 B3
Groves Nook DE73 ...232 C1
Grundy Ave NG16 ...171 B4
Grundy Nook S80 ...82 A3
Grundy Rd S45 ...131 B2
Grunmore Dr DE13 ...240 C1
Guernsey Rd S2 ...43 A4
Guide Post DE56 ...168 B1
Guildford Ave
Chesterfield S40 ...114 B4
Mansfield Woodhouse
NG19 ...136 B3
Sheffield S2 ...43 B4
Swadlincote DE11 ...256 C3
Guildford Cl S2 ...43 B4
Guildford Dr S2 ...43 B4
Guildford Rise S2 ...43 C4
Guildford St ST4 ...269 C2
Guildford View S2 ...43 C4
Guildford Way S2 ...43 C4
Guildhall Dr NG16 ...160 C1
Guilford Cl S45 ...131 C2
Guilford La S45 ...131 C2
Guinea Cl NG10 ...236 A4
Guinevere Ave DE13 ...240 C1
Gun La DE56 ...168 B1
Gun Rd SK6 ...16 B1
Gunby Hill DE12 ...261 C1
Gunhills La DE56 ...189 C3
Gunnel Cl ST16 ...269 A3
Gurney Ave DE23 ...231 B3
Gutersloh Ct NG9 ...223 C4
Guy Cl NG9 ...223 C3
Gypsy La Creswell S80 ...81 C1
Draycott DE72 ...221 C1

H

Hackney La S18 ...75 C1
Hackney Rd DE4 ...143 A4
Hackthorne Rd S8 ...43 A2
Haddon Ave S43 ...81 A2
Haddon Cl Alfreton DE55 158 C2
Bullbridge DE56 ...168 A3
Chesterfield S40 ...95 B1
Derby DE22 ...204 B2
Dronfield S18 ...57 A1
West Hallam DE7 ...207 C4
Haddon Ct DE6 ...185 B4
Haddon Dr
Bakewell DE45 ...109 C2
Derby DE22 ...204 B2
Derby, Mickleover DE3 ..217 C2
Derby, Spondon DE21 ...220 C2
Little Eaton DE21 ...191 B1
Haddon Gn 11 SK13 ...9 B1
Haddon Hall★ DE45 ...110 A1
Haddon Lea 10 SK13 ...9 B1
Haddon Nurseries DE7 .194 C2
Haddon Pl
Shirebrook NG20 ...119 B3
Staveley S43 ...97 B4
Haddon Rd
Bakewell DE45 ...109 C2
Buxton SK17 ...85 B4
Mansfield NG18 ...268 B4
North Wingfield S42 ...132 A4
Haddon St Derby DE23 ..218 C1
Ilkeston DE7 ...194 C2
Tibshelf DE55 ...148 A3
Haddon Way NG10 ...235 C2
Hade La SK17 ...106 C4
Hades La SK17 ...88 A2
Hadfield CE Jun Sch SK13 9 C2
Hadfield Ind Est SK13 ...9 C3
Hadfield Inf Sch SK13 ...9 C3
Hadfield Pl SK13 ...17 B4
Hadfield Rd SK13 ...9 C2
Hadfield Sq 1 SK13 ...17 B4
Hadfield St SK13 ...17 B4
Hadfield Sta SK13 ...10 A3
Hadfields Ave SK14 ...9 B3
Hadleigh Cl 2 NG9 ...223 C1
Hadley La DE6 ...186 C4
Hadley St DE7 ...209 A3
Hadley's Ct DE12 ...262 B2
Hadstock Cl NG10 ...223 A2
Hady Cres S41 ...96 B2
Hady Hill S41 ...96 B1
Hady La S41 ...96 B1
Hady Prim Sch S41 ...96 B1
Hag Bank La SK12 ...32 B4
Hagg La Dale Abbey DE7 .207 B2
Windley DE56 ...177 B1
Hague Ave S21 ...79 A4
Hague Bar Prim Sch
SK22 ...32 C4
Hague Bar Rd SK22 ...33 A4
Hague Fold Rd SK22 ...32 C4
Hague La S21, S43 ...79 A3
Hague Rd SK14 ...16 A4
Hague St SK13 ...17 B4
Haig Meml Homes S8 ...57 A4
Haig St DE24 ...232 C4
Haigh Moor Rd S13 ...44 C4
Haigh Moor Wlk S13 ...44 C4
Hailsham Cl DE3 ...217 B2
Haines Cl DE24 ...231 C2
Halcyon App S42 ...115 B1
Halcyon Cl S12 ...44 C2
Haldane Cl S80 ...81 C1
Haldane Cres S44 ...98 C1
Halesworth Cl S40 ...114 A4
Haley Cl NG16 ...195 B3
Half Acre La S18 ...76 B4
Half Croft S43 ...96 C4
Halfmoon La DE6 ...165 A2
Halfway Ctr S20 ...59 C4
Halfway Dr S20 ...59 C4
Halfway Gdns S20 ...59 C4
Halfway Inf Sch S20 ...59 C4
Halfway Jun Sch S20 ...59 C3
Halifax Cl Derby DE21 ..205 B1
Hilton DE65 ...228 C1
Halifax Pl NG1 ...268 B1
Hall Bank Buxton SK17 ..85 A4
Hartington SK17 ...137 C3
Hall Cl Barlow S42 ...94 C4
Dronfield S18 ...56 B1
Mottram in L SK14 ...9 A3
Hall Ct DE7 ...207 C4
Hall Dale View DE4 ...127 B2
Hall Dr Doveridge DE6 ..211 A1
Sandiacre NG10 ...223 A3
Hall Dyke DE21 ...220 B3
Hall End La DE45 ...108 C4
Hall Farm Cl
Castle Donington DE74 ..247 A2
Swadlincote DE11 ...256 B2
Hall Farm Rd
Duffield DE56 ...190 C1
Swadlincote DE11 ...256 B2
Hall Gate View S33 ...51 A4
Hall Gdns
Castle Donington DE74 ..247 B2
Marchington ST14 ...224 C1
Hall Green Ave DE13 ...240 C1
Hall La Ashbourne DE6 ..173 B1
Brailsford DE6 ...202 A3
Brinsley NG16 ...182 B3
Donisthorpe DE12 ...265 C4
Doveridge DE6 ...224 A4
Mayfield DE6 ...183 A4
Nether Heage DE56 ...168 B2
Newton DE55 ...148 A2
Shirley DE6 ...200 B4
Staveley S43 ...78 B2
Taddington SK17 ...88 A2
Tideswell SK17 ...69 C2
Willington DE65 ...242 A3
Hall Leys La DE73 ...245 B1
Hall Meadow Croft S20 ..59 C3
Hall Meadow Dr S20 ...59 C3
Hall Meadow Gr S20 ...59 C3
Hall Meadow Rd SK13 ...10 B1
Hall Pk DE73 ...244 A3
Hall Rd Aldercar NG16 ..182 B2
Brimington S43 ...96 C4
Marchington ST14 ...224 C1
Rolleston DE13 ...239 C2
Hall Rise Ashbourne DE6 .173 B2
Darley Dale DE4 ...127 B2
Hall St Alfreton DE55 ...159 A2
Derby DE24 ...233 A4
New Mills SK22 ...33 A4
Swadlincote DE11 ...256 A1
Hall Terr S45 ...131 B2
Hall The DE4 ...154 B3
Hall View S41 ...95 C3
Hall View Cottage Herb
Gdn★ S45 ...132 C2
Hall Wlk S42 ...115 B1
Hall's Ct SK13 ...10 B1
Hall's Row 1 S40 ...95 B1
Hallahan Gr ST4 ...269 B2
Hallam Ct S18 ...76 A4
Hallam Fields DE74 ...247 A1
Hallam Fields Jun Sch
DE7 ...208 C3
Hallam Fields Rd DE7 ..209 A2
Hallam Way DE7 ...207 B4
Hallamway NG19 ...136 B1
Hallcliff La S42 ...93 C1
Hallcroft Ave DE12 ...262 A2
Hallcroft Rd 6 DE7 ...208 C4
Halldale La DE4 ...127 C2
Hallfield Cl S42 ...115 A2
Hallfield Rd DE55 ...148 A2
Hallfieldgate La DE55 ..146 B1
Hallfields Rd DE15 ...255 B2
Hallfields Rise DE55 ...146 B1
Hallflash La S44 ...116 A4
Hallgate Cl DE21 ...206 B2
Hallgate La S45 ...132 A1
Hallington Dr DE75 ...181 B1
Hallmoor Rd DE4 ...127 B2
Hallowes Ct S18 ...57 A1
Hallowes Dr S18 ...76 B4
Hallowes La S18 ...76 A4
Hallowes Rise S18 ...76 B4
Halls La NG16 ...195 A4
Halls Rd NG9 ...223 B3
Hallside Ct S20 ...59 B3
Hallsteads SK17 ...47 C1
Hallsteads Cl SK17 ...47 C1
Hallum Ct DE7 ...194 C2
Hallworth Wlk S21 ...58 C1
Hallyburton Cl S2 ...43 B3
Hallyburton Dr S2 ...43 B3
Hallyburton Rd S2 ...43 B3
Halstead Cl NG19 ...136 C1
Halsteads The DE6 ...163 A1
Halstock Dr DE24 ...233 B4
Halton Cl S41 ...76 C1
Hamble Cl NG19 ...136 B2
Hambledon Cl S40 ...95 B3
Hambledon Dr DE24 ...231 B1
Hambleton Ave S42 ...131 C3
Hambleton Cl
Ashbourne DE6 ...185 B4
2 Long Eaton NG10 ...223 A1
Hamblin Cres DE24 ...231 C2
Hamill Cl S42 ...131 C4
Hamilton Cl
Beeston NG9 ...223 C1
Derby DE3 ...217 C2
Hamilton Dr
Nottingham NG7 ...268 A1
Swadlincote DE11 ...256 B3
Hamilton Fields DE15 ..248 A1
Hamilton Gr DE11 ...256 B3
Hamilton Rd
Burton u T DE15 ...248 A1
Derby DE23 ...218 C1
Derby, Spondon DE21 ...220 C3
Long Eaton NG10 ...223 B1
Hamilton St ST4 ...269 C1
Hamilton Terr DE65 ...242 A3
Hamlet La DE55 ...160 A3
Hamlet The Heanor DE75 181 C2
South Normanton DE55 ..160 A3
Hammer Leys DE55 ...160 B2
Hammersmith DE5 ...169 B2
Hammersmith Sta★
DE5 ...169 B2
Hammonds Ct DE4 ...165 C4
Hampden Ho DE15 ...254 C3
Hampden St Derby DE23 232 A4
Eastwood NG16 ...195 B4
Heanor NG16 ...182 A2
Nottingham NG1 ...268 A2
Hampshire Cl SK13 ...17 C4
Hampshire Ct NG16 ...171 A2
Hampshire Dr NG10 ...223 A3
Hampshire Rd DE21 ...219 B4
Hampstead Dr DE22 ...218 A3
Hampton Cl
Beeston NG9 ...223 C2
Derby DE21 ...220 C3
West Hallam DE7 ...207 B4
Hampton Ct DE75 ...181 B1
Hampton St S41 ...115 B4
Hanbury Ave DE65 ...227 B1
Hanbury Cl
Chesterfield S40 ...95 A3
Dronfield S18 ...56 C1
Hanbury Hill DE13 ...238 A3
Hanbury Rd DE21 ...219 C3
Hanchurch Cl DE15 ...248 A2
Hancock St ST4 ...269 C2
Hand's Rd DE75 ...182 A1
Handby St S41 ...115 B4
Handel St Derby DE24 ..232 B4
Nottingham NG1,NG3 ..268 C2
Handford Ct DE22 ...218 B3
Handford St DE22 ...218 B3
Handley Arc NG18 ...268 B4
Handley Ct S43 ...77 B2
Handley La
Clay Cross S45 ...131 A1
Pilsley DE45 ...91 A1
Shirland S45 ...145 C4
Handley Rd S43 ...77 B3
Handsacre Cl DE11 ...255 C2
Handyside St DE1 ...267 B4
Hangar Hill S80 ...82 A3
Hanger Bank DE72 ...246 A4
Hanley Cl SK12 ...32 B3
Hanley St 10 NG1 ...268 A2
Hannage Way DE4 ...165 C4
Hanover Sq DE22 ...218 A3
Hansard Gate DE21 ...267 D3
Hanslynn DE72 ...233 C2
Hanstubbin Rd NG16 ...171 C3
Hanwell Way DE22 ...218 A3
Harbin Rd DE12 ...253 B1
Harbord Cl DE6 ...185 A4
Harborough Ave S2 ...44 A4
Harby Ave NG19 ...136 B3
Harcourt Cl S41 ...115 B4
Harcourt Pl DE74 ...247 A2
Harcourt Rd DE14 ...253 C4
Harcourt St Derby DE1 ..267 B2
Mansfield NG18 ...268 C3
Hard La S26 ...61 C4
Hardacre Cl DE73 ...252 A4
Hardhurst Rd
Derby DE24 ...233 A3
Unstone S18 ...76 C3
Hardie Ave DE55 ...160 A3
Hardie Pl S43 ...97 B4
Harding Terr ST4 ...269 B1
Harding's Cl DE6 ...165 A1
Harding's La SK17 ...138 A3
Hardinge St ST4 ...269 C1
Hardmeadow La S45 ..130 A1
Hardstaff Homes The
NG19 ...136 A2
Hardstoft Rd S45 ...132 C1
Hardwick Ave
Chesterfield S43 ...77 B2
Derby DE22 ...204 B2
Glapwell S44 ...134 A4
Shirebrook NG20 ...119 C2
West Hallam DE7 ...207 C4
Hardwick Cl
Blackwell DE55 ...147 B1
Clowne S43 ...81 A2
Dronfield S18 ...57 B1
Holmewood S42 ...132 C4
Ripley DE5 ...169 B2
Hardwick Ct
Long Eaton NG10 ...235 C2
South Normanton DE55 ..160 B3
5 Staveley S43 ...78 C1
Hardwick Dr Derby DE3 .217 C1
Long Duckmanton S44 ...97 B2
Hardwick Hall★ S44 ...133 C2
Hardwick Inf & Jun Schs
DE23 ...219 A1
Hardwick La S45 ...129 B3
Hardwick Mount SK17 ..85 B4
Hardwick Old Hall★
S44 ...133 C2
Hardwick Park Nature Wlk★
S44 ...133 B2
Hardwick Pk★ S44,
NG17 ...133 C3
Hardwick Pl DE7 ...208 B3
Hardwick Rd NG7 ...268 A1
Hardwick Sq E SK17 ...85 B4
Hardwick Sq N SK17 ...85 B4
Hardwick Sq S SK17 ...85 A4
Hardwick Sq W SK17 ...85 A4
Hardwick St Buxton SK17 .85 A4
Chesterfield S41 ...266 B4
Derby DE24 ...232 B4
Langwith NG20 ...119 C4
Mansfield NG18 ...268 C4
Shirebrook NG20 ...120 A2
Tibshelf DE55 ...148 A4
Hardwick View Rd S42 .132 C4
Hardwick's Yd S40 ...95 C1
Hardy Barn DE75 ...194 A4
Hardy Cl Kimberley NG16 195 C4
Long Eaton NG10 ...236 B3
Hardy Cres DE5 ...181 A4
Hardy Pl NG19 ...268 A4
Hardy St Alfreton DE55 ..158 C3
Kimberley NG16 ...195 C4
Hardybarn La SK17 ...86 B4
Harebell Cl Derby DE21 .206 A2
Swadlincote DE11 ...256 C2
Harehedge La DE13 ...240 A1
Harehill Cres S42 ...114 B2
Harehill Ct S40 ...114 C4
Harehill Rd S40 ...114 C4
Hareholme St NG19 ...268 B4
Harepit Cl DE24 ...233 A3
Harewood Cl DE56 ...179 B3
Harewood Cres S42 ...131 A3
Harewood Ct NG10 ...223 A2
Harewood Lo SK14 ...16 A4
Harewood Rd
Derby DE22 ...204 B2
Holymoorside S42 ...113 B3
Hargate Hill La SK13 ...16 C4
Hargate Rd
Burton u T DE15 ...248 B1
Buxton SK17 ...84 C3
Hargrave Ave DE72 ...221 B3
Hargreaves Cl DE23 ...231 A3
Hargreaves La ST17 ...269 A3
Harlaxton Dr
Long Eaton NG10 ...237 A4
Nottingham NG7 ...268 A1
Harlaxton Wlk 8 NG3 ...268 B2
Harlech Cl Derby DE21 ..221 A3
Ilkeston DE7 ...194 B2
Harlequin Ct NG16 ...182 B2
Harlesden Ave DE22 ...218 A4
Harlesthorpe Ave S43 ...80 C3
Harlesthorpe La S43 ...80 C3
Harlow Cl Derby DE24 ..232 C2
Mansfield Woodhouse
NG19 ...136 B3
Harlow Ct DE7 ...207 B4
Harnett Cl NG1 ...268 B1
Harold Ave NG16 ...182 A2
Harold St NG2 ...268 C1
Harperhill Cl S40 ...114 C4
Harpfield Rd ST4 ...269 A1
Harpole Cl DE55 ...169 C4
Harport Dr S45 ...131 C1
Harpswell Cl DE22 ...204 C1

Harpur Ave Derby DE23 .231 A4
Ticknall DE73 ....251 B1
Harpur Hill Prim Sch
SK17 ....85 B2
Harpur Hill Rd SK17 ....85 B2
Harpur-Crewe Cotts
DE6 ....149 B2
Harrier Rd DE56 ....179 B3
Harrier Way DE24 ....231 C2
Harriet St DE23 ....219 A2
Harriett St NG9 ....223 B4
Harrimans Dr DE72 ..235 C4
Harringay Gdns DE21 .218 B3
Harrington Ave DE72 ..221 B1
Harrington Jun Sch
NG10 ....223 A1
Harrington Rd
Derby DE23 ....218 B1
Sheffield S2 ....43 A4
Harrington St
Derby, Allenton DE24 ...232 C3
Derby, Normanton DE23 .232 A4
Draycott DE72 ....235 A4
Long Eaton NG10 ....236 A3
Mansfield NG18 ....268 B3
Harris Ave DE5 ....169 B1
Harris Cl DE5 ....169 B1
Harris Rd Buxton SK17 ..85 B2
Stafford ST16 ....269 C4
Harris St ST4 ....269 C1
Harrison Cl DE14 .....254 A4
Harrison Dr DE4 ......154 C1
Harrison La
Ringinglow S10 ....42 C4
Tibshelf DE55 ....147 C3
Harrison Rd
Mansfield NG18 ....268 A3
Stapleford NG9 ....223 B4
Harrison St DE22 .....218 C2
Harrison Way DE4 ....127 A3
Harrogate Cres DE21 .205 B1
Harrop La S10 ....42 C3
Harrop White Rd NG18,
NG19 ....268 A4
Harrots La SK17 ....137 B3
Harrow Dr
Burton u T DE14 ....254 B4
Ilkeston DE7 ....209 A2
Harrow Rd DE11 ......256 A4
Harrow St DE24 ......219 C1
Harrowby St ST16 ....269 C4
Hart Ave NG10 ....223 A3
Hart Lea 3 NG10 ......223 A3
Hartfield Cl S41 ......115 A4
Hartford Cl S8 ....43 A2
Hartford Rd S8 ....43 A2
Harthill Field Rd S26 ...62 A2
Harthill La S43,S26 ...61 C1
Harthill Prim Sch S26 ..61 C3
Harthill Rd Sheffield S13 .44 A4
Thorpe Salvin S80 ......62 B4
Hartill St ST4 ....269 C2
Hartington CE Prim Sch
SK17 ....137 B3
Hartington Cl DE7 ....207 C4
Dronfield S18 ....57 A1
Hartington Ct Clowne S43 .81 A2
Hartington Dr
Chinley SK23 ....34 C1
Creswell S80 ....81 B1
Hartington Hall YH ★
SK17 ....137 C3
Hartington Ind Est S43 .78 C2
Hartington Pl DE7 ....194 C3
Hartington Rd
Buxton SK17 ....85 A4
Chesterfield S41 ....96 B1
Dronfield S18 ....57 A1
Hartington St
Derby DE1, DE23 ....267 B1
Langwith NG20 ....119 C4
Hartington View S43 ...78 C2
Hartington Way DE3 ..217 B1
Hartland Dr DE23 ....231 C3
Hartland Way S41 .....77 A1
Hartley St S2 ....43 A4
Hartopp Ave S2 ....43 B3
Hartopp Cl S2 ....43 B3
Hartopp Dr S2 ....43 B3
Hartopp Rd S2 ....43 B3
Hartshay Hill DE5 ....169 B1
Hartshill Rd
Hartshorne DE11 ......257 A2
Stoke-on-T ST4 ....269 A2
Hartshorne CE Prim Sch
DE11 ....257 A3
Hartshorne Rd
Derby DE23 ....231 B3
Repton DE65 ....249 C4
Woodville DE11 ....256 C2
Hartside Cl 9 S40 ......95 B3
Hartside Gdns 1 NG10 .236 A4
Hartside Way DE75 ...182 A1
Hartwell St NG3 ......268 B2
Hartwood Dr NG9 .....209 B1
Harvest Hill DE11 .....256 A4
Harvest Way Derby DE21 206 B2
2 Old Brampton S42 .....95 A3
Harvester Cl DE5 .....169 B1
Harvey Clough Mews S8 43 A4
Harvey Clough Rd S8 ...43 A4
Harvey Croft NG9 .....209 B2
Harvey Ct S44 ....98 C1
Harvey Pl ST14 ....210 A1

Harvey Rd
Burton u T DE14 ....254 A4
Castle Donington DE74 .247 A1
Chesterfield S41 ....96 C1
Derby DE24 ....232 C3
Harwood Ave DE14 ...253 C4
Harwood Cl S2 ....43 A4
Hasgill Cl DE21 ....206 B2
Haslam Cres S8 ....56 C3
Haslam Ct S44 ....98 C1
Haslam St NG7 ....268 A1
Haslam's La DE21,DE22 205 A1
Hasland Hall Com Sch
S41 ....115 B4
Hasland Inf Sch S41 ..115 B4
Hasland Jun Sch S41 ..115 B4
Hasland Rd S41 ....115 B4
Haslemere Ct DE23 ...219 A1
Haslemere Rd NG10 ..236 A4
Haslin Rd SK17 ....85 B1
Hassall Rd DE65 ......227 B1
Hassock La N DE75 ...194 A4
Hassock La S DE7,DE75 194 B3
Hassocky La S44,S42 ...116 A3
Hassop Cl Chesterfield S41 95 B3
Dronfield S18 ....57 B1
Hassop Rd Calver S32 ..72 A1
Derby DE21 ....220 A4
Hassop DE45 ....90 B1
Staveley S43 ....78 C2
Hastilar Cl S2 ....44 A4
Hastilar Rd S2 ....44 A4
Hastilar Rd S S13 .....44 B4
Hasting St DE74 ....247 A1
Hastings Cl
Breedon on t H DE73 ...252 C1
Chesterfield S41 ....95 B3
Hastings Rd Buxton SK17 .85 B2
Swadlincote DE11 ......256 A2
Hastings St DE23 .....219 A1
Haston Dr DE55 ....170 A4
Hatchmere Cl DE21 ...206 A1
Hatfield Ave NG10 ....223 A2
Hatfield Rd DE24 .....232 C3
Hathaway Cl S42 ......131 A3
Hathern Cl Calow S43 ..96 C2
Derby DE23 ....231 C3
Long Eaton NG10 ......236 A3
Hathersage Ave
Derby DE23 ....231 C4
Long Eaton NG10 ......235 C3
Hathersage Cres SK13 ..9 C1
Hathersage Dr
Glossop SK13 ....17 C4
Somercotes DE55 ......170 A4
Hathersage Rd
Bamford S33 ....40 A1
Totley S11 ....54 B3
Hathersage Sta S32 ...53 A4
Hatherton St ST16 ....269 C4
Hatton Cl S18 ....75 B4
Hatton Crofts NG10 ..236 B3
Hatton Ct DE73 ....252 A4
Hatton Dr S40 ....95 A3
Haulton Dr DE74 ......247 A2
Havelock Gdns NG3 ..268 B2
Havelock Rd DE23 ....232 A4
Havelock St Ilkeston DE7 208 C4
Ripley DE5 ....169 C1
Haven Baulk Ave DE23 .230 C4
Haven Baulk La DE23 ..230 C4
Haven Ct DE24 ....233 B3
Havenwood Gr DE23 ..231 B3
Havercroft Tr S21 ......60 A4
Hawfield La
Burton u T DE15 ....248 B2
Newton Solney DE15 ...248 C2
Hawk Green Rd SK6 ...23 A2
Hawk Rd S32 ....33 C4
Hawk's Dr DE15 ....248 B2
Hawke St DE22 ....218 B3
Hawkeshead Ave S18 ..56 C1
Hawkhill Rd S32 ....71 B3
Hawking La S44 ......133 A4
Hawkinge Ho 8 S41 ...95 B3
Hawkins Ct DE7 ......194 C2
Hawkins Dr DE56 .....168 A2
Hawkins St S14 ....269 C1
Hawksdale Cl DE73 ...233 A1
Hawkshead Ave DE21 .205 B1
Hawkshead Rd SK13 ...10 C2
Hawksley Ave S40 .....95 C2
Hawksley Dr
Darley Dale DE4 ....127 A2
Rolleston DE13 ....240 A2
Hawksway S21 ....59 A2
Hawksworth St NG3 ..268 C2
Hawley St S18 ....58 A1
Hawleys Cl DE4 ....143 C3
Hawthorn Ave
Breaston DE72 ....235 C4
Creswell S80 ....81 C1
Derby DE24 ....233 A4
Glapwell S44 ....134 A4
Mastin Moor S43 ....79 B2
Netherseal DE12 ......264 C4
Ripley DE5 ....180 B4
Stapleford NG9 ....223 B3
Hawthorn Bank
Glossop SK13 ....9 C2
New Mills SK22 ....33 A4
Hawthorn Cl
Ashbourne DE6 ....185 B4
Chinley SK23 ....34 C1
Clowne S43 ....80 B2
Denstone ST14 ....196 C3
Doveridge DE6 ....211 A1
Hilton DE65 ....228 B1

Hawthorn Cl continued
Hope S33 ....39 A2
Mansfield Woodhouse
NG19 ....136 C3
Hawthorn Cr DE65 ....230 B1
Hawthorn Cres DE15 ..254 C4
Hawthorn Dr DE4 .....155 A3
Hawthorn Gr SK14 ....9 B3
Hawthorn Hill S43 .....78 C3
Hawthorn Rd
Castle Donington DE74 .247 A3
Eckington S21 ....59 A1
Hawthorn Rise DE11 ..255 C4
Hawthorn St DE24 ....232 B4
Hawthorn Way ST17 ..269 C3
Hawthorne Ave
Borrowash DE72 ....221 B1
Dronfield S18 ....57 A2
Long Eaton NG10 ......236 B3
Shirebrook NG20 ......119 B2
Shirland DE55 ....146 B3
Stoke-on-T ST4 ....269 A1
Tibshelf DE55 ....148 A4
Hawthorne Cl
Barlborough S43 ......80 A3
Kilburn DE56 ....179 C1
Killamarsh S21 ....60 B3
Shirland DE55 ....145 B4
Hawthorne Rd NG16 ..160 B2
Hawthorne Rise NG16 .195 A2
Hawthorne St S40 ....266 B1
Hawthorne Way S42 ...94 C3
Hawthornes Ave DE55 159 C3
Hawthorns The
Belper DE56 ....179 B3
Chapel-en-le-F SK23 ...47 A2
Little Eaton DE21 ......205 B4
Hawton Cl NG19 ......135 C1
Hawtrey Gdns DE24 ..233 A3
Haxby Cl S13 ....44 C3
Haxby Pl S13 ....44 C3
Haxby St S13 ....44 C3
Hay La Ashover S45 ...145 A4
Scropton DE65 ....226 C3
Spout DE4 ....166 B3
Hay Wain La DE11 ....256 A4
Haybrook Ct S17 ....55 C3
Haycroft Cl NG19 .....136 C3
Haycroft Gdns DE55 ..231 A4
Haydock Cl
Burton u T DE14 ....254 A4
Kimberley NG16 ....195 C4
Haydock Park Rd DE24 232 C4
Hayes Ave
Breaston DE72 ....235 A4
Derby DE23 ....231 B4
Hayes Cl Pinxton NG16 .160 B2
West Hallam DE7 ......207 C4
Hayes Con Ctr The
DE55 ....170 A4
Hayes Cres DE55 .....169 C4
Hayes Ct S20 ....59 C3
Hayes Dr S20 ....59 C3
Hayes Farm Ct DE73 ..251 A2
Hayes La DE55 ....169 C4
Hayes The DE65 ......230 B1
Hayes Wood Rd DE7 ..193 A4
Hayfield Cl Belper DE56 .179 A3
Dronfield S18 ....56 B1
Staveley S43 ....78 C2
Wingerworth S42 ......114 C2
Hayfield Cres S12 .....44 B2
Hayfield Dr S12 ....44 B2
Hayfield Gdns DE23 ..231 A3
Hayfield Pl S12 ....44 B2
Hayfield Prim Sch SK22 .25 B2
Hayfield Rd
Chapel-en-le-F SK23 ...47 A4
Chinley SK23 ....35 A2
New Mills SK22 ....24 C1
Hayfield Rd E SK23 ...47 B3
Hayfield View S21 .....59 B2
Hayfield Vistor Ctr ★
SK22 ....25 B1
Hayford Way S43 .....78 C1
Hayley Croft DE56 ....190 C1
Havling Cl DE7 ....194 B2
Haynes Ave NG9 ......209 B3
Hays Cl DE7 ....194 B1
Hays La DE6 ....164 C1
Hays The DE65 ....227 B1
Haywards Cl SK13 .....10 B2
Haywood Cl DE24 ....233 A3
Haywood St NG2 .....268 C1
Hayworth Rd NG10 ...223 B3
Hazel Ave Derby DE23 .231 B3
Killamarsh S21 ....60 B3
Pilsley S45 ....132 A2
Hazel Cl Ashbourne DE6 .185 B4
Dronfield S18 ....76 A1
Findern DE65 ....230 C1
Heanor DE75 ....181 B1
Stoke-on-T ST4 ....269 A1
Swadlincote DE11 .....256 A3
Hazel Cres NG20 .....119 B2
Hazel Ct S18 ....76 A1
Hazel Dr Chesterfield S40 114 C4
Derby DE21 ....221 A3
Wingerworth S42 ......115 A2
Hazel Gr Calver S32 ...72 B1
Duffield DE56 ....190 C2
Mansfield Woodhouse
NG19 ....136 A3
Mastin Moor S43 ....79 B2
Matlock DE4 ....143 B3

Hazel Gr continued
South Normanton DE55 .160 A3
Hazel Rd S21 ....59 B1
Hazelbadge Cres S12 ..44 C2
Hazelby Rd S80 ....100 C4
Hazeldene Cl DE56 ....190 C3
Hazeldene Cotts DE56 .178 B3
Hazelhurst S41 ....115 B3
Hazelhurst Ave S41 ...96 A3
Hazelhurst La S41 .....96 A3
Hazelmere Rd S80 ....81 B2
Hazelrigg Cl DE74 ....246 C2
Hazeltree Cl DE5 .....180 B4
Hazelwood Cl 7 S18 ..56 B1
Hazelwood Hill DE56 ..190 B4
Hazelwood Rd
Burton u T DE15 ....254 C3
Derby DE21 ....219 C4
Duffield DE56 ....190 B3
Hazlebarrow Cl S8 ....57 B3
Hazlebarrow Cres S8 ..57 B4
Hazlebarrow Ct S8 ....57 A4
Hazlebarrow Dr S8 ....57 A4
Hazlebarrow Gr S8 ....57 B4
Hazlebarrow Rd S8 ....57 A4
Hazlehurst La S8 ......57 C4
Hazletarrow Prim Schs
S8 ....57 B3
Hazlewood Dr S43 ....80 A3
Headingley Ct DE23 ..231 B4
Headland Cl S43 ......96 C4
Headland Rd S43 ......96 C4
Heage La DE65 ....229 B4
Heage Prim Sch DE56 .168 B1
Heage Rd DE5 ....169 B1
Healaugh Way S40 ...115 A4
Heale St S43 ....80 C2
Heanor Gate Ind Est
DE75 ....193 B4
Heanor Gate Rd DE75 .193 B4
Heanor Gate Sch DE75 181 B4
Heanor Ho DE21 ......220 C2
Heanor Langley Mill &
District Meml Hosp
DE75 ....181 C1
Heanor Rd Codnor DE5 .181 A4
Denby DE5 ....181 A2
Heanor, Loscoe DE75 ..181 B2
Ilkeston DE7 ....194 B2
Smalley DE7,DE75 .....193 A4
Hearthcote Rd DE11 ..256 A2
Hearthstone La DE4 ..143 B1
Heath Ave Derby DE23 .218 B3
Killamarsh S21 ....60 B3
Heath Cross ST14 ....210 A1
Heath Ct Chesterfield S40 115 A4
Derby DE24 ....231 C2
Heath Fields Prim Sch
DE65 ....227 B1
Heath Gdns DE72 ....236 A4
Heath Gr SK17 ....85 B3
Heath La
Blackfordby DE11 ......257 B1
Findern DE65 ....242 B4
Hartshorne DE11 ......257 C2
Smisby LE65 ....258 A3
Ticknall LE65 ....258 A2
Heath Park Rd SK17 ...85 B3
Heath Prim Sch S44 ..116 C1
Heath Rd
Burton u T DE15 ....254 C4
Glossop SK13 ....10 B1
Holmewood S44 ....116 C1
Holmewood, Williamthorpe
S42 ....132 C4
Ripley DE5 ....169 C1
Uttoxeter ST14 ....210 A1
Heath St SK17 ....85 A3
Heath View SK17 .....85 C1
Heath Way DE65 .....227 B1
Heathcoat St NG1 ....268 B2
Heathcote Cl DE24 ...233 B3
Heathcote Dr S41 .....115 C4
Heather Ave S44 .....116 C1
Heather Bank Cl 7 SK13 17 A4
Heather Cl
Burton u T DE14 ....254 A4
Calow S44 ....97 A2
Derby DE24 ....231 B1
Mansfield NG18 ....268 B3
South Normanton DE55 .160 A2
Swanwick DE55 ....170 A4
Heather Cres
Breaston DE72 ....235 C4
Derby DE23 ....231 B3
Heather Ct DE75 .....182 A1
Heather Gdns S41 ....115 C4
Heather Lea Ave S17 ..55 B4
Heather Lea Pl S17 ...55 B4
Heather Vale S41 .....115 C4
Heather Vale Cl S41 ..115 C4
Heather Way S42 .....113 B4
Heatherley Dr NG19 ..136 C1
Heatherley Prim Sch
NG19 ....136 C1
Heathermead Cl DE21 .205 C1
Heathervale Rd S41 ...115 B4
Heathfield DE4 ....143 B3
Heathfield Ave
Chesterfield S40 ....95 B2
Ilkeston DE7 ....209 A4
Heathfield Cl
Dronfield S18 ....75 C4
Wingerworth S42 ......115 A4

Heathfield Gdns
Buxton SK17 ....85 A4
Tibshelf DE55 ....148 A4
Heathfield Nook Rd
SK17 ....85 C1
Heathfield Rd S12 ....44 B2
Heathlands Dr ST14 ..210 A1
Heathley Mews DE14 .254 B4
Heaton 20 S18 ....56 B1
Heaton St S40 ....95 B1
Heavygate La DE56 ...177 C4
Hebden Cl DE23 ......230 C3
Hebden Dr SK13 ......17 C4
Hebrides Cl DE24 ....231 B2
Hedderley Wlk 14 NG3 268 B2
Heddon Bar NG19 ....136 C2
Hedge Gr DE11 ....256 A4
Hedgebank Ct DE21 ..206 B2
Hedgerow Gdns DE21 .206 B2
Hedges Dr DE7 ....209 A3
Hedingham Way DE3 ..230 B4
Hedley Cl DE55 ....170 A4
Hedley Dr S43 ....96 B4
Heeley Arches S2 .....43 A4
Heeley Bank Rd S2 ...43 A4
Heeley City Farm ★ S2 .43 A4
Heeley Gn S2 ....43 A3
Heigham Cl DE24 ....232 B2
Heights of Abraham ★
DE4 ....143 A1
Heights of Abraham Cable
Car ★ DE4 ....143 A1
Helmsdale Cl NG18 ..268 C3
Helmsley Ave S20 ....59 C4
Helmsley Cl S41 ......95 B4
Helmton Dr S8 ....43 A2
Helmton Rd S8 ....43 A1
Helpston Cl DE55 ....147 B1
Helston Cl
Chesterfield S41 ....115 A4
Derby DE24 ....233 A3
Linton DE12 ....261 B3
Helvellyn Way 7 NG10 223 A3
Heming Ave S45 ......132 B1
Hemington Ct DE74 ..247 B2
Hemington Hill DE74 ..247 B2
Hemington La DE74 ..247 C3
Hemington Sch DE74 .247 B2
Hemlock Ave
Long Eaton NG10 ......223 B4
Stapleford NG9 ....223 C4
Hemlock Cl DE21 .....206 B2
Hemlock La DE7 ......208 B3
Hemp Yd DE6 ....165 A1
Hemper Gr S8 ....56 B4
Hemper La S8 ....56 B3
Hemsley Dr NG16 ....182 C3
Hemsworth Prim Sch
S14 ....43 B1
Hemsworth Rd S8 ....43 B1
Hendon Way DE22 ...218 A3
Henley Ave S8 ....57 B4
Henley Gdns NG9 ....209 C1
Henley Gn DE22 ......217 C3
Henley Way DE7 .....207 B4
Henmore Pl DE6 .....173 B1
Henmore Trad Est DE6 173 A1
Hennymoor Cl S80 ...82 A3
Hennymoor La S80 ...82 A3
Henry Ave
Mansfield Woodhouse
NG19 ....136 A3
Matlock DE4 ....143 B3
Henry Bradley Inf Sch
S43 ....96 C4
Henry Cres DE55 .....159 B3
Henry Prince CE Fst Sch The
DE6 ....184 B4
Henry St Chesterfield S41 96 A4
Derby DE1 ....267 A4
Eckington S21 ....59 B2
Glossop SK13 ....10 B1
Grassmoor S42 ....115 C2
Nottingham NG2 ......268 C1
Ripley DE5 ....169 B1
Henshaw Ave DE7 ....208 B3
Henshaw Pl DE7 .....194 C2
Herbert Rd ST17 .....269 B3
Herbert St
Burton u T DE15 ....248 A2
Fenton S14 ....269 C1
Mansfield NG18 ....268 C3
Herbert Strutt Prim Sch
DE56 ....178 C1
Herdings Ct S12 ......44 A2
Herdings Leighton Rd
S12 ....44 A2
Herdings Pk S14 ......43 C1
Herdings Prim Sch S14 .43 C1
Herdings Rd S12 ......44 A2
Herdings View S12 ...44 A2
Hereford Ave NG19 ..136 B3
Hereford Cl SK17 .....85 B2
Hereford Cres DE11 ..256 B3
Hereford Dr S43 ......96 C4
Hereford Rd Buxton SK17 85 B2
Derby DE21 ....219 B4
Hereward's Rd S14 ...43 B1
Herewood Cl NG20 ...119 C2
Heritage Com Sch S43 .80 B2
Heritage Dr S43 ......80 B3
Heritage Way DE15 ..248 A1
Hermitage Ave
Borrowash DE72 ......221 B1
Mansfield NG18 ....268 A3
Somercotes DE55 .....170 B3
Hermitage Ct DE21 ..206 A1

Her – Hol 289

Hermitage Gdns 1 ST14 210 A1
Hermitage La
Mansfield NG18 268 A3
Mayfield DE6 184 A3
Hermitage Park Way 7 DE11 256 A4
Hermitage Sq 6 NG2 268 C1
Hermitage Wlk
Ilkeston DE7 208 C3
Nottingham NG7 268 A1
Hermon St 33 NG7 268 A2
Hernstone La SK17 49 A1
Heron Dr DE11 256 C2
Heron Way DE3 218 A1
Heronswood Dr DE21 220 B3
Herriot Dr S40 266 C1
Heskey Cl NG3 268 B2
Heskey Wlk 7 NG3 268 B2
Hessey St S13 44 C3
Hewers Holt S43 80 A3
Hewett St NG20 120 B3
Hewitt Pl S26 61 C3
Hexham Ave DE7 209 A2
Hexham Wlk DE21 205 C1
Hey St NG10 236 B2
Heyden Bank SK13 9 B1
Heyden Terr SK13 9 B1
Heydon Cl DE56 179 A3
Heyford Ct DE75 182 A1
Heysbank Rd SK12 32 B3
Heyward St NG18 268 C4
Heywood St
Brimington S43 96 C4
Mansfield NG18 268 C4
Heywood View S43 80 B3
Heywood Villas 8 S43 96 C4
Heyworth Rd SK23 47 B3
Heyworth St DE22 218 B3
Hibbert Rd NG18 268 C4
Hibbert St SK22 33 A3
Hickings La NG9 223 C4
Hickingwood La S43 81 A3
Hickinwood Cres S43 80 C3
Hickleton Cl DE5 169 B1
Hickling Cl DE24 232 B2
Hickling Ct NG18 268 C4
Hickton Rd DE55 169 C3
Hide La SK17 137 C4
Hide Pl ST4 269 B2
Hide St ST4 269 B2
Hides Gn S44 99 A1
Higg La DE56 167 A3
Higger La S32 52 C4
Higgins Rd DE11 255 C3
Higgott Cl DE14 254 A4
High Bank DE5 180 C1
High Bank Rd DE15 248 A2
High Cross
Hartington SK17 137 C3
Linton DE11 261 C4
High Cross St 28 NG1 268 B2
High Ct DE4 143 B3
High Edge Dr DE56 179 C4
High Edge Mews DE56 179 A3
High Gr Belper DE56 179 B2
Mansfield NG19 136 C1
High Hazel Cl S45 131 C2
High Hazel Wlk S45 131 C2
High Hazels Rd S43 80 A3
High Hill Rd SK22 24 B1
High Holborn DE7 194 C2
High Holborn Rd DE5 170 A1
High La Broadbottom SK13 16 C4
Holloway, Dethick Common DE4 144 C1
Holloway, Upper Holloway DE4 156 B3
Holymoorside S42 113 C3
Sheffield S12 44 C1
High La Central DE7 193 C1
High La E DE7 208 A4
High La W DE7 193 C1
High Lea Rd SK22 33 A4
High Leys Rd S43 80 C1
High Mdws SK13 17 A4
High Meadow Cl DE5 180 B4
High Pavement
Belper DE56 179 A2
Nottingham NG1 268 B1
High Pk ST16 269 A3
High Rd DE55 157 C2
High Ridge
Mansfield NG19 136 C1
Matlock DE4 143 B4
High Spania NG16 195 C4
High St Alfreton DE55 159 A2
Alfreton, Riddings DE55 170 B3
Apperknowle S18 58 A1
Barlborough S43 80 A4
Belper DE56 179 A2
Bolsover S44 99 A1
Bonsall DE4 142 B1
Brimington S43 96 C4
Brinsley NG16 171 B1
Buxton SK17 85 A4
Calver S32 72 A1
Castle Donington DE74 247 A1
Chapel-en-le-F SK23 47 A3
Chesterfield S41,S43 77 B2
Chesterfield, Stonegravels S40 266 B3
Clay Cross S45 131 B2
Clowne S43 80 B2
Codnor DE5 181 A4
Derby DE73 233 A1
Dore S17 55 B4
Doveridge DE6 211 A1
High St *continued*
Dronfield S18 57 A1
Eckington S21 59 B2
Heanor, Loscoe DE75 181 B2
Heanor, Newlands DE75 181 C1
Ilkeston DE7 208 C4
Kilburn DE56 192 A4
Killamarsh S21 60 B3
Kimberley NG16 195 C3
Linton DE12 261 B3
Long Eaton NG10 236 C4
Longnor SK17 121 B3
Mansfield Woodhouse NG19 136 B2
Marchington ST14 224 C1
Melbourne DE73 252 A4
Mosborough S20 59 B4
New Mills SK22 33 B4
Nottingham NG1 268 B1
Pilsley DE45 91 B2
Pleasley NG19 135 A3
Repton DE65 242 B1
Ripley DE5 169 B1
Rocester ST14 196 C2
Somercotes DE55 170 B4
South Normanton DE55 160 A3
Stapleford NG9 223 C4
Staveley S43 78 C1
Stonebroom DE55 147 A2
Stoney Middleton S32 71 C2
Swadlincote, Church Gresley DE11 256 B2
Swadlincote, Newhall DE11 256 A3
Swanwick DE55 169 C4
Tibshelf DE55 148 A4
Ticknall DE73 251 A2
Tideswell SK17 69 B2
Tutbury DE13 239 B3
Whitwell S80 81 C3
Woodville DE11 256 C1
High St E SK13 10 B1
High St W SK13 10 A1
High Tor★ DE4 143 A2
High Tor Rd DE4 143 A1
High Trees S17 55 B4
High View Cl S41 96 B1
High View Rd DE55 160 B4
High View Sch & Tech Ctr DE21 205 C1
High Wood Bank DE56 179 B1
High Wood Fold SK6 23 B4
Higham La Compstall SK14 15 A4
Stonebroom DE55 146 C2
Highashes La S45 113 C1
Highbank SK13 9 C4
Highbank Rd SK13 17 C4
Highbury Cl DE22 217 C3
Highbury Rd S41 95 C3
Highcliffe Ave NG20 119 B2
Highcroft Cl NG10 236 C3
Higher Albert St S41 266 B4
Higher Barn Rd SK13 9 C2
Higher Dinting SK13 10 A1
Higher Halsteads SK17 47 C2
Higher La SK12 32 C1
Higher Sq SK13 10 A4
Highfield DE45 108 C4
Highfield Ave
Chesterfield S41 95 C3
Dove Holes SK17 47 C1
Mansfield NG19 136 A1
Shirebrook NG20 119 B3
Highfield Cl
Bakewell DE45 109 B3
Heanor DE75 181 A3
Mansfield NG19 136 A1
Highfield Cotts DE21 219 C3
Highfield Ct SK14 9 A2
Highfield Dr
Bakewell DE45 109 B3
Ilkeston DE7 208 A3
Matlock DE4 143 B3
South Normanton DE55 160 A3
Highfield Gdns
Derby DE22 218 C4
Hollingworth SK14 9 B3
Highfield Hall Prim Sch S41 95 C3
Highfield La
Chesterfield S41 95 C3
Derby DE21 219 C3
Hartington SK17 137 C3
Weston Underwood DE6 188 C3
Highfield Mews DE21 219 C3
Highfield Pl S2 43 A4
Highfield Prim Sch NG10 223 B1
Highfield Rd
Ashbourne DE6 185 A4
Belper DE56 178 C1
Bolsover S44 99 A1
Chesterfield S41 266 A4
Derby DE22 218 C4
Derby, Littleover DE23 231 B4
Glossop SK13 17 B4
Hayfield SK22 25 B2
Hulland Ward DE6 175 C2
Kilburn DE56 191 C4
Little Eaton DE21 205 B4
Marple SK6 23 A3
Swadlincote DE11 256 A2
Swanwick DE55 169 B4
Highfield St
Long Eaton NG10 223 B1
Swadlincote DE11 256 A2
Highfield Terr
Chesterfield S41 95 C3
Highfield Terr *continued*
New Mills SK22 33 B4
Highfield View Rd S41 95 C3
Highfield Way
Mansfield NG18 268 B3
Ripley DE5 180 B4
Highfields Buxton SK17 67 A3
Codnor DE5 181 A4
Highfields Cres S18 76 A4
Highfields Dr
Holmewood S42 132 B4
Linton DE12 261 B3
Highfields Lower Sch DE4 143 B2
Highfields Rd S18 76 A4
Highfields Sch DE4 143 C4
Highfields Way S42 132 B4
Highgate Cl S43 77 B2
Highgate Dr Dronfield S18 76 B4
Ilkeston DE7 194 B2
Highgate Gn DE22 218 A3
Highgate La S18 76 B4
Highgate Rd SK22 25 C1
Highgrove Cl
Burton u T DE13 240 B1
Heanor DE75 181 B1
Highgrove Dr DE73 232 C1
Highland Cl Buxton SK17 85 B3
Mansfield Woodhouse NG19 136 B2
Highland Rd S43 77 B2
Highlands Dr DE15 248 A2
Highlands Pl S41 76 C1
Highlightley La S18 75 B3
Highlow Cl S40 95 B3
Highstairs La DE55 146 B4
Highstones Gdns SK13 10 C1
Highstool La SK17 106 A3
Highurst Ct 21 NG7 268 A2
Highurst St NG7 268 A2
Highview SK13 17 A4
Highway La DE6 151 C1
Highwood Ave DE56 179 B1
Highwood Cl SK13 17 A4
Highwood La S80 81 B3
Highwood Pl S21 59 B2
Higson Ave ST4 269 B2
Hilary Cl DE56 179 C3
Hilcote La DE55 148 A1
Hilcote St DE55 160 A3
Hilderstone Cl DE24 233 B3
Hill Brow DE1 267 B2
Hill Cl Derby DE21 220 C2
Stanley DE7 193 A1
Turnditch DE56 177 A1
Hill Crest Crich DE4 157 A1
Shirebrook NG20 119 B2
Hill Crest Cotts DE4 142 C4
Hill Crest Rd DE21 219 B4
Hill Cross DE45 108 C4
Hill Cross Ave DE23 231 B4
Hill Cross Dr DE23 231 A4
Hill Dr DE13 238 A2
Hill Fields DE55 160 A2
Hill Gr S43 78 A2
Hill Head S33 51 A4
Hill La S32 52 C4
Hill Nook Cl DE73 233 A1
Hill Park Cl DE23 218 A1
Hill Pond Ave SK22 24 B1
Hill Rd Ashover S45 129 C2
Eckington S21 59 C2
Heanor DE75 181 B1
Hill Rise NG9 209 B2
Hill Rise Cl DE23 231 B4
Hill Sq The DE22 205 A1
Hill St Burton u T DE15 254 C4
Clay Cross S45 131 B2
Donisthorpe DE12 262 C1
Pleasley NG19 135 A3
Ripley DE5 169 B2
Stoke-on-T ST4 269 B2
Swadlincote DE11 255 C3
Swadlincote, Church Gresley DE11 256 B2
Hill The Derby DE22 205 A1
Glapwell S44 118 A1
Hill Top Bolsover S44 99 A1
Castle Donington DE74 247 A1
Derby DE21 205 C2
Hill Top Ave NG20 119 C2
Hill Top Inf Sch DE6 185 B4
Hill Top Rd DE55 170 B3
Hill Top Rise SK23 45 B4
Hill View Duffield DE56 190 B2
Repton DE65 242 C1
Whaley Bridge SK23 45 B4
Hill View Cl DE7 192 A4
Hill View Gr DE21 220 C3
Hill View Rd S43 96 C4
Hillary Pl DE7 208 A3
Hillberry DE5 170 A1
Hillberry Rise S40 114 C3
Hillcliff La DE56 176 C1
Hillcrest DE13 239 A3
Hillcrest Ave
Burton u T DE15 248 A2
Hulland Ward DE6 175 C2
South Normanton DE55 160 A2
Hillcrest Dr Codnor DE5 181 A4
Kilburn DE56 192 A4
Hillcrest Gr S43 78 C2
Hillcrest Rd S41 115 B4
Hillcreste Dr DE73 232 C2
Hillcroft Dr DE72 221 B2
Hillend SK14 9 A1
Hillend La SK14 9 A1
Hillfield La DE13 240 C1
Hillfield Rd NG9 209 C1
Hillfoot Rd S17 55 B3
Hillhead La SK17 85 C1
Hillhouses La S42 114 C2
Hillman Dr S43 97 B4
Hillmoor St NG19 135 B2
Hillock The S32 72 C1
Hills Croft DE6 164 A1
Hills Rd DE72 235 B4
Hills The S33 51 A3
Hillsdale Rd DE15 248 A3
Hillside Ashover S45 130 A2
Buxton SK17 85 B2
Castle Donington DE74 247 A2
Chinley SK23 47 A4
Curbar S32 72 C1
Findern DE65 230 B1
Holloway DE4 156 A3
Langley Mill NG16 182 A2
Middleton (Nr Wirksworth) DE4 154 B2
Mosborough S20 59 B4
Tutbury DE13 239 B3
Whitwell S80 81 C3
Hillside Ave
Ashbourne DE6 173 B2
Derby DE21 220 A3
Dronfield S18 76 A4
Hillside Cl Disley SK12 32 C3
Glossop SK13 9 C2
Whitwell S80 81 C3
Hillside Cres DE21 220 C2
Hillside Ct DE73 252 C1
Hillside Dr
Chesterfield S40 95 B1
Long Eaton NG10 236 A4
Mastin Moor S43 79 B2
Hillside Gdns DE11 255 C1
Hillside Gr Marple SK6 15 A1
Sandiacre NG10 223 A3
Hillside La DE4 152 C1
Hillside Rd Derby DE21 220 C2
Linton DE12 261 B4
Hillside Rise DE56 178 C1
Hillside View SK22 33 A4
Hillsway Derby DE23 218 A1
Derby, Chellaston DE73 232 C2
Shirebrook NG20 119 B2
Hilltop DE56 168 A4
Hilltop Cl S44 118 A1
Hilltop La Belper DE56 179 C1
Thurvaston DE6 215 B3
Hilltop Rd Ashover S45 129 C3
Chesterfield S41 77 A1
Dronfield S18 76 A4
Glossop SK13 10 A2
Pinxton NG16 160 B2
Wingerworth S42 114 B2
Hilltop Way S18 76 A4
Hilltops View DE4 143 B3
Hillview Ct NG19 136 B2
Hillwood Dr SK13 17 C4
Hilton Cl Derby DE3 217 B1
Long Eaton NG10 235 C2
Swadlincote DE11 256 A4
Hilton Gdns DE72 246 A4
Hilton Park Dr DE55 170 B4
Hilton Prim Sch DE65 228 B1
Hilton Rd Disley SK12 32 A4
Egginton DE65 241 A4
Etwall DE65 229 A2
Stoke-on-T ST4 269 A2
Hincley Ct DE4 110 C1
Hind Ave DE72 235 B4
Hindersitch La DE4 156 B1
Hindscarth Cres DE3 217 C1
Hinton Gr SK14 15 A4
Hipley Cl S40 95 A3
Hipper St S40 266 B2
Hipper St S S40 266 B2
Hipper St W S40 95 C1
Hirst Ct 24 NG7 268 A2
Hixon's La DE7 208 A1
Hoades St S42 131 B4
Hoargate La DE6 200 C1
Hob Hill DE56 190 A4
Hob Hill Mdws SK13 17 B4
Hob Hurst's Ho★ DE45 111 C4
Hob La Kirk Ireton DE6 176 B4
Totley S18 55 C1
Hobart Cl
Burton u T DE15 248 B1
Derby DE3 217 C1
Hobart Dr NG9 209 C1
Hobhouse Rd NG19 135 B1
Hobkirk Dr DE24 231 C1
Hobsic Cl NG16 182 B4
Hobsic La NG16 171 C4
Hobson Dr DE7 208 C3
Hobson Moor Rd SK14 9 A4
Hockerley Ave SK23 45 B4
Hockerley Cl SK23 45 B4
Hockerley La SK23 45 B4
Hockley NG1 268 B1
Hockley La Ashover S45 130 A1
Wingerworth S42 115 A2
Hockley Way DE55 159 A1
Hodder Cl DE4 156 C1
Hodge Beck Cl DE24 233 B3
Hodge Fold SK14 15 C4
Hodge La Ashover S45 128 C4
Broadbottom SK14 15 C4
Marchington ST14 224 A1
Hodmire La S44 133 C4
Hodthorpe Cl DE21 206 A1
Hodthorpe Prim Sch S80 82 B3
Hogarth Cl NG9 223 C3
Hogarth Rd SK6 23 A4
Hogarth Rise S18 75 C4
Hogarth St NG3 268 C2
Hoggbarn La DE75,NG16 181 B3
Hoggs Field NG16 182 C1
Hogshaw Villas Rd 1 SK17 85 B4
Hoillant Sq DE6 175 C2
Holbeach Dr S40 114 C4
Holbeck Ave S44 99 B1
Holbeck Cl S41 266 C4
Holbeck La S80 101 B4
Holbeck St S80 81 B1
Holbein Cl S18 75 C4
Holborn Ave NG2 268 C1
Holborn Dr DE22 218 A4
Holborn View DE5 170 A1
Holbrook Ave
Mosborough S20 59 C4
North Wingfield S42 132 A4
Holbrook CE Prim Sch DE56 191 B4
Holbrook Centre For Autism DE56 191 B3
Holbrook Cl
Chesterfield S40 114 B4
Pleasley NG19 135 A3
Holbrook Dr S13 44 A4
Holbrook Gn S20 60 A4
Holbrook Pl S43 97 B3
Holbrook Rd
Belper DE56 178 C1
Derby DE24 233 A3
Sheffield S13 44 A4
Holbrook St DE75 182 A1
Holbrook View DE56 192 A4
Holbrook Way S42 132 A4
Holburn Ave S18 57 A1
Holcombe St DE23 219 A1
Holden Ave DE72 246 A4
Holden Ct 28 NG7 268 A2
Holden Gdns NG9 223 C3
Holden St
Mansfield NG18 268 B3
Nottingham NG7 268 A2
Holderness Cl DE24 231 B1
Holdings The DE11 256 A1
Holdon Croft DE12 260 B3
Holestone Gate Rd S45 129 B1
Holker Ave SK17 85 B4
Holkham Cl DE7 194 B2
Holland Cl DE55 146 C3
Holland Mdw NG10 236 B3
Holland Pl 8 S2 43 A4
Holland Rd
Chesterfield S41 76 C1
Sheffield S2 43 A4
Hollens Way S40 95 A3
Hollies Cl Clifton DE6 184 C3
Dronfield S18 76 B4
Newton Solney DE15 248 C4
Hollies Cres NG7 268 A1
Hollies Dr SK6 23 A3
Hollies Farm Cl DE73 244 C2
Hollies La DE6 198 B2
Hollies Rd DE22 204 B2
Hollies The
Eastwood NG16 182 C1
Repton DE65 243 A1
Sandiacre NG10 223 A3
Hollin Cl S41 95 B4
Hollin Cross La SK13 17 B4
Hollin Dr SK23 47 A3
Hollin Hill S43 81 A2
Hollindale Dr S12 44 B3
Hollington Cl 6 DE21 219 C4
Hollingwood Cres S43 78 A1
Hollingwood Prim Sch S43 78 A1
Hollingworth Ave NG10 223 A2
Hollingworth Prim Sch SK14 9 B3
Hollinhey Terr SK14 9 B3
Hollins Ave SK17 85 A4
Hollins Bank SK13 9 B1
Hollins Cl SK13 9 B1
Hollins Gdns SK13 9 B1
Hollins Head S8 43 A2
Hollins Ind Pk SK13 10 A3
Hollins La Crich DE4 157 A2
Marple SK6 23 B4
Hollins Mews SK13 9 B1
Hollins Mt SK6 23 A4
Hollins Spring Ave S18 76 A4
Hollins Spring Rd S18 76 A4
Hollins St SK17 85 A3
Hollins The DE4 156 A3
Hollins Wood Cl DE4 156 A3
Hollinsclough CE Prim Sch SK17 104 B1
Hollinsclough Rake SK17 104 A1
Hollinsend S12 44 A2
Hollinsend Ave S12 44 B3
Hollinsend Pl S12 44 B3
Hollinsend Rd S12 44 A3
Hollinsmoor Rd SK6,SK22 24 B4
Hollinwood Rd
Disley SK12 32 B3
Marple SK6 23 A1
Hollis La Chesterfield S41 266 C2
Denstone ST14 196 A3
Hollis St DE24 233 A4
Hollow Cres DE15 248 B2
Hollow Gate S33 51 A4

Hollow La
Burton u T DE15 ....248 B2
Mayfield DE6 ....172 B1
Mosborough S20 ....59 C3
Hollow of the Moor SK17 87 C2
Hollow Rd DE73 ....252 C1
Hollow Stone NG1 .....268 B1
Hollow The Bamford S33 ..40 A2
Castle Donington DE74 ...247 A2
Derby, Littleover DE23 ...231 B4
Derby, Mickleover DE3 ...230 B4
Holloway DE4 ....156 A3
Roston DE6 ....197 C3
Holloway Rd Derby DE24 232 C3
Duffield DE56 ....190 C2
Hollowford Rd S33 ......38 A2
Hollowford Training & Conference Ctr S33 ....38 A2
Hollowood Ave DE23 ....231 B4
Hollows The NG10 ......237 A4
Holly Ave Breaston DE72 .222 C1
Ripley DE5 ....180 B4
Holly Bank Glossop SK13 ..17 C4
Hollingworth SK14 ....9 B3
Holly Bank Ct DE4 .....156 C1
Holly Brook Way DE4 ...230 C3
Holly Bush La DE56 ....191 A4
Holly Cl Ashbourne DE6 .185 B4
Draycott DE72 ....235 A4
Killamarsh S21 ....60 B3
Holly Ct Aston-on-T DE72 .246 A4
Derby DE3 ....217 B1
Mansfield NG19 ....136 C1
Woodville DE11 ....256 C1
Holly Gdns S12 ....44 B3
Holly Gn DE15 ....254 C4
Holly Gr Sheffield S12 ...44 B3
Swanwick DE55 ....169 C4
Holly Hill Rd NG16 ....171 C3
Holly House Sch S41 ....77 A2
Holly La
Alderwasley DE56 ....167 B2
Tansley DE4 ....144 C4
Holly Rd Kimberley NG16 .195 C4
Mansfield NG19 ....136 C1
Uttoxeter ST14 ....210 A1
Holly St DE15 ....254 C4
Hollybank Ave S12 ......44 B3
Hollybank Cl Sheffield S12 44 B3
Swadlincote DE11 ....256 C4
Hollybank Cres
Sheffield S12 ....44 B3
Stoke-on-T ST4 ....269 B1
Hollybank Dr S12 ....44 B3
Hollybank Rd S12 ....44 B3
Hollybank Way S12 ......44 B3
Hollybrook Way DE23 ...230 C3
Hollybush Cl DE12 .....264 C4
Hollyhock Way DE14 ...253 C3
Hollyhouse Dr DE55 ....160 A3
Hollyhurst La DE6 ......212 A3
Hollyhurst Row DE55 ...170 C3
Hollymoor Dr DE73 ......232 C1
Hollythorpe Cl S41 .....115 B4
Hollythorpe Cres S8 ....43 A2
Hollythorpe Rd S8 ......43 A2
Hollythorpe Rise S8 ....43 A2
Hollywell Ave DE5 ......181 A4
Hollywell Prim Sch
NG16 ....195 C4
Hollywood Rd SK6 ....23 C4
Holm Ave DE21 ....205 A4
Holm Cl S18 ....56 B1
Holm La DE55 ....158 A2
Holme Bank DE6 ....184 B4
Holme Cl Hatton DE65 ...227 B1
Holloway DE4 ....156 A3
Ilkeston DE7 ....194 B1
Holme Croft DE7 ....207 C4
Holme Farm Ave DE15 ..254 C4
Holme Hall Cres S40 ....95 A3
Holme Hall Prim Sch
S40 ....95 A3
Holme Lea [2] NG10 ....223 A3
Holme Park Ave S41 ....95 B4
Holme Rd Chesterfield S41 96 A3
Matlock Bath DE4 ....143 A4
Holme Woods La HD7 .....2 C1
Holmebank Cl S40 ....95 C2
Holmebank E S40 ....95 C2
Holmebank View S40 .....95 C2
Holmebank W S40 ....95 C2
Holmebrook View S41 ....95 B3
Holmefield Cres DE7 ....209 A4
Holmefield Rd S80 ....82 A3
Holmes Cl NG16 ....182 A2
Holmes Cl DE11 ....256 A3
Holmes Rd DE72 ....235 B4
Holmes St Derby DE23 ...219 A1
Heanor DE75 ....181 B1
Holmesdale Cl S18 ....57 B2
Holmesdale Rd S18 ......57 B2
Holmesfield Cl DE4 .....144 A3
Holmesfield Dr
Derby DE3 ....217 C1
Shipley DE75 ....194 A4
Holmesfield Rd S18 .....56 A1
Holmewood Bsns Pk
S42 ....116 B1
Holmewood Rd NG16 ....195 A4
Holmewood Ind Est
S42 ....132 C4
Holmewood Ind Pk S42 116 B1

Holmfield Buxton SK17 ...84 C3
Derby DE23 ....231 C4
Holmgate Prim Sch
S45 ....131 A2
Holmgate Rd S42 ....130 C2
Holmley Bank S18 ....57 A2
Holmley La S18 ....57 A2
Holmoak Cl DE21 ....206 A2
Holmshaw Dr S13 ....44 C4
Holmshaw Gr S13 ....44 C4
Holmwood Terr [2] SK17 ..85 B4
Holrold Ho DE24 ....219 B1
Holroyd Ave NG2 ....268 C1
Holt Ave DE24 ....233 B3
Holt Dr DE4 ....142 C4
Holt La Holloway DE4 ...156 A4
Matlock DE4 ....143 A3
Holt Rd DE4 ....127 C1
Holt's La DE13 ....239 A3
Holtlands Dr DE24 .....232 C3
Holy Rosary RC Prim Sch
DE15 ....248 A2
Holy Trinity CE Prim Sch
DE4 ....155 A4
Holyhead Dr DE21 ......206 A2
Holymoor Rd S42 ....113 C4
Holyoake Ave S13 ....44 C4
Holyoake Dr NG10 ......236 C4
Holyrood Cl DE21 ......221 A3
Holywell DE45 ....109 B3
Holywell La DE45 ......125 A3
Holywell Rd DE7 ....194 B2
Holywell St S41 ....266 B3
Home Farm Cl DE21 ....221 B3
Home Farm Ct DE11 ....255 B1
Home Farm Dr DE22 ....205 A2
Home Fm Ct NG16 ......171 B3
Homecroft Dr NG16 ....171 C1
Homefields Prim Sch
DE73 ....232 C1
Homeport Mews S41 ....266 B4
Homer Dr SK6 ....23 A4
Homestead Cl DE56 ....179 A1
Homestead Rd SK12 .....32 B3
Homestead Way SK23 ....47 B3
Honeycroft Cl DE56 ....179 A1
Honeycroft Ct DE55 ....160 A2
Honeyfield Dr DE5 .....180 C4
Honeysuckle Cl DE11 ...256 A3
Honeysuckle View
DE15 ....255 A4
Honeywall DE4 ....269 B2
Honeywall Ho ST4 .....269 B2
Honeywall La DE6 ......183 C4
Honingham Rd DE7 .....194 B2
Hook La ST14 ....210 A3
Hoole St S41 ....115 B4
Hooley Cl NG10 ....236 A3
Hooley St NG16 ....171 C3
Hoon Rd DE65 ....239 B4
Hoonwell La DE6 ......175 C3
Hooton St NG3 ....268 C2
Hop Inge The S26 ......61 C3
Hope Ave DE3 ....217 B1
Hope Dr NG7 ....268 A1
Hope Prim Sch S33 ......39 A2
Hope Rd S33 ....39 B1
Hope St Chesterfield S40 .95 C2
Derby DE1 ....267 C2
Glossop SK13 ....10 C1
[10] Ilkeston DE7 ....208 C4
Mansfield NG18 ....268 C3
Melbourne DE73 ....252 A4
Hope Terr DE4 ....143 A1
Hope Valley Coll S33 ...38 C2
Hopedale Rd S12 ....44 B2
Hopefield Ave S12 ......44 B2
Hopetoun St DE23 .....232 A4
Hopewell Rd DE4 ......143 B3
Hopewell Wlk DE7 .....194 C3
Hopkins Ct NG16 ......182 C2
Hopmeadow Way DE15 .248 A1
Hopping Hill DE56 .....190 C4
Hopping Hill Terr E
DE56 ....191 A4
Hopping Hill Terr W
DE56 ....191 A4
Hopping La DE45 ......125 A2
Hopton Cl Derby DE21 ..206 A1
Ripley DE5 ....169 C1
Hoptonwood Cl DE4 ....154 B2
Hopwell Rd DE72 ......222 A1
Horace Ave NG9 ....223 B3
Hordern Cl SK13 ....10 C1
Horderns La SK23 ....47 A3
Horderns Park Rd SK23 .47 A3
Horderns Rd SK23 ....47 A3
Horeston Cotts DE7 ....192 A4
Hornbeam Cl
Derby DE21 ....205 C1
Ilkeston DE7 ....209 A4
Hornbeams The [2]
ST14 ....210 A1
Hornby Row ST4 ....269 B2
Horncastle Rd DE21 ....205 B1
Horner Rd [11] S7 ....43 A4
Hornscroft Rd S44 ......99 A1
Hornsea Rd DE21 ......205 B1
Hornthorpe Rd S21 ......59 B1
Horridge St DE7 ....194 C2
Horse Fair Ave SK23 ....47 A3
Horse Shoes The DE74 ..247 B2
Horsecroft Cl DE7 .....194 B1
Horsehead La DE4 ....99 B1
Horseshoe Ave SK17 ....47 C1
Horsewood Rd S40 .....114 A4

Horsley CE Prim Sch
DE21 ....191 C3
Horsley Cl S40 ....95 A3
Horsley Cres
Holbrook DE56 ....191 B4
Langley Mill NG16 ......182 A2
Horsley La DE21 ....191 C3
Horsley Rd DE21,DE56 ..191 C3
Horsley Woodhouse Prim Sch
DE7 ....192 B3
Horsleygate La S18 ......74 C4
Horsleygate Rd S17,S18 .74 A4
Horton Cl
[28] Mosborough S20 ....59 C4
Swanwick DE55 ....169 C4
Horton Dr S20 ....59 C4
Horton St DE23 ....219 B1
Horwood Ave DE23 .....218 B1
Hoselett Field Rd NG10 236 C3
Hospital La DE3 ....230 A4
Hoten Rd NG2 ....268 C1
Houfton Cres S44 ....98 C2
Houfton Rd S44 ....98 C2
Houghton Ave DE7 .....194 B2
Houghton Cl SK22 ....25 B1
Houghton Ct DE21 .....205 C1
Houldsworth Cres S44 ...98 C1
Houldsworth Dr S41 .....96 C1
Hoult St DE22 ....218 B2
Houndkirk Rd S11 ....54 B4
Hounds Gate NG7 ......268 B1
Hounslow Rd DE22 .....218 A3
Houston Cl DE21 ....220 A3
Hoveton Cl DE24 ....232 B2
How La S33 ....38 B2
Howard Cl Glossop SK13 .10 A1
[11] Long Eaton NG10 ....223 C1
Howard Ct [1] NG7 ....268 A2
Howard Dr
Chesterfield S41 ....77 A1
North Wingfield S42 ....131 C3
Howard Rd NG19 ....268 A4
Howard St Derby DE23 ..218 C1
Glossop SK13 ....10 B1
Nottingham NG1 ....268 B2
Howards Mdw SK13 .....17 A4
Howarth Cl NG10 ......236 A4
Howden Cl Derby DE3 ...217 B1
Staveley S43 ....78 C1
Howden Rd SK22 ....24 B1
Howe St DE22 ....218 B3
Howells Pl S43 ....79 A2
Howitt Cres ST14 ......210 A1
Howitt St Heanor DE75 ..181 C1
Long Eaton NG10 ....236 C4
Howth Cl DE21 ....220 A2
Hoylake Ave S40 ....114 B4
Hoylake Cl NG19 ......136 C3
Hoylake Ct DE3 ....217 B2
Hoylake Dr DE3 ....217 B2
Hoyland Ct DE56 ......179 C3
Hubert Shaw Cl DE24 ..232 C2
Huckerby Rd DE7 ......194 B1
Hucklow Ave
Chesterfield S40 ....266 A1
North Wingfield S42 ....132 A4
Staveley S43 ....97 B4
Hucklow Ct DE21 ......206 A2
Hucklow Fold [9] SK13 ...9 B1
Hucknall Ave S40 ....95 B2
Hudson Cl S26 ....61 C4
Hudson Mount S44 .....118 A4
Hudson St NG3 ....268 C2
Hudson Way DE24 ......219 B2
Hufton's Ct DE75 ......194 A4
Hufton's Dr DE75 ......194 A4
Hugh La S33 ....51 A4
Hugh St SK13 ....10 A1
Hulland CE Prim Sch
DE6 ....175 C2
Hulland St DE1 ....267 D1
Hulland View DE22 ....204 B1
Hulme St ST4 ....269 A2
Humber Cl DE24 ....233 B3
Humber Rd NG10 ......223 B1
Humbleton Dr DE22 ....218 A3
Humphrey Rd S8 ....56 C4
Hundall La
Chesterfield S41 ....77 A2
Unstone S18 ....77 A2
Hunger La DE6 ....188 C2
Hungerhill La S42,S45 ..113 A2
Hungry La Bradwell S33 ..51 A3
Hathersage S32 ....53 A4
Hunloke Ave S40 ....95 C1
Hunloke Cres S40 ....95 C1
Hunloke Park Prim Sch
S42 ....115 A2
Hunloke Rd S42 ....132 C2
Hunloke View S42 ......115 A2
Hunsdon Rd S21 ....59 B2
Hunstone Ave S8 ....57 A4
Hunt Ave DE75 ....181 C1
Hunt La S45 ....145 A4
Hunter Dr DE56 ....191 C4
Hunter Rd DE56 ....179 B3
Hunter's La S13 ....44 B3
Hunters Croft DE24 ....231 C1
Hunters Dr ST4 ....269 A1
Hunters Gn SK23 ....34 C1
Hunters La SK13 ....16 C4
Hunters Way DE7 ......269 B1
Huntingdon Ave S44 ....99 A1
Huntingdon Ct DE73 ...252 A4
Huntingdon Dr
Castle Donington DE74 ..247 A2
Nottingham NG7 ....268 A1
Huntingdon Gn DE21 ...219 B3

Huntingdon Prim Sch
NG3 ....268 B2
Huntingdon Rd DE15 ...254 B4
Huntingdon St NG3 ....268 B2
Huntingdon Way [4]
NG9 ....223 C1
Huntingdon Wlk [4]
NG10 ....223 A3
Huntley Ave Derby DE21 .220 C3
Stoke-on-T ST4 ....269 B1
Huntley Cl S43 ....97 A4
Hunts La DE12 ....264 C4
Hunts Row DE55 ......157 C2
Huntsman Rd S43 ....78 C1
Huntspill Rd DE65 .....228 C1
Hurdlow Gn [14] SK13 ...9 B1
Hurdlow Mews [15] SK13 ..9 B1
Hurds Hollow DE4 .....143 A3
Hurker Rise DE4 ......143 B4
Hurl Dr S12 ....43 A3
Hurley Ct DE7 ....207 C4
Hurlfield Ave S12 ......44 A3
Hurlfield Ct S12 ....44 A3
Hurlfield Dr S12 ....44 A3
Hurlfield Hill S14 ......43 C3
Hurlfield Rd S12 ....43 C3
Hurst Dr Burton u T DE13 .240 C1
Stanley DE7 ....207 B3
Hurst La DE55 ....146 A3
Hurst Lea Rd SK22 ......33 B4
Hurst Rd SK13 ....10 C1
Hurst Rise DE4 ....143 B3
Hurstbrook Cl SK13 ....10 C1
Hurstclough La S32 .....40 B1
Huss's La NG10 ....236 C4
Hutchings Cres S43 .....80 B3
Hutchinson Gn [12] NG3 268 B2
Huthwaite La DE55 ....148 B1
Hutmoor Butts DE45 ...107 A2
Hutton St Derby DE24 ..232 C3
Nottingham NG2 ....268 C1
Huxley Cl DE23 ....231 C4
Hyde Bank Ct SK22 ......33 B4
Hyde Bank Rd SK22 .....33 B4
Hyde Park Rd DE22 ....218 A3
Hyde Rd SK14 ....9 A2
Hydro Cl DE45 ....91 C3
Hylton Cl DE14 ....254 A4
Hyndley Rd S44 ....98 C2

I

Ian Ave DE4 ....165 C4
Ians Way S40 ....95 B2
Ibbotsons Croft S32 .....53 A4
Ibsley Cl DE24 ....233 B3
Ida's Rd S21 ....59 B2
Ilam Cl S43 ....97 B3
Ilam Ct DE6 ....185 B4
Ilam Sq DE7 ....194 C3
Ilford Cl DE7 ....194 B2
Ilford Rd DE22 ....218 A3
Ilford Wlk DE22 ......218 A3
Ilion St NG19 ....135 C1
Ilkeston Com Hospl
DE7 ....194 B2
Ilkeston Rd Heanor DE75 193 C2
Nottingham NG7 ....268 A2
Sandiacre DE7,NG9 ....223 B2
Smalley DE7 ....192 C1
Stanton-by-D DE7 ......208 C2
Stapleford NG9 ....209 C1
Trowell NG9 ....209 B3
Ilkeston Sch DE7 ......208 B4
Immingham Gr S43 ......78 B1
Imperial Ct DE22 ......204 B3
Imperial Rd DE4 ......143 A3
Inchwood Cl [7] NG9 ...223 C1
Independent Hill DE55 ..158 C2
Industrial St [8] DE23 ..219 A1
Infirmary Rd S41 ......266 C4
Ingestre Rd ST17 ......269 B3
Ingham Dr DE3 ....230 B4
Ingham Rd NG10 ......223 B1
Ingle Cl DE21 ....220 C3
Ingle's Channel [7] DE56 178 C2
Ingleborough Gdns [8]
NG10 ....236 A4
Ingleby Ave DE23 ......231 C4
Ingleby Cl
[16] Dronfield S18 ....56 B1
Swadlincote DE11 ....256 A2
Ingleby La DE73 ....251 A3
Ingleby Rd
Barrow-u-T DE73 ....244 B2
Long Eaton NG10 ......235 C2
Ingledew Cl DE21 .....205 C1
Inglefield Rd DE7 .....209 A3
Ingleton Rd S41 ....115 A4
Inglewood ST17 ....269 A3
Inglewood Ave DE3 ....217 B2
Inglis St ST4 ....269 C2
Ingliston Cl [10] DE24 ..233 B3
Inkerman Rd NG16 ....171 C3
Inkerman St NG16 .....171 C3
Inkersall Dr S20 ....59 C4
Inkersall Green Rd S43 ..97 A4
Inkersall Prim Sch S43 ..97 A4
Inkersall Rd S43 ....97 C4
Inn La DE22 ....204 A4
Inns La DE55 ....157 C2
Institute La DE55 ......159 A2
Instow Dr DE23 ....231 B3
Instow Rise NG3 ......268 B2
Intake Ave NG18 ......268 A3

Intake Farm Fst Sch
NG19 ....268 A4
Intake La Bakewell DE45 109 C2
Cromford DE4 ....155 A3
Holloway DE4 ....155 C2
Intake Prim Sch S12 ....44 A3
Intake Rd S44 ....98 C2
Intakes La DE56 ....188 B4
Inverary Cl DE24 ......231 C2
Invernia Cl DE24 ......231 C3
Iona Cl Derby DE24 ....231 C2
Tibshelf DE55 ....147 C3
Iona Dr NG9 ....209 B1
Ireland Cl S43 ....78 C1
Ireland Ind Est S43 .....97 C4
Ireland St S43 ....78 C1
Ireton St NG7 ....268 A2
Iron Cliff Rd S44 ....98 C2
Iron Gate DE1 ....267 B3
Irongate S40 ....266 B3
Ironside Cl S14 ....43 B2
Ironside Pl S14 ....43 B2
Ironside Rd S14 ....43 B2
Ironside Wlk S14 ....43 B1
Ironville & Codnor Park Prim Sch NG16 ....170 C2
Ironwalls La DE13 .....239 B3
Irvine Cl DE24 ....231 B2
Irving Pl DE24 ....232 C4
Isaac's La NG9 ....223 B4
Isabella St NG1 ....268 B1
Island The NG16 ......182 C1
Islay Cl NG9 ....209 B2
Islay Rd DE24 ....231 C2
Isleworth Dr DE22 .....217 C3
Ismay Rd DE21 ....219 C3
Ivan Brook Cl [17] S18 ..56 B1
Ivanhoe Cl S42 ....115 B1
Ivanhoe Ct [3] S41 .....96 C1
Ivatt Dr NG2 ....268 C1
Iveagh Wlk DE55 ......170 C3
Ivonbrook Cl DE4 .....142 A4
Ivy Cl Chesterfield S41 ..77 A1
Donisthorpe DE12 ......262 C1
Willington DE65 ....242 A3
Ivy Ct Derby DE3 ......217 B1
Egginton DE65 ....241 A3
Hilton DE65 ....228 B1
Sheffield S8 ....43 B1
Ivy Gr DE5 ....169 B1
Ivy House Specl Sch
DE23 ....219 B1
Ivy La Eastwood NG16 ..182 C1
Elton DE4 ....140 C3
Ivy Lodge Cl DE15 .....254 C4
Ivy Spring Cl S42 ......115 A2
Ivy Sq DE23 ....219 B1
Ivycroft SK13 ....9 C2
Ivyside Cl S21 ....60 B3
Ivyside Gdns S21 ....60 B3

J

Jack Ashley Ct ST4 ....269 C1
Jack's La ST14 ....224 C1
Jackass La DE56 ....167 A2
Jacklin Cl DE14 ....254 A3
Jacksdale Cl DE22 .....204 B1
Jacksdale Prim Sch
NG16 ....171 A2
Jackson Ave Derby DE3 .218 A1
Ilkeston DE7 ....208 C4
Sandiacre NG10 ....223 A3
Tupton S42 ....131 B4
Jackson Cl DE12 ......262 C4
Jackson Rd
Bramley-Vale S44 ......117 C1
Clay Cross S45 ....131 C2
Matlock DE4 ....143 A3
Jackson St Derby DE22 .218 C2
Glossop SK13 ....17 B4
Glossop, Padfield SK13 ...10 B3
Mottram in L SK14 ......9 A2
Jackson Tor Rd DE4 ...143 A3
Jackson's La
Heage DE56 ....179 B4
Ripley DE5 ....180 B4
Jacksons Edge Rd SK12 .32 A3
Jacksons La Belper DE56 190 C4
Etwall DE65 ....229 B1
Jackys La S26 ....61 C3
Jacobean Ct DE15 .....248 B2
Jagger's La S32 ....52 C4
Jaggers La DE4,S45 ....128 C3
Jago Ave S43 ....81 A2
James Andrew Cl S8 ....56 C4
James Andrew Cres S8 ..56 C4
James Andrew Croft S8 .56 C4
James Ave DE55 ....170 B4
James Cl DE1 ....218 C3
James St Chesterfield S41 .96 A3
[3] Glossop SK13 ....17 B4
Kimberley NG16 ....195 C3
Somercotes DE55 ......170 B4
Stoke-on-T ST4 ....269 B1
Swadlincote DE11 ......256 B3
James's La DE6 ....215 B1
Jane La SK23 ....34 A1
Jap La DE45 ....110 C4
Jardine Ct DE72 ......235 A4
Jardines La ST14 ......196 B2
Jarnett The SK17 ......107 A4
Jarvey's La DE22 ......217 C4
Jarvis Ct DE24 ....231 C1
Jarvis Rd DE24 ....231 C1
Jasmin Cl NG20 ....119 B3

Jasmine Cl
Burton u T DE15 . . . . . . .255 A4
Derby DE21 . . . . .220 A3
Swanwick DE55 . . . . . . .169 C4
Jasmine Ct DE75 . . . . . . .182 A1
Jasmine Dr DE55 . . . . . . .148 A4
Jaspers La DE4 . . . . .153 A1
Jaunty Ave S12 . . . . .44 B2
Jaunty Cl S12 . . . . .44 A2
Jaunty Cres S12 . . . . .44 A2
Jaunty Dr S12 . . . . .44 A2
Jaunty La S12 . . . . .44 A2
Jaunty Mount S12 . . . . . . .44 A2
Jaunty Pl S12 . . . . .44 B2
Jaunty Rd S12 . . . . .44 B2
Jaunty View S12 . . . . .44 A2
Jaunty Way S12 . . . . .44 A2
Jaw Bones Hill S40 . . . . . .115 A4
Jawbone La DE73 . . . . . . .252 B4
Jebb Gdns S40 . . . . .95 B1
Jebb's La
Idridgehay DE56 . . . . . .176 C4
Shottle DE56 . . . . .177 A4
Jedburgh Cl Derby DE24 231 C1
Nottingham NG3 . . . . . . .268 B2
Jefferson Pl DE24 . . . . . . .232 C4
Jeffery St S2 . . . . .43 A3
Jeffrey La S33 . . . . .51 A3
Jeffries Ave DE4 . . . . .156 C1
Jeffries La DE4 . . . . .156 C1
Jellicoe St NG20 . . . . . . .101 A1
Jemison Cl DE23 . . . . . . .230 C4
Jenford St DE18 . . . . .268 A3
Jennison St NG19 . . . . . . .136 A1
Jenny's Ct DE56 . . . . .179 B3
Jephson Rd DE14 . . . . . . .254 A4
Jepson Rd S41 . . . . .115 B4
Jeremy Cl ST4 . . . . .269 A1
Jermyn Ave S12 . . . . .44 C2
Jermyn Cl S12 . . . . .44 C2
Jermyn Cres S12 . . . . .44 C2
Jermyn Dr S12 . . . . .44 C2
Jermyn Way S12 . . . . .44 C2
Jerningham St ST16 . . . . .269 A4
Jersey Gdns NG3 . . . . . . .268 C2
Jersey Rd S2 . . . . .43 A4
Jervis Ct DE7 . . . . .194 C2
Jervis Pl S43 . . . . .97 A3
Jesses La DE56 . . . . .178 B4
Jessop Ave NG16 . . . . . . .170 C2
Jessop Dr DE24 . . . . .231 C1
Jessop St Codnor DE5 . . .181 A4
Ripley DE5 . . . . .181 A4
Jill Iain Ct NG9 . . . . .223 C3
Jinny Cl DE65 . . . . .239 B4
Joan Ave DE75 . . . . .181 C1
Joan La S33 . . . . .40 B2
Jodrell Ave DE56 . . . . . . .179 B2
Jodrell Mdw SK23 . . . . . . .45 C4
Jodrell Rd SK23 . . . . .45 B4
Jodrell St SK22 . . . . .33 A4
John Bank La DE45 . . . . . .108 C4
John Berrysford Cl
DE21 . . . . .219 C3
John Carroll Ct NG3 . . . . .268 C2
John Dalton St SK13 . . . . . .9 C3
John Davies Prim Sch
NG17 . . . . .148 C2
John Duncan Sch SK17 . . .66 A1
John Eaton's Almshouses
S8 . . . . .43 A1
John F Kennedy Gdns
DE21 . . . . .220 B3
John Flamsteed Com Sch
DE5 . . . . .180 A1
John Kennedy Rd SK14 . . . .9 A2
John King Inf Sch NG16 160 B2
John King Workshop Mus ★
NG16 . . . . .160 B2
John Lombe Dr DE1 . . . . .219 A4
John O'Gaunts Way
DE56 . . . . .179 B2
John of Rolleston Prim Sch
DE13 . . . . .240 B2
John Port Cl DE65 . . . . . .229 B2
John Port Sch DE65 . . . . .229 A2
John St Alfreton DE55 . . . .159 A4
Brimington S43 . . . . .96 C4
Chesterfield S40 . . . . . . .95 C2
Clay Cross S45 . . . . .131 B2
Clowne S43 . . . . .80 B2
Compstall SK6 . . . . .15 A2
Creswell S80 . . . . .81 C1
Derby DE1 . . . . .267 C2
Eckington S21 . . . . .59 B2
Glossop SK13 . . . . .17 B4
Heanor DE75 . . . . .181 B4
Ilkeston DE7 . . . . .194 C1
Marple SK6 . . . . .23 A3
Matlock DE4 . . . . .143 A3
North Wingfield S42 . . . .131 C4
Somercotes DE55 . . . . . .170 B4
Stafford ST16 . . . . .269 C4
Swadlincote DE11 . . . . . .255 C4
Swadlincote, Albert Village
DE11 . . . . .256 B1
Swadlincote, Lower Medway
DE11 . . . . .256 B3
John Turner Rd DE4 . . . .127 B2
John Woodhead Ct
NG19 . . . . .268 A4
Johnnygate La S18 . . . . . .75 A2
Johnson Ave DE24 . . . . . .232 C4
Johnson Dr DE75 . . . . . . .181 C1
Johnson La
Idridgehay DE56 . . . . . .176 C4
Monyash DE45 . . . . .107 C3
Johnson Rd ST14 . . . . . . .210 A1

Johnson St SK23 . . . . .45 C4
Johnson Way SK23 . . . . . . .47 B3
Johnstone Cl S40 . . . . . . .266 A1
Jolly La DE6 . . . . .175 A4
Jones St S13 . . . . .10 A3
Jordan Ave DE13 . . . . . . .240 C1
Jordan St S13 . . . . .10 C1
Jordanthorpe Gn S8 . . . . . .57 B3
Jordanthorpe Parkway
S8 . . . . .57 B3
Jordanthorpe View S8 . . . . .57 B4
Joseph Fletcher Dr S42 114 C1
Joseph St Belper DE56 . . .178 C2
Derby DE23 . . . . .219 A1
Eckington S21 . . . . .59 B2
Marple SK6 . . . . .23 A3
Joseph Wright Terr
DE1 . . . . .267 B2
Joyce Ave NG9 . . . . .223 C2
Jubalton Cl DE24 . . . . . . .232 C3
Jubilee Ave DE5 . . . . .169 B1
Jubilee Cl DE73 . . . . .252 A4
Jubilee Cotts S44 . . . . . . .97 A1
Jubilee Ct Clowne S43 . . .81 A2
Whitwell S80 . . . . .81 C3
Jubilee Ct Belper DE56 . . .179 A1
Wirksworth DE4 . . . . . . .165 C4
Jubilee Gdns
New Mills SK22 . . . . .33 B4
Whitwell S80 . . . . .81 C3
Jubilee Pl S80 . . . . .81 C3
Jubilee Rd
Chapel-en-le-F SK23 . . . .47 A3
Derby DE24 . . . . .232 C2
Whitwell S80 . . . . .81 C3
Jubilee Sq DE6 . . . . .184 B4
Jubilee St
Kimberley NG16 . . . . . . .195 C4
New Mills SK22 . . . . .33 B4
Nottingham NG2 . . . . . . .268 C1
Jubilee Terr DE12 . . . . . . .262 C1
Judith Gr ST4 . . . . .269 C1
Judson Ave NG9 . . . . .223 C2
Judy Hill DE4 . . . . .127 C1
Julia Cres DE55 . . . . .146 C2
Julian Cl DE7 . . . . .209 A3
Julie Ave DE75 . . . . .182 A1
Jumble Rd S11 . . . . .42 C1
Junction Rd NG10 . . . . . . .237 A3
Junction St DE1 . . . . .218 C2
Juniper Ct NG16 . . . . .195 B4
Juniper Rise S21 . . . . .60 B3
Jura Ave DE5 . . . . .169 B1
Jury St DE1 . . . . .267 A3

K

Katherine Dr NG9 . . . . . . .223 C2
Katrine Wlk DE24 . . . . . . .231 C3
Kay Dr DE11 . . . . .255 C3
Kean Pl DE24 . . . . .232 C4
Kearsley Rd S2 . . . . .43 A4
Keary St ST4 . . . . .269 B1
Keats Ave DE55 . . . . .218 A1
Keats Dr DE11 . . . . .256 B3
Keats Rd Chesterfield S41 .95 C4
Stonebroom DE55 . . . . . .146 C2
Keats Way S42 . . . . .115 C2
Keats Wlk DE55 . . . . .146 C2
Keble Cl Burton u T DE15 .248 B1
Derby DE1 . . . . .267 C1
Kedleston Cl
Burton u T DE13 . . . . . .240 B1
Chesterfield S41 . . . . . . .95 B3
Derby DE22 . . . . .204 B3
Long Eaton NG10 . . . . . .236 A3
Ripley DE5 . . . . .169 B2
Kedleston Ct
Staveley S43 . . . . .78 C1
Tibshelf DE55 . . . . .148 A3
Kedleston Dr DE7 . . . . . . .194 B2
Kedleston Gdns DE1 . . . . .267 A4
Kedleston Hall ★ DE22 . .203 C3
Kedleston Old Rd DE22 . .218 B4
Kedleston Rd Buxton SK17 85 B4
Quarndon DE22 . . . . . . .204 A3
Weston Underwood DE22 .203 C4
Kedleston St DE1 . . . . . . .267 A4
Kedlestone Cl NG17 . . . . .148 C1
Keeling La DE4 . . . . .126 A1
Keepers La S18 . . . . .75 C2
Kegworth Ave DE23 . . . . .231 B3
Keilder Ct S40 . . . . .95 B1
Kelburn Ave S40 . . . . .95 B1
Keldeston Cl S41 . . . . .95 B4
Keldholme La DE24 . . . . .233 B3
Kelgate S20 . . . . .59 B3
Kelham Gn NG3 . . . . .268 C2
Kelham Rd NG19 . . . . . . .268 A4
Kelham Way NG16 . . . . . .182 C2
Kelmoor Rd DE24 . . . . . . .233 A4
Kelsons Ave S17 . . . . .85 B3
Kelstedge La S45 . . . . . . .129 B3
Kelvedon Dr S42 . . . . .231 A3
Kelvedon Gdns NG3 . . . . .268 C2
Kelvin Cl NG9 . . . . .223 B3
Kemble Pl DE24 . . . . .232 C4
Kemp Cl S21 . . . . .60 B3
Kemp Rd SK6 . . . . .23 A2
Kempton Cl NG16 . . . . . . .195 C4
Kempton Park Rd DE24 .232 B4
Kempton Rd DE15 . . . . . .248 A2
Kendal Cl SK17 . . . . .85 B2
Kendal Dr S18 . . . . .56 C1
Kendal Rd S41 . . . . .95 C4

Kendal Wlk DE21 . . . . . . .205 B1
Kendon Ave DE23 . . . . . . .231 C3
Kendray St S43 . . . . .79 B3
Kendricks Cl DE11 . . . . . .257 A4
Kenilworth Ave DE23 . . . . .231 C4
Kenilworth Ct
Chesterfield S41 . . . . . . .96 A3
Nottingham NG7 . . . . . . .268 A1
Kenilworth Dr DE7 . . . . . .208 B3
Kenilworth Rd
Nottingham NG7 . . . . . . .268 A1
Ripley DE5 . . . . .169 B1
Kenmere Cl S45 . . . . .131 B1
Kenmore Cl NG19 . . . . . . .268 A3
Kenmore Gdns NG3 . . . . .268 C2
Kennack Cl DE55 . . . . . . .160 B3
Kennedy Cl
Long Eaton NG10 . . . . . .236 B3
Mansfield Woodhouse
NG19 . . . . .136 B2
Kennedy Dr NG9 . . . . . . .209 C1
Kennet Paddock NG19 .136 B2
Kennet Vale S40 . . . . .95 B3
Kennett Gr SK17 . . . . .84 C3
Kenning St S45 . . . . .131 B2
Kenninghall Cl S2 . . . . . . .43 B4
Kenninghall Dr S2 . . . . . . .43 B4
Kenninghall Pl S2 . . . . . . .43 B4
Kenninghall Rd S2 . . . . . . .43 B4
Kensal Rise DE22 . . . . . . .218 A3
Kensington Ave DE75 . . . .181 B1
Kensington Cl NG19 . . . . .136 C3
Kensington Gdns DE7 . . .208 C4
Kensington Jun Sch
DE7 . . . . .209 A4
Kensington Rd
Burton u T DE15 . . . . . .248 B1
Sandiacre NG10 . . . . . . .223 A2
Kensington St
Derby DE1 . . . . .267 A3
Ilkeston DE7 . . . . .208 C3
Kent Ave NG16 . . . . .171 A2
Kent House Cl S12 . . . . . . .58 C4
Kent Rd Burton u T DE15 .254 C3
Eastwood NG16 . . . . . . .195 B4
Glossop SK13 . . . . .10 B1
Sheffield S8 . . . . .43 A3
Kent St Chesterfield S41 .115 B4
Derby DE21 . . . . .219 B4
Nottingham NG1 . . . . . . .268 B2
Kent's Bank Rd SK17 . . . .85 B3
Kentmere Cl S18 . . . . .56 C1
Kentwood Rd NG2 . . . . . .268 C1
Kenwell Dr S17 . . . . .56 A3
Kenyon Rd S41 . . . . .96 C1
Keppel Ct DE7 . . . . .194 C2
Kepple Gate DE5 . . . . . . .180 C4
Kernel Cl DE23 . . . . .231 A4
Kerry Dr DE7 . . . . .192 C3
Kerry St DE21 . . . . .219 B4
Kerry's Yd DE56 . . . . .191 C4
Kershaw St S13 . . . . .17 B4
Kershope Dr DE21 . . . . . .206 A2
Kerwin Cl S17 . . . . .55 B4
Kerwin Dr S17 . . . . .55 B4
Kerwin Rd S17 . . . . .55 B4
Kestrel Cl Burnaston DE3 230 A4
Ilkeston DE7 . . . . .208 C2
Killamarsh S21 . . . . .60 A4
Marple SK6 . . . . .23 A2
Kestrel Ct DE24 . . . . .231 C1
Kestrel Dr S21 . . . . .59 A2
Kestrel Hts NG16 . . . . . . .170 C2
Kestrel Way DE55 . . . . . . .148 B2
Kestrels Croft DE24 . . . . .231 C2
Keswick Ave DE23 . . . . . .231 C3
Keswick Cl Bolsover S44 . .98 C1
Ilkeston DE7 . . . . .208 B3
Keswick Ct NG10 . . . . . . .223 A1
Keswick Dr S41 . . . . .95 B4
Keswick Pl S18 . . . . .56 B1
Keswick Rd S42 . . . . .268 C1
Ketton Ave S8 . . . . .43 A2
Kevin Cl DE21 . . . . .220 A4
Kew Cres Heanor DE75 . .182 A1
Sheffield S12 . . . . .44 A1
Kew Gdns DE22 . . . . .218 A3
Key St NG3 . . . . .268 C2
Keyhaven Cl DE21 . . . . . .219 B4
Keynsham Cl DE24 . . . . . .232 C4
Keys Rd DE55 . . . . .159 A1
Keys St DE1 . . . . .267 C4
Keyworth Cl NG19 . . . . . .268 A4
Kibworth Cl
Chesterfield S41 . . . . . . .115 B4
Derby DE21 . . . . .220 A4
Kidd Rd SK13 . . . . .17 C3
Kidsley Cl S40 . . . . .95 A3
Kilbourn St NG1 . . . . .268 B2
Kilbourne Rd DE56 . . . . . .179 B2
Kilburn Dr DE7 . . . . .194 B2
Kilburn Inf & Jun Schs
DE56 . . . . .191 C4
Kilburn La DE56 . . . . .179 C2
Kilburn Rd S18 . . . . .56 B1
Kilburn Toll Bar DE56 . . . .179 C1
Kilburn Way DE11 . . . . . . .255 C3
Kilby Ho NG10 . . . . .236 C4
Kildale Gdns S20 . . . . .59 B4
Kildare Rd DE24 . . . . .220 A2
Kildonan Gr S12 . . . . .44 B2
Killamarsh Inf Sch S21 . . .60 C4
Killamarsh La S21,S26 . . .61 A3
Killingworth Ave DE24 . . .231 C2
Killis La Belper DE56 . . . .179 B1

Killis La continued
Holbrook DE56 . . . . .191 B4
Kilmory Fold SK13 . . . . . . .10 C2
Kiln Bent Rd HD9 . . . . .3 A3
Kiln Cl DE7 . . . . .193 C1
Kiln Croft DE65 . . . . .229 B2
Kiln Hill S18 . . . . .57 B2
Kiln La Glossop SK13 . . . .10 A3
Parwich DE6 . . . . .151 B2
Kiln Way DE11 . . . . .256 B2
Kilnsey Ct DE23 . . . . .230 C3
Kilverston Rd NG10 . . . . . .223 A3
Kilvington Ave S13 . . . . . . .44 A4
Kilvington Cres S13 . . . . . .44 A4
Kilvington Rd S13 . . . . . . .44 A4
Kimberley Cl NG16 . . . . . .195 C3
Kimberley Dr DE15 . . . . . .248 B2
Kimberley Prim Sch
NG16 . . . . .195 C3
Kimberley Rd DE72 . . . . .221 A1
Kinder Cl SK13 . . . . .17 A4
Kinder Cres DE56 . . . . . . .168 A3
Kinder Dr SK6 . . . . .23 A3
Kinder Gr S17 . . . . .85 A3
Kinder Rd Hayfield SK22 . .25 C1
Staveley S43 . . . . .97 A3
Kinder Row S22 . . . . .25 C1
Kinder View S22 . . . . .33 B4
Kinder Way S17 . . . . .85 C4
Kinder Wlk DE22 . . . . . . .218 C2
Kinderlee Way SK13 . . . . .16 A3
King Alfred St DE22 . . . . .267 A2
King Charles Ct S13 . . . . .17 B4
King Charles St NG1 268 C1
King Ecgbert Lower Sch
S17 . . . . .55 B3
King Ecgbert Rd S17 . . . . .55 C3
King Ecgbert Upper Sch
S17 . . . . .55 C3
King Edward Ave SK13 . . .10 B1
King Edward Fst Sch
NG18 . . . . .268 C3
King Edward Gdns
NG10 . . . . .223 A3
King Edward St
Nottingham NG1 . . . . . . .268 B2
Sandiacre NG10 . . . . . . .223 A3
Shirebrook NG20 . . . . . . .119 C2
Wirksworth DE4 . . . . . . .166 A4
King Edward VI High Sch
ST17 . . . . .269 A3
King George Ave DE7 . . .208 C4
King George St
Wessington DE55 . . . . . .157 C4
Wirksworth DE4 . . . . . . .165 C4
King John's Arc
NG1 . . . . .268 B1
King St Alfreton DE55 . . . .158 C2
Ashbourne DE6 . . . . . . .173 B1
Bakewell DE45 . . . . .109 B3
Belper DE56 . . . . .178 C2
Brimington S43 . . . . .77 C1
Broadbottom SK14 . . . . .16 A4
Burton u T DE14 . . . . . .254 B4
Clay Cross S45 . . . . .131 B2
Clowne S43 . . . . .80 C2
Creswell S80 . . . . .81 C1
Creswell, Hodthorpe S80 . .82 B3
Derby DE1 . . . . .267 B4
Duffield DE56 . . . . .190 C2
Eastwood NG16 . . . . . . .182 C1
Glossop SK13 . . . . .17 B4
Hollingworth SK14 . . . . . .9 B3
Ilkeston DE7 . . . . .194 C1
Long Eaton NG10 . . . . . .236 B4
Mansfield NG18 . . . . . . .268 C4
Mansfield Woodhouse
NG19 . . . . .136 B1
Market Warsop NG20 . . . .120 B3
Middleton (Nr Wirksworth)
DE4 . . . . .154 B3
Nottingham NG1 . . . . . . .268 B2
Pinxton NG16 . . . . .160 B2
South Normanton DE55 . .159 C3
Tibshelf DE55 . . . . .148 A4
King St S S40 . . . . .115 A4
King William Ctr NG16 . .170 C2
King William St NG16 . . . .170 C2
King's Cl S17 . . . . .85 B4
King's Mead Cl DE1 . . . . .267 A4
King's Mead Wlk DE1 . . . .267 A4
King's Mills La DE72 . . . .245 C3
King's Pl NG1 . . . . .268 B1
King's Rd S17 . . . . .85 B4
King's Wlk NG1 . . . . .268 B2
Kingfisher Ave DE11 . . . . .256 C2
Kingfisher Cl DE3 . . . . . . .230 A4
Kingfisher Ct DE7 . . . . . . .208 C2
Kingfisher Ho S41 . . . . . . .77 A2
Kingfisher Mews SK6 . . . .23 A3
Kingfisher Wlk DE24 . . . . .231 C1
Kings Cl Carsington DE4 .164 C4
Clowne S43 . . . . .80 C2
Creswell S80 . . . . .81 C1
Heanor DE75 . . . . .181 B1
Kings Coppice S17 . . . . . .55 B3
Kings Croft DE22 . . . . . . .204 C2
Kings Ct DE1 . . . . .267 B4
Kings Dr Brinsley NG16 . .182 C4
Derby DE3,DE23 . . . . . . .218 A3
Kings Gate DE74 . . . . . . .247 C2
Kings Hill S43 . . . . .153 A1
Kings Mews S21 . . . . .59 C2
Kings Rd Sandiacre NG10 223 A3
Swadlincote DE11 . . . . . .256 A1
Kings Way S80 . . . . .82 B2
Kingsbury Cl DE15 . . . . . .248 A2

Kingsbury Rd DE22 . . . . .218 A3
Kingsclere Ave DE21 . . . .206 A1
Kingscroft S17 . . . . .55 C4
Kingsdale Cl NG10 . . . . . .236 A3
Kingsdale Gr DE73 . . . . . .244 C4
Kingsfield Ind Est DE4 . . .165 C3
Kingsfield Rd DE4 . . . . . . .165 C4
Kingsgate S32 . . . . .72 B1
Kingsland Cl DE21 . . . . . .205 C1
Kingsley Ave
Chesterfield S40 . . . . . . .114 C4
Mansfield Woodhouse
NG19 . . . . .136 B3
Kingsley Cl NG19 . . . . . . .136 B3
Kingsley Cres
Long Eaton NG10 . . . . . .236 A2
Stonebroom DE55 . . . . . .146 C2
Kingsley Ct NG19 . . . . . . .136 B3
Kingsley Rd DE22 . . . . . . .204 B2
Kingsley St DE24 . . . . . . .231 C3
Kingsmead Ave NG9 . . . . .209 B1
Kingsmead Hospl ST16 . .269 B4
Kingsmead Ind Est
DE22 . . . . .218 B3
Kingsmede Ave S40 . . . . .95 B1
Kingsmoor Fields SK13 . . .10 B2
Kingsmoor Rd SK13 . . . . .10 B1
Kingsmuir Rd DE3 . . . . . .217 B2
Kingsthorpe Cl NG19 . . . .136 C1
Kingston Ave
Ilkeston DE7 . . . . .209 A2
Stafford ST16 . . . . .269 C4
Kingston Ct DE7 . . . . .207 C3
Kingston Rd
Burton u T DE15 . . . . . .248 B1
Mansfield NG18 . . . . . . .268 C4
Kingston Row ST16 . . . . .269 C4
Kingston St DE1 . . . . .218 C4
Kingsway
Burton u T DE14 . . . . . .254 A4
Derby DE22 . . . . .218 A3
Heanor DE75 . . . . .181 B1
Ilkeston DE7 . . . . .209 A3
Stafford ST16 . . . . .269 A3
Stoke-on-T ST4 . . . . . . .269 B2
Kingsway Cres DE56 . . . .192 B3
Kingsway Hospl DE22 . . .218 A2
Kingsway Ind Pk DE22 . . .218 B3
Kingsway Park Cl DE22 . .218 B3
Kingsway Ret Pk DE22 . . .218 B3
Kingswood Ave DE56 . . . .179 B3
Kingswood Cl S41 . . . . . . .95 B4
Kinross Ave DE21 . . . . . . .219 B2
Kintyre Dr DE24 . . . . .231 B2
Kinver Cl DE6 . . . . .184 C4
Kinver Rd DE15 . . . . .248 A2
Kipling Cl S18 . . . . .76 B1
Kipling Dr DE3 . . . . .217 B1
Kipling Rd S41 . . . . .95 C4
Kipling St NG18 . . . . . . .268 B4
Kipps St NG1 . . . . .268 B2
Kirby La DE4 . . . . .142 C4
Kirk Cl DE5 . . . . .180 B4
Kirk Dale Ave DE21 . . . . .220 C4
Kirk Hallam Com Tech Coll
DE7 . . . . .208 B3
Kirk Ireton CE Prim Sch
DE6 . . . . .165 A1
Kirk Langley CE Prim Sch
DE6 . . . . .202 C1
Kirk Leys Ave N DE21 . . .220 C2
Kirk Leys Ave S DE21 . . .220 C2
Kirk St DE1 . . . . .219 A4
Kirk's La DE56 . . . . .179 A2
Kirkby Ave Ilkeston DE7 . .208 C3
Sheffield S12 . . . . .44 A2
Kirkby Dr S12 . . . . .44 A2
Kirkby Rd S12 . . . . .44 A2
Kirkby View S12 . . . . .44 A2
Kirkby Way S12 . . . . .44 A2
Kirkcroft Ave S21 . . . . . . .60 B4
Kirkcroft Dr S21 . . . . .60 B3
Kirkcroft La S21 . . . . .60 B3
Kirkdale Cl S40 . . . . .115 A4
Kirkdale Gdns NG10 . . . . .236 A3
Kirkdale Rd NG10 . . . . . . .236 A3
Kirkewhite Ave NG10 . . . .236 B4
Kirkewhite Ho NG10 . . . . .236 B4
Kirkfield Dr DE72 . . . . . . .235 B4
Kirkham Cl DE75 . . . . . . .181 B1
Kirkham Dr NG9 . . . . .223 C1
Kirkham La DE56 . . . . . . .168 A4
Kirkham St ST4 . . . . .269 B1
Kirkhill Sch S2 . . . . .43 B4
Kirkistown Cl DE24 . . . . . .233 B3
Kirkland Ave NG18 . . . . . .268 A3
Kirkland Cl ST4 . . . . .269 B1
Kirkland Way
Derby DE24 . . . . .231 B2
Swadlincote DE11 . . . . . .256 A1
Kirkley Dr DE75 . . . . .181 B1
Kirkman Rd DE75 . . . . . . .181 B1
Kirkstead Cl Derby DE21 206 A1
Pinxton NG16 . . . . .160 B2
Kirkstead Jun Sch
NG16 . . . . .160 B2
Kirkstead Rd NG16 . . . . . .160 B2
Kirkstone Ave DE75 . . . . .182 A1
Kirkstone Ct NG10 . . . . . .223 A1
Kirkstone Rd Buxton SK17 85 B2
Chesterfield S41 . . . . . . .95 B4
Kirton Ave NG10 . . . . . . .236 B4
Kishfield La SK23 . . . . . . .45 A3
Kitchener Ave DE23 . . . . .231 C4

Kitchener Dr NG18 ....268 C3
Kitchener Terr NG20 ....101 A1
Kitson Ave NG16 ....171 B2
Knab Rd DE4 ....127 C2
Knabhall La DE4 ....144 B3
Knapp Ave NG16 ....182 C1
Knifesmithgate S40 ....266 B3
Knight Ave ST16 ....269 C4
Knight's La Bretby DE15 ...249 A3
Repton DE15 ....249 A3
Knighton Ct S42 ....131 C3
Knighton St S42 ....131 C3
Knights Cl Beeston NG9 ...223 C1
Derby DE22 ....231 C1
Knights Ct 3 DE13 ....240 C1
Knightsbridge DE22 ....218 A3
Knightwake Rd SK22 ......33 A4
Kniveton CE Prim Sch
DE6 ....163 B1
Kniveton La DE6 ....174 B2
Kniveton Pk DE7 ....208 B4
Knob Fields DE11 ....261 C4
Knob La DE4 ....166 B3
Knoll Cl DE23 ....231 A4
Knoll St S22 ....33 A4
Knoll The Chesterfield S40 .94 C1
Dronfield S18 ....57 B2
Mansfield NG18 ....268 A3
Shirebrook NG20 ....119 B2
Swadlincote DE11 ....256 A3
Tansley DE4 ....144 A3
Knowes Cl SK17 ....85 C4
Knowes Cres SK17 ....85 B4
Knowl Ave DE56 ....178 C3
Knowle Ave SK23 ....47 A3
Knowle Gn S17 ....55 B4
Knowle Rd SK6 ....23 B3
Knowle St ST4 ....269 B2
Knowle Top S20 ....59 C4
Knowles Hill DE13 ....240 A2
Knowles Pl DE4 ....143 B2
Knutsford Gn DE21 ......205 B1
Kye La S26 ....61 C3
Kyle Gr DE21 ....206 A2
Kynance Cl Derby DE24 ...233 B3
South Normanton DE55 ...160 B3
Kynnersley Croft ST14 ...210 A1

L

Laburnam Cl S80 ....81 C1
Laburnham Ct S44 ....97 A2
Laburnum Ave NG20 .....119 C3
Laburnum Cl Bolsover S44 99 B1
Darley Dale DE4 ....127 C2
Sandiacre NG10 ....223 A4
South Normanton DE55 ...160 A4
Laburnum Cres
Derby DE22 ....204 B2
Swanwick DE55 ....170 A4
Laburnum Gr
Derby DE22 ....218 A3
Killamarsh S21 ....60 B3
Mansfield Woodhouse
NG19 ....136 A2
Laburnum Rd
Burton u T DE15 ....254 C3
Swadlincote DE11 ....256 A3
Laburnum St S43 ....78 A1
Laburnum Way DE65 ....229 B2
Lace Way NG1 ....268 C1
Laceby Rd NG19 ....136 C2
Lacey Cl DE7 ....194 B2
Lacey Fields Rd DE75 ....182 A1
Ladbroke Gdns DE22 ....217 C3
Ladies Spring Dr S17 ....56 A4
Ladies Spring Gr S17 ....56 A4
Ladle End La DE12 ....253 B1
Lady Bank View S21 ....59 B2
Lady Field Rd S80 ....62 B4
Lady Grove Rd DE4 .....127 C1
Lady Lea Rd DE21,DE7 ..192 A3
Lady Ley Hill DE21 ......192 A3
Lady Manners Sch DE45 109 B2
Lady Mantle Cl DE73 ....232 C1
Lady Meadow Cl ST14 ...196 C3
Ladybank Rd Derby DE3 217 B1
Mosborough S20 ....59 B3
Ladybower Cl DE11 .....256 A1
Ladybower Dr 9 S17 ....56 A3
Ladybower Dr S32 ......53 A4
Ladybower La S43 ......97 B4
Ladybower Rd DE21 ....220 C2
Ladybrook La NG18 .....268 A4
Ladybrook Pl NG19 .....268 A4
Ladycroft SK17 ....66 B1
Ladycroft Paddock
DE22 ....204 C2
Ladycross Inf Sch NG10 223 A4
Ladyfields DE11 ....256 A3
Ladyfields Way DE11 ...255 C3
Ladyflatts Rd DE4 ......165 C4
Ladygrove Cotts DE23 ..219 A2
Ladylea Rd NG10 ....236 A2
Ladypit Rd SK23 ....33 C2
Ladysmith Rd DE72 ....221 A1
Ladythorne Ave SK6 ....23 A3
Ladywell Cl DE13 ......240 C1
Ladywell Ct DE56 ......179 A2
Ladywood Ave DE56 ...179 A3
Ladywood Dr S41 ......95 B4
Ladywood Prim Sch
DE7 ....208 B3

Ladywood Rd DE7 ......208 B3
Lake Ave Heanor DE75 ...181 B2
Mansfield NG19 ....268 A4
Lake Dr Derby DE23 .....231 C4
Doveridge DE6 ....211 A1
Lake Lands S42 ....114 C1
Lake Side Doveridge DE6 211 A1
Glossop SK13 ....10 A3
Lake View SK23 ....33 B2
Lakeside Ashbourne DE6 .173 B1
Bakewell DE45 ....109 A4
Wingerworth S42 ....114 C1
Lakeside Ave NG10 .....236 B2
Lakeside Cl S41 ....77 B2
Lakeside Cres NG16 ....236 B3
Lakeside Dr DE23 ......231 A4
Lakeside Inf Sch NG10 .236 B3
Lamartine Ct 17 NG3 ...268 B2
Lamartine St NG3 ......268 B2
Lamb Cres DE5 ....169 C1
Lamb Hill Cl S13 ....44 B4
Lambcroft Rd NG16 ....160 B2
Lambe Ct DE23 ....267 C1
Lambgates SK13 ....10 A3
Lambhouse La DE56 ....177 C3
Lambley Dr DE22 ....204 B1
Lambourn Ct DE22 .....205 A2
Lambourn Dr DE22 .....205 A2
Lambourne Ave DE6 ...185 B4
Lambpart La S33 ....50 B3
Lambrook Cl DE3 ......217 B1
Lambton Cl DE7 ....194 C2
Lammascote Rd ST16 ..269 B4
Lampad Cl DE73 ......252 A4
Lampeter Cl DE21 .....206 A1
Lanark St DE21 ....219 C4
Lancaster Ave
Sandiacre NG10 ....223 A2
Stapleford NG9 ....223 C4
Lancaster Dr Hilton DE65 228 C1
Tutbury DE13 ....239 A3
Lancaster Rd S41 ......95 C4
Lancaster Rise DE56 ...179 A3
Lancaster Sports Ctr
DE1 ....267 B4
Lancaster St S44 ......117 C1
Lancaster Wlk DE21 ...221 A3
Lancelot Cl S40 ....114 B4
Lancelot Dr DE13 ......240 C1
Lancing Rd S2 ....43 A4
Landau Forte Coll DE1 .267 C4
Lander La DE56 ....179 A2
Landmere Cl DE7 .....194 B2
Landon Cl S40 ....114 A4
Landsdown Gr NG10 ..223 C1
Landseer Cl Dronfield S18 .56 C1
Sheffield S14 ....43 B1
Landseer Dr Marple SK6 ..23 B4
Sheffield S14 ....43 C1
Landseer Pl S14 ......43 C1
Landseer Wlk S14 ....43 C1
Lane Head Longnor SK17 121 A4
Stoney Middleton S32 ...71 B2
Tideswell SK17 ....69 B3
Lane Head Rd Totley S17 ..55 B2
Whaley Bridge SK23 ...45 B3
Lane The Awsworth NG16 195 B2
Killamarsh S21 ....60 B1
Youlgreave DE4 ....126 B3
Lanes The DE4 ....155 A2
Lanesend Cotts SK23 ...46 A4
Laneside Ave NG9 .....223 C1
Laneside Cl SK23 .....47 A3
Laneside Rd
New Mills SK22 ....33 C4
New Mills, Rowarth SK22 ..34 C2
Laneward Cl DE7 .....194 B2
Lang Rd DE24 ....232 C3
Langdale Cl S40 ......94 C3
Langdale Dr Derby DE21 205 B1
Dronfield S18 ....57 B2
Long Eaton NG10 ......236 A3
Langdale Sq S43 ......96 B4
Langdon Cl 3 NG10 ...223 A1
Langen Ct NG10 ......236 C3
Langer Cl DE14 ......254 A3
Langer La
Chesterfield S40, S42 ...114 C3
Wingerworth S40, S42 ..114 C3
Langerfield Ave S40 ...115 A4
Langford Rd Derby DE3 217 B2
Mansfield NG18 ....268 A3
Langham Pl NG18 ....268 A4
Langhurst Ct S40 .....95 B2
Langhurst Rd S40 ....95 B2
Langley Ave Ilkeston DE7 194 B3
Somercotes DE55 .....170 B4
Langley Bsns Pk NG16 .182 A1
Langley Cl
3 Chesterfield S40 ....95 A3
Mansfield NG19 ....135 C1
Langley Ct SK13 ....10 A3
Langley Dr SK13 ......17 C4
Langley Inf Sch DE75 ..182 A1
Langley Mill CE Inf Sch
NG16 ....182 A2
Langley Mill Jun Sch
NG16 ....182 A2
Langley Mill Sta NG16 ..182 A2
Langley Pk NG16 ......182 A2
Langley Rd DE21 ......220 C2
Langley St DE22 ......218 B3
Langsett Ave 21 SK13 ...9 B1
Langsett Gn 20 SK13 ...9 B1
Langsett La SK13 .....9 B1
Langsett Terr 19 SK13 ..9 B1
Langstone Ave S44 ...99 B1

Langton Hollow NG16 ..171 B3
Langtree Ave S41 ......77 A1
Langwith Bassett Prim Sch
NG20 ....119 C3
Langwith Dr NG20 .....100 C1
Langwith Maltings
NG20 ....119 C4
Langwith Rd
Bolsover S44 ....118 B4
Shirebrook NG20 ......119 C3
Langwith Whaley Thorns Sta
NG20 ....100 C1
Lansbury Ave
Mastin Moor S43 ......79 A2
Pilsley S45 ....132 B1
Lansbury Dr DE55 .....160 A3
Lansbury Rd S21 ......59 B2
Lanscombe Park Rd
DE22 ....204 C1
Lansdowne Ave S41 ...95 C3
Lansdowne Rd
Branston DE14 ....253 C4
Brimington S43 ....96 A4
Buxton SK17 ....66 A1
Swadlincote DE11 .....256 A2
Lansing Gdns DE21 ...220 A3
Lant La DE4 ....144 A4
Lantern Gr DE3 ....217 B2
Lantern Pike View SK22 .25 A1
Lantern View SK22 ....24 A1
Lapwing Cl DE24 .....231 C1
Larch Ave Killamarsh S21 .60 B3
Mansfield Woodhouse
NG19 ....136 A3
Ripley DE5 ....169 B1
Shirebrook NG20 ......119 B2
Larch Cl DE22 ....204 B2
Larch Cres NG16 .....182 C1
Larch Dr NG10 ....223 A4
Larch Rd Eckington S21 .59 A1
Kilburn DE56 ....192 A4
Swadlincote DE11 .....255 C3
Larch Way
Chesterfield S40 ......95 B3
Glossop SK13 ....17 C4
Larchdale Cl DE55 ....160 A2
Larges St DE1 ....218 C3
Lark Cl DE23 ....231 B3
Lark Hill DE3 ....230 A4
Lark Hill Cotts SK22 ...33 A4
Larkdale St NG7 .....268 A2
Larkfields Cres DE55 ..169 C4
Larkhill DE55 ....169 C4
Larkhill Cl DE55 ......169 C4
Larkhill Cres DE24 ...231 C2
Larkin Cl DE24 ......232 A2
Larklands Ave DE7 ...209 A4
Larklands Inf Sch DE7 209 A4
Larkspur Cl
Mansfield NG19 ......136 B1
South Normanton DE55 .160 A2
Larkspur Ct DE21 ....206 A2
Larkstone La DE6 ....149 A1
Larpit Gn S80 ....82 A3
Lascelles Rd SK17 ....85 A4
Lashley Cl DE21 ......205 C1
Latham Cl DE15 .....248 B1
Lathbury Cl DE21 ....205 B1
Lathkil Dr DE55 ......159 C3
Lathkil Gr SK17 ......85 B4
Lathkill Ave Derby DE24 233 B4
Ilkeston DE7 ....194 C3
Staveley S43 ....97 B3
Lathkill Cl Sheffield S13 ..44 B4
West Hallam DE7 .....207 C4
Lathkill Dale DE11 ....255 C1
Lathkill Dale National Nature
Reserve ★ DE45 ....124 B4
Lathkill Dr
Ashbourne DE6 ....185 C4
Ripley DE5 ....180 B3
Selston NG16 ....171 C4
Lathkill Gr
Clay Cross S45 ....131 B1
Tibshelf DE55 ....147 C3
Lathkill Rd Derby DE21 .219 C4
Sheffield S13 ....44 B4
Lathkilldale Cres NG10 236 A3
Latimer Cl DE23 .....230 C4
Latimer St DE24 .....232 B3
Latrigg Cl DE3 ....217 C1
Lauder Cl DE24 ....231 C1
Launceston Rd DE24 .233 A3
Laund Ave DE56 .....179 A3
Laund Cl DE56 ......179 B3
Laund Farm DE56 ...179 B3
Laund Hill DE56 .....179 A3
Laund Nook DE56 ...179 A3
Launds Ave NG16 ...171 B4
Laurel Ave
Long Duckmanton S44 ..97 B2
Mansfield NG18 ......268 C3
Mansfield Woodhouse
NG19 ....136 C1
Ripley DE5 ....169 B1
Laurel Cl Eckington S21 ..59 B1
Shirebrook NG20 .....119 B3
Swanwick DE55 ......170 A4
Laurel Cres
Brimington S43 ....78 A1
Long Eaton NG10 .....236 B3
Smalley DE7 ....192 C3
Laurel Dr
Aston-on-T DE72 .....246 A4
Killamarsh S21 ....60 B3
Laurel Garth Cl S41 ..77 A2
Laurel Gr
Burton u T DE15 .....254 C3

Laurel Gr continued
South Normanton DE55 ..160 A2
Laurence Cl S41 ......77 A1
Laurie Pl DE24 ....232 C4
Lavant Ct 6 S43 .....96 C4
Lavender Cl
Burton u T DE14 ......254 A4
Lavender Gdns DE75 ..182 A1
Lavender Rd DE55 ....170 A4
Lavender Row DE22 ..204 C1
Laverdene Ave S17 ...55 C2
Laverdene Cl S17 ....55 C2
Laverdene Dr S17 ....55 C2
Laverdene Rd S17 ....55 C3
Laverdene Way S17 ..55 C3
Laverick Rd NG16 ....171 A2
Laverock Cl NG16 ....195 C3
Laverstoke Ct DE22 ..218 C2
Lawman Gdns DE55 ..158 C2
Lawman Mews DE55 ..159 A2
Lawn Ave Derby DE22 .204 B1
Etwall DE65 ....229 B3
Lawn Cl DE55 ....181 C1
Lawn Heads Ave DE23 .218 B3
Lawn Mill Rd NG16 ...195 C4
Lawn Prim Sch DE22 ..204 B1
Lawn Rd ST17 ....269 A3
Lawn The S18 ....57 A1
Lawn Villas S44 ......97 A1
Lawnfold SK13 ....9 C2
Lawnlea Cl DE23 .....231 C3
Lawns Dr DE11 ....256 A4
Lawns The
Aston-on-T DE72 .....246 A4
Rolleston DE13 ....240 A2
Uttoxeter ST14 ....210 A1
Lawnside DE21 ......220 C3
Lawnswood Cl DE23 ..231 B4
Lawrence Ave
Awsworth NG16 ......195 B2
Breaston DE72 ....235 B4
Derby DE21 ....220 A4
Eastwood NG16 ......182 C1
Holmewood S42 .....116 B1
Mansfield Woodhouse
NG19 ....136 A2
Ripley DE5 ....180 B4
Lawrence Dr NG16 ...182 B4
Lawrence St Derby DE23 231 C4
Long Eaton NG10 .....236 B4
Sandiacre NG10 ......223 A4
Stafford ST17 ....269 B3
Stapleford NG9 ......223 B3
Lawson Ave NG10 ...236 C4
Lawson St NG7 ......268 A2
Laxfield Cl S40 ......114 B4
Layton Ave NG18 ....268 B4
Layton Burroughs 8
NG18 ....268 B4
Layton Dr S41 ....77 A1
Lea Cl DE22 ....204 C2
Lea Cres DE55 ......170 B3
Lea Ct S41 ....266 B4
Lea Dr
Derby, Chaddesden DE21 .219 C3
Derby, Mickleover DE3 ..217 C2
Lea Gdns★ DE4 .....156 A4
Lea La NG16 ....171 C3
Lea Main Rd DE4 ....156 A4
Lea Moor Rd DE4 ...156 C4
Lea Prim Sch DE4 ...156 A4
Lea Rd Cromford DE4 155 B3
Dronfield S18 ....57 A1
Hayfield SK22 ....25 B2
Holloway DE4 ....156 A4
Lea St S22 ....33 A4
Lea Vale DE55 ......160 A2
Lea Wood Croft DE4 156 A3
Leabrook Rd S18 ....56 B1
Leabrooks Ave NG19 .136 B3
Leabrooks Rd DE55 ..170 B4
Leacroft Rd Derby DE23 219 A1
Winster DE4 ....141 B3
Leadale Ave DE55 ...170 A4
Leadale Cres NG19 ..136 C3
Leadbeater Ave ST4 ..269 A1
Leadbeater Rd S12 ..44 A2
Leafenden Cl DE22 ..205 A2
Leafgreen La DE23 ..231 B3
Leafield Rd SK12 ....32 B3
Leafy La DE75 ....181 C1
Leake St DE22 ....218 B3
Leam Glen NG19 ....136 B1
Leamington Cl DE23 .218 B1
Leamington Dr DE55 .160 A3
Leamington Rd DE14 .253 C4
Leamington St DE5 ..169 C1
Leamoor Ave DE55 ..170 A4
Lean Town SK13 .....17 B3
Leander Cl DE23 ....231 B4
Leander Ct 13 S43 ..78 C1
Leander Rise DE15 ..255 A4
Leaper St DE1 ....218 C3
Leapley La DE6 .....199 B2
Leas Ave NG19 ......135 A3
Leas Park Jun Sch
NG19 ....136 B2
Leas Rd NG19 ......136 B2
Leashaw DE4 ....156 B2
Leashaw Rd DE4 ...156 B2
Leaside Rd ST4 ....269 A1
Leason St S4 ....269 C1
Leather St DE4 .....126 C2
Leathersley La DE6,DE65 226 B1
Leaway The NG20 ..119 B2
Leawood Gdns DE21 .206 A2
Leawood Pump Ho★
DE4 ....155 C2

Leawood Rd DE11 ....256 B4
Leche Croft DE56 ....179 B2
Lechlade Cl DE7 .....207 B4
Ledbury Chase DE24 .231 B1
Ledbury Pl DE21 .....205 B1
Ledo Ave DE5 ....169 B1
Lee Cres DE7 ....209 A4
Lee Dale SK17 ......85 B2
Lee Farm Cl DE73 ..232 C1
Lee Head SK13 .....16 B3
Lee La DE75 ....182 A1
Lee Mount SK13 ...17 B4
Lee Rd S41 ....96 C1
Lee Vale Dr SK13 ..16 B4
Leebangs Rd SK14 ..16 A4
Leech Ct NG16 ....195 A4
Leedhams Croft DE12 259 B4
Leeds Pl DE1 ......267 D2
Leeds Rd S81 ......63 C4
Leefield Rd SK23 ..47 A3
Leek Rd Buxton SK17 ..84 C3
Longnor SK17 ....121 A3
Stoke-on-T ST4 .....269 C2
Leeming La NG19, NG20 136 C4
Leeming La N NG19 ..136 C3
Leeming La S NG19 ..136 B1
Leeming Pk NG19 ...136 B2
Leeming St NG18 ...268 B4
Leen Valley Dr NG20 .119 B2
Lees Brook Com Sch
DE21 ....220 A4
Lees Brook Ho DE21 .220 A4
Lees Hall Ave S8 ....43 A3
Lees Hall Pl S8 .....43 A3
Lees Hall Rd S8 ....43 A3
Lees Hill St NG2 ...268 C1
Lees House Ct S8 ..43 A3
Lees La DE55 ......159 C3
Lees Nook S8 .....43 A3
Lees Rd DE4 ......126 C2
Lees Row SK13 ....10 B3
Lees The DE72 ....233 B3
Leese St S4 ....269 B2
Leeside Rd S33 ....40 B2
Leeswood Cl S41 ..95 B4
Leeway DE21 ......220 B2
Legh Rd SK12 .....32 A3
Leicester Dr SK13 ..17 C4
Leicester Ho 2 NG9 .223 C4
Leicester St
Burton u T DE14 ....254 A4
Derby DE22 ....218 C2
Long Eaton NG10 ....236 C3
Leigh Rd NG9 ......223 C2
Leigh Way S42 .....131 C4
Leighton Dr Marple SK6 ..23 B4
Sheffield S14 ....43 C2
Leighton Pl S14 ....43 C2
Leighton Rd S14 ...43 C2
Leighton St NG3 ...268 C2
Leighton View S2 ..43 C3
Leisure La SK17 ....137 C3
Leman St DE22 ....218 C2
Lemont Rd S17 ....55 C2
Leniscar Ave DE75 .181 B2
Lennox St NG1 ....268 B2
Lens Rd DE22 .....204 B1
Lenthall Inf Sch S18 ..57 A2
Lenton Ave Derby DE21 .219 C3
Nottingham NG7 ....268 A1
Lenton Rd NG7 ....268 A1
Lenton St NG10 ...223 B4
Leominster Dr DE21 .206 A1
Leonard Cheshire Cl
DE75 ....182 A1
Leonard Cl Derby DE23 .267 B1
Sheffield S2 ....44 A4
Leonard St DE1 ....267 C1
Leopold St Derby DE1 .267 B2
Long Eaton NG10 ...236 B4
Leslie Ave NG16 ...195 C3
Leslie Cl DE23 .....230 C4
Lesser La Buxton SK17 ..85 C4
Chapel-en-le-F SK23 .46 C1
Level La SK17 ......84 B3
Leven Cl DE24 .....231 C1
Levens Way S41 ...95 C4
Leveret Cl DE73 ...233 A1
Leverton Rd NG19 ..268 A4
Lewcote La DE7 ...194 A1
Lewis Cl NG3 ......268 B2
Lewis St Derby DE23 .218 C1
Stoke-on-T ST4 ....269 B2
Lewiston Rd DE21 ..220 A3
Lexington Rd DE21 .220 B3
Ley Ave DE55 .....159 A2
Ley Croft Hatton DE65 ..227 B1
Mansfield Woodhouse
NG19 ....136 B3
Ley Gdns DE55 ....159 A2
Ley La
Mansfield Woodhouse
NG19 ....136 B2
Marple SK6 ....23 B4
Leyburn Cl
Chesterfield S40 ....95 C3
Swadlincote DE11 ..256 A1
Leycote Way DE56 .179 A3
Leyfield Rd S17 ...55 B4
Leygate View SK22 .33 A4
Leyland Cl NG9 ...223 C1
Leyland Ct DE1 ...218 C4
Leyland Gdns DE1 ..218 C4
Leyland St DE1 ....218 C4
Leylands DE22 ....218 C4
Leylands La SK14 ..15 C4
Leys Ct DE56 .....179 B2
Leys Field Gdns DE73 .233 A1

Leys Jun Sch DE55 .....159 B2
Leys La DE4 .....154 A4
Leys The
　Little Eaton DE21 ....191 B1
　Swadlincote DE11 .....255 C3
Leyton Ct S43 .....77 B2
Leytonstone Dr DE22 .218 A3
Lichfield Ave DE11 .....256 C3
Lichfield Cl NG9 .....223 C2
Lichfield Ct ST17 .....269 B3
Lichfield Dr DE24 .....233 A4
Lichfield Rd
　Branston DE13,DE14 .....253 B2
　Chesterfield S40 .....114 B4
　Stafford ST17 .....269 B3
Lichford Rd S2 .....43 B3
Lickpenny La DE4 .....144 C2
Lid La DE6 .....197 C4
Liddle St S41 .....269 B1
Lidgate Cl DE3 .....217 B1
Liffs Rd DE6,SK17 .....150 B4
Light Alders La SK12 .....32 A3
Lightfoot Rd ST14 .....210 A1
Lightwood Ave 3 SK17 ..85 B4
Lightwood La
　Chesterfield S21 .....77 C4
　Sheffield S8 .....43 C1
Lightwood Rd
　Buxton SK17 .....66 A1
　Eckington S21 .....58 C1
Lilac Ave DE22 .....218 A3
Lilac Cl Derby DE24 .....233 A3
　Holmewood S44 .....116 C1
Lilac Ct DE24 .....233 A3
Lilac Gr Bolsover S44 ....99 B1
　Burton u T DE15 .....254 C3
　Glapwell S44 .....134 A4
　Heanor DE75 .....181 C1
　Market Warsop NG20 ...120 C4
　Shirebrook NG20 .....119 C3
　South Normanton DE55 .160 A2
Lilac Mews DE7 .....194 B2
Lilac St S43 .....78 A1
Lilac Way Derby DE22 ..204 B1
　Shirland DE55 .....146 B1
Lilian Prime Cl DE24 .....233 A4
Lilley St DE24 .....233 A3
Lillymede Cl S40 .....114 C3
Lilybank Cl DE4 .....143 B3
Lilypools The DE73 .....252 A4
Limb La S17 .....55 B4
Limbersitch La DE65 .....227 C3
Lime Ave Derby DE1 .....267 A1
　Derby, Breadsall Hilltop
　DE21 .....205 B1
　Duffield DE56 .....190 C3
　Langley Mill NG16 .....182 B1
　New Mills SK22 .....24 B1
　Ripley DE5 .....169 B1
　Staveley S43 .....78 C1
Lime Cl Calow S44 .....97 A2
　Doveridge DE6 .....224 A4
　Hatton DE65 .....227 B1
　Pinxton NG16 .....160 B2
Lime Cres Belper DE56 ..179 A1
　Market Warsop NG20 ...120 C4
Lime Croft DE22 .....204 C2
Lime Gr Ashbourne DE6 .185 B4
　Burton u T DE15 .....254 C3
　Darley Dale DE4 .....127 B2
　Derby DE21 .....220 A3
　Draycott DE72 .....234 C4
　Long Eaton NG10 .....236 B4
　Sandiacre NG10 .....223 A3
　South Normanton DE55 .160 A3
　Stapleford NG9 .....223 B3
Lime Grove Ave DE4 .....143 B3
Lime Grove Wlk DE4 ....143 B3
Lime Kiln La Marple SK6 ..23 A3
　Turnditch DE56 .....189 A4
Lime La Derby DE21 .....206 A2
　Morley DE7,DE21 .....206 B3
Lime Rd S21 .....59 A1
Lime St Ilkeston DE7 .....208 C4
　Stoke-on-T ST4 .....269 B1
Lime Terr NG10 .....236 B4
Lime Tree Ave
　Darley Dale DE4 .....127 A2
　Glapwell S44 .....134 A4
　Killamarsh S21 .....60 B3
　Mansfield Woodhouse
　NG19 .....136 A3
　Swadlincote DE11 .....256 A4
Lime Tree Bsns Pk DE4 .143 B2
Lime Tree Gr
　Clay Cross S45 .....131 C1
　Long Duckmanton S44 ....97 B2
Lime Tree Pl NG18 .....268 C3
Lime Tree Rd DE7 .....208 C4
Limecroft View S42 .....115 A2
Limedale Ave DE21 .....206 A2
Limekiln Fields Rd S44 ..99 A2
Limekiln Way S43 .....80 B2
Limekilns The DE73 .....252 C1
Limerick Rd DE21 .....220 C2
Limes Ave Derby DE3 ....217 B1
　Whaley Thorns NG20 ...101 A1
Limes Cl The DE4 .....143 B3
Limes Cres NG20 .....119 B3
Limes Pk DE5 .....169 B1
Limes The
　Barton in F NG11 .....237 C3
　Mapperley DE7 .....193 C2
Limestone Cl DE11 .....257 A2
Limestone Terr NG19 ...136 A2
Limetree Cl S43 .....96 C3
Limetree Ct DE7 .....208 B3

Limetree Rise DE7 .....208 B3
Limmen Gdns NG3 .....268 C2
Limpenny St NG7 .....268 A2
Linacre Ave S45 .....131 B1
Linacre Way SK13 .....17 C4
Linacre Resr Nature Trail★
　S42 .....94 B3
Linacres Dr DE73 .....233 A1
Linbery Cl DE55 .....158 A2
Lincoln Ave Derby DE24 .233 A4
　Sandiacre NG10 .....223 A2
Lincoln Cir NG7 .....268 A1
Lincoln Cl
　Stapleford NG9 .....209 C1
　Tibshelf DE55 .....148 A3
Lincoln Dr NG19 .....136 B2
Lincoln Gn DE73 .....232 C1
Lincoln Rd DE15 .....254 B4
Lincoln St Alfreton DE55 .158 C2
　Chesterfield S40 .....115 A4
　Nottingham NG3 .....268 B1
　Tibshelf DE55 .....148 A3
Lincoln Way
　5 Glossop SK13 .....17 C4
　North Wingfield S42 .....131 C3
　Swadlincote DE11 .....256 C3
Lindale Rd S41 .....76 B1
Lindale Way DE73 .....233 A1
Linden Ave
　Chesterfield S40 .....95 A1
　Clay Cross S45 .....131 B1
　Dronfield S18 .....57 A2
Linden Cl DE56 .....192 A4
Linden Ct S45 .....131 B1
Linden Dr S41 .....115 B3
Linden Gr Matlock DE4 ..143 B3
　Sandiacre NG10 .....223 A4
　Shirebrook NG20 .....119 C2
　Stapleford NG9 .....223 C3
Linden Park Gr S40 .....95 B2
Linden Rd S80 .....81 C1
Linden St
　Mansfield NG19 .....136 A1
　Shirebrook NG20 .....119 C2
Linden Way SK6 .....32 A4
Lindford Cl DE21 .....205 C2
Lindisfarne Cl 8 DE24 ..231 B2
Lindisfarne Ct 5 S40 ....95 A4
Lindisfarne Dr S18 .....76 A4
Lindley St
　Mansfield NG18 .....268 B4
　Selston NG16 .....171 B3
Lindon Dr DE24 .....233 B3
Lindrick Cl Derby DE3 ...217 C1
　Mansfield Woodhouse
　NG19 .....136 B3
Lindrick Gdns S40 .....114 B4
Lindsay Cl NG18 .....268 B3
Lindsey Cl DE21 .....219 C3
Lindum Gr 7 NG2 .....268 C1
Lindway La DE55 .....145 A1
Line Ct DE15 .....254 C4
Lingfield Rd DE14 .....253 C4
Lingfield Rise DE3 .....217 B2
Lingfoot Ave S8 .....57 A4
Lingfoot Cl S8 .....57 B3
Lingfoot Cres S8 .....57 B3
Lingfoot Dr S8 .....57 B3
Lingfoot Pl S8 .....57 B3
Lingfoot Wlk S8 .....57 B3
Linglongs Ave SK23 .....45 A3
Linglongs Rd SK23 .....45 B3
Lings Cres S42 .....132 A4
Linkmel Rd NG16 .....182 B2
Links Cl DE24 .....231 C2
Links Rd
　Chapel-en-le-F SK23 ....46 C3
　Dronfield S18 .....76 A4
Linley La S12 .....44 B3
Linmell St NG3 .....268 C2
Linnet Cl DE21 .....220 C3
Linnet Hill DE3 .....230 B4
Linnet Ho S41 .....77 A2
Linscott Cl S41 .....95 B4
Linshaws Rd HD9 .....3 C1
Linton Heath DE12 .....261 C3
Linton Prim Sch DE12 ..261 B1
Linton Rd
　Chesterfield S40 .....114 B4
　Linton DE11 .....261 C2
　Rosliston DE12 .....260 C3
Linwood Cres NG16 .....182 C1
Linwood Ct NG19 .....136 C2
Lion St ST4 .....269 B4
Lionel St DE22 .....204 A3
Lipp Ave S21 .....60 B4
Liskeard Dr DE22 .....204 C3
Lismore Ct 5 DE24 .....231 B2
Lismore Gr SK17 .....85 A4
Lismore Pk SK17 .....85 A4
Lismore Rd Buxton SK17 .85 A4
　Sheffield S8 .....43 A3
Lissett Ave 4 DE7 .....208 C4
Lister Ave S12 .....44 A2
Lister Cl Derby DE3 .....218 A2
　Sheffield S12 .....44 A2
Lister Cres S12 .....44 A2
Lister Dr S12 .....44 A2
Lister Gate NG1 .....268 B1
Lister Pl S12 .....44 A2
Lister Way S12 .....44 A2
Liston Dr DE22 .....218 C4
Litchen Cl DE7 .....194 C1
Litchfield Cl NG10 .....237 A4
Litchurch La DE24 .....219 B1

Litchurch St DE1 .....267 C1
Little Acre NG19 .....136 C3
Little Bolehill DE4 .....155 A1
Little Breck DE55 .....160 A2
Little Bridge St DE1 .....218 C3
Little Brind Rd S40 .....95 A4
Little Cl DE11 .....256 A3
Little Eaton Prim Sch
　DE21 .....205 B4
Little Edge S32 .....71 B4
Little Fen DE55 .....147 C3
Little Hallam Hill DE7 ..208 C3
Little Hallam La DE7 ....209 A3
Little La
　Ashford in t W DE45 .....89 C1
　Heanor DE5 .....181 A2
　Kimberley NG16 .....195 C3
　Pleasley NG19 .....135 A3
　Sheffield S12 .....44 A3
　Shirebrook NG20 .....119 B2
　Sutton in A NG17 .....148 C1
　Thorpe Salvin S80 .....63 A3
　Tideswell SK17 .....69 C2
Little London DE4 .....156 A3
Little Longstone Cl DE3 217 C1
Little Lunnon NG11 .....237 C3
Little Meadow Rd DE73 233 A1
Little Moorside DE72 ...246 A4
Little Morton Rd S42,
　S45 .....132 A3
Little Norton Ave S8 ....57 A4
Little Norton Dr S8 .....57 A4
Little Norton La S8 .....57 A4
Little Norton Way S8 ....57 A4
Little Robins Ct S18 ....268 A3
Little Thorn Ind Est
　DE11 .....256 C1
Little Wood Dr S12 .....44 A2
Little Wood Rd S12 .....44 A2
Little Woodbury Dr
　DE23 .....230 C3
Littlebrook Cl SK13 .....10 A2
Littledale Cl DE21 .....206 B2
Littlefield La
　Ellastone DE6 .....183 A1
　Snelston DE6 .....184 A2
Littlefield Rd DE65 .....227 B4
Littlefields SK14 .....9 A2
Littlemoor
　Chesterfield S41 .....95 B4
　Eckington S21 .....59 C2
Littlemoor Cres S41 .....95 B4
Littlemoor Ctr 2 S41 ....95 C4
Littlemoor La DE4 .....143 C1
Littlemoor Rd SK14 .....9 A1
Littleover Com Sch
　DE23 .....230 C4
Littleover Cres DE23 ...218 B1
Littleover La DE23 .....231 C4
Littleton St S16 .....269 C4
Littlewell La DE7 .....208 C1
Littlewood La NG19 .....136 A3
Littleworth NG18 .....268 C3
Litton Bank 16 SK13 .....9 C1
Litton CE Prim Sch SK17 69 C2
Litton Cl Belper DE56 ...179 A3
　Ilkeston DE7 .....194 C2
　Staveley S43 .....97 B4
Litton Dr DE21 .....220 C2
Litton Gdns 15 SK13 .....9 C1
Litton Mews SK13 .....9 C1
Litton Rd NG19 .....136 C2
Liverpool Rd ST4 .....269 B2
Liverpool St
　5 Derby DE21 .....219 C4
　Nottingham NG3 .....268 C2
Liversage Pl DE1 .....267 C2
Liversage Rd DE1 .....267 C2
Liversage St DE1 .....267 C2
Livingstone Rd DE23 ...218 C1
Lloyd St Derby DE22 .....218 B3
　Stafford ST16 .....269 B4
Loads Rd S42 .....113 A4
Loadshead La S42 .....112 B4
Lochinvar Cl DE21 .....220 C2
Lock Cl DE7 .....208 B3
Lock La Long Eaton NG10 236 B4
　Sandiacre NG10 .....223 B2
Locke Way ST16 .....269 C4
Lockington Cl DE73 .....232 C1
Lockington Rd DE74 ....247 B3
Locko Ct DE21 .....220 B3
Locko La S45 .....132 C2
Locko Rd DE21 .....220 C4
Lockoford La
　Chesterfield, Stonegravels
　S41 .....96 A3
　Chesterfield, Tapton S41 ..96 B3
Lockoford Rd S41 .....96 A3
Lockside SK6 .....23 A3
Locksley Ho NG3 .....268 C2
Lockton Ave DE75 .....193 C4
Lockwood Rd DE22 .....204 B3
Locomotive Way DE24 ..219 B2
Lode La DE6 .....149 C2
Lodge Ave DE6 .....185 A4
Lodge Bank SK13 .....10 A3
Lodge Cl Calow S43 .....97 A2
　Duffield DE56 .....190 C2
　Etwall DE65 .....229 B2
Lodge Ct DE6 .....9 A2
Lodge Dr Belper DE56 ...178 C3
　Wingerworth S42 .....115 A2
Lodge Est DE7 .....208 C1
Lodge Farm Chase DE6 185 A4
Lodge Farm Cl S40 .....114 B4
Lodge Hill DE13 .....239 C2

Lodge La Aldercar NG16 .181 C4
　Alstonefield DE6 .....149 A2
　Derby DE1 .....267 A4
　Derby, Spondon DE21 ...220 A2
　Mackworth DE6,DE22 ...203 B3
　Shottle DE56 .....177 B4
Lodge Mews DE72 .....246 A4
Lodge Moor Rd S10 .....42 C4
Lodge Pl S43 .....97 B3
Lodge Rd Eastwood NG16 195 A4
　Long Eaton NG10 .....236 B3
　Mapperley DE7 .....193 C2
　Netherseal DE12 .....261 B1
　Stoke-on-T ST4 .....269 A2
Lodge St DE7 .....235 A4
Lodge The Glossop SK13 ..10 A3
　Tideswell SK17 .....69 B1
Lodge Way DE3 .....217 B1
Lodge Wlk S43 .....97 B3
Lohengrin Ct 1 DE13 ...240 C1
Lombard St DE22 .....217 C3
Lomond Ave DE24 .....231 C1
London Rd Buxton SK17 ..85 B3
　Castle Donington DE72 .247 A4
　Derby DE23,DE24 .....219 B3
　Nottingham NG2 .....268 B1
　Shardlow DE72 .....234 C1
　Sheffield, Heeley S2 .....43 A3
　Sheffield, Highfield S2 ...43 A4
　Stoke-on-T ST4 .....269 A4
London Rd S S2 .....43 A4
London St S43 .....77 B2
Long Acre View S20 .....60 A4
Long Bridge La DE24 ....232 A4
Long Croft DE72 .....246 A4
Long Eaton Com Sch
　NG10 .....236 B4
Long Eaton Com Sch (Lower
　Site) NG10 .....236 C4
Long Eaton Sta NG10 ...236 A3
Long Field Grange S41 ..95 B3
Long Hill Darley Dale DE4 127 B2
　Whaley Bridge SK17, SK23 .65 B3
Long La Alstonefield DE6 .149 A2
　Ashover S42 .....130 A3
　Broadbottom SK13 .....16 B4
　Chapel-en-le-F SK23 .....47 A2
　Chesterfield S21 .....77 B4
　Holloway DE4 .....156 A3
　Killamarsh S21 .....60 C3
　Kirk Langley DE6 .....202 A1
　Longford DE6 .....200 C1
　Shipley DE75 .....194 C4
　Shirebrook NG20 .....119 C2
　Taddington SK17 .....87 C3
　Thurvaston DE6 .....201 B1
　Whaley Bridge SK23 .....46 B2
Long Lane CE Prim Sch
　DE6 .....201 C1
Long Mdw
　Great Cubley DE6 .....198 C1
　Mansfield Woodhouse
　NG19 .....136 B3
Long Meadow Rd DE55 .158 C2
Long Rake DE45 .....123 B2
Long Row Belper DE56 ..178 C2
　Nottingham NG1 .....268 B1
　Shardlow DE72 .....235 A1
Long Row Prim Sch
　DE56 .....178 C2
Long Row W NG1 .....268 B1
Long Shambles S40 .....266 B3
Long Sleets DE55 .....160 A2
Long St DE15 .....254 C4
Longacre Rd S18 .....76 A4
Longacre Way S20 .....60 A4
Longbourne Ct NG19 ...136 C1
Longbow Cl DE13 .....240 B1
Longbow Gr DF13 .....240 B1
Longbridge La
　Buxton SK17 .....67 A2
　Heanor DE75 .....181 B2
Longcliff Wlk 16 S41 ....95 B3
Longclough Dr SK13 .....17 A4
Longcourse La S44 .....98 A1
Longcroft Ave S18 .....56 B1
Longcroft Cl S18 .....56 B4
Longcroft Cres 2 S18 ...56 B1
Longcroft Rd S40 .....114 C4
Longcroft Rd S18 .....56 B1
Longcroft View S80 .....82 A3
Longdale NG19 .....136 C1
Longdale Dr SK14 .....9 A2
Longdale Gdns SK14 .....9 A2
Longden Cl NG9 .....209 C1
Longden St NG3 .....268 C2
Longdendale High Sch
　SK14 .....9 B3
Longdons Row DE21 ....220 B3
Longedge Gr S42 .....115 A2
Longedge La S42 .....114 C2
Longedge Rise S42 .....115 A2
Longfield Cres DE7 .....208 C3
Longfield La DE7 .....208 C3
Longfield Rd ST4 .....269 B4
Longford CE Prim Sch
　DE6 .....214 B2
Longford Cl Derby DE22 .204 B1
　8 Sheffield S17 .....56 A3
Longford Cres S17 .....56 A3
Longford Dr S17 .....55 C2
Longford La DE6 .....214 C4
Longford Rd S17 .....56 A2
Longford Spinney S17 ...55 C2
Longford St DE22 .....218 C4
Longhedge La
　Burton u T DE13 .....239 C1
　Pleasley NG19 .....134 C3

Longhurst La SK6 .....23 B3
Longhurst View S80 .....81 C3
Longlands S44 .....99 A1
Longlands Dr SK22 .....33 A4
Longlands La DE65 .....230 B1
Longlands Rd
　New Mills SK22 .....33 A4
　Swadlincote DE11 .....256 B4
Longlands Villas DE56 .167 C2
Longley La DE21 .....220 B3
Longload La DE4 .....154 C3
Longmeade Dr SK23 .....47 A2
Longmoor Gdns 11
　NG10 .....223 A1
Longmoor La
　Breaston DE72 .....222 C1
　Sandiacre NG10 .....223 A2
Longmoor Prim Sch
　NG10 .....223 B2
Longmoor Rd
　Glossop SK13 .....17 A4
　Long Eaton NG10 .....223 A1
Longnor Craft Ctr★
　SK17 .....121 B3
Longnor Gn SK13 .....9 B1
Longnor Mews SK13 .....9 B1
Longnor Way SK13 .....9 B1
Longreave La DE45 .....90 B2
Longrose La DE6 .....163 A1
Longshaw Cl
　North Wingfield S42 .....131 C3
　Staveley S43 .....97 B4
Longshaw Estate Cntry Pk★
　S32 .....54 A2
Longside Rd S42 .....112 C3
Longson Rd SK23 .....47 B3
Longster La NG20,NG19 .120 B2
Longstock Cl DE21 .....205 C1
Longstone CE Prim Sch
　DE45 .....89 C2
Longstone Cres S12 .....44 B2
Longstone La DE45 .....89 C1
Longstone Rise DE56 ...179 A3
Longstone Wlk DE1 .....267 A4
Longthorpe Cl DE23 ....231 A4
Longwalls La DE56 .....178 B3
Longwood Inf Sch NG16 160 B1
Longwood Rd NG16 .....160 C3
Lons Inf Sch DE5 .....169 B1
Lonsdale Dr NG9 .....223 C1
Lonsdale Gr DE4 .....142 C4
Lonsdale Pl DE22 .....218 B2
Lonsdale Rd
　Burton u T DE14 .....254 A4
　Pilsley S45 .....132 A1
Lonsdale St ST4 .....269 B1
Loom Cl DE56 .....179 B3
Loosemore Dr S12 .....43 C3
Lord Haddon Rd DE7 ...194 C1
Lord Nelson St NG2 .....268 C1
Lord Roberts Rd S40 ....266 B1
Lord St Derby DE24 .....232 B4
　Glossop SK13 .....10 B1
　Hollingworth SK14 .....9 B2
　Mansfield NG18 .....268 B3
　Nottingham NG2 .....268 C1
Lords Cl S44 .....99 A1
Lordship La S44 .....269 C2
Lordsmill St S41 .....266 C2
Lorien Ct S44 .....269 B2
Lorne Ct S18 .....56 B1
Lorne St DE22 .....218 C2
Lorraine Cl DE24 .....232 C2
Loscoe CE Prim Sch
　DE75 .....181 B1
Loscoe Grange DF75 .....181 B2
Loscoe Rd Derby DE21 ..206 A1
　Heanor DE75 .....181 B1
Loscoe-Denby La DE5,
　DE75 .....181 A2
Losehill Hall Study Ctr★
　S33 .....38 B2
Losk Cnr S44 .....118 C2
Losk La S44 .....118 C2
Lothian Pl
　Castle Donington DE74 .247 A2
　Derby DE21 .....219 B4
Lothlorien Cl DE23 .....231 A4
Loudon St DE23 .....219 A2
Loudoun Pl DE74 .....247 A2
Loughborough Ave NG2 268 C1
Loundes Rd S18 .....76 C3
Loundsley Cl S42 .....94 C2
Loundsley Green Rd S40 .95 B3
Lount La DE13 .....239 C1
Lousie Greaves La DE21 220 C3
Louvain Rd DE22,DE23 ..218 B1
Louwil Ave NG19 .....136 C3
Lovatt Cl DE13 .....240 C1
Lovatt St ST4 .....269 B2
Love La DE55 .....147 B2
Loveys Croft DE73 .....252 C1
Low Cl DE6 .....189 A1
Low Comm S21 .....79 B4
Low Lea Rd SK6 .....23 A3
Low Leighton Rd SK22 ..33 B4
Low Mdw SK23 .....45 B4
Low Pavement
　Chesterfield S40 .....266 B3
　5 Nottingham NG1 .....268 B1
Low's La DE7 .....209 A1
Lowburn Rd S13 .....44 A4
Lowdham St NG3 .....268 C1
Lowe St Derby DE24 .....232 C3
　Stoke-on-T ST4 .....269 B2

Lowedges Cres S8 ......56 C3
Lowedges Dr S8 ......56 C3
Lowedges Pl S8 ......57 A3
Lowedges Prim Sch S8 .56 C3
Lowedges Rd S8 ......56 C3
Lower Bagthorpe NG16 .171 C2
Lower Bank SK13 ......17 A4
Lower Barn Rd SK13 ......9 C2
Lower Bloomsgrove Rd
DE7 ....194 C1
Lower Brook St NG10 ..236 C4
Lower Burch Pl S32 .....71 C3
Lower Chapel St
🖽 Ilkeston DE7 ......194 C1
Stonebroom DE55 .....147 A2
Lower Clara Mount Rd
DE75 ....182 A1
Lower Cres ST4 ......269 A2
Lower Dale Rd DE23 ...218 C1
Lower Dr DE55 ......169 B4
Lower Dunstead Rd
Aldercar NG16 ......182 A2
Langley Mill NG16 ......182 A2
Lower Eaves View SK23 .47 B3
Lower Eldon St NG2 ...268 C1
Lower Eley St DE1 .....267 A1
Lower Fold SK6 ......23 A4
Lower Gladstone St
DE75 ....181 C1
Lower Gn DE65 ......230 B1
Lower Granby St DE7 ..194 C1
Lower Greenshall La
SK12 ....32 C3
Lower Grove Rd S40 ..266 A3
Lower Hague S22 ......32 C4
Lower Hall Cl DE56 ...191 B3
Lower Hardwick St 🖽
SK17 ....85 A4
Lower High St DE13 ..239 B4
Lower La S23 ......34 B1
Lower Macclesfield Rd
SK23 ....45 C3
Lower Mantle Cl S45 ..131 B2
Lower Maples DE75 ...194 A4
Lower Market St SK14 ..16 A4
Lower Middleton St
DE7 ....195 A1
Lower Nelson St DE75 .181 B1
Lower Orchard St NG9 .223 B4
Lower Park St NG9 ...223 B3
Lower Parliament St
NG1 ....268 B1
Lower Rd DE22 ......217 C4
Lower Smithy La SK17 ..88 A2
Lower Somercotes
DE55 ....170 C4
Lower Sq SK13 ......10 A4
Lower St DE6 ......224 A4
Lower Stanton Rd DE7 .208 C3
Lower Strines Rd SK6 ..23 A3
Lower Terr Rd SK17 ....69 C4
Lower Whitworth Rd
DE7 ....208 C3
Lowerlea SK12 ......32 B3
Lowery Dr SK6 ......23 A4
Lowes Hill DE5 ......169 B2
Lowes La DE73 ......244 B4
Lowfield Ave S12 ......58 C4
Lowfield Ct 🖽 S2 .....43 A4
Lowfield Prim Sch S2 ..43 A4
Lowfields S43 ......79 A1
Lowgates S43 ......79 A1
Lowlands Lea DE75 ...181 C1
Lowlands Rd DE56 ...179 A2
Lowndes Cl ST4 ......269 A1
Lowry Ct SK14 ......9 A2
Lowry Dr S18 ......56 C1
Lows Ct DE73 ......233 A1
Lowside S32 ......72 A1
Lowside Cl S32 ......72 A1
Loxley Cl Chesterfield S40 .95 A2
Derby DE21 ....206 A1
Loxley La S80 ......82 A3
Loxton Ct DE3 ......217 B2
Loyne Cl DE24 ......231 C1
Lucas La DF65 ......228 C1
Lucas Rd S41 ......95 C3
Lucas Terr SK22 ......25 B2
Luccombe Dr DE24 ...233 B3
Lucerne Rd DE21 ...206 B2
Ludborough Wlk NG19 .136 C2
Ludgate St DE13 ...239 B3
Ludgate Wlk DE22 ...217 C3
Ludham Cl S41 ......95 C4
Ludham Gdns S41 ......95 C4
Ludlam Ave NG16 ...195 A4
Ludlow Cl DE21 ......220 C3
Ludworth Prim Sch SK6 .23 A4
Luke La DE6 ......201 C4
Lukesland Ave ST4 ...269 A1
Lullington Mews DE12 .262 A2
Lullington Rd
Clifton Campville B79 ...263 C2
Overseal DE12 ......262 A2
Lulworth Cl DE23 ...231 B3
Lulworth Ct NG16 ...195 C4
Lum's Hill Rise DE4 ...143 B3
Lumb La Hazelwood DE56 178 B2
Northwood DE4 ......127 A3
Lumber La DE6 ......176 B1
Lumford Cotts DE45 ...109 B4
Lumsdale Cres DE4 ...143 B3
Lumsdale Rd
Matlock DE4 ......143 C3
Staveley S43 ......97 B4

Luna Croft S12 ......43 C1
Lundie Cl DE24 ......231 B1
Lundy Rd S18 ......76 A4
Lune Mdw NG19 ...136 C2
Lunness Ct NG18 ...268 C3
Lupin Cl DE21 ......206 B2
Lupin Way S44 ......97 A2
Lupton Cres S8 ......56 C3
Lupton Dr S8 ......56 C3
Lupton Rd S8 ......56 C3
Lupton Wlk S8 ......57 A3
Lwr Bank CI SK13 ......9 C2
Lychgate Cl DE21 ...205 B1
Lydden Cl S43 ......96 C4
Lydford Ave S41 ......77 A1
Lydford Rd DE55 ...159 A3
Lydgate S32 ......71 C3
Lydgate Dr S42 ......114 C2
Lydia Gdns NG16 ...182 C1
Lydstep Cl DE21 ...206 B1
Lyle Cl NG16 ......195 C4
Lyme Park* SK12 ......32 A3
Lyme Park Ctry Pk SK12 .32 A1
Lyme Pk SK23 ......34 C1
Lyme Rd SK12 ......32 A3
Lymefield Terr SK14 ...16 A4
Lymewood Dr SK12 ...32 B3
Lynam Cl S45 ......131 C2
Lynam Rd DE55,DE56 ..168 B4
Lynam St ST4 ......269 B2
Lyncroft Ave DE5 ...169 C1
Lyndale Dr DE5 ......181 A4
Lynden Ave NG10 ...236 B3
Lyndhurst Gr DE21 ...220 A3
Lyndhurst Rd NG2 ...268 C1
Lyndhurst St DE23 ...219 A1
Lyne Ave SK13 ......17 A4
Lynholmes Rd DE4 ...143 B3
Lynmouth Dr DE7 ...194 B2
Lynne Cl SK13 ......17 C4
Lynton Cl DE5 ......169 B2
Lynton Rd DE56 ...168 A2
Lynton St DE22 ......218 C2
Lynwood Cl
Branston DE14 ......253 C4
🖽 Dronfield S18 ......56 B1
Lynwood Rd
Branston DE14 ......253 C4
Derby DE24 ......231 C2
Lytham Cl DE21 ...205 B1
Lyttelton St DE22 ...218 B3
Lytton Cl NG3 ......268 C2
Lytton St ST4 ......269 C2

M

M1 Commerce Pk S44 ..98 C4
Macaulay St DE24 ...232 A3
Macclesfield Main Rd
SK17 ....84 B3
Macclesfield Old Rd
SK17 ....84 B3
Macclesfield Rd
Buxton SK17 ......85 A3
Whaley Bridge SK23 ....45 B3
Macdonald Cl S42 ...115 C2
Macdonald Sq DE7 ...208 B3
Machins Cl S18 ......57 A1
Mackenzie St DE22 ...218 B3
Mackinley Ave NG9 ...209 C1
Macklin Cl DE1 ......267 B3
Mackworth Cl DE11 ...256 A4
Mackworth Coll DE22 .218 A3
Maclagan St S14 ...269 B1
Macready Pl DE24 ...232 C4
Macworth Rd DE1 ...218 C3
Maddock La DE4 ......153 A1
Madehurst Gdns S2 ...43 A4
Madehurst Rd S2 ......43 A4
Madehurst Rise S2 ...43 A4
Madehurst View S2 ...43 A4
Madeley Cl DE3 ......217 B1
Madeley St DE23 ...219 A1
Madford Ret Pk ST16 .269 A4
Madin Dr S43 ......97 A3
Madin St Chesterfield S41 266 B4
Tupton S42 ......131 B4
Madison Ave DE21 ...219 C4
Madras Rd DE15 ...248 B2
Maesfield Dr ST17 ...269 A3
Mag La Creswell NG20 .100 B3
Idridgehay DE56 ......176 B3
Magnolia Way DE55 ...170 A4
Magson St NG3 ......268 C2
Maguire Ave SK13 ......10 A3
Maid Marian Way NG1 .268 B1
Maiden La 🖽 NG1 ...268 B1
Maidstone Dr DE24 ...232 C3
Maidwell Cl DE56 ...179 B3
Main Ave Derby DE22 ...204 C3
Totley S17 ......55 C2
Main Dr S42 ......114 C1
Main Rd Bamford S33 ...40 A2
Bradwell S33 ......51 A4
Brailsford DE6 ......201 C4
Chesterfield S21 ......77 B4
Crich DE4 ....156 B1
Eckington S21 ......58 C2
Elvaston DE72 ......234 A3
Flagg SK17 ....106 C3
Grindleford S32 ......72 B4
Hathersage S32 ......53 A4
Heath S44 ....117 A1
Holmesfield S18 ......75 A4
Old Brampton S42 ......94 C4
Renishaw S21 ......79 A4
Ripley DE5 ......169 A2

Main Rd continued
Ripley, Pentrich DE5 ...169 B3
Sheffield S12 ......58 C4
Shirland DE55 ......146 B1
Smalley DE7 ......192 C2
Somercotes DE55 ...170 C3
Stonebroom DE55 ...147 A3
Sudbury DE6 ......225 C3
Sudbury, Aston DE6 ...226 A2
Taddington SK17 ......88 A2
Underwood Green NG16 .171 C1
Unstone S18 ......76 C4
Wensley DE4 ......127 B1
Westwood NG16 ...171 A2
Whaley Thorns NG20 ...101 A1
Main St Awsworth NG16 .195 B3
Blackfordby DE11 ...257 B1
Bolsover S44 ......117 C4
Branston DE14 ......253 C4
Branston, Tatenhill DE13 .253 A4
Breaston DE72 ......235 B4
Breedon on t H DE73 ..252 C1
Brinsley NG16 ......171 B1
Burnaston DE65 ......229 C3
Burton u T, Stapenhill
DE15 ....254 C4
Burton u T, Stretton DE13 .240 C1
Caldwell DE12 ......260 C4
Calver S32 ......72 B1
Castle Donington DE74 .247 B3
Chelmorton SK17 ...106 A4
Church Broughton DE65 .227 A4
Clifton Campville B79 ...263 C1
Coton in t E DE12 ...260 B2
Eastwood NG16 ......182 C1
Egginton DE65 ......241 A3
Elton DE4 ......140 C4
Elvaston DE72 ......234 B3
Etwall DE65 ......229 A2
Findern DE65 ......230 B1
Great Longstone DE45 ..90 A2
Hartshorne DE11 ...257 A3
Hilton DE65 ......228 B1
Horsley Woodhouse DE7 .192 B3
Kimberley NG16 ......195 C3
Kirk Ireton DE6 ......165 A1
Linton DE12 ......261 B3
Lockington DE74 ...247 C3
Long Eaton NG10 ...236 C4
Longford DE6 ......214 B4
Mapperley DE7 ......193 C2
Melbourne DE73 ...245 B1
Melbourne, Wilson DE73 .252 C3
Middleton (Nr Wirksworth)
DE4 ....154 B2
Moira DE11 ......256 B1
Netherseal DE12 ...264 C4
Newton DE55 ......148 A2
Newton Solney DE15 ..248 C4
Over Haddon DE45 ...109 A1
Overseal DE12 ......262 A2
Palterton S44 ......118 A3
Repton DE65 ......242 B1
Rosliston DE12 ......260 B3
Scarcliffe S44 ......118 C3
Shirebrook NG20 ...119 B2
Smisby LE65 ......257 C2
South Normanton DE55 .160 A3
Stanton-by-D DE7 ...222 C4
Sutton in A NG17 ...148 C2
Swadlincote DE11 ...255 C3
Ticknall DE73 ......251 A2
Ticknall, Milton DE65 ...243 A1
Walton-on-T DE12 ...253 B1
Weston-on-T DE72 ...245 C3
Whaley Thorns NG20 ...101 A1
Winster DE4 ......141 B3
Maine Dr DE21 ......220 A3
Mais Cl DE4 ......144 A3
Maize Cl DE3 ......231 A3
Makeney Rd Belper DE56 191 B3
Duffield DE56 ......190 C1
Holbrook DE56 ......191 B3
Malbon's Yd DE6 ...173 B1
Malcolm Gr DE23 ...230 C4
Malcolm St DE23 ...219 A1
Malham Cl S40 ......95 B3
Malham Gdns S20 ...59 B4
Malham Gr S20 ......59 C4
Malham Rd DE23 ...230 C3
Malia Rd S41 ......96 B3
Malin Cl DE24 ......233 A4
Malinder Cl S21 ......60 B3
Malinscommon La DE56 166 B2
Malkin St S41 ......266 C3
Mallard Cl Killamarsh S21 .60 A4
Shirebrook NG20 ...119 C2
Mallard Ct 🖽 S43 ......78 C1
Mallard Wlk DE3 ...230 B4
Mallory Cl S41 ......76 C2
Malmas Rd DE4 ......143 A3
Malson Way S41 ......95 C3
Malt Mill La ST16 ...269 B4
Maltby Ave DE55 ...146 C3
Maltby Cl 🖽 DE22 ...204 C1
Malthouse La
Eastwood NG16 ......182 C1
Wirksworth DE4 ......154 C2
Malthouse Ct DE6 ...173 B1
Malthouse La
Ashover S45 ......129 C2
Hatton DE65 ......227 A4
Nether Heage DE56 ...168 A1
Stoney Middleton S32 ...72 B3
Malthouse Rd
Ilkeston DE7 ......208 C2

Malthouse Rd continued
Whitwell S80 ......82 A3
Maltings The
Ashbourne DE6 ......173 A1
Burton u T DE15 ...248 A1
Shardlow DE72 ......235 A1
Maltmill La NG1 ...268 B1
Malton Pl DE21 ......205 B1
Malvern Ave DE15 ...248 A1
Malvern Cl DE3 ......217 B2
Malvern Gdns
🖽 Long Eaton NG10 ...236 A4
Matlock DE4 ......143 A3
Malvern Rd S40 ......95 C2
Malvern Rise SK13 ...10 A3
Malvern Way DE21 ...205 B1
Manchester La DE11 ..257 B3
Manchester Rd
Buxton SK17 ......65 C1
Chapel-en-le-F SK23 ...46 C3
Glossop SK13,SK14 ......9 C4
Tideswell SK17 ......69 A3
Manchester St
Derby DE22 ......218 B3
Long Eaton NG10 ...236 B3
Manifold Ave
Ashbourne DE6 ......173 A1
Staveley S43 ......97 B4
Manifold Dr Derby DE24 .233 A4
Selston NG16 ......171 C4
Manitoba Way NG16 ...171 C4
Manknell Rd S41 ......96 A4
Manners Ave DE7 ...194 B1
Manners Cl SK23 ......34 C1
Manners Ind Est DE7 ..194 B1
Manners Rd DE7 ...194 C1
Manners St DE7 ...209 A3
Manning View DE7 ...194 C1
Mannion Cres NG10 ...236 A3
Manor Ave Brimington S43 96 C4
Derby DE23 ......218 B2
🖽 Nottingham NG2 ...268 C1
Stapleford NG9 ......223 B4
Manor Bglws S18 ......56 C1
Manor Cl Belper DE56 ...179 A1
Brassington DE4 ......153 A1
Newton DE55 ......148 A2
Pilsley S45 ......132 B1
Swadlincote DE15 ...255 A3
Manor Coll S40 ......266 A3
Manor Comp Sch NG19 .136 B3
Manor Court Rd S44 ...98 C2
Manor Cres
Burton u T DE15 ...255 A3
Chesterfield S40 ......95 B2
Dronfield S18 ......56 C1
Manor Croft
Branston DE13 ......253 A4
Ripley DE5 ......169 B2
Manor Ct
Barrow u T DE73 ...244 A3
Breaston DE72 ......235 C4
Clowne S43 ......80 C2
Somercotes DE55 ...170 C4
South Wingfield DE55 ..157 C2
Manor Ct St ST4 ......269 A1
Manor Dr Brimington S43 .96 C4
Chesterfield S40 ......95 B2
Netherseal DE12 ...264 C3
Manor Farm Ct S80 ...81 C3
Manor Farm Mews
Aston-on-T DE72 ...246 A4
Burnaston DE65 ......229 C3
Long Duckmanton S44 ...98 A2
Manor Farm Rd DE72 ..246 A4
Manor Fields Dr DE7 ..208 B4
Manor Gr S43 ......96 C3
Manor House Rd NG10 .236 C3
Manor Inf Sch S43 ......96 C3
Manor Leigh DE72 ...235 C4
Manor Park Ct DE3 ...218 A2
Manor Park Rd SK13 ...10 C1
Manor Park View SK13 ..10 C1
Manor Park Way DE3 ..218 A2
Manor Pk DE72 ......221 A1
Manor Rd Ashbourne DE6 173 B2
Barlborough S43 ......80 A4
Barton in F NG11 ...237 C3
Belper DE56 ......178 C2
Borrowash DE72 ...221 A1
Calow S43 ......96 C3
Chesterfield S40 ......95 B2
Derby DE23 ......218 B1
Derby, Chellaston DE73 .232 C1
Eastwood NG16 ......182 C1
Harthill S26 ......61 C4
Ilkeston DE7 ......194 C1
Killamarsh S21 ......60 C3
Mansfield Woodhouse
NG19 ....136 A2
South Wingfield DE55 ..157 C2
Swadlincote DE15 ...255 A3
Whaley Bridge SK23 ...45 C3
Manor St Glossop SK13 ...10 B1
Nottingham NG2 ...268 C1
Manor Top, Elm Tree
S12 ....44 A3
Manor View S20 ......59 C4
Manor View Cotts DE45 .89 C2
Manse Ave S80 ......100 B4
Manse Cl S80 ......100 B4
Mansell Cl ST16 ...269 A3
Mansfeldt Cres S41 ...95 C3
Mansfeldt Rd S41 ...95 C3
Mansfield Cl DE11 ...256 B1
Mansfield Comm Hospl
NG18 ....268 B3
Mansfield Dr S12 ......44 B3

Mansfield Gr NG1 ...268 A2
Mansfield Rd
Alfreton DE55 ......159 A2
Bramley-Vale S44 ...117 C1
Brinsley NG16 ......182 C2
Chesterfield S41 ......115 C3
Clowne S80 ......80 C1
Creswell S80 ......81 C1
Derby DE1,DE21 ...219 A4
Eastwood NG16 ......182 C2
Glapwell NG19,S44 ...134 B4
Heanor DE75 ......182 A1
Heath S44 ......117 A2
Holmewood S42 ...116 B2
Killamarsh S21, S26 ...60 C3
Mansfield Woodhouse
NG19 ....136 B3
Market Warsop NG20 ..120 C3
Nottingham NG1 ...268 B2
Palterton S44 ......118 A3
Scarcliffe S44 ......118 B3
Selston NG16 ......171 C1
Sheffield S12 ......44 B3
South Normanton DE55 .160 B3
Tibshelf DE55 ......148 A4
Whitwell S80 ......82 C4
Mansfield St Derby DE1 .267 B5
Somercotes DE55 ...170 B4
Mansfield Sta NG18 ...268 B3
Mansfield Woodhouse Sta
NG19 ....136 A2
Mansfields Croft DE65 .229 A2
Manton Cl
🖽 Burton u T DE13 ...240 C1
Swadlincote DE11 ...255 C3
Manvers Ave DE5 ...169 C1
Manvers Ct NG20 ...120 A2
Manvers Rd S44 ......97 A2
Manvers St
🖽 Mansfield NG18 ...268 B4
Mansfield Woodhouse
NG19 ....136 A2
Market Warsop NG20 ..120 A2
Nottingham NG2 ...268 C1
Ripley DE5 ......169 C1
Manystones La DE4 ...153 A2
Maple Ave Derby DE23 .231 B3
Disley SK12 ......33 A3
Ripley DE5 ......180 B4
Sandiacre NG10 ...223 A4
Maple Cl Doveridge DE6 .211 A4
Mansfield NG19 ...136 C1
Maple Ct ST17 ......269 A3
Maple Dr Ashbourne DE6 .185 B4
Aston-on-T DE72 ...246 A4
Belper DE56 ......179 A1
Creswell S80 ......81 C1
Derby DE73 ......233 A1
Derby, Boulton DE24 ...233 A3
Killamarsh S21 ......60 B3
South Normanton DE55 .160 A2
Maple Gdns DE75 ...181 B3
Maple Gr Breaston DE72 .235 C4
Burton u T DE15 ...254 C3
Derby DE22 ......204 B3
Glapwell S44 ......134 A4
Maple Rd DE11 ......256 A3
Maple St S43 ......97 A4
Maple View DE4 ......143 B2
Maple Way
Branston DE14 ......253 C4
Burton u T DE14 ...254 A4
Selston NG16 ......171 C4
Maplebeck Ct DE1 ...267 B5
Maples The DE75 ...194 A4
Mapletoft Ave NG19 ...136 A3
Mapleton Ave DE21 ...205 C1
Mapleton Rd
Ashbourne DE6 ......173 A1
Draycott DE72 ......235 A4
Mapperley CE Prim Sch
DE7 ....193 C2
Mapperley La DE7 ...193 C1
Mapperley Rd 🖽 S18 ...56 B1
Marchington CE DE22 .204 C1
Marchwood Cl S40 ......95 C2
Marchwood Ct ST4 ...269 A1
Marcus St DE1 ......219 A4
Mardale Cl S41 ......76 C1
Maree Cl DE24 ......231 C2
Marfleet Cl DE3 ......217 B2
Margaret Ave
Derby DE21 ......219 C3
Ilkeston DE7 ......208 C4
Long Eaton NG10 ...223 C4
Sandiacre NG10 ...223 A2
Margaret St DE1 ...267 B5
Margery Cl DE6 ......185 A4
Margreave Rd DE21 ...219 C4
Marham Cl NG2 ......268 C1
Marigold Cl DE21 ...206 A2
Marigold Pl DE11 ...256 C2
Marina Dr
Derby, Allenton DE24 ...232 C2
Derby, Spondon DE21 ..220 B3
Marina Rd DE7 ......193 C4
Marion Ct SK17 ......85 B3
Maris Cl NG7 ......268 A1
Marjorie Rd DE21 ...219 C4
Marjory La DE6,DE65 ..213 B2
Mark St NG10 ......223 B3
Mark's Cl DE23 ......231 B3
Markeaton La DE22 ...218 A4
Markeaton Prim Sch
DE22 ....218 C4
Markeaton St DE22 ...218 C4
Market Arc SK13 ......10 B1

Market Cl
Shirebrook NG20 ......119 C2
South Normanton DE55 ...160 A3
Market Pl Alfreton DE55 ..158 C2
Alfreton, Riddings DE55 ..170 C3
Ashbourne DE6 ....173 B1
Belper DE56 ....179 A2
Bolsover S44 ....99 A1
5 Buxton SK17 ....85 A4
Castleton S33 ....38 B1
Chapel-en-le-F SK23 ...47 A3
Chesterfield S40 .....266 B3
Codnor DE5 ....181 A4
Compstall SK6 ....15 A1
Crich DE4 ....156 C1
Cromford DE4 ....155 A3
Hartington SK17 .....137 B3
Ilkeston DE7 ....208 C4
Ironville NG16 ....170 C2
Long Eaton NG10 .....236 C4
Longnor SK17 ....121 A3
Mansfield NG18 ......268 B4
Mansfield Woodhouse
NG19 ....136 B2
Melbourne DE73 .....252 A4
Mottram in L SK14 .....9 A2
Ripley DE5 ....169 B1
Somercotes DE55 ....170 B4
South Normanton DE55 .160 A3
Staveley S43 ....78 C1
Sutton in A NG17 ....148 C2
Tideswell SK17 ....69 B2
Wirksworth DE4 .....165 C1
Market Sq
10 Stafford ST16 .....269 B4
Tideswell SK17 ....69 B2
Market St Bakewell DE45 109 B3
Broadbottom SK14 ....16 A4
Buxton SK17 ....85 A4
Castle Donington DE74 .247 A2
Chapel-en-le-F SK23 ...47 A3
Clay Cross S45 ......131 B2
Disley SK12 ....32 B3
Draycott DE72 ......235 A4
Eckington S21 ....59 B2
Glossop SK13 ....10 B1
Hayfield SK22 ....25 B2
Heanor DE75 ....181 C1
Hollingworth SK14 .....9 B3
Ilkeston DE7 ....208 C4
Ironville NG16 ....170 C2
Mansfield NG18 ......268 B4
Mottram in L SK14 .....9 A2
New Mills SK22 ....33 A4
Nottingham NG1 .....268 B1
Shirebrook NG20 .....119 C2
South Normanton DE55 .160 A3
Stafford ST16 ....269 B4
Staveley S43 ....78 C1
Sutton in A NG17 ....148 C2
Swadlincote DE11 ....256 A2
Whaley Bridge SK23 ...45 C4
Markham Cres S43 .....78 C1
Markham Ct Derby DE21 205 A2
Long Duckmanton S44 ..98 A3
Markham La S44 ....98 A2
Markham Rd
Chesterfield S40 .....266 B2
Long Duckmanton S44 ..98 A3
Markham Rise S45 ....131 A2
Markland Ave S43 .....81 A2
Markland Cres S43 ....81 A2
Markland La S80,S43 ...81 A1
Markland View S80 ....81 B2
Marlborough Cres DE15 255 A4
Marlborough Dr DE56 .179 B3
Marlborough Rd
Breaston DE72 ....235 B4
Buxton SK17 ....85 A4
Derby DE24 ....232 B4
Long Eaton NG10 ....223 C1
Mansfield NG19 .....135 C1
Marlborough St ST4 ..269 C1
Marlow Brow SK13 ....10 A2
Marlow Cres DE7 ....207 B4
Marlow Dr DE14 .....254 A4
Marlow St 5 Buxton SK17 85 B4
5 Glossop SK13 ......10 A3
Marlowe Ct DE23 ....231 C3
Marlpit La Bolsover S44 .99 B2
Denstone ST14 ......196 B3
Ellastone DE6 ....183 A4
Sutton on t H DE6 ...228 A4
Marlpool Inf Sch DE75 .194 A4
Marlpool Jun Sch DE75 182 A1
Marple Rd SK13 ....16 A3
Marple Sq 5 NG3 ....268 B2
Marple Sta SK6 ....23 A4
Marples Ave NG19 ....136 C3
Marquis Ct DE12 .....262 C3
Marquis Dr DE12 .....262 C3
Marriott Ave NG18 ...268 A4
Marrison Dr S21 ......60 B3
Marsden Cl DE56 ....190 C2
Marsden Pl 2 S40 ....95 B1
Marsden Row S33 .....40 A2
Marsden St
Chesterfield S40 .....266 B3
Derby DE24 ....232 C4
Glossop SK13 ....10 B1
Marsh Ave Dronfield S18 .57 A2
Hope S33 ....38 C2
Marsh Cl S20 ....59 B3
Marsh Green La S45 ..129 C2
Marsh Hall La S43 ....46 C3
Marsh Hollow DE6 ...200 C3
Marsh La Belper DE56 .179 A3
Mayfield DE6 ....183 B4

Marsh La continued
New Mills SK22,SK23 ...33 B3
Marsh Lane Cres DE56 .179 A2
Marsh Lane Prim Sch
S21 ....58 C2
Marsh Lane Trad Est
SK22 ....33 B4
Marsh View S21 ....59 A1
Marshall Dr 1 NG9 ..223 C4
Marshall St
Alfreton DE55 ....159 A2
Heanor DE75 ....181 C1
Marsham Dr SK6 ......23 A4
Marshaw Cl DE3 .....217 C1
Marshes The S33 ......38 C2
Marshfield Gr S43 .....79 A1
Marshgreen Cl DE24 .233 B3
Marston Cl SK17 .....106 A4
Marston Brook DE56 .228 C1
Marston Cl Belper DE56 .179 B3
Derby DE23 ....231 B3
Dronfield S18 ....75 B4
Marston Cres S17 .....55 C3
Marston La
Doveridge DE6 ......211 B2
Hatton DE65 ....239 B4
Marston on D DE65 ..228 A1
Marston Montgomery Prim
Sch DE6 ....211 C4
Marston Old La DE65 .239 B4
Marston Rd DE65 ....240 A4
Marston Rise DE15 ...254 C4
Martin Cl S21 ....59 B2
Martin Dr Derby DE21 .220 A4
Stafford ST16 ....269 A4
Martin Rise S21 ....59 B2
Martin St ST16 ......269 B4
Martin's La DE13 ....238 A2
Martindale Ct DE56 ..179 B3
Martins La S42 ......131 A4
Martlet Ave SK12 .....32 B3
Marx Ct S45 ....131 B2
Mary Ann St S41 ......76 C2
Mary Devonshire Cotts
DE45 ....91 B1
Mary Howitt Inf Sch
DE75 ....181 B1
Mary St Eckington S21 ..59 B2
Whaley Thorns NG20 ..101 A1
Mary Swanwick Prim Sch
S41 ....77 A2
Maryfield Wlk ST4 ...269 A2
Maryland Ct
Stapleford NG9 .....209 C1
Swadlincote DE11 ....256 A4
Maryland Rd DE21 ...220 A3
Marylebone Cres DE22 .218 A3
Masefield Ave
Derby DE23 ....231 C4
Holmewood S42 .....116 B1
Swadlincote DE11 ....256 B3
Masefield Rd S13 .....44 B4
Mason Cres S13 ......44 B4
Mason Gr S13 ....44 B4
Mason Rd DE7 ......194 B1
Mason St S80 ....81 C3
Masonic Pl NG1 .....268 A2
Masons Gr SK13 ......10 A3
Massey Gdns NG3 ...268 C2
Masson Cl S40 ....95 B3
Masson Rd DE4 .....143 A1
Masson Shopping Village
DE4 ....155 A4
Masson Wlk DE22 ...218 C2
Masterson St ST4 ...269 C1
Mastin Ave S43 ....80 B4
Mather's Way S42 ...115 B1
Matlock Ave NG18 ...268 B4
Matlock Bath Sta DE4 .143 A1
Matlock Ct
Long Eaton NG10 ....235 C3
31 Nottingham NG1 ..268 B2
Matlock Dr S43 ....97 B3
Matlock Gdns 11 SK13 ..9 C1
Matlock Gn DE4 .....143 B2
Matlock Ho DE21 ....220 C2
Matlock Pl 12 SK13 ...9 C1
Matlock Rd
Ambergate DE56 ....167 C2
Ashover S42,S45 ....113 C2
Belper DE56 ....178 C4
Brackenfield DE55 ...145 B1
Derby DE21 ....205 C1
Holymoorside S40,S42 .114 A4
Wessington DE55 ...157 C4
Matlock Riverside Sta*
DE4 ....143 A4
Matlock St DE45 ....109 B3
Matlock Sta DE4 ....143 A4
Matt Orch DE55 .....160 A2
Mattersey Ct NG19 ..136 A1
Matthew Cl SK13 ......9 C4
Matthew Holland Comp Sch
NG16 ....171 C4
Matthew Kirtley Mus*
DE5 ....170 A2
Matthew St DE24 ...232 C3
Matthew Way DE23 .230 C4
Matthews Ct NG9 ...209 C1
Matthews Fold S8 .....43 B1
Matthews La S8 ....43 B1
Maude St S21 ....59 B2
Maugerhay S8 ....43 B1
Maunleigh NG19 ....136 C1
Mawfa Ave S14 ....43 B1
Mawfa Cres S14 ......43 B1
Mawfa Dr S14 ....43 B1
Mawfa Rd S14 ....43 B1

Mawfa Wlk S14 ....43 B1
Mawkin La NG16 .....160 C3
Maws La NG16 ......195 C4
Max Rd DE21 ....219 C4
Maxey Pl S8 ....43 A3
Maxtoke Rd NG7 ....268 A1
Maxwell Ave DE22 ...218 B4
Maxwell Pl ST4 .....269 A2
Maxwell St DE72 ....235 C4
May Ave S41 ....77 B2
May S DE7 ....194 B2
May St Derby DE22 ..218 C2
Ilkeston DE7 ....194 C2
Maybank Cl SK23 .....35 A1
Mayfair DE11 ....255 C3
Mayfair Ave NG18 ...268 C3
Mayfair Cres DE22 ..217 C3
Mayfield Ave
Heanor DE75 ....181 C1
Kilburn DE56 ....192 A4
Mayfield DE6 ....184 B4
Mayfield Dr
Burton u T DE15 ....255 A4
North Wingfield S42 .131 C3
Stapleford NG9 .....209 C1
Mayfield Gr NG10 ...223 C1
Mayfield Pl W ST4 ..269 A1
Mayfield Rd
Burton u T DE15 ....248 A2
Chesterfield S40 .....95 B1
Derby DE21 ....219 C4
Marple SK6 ....15 A1
Ringinglow S10 ....42 C4
Mayfield Terr
Hathersage S32 ....53 A4
Mayfield DE6 ....184 B3
Mayflower Ct
Sheffield S12 ....44 A3
Shirebrook NG20 ....119 C2
Mayflower Rd NG16 .195 A4
Mayhall Ave NG19 ...136 A2
Maylands DE72 .....221 A1
Maylands Ave DE72 .235 C4
Maynard Rd
Chesterfield S40 .....266 A1
Nether Padley S32 ....53 B1
Maynestone Rd SK23 ..34 C3
Maypole Hill DE11 ..256 A3
Maypole La DE21 ....230 C4
McAdam Cl DE15 ....248 A1
McAuley St DE1 .....267 B4
McGough Mews DE24 .232 A3
McGregor's Way S40 .115 A4
McMahon Ave S43 ....97 A3
McNeil Gr DE72 ....235 A4
Mead Cl DE24 ......231 C2
Mead Cres DE15 ....255 A4
Mead Wlk DE15 ....255 A3
Meadow Ave Buxton SK17 .67 A3
Codnor DE5 ....181 A4
Mansfield NG18 ....268 C3
Meadow Bank
Glossop SK13 ....16 C4
Hollingworth SK14 ....9 B3
Mansfield Woodhouse
NG19 ....136 C3
South Normanton DE55 .160 A4
Meadow Brook Cl DE23 230 C3
Meadow Cl
Barlborough S43 .....80 B3
Bolsover S44 ....118 A4
Breaston DE72 .....235 C4
Chesterfield S43 ......77 B1
Derby DE21 ....220 C2
Dove Holes SK17 .....47 C1
Draycott DE72 ......235 A4
Dronfield S18 ....57 B2
Eastwood NG16 ....182 C2
Findern DE65 ....230 B1
Horsley Woodhouse DE7 .192 B3
Repton DE65 ....242 C1
Stoney Middleton S32 .72 A2
Tibshelf DE55 ......148 A4
Whaley Bridge SK23 ...45 B4
Meadow Cotts NG19 .136 B2
Meadow Cres
Castle Donington DE74 .247 A1
Mosborough S20 ......59 A4
Meadow Croft S42 ..132 B4
Meadow Ct Belper DE56 .178 C2
Chesterfield S43 ......77 B2
Kilburn DE56 ....192 A4
South Normanton DE55 .159 C2
Meadow Dr S43 ....78 C1
Meadow Farm Com Prim Sch
DE21 ....220 A2
Meadow Gdns DE75 .182 A1
Meadow Gr
Newton DE55 ....148 A2
Totley DE55 ....55 B2
Meadow Grove Rd S17 .55 B2
Meadow Head Ave S8 ..56 C4
Meadow Head Dr S8 ..56 C4
Meadow La
Burton u T DE13 ....248 A4
Derby DE1, DE21 ...267 D3
Derby, Chaddesden DE21 .219 C3
Disley SK12 ....32 B3
Dove Holes SK17 .....47 C1
Long Eaton NG10 ....236 C4
Newton DE55 ....159 C4
Nottingham NG2 ....268 C1
Repton DE65 ....243 A2
Roston DE6 ....197 B4
Swadlincote DE11 ...256 A3
Tideswell SK17 ....69 A1

Meadow Lane Ind Est
DE55 ....159 A3
Meadow Nook DE24 .233 B3
Meadow Rd
Awsworth NG16 .....195 B3
Clay Cross S45 .....131 A3
Derby DE1 ....267 C3
Derby, Wilmorton DE21,
DE24 ....219 A2
Ripley DE5 ....169 C1
Meadow Rise
Brassington DE4 ....153 A1
Church Broughton DE65 .227 A4
Glossop SK13 ....16 C4
Old Brampton S42 ....94 C2
Meadow St Ilkeston DE7 .194 C1
Ironville NG16 ....170 C3
New Mills SK22 ....33 B4
Meadow Vale DE56 ..190 B2
Meadow View
Belper DE56 ....178 C2
Bolsover S43 ....80 C2
Chesterfield S40 ....114 A4
Darley Dale DE4 ....142 C4
Doveridge DE6 .....224 B4
Holmewood S42 ....132 B4
Rolleston DE13 .....240 B2
South Wingfield DE55 .157 C3
Meadow View Cl DE21 .206 A2
Meadow View Rd
Sheffield S8 ....56 C4
Swadlincote DE11 ...255 C3
Meadow Way
Derby DE73 ....233 A1
Swadlincote DE11 ...256 A3
Meadowbank Way
NG16 ....182 B2
Meadowbrook Ind Est
S20 ....60 A4
Meadowcroft SK14 ....9 A2
Meadowcroft Gdns S20 .59 C4
Meadowcroft Glade S20 .59 C4
Meadowcroft Rise S20 .59 C4
Meadowfield SK23 ....45 B4
Meadowfield Cl SK13 ...9 C2
Meadowgrass Cl DE23 .231 A1
Meadowhead S8 ......57 A4
Meadowhead Sch S8 ..57 A3
Meadowhead Sec Sch
S8 ....57 A4
Meadowhill Rd S41 .115 B4
Meadowlands S44 .....99 B1
Meadowlark Gr DE21 .206 A1
Meadows Com Sch The
S41 ....77 A2
Meadows Croft DE56 .190 B2
Meadows Dr S43 ......97 C4
Meadows Ind Est The
DE21 ....219 B3
Meadows Prim Sch
DE56 ....190 B2
Meadows Rd SK22 ....25 B1
Meadows The
Chesterfield S42 ......94 C3
Dove Holes SK17 .....47 C1
Great Longstone DE45 .90 A2
Heanor DE75 ....181 C1
Old Brampton S42 ....95 A3
Swanwick DE55 ....169 C4
Uttoxeter ST14 .....210 A1
Meadowside Disley SK12 .33 A3
Mayfield DE6 ....184 B3
Whaley Bridge SK23 ...45 B4
Meadowside Cl
Shirley DE6 ....200 B4
Wingerworth S42 ...115 A4
Meads The S8 ....57 A4
Meadway DE7 ....55 B4
Meadway The S17 .....55 B4
Meakin St S41 ......115 B4
Meal Hill Rd HD7 ......2 C4
Meal St S42 ....33 B4
Mear Dr DE72 ......221 A1
Mear Greaves La DE15 .248 A2
Mease La DE7 ....263 A1
Mease The DE65 ....228 C1
Measham Rd
Donisthorpe DE12 ...265 B3
Moira DE12 ....262 C2
Stretton en le F DE12 .265 C1
Meath Ave DE21 ....220 B2
Meden Ave NG16 ...134 C4
Meden Cl NG19 .....135 A3
Meden Ct NG19 .....135 A3
Meden Rd NG19 ....136 B2
Meden Sq NG19 ....135 A3
Medina Cl DE24 ....233 B3
Medlock Cl S40 .....114 A4
Medlock Rd S40 ....114 B4
Medway Dr DE22 ...205 A2
Meerbrook Cl DE21 .206 A1
Meerbrook Pl DE7 ..208 B3
Meersbrook Park Rd S8 .43 A4
Meersbrook Rd S8 ....43 A4
Megaloughton La DE21 .220 B2
Megdale DE4 ....143 A3
Melandra Castle Rd SK13 .9 B1
Melandra Ct DE22 ..218 C2
Melandra Rd SK13 ....9 C2
Melanie Cl S14 ....43 A4
Melbourn Cl DE56 ..190 C2
Melbourne Ave
Burton u T DE15 ....248 A1
Dronfield S18 ....56 A1
Melbourne Cl
Belper DE56 ....179 B1
Derby DE22 ....204 B1
Derby, Mickleover DE3 .217 C2

Melbourne Ct
Long Eaton NG10 ....235 C2
8 Staveley S43 ....78 C1
Melbourne Hall* DE73 252 A4
Melbourne Hall & Gdns*
DE73 ....252 A4
Melbourne Ho DE21 ..220 C2
Melbourne Inf Sch
DE73 ....252 A4
Melbourne Jun Sch
DE73 ....252 A4
Melbourne La
Breedon on t H DE73 .252 C1
Ticknall DE73 ......251 B3
Melbourne Rd NG9 ..209 C1
Melbourne St Derby DE1 267 B1
Mansfield Woodhouse
NG19 ....136 B3
Melbreak Cl DE3 ....217 C1
Melfort Cl DE24 .....231 C1
Meliden Way ST4 ...269 A1
Melling Cl S40 ......114 C4
Melling Ct S40 ......114 C4
Mellington Cl S8 ......43 B1
Mellor Dr ST14 .....210 A1
Mellor La Barlow S18 ..75 C1
Chapel-en-le-F SK23 ...47 A3
Mellor Prim Sch SK6 ..23 B3
Mellor Rd
Burton u T DE14 ....254 A4
New Mills SK6,SK22 ...24 B2
Mellor St DE24 .....232 C3
Mellor Way S40 .....115 A4
Mellor's La DE56 ...191 B3
Melrose Ave NG18 ..268 C3
Melrose Cl
Chesterfield S40 ......95 B2
Derby DE24 ....231 C1
Melrose Ct 7 S41 ....96 A3
Meltham La S41 ......96 A3
Melville Ave Derby DE23 .231 B3
Melbourne DE73 ....252 A4
Melton Ct
Sandiacre NG10 ....223 A3
Somercotes DE55 ...170 B3
Melville Cl DE6 .....175 C2
Melville Cres S43 .....96 C2
Melville Ct DE65 ....229 A2
Melville Gdns NG3 ..268 C2
Mclville St NG1 .....268 B1
Memorial Croft DE4 .154 C2
Memorial Rd DE22 ..204 B2
Mendip Cl 1 NG10 ..223 A1
Mendip Cres S40 .....95 A2
Mendip Ct DE21 ....205 C2
Menin Rd DE22 .....204 B1
Mentmore Cl DE55 .170 A4
Mercaston Cl S40 ....95 A3
Mercaston La
Hulland Ward DE6 ...188 A2
Mackworth DE6,DE22 ...203 A4
Mercaston Rd DE21 .219 C4
Mercer Cres DE55 ..159 B2
Merchant Ave DE21 .220 B2
Merchant St Derby DE22 218 C3
Shirebrook NG20 ....120 A2
Mercia Cl
Eastwood NG16 ....195 A4
Hatton DE65 ....239 B4
Mercia Dr Borr S17 ...55 C3
Willington DE65 ....242 A3
Mercian Cl DE7 .....194 C1
Mercian Mews DE21 .220 B2
Mereoak La DE11,DE73 .257 C4
Meredith Ct NG9 ...209 C1
Meridian Cl DE7 ....194 C2
Merion Gr DE23 ....218 A1
Merlin Cl DE56 .....179 B3
Merlin Cres DE14 ...253 C4
Merlin Gn DE21 ....231 B2
Merlin Way
Burnaston DE3 .....230 A4
Ilkeston DE7 ....208 C2
Woodville DE11 ....256 C2
Merrial Cl DE45 ....109 B2
Merrick Cl S40 ....95 B3
Merridale Rd DE23 .231 B4
Merrill Coll DE24 ...232 C2
Merrill Coll (Lower Site)
DE24 ....232 C3
Merrill Way DE24 ..232 B3
Merrybower Cl DE21 .231 B2
Merrydale Rd DE15 .255 A4
Mersey Bank Rd SK13 ..9 C2
Merthyr Ct DE21 ...206 A1
Merton Ct NG9 .....209 C1
Mervyn Rd DE15 ....248 A2
Metcalfe Cl DE24 ...233 A4
Metcalfe Way S21 ....60 B3
Meteor Ctr The DE21 .205 B1
Methley Cl S12 ....43 C3
Metro Ave DE55 ....148 A2
Mettesford DE4 .....143 B3
Meverill Rd SK17 .....69 B3
Mevril Rd SK23 ......45 C2
Mewies Cl DE12 ....253 B1
Mews The DE73 ....252 A4
Meynell Cl
Burton u T DE15 ....248 A1
Chesterfield S40 ......95 B1
Meynell Ct DE22 ....204 B1
Meynell Rd DE15 ...248 A1
Meynell Rise DE6 ...173 B2
Meynell St Derby DE23 .218 C1
Swadlincote DE11 ...256 A1

Meynell Way S21 ....60 B3
Meyrick Rd ST17 ......269 B3
Michael Cl S42 ....115 A3
Michael House-Rudolf
 Steiner Sch DE75 ....194 A3
Michael's La DE6 ......183 B3
Michelle Cl DE24 ......231 B2
Michigan Cl DE21 ......220 B3
Michlow Cl S33 ....51 A4
Michlow Dr S33 ....51 A4
Michlow La S33 ....51 A4
Mickover Manor DE3 ..217 B1
Micklebring Cl DE5 ....169 B1
Micklecroft Gdns DE23 .230 C4
Mickledon Cl **3** NG10 .236 A4
Mickleover Prim Sch
 DE3 ....217 B1
Mickleross Cl DE3 .....217 B2
Mickleton Cl DE11 .....256 A1
Mickley Est DE55 ......146 B3
Mickley Inf Sch DE55 ..146 B2
Mickley La Shirland DE55 146 B3
 Totley S17 ....55 C2
Middle Cl DE11 ....256 A2
Middle Friars ST17 ....269 B3
Middle Hay Cl S14 ......43 C2
Middle Hay Pl S14 ......43 C2
Middle Hay Rise S14 ....43 C2
Middle Hay View S14 ....43 C2
Middle Hill NG1 ....268 B1
Middle La Clay Cross S45 131 C2
 Crich DE4 ....156 B1
Middle Ox Cl S20 ....59 C3
Middle Ox Gdns S20 .....59 C3
Middle Pavement
 Chesterfield S40 .....266 B3
 6 Nottingham NG1 ...268 B1
Middle Rd S42 ....114 C1
Middle Shambles S40 ..266 B3
Middle St Bolsover S44 ..99 A1
 Bolsover, Hillstown S44 .118 B4
Middlebeck Cl DE73 ....232 C1
Middlecroft L Ctr S43 ...97 B4
Middlecroft Rd S43 .....97 B4
Middlefield Cl S17 ......55 B4
Middlefield Croft S17 ...55 B4
Middlegate Field Dr S80 82 A3
Middleton Ave
 Codnor DE5 ....181 A3
 Derby DE23 ....218 B1
Middleton Dr S43 ....97 A3
Middleton La S32 ....71 B2
Middleton Prim Sch
 DE4 ....154 B2
Middleton Rd
 Ilkeston DE7 ....209 A3
 Mansfield Woodhouse
 NG19 ....136 B3
Middleton St
 Awsworth NG16 ....195 B2
 Cossall DE7 ....195 A1
 Derby DE23 ....219 A1
Middleton Top Visitor's Ctr★
 DE4 ....154 B2
Middletown Mdws S43 ..80 A3
Midhill Rd S2 ....43 A4
Midland Ave NG9 ......223 B3
Midland Ct S41 ....115 A4
Midland Pl DE1 ....267 D2
Midland Railway Ctr★
 DE5 ....169 C2
Midland Rd Derby DE1 .267 D1
 Eastwood NG16 ....182 C1
 Heanor DE75 ....181 C1
 Swadlincote DE11 ....256 A2
Midland Road Ind Est
 DE11 ....256 A3
Midland St NG10 ......236 C4
Midland Terr
 Ambergate DE56 ......167 C2
 Barrow Hill S43 ....78 A2
 Blackwell DE55 ....147 B1
 Chesterfield S41 .....115 A4
 New Mills SK22 ....33 B4
Midland View S42 .....131 C4
Midland Way S43 ....80 A3
Midway DE22 ....204 C1
Midway Ctr S45 ....131 B2
Midway Rd DE11 ......256 B3
Midworth St NG18 ....268 B3
Mikado Rd NG10 ......236 B3
Milbank Cl DE22 ......217 C3
Milburn Gdns DE21 ...206 A2
Milbury Cl DE21 ......205 C1
Mile Ash La DE22 .....204 C1
Milford DE45 ....109 B3
Milford Ave NG10 ....223 B4
Milford Com Prim Sch
 DE56 ....190 C4
Milford Ct DE56 ......109 B3
Milford Dr DE7 ....194 B2
Milford Rd Duffield DE56 190 C2
 Staveley S43 ....97 B3
Milford St DE1 ....218 C4
Milken La S45 ....130 A2
Mill Acre Cl DE7 .....194 B1
Mill Brow
 Broadbottom SK14 .....16 A4
 Marple SK6 ....23 B4
Mill Brow Rd SK6 ......23 C4
Mill Cl Borrowash DE72 .221 B1
 Findern DE65 ....230 B1
 Kilburn DE56 ....192 A4
 Newton Solney DE15 ..248 C4
 Swadlincote DE11 ....256 B3

Mill Cl continued
 Swanwick DE55 ......169 C4
Mill Cliff SK17 ....85 B4
Mill Cres Whitwell S80 ..82 A3
 Wingerworth S42 .....115 B2
Mill Croft DE3 ....217 B2
Mill Farm Cl S32 ....72 B1
Mill Fleam DE65 ......228 C1
Mill Gn Shardlow DE72 .235 A1
 Staveley S43 ....78 C1
Mill Green Cl DE12 ....260 B2
Mill Hill Sch DE5 .....180 C4
Mill Hill Elvaston DE24 .233 B2
 Long Duckmanton S44 .117 A3
Mill Hill Cl DE5 ....169 C1
Mill Hill Dr DE15 .....248 A2
Mill Hill La
 Breaston DE72 ....222 C1
 Burton u T DE15 .....248 A2
 Derby DE1, DE23 .....267 A1
Mill Hill Rd DE23 .....267 A1
Mill Holme DE55 ......160 A2
Mill La Ashbourne DE6 .173 C1
 Barlow S18 ....75 B2
 Belper DE56 ....179 A2
 Bolsover S44 ....99 A2
 Bolsover, Shuttlewood S44 .98 C4
 Bradbourne DE6 ......163 A1
 Castleton S33 ....38 B2
 Chesterfield S40 ......95 B1
 Clay Cross S42, S45 ..130 C3
 Codnor DE5 ....181 A4
 Cossall NG16 ....195 B1
 Derby DE3 ....217 B2
 Doveridge DE6 ....211 A1
 Dronfield S18 ....57 A1
 Ellastone DE6 ....183 A1
 Eyam S32 ....71 C3
 Grassmoor S42 ......115 B2
 Hartington SK17 .....137 B3
 Heath S44 ....117 A1
 Hilton DE65 ....228 B1
 Holloway DE4 ....156 A3
 Holmesfield S18 ......74 C3
 Holmewood S44 .....133 B4
 Pinxton NG16 ....160 B1
 Renishaw S21 ....60 A1
 Roston DE6 ....197 B4
 Sandiacre NG10 ......223 B3
 Scropton DE65 ....226 C1
 Scropton, Foston DE65 .226 B4
 Shirley DE6 ....200 B4
 Sutton in A NG17 ....148 C1
 Totley S17 ....55 C3
 Whitwell S80 ....82 A3
Mill Meadow Way DE65 229 A2
Mill Moor Cl DE73 ....232 C1
Mill Rd Cromford DE4 ..155 A3
 Heanor DE75 ....194 A4
 Stapleford NG9 ......223 B4
Mill Row DE21 ....220 B3
Mill St Bakewell DE45 ..109 B3
 Barlow S18 ....75 B2
 Belper DE56 ....179 A2
 Chesterfield S41 .....266 C3
 Clowne S43 ....80 C2
 Coton in t E DE12 ....260 B2
 Derby DE1 ....218 C3
 Glossop SK13 ....10 B1
 Hayfield SK22 ....25 B2
 Ilkeston DE7 ....194 C1
 Mansfield NG18 ......268 C1
 Rocester ST14 ....197 A2
 Stafford ST16 ....269 B4
 Stoney Middleton S32 ..72 A2
Mill Stream Cl S40 .....95 B1
 Whitwell S80 ....82 A3
Mill Wlk Bolsover S44 ...99 A2
 Whitwell S80 ....82 A3
Mill Yd DE55 ....170 B4
Millash La S80 ....82 A2
Millbank Heanor DE75 .194 A4
 Stafford ST16 ....269 B4
Millbank Ave DE56 ....179 A1
Millbank Cl DE7 ......194 B2
Millbank Dr ST14 .....197 A2
Millbrook SK14 ....9 C3
Millcross La S18 ....75 C2
Milldale Ave SK17 .....84 C3
Milldale Cl
 Chesterfield S40 ......95 B3
 Ripley DE5 ....180 B3
Milldale Ct
 Ashbourne DE6 ......185 B4
 Belper DE56 ....179 A2
Milldale Rd Derby DE21 .220 C2
 Long Eaton NG10 ....236 A3
 Totley S17 ....55 C3
Milldam La DE6 ....186 C4
Millenium Ave DE12 ..262 C3
Millennium Cl DE7 ....194 C2
Millennium Way
 Chesterfield S41 ......76 C1
 Derby DE21 ....219 C2
Miller Ave S43 ....79 B2
Millers Dale Cl DE56 ..179 B3
Millers Gn DE4 ....165 C3
Millers La DE55 ......145 C1
Millersdale Ave DE7 ..194 C3
Millersdale Cl DE15 ..248 A3
Millersdale Way SK17 ..85 A3
Millfield DE72 ....235 A1
Millfield Croft **10** DE11 .256 A4
Millfield Rd Ilkeston DE7 209 A4
 Kimberley NG16 .....195 C4
Millfield St DE11 .....257 A1
Millhouse Ct DE72 ....235 A4

Millom Pl DE21 ......205 B1
Millpool Cl DE11 .....257 A4
Mills Ct DE4 ....235 A4
Mills Ct DE4 ....156 C1
Millstone Cl **21** S18 ...56 B1
Millstone La
 Ashford in t W DE45 ..108 C4
 Ripley DE5 ....169 B4
Millthorpe La S18 ......75 A3
Milltown SK13 ....10 B1
Millview Cl NG2 ......268 C1
Millway NG19 ....136 B1
Millway La DE6 ......149 C2
Milnbank Ave SK17 ....85 B4
Milner Ave Codnor DE5 .181 A4
 Draycott DE72 ....235 A4
Milner Rd NG10 ......236 B4
Milnhay Rd NG16 .....182 B1
Milton Ave Alfreton DE55 159 B2
 Ilkeston DE7 ....194 C1
 Shirland DE55 ....146 B2
 Swadlincote DE11 ....256 B3
Milton Cres S40 ......115 A4
Milton Ct SK17 ....85 A4
Milton La SK23 ....46 A3
Milton Pl S43 ....78 C1
Milton Rd Derby DE3 ..217 B2
 Ilkeston DE7 ....194 C2
 Repton DE65 ....242 B1
Milton St Derby DE22 ..218 B2
 Ilkeston DE7 ....194 C2
 Long Eaton NG10 ....236 B4
 Mansfield NG18 .....268 B4
 Nottingham NG1 .....268 B1
Milton Terr NG10 .....236 B4
Milward Rd DE75 .....181 B1
Mimosa Cres DE23 ....231 C3
Miners Hill DE4 ......153 A1
Minimum Terr S40 ....266 A2
Minshall Ct ST4 ......269 C1
Minshall St ST4 ......269 C1
Minster Rd DE21 .....205 C1
Minster Way DE55 ....169 C4
Mint Gr NG10 ....236 A4
Minton Rd DE74 .....246 C2
Minton St ST4 ....269 C2
Mires La
 Great Longstone DE45 ..90 A4
 Tideswell SK17 ....70 A2
Mires The
 Alstonefield DE6 .....149 A2
 Birchover DE4 ....126 A1
Miriam Ave S40 ......114 A4
Miry La DE65 ....227 B2
Misterton Cl DE22 ....204 C1
Misterton Ct NG19 ...136 A1
Mitcham Wlk DE22 ...218 A3
Mitchell Ave NG16 ...182 A4
Mitchell St Clowne S43 ..80 C2
 Long Eaton NG10 ....236 C4
Mitchell Terr DE7 ....209 A3
Mitchell Villas S43 ....77 C2
Mitchell Way S43 .....77 C2
Mitre Dr DE65 ....242 B1
Moat Bank DE15 .....248 B1
Moat St DE11 ....256 A1
Moat The DE74 ......247 A2
Model Village S80 ....100 C4
Model Village Prim Sch
 NG20 ....119 C2
Moffatt Rd S2 ....43 A4
Moira Cl DE21 ....220 A4
Moira Dale DE74 .....247 B2
Moira Furnace Mus★
 DE12 ....262 C2
Moira Rd
 Donisthorpe DE12 ...262 C1
 Moira DE11 ....262 C4
 Overseal DE12 ......262 A3
 Woodville DE11 .....256 C1
Moira St DE73 ....252 A4
Moisty La
 Marchington ST14 ...224 B3
 Stoney Middleton S32 ..71 A2
Molineux Ave S43 .....78 C1
Molineux St DE23 ....219 A1
Molloy Pl S8 ....43 A3
Molloy St S8 ....43 A3
Molyneaux Bsns Pk
 DE4 ....127 A2
Monarch Dr DE21 ....206 B2
Monarch Way DE75 ..181 B1
Moncreiff Dr DE13 ...241 A1
Moncrieff Cres DE21 .220 A4
Mondello Dr DE24 ....233 B3
Monk Rd DE55 ....159 A1
Monk St Derby DE22 ..267 A2
 Tutbury DE13 ....239 B4
Monk's Rd SK13 ....17 A2
Monks Cl Derby DE24 .231 B2
 Ilkeston DE7 ....209 A4
Monks Way S81 ....63 C4
Monks' Rd SK13 ....16 C3
Monksdale Cl SK17 ....69 A2
Monksdale La SK17 ...68 C1
Monkton Cl DE7 .....194 B2
Monkwood Rd S41 .....95 B4
Monmouth St DE21 ..219 B3
Monnies End S43 ......80 B3
Monpelier Cl DE14 ...254 A4
Monsal Ave SK17 ......85 A4
Monsal Cres Staveley S43 .97 B3
 Tibshelf DE55 ....147 C3
Monsal Dr Derby DE21 .220 C2
 South Normanton DE55 .159 C3
Monsal Gr SK17 ....85 A4
Monsaldale Cl
 Burton u T DE15 .....248 A1

Monsaldale Cl continued
 Long Eaton NG10 ....236 A3
Monsall Ave DE7 .....194 C3
Monsdale La DE6 .....151 C1
Monsom La DE65 .....242 B2
Montagu St SK6 ....15 A1
Monteith Pl DE74 ....247 A2
Montford Mews DE74 247 A2
Montfort St **27** NG7 ..268 A2
Montgomery Cl DE21 .228 C1
Montgomery St NG7 ..268 A2
Montpelier DE22 .....204 B4
Montpelier Pl SK17 ....66 B1
Montpelier Rd DE56 ..167 C2
Montrose Cl DE24 ....231 C2
Montrose Ct NG9 ....209 C1
Montrose **12** S18 ....56 B1
Montrose Sq NG19 ...136 A3
Monument Hill NG10 .170 C2
Monument La NG16 ..170 C2
Monyash CE Prim Sch
 DE45 ....107 B1
Monyash Cl Derby DE21 .220 A4
 Ilkeston DE7 ....194 C2
 Staveley S43 ....97 B4
Monyash **18** SK13 .....9 B1
Monyash Mews **16** SK13 .9 B1
Monyash **17** SK13 ......9 B1
Monyash Rd
 Bakewell DE45 ......109 B3
 Over Haddon DE45 ..109 A1
Monyash Way DE56 ..179 A3
Moonpenny Way S18 ...57 A1
Moor Cres S20 ....59 B4
Moor Dr DE24 ....233 A3
Moor End DE21 ......220 C3
Moor End Rd SK6 ......24 A3
Moor Farm Ave S20 ....59 B4
Moor Farm Garth S20 ..59 B4
Moor Farm Rd E DE6 ..185 C4
Moor Farm Rd W DE6 .185 C4
Moor Farm Rise S20 ...59 B4
Moor Furlong DE13 ..240 C1
Moor La Aston-on-T DE72 246 A4
 Barrow u T DE73 .....244 A4
 Bolsover S44 ....99 A1
 Bonsall DE4 ....142 A1
 Calow S44 ....116 B4
 Dale Abbey DE7 .....207 C1
 Darley Dale DE4 .....127 B2
 Derby DE24 ....232 B3
 Elton DE4 ....140 C3
 Flagg DE45 ....106 C2
 Kirk Ireton DE6 .....165 A2
 Kirk Langley DE6 ....202 C1
 Little Eaton DE21 ...191 C1
 Mansfield NG18 .....268 A3
 Ockbrook DE72 .....221 B3
 Osmaston DE6 ......185 C3
 Scarcliffe S44 ....119 A4
 Taddington SK17 .....87 C1
 Youlgreave DE45 ....125 C3
Moor Lane Fst Sch
 NG18 ....268 A3
Moor Rd Ashover S45 .129 C2
 Breadsall DE7,DE21 ..205 C3
 Brinsley NG16 ......182 C4
 Great Longstone DE45 ..89 C3
Moor Rise DE56 ......191 B4
Moor St Derby DE21 ..220 C3
 Mansfield NG18 .....268 B3
Moor The Brinsley NG16 .182 B4
 Middleton (Nr Wirksworth)
 DE4 ....154 B2
Moor Valley S20 ....44 C1
Moor View Rd S43 .....79 A1
Mooracre La S44 ....99 B1
Moorbridge La NG9 ..209 B1
Moorbrook La S33 .....50 C4
Moore Cl S42 ....116 B1
Moore St DE23 ....219 A2
Mooredge Rd DE4 ....143 B3
Mooredge Rd DE4 ....157 A1
Moorend DE4 ....111 B2
Moores Ave NG10 ....223 B4
Moorfield DE4 ....143 B4
Moorfield Ave
 Bolsover S44 ....99 A1
 Holbrook DE56 ......191 B4
Moorfield Cres **5** NG10 223 A3
Moorfield Ct NG9 ....209 C1
Moorfield La NG20 ...100 C2
Moorfield Prec SK14 ...9 B3
Moorfield Sq S44 ......99 A1
Moorfield St SK14 .....9 B3
Moorfield Terr SK14 ...9 B3
Moorfields Ave NG16 .182 C2
Moorgate DE22 ......217 C3
Moorgate Ave NG19 ..134 C4
Moorgate Cres S18 ....76 A4
Moorgate St NG7 ....268 A2
Moorhaigh La NG19 ..135 A2
Moorhall DE45 ....109 A3
Moorhay Cl S41 ....95 A4
Moorhead Ave DE24 ..232 C3
Moorhead Prim Sch
 DE24 ....232 C3
Moorings The SK12 ....32 C3
Moorland Ave NG9 ...223 B3
Moorland Cl NG19 ...268 A4
Moorland Dr S44 .....116 C1
Moorland La NG19 ...268 A4
Moorland Rd Derby DE3 217 B2
 Hathersage S32 ......53 A4
Moorland Terr S42 ...144 A2
Moorland View
 Apperknowle S18 .....58 A1
 Sheffield S12 ....44 A1

Moorland View Rd S40 ..95 B1
Moorlands Cl NG10 ...223 A1
Moorlands Dr DE6 ...184 B4
Moorlands La
 Bonsall DE4 ....142 A2
 Stoney Middleton S32 ..72 B3
Moorlawn Ave S42 ...113 C4
Moorpark Ave S40 ...114 B4
Moorpool Cres DE56 .191 B4
Moorside Dr
 Cromford DE4 ....155 A3
 Glossop SK13 ....17 A4
 Mosborough S20 ......59 B4
Moorside Cres DE24 ..231 C2
Moorside Gdns DE72 .234 B1
Moorside La DE56 ....191 B4
Moorsyde Rd S17 .....269 A1
Moorthorpe Gdns S20 .44 C1
Moorthorpe Gn S20 ...44 C1
Moorthorpe Way S20 ..44 C1
Moortop Rd S21 ....58 C4
Moorview Cl
 Brimington S43 ....96 B4
 Wingerworth S42 ....115 A2
Moorview Ct **14** S17 ..56 A3
Moorway DE21 ....205 C2
Moorway Croft DE23 .231 A4
Moorway La DE23 ....231 A4
Moorways Sports Ctr
 DE24 ....232 B3
Moorwinstow Croft S17 .55 C4
Moorwood Ave S17 ....55 B1
Moorwoodmoor La
 DE55 ....157 B3
Moray Ct S16 ....195 C4
Moray Pl S18 ....56 B1
Mordaunt Rd S2 ....43 C3
Morden Gn DE22 ....218 A3
Morden Rd NG16 ....195 B4
Morefern Dr DE21 ...205 C1
Moreland Ct **9** NG2 .268 C1
Moreland Pl **10** NG2 .268 C1
Moreland St NG2 ....268 C1
Morland Cl S14 ....43 C2
Morland Dr S14 ....43 C2
Morland Pl S14 ....43 C2
Morland Rd Hayfield SK22 25 A1
 Sheffield S14 ....43 C1
Morledge DE1 ....267 C3
Morleston St DE23 ...267 C1
Morley Almshouses La
 DE7 ....206 A4
Morley Ave S40 ....95 B2
Morley Cl Belper DE56 .179 C3
 Dronfield S18 ....56 B1
Morley Ct NG3 ......268 C2
Morley Dr DE7 ....194 B2
Morley La
 Little Eaton DE7, DE21 .205 C4
 Stanley DE7 ....207 A3
Morley Prim Sch DE7 .206 B4
Morley Rd DE21 .....220 A4
Morley St Derby DE22 .218 B3
 Glossop SK13 ....17 B4
Morleyfields Cl DE5 ..169 C1
Morlich Dr DE24 .....231 C3
Morningside Cl DE24 .232 B2
Mornington Cl NG10 .223 B3
Mornington Cres DE22 .218 A3
Mornington Rd S42 ..132 B4
Mornington Rise DE4 .143 B4
Morpeth Gdns DE21 ..205 B3
Morrell Wood Dr DE56 .179 B3
Morris Ave S41 ....95 C3
Morris Dr S41 ....95 C3
Mortimer St DE24 ...232 B4
Mortimer Wilson Sch
 DE55 ....159 A2
Morton Ave S45 .....131 A2
Morton Gdns S20 .....59 C3
Morton La S21 ....58 B1
Morton Mt S20 ....59 C4
Morton Prim Sch DE55 147 A3
Morton Rd Pilsley S45 .147 B4
 Shirland DE55 ......146 B3
Morton St NG19 .....135 C2
Morven Ave Bolsover S44 99 A1
 Mansfield Woodhouse
 NG19 ....136 A1
Morven St S80 ....100 C4
Mosborough Hall Farm
 S20 ....59 B3
Mosborough Moor S20 .59 A4
Mosborough Prim Sch
 S20 ....59 B3
Mosbrough Rd S13 ....44 A4
Moscar Cross Rd S6 ...31 C3
Mosedale Cl DE24 ...232 C4
Moseley St DE5 ......169 B1
Moses La DE7 ....206 C4
Moses View S81 ....63 C4
Mosley Dr ST14 .....210 A1
Mosley Rd SK17 ....85 A3
Moss Dr S21 ....60 B3
Moss Edge Rd HD9 .....2 B3
Moss La Broadbottom SK14 15 C4
 Hulland Ward DE6 ...175 C2
 Ripley DE5 ....169 B2
Moss Rd Ilkeston DE7 .208 C4
 Totley S17 ....55 A2
Moss Rise Pl S21 ......59 B2
Moss St Derby DE22 ..218 C2
 Hollingworth SK14 ....9 B3
Moss View S20 ....59 B3
Moss View Rd S23 ....47 B3
Moss Way S20 ....59 B4
Mossbank Cl SK13 ....9 C2

Mossborough Hall Dr
S20 ....59 C3
Mossbrook Sch S8 ...57 B4
Mosscar Cl NG20 ...120 C1
Mossdale Ave S20 ...59 B4
Mossvale Dr DE23 ...231 A3
Moston Wlk S40 ...114 C3
Mostyn Ave DE23 ...218 B1
Mottistone Cl DE24 ...233 B3
Mottram CE Prim Sch
SK14 ....9 A2
Mottram Fold SK14 ...9 A2
Mottram Old Rd SK14 ...15 A3
Mottram Rd
Broadbottom SK14 ...16 A4
Mottram in L SK14 ...9 A2
Mouldridge La DE4 ...139 C1
Moult Ave DE21 ...220 C2
Moulton Cl Belper DE56 ...179 B3
Swanwick DE55 ...169 C4
Mound Rd S40 ...266 B1
Mounfield Pl ST4 ...269 C4
Mount Ave ST4 ...269 C4
Mount Carmel St DE23 ...267 A1
Mount Cres DE55 ...160 A4
Mount Hooton Rd NG7 ...268 A2
Mount Milner NG18 ...268 C3
Mount Pleasant
Ashford in t W DE45 ...108 C4
Castle Donington DE74 ...247 A4
Cromford DE4 ...155 A4
Ilkeston DE7 ...194 C2
Mansfield NG18 ...268 B4
Ripley DE5 ...169 B1
Somercotes DE55 ...170 B4
Mount Pleasant CE Prim Sch
ST4 ....269 A2
Mount Pleasant Ct S32 ...72 B4
Mount Pleasant Dr
Belper DE56 ...178 C3
Heage DE56 ...179 C4
Mount Pleasant La
DE12 ....265 A4
Mount Pleasant Rd
Grindleford S32 ...72 B4
Linton DE11 ...261 C4
Repton DE65 ...242 C1
Swadlincote DE11 ...256 A1
Mount Rd Bretby DE15 ...249 A2
Compstall SK14 ...15 A3
Hartshorne DE11 ...257 A2
Linton DE11 ...261 B4
Mount Row ST16 ...269 B4
Mount Sch for Deaf The
ST4 ....269 A2
Mount St Breaston DE72 ...235 C4
Burton u T DE15 ...248 A1
Derby DE1 ...267 B1
Glossop SK13 ...17 B4
Heanor DE75 ...181 C1
Mansfield NG19 ...268 B4
Nottingham NG1 ...268 A1
3 Stafford ST16 ...269 B4
Stapleford NG9 ...223 C4
Mount St Mary's RC Coll
S21 ....60 B1
Mount The NG9 ...223 B3
Mount View Ave S8 ...43 A2
Mount View Cl NG18 ...268 C3
Mount View Gdns S8 ...43 A2
Mount View Rd S8 ...43 A2
Mountbatten Cl DE7 ...194 C2
Mountcastle St S41 ...95 C4
Mountcastle Wlk S41 ...95 C4
Mountfield Ave NG10 ...223 C4
Mountfield Way DE24 ...233 B2
Mountford Ave DE4 ...165 C4
Mountford Cl DE21 ...206 A1
Mountford Croft S17 ...55 B2
Mouselow Cl SK13 ...9 C2
Mowbray Ct 16 NG3 ...268 B2
Mowbray St DE24 ...232 B4
Moy Ave DE24 ...231 C1
Moyne Gdns DE73 ...245 A4
Mudhurst La SK12 ...32 C2
Mugginton CE Prim Sch
DE6 ....188 C1
Muirfield Cl S41 ...96 A3
Muirfield Dr DE3 ...217 C1
Muirfield Way NG19 ...136 C3
Mulberries Ct DE22 ...204 C2
Mulberry Cl Belper DE56 ...179 A2
Wingerworth S42 ...115 A4
Mulberry Mews DE5 ...180 B3
Mulberry Rd S21 ...59 C4
Mulberry Way
Hilton DE65 ...228 C2
Killamarsh S21 ...60 A3
Weston-on-T DE72 ...246 A3
Mull Cl 9 DE24 ...231 B2
Mullion Pl DE24 ...233 A3
Mumford Dr DE6 ...185 B4
Mundella Pl S8 ...43 A2
Mundella Prim Sch S8 ...43 A2
Mundy CE Jun Sch
DE75 ....181 C1
Mundy Cl DE1 ...218 C3
Mundy St Derby DE1 ...218 C3
Heanor DE75 ...181 C1
Ilkeston DE7 ...194 C1
Mundy's Dr DE75 ...193 C4
Munro Cl S21 ...60 B3
Munro Ct DE24 ...231 C2
Munslow Cl S41 ...269 B1
Munster Terr ST4 ...269 A1
Murray Park Com Sch
DE3 ....217 C2
Murray Rd Derby DE3 ...217 C2

Murray Rd continued
Killamarsh S21 ...60 C4
Murray St Derby DE24 ...232 C4
Mansfield NG18 ...268 B3
Murrayfield Dr S20 ...59 C3
Mus of Costumes & Textiles★
NG7 ....268 A1
Mus of Nottingham Lace★
NG1 ....268 B1
Musard Pl S43 ...78 B1
Musard Way S21 ...60 B3
Muse La Boylestone DE6 ...213 A1
Church Broughton DE6 ...226 A4
Musgrave Ho S33 ...40 A2
Mushroom Farm Ct
NG16 ....182 B2
Mushroom La DE11 ...262 B4
Muskham Ave DE7 ...194 C2
Muskham Ct NG19 ...136 A1
Musters St NG20 ...120 A2
Muswell Rd DE22 ...217 C3
Mycock La DE45 ...106 C3
Myers Cl DE24 ...231 C2
Mynd The NG19 ...136 C3
Mynors St ST16 ...269 C4
Myrtle Ave
Long Eaton NG10 ...236 B3
Stapleford NG9 ...223 C3
Myrtle Cl NG20 ...119 B3
Myrtle Gr S43 ...78 A1
Myrtle Rd S2 ...43 A4
Myrtle Springs S12 ...43 C3
Myrtle Springs Sch S12 ...43 C3
Mytham Bridge S33 ...40 A1

N

Nabb La ST14 ...196 A2
Nailers Way DE56 ...179 B3
Nailor La DE4 ...142 B2
Nairn Ave DE21 ...219 B4
Nairn Cl DE24 ...231 B2
Nairn Dr S18 ...56 B1
Namur Cl DE22 ...218 B2
Nan Gell's Hill DE4 ...155 A4
Napier Cl DE3 ...217 C2
Napier St Derby DE22 ...218 B3
Fenton ST4 ...269 C1
Narlow La DE6 ...161 C1
Narrow La ST14 ...196 B3
Narrowleys La S45 ...129 C2
Naseby Cl DE3 ...217 B2
Naseby Dr NG10 ...236 C2
Naseby Rd DE56 ...179 B2
Nathaniel Rd NG10 ...236 C3
National Stone Ctr★
DE4 ....154 C2
National Tramway Mus★
DE4 ....156 C1
Navan Rd S2 ...44 A4
Neal Ct NG16 ...182 A2
Neale Bank S43 ...96 A4
Neale St NG10 ...236 C4
Near Mdw NG10 ...236 C3
Nearwell Cl SK23 ...46 C3
Nearwood Dr DE21 ...205 C2
Needham St DE5 ...181 A4
Needwood Ave NG9 ...209 B1
Needwood Ct DE13 ...239 B3
Neighwood Cl NG9 ...223 C1
Neilson St DE24 ...232 C4
Nelper Cres DE7 ...209 A3
Nelson Cl DE3 ...217 C2
Nelson Pl LE65 ...257 C2
Nelson Rd ST4 ...269 A2
Nelson St
Burton u T DE15 ...248 B2
Chesterfield S41 ...96 A3
Derby DE1 ...267 D1
Fenton ST4 ...269 C1
Ilkeston DE7 ...194 C2
Long Eaton NG10 ...236 B3
Nottingham NG1 ...268 B1
Swadlincote DE11 ...256 A3
Nene Cl DE13 ...240 B1
Nene Way DE65 ...240 C4
Nesbit St S44 ...118 A4
Nesfield Cl
Chesterfield S41 ...95 B4
Derby DE24 ...233 B4
Nesfield Ct DE7 ...194 C1
Nesfield Rd DE7 ...194 C1
Ness Wlk DE22 ...204 C2
Nether Ave S21 ...60 B3
Nether Blindlow La
SK17 ....106 A3
Nether Cl Duffield DE56 ...190 C3
Eastwood NG16 ...182 C2
Swanwick DE55 ...169 C4
Wingerworth S42 ...115 A1
Nether Croft Cl 10 S43 ...96 C4
Nether Gdns DE4 ...165 C4
Nether La
Brassington DE4 ...163 C4
Hazelwood DE56 ...190 A4
Holbrook DE56 ...191 B3
Kirk Ireton DE6 ...176 A4
Nether Springs Rd S44 ...98 C2
Nether Thorpe Rd S80 ...63 A3
Nether Way DE4 ...127 B2
Netherclose St 1 DE23 ...219 A1
Nethercroft La S45 ...131 C2
Netherdene Rd S18 ...57 A1
Netherfield Cl
Ashbourne DE6 ...185 C1
Staveley S43 ...79 C1

Netherfield La DE72,
DE74 ....247 C4
Netherfield Rd
Chapel-en-le-F SK23 ...47 B3
Chesterfield S40 ...114 A4
Long Eaton NG10 ...236 B3
Sandiacre NG10 ...223 A2
Netherfields Cres S18 ...76 A4
Nethergreen Ave S21 ...60 B4
Nethergreen Ct S21 ...60 B4
Nethergreen Gdns S21 ...60 B4
Netherleigh Ct S40 ...95 A2
Netherleigh Rd S40 ...95 A2
Nethermoor Ave S21 ...60 B4
Nethermoor Ct S21 ...60 B4
Nethermoor Cotts DE55 147 B3
Nethermoor Dr S21 ...60 B4
Nethermoor La S21 ...60 B4
Nethermoor Rd
Tupton S42 ...131 B4
Wingerworth S42 ...115 A1
Netherseal Rd
Clifton Campville B79 ...263 C1
Netherseal DE12 ...264 C2
Netherside S33 ...51 A4
Netherside Dr DE73 ...233 A1
Netherthorpe S43 ...79 A1
Netherthorpe Cl
Killamarsh S21 ...60 B4
Staveley S43 ...78 C1
**Netherthorpe Flash Nature
Reserve**★ S43 ...79 A1
Netherthorpe La S21 ...60 B4
Netherthorpe Rd 11 S43 ...78 C1
Netherthorpe St S43 ...79 A1
Netherwood Ct DE22 ...204 B3
Nettlefold Cres DE73 ...245 A1
Nettleton Ct SK17 ...85 B3
Nettleworth Inf Sch
NG19 ....136 B2
Neville Cl DE13 ...240 A2
Nevinson Ave S21 ...231 B4
Nevinson Dr DE23 ...231 B4
Nevis Cl Chesterfield S40 ...95 B2
Derby DE24 ...231 B1
New Barlborough Cl S43 80 B3
New Bath Rd DE4 ...155 A4
New Beetwell St S40 ...266 B2
New Bolsover Prim Sch
S44 ....98 C1
New Breck Rd DE56 ...179 A2
New Church St S33 ...51 A4
New Cl S32 ...71 B3
New Cotts NG20 ...101 C2
New Derby Rd NG16 ...182 B1
New Eaton Rd NG9 ...223 C3
New England Way NG19 135 B2
New Fall St NG17 ...148 C2
New Garden St ST17 ...269 B3
New Hall Rd S40 ...95 B1
New High St NG17 ...85 B4
New Horwich Rd SK23 ...45 C4
New Inn La DE21 ...205 B4
New La Bradwell S33 ...50 C3
Hilcote DE55 ...148 B1
New Lane Galleries
DE55 ....159 A2
New Lawn Rd DE7 ...208 C4
New Linden St NG20 ...120 A1
New Lumford DE45 ...109 B4
New Market St SK17 ...85 A3
New Mill La NG19 ...136 C2
New Mills Central Sta
SK22 ....33 A4
New Mills Newtown Sta
SK22 ....33 A3
New Mills Prim Sch
SK22 ....33 A4
New Mills Rd
Broadbottom SK13 ...16 A2
Hayfield SK22 ...25 A2
New Mills Sch SK22 ...33 B4
New Mount Cl DE23 ...231 B3
New Queen St S41 ...266 B4
New Rd Apperknowle S18 ...58 A1
Bamford S33 ...40 A3
Barlborough S43 ...80 A4
Barton in F NG11 ...237 C3
Belper DE56 ...178 C2
Boylestone DE6 ...213 A2
Bradwell S33 ...51 A2
Chapel-en-le-Frith SK23 ...34 A1
Coton in t DE12 ...260 B2
Crich DE4 ...168 A4
Derby DE22 ...205 A1
Eyam S32 ...71 C3
Glossop SK13 ...9 C4
Grindleford S32 ...72 A3
Heage DE56 ...179 B4
Hilton DE65 ...228 C1
Holmesfield S18 ...75 A3
Holymoorside S42 ...113 B4
Idridgehay DE56 ...176 C2
Ironville NG16 ...170 C2
Middleton (Nr Wirksworth)
DE4 ....154 A3
Ridgeway DE56 ...156 B1
Somercotes NG16, DE55 ...170 B1
Stapleford NG9 ...209 B1
Swadlincote DE11 ...255 C3
Uttoxeter ST14 ...210 A1
Weston Underwood DE6 ...188 B1
Whaley Bridge SK23 ...45 C4
Whaley Bridge, Bridgemont
SK23 ....33 C1
Wingerworth S42 ...114 C2

New Rd continued
Wirksworth DE4 ...155 A2
Woodville DE11 ...256 C1
Youlgreave DE45 ...125 B3
Flash SK17 ...103 A2
New Rd (Baslow Rd)
DE45 ....108 C4
New Row NG16 ...171 A3
New Sq S40 ...266 B3
New St Alfreton DE55 ...159 A2
Bakewell DE45 ...109 B3
Bolsover S44 ...99 A2
Broadbottom SK14 ...16 A4
Buxton SK17 ...67 A3
Chesterfield S40 ...266 B2
Derby DE1 ...267 C2
Donisthorpe DE12 ...262 C1
Draycott DE72 ...235 A4
Grassmoor S42 ...115 C2
Hilcote DE55 ...160 B4
Little Eaton DE21 ...205 B4
Long Eaton NG10 ...236 C4
Matlock DE4 ...143 B3
Mosborough S20 ...60 A4
New Mills SK22 ...33 B4
Newton DE55 ...148 A2
North Wingfield S42 ...131 C3
Ockbrook DE72 ...221 B2
Pilsley S45 ...132 B1
Ripley DE5 ...169 C1
Rosliston DE12 ...260 B3
Shirland DE55 ...146 B1
Somercotes DE55 ...170 B4
South Normanton DE55 ...160 A3
Stafford ST16 ...269 A4
Stanley DE7 ...207 B3
Stonebroom DE55 ...147 A3
Sutton in A NG17 ...148 C2
Swadlincote DE11 ...256 A1
Swanwick DE55 ...169 C4
Whitwell S80 ...81 C3
New St Bus Link S20 ...60 A4
New Station Rd S44 ...99 A1
New Terr Pleasley NG19 ...134 C3
Sandiacre NG10 ...223 A3
New Tythe St NG10 ...236 C4
New Westwood NG16 ...171 B3
**New Whittington Com Prim
Sch** S43 ...77 B2
New Wye St SK17 ...85 B4
New Zealand La DE56 ...190 C1
New Zealand Sq DE22 ...218 B3
Newark S20 ...59 C4
Newark Ave 3 NG2 ...268 C1
Newark Cres DE21 ...268 C1
Newark Rd DE21 ...205 B1
Newark St NG2 ...268 C1
Newbarn Cl NG20 ...119 B1
Newbery Ave NG10 ...236 C3
Newbold Ave
Borrowash DE72 ...221 B1
Chesterfield S41 ...95 C3
Newbold Back La S40 ...95 B3
Newbold CE Prim Sch
S41 ....95 C4
Newbold Com Sch
Chesterfield S41 ...95 C3
Chesterfield, Newbold S41 ...95 B3
Newbold Cl 1 S41 ...95 B4
Newbold Dr
Castle Donington DE74 ...247 A3
Chesterfield S41 ...95 C3
Newbold Rd S40 ...95 C3
Newborough Rd DE24 ...233 B3
Newbound La NG17 ...134 B1
Newboundmill La NG19 135 A3
Newbridge Cl DE7 ...207 B4
Newbridge Cres DE24 ...232 C2
Newbridge Dr S43 ...96 B4
Newbridge La S41 ...77 A1
Newbridge Rd DE56 ...168 A1
Newbridge St S41 ...77 A1
Newburgh Terr S32 ...72 B1
Newbury Dr DE13 ...240 B1
Newbury St DE24 ...232 C4
Newby Cl DE15 ...248 A1
Newby Rd S41 ...95 B4
Newcastle Cir NG7 ...268 A1
Newcastle Ct NG7 ...268 A2
Newcastle La ST4 ...269 A1
Newcastle Rd ST4 ...269 A1
Newcastle St
2 Mansfield NG18 ...268 B4
Mansfield Woodhouse
NG19 ....136 A2
Sutton in A NG17 ...148 C2
Newchase Bsns Pk
DE23 ....219 B1
Newdigate St
Derby DE23 ...232 A4
Ilkeston DE7 ...209 A3
Kimberley NG16 ...195 C3
Nottingham NG7 ...268 A2
West Hallam DE7 ...207 B3
Newdigate Villas 17
NG7 ....268 A2
Newell Way DE4 ...127 B2
Newfield Cres DE7 ...55 B4
Newfield Croft S17 ...55 B4
Newfield Farm Cl S14 ...43 C3
Newfield Green Rd S2 ...43 B4
Newfield La S17 ...55 B4
Newfield Rd DE15 ...248 C4
Newfield Sec Sch S8 ...43 B2
Newgate Cl DE73 ...233 A1
Newgate Fst Sch NG18 ...268 C4

Newgate La NG18 ...268 C4
Newhall Com Jun Sch
DE11 ....255 C3
Newhall Inf Sch DE11 ...255 C4
Newhall Rd DE11 ...256 B1
Newham Ave DE5 ...169 B1
Newham Cl DE75 ...182 A1
Newhaven Ave NG19 ...136 A2
Newhaven Cl S40 ...95 A1
Newhaven Rd DE21 ...220 A3
Newhay DE13 ...240 C1
Newholme Hospl DE45 ...109 C4
Newland Dale S41 ...266 B4
Newland Gdns S41 ...95 C3
Newland St DE1 ...267 A3
Newlands Ave
Chesterfield S40 ...95 B2
Sheffield S12 ...44 A3
Newlands Cl Ripley DE5 ...169 C1
Swadlincote DE11 ...256 A1
Newlands Cres S12 ...44 A3
Newlands Dr Glossop SK13 ...9 C2
Heanor DE75 ...181 C2
Sheffield S12 ...44 A3
Newlands Gr S12 ...44 A3
Newlands Inn Sta DE55 ...170 A4
Newlands Rd
Sheffield S12 ...44 A3
Somercotes S12 ...170 B2
Newlyn Dr Derby DE23 ...231 C4
South Normanton DE55 ...160 B3
Newlyn Pl S8 ...43 A2
Newman Dr DE14 ...254 A4
Newmanleys Rd NG16 ...194 C4
Newmanleys Rd S NG16 194 C4
Newmarket Ct DE21 ...219 C1
Newmarket Dr DE24 ...232 C4
Newmarket La S45 ...130 C2
Newmarket Way NG9 ...223 C3
Newness Ct DE4 ...143 B3
Newport Cres NG19 ...135 C1
Newport Ct DE24 ...233 C4
Newport Rd ST16,ST17 ...269 A3
Newquay Pl DE24 ...233 C4
Newshaw La SK13 ...9 C2
Newstead Ave
Derby DE21 ...219 C3
Sheffield S12 ...44 C2
Newstead Cl
5 Dronfield S18 ...56 B1
Sheffield S12 ...44 C2
Newstead Dr S12 ...44 C1
Newstead Gr
Nottingham NG1 ...268 B4
Sheffield S12 ...44 C2
Newstead Pl S12 ...44 C1
Newstead Rd
Long Eaton NG10 ...223 B2
Sheffield S12 ...44 C1
Newstead Rd N DE7 ...194 B2
Newstead Rd S DE7 ...194 B2
Newstead Rise S41 ...44 C1
Newstead Terr SK17 ...85 A3
Newstead Way S41 ...44 C1
Newthorpe Comm
NG16 ....195 A4
Newton Cl Belper DE56 ...179 B3
Newton Solney DE15 ...248 A4
Newton Dr NG9 ...223 C3
Newton La DE15 ...248 C4
Newton Leys LE15 ...248 B2
Newton Park Cl 2
DE11 ....256 A4
Newton Prim Sch DE55 ...148 A2
Newton Rd
Burton u T DE15 ...248 A3
Tibshelf DE55 ...147 C2
Newton Solney CE Inf Sch
DE15 ....248 C4
Newton St S18 ...268 C3
Newton's La NG16 ...195 A4
Newton's Wlk DE22 ...218 C4
Newtondale Ave NG19 ...136 C3
Newtons Croft Cres S43 ...80 A3
Newtonwood La DE55,
NG17 ....148 B3
Newtown Prim Sch SK22 33 A3
Nicholas Cl DE21 ...220 C3
Nicholas St S41 ...115 B4
Nicholls St ST4 ...269 B1
Nicholson Ct SK17 ...69 B2
Nicholson Pl S8 ...43 A3
Nicholson Rd S8 ...43 A3
Nicholson's Row NG20 ...119 C2
Nicklaus Ct DE14 ...254 A4
Nicola Gdns DE23 ...231 B2
Nicolas Cl SK17 ...85 C2
Nidderdale Ct 7 DE24 ...233 B3
Nields Way SK6 ...23 B2
Nightingale Ave NG19 ...135 C2
Nightingale Cl
Clay Cross S45 ...131 C1
Holloway DE4 ...155 C3
Ripley DE5 ...169 B1
Nightingale Dr
Mansfield NG19 ...135 C2
Woodville DE11 ...256 C2
Nightingale Inf Sch
DE24 ....232 B4
Nightingale Jun Sch
DE24 ....232 B4
Nightingale Rd DE24 ...232 B4
Nile St NG1 ...268 B2
Nine Corners NG16 ...195 C3

Nine Ladies Stone Circ★
DE4 . . . . **126** B2
Ninelands Rd S32 . . . . . . **53** A4
Nix's Hill DE55 . . . . **159** A1
No Man's Heath Rd
DE12 . . . . **264** C2
No Man's La DE7,DE27 . .**222** B4
Nobel Cl S80 . . . .**81** B1
Noble St DE1 . . . .**267** D1
Nodder Rd S13 . . . .**44** B4
Nodin Hill La DE56 . . . . **168** A2
Noel St Derby DE22 . . . . . .**218** B3
Mansfield NG18 . . . .**268** B4
Noel-Baker Com Sch
DE24 . . . . **232** C2
Nook End Rd DE75 . . . . . .**181** B1
Nook La S44 . . . .**97** A2
Nook The
Barrow u T DE73 . . . . . .**244** A3
Heanor DE75 . . . .**181** B2
Holbrook DE56 . . . .**191** B4
Shirebrook NG20 . . . .**119** B2
Stoney Middleton S32 . . . .**72** A2
Nooning La DE72 . . . .**234** C4
Norbriggs Prim Sch S43 . .**79** A2
Norbriggs Rd S43 . . . .**79** B1
Norburn Dr S21 . . . .**60** B3
Norbury CE Prim Sch
DE6 . . . . **197** C4
Norbury Cl
Chesterfield S40 . . . .**95** A3
Derby DE21 . . . .**204** B1
Dronfield S18 . . . .**56** B1
Sheffield S8 . . . .**56** C4
Norbury Cres DE23 . . . . . .**231** B3
Norbury Ct DE22 . . . .**204** B1
Norbury Hollow DE6 . . . .**183** B1
Norbury Way
Belper DE56 . . . .**179** B3
Sandiacre NG10 . . . .**223** A3
Norfolk Ave S42 . . . .**115** C1
Norfolk Cl S40 . . . .**114** A4
Norfolk Ct NG19 . . . .**136** C3
Norfolk Dr NG18 . . . .**268** B4
Norfolk Gdns DE22 . . . . . .**218** C4
Norfolk Mid Sch S2 . . . . . .**43** C4
Norfolk Prim Sch S2 . . . . .**43** C4
Norfolk Rd
Burton u T DE15 . . . .**254** B4
Long Eaton NG10 . . . .**223** C1
Norfolk Sq SK13 . . . .**10** B1
Norfolk St Derby DE23 . . .**219** A1
Glossop SK13 . . . .**10** B1
Norfolk Wlk NG10 . . . .**223** A3
Norgreave Way S20 . . . . . .**59** C4
Norman Ave DE23 . . . .**231** C4
Norman Cl NG3 . . . .**268** B2
Norman Cres DE7 . . . .**194** C2
Norman Keep DE13 . . . . . .**239** B3
Norman Rd Ripley DE5 . . . .**169** B1
Somercotes DE55 . . . .**170** C4
Tutbury DE13 . . . .**239** C3
Norman St Ilkeston DE7 . . .**194** C2
Kimberley NG16 . . . .**195** C4
Normandy Rd DE65 . . . . . .**228** C1
Normanhurst Pk DE4 . . . .**127** C1
Normanton Ave DE55 . . . .**159** B2
Normanton Gr S13 . . . .**44** C3
Normanton Hill S12,S13 . . .**44** B3
Normanton Jun Sch
DE23 . . . . **231** C4
Normanton La DE23 . . . . .**231** A4
Normanton Lodge DE23 **231** C4
Normanton Rd DE1,
DE23 . . . . **267** B1
Normanton Spring Ct
S13 . . . .**44** C3
Normanton Spring Rd
S13 . . . .**44** C3
Normanton Village Inf Sch
DE23 . . . . **231** C4
North Ave
Ashbourne DE6 . . . .**173** A1
Derby DE3 . . . .**217** C1
Derby, Darley Abbey DE22 **205** A2
Sandiacre NG10 . . . .**223** A3
North Brook Rd SK13 . . . . . .**9** C2
North Castle St ST16 . . . . .**269** A4
North Church St
Bakewell DE45 . . . .**109** B3
30 Nottingham NG1 . . . .**268** B2
North Circus St NG1 . . . . .**268** A1
North Cl Derby DE3 . . . . . .**217** C2
Glossop SK13 . . . .**9** C4
South Normanton DE55 . .**159** C3
Unstone S18 . . . .**76** C3
Willington DE65 . . . .**242** A3
North Cres Killamarsh S21 **60** C4
Long Duckmanton S44 . . . .**98** A3
North Derbyshire Tertiary
Coll S43 . . . .**80** C2
North Derbyshire Tertiary
Coll (markland Campus)
S80 . . . .**81** C2
North End DE4 . . . .**154** C1
North Farm Cl S26 . . . .**61** C4
North Gr S44 . . . .**98** A3
North La
Belper, Farnah Green
DE56 . . . .**178** B1
Belper, Milford DE56 . . . .**190** C4
Brailsford DE6 . . . .**187** C2
Old Brampton S42 . . . .**94** B2
North Leys DE6 . . . .**173** A1
North Moor View S43 . . . . .**96** C4

North Par Derby DE1 . . . .**267** B4
Matlock Bath DE4 . . . . . .**143** A1
North Rd Buxton SK17 . . . .**66** B1
Calow S44 . . . .**96** C2
Clowne S43 . . . .**80** C2
Glossop SK13 . . . .**10** B2
Hayfield SK22 . . . .**25** B2
Long Eaton NG10 . . . .**236** B3
Nottingham NG7 . . . .**268** A1
North Row DE22 . . . .**205** A1
North Sherwood St
NG1 . . . . **268** B2
North St Alfreton DE55 . . .**159** A2
Blackwell DE55 . . . .**147** C1
Bramley-Vale S44 . . . .**117** B1
Burton u T DE15 . . . .**248** A2
Clay Cross S45 . . . .**131** C3
Cromford DE4 . . . .**155** A3
Derby DE1 . . . .**267** B5
9 Ilkeston DE7 . . . .**194** C1
Langley Mill NG16 . . . . . .**182** A2
Market Warsop NG20 . . . .**120** B2
Melbourne DE73 . . . .**252** A4
North Wingfield S42 . . . . .**131** C3
Pinxton NG16 . . . .**160** B2
Somercotes DE55 . . . .**170** B3
South Normanton DE55 . .**159** C3
Stoke-on-T ST4 . . . .**269** B2
Swadlincote DE11 . . . .**256** A3
Whaley Thorns NG20 . . . .**101** A1
North Staffordshire Hospl Ctr
(Outpatients Dept)
ST4 . . . . **269** A2
North Staffordshire Medical
Inst ST4 . . . .**269** A2
North Staffordshire Royal
Infmy ST4 . . . .**269** A2
North Terr S41 . . . .**115** A4
North View Crich DE4 . . . .**168** A4
Derby DE23 . . . .**218** B1
North View St S44 . . . .**98** C1
North Walls ST16 . . . .**269** B4
North Wingfield Inf & Jun
Sch S42 . . . .**131** C4
North Wingfield Rd S42 **115** C2
Northacre Rd DE21 . . . . . .**206** A1
Northam Dr DE5 . . . .**169** B2
Northampton St NG3 . . . .**268** C2
Northcliffe Rd DE6 . . . . . .**173** A4
Northcote Ave
Sheffield S8 . . . .**43** A4
Stoke-on-T ST4 . . . .**269** B2
Northcote Rd S2 . . . .**43** A4
Northcote St S2 . . . .**43** A4
Northedge La S42 . . . .**130** A4
Northern Ave S2 . . . .**43** C4
Northern Comm S18 . . . . . .**56** A1
Northern Dr NG9 . . . .**209** B2
Northern Rd DE75 . . . .**181** B1
Northfield Derby DE24 . . .**231** B2
Kilburn DE56 . . . .**179** C1
Northfield Ave
Ilkeston DE7 . . . .**194** C1
Long Eaton NG10 . . . .**236** A2
Mansfield Woodhouse
NG19 . . . .**136** A3
Rocester ST14 . . . .**197** A2
Northfield Cl ST14 . . . . . .**210** A1
Northfield Cres NG9 . . . . .**223** C2
Northfield Jun Sch S18 . . .**57** B2
Northfield La
Mansfield Woodhouse
NG19 . . . .**135** C2
Mansfield Woodhouse
NG19 . . . .**136** A3
Palterton S44 . . . .**118** B3
Northfield Pk NG19 . . . . .**136** A3
Northfield Prim Sch
NG19 . . . .**136** A3
Northfield Rd NG9 . . . . . .**223** C2
Northfields Clowne S43 . .**80** C2
Long Eaton NG10 . . . .**236** A2
Northgate St **6** DE7 . . . .**194** C1
Northlands S26 . . . .**61** C4
Northmead Dr DE3 . . . . . .**218** A2
Northmoor Cl **12** S43 . . . .**96** C4
Northside S42 . . . .**115** B1
Northumberland Cl
NG3 . . . . **268** B2
Northumberland Rd
DE15 . . . . **254** B4
Northumberland St
DE23 . . . . **218** C1
Northway Dr DE1 . . . .**218** C2
Northwood Ave
Darley Dale DE4 . . . .**127** B2
Derby DE21 . . . .**219** C4
Northwood La
Ellastone DE6 . . . .**183** B2
Northwood DE4 . . . .**127** A3
Northwood Rise DE6 . . . .**185** A4
Northwood St NG9 . . . . . .**223** B4
Norton Ave Bolsover S44 . .**98** C3
Chesterfield S40 . . . .**114** A4
Sheffield S8,S12,S14 . . . . .**43** C1
Norton Church Glebe S8 **43** B1
Norton Church Rd S8 . . . . .**43** A1
Norton Free Sch S8 . . . . . .**43** B1
Norton Green Cl S8 . . . . . .**43** A1
Norton Hall Cl S8 . . . .**43** A1
Norton La S8 . . . .**57** A4
Norton Lawns S8 . . . .**43** B1
Norton Lees Cl S8 . . . .**43** A1
Norton Lees Cres S8 . . . . .**43** A1
Norton Lees Glade S8 . . . .**43** A1
Norton Lees La S8 . . . .**43** A1
Norton Lees Rd S8 . . . .**43** A1
Norton Lees Sq S8 . . . .**43** A1

Norton Mews S8 . . . .**43** B1
Norton Park Ave S8 . . . . . .**57** A4
Norton Park Cres S8 . . . . .**57** A4
Norton Park Dr S8 . . . .**57** A4
Norton Park Rd S8 . . . .**57** A4
Norton Park View S8 . . . . .**57** A4
Norwell Ct NG19 . . . .**136** A1
Norwich Cl NG19 . . . .**136** B3
Norwich St DE21 . . . .**219** B4
Norwood Ave S41 . . . .**115** C3
Norwood Cl
Chesterfield S41 . . . .**115** C3
Derby DE22 . . . .**218** A3
Norwood Cres S21 . . . .**60** C4
Norwood Ind Est S21 . . . . .**60** C4
Norwood Pl S21 . . . .**60** C4
Notintone NG2 . . . .**268** C1
Nottingham Canal Nature
Reserve The★ DE7,
NG16 . . . . **195** B1
Nottingham Castle★
NG7 . . . . **268** A1
Nottingham Cl S42 . . . . . .**115** A2
Nottingham Dr S42 . . . . . .**115** A2
Nottingham High Sch
NG1 . . . . **268** A2
Nottingham High Sch for
Girls NG1 . . . .**268** A2
Nottingham La NG16 . . . .**170** C3
Nottingham Midland Sta
NG1 . . . . **268** B1
Nottingham Rd
Alfreton DE55 . . . .**159** A1
Ashby-de-la-Z LE65 . . . . .**258** C1
Belper DE56 . . . .**179** A2
Borrowash DE72 . . . .**221** B1
Breedon on t H DE73 . . . .**252** B1
Codnor DE5,NG16 . . . . . .**181** B4
Derby DE1, DE21 . . . .**267** C4
Derby, Chaddesden DE21 .**219** C3
Derby, Spondon DE21 . . . .**220** C2
Eastwood, Bailey Grove
NG16 . . . .**182** C1
Eastwood, Giltbrook NG16 **182** C1
Ilkeston DE7 . . . .**209** A3
Long Eaton NG10 . . . .**236** C4
Mansfield NG18 . . . .**268** B4
Ripley DE5 . . . .**169** C1
Selston NG16 . . . .**171** C3
Somercotes DE55 . . . .**159** A1
Stapleford, Stanton Gate
NG9 . . . .**223** C4
Tansley DE4 . . . .**144** A2
Trowell NG9 . . . .**209** C3
Nottingham Sta NG1 . . . .**268** B1
Nottingham Trent Univ
NG1 . . . . **268** A2
Nowill Ct **4** S8 . . . .**43** A3
Nowill Pl **5** S8 . . . .**43** A3
Nugent Gdns NG3 . . . . . .**268** C2
Nun's St DE1 . . . .**218** C3
Nunbrook Gr SK17 . . . .**85** B4
Nunn Brook Rd NG17 . . . .**148** C1
Nunn Brook Rise NG17 . . .**148** C1
Nunn Cl NG17 . . . .**148** C1
Nunsfield Dr DE24 . . . . . .**233** A4
Nursery Ave
Sandiacre NG10 . . . .**222** C3
West Hallam DE7 . . . .**207** C4
Nursery Cl
Borrowash DE72 . . . .**221** A1
2 Glossop SK13 . . . .**17** B4
Swadlincote DE11 . . . .**256** A3
Nursery Croft DE4 . . . . . .**165** C3
Nursery Ct NG18 . . . .**268** C4
Nursery Dr Bolsover S44 . .**98** C1
Buxton SK17 . . . .**66** B1
Nursery Gdns DE55 . . . . . .**160** B2
Nursery Hollow DE7 . . . .**208** C3
Nursery La SK17 . . . .**84** C3
Nursery St
Mansfield NG18 . . . .**268** C4
Stoke-on-T ST4 . . . .**269** B1
Nutbrook Cres DE7 . . . . . .**208** B2
Nuthall Cir DE7 . . . .**208** B2
Nuttall Cl DE55 . . . .**158** C2
Nuttall St DE55 . . . .**158** C2
Nuttall Terr S44 . . . .**117** B1
Nutwood Cl DE22 . . . .**205** C2

O

Oadby Dr S41 . . . .**115** B4
Oadby Rise DE23 . . . .**231** C4
Oak Apple Cres DE7 . . . . .**208** C3
Oak Ave Aldercar NG16 . . .**182** A3
Disley SK12 . . . .**33** A3
Mansfield NG18 . . . .**268** C4
Ripley DE5 . . . .**180** B4
Sandiacre NG10 . . . .**223** A4
Shirebrook NG20 . . . .**119** B2
Oak Bank SK12 . . . .**33** A3
Oak Bank Ave S41 . . . .**77** A1
Oak Bank Cl NG18 . . . . . .**268** B4
Oak Cl Brimington S43 . . . .**96** B4
Chapel-en-le-F SK23 . . . . .**47** B3
Derby DE22 . . . .**204** C2
Duffield DE56 . . . .**190** C1
Killamarsh S21 . . . .**60** B3
Linton DE11 . . . .**261** C4
Mottram in L SK14 . . . .**9** A3
Oak Cres Ashbourne DE6 . .**185** B4
Derby DE23 . . . .**231** B4
Wingerworth S42 . . . .**114** C2

Oak Dr Alfreton DE55 . . . .**159** A2
Derby DE3 . . . .**217** C1
Derby, Boulton DE24 . . . .**233** A3
Doveridge DE6 . . . .**211** A1
Eastwood NG16 . . . .**182** C1
Hilton DE65 . . . .**228** B1
Oak La DE6 . . . .**212** B2
Oak Lodge Dr NG16 . . . . .**195** C4
Oak Rd Denstone ST14 . . .**196** B3
Elvaston DE72 . . . .**233** C2
Grassmoor S42 . . . .**115** C2
Matlock DE4 . . . .**143** B3
Sheffield S12 . . . .**44** A1
Oak Sq DE11 . . . .**255** C1
Oak St Brimington S43 . . . .**78** A1
Derby DE23 . . . .**219** A1
Glossop SK13 . . . .**10** B1
Mosborough S20 . . . .**59** B4
Sheffield S8 . . . .**43** A4
Swadlincote DE11 . . . .**256** C1
Oak Tree Ave S44 . . . .**134** A4
Oak Tree Cl S44 . . . .**97** B2
Oak Tree Cotts S44 . . . . . .**97** A1
Oak Tree Cres NG19 . . . . .**136** A2
Oak Tree Ct DE72 . . . .**221** B1
Oak Tree Gdns DE4 . . . . .**144** A2
Oak Tree Rd S43 . . . .**80** C1
Oakamoor Cl S40 . . . .**95** A3
Oakbank Ct S17 . . . .**55** C3
Oakdale Cl S45 . . . .**131** C1
Oakdale Gdns DE21 . . . . .**206** A2
Oakdale Rd DE55 . . . .**160** A2
Oakdell S18 . . . .**57** B2
Oakerthorpe Rd DE4 . . . .**155** A1
Oakes Cl DE55 . . . .**170** B4
Oakes Park Specl Sch
S8 . . . .**43** B1
Oakes Park View S14 . . . . .**43** B1
Oakes The SK13 . . . .**17** A4
Oakes's Row NG16 . . . . . .**170** C3
Oakfield Ave S40 . . . .**95** A1
Oakfield Ct DE7 . . . .**193** A1
Oakfield Dr NG10 . . . .**223** A2
Oakfield Rd Glossop SK13 . .**9** C2
Stapleford NG9 . . . .**223** B3
Oakfields DE23 . . . .**238** A2
Oakham Cl DE21 . . . .**205** B1
Oakham Way DE7 . . . .**194** C2
Oakhill Rd S18 . . . .**57** B2
Oakhurst Cl DE56 . . . .**178** B3
Oakland Ave
Long Eaton NG10 . . . .**236** B3
Sutton in A NG17 . . . .**148** C1
Oakland Cres DF55 . . . . . .**170** B3
Oakland St DE55 . . . .**159** A2
Oakland Terr NG10 . . . . . .**236** B3
Oaklands Ave
Derby DE23 . . . .**231** B3
Heanor DE75 . . . .**182** A1
Marple SK6 . . . .**23** B4
Oaklands Cl DE5 . . . .**180** B1
Oaklands Rd DE65 . . . . . .**229** B2
Oaklands The DE55 . . . . . .**160** A2
Oaklands Way DE73 . . . . .**252** A4
Oaklea SK17 . . . .**85** B3
Oaklea Way S42 . . . .**131** C4
Oakleigh Ave
Derby DE21 . . . .**219** C3
Mansfield Woodhouse
NG19 . . . .**136** C2
Swadlincote DE11 . . . .**255** C3
Oakley Ave S40 . . . .**95** C2
Oakley's Rd NG10 . . . .**236** C4
Oakley's Rd W NG10 . . . . .**236** B3
Oakmeadows DE55 . . . . . .**160** A2
Oakover Dr DE22 . . . .**204** B1
Oakridge DE21 . . . .**220** A4
Oakridge Cl NG19 . . . .**136** C1
Oaks Ave Creswell S80 . . .**100** B4
Hayfield SK22 . . . .**25** B1
Oaks Farm La S44 . . . .**97** A1
Oaks La Ashover S45 . . . . .**129** B3
Old Brampton S18,S42 . . . .**94** A4
Oaks Rd DE65 . . . .**242** A4
Oaks The DE21 . . . .**205** B4
Oaksedge La DE4 . . . .**144** A3
Oakside Way DE21 . . . . . .**206** A2
Oakstedge La S45 . . . .**145** A4
Oaktree Ave DE24 . . . .**232** A4
Oaktree Cl DE55 . . . .**170** A4
Oaktree Rd DE55 . . . .**148** B1
Oakwell Cres DE7 . . . .**208** C4
Oakwell Dr Crich DE4 . . . .**156** C1
Ilkeston DE7 . . . .**208** C4
Oakwood SK13 . . . .**16** C4
Oakwood Cl Derby DE65 . .**231** B1
Hatton DE65 . . . .**239** B4
Oakwood District Ctr
DE21 . . . . **206** A1
Oakwood Dr
Darley Dale DE4 . . . .**142** C4
Derby DE21 . . . .**206** A1
Oakwood Inf Sch DE24 . . .**233** A3
Oakwood Jun Sch DE24 **233** A3
Oakwood Rd SK12 . . . .**32** B3
Oakworth Cl S20 . . . .**59** C3
Oakworth Dr S20 . . . .**59** B3
Oakworth Gr S20 . . . .**59** B3
Oakworth View S20 . . . . . .**59** B3
Oardale Rd NG18 . . . .**268** A4
Oat Hill DE4 . . . .**165** C4
Oats Orch S20 . . . .**59** B3
Occupation Cl S43 . . . .**80** A3
Occupation La
North Wingfield S42 . . . . .**131** C4
Sheffield S12 . . . .**44** C2
Woodville DE11 . . . .**256** C1

Occupation Rd
Chesterfield S41 . . . .**95** C4
Moira DE11 . . . .**262** B4
New Houghton NG19 . . . .**134** C4
Ochbrook Ct DE7 . . . .**194** C2
Ockbrook Sch DE72 . . . . .**221** B1
Oddfellow Terr DE55 . . . .**109** B3
Oddfellows Cotts **8**
SK17 . . . .**85** A4
Oddfellows Rd S32 . . . . . .**53** A4
Oddfellows Row S32 . . . . .**53** A4
Oddfellows Terr S32 . . . . .**53** A4
Oddford La DE4 . . . .**127** B3
Odom Ct S2 . . . .**43** A3
Offcote Cres DE6 . . . .**173** B2
Offerton Ave DE23 . . . . . .**231** C4
Offridge Cl S43 . . . .**80** C1
Ogden St S43 . . . .**80** C1
Ogdon Ct NG3 . . . .**268** C2
Ogle Dr NG7 . . . .**268** A1
Ogston La DE55 . . . .**146** A2
Ogston New Rd DE55 . . . .**145** C2
Okeover Ave DE6 . . . .**173** B1
Oker Ave DE4 . . . .**127** A2
Oker Dr DE4 . . . .**127** A2
Oker La DE4 . . . .**142** B3
Oker Rd DE4 . . . .**142** B3
Oker Terr DE4 . . . .**142** A4
Old Bakery Cl S41 . . . .**77** A1
Old Bank DE4 . . . .**184** B4
Old Barn Cl DE21 . . . .**205** B4
Old Brick Works La S41 . . .**96** A3
Old Chester Rd DE1 . . . . .**219** A4
Old Church La DE22 . . . . .**204** B3
Old Coach Rd DE4 . . . . . .**143** C2
Old Coalpit La SK17 . . . . . .**86** C1
Old Colliery La S42 . . . . . .**132** C4
Old Coppice Side DE75 . . .**193** C4
Old Dam La SK17 . . . .**49** B2
Old Derby Rd
Ashbourne DE6 . . . .**185** B4
Eastwood NG16 . . . .**182** B2
Old End DE12 . . . .**265** C4
Old Forge Bsns Pk **16** S2 **43** A4
Old Forge Cl DE65 . . . . . .**241** A3
Old Gate HD7 . . . .**2** C4
Old Gate Ave DE72 . . . . . .**245** C4
Old Hackney La DE4 . . . .**142** C4
Old Hall Ave Derby DE23 **218** A1
Derby, Alvaston DE24 . . . .**233** A4
Duffield DE56 . . . .**190** C2
Whaley Bridge SK23 . . . . .**45** C2
Old Hall Cl
Darley Dale DE4 . . . .**127** B3
Glossop SK13 . . . .**10** B1
Old Hall Ct DE55 . . . .**169** C4
Old Hall Dr DE65 . . . .**242** A3
Old Hall Gdns
Stoney Middleton S32 . . . .**72** A4
Swadlincote DE11 . . . .**256** A1
Old Hall Jun Sch S40 . . . . .**95** B1
Old Hall La
Church Broughton DE65 . .**227** A4
Marple SK6 . . . .**23** B3
Mottram in L SK14 . . . .**9** A3
Whitwell S80 . . . .**81** C3
Old Hall Mills Bsns Pk
DE21 . . . . **205** A4
Old Hall Rd
Chesterfield S40 . . . .**95** B2
Derby DE23 . . . .**218** B1
Old Hall Sq **3** SK13 . . . . . .**10** A3
Old Hartshay Hill DE5 . . .**169** B4
Old Hay Gdns S17 . . . .**55** B3
Old Hay La S17 . . . .**55** B3
Old Highcliff La DE56 . . . .**177** A2
Old Hill DE6 . . . .**173** B1
Old House Mus★ DE45 . . .**109** B3
Old House Rd S40 . . . .**95** B3
Old Houses S41 . . . .**96** B4
Old La Derby DE22 . . . . . .**205** A1
Mosborough S20 . . . .**60** A4
Shottle DE56 . . . .**177** A3
Wirksworth DE4 . . . .**154** C1
Old Lenton St NG1 . . . . . .**268** B2
Old Lime Ct DE4 . . . .**143** B3
Old Longhill Rd SK17 . . . . .**65** C2
Old Manor Rd NG19 . . . . .**136** B2
Old Mansfield Rd DE21 . .**205** B1
Old Market Pl
Mansfield NG18 . . . .**268** B4
South Normanton DE55 . .**160** A3
Old Market Sq NG1 . . . . . .**268** B1
Old Mill Cl Duffield DE56 **190** C2
Pilsley DE55 . . . .**132** B1
Old Mill Dr S40 . . . .**95** A4
Old Mill La Calver S32 . . . .**72** B4
Mansfield NG19 . . . .**136** C1
Old Park Ave S8 . . . .**56** B4
Old Park Rd S8 . . . .**56** B4
Old Peveril Rd S44 . . . .**98** A2
Old Pit La DE7 . . . .**193** A3
Old Pond The DE75 . . . . .**194** A4
Old Post Office Row S33 **40** A2
Old Quarry Cl S43 . . . .**80** B3
Old Rd Branston DE14 . . . .**253** C4
Buxton SK23 . . . .**65** B3
Chesterfield S40 . . . .**95** B2
Darley Dale DE4 . . . .**127** B1
Glossop SK13 . . . .**10** A4
Heage DE56 . . . .**179** C2
Mottram in L SK14 . . . .**9** A3
Whaley Bridge, Furness Vale
SK23 . . . .**33** B2
Whaley Bridge, New Horwich
SK23 . . . .**45** C2
Old School Cl
Bramley-Vale S44 . . . .**117** B1

Old School Cl *continued*
Tideswell SK17 69 B2
Old School La
Awsworth NG16 195 B3
Chesterfield S44 96 C1
Pleasley NG19 135 A3
Old School Mews DE72 246 A4
Old Ship La S40 266 B3
Old St SK14 16 A4
Old Station Cl
Darley Dale DE4 126 C4
Etwall DE65 229 A2
Old Station Yd S43 96 B4
Old Storth La DE55 160 A2
Old Swanwick Colliery Rd
DE55 158 C1
Old Tennis Cts The SK17 85 A4
Old Terr NG19 134 C2
Old Vicarage Cl DE23 218 B1
Old Vicarage La DE22 204 B3
Old Vicarage Sch The
DE22 205 A2
Old Whieldon Rd ST4 269 C1
Old Whittington La S18 76 C3
Oldbury Cl DE21 206 A1
Olde Derwent Ave DE4 143 A2
Oldfield Dr DE11 256 B3
Oldfield La
Egginton DE65 241 A4
Hognaston DE6 164 A1
Kirk Ireton DE6 164 C1
Snelston DE6 184 A2
Wensley DE4 142 A4
Oldhay Cl S17 55 B3
Oldicote La DE15 248 C2
Oldknow Rd SK6 23 A3
Oldmill St ST4 269 C2
Oldridge Cl S40 95 A3
Oldwell Cl S17 55 B2
Olga Rd NG3 268 C2
Olive Ave
Long Eaton NG10 223 C1
Shirebrook NG20 119 B3
Olive Cres S12 44 A1
Olive Gr DE21 219 C3
Olive Grove Rd S2 43 A4
Olive Rd S20 59 B4
Olive St DE22 218 C2
Olive Terr SK14 16 A4
Oliver Cl Heanor DE75 182 A1
Nottingham NG7 268 A2
Oliver Lodge Ho ST4 269 B2
Oliver Rd Ilkeston DE7 208 B3
Stoke-on-T ST4 269 A2
Oliver St NG7 268 A2
Olivet Rd S8 43 A2
Olivier St DE23 219 A1
Ollersett Ave SK22 33 B4
Ollersett La SK22 24 C1
Olton Rd DE3 217 B2
Onslow Rd DE3 217 C2
Onward Cotts SK17 85 B4
Opal Cl DE21 206 A1
Openacre NG16 170 C2
Openwood Rd DE56 179 C2
Openwoodgate DE56 179 B2
Orange Cl NG20 119 C3
Orange St DE55 159 A2
Orby Cl NG3 268 C2
Orchard Ave
Castle Donington DE74 247 A2
Whaley Bridge SK23 45 B4
Orchard Bsns Pk
Ilkeston DE7 194 B1
Sandiacre NG10 223 B3
Orchard Cl
Barlborough S43 80 A4
Belper DE56 191 A4
Bolsover S44 99 A1
Breaston DE72 235 C4
Clowne S43 80 C2
Derby DE23 231 B4
Elvaston DE24 233 B2
Hilton DE65 228 B1
Melbourne DE73 252 A4
Ockbrook DE72 221 B2
Ripley DE5 181 A4
Shirebrook NG20 119 C3
Sudbury DE6 225 C3
Uttoxeter ST14 210 A1
Walton-on-T DE12 253 B1
West Hallam DE7 207 C4
Willington DE65 242 A3
Orchard Com Prim Sch
DE74 247 A2
Orchard Cotts DE56 190 C2
Orchard Cres
Glapwell S44 134 A4
Swanwick DE55 169 B4
Orchard Ct Derby DE21 220 C3
Doveridge DE6 211 A1
Langley Mill NG16 182 A2
South Normanton DE55 159 C2
Orchard Dr Creswell S80 81 C1
Gamesley SK13 9 C1
Orchard La DE6 185 B1
Orchard Lee S26 61 C3
Orchard Pl S21 60 B3
Orchard Rd Compstall SK6 15 A1
Darley Dale DE4 142 C4
Matlock Bath DE4 143 A1
Somercotes DE55 170 B3
Whaley Bridge SK23 45 B4
Orchard Rise DE75 181 C1
Orchard Sq 26 S18 56 B1
Orchard St Derby DE1 267 A4
Derby, Mickleover DE3 217 B1
Ilkeston DE7 208 C4
Orchard St *continued*
Kimberley NG16 195 C3
Langley Mill NG16 182 A2
Long Eaton NG10 236 C4
Mansfield NG19 136 A1
Stafford ST17 269 B3
Stapleford NG9 223 B4
Swadlincote DE11 255 C3
Orchard The
Belper DE56 179 A2
Codnor DE5 170 A1
Disley SK12 32 B3
Horsley Woodhouse DE7 192 B3
Stanton-by-D DE7 222 C4
Uttoxeter ST14 210 A2
Youlgreave DE45 125 B3
Orchard View
Bolsover S44 117 C4
Mansfield Woodhouse
NG19 136 A2
Orchard View Rd S40 95 B2
Orchard Way
Derby DE73 232 C1
Sandiacre NG10 223 A2
Orchards The
Derby DE22 204 B2
Westwood NG16 171 A2
Orchards Way S40 95 B1
Orchid Cl
Burton u T DE15 255 A4
Calow S44 97 A2
Orchid Way NG20 119 B2
Ordish Ave DE21 219 C3
Ordley La DE6 183 C4
Oregon Way DE21 220 B3
Orford Ave SK12 32 B3
Organ Way SK14 9 B3
Oriel Cl DE1 267 C1
Oriel St ST4 269 B2
Orkney Cl DE24 231 B2
Orly Ave DE74 247 A1
Ormesby Cl S18 56 B1
Ormond Cl
Chesterfield S40 114 A4
Sheffield S8 57 A3
Ormond Dr S8 57 A3
Ormond Rd S8 57 A4
Ormond Way S8 57 A4
Ormonde St NG16 182 A2
Ormonde Terr NG16 182 A2
Ormsby Rd S41 95 C4
Ormskirk Rise DE21 220 C2
Orpean Way NG9 223 C1
Orpen Dr S14 43 C1
Orpen Way S14 43 C1
Orton Way DE56 179 A3
Orwins Cl 5 S41 95 B4
Osborne Cl NG10 223 A2
Osborne Croft S26 61 C3
Osborne Pl SK13 10 A3
Osborne Rd Derby DE23 219 B2
Stoke-on-T ST4 269 A2
Osborne St DE15 248 A2
Osmaston CE Prim Sch
DE6 185 C2
Osmaston Cl NG10 235 C3
Osmaston Park Ind Est
DE24 232 C4
Osmaston Park Rd
DE23,DE24 232 B4
Osmaston Rd DE23,DE24 219 A1
Osmaston St NG10 223 B3
Osmaston Pk Ind Est
DE24 219 B1
Osmond Rd S21 59 B2
Osprey Cl
Burton u T DE15 248 B2
Derby DE24 231 C1
Ossington Cl NG1 268 B2
Osterly Gn DE22 218 A3
Ostrich La DE6 163 A1
Oswestry Cl DE21 206 A2
Otter St DE1 219 A4
Otterburn Dr DE22 204 B1
Oulton Cl DE24 232 B2
Oundle Dr Ilkeston DE7 209 A4
Mansfield NG19 135 B1
Our Lady's RC Prim Sch
ST4 269 C1
Ousley La DE6 183 B3
Out La S42,S44 132 C3
Outfield Rd DE15 254 C4
Outgang La
Mansfield Woodhouse
NG19 136 B2
Pleasley NG19 135 B3
Outlands Rd S33 50 C3
Outram Ct DE5 169 C1
Outram Dr DE11 256 B2
Outram Rd S41 95 C3
Outram St DE5 169 C1
Outram Way DE24 231 C1
Outseats Dr DE55 159 A2
Oval Ct DE23 231 B4
Oval The ST17 269 B3
Over Haddon Craft Ctr*
DE45 109 A1
Over Hill Rd SK22,SK23 34 A3
Over La Baslow DE45 91 C3
Belper DE56 179 C3
Hazelwood DE56 178 A1
Over Rd DE45 91 C3
Overcroft Rise S17 55 B2
Overdale DE4 143 B3
Overdale Ave SK17 85 B4
Overdale Cl NG10 236 A3
Overdale Gdns S17 55 B3
Overdale Rd Derby DE23 218 C1
Overdale Rd *continued*
New Mills SK12 32 C3
Overdale Rise S17 55 B3
Overend Cl S14 43 B2
Overend Dr S14 43 B2
Overend Rd S14 43 B2
Overend Way S14 43 B2
Overlees S18 75 B2
Overmoor View DE55 148 A4
Overseal Manor Sch
DE12 262 A2
Overseal Prim Sch
DE12 262 A2
Oversetts Ct DE11 255 C3
Oversetts Rd DE11 255 C3
Overstone Cl DE56 179 B2
Overton Cl S43 78 C2
Owen Ave NG10 237 A3
Ower Bar Rd S17 54 A2
Owers Ave DE75 193 C4
Owlcotes View S44 118 A4
Owler Car La S18 57 C3
Owlers La DE23 218 B1
Owlston Cl NG16 182 C2
Owlswick Cl DE23 231 A4
Owlthorpe Ave S20 59 A4
Owlthorpe Cl S20 59 A4
Owlthorpe Dr S20 59 A4
Owlthorpe Gr S20 59 A4
Owlthorpe La S20 59 A4
Owlthorpe Rise S20 59 A4
Ox Cl S45 131 B2
Ox Close Ave S17 56 A3
Ox Hill S20 60 A3
Oxbury Rd NG16 195 C4
Oxclose Dr S18 56 B1
Oxclose La
Alsop en le D DE6 150 B1
Dronfield S18 56 B1
Mansfield NG19 135 B2
Mansfield Woodhouse
NG19 136 A2
Oxclose Park Rd S20 59 C3
Oxclose Park Rd N S20 59 C4
Oxcroft Est S44 99 B4
Oxcroft La Bolsover S44 99 A3
Elmton S44 99 C4
Oxcroft Way S43 80 A3
Oxenhope Cl DE23 230 C4
Oxford Cl S43 96 C4
Oxford Cres ST4 269 B2
Oxford St Blackwell DE55 147 C1
Bramley-Vale S44 117 C1
Derby DE1 267 C1
Derby, Spondon DE21 220 C3
Eastwood NG16 182 C1
12 Ilkeston DE7 208 C4
Long Eaton NG10 236 B4
Mansfield Woodhouse
NG19 136 B1
Nottingham NG1 268 A1
Ripley DE5 169 B1
Stoke-on-T ST4 269 B2
Swadlincote DE11 256 A1
Oxley Rd DE15 248 A2
Oxmead DE6 184 B4
Oxpasture La NG20 100 A3
Oxton Cl NG19 268 A4
Oxton Rake Rd S18 94 A4
Oxwich Ct DE21 206 A1
Ozier Holt NG10 236 B3

P

Pack Horse Rd DE73 252 A4
Packenham Bvd DE65 227 A2
Packer's Row S40 266 B3
Packman La S26 62 B3
Paddock Cl
Castle Donington DE74 246 C2
Wingerworth S42 114 C2
Paddock Cres S2 43 C3
Paddock Croft DE21 205 C1
Paddock La SK23 45 C3
Paddock The
Blackwell DE55 147 C1
Bolsover S44 99 A1
Burton u T DE15 248 A2
Buxton SK17 84 C4
Elvaston DE24 233 B2
Glossop SK13 9 C3
Holbrook DE56 191 B3
Hollingworth SK14 9 C3
Ockbrook DE72 221 B2
Pleasley NG19 135 A3
Rolleston DE13 240 A2
Whaley Bridge SK23 45 C3
Paddock Way S18 57 A2
Paddocks Cl NG16 160 B2
Paddocks The
Mansfield Woodhouse
NG19 136 C3
Pilsley S45 132 B1
Sandiacre NG10 223 A3
Staveley S43 79 B2
Sutton in A NG17 148 C1
Swadlincote DE11 255 C3
Paddocks View NG10 236 A4
Padfield Com Prim Sch
SK13 10 A3
Padfield Gate SK13 17 B4
Padfield Main Rd SK13 10 B3
Padget High Sch DE14 254 A4
Padley Cl Derby DE22 205 A3
Ripley DE5 169 B2
Padley Hill
Mansfield NG18 268 B3
Padley Hill *continued*
Nether Padley S32 53 C1
Padley Rd S32 53 B1
Padley Way S42 131 C3
Padley Wood La S45 147 A4
Padley Wood Rd S45 132 B1
Padstow Cl DE24 231 B2
Padstow Rd DE24 233 B3
Painter's La DE6 186 A3
Painters Way
Darley Dale DE4 127 B1
Winster DE4 141 B3
Paisley Cl S43 97 B4
Palace La DE56 166 B1
Palace Rd SK17 85 A4
Palatine Gr DE23 230 C4
Palatine St NG7 268 A1
Palerow La DE56 166 C2
Palissy Cl DE11 256 B2
Pall Mall DE21 205 C2
Palladium Dr DE23 231 A3
Palm Cl DE23 218 A1
Palmbourne Ind Pk
ST16 269 A4
Palmer Cl
Burton u T DE14 254 A4
Stafford ST16 269 C4
Palmer Cres S18 57 A1
Palmer Dr
Stapleford NG9 223 B3
Swanwick DE55 169 C4
Palmersgate S40 266 B3
Palmerston Ct DE73 252 A4
Palmerston Gdns NG3 268 B2
Palmerston St
Derby DE23 218 C1
Underwood Green NG16 171 C1
Westwood NG16 171 B2
Palterton La S44 117 B3
Palterton Prim Sch S44 118 A3
Pankhurst Pl S45 131 B2
Panton Cl ST16 269 C4
Parade The DE3 217 B1
Paradise St SK13 10 A3
Parcel Terr DE22 218 B3
Pares Way DE72 221 B3
Pargate Cl DE5 180 B3
Park Ave Ashbourne DE6 173 B1
Awsworth NG16 195 A3
Castle Donington DE74 246 C2
Darley Dale DE4 127 B2
Dronfield S18 57 A1
Eastwood NG16 182 C2
Glapwell S44 118 B1
Holmesfield S18 75 A4
Ilkeston DE7 208 C4
Mansfield NG18 268 C4
Mansfield Woodhouse
NG19 136 B2
Ripley DE5 169 C1
Scropton DE65 227 A3
Shirebrook NG20 119 C2
Stanley DE7 207 B3
Uttoxeter ST14 210 A1
Whaley Bridge SK23 33 B2
Park Cl Belper DE56 179 A1
Chesterfield S40 115 A4
Glossop SK13 10 B1
Linton DE12 261 B3
Little Eaton DE21 205 A4
Matlock DE4 143 B2
Pinxton NG16 160 B1
Shirland DE55 146 C1
Stanton-by-D DE7 222 C4
Park Cotts DE4 127 A3
Park Cres
Chapel-en-le-F SK23 47 A3
Doveridge DE6 211 A1
Eastwood NG16 182 C2
Glossop SK13 10 A2
Heage DE56 179 C4
Ilkeston DE7 209 A4
Stafford ST17 269 B3
Whaley Bridge SK23 33 B2
Park Ct Heanor DE75 181 C1
Mansfield NG18 268 C4
Swadlincote DE11 256 B3
Park Dene Dr SK13 10 B1
Park Dr Chesterfield S41 266 C1
Derby DE23 218 B1
Ilkeston DE7 208 C4
Nottingham NG7 268 A1
Sandiacre NG10 223 A2
Swanwick DE55 169 C3
Park Edge S32 52 C4
Park Farm S18 56 B1
Park Farm Ctr DE22 204 B1
Park Farm Dr DE22 204 B1
Park Farm Mews S21 60 B1
Park Gr DE22 218 C4
Park Grange S2 43 B4
Park Grange Cl S2 43 B4
Park Grange Dr S2 43 B4
Park Grange Mount S2 43 B4
Park Grange Rd S2 43 B4
Park Grange View S2 43 B4
Park Hall Ave S40,S42 114 A4
Park Hall Cl S40 114 A4
Park Hall Gdns
Chesterfield S40 114 A4
Mansfield Woodhouse
NG19 136 B3
Park Hall La DE7 207 B4
Park Hall Rd Denby DE5 180 A2
Mansfield Woodhouse
NG19 136 B3
Park Head Rd DE4 143 A3
Park Hill Awsworth NG16 195 A3
Park Hill *continued*
Eckington S21 59 C2
Park Hill Cl SK22 24 B1
Park Hill Dr DE23 231 C4
Park Ho DE56 179 A2
Park House Prim Sch
S45 132 A2
Park Jun & Inf Schs The
NG20 119 C3
Park La Hayfield SK22 25 B3
Castle Donington DE74 246 C2
Chesterfield S41 95 C4
Darley Dale DE4 127 B1
Derby, Allestree DE22 204 C2
Derby, Normanton Park
DE23 218 B1
Heage DE56 179 C4
Holbeck NG20,S80 101 B3
Mansfield NG18 268 B3
Over Haddon DE45,DE4 110 B1
Pinxton NG16 160 B1
Ripley DE5 169 A4
Shirland DE55 158 C4
Shirley DE6 200 B4
South Wingfield DE55 157 B1
Tutbury DE13 239 A3
Weston-on-T DE72 245 C2
Youlgreave DE4 126 B3
Park Leys Ct DE21 220 C2
Park Mews
Mansfield Woodhouse
NG19 136 B2
Somercotes DE55 170 B3
Park Mill Dr DE55 159 B4
Park Pale The DE13 239 B3
Park Ravine NG7 268 A1
Park Rd Ashbourne DE6 173 B1
Bakewell DE45 109 B3
Belper DE56 179 A1
Buxton SK17 85 A4
Chapel-en-le-F SK23 47 A3
Chesterfield S40 266 B2
Chesterfield, Queen's Park
S40 266 A1
Derby DE3 217 B1
Derby, Spondon DE21 220 B3
Donisthorpe DE12 262 C1
Duffield DE56 190 B2
Glossop SK13 10 A2
Heage DE56 179 C4
High Lane SK12 32 A3
Holmewood S42 116 C1
Ilkeston DE7 208 C4
Linton DE12 262 A3
Mansfield Woodhouse
NG19 136 A2
New Mills SK22 33 B4
Nottingham NG7 268 A1
Over Haddon DE45 110 A1
Ripley DE5 169 C1
Shirebrook NG20 119 C3
Stapleford NG9 223 C4
Swadlincote DE11,DE15 255 B3
Swadlincote, Church Gresley
DE11 256 B1
Tupton S42 131 B4
Whaley Bridge SK23 45 B3
Park Rise S18 75 A4
Park Row Clay Cross S45 131 B2
Nottingham NG1 268 A1
Park Side Belper DE56 179 A2
Somercotes DE55 170 B4
Park Spring Cl S2 43 B4
Park Spring Dr S2 43 B4
Park Spring Gr S2 43 B4
Park Spring Pl S2 43 B4
Park Spring Way S2 43 B4
Park St Alfreton DE55 158 C2
Barlborough S43 80 A4
Breaston DE72 235 C4
Chesterfield S40 115 A4
Derby DE1 267 D2
Heanor DE75 181 B1
Long Eaton NG10 223 B1
Mansfield Woodhouse
NG19 136 A2
Ripley DE5 169 C1
Stafford ST17 269 B3
Stapleford NG9 223 B3
Swadlincote DE11 256 A3
Uttoxeter ST14 210 B1
Wessington DE55 157 C4
Park Terr Northwood DE4 127 A3
Nottingham NG1 268 A1
Park The Darley Dale DE4 127 B2
Ironville NG16 170 C2
Mansfield NG18 268 C4
Mayfield DE6 184 B4
Park Valley NG7 268 A1
Park View
Aston-on-T DE72 246 A4
Bakewell DE45 109 B3
Barlborough S43 80 A4
Chesterfield S41 115 B4
Clowne S43 80 C3
Heanor DE75 181 B1
Pleasley NG19 135 A3
Somercotes DE55 170 B3
Whaley Thorns NG20 100 C1
Park View Ave S20 59 C4
Park View Cl DE22 204 C2
Park View Ct
22 Nottingham NG3 268 B2
Sheffield S8 43 A1
Park View Dr SK23 47 A3

Park View Ho DE21 . . . . .219 B3
Park View Rise SK22 . . . .24 B1
Park View Way NG18 . . . .268 C3
Park Way DE65 . . . . .229 B2
Park Wharf NG7 . . . . .268 A1
Parker Ave S44 . . . . .96 C2
Parker Cl DE1 . . . . .267 A4
Parker Ctr DE21 . . . . . . .219 A4
Parker Gdns NG9 . . . . . .223 C4
Parker St DE1 . . . . .218 C4
Parker's Croft Rd ST17 .268 A4
Parker's La NG19 . . . . . .136 B2
Parkers Cl DE11 . . . . . . .257 A1
Parkers La S17 . . . . .55 B4
Parkfield Cl S2 . . . . .43 A4
Parkfield Cres DE21 . . . .265 C1
Parkfield Ct SK17 . . . . . .85 C4
Parkfield La DE6 . . . . . . .184 B2
Parkfields Dr DE22 . . . . .218 C4
Parkfields View DE56 . . .179 C4
Parkgate Cl S20 . . . . . . .59 A4
Parkgate Croft S20 . . . . .59 A4
Parkgate Dr S20 . . . . . . .59 A4
Parkgate La S21,S43 . . . .77 C3
Parkham Rd NG16 . . . . . .195 C4
Parkhill La S21 . . . . .60 B1
Parkhouse Cl S45 . . . . . .131 A2
Parkhouse Dr S45 . . . . . .159 C3
Parkhouse Rd S45 . . . . . .132 A2
Parkin St DE55 . . . . .159 A2
Parkland Ave SK22 . . . . .24 B1
Parkland Dr S42 . . . . . . .115 A1
Parklands Dr DE73 . . . . .245 A4
Parklands Inf Sch NG10 223 A1
Parks Ave S45 . . . . .157 C2
Parkside Buxton SK17 . . .85 A4
 Chesterfield S41 . . . . . .96 A4
 Heage DE56 . . . . .179 C4
Parkside Ave NG10 . . . . .236 A4
Parkside Cl NG16 . . . . . .170 C2
Parkside Com Jun Sch
 DE6 . . . . .173 B1
Parkside Com Sch S40 .266 A2
Parkside Dr
 Ironville NG16 . . . . . . .170 C2
 Long Eaton NG10 . . . . .236 A4
Parkside La SK6 . . . . . . .23 B3
Parkside Rd DE21 . . . . . .220 C4
Parkside Sh Ctr S21 . . . .60 B4
Parkside View S40 . . . . .95 A3
Parkstone Ct DE3 . . . . . .217 B1
Parkstone Delph S12 . . . .44 A1
Parkview DE21 . . . . .205 B4
Parkview Prim Sch
 DE21 . . . . .206 A1
Parkville Cl SK17 . . . . . .85 B3
Parkway Derby DE73 . . . .232 C1
 New Mills SK22 . . . . . .24 B1
 Whitwell S80 . . . . .82 A3
Parkway Ct S8 . . . . .56 C4
Parkway The DE4 . . . . . .127 B2
Parkwood Sch DE55 . . . .158 C2
Parliament Cl DE22 . . . . .218 C2
Parliament Rd NG19 . . . .268 A4
Parliament St
 Derby DE22 . . . . .218 C2
 Swadlincote DE11 . . . . .255 C3
Parr Ct 12 NG7 . . . . .268 A2
Parson's Wlk B79 . . . . . .263 C1
Parsonage Cl S20 . . . . . .59 B3
Parsonage Croft DE45 . .109 B3
Parsonage Gdns SK6 . . .23 A2
Parsons Cl
 Hartington SK17 . . . . . .137 B3
 Swadlincote DE11 . . . . .256 A1
Parsons Gate S33 . . . . . .40 A3
Parsons Gr DE5 . . . . . . .180 B1
Parsons La S33 . . . . .39 B2
Parthenon Cl NG19 . . . . .134 C3
Partington Cl SK13 . . . . .10 C1
Partington Pk SK13 . . . . .10 B2
Partridge Cl S21 . . . . . . .59 A2
Partridge Dr DE11 . . . . . .256 C2
Partridge Way DE3 . . . . .218 A2
Parture Gr S21 . . . . .59 B2
Parwich Cl S40 . . . . .95 A3
Parwich La DE4 . . . . .151 C4
Parwich Prim Sch DE6 .151 B1
Parwich Rd S42 . . . . . . .131 C3
Pasteur Ave DE5 . . . . . . .169 B1
Pasture La
 Brassington DE4,DE6 . .152 B1
 Flagg SK17 . . . . .106 B3
 Hilcote DE55 . . . . .148 B1
 Long Eaton NG10 . . . . .237 A3
 Stonebroom DE55 . . . . .147 A2
Pasture Rd NG9 . . . . . . .209 B1
Pastures Ave DE23 . . . . .230 C4
Pastures Hill DE23 . . . . .231 A4
Pastures The
 Duffield DE56 . . . . . . .190 C2
 Eastwood NG16 . . . . . .195 A4
 Mansfield Woodhouse
  NG19 . . . . .136 C3
 Repton DE65 . . . . .242 B1
 Swadlincote DE11 . . . . .255 C3
 Weston-on-T DE72 . . . .245 C3
Patchwork Row NG20 . . .119 C2
Paterson Ave DE21 . . . . .220 A3
Patmore Sq DE23 . . . . . .231 C4
Paton Gr S43 . . . . .96 B4
Patrick Cl DE12 . . . . .261 B3
Patten Ct DE24 . . . . .232 A3
Patterdale Cl 3 S18 . . . .56 C1
Patterson Pl NG18 . . . . .268 C4

Pattison St S44 . . . . .98 C3
Paulet High Sch DE15 . .254 C4
Paulson's Dr NG18 . . . . .268 B4
Pavilion Cl S43 . . . . .80 C1
Pavilion GdnsBuxton SK17 85 A4
 New Houghton NG19 . . .134 C4
Pavilion Rd Derby DE23 .231 B4
 Ilkeston DE7 . . . . .194 C3
Pavilion Workshops
 S42 . . . . .116 B1
Paxton Cl Derby DE3 . . .217 B1
 Matlock DE4 . . . . .143 A3
Paxton Ct S14 . . . . .43 C2
Paxton Gdns NG3 . . . . . .268 C2
Paxton Rd S41 . . . . .96 B3
Payler Cl S2 . . . . .44 A4
Payne St DE22 . . . . .218 B3
Peach Ave Selston NG16 .171 C3
 South Normanton DE55 .160 A4
Peach St Derby DE22 . . .218 B3
 Heanor DE75 . . . . .181 B1
Peachey St NG1 . . . . . . .268 B3
Peacock Cl Glossop SK13 .9 C2
 Killamarsh S21 . . . . . . .60 B3
Peacock Gr DE23 . . . . . .231 A3
Peacock Pl DE7 . . . . . . .194 B2
Peacock St NG18 . . . . . .268 B3
Peacock Way DE55 . . . . .169 C4
Peacroft Ct DE65 . . . . . .228 B1
Peacroft La DE65 . . . . . .228 B1
Peafield La NG19 . . . . . .136 C2
Peafield Lane Prim Sch
 NG19 . . . . .136 C2
Peak Ave DE55 . . . . .170 A3
Peak Cavern ★ S33 . . . . .38 A1
Peak Cl S45 . . . . .132 B1
Peak Dale Prim Sch
 SK17 . . . . .67 A3
Peak District Mus of
 Mining ★ DE4 . . . . . . .143 A1
Peak Dr DE23,DE24 . . . . .232 A4
Peak Forest CE Prim Sch
 SK17 . . . . .49 A2
Peak Ho SK13 . . . . .10 A3
Peak Pl S43 . . . . .97 B4
Peak Rd SK22 . . . . .33 B4
Peak Rly ★ DE4 . . . . . . .143 A3
Peak The SK20 . . . . .119 C2
Peak View Clowne S43 . .80 B3
 South Normanton DE55 .159 C3
Peak View Dr DE6 . . . . . .173 B1
Peak View Rd S40 . . . . . .95 B3
Peakdale Cl
 Long Eaton NG10 . . . . .236 A3
 Ripley DE5 . . . . .180 B3
Peakdale Cres DE55 . . . .44 C3
Peakdale Rd Glossop SK13 .9 C2
 Marple SK6 . . . . .23 A2
Peakland View DE4 . . . . .127 A2
Peaknaze Cl SK13 . . . . . .17 A4
Peaktor La DE4 . . . . .126 C4
Pear Tree Ave
 Ripley DE5 . . . . .180 B4
 Swadlincote DE11 . . . . .255 C4
 Wingerworth S42 . . . . .114 C2
Pear Tree Cl
 Brimington S43 . . . . . .97 A4
 Glossop SK13 . . . . .9 C2
 Hartshorne DE11 . . . . .257 A4
 Killamarsh S21 . . . . . . .60 B3
 Marple SK6 . . . . .23 A4
Pear Tree Com Jun Sch
 DE23 . . . . .219 A1
Pear Tree Cres DE23 . . .232 A4
Pear Tree Dr
 Linton DE12 . . . . .261 B3
 Shirebrook NG20 . . . . .119 C3
Pear Tree Rd S45 . . . . . .132 B1
Pear Tree St DE23 . . . . . .219 A1
Pearce La S42 . . . . .114 B2
Pearl Bank DE6 . . . . . . .211 C4
Pearl Cl DE21 . . . . .206 A1
Pearl Way SK14 . . . . .9 A1
Pearson Croft S41 . . . . . .95 B3
Peartree Ct DE74 . . . . . .247 A3
Peartree Ct DE21 . . . . . .205 B1
Peartree La NG17 . . . . . .134 A1
Peartree Sta DE23 . . . . .232 A4
Peas Hill Rd NG3 . . . . . .268 B2
Pease Hill DE55 . . . . . . .159 A2
Peasehill DE5 . . . . .180 C4
Peasehill Rd DE5 . . . . . .180 C4
Peasunhurst La S45 . . . .113 A1
Peat La DE4,DE56 . . . . . .166 B2
Peatburn Ave DE75 . . . . .181 B1
Peatfield Ct NG9 . . . . . . .209 B1
Peatfield Rd
 Killamarsh S21 . . . . . . .60 C4
 Stapleford NG9 . . . . . .209 B1
Peats Cl DE6 . . . . .165 A1
Peckham Gdns DE22 . . .218 A3
Pedley Ave 1 S20 . . . . . .59 C4
Pedley Dr 2 S20 . . . . . . .59 C4
Pedley St DE7 . . . . .208 C4
Peebles Cl DE24 . . . . . . .231 C1
Peel Cres NG19 . . . . . . .135 B1
Peel Gdns S18 . . . . .56 C1
Peel Rd NG19 . . . . .268 A4
Peel St Derby DE22 . . . .218 B3
 Glossop SK13 . . . . .10 B3
 Langley Mill NG16 . . . . .182 A2
 Long Eaton NG10 . . . . .236 C4
 Nottingham NG1 . . . . . .268 A2
 South Normanton DE55 .160 A3
 Stafford ST16 . . . . .269 A4
Peers Cl DE21 . . . . .206 A1
Peet St DE22 . . . . .218 C2

Pegasus Sch DE12 . . . . .260 C4
Pegasus Way DE65 . . . . .228 C1
Peggars Cl S43 . . . . .80 A3
Peggs Wlk DE23 . . . . . . .231 C4
Pegwell Cl DE23 . . . . . . .231 B4
Pelham Ave DE7 . . . . . . .194 C1
Pelham Cres NG7 . . . . . .268 A1
Pelham St Derby DE22 . .218 C2
 Ilkeston DE7 . . . . .194 C1
 Mansfield NG18 . . . . . .268 C4
 15 Nottingham NG1 . . . .268 B1
Pemberton St NG1 . . . . .268 B1
Pemberton The S45 . . . . .160 A2
Pembleton Dr NG19 . . . .135 B1
Pembrey Cl NG9 . . . . . . .209 B1
Pembroke Cl 7 S40 . . . . .95 B1
Pembroke St 6 S41 . . . . .95 C4
Pembroke Rd
 Dronfield S18 . . . . .76 A4
 Shireoaks S81 . . . . .63 C4
Pembroke St DE21 . . . . .219 B4
Pen Cl DE55 . . . . .148 A2
Penalton Cl DE24 . . . . . .232 C3
Pencroft Gr DE23 . . . . . .231 B3
Pendean Cl DE55 . . . . . .147 C1
Pendennis Cl DE24 . . . . .233 A3
Pendine Cl DE55 . . . . . . .160 B3
Pendlebury Dr DE3 . . . . .217 C1
Pendleside Way DE23 . . .230 C4
Pendleton La DE56 . . . . .166 C4
Penfold Way DE55 . . . . .147 A3
Penge Rd DE22 . . . . .218 A4
Penhaligan's Cl DE73 . . .232 C1
Penine View DE56 . . . . . .179 C4
Peniston Rise DE73 . . . . .252 A4
Penistone Gdns S45 . . . .131 B1
Penkhull Inf Sch ST4 . . .269 B2
Penkhull New Rd ST4 . . .269 B1
Penkhull Terr ST4 . . . . . .269 B1
Penkridge Rd DE11 . . . . .256 A1
Penkville St ST4 . . . . . . .269 B1
Penmore Cl S41 . . . . . . .115 B4
Penmore Gdns S41 . . . . .96 B3
Penmore La S41 . . . . . . .115 B4
Penmore St S41 . . . . . . .115 B4
Penn La DE73 . . . . .252 A4
Penn Moor Cl NG10 . . . .236 A3
Penn St DE56 . . . . .179 A2
Penncroft Dr S45 . . . . . .131 B1
Penncroft La S45 . . . . . .131 B1
Pennie Cl NG10 . . . . .236 B2
Penniment La NG19 . . . . .135 A1
Pennine Ave DE55 . . . . . .170 B4
Pennine Cl
 Long Eaton NG10 . . . . .223 A1
 Mansfield Woodhouse
  NG19 . . . . .136 B2
 Newton DE55 . . . . .148 A2
 Sutton in A NG17 . . . . .148 C2
 Tibshelf DE55 . . . . .147 C3
Pennine Dr Selston NG16 171 C4
 South Normanton DE55 .159 C3
Pennine Rd SK13 . . . . . . .17 A4
Pennine View S44 . . . . . .118 A3
Pennine Way
 Chesterfield S40 . . . . . .95 B3
 Grassmoor S42 . . . . . .115 C2
 Swadlincote DE11 . . . . .256 A2
Pennine Way Jun Sch
 DE11 . . . . .256 A1
Penns Rd S2 . . . . .43 B3
Penny Acres Prim Sch
 S18 . . . . .74 C1
Penny Engine La S21 . . . .59 C2
Penny Gn S80 . . . . .82 A3
Penny La S17 . . . . .55 B3
Penny Long La DE22 . . . .218 C4
Pennycroft Cl DE23 . . . . .231 A4
Pennycroft La ST14 . . . . .210 B1
Pennycroft Rd ST14 . . . .210 A1
Pennycrofts ST16 . . . . . .269 B4
Pennycrofts Ct ST16 . . . .269 B4
Pennyfields Bvd NG10 . .236 A4
Pennyfoot St NG1 . . . . . .268 C1
Pennytown Ct DE55 . . . . .159 B1
Pennyunk La DE45 . . . . . .89 C1
Pennywell Dr S42 . . . . . .113 B4
Penrhyn Ave DE23 . . . . . .218 B1
Penrhyn Cl NG3 . . . . .268 B2
Penrith Pl DE21 . . . . .205 B1
Penrose Cres S44 . . . . . .97 B2
Penryn Cl DE55 . . . . .160 B3
Pentagon The DE21 . . . . .219 B3
Pentewen Cl DE22 . . . . . .204 C1
Penthorpe Cl S12 . . . . . .44 A3
Pentland Cl
 5 Chesterfield S40 . . . .95 B3
 Derby DE21 . . . . .206 A1
Pentland Gdns NG10 . . . .223 A1
Pentland Rd S18 . . . . . . .56 B1
Pentrich Rd Ripley DE5 . .169 B1
 Swanwick DE55 . . . . . .169 B4
Pentridge Dr DE7 . . . . . .194 B2
Penzance Rd DE24 . . . . .233 A3
People's Coll The
 Nottingham, Castle Lock
  NG1 . . . . .268 B1
 Nottingham, Sneinton NG3 268 C2
Pepper La DE7 . . . . .208 C1
Pepper St NG1 . . . . .268 B1
Percy St Derby DE22 . . . .218 C2
 Ilkeston DE7 . . . . .208 C4
Percy Wood Cl
 DE65 . . . . .228 B1
Peregrine Cl
 Burton u T DE15 . . . . . .248 B2
 3 Derby DE24 . . . . . . .231 B2
Peregrine Way S26 . . . . .61 C3

Perlethorpe Ave
 Mansfield NG19 . . . . . .136 A1
 Nottingham NG2 . . . . . .268 C1
Perrymount Ct ST4 . . . . .269 A1
Pershore Dr DE14 . . . . . .254 A4
Perth Cl Burton u T DE15 .248 B1
 Derby DE3 . . . . .217 C2
 Mansfield Woodhouse
  NG19 . . . . .136 B3
Perth Dr NG9 . . . . .209 C1
Perth St Derby DE21 . . . .205 B1
 Nottingham NG3 . . . . . .268 B2
Peter Baines Ind Est
 DE22 . . . . .267 A1
Peter More Hill S80 . . . . .81 C2
Peter St Ashbourne DE6 .173 B1
 Glossop SK13 . . . . .10 A3
Peterborough St DE21 . .219 C4
Peterdale Cl S43 . . . . . . .96 C4
Peterdale Rd S43 . . . . . .96 C4
Peterhouse Terr 2
 DE23 . . . . .219 A1
Peterlee Pl DE24 . . . . . .233 A3
Peters Ave S45 . . . . .131 A2
Peters Ct DE65 . . . . .227 B1
Petersgate NG10 . . . . . .223 A1
Petersgate Cl NG10 . . . .223 A1
Petersham Ct 5 NG10 . .223 A1
Petersham Dr DE24 . . . . .233 A3
Petersham Rd NG10 . . . .223 A1
Peterway DE55 . . . . .170 B4
Pettifor Terr DE55 . . . . . .147 B1
Petty Close La DE6 . . . . .202 B1
Pettyclose La S41,S43 . . .96 B3
Petworth Ave NG9 . . . . . .223 C2
Pevensey Ave S41 . . . . . .95 C3
Pevensey Ct S41 . . . . . . .95 C4
Peveril Ave
 Borrowash DE72 . . . . . .221 B1
 New Mills SK22 . . . . . . .24 B1
Peveril Castle ★ S33 . . . .38 B1
Peveril Cl Castleton S33 .38 B1
 Darley Dale DE4 . . . . . .127 B2
 Somercotes DE55 . . . . .170 B3
Peveril Cres
 Long Eaton NG10 . . . . .235 C3
 West Hallam DE7 . . . . .207 C4
Peveril Ct 1 Glossop SK13 17 C4
 Ripley DE5 . . . . .169 B1
Peveril Dr Ilkeston DE7 . .194 B1
 Nottingham NG7 . . . . . .268 A1
 Somercotes DE55 . . . . .170 B3
Peveril Gdns SK12 . . . . . .33 A3
Peveril Mews SK12 . . . . .33 A3
Peveril Rd Buxton SK17 . .85 B4
 Castleton S33 . . . . .38 B1
 Chesterfield S41 . . . . . .95 C4
 Eckington S21 . . . . .59 C2
 Tibshelf DE55 . . . . .147 C3
Peveril St DE24 . . . . .232 B3
Peverill Rd S44 . . . . .98 C2
Pewit Cl S42 . . . . .132 B4
Pewit La Pilsley DE55 . . .147 B3
 Tibshelf DE55 . . . . .147 B3
Pheasant Field Dr DE21 221 A3
Pheasant Hill NG19 . . . . .136 A1
Philip Howard Rd SK13 . .17 B4
Philips Croft DE56 . . . . . .190 C2
Philipway DE55 . . . . .170 B4
Phoenix St S12 . . . . .44 C1
Phoenix Rd S12 . . . . .44 C1
Phoenix St DE1 . . . . .267 B4
Phyllis Gr NG10 . . . . .236 C4
Pic Tor La DE4 . . . . .143 A2
Piccadilly La DE6 . . . . . .172 B1
Piccadilly Rd S41 . . . . . .96 B2
Pickard La DE55 . . . . . . .168 B1
Pickering Ave NG16 . . . . .182 C1
Pickering Rise DE21 . . . .205 B1
Pickford Pl SK23 . . . . . . .47 A3
Pickleys La DE6 . . . . .224 B4
Pickton Cl S40 . . . . .95 B1
Pictor Gr SK17 . . . . .85 B4
Pictor Rd SK17 . . . . .85 B4
Piddocks Rd DE15 . . . . . .255 A3
Pig La DE4 . . . . .111 A2
Pighills La S18 . . . . .57 A3
Pike Cl S40 . . . . .95 A3
Pike View Cl SK23 . . . . . .34 C1
Pike's La SK13 . . . . .17 A4
Pilcher Gate NG1 . . . . . .268 B1
Pilgrim Cl S81 . . . . .63 C4
Pilgrim Pl ST16 . . . . .269 B4
Pilgrim St ST16 . . . . .269 B4
Pilgrims Way DE24 . . . . .231 B2
Pilhough La DE4 . . . . . . .126 B3
Pilhough Rd DE4 . . . . . . .126 B4
Pilkington's Yd S21 . . . . .59 C2
Pillar Butts DE4 . . . . .165 C4
Pilsley CE Prim Sch
 DE45 . . . . .91 B1
Pilsley Cl DE56 . . . . .179 B3
Pilsley Prim Sch S45 . . .132 B1
Pilsley Rd
 Clay Cross S45 . . . . . .131 C2
 Stonebroom DE55 . . . . .147 A3
Pimlico Derby DE22 . . . . .218 A3
 Ilkeston DE7 . . . . .208 C4
Pimm's Rd DE6 . . . . .217 A4
Pinch The DE6 . . . . .150 A1
Pinchom's Hill Rd DE56 179 A2
Pincot St SK22 . . . . .33 B4
Pindale Ave S43 . . . . . . .97 B4
Pindale Rd S33 . . . . .38 C1
Pinder St NG1 . . . . .268 B1
Pine Ave NG16 . . . . .182 A2
Pine Cl Burton u T DE14 .254 A4

Pine Cl continued
 Creswell S80 . . . . .81 C1
 Derby DE21 . . . . .220 A2
 Etwall DE65 . . . . .229 B2
 Killamarsh S21 . . . . . . .60 B3
 Mansfield Woodhouse
  NG19 . . . . .136 B3
 Ripley DE5 . . . . .169 B1
 Shirebrook NG20 . . . . .119 C3
 Smalley DE7 . . . . .192 C3
Pine Croft DE6 . . . . .185 B4
Pine Gr DE11 . . . . .255 C3
Pine St S43 . . . . .97 A4
Pine Tree Wlk NG16 . . . .182 B1
Pine View Chesterfield S40 95 A2
 Clay Cross S45 . . . . . .131 C2
Pine Wlk DE11 . . . . .261 C4
Pinecroft Ct DE21 . . . . . .206 A3
Pinegreaves Dr DE73 . . .233 A1
Pines The DE72 . . . . .235 A4
Pinewood DE5 . . . . .181 A4
Pinewood Cl DE55 . . . . .159 B2
Pinewood Rd
 Belper DE56 . . . . .178 C3
 Burton u T DE15 . . . . . .254 C3
 Matlock DE4 . . . . .143 A4
Pinfold SK13 . . . . .9 C2
Pinfold Cl
 Holymoorside S42 . . . . .113 C4
 Repton DE65 . . . . .242 B1
 Tutbury DE13 . . . . .239 B3
Pinfold Cres SK17 . . . . . .69 B2
Pinfold Hill S32 . . . . .72 C1
Pinfold La Bradley DE6 . .187 A4
 Repton DE65 . . . . .242 B1
 Stapleford NG9 . . . . . .223 C4
Pinfold Rd S21 . . . . .59 B2
Pinfold St S21 . . . . .59 B2
Pinfold The Belper DE56 .179 B3
 Elvaston DE72 . . . . . . .233 C2
 Glapwell S44 . . . . .118 A1
 Middleton DE45 . . . . . .124 C2
Pinfold View DE45 . . . . . .109 B3
Pingle DE22 . . . . .204 C2
Pingle Cres DE56 . . . . . .178 C3
Pingle Farm Rd DE11 . . .255 C2
Pingle Grange S43 . . . . . .96 C4
Pingle La Belper DE56 . .178 C3
 Carsington DE4 . . . . . .164 C4
Pingle Rd S21 . . . . .60 C4
Pingle Sch DE11 . . . . . . .256 A3
Pingle The DE21 . . . . . . .220 C2
 Long Eaton NG10 . . . . .236 B4
 Melbourne DE73 . . . . . .252 A4
Pinglehill Way DE73 . . . .233 A1
Pingott La SK13 . . . . .10 A3
Pintail Dr DE24 . . . . .231 B2
Pinxton Gn NG16 . . . . . .160 C2
Pinxton La
 Kirby-in-A NG17 . . . . . .160 C3
 South Normanton DE55 .160 B3
Piper Ave S45 . . . . .131 C2
Piper La S42 . . . . .94 C2
Pipeyard La S21 . . . . . . .59 B1
Pippenwell Rd SK17 . . . .106 A4
Pippin Hill DE5 . . . . .180 C1
Pit Close La DE73 . . . . . .233 A1
Pit La Codnor DE5 . . . . . .181 A4
 Crich DE4,DE55 . . . . . .157 A3
 Ripley DE5 . . . . .169 C1
 Sheffield S2 . . . . .44 A4
 Shipley DE75 . . . . .194 A3
 Shirland DE55 . . . . . . .158 A4
 Stonebroom DE55 . . . . .147 A3
Pitch Cl S43 . . . . .80 C1
Pitt Hill NG20 . . . . .100 C1
Pitt St S21 . . . . .59 B1
Pittar St DE22 . . . . .267 A2
Pittlemere La SK17 . . . . .50 C1
Pittywood Rd DE4 . . . . . .165 C4
Placket La DE4 . . . . .141 B4
Plackett Cl
 Breaston DE72 . . . . . . .235 B4
 Stapleford NG9 . . . . . .223 C4
Plain The DE6 . . . . .201 C4
Plains La DE56 . . . . .178 A2
Plainspot Rd NG16 . . . . .171 C1
Plaistow Green Rd DF4 .156 C1
Plant La NG10 . . . . .236 A2
Plantagenet Ct 18 NG3 .268 B2
Plantagenet St NG3 . . . .268 B2
Plantain Gdns DE23 . . . .231 B3
Plantation Cl S80 . . . . . .81 C2
Plantation Rd S8 . . . . . . .43 C4
Plantations The 9
 NG10 . . . . .236 A4
Plantin Rise S20 . . . . . . .59 C4
Plantin The S20 . . . . .59 C4
Platt St Glossop SK13 . . .10 A3
 Pinxton NG16 . . . . .160 B1
Platts Ave DE75 . . . . . . .181 B1
Pleasant Ave S44 . . . . . .118 A4
Pleasant Cl S12 . . . . .44 A3
Pleasant Pl S40 . . . . .95 B2
Pleasant Rd S12 . . . . . . .44 A3
Pleasant View SK6 . . . . . .15 A2
Plimsoll St DE22 . . . . . . .218 B3
Plough Gate DE22 . . . . . .204 C1
Plough La NG1 . . . . .268 C1
Ploughfield Cl DE23 . . . .231 A4
Plover Ave DE11 . . . . . . .256 C2
Plover Ct DE3 . . . . .230 A4
Plover Way S44 . . . . .96 C2
Plowman Ct NG9 . . . . . . .223 B3
Plowright Cl S14 . . . . . . .43 B3
Plowright Dr S14 . . . . . . .43 B3
Plowright Mount S14 . . . .43 B3

Plowright Way S14 . . . . . .43 B3
Plucksbridge Rd SK6 . . . .23 A2
Plumbley Hall Mews S20 59 B3
Plumbley Hall Rd S20 . . .59 B3
Plummer Rd DE11 . . . . . .256 A3
Plumptre Cl NG16 . . . . . .182 C1
Plumptre Pl **11** NG1 . . . . .268 B1
Plumptre Sq NG1 . . . . . . .268 B1
Plumptre St NG1 . . . . . . .268 B1
Plumptre Way NG16 . . . .182 C1
Plumtre Rd NG16 . . . . . . .182 A3
Plymouth Ave NG16 . . . .160 C1
Pocknedge La S42 . . . . . .113 B4
Pole La Marple SK22 . . . . .24 A2
New Mills SK22, SK6 . . . . .24 A2
Pole's Rd DE6 . . . . .217 A4
Pollard Dr NG18 . . . . .268 C4
Pollards Oaks DE72 . . . . .221 B1
Polly Froggat La S32 . . . .72 A1
Polyfields La S44 . . . . . . .118 A4
Pond La Tupton S42 . . . . .131 B4
Wingerworth S42 . . . . .114 C2
Pond Rd DE56 . . . . .191 B4
Pond St S40 . . . . .266 B2
Pondwell Cnr S43 . . . . . . .96 C4
Pondwell Dr S43 . . . . .96 C4
Ponsonby Terr DE1 . . . . .218 C3
Pontefract St DE24 . . . . .232 B4
Pontypool Cl DE21 . . . . . .206 A1
Pool Cl Elvaston DE24 . . .233 B2
Pinxton NG16 . . . . .160 B1
Pool Rd DE73 . . . . .252 B3
Pool St DE11 . . . . .256 B1
Pool's La S21 . . . . .77 B4
Poolar Terr NG16 . . . . . . .171 C3
Poole St DE24 . . . . .232 C3
Poole's Cavern★ SK17 . .85 A3
Pools Brook Ctry Pk★
S43 . . . . .79 A1
Poolsbrook Ave S43 . . . . .98 A4
Poolsbrook Country Pk★
S43 . . . . .97 C4
Poolsbrook Cres S43 . . . .98 A4
Poolsbrook Prim Sch
S43 . . . . .98 A4
Poolsbrook Rd S44 . . . . . .98 A3
Poolsbrook Sq S43 . . . . . .98 A4
Poolsbrook View S43 . . . .98 A4
Pope Carr Rd DE4 . . . . .143 B3
Popham St NG1 . . . . .268 B1
Poplar Ave
Chesterfield S40 . . . . .95 A1
Derby DE21 . . . . .220 C3
Moira NG16 . . . . .262 C1
New Mills SK22 . . . . .24 B1
Ripley DE5 . . . . .180 B4
Sandiacre NG10 . . . . .223 A4
Swadlincote DE11 . . . . . . .256 A3
Poplar Cl Derby DE24 . . .233 A4
Dronfield S18 . . . . .76 B4
Killamarsh S21 . . . . .60 B3
Poplar Cres DE6 . . . . . . .185 A4
Poplar Dr
Chesterfield S42 . . . . .115 B1
Glapwell S44 . . . . .134 A4
Pleasley NG19 . . . . .135 A2
Poplar Nook DE22 . . . . . .204 C2
Poplar Rd Breaston DE72 235 C4
Eckington S21 . . . . .59 B1
South Normanton DE55 . .160 A4
Poplar Row DE22 . . . . . . .205 A1
Poplar St
Mansfield Woodhouse
NG19 . . . . .136 B2
Nottingham NG1 . . . . .268 C1
Poplar Terr SK23 . . . . . . .47 A4
Poplar Way High Lane SK6 32 A4
Ilkeston DE7 . . . . .208 B3
Poplars The Derby DE22 .204 C2
Whitwell S80 . . . . .82 A3
Poppy Cl NG16 . . . . .119 B2
Poppy Gdns DE55 . . . . . .148 A4
Porlock Cl **2** NG10 . . . . .236 A4
Porlock Ct DE21 . . . . .206 A1
Port Way DE21,DE56 . . . .191 B3
Porteous Cl DE4 . . . . . . .127 B2
Porter La DE4 . . . . .154 C2
Porter Rd DE23 . . . . .218 C1
Porter St S43 . . . . .78 C1
Porter's La Derby DE21 . .205 C2
Findern DE65 . . . . .230 B1
Porterhouse Rd DE5 . . . .169 C1
Porters Farm Ct ST14 . .224 C1
Porthcawl Pl DE21 . . . . . .206 B1
Portico Rd DE23 . . . . .231 A3
Portland Ave Bolsover S44 99 A1
Burton u T DE14 . . . . .254 A4
Creswell S80 . . . . .81 C1
Portland Cl DE3 . . . . .217 B1
Portland Cres
Bolsover S44 . . . . .99 A1
Mansfield Woodhouse
NG19 . . . . .136 B2
Stapleford NG9 . . . . .223 C3
Portland Ct Mews NG19 136 B2
Portland Gr SK23 . . . . . . .34 C1
Portland Rd
Beeston NG9 . . . . .223 C1
Eastwood NG16 . . . . .195 A4
Ilkeston DE7 . . . . .194 C2
Long Eaton NG10 . . . . . . .236 A2
New Mills SK22 . . . . .24 B1
Nottingham NG7 . . . . .268 A2
Shirebrook NG20 . . . . . . .119 C2
Whaley Thorns NG20 . . . .101 A1
Portland Ret Pk NG18 . .268 B3
Portland Sq DE45 . . . . . .109 B3

Portland St Clowne S43 . .81 A2
Derby DE23 . . . . .232 A4
Etwall DE65 . . . . .229 A2
Mansfield NG18 . . . . .268 B3
Mansfield Woodhouse
NG19 . . . . .136 B2
New Houghton DE19 . . . .135 A4
Whitwell S80 . . . . .81 C3
Portland Terr NG20 . . . .101 A1
Portman Chase DE24 . . .231 B1
Portreath Dr DE22 . . . . . .204 C2
Portway Cl DE22 . . . . . . .205 A2
Portway Dr DE13 . . . . . . .239 B3
Portway Inf Sch DE22 . .204 C2
Portway Jun Sch DE22 .204 C2
Post St SK13 . . . . .10 A3
Postern St **4** NG1 . . . . . .268 A1
Postmans La S42 . . . . . . .116 B2
Posy La DE72 . . . . .246 A4
Potato Pit Hill DE7 . . . . .208 A1
Potlocks The DE65 . . . . .242 B3
Potter Rd SK13 . . . . .9 C2
Potter St Derby DE21 . . .220 B2
Melbourne DE73 . . . . .252 A4
Potters Cl S41 . . . . .77 B1
Potters Croft
Clifton Campville B79 . . . .263 C1
Swadlincote DE11 . . . . . . .256 A3
Potters La DE4,DE55 . . . .157 A3
Potters Nook S81 . . . . . . .63 C4
Potters Way DE7 . . . . . . .209 A4
Pottery Cl DE56 . . . . .179 B3
Pottery La DE5 . . . . .180 B2
Pottery La E S41 . . . . .96 A4
Pottery La W S41 . . . . . . .96 A4
Pottery Prim Sch DE56 .179 B2
Poulson St ST4 . . . . .269 B2
Poulter Ctry Pk NG20 . .100 C1
Poulter St NG20 . . . . .100 C1
Poulton Dr NG2 . . . . .268 C1
Poultry NG1 . . . . .268 B1
Powell Dr S21 . . . . .60 B3
Powell St DE23 . . . . .218 C1
Pown St SK17 . . . . .137 A3
Powtrell Pl DE7 . . . . .209 A4
Poynter Cl DE75 . . . . .181 B1
Poynton Wood Cres S17 .56 A3
Poynton Wood Glade
S17 . . . . .56 A3
Poyser Ave DE21 . . . . . . .220 A4
Poyser La DE6 . . . . .203 A1
Pratt Cl NG19 . . . . .135 B1
Pratthall La DE4 . . . . .166 A3
Premier Ave DE6 . . . . . . .185 A4
Prescot Cl DE3 . . . . .217 B1
Prescott Ave ST16 . . . . . .269 C4
Press La S42 . . . . .130 B3
Prestbury Cl DE21 . . . . . .206 A1
Preston Ave DE55 . . . . . .159 A2
Preston St **15** S8 . . . . .43 A4
Prestwold Way S41 . . . . .115 B4
Prestwood Cl ST17 . . . . .269 B3
Prestwood La ST14 . . . . .196 C1
Prestwood Park Dr
DE11 . . . . .256 B3
Pretoria St S44 . . . . .98 C1
Previn Gdns NG3 . . . . . . .268 C2
Pride Park Stad (Derby FC)
DE24 . . . . .219 C2
Pride Parkway DE1,DE21 219 B2
Priestcliffe Rd SK17 . . . .87 C2
Priestfield Gdns S41 . . . .95 A4
Priestland Ave DE22 . . . .220 B2
Priestley Ave DE55 . . . . .146 B3
Primary Cl DE56 . . . . .179 A2
Prime Ind Est DE23 . . . . .219 B1
Prime Ind Pk DE23 . . . . .219 B1
Prime Parkway DE1 . . . . .267 C5
Primrose Ave NG16 . . . .171 C1
Primrose Cl Derby DE21 .205 C2
Killamarsh S21 . . . . .60 C4
South Normanton DE55 . .160 A4
Primrose Cotts DE72 . . .222 B2
Primrose Cres **1** SK13 . .17 A4
Primrose Ct SK22 . . . . . . .25 B2
Primrose Dr
Burton u T DE14 . . . . .254 A4
Morley DE7 . . . . .206 B4
Primrose Hill
Blackwell DE55 . . . . .147 C1
Glossop SK13 . . . . .17 A4
Primrose La Hayfield SK22 25 B3
Glossop SK13 . . . . .17 A4
Killamarsh S21 . . . . .60 C4
Marple SK6 . . . . .24 A2
Primrose Mdw DE11 . . . .256 A4
Primrose Rise NG16 . . . .195 A4
Primrose St DE7 . . . . .194 C2
Primrose Terr **2** SK13 . .17 A4
Primrose Way NG20 . . . .119 C3
Primula Way DE23 . . . . . .231 B2
Prince Charles Ave
DE22 . . . . .218 A3
Prince Edward Prim Sch
S2 .44 A4
Prince of Wales Rd S2 . .44 A4
Prince St Ilkeston DE7 . .194 C2
Long Eaton NG10 . . . . . . .236 B4
Prince's Rd SK17 . . . . . . .85 A4
Princes Dr DE23 . . . . .218 A1
Princes Rd Chinley SK23 .34 C1
Stoke-on-T ST4 . . . . .269 A2
Princes St Derby DE23 . .219 A1
Mansfield NG18 . . . . .268 B3
4 Stafford ST16 . . . . .269 B4
Princess Ave
Linton DE12 . . . . .261 B3

Princess Ave continued
South Normanton DE55 . .160 A3
Princess Cl Heanor DE75 181 B1
Woodville DE11 . . . . .256 C1
Princess Ct S2 . . . . .44 A4
Princess Dr
Borrowash DE72 . . . . .221 A1
Sandiacre NG10 . . . . .223 A2
Princess Pl S45 . . . . .131 B1
Princess Rd Dronfield S18 57 A1
Uttoxeter ST14 . . . . .210 A1
Princess St
Brimington S43 . . . . .96 C4
Chesterfield S40 . . . . .266 A4
Eastwood NG16 . . . . .182 C2
Glossop SK13 . . . . .17 B4
Long Eaton NG10 . . . . . . .236 B4
Swadlincote DE11 . . . . . . .261 C4
Princess Way DE13 . . . . .240 C1
Printers Fold SK14 . . . . . .9 B3
Printers Pk SK14 . . . . .9 C3
Priors Barn Cl DE72 . . . .221 B1
Prioryway Rd DE72 . . . . .221 B1
Priorway Gdns DE72 . . . .221 B1
Priory Cl Derby DE73 . . . .245 A4
Ilkeston DE7 . . . . .208 B3
Swadlincote DE11 . . . . . . .256 A3
Tutbury DE13 . . . . .239 A3
Yeaveley DE6 . . . . .199 B3
Priory Ct S26 . . . . .61 C3
Priory Gdns Derby DE21 .205 C2
Swanwick DE55 . . . . .170 A4
Priory Lands DE13 . . . . . .240 C1
Priory Rd Alfreton DE55 .159 A3
Eastwood NG16 . . . . .182 C1
Mansfield Woodhouse
NG19 . . . . .136 A2
Priory Sq NG19 . . . . .136 A2
Pritchard Dr NG9 . . . . . . .223 C3
Pritchett Dr DE23 . . . . . . .230 C4
Private St DE7 . . . . .78 A1
Progress Ct DE45 . . . . . . .109 B3
Prospect Ave DE55 . . . . .159 C3
Prospect Ct
13 Sheffield S17 . . . . .56 A3
Sutton in A NG17 . . . . . . .148 C1
Prospect Dr Belper DE56 178 C1
Matlock DE4 . . . . .143 A4
Sheffield S17 . . . . .55 C3
Shirebrook NG20 . . . . . . .119 C2
Prospect Gdns DE55 . . . .169 C4
Prospect Pl **5** S17 . . . . .56 A3
Prospect Rd
Chesterfield S41 . . . . .76 C1
Denby DE5 . . . . .180 A1
Dronfield S18 . . . . .57 B2
Heanor DE75 . . . . .194 A4
Pilsley S45 . . . . .132 B1
Sheffield, Lowfield S2 . . . .43 A4
Sheffield, Totley Rise S17 .56 A3
Stafford ST16 . . . . .269 B4
Prospect St
Alfreton DE55 . . . . .159 A2
Mansfield NG18 . . . . .268 C3
Prospect Terr
Chesterfield S40 . . . . .95 C2
Crich DE4 . . . . .168 A4
Providence Ct DE11 . . . . .256 C1
Providence Pl
Alfreton DE55 . . . . .158 C2
12 Ilkeston DE7 . . . . .194 C1
Providence Rd NG16 . . . .171 A2
Providence St DE5 . . . . . .180 C4
Provident St **9** DE23 . . .219 A1
Pryor Mede S26 . . . . .61 C3
Pudding Bag La S45 . . . .129 C4
Pulborough Gdns DE23 .231 A3
Pullman Cl S43 . . . . .78 C2
Pullman Rd Derby DE21 .219 C2
Nottingham NG2 . . . . .268 C1
Pump Cl DE4 . . . . .143 B2
Pump La DE6 . . . . .224 A4
Pump St ST4 . . . . .269 B2
Purbeck Ave S40 . . . . . . .95 B2
Purbeck Cl
Long Eaton NG10 . . . . . . .236 A4
Mansfield Woodhouse
NG19 . . . . .136 B3
Purchase Ave DE75 . . . . .181 B1
Purdy Mdw NG10 . . . . . . .235 C3
Purseglove Dr SK17 . . . . .69 B2
Purseglove Rd SK17 . . . .69 B2
Putney Cl DE22 . . . . .217 C3
Pybus St DE22 . . . . .218 C3
Pye Bridge Ind Est
DE55 . . . . .170 C3
Pye Hill Rd NG16 . . . . . . .171 A2
Pyegrove SK13 . . . . .10 C1
Pyegrove Rd SK13 . . . . . .10 C1
Pykestone Cl DE21 . . . . .205 C1
Pym Leys NG10 . . . . .235 C3
Pym St NG3 . . . . .268 C2
Pym Wlk NG3 . . . . .268 C2
Pynot Rd S41 . . . . .77 A1
Pytchley Cl DE56 . . . . . . .179 B2

Q

Quadrant The
Buxton SK17 . . . . .85 A4
Totley S17 . . . . .55 C3
Quaker Cl DE73 . . . . .252 A4
Quaker La NG18 . . . . .268 B3
Quaker Way NG18 . . . . . .268 B4
Quantock Cl DE24 . . . . . .231 B1
Quantock Rd NG10 . . . . .223 A1

Quantock Way S40 . . . . . .95 A3
Quarn Dr DE22 . . . . .204 B2
Quarn Gdns DE1 . . . . . . .218 C4
Quarn St DE1 . . . . .218 C4
Quarn Way DE1 . . . . .218 C3
Quarndon Hts DE22 . . . .204 B2
Quarndon View DE22 . . .204 B1
Quarry Ave ST4 . . . . .269 A2
Quarry Bank DE4 . . . . . . .143 A4
Quarry Bank Rd S41 . . . .96 B1
Quarry Berry La DE12 . . .264 C1
Quarry Cl SK13 . . . . .10 B1
Quarry Hill Eckington S21 .58 B1
Mosborough S20 . . . . .59 A4
Stanton-by-D DE7 . . . . . . .223 A4
Quarry Hill Ind Est DE7 .209 A2
Quarry Hill Ind Pk DE7 .208 C3
Quarry Hill Rd DE7 . . . . .208 C3
Quarry La Alton S42 . . . . .130 C3
Brackenfield DE55 . . . . . . .145 B3
Chesterfield S40 . . . . .95 B1
Mansfield NG18 . . . . .268 B1
Matlock DE4 . . . . .143 C4
Stonebroom DE55 . . . . . .146 C2
Quarry Rd
Apperknowle S18 . . . . .58 A1
Belper DE56 . . . . .178 C1
Bolsover S44 . . . . .99 A2
Hayfield SK22 . . . . .24 C1
Killamarsh S21 . . . . .60 B4
Morley DE7 . . . . .192 A1
New Mills SK22 . . . . .33 B4
Somercotes DE55 . . . . . . .170 B4
Stoke-on-T ST4 . . . . .269 A2
Totley S17 . . . . .55 C3
Quarry Vale Gr S12 . . . . .44 B2
Quarry Vale Rd S12 . . . . .44 B2
Queen Anne St ST4 . . . . .269 B2
Queen Elizabeth CE Comp
Sch NG19 . . . . .136 A1
Queen Elizabeth DE6 173 A1
Queen Elizabeth Way
DE7 . . . . .208 B3
Queen Elizabeth's Gram Sch
DE6 . . . . .173 B2
Queen Elizabeth's Lower Sch
Department DE6 . . . . . . .185 C4
Queen Mary Cl S2 . . . . . .44 A4
Queen Mary Cres S2 . . . .44 A4
Queen Mary Ct DE1 . . . .218 C4
Queen Mary Gr S2 . . . . . .43 C4
Queen Mary Mews S2 . .44 A4
Queen Mary Rd
Chesterfield S40 . . . . .95 A1
Sheffield S2 . . . . .44 A4
Queen St Belper DE56 . .179 A2
Brimington S43 . . . . .77 C1
Chesterfield S40 . . . . .266 A4
Clay Cross S45 . . . . .131 B2
Creswell S80 . . . . .81 C1
Derby DE1 . . . . .267 B4
Eckington S21 . . . . .59 C2
Glossop SK13 . . . . .17 A4
Glossop, Hadfield SK13 . .10 A2
Ilkeston DE7 . . . . .208 C4
Ironville NG16 . . . . .170 C2
Langley Mill NG16 . . . . . .182 B2
Long Eaton NG10 . . . . . . .236 C4
Longnor SK17 . . . . .121 A3
Mansfield NG18 . . . . .268 B1
Marple SK6 . . . . .23 A3
Middleton (Nr Wirksworth)
DE4 . . . . .154 B3
Mosborough S20 . . . . .59 B4
29 Nottingham NG1 . . . . .268 B2
Pilsley S45 . . . . .132 B1
Pinxton NG16 . . . . .160 B2
Ripley DE5 . . . . .181 A4
Somercotes DE55 . . . . . . .170 B4
South Normanton DE55 . .159 C3
Staveley S43 . . . . .97 B4
Swadlincote DE11 . . . . . . .256 A1
Tideswell SK17 . . . . .69 B2
Queen St N S41 . . . . .96 A4
Queen Victoria Rd
Totley S17 . . . . .55 C3
Tupton S42 . . . . .115 B1
Queen's Ave SK17 . . . . . .85 B4
Queen's Bridge Rd NG2 268 B1
Queen's Ct S41 . . . . .266 A4
Queen's Dr Belper DE56 .178 C3
Glossop SK13 . . . . .10 C1
Ilkeston DE7 . . . . .208 C4
Swadlincote DE11 . . . . . . .256 A3
Queen's Park Sports Ctr
S40 . . . . .266 A4
Queen's Rd Buxton SK17 .85 B4
Nottingham NG2 . . . . .268 B1
Stoke-on-T ST4 . . . . .269 A2
Queen's Sq NG16 . . . . . .182 C1
Queen's Way S42 . . . . . . .115 B1
Queen's Wlk Tupton S42 .115 B1
Whaley Thorns NG20 . . . .101 A1
Queens Ave Heanor DE75 181 B1
Ilkeston DE7 . . . . .209 A3
Stanley DE7 . . . . .207 B3
Queens Ct
Burton u T DE14 . . . . .254 A4
Creswell S80 . . . . .81 C1
Draycott DE72 . . . . .235 A4
Derby DE22 . . . . .218 C3
Queens Dr Brinsley NG16 182 C4
Derby DE23 . . . . .218 B1
Sandiacre NG10 . . . . .223 A4
Queens Gr **12** NG1 . . . . .268 B1
Queens L Ctr DE1 . . . . . .267 B4
Queens Rd Creswell S80 .82 C3

Queens Rd continued
Sheffield S2 . . . . .43 A4
Queens Rd N NG16 . . . . .182 C1
Queens Rd S NG16 . . . . .182 C1
Queens Ret Pk S2 . . . . . .43 A4
Queens Rise S13 . . . . . . .239 B3
Queens Wlk S42 . . . . .116 C1
Queensbury Chase
DE23 . . . . .231 A3
Queensferry Gdns DE24 232 C2
Queensgate Dr DE73 . . .244 C4
Queensland Cl DE3 . . . . .217 C2
Queensland Cres DE15 .248 B1
Queensview Dr DE5 . . . . .181 A4
Queensville Ave ST17 . . .269 C3
Queensville Bridge
ST17 . . . . .269 C3
Queensway
Castle Donington DE74 . .246 C2
Derby DE22 . . . . .204 C1
Holmewood S42 . . . . .116 C1
Melbourne DE73 . . . . .252 A4
Pilsley S45 . . . . .132 B1
Stafford ST16 . . . . .269 B4
Stoke-on-T ST4 . . . . .269 C1
Stonebroom DE55 . . . . . .146 C2
Queenville ST17 . . . . .269 C3
Quenby La DE5 . . . . .169 C1
Quentin Rd SK23 . . . . . . .47 B3
Quick Cl DE73 . . . . .252 A4
Quick Hill Rd DE24 . . . . .231 B1
Quillings Way DE72 . . . . .221 B1
Quilow La DE6 . . . . .185 C2
Quixhill Bank ST14 . . . . .196 C4
Quixhill Cl DE6 . . . . .185 A4
Quixhill La ST14 . . . . .196 B4
Quoit Gn S18 . . . . .57 C3
Quorn Cl DE15 . . . . .248 A1
Quorn Dr **5** S40 . . . . . . .95 A3
Quorn Rise DE23 . . . . . . .231 C3
Quorndon Cres NG10 . . .236 B3

R

Rabown Ave DE23 . . . . . .231 B4
Racecourse Ind Est
DE21 . . . . .219 B4
Racecourse Mount S41 . .95 C4
Racecourse Rd S41 . . . . .95 C4
Racester Way S42 . . . . . .131 C3
Rad Mdws NG10 . . . . . . .236 B3
Radbourne Gate DE3 . . .217 B3
Radbourne La DE22 . . . . .217 C3
Radbourne Rd NG2 . . . . .268 C1
Radbourne St
Derby DE22 . . . . .218 B3
Mansfield Woodhouse
NG19 . . . . .136 C2
Radburn Ct NG9 . . . . .209 C4
Radcliffe Ave DE21 . . . . .219 C4
Radcliffe Dr DE22 . . . . . .218 B2
Radford St DE7 . . . . .192 C3
Radford St Derby DE24 . .232 C4
1 Mansfield NG18 . . . . . .268 C3
Radmanthwaite Rd
NG19 . . . . .135 B2
Radnor Pl NG19 . . . . .135 B2
Radnor St NG3 . . . . .219 B4
Radstock Gdns DE21 . . .205 C1
Radstone Cl DE21 . . . . . .206 A1
Raeburn Cl S14 . . . . .43 C1
Raeburn Dr Beeston NG9 223 C1
Marple SK6 . . . . .23 A4
Raeburn Pl S14 . . . . .43 C2
Raeburn Rd S14 . . . . .43 C2
Raeburn Way S14 . . . . . . .43 C1
Raglan Ave DE22 . . . . . . .218 B3
Raglan St Alfreton DE55 .159 A2
Fenton ST4 . . . . .269 C1
Raglan Wlk DE22 . . . . . . .269 C1
Railway Ave S80 . . . . .100 B4
Railway Cotts
Derby DE73 . . . . .243 A4
Egginton DE65 . . . . .241 A4
Holmewood S42 . . . . .116 C1
Kimberley NG16 . . . . .195 C3
Railway Row NG16 . . . . . .170 C2
Railway Side DE11 . . . . . .256 A1
Railway St Glossop SK13 .10 B1
Glossop, Hadfield SK13 . .10 A3
Stafford ST16 . . . . .269 A4
Railway Terr Buxton SK17 .85 B4
Chesterfield S41 . . . . .115 A4
Derby DE1 . . . . .267 D2
Disley SK12 . . . . .32 B3
Rain's La DE4 . . . . .154 B2
Rainham Gdns DE24 . . . .233 A3
Rainier Dr DE21 . . . . .220 A3
Rake Head Rd HD7 . . . . .2 C4
Rake La DE45 . . . . .124 B2
Rake The DE45 . . . . .123 A4
Rakes La DE6 . . . . .162 A3
Rakes Rd DE45 . . . . .107 B1
Raleigh Cl DE7 . . . . .194 C2
Raleigh Rd
Mansfield NG19 . . . . .268 A4
Sheffield S2 . . . . .43 A3
Raleigh Sq **18** NG7 . . . . .268 A2
Raleigh St Derby DE22 . .218 B3
Nottingham NG7 . . . . .268 A2
Ralph Dr DE55 . . . . .170 B4
Ralph Rd S43 . . . . .79 A1
Ralston Croft S20 . . . . . . .59 C3
Ralston Ct S20 . . . . .59 B3

Ralston Gr S20 ....59 B3
Ralston Pl S20 ....59 B3
Rambler Cl DE11 .....256 A3
Ramblers Dr DE21 ....206 B2
Ramper Ave S43 ....80 C1
Ramscliff Ave DE12 ...265 C4
Ramsdean Cl DE21 ....219 B4
Ramsden Cl SK13 ....10 B1
Ramsden La HD9 ....3 A4
Ramsden Rd HD9 ....3 B4
Ramsey Ave S40 ....95 B1
Ramsey Cl NG9 ....209 C1
Ramsey St ST4 ....269 C1
Ramshaw Cl 6 S41 .....95 B4
Ramshaw Rd S18 ....76 C3
Ramshaw Way DE22 ...218 C2
Ranby Wlk NG3 ....268 C2
Randall Dr DE11 .....256 A2
Randall Pl S2 ....43 A4
Randall St S21 ....59 A1
Randolph Rd DE23 ....231 C4
Ranelagh Gdns DE22 ..218 A4
Raneld Mount S40 ....114 B4
Rangemoor La DE6 ....183 B3
Rangemore Cl DE3 ....217 C2
Ranmoor Cl S41 ......115 B4
Ranmoor Hill S32 .....52 C4
Ranmoor La S32 ....52 C4
Rannoch Cl Derby DE22 ..204 C2
Derby, Spondon DE21 ...220 C3
Rannoch Dr NG19 .....268 A3
Ranworth Cl DE24 ....232 B2
Ratcliffe Ave DE14 ...254 A4
Ratcliffe Gate DE18 ..268 C3
Ratcliffe St NG16 ....182 C1
Rauche Ct DE23 ......267 C1
Raven Ave DE55 ......147 C3
Raven Cl DE55 ....170 B3
Raven Oak Cl DE56 ...179 A2
Raven St DE22 ....218 C2
Ravencar Rd S21 ......59 A2
Ravenscourt Rd DE22 .218 B3
Ravenscroft Ave S13 ...44 C4
Ravenscroft Cl S13 ....44 C4
Ravenscroft Cres S13 ..44 C4
Ravenscroft Ct S13 ....44 C4
Ravenscroft Dr
  Derby DE21 ....219 C3
  Sheffield S13 ....44 C4
Ravenscroft Oval S13 ..44 C4
Ravenscroft Pl S13 ....44 C4
Ravenscroft Rd S13 ...44 C4
Ravenscroft Way S13 ..44 C4
Ravensdale Ave
  Long Eaton NG10 ....223 A1
  Mansfield NG18 .....268 C4
Ravensdale Cl S43 ....97 B3
Ravensdale Inf & Jun Schs
  DE3 ....217 C2
Ravensdale Rd
  Derby DE22 ....204 B2
  Dronfield S18 ....56 B1
  Mansfield NG18 .....268 C4
Ravenside Ret Pk S40 .266 B2
Ravenstor Rd DE4 ....154 C1
Ravenswood Rd S40 ...95 A3
Rawdon Cl DE74 .....247 A2
Rawdon Rd DE12 .....262 C4
Rawdon Side DE11 ...256 B2
Rawdon St DE23 .....218 C1
Rawlins Ct S18 ....57 B2
Rawlinson Ave DE23 ..232 A4
Rawson Gn DE56 .....179 C1
Ray St DE75 ....181 C1
Ray's Ave DE75 ......181 C1
Rayleigh Ave S43 .....96 B4
Raynald Rd S2 ....44 A4
Rayneham Rd DE7 ....194 B2
Raynesway DE21 .....220 A1
Raynesway Park Dr
  DE21 ....220 A1
Reader St DE21 ......220 C3
Rebecca St ST4 ......269 B4
Recreation Cl
  Blackwell DE55 .....147 C1
  Clowne S43 ....80 C2
Recreation Dr NG20 ..119 C1
Recreation Gd (Chesterfield
  FC) The S40 ....266 A4
Recreation Rd Calow S43 ..96 C3
  New Houghton NG19 ..134 C4
  Sandiacre NG10 .....223 A3
  Shirebrook NG20 ....119 C2
  Tideswell SK17 ....69 B2
  Wirksworth DE4 .....165 C4
Recreation St
  Long Eaton NG10 ....236 C4
  Mansfield NG18 .....268 C4
Recreation Terr NG9 ..223 B3
Recreation View NG20 .119 C3
Rectory Cl
  Breedon on t H DE73 .252 C1
  Eckington S21 ....59 C2
  Long Duckmanton S44 .98 A2
Rectory Dr S42 ......114 C2
Rectory Farm Mews
  DE72 ....245 C2
Rectory Gdns
  Aston-on-T DE72 ....246 A4
  Harthill S26 ....61 C3
  Killamarsh S21 ......60 B3
Rectory La
  Breadsall DE21 .....205 D3
  Kirk Ireton DE6 .....165 A1
  Stretton en le F DE12 .265 C1

Rectory Mews DE65 ..241 A2
Rectory Pl NG11 .....237 C3
Rectory Rd
  Breaston DE72 ......235 C4
  Clowne S43 ....80 C2
  Killamarsh S21 ......60 B3
  Long Duckmanton S44 .98 A2
  Staveley S43 ....78 C1
Reculver Ct DE23 ....231 B4
Red Barn Cl DE55 ....148 A2
Red Hill DE4 ....144 B2
Red Hill La DE4 .....144 B2
Red La Belper DE56 ..191 A3
  Brinsley NG16 ......171 C1
  Disley SK12 ....32 B3
  Repton DE65 ....249 C3
  South Normanton DE55 .159 C2
Red Lion Hill DE4 ...153 A1
Red Lion Sq DE75 ....181 C1
Red Lion St ST16 ....269 B4
Redacre Ct S44 ....99 B1
Redbarn La DE55 ....148 A2
Redbrook Ave S41 ...115 A4
Redbury Cl DE1 .....218 C2
Redcar Gdns DE21 ...205 B1
Redcliffe Rd NG18 ...268 C3
Reddish Ave S43 ......80 C1
Reddish La S43 ....45 B3
Reddish Rd SK23 ......45 B3
Redens The NG10 ....236 A2
Redfern Ave DE5 ....169 C1
Redfern Cl SK13 ......10 A3
Redfern St ST14 .....210 A1
Redfern St S42 ......131 B4
Redgap La SK17 ....86 A4
Redgate SK13 ....10 B2
Redgate Cl NG19 ....268 A4
Redgate Sch NG19 ...268 A4
Redgate St
  Mansfield NG19 .....268 A4
  Pinxton NG16 ....160 B1
Redgrave Dr ST16 ...269 A3
Redgrove Way S40 ...114 B4
Redhill Ct DE56 .....179 A1
Redhill La DE13 .....239 A3
Redhill Lodge Rd 6
  DE11 ....256 A4
Redhill Prim Sch DE72 .221 B3
Redhouse Cl S43 ......77 B2
Redhouse La SK12 ....32 C4
Redhouse Stables Working
Carriage Mus★ DE4 .127 B1
Redland Ct Derby DE24 .231 C2
  Ilkeston DE7 ....194 C2
Redmires Dr DE73 ...233 A1
Redmires Rd S10 .....42 A4
Redmoor Cl
  Burton u T DE15 ....248 A2
  Codnor DE5 ....170 A1
Redmoor La Disley SK12 ..33 A2
  New Mills SK22 ......33 A3
Rednall Cl S40 ....95 A3
Redruth Pl DE24 ....233 B3
Redshaw St DE1 .....218 C4
Redstart Cl DE21 ....220 C3
Redthorn Rd S13 .....44 C4
Redvers Buller Rd S40 .266 B1
Redway Croft DE23 ..252 A4
Redwing Croft DE23 .231 B4
Redwood Cl S43 ......97 A4
Redwood Dr DE15 ...255 A4
Redwood Inf Sch DE24 .231 C2
Redwood Jun Sch DE24 .231 C2
Redwood Rd DE24 ...231 C2
Reedman Rd NG10 ...236 A2
Reeves Ave S45 .....132 B1
Reeves Rd DE23 .....219 A1
Regal Gate DE73 ....244 C4
Regency Ct Derby DE23 .231 B4
  Glossop SK13 ....10 B1
Regent Ct Ironville NG16 .170 C2
  Swadlincote DE11 ...256 A1
Regent St Clowne S43 ..80 B2
  Derby DE1 ....267 C1
  Glossop SK13 ....10 B1
  Glossop, Padfield SK13 .10 A3
  Ilkeston DE7 ....208 C4
  Kimberley NG16 ....195 C3
  Langley Mill NG16 ..182 A2
  Long Eaton NG10 ...236 B4
  Mansfield NG18 .....268 B4
  Nottingham NG1 ....268 A1
  Stapleford NG10 ....223 B3
  Stoke-on-T ST4 ....269 B1
  Swadlincote DE11 ...256 A1
Reginald Rd N DE21 ..219 C4
Reginald Rd S DE21 ..219 C3
Reginald St DE23 ....219 A1
Regis Cl DE21 ....206 A1
Registry St ST4 .....269 B2
Reigate Dr DE22 ....218 A4
Reigate Prim Sch DE22 .217 C4
Rembrandt Dr S18 ....56 C1
Rempstone Dr S41 ...115 B4
Renals St DE23 ......267 B1
Reney Ave S8 ....56 B3
Reney Cres S8 ....56 B3
Reney Dr S8 ....56 B3
Reney Rd S8 ....56 C4
Reney Wlk S8 ....56 B3
Renfrew Ct NG19 ....268 A3
Renfrew St DE21 .....219 C4
Renishaw Hall Mus & Craft
  Ctr★ S21 ....59 C1
Renishaw Prim Sch S21 .79 A4
Renishaw Rd S43 .....79 B2
Renshaw Dr DE11 ...255 C3
Rent Cl S41 ....95 C3

Repton Ave DE23 ....218 B1
Repton Cl S40 ....95 A3
Repton Ct NG19 .....136 C2
Repton Dr DE7 ......209 A4
Repton Pl 3 S18 .....56 B1
Repton Prep Sch DE65 .243 B1
Repton Prim Sch DE65 .242 C1
Repton Rd
  Hartshorne DE11 ...256 C4
  Long Eaton NG10 ...235 C2
  Newton Solney DE15 .248 C4
  Willington DE65 ....242 A3
Repton Sch DE65 ....242 B2
Reservoir Hill DE12 ..262 B3
Reservoir Rd SK23 ....45 B4
Reservoir Terr S40 ...95 C2
Resthaven DE11 .....256 A3
Retford Cl DE21 .....205 B1
Revill Cl DE7 ....194 B1
Revill Cres NG9 ....223 C4
Revolution House Mus★
  S41 ....77 A1
Reynard Cres S21 .....79 A4
Reynards La SK17 ...137 C2
Reynolds Ave DE5 ...169 C1
Reynolds Cl S18 ......75 C4
Reynolds Dr SK6 .....23 A4
Rhodes Ave S41 ......95 C3
Rhodes Cotts S43 ....80 C2
Rhodes Ho DE15 ....248 B2
Rhodes St SK13 ......10 A3
Rhodes Wlk NG18 ...268 A3
Rhodesia Rd S40 .....95 B1
Rhodeswood Dr SK13 .10 A3
Rhuddlan Pl SK23 ....34 B1
Ribblesdale DE7 ....208 B3
Ribblesdale Cl DE22 .204 B1
Ribblesdale Dr S12 ...59 A4
Ribblesdale Rd NG10 .236 A3
Riber Ave DE55 .....170 B4
Riber Bank 17 SK13 ...9 C1
Riber Cl Long Eaton NG10 .236 B3
  Staveley S43 ....97 B3
  West Hallam DE7 ...207 C4
Riber Cres S42 ......131 A3
Riber Fold SK13 ......9 C1
Riber Gn SK13 ....9 C1
Riber Rd Holloway DE4 .156 A4
  Matlock DE4 ....143 B1
Riber Terr S40 ......266 A2
Riber View Cl DE4 ...144 A3
Richard La SK17 ......69 B2
Richard Wakefield CE Prim
  Sch DE13 ....239 B3
Richards Ave ST16 ..269 C4
Richards Ct S8 ....43 A4
Richards Rd S2 ....43 A4
Richardson Dr DE7 ..192 C3
Richardson Endowed Prim
  Sch DE7 ....192 C3
Richardson St DE22 ..218 B3
Richardsons La DE55 .170 B3
Richmond Ave
  Derby DE23 ....231 B4
  Ilkeston DE7 ....194 C2
  Long Eaton DE72 ...236 A4
  Sandiacre NG10 ....223 A2
  Sheffield S13 ....44 C4
Richmond Cl
  Chesterfield S40 ...114 C4
  Derby DE23 ....231 A4
  Glossop SK13 ....10 A3
  West Hallam DE7 ...207 B4
Richmond Ct
  Repton DE65 ....242 B1
  Sheffield S13 ....44 B4
Richmond Dr
  Duffield DE56 ......190 B3
  Mansfield Woodhouse
    NG19 ....136 B1
Richmond Gr S13 ....44 C4
Richmond Hall Ave S13 ..44 B4
Richmond Hall Cres S13 .44 B4
Richmond Hall Dr S13 ..44 B4
Richmond Hall Rd S13 .44 B4
Richmond Hall Way S13 .44 B4
Richmond Hill Rd S13 ..44 B4
Richmond Park Rd S13 .44 C4
Richmond Pl S13 .....44 B4
Richmond Rd
  Derby, Chaddesden DE21 .219 C3
  Derby, Rose Hill DE23 .219 A1
  Sheffield S13 ....44 B4
Richmond St ST4 ....269 B2
Richworth Rd S13 ....44 C4
Rick St NG1 ....268 B2
Ricroft Rd SK6 ....15 A2
Ridd Way S42 ....115 A2
Riddings DE22 ......204 C2
Riddings Cl S2 ....44 A4
Riddings Croft S41 ...95 B3
Riddings Inf Sch DE55 .170 B3
Riddings Jun Sch DE55 .170 B3
Riddings La S32 ......72 B2
Riddings St DE22 ...218 C2
Riddle St DE4 ....126 B3
Ridge Ave SK6 ....23 A2
Ridge Cl SK13 ....9 C2
Ridge Cres SK6 ....23 A2
Ridge End Fold SK6 ..23 A1
Ridge La
  Chapel-en-le-F SK23 ..65 B4
  Chapel-en-le-F, Combs
    SK23 ....46 C1
Ridge Rd Eckington S21 .58 C1
  Marple SK6 ....23 A2
Ridge The
  Blackwell DE55 .....147 C1

Ridge The continued
  Marple SK6 ....23 A2
Ridge Top La SK22 ...25 B1
Ridgedale Rd S44 ...118 A4
Ridgedale View S43 ..169 B1
Ridgehill Ave S12 ....44 A3
Ridgehill Gr S12 .....44 A3
Ridgeway Derby DE73 .245 A4
  Dronfield S18 ....57 B2
  Heanor DE75 ....193 C4
Ridgeway Ave
  Bolsover S44 ....99 B1
  Derby DE23 ....231 B3
Ridgeway Craft Ctr★
  S18 ....58 C4
Ridgeway Cres S12 ...44 A3
Ridgeway Dr
  Ilkeston DE7 ....208 A3
  Sheffield S12 ....44 A3
Ridgeway Inf Sch DE23 .231 B3
Ridgeway La DE56 ...168 B2
Ridgeway Moor S12 ..58 C3
Ridgeway Prim Sch S12 .58 C4
Ridgeway Rd
  Burton u T DE15 ...254 C4
  Sheffield S12 ....44 A2
Ridgeway St NG3 ...268 C2
Ridgeway The S12 ....32 B3
Ridgeways The SK22 ..25 B1
Ridgewood Ct DE21 .205 C1
Ridgewood Dr DE4 ..155 B3
Ridgway S43 ....80 C1
Ridgway W S43 ....80 C1
Riding Bank DE73 ...251 C3
Ridings Rd SK13 ......9 C3
Ridings The
  Mansfield NG19 ....136 C1
  Ockbrook DE72 ....221 B3
Ridley St S44 ....99 C1
Ridley Wlk ST4 .....269 C1
Rigga La DE56 ......191 A1
Riggott's Way S42 ....94 C4
Riggs La DE6 ....212 A4
Rigley Ave 19 DE7 ..194 C1
Rigsby Ct DE3 ......217 B2
Riley Ave DE55 .....157 B4
Riley Back La S32 ....71 C4
Riley La DE5 ....169 A3
Rimsdale Cl DE24 ...231 C2
Ring-o-Bells La SK12 .32 B3
Ringer La S43 ....80 C2
Ringer Way S43 ......80 C2
Ringinglow Rd S10,S11 .42 C2
Ringstone Way SK23 ..45 B4
Ringwood Ave
  Chesterfield S41 .....95 C4
  Compstall SK14 ......15 A4
  Staveley S43 ....97 B4
Ringwood Cl 4 DE21 .219 C4
Ringwood Rd S43 ....96 C4
Ringwood View 14 S43 .96 C4
Rink Dr DE11 ....256 A2
Ripley Ho DE21 .....220 C2
Ripley Hospl DE5 ...169 B1
Ripley Inf Sch DE5 ..180 B4
Ripley Jun Sch DE5 ..180 B4
Ripley Rd DE56 .....168 B3
Ripon Cres DE21 ....219 C4
Ripon Gdns SK17 ....85 B3
Risborrow Cl DE65 ..229 B2
Rise The Derby DE22 .204 C1
  Swadlincote DE11 ..255 C3
  Whaley Bridge SK23 .45 B3
Rises The SK13 ....9 C3
Risley Ct DE7 ......194 C2
Risley La DE72 .....222 B1
Risley Lower Gram CE Prim
  Sch DE72 ....222 C1
Ritson Cl NG3 ......268 B2
Rivenhall Cl DE23 ...230 C4
River St DE1 ....267 C4
River View
  Aldercar DE55 .....171 A3
  Belper DE56 ....190 C4
  Chesterfield S40 ...115 A4
  Longnor SK17 ....121 A3
  Tideswell SK17 ......88 B4
Riverbank DE4 ......110 C1
Riverbank The DE65 .242 A3
Riverbank Way SK13 .17 C4
Rivercroft Cl ST14 ..197 A2
Riverdale S32 ....72 B4
Riverdale Cl DE15 ...248 A3
Rivermead Ho DE1 ..267 B5
Riversdale Rd S18 ...168 A2
Riversfield Dr ST14 ..196 C2
Riverside Baslow DE45 .91 B3
  Walton-on-T DE12 ..253 B1
Riverside Cl Calver S32 .72 B1
  Glossop SK13 ....10 B1
Riverside Cres S42 ..113 C4
Riverside Croft S32 ..72 B1
Riverside Ct
  Ambergate DE56 ...167 C2
  Baslow DE45 ....91 C3
  Derby DE24 ....219 B2
Riverside Dr
  Branston DE14 .....253 C4
  Calver S32 ....72 B1
Riverside L Ctr ST16 .269 B4
Riverside Rd DE21 ..219 B3
Riverside Way
  Bolsover S44 ....98 C3
  Mansfield Woodhouse
    NG19 ....136 B3
Riverview Cotts 5 SK13 .17 B4
Riverway ST16,ST17 ..269 B4
Rivington Rd 3 NG9 ..223 C1

Roadmeadow Cl DE6 .185 B4
Robert Ave NG18 ....268 A3
Robert Cl S18 ....76 C3
Robert Rd S8 ....57 A4
Robert St DE1 ......267 C4
Robert Sutton RC High Sch
  DE15 ....255 A4
Roberts Ave NG17 ...148 C1
Roberts Dr DE55 ....159 A2
Roberts St Ilkeston DE7 .209 A3
  Nottingham NG2 ...268 C1
Robertson Rd SK17 ..85 A3
Robertson's Ave S44 .98 A2
Robey Dr NG16 .....182 C2
Robian Way DE11 ...256 A2
Robin Croft S40 .....114 C4
Robin Croft Rd DE22 .204 C2
Robin Hood Chase NG3 .268 B2
Robin Hood Cl NG16 .182 C1
Robin Hood Ind Est 1
  NG3 ....268 C2
Robin Hood Pl DE11 .256 B1
Robin Hood Prim Sch
  NG19 ....136 A2
Robin Hood Rd DE4 .156 B1
Robin Hood St NG3,NG7 .268 B2
Robin Hood Terr 20
  NG3 ....268 B2
Robin Rd DE1 ......218 C4
Robin's Cross La DE65 .249 C4
Robina Cl DE21 .....206 B2
Robina Dr NG16 ....195 B4
Robincroft Rd S42 ..114 B2
Robinettes La NG16 .195 B3
Robinlands La S33 ...38 A2
Robins Cl 16 DE72 ...233 B3
Robinscross DE72 ...221 A1
Robinson Ind Est DE23 .219 A1
Robinson Rd DE11 ..256 A3
Robinson Way S21 ...60 B3
Robinson's Hill DE73 .251 C3
Robinwood Lodge 18
  SK13 ....9 C1
Robridding Rd S45 ..129 A2
Robson Dr DE24 ....233 A4
Roby Lea DE74 .....246 C2
Roche 17 S20 ....59 C4
Rochester Cl
  Derby DE24 ....233 A3
  Long Eaton NG10 ..236 A4
Rochley Cl DE21 ....205 C1
Rock Bank Buxton SK17 .85 B2
  Whaley Bridge SK23 .45 C3
Rock Cres S45 ......131 A3
Rock Ct NG18 ......268 C4
Rock Dr NG7 ....268 A1
Rock Hill NG18 .....268 C3
Rock Ho DE4 ....155 A3
Rock House Cl DE55 .147 C3
Rock La S44 ....116 C3
Rock Mill Bsns Pk S32 .71 C2
Rock Side NG16 ....195 C3
Rock St Mansfield NG18 .268 C3
  New Mills SK22 ......33 B4
Rock Terr Bakewell DE45 .109 B3
  Buxton SK17 ....85 A3
Rock Valley NG18 ...268 C4
Rock View SK17 ......88 C4
Rockbourne Cl DE24 .233 B3
Rockcliffe Cl DE11 ..256 A1
Rockeries The DE56 .168 C1
Rockfield Rd SK17 ...85 B4
Rockford Ct NG9 ...209 C4
Rockhall Terr SK22 ..25 C1
Rockhouse Rd DE24 .233 A3
Rockingham 16 S20 ..59 C4
Rockingham Cl
  Chesterfield S40 .....95 B2
  Derby DE22 ....205 A2
  4 Dronfield S18 ....56 B1
Rocklands The NG20 .119 C2
Rockley Cl S40 ......114 C4
Rockley Way NG20 ..119 C2
Rocks The DE4 .....144 A3
Rockside Stps DE4 ..143 B3
Rockside View DE4 ..143 B4
Rockvale Terr DE4 ..143 A3
Rockvale Villas DE4 .143 A1
Rod Moor Rd S18 ....56 A2
Roden St NG3 ......268 C2
Rodge Croft S41 .....77 A2
Rodger's La DE55 ...159 A3
Rodknoll La S42 .....93 B1
Rodney Cl DE65 ....228 C1
Rodney Way DE7 ...194 C2
Rodney Wlk DE23 ..230 C4
Rodsley Cl S40 ....95 A3
Rodsley Cres DE23 ..231 B3
Rodsley La Rodsley DE6 .199 C3
  Yeaveley DE6 ......199 C3
Rodwood Ave S43 ...80 C4
Roe Cross Ind Est SK14 ..9 A3
Roe Cross Rd SK14 ..9 A3
Roe Farm La DE21 ..219 C4
Roe Farm Prim Sch
  DE21 ....219 C4
Roe Wlk DE23 ......219 A1
Roe's La DE4 ....157 A1
Roebuck Pl SK23 ....47 A3
Roebuck St ST4 ....269 C2
Roecar Cl S41 ....77 A1
Roehampton Dr
  Derby DE22 ....218 A4
  Stapleford NG9 ....209 B1
Rogers Ave S80 ......81 B1
Rogers Ct DE65 .....227 B1
Rogerstone Ave ST4 .269 A1
Rolaine Cl NG19 ....136 B2

Rolleston Cres NG16 195 C4
Rolleston Dr NG16 195 A4
Rolleston La DE13 239 B3
Rollins La SK6 15 A1
Roman Bank NG19 136 B2
Roman Rd DE1 219 A4
Roman Way DE72 221 B1
Romeley Cres S43 80 B2
Romford Way S43 78 A2
Romley Cl DE11 256 B3
Romney Dr S18 56 C1
Romney Gdns S2 43 A3
Romorantin Pl NG10 236 C4
Romsley Cl DE3 217 B2
Rona Cl Derby DE24 231 C2
Mansfield NG18 268 A3
Ronald Cl DE23 230 C4
Rood La Clowne S43 80 C2
Idridgehay DE56 176 C3
Rookery The NG18 268 B4
Roosevelt Ave
Derby DE21 220 A3
Long Eaton NG10 236 B3
Rooth St NG18 268 B3
Rope Cl DE4 165 C4
Roper Ave DE75 193 C4
Roper Hill S10 42 B4
Ropewalk Ct 36 NG1 268 A2
Ropewalk Ind Ctr DE7 195 A1
Ropewalk The
Heanor DE75 193 C4
Ilkeston DE7 195 A1
Nottingham NG1 268 A1
Stanley DE7 193 A1
Rosamond Ave S17 56 A3
Rosamond Cl S17 56 A3
Rosamond Dr S17 56 A3
Rosamond Glade S17 56 A3
Rosamond Pl S17 56 A3
Rosamond's Ride DE23 231 B4
Rose Ave
Borrowash DE72 221 B1
Burton u T DE13 241 A1
Calow S44 97 A2
Clowne S43 81 A3
Ilkeston DE7 194 C1
Rose Bank Cl SK14 9 B3
Rose Cottage Dr NG17 148 C1
Rose Cotts S41 96 B1
Rose Cres S43 79 B2
Rose Ct Clay Cross S45 131 A2
Long Eaton NG10 223 A1
Rose End Ave DE4 155 A3
Rose Hill Chesterfield S40 266 B3
Mosborough S20 59 A4
Stafford ST16 269 A4
Swadlincote DE11 256 C2
Rose Hill Ave S20 59 A4
Rose Hill Cl S20 59 A4
Rose Hill Dr S20 59 A4
Rose Hill E S40 266 B3
Rose Hill Mews S20 59 A4
Rose Hill St DE23 219 A1
Rose Hill W S40 266 A3
Rose La
Mansfield Woodhouse NG19 136 B2
Ticknall DE73 251 A2
Rose Tree La DE11 255 C4
Rose Valley DE11 256 A3
Rose Way S21 60 B3
Rose Wood Cl S41 95 B4
Roseberry Ct DE21 206 A1
Rosebery Hill NG18 268 C3
Rosecroft Gdns DE11 256 B2
Rosedale Ave
Chesterfield S40 115 A4
Derby DE24 233 A3
Rosedale Cl NG10 236 A3
Rosedale View S40 114 A4
Rosedale Way NG19 136 C1
Rosegarth Cl S41 96 B1
Roseheath Cl DE23 231 C3
Rosehill Ct S44 99 A1
Rosehill Inf Sch DE23 219 A2
Rosehill Sch NG3 268 C2
Roseleigh Cres DE11 255 C3
Rosemary Ave NG18 268 B4
Rosemary Dr DE24 233 A3
Rosemary St NG18,NG19 268 B4
Rosemoor La DE21 206 A1
Rosemount Ct DE22 204 B2
Rosengrave St DE1 267 B2
Rosette Cl DE21 206 B2
Rosewood Cl
Derby DE24 233 B4
South Normanton DE55 160 A4
Rosewood Cres DE75 182 A1
Rosewood Gdns ST16 269 A4
Rosewood Rd DE15 254 C3
Rosier Cres DE55 170 A4
Rosling Way S44 97 B1
Rosliston CE Prim Sch
DE12 260 B3
Rosliston Forestry Ctr★
DE12 260 B4
Rosliston Rd
Burton u T DE15 254 C4
Swadlincote DE15 254 B2
Walton-on-T DE12 259 C4
Rosliston Rd S DE15 254 C3
Roslyn Cres S32 53 A4
Roslyn Rd S32 53 A4
Ross Wlk DE21 205 C1
Rossell Dr NG9 223 C3
Rossendale DE7 194 C2
Rossendale Cl S40 114 C4
Rosser Ave S12 43 C1
Rossington Dr DE23 230 C3
Rossington Rd NG2 268 C2
Rosslyn Gdns DE24 233 A3
Roston Cl 10 S18 56 B1
Rothay Cl S18 75 C4
Rothbourne Croft DE6 151 B1
Rothbury Ave NG9 209 B1
Rothbury Pl DE21 205 C1
Rother Ave S43 96 B4
Rother Cl S40 114 C4
Rother Croft S42 131 B4
Rother Jun Sch S40 115 A4
Rother St S45 132 B1
Rother Valley Way S20 60 A4
Rother Way S41 96 A3
Rotherham Cl S21 60 C4
Rotherham Rd
Barlborough S43 61 B1
Bolsover S44 99 C1
Clowne S43 80 C3
Killamarsh S21 60 C4
Mosborough S20 59 C3
New Houghton NG19 134 C4
Scarcliffe S44 118 B4
Shirebrook S44 118 B2
Rotherham Rd N S20 59 C4
Rotherside Rd S21 59 C2
Rothervale Rd S40 115 A4
Rotherwood Dr ST17 269 A3
Rotherwood Gdns ST16 269 A4
Rotherwood Rd S21 60 C4
Rothesay Cl DE24 231 C2
Rothey Gr S40 94 C3
Rothley Ave NG3 268 C2
Rothwell La DE56 179 A2
Rothwell Rd DE3 217 B2
Rothwell St ST4 269 A1
Rough Heanor Rd DE3 218 A1
Rough La DE6 186 B3
Roughpiece La DE4 166 B3
Roughton Cl DE3 230 B4
Round Hill Cl SK13 9 C2
Round Way SK22 33 B4
Roundhouse Rd DE24 219 B2
Rouse Cl ST16 269 A3
Rouse St S45 132 B1
Routh Ave DE74 247 A1
Row The DE4 156 A4
Rowan Ave Ripley DE5 180 B4
Stapleford NG9 209 C1
Rowan Cl Creswell S80 81 C1
Darley Dale DE4 127 A2
Derby, Cherrytree Hill DE21 220 A3
Derby, Sinfin DE24 231 B2
Ilkeston DE7 208 C3
Mansfield NG19 136 B1
Rowan Croft NG17 148 C2
Rowan Dr Kilburn DE56 192 A4
Selston NG16 171 B4
Shirebrook NG20 119 B3
Shirland DE55 146 B1
Rowan Park Cl DE23 231 B4
Rowan Rd Eckington S21 59 B1
Mastin Moor S43 79 B2
Rowan Sch The S17 55 C3
Rowan Tree Cl
Ashbourne DE6 185 B4
Killamarsh S21 60 B3
Rowan Tree Dell S17 55 C2
Rowan Tree Rd S21 60 A3
Rowan Wlk SK13 9 C2
Rowarth Ave 7 SK13 9 B1
Rowarth Fold 6 SK13 9 B1
Rowbury Dr DE15 248 A1
Rowdale Cres S12 44 B3
Rowditch Ave DE22 218 B2
Rowditch Cotts DE1 218 B2
Rowditch Pl DE22 218 B2
Rowena Cl DE24 232 C4
Rowland Ct DE55 158 C2
Rowland Rd 1 S2 43 A4
Rowland St
Alfreton DE55 159 A2
Derby DE24 232 C3
Rowley Ave ST17 269 A3
Rowley Ct DE11 256 A2
Rowley Gdns DE23 231 B4
Rowley Hall Dr ST17 269 A3
Rowley La DE23 231 B4
Rowsley Ave Derby DE23 231 B4
Long Eaton NG10 236 A3
Rowsley CE Prim Sch
DE4 126 C4
Rowsley Cres S43 97 B4
Rowsley Gr SK13 9 C1
Rowsley Mews SK13 9 C1
Rowsley South Sta★
DE4 127 A3
Rowthorne Ave DE55 170 A4
Rowthorne La
Ault Hucknall S44 134 A4
Glapwell S44 134 A4
Rowton Grange Rd SK23 47 A3
Roxburgh Ave DE21 219 C4
Roxton Ave S8 56 C4
Roxton Ct NG16 195 C4
Royal Albert Ct 5 NG7 268 A2
Royal App DE73 244 C4
Royal Ave NG10 223 B1
Royal Cl DE72 221 A1
Royal Croft Dr DE45 91 C3
Royal Crown Derby Visitor Ctr★ D23 267 C1
Royal Gate DE56 179 B2
Royal Gr DE21 206 B2
Royal Hill Rd DE21 220 B3
Royal Oak Pl DE45 109 B3
Royal Rd SK12 32 B3
Royal Sch for the Deaf
DE22 218 B3
Royal Standard Ho NG1 268 A1
Royal Way DE24 219 C2
Royale Cl S21 59 C2
Roydon Cl DE3 217 B2
Royle Ave SK13 10 B1
Royston Cl
Ashbourne DE6 185 B4
Chesterfield S40 114 A4
Royston Dr DE56 179 B3
Rubens Cl Dronfield S18 56 C1
Marple SK6 23 B4
Ruby Paddocks NG16 195 C3
Rudyard Ave DE21 220 C3
Rufford Ave NG18 268 C4
Rufford Cl S40 95 C1
Rufford Dr NG19 136 C2
Rufford Rd NG10 236 A2
Ruffstone Cl DE56 191 B4
Rugby Ave DE55 159 B2
Rugby Cl DE14 254 B4
Rugby St DE24 219 C1
Rugeley Ave NG10 237 A4
Ruislip Cl NG16 195 C4
Runnymede Ct 19 NG7 268 A2
Rupert Rd DE21 220 A4
Rupert St Ilkeston DE7 195 A1
Pilsley S45 132 A2
Rush Leys NG10 236 B3
Rushcliffe Ave DE21 219 C3
Rushcliffe Gdns DE21 219 C3
Rushdale Ave
Derby DE23 231 B3
Sheffield S8 43 A3
Rushdale Mount S8 43 A3
Rushdale Rd S8 43 A3
Rushdale Terr S8 43 A3
Rushen Mount S40 114 C3
Rushes The Glossop SK13 9 C2
Mansfield Woodhouse NG19 136 B3
Rushleigh Ct S17 55 B4
Rushley Ave S17 55 B4
Rushley Cl S17 55 B4
Rushley Dr S17 55 B4
Rushley Rd S17 55 B4
Rushpool Ave NG19 136 B2
Rushpool Cl NG19 136 C1
Rushton Dr SK6 23 A3
Rushup Cl DE22 205 A3
Rushup La SK17,SK23 48 B4
Rushy La NG10,DE72 222 C3
Rushycroft SK14 9 A2
Rusk The S43 80 A3
Ruskin Ave NG10 236 A3
Ruskin Rd Derby DE1 218 C4
Mansfield NG19 135 B1
Ruskin Sq S8 43 A3
Ruskin Way DE23 231 A4
Russel St ST16 269 A4
Russell Gdns S42 131 A3
Russell Pl NG1 268 A2
Russell St Compstall SK6 15 A2
Derby DE24 219 B1
Long Eaton NG10 223 B1
Nottingham NG7 268 A2
Swadlincote DE11 256 B2
Russet Cl Derby DE21 206 A1
Hatton DE65 227 B1
Russet Ct DE23 218 C1
Ruston Cl Chesterfield S40 95 A3
Swadlincote DE11 256 A2
Tutbury DE13 239 B3
Rutherford Dr DE21 205 C1
Rutherford Pl ST4 269 A2
Ruthyn Ave S43 80 A4
Rutland Ave Bolsover S44 99 A1
Borrowash DE72 221 B1
Matlock DE4 143 B3
Ripley DE5 181 A4
Rutland Cl DE15 254 B3
Rutland Ct Ilkeston DE7 194 B1
Matlock DE4 143 B3
Rutland Dr DE3 217 C2
Rutland Gr NG10 223 B3
Rutland Pl DE56 168 A3
Rutland Rd
Chesterfield S40 266 A3
Westwood NG16 171 B2
Rutland Sq DE45 109 B3
Rutland St
Chesterfield S41 77 A1
Derby DE23 219 A1
Ilkeston DE7 194 C1
Mansfield NG18 268 C3
Matlock DE4 143 B3
6 Nottingham NG1 268 A1
Rutland Terr Barlow S18 75 C2
Ilkeston DE7 194 C1
Rutland Way SK23 34 B1
Ryal Cl DE72 221 B3
Ryan Cl DE24 231 C2
Rycroft CE Mid Sch
ST14 196 C2
Rycroft Rd DE74 247 B3
Rydal Ave NG10 223 A1
Rydal Cl Derby DE22 204 C2
Dronfield S18 56 B1
Rydal Cres S41 95 C4
Rydal Ho ST16 269 B4
Rydal Way S45 131 A2
Ryder Cl DE11 255 C1
Rye Butts DE73 232 C1
Rye Cl DE21 205 C2
Rye Cres S45 131 B2
Rye Flatt La S40 95 B1
Rye Flatts La DE65 227 B1
Ryecroft DE4 127 B1
Ryecroft Glen Rd S17 56 A4
Ryecroft St NG9 223 C4
Ryecroft View S17 55 B4
Ryedale Gdns DE23 231 B3
Ryegrass Cl DE56 179 B2
Ryegrass Rd DE21 206 B1
Ryehill Ave S40 95 A1
Ryemere Cl NG16 182 C1
Ryemere Ct NG16 182 C1
Rykneld Cl DE23 230 C3
Rykneld Ct S45 131 B2
Rykneld Dr DE23 230 C4
Rykneld Prim Sch DE14 253 C4
Rykneld Rd DE23 230 C3
Rykneld Rise S42 115 A2
Rykneld Sq S40 266 B3
Rykneld Way DE23 230 C3
Ryknield Hill DE5 180 A1
Ryknield Rd DE56,DE7 192 A4
Rylah Hill S44 118 A3
Rymill Dr DE21 205 C1
Ryton Way DE65 240 B4

S

Sabine St ST17 269 B3
Sacheveral La DE4 140 C2
Sacheverall Ave NG16 160 B2
Sacheverel St DE1 267 B2
Sackerville Tr S21 60 A4
Sackville Cl S40 114 A4
Sackville St DE23 231 C4
Saddlers Cl NG19 136 C1
Saddleworth Ct 4 NG3 268 B2
Saddleworth Wlk DE24 232 C2
Sadler Gate DE1 267 B3
Sadler St NG19 268 A4
Saffron Dr DE21 206 A1
Sage Dr DE11 256 C2
Saint Philip Howard Comp
Sch SK13 10 A1
St Agnes Ave DE22 204 B2
St Aidan's Ave S2 43 B4
St Aidan's Dr S2 43 C4
St Aidan's Pl S2 43 C4
St Aidan's Rd S2 43 C4
St Aidan's Way S2 43 C4
St Alban's RC Prim Sch
DE21 219 C3
St Albans Cl
Holmewood S42 132 C4
Long Eaton NG10 236 C3
St Albans Pl SK22 33 B4
St Albans Rd DE22 218 B2
St Albans St SK22 33 B4
St Alkmund's Cl DE56 190 C2
St Alkmund's Way DE1 267 B4
St Alkmunds Way DE56 190 C2
St Andrew St NG18 268 C3
St Andrew's CE Jun Sch
SK13 9 C2
St Andrew's CE Prim Sch
Dronfield S18 56 B1
Stanley DE7 207 A3
St Andrew's CE Sch
B79 263 C1
St Andrew's Cl B79 263 C1
St Andrew's Dr
Ilkeston DE7 208 C4
Swanwick DE55 169 C4
St Andrews Cl DE55 170 A4
St Andrews Ct SK13 10 A2
St Andrews Rise S40 114 B4
St Andrews Specl Sch
DE21 205 C1
St Andrews View DE21 205 C1
St Andrews Wlk SK22 33 B4
St Ann's Cl SK23 46 C3
St Ann's St NG1 268 B2
St Ann's Valley NG3 268 C2
St Ann's Way NG3 268 B2
St Ann's Well Rd NG3 268 B2
St Anne's CE Prim Sch
DE45 91 C3
St Anne's Cl Baslow DE45 91 C3
Derby DE1 218 C3
St Anne's La DE74 247 A2
St Anne's RC Prim Sch
SK17 66 A1
St Anne's Well (Micrarium)★
SK17 85 A4
St Annes St SK14 16 A4
St Anselm's Sch DE45 109 B3
St Augustine St DE23 218 C1
St Augustines Ave S40 115 A4
St Augustines Cres S40 115 A4
St Augustines Dr S40 266 B1
St Augustines Mount
S40 266 B1
St Augustines Rd S40 115 A4
St Augustines Rise S40 115 A4
St Austin's RC Prim Sch
ST17 269 B3
St Barnabas Ho 6 S2 43 A4
St Barnabas La 4 S2 43 A4
St Barnabas Rd 5 S2 43 A4
St Barnabus Cath NG1 268 A1
St Bartholomew's CE Prim
Sch SK17 121 A4
St Benedict RC Sch
DE22 204 C1
St Benedicts Ct S2 43 B4
St Bride's Wlk DE22 218 A3
St Catherine St NG18 268 C3
St Catherine's Rd DE11 255 C3
St Catherines Prep Sch
SK6 23 A4
St Cecilia Gdns NG3 268 B2
St Chad's CE Inf Sch
DE23 218 C2
St Chad's Cl
Denstone ST14 196 B3
Draycott DE72 235 A4
St Chad's Pl 12 ST16 269 B4
St Chad's Rd Derby DE23 218 C1
Nottingham NG3 268 C2
St Charles Cl SK13 9 C3
St Charles RC Prim Sch
SK13 9 C3
St Christopher Ave ST4 269 A1
St Christopher St NG2 268 C1
St Clare's Cl DE22 218 B1
St Clare's Specl Sch
DE3 218 A1
St Cuthbert's Rd
Derby DE22 218 B2
Nottingham NG3 268 C2
St David's Cl DE22 218 B2
St David's Rise S40 114 B4
St Davids Rd B79 263 C1
St Dominics Ind Jun Sch
ST4 269 A2
St Edmund's Ave NG19 136 B2
St Edmund's Cl DE22 204 C2
St Edmunds CE Prim Sch
NG19 136 B2
St Edward's Prim CE Sch
DE74 247 A2
St Edward's RC Prim Sch
DE11 256 A3
St Edward's Rd DE74 247 A1
St Edwards Ct DE11 255 C3
St Elizabeth Cl S2 43 A4
St Elizabeth's RC Prim Sch
DE56 178 C3
St Elphin's Sch DE4 127 C1
St Francis Ley Ind Pk
DE23 219 A1
St George's CE Prim Sch
DE11 256 A1
St George's Pl 1 DE56 178 C2
St George's RC Prim Sch
DE23 231 B4
St George's Rd ST17 269 C3
St Georges Dr 6 NG9 223 C1
St Georges Hospl ST16 269 B4
St Georges Rd SK22 33 B4
St Giles CE Prim Sch
DE4 143 B2
St Giles CE Sch S21 60 B3
St Giles Cl S40 115 A4
St Giles Rd DE23 218 C1
St Giles Specl Sch DE21 205 B1
St Giles Wlk DE4 143 B2
St Helen's Cl
Chesterfield S41 266 B4
Darley Dale DE4 127 A2
Grindleford S32 72 B4
St Helen's Cres NG9 209 B2
St Helen's Croft S32 72 B4
St Helen's Dr NG16 171 B4
St Helen's La DE4 166 A4
St Helen's St
Chesterfield S41 266 B4
Derby DE1 267 A4
Nottingham NG7 268 A2
St Helens Ave NG16 160 B2
St Hugh's Cl DE22 205 A1
St James Ave DE7 209 A4
St James CE Prim Sch
SK13 17 A4
St James Cl Belper DE56 179 B2
Chesterfield S41 96 B1
Glossop SK13 17 B4
Willington DE65 242 B3
St James Ct
Ashbourne DE6 173 B2
Sandiacre NG10 223 A2
St James Sq
Chesterfield S40 266 B3
Chesterfield S40 266 B3
St James' CE Inf Sch
DE23 267 C1
St James' CE Jun Sch
DE23 219 A2
St James' Dr NG16 182 B4
St James' Sq SK22 33 B4
St James' St
9 Buxton SK17 85 A4
Derby DE1 267 B3
Derby, Rose Hill DE23 219 A1
St James' Terr SK17 85 A4
St James's Ct SK17 85 B2
St James's St
Nottingham NG1 268 A1
Stapleford NG9 223 B3
St James's Terr
5 Nottingham NG1 268 A1
Stapleford NG9 223 B3
St John Fisher RC Prim Sch
DE24 233 B4
St John Houghton RC Sch
DE7 208 B3
St John St Hayfield SK22 25 B1
Mansfield NG18 268 B4
St John's Ave DE21 220 A3
St John's CE Mid Sch
NG18 268 B4
St John's CE Prim Sch
Belper DE56 179 A3

St John's CE Prim Sch
continued
Ripley DE5 ....169 C1
Stafford ST16 ....269 C4
Stapleford NG9 ....223 C4
St John's Cl
Brinsley NG16 ....171 B1
Derby DE22 ....204 B2
St John's Dr Derby DE21 220 A3
Kilburn DE56 ....192 A4
Swadlincote DE11 .....255 C3
St John's Mount S41 ...95 C4
St John's Pl NG18 ....268 B4
St John's Rd
Belper DE56 ....179 A2
Buxton SK17 ....85 A4
Chesterfield S41 ......95 C4
Dronfield S18 ....76 C4
Ilkeston DE7 ....209 A4
Matlock Bath DE4 ....143 A2
Smalley DE7 ....192 C3
Stafford ST17 ....269 B3
Tideswell SK17 ....69 B2
St John's St
Ashbourne DE6 ....173 B1
Long Eaton NG10 .....236 B4
Wirksworth DE4 ......165 C4
St John's Terr DE1 ...218 C3
St John's Wlk ST16 ..269 C4
St Johns Cl Bamford S33 .40 A2
Chesterfield S40 ......114 A4
Ripley DE5 ....169 C1
St Johns Pl S43 ......78 B1
St Johns Rd S43 .....78 B1
St Johns Road Bsns Ctr 🖫
S41 ....95 C4
St John's Cres S43 ...80 C2
St Joseph's Convent Day
Sch S41 ....266 A4
St Joseph's Prep Sch
NG1 ....268 A4
St Joseph's RC Prim Sch
Derby DE23 ....267 A1
Matlock DE4 ....143 B3
Shirebrook NG20 .....119 C3
Staveley S43 ....97 B4
St Joseph's St DE4 ...143 B3
St Katherine's La DE4 ..110 C1
St Laurence CE Prim Sch
NG10 ....236 B3
St Laurence Ct NG10 ..236 C3
St Lawrence Ave S44 ..118 B4
St Lawrence Cl DE75 ..181 C1
St Lawrence Rd S42 ..131 C3
St Lawrence View S80 ..81 C3
St Leonard's Ave ST17 .269 C3
St Leonard's Prim Sch
ST17 ....269 C3
St Leonards Dr S41 ...96 B1
St Leonards Pl DE55 ..146 C1
St Luke's CE Prim Sch
SK13 ....10 B1
St Luke's Sch S81 .....63 C4
St Luke's St NG3 .....268 C2
St Lukes Ct 🖫 S41 ....95 C4
St Margaret St NG18 ..268 C3
St Margaret's Dr S40 ..268 A4
St Margaret's RC Prim Sch
SK13 ....16 B4
St Mark's Cl DE4 .....155 B4
St Mark's Rd
Chesterfield S40 ......95 C4
Derby DE21 ....219 B3
St Marks St NG1,NG3 ..268 B2
St Martin's Cl S41 ....95 B3
St Martin's Pl 🖫 ST16 .269 B4
St Martin's Rd SK6 ....23 A3
St Martin's Specl Sch
DE24 ....232 C4
St Martin's Wlk S80 ...82 B3
St Martins Ct DE55 ...158 C2
St Mary & All Saints Church
(Crooked Spire)★ S40 266 B3
St Mary St DE7 ....208 C4
St Mary's Ave DE72 ...235 A4
St Mary's CE Fst Sch
ST14 ....210 A1
St Mary's Cl Belper DE24 233 A3
Newton Solney DE15 ...248 C4
St Mary's Cres ST14 ...210 A1
St Mary's Ct DE1 .....267 B4
St Mary's Dr DE13 ...240 C1
St Mary's Gate
Chesterfield S41 ......266 C3
Derby DE1 ....267 B3
Nottingham NG1 ......268 B1
🖫 Stafford ST16 ......269 B4
Wirksworth DE4 ......165 C4
St Mary's Gr 🖫 ST16 ..269 B4
St Mary's Pl
Chesterfield S41 ......266 C3
🖫 Nottingham NG1 ...268 B1
St Mary's Pl 🖫 ST16 ..269 B4
St Mary's RC High Sch
S41 ....95 A4
St Mary's RC Prim Sch
Chesterfield S40 ......266 A4
Derby DE1 ....267 B4
Glossop SK13 ....17 B4
Marple SK6 ....23 A4
New Mills SK22 ....33 A4
St Mary's Rd Disley SK12 .32 B3
Glossop SK13 ....17 B4
New Mills SK22 ....33 A4
St Mary's Wlk NG16 ..171 A2

St Marys Wharf Rd DE1 219 A4
St Matthew's St DE14 ..254 B4
St Matthew's Wlk 🖪
DE22 ....204 C1
St Matthias Rd NG3 ...268 C2
St Mawes Cl DE22 ....204 B2
St Mellion Cl DE3 .....217 C1
St Michael's CE Prim Sch
S32 ....53 C4
St Michael's Cl
Holbrook DE56 ....191 B3
Shirley DE6 ....200 B4
Willington DE65 ......242 A3
St Michael's Dr
South Normanton DE55 ..160 A4
Stretton en le F DE12 ..265 C1
St Michael's La DE1 ...267 B4
St Michaels Cl Crich DE4 156 C1
Derby DE24 ....233 B4
St Michaels View
Derby DE24 ....233 B4
Selston NG16 ....171 C3
St Nicholas Cl DE21 ...204 B1
St Nicholas Pl DE1 ....267 A4
St Nicholas St NG1 ....268 B1
St Norbert Dr DE7 ....208 B2
St Oswald Cres DE6 ...173 B1
St Oswald's CE Inf Sch
DE6 ....173 A1
St Oswald's Hospl DE6 .173 A1
St Pancras Way DE1 ...267 C5
St Patrick's Pl 🖪 ST16 .269 B4
St Patrick's St 🖪 ST16 .269 B4
St Paul's CE Prim Sch
ST17 ....269 B3
St Paul's Rd DE1 ......219 A4
St Pauls Ave S41 .....115 B3
St Pauls Ct NG16 ......195 C3
St Peter & St Paul Sch
S41 ....115 B4
St Peter & St Paul's Sch
S41 ....96 B2
St Peter's CE Fst Sch
ST14 ....224 C1
St Peter's CE High Sch
ST4 ....269 A2
St Peter's CE Jun Sch
DE23 ....218 B1
St Peter's CE Prim Sch
DE12 ....264 C1
St Peter's Churchyard
DE1 ....267 B3
St Peter's Cl DE56 ....179 A2
St Peter's Gate NG1 ...268 B1
St Peter's Rd Buxton SK17 .66 B1
Derby DE73 ....233 A1
Thorpe Salvin S80 .....62 C4
St Peter's Sq NG1 ....268 B1
St Peter's St DE1 .....267 B3
St Peter's Way NG18 ..268 C3
St Peters Cl
Long Duckmanton S44 ..98 A2
Stoke-on-T ST4 ....269 B2
St Peters Croft DE56 ..179 A2
St Philip Howard RC Sch
SK13 ....17 A4
St Philip Neri's RC Prim Sch
NG18 ....268 B4
St Philip's Dr S41 .....115 A4
St Philomena's Convent Prim
Sch DE1 ....267 B4
St Quentin Cl
Derby DE22 ....218 B2
🖫 Sheffield S17 ....56 A3
St Quentin Dr S17 .....56 A3
St Quentin Mount S17 ..56 A3
St Quentin Rise S17 ...56 A3
St Quentin View S17 ...56 A3
St Ronan's Ave DE56 ..190 C1
St Stephen's Ave 🖪
NG2 ....268 C1
St Stephen's Cl DE23 ..231 B3
St Stephen's Ct DE11 ..256 C2
St Stephen's Rd NG2 ..268 C1
St Stephens DE72 .....221 A1
St Swithin's Cl DE22 ...218 B2
St Theresa's RC School
S2 ....43 C4
St Thomas Aquinas RC Prim
Sch ST4 ....269 A2
St Thomas Cl DE55 ...147 C3
St Thomas More RC Sch
SK17 ....85 A4
St Thomas of Canterbury
Prim Sch S8 ......56 C4
St Thomas Pl ST4 .....269 A1
St Thomas RC Prim Sch
DE7 ....208 C4
St Thomas Rd DE23 ...219 A1
St Thomas St ST16 ....269 C4
St Thomas' St S40 .....95 B1
St Vincent Cl NG10 ...236 C3
St Werburgh's CE Prim Sch
Derby DE21 ....220 B3
Hanbury DE13 ....238 A2
St Werburgh's View
DE21 ....220 B3
St Wilfrid's Rd
Sheffield S2 ....43 A4
West Hallam DE7 .....207 C4
St Wystan's Rd DE22 ..218 B2
St Wystans Sch DE65 ..242 B1
Salcey Cl DE55 ....169 C4
Salcey Dr NG9 ....209 B1
Salcey Sq 🖪 S40 .....95 B1
Salcombe Rd DE55 ...159 B3
Sale & Davys CE Sch
DE73 ....244 A3

Sale St DE23 ....219 A1
Sales Ave S42 ....131 B4
Sales La DE15 ....248 B2
Salford Gdns NG3 .....268 B2
Salisbury Ave
Burton u T DE15 ......248 B2
Chesterfield S41 ......95 C4
Dronfield S18 ....76 A4
Salisbury Cl NG19 ....136 B2
Salisbury Cres S41 ....95 C4
Salisbury Dr Belper DE56 179 B3
Stafford ST16 ....269 C4
Swadlincote DE11 .....256 C3
Salisbury La DE73 ....242 A4
Mansfield NG19 ......268 A4
Stafford ST16 ....269 C4
Salisbury St Derby DE23 267 B1
Glossop SK13 ....10 A3
Long Eaton NG10 .....236 C4
Sallyfield La DE6 .....183 C4
Sallywood Cl DE24 ....231 B1
Salmond Ave ST16 ....269 C4
Salt Ave ST17 ....269 B3
Salt Rd ST17 ....269 B3
Saltburn Cl DE21 .....205 B1
Salter Cl DE74 ....246 C2
Saltergate S40 ....266 B3
Saltergate La S30 .....40 B1
Salters La DE4 ....142 C2
Salvin Cres S43 ....80 C2
Samantha Ct DE21 ...206 A1
Sampson's La NG19 ...135 A2
Samuel Brunts Way
NG18 ....268 C4
Samuel Cl
Mansfield NG19 ......268 A4
Sheffield S2 ....43 B4
Samuel Ct DE5 ....180 B4
Samuel Dr S2 ....43 B4
Samuel Pl S2 ....43 B4
Samuel Rd S2 ....43 B4
Samuel St SK14 ....9 B2
Sand La DE6 ....211 A4
Sandalwood Cl DE24 ..233 B4
Sandalwood Rd DE15 ..254 C3
Sandbach Cl DE21 ....206 A1
Sandbed La DE56 .....179 B1
Sandby Croft S14 .....43 C1
Sandby Cl S14 ....43 C1
Sandby Dr Marple SK6 ..23 A4
Sheffield S14 ....43 C1
Sandcliffe Pk DE11 ...256 C4
Sandcliffe Rd DE11 ...256 B3
Sandcroft Cl DE11 ....256 B3
Sandcroft Rd DE21 ...220 C3
Sanderling Heath DE3 ..230 A4
Sanders Cl DE7 ......194 B1
Sanderson Rd DE21 ...220 A3
Sandfield Cl DE21 ....220 A4
Sandfield Rd 🖪 NG9 ..223 C1
Sandford Ave NG10 ...236 C4
Sandford Brook DE65 ..228 C1
Sandgate Ave NG19 ...136 B2
Sandgate Cl DE24 ....233 B4
Sandgate Rd NG19 ....136 B2
Sandhall La DE5 ......169 B1
Sandhill La
Broadbottom SK6 .....16 A1
Marple SK6 ....15 C1
Sandhills Rd S44 .....99 B1
Sandiacre Rd NG9 ....223 B3
Sandiway
Chesterfield S40 ......114 B4
Glossop SK13 ....17 C4
Sandlands The DE11 ..256 B3
Sandlands Way NG19 ..136 C1
Sandown Ave DE3 ....217 B2
Sandown Cl
Burton u T DE14 ......254 A4
Eckington S21 ....59 A2
Sandown Rd
Beeston NG9 ....223 C1
Derby DE24 ....232 C4
Sandringham Ave DE15 .248 A1
Sandringham Cl S44 ...97 A2
Sandringham Ct
Buxton SK17 ....85 A4
Mansfield Woodhouse
NG19 ....136 A3
Sandringham Dr
Derby DE21 ....220 C3
Heanor DE75 ....181 B1
Mansfield Woodhouse
NG19 ....136 A3
Sandringham Ho DE24 .219 B1
Sandringham Pl DE7 ..208 B3
Sandringham Rd
Calow S44 ....97 A2
Derby DE21 ....205 C1
Mansfield Woodhouse
NG19 ....136 B2
Nottingham NG2 .....268 C1
Sandiacre NG10 ......223 B2
Sands Cl S14 ....43 C2
Sandstone Ave S40 ...114 A4
Sandwell Cl NG10 ....236 A3
Sandwood Cl DE55 ...148 A2
Sandy Cl S80 ....81 C3
Sandy La
Broadbottom SK13 .....16 A1
Caldwell DE12 ....261 A4
Crich DE4 ....167 C4
Hursley DE21,DE7 .....192 A2
Mansfield NG18 ......268 C4
Matlock DE4 ....143 B4

Sandybank Cl SK13 .....9 C2
Sandybrook Cl DE6 ...173 B2
Sandycliffe Cl NG19 ..136 C1
Sandyford Ct ST16 ...269 B4
Sandyford La DE56 ...166 C2
Sandyhill Cl DE73 ....233 A1
Sandypits La DE65 ...229 B2
Sanforth St S41 ....96 A3
Sankey Dr DE21 ......256 B1
Santolina Dr DE21 ...205 C1
Sapperton Cl DE23 ...231 B3
Sapperton La DE65 ...213 C1
Sappertonfield La DE6,
DE65 ....213 B2
Sapphire Dr DE5 .....180 A1
Sarah Cl DE55 ....170 B4
Sargent Gdns NG3 ....268 C2
Sark Rd 🖫 S2 ....43 A4
Sash St ST16 ....269 B4
Saundby Ave NG19 ...135 B1
Saundersfoot Way DE21 .206 B1
Savage La S17 ....55 B4
Saville Cl NG9 ....223 C4
Saville House Sch NG19 136 A2
Saw Pit Ind Est DE55 ..148 B3
Saw Pit La DE55 ......148 A3
Sawley Jun & Inf Schs
NG10 ....236 B4
Sawley Rd
Breaston DE72 ....235 C3
Draycott DE72 ....235 A4
Sawmand Cl NG10 ...236 A4
Sawmills Ind Pk DE75 .181 B2
Sawpit La DE65 ......227 B1
Saxon Cl
Breedon on t H DE73 ..252 C1
Burton u T DE15 ......254 C4
Saxon Croft DE65 ....242 B4
Saxon Gr DE65 ....242 A3
Saxon Rd S8 ....43 A4
Saxon St DE15 ....254 C4
Saxondale Ave DE3 ...217 B2
Saxton Ave DE75 .....181 C1
Scalby Cl NG18 ......182 B1
Scaliot Cl SK22 ....33 A4
Scalpcliffe Rd DE15 ...248 A1
Scarborough Ave DE7 ..208 C4
Scarborough Rise DE21 205 B1
Scarborough St NG3 ...268 B2
Scarcliffe Cl DE24 ....232 C2
Scarcliffe La NG20 ....119 B4
Scarcliffe Prim Sch
S44 ....118 C3
Scarcliffe St NG18 ....268 C4
Scarcliffe Terr NG20 ..101 A1
Scargill CE Prim Sch
DE7 ....207 B4
Scargill Rd DE7 ......207 C4
Scargill Wlk NG16 ....182 C2
Scarsdale Ave
Derby, Allestree DE22 ..204 B2
Derby, Littleover DE23 ..218 B1
Scarsdale Cl S18 ......76 A4
Scarsdale Cres S43 ...96 B4
Scarsdale Cross S18 ..57 A1
Scarsdale Hospl S40 ..266 B4
Scarsdale Pl 🖪 SK17 ..85 C4
Scarsdale Rd
Chesterfield S41 ......96 A4
Dronfield S18 ....57 A1
Duffield DE56 ....190 C2
Scarsdale St S44 .....117 C4
Scarthin DE4 ....155 A3
Schofield Ct S44 ......110 C1
School Ave S20 ....59 C4
School Board La S40 ...95 C2
School Cl Blackwell DE55 147 B1
Darley Dale DE4 ......127 B2
Fenny Bentley DE6 ....162 A1
Moira DE11 ....256 B1
Mosborough S20 ......59 C4
Newton DE55 ....148 A2
Shirland DE55 ....146 B1
Stonebroom DE55 .....146 C2
School Croft DE55 ....170 B3
School House Hill DE56 168 B1
School La Ashbourne DE6 173 A1
Baslow DE45 ....91 C3
Beeley DE4 ....111 A4
Brackenfield DE55 ....145 B1
Castle Donington DE74 ..247 A2
Compstall SK6 ....15 A2
Crich DE4 ....157 A1
Darley Dale DE4 ......126 C4
Derby DE73 ....233 A1
Dronfield S18 ....57 A1
Eckington S21 ....58 C2
Hassop DE45 ....90 C3
Hathersage S32 ....53 A4
Heage DE56 ....168 B1
Long Duckmanton S44 ..97 B2
Mansfield Woodhouse
NG19 ....136 B2
Old Brampton S42 ....93 C2
Ripley DE5 ....169 B1
Rolleston DE13 ....240 A2
Sheffield, Greenhill S8 ..56 C4
Sheffield, Norton S8 ...57 B4
South Normanton DE55 ..160 A2
Stanton-by-D DE7,NG10 ..222 C4
Sudbury DE6 ....225 C2
Taddington SK17 ......87 C2
Youlgreave DE4 ......126 B3
School Lane Cl S8 ....43 B1
School Rd Buxton SK17 ..67 A3
Chesterfield S41 ......96 A4
Matlock DE4 ....143 B3
Uttoxeter ST14 ......210 A1

Sandbank Cl SK13 ......9 C2
School Sq DE7 ....207 C4
School St Eckington S21 ..59 B2
Moira DE12 ....262 C1
Mosborough S20 .....59 B4
Swadlincote DE11 ....256 A1
Schoolpiece La DE65 ..227 C4
Scothces The DE56 ...178 C3
Scotia Cl S2 ....43 C4
Scotia Dr S2 ....43 C4
Scotland St S80 ......81 C3
Scotswood Rd NG16 ..136 A3
Scott Cl S42 ....115 C2
Scott Cres DE55 .....146 C2
Scott Dr Belper DE56 ..179 C3
Marple SK6 ....23 A4
Somercotes DE55 .....170 B4
Scott St Derby DE23 ...218 C1
Whaley Thorns NG20 ..101 A1
Scotts The DE11 .....261 B4
Scowerdons Cl S12 ...44 C3
Scowerdons Dr S12 ...44 C3
Scratta La S80 ....63 B1
Screetham La DE4 ....112 B1
Scropton Old Rd DE65 .239 B4
Scropton Rd DE65 ....239 A4
Scropton Wlk DE24 ...232 C2
Sea Breeze Terr S13 ..44 C4
Seaburn Rd NG9 .....223 C1
Seaford Way DE7 ....194 C3
Seagrave Ave S12 .....44 A2
Seagrave Cl DE21 ....220 A4
Seagrave Cres S12 ...44 A2
Seagrave Dr
Chesterfield S41 ......115 B4
Sheffield S12 ....44 A2
Seagrave Rd S12 .....44 A2
Seal View DE12 ......261 B3
Seale St DE1 ....267 B5
Sealey Cl DE65 ....242 B3
Seals Rd DE12 ....262 C1
Sealwood La
Linton DE12 ....261 C2
Overseal DE12 ....261 C3
Seamer Rd NG16 ....195 C4
Seanor La S45 ....132 A2
Searl St DE1 ....218 C3
Searle Ave ST16 .....269 A3
Searson Ave S44 ......99 A1
Searston Ave S42 ....132 B4
Seascale Cl DE21 .....205 B1
Seaton Cl DE3 ....217 B2
Sebastion Cl SK6 .....23 A4
Second Ave
Branston DE14 ....253 C4
Derby DE73 ....245 A4
Risley DE72 ....222 C3
Sedbergh Cres S41 ...95 B4
Sedgebrook Cl DE21 ..205 C1
Sedgebrook St NG19 ..136 C2
Sedgefield Gn DE3 ...217 B1
Sedgefield Rd
Branston DE14 ....253 C4
Burton u T DE14 .....254 A4
Sedgemoor Cl S40 ...95 A2
Sedgemoor Rd NG10 ..236 C3
Sedgemoor Way DE23 .231 A3
Sedgley Ave NG2 ....268 C2
Sedgwick Cl NG16 ...160 B1
Sedgwick St
Langley Mill NG16 ....182 A2
Westwood NG16 .....171 A2
Seely Rd NG7 ....268 A2
Sefton Ave NG9 ......223 C4
Sefton Cl DE15 ......248 A1
Sefton Rd DE21 ......219 C3
Sefton St SK13 ....17 B4
Selborne St DE24 ....219 B1
Selby Cl Beeston NG9 ..223 C2
Chesterfield S40 ......114 B4
Selhurst Rd S41 ......95 C3
Selina Cl DE74 ....247 A2
Selina St DE73 ....252 A4
Selkirk St DE21 ......219 C4
Selly Oak Gr S8 ......57 B3
Selly Oak Rd S8 ......57 B3
Selmer Ct S43 ....96 B4
Selston CE Inf Sch
NG16 ....171 C3
Selston Rd NG16 .....171 A3
Selworthy Cl DE21 ...206 A1
Selwyn St Bolsover S44 ..118 B4
Derby DE22 ....218 B3
Stoke-on-T ST4 ......269 B1
Senners La SK17 ......87 A1
Serina Ave DE23 .....231 B4
Serlby Dr S26 ....61 C3
Serlby La S26 ....61 C3
Serlby Rise NG3 ......268 C2
Serpentine Wlk S8 ...57 A4
Setcup La S21 ....59 B1
Sett Cl SK22 ....33 A4
Settlement The DE72 .221 B3
Setts Way S42 ....115 A2
Seven Arches Way ST4 .269 C2
Seven Oaks Rd DE7 ..209 A1
Sevenoaks Ave DE22 .217 C3
Severals NG9 ....223 C4
Severn Cl DE13 ......240 B1
Severn Cres S42 .....132 A3
Severn Sq DE55 .....159 A2
Severn St DE24 ......232 C4
Severnale Cl DE22 ...205 A3
Severnlands Dr DE24 ..233 B4
Sewell Rd S20 ....59 C3
Sexton St SK13 ....9 C4
Seymour Cl DE22 ....218 B3
Seymour Ct 🖪 NG7 ...268 A2
Seymour La S43 ......79 B1

Seymour Rd NG16 .....182 C1
Seymour St NG3 ....268 C2
Shacklecross Cl DE72 .221 B1
Shady Gr DE65 ....228 B1
Shaef Cl DE65 ....228 C1
Shaftesbury Ave
  Chesterfield S40 ......95 B2
  Long Eaton NG10 .....236 A2
  Mansfield NG19 ......135 C1
  Sandiacre NG10 ......223 A3
Shaftesbury Cres DE23 219 A1
Shaftesbury St DE23 .219 A1
Shaftesbury St S DE23 219 A1
Shafton Cl S45 ....131 C2
Shafton Wlk S45 ......131 C2
Shakespeare Ave
  Creswell S80 ....81 B1
  Mansfield Woodhouse
    NG19 ....136 A2
  Shirland DE55 ....146 B2
Shakespeare Cl
  Clay Cross S42 ....131 A3
  Repton DE65 ....242 B1
  Swadlincote DE11 ...256 B3
Shakespeare Cres S18 ..76 B4
Shakespeare Ct DE6 ..173 A1
Shakespeare Dr DE55 .159 A2
Shakespeare Mdw DE21 242 B1
Shakespeare Rd NG16 .195 B3
Shakespeare St
  Derby DE24 ....232 A3
  Grassmoor S42 ....115 C2
  Holmewood S42 ......116 B1
  Long Eaton NG10 .....223 B1
  Nottingham NG1 ......268 B2
Shakespeare Villas NG1 268 B2
Shaldon Dr DE55 .....218 B1
Shalfleet Dr DE24 ....233 B3
Shallcross Ave SK23 ...45 C2
Shallcross Cres SK23 ..45 C2
Shallcross Rd SK23 ....45 C2
Shambles The S40 ....266 B3
Shamrock Pl S43 ....79 B2
Shamrock St DE23 ...218 C1
Shandwick Ct 14 DE24 .231 C1
Shanklin Dr NG9 .....223 B4
Shannon Cl DE23 .....231 B1
Shannon Sq DE21 ....220 A2
Shap Cl 7 S40 ....95 B3
Shardlow Prim Sch
  DE72 ....234 C1
Shardlow Rd
  Aston-on-T DE72 .....246 A4
  Derby DE24,DE74 ....233 A3
Sharman Cl
  Apperknowle S18 .....58 A1
  Stoke-on-T ST4 ......269 A2
Sharman Wlk S18 ......58 A1
Sharp Cl Ilkeston DE7 .208 B3
  Long Eaton NG10 .....236 B3
Sharpe Ave S8 ....56 C4
Sharpswood Manor
  DE11 ....256 C2
Sharrard Cl S12 ....44 A3
Sharrard Dr S12 ....44 A3
Sharrard Gr S12 ....44 A3
Sharrard Rd S12 ....44 A3
Shatton La S32,S33 ....51 C4
Shaw La Belper DE56 .191 A4
  Glossop SK13 ....9 C2
  Holloway DE4 ....156 B4
  Marston Montgomery DE6 198 A1
Shaw St Chesterfield S41 .96 A4
  Derby DE22 ....218 C3
  Dronfield S18 ....57 B2
  Glossop SK13 ....17 B4
  Holmewood S42 ......116 B1
  Mottram in L SK14 .....9 A2
  Somercotes DE55 ....170 B3
Shaw St E DE7 ....209 A3
Shaw St W DE7 ....209 A3
Shaw Wood View DE55 .157 C2
Shaw's Row S40 ....95 B1
Shaw's Yd DE56 ......191 C4
Shawcroft DE6 ....173 B1
Shawcroft Ave DE55 .170 B3
Shawfield Rd SK13 .....9 C2
Shaws Gn DE22 ......218 C3
Shaws Hill DE4 ......156 B4
Sheaf Bank S2 ....43 A4
Sheardhall Ave SK12 ..32 C3
Sheards Cl 7 S18 ......56 C1
Sheards Dr S18 ....56 C1
Sheards Way S18 .....56 C1
Shearsby Dr NG9 ....136 C1
Shearwater Cl DE23 .231 B4
Sheepbridge La
  Chesterfield S41 ......76 C1
  Mansfield NG18 .....268 A3
Sheepcote Rd S21 .....60 B3
Sheephill Rd S11 ......42 C1
Sheeplea La S45 .....129 C4
Sheepwash La S45 ...145 A4
Sheet Stores Ind Est
  NG10 ....236 B3
Sheffield Coll Norton Ctr
  S8 ....57 A4
Sheffield Pl DE1 .....267 D2
Sheffield Rd Baslow DE45 92 A4
  Chapel-en-le-F SK23 ...47 C4
  Chesterfield S41 ......96 A3
  Creswell S80,S43 ......81 B2
  Dronfield S18 ....56 C2
  Glossop SK13 ....10 C1
  Hathersage S32 ....53 A4
  Killamarsh S21 ....60 B4
  Mosborough S20 ......59 C3
  Renishaw S21, S43 ....79 B4

Sheffield Rd continued
  Sheffield S12 ....44 C1
  Unstone S18,S41 ......76 C2
Shelburne St ST4 ....269 B1
Shelden Cl SK13 ....9 B1
Shelden Fold SK13 .....9 B1
Shelden Pl SK13 ....9 B1
Sheldon Cl NG10 ....223 A2
Sheldon Ct DE24 ....232 C2
Sheldon Gdns DE4 ...156 C1
Sheldon Mews SK13 ...9 B1
Sheldon Rd
  Chesterfield S40 ......95 A3
  Heanor DE75 ....181 B3
Shelford Cl DE3 .....217 B2
Shelford Hill NG19 ..268 A3
Shelford La DE4 .....156 A4
Shelley Ave NG19 ...136 A2
Shelley Dr Derby DE24 .232 A3
  Dronfield S18 ....76 B4
Shelley Gr DE55 .....146 C2
Shelley St S42 ....116 B1
Shelly Rd DE11 ......256 B3
Shelmory Cl DE24 ...232 C3
Shelton Cl NG19 ....135 C1
Shelton Dr DE24 ....232 C2
Shelton Jun & Inf Sch
  DE24 ....232 B2
Shelton Old Rd ST4 .269 C1
Shelton St NG3 ......268 B2
Shenington Way DE21 .206 A1
Shepherd St DE21 ...218 B1
Shepherd's La DE73 .251 B3
Shepherd's Row S18 ..77 A4
Shepley St
  Chesterfield S40 ......95 B1
  Glossop SK13 ....10 C1
  Glossop, Hadfield SK13 ..9 C2
Shepley's Yd S40 ....266 B3
Sheppard St ST4 ....269 B1
Shepton Cl DE7 .....194 B2
Sheraton Way SK17 ...66 A1
Sherbourne Ave S41 ..95 C4
Sherbourne Dr
  Belper DE56 ....179 B3
  Burton u T DE14 ....254 A4
Sherbrook Gr SK17 ...85 B3
Sherbrook Lodge (Youth
  Hostel) * SK17 ....85 B3
Sherbrooke Rd SK12 ..32 B3
Sheridan La NG9 ....209 C1
Sheridan Ctr ST16 ..269 B4
Sheridan St Derby DE24 231 C3
  Stafford ST16 ....269 C4
Sheriff Dr DE4 ......143 A3
Sheriffs Way NG2 ...268 B1
Sheringham Dr NG18 .268 C3
Sherman Ct DE65 ...228 C1
Sherrton Ct DE21 ...206 A1
Sherwin Cl NG3 .....268 B2
Sherwin Rd NG9 ....209 C1
Sherwin St DE22 ....218 C4
Sherwin Wlk 2 NG3 .268 B2
Sherwood Ave
  Borrowash DE72 ....221 B1
  Creswell S80 ....81 B1
  Derby, Chaddesden DE21 219 C4
  Derby, Littleover DE23 .231 B3
  Hope S33 ....39 A2
  Pinxton NG16 ....160 B2
  Shirebrook NG20 ....119 C2
Sherwood Chase S17 .55 C3
Sherwood Copse SK17 .69 B2
Sherwood Ct NG19 ..136 A1
Sherwood Dr NG20 .119 C2
Sherwood Fold SK13 .16 B2
Sherwood Foresters
  Regiment Meml * DE4 156 C2
Sherwood Hall L Ctr
  DE4 ....143 B2
Sherwood Pl 15 S18 ..56 B1
Sherwood Rd Buxton SK17 85 B3
  Dronfield S18 ....56 B1
  Killamarsh S21 ....60 C4
  Matlock DE4 ....143 B2
  Tideswell SK17 ....69 B2
Sherwood Rise
  Eastwood NG16 .....182 C1
  Mansfield Woodhouse
    NG19 ....136 C2
Sherwood St
  Bolsover S44 ....117 C4
  Chesterfield S40 ....266 C1
  Derby DE22 ....218 C2
  Mansfield NG18 .....268 B2
  Mansfield Woodhouse
    NG19 ....136 A1
  Newton DE55 ....148 A2
  Shirland DE55 ......146 B3
  Somercotes DE55 ....170 B4
  Sutton in A NG17 ...148 C2
Shetland Cl Derby DE21 219 B4
  Mansfield NG19 .....136 C1
Shetland Rd Dronfield S18 76 A4
  Tibshelf DE55 ....147 C3
Shields Cres DE74 ..246 C2
Shieling The DE65 ...227 B1
Shilling Way NG10 ...236 A4
Shiloh Rd SK22,SK6 ...24 C3
Shilton Cl ST4 ......269 A1
Shining Cliffe YH *
  DE56 ....167 B3
Shinwell Ave S43 .....97 A4
Shipley Cl DE14 .....254 A4
Shipley Common La
  DE7 ....194 B2

Shipley Country Park Visitor
  Ctr * DE75 ....193 C3
Shipley Ct DE7 ......194 B1
Shipley Ctry Pk * DE7 .194 A2
Shipley La DE7,DE75 .193 C3
Shipley Wlk DE24 ...232 C2
Shipman Ct S20 ....59 B4
Shirburn Ave NG18 .268 C4
Shire Hill Hospl SK13 ..10 C2
Shire La S44 ....116 C2
Shire Way SK13 ....10 C2
Shirebrook Bsns Pk
  NG20 ....119 C1
Shirebrook Com Sch
  NG20 ....119 B3
Shirebrook Dr SK13 ..17 C4
Shirebrook Rd S8 .....43 A3
Shirebrook Sta NG20 .120 A2
Shiregate Gdns DE23 .231 B1
Shireoaks DE56 .....178 B3
Shireoaks Cl DE23 ..231 B4
Shireoaks Comm S81 .63 C4
Shireoaks Rd
  Dronfield S18 ....57 B1
  Shireoaks S80 ....63 C3
Shireoaks Row S81 ...63 C4
Shireoaks Sta S81 ....63 C4
Shires The NG19 ....136 C1
Shirland Prim Sch DE55 146 B1
Shirland St S41 .....266 B4
Shirley Cl
  Castle Donington DE74 247 A2
  Chesterfield S40 ......95 A3
  Hope S33 ....39 A2
Shirley Cres DE72 ...235 B4
Shirley La DE6 ......200 A3
Shirley Pk DE72 .....246 A4
Shirley Rd Derby DE21 .205 C1
  Ripley DE5 ....169 B1
  Swanwick DE55 ....169 C4
Shirley St NG10 .....236 A2
Shop La DE56 ....168 B1
Shop Stones DE72 ..221 B3
Shoreham St S2 ....43 A4
Short Ave DE22 .....204 C3
Short Brook Prim Sch
  S20 ....59 C4
Short Cl S42 ....113 B4
Short Hill
  Breedon on t H DE73 .252 C3
  Nottingham NG1 ....268 B1
Short La DE74 ......246 C2
Short Lands DE56 ...179 A2
Short Row 4 DE56 ...178 C2
Short St Belper DE56 .179 A2
  Burton u T DE15 ....254 C4
Short Street Com Inf Sch
  DE15 ....254 C4
Shortbrook Bank 19 S20 .59 C4
Shortbrook Cl 14 S20 .59 C4
Shortbrook Croft 12 S20 .59 C4
Shortbrook Dr 18 S20 .59 C4
Shortbrook Rd S20 ...59 C4
Shortbrook Way 21 S20 .59 C4
Shortbrook Wlk 15 S20 .59 C4
Shortheath DE12 ....262 B2
Shortheath Rd DE12 .262 C2
Shortlands The DE4 .143 A2
Shorts La S17 ....55 A3
Shortwood Cl NG1 ..268 B1
Shorwell Gdns DE24 .233 B3
Shottle Wlk DE24 ...232 C2
Shotwood Cl DE13 ..240 A4
Shotwoodhill La DE13 240 A3
Shrewsbury Rd
  Burton u T DE13 ....240 C1
  Stafford ST17 ....269 B3
Shrewsbury St S18 ...10 B1
Shropshire Ave
  Derby DE21 ....219 C4
  Westwood NG16 ....171 B2
Shropshire Dr SK13 ..17 C4
Shrubbery The DE11 .257 A1
Shuckstone La DE4 .156 C3
Shudehill Cl SK22 ....25 B2
Shunters Drift S43 ...80 A3
Shuttlewood Rd S44 ..99 A2
Shutts La DE45 .....109 B2
Sibthorpe St NG18 ..268 B3
Sickleback La S18 ....57 C2
Sickleholme S33 ......40 A1
Siddals La DE22 ....204 C2
Siddals Rd DE1 .....267 C2
Siddals St DE15 ....248 A2
Siddons St DE24 ....233 A4
Side End La SK23 .....45 A1
Sides La DE6 ....184 A3
Sideway Rd ST4 ....269 B1
Sidings The Derby DE21 220 A2
  Kimberley NG16 ....195 C3
Sidings Way DE55 ...147 B1
Sidlaw Cl 6 S40 ......95 B3
Sidmouth Cl DE24 ..233 B4
Sidney Cl DE3 ......217 C2
Sidney St Derby DE1 .267 C1
  Kimberley NG16 ....195 C3
  Long Eaton NG10 ...236 B3
Siemens St ST17 ....269 B3
Silk Hill SK23 ....45 C4
Silk Mill La DE13 ...239 B3
Silk St SK13 ....10 C1
Silken Holme DE55 .160 A2
Silkstone Cres S12 ...44 C2
Silkstone Pl S12 ......44 C2
Silkstone Rd S12 .....44 C2

Sillitoe Pl ST4 ......269 B1
Silver Birch Cres DE55 .159 B4
Silver Hill Rd DE23 .219 A1
Silver La Elvaston DE72 234 A3
  Marchington ST14 ...224 C1
Silver Mill Rd S2 .....43 A4
Silverburn Dr SK13 ..206 A1
Silverdale NG9 .....223 C3
Silverdale Ave NG19 .136 A2
Silverdale Cl
  Chesterfield S41 ......76 C1
  Derby DE73 ....233 A1
Silverhill Cl DE13 ...240 B1
Silverhill La DE55 ...148 C4
Silverhill Prim Sch DE3 217 B2
Silverhill Rd DE21 ...220 C2
Silverlands SK17 .....85 B4
Silverlands Cl SK17 ..85 B4
Silverlands Pk SK17 ..85 B4
Silverton Dr DE24 ..231 B1
Silvey Gr DE21 .....220 B2
Simcoe Leys DE73 ..233 A1
Simcrest Ave S21 .....60 B3
Simmondley Gr SK13 ..17 A4
Simmondley La SK13 .17 A4
Simmondley New Rd
  SK13 ....17 A4
Simmondley Prim Sch
  SK13 ....17 A4
Simon Fields Cl DE7 .193 A1
Simonburn Ave ST4 .269 A2
Simons Cl SK13 ......17 A4
Simons Wlk SK13 ....17 A4
Simpson St DE24 ...232 C3
Sims Ave DE21 .....218 C3
Sims Croft S41 ....77 B2
Sinclair Cl Derby DE24 231 C2
  Heanor DE75 ....193 B4
Sinder Ave DE11 ...256 A3
Sinfin Ave DE24 ....232 B2
Sinfin Com Sch DE24 231 C2
Sinfin Fields Cres DE24 232 B3
Sinfin La
  Barrow u T DE73 ....244 A3
  Derby DE23,DE24 ...231 C2
Sinfin Moor La DE73 .232 C1
Sinfin Prim Sch DE24 231 C3
Sir Frank Whittle Rd
  DE21 ....219 B4
Sir Harold Jackson Prim Sch
  S17 ....56 A3
Sir Henry's La DE73 .252 A2
Sir Joseph's La DE4 .127 A2
Sir William Hill Rd S32 71 B4
Sir William Terr S32 ..72 B4
Siskin Cl DE3 ....230 A4
Siskin Dr DE24 .....231 B2
Sisley Ave NG9 .....223 C3
Sister's La DE72 ....221 B3
Sitch La Hayfield SK22 ..24 C2
  Kirk Ireton DE4 ....165 A2
Sitch Rd DE4 ....142 B4
Sitwell 20 S20 ....59 C4
Sitwell Ave S40 ....266 A1
Sitwell Cl DE21 .....220 B2
Sitwell Dr DE56 ....192 A4
Sitwell Grange La
  Pilsley S45 ....147 B4
  Tibshelf S45 ....147 B4
Sitwell St Derby DE1 .267 B2
  Derby, Spondon DE21 220 C2
  Eckington S21 ....59 B2
Sitwell Villas DE55 .146 C3
Skardu Ct 1 DE24 ..268 C1
Skeavington's La DE7 194 C1
Skegby La NG18, NG19 268 A3
Skegby Mount NG18 .268 A3
Skeldale Dr S40 ....115 A4
Skelton Rd S8 ....43 A3
Skelwith Cl S41 ......95 B4
Sketchley St NG3 ...268 C2
Ski 2000 Ilkeston DE7 195 A1
Skiddaw Cl 11 S40 ...95 B3
Skiddaw Dr DE3 ....217 C1
Skinner St S80 ....81 B1
Skinners Way DE11 .256 B3
Skipton Cl DE7 .....194 B2
Skipton Gn DE21 ...205 B1
Skye Gdns DE55 ....147 C3
Skylark Way DE24 ..231 B2
Slack La Ashover S45 129 B1
  Brailsford DE6 ....187 B1
  Chesterfield S40 ......95 A2
  Derby, Allestree DE22 204 A3
  Derby, New Zealand DE22 218 B3
  Hartshorne DE11 ....257 A3
  Mayfield DE6 ....184 B4
  Nether Heage DE56 168 B2
  Ripley DE5 ....169 B1
  Somercotes DE55 ....170 A3
  Wessington DE55 ....157 B4
Slack Rd DE7 ....193 C2
Slack's La S45 ......132 B1
Slackey La DE12 ....262 B2
Slacks Cott SK17 .....84 C3
Slacks La S20 ....25 B3
Slade Cl Etwall DE65 .229 B2
  Ilkeston DE7 ....209 A3
  South Normanton DE55 160 A2
Slade Fields ST14 ...210 A3
Slade Hollow La DE6 .201 A2
Slade La DE6 ....202 C4
Slag La S43 ....77 B3
Slaidburn Cl DE3 ...217 C1
Slaley La DE4 ......154 B4
Slaley View Rd S43 ..80 B3
Slaney Cl DE24 .....232 C4

Slant Cl SK13 ....17 C4
Slant La NG19 ......136 A2
Slant The NG20 ....119 B2
Slate St S2 ....43 A4
Slatelands Ave SK13 .17 A4
Slatelands Rd SK13 ..17 A4
Slatepit La S18,S42 ..93 B4
Slater Ave DE22 ....218 C3
Slater Cres DE4 ....165 C4
Slater St S45 ....131 B2
Slayley Hill S43 ......80 B2
Slayley View S43 .....80 B3
Slaypit La S80 ....62 B3
Sledgegate La DE4 .156 A4
Sledmere Cl DE24 ..233 B3
Sleepy La DE73 .....245 B1
Sleetmoor La DE55 .170 A4
Sleights La NG16 ...160 B1
Slessor Rd ST16 ....269 C4
Slindon Croft DE24 .233 B3
Slipperlow La SK17 ..87 C1
Sloade La S12 ....58 C3
Sloane Rd DE22 ....218 A3
Small Gate NG19 ...136 C1
Small Knowle End S33 .67 B3
Small Meer DE73 ...232 C1
Small Thorn Pl DE11 .256 C1
Smalldale Cotts SK17 .67 B4
Smalldale Head Rd S33 .50 C4
Smalldale Rd Buxton SK17 67 B4
  Sheffield S12 ....44 B2
Smalley Dr DE21 ....206 A2
Smalley Mill Rd DE21,
  DE7 ....192 A2
Smallman St ST16 ..269 A4
Smeath Rd NG16 ...171 C1
Smeckley Wood Cl S41 .76 B2
Smedley Ave
  Ilkeston DE7 ....209 A4
  Somercotes DE55 ...159 B1
Smedley Ct DE65 ...241 A3
Smedley Pl SK13 .....10 C1
Smedley St DE4 ....143 A3
Smedley St E DE4 ..143 B3
Smedley St W DE4 .143 A3
Smedley's Ave NG10 .223 A3
Smeeton St DE75 ..182 A1
Smelter Wood Ave S13 .44 C4
Smelter Wood Cl S13 .44 C4
Smelter Wood Cres S13 44 C4
Smelter Wood Ct S13 .44 C4
Smelter Wood Dr S13 .44 C4
Smelter Wood La S13 .44 C4
Smelter Wood Pl S13 .44 C4
Smelter Wood Rd S13 .44 C4
Smelter Wood Rise S13 44 C4
Smelter Wood Way S13 44 C4
Smeltinghouse La S18 .75 C2
Smisby Rd LE65 ....258 A1
Smisby Way DE24 ..232 C2
Smith Ave Codnor DE5 .170 A4
  Melbourne DE73 ....245 A1
  Staveley S43 ....97 B4
Smith Cres S41 ....96 B1
Smith Dr NG16 .....182 A2
Smith Rd DE4 ......143 A4
Smith-Hall La DE6 ..188 A4
Smithbrook Cl SK23 ..47 B3
Smithfield Ave
  Chesterfield S41 ....115 B4
  Trowell NG9 ....209 B2
Smithfield Rd S12 ...44 A2
Smithpool Rd ST4 ..269 C1
Smithson Ave S44 ...99 A1
Smithurst Rd NG16 .195 A4
Smithy Ave S45 ....131 B2
Smithy Brook Rd S21 .79 B2
Smithy Cl Glossop SK13 .10 B1
  Parwich DE6 ....151 B1
Smithy Croft S18 .....56 B1
Smithy Fold SK13 ...10 B1
Smithy Hill S33 ....51 A4
Smithy Knoll Rd S32 .72 C1
Smithy La
  Clifton Campville B79 .263 C1
  Marple SK6 ....15 C1
  Taddington SK17 ....88 A2
Smithy Mdws S32 ...51 A4
Smithy Pl S42 ......115 C1
Smithy Row NG1 ...268 B2
Smuse La DE4 ......143 C2
Snake La DE56 .....190 C2
Snake Rd S33 ....28 B4
Snake Woodland Forest
  Walk * S33 ....19 C2
Snape Hill S18 ....57 A1
Snape Hill Dr S18 ....57 A2
Snape Hill La S18 ....57 A1
Snapehill Cl S18 .....57 A2
Snapehill Cres S18 ..57 A2
Snapes La DE6 .....184 A1
Sneinton Bvd NG2 ..268 C1
Sneinton CE Prim Sch The
  NG2 ....268 C1
Sneinton Dale NG2 .268 C1
Sneinton Hermitage
  NG2 ....268 C1
Sneinton Hollows NG2 268 C1
Sneinton Rd NG2 ...268 C1
Snelsmoor La DE73 .233 C4
Snelston Cl S18 ......56 B1
Snelston Cres DE23 .218 B3
Snipe Cl S42 ....113 C4
Snipesmoor La DE6 .185 C2
Snitterton Rd DE4 ..143 A3

Snow Hill ST16 ....**269** B4
Snowberry Ave DE56 ..**179** A4
Snowdon La S21 ....**58** A2
Snowdrop Valley DE4 ..**168** A4
Snowfield View DE4 ....**165** C3
Snows Yd ST16 ....**269** A4
Soaper La S18 ....**57** A1
Soarbank Cl NG16 .....**195** C4
Society Pl DE23 ....**219** A1
Soft Water La S33 ....**51** A4
Solney Cl DE55 ....**255** C2
Soloman Pk NG16 ......**195** A1
Soloman Rd DE7 ....**195** A1
Solomons View SK17 ....**85** B4
Solway Cl DE21 ....**206** A1
Solway Rise S18 ....**56** B1
Somerby Way DE21 ....**205** C1
Somercotes Hill DE55 ..**170** B4
Somercotes Inf Sch
DE55 ....**170** B4
Somercotes Rd S12 ......**44** B3
Somerlea Park Jun Sch
DE55 ....**170** B4
Somerleyton Dr DE7 ...**209** A2
Somersal Cl DE24 ......**232** C2
Somersall Cl S40 ....**95** A1
Somersall La S40 ....**95** A1
Somersall Park Rd S40 ..**95** A1
Somersall St NG19 .....**268** A4
Somersall Willows S40 ..**95** A1
Somersby Ave S40 ......**114** A4
Somerset Cl Buxton SK17 **85** B2
Long Eaton NG10 ......**237** A4
Somerset Dr S43 ....**97** A4
Somerset Rd DE15 .....**254** B3
Somerset St DE21 ......**219** B4
Somme Rd DE22 ....**204** A2
Sookholme Cl NG20 ....**119** C2
Sookholme La NG20,
NG19 ....**120** C3
Sookholme Rd
Market Warsop NG20 ...**120** C2
Shirebrook NG20 ......**119** C2
Soresby St S40 ....**266** B3
Sorrel Dr DE11 ....**256** C2
Sough La Bolehill DE4 ..**155** A1
Taddington SK17 ....**87** B1
Wirksworth DE4 ....**154** C1
Sough Rd DE55 ....**160** A4
Soughley La S10 ....**42** B4
South Ave Buxton SK17 ..**85** A4
Dorby DE23 ....**218** B1
Derby, Chellaston DE73 ..**232** C2
Derby, Darley Abbey DE22 **205** A2
Derby, Spondon DE21 ...**220** C2
Shirebrook NG20 ......**119** C2
South Brae Cl DE23 ...**231** B4
South Broadway St
DE14 ....**254** B4
South Church St DE45 ..**109** B3
South Cl Glossop SK13 ...**9** C4
Unstone S18 ....**76** C3
South Cres Bolsover S44 ..**99** A1
Killamarsh S21 ....**60** C4
Long Duckmanton S44 ...**98** A3
South Ct S17 ....**55** C4
South Darley CE Prim Sch
DE4 ....**142** A4
South Dr
Derby, Chellaston DE73 ..**232** C2
Derby, Cherrytree Hill
DE21 ....**220** A3
Derby, Litteover DE3 ....**218** A1
Derby, Little Chester DE1 **218** C4
Swadlincote DE11 ......**255** C3
South East Derbyshire Coll
Heanor DE75 ....**181** C1
Ilkeston DE7 ....**208** C3
South Farm Ave S26 ....**61** C3
South Head Dr SK23 ....**47** B4
South Hill Rolleston DE13 **240** B2
Shirland DE55 ....**145** C4
South Hill La DE55 ....**145** C3
South Lodge Ct S40 .....**95** A2
South Marlow St SK13 ...**10** A2
South Oak St DE14 ....**254** A4
South Par
Matlock DE4 ....**143** A1
3 Nottingham NG1 ...**268** B1
South Park Ave DE4 ...**127** C4
South Pl
Chesterfield, Brampton S40 **95** B1
Chesterfield, Stonegravels
S40 ....**266** B2
Ripley DE5 ....**169** B4
South Rd NG7 ....**268** A1
South Sherwood St
NG1 ....**268** B2
South St Ashbourne DE6 **173** B1
Blackwell DE55 ....**147** C1
Buxton SK17 ....**85** A4
Chesterfield S40 ....**266** B2
Derby DE1 ....**218** C3
Draycott DE72 ....**235** A4
Eastwood, Bailey Grove
NG16 ....**182** C1
Eastwood, Giltbrook NG16 **195** B4
Ilkeston DE7 ....**208** C4
Long Eaton NG10 ......**236** C4
Melbourne DE73 ....**252** A4
Mosborough S20 ....**59** B3
Pilsley S45 ....**132** B1
Somercotes DE55 ......**170** B4
South Normanton DE55 **160** A3
Stafford ST16 ....**269** A4

South St continued
Swanwick DE55 ....**169** C4
Woodville DE11 ....**257** A1
South St N S43 ....**77** B2
South Terr ST4 ....**269** B1
South Uxbridge St
DE14 ....**254** A4
South View Bamford S33 ..**40** A2
Derby DE23 ....**218** B1
Mayfield DE6 ....**184** B3
Mosborough S20 ....**60** A4
New Mills SK22 ....**33** A4
Pilsley DE45 ....**91** B1
Whitwell S80 ....**81** C3
South View Rd SK13 ....**17** C4
South View Wlk ST14 ..**196** C2
South Walls ST16 .....**269** B4
South Wingfield Prim Sch
DE55 ....**157** C2
South Wolf St ST4 ....**269** B2
Southampton La NG3 ..**268** C2
Southard's La S80 ....**62** C3
Southbourne Ct S17 .....**55** B3
Southbrook Cl SK13 ......**9** C2
Southcote Dr S18 ....**56** B1
Southcroft Alfreton DE55 **159** A2
Buxton SK17 ....**85** A4
Derby DE23 ....**231** B2
Southdown Ave S40 .....**95** B3
Southdown Cl DE24 ....**231** B1
Southend S42 ....**115** C1
Southey St NG7 ....**268** A2
Southfield Ave S41 .....**115** B3
Southfield Cl S80 ....**81** C3
Southfield Dr
Dronfield S18 ....**76** B1
South Normanton DE55 **160** B3
Southfield Ind Site S80 ..**82** A2
Southfield La S80 ....**82** A2
Southfield Mount S18 ...**76** B1
Southfields Clowne S43 ..**80** C2
Long Eaton NG10 ......**236** C4
Southfields Ave NG16 ..**160** B2
Southgate S21 ....**59** C2
Southgate Cl DE3 ......**217** B2
Southgate Cres S43 .....**80** C3
Southgate Ct S21 ....**59** C2
Southgate Inf Sch DE24 **232** C4
Southgate Way S43 ......**78** A2
Southmead Way DE3 ...**218** A2
Southmoor Cl S43 ......**96** C2
Southwark Cl DE22 ....**218** A3
Southwell Rd NG1 .....**268** B1
Southwell Rise NG16 ..**195** A4
Southwood Ave S18 .....**76** A4
Southwood Dr S43 ......**80** C2
Southwood St DE24 ....**232** C4
Southworth Rd DE73 ..**252** C1
Sovereign Gr NG10 ....**236** A4
Sovereign Dr DE14 ....**254** A4
Sovereign Way
Derby DE21 ....**206** B2
Heanor DE75 ....**181** B1
Sowbrook Brook DE7 ..**208** B3
Sowbrook La DE7 ......**208** C2
Sowter Rd DE1 ....**267** B4
Sowters Row S40 ......**266** B3
Spa Brook Cl S12 ....**44** C2
Spa Brook Dr S12 ......**44** C3
Spa Croft DE55 ....**147** C3
Spa La
Chesterfield, Hady S41 ..**266** C2
Chesterfield, Stonegravels
S41 ....**266** C3
Derby DE1 ....**267** A1
Spa View Ave S12 ......**44** C2
Spa View Dr S12 ....**44** C2
Spa View Pl S12 ....**44** C2
Spa View Rd S12 ....**44** C2
Spa View Terr S12 .....**44** C2
Spa View Way S12 .....**44** C2
Spalden Ave DE6 ......**173** B2
Spalding Rd NG3 ......**268** C2
Spang La NG17 ....**148** C2
Spaniel Row **4** NG1 ..**268** B1
Spanker La DE56 ......**168** A1
Spanker Terr DE56 ....**168** B1
Spark St ST4 ....**269** B2
Spark Terr ST4 ....**269** B2
Sparrow Cl Derby DE24 **231** B2
Ilkeston DE7 ....**209** A3
Sparrowbusk Cl S43 ....**80** C3
Speedwell SK13 ....**9** C4
Speedwell Cl
Derby DE21 ....**206** B2
Glossop SK13 ....**9** C4
Woodville DE11 ....**256** C2
Speedwell Ind Est S43 ..**78** C1
Speedwell Inf Sch S43 ..**78** C1
Speedwell La NG16 ....**195** C3
Speetley View S43 ......**80** A4
Speighthill Cres S42 ...**114** C2
Spenbeck Dr DE22 ....**205** A3
Spencer Ave
Belper DE56 ....**179** A2
Derby DE24 ....**232** B2
Sandiacre NG10 ....**223** A3
Staveley S43 ....**79** A1
Spencer Cl
Ashbourne DE6 ....**185** B4
Burton u T DE13 ....**240** B1
Spencer Cres NG9 .....**223** C4
Spencer Dr DE55 ......**170** B4
Spencer Gr SK17 ......**85** A3
Spencer Rd Belper DE56 **179** A2
Buxton SK17 ....**85** A3
Chapel-en-le-F SK23 ....**46** C3
Sheffield S2 ....**43** A4

Spencer Rd continued
Stoke-on-T ST4 ....**269** C2
Spencer St Bolsover S44 **117** C4
Chesterfield S40 ....**266** B4
Derby DE24 ....**233** A4
Mansfield NG18 ....**268** B3
Stanley DE7 ....**193** A1
Spend La DE6 ....**161** C1
Sperry Cl NG16 ....**171** C3
Spilsbury Cl DE65 .....**242** B3
Spindletree Dr DE21 ...**205** C1
Spinkhill Ave S13 ....**44** B4
Spinkhill Dr S13 ....**44** B4
Spinkhill Immaculate
Conception Prim Sch
S21 ....**60** B1
Spinkhill La S21 ....**60** A1
Spinkhill Rd
Killamarsh S21 ....**60** C2
Sheffield S13 ....**44** B4
Spinnerbottom SK22 ....**24** C1
Spinners Way DE56 ....**179** B3
Spinney Cl Derby DE22 **205** A1
Glossop SK13 ....**10** B1
Mansfield Woodhouse
NG19 ....**136** C3
Spinney Cres NG9 .....**223** C2
Spinney Dr S13 ....**44** B1
Spinney Hill DE73 .....**252** A4
Spinney Lodge
Repton DE65 ....**242** B1
Tutbury DE13 ....**238** C3
Spinney Rd
Branston DE14 ....**253** C4
Derby DE22 ....**218** C2
Ilkeston DE7 ....**208** C3
Long Eaton NG10 ......**223** B1
Spinney Rise NG9 .....**223** C2
Spinney The
Belper DE56 ....**179** A3
Borrowash DE72 ....**221** B1
Brailsford DE6 ....**201** C4
Castle Donington DE74 .**247** A2
Ilkeston DE7 ....**208** C3
Ripley DE5 ....**169** B2
Shirebrook NG20 ......**119** B2
Stanton-by-D NG10 ....**222** C4
Spinneybrook Way DE3 **217** B3
Spire Hollin SK13 ......**10** B1
Spital Gdns S41 ....**96** B1
Spital La S41 ....**96** B1
Spitalbrook S41 ....**96** B1
Spitewinter La S18,S42 ..**93** B1
Spittal DE74 ....**247** A2
Spittal Gn S44 ....**118** A4
Spittal Hill DE74 ......**247** A2
Spode St ST4 ....**269** B1
Spondon Sta DE21 ....**220** B2
Spooner Dr S21 ....**60** B3
Spooner La S32 ....**72** B3
Spoonley Wood Ct
DE23 ....**230** C4
Sporton Cl DE55 ......**160** A4
Sporton La DE55 ......**160** A4
Spotswood Cl S14 ......**43** C2
Spotswood Dr S14 .....**43** C3
Spotswood Mount S14 ..**43** C3
Spotswood Pl S14 ......**43** B2
Spotswood Rd S14 .....**43** B2
Spout La Spout DE56 ..**166** B2
Tansley DE4 ....**144** A2
Spridgeon Cl **18** NG10 **223** A1
Spring Bank Buxton SK17 **67** B2
Great Longstone DE45 ...**90** A2
Spring Bank Rd
Chesterfield S40 ....**266** A3
New Mills SK22 ....**33** B4
Spring Cl Belper DE56 ..**178** C3
Bradwell S33 ....**51** A4
Breaston DE72 ....**235** B4
Renishaw S21 ....**79** B4
Swadlincote DE11 ......**256** A1
Wirksworth DE4 ....**154** C1
Spring Cl Dell S14 ......**43** C2
Spring Cl Mount S14 ....**43** C2
Spring Cl View S14 .....**43** C2
Spring Cottage Rd
DE12 ....**262** B3
Spring Ct Mews SK14 ....**9** B3
Spring Dale Gdns NG9 .**209** D2
Spring Garden Terr
DE7 ....**194** C1
Spring Gardens Ctr The
SK17 ....**85** A4
Spring Gdns Buxton SK17 **85** B4
Derby DE21 ....**219** C4
Glossop SK13 ....**10** A3
Spring Hill
Kimberley NG16 ....**195** C3
Mansfield Woodhouse
NG19 ....**136** A2
Whitwell S80 ....**82** A3
Spring Hollow DE56 ...**190** B4
Spring House Cl S42 ....**94** C3
Spring La Elmton S80 ...**99** C3
Heanor DE75 ....**181** C1
Sheffield S2 ....**43** C4
Sheffield S2 ....**43** C4
Shireoaks S80,S81 ......**63** C3
Spring Mount SK22 ....**33** B4
Spring Pl S40 ....**266** B3
Spring Rd DE55 ....**170** C3
Spring Rise SK13 ....**16** C4
Spring St
Broadbottom SK14 .....**16** A4
Derby DE22 ....**218** C2
Glossop SK13 ....**10** A1

Spring St continued
Hollingworth SK14 ......**9** B3
Swadlincote DE11 ......**262** A4
Whitwell S80 ....**82** A3
Spring The NG10 ......**236** B3
Spring Vale Rd
Brimington S43 ....**96** C4
Hayfield SK22 ....**25** C1
Spring Water Dr SK13 ...**9** C2
Spring Wood Cl S41 ....**95** B4
Springbank S13 ....**9** C3
Springdale Ct DE3 .....**217** C1
Springfarm Rd DE15 ..**248** A3
Springfield
Broadbottom SK13 .....**16** B3
Derby DE23 ....**218** A1
Springfield Ave
Ashbourne DE6 ....**185** B4
Chesterfield S40 ....**95** B2
Heanor DE75 ....**181** A3
Long Eaton NG10 ......**236** C4
Sandiacre NG10 ....**223** A2
Shirebrook NG20 ......**119** C3
Springfield Cl Clowne S43 **80** C2
Crich DE4 ....**157** A1
Eckington S21 ....**59** B2
Glossop SK13 ....**9** C2
Swadlincote DE11 ......**256** A3
Springfield Cres
Bolsover S44 ....**98** C2
Somercotes DE55 ......**170** B4
Springfield Ct NG9 ....**209** C1
Springfield Dr DE56 ...**190** B2
Springfield Gdn DE7 ..**194** C1
Springfield Jun Sch
DE11 ....**256** B3
Springfield Prim Sch
Derby DE21 ....**220** B3
Stoke-on-T ST4 ....**269** A1
Springfield Rd Barlow S18 **75** B2
Bradwell S33 ....**51** A4
Derby, Chellaston DE73 **232** C1
Derby, Cherrytree Hill
DE21 ....**220** A3
Etwall DE65 ....**229** A2
Holmewood S42 ....**132** C4
Repton DE65 ....**242** B1
Swadlincote DE11 ......**256** A3
Springfield Rise DE4 ..**143** B3
Springfield Terr
Burton u T DE15 ....**248** A1
Hayfield SK22 ....**25** B1
Ripley DE5 ....**169** C1
Springfield View DE5 ..**169** B1
Springfields Rd ST4 ...**269** A1
Springhill DE11 ....**257** A4
Springhill Way DE5 ...**181** A4
Springmeadow SK13 ....**16** B4
Springvale Cl S45 .....**131** B1
Springvale Rd S45 ....**131** B1
Springwell Com Sch S43 **97** B4
Springwell Hill S21 .....**77** C3
Springwell Park Dr S43 ..**97** B4
Springwell St NG17 ...**148** C1
Springwood SK13 ......**16** C4
Springwood Ct S43 .....**77** B2
Springwood Dr DE21 ..**206** A1
Springwood Farm Rd
DE11 ....**256** A4
Springwood Gdns DE56 **179** A4
Springwood Rd S8 ......**43** A3
Springwood St S42 ....**116** A2
Sprinkswoods La DE6 ..**184** C3
Spruce Ave NG16 .....**171** B3
Spruce Rise S21 ....**60** B3
Spurr St S2 ....**43** A4
Square The Bretby DE15 **249** A2
Buxton SK17 ....**85** A4
Clay Cross S45 ....**131** C2
Derby DE3 ....**217** B1
Derby, Darley Abbey DE22 **205** A1
Eyam S32 ....**71** C3
Marchington ST14 .....**224** C1
Monyash DE45 ....**107** A1
Squires La S33 ....**38** B2
Squires View S43 ......**269** C2
Squires Way DE23 ....**231** A4
Squirrel La DE12 ......**252** C2
Squirrel Wlk DE12 ....**262** A2
Stable Cl DE4 ....**156** A3
Stable La DE6 ....**149** A1
Stable Mews DE11 ....**256** C1
Stables Ct S44 ....**99** B1
Stables St DE22 ....**218** B3
Stacey Rd NG19 ......**135** B1
Staden Bsns Pk SK17 ..**85** C3
Staden La SK17 ....**85** C2
Stadium Ind Pk NG10 .**236** C4
Stadium View DE24 ...**219** C2
Stadmoor Ct DE73 ....**232** C1
Staffa Dr DE55 ....**147** C3
Stafford Cl
1 Dronfield S18 ....**56** B1
6 Glossop SK13 ......**17** C4
Smalley DE7 ....**192** C3
Stafford Coll ST16 ....**269** A4
Stafford Coll (The Oval
Annexe) ST17 ....**269** B3
Stafford Cres DE4 ....**165** C4
Stafford St Derby DE1 .**267** A3
Long Eaton NG10 ......**236** C4
Mansfield NG19 ....**268** A4
New Mills SK22 ....**24** C1
Stafford ST16 ....**269** A4
Stafford Sta ST16 ....**269** A4
Staffordshire General Hospl
ST16 ....**269** C4

Staffordshire Univ Stoke
(Campus) ST4 ....**269** C2
Staines Cl DE3 ....**217** B1
Stainforth St NG19 ....**136** B1
Stainsbro' La DE4,DE6 .**165** A3
Stainsby Ave
Heanor DE75 ....**193** C4
Horsley Woodhouse DE7 **192** C3
Stainsby Cl S42 ....**132** C4
Stainsby Gr NG17 .....**148** C3
Stainsby Mill ★ S44 ..**133** B4
Staithes Wlk DE21 ....**205** B1
Staker La S3 ....**230** B3
Stalybridge Ctry Pk ★
SK15 ....**4** A2
Stalybridge Rd SK14 ....**9** A2
Stamer St ST4 ....**269** B1
Stamford Cl NG10 ....**236** C2
Stamford St
Awsworth NG16 ....**195** B2
Derby DE24 ....**232** B3
Heanor DE75 ....**181** C1
3 Ilkeston DE7 ....**194** C1
Stamps Cl DE15 ......**248** B2
Stanage Gn DE23 .....**217** C1
Stanage Rise S12 ....**44** C3
Stanage Way S40 ......**94** C3
Stancliffe Ave DE4 ...**127** B2
Stancliffe Hall Sch DE4 **127** A3
Stancliffe View DE4 ..**127** A2
Stand Park Ind Est S41 ..**96** A4
Stand Rd S41 ....**95** C4
Standard Hill **7** NG1 .**268** C4
Standard St ST4 ......**269** C1
Standing Butts Cl DE12 **259** B4
Standlow La DE6 ......**163** B1
Stanedge Rd DE45 ....**109** A3
Stanford Rd S18 ....**56** B1
Stanford St NG1 ......**268** B1
Stanford Way S40 ....**114** A4
Stanhope Glade DE15 ..**256** A4
Stanhope Rd Derby DE3 **217** C2
Sheffield S12 ....**44** B3
Swadlincote DE11 ......**256** A2
Stanhope St
Bramley-Vale S44 .....**117** C1
Burton u T DE15 ....**248** A2
Derby DE23 ....**219** A1
Ilkeston DE7 ....**209** A3
Long Eaton NG10 ......**236** B4
Nottingham NG1 ......**268** B1
Stanton-by-D NG10 ....**222** C4
Stanier Way Derby DE21 **220** A2
Renishaw S21 ....**79** A4
Staniforth Ave S21 .....**59** A2
Stanleigh Gdns DE12 ..**265** C4
Stanleigh Rd DE12 ....**262** A2
Stanley Ave Ripley DE5 **169** C1
Staveley S43 ....**97** A4
Stanley Cl Derby DE22 **218** C4
Ilkeston DE7 ....**208** C4
Netherseal DE12 ......**264** C4
Woodville DE11 ....**256** C2
Stanley Comm Prim Sch
DE7 ....**193** A1
Stanley Cres ST14 ....**210** A1
Stanley Ct NG16 ......**182** C1
Stanley Dr NG9 ....**209** C1
Stanley Hall La SK12 ...**32** B3
Stanley La S44,NG17 ..**133** B1
Stanley Matthews Sports Ctr
ST4 ....**269** C2
Stanley Pl NG1 ....**268** B4
Stanley Rd
Derby, Allenton DE24 ..**232** C4
Derby, Cherrytree Hill
DE21 ....**220** A3
Sheffield S8 ....**43** A3
Stoke-on-T ST4 ....**269** A2
Stanley St Chesterfield S41 **96** B1
Derby DE22 ....**218** B3
Ilkeston DE7 ....**208** C4
Killamarsh S21 ....**60** B4
Long Eaton NG10 ......**236** C4
Somercotes DE55 ......**170** B4
Swadlincote DE11 ......**256** B2
Stanshope La DE6 .....**149** B1
Stanstead Rd DE3 ....**217** B2
Stanton Ave DE56 ....**179** A4
Stanton Cl DE4 ....**127** A2
Stanton Cres S12 ....**44** B2
Stanton Gate DE7 ....**209** B1
Stanton Hill DE73 ....**251** B3
Stanton La DE6 ....**172** A1
Stanton Moor View
DE4 ....**142** C4
Stanton Pl
Mansfield NG18 ....**268** B4
New Houghton NG19 ..**134** C4
Stanton Prim Sch DE15 **255** A3
Stanton Rd
Ashbourne DE6 ....**185** B4
Burton u T DE15 ....**254** C4
Ilkeston DE7 ....**208** C4
Sandiacre NG10 ....**223** A4
Stanton St Derby DE23 **218** C1
New Houghton NG19 ..**134** C4
Stanton Vale Specl Sch
DE7 ....**208** C3
Stanton View DE45 ...**109** B3
Stanton-in-Peak CE Prim
Sch DE4 ....**126** B3
Stantonhall La DE4 ..**126** B4
Stanwood Dr S40 .....**114** A4
Stanyforth St SK13 ....**10** A2
Stapleford La NG9 ....**223** C2
Stapleford Rd
Stapleford NG9 ....**209** B2

Sta – Swi 307

Stapleford Rd *continued*
Trowell NG9 209 B2
Stapleton Rd DE7 194 C2
Starch La NG10 223 B4
Starcross Ct DE3 217 B2
Starkholmes Rd DE4 143 B1
Starkie Ave DE74 246 C2
Start La SK23 45 A4
Starth La DE4 144 A2
Starthe Bank DE75 181 C1
Statham Ave S42 131 B4
Statham St DE22 218 C4
Station App
Ambergate DE56 167 C2
Buxton SK17 85 A4
Derby DE1 267 C2
Duffield DE56 190 C2
Hathersage S32 53 A4
Station Back La S41 266 C3
Station Cl DE73 232 C1
Station Cotts NG19 135 A3
Station Ct 10 DE7 194 C1
Station Dr DE12 262 C2
Station Hill NG19 136 A2
Station La
Apperknowle S18 58 A1
Chesterfield S41,S43 77 B1
Codnor DE5 181 A3
Thornhill S33 40 A1
Walton-on-T DE12 253 B1
Station La Ind Est S41 77 A1
Station New Rd S42 131 B4
Station Rd
Ashbourne DE6 173 A1
Awsworth NG16 195 B3
Bakewell DE45 109 C3
Bamford S33 40 A1
Barrow Hill S43 78 A2
Bolsover S44 98 C1
Borrowash DE72 221 A1
Breadsall DE21 205 C2
Brimington S43 96 B4
Brimington, Hollingwood S43 78 A1
Burton u T DE13 253 A1
Buxton SK17 85 B4
Castle Donington DE74 247 B3
Castle Doninmton DE74 247 A3
Chapel-en-le-F SK23 47 A3
Chapel-en-le-Frith SK23 34 A1
Chesterfield S41 266 C3
Chesterfield, Old Whittington S41 77 A1
Chinley SK23 34 B1
Clowne S43 80 C2
Darley Dale DE4 127 B1
Denby DE5 180 A2
Derby DE3 217 B2
Derby, Chellaston DE73 232 C1
Derby, Spondon DE21 220 B2
Dove Holes SK17 47 C1
Draycott DE72 235 A4
Duffield DE56 190 C2
Eckington S21 59 C2
Glossop SK13 10 A3
Great Longstone DE45 89 C2
Hathersage S32 53 A4
Hatton DE65 239 B4
Hayfield SK22 25 B1
Hayfield, Birch Vale SK22 25 A1
Hope S33 39 A2
Ilkeston DE7 194 C1
Ironville NG16 170 C2
Killamarsh S21 60 A3
Killamarsh, Spinkhill S21 60 B1
Kimberley NG16 195 C3
Langley Mill NG16 182 A1
Little Eaton DE21 205 B4
Long Eaton NG10 236 C4
Mansfield NG18 268 B3
Marple SK6 23 A4
Marple, Strines SK6,SK22 23 B1
Melbourne DE73 252 B4
Mosborough S20 59 C4
New Mills SK22 33 A4
North Wingfield S42 131 C3
Pilsley S45 132 B1
Rolleston DE13 240 B2
Sandiacre NG10 223 B3
Scarcliffe S44 118 C3
Selston NG16 160 C1
Shirebrook NG20 119 C3
Stafford ST16 269 A3
Stanley DE7 207 B3
Stoke-on-T ST4 269 B2
Stonebroom DE55 147 A3
Tibshelf DE55 147 C3
West Hallam DE7 207 B4
Whaley Bridge SK23 33 B2
Whitwell S80 82 A3
Woodville DE11 256 C1
Station St
Ashbourne DE6 173 A1
Cossall DE7 195 A1
Glossop SK13 10 B1
Long Eaton NG10 236 C4
Mansfield NG18 268 B3
Mansfield Woodhouse NG19 136 A2
Nottingham NG2 268 B1
Swadlincote DE11 261 C4
Station View NG20 119 C2
Station Wlk 6 SK17 85 B4
Staunton Ave DE23 231 C3
Staunton Cl DE74 247 A2
Staunton Harold Resr Visitor Ctr* DE73 251 C3
Staunton La DE73 251 A1
Staveley Cl DE24 232 C2
Staveley Jun Sch S43 78 C1
Staveley La
Barrow Hill S21,S43 78 A3
Eckington S21 59 C1
Staveley Rd
Chesterfield S43 77 C2
Long Duckmanton S44 97 C2
Poolsbrook S43 98 A4
Sheffield S8 43 A4
Staverton Dr DE3 217 B2
Stead Mews S21 59 B2
Stead St S21 59 B2
Steam Mill La DE5 181 A4
Steel La S44 99 A1
Steel St ST4 269 A2
Steel's La S44 118 A3
Steele Ave S43 97 A3
Steele Ct SK17 85 A4
Steep La S42 114 A2
Steep Turnpike DE4 143 B3
Steeping Cl S43 96 C4
Steeple Cl DE21 205 C1
Steeple End Fold SK22 25 B1
Steeple Grange DE4 154 C2
Steeple Grange Light Rly* DE4 154 C2
Steeplegate S40 266 B3
Steetley La S80 63 C2
Stella St NG18 268 B3
Stenson Ave DE23 231 C3
Stenson Ct DE5 169 C1
Stenson Fields Prim Com Sch DE24 231 B1
Stenson Rd DE23, DE24 231 B2
Stenton Rd S8 56 C4
Stephens Rd DE14 254 A4
Stephenson Pl
Chesterfield S40 266 B3
Clay Cross S45 131 A2
Stephenson Rd S43 78 C1
Stephensons Way DE21 220 A2
Stepping Cl DE22 218 C3
Stepping La DE22 218 C3
Sterland St S40 95 C2
Sterling Cl DE5 180 A1
Sterndale Cl SK17 69 C2
Sterndale La SK17 69 C2
Sterndale Moor SK17 105 C3
Sterndale Rd NG10 236 A3
Sterry Cl S43 80 C1
Steven Cl NG9 223 C2
Stevenage Cl DE24 232 C3
Stevens La DE72 235 B4
Stevens Rd NG10 223 A3
Stevenson Ave DE72 235 A4
Stevenson Jun Sch NG9 223 C4
Stevenson Pl DE23 231 A4
Stevenson Rd DE6 224 A4
Steward Gate S33 40 A3
Stewart Cl
Burton u T DE14 254 A3
Derby DE21 220 C3
Stewart St Fenton ST4 269 C1
Somercotes DE55 170 B3
Stile Croft DE4 154 B3
Stiles Cl SK13 9 C3
Stiles Rd DE24 233 A4
Stillman Cl S41 115 B4
Stinting La
Mansfield NG19 136 C1
Shirebrook NG20 119 B1
Stirland St DE5 170 A1
Stirling Ave NG19 268 A3
Stirling Cl DE21 219 B4
Stirling Gr NG16 195 C4
Stock La ST14 224 B1
Stockbrook Rd DE22 218 B2
Stockbrook St DE22 218 C2
Stockdove Cl DE24 231 B2
Stocker Ave DE24 233 B4
Stockley La S44 117 C1
Stockley View S44 118 A4
Stockport Rd SK6 23 A3
Stocks Brow SK13 10 A4
Stocks Green Ct S17 55 B2
Stocks Green Dr S17 55 B2
Stocks Rd NG16 195 C4
Stocks The SK13 10 A4
Stockton Dr SK23 34 C1
Stockwell Ct
Chesterfield S40 114 C4
Mansfield NG18 268 B3
Stockwell Gate NG18 268 B3
Stoddard Dr DE75 181 C1
Stoke Bsns Pk ST4 269 B1
Stoke Cl DE56 179 C3
Stoke Rd ST4 269 B2
Stoke Recn Ctr ST4 269 B1
Stoke-on-Trent Sta ST4 269 B2
Stollard St S45 131 B2
Stone Bench Way SK17 85 C4
Stone Bridge Rd NG3 268 C2
Stone Cl Derby DE21 220 C3
Dronfield S18 57 B2
Stone Cotts DE6 184 C4
Stone Cross Ct NG18 268 B4
Stone Cross La NG18 268 B4
Stone Furlong Rd DE45 91 C3
Stone Hill Rd DE23 218 C1
Stone La S43 77 B2
Stone Mdws NG10 236 C3
Stone Rd S18 57 B2
Stone Row
Chesterfield S40 95 B1
Marple SK6 23 A3
Stone St Mosborough S20 59 B4
Stoke-on-T ST4 269 B2
Stonebench La SK17 106 B2
Stonebridge Ct Ind Est 2 NG3 268 C2
Stonebridge La NG20 120 C2
Stonebroom La DE55 147 A3
Stonebroom Prim Sch DE55 147 A2
Stonebroom Wlk DE24 232 C2
Stonechat Cl DE3 218 A2
Stonecliff Terr SK17 85 B4
Stonecroft Rd S17 55 C3
Stonedale Cl S20 59 B4
Stonegravels Croft S20 59 C3
Stonegravels La S41 96 A3
Stonegravels Way S20 59 C3
Stoneheads SK23 45 B4
Stoneheads Rise SK23 45 B4
Stonehill DE74 247 A1
Stoneholes Dr S45 131 C1
Stoneleigh St 20 NG7 268 A2
Stoneleigh Way DE55 169 C4
Stoneley Cl S12 44 A1
Stoneley Cres S12 44 A1
Stoneley Dell S12 44 A1
Stoneley Dr S12 44 A1
Stonelow Cres S18 57 B1
Stonelow Gn S18 57 A1
Stonelow Jun Sch S18 57 B1
Stonelow Rd S18 57 B1
Stonepit La DE6 164 A2
Stoneridge SK13 9 C3
Stonerows La S45 145 B3
Stones The S33 38 A1
Stonesby Cl DE21 205 C1
Stonesdale Ct 1 DE24 233 B3
Stonewell La SK17 137 B3
Stoney Cl DE45 109 B2
Stoney Cross DE21 220 C2
Stoney Flatts Cres DE21 220 A4
Stoney Gate Rd DE21 220 B2
Stoney Hill DE4 155 A1
Stoney La Ashover S42 130 B2
Brinsley NG16 182 B3
Derby DE21 220 C3
Hognaston DE6 164 A1
Selston NG16 171 C4
Stretton en le F DE12 265 C1
Trowell NG9 209 A3
Stoney Middleton CE Prim Sch S32 71 C2
Stoney St NG1 268 B1
Stoney Way DE4 143 B2
Stoney Wood Dr DE4 156 B1
Stoneycroft La S42 114 A3
Stoneydale Cl DE11 255 C3
Stoneyfield Bank DE56 179 A3
Stoneyland Dr SK22 33 A4
Stony La DE56 191 B3
Stony Ridge Rd S17 54 B3
Stonyhurst Ct DE24 232 C2
Stoodley Pike Gdns DE22 204 B1
Stoops Cl S40 95 B3
Stoppard Cl DE7 194 B1
Storer La DE4 166 A2
Stores Rd DE21 219 A4
Storforth La S41 115 A4
Storforth Lane Terr S41 115 B4
Storforth Lane Trad Est S40 115 A4
Stormont Cl DE55 160 A2
Stornoway Cl 11 DE24 231 B2
Storrs Rd S40 95 A1
Stort Sq NG19 136 B1
Storth Bank SK13 16 C4
Storth La DE55 160 A2
Storth Meadow Rd SK13 16 C4
Storthfield Way DE55 160 A2
Stour Cl Brimington S43 96 C4
Hilton DE65 240 C4
Stourdale Cl NG10 236 A3
Stourport Dr DE73 233 A2
Stow Ct NG19 136 C2
Stowmarket Dr DE21 219 B4
Stradbroke Ave S13 44 B4
Stradbroke Cl S13 44 C4
Stradbroke Cres S13 44 C4
Stradbroke Dr S13 44 C4
Stradbroke Pl S13 44 C4
Stradbroke Prim Sch S13 44 B4
Stradbroke Rd S13 44 C4
Stradbroke Rise S40 114 B4
Stradbroke Way S13 44 C4
Stradbroke Wlk S13 44 B4
Strand DE1 267 B3
Strand Arc DE1 267 B3
Stranfaer Cl DE55 170 A4
Stranraer Cl NG19 136 B3
Stratford Cl DE65 242 B1
Stratford Rd DE21 205 B1
Stratford St DE7 194 C2
Strathallan Cl DE4 127 B2
Strathaven Ct DE21 220 C3
Strathglen Cl NG16 195 C4
Strathmore Ave DE24 233 A3
Stratton Rd S44 99 A1
Straw La DE55 146 B4
Strawberry Bank NG17 148 C2
Strawberry La
Blackfordby DE11 257 A1
Rosliston DE12 260 B3
Strawberry Lee La S17 55 A3
Streatham Rd DE22 218 A3
Street Farm Cl S26 61 C3
Street Forest Walks The* SK17 64 C2
Street La DE5 180 A3
Street Lane Prim Sch DE5 180 A3
Street The SK10,SK17 64 B3
Streetfield Cres S20 59 B3
Streetfield La S20 59 C3
Streetfields S20 59 C3
Strelley Ave DE5 180 B4
Stretfield Rd S33 39 A1
Strettea La DE55 146 B1
Stretton Brook Sch DE13 240 B1
Stretton Cl DE3 217 B1
Stretton Handley CE Prim Sch DE55 145 B4
Stretton Rd
Clay Cross S45 131 B1
Shirland DE55 146 B4
Stonebroom DE55 146 C3
Stretton View DE12 265 C3
Striding Edge Cl 8 NG10 223 A1
Strines Rd Marple SK6 23 A2
New Mills SK6 32 B4
Strines Sta SK6 23 B1
Stroma Cl DE24 231 C2
Strutt St Belper DE56 178 C2
Derby DE23 219 A1
Stuart Cl S41 96 B3
Stuart St DE1 267 B4
Stubben Edge La S45 130 B1
Stubbin Wood Sch NG20 119 C3
Stubbing Rd S40 114 C4
Stubbins La SK23 34 B1
Stubbins Wood NG20 119 C3
Stubbins Wood La NG20 119 C3
Stubley Cl S18 56 C2
Stubley Croft S18 56 C1
Stubley Dr S18 56 C1
Stubley Hollow S18 56 C2
Stubley La S18 56 C1
Stubley Pl S18 56 C1
Stubwood Hollow ST14 196 B3
Stubwood La ST14 196 B2
Studbrook Cl DE74 246 C2
Studfarm Cl DE73 252 C1
Studland Cl NG19 136 B3
Sturge Croft S2 43 A3
Sturges La DE72 233 C2
Sturgess St ST4 269 B1
Sturston Rd DE6 173 B1
Stychfields ST17 269 B3
Sudbury Ave
Ilkeston DE7 209 A4
Sandiacre NG10 223 A3
Sudbury Cl
Chesterfield S40 95 A3
Derby DE1 218 C3
Sudbury Ct NG10 235 C2
Sudbury Dr NG17 148 C1
Sudbury Hall & Mus of Childhood* DE6 225 B3
Sudbury Mews NG16 182 C1
Sudbury Pk DE6 225 B4
Sudbury Prim Sch DE6 225 C2
Sudbury St DE1 218 C3
Sudhall Cl S41 95 B4
Suff La NG16 160 B2
Suffolk Ave DE21 219 C4
Suffolk Rd DE15 254 B4
Sugworth Rd S6 31 C3
Sulleys Field DE22 204 B4
Summer Cross SK17 69 A2
Summer Dr DE4 165 C4
Summer La Totley S17 55 B2
Wirksworth DE4 165 C4
Summer Leys La NG2 268 B1
Summer St ST4 269 B1
Summer Wood Ct DE23 231 B4
Summerbottom SK14 16 A4
Summerbrook Ct DE22 218 C2
Summerfield Cres S43 96 C4
Summerfield Rd
Chesterfield S40 266 A1
Dronfield S18 57 A2
Summerfields Way DE7 194 B2
Summerfields Way S DE7 194 B1
Summerley Lower Rd S18 57 C1
Summerley Rd S18 57 C1
Summerskill Gn S43 97 B4
Summerwood La S18 56 C2
Summerwood Pl 8 S18 56 C1
Summit Dr NG20 119 C2
Sumner St SK13 17 B4
Sumners Pl SK13 10 A1
Sun La DE4 156 C1
Sun St Derby DE22 267 A2
Woodville DE11 256 C1
Sunart Cl DE24 231 C1
Sunbourne Ct 4 NG7 268 A2
Sundew Cl DE21 220 C2
Sundown Ave DE23 231 B3
Sundown Cl SK22 33 A4
Sundown Pl S13 44 C4
Sundown Rd S13 44 C4
Sunflower Cl NG20 119 B2
Suningdale Cl DE13 240 B1
Sunlaws St SK13 17 A4
Sunlea Cres NG9 223 C3
Sunningdale Ave
Derby DE21 220 B3
Heanor DE75 193 C4
Sunningdale Cl S40 114 C4
Sunningdale Dr
Glossop SK13 10 C1
Ilkeston DE7 208 A3
Sunningdale Rise S40 114 B4
Sunninghill Cl DE7 207 B4
Sunny Bank
Great Longstone DE45 90 A2
Mayfield DE6 184 B4
Tibshelf DE55 147 C3
Sunny Bank Gdns DE56 178 C1
Sunny Bank La SK17 69 B2
Sunny Banks 3 SK13 17 A4
Sunny Brook Cl S43 80 C2
Sunny Gr DE21 220 A3
Sunny Hill DE56 190 C4
Sunny Springs S41 266 B4
Sunnybank DE4 110 C1
Sunnyfield SK17 85 C1
Sunnyhill Ave DE23 231 C3
Sunnyhill Inf Sch DE23 231 C4
Sunnyside
Swadlincote DE11 255 C4
Whitwell S80 82 A3
Sunnyside Rd ST14 210 A1
Sunnyvale Ave S17 55 B2
Sunnyvale Rd S17 55 B2
Surbiton Cl DE22 218 A3
Surbiton Ct DE7 207 B4
Surgery La DE4 157 A1
Surrey Dr NG19 268 A4
Surrey St Derby DE22 218 B3
Glossop SK13 10 B1
Sussex Cir DE21 219 C4
Sussex Cl NG16 195 A4
Sussex Rd DE15 254 C3
Sussex Way NG10 223 A3
Sutherland Rd DE23 219 A1
Sutherland St ST4 269 C1
Sutton Ave DE73 232 C2
Sutton Cl DE22 218 B3
Sutton Cres S43 97 B4
Sutton Ct NG16 182 C1
Sutton Dr Derby DE24 232 C2
Stoke-on-T ST4 269 A1
Sutton Hall Rd S44 117 C4
Sutton La Etwall DE65 229 A3
Hatton DE65 227 C2
Hilton DE65 228 B2
Long Duckmanton S44 116 C4
Sutton Rd
Church Broughton DE65 227 B4
Mansfield NG18 268 A3
Sutton in A NG17 148 C2
Sutton Road Fst Sch NG18 268 A3
Sutton Scarsdale Hall* S44 117 A3
Sutton View S44 118 A4
Sutton Way SK13 10 A3
Suttons La SK6 23 A3
Swaddale Ave S41 96 A3
Swaddale Cl S41 96 A3
Swadlincote La DE11 255 C1
Swadlincote Rd DE11 256 C2
Swadlincote Ski Ctr DE11 256 B2
Swaines Mdw DE4 165 B4
Swalebank Cl S40 115 A4
Swaledale Ct 2 DE24 233 B3
Swallow Cl DE3 218 A2
Swallow House Cres SK22 25 B2
Swallow House La SK22 25 B2
Swallow Rd DE11 256 C2
Swallowdale Rd DE24 231 B2
Swan Cl ST16 269 A3
Swan La NG19 136 A2
Swan St ST4 269 B2
Swanbourne Cl S41 96 B1
Swanmore Rd DE23 231 A4
Swann Yd NG17 148 C2
Swanson Ave NG17 148 C2
Swanwick Ave NG20 119 C2
Swanwick Gdns DE21 206 A1
Swanwick Hall Sch DE55 169 C4
Swanwick Hill DE55 169 C4
Swanwick Junc Sta DE5 170 A3
Swanwick Prim Sch DE55 169 B3
Swanwick Rd DE55 170 A4
Swanwick St S41 77 A1
Swarkestone Dr DE23 231 B3
Swarkestone Rd
Barrow u T DE73 244 A3
Derby DE73 244 C4
Swathwick Cl S42 114 C2
Swathwick La S42 114 B2
Swayfield Cl DE3 217 B2
Sweetbriar Cl DE24 233 A3
Swift Cl Derby DE3 218 A2
Woodville DE11 256 C2
Swift Ct NG16 182 C1
Swinburne St Derby DE1 267 B1
Nottingham NG3 268 C2
Swinderby Dr DE21 206 A1
Swindon Cl NG16 195 B4
Swiney Way NG9 223 C1
Swinger La S45 129 B4
Swinney Bank DE56 179 A3
Swinney La DE56 179 A3
Swinscoe Hill DE6 172 A1
Swinscoe Way S40 95 A3

Swinson Cl ST14 ....197 A2
Swithland Cl S41 ....115 B4
Sycamore Ave
  Chesterfield S40 ....95 C1
  Creswell S80 ....81 C1
  Derby DE22 ....204 B2
  Dronfield S18 ....57 A2
  Findern DE65 ....230 C1
  Glapwell S44 ....134 A4
  Ripley DE5 ....180 B4
  Swadlincote DE11 ....256 A4
Sycamore Cl Bolsover S44 99 B1
  Burton u T DE15 ....254 C3
  Buxton SK17 ....66 A1
  Etwall DE65 ....229 B2
  Linton DE12 ....261 B3
  Mapperley DE7 ....193 C2
  New Mills SK22 ....24 C1
  Pinxton NG16 ....160 B2
  Selston NG16 ....171 B4
  Shirland DE55 ....146 B2
Sycamore Cotts DE6 ....151 B1
Sycamore Cres NG10 ....223 A4
Sycamore Ct Derby DE21 220 C3
  Willington DE65 ....242 A3
Sycamore Dr Calow S44 ....96 C2
  Ilkeston DE7 ....209 A4
  Killamarsh S21 ....60 B3
Sycamore Jun & Inf Schs
  NG3 ....268 B2
Sycamore La
  Barlborough S43 ....80 A3
  Brimington S43 ....78 A1
Sycamore Rd
  Awsworth NG16 ....195 B3
  Brimington S43 ....78 A1
  Burton u T DE15 ....254 C3
  Castle Donington DE74 ....247 A3
  Chapel-en-le-F SK23 ....47 A2
  Hayfield SK22 ....24 C1
  Long Eaton NG10 ....236 B3
  Mansfield Woodhouse
    NG19 ....136 B3
  Matlock DE4 ....143 A3
  Mayfield DE6 ....184 B4
Sycamore St
  Market Warsop NG20 ....120 C3
  Mosborough S20 ....59 B4
Sycamore Terr SK22 ....25 B2
Sycamores The
  Eastwood NG16 ....182 C1
  Glossop SK13 ....9 C2
  South Normanton DE55 ....160 A3
Syda La S42 ....93 C1
Syday La S21 ....79 C4
Sydenham Rd DE22 ....218 A4
Sydney Cl NG19 ....136 B3
Sydney St Chesterfield S40 95 C2
  Draycott DE72 ....235 A4
Sydnope Hill DE4 ....128 A3
Syerscote La B79 ....263 A1
Sylvan Cl S41 ....266 C1
Sylvan Cliff SK17 ....85 B4
Sylvan Dr S42 ....131 A3
Sylvan Pk SK17 ....85 B4
Sylvester St NG18 ....268 A3
Sylvia Rd S18 ....76 B3
Sywell Cl DE55 ....169 C4

T

Tabley Gdns SK6 ....23 A2
Taddington & Priestcliffe CE
  Sch SK17 ....87 C2
Taddington Cl 3 DE21 ....219 C4
Taddington Rd
  Chesterfield S40 ....95 A3
  Derby DE21 ....205 C1
Taft Ave NG10 ....223 A3
Tagg La DE45 ....107 A1
Taggs Knoll S33 ....40 A2
Taghole La DE6 ....188 C1
Tailby Dr DE65 ....242 A3
Talbot Cres S41 ....115 B4
Talbot Dr NG9 ....209 B1
Talbot Pl DE12 ....265 C4
Talbot Rd Glossop SK13 ....10 B1
  Stafford ST17 ....269 B3
Talbot St
  Chesterfield S41 ....115 B4
  Derby DE1 ....218 C3
  Glossop SK13 ....10 B1
  Nottingham NG1 ....268 A2
  Pinxton NG16 ....160 B1
  Swadlincote DE11 ....256 A1
Talgarth Cl DE21 ....206 B1
Tamar Ave DE22 ....204 B2
Tamworth Rd
  Castle Donington DE72,
    NG10 ....235 C1
  Long Eaton NG10 ....236 B3
  Stretton en le F DE12 ....265 C1
Tamworth St DE12 ....190 C2
Tamworth Terr DE56 ....190 C2
Tanner's La DE65 ....242 B2
Tansley Ave DE7 ....193 A1
Tansley Dr S40 ....95 A3
Tansley House Gdns
  DE4 ....144 A2
Tansley Prim Sch DE4 ....144 A2
Tansley Rd S42 ....131 C4
Tansley Rise DE21 ....205 C1
Tansley Way S43 ....97 B3
Tants Mdw DE56 ....191 C3

Tantum Ave DE75 ....181 B2
Tanyard Cl DE74 ....247 A2
Tap La S40 ....266 A3
Taplow Cl DE3 ....217 B1
Tapton La S41 ....266 C3
Tapton Lock Hill S41 ....96 A3
Tapton Terr S41 ....266 C4
Tapton Vale S41 ....96 B3
Tapton View Rd S41 ....95 C3
Tapton Way S44 ....96 C2
Tarina St DE7 ....233 A1
Tarnside Fold 6 SK13 ....17 A4
Tarporley Gr ST4 ....269 A1
Tasman Cl DE3 ....217 C2
Tatenhill La
  Branston DE14 ....253 B4
  Branston, Tatenhill DE13 ....253 A4
Tatham's La DE7 ....194 C1
Tattersall Wlk NG19 ....136 C2
Tattershall Dr NG7 ....268 A1
Tattle Hill DE7 ....207 C1
Taunton St DE24 ....233 B4
Tavern Rd SK13 ....9 C2
Taverners Cres DE23 ....231 B4
Tavistock Ave DE5 ....169 B1
Tavistock Cl DE24 ....231 B2
Tavistock Sq DE55 ....159 A3
Tawney Croft DE4 ....144 A2
Tawny Way DE23 ....231 B4
Taxal & Fernilee CE Prim Sch
  SK23 ....45 B3
Taxal Ctr The SK23 ....45 B3
Taxal Moor Rd SK23 ....45 B2
Tay Cl Derby DE24 ....231 B1
  Dronfield S18 ....56 B1
Tay Wlk DE22 ....204 C2
Taylor Cres
  Chesterfield S41 ....96 B1
  Stapleford NG9 ....223 C4
Taylor La DE75 ....181 B2
Taylor St Derby DE24 ....219 C1
  Hollingworth SK14 ....9 B2
  Ilkeston DE7 ....194 C1
Taylor's La Spout DE4 ....166 A2
  Trusley DE6 ....215 C3
Taylors La ST14 ....196 B2
Tayside Cl DE24 ....231 B2
Teal Cl NG20 ....119 B2
Tealby Wlk NG19 ....136 C2
Tean Cl DE15 ....248 A1
Teasel Dr DE11 ....256 C2
Tedder Ave SK17 ....85 B2
Tedgness Rd S32 ....53 C1
Tedworth Ave DE24 ....231 B1
Teesdale Rd
  Long Eaton NG10 ....236 A3
  Mosborough S12 ....58 C4
Telegraph St ST17 ....269 B3
Telford Cl DE3 ....217 C1
Telford Cres S43 ....78 C1
Telford Rd SK6 ....23 A2
Telmah Cl DE13 ....240 B1
Temperance Hill DE55 ....145 C4
Temperance Sq SK14 ....9 A2
Temperance St SK14 ....16 A4
Templar Cl DE24 ....231 B2
Temple Ave SK13 ....10 B3
Temple Ct SK17 ....85 A3
Temple Normanton Bsns Pk
  S41 ....116 A2
Temple Normanton Prim Sch
  S42 ....116 B2
Temple Rd Buxton SK17 ....85 A3
  Fenton ST4 ....269 C1
  Glossop SK13 ....10 B3
Temple View SK17 ....85 B4
Temple Wlk DE4 ....143 A1
Templebell Cl DE23 ....231 A1
Ten Foot Cl SK13 ....10 A1
Tenant St DE1 ....267 B3
Tenby Dr DE21 ....206 B1
Tennessee Rd DE21 ....220 A4
Tennis Dr NG7 ....268 A1
Tennyson Ave
  Chesterfield S40 ....266 A3
  Mansfield Woodhouse
    NG19 ....136 B1
  Swadlincote DE11 ....256 B3
Tennyson Rd S81 ....81 B1
Tennyson Sq NG16 ....195 B2
Tennyson St Derby DE24 ....232 B4
  Holmewood S42 ....116 B1
  Ilkeston DE7 ....194 C2
  7 Mansfield NG18 ....268 B4
  Nottingham NG7 ....268 A2
  Shirland DE55 ....146 B3
Tennyson Way S42 ....115 C2
Tenter Cl NG10 ....236 B3
Tenter La Heage DE56 ....168 B1
  Mansfield NG18 ....268 B3
Tenterbanks ST16 ....269 A4
Tern Ave DE11 ....256 C2
Terr The DE21 ....219 C4
Terrace La NG19 ....134 C3
Terrace Rd Buxton SK17 ....85 A4
  Chapel-en-le-F SK23 ....47 A3
  Mansfield NG18 ....268 C4
  Tideswell SK17 ....69 B2
Terrace The DE4 ....143 C4
Terret Gr SK17 ....84 B3
Terrey Rd S17 ....55 C3
Terry Pl DE24 ....232 C4
Tetford Wlk NG19 ....136 C2
Teversal Ave NG17 ....135 A2
Tevery Cl NG9 ....223 C4
Teviot Pl DE21 ....206 A1

Tewkesbury Ave NG19 ....136 B2
Tewkesbury Cres DE21 ....219 B4
Tewkesbury Dr NG16 ....195 C4
Tewkesbury Rd NG10 ....236 C3
Thackeray Rd DE55 ....146 C2
Thackeray St DE24 ....232 A3
Thame Ct 5 S43 ....96 C4
Thames Cl DE22 ....217 C3
Thanet Dr DE24 ....233 A3
Thanet St S45 ....131 B2
Thatch Cl DE22 ....204 C1
Thatchers La DE4 ....144 A2
Theatre La S41 ....266 C3
Theatre Sq NG1 ....268 B2
Theatre Yd S40 ....266 B3
Thickley Cl NG20 ....119 C2
Thirlmere Ave DE22 ....204 C2
Thirlmere Cl 9 NG10 ....223 A1
Thirlmere Dr S18 ....57 A1
Thirlmere Rd
  Chesterfield S41 ....95 B4
  Long Eaton NG10 ....223 A1
Thirlwell Rd S8 ....43 A3
Thirsk Pl DE24 ....232 B4
Thirteen Row S44 ....118 A3
Thistle Cl NG16 ....195 A4
Thistle Green Cl DE75 ....182 A1
Thistle Rd DE7 ....209 A2
Thistledown Cl DE22 ....205 A1
Thistley Hough S17 ....44 A4
Thistley Hough High Sch
  ST4 ....269 A1
Thomas Cl NG3 ....268 B2
Thomas Cook Cl DE73 ....252 A4
Thomas St Compstall SK6 ....15 A1
  Glossop SK13 ....10 C1
Thompson Cl S41 ....96 A4
Thompson St
  Chesterfield S41 ....96 A4
  Langley Mill NG16 ....182 A2
Thomson Dr DE5 ....181 A4
Thoresby Ave
  Nottingham NG2 ....268 C1
  Shirebrook NG20 ....119 C2
Thoresby Cl Derby DE21 ....206 A1
  Ripley DE5 ....169 C1
Thoresby Cres DE72 ....234 C4
Thoresby Pl S43 ....97 B3
Thoresby Rd
  Long Eaton NG10 ....236 B3
  Mansfield Woodhouse
    NG19 ....136 A2
Thoresby St NG18 ....268 B4
Thoresey Ave S43 ....81 A2
Thorn Ave NG19 ....135 C1
Thorn Cl Buxton SK17 ....85 C4
  Derby DE22 ....204 B2
Thorn Dr NG16 ....195 A4
Thorn St Derby DE23 ....218 C1
  Woodville DE11 ....256 C1
Thorn Street Mews
  DE11 ....256 C1
Thorn Tree Gdns NG16 ....182 C2
Thorn Tree La DE11,
  DE15 ....255 C4
Thornborough Cl S2 ....43 B4
Thornborough Pl S2 ....43 B4
Thornborough Rd S2 ....43 B4
Thornbridge Ave S12 ....44 B2
Thornbridge Cl S12 ....44 B2
Thornbridge Cres
  Chesterfield S40 ....115 A3
  Sheffield S12 ....44 C2
Thornbridge Dr S12 ....44 B2
Thornbridge Education Ctr
  DE45 ....89 C1
Thornbridge Gr S12 ....44 B2
Thornbridge Gr S12 ....44 C2
Thornbridge La S12 ....44 B2
Thornbridge Pl S12 ....44 B2
Thornbridge Rise S12 ....44 B2
Thornbridge Way S12 ....44 C2
Thornbrook Cl SK23 ....47 B3
Thornbrook Rd SK23 ....47 B3
Thornburrow Dr ST4 ....269 A2
Thorncliffe Ave DE4 ....127 A3
Thorncliffe Rd SK13 ....9 C2
Thorndene Cl S41 ....96 A3
Thorndike Ave DE24 ....233 A4
Thorndon Cl DE3 ....230 B4
Thorndon Way S40 ....114 B4
Thorne Cl S42 ....94 C2
Thornecliffewood SK14 ....9 B1
Thornell Cl SK23 ....47 B3
Thornescroft Gdns
  DE14 ....254 A4
Thorness Cl DE24 ....233 B3
Thornewill Dr DE13 ....240 C1
Thorneywood Rd NG10 ....236 C4
Thornfield Ave S40 ....95 A1
Thornfield Ct S41 ....96 A3
Thornhill La S33 ....39 C2
Thornhill Rd
  Derby, California DE22 ....218 B2
  Derby, Littleover DE23 ....218 B1
Thornsett S32 ....24 C1
Thornsett Ave SK17 ....85 C4
Thornsett Cl SK17 ....85 C4
Thornsett Gdns S17 ....55 C4
Thornsett Prim Sch SK22 ....24 C2
Thornsett Trad Est SK22 ....24 C1
Thornton Pl S18 ....56 B1
Thornton Rd ST4 ....269 C2
Thorntree Cl DE72 ....222 C1
Thorntree Cotts DE4 ....154 C1
Thorntree Ct S40 ....114 C4
Thorntree La DE1 ....267 B3
Thornway SK6 ....32 A4
Thornwood Ct SK17 ....85 A4

Thoroton St 7 NG7 ....268 A2
Thorp Cl S2 ....43 A4
Thorpe Ave Dronfield S18 ....57 B2
  Whitwell S80 ....81 C3
Thorpe Cl
  Burton u T DE15 ....248 B1
  10 Chesterfield S41 ....95 C4
  Stapleford NG9 ....223 B4
Thorpe Croft DE55 ....156 A3
Thorpe Dr DE3 ....217 C2
Thorpe Downs Rd DE11 ....256 A1
Thorpe House Ave S8 ....43 A2
Thorpe House Rd S8 ....43 A2
Thorpe House Rise S8 ....43 A2
Thorpe La S80,S81 ....63 B3
Thorpe Leys NG10 ....236 B3
Thorpe Rd
  Eastwood NG16 ....182 C2
  Harthill S26 ....62 A4
Thorpe St Glossop SK13 ....10 C1
  Ilkeston DE7 ....194 C2
Thorpe Way DE56 ....179 A3
Thorpe's Rd
  Heanor DE75 ....181 B1
  Shipley DE75 ....193 B4
Thorpelands Way NG19 ....136 C1
Thorpelands Dr DE22 ....204 C1
Thorpleigh Rd S43 ....79 A1
Three Gates DE56 ....178 C1
Thrift Rd DE14 ....254 A4
Throstle Nest Way DE4 ....201 C4
Thrumpton Ave NG10 ....237 A4
Thrumpton Hall* NG11 237 A2
Thrushton Cl DE65 ....230 B1
Thruxton Cl DE24 ....233 B3
Thunderpit La S32 ....71 A2
Thurcaton Way DE55 ....148 A2
Thurcroft Cl DE22 ....218 B1
Thurgarton St DE6 ....173 B1
Thurgarton St NG2 ....268 C1
Thurland St 16 NG1 ....268 B1
Thurlby Ct NG19 ....136 C2
Thurlow Ct DE21 ....206 A1
Thurman St DE7 ....209 A3
Thurrows Way DE73 ....233 A1
Thurstan Ave S8 ....56 C4
Thurston Ave DE55 ....170 B4
Thurstone Furlong
  DE73 ....232 C1
Thurvaston Rd DE6 ....197 C1
Thyme Cl DE23 ....231 B2
Tiber Cl 12 DE24 ....233 B3
Tibshelf Inf Sch DE55 ....148 A4
Tibshelf Rd
  Blackwell DE55 ....147 B1
  Holmewood S42 ....132 C4
Tibshelf Sch DE55 ....148 A4
Tickham Ave DE24 ....231 B1
Ticknall La
  Denby DE5,DE56 ....180 A1
  Hartshorne DE11 ....257 A4
Ticknall Wlk DE23 ....231 C3
Tideswell Bank 14 SK13 ....9 C1
Tideswell Ct S43 ....97 B4
Tideswell Ct NG18 ....268 C4
Tideswell Gn DE11 ....255 C3
Tideswell La S32 ....71 A3
Tideswell Rd DE21 ....205 C1
Tiger Yd DE6 ....173 A1
Tilbury Pl DE24 ....233 A3
Tilford Gdns NG9 ....223 C3
Tiller Ct DE23 ....231 A3
Tillotson Cl S8 ....43 A3
Tillotson Rise S8 ....43 A3
Tilson Ave ST4 ....269 A2
Tilton Gr DE7 ....208 B3
Timber La S45 ....132 C3
Timberfields Rd ST16 ....269 A4
Timbersbrook Cl DE21 ....206 A1
Timsbury Ct DE21 ....205 C1
Tinderbox La DE65 ....229 C3
Tinker Croft DE7 ....208 C4
Tinkerley La DE6 ....165 B1
Tinkley La S42 ....130 B2
Tinsell Brook DE65 ....228 C1
Tinsley Rd DE756,NG16 ....182 B3
Tintagel Cl
  Burton u T DE13 ....240 C1
  5 Derby DE23 ....219 A1
Tintwistle CE Prim Sch
  Glossop SK13 ....10 A4
  Glossop SK13 ....9 C3
Tip Tree Cl NG16 ....195 C4
Tipnall Rd DE74 ....247 A2
Tipper's La DE65 ....227 A4
Tippett Ct NG3 ....268 C2
Tipping St ST16 ....269 B4
Tiree Cl Derby DE24 ....231 C2
  Stapleford NG9 ....209 B1
Tibshelf DE55 ....147 C3
Tissington Cl S40 ....95 A3
Tissington Dr DE21 ....206 A2
Tissington Terr 15 SK13 ....9 B1
Titchfield Ave NG19 ....136 B2
Titchfield St Creswell S80 ....81 C1
  Mansfield NG19 ....268 B4
  Whitwell S80 ....81 C2
Tithe Barn Cl SK17 ....69 B2
Tithe Barn Rd ST16 ....269 C4
Tithebarn La DE6 ....215 B3
Titterton St ST4 ....269 C1
Tiverton Cl DE3 ....217 B2
Tivoli Gdns DE1 ....218 C4
Tixall Rd DE14 ....269 C4
Toadmoor La DE56 ....167 C2
Tobermory Way DE24 ....231 B2

Todbrook Cl SK23 ....45 B3
Todd St SK13 ....17 B4
Tolkien Way ST4 ....269 B2
Toll Bar Ave S12 ....43 C3
Toll Bar Cl S12 ....43 C3
Toll Bar Dr S12 ....43 C3
Toll Bar Rd S12 ....43 C3
Toll House Mead S20 ....59 B4
Tollbridge Rd S43 ....79 A1
Tollemache Cl SK14 ....9 A3
Tollemache Rd SK14 ....9 A3
Tollgate Cotts DE6 ....184 C4
Tollhouse Hill 39 NG1 ....268 A2
Tom Brads Croft S43 ....45 C4
Tom La
  Chapel-en-le-F SK23 ....46 B3
  Staveley S44 ....97 C3
Tomlinson Ct DE24 ....232 C4
Tomlinson Ind Est DE21 ....205 B1
Tomlinsons Cotts DE21 ....205 B1
Tomwood Rise SK13 ....16 B3
Tonbridge Dr DE24 ....233 A3
Tonge La DE73 ....252 C2
Tongue La SK17 ....85 C2
Tongue La Ind Est SK17 ....85 C4
Tontine Rd S40 ....266 B2
Toothill La NG18 ....268 C4
Toothill Rd NG18 ....268 B4
Top Farm Ct DE56 ....191 C4
Top Fingle Cl S43 ....96 C4
Top Hag La DE56 ....168 A3
Top La Crich DE4 ....156 B1
  Mansfield NG19 ....135 A2
  Old Brampton S42 ....93 C2
  Shottle DE56 ....166 B1
Top Lons DE6 ....176 A4
Top Manor Cl DE72 ....221 B3
Top Mdw DE11 ....256 A4
Top Rd Calow S44 ....97 A2
  Wingerworth S42 ....114 B1
Top Row NG16 ....171 A3
Tophill La DE4 ....153 B4
Tophole Rd S33 ....50 C2
Topley Gdns DE21 ....205 C1
Toppham Dr S8 ....56 C3
Toppham Rd S8 ....56 C3
Toppham Way S8 ....56 C3
Topshill La DE6 ....165 A1
Tor Ave DE55 ....170 B3
Tor Cl DE4 ....143 A1
Tor Rise DE4 ....143 A2
Tor View Rise DE4 ....155 A3
Torksey Wlk NG19 ....136 C2
Torr St SK17 ....85 A4
Torr Top St SK22 ....33 B4
Torrance Cl DE14 ....254 A4
Torrani Way S42 ....131 C4
Torridon Cl DE24 ....231 C2
Torrs Valley SK22 ....33 B4
Torrvale Rd SK22 ....33 A4
Tors The DE4 ....156 C1
Torside Way SK13 ....10 A3
Torwood Dr S8 ....56 C4
Totley All Saints CE Prim Sch
  S17 ....55 B2
Totley Brook Cl S17 ....55 B3
Totley Brook Croft S17 ....55 B3
Totley Brook Glen S17 ....55 B3
Totley Brook Gr S17 ....55 B3
Totley Brook Rd S17 ....55 C3
Totley Brook Way S17 ....55 B3
Totley Cl SK13 ....9 B1
Totley Gdns SK13 ....9 B1
Totley Gn 24 SK13 ....9 B1
Totley Grange Cl S17 ....55 B2
Totley Grange Dr S17 ....55 B2
Totley Grange Rd S17 ....55 B2
Totley Hall Croft S17 ....55 B2
Totley Hall Dr S17 ....55 B2
Totley Hall La S17 ....55 B2
Totley Hall Mead S17 ....55 B2
Totley La S17 ....56 A3
Totley Laurels 25 SK13 ....9 B1
Totley Mews SK13 ....9 B1
Totley Mnt S43 ....96 B4
Totley Pl SK13 ....9 B1
Totley Prim Sch S17 ....55 B2
Toton Banks Road Inf Sch
  NG9 ....223 C1
Toton Bispham Drive Jun Sch
  NG9 ....223 C1
Toton La NG9 ....223 C3
Toulmin Dr DE11 ....256 A2
Tower Bsns Pk S45 ....131 B2
Tower Cl Sheffield S2 ....43 B4
  Somercotes DE55 ....170 B4
Tower Cres S44 ....118 A4
Tower Dr S2 ....43 B4
Tower Rd
  Burton u T DE15 ....248 A1
  Hartshorne DE11 ....257 A3
Tower St DE24 ....232 B4
Tower View Prim Sch
  DE15 ....248 B2
Towers La S32 ....40 C1
Towle Cl DE72 ....221 B1
Towle St NG10 ....236 A2
Towles Pastures DE74 ....247 A2
Town End
  Apperknowle S18 ....58 A4
  Bolsover S44 ....99 A1
  Buxton SK17 ....66 C1
  Shirland DE55 ....146 B2
Town End Jun Sch
  DE55 ....147 C3
Town End Rd DE72 ....235 A4
Town Fold SK6 ....23 A4
Town Gate S33 ....51 A4

Town Hall Yd DE6 . . . . . .173 B1
Town Head DE6 . . . . .173 B1
Town La Bradwell S33 . . . . . .51 A4
  Broadbottom SK13 . . . . . .16 B3
  Newton DE55 . . . . .148 A2
Town St Brassington DE4 .153 A1
  Duffield DE56 . . . . .190 C2
  Holbrook DE56 . . . . .191 B3
  Marple SK6 . . . . .23 A4
  Pinxton NG16 . . . . .160 C2
  Sandiacre NG10 . . . . . . .223 A3
Town The DE21 . . . . .205 B4
Town View NG16 . . . . . . .195 C4
Townfield La S33 . . . . .39 C1
Townhead S32 . . . . .71 B3
Townhead La S33 . . . . .39 C2
Townhead Rd S17 . . . . .55 B4
Townscliffe La SK6 . . . . . . .23 B3
Townsend Gr DE73 . . . . . .233 A1
Townside Cl NG10 . . . . . .236 A2
Towson Ave NG16 . . . . . .182 B1
Trade St ST4 . . . . .269 B2
Trafalgar Rd
  Long Eaton NG10 . . . . . . .236 B3
  Stoke-on-T ST4 . . . . .269 A2
Trafalgar Sq NG10 . . . . . .236 C4
Trafalgar Terr NG10 . . . . .236 C4
Traffic St Derby DE1 . . . . .267 C2
  Nottingham NG2 . . . . . . .268 B1
Traffic Terr
  Barrow Hill S43 . . . . .78 A2
  Chesterfield S41 . . . . . . .115 A4
Trafford Way DE23 . . . . . .231 B4
Tranmere Ave S45 . . . . . .131 C4
Transvaal Terr S44 . . . . . .118 A3
Travers Ct ST4 . . . . .269 C1
Travers Rd NG10 . . . . . . .223 A3
Travey Rd S2 . . . . .44 A4
Treak Cliff Cavern★ S33 .37 C2
Tredcroft St S17 . . . . .17 A4
Tredegar Dr DE21 . . . . . . .206 A1
Treeneuk Cl S40 . . . . .95 A2
Trefoil Ct DE23 . . . . .231 A4
Tregaron Cl DE21 . . . . . . .206 B1
Tregony Way DE24 . . . . . .231 B2
Trelawney Rd S45 . . . . . . .131 B2
Trenchard Ave ST16 . . . . .269 C4
Trenchard Dr SK17 . . . . . . .85 B2
Trent Ave Buxton SK17 . . . .85 A3
  Willington DE65 . . . . .242 B3
Trent Bridge Ct DE23 . . . .231 B4
Trent Cl Derby DE65 . . . . .231 B1
  Willington DE65 . . . . .242 B3
Trent Coll NG10 . . . . .236 B4
Trent Dr DE23 . . . . .231 B3
Trent Gr Alfreton DE55 . . .159 A1
  Dronfield S18 . . . . .57 A2
Trent Ho NG10 . . . . .236 A4
Trent La
  Castle Donington DE74 . .247 A3
  Long Eaton NG10 . . . . . . .236 C3
  Melbourne DE73 . . . . . . .245 B1
  Newton Solney DE15 . . . .248 C4
  Nottingham NG2 . . . . . . .268 C4
  Weston-on-T DE72 . . . . . .245 C2
Trent Lane Ind Est
  DE74 . . . . .247 A3
Trent Rd Ilkeston DE7 . . . .208 B2
  Nottingham NG2 . . . . . . .268 C1
Trent Rise DE21 . . . . .220 C2
Trent St Derby DE24 . . . . .233 A4
  Long Eaton NG10 . . . . . . .236 C4
  Nottingham NG1,NG2 . . .268 C1
Trent Valley Rd ST4 . . . . .269 A1
Trent Wlk NG19 . . . . .136 C4
Trenton Dr NG10 . . . . . . .237 A4
Trenton Gn DE21 . . . . . . .220 A3
Trenton Green Dr DE21 .220 A3
Tresillian Cl DE22 . . . . . . .204 C1
Tressall Cl DE7 . . . . .209 A4
Trevelyn Cl DE15 . . . . . . .248 B1
Treveris Cl DE21 . . . . .220 C2
Trevone Ave NG9 . . . . . . .223 C3
Trevose Cl S40 . . . . .114 B4
Triangle The DE7 . . . . . . .209 A3
Trickett Cl S33 . . . . .38 C1
Trinity Cl
  Chesterfield S40 . . . . . . .266 A4
  Ilkeston DE7 . . . . .194 C2
Trinity Ct S41 . . . . .266 A4
Trinity Gr DE11 . . . . .256 A2
Trinity Mews S41 . . . . . . .266 A4
Trinity Sq NG1 . . . . .268 B2
Trinity St DE1 . . . . .267 C2
Trinity View NG10 . . . . . .236 C4
Trinity Wlk 27 NG1 . . . . .268 B2
Trinkey La S32 . . . . .72 A2
Tristram Gr DE13 . . . . . . .240 C1
Troon Cl Burton u T DE13 .240 B1
  Chesterfield S40 . . . . . . .114 B4
  Derby DE23 . . . . .231 A4
  Kimberley NG16 . . . . .195 C4
Trot La SK17 . . . . .70 A3
Trough La NG16 . . . . .195 C4
Troughbrook Hill S43 . . . . .97 A4
Troughbrook Rd S43 . . . . .78 A1
Troutbeck Gr DE23 . . . . . .231 A4
Trowbridge Cl DE21 . . . . .205 C1
Trowell Ave DE7 . . . . .209 A4
Trowell CE Prim Sch
  NG9 . . . . .209 B2
Trowell Gr
  Long Eaton NG10 . . . . . . .223 B1
  Stapleford NG9 . . . . .209 B2
Trowell Park Dr NG9 . . . .209 B1
Trowell Rd NG9 . . . . .209 B1
Trowels La DE22 . . . . .218 B2
Trueman St DE7 . . . . .194 C2

Truman Cl NG3 . . . . .268 B2
Truman St Cossall DE7 . . .195 A1
  Kimberley NG16 . . . . .195 B4
Truro Cl DE11 . . . . .256 C3
Truro Cres DE21 . . . . .219 C4
Trusley Gdns DE23 . . . . . .231 B3
Trusley Wlk NG19 . . . . . .136 C2
Trustley Cl DE14 . . . . .254 A4
Tuckers La NG18,NG19 . .268 A4
Tudor Cl
  Long Eaton NG10 . . . . . . .223 C1
  Stoke-on-T ST4 . . . . .269 B1
Tudor Ct Derby DE22 . . . .204 C2
  10 Nottingham NG7 . . . .268 A2
Tudor Falls DE75 . . . . .181 C2
Tudor Field Cl DE73 . . . . .233 A1
Tudor Pl DE7 . . . . .208 B3
Tudor Rd DE21 . . . . .220 A3
Tudor Rise B79 . . . . .263 C1
Tudor St 10 S43 . . . . .78 C1
Tudor Way DE11 . . . . .256 A3
Tudorhouse Cl DE11 . . . . .256 A4
Tuffolds Cl S2 . . . . .44 A4
Tufnell Gdns DE22 . . . . . .218 A4
Tulip Rd NG16 . . . . .195 A3
Tulla Cl DE24 . . . . .231 C1
Tullis Cl ST16 . . . . .269 A3
Tumbling Hill DE56 . . . . . .168 C1
Tunicliffe Cl DE11 . . . . . . .256 B2
Tunnel Rd NG7 . . . . .268 A1
Tunnel Yd DE6 . . . . .173 A1
Tunstall Gn S40 . . . . .95 B1
Tunstall Way S40 . . . . .95 B1
Tuphall Cl DE73 . . . . .233 A1
Tupton Hall Sch S42 . . . . .131 B4
Tupton Moor Cl S42 . . . . .115 B1
Tupton Prim Sch S42 . . . .115 B1
Tupton Way S42 . . . . .116 B1
Turf Lea Rd SK6 . . . . .23 A1
Turlowfields La DE6 . . . . .175 B4
Turnberry Cl
  Chesterfield S40 . . . . . . .114 B4
  Ilkeston DE7 . . . . .194 B1
Turnbull Cl S40 . . . . .266 A1
Turnbury Cl DE14 . . . . . . .254 A4
Turncliffe Cl SK17 . . . . . . .84 C3
Turnditch CE Prim Sch
  DE56 . . . . .177 A1
Turner Ave NG16 . . . . . . .182 A2
Turner Cl 4 Dronfield S18 . 56 C1
  Stapleford NG9 . . . . .223 C3
Turner Dr
  Eastwood NG16 . . . . .195 A4
  Staveley S43 . . . . .97 A4
Turner Rd NG10 . . . . .236 B2
Turner St DE24 . . . . .232 C3
Turners La DE55 . . . . .170 A4
Turnlee Cl S13 . . . . .17 B4
Turnlee Dr SK13 . . . . .17 B4
Turnlee Rd SK13 . . . . .17 B4
Turnley Rd DE55 . . . . .160 B3
Turnoaks Bsns Pk S40 . . .115 A3
Turnoaks La S40 . . . . .115 A4
Turnpike Cl
  Alfreton DE55 . . . . .158 C1
  Matlock DE4 . . . . .143 B3
Turton Cl DE6 . . . . .182 A2
Tutbury & Hatton Sta
  DE65 . . . . .239 B4
Tutbury Castle★ DE13 . . .239 A4
Tutbury Rd DE13 . . . . .240 A1
Tuxford Cl DE21 . . . . .206 A1
Tuxford Wlk NG3 . . . . . . .268 C2
Twayblade DE14 . . . . .254 A4
Twentylands DE13 . . . . . .240 B2
Twentywell Dr S17 . . . . . . .56 A3
Twentywell La S17 . . . . . . .56 A3
Twentywell Rd S17 . . . . . . .56 A3
Twentywell Rise S17 . . . . . .56 A3
Twentywell View S17 . . . . .56 A3
Twickenham Cl S20 . . . . . .59 C3
Twickenham Cres S20 . . . .59 C3
Twickenham Ct S20 . . . . . .59 C3
Twickenham Dr DE22 . . . .218 A3
Twickenham Glade S20 . . .59 C3
Twickenham Glen S20 . . . .59 C3
Twickenham Gr S20 . . . . . .59 C3
Twiggs Row DE4 . . . . .143 A4
Twin Oaks Cl DE23 . . . . . .230 C4
Twisses Bank DE6 . . . . . . .213 A1
Twyford Cl Heanor DE75 .193 B4
  Swadlincote DE11 . . . . . .255 C1
  West Hallam DE7 . . . . . . .207 B4
  Willington DE65 . . . . .242 B3
Twyford Rd
  Barrow u T DE73 . . . . . . .244 B3
  Long Eaton NG10 . . . . . . .235 C2
  Willington DE65 . . . . .242 A3
Twyford St DE23 . . . . .267 B1
Tylney Rd S40 . . . . .114 A4
Tyndale Chase DE24 . . . . .231 B1
Tyndall Pl ST4 . . . . .269 A2
Tynedale Cl NG10 . . . . . . .236 A3
Tynefield Ct DE65 . . . . . . .229 A1
Tynefield Mews DE65 . . . .229 A1
Tynsel Parkes CE Fst Sch
  ST14 . . . . .210 A1
Tythe The DE11 . . . . .256 A4

U

Uffa Magna DE3 . . . . .217 B1
Uldale Gr DE11 . . . . .256 B1
Ulley Cres S13 . . . . .44 A4
Ulley Rd S13 . . . . .44 A4
Ullswater Ave S20 . . . . . . .59 C3
Ullswater Cl Derby DE21 .205 B1

Ullswater Cl continued
  Dronfield S18 . . . . .56 C1
  Mosborough S20 . . . . .59 C3
Ullswater Dr Derby DE21 220 C3
  Dronfield S18 . . . . .56 C1
Ullswater Pk 6 S18 . . . . .56 C1
Ullswater Pl S18 . . . . .56 C1
Ulster Terr ST4 . . . . .269 B1
Ulverston Rd S41 . . . . .95 B4
Underhall DE4 . . . . .127 B1
Underhill Ave DE23 . . . . . .231 C4
Underhill Cl DE23 . . . . . . .231 C3
Underhill Rd S43 . . . . .80 C1
Underpass The DE1 . . . . . .267 C4
Undertown La DE6 . . . . . .197 B3
Underwood CE Prim Sch
  NG16 . . . . .171 C1
Underwood Terr DE4 . . . .143 A4
Union Rd Ilkeston DE7 . . .208 C3
  New Mills SK22 . . . . .33 B4
  Nottingham NG1,NG3 . . .268 B2
  Swadlincote DE11 . . . . . .256 A3
Union St Ashbourne DE6 .173 A1
  Glossop SK13 . . . . .17 B4
  Harthill S26 . . . . .61 C3
  Long Eaton NG10 . . . . . . .236 C4
  Mansfield NG18 . . . . .268 B4
  Melbourne DE73 . . . . . . .252 A4
  South Normanton DE55 . .159 C3
Unity Cl DE11 . . . . .256 A2
Unity Prim Sch NG7 . . . . .268 A2
Unity Wlk S13 . . . . .17 B4
Univ of Derby DE22 . . . . .204 B1
Univ of Derby (Buxton
  Campus) SK17 . . . . .85 B2
Univ of Derby (Sch of Art &
  Design) DE1 . . . . .267 B2
Univ of Sheffield SK17 . .104 C4
Univ of Sheffield (Research
  Labs) SK17 . . . . .85 A1
Unstone Dronfield By-Pass
  S18 . . . . .75 C4
Unstone Hill S18 . . . . .76 B4
Unstone Jun Sch S18 . . . . .76 C4
Unstone Rd S41 . . . . .76 C2
Unstone St Mary's Inf Sch
  S18 . . . . .76 B4
Unthank La S18 . . . . .74 B2
Upchurch Cl DE3 . . . . . . .217 B2
Upland Rise S40 . . . . .95 B1
Uplands Ave DE23 . . . . . .231 B3
Uplands Gdns DE23 . . . . .218 C1
Uplands Rd
  Compstall SK14 . . . . .15 A3
  Glossop SK13 . . . . .17 B4
Upper Albert Rd S8 . . . . . .43 A3
Upper Bainbridge St
  DE23 . . . . .219 A2
Upper Barn Cl DE75 . . . . .181 C1
Upper Blindlow La
  SK17 . . . . .106 A3
Upper Boundary Rd
  DE22 . . . . .218 C2
Upper College St 37
  NG1 . . . . .268 A2
Upper Cres ST4 . . . . .269 A2
Upper Croft
  Clay Cross S45 . . . . .131 C2
  Tupton S42 . . . . .131 B4
Upper Croft Cl S43 . . . . . . .96 C4
Upper Dale Rd DE23 . . . . .218 C1
Upper Dunstead Rd
  NG16 . . . . .182 A2
Upper Eldon St NG2 . . . . .268 C1
Upper End Rd SK17 . . . . . .67 B2
Upper Furlong ST4 . . . . . .269 C1
Upper Greenhill Gdns
  DE4 . . . . .143 B3
Upper Hall Cl DE56 . . . . . .191 B3
Upper Hollow DE23 . . . . .218 B1
Upper King St S43 . . . . . . .77 C1
Upper La DE6 . . . . .175 C2
Upper Mantle Cl S45 . . . .131 C2
Upper Marehay Rd DE5 180 B3
Upper Moor St S40 . . . . . .95 A1
Upper Nelson St DE75 . . .181 B1
Upper Newbold Cl S40 . . .95 A4
Upper Orchard St 8
  NG9 . . . . .223 C4
Upper Parliament St
  NG1 . . . . .268 B2
Upper School La S18 . . . . .76 A4
Upper Town La DE4 . . . . .126 A1
Upper Valley Rd S8 . . . . . .43 A3
Upper Wellington St
  NG10 . . . . .223 B1
Upper Yeld Rd DE45 . . . . .109 B2
Uppermoor Rd DE24 . . . .232 C3
Upperthorpe Rd S21 . . . . .60 B3
Upperthorpe Villas S21 . .60 B3
Uppertown La DE4 . . . . . .142 B1
Upperwood Rd DE4 . . . . .143 A1
Upton Cl DE75 . . . . .182 A1
Upton Mount NG19 . . . . .135 C1
Upwood Cl S40 . . . . .95 A3
Upwoods Rd DE6 . . . . . . .211 A1
Utah Cl DE55 . . . . .228 C1
Uttoxeter New Rd DE22 218 B2
Uttoxeter Old Rd DE22 . .218 C2
Uttoxeter Rd Derby DE3 .217 C1
  Hatton DE65 . . . . .227 A1
  Hilton DE65 . . . . .228 B1
  Scropton, Foston DE65 . .226 C2
  Scropton, HM Detention Ctr
  DE65 . . . . .226 B2
Uxbridge St DE14 . . . . . . .254 B4

V

Vale Cl Bolsover S44 . . . . . .99 A1
  Dronfield S18 . . . . .57 A1
Vale Dr NG20 . . . . .119 C1
Vale House Dr SK13 . . . . . .10 A3
Vale Mills DE22 . . . . .218 C2
Vale Rd Hartshorne DE11 .257 A2
  Mansfield Woodhouse
  NG19 . . . . .136 A2
  Swadlincote DE11 . . . . . .256 A3
Vale St ST4 . . . . .269 B2
Vale The DE7 . . . . .194 C2
Valemount SK13 . . . . .10 A3
Valentine Ave NG16 . . . . .171 C4
Valerian Cl SK17 . . . . .85 B4
Valerie Rd DE72 . . . . .246 A4
Vallance St NG19 . . . . . . .136 A2
Valley Cl S45 . . . . .132 A2
Valley Dr
  Chapel-en-le-F SK23 . . . . .47 B3
  Killamarsh S21 . . . . .60 B4
Valley Gdns SK14 . . . . .15 C4
Valley Ho NG7 . . . . .268 A1
Valley Rd Barlow S18 . . . . .75 B2
  Bolsover S44 . . . . .118 A4
  Broadbottom SK14 . . . . . .15 C4
  Chesterfield S41 . . . . .96 B1
  Clay Cross S45 . . . . .131 A2
  Derby DE23 . . . . .218 B1
  Derby, Cherrytree Hill
  DE21 . . . . .220 A3
  Glossop SK13 . . . . .16 C4
  Hayfield SK22 . . . . .25 C1
  Ilkeston DE7 . . . . .208 C3
  Killamarsh S21 . . . . .60 B4
  Kimberley NG16 . . . . .195 B4
  Mastin Moor S43 . . . . .79 B2
  Overseal DE12 . . . . .262 A2
  Sheffield S8 . . . . .43 A3
  Shirebrook NG20 . . . . . . .119 C3
Valley Rise Barlow S18 . . . .75 B2
  Swadlincote DE11 . . . . . .256 A3
Valley View Belper DE56 .179 A1
  Ilkeston DE7 . . . . .208 C3
Valley View Cl
  Chesterfield S41 . . . . . . .115 C4
  Eckington S21 . . . . .59 B1
Valley View Dr DE7 . . . . . .193 A1
Valley View Rd DE55 . . . . .170 B2
Valley View Wlk ST14 . . .197 A2
Vancouver Ave DE21 . . . . .220 B2
Vancouver Dr DE15 . . . . . .248 B2
Vanguard Rd NG10 . . . . . .236 B3
Vanguard Trad Est S40 . .115 A4
Varley St DE24 . . . . .232 B3
Vaughan Pl NG20 . . . . . . .119 C3
Vaughan Rd SK23 . . . . .45 C3
Vaughan Way ST17 . . . . . .269 A3
Vauxhall Ave DE22 . . . . . .218 A4
Ventura Ct SK22 . . . . .24 B1
Venture Cres DE55 . . . . . .159 A1
Venture Way S41 . . . . .76 C1
Verbena Dr DE23 . . . . . . .231 B2
Vere Cl DE65 . . . . .242 A3
Vermont Dr DE21 . . . . . . .220 B3
Verney St NG19 . . . . .134 C4
Verney Way NG19 . . . . . .134 C4
Vernon Cotts S43 . . . . . . .170 A4
Vernon Ct Bakewell DE45 109 B3
  Shirebrook NG20 . . . . . . .120 C3
Vernon Dr
  Bakewell DE45 . . . . .109 A4
  Derby DE21 . . . . .220 C2
Vernon Gn DE45 . . . . .109 A4
Vernon Rd
  Chesterfield S40 . . . . .95 B2
  Dore S17 . . . . .55 C3
  Stoke-on-T ST4 . . . . .269 B1
Vernon Rise S42 . . . . .115 C1
Vernon St Derby DE1 . . . .218 C3
  Ilkeston DE7 . . . . .194 C2
  38 Nottingham NG1 . . . .268 A2
  Shirebrook NG20 . . . . . . .120 C3
Vernongate DE1 . . . . .218 C3
Veronica Dr NG16 . . . . . . .195 B4
Vestry Rd DE21 . . . . .205 C2
Vetchfield Cl DE24 . . . . . .231 C1
Via Gellia Rd DE4 . . . . . . .154 C2
Vicar La Chesterfield S40 .266 B3
  Tibshelf DE55 . . . . .148 A3
Vicarage Ave
  Derby DE23 . . . . .218 C1
  Ilkeston DE7 . . . . .194 B2
Vicarage Cl Belper DE56 .179 A1
  Burton u T DE15 . . . . .248 C1
  Heath S44 . . . . .117 A1
  Holmesfield S18 . . . . .75 A4
  Nottingham NG3 . . . . . . .268 B2
  Shirebrook NG20 . . . . . . .119 C2
  Smalley DE7 . . . . .192 C3
  Swanwick DE55 . . . . .169 C4
Vicarage Ct DE3 . . . . .217 C1
Vicarage Dr Derby DE21 .220 A4
  Uttoxeter ST14 . . . . .210 A2
Vicarage Gdns
  Clay Cross S45 . . . . .131 B1
  Heanor DE75 . . . . .181 C1
  Swadlincote DE11 . . . . . .256 B2
Vicarage La
  Ashford in t W DE45 . . . .108 C4
  Darley Dale DE4 . . . . .110 C1
  Dore S17 . . . . .55 B4
  Duffield DE56 . . . . .190 C2
  Hayfield SK22 . . . . .25 B1
  Ironville NG16 . . . . .170 C2
  Little Eaton DE21 . . . . . . .205 B4

Vicarage Mews DE55 . . . .170 C3
Vicarage Rd Belper DE56 190 C4
  Derby DE3 . . . . .217 B1
  Derby, Chellaston DE73 . .232 C1
  Stoke-on-T ST4 . . . . .269 A2
  Swadlincote DE11 . . . . . .256 B2
  Woodville DE11 . . . . .256 C1
Vicarage St DE7 . . . . .194 B2
Vicarage Way S17 . . . . . . .269 A3
Vicarage Wlk DE12 . . . . . .260 B3
Vicarwood Ave
  Derby DE22 . . . . .204 C2
  Holbrook DE56 . . . . .191 B4
Victor Ave DE22 . . . . .218 C4
Victor Cres NG10 . . . . . . .223 B2
Victor Rd S17 . . . . .55 C4
Victoria Ave
  Borrowash DE72 . . . . . . .221 A1
  7 Buxton SK17 . . . . .85 B4
  Draycott DE72 . . . . .235 A4
  Glossop SK13 . . . . .10 A3
  Nottingham NG2 . . . . . . .268 C1
  Staveley S43 . . . . .79 A2
Victoria Cl DE3 . . . . .217 C2
Victoria Cotts DE55 . . . . .159 B1
Victoria Cres NG16 . . . . . .170 C2
Victoria Ct Ilkeston DE7 . .194 C1
  Long Eaton NG10 . . . . . . .236 B4
  Mansfield NG18 . . . . .268 B3
  Matlock DE4 . . . . .143 B3
Victoria Ctr NG1 . . . . .268 C2
Victoria Dr DE55 . . . . .147 C1
Victoria Gr S43 . . . . .96 C3
Victoria Hall Gdns DE4 . .143 B3
Victoria Ho S80 . . . . .81 C1
Victoria Park Rd
  Buxton SK17 . . . . .85 B4
  Calow S43 . . . . .96 C3
Victoria Rd Bamford S33 . . .40 A2
  Draycott DE72 . . . . .235 A4
  Pinxton NG16 . . . . .160 B2
  Ripley DE5 . . . . .169 B1
  Sandiacre NG10 . . . . .223 A3
  Selston NG16 . . . . .171 C3
  Stafford ST16 . . . . .269 A4
  Stoke-on-T ST4 . . . . .269 C2
Victoria Sq DE6 . . . . .173 B1
Victoria St Alfreton DE55 159 A2
  Bolsover S44 . . . . .118 A4
  Brimington S43 . . . . .77 C1
  Castle Donington DE74 . .247 A3
  Chesterfield S41 . . . . . . .266 B4
  Clay Cross S45 . . . . .131 B2
  Creswell S80 . . . . .81 C1
  Derby DE1 . . . . .267 B3
  Dronfield S18 . . . . .56 C1
  Glossop SK13 . . . . .17 B4
  Ilkeston DE7 . . . . .194 C1
  Ironville NG16 . . . . .170 C2
  Langley Mill NG16 . . . . . .182 B2
  Long Eaton NG10 . . . . . . .236 A3
  Melbourne DE73 . . . . . . .252 A4
  New Mills SK22 . . . . .33 A3
  Nottingham NG1 . . . . . . .268 B1
  Ripley DE5 . . . . .169 C1
  Shirebrook NG20 . . . . . . .119 C3
  Somercotes DE55 . . . . . .170 B4
  South Normanton DE55 . .160 A3
  Stafford ST16 . . . . .269 B4
  Stapleford NG9 . . . . .223 B4
Victoria St N S41 . . . . .76 C1
Victoria St W S40 . . . . .95 B1
Victoria Terr
  Great Longstone DE45 . . . .89 C2
  Tibshelf DE55 . . . . .148 A4
Victoria Wlk S42 . . . . .115 B1
Victory Ave DE5 . . . . .169 C1
Victory Cl NG10 . . . . .236 B3
Victory Dr NG19 . . . . .136 C1
Victory Rd DE24 . . . . .232 A3
View Rd S2 . . . . .43 A4
Viewdales Cl DE6 . . . . . . .175 C2
Viking Bsns Ctr DE11 . . . .256 C2
Vikinglea Cl S2 . . . . .44 A4
Vikinglea Dr S2 . . . . .44 A4
Villa St Draycott DE72 . . . .235 A4
  Stoke-on-T ST4 . . . . .269 B1
Villa The SK14 . . . . .9 A3
Village Cl DE56 . . . . .190 C2
Village St DE23 . . . . .231 C4
Village The
  Dale Abbey DE7 . . . . .207 C1
  West Hallam DE7 . . . . . . .207 C4
Villas Rd Bolsover S44 . . . .98 C1
  Toadmoor DE56 . . . . .167 C2
Villas The Bolsover S44 . . . .99 A1
  Stoke-on-T ST4 . . . . .269 B1
  Whaley Thorns NG20 . . . .101 A4
Villiers Cl S2 . . . . .43 C3
Villiers Dr S2 . . . . .43 C3
Vincent Ave Derby DE21 .220 C2
  Ilkeston DE7 . . . . .208 C4
Vincent Cl DE56 . . . . .192 A4
Vincent Cres S40 . . . . .95 A1
Vincent La S40 . . . . .95 A1
Vincent St DE23 . . . . .218 C1
Vine Cl DE23 . . . . .231 C4
Vine Cres NG10 . . . . .223 A3
Vine Farm Cl DE7 . . . . . . .208 B3
Vine Row ST4 . . . . .269 B1
Vinebank St S14 . . . . .269 B1
Vineyard Terr DE4 . . . . . . .127 C2
Viola Cl DE21 . . . . .206 B2
Violet Ave NG16 . . . . .195 A4

Violet Cl
Donisthorpe DE12 ......262 C1
Shirebrook NG20 ......119 B2
Violet La DE15 ......254 C4
Violet Lane Inf Sch
DE15 ......254 C4
Violet St DE23 ......218 C2
Violet Way DE15 ......255 A4
Virginsalley La DE6 ......184 B1
Vista The NG9 ......223 C3
Vivian St Bolsover S44 ......98 C3
Derby DE1 ......219 A4
Vulcan St DE23 ......219 A1
Vyse Dr NG10 ......236 B3

W

Wade Ave Derby DE23 ...218 B1
Ilkeston DE7 ......209 A4
Wade Dr DE3 ......217 C1
Wade St DE23 ......218 B1
Wadebridge Gr DE24 ...233 B3
Wadham St ST4 ......269 B2
Wadhurst Gdns NG3 ...268 B2
Wadsworth Ave S12 ......44 B3
Wadsworth Cl S12 ......44 B3
Wadsworth Dr S12 ......44 B3
Wadsworth Rd
Sheffield S12 ......44 B3
Stapleford NG9 ......223 C4
Wagstaff La NG16 ......171 B3
Wagtail Cl DE24 ......231 B2
Wain Ave S42 ......132 A4
Wain Dr ST4 ......269 A1
Wain Way S42 ......132 A4
Wainfleet Cl DE7 ......194 B2
Waingroves Prim Sch
DE5 ......181 A4
Waingroves Rd
Codnor DE5 ......181 A4
Ripley DE5 ......181 A4
Wainhouse Brow SK22 ...25 B2
Wains Cl SK17 ......47 C1
Wainwood Rise ST4 ...269 A1
Wainwright Ave S13 ......44 B4
Wainwright Cres S13 ......44 B4
Wakami Cres DE73 ......233 A2
Wakefield Ave DE13 ...239 A3
Wakefield Croft DE7 ...194 B2
Wakefield Ct DE74 ......247 B2
Wakclyn Cl DE72 ......234 C1
Walbrook Rd DE23 ......218 C1
Walcote Cl DE56 ......179 B3
Walden Rd S2 ......43 A4
Waldene Dr DE24 ......233 A3
Waldley La DE6 ......211 B4
Waldorf Ave DE24 ......233 A4
Waldorf Cl DE24 ......233 A4
Walford Rd Killamarsh S21 60 B3
Rolleston DE13 ......240 B2
Walgrave Cl DE56 ......179 A3
Walgrove Rd S40 ......95 C1
Walgrove Rd S40 ......95 B1
Walk Cl DE72 ......235 A4
Walk Mill Rd SK22 ......25 B1
Walk The DE56 ......192 A4
Walkdale Brow SK13 ......17 A4
Walkden St NG18 ......268 B4
Walker Ave DE5 ......169 C1
Walker Brow SK17 ......47 C1
Walker Cl DE7 ......209 A2
Walker Gr NG9 ......223 C3
Walker La DE1 ......267 A4
Walker St Glossop SK13 ...10 A4
Nottingham NG2 ......268 C1
Walkers Ave NG16 ......182 C3
Walkers La S21 ......60 B3
Wall Ditch DE6 ......149 A1
Wall Rd DE14 ......254 A4
Wall St Buxton SK17 ......85 B4
Ripley DE5 ......169 B1
Wallace Gdns 8 NG9 ...223 C1
Wallace St DE23 ......218 B1
Wallfields Cl DE65 ......230 B1
Wallis Cl DE72 ......235 A4
Wallis Rd NG18 ......268 C4
Walls La S80 ......81 A4
Walnut Ave Derby DE24 ...233 A4
Shireoaks S81 ......63 C4
Walnut Cl
Aston-on-T DE72 ......246 A4
Barrow u T DE73 ......244 A3
Burnaston DE65 ......229 C3
Derby DE73 ......245 A4
Ilkeston DE7 ......209 A4
Repton DE65 ......243 A1
Swadlincote DE11 ......256 A3
Walnut Dr S21 ......60 B3
Walnut Rd DE56 ......179 A2
Walnut St DE24 ......232 B4
Walpole St DE21 ......219 B3
Walseker La S26 ......61 B4
Walsham Ct DE21 ......205 B1
Walter Evans CE Prim Sch
DE22 ......204 C1
Walter St Derby DE1 ......218 C4
Draycott DE72 ......234 C4
Nottingham NG7 ......268 A2
Walters Cres NG16 ......171 B3
Waltham Ave DE24 ......232 A4
Walthamstow Dr DE22 ...218 A3
Waltheof Rd S2 ......44 A4
Walton Ave Derby DE24 ...232 C2
Nottingham NG3 ......268 C2

Walton Back La
Chesterfield S40 ......114 A4
Holymoorside S42 ......113 C4
Walton Cl
Chesterfield S40 ......114 A4
Dronfield S18 ......56 B1
Swadlincote DE11 ......256 A2
Walton Cres
Ashbourne DE6 ......173 B1
Chesterfield S40 ......95 C1
Fenton ST4 ......269 C1
Walton Ct Sheffield S8 ...56 C4
West Hallam DE7 ......207 B4
Walton Dr
Chesterfield S40 ......95 C1
Derby DE23 ......231 C4
Walton Drive Ct S40 ......95 C1
Walton Fields Rd S40 ...95 B1
Walton Hill DE74 ......247 A2
Walton Holymoorside Prim
Sch S42 ......113 B4
Walton Hospl S40 ......114 C4
Walton Rd
Chesterfield S40 ......95 B1
Derby DE21 ......219 C3
Swadlincote DE15 ......254 B3
Walton St NG10 ......223 B1
Walton Way S42 ......114 C2
Walton Wlk S40 ......95 C1
Walton-on-Trent CE Prim
Sch DE12 ......259 B4
Wansbeck St 22 NG7 ...268 A2
Wansfell Cl DE7 ......217 C1
Wapentake La DE6 ......165 B1
Warburton Cl S2 ......43 B4
Warburton Gdns S2 ......43 B4
Warburton Rd S2 ......43 B4
Ward Dr DE55 ......170 B4
Ward La Barlborough S43 ...80 A4
Disley SK12 ......32 C2
Ward Pl Mansfield NG18 ...268 A3
Sheffield S2 ......43 A4
Ward St Derby DE22 ......218 C2
Tupton S42 ......131 B4
Ward's La Breaston DE72 235 B4
King's Newton DE73 ......245 A1
Melbourne DE73 ......244 C2
Ward's Yd S40 ......266 B2
Wardgate Way S40 ......95 A3
Wardlow Ave DE21 ......220 A4
Wardlow Cl S40 ......114 C4
Wardlow Fold 28 SK13 ...9 B1
Wardlow Mews SK13 ...9 B1
Wardlow Rd
Ilkeston DE7 ......194 C2
Sheffield S12 ......44 B3
Wardlow Wlk 22 SK13 ...9 B1
Wardwick DE1 ......267 B3
Warehouse La S33 ......38 B2
Warhurst Fold 2 SK13 ...10 A3
Warmbrook DE4 ......165 C4
Warmbrook Jun Sch
SK23 ......47 B3
Warmbrook Rd SK23 ......47 B3
Warminster Cl S8 ......43 A2
Warminster Cres S8 ......43 A2
Warminster Dr S8 ......43 A2
Warminster Gdns S8 ...43 A2
Warminster Pl S8 ......43 A1
Warminster Rd S8 ......43 A2
Warmwells La DE5 ......180 B3
Warner St
Chesterfield S41 ......266 C1
Derby, Mickleover S18 ...217 B1
Derby, St Luke's DE22 ...218 C2
Warney Rd DE4 ......127 B1
Warren Ave NG9 ......223 B4
Warren Ave Extension
NG9 ......223 B4
Warren Cl
Burton u T DE13 ......240 C1
Pilsley S45 ......132 C1
Warren Cres S21 ......58 C1
Warren Ct NG9 ......223 B4
Warren Dr DE12 ......261 B3
Warren La
Branston DE14 ......253 C4
Castle Donington DE74,
NG10 ......236 A1
Warren Lea SK6 ......15 A1
Warren Rise S18 ......57 B2
Warren St DE24 ......232 C4
Warren Wlk S21 ......58 C1
Warrendale Ct DE73 ......233 A1
Warser Gate NG1 ......268 B1
Warsop Rd NG19 ......136 B2
Warwick Ave DE23 ......218 B1
Warwick Cl
Branston DE14 ......253 C4
Glossop SK13 ......17 C4
Swadlincote DE11 ......256 C3
Warwick Dr DE7 ......194 B2
Warwick Gdns DE56 ......179 B3
Warwick Rd
Long Eaton NG10 ......237 A4
Somercotes DE55 ......159 B1
Warwick St
Chesterfield S40 ......115 A4
Derby DE24 ......219 B1
Wasdale Ave S20 ......59 C3
Wash Gn DE56, DE4 ......166 A4
Wash Hills Cl DE4 ......153 A1
Wash House La S40 ......95 B1
Washbrook La NG16 ......161 C2
Washford Rd DE65 ......240 C4
Washhouse Bottom SK17 69 C4
Washington Ave DE21 ...220 A3
Washington Cl DE73 ......252 A4

Washington Cotts DE72 221 B1
Washington Dr NG9 ......209 C1
Wasnidge Cl NG3 ......268 B2
Wasnidge Wlk 15 NG3 ...268 B2
Watburn Rd SK22 ......24 B1
Watchorn Cl DE11 ......256 B3
Watchorn Cotts DE55 ...158 C2
Watchorn La DE55 ......158 C1
Water La Bakewell DE45 109 B3
Bamford S33 ......40 A2
Bolsover S44 ......117 C4
Cromford DE4 ......155 A3
Eyam S32 ......71 C3
Hollingworth SK14 ......9 B3
Mansfield NG19 ......135 C4
Middleton (Nr Wirksworth)
DE4 ......154 B3
Shirebrook NG19 ......118 C1
South Normanton DE55 ...160 A3
Tideswell SK17 ......68 C3
Wirksworth DE4 ......165 C4
Water Mdws The DE73 ...244 B3
Water Meadow La S40 ...95 A4
Water Orton Cl NG9 ......223 C2
Water St Bakewell DE45 109 B3
Buxton SK17 ......85 A4
Glossop SK13 ......10 C1
Stafford ST16 ......269 B4
Stoke-on-T ST4 ......269 B1
Watercress La S45 ......131 B1
Waterdown Cl NG19 ......136 B3
Waterfoots Cl SK14 ......9 A2
Waterford Dr DE21 ......220 A2
Watergo La DE23 ......230 C4
Watering La DE56 ......191 B3
Wateringbury Gr 9 S43 .78 C1
Waterloo Cl DE55 ......160 B4
Waterloo Cres NG7 ......268 A2
Waterloo Ct DE1 ......267 C5
Waterloo La NG9 ......209 C3
Waterloo Pl DE11 ......256 A2
Waterloo Prom NG7 ......268 A2
Waterloo Rd
Matlock Bath DE4 ......143 A1
Nottingham NG7 ......268 A2
Waterloo St
Bramley-Vale S44 ......117 C1
Clay Cross S45 ......131 B2
Watermeade S21 ......59 A1
Watermeadow Rd DE24 233 A3
Watermeadows The
NG10 ......236 A4
Waterpark Rd DE6 ......224 A4
Waters Edge SK6 ......23 A4
Waters Edge La SK23 ...47 B3
Waterside
Burton u T DE15 ......254 C4
Glossop SK13 ......10 A3
Ironville NG16 ......170 C2
Marple SK6 ......23 A4
Waterside Bsns Pk SK13 .9 C3
Waterside Cl
Derby DE22 ......205 A1
Sandiacre NG10 ......223 A4
Waterside Com Jun Sch
DE15 ......254 C4
Waterside Rd
Burton u T DE15 ......254 B4
Disley SK12,SK22 ......32 C4
Waterswallows La SK17 .66 C2
Waterswallows Mews
SK17 ......66 C1
Waterswallows Rd SK17 .66 C1
Waterthorpe Cl 9 S20 ...59 C4
Waterthorpe Cres S20 ...59 C4
Waterthorpe Gdns 6
S20 ......59 C4
Waterthorpe Glade S20 .59 C4
Waterthorpe Glen 8
S20 ......59 C4
Waterthorpe Rise 7 S20 59 C4
Waterway The NG10 ......223 B2
Watery La Bretby DE15 .249 B2
Clifton DE6 ......184 C4
Ellastone DE6 ......183 A2
Scropton DE65 ......226 C1
Swadlincote DE55 ......255 B3
Thurvaston DE6 ......215 B3
Watford Bridge Ind Est
SK22 ......24 B1
Watford Bridge Rd SK22 .24 B1
Watford La SK22 ......24 B1
Watford Rd Buxton SK17 ...84 C4
New Mills SK22 ......24 B1
Watford St ST4 ......269 C2
Watkin Ave SK13 ......9 C2
Watkin St Fenton ST4 ...269 C1
Nottingham NG1,NG3 ...268 B2
Watkinson St DE75 ......181 B1
Watnall Cres NG19 ......268 A4
Watson Ave
Heanor DE75 ......181 C1
Mansfield NG18 ......268 C4
Watson La S42 ......114 B2
Watson Rd DE7 ......194 B1
Watson St Derby DE1 ......218 C3
Derby, Markeaton DE1 ...218 C4
Stoke-on-T ST4 ......269 B2
Watten Cl DE24 ......231 C1
Watts Gn DE45 ......108 C4
Waveney Cl DE22 ......205 A3
Waverley Ct 2 S41 ......96 A1
Waverley House Sch
NG7 ......268 A2
Waverley St Derby DE24 .232 B4
Long Eaton NG10 ......236 C4
Nottingham NG1,NG7 ...268 A2

Waverley St *continued*
Tibshelf DE55 ......148 A4
Wayfaring Rd DE21 ......206 A1
Wayford Ave S41 ......266 C1
Wayside S43 ......96 B4
Wayside Cl S42 ......132 A4
Wayside Ct S43 ......96 B4
Wayzgoose Dr DE21 ......219 B3
Weaddow La DE45 ......124 C1
Weakland Cl S12 ......44 C2
Weakland Cres S12 ......44 C2
Weakland Dr S12 ......44 C2
Weakland Way S12 ......44 C2
Weather Hill La HD9 ......3 C4
Weathern Field DE12 ...261 B3
Weaver Cl
Ashbourne DE6 ......185 B4
Crich DE4 ......156 C1
Weaver Rd ST14 ......210 A1
Weavers Cl Belper DE56 .179 B3
Borrowash DE72 ......221 B1
Weavers Croft DE5 ......180 C4
Weavers Ct S14 ......9 A2
Weavers Gn DE3 ......217 B1
Weavers The ST14 ......196 B3
Weaving Ave S33 ......38 B1
Webbs Orch SK23 ......45 B4
Webster Ave NG16 ......182 C1
Webster Croft S41 ......77 A1
Webster Ct S40 ......95 C3
Webster St DE1 ......267 A2
Webster's Terr DE4 ......143 B2
Wedgewood Cl DE15 ...248 A1
Wedneshough SK14 ......9 B3
Weekday Cross NG1 ......268 B1
Weighbridge Rd NG18 ...268 C3
Weightman Dr NG16 ......195 A4
Weir Bank DE15 ......254 C3
Weirfield Rd DE22 ......205 A1
Weirside DE6 ......184 B4
Welbeck Ave Buxton SK17 .85 B3
Ilkeston DE7 ......208 B3
Welbeck Cl
23 Dronfield S18 ......56 B1
Nottingham NG3 ......268 C2
Staveley S43 ......97 B3
Welbeck Ct Clowne S43 ...80 C2
7 Staveley S43 ......78 C1
Welbeck Dr S42 ......114 C2
Welbeck Gdns NG9 ......223 C2
Welbeck Gr DE22 ......204 C1
Welbeck Rd Bolsover S44 ...99 A1
Long Eaton NG10 ......223 B2
Mansfield Woodhouse
NG19 ......136 B2
Welbeck St Creswell S80 .81 C1
Mansfield NG18 ......268 B4
Whitwell S80 ......82 A3
Welbeck Wlk 3 NG3 ...268 B2
Welbeck Workshops 6
NG3 ......268 B2
Welbury Gdns S20 ......59 C3
Welby St ST4 ......269 C1
Welch Ave NG9 ......223 C4
Welch St S14 ......269 B2
Welfare Ave S40 ......95 B2
Welfare Cl NG20 ......119 C2
Welfitt Gr NG20 ......101 A1
Well Banks DE6 ......165 A1
Well Cl DE6 ......175 C2
Well Gate SK13 ......10 C1
Well La Belper DE56 ......190 C4
Blackfordby DE11 ......257 A1
Holymoorside S42 ......112 C4
Repton DE65 ......242 B1
Shirland DE55 ......146 B3
Well Rd S8 ......43 A3
Well Row SK14 ......16 A4
Well Spring Cl 11 S43 ...96 C4
Well St Brassington DE4 ...152 C1
Derby DE1 ......267 B5
Elton DE4 ......140 C4
New Mills SK22 ......33 A4
Ripley DE5 ......169 B1
Well Yd Belper DE56 ......179 A3
DE56 ......191 B3
Welland Cl
Burton u T DE15 ......248 A3
Derby DE1 ......217 B2
Welland Ct NG3 ......268 C2
Welland Rd DE65 ......228 B1
Wellcarr Rd S8 ......43 A1
Wellcroft DE4 ......126 A1
Wellcroft Cl NG18 ......268 C4
Welldon St DE5 ......181 A2
Weller St ST4 ......269 C1
Wellesley Ave DE23 ......231 B4
Wellfield DE4 ......143 B4
Wellfield Cl S12 ......44 C1
Wellfield St S14 ......143 B3
Wellgate La DE45 ......109 A1
Wellhead Rd 3 S8 ......43 A3
Wellington Cir 1 NG1 ...268 B1
Wellington Cl DE4 ......143 B4
Wellington Cres DE1 ......267 D2
Wellington Ct 9 DE56 ...178 C2
Wellington Mews DE55 .146 B1
Wellington Pl NG16 ......182 C1
Wellington Rd DE14 ......253 C4
Wellington Sq 32 NG7 ...268 A2
Wellington St
Chesterfield S43 ......77 B2
Derby DE1 ......267 C4
Eastwood NG16 ......182 C2
Heanor DE75 ......181 B2
Long Eaton NG10 ......223 B1
Matlock DE4 ......143 B3

Wellington St *continued*
Nottingham NG3 ......268 B2
Ripley DE5 ......169 C1
Stapleford NG9 ......223 B3
Wellington Terr 31 NG7 .268 A2
Wellington Villas 30
NG7 ......268 A2
Wells Cl NG19 ......136 B2
Wells Ct DE23 ......230 C4
Wells Rd DE3 ......217 C1
Wells St S44 ......118 B4
Wellspring Cl
Barlborough S43 ......80 A3
Wingerworth S42 ......115 A2
Wellspring Dale NG9 ...223 C3
Wellwood Rd DE11 ......256 A3
Wellwyn Ct S12 ......44 A2
Welney Cl DE3 ......230 B4
Welshpool Pl S40 ......95 B2
Welshpool Rd DE21 ......205 B1
Welton Ave DE56 ......179 A3
Welwyn Ave Derby DE22 .204 B3
Derby, Alleton DE24 ......232 C2
Mansfield Woodhouse
NG19 ......136 C2
Welwyn Cl
Chesterfield S40 ......95 B3
Sheffield S12 ......44 A2
Welwyn Rd S12 ......44 A2
Wembley Gdns DE22 ......218 A3
Wendover Cl DE3 ......217 B1
Wenham La NG17 ......148 C1
Wenlock Cl
Chesterfield S40 ......95 B3
Derby DE3 ......217 C1
Eastwood NG16 ......195 B4
Wenlock Cres S40 ......95 B2
Wenlock Dr S42 ......115 C2
Wensley Dr DE21 ......220 C2
Wensley Rd
North Wingfield S42 ......131 C3
Winster DE4 ......141 B3
Wensley Way S43 ......97 B4
Wensleydale Cl NG19 ...136 C1
Wensleydale Rd NG10 ...236 A3
Wensleydale Wlk DE24 233 B4
Wentworth Ave S40 ......114 C4
Wentworth Cl Derby DE3 217 C1
Mansfield NG19 ......136 C1
Wentworth Croft DE75 ...182 A2
Wentworth Ct NG16 ......195 C3
Wentworth Dr DE13 ......240 B4
Wentworth Rd S18 ......56 B1
Wentworth St DE7 ......195 A4
Werburgh Cl DE21 ......220 B2
Werburgh St DE22 ......218 C2
Werneth Low Cntry Pk
SK14 ......15 A4
Werneth Low Rd SK14 ...15 A3
Werneth Rd SK13 ......17 A4
Wesley Ct SK23 ......47 B3
Wesley La DE72 ......221 B1
Wesley Pl NG9 ......223 C4
Wesley Rd
Ambergate DE56 ......167 C2
Derby DE24 ......233 A3
Stonebroom DE55 ......146 C2
Wesley St Glossop SK13 ...10 A4
Glossop, Hadfield SK13 ...10 A3
Ilkeston DE7 ......194 C2
Langley Mill NG16 ......182 C2
Wesleyan Chapel La
SK17 ......88 A2
Wesleyan Chapel Wlk
NG9 ......223 B4
Wessex Dr NG16 ......195 A4
Wessex Gdns S17 ......55 B3
Wessington Bank 1 SK13 .9 C1
Wessington Dr S43 ......97 B4
Wessington Gn 2 SK13 ...9 C1
Wessington La DE55 ......158 C2
Wessington Mews
Derby DE22 ......204 C1
Gamesley SK13 ......9 C1
Wessington Prim Sch
DE55 ......157 C4
West Ave Derby DE1 ......267 A4
Derby, Chellaston DE73 ...232 C2
Draycott DE72 ......234 C4
Hilton DE65 ......228 B1
Ripley DE5 ......169 B1
Sandiacre NG10 ......223 C4
Stapleford NG9 ......223 C4
Stoke-on-T ST4 ......269 C2
West Bank
Matlock Bath DE4 ......143 A1
Stoke-on-T ST4 ......269 B1
Toadmoor DE56 ......168 A1
Winster DE4 ......141 A3
West Bank Ave
Crich DE4 ......156 C1
Derby DE22 ......218 C4
Mansfield NG18, NG19 ...268 B4
West Bank Cl DE22 ......218 C4
West Bank Lea NG19 ...136 A1
West Bank Link NG19 ...136 A1
West Bank Rd DE22 ......204 C3
West Bank Wynd NG18 ...268 B4
West Bars S40 ......266 A3
West Cl Derby DE22 ......204 C1
Stafford ST16 ......269 C4
West Cres
Long Duckmanton S44 ...98 A3
Matlock DE4 ......143 A3
West Croft Ave DE23 ......231 B3
West Croft Cl DE45 ......125 A3
West Croft Ct S43 ......97 A3
West Croft Dr S43 ......97 A3

West Dr Derby DE3 .217 B1
Doveridge DE6 .211 A1
Glossop SK13 .9 C4
West Edge Cl S45 .129 B2
West End Alfreton DE55 .159 A2
Barlborough S43 .80 A4
Brassington DE4 .152 C1
Broadbottom SK14 .15 C4
Elton DE4 .140 C3
Pinxton NG16 .160 B2
Wirksworth DE4 .165 C4
West End Cl DE55 .159 A2
West End Cres DE7 .208 B4
West End Dr
Ilkeston DE7 .208 B4
Shardlow DE72 .234 C1
West End St NG9 .223 B3
West End View S21 .59 B1
West Gate Holme HD9 .3 C4
Long Eaton NG10 .236 C4
Mansfield NG18 .268 B4
West Gr DE24 .232 B3
West Hill Codnor DE5 .181 A4
Mansfield NG18 .268 B4
West Hill Ave NG18 .268 B4
West Hill Dr NG18 .268 B4
West Hill Pk NG19 .136 A2
West Hill Way NG18 .268 B4
West Lawn DE65 .230 B1
West Lea Barlborough S43 .80 B2
Chesterfield S40 .95 A1
West Lea Cotts S43 .80 B2
West Lees Rd S33 .40 A2
West Nottinghamshire Coll
NG18 .268 B4
West Par ST4 .269 C1
West Park Com Sch
DE21 .220 B3
West Park Rd DE22 .218 C4
West Rd Buxton SK17 .85 A3
Derby DE21 .220 B3
West Row DE22 .205 A1
West Service Rd DE21 .220 A2
West St Bramley-Vale S44 117 B1
Burton u T DE15 .248 A2
Chesterfield S40 .266 A4
Clay Cross S45 .131 A2
Clowne S43 .81 A3
Creswell S80 .81 B1
Dronfield S18 .56 C1
Eckington S21 .59 B1
Glossop SK13 .9 C4
Heanor DE75 .181 B1
Ilkeston DE7 .208 C4
Langley Mill NG16 .182 A2
Market Warsop NG20 .120 B2
Nottingham NG2 .268 C1
Somercotes DE55 .170 B3
South Normanton DE55 .159 C3
Stonebroom DE55 .146 C2
Swadlincote DE11 .256 A2
Whaley Thorns NG20 .101 A2
West Terr 8 DE7 .194 C1
West View
Barlborough S43 .80 A3
Bolsover S44 .118 A4
Mayfield DE6 .184 B3
Rocester ST14 .197 A2
Staveley S43 .78 B1
West View Ave DE23 .231 A4
West View Cl S17 .55 C3
West View La S17 .55 C3
West View Rd S41 .95 C3
West Way
Somercotes DE55 .159 B1
Stafford ST17 .269 A3
West Way Gn ST17 .269 A3
Westacre Dr DE11 .255 C1
Westbank Cl S18 .57 A2
Westbank Ct S18 .57 B2
Westbourne Ave DE55 .147 A2
Westbourne Cl NG19 .136 C2
Westbourne Gr S40 .95 A2
Westbourne Pk DE22 .217 C4
Westbridge Rd S43 .80 A4
Westbrook Cl
Chapel-en-le-F SK23 .47 B3
Chesterfield S40 .94 C1
Westbrook Dr S40 .94 C1
Westbrook Specl Sch
NG10 .236 B4
Westbury Gdns DE56 .179 B3
Westbury St DE22 .218 C2
Westby La NG16 .195 B2
Westcroft Cres S20 .59 C4
Westcroft Dr S20 .59 C4
Westcroft Gdns S20 .59 C4
Westcroft Glen S20 .59 C4
Westcroft Gr S20 .59 C4
Westcross Ave NG9 .223 C4
Westdale Cl NG10 .236 A3
Westdale Rd
Mansfield NG19 .136 A1
Westwood NG16 .171 B2
Westdene Ave DE24 .232 B3
Westerlands NG9 .223 C3
Western Ave DE55 .169 B4
Western Dr DE75 .193 C4
Western La SK23 .46 A4
Western Rd Derby DE3 .217 C1
Derby, Rose Hill DE23 .219 A2
Western St 24 NG1 .268 B2
Western Terr NG7 .268 A1
Western View DE45 .90 A2
Western Villas DE56 .167 C2
Westfield Ave
Chesterfield S40 .95 A1
Heanor DE75 .181 C1
Westfield Bank S43 .80 A4
Westfield Cl
Chesterfield S40 .95 A1
Ilkeston DE7 .208 B3
Mansfield NG19 .268 A4
Westfield Cres S20 .59 B4
Westfield Ctr S20 .59 C4
Westfield Dr
Blackwell DE55 .147 C1
Ilkeston DE7 .194 B1
Mansfield NG19 .268 A4
Westfield Gdns S40 .95 A1
Westfield Inf Sch S40 .95 A1
Westfield La
Barlborough S43 .79 C4
Chesterfield S21 .77 C4
Mansfield NG19 .268 A4
Westfield Northway S20 .59 C4
Westfield Rd
Dronfield S18 .76 B4
Killamarsh S21 .60 B3
Swadlincote DE11 .256 A3
Westfield Sch S20 .59 B4
Westfield Southway S20 .59 C4
Westgate St NG3 .268 C2
Westgreen Ave DE24 .232 B3
Westhall Rd DE3 .217 B2
Westhead Ave ST16 .269 C4
Westhill La S42 .115 C2
Westhorpe Ave NG3 .268 C2
Westhorpe Dr NG10 .236 B4
Westhouses Prim Sch
DE55 .147 B1
Westland Dr NG16 .160 B2
Westland Gdns S20 .59 B4
Westland Gr 3 S20 .59 C4
Westland Rd S20 .59 C4
Westland St ST4 .269 B2
Westlands The ST14 .196 B3
Westlea View S43 .80 B2
Westleigh NG19 .136 B3
Westleigh Ave DE22 .218 B3
Westleigh Ct S40 .95 C3
Westley Cres DE21 .191 B1
Westminster Ave NG10 .223 B3
Westminster St DE24 .232 C4
Westmoor Rd S43 .96 C2
Westmorland Cl DE21 .219 B3
Westmorland Way
NG16 .171 A2
Weston Bank DE6 .197 C1
Weston Cl S40 .95 A3
Weston Cres NG10 .235 C2
Weston Ct DE72 .245 C2
Weston Park Ave DE24 .232 C2
Weston Park Gdns
DE24 .232 B2
Weston Rd
Aston-on-T DE72 .246 A4
Stafford ST16 .269 C4
Weston-on-T DE72 .245 C3
Weston Rise DE73 .245 A4
Weston Spot Cl DE5 .180 B4
Weston St Heanor DE75 .194 A4
Swadlincote DE11 .256 A2
Weston-on-Trent CE Prim
Sch DE72 .245 C2
Westthorpe Fields Rd
S21 .60 B2
Westthorpe Rd S21 .60 B3
Westward Cl ST14 .210 A1
Westwell Pl S20 .59 B3
Westwick Cres S8 .56 B4
Westwick Gr S8 .56 C4
Westwick La S42 .94 B1
Westwick Pk S41 .76 B2
Westwick Rd S8 .56 C4
Westwick St DE7 .209 A3
Westwood Ave S43 .97 B4
Westwood Cl S43 .97 B3
Westwood Dr
Derby DE24 .232 B3
Staveley S43 .97 B3
Westwood Dr Gdns S43 .97 A3
Westwood La S43 .96 C2
Westwood Pk DE11 .255 C3
Westwood Rd Calow S44 .97 A2
Nottingham NG2 .268 C1
Wetherby Cl NG16 .195 C4
Wetherby Ct DE14 .253 C4
Wetherby Rd DE24 .232 C4
Wetherel Rd DE15 .248 B1
Wetlands La S43,S44 .96 C2
Weyacres DE72 .221 B1
Weybridge Cl DE7 .207 B4
Whaley Bridge Prim Sch
SK23 .45 C4
Whaley Bridge Sta SK23 .45 C4
Whaley Comm S44 .100 B2
Whaley La SK23 .45 B4
Whaley Rd NG20 .100 C1
Whaley Thorns Heritage
Ctr* NG20 .101 A2
Whaley Thorns Prim Sch
NG20 .101 A2
Whalley Ave ST4 .269 A1
Wharf Ct SK23 .45 C4
Wharf Hos DE13 .253 A1
Wharf La
Chesterfield S41 .266 B4
Staveley S43 .78 C2
Wharf Pl ST4 .269 C2
Wharf Rd
Nottingham NG7 .268 A1
Pinxton NG16 .160 B1
Whaley Bridge SK23 .45 C4
Wharf The DE72 .235 A1
Wharfdale Rd NG10 .236 A3
Wharfedale Cl DE22 .205 A2
Wharmby Ave NG19 .135 B2
Wharncliffe Cl SK13 .9 C2
Wharncliffe Rd DE7 .208 C4
Whatstandwell Sta DE4 156 B1
Wheal La SK17 .107 B4
Wheatbridge Rd S40 .266 A3
Wheatbridge Ret Pk
S40 .266 A2
Wheatcroft SK13 .9 C2
Wheatcroft Cl
Clay Cross S45 .131 B1
Wingerworth S42 .115 A2
Wheatcroft La DE4 .156 C4
Wheatcroft Way DE21 .205 B1
Wheatfield Cres NG19 .136 C3
Wheatfield Way S42 .94 C3
Wheatfields SK23 .47 B4
Wheathill Cl Calow S43 .96 C2
Chesterfield S42 .94 C3
Wheathill Gr DE23 .231 A3
Wheathill La S41 .96 B2
Wheatland Cl DE24 .231 B1
Wheatlands DE11 .256 A4
Wheatlands La DE45 .91 B3
Wheatlands Rd
Burton u T DE15 .254 C4
Wingerworth S42 .114 C2
Wheatley Ave
Somercotes DE55 .159 B1
Stoke-on-T ST4 .269 A1
Wheatley Cl NG19 .136 C1
Wheatley Gdns DE4 .127 B1
Wheatley La DE15 .248 B2
Wheatley Rd DE4 .127 B2
Wheatsheaf Cl DE21 .206 B1
Wheatsheaf La DE4 .156 C1
Wheatsheaf Rd SK23 .45 C3
Wheeldon Ave
Belper DE56 .179 A2
Derby DE22 .218 C4
Wheeldon Cres S43 .96 B4
Wheeldon Way DE6 .175 C2
Wheeler Gate NG1 .268 B1
Wheelwright Way DE24 .219 B2
Whenby Cl DE3 .217 B1
Whernside Cl DE24 .233 B3
Wheston Bank SK17 .69 A3
Whetmorhurst Rd SK6 .23 C2
Whieldon Cres ST4 .269 C1
Whieldon Rd ST4 .269 C1
Whilton Cres DE7 .207 B4
Whilton Ct DE56 .179 B2
Whinacre Cl S8 .57 A3
Whinacre Pl S8 .57 A3
Whinacre Wlk S8 .57 A3
Whinbush Ave DE24 .232 C3
Whinney Bank NG19 .136 B2
Whinney Hill NG19 .136 B2
Whistlestop Cl DE3 .217 B2
Whiston St DE23 .219 A1
Whitaker Gdns DE23 .218 C1
Whitaker Mews ST14 .196 C2
Whitaker Rd DE23 .218 C1
Whitaker St DE23 .219 A1
Whitburn Rd NG9 .223 C2
Whitby Ave DE21 .205 B1
Whitcombe Pl DE5 .169 B1
White Edge Cl S40 .95 B3
White Edge Dr DE45 .91 C3
White Gate Rd HD9 .3 B4
White Gates DE5 .181 A4
White Hart St NG18 .268 B4
White Hart Yd DE56 .191 C4
White Horse La DE55,
S45 .145 B4
White Knowle Cl SK17 .85 B3
White Knowle Pk SK17 .85 B3
White Knowle Rd SK17 .85 B3
White La Sheffield S12 .44 A2
Sheffield S12 .44 B1
Shottle DE56 .177 B2
White Leas S40 .95 A2
White Leas Ave S42 .132 A4
White Lion Sq DE7 .208 C4
White Lion St ST17 .269 B3
White Lodge La DE45 .91 C3
White Rd New Mills SK22 .24 B1
Staveley S43 .79 A2
White St DE22 .218 C4
White Thorns Cl S8 .57 A3
White Thorns Dr S8 .57 A3
White Thorns View S8 .57 A3
White Tor Rd DE4 .143 B1
White's La DE55 .170 A4
Whitebank Cl S41 .266 C1
Whitecarr La DE55,S45 .145 A2
Whitecotes Cl S40 .114 C4
Whitecotes La S40 .114 C4
Whitecotes Pk S40 .114 C4
Whitecotes Prim Sch
S40 .114 C4
Whitecroft Rd SK6 .23 B1
Whitecross Ave SK17 .69 B2
Whitecross Gdns DE1 .218 C4
Whitecross Rd SK17 .69 B3
Whitecross St DE1 .218 C3
Whitefield La
Ashover S45 .129 A3
Chelmorton SK17 .106 B4
Whitegates Way NG17 .148 C1
Whitehall Terr SK23 .34 B1
Whitehaven Gr DE73 .233 A2
Whitehead Cl DE7 .194 B1
Whitehead Dr NG16 .182 B4
Whitehead St 12 S43 .78 C1
Whitehough Head La
SK23 .46 C4
Whitehouse Cl DE24 .232 B2
Whitehouse Rise DE56 .178 C3
Whitehouses S41 .266 C1
Whitehurst St DE24 .232 B4
Whitelea La DE4 .144 A3
Whiteleas Rd SK23 .45 B2
Whiteley Rd DE5 .180 C4
Whitelow La Dore S17 .55 A4
Ible DE4 .153 C4
Whitely Cl 6 NG9 .223 C4
Whitemoor Hall DE56 .179 B3
Whitemoor La DE56 .179 B3
Whites Cl DE55 .159 A1
Whites Croft View S43 .80 A3
Whitesmead Cl SK12 .32 B3
Whiteway DE22 .204 C1
Whitewell Gdns DE24 .233 B3
Whitewells La DE56 .178 B4
Whitewells Rd DE56 .167 C1
Whitewood Way DE4 .143 A2
Whitfield Ave SK13 .17 B4
Whitfield Cross SK13 .17 B4
Whitfield La DE45 .124 C1
Whitfield Pk SK13 .17 B4
Whiting Ave 5 NG9 .223 C1
Whiting St S8 .43 A3
Whitle Bank Rd SK22 .24 A1
Whitle Rd SK22 .24 B1
Whitley Way DE6 .185 C4
Whitmore Ave S42 .115 C1
Whitmore Rd DE21 .219 C3
Whitstable Cl DE23 .231 B4
Whittaker La DE21 .191 B1
Whitting Mews S41 .76 C1
Whitting Valley Rd S41 .77 A1
Whittington Hill S41 .77 A1
Whittington La S18 .76 C3
Whittington Rd S43 .77 C2
Whittington St DE24 .232 B3
Whittington Way S41 .77 A1
Whittlebury Dr DE23 .230 C4
Whitwell Cl 3 SK13 .9 B1
Whitwell Fold 1 SK13 .9 B1
Whitwell Gn 2 SK13 .9 B1
Whitwell Prim Sch S80 .82 A3
Whitwell Rd S80 .63 A2
Whitwell Sta S80 .82 A3
Whitworth Ave DE4 .127 B2
Whitworth Hospl DE4 .142 C4
Whitworth Rd
1 Chesterfield S41 .96 A3
Darley Dale DE4 .127 A2
Ilkeston DE7 .208 C3
Northwood DE4 .127 A2
Whysall St DE75 .181 C1
Whyteleafe Gr DE21 .206 A1
Wickersley Cl 1 DE22 .204 C1
Wickets The DE15 .254 C4
Wickfield Cl S12 .44 C3
Wickfield Dr S12 .44 C3
Wickfield Gr S12 .44 C2
Wickfield Pl S12 .44 C3
Wickfield Rd S12 .44 C3
Wickins Pl S43 .79 A2
Wicksteed Cl DE56 .179 B3
Widdop Cl S13 .44 B4
Widdop Croft S13 .44 B4
Widdybank Cl DE22 .204 B1
Wideshaft DE11 .256 B2
Widmerpool St NG16 .160 B1
Wigley Cl NG3 .268 C2
Wigley Prim Sch S42 .93 C2
Wigley Rd S43 .97 B3
Wigmore Cl DE3 .217 B2
Wilberforce Rd NG19 .135 B1
Wilbury Dr S12 .44 A3
Wilcox Ave NG19 .136 A3
Wilcox Ho DE21 .219 B3
Wild Hill NG17 .148 C4
Wild La DE4,DE55 .157 A2
Wild St DE22 .218 B3
Wildaygreen La S18 .75 A1
Wilderbrook La DE56 .178 A4
Wilders Lea Ct DE56 .179 A1
Wildersley Rd DE56 .179 A1
Wildhay La DE6 .183 B4
Wildman St NG7 .268 A2
Wildpark La DE6 .202 B3
Wildsmith St DE24 .233 A4
Wilford Rd NG2 .268 B1
Wilford St NG2 .268 B1
Wilfred Pl ST4 .269 A2
Wilfred St DE23 .219 A1
Wilhallow La NG16 .171 C1
Wilkin Hill S18 .75 C1
Wilkins Dr DE24 .232 C4
Wilkinson Cl
Chesterfield S40 .115 A3
Pleasley NG19 .135 A3
Wilkinson Dr S43 .97 A4
Will Shore's La DE4 .142 B3
Willcock Rd DE14 .254 A4
Willersley Ct 3 S41 .95 B4
Willersley Ho NG10 .236 A3
Willersley La
Matlock DE4 .143 B1
Matlock Bath DE4 .155 B4
Willesden Ave DE22 .218 A4
Willetts Rd DE21 .220 A4
William Allitt Sch DE11 .255 C4
William Ave NG16 .182 C1
William Booth Inf Sch
NG2 .268 C1
William Cl S20 .59 B3
William Cres S20 .59 B3
William Gilbert Endowed
Prim Sch DE56 .190 C2
William Howitt Jun Sch
DE75 .181 B1
William Levick Prim Sch
S18 .56 B1
William Lilley Inf Sch
NG9 .223 B3
William Nadin Way
DE11 .255 C2
William Newton Cl
DE65 .241 A3
William Rd NG9 .223 B4
William Rhodes Prim Sch
S40 .266 A1
William Shrewsbury Prim
Sch DE13 .240 C1
William St Belper DE56 .178 C2
Chesterfield S41 .96 A3
Derby DE1 .218 C3
Eckington S21 .59 B2
Long Eaton NG10 .223 B1
William St N S41 .76 C1
Williams Cl DE55 .170 B3
Williamson Ave SK17 .66 B1
Williamson Cres SK23 .45 B4
Williamson Rd SK23 .45 B4
Williamson St NG19 .268 A4
Williamthorpe Cl S42 .132 A4
Williamthorpe Ind Pk
S42 .116 B1
Williamthorpe Rd S42 .132 A4
Willington Prim Sch
DE65 .242 A3
Willington Rd
Etwall DE65 .229 B2
Findern DE65 .242 B4
Repton DE65 .242 A2
Willington Sta DE65 .242 A3
Willn St DE23 .218 C1
Willoughby Ave NG10 .223 B2
Willoughby Cl DE72 .235 C4
Willoughby Ct DE72 .222 B2
Willoughby Ho DE11 .256 B2
Willoughby St DE7 .195 A1
Willow Ave
Long Eaton NG10 .223 B1
Ripley DE5 .180 B4
Shirebrook NG20 .119 B3
Stapleford NG9 .223 B3
Willow Brook Cl DE65 .228 B1
Willow Cl Alfreton DE55 .159 A3
Aston-on-T DE72 .246 A4
Creswell S80 .81 C1
Derby DE72 .204 C1
Heanor NG16 .182 A2
Pilsley S45 .132 B1
South Normanton DE55 .160 A3
Stanley DE7 .193 A1
Willow Croft DE24 .233 B2
Willow Ct Ashbourne DE6 185 B4
Calow S44 .97 A2
Swadlincote DE11 .256 B2
Willow Dr
Chapel-en-le-F SK23 .47 A3
Mastin Moor S43 .79 B2
Swadlincote DE11 .255 C4
Willow Farm Bsns Pk
DE74 .247 A3
Willow Farm Ct DE65 .230 B1
Willow Garth Rd S41 .95 B4
Willow Gr Belper DE56 .179 A1
Willington DE65 .242 A3
Willow Ho DE21 .219 B3
Willow Meadow Rd DE6 185 B4
Willow Park Way DE72 .246 A4
Willow Pl DE15 .254 C4
Willow Rd
Castle Donington DE74 .247 A3
Killamarsh S21 .60 B3
Willow Rise NG10 .223 A3
Willow Row DE1 .267 A4
Willow St DE55 .146 B1
Willow Terr S43 .80 C1
Willow Way DE4 .127 A2
Willowbath La DE4 .165 C4
Willowbrook Grange
DE73 .233 A1
Willowcroft Rd DE21 .220 C2
Willowdale Ave ST4 .269 C1
Willowfields DE65 .228 B1
Willowherb Cl DE24 .231 C1
Willowpit La DE65 .228 C3
Willows Ave DE55 .159 A3
Willows Ct DE5 .169 B1
Willows The
Hulland Ward DE6 .175 C2
Pleasley NG19 .135 A3
Willowsend Cl DE65 .230 B1
Willridding La DE6 .183 B4
Willson Ave DE23 .231 B4
Willson Rd DE23 .231 B4
Wilmans Wlk SK13 .10 A3
Wilmington Ave DE24 .233 A3
Wilmore Rd DE24 .232 A3
Wilmorton Com Prim Sch
DE24 .219 C1
Wilmorton Tertiary Coll
DE24 .219 C1
Wilmot Ave Derby DE21 .219 C3
Weston-on-T DE72 .245 C3
Wilmot Dr DE7 .192 C3
Wilmot Ho NG10 .236 A3
Wilmot Rd Belper DE56 .179 A2
Swadlincote DE11 .256 A2
Wilmot St Derby DE1 .267 B2
Heanor DE75 .181 C1

Wilmot St *continued*
Ilkeston DE7 . . . .**194** C1
Long Eaton NG10 . . . . . .**236** A3
Matlock DE4 . . . .**143** A3
Wilmslow Dr DE21 . . . . .**206** A1
Wilne Ave NG10 . . . .**236** A2
Wilne Cl NG10 . . . .**235** C2
Wilne La Breaston DE72 .**235** B2
Shardlow DE72 . . . .**235** A1
Wilne Rd Draycott DE72 .**235** A3
Long Eaton NG10 . . . . . .**235** C2
Wilshaw Cl SK23 . . . .**47** B3
Wilson Ave
Blackwell DE55 . . . .**147** C1
Clowne S43 . . . .**80** C3
Heanor DE75 . . . .**181** A2
Wilson Cl Burnaston DE3 .**230** B4
Clay Cross S45 . . . .**131** B1
Wilson Dr DE55 . . . .**170** B4
Wilson La S44 . . . .**117** A1
Wilson Pl S8 . . . .**43** A4
Wilson Rd Derby DE21 . .**219** C4
Dronfield S18 . . . .**57** B2
Eastwood NG16 . . . .**182** C1
Wilson Rise DE73 . . . . . .**252** C3
Wilson St Alfreton DE55 .**159** A2
Derby DE1 . . . .**267** B2
Dronfield S18 . . . .**76** A4
Mansfield NG19 . . . .**135** B1
Pinxton NG16 . . . .**160** B2
Wilson's Terr SK13 . . . . . .**17** A4
Wilsthorpe Com Sch
NG10 . . . .**223** A1
Wilsthorpe Rd
Breaston DE72 . . . .**235** C4
Derby DE21 . . . .**220** A4
Long Eaton NG10 . . . . . .**236** A3
Wilton Cl DE24 . . . .**231** B1
Wilton Pl DE7 . . . .**194** C1
Wilton St 7 DE7 . . . . . .**194** C1
Wiltshire Ave S43 . . . . . .**95** C4
Wiltshire Dr SK13 . . . . . .**17** C4
Wiltshire Rd DE21 . . . . .**219** C4
Wimbledon Rd DE22 . . . .**218** A4
Wimborne Cres S41 . . . . .**95** C4
Wimbourne Dr DE73 . . . .**233** A1
Wimpole Gdns DE22 . . . .**218** A3
Wimsey Way DE55 . . . . .**159** A1
Wincanton Cl DE24 . . . . .**219** B1
Winchcombe Dr DE15 . . .**248** A1
Winchcombe Way DE21 .**206** A1
Winchester Cl S42 . . . . . .**131** C3
Winchester Cres DE7 . . . .**209** A4
Winchester Dr
Burton u T DE14 . . . .**254** A4
Linton DE12 . . . .**261** B3
Mansfield Woodhouse
NG19 . . . .**136** B2
Swadlincote DE11 . . . . . .**256** B3
Winchester Rd S41 . . . . . .**95** C4
Windermere Ave
Dronfield S18 . . . .**56** C1
Ilkeston DE7 . . . .**208** B3
Windermere Cres DE22 . .**204** C2
Windermere Dr DE21 . . .**220** C3
Windermere Gdns
NG10 . . . .**223** A1
Windermere Ho ST16 . . .**269** B4
Windermere Rd
Chesterfield S41 . . . .**95** B4
Clay Cross S45 . . . .**131** A2
Long Eaton NG10 . . . . . .**223** A1
Winders Cnr S43 . . . .**80** A3
Windlea Rd DE55 . . . . . .**170** B3
Windley Dr DE7 . . . .**194** B2
Windley La
Idridgehay DE56 . . . .**176** C3
Turnditch DE56 . . . .**177** A1
Windley DE56 . . . .**189** C4
Windmill Ave DE56 . . . . .**192** A4
Windmill Cl Bolsover S44 .**99** A2
Castle Donington DE74 . . .**247** A1
Elvaston DE24 . . . .**233** B2
Nottingham NG3 . . . .**268** C2
Ockbrook DE72 . . . .**221** B3
4 Uttoxeter ST14 . . . . .**210** A1
Windmill Dr ST14 . . . . . .**224** C2
Windmill Greenway S20 .**59** C3
Windmill Hill La DE22 . .**218** B3
Windmill La
Alderwasley DE56 . . . . . .**166** C3
Ashbourne DE6 . . . .**173** B2
Belper DE56 . . . .**179** A2
Eyam S32 . . . .**71** B3
Mansfield NG18 . . . .**268** C4
Nottingham NG2,NG3 . . .**268** C2
Snelston DE6 . . . .**184** C1
Unstone S18 . . . .**77** A3
Windmill Rd DE65 . . . . . .**229** A2
Windmill Rise
Belper DE56 . . . .**179** A3
Somercotes DE55 . . . . . .**170** B4
South Normanton DE55 . .**159** C3
Windmill St DE11 . . . . . .**256** A1
Windmill View DE56 . . . .**179** C4
Windrush Cl DE22 . . . . . .**205** A3
Windrush Ct 7 S43 . . . . .**96** C4
Windses Est S32 . . . .**53** B1
Windsmoor Rd NG16 . . . .**182** B4
Windsmoor St S14 . . . . . .**44** A2
Windsor Ave Derby DE23 .**231** A4
Melbourne DE73 . . . .**252** A4
Windsor Cl
Ashbourne DE6 . . . .**173** B2

Windsor Cl *continued*
Borrowash DE72 . . . .**221** B1
4 Chesterfield S40 . . . . .**95** B1
Heanor DE75 . . . .**181** C2
Swadlincote DE11 . . . . . .**256** A3
Swanwick DE55 . . . .**170** A4
Trowell NG9 . . . .**209** A3
Windsor Cres
Ilkeston DE7 . . . .**208** C2
Stapleford NG9 . . . .**223** C4
Windsor Ct Derby DE3 . .**217** B1
Long Eaton NG10 . . . . . .**236** C4
Sandiacre NG10 . . . .**223** A2
West Hallam DE7 . . . . . .**207** B4
Windsor Dr Derby DE21 .**221** A3
Dronfield S18 . . . .**56** B1
Wingerworth S42 . . . . . .**114** C2
Windsor Gdns NG18 . . . .**268** C3
Windsor Park Rd SK17 . . .**85** B4
Windsor Rd Buxton SK17 . .**85** B4
Linton DE12 . . . .**261** B3
Mansfield NG18 . . . .**268** C3
Uttoxeter ST14 . . . .**210** A1
Windsor St NG9 . . . .**223** C4
Windsor Wlk S41 . . . .**96** B1
Windy Fields Rd S42 . . . .**113** B4
Windy House La S2 . . . . . .**44** A4
Windy La DE21 . . . .**191** B1
Windyridge SK17 . . . . . .**121** A3
Winfield Gr SK6 . . . .**15** A1
Wingerworth Ave S8 . . . . .**56** B4
Wingerworth Cotts S42 **115** C2
Wingerworth Park Rd
DE21 . . . .**220** C3
Wingerworth St S42 . . . .**115** C2
Wingfield Cl S18 . . . .**56** B1
Wingfield Cres S12 . . . . . .**44** B3
Wingfield Dr Derby DE21 **205** C1
Ilkeston DE7 . . . .**194** B2
Wingfield Gr SK13 . . . . . .**17** C4
Wingfield Rd
Alfreton DE55 . . . .**158** C2
Tupton S42 . . . .**131** B4
Wingfield View S45 . . . . .**131** C2
Winhill Rd SK22 . . . .**24** B1
Winkburn Rd NG18,
NG19 . . . .**268** A4
Winn La DE6 . . . .**174** C4
Winnat Pl S43 . . . .**97** B4
Winnats S33 . . . .**37** C1
Winnats Cl
Chesterfield S40 . . . .**95** B3
Glossop SK13 . . . .**17** C4
Winney Hill S26 . . . .**61** C3
Winney La S26 . . . .**61** C2
Winnington Rd SK6 . . . . .**23** A4
Winshill Inf Sch DE15 . .**248** A2
Winslow Ave SK14 . . . .**9** A1
Winslow Gn DE21 . . . . . .**220** B3
Winster CE Prim Sch
DE4 . . . .**141** B3
Winster Cl Belper DE56 . .**179** A3
Clay Cross S42 . . . .**131** A3
Winster Ct S41 . . . .**96** A3
Winster Gn DE11 . . . .**255** C3
Winster Gr SK17 . . . .**85** C4
Winster La DE4 . . . .**140** C4
Winster Market Ho ★
DE4 . . . .**141** B3
Winster Mews SK13 . . . . . .**9** C1
Winster Rd Derby DE21 . .**205** C1
Staveley S43 . . . .**97** B4
Winster Sq SK17 . . . .**85** C4
Winster Way NG10 . . . . .**235** C3
Winston Cl NG9 . . . .**223** C4
Winter Closes NG16 . . . .**171** C1
Winterbourne Dr NG9 . .**209** C1
Wintercroft La DE6 . . . . .**161** C1
Wintergreen Dr DE23 . . .**230** C3
Winton Sq ST4 . . . .**269** C2
Wintonfield St ST4 . . . . .**269** C2
Wire La DE55 . . . .**148** A2
Wirksmoor Rd SK22 . . . .**33** A4
Wirksworth CE Inf Sch
DE4 . . . .**165** C4
Wirksworth Hall Gdns
DE4 . . . .**165** C4
Wirksworth Ind Ctr DE4 **154** C2
Wirksworth Inf Sch
DE4 . . . .**154** C1
Wirksworth Jun Sch
DE4 . . . .**155** A1
Wirksworth Rd
Duffield DE56 . . . .**190** A2
Holloway DE4 . . . .**156** A1
Idridgehay DE56 . . . .**176** C3
Ilkeston DE7 . . . .**208** B2
Kirk Ireton DE6 . . . .**165** A1
Shottle DE56 . . . .**177** B2
Wisbech Cl S40 . . . .**114** C4
Wisgreaves Rd DE24 . . . .**232** C4
Wishing Stone Way
DE4 . . . .**143** C3
Witham Cl
Chesterfield S41 . . . .**96** B3
Hilton DE65 . . . .**228** C1
Witham Ct S40 . . . .**95** B2
Witham Dr DE23 . . . .**231** B3
Witney Cl DE24 . . . .**232** B4
Witney St S8 . . . .**43** A4
Wittering Cl NG10 . . . . .**236** C3
Witton Ct DE24 . . . .**231** B2
Woburn Cl
Blackwell DE55 . . . .**147** C1
Swanwick DE55 . . . .**169** C4
Woburn Cotts DE4 . . . . .**143** A4
Woburn Croft NG10 . . . .**223** A2
Woburn Ct DE55 . . . .**147** C1

Woburn La NG19 . . . . . .**135** B2
Woburn Pl Derby DE22 . .**218** A3
Mansfield NG19 . . . .**135** B2
Woburn Rd NG19 . . . . . .**135** B2
Wolds Rd DE4 . . . .**143** B3
Wolds Rise DE4 . . . .**143** B4
Wolfa St DE22 . . . .**218** C2
Wolfcote Cl S45 . . . .**131** B1
Wolfe Cl S40 . . . .**95** B1
Wolfe St ST4 . . . .**269** B1
Wolfscote Dale DE11 . . .**255** C1
Wollaton Ave S17 . . . .**56** A3
Wollaton Dr 7 S17 . . . . . .**56** A3
Wollaton Rd Derby DE21 **219** C4
Sheffield S17 . . . .**56** A3
Wollaton Rd S DE21 . . . .**205** C1
Wollaton St NG1 . . . .**268** A2
Wollen Cl S80 . . . .**81** C1
Wolseley Rd S8 . . . .**43** A4
Wolverhampton Rd
ST17 . . . .**269** B3
Wolverley Grange DE24 **233** B3
Wood Ave Creswell S80 . . .**81** B1
Sandiacre NG10 . . . .**223** A3
Wood Cl S42 . . . .**114** B2
Wood Croft DE23 . . . . . .**231** B4
Wood End DE4 . . . .**156** A3
Wood End Rd DE75 . . . . .**181** C1
Wood Farm La DE11 . . . .**256** C2
Wood Gdns SK22 . . . .**25** B2
Wood La Belper DE56 . . . .**190** C4
Creswell S80 . . . .**100** B4
Hanbury DE13 . . . .**238** A2
Hayfield SK22 . . . .**25** B2
Holloway DE4 . . . .**144** A1
Horsley Woodhouse DE7 . .**192** B3
Ible DE4 . . . .**153** C3
Idridgehay DE6,DE56 . . .**176** C4
Kniveton DE6 . . . .**163** A1
Market Warsop NG20 . . .**120** C4
Pleasley NG20 . . . .**119** C1
Ripley DE5 . . . .**169** A2
Scarcliffe S44 . . . .**118** C3
Shirebrook NG20 . . . . . .**119** C1
Swadlincote DE11 . . . . . .**256** A4
Wood Nook Cl NG16 . . . .**171** C3
Wood Rd
Derby, Chaddesden DE21 .**220** A4
Derby, Oakwood DE21 . . .**205** C1
Derby, Spondon DE21 . . .**221** A3
Wood St Alfreton DE55 . .**159** B3
Codnor DE5 . . . .**181** A4
Derby DE1 . . . .**267** C4
Eastwood NG16 . . . .**182** C2
Glossop SK13 . . . .**17** B4
Hollingworth SK14 . . . .**9** B3
Holmewood S42 . . . .**116** C1
Ilkeston DE7 . . . .**194** C1
Mansfield NG18 . . . .**268** B4
New Mills SK22 . . . .**33** A4
Nottingham NG7 . . . .**268** A2
Ripley DE5 . . . .**169** B1
Somercotes DE55 . . . . . .**170** B4
Swadlincote DE11 . . . . . .**256** A1
Wirksworth DE4 . . . .**165** C4
Wood St N DE55 . . . .**159** B3
Wood View S21 . . . .**79** A4
Wood's Hospl SK13 . . . . . .**10** B2
Woodale Cl DE23 . . . .**230** C3
Woodall La S26 . . . .**61** B3
Woodall Rd S21 . . . .**60** C3
Woodbeck Ct DE21 . . . . .**206** A1
Woodberry Ave ST4 . . . . .**269** A4
Woodberry Cl ST4 . . . . . .**269** A1
Woodbine Terr SK23 . . . .**47** A3
Woodbine Way DE14 . . . .**253** C3
Woodborough Rd
Mansfield NG19 . . . .**135** C1
Nottingham NG3 . . . .**268** B2
Woodbourne Rd SK22 . . .**33** A4
Woodbridge Cl DE73 . . . .**232** C1
Woodbridge Jun Sch
DE55 . . . .**159** A2
Woodbridge Rise S40 . . .**114** A4
Woodbrook SK23 . . . .**45** C4
Woodbrook Ct S43 . . . . . .**45** C4
Woodchester Dr DE24 . . .**233** B3
Woodcock Gr SK13 . . . . . .**10** C1
Woodcock Rd SK13 . . . . . .**11** A1
Woodcock Sq DE3 . . . . . .**230** B4
Woodcote Way DE23 . . . .**231** A4
Woodfall La DE22 . . . . . .**189** C2
Woodfield Cl SK13 . . . .**9** C3
Woodfield Dr Ripley DE5 .**181** A4
Swadlincote DE11 . . . . . .**256** B3
Woodfield Rd
Pinxton NG16 . . . .**160** B2
South Normanton DE55 . .**159** C2
Woodford Rd DE22 . . . . .**218** A4
Woodford Way S43 . . . . . .**78** A2
Woodgate Ct 29 NG7 . . .**268** A2
Woodgate Dr DE73 . . . . .**233** A1
Woodhall Dr DE23 . . . . . .**230** C4
Woodhead La S45 . . . . . .**130** B1
Woodhead Rd
Glossop SK13 . . . .**10** B3
Glossop, Tintwistle SK13 . .**10** A4
Holme HD7 . . . .**2** C3
Sheffield S2 . . . .**43** A4
Woodhouse Ct NG19 . . . .**136** B1
Woodhouse La
Barlborough S43 . . . .**79** C3
Bolsover S44 . . . .**98** C2
Darley Dale DE4 . . . .**126** C4
Mastin Moor S43 . . . .**79** B3
Scropton DE65 . . . .**226** C4
South Normanton DE55 . .**159** C3
Winster DE4 . . . .**141** B3

Woodhouse Rd
Kilburn DE56,DE7 . . . . . .**192** A4
Mansfield NG18 . . . .**268** B4
Sheffield S12 . . . .**44** A3
Woodhouse St
Nottingham NG3 . . . .**268** C2
Stoke-on-T ST4 . . . .**269** B1
Swadlincote DE11 . . . . . .**256** B2
Woodhouse West Prim Sch
S13 . . . .**44** C4
Woodhurst Cl DE21 . . . .**219** B4
Woodland Ave
Borrowash DE72 . . . .**221** B1
Ilkeston DE7 . . . .**194** B2
Sutton in A NG17 . . . . . .**148** C2
Woodland Dr
Scropton DE6 . . . .**226** B2
Sheffield S44 . . . .**44** A1
Woodland Gr
Barlborough S43 . . . .**80** A3
Clowne S43 . . . .**81** B1
Mansfield Woodhouse
NG19 . . . .**136** B2
Woodland Pl S17 . . . .**55** C3
Woodland Rd
Derby DE22 . . . .**218** C4
Sheffield S8 . . . .**43** A2
Swadlincote DE15 . . . . . .**255** A2
Woodland View Dore S17 .**56** A4
Sheffield S32 . . . .**44** A1
Whaley Bridge SK23 . . . . .**45** C1
Whaley Thorns NG20 . . . .**101** A2
Woodland Views ST14 . .**224** C1
Woodland Way
Clay Cross S45 . . . .**131** A4
Eastwood NG16 . . . .**182** C1
Woodland Wlk S40 . . . . . .**94** C3
Woodlands Brimington S43 **96** B4
Great Longstone DE45 . . .**89** C2
Wirksworth DE4 . . . .**165** C4
Woodlands Ave
Breaston DE72 . . . .**235** C4
Derby DE24 . . . .**232** C2
Woodlands Brow DE6 . . .**173** B2
Woodlands Cl
Glossop SK13 . . . .**9** C3
Little Eaton DE21 . . . . . .**205** A4
Melbourne DE73 . . . .**252** A4
Thorpe DE6 . . . .**161** B1
Woodlands Com Sch
DE22 . . . .**204** B2
Woodlands Cres DE12 . .**262** A2
Woodlands Gr S42 . . . . . .**131** C3
Woodlands La
Dorby DE73 . . . .**245** A4
Quarndon DE22 . . . .**204** B3
Woodlands Rd
Chapel-en-le-F SK23 . . . . .**47** A2
Derby DE22 . . . .**204** C3
High Lane SK12 . . . .**32** A3
New Mills SK22 . . . .**33** A4
Overseal DE12 . . . .**262** A2
Woodlands The
Branston DE13 . . . .**253** A4
Mansfield NG19 . . . .**136** A1
Melbourne DE73 . . . .**252** A4
Whaley Thorns NG20 . . . .**101** A2
Woodlands Way DE73 . . .**252** A4
Woodlands Yd DE73 . . . .**245** A4
Woodlea Gr DE21 . . . . . .**205** B4
Woodlea Rd SK13 . . . .**17** C4
Woodleigh Cl S40 . . . .**94** C3
Woodmans Croft DE65 . .**227** B1
Woodmere Dr S41 . . . .**77** B2
Woodminton Dr DE73 . . .**232** C2
Woodnook Cl S42 . . . .**95** A4
Woodnook La S42 . . . .**94** C3
Woodnook Way S42 . . . . . .**94** C3
Woodpecker Hill DE7 . . .**208** A1
Woodrising Cl DE21 . . . .**206** A3
Woodroffe Wlk DE23 . . .**231** C4
Woodrove Ave S13 . . . . . .**44** A4
Woodrove Cl S13 . . . .**44** A4
Woods La
Burton u T, Stapenhill
DE15 . . . .**254** C4
Burton u T, Stapenhill
DE15 . . . .**254** C4
Derby DE22 . . . .**267** A1
Woods Mdw DE72 . . . . . .**233** B3
Woodseats La S13 . . . .**16** A3
Woodshop La DE73 . . . . .**244** B3
Woodside Buxton SK17 . . .**85** B4
Eastwood NG16 . . . .**182** C1
Horsley DE7 . . . .**192** C4
Woodside Ave
Holmesfield S18 . . . .**75** A4
Killamarsh S21 . . . .**60** C4
Ripley DE5 . . . .**180** B4
Woodside Cl
Bakewell DE45 . . . .**109** B3
Chesterfield S40 . . . .**95** A4
Woodside Cres
Ilkeston DE7 . . . .**194** B3
Long Eaton NG10 . . . . . .**236** A3
Woodside Dr
Bakewell DE45 . . . .**109** B3
Derby DE22 . . . .**205** A2
Woodside Pl S45 . . . .**131** C2
Woodside Rd
Sandiacre NG10 . . . .**223** A3
Shirebrook NG20 . . . . . .**119** C3
Shireoaks S81 . . . .**63** C4
Woodside St S22 . . . .**33** A3
Woodside View S18 . . . . . .**75** A4
Woodsome Pk S42 . . . . . .**116** B1
Woodsorrel Dr DE21 . . . .**206** A1
Woodstock Cl DE22 . . . . .**204** B2

Woodstock Ct 5 S41 . . . .**96** A3
Woodstock Dr S41 . . . . . .**115** B4
Woodstock Rd NG9 . . . . .**223** C2
Woodstock Rise S41 . . . .**115** B4
Woodthorpe Ave
Clay Cross S45 . . . .**131** A2
Derby, Allenton DE24 . . . .**232** C2
Derby, Chaddesden DE21 .**219** C3
Woodthorpe CE Prim Sch
S43 . . . .**79** B1
Woodthorpe Cl
Bolsover S44 . . . .**98** C4
Sheffield S2 . . . .**44** A4
Woodthorpe Com Prim Sch
S13 . . . .**44** B4
Woodthorpe Cres S13 . . .**44** B4
Woodthorpe Rd
Bolsover S44 . . . .**98** C4
Sheffield S13 . . . .**44** B4
Staveley S43 . . . .**79** B1
Woodvale Cl S40 . . . .**114** A4
Woodview Cl S42 . . . .**114** C1
Woodview Rd DE11 . . . . .**255** C3
Woodville CE Jun Sch
DE11 . . . .**256** C1
Woodville Inf Sch DE11 **256** C1
Woodville Rd
Hartshorne DE11 . . . . . .**257** A3
Overseal DE12 . . . .**262** A4
Woodward Way DE11 . . .**256** B2
Woodward's Pl DE11 . . . .**256** B2
Woodwards Cl DE72 . . . .**221** B1
Woodyard La DE65 . . . . .**226** C3
Woolaton La SK17 . . . . . .**138** C3
Wooley Cl S42 . . . .**131** A4
Wooliscroft Cl DE7 . . . . .**194** B1
Woolley Bridge Rd SK13 . .**9** B2
Woolley Cl SK14 . . . .**9** B2
Woolley La SK14 . . . .**9** B2
Woolley Mill La SK13 . . . . .**9** C4
Woolley Rd DE4 . . . .**143** A3
Woolley Yd DE4 . . . .**141** B3
Woolpack La NG1 . . . . . .**268** A2
Woolrych St DE23 . . . . . .**218** C1
Woolsthorpe Cres DE7 . .**208** B3
Woosnam Cl DE14 . . . . . .**254** A3
Worcester Ave NG19 . . . .**136** B3
Worcester Cres DE21 . . .**219** C4
Worcester Gr S13 . . . .**17** C4
Worcester Mews NG19 . .**136** B3
Worcester Rd DE15 . . . . .**254** C3
Wordsworth Ave
Derby DE24 . . . .**231** C3
Mansfield Woodhouse
NG19 . . . .**136** A2
Swadlincote DE11 . . . . . .**256** B3
Wordsworth Dr DE24 . . .**232** A4
Wordsworth Pl S18 . . . . . .**76** B4
Wordsworth Rd
Awsworth NG16 . . . .**195** B3
Chesterfield S41 . . . .**95** C4
Works La S44 . . . .**97** A2
Works Rd S43 . . . .**78** A1
Worksop Rd
Mastin Moor S43 . . . .**79** B2
Nottingham NG3 . . . .**268** C2
Thorpe Salvin S80 . . . .**62** C4
Whitwell S80 . . . .**81** C3
Worrall Ave NG10 . . . . . .**223** C1
Worthington La DE73 . . .**252** C1
Wortley Ave NG9 . . . .**209** B2
Wortley Cl DE7 . . . .**209** A4
Wortley Ct S33 . . . .**51** A4
Wragley Way DE24 . . . . .**231** B1
Wray Cl NG3 . . . .**268** C2
Wreakes La S18 . . . .**56** C1
Wren Cl DE11 . . . .**256** C2
Wren Nest Rd SK13 . . . . .**10** A1
Wren Nest Terr SK13 . . . .**10** B1
Wren Park Cl
Belper DE56 . . . .**178** B3
Chesterfield S40 . . . .**114** C4
Findern DE65 . . . .**230** B1
Sheffield S12 . . . .**58** C4
Wren Park Prim Sch
DE3 . . . .**218** A4
Wren Way DE3 . . . .**230** A4
Wrenpark Rd S42 . . . . . .**114** B2
Wretham Cl DE3 . . . .**230** B4
Wright Ave DE5 . . . .**169** C1
Wright St DE5 . . . .**181** A4
Wroxham Ct DE24 . . . . . .**232** B2
Wulfric Cl S2 . . . .**43** C4
Wulfric Pl S2 . . . .**43** C4
Wulfric Rd Eckington S21 .**59** B2
Sheffield, Deep Pit S2 . . . .**43** C4
Sheffield, Manor Estate S2 .**44** A4
Wyaston Cl DE22 . . . .**204** C1
Wyaston Gdns DE6 . . . . .**185** B3
Wyaston Rd DE6 . . . .**185** B3
Wyatts Way DE5 . . . .**169** C2
Wybersley Rd SK6 . . . . . .**32** A4
Wychwood Dr NG9 . . . . .**209** B3
Wycliffe Rd DE55 . . . . . .**159** A2
Wycombe Grange NG19 **136** C1
Wye Bank DE45 . . . .**109** C2
Wye Bank Gr DE45 . . . . .**109** C2
Wye Croft Ct DE45 . . . . .**109** B3
Wye Dale DE11 . . . .**255** C1
Wye Gr SK17 . . . .**85** A4
Wye Head Cl SK17 . . . . . .**84** C4
Wye St Buxton SK17 . . . . .**85** B4
Derby DE24 . . . .**233** A4
Wye Terr DE4 . . . .**126** C4
Wyedale Cl
Bakewell DE45 . . . .**109** C2
Buxton SK17 . . . .**85** A4
Wyedale Cres DE45 . . . . .**109** C2

Wyedale Ct **5** S41 ......95 C4
Wyedale Dr DE45 ......109 C2
Wyedale View DE45 ....109 C2
Wyelands Cl SK17 ......84 C4
Wyming Brook Dr S10 ...42 A4
Wynd The S21 ....79 B4
Wyndale Dr DE7 ......208 B3
Wyndham Cres DE15 ..248 B2
Wyndham St DE24 ....233 A4
Wynton Ave DE24 .....232 C4
Wyntor Ave DE4 ......141 B3
Wynward Cl DE7 ......194 B2
Wysall Cl NG19 ....135 C1
Wystan Ct DE65 ....242 B1
Wyston Brook DE65 ...228 B1
Wythburn Rd S41 ......95 B4
Wyver La DE56 ....178 C3
Wyvern Ave NG10 .....236 B3
Wyvern Bsns Pk DE21 ..220 A2
Wyvern Cl
  Eastwood NG16 .....195 A4
  Matlock DE4 ....143 A3
Wyvern Gdns S17 ......55 C3
Wyvern Way DE21 ....220 A2
Wyvernside DE21 .....219 C2

Y

Yard Cl DE11 ....256 A2
Yardley Cl DE55 ......169 C4
Yardley Way DE56 ....179 B2
Yarncliff Cl S40 ....95 B3
Yarrow Cl DE24 ......231 C1
Yarwell Cl DE21 ......205 B1
Yates Ave DE72 ......246 A4
Yates Rd SK22 ....33 B4
Yates St DE23 ....219 A1
Yeaman St ST4 ......269 B1
Yeardsley Ave SK23 ...33 B2
Yeardsley Gn SK23 ....45 B4
Yeardsley La SK23 ....33 B2
Yeld Cl DE45 ....109 B2
Yeld Rd DE45 ....109 B3
Yeld The DE45 ....109 B3
Yeldersley Cl S40 .....95 A3
Yeldersley La
  Brailsford DE6 ......187 A1
  Osmaston DE6 ......186 C3
Yelt La DE6 ....224 B4
Yeoman Park Specl Sch
  NG19 ....136 B2

Yeoman St DE4 ....142 B1
Yeovil Cl DE24 ......233 B4
Yerley Hill DE6 ....172 B3
Yew Tree Ave DE72 ..221 B3
Yew Tree Cl Ashover S45 129 C2
  Darley Dale DE4 ....127 A2
Yew Tree Cotts DE72 ..222 C2
Yew Tree Dr
  Chesterfield S40 ....114 A4
  Clay Cross S42 .....131 A3
  Killamarsh S21 ......60 B3
  Shirebrook NG20 ...119 B3
  Sutton in A NG17 ...148 C1
Yew Tree Gdns DE12 ..260 B3
Yew Tree Hill DE4 ...156 A3
Yew Tree La Bradley DE6 186 C4
  Elvaston DE72 ......233 C2
Yew Tree Rd
  Hatton DE65 ....227 B1
  Rosliston DE12 .....260 B3
  Swadlincote DE11 ...255 C4
Yewdale Gr DE21 ....206 B2
Yews Cl DE73 ....233 A1
Yewtree Cl DE24 ....233 B4
Yewtree Cres DE15 ..254 C4
Yokecliffe Ave DE4 ..165 C4

Yokecliffe Cres DE4 ...165 C4
Yokecliffe Dr DE4 ....165 C4
Yokecliffe Hill DE4 ..165 C4
York Ave Sandiacre NG10 223 A3
  Westwood NG16 ....171 A2
York Cl DE11 ....256 B3
York Cres S44 ....117 C1
York Pl
  North Wingfield S42 ..132 A4
  Shireoaks S81 ....63 C4
York Rd Derby DE21 ..219 C4
  Long Eaton NG10 ...223 B1
  Shirebrook NG20 ...119 C2
  Swadlincote DE11 ..256 A1
York St Chesterfield S41 115 B4
  Derby DE1 ....218 C3
  Glossop SK13 ....10 C1
  Mansfield NG18 ....268 B3
  Nottingham NG1 ...268 C2
York Terr Glossop SK13 ..17 B4
  Pinxton NG16 ......160 B1
Yorke St NG19 ....136 A1
Yorkshire Way SK13 ..17 C4
Youlgreave Cl DE21 ..205 C1
Youlgreave Cres SK13 ..9 B1
Youlgreave Dr S12 ...44 B3

Youlgreave YH★ DE45 ..125 B3
Young St DE23 ......218 C1
Younger St ST4 ......269 C1
Yoxall Ave ST4 ......269 A2
Ypres Rd DE22 ....204 B1

Z

Zetland Cres DE24 ....231 B1

Any feature in this atlas can be given a unique reference to help you find the same feature on other Ordnance Survey maps of the area, or to help someone else locate you if they do not have a Street Atlas.

The grid squares in this atlas match the Ordnance Survey National Grid and are at 1 kilometre intervals. The small figures at the bottom and sides of every other grid line are the National Grid kilometre values (**00** to **99** km) and are repeated across the country every 100 km (see left).

To give a unique National Grid reference you need to locate where in the country you are. The country is divided into 100 km squares with each square given a unique two-letter reference. Use the administrative map to determine in which 100 km square a particular page of this atlas falls.

The bold letters and numbers between each grid line (**A** to **C**, **1** to **4**) are for use within a specific Street Atlas only, and when used with the page number, are a convenient way of referencing these grid squares.

Example   The railway bridge over DARLEY GREEN RD in grid square A1

Step 1: Identify the two-letter reference, in this example the page is in **SP**

Step 2: Identify the 1 km square in which the railway bridge falls. Use the figures in the southwest corner of this square: Eastings **17**, Northings **74**. This gives a unique reference: **SP 17 74**, accurate to 1 km.

Step 3: To give a more precise reference accurate to 100 m you need to estimate how many tenths along and how many tenths up this 1 km square the feature is. This makes the bridge about **8** tenths along and about **1** tenth up from the southwest corner.

This gives a unique reference: **SP 178 741**, accurate to 100 m.

Eastings (read from left to right along the bottom) come before Northings (read from bottom to top). If you have trouble remembering say to yourself "Along the hall, THEN up the stairs"!

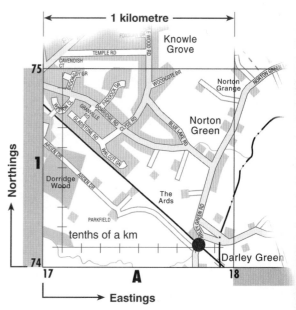

Name and Address	Telephone	Page	Grid reference

Addresses

Name and Address	Telephone	Page	Grid reference

Street Atlases from Philip's

Philip's publish an extensive range of regional and local street atlases which are ideal for motoring, business and leisure use. They are widely used by the emergency services and local authorities throughout Britain.

Key features include:

◆ Superb county-wide mapping at an extra-large scale of 3½ inches to 1 mile, or 2½ inches to 1 mile in pocket editions

◆ Complete urban and rural coverage, detailing every named street in town and country

◆ Each atlas available in two handy sizes – standard spiral and pocket paperback

'The mapping is very clear... great in scope and value'
★★★★ BEST BUY   AUTO EXPRESS

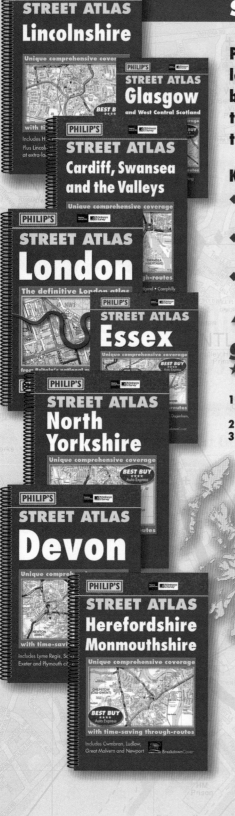

1 Anglesey, Conwy and Gwynedd
2 Bedfordshire
3 Berkshire
4 Birmingham and West Midlands
5 Bristol and Bath
6 Buckinghamshire
7 Cambridgeshire
8 Cardiff, Swansea and The Valleys
9 Cheshire
10 Cornwall
11 Cumbria
12 Denbighshire, Flintshire and Wrexham
13 Derbyshire
14 Devon
15 Dorset
16 County Durham and Teesside
17 Edinburgh and East Central Scotland
18 Essex
19 North Essex
20 South Essex
21 Fife and Tayside
22 Glasgow and West Central Scotland
23 Gloucestershire
24 North Hampshire
25 South Hampshire
26 Herefordshire and Monmouthshire
27 Hertfordshire
28 Isle of Wight
29 East Kent
30 West Kent
31 Lancashire
32 Leicestershire and Rutland
33 Lincolnshire
34 London
35 Greater Manchester
36 Merseyside
37 Norfolk
38 Northamptonshire
39 Nottinghamshire
40 Oxfordshire
41 Shropshire
42 Somerset
43 Staffordshire
44 Suffolk
45 Surrey
46 East Sussex
47 West Sussex
48 Tyne and Wear and Northumberland
49 Warwickshire
50 Wiltshire and Swindon
51 Worcestershire
52 East Yorkshire and Northern Lincolnshire
53 North Yorkshire
54 South Yorkshire
55 West Yorkshire

How to order

The Philip's range of street atlases is available from good retailers or directly from the publisher by phoning 01903 828503

Breakdown cover from £35

No wonder almost 5 million motorists have found their route to Green Flag.

With Green Flag Motoring Assistance, not only could you save money on your breakdown cover, but you can rely on a totally professional, fast service, when you need it most.

- 24hr assistance, 365 days a year
- 6,000 breakdown specialists nationwide
- 39 mins average response time*
- Priority response for vulnerable callers

Green Flag
motoring assistance

Call 0845 246 2445
or buy online at www.greenflag.com

*Figures based on 222,277 customer questionnaires Jan 03 to Dec 03. Response times may vary. Green Flag Motoring Assistance is a trading name of Direct Line Insurance plc, 3 Edridge Road, Croydon, Surrey CR9 1AG. Members of the General Insurance Standards Council. Subject to underwriting criteria. Calls may be monitored and recorded.